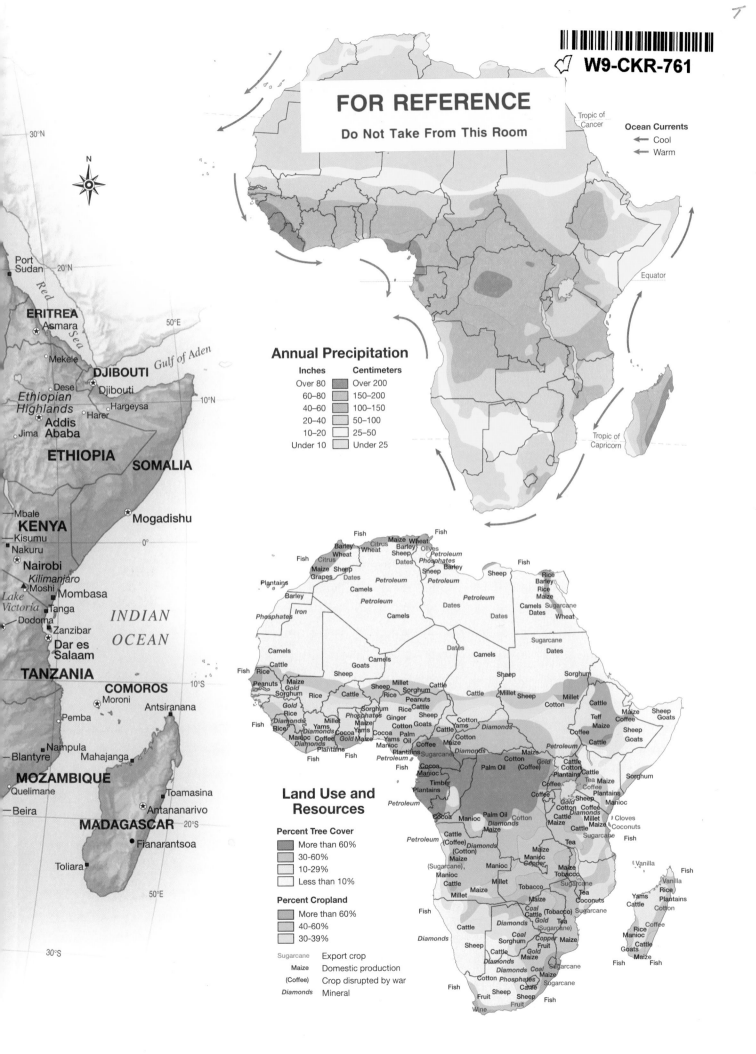

FOR REFERENCE

Do Not Take From This Room

W9-CKR-761

NEW ENCYCLOPEDIA OF

AFRICA

NEW ENCYCLOPEDIA OF

AFRICA

Volume 3

Ibadan–Mzilikazi

John Middleton

EDITOR IN CHIEF

Joseph C. Miller

EDITOR

CHARLES SCRIBNER'S SONS
A part of Gale, Cengage Learning

GALE
CENGAGE Learning·

Detroit • New York • San Francisco • New Haven, Conn • Waterville, Maine • London

New Encyclopedia of Africa

John Middleton, Editor in Chief
Joseph C. Miller, Editor

NEW ENCYCLOPEDIA OF AFRICA

John Middleton, editor in chief ; Joseph C. Miller, editor.
p. cm.
Includes bibliographical references and index.
ISBN 978-0-684-31454-9 (set : alk. paper)
ISBN 978-0-684-31455-6 (vol. 1 : alk. paper)
ISBN 978-0-684-31456-3 (vol. 2 : alk. paper)
ISBN 978-0-684-31457-0 (vol. 3 : alk. paper)
ISBN 978-0-684-31458-7 (vol. 4 : alk. paper)
ISBN 978-0-684-31459-4 (vol. 5 : alk. paper)
Africa—Encyclopedias. Middleton, John, 1921-
Miller, Joseph Calder.
Title.

DT2.N48 2008
960.03—dc22

2007021746

ISBN-10:

0-684-31454-1 (set)
0-684-31455-X (vol. 1)
0-684-31456-8 (vol. 2)
0-684-31457-6 (vol. 3)
0-684-31458-4 (vol. 4)
0-684-31459-2 (vol. 5)

This title is also available as an e-book.
ISBN-13: 978-0-684-31557-7; ISBN-10: 0-684-31557-2
Contact your Gale representative for ordering information.

Printed in the United States of America
2 3 4 5 6 7 14 13 12 11 10 09 08

EDITORIAL BOARD

Joseph Harris
Howard University
Historian

Goran Hyden
University of Florida
Political scientist,
East Africa

Ali Mazrui
State University of New York,
Binghamton
Political scientist,
East Africa

Sally Falk Moore
Harvard University
Anthropologist, lawyer, East
Africa

V. Y. Mudimbe
Duke University
Philosopher, novelist, poet,
Central Africa

Roland Oliver
School of Oriental and African
Studies, University of London
Historian

Abdul Sheriff
Zanzibar Indian Ocean Research
Institute
Historian, East Africa

Wim Van Binsbergen
University of Leiden,
Netherlands
Anthropologist, philosopher,
Southern Africa

Jan Vansina
University of Wisconsin
Historian, Central Africa

CONSULTANTS

Kelly Askew
University of Michigan
Anthropologist, musicologist,
East Africa

Karin Barber
University of Birmingham
Historian, West Africa

Julia Clancy-Smith
University of Arizona
Historian, North Africa

Mamadou Diouf
Columbia University
Anthropologist, historian, West
Africa

Toyin Falola
University of Texas, Austin
Historian, West Africa

Richard Fardon
School of Oriental and African
Studies, University of London
Anthropologist, Central Africa

Gillian Feeley-Harnik
University of Michigan
Anthropologist, Madagascar

Peter Geschiere
University of Amsterdam
Anthropologist, Central Africa

Michelle Gilbert
Sarah Lawrence College
Art historian, West Africa

Jane Guyer
Johns Hopkins University
Historian, West Africa

Andrew Hill
Yale University
Paleontologist, East Africa

Michael Lambek
University of Toronto
Anthropologist, East Africa

George Nelson
University of Liverpool
Medicine, East/West Africa

Kimani Njogu
Twaweza Communications,
Nairobi
Director, linguist, East Africa

John Peel
School of Oriental and African
Studies, University of
London
Anthropologist, West Africa

Paul Richards
Wageningen University and
Research Centre,
Netherlands
Geographer, West Africa

Janet Roitman
University of Paris
Anthropologist,
Central Africa

Parker Shipton
Boston University
Anthropologist, East Africa

Thomas Spear
University of Wisconsin
Historian, East Africa

Dorothy Woodson
Yale University
Librarian, Africa

IBADAN. Ibadan, the capital of the southwestern Nigerian state of Oyo, reflects both its traditional and its modern heritages. It has indigenous quarters, where the descendants of the nineteenth-century Ibadan warriors live, and modern sections, occupied largely by the elite attracted to the city by business. The city's growth since the 1980s has been rapid, and the population in 2000 was estimated at more than 3 million. As a result of such rapid growth, the city' ability to provide services has been severely strained, and unemployment is high.

The city originated as a military camp about 1829. In the following years Ibadan became the most powerful city-state in Yorubaland. Unlike other Yoruba towns, where upward mobility depended on hereditary status, Ibadan created an open society where advancement depended on talent. The system attracted many people with administrative and military skills.

Ibadan achieved a memorable victory in 1840 when, at a battle near Osogbo, it checked the expansion of Fulani power based in Ilorin to the north. Ibadan subsequently saw itself as the savior of Yorubaland. Ibadan established its hegemony over eastern Yorubaland between 1851 and 1855. However, by 1877 the resentment of Ibadan's oppressive rule had generated an anti-Ibadan alliance which precipitated the Kiriji War. Peace was not achieved until the British intervened in 1886. In 1893 the British imposed a treaty of friendship on Ibadan, which was subsequently absorbed into the colonial state.

In spite of the military threat of Muslim Fulani expansionism following the Sokoto jihad, Islam took root firmly in the mid-nineteenth century, preceding Christianity by a few decades. The development of Western education among the indigenous population of Ibadan has been slow until the early twenty-first century. Politics in the city has a volatile character. Most of the successful politicians have been demagogues.

The majority of the people of Ibadan have been, and still are, peasant farmers, self-employed traders, and craftsmen. A few work as clerks and laborers for the government and for business houses. Modern Ibadan is regarded as the intellectual center of Nigeria. Its university, established by the British in 1948, was the first in Nigeria and is respected worldwide. The colonial administration provided railways and an airport, while self-government in the 1950s brought radio and television stations and industries. Markets such as Oje, Agbeni, and Oja'ba are very important for the sale of every conceivable kind of locally made cloth, beads, and consumer items.

See also **'Abd al-Qādir; Nigeria.**

BIBLIOGRAPHY

Adelugba, Dapo, et al., eds. *Ibadan Meslogo: A Celebration of a City, Its History, and People.* Ibadan, Nigeria: Bookcraft Ltd./The Association of Nigerian Authors, 2001.

Falola, Toyin. *The Political Economy of a Pre-Colonial African State: Ibadan, 1830–1900.* Ile-Ife, Nigeria: University of Ife Press, 1984.

Lloyd, Peter Cutt; A. L. Mabogunje; and Bolande Awe; eds. *The City of Ibadan.* Cambridge, U.K.: Cambridge University Press, 1967.

OLUTAYO ADESINA

IBN BATTUTA, MUHAMMAD IBN ABDULLAH

(1304–c. 1368). The North African Muslim traveler Muhammad ibn Abdullah Ibn Battuta was born and raised in the Marinid principality (in present-day Morocco). Ibn Battuta departed at the age of twenty-one for a pilgrimage to the holy places of Islam in Arabia. This was to be the beginning of almost three decades (1325–1353) spent traveling all over the known world of the time. The "traveler of the century," as he became known to his contemporaries, traveled from Spain to South East Asia, and from the Russian steppes to the northern fringes of Black Africa, only stopping for a few years at some places (Delhi, the Maldives Islands, and Mecca) to set up as a judge and an office holder at rulers' court.

After he returned home, the account of this exceptional experience was written down and embellished by an official scribe of the Marinids, Ibn Djuzayy. This book in Arabic is commonly known as the *Rihla,* or "account of a journey." Although some doubts have been cast onto the authenticity of the most peripheral parts of the travels (to the Volga River or to China, for instance), or on the way these travels were recalled and recounted, the documentary value of the *Rihla* for the fourteenth-century Muslim world is outstanding. Of peculiar interest is Ibn Battuta's tacit agenda of making inventories and describing Muslim sanctuaries and legal systems as well as princes' courts and etiquette, depicting the Muslim community both in its unity and diversity, and thus resuscitating in a literary way the defunct caliphate of the previous centuries. Although possibly not entirely first-hand, Ibn Battuta's account of the kingdom of Mali is a vivid description of the *mansa* (king) Suleyman, his court and capital, and the political organization of the country.

See also **Morocco, History of (1000 to 1900); Travel and Exploration.**

BIBLIOGRAPHY

Dunn, Ross E. *The Adventures of Ibn Battuta: a Muslim Traveler of the 14th Century.* Berkeley and London: University of California Press, 2005.

Gibb, H. A. R. (continued by C. F. Beckingham). *The Travels of Ibn Battûta, A.D. 1325–1354.* 4 vols. Cambridge, U.K.: Cambridge University Press (for Hakluyt Society), 1958–1994.

FRANÇOIS-XAVIER FAUVELLE-AYMAR

IBN KHALDUN, ABD AL-RAHMAN

(1332–1406). Born in Tunis, Ibn Khaldun received a classical *madrasa* education there that included the study of the Qur'an, the sayings of the Prophet (*hadith*), Arab-Muslim philosophy, and the Arabic language. A combination of political disorder and the Black Death, which ravaged much of Europe and North Africa in the middle of the fourteenth century, motivated him to set out for Fez, which was at the time the region's most outstanding intellectual center. Often seen as a precursor of modern sociology, Ibn Khaldun was also an inheritor of the rationalist intellectual tradition that includes Aristotle and a succession of Greco-Islamic thinkers. After retiring in 1375 from the tumultuous politics of his era—Muslim rule in Spain was rapidly disintegrating—he wrote the *Muqaddima* (Introduction to History), a vast work that explores the nature of society, social organization, and dynastic change, often invoking as examples the societies and states of his day. Ibn Khaldun's approach to writing has been compared in style to that of the French historian Marc Bloch (1886–1944), cofounder of the *Annales* tradition of history, which emphasizes the underlying structure of society and of social relations over the narrative of surface events.

See also **History and the Study of Africa.**

BIBLIOGRAPHY

Dale, Stephen Frederic. "Ibn Khaldun: The Last Greek and the First *Annaliste* Historian." *International Journal of Middle East Studies* 38 (2006): 431–451.

Ibn Khaldun. *The* Muqaddimah: *An Introduction to History,* trans. Franz Rosenthal. 2nd edition. Princeton, NJ: Princeton University Press, 1967.

DALE F. EICKELMAN

IDRIS, AHMAD IBN (1749–1837).
The Moroccan teacher, mystic, and Muslim leader Ahmad ibn Idris was born in northern Morocco into a family that claimed descent from the Prophet Muhammad. He studied at the Qarawiyyin mosque school in Fez. His principal Sufi affiliation (*tariqa*) was the Shadhiliyya; his most important spiritual master was Abd at-Wahhab al-Tazi.

About 1798 Ibn Idris left Morocco and, after a short stay in Egypt, settled in Mecca, where he lived for the next thirty years, except for several visits to upper Egypt. In 1828, allegedly after public disagreements with other scholars in Mecca, he moved to Asir (part of present-day Saudi Arabia) and settled in the town of Sabyā, where he died and was buried.

Ibn Idris wrote very little—only some letters and lecture notes survive—and he did not establish a Sufi brotherhood. His importance lies in his role as teacher and spiritual guide to a number of students who established Sufi brotherhoods in Africa. His principal student was an Algerian, Muhammad ibn Ali al-Sanusi (1787–1859), who founded the Sanusiyya brotherhood in Libya and the central Sahara. The Sanusiyya led Libyan resistance to the Italian colonial occupation, and a grandson of al-Sunusi became King Idris I of independent Libya after World War II.

A second student was the Meccan Muhammad Uthman al-Mirghani (1793–1852), who had a complex relationship with his master. Al-Mirghani spread his order, the Khatmiyya, throughout the Nilotic Sudan. The Mirghani family played (and still plays) an important role in Sudanese politics during the Anglo-Egyptian Condominium period (1898–1956) through its political party, the Democratic Unionist Party.

A third student was the Sudanese Ibrahim al-Rashid (1813–1874), from whom stemmed a number of brotherhoods widespread in northeast Africa and beyond. The Rashidiyya remained largely a Sudanese order, but an offshoot founded by Ibrahim's nephew, Muhammad Salih, dominated northern Somalia and also found its way to Malaysia and Thailand. A prominent member of the Salihiyah in Somalia was Muhammad 'Abdallah Hasan (1856–1920), a Sufi poet who led a resistance movement against Ethiopian, British, and Italian aggression. Another student of Ibrahim al-Rashid was the Egyptian Muhammad ibn Ahmad al-Dandarawi (1839/40–1910/11), who established the Dandarawiyya, which is found in Southeast Asia.

In 1908 a great-grandson of Ibn Idris, Muhammad ibn Ali al-Idrisi (1876–1923), established a small state in Asir that survived until its peaceful incorporation into Saudi Arabia in 1932. The descendants of Ibn Idris live in Egypt and the Sudan, leading a small order known as the Idrisiyya or Ahmadiyya.

See also **Fez; Hasan, Muhammad 'Abdallah; Islam.**

BIBLIOGRAPHY

Ibn Idris, Ahmad. *The Exoteric Ahmad Ibn Idris: A Sufi's Critique of the Madhahib and the Wahhabis: Four Arabic Texts with Translation and Commentary*, ed. Bernd Radtke et al. Boston: Brill, 2000.

O'Fahey, Rex S. *Enigmatic Saint: Ahmad ibn Idris and the Idrisi Tradition*. Evanston, IL: Northwestern University Press, 1990.

Thamassen, Einar, and Bernd Radke, eds. *The Letters of Ahmad ibn Idris*. Evanston, IL: Northwestern University Press, 1993.

R. S. O'FAHEY

IFE (ILE-IFE).
Located in Osun State in southwestern Nigeria and with a population of about half a million people, the Yoruba city of Ife is world famous for three main reasons. First, it is the site of Obafemi Awolowo University, one of Africa's leading institutions whose emeritus professor (Wole Soyinka) won the Nobel Prize in Literature in 1986—the first African to be so honored. Second, the city (occupied as early as the fourth century BCE) is an archaeological gold mine, yielding a large number of naturalistic stone, terra-cotta, and brass sculptures dating between the eleventh and fifteenth centuries CE and attesting to a period of advanced cultural development and economic prosperity. Third, Yoruba oral traditions regard Ife as the center of creation from where not only the Yoruba but also all of humankind originated and dispersed to different parts of the world. Hence the city's full name, Ile-Ife, means Center of Dispersal.

The city's importance in local and national politics in the early twenty-first century derives essentially from this Edenic past and from its reputation as the cradle of Yoruba culture. A major attraction is the cycle of festivals commemorating creation and major events in Yoruba history. These festivals are presided over by the king (*Ooni*) of Ife, who claims direct descent from Oduduwa, the divine ancestor who allegedly created land out of the primordial sea at Ife and established a ruling dynasty to which other Yoruba kings trace their rights to wear the beaded crown. However, the ritualized mock battles associated with some of Ife festivals strongly suggest that, some time in the past, an invading group (apparently led by a culture hero later identified as Oduduwa) invaded Ife, conquered, and intermarried with the aboriginal population to create the complex culture now called the Yoruba.

See also **Festivals and Carnivals; Soyinka, Wole.**

BIBLIOGRAPHY

Adedeji, Joel A. "Folklore and Yoruba Drama: Obatala as a Case Study." In *African Folklore*, ed. Richard M. Dorson. Bloomington: Indiana University Press, 1972.

Akinjogbin, Isaac A., ed. *The Cradle of a Race: Ife from the Beginning to 1980*. Port Harcourt, Nigeria: Sunray, 1992.

Smith, Robert S. *Kingdoms of the Yoruba*. Madison: University of Wisconsin Press, 1988.

Willett, Frank. *Ife in the History of West African Sculpture*. London: Thames and Hudson, 1967.

BABATUNDE LAWAL

ILORI, ADAM ABDULLAHI AL-

(1917–1992). Of northern Yoruba ancestry, the Nigerian scholar Adam Abdullahi al-Ilori was brought up and educated in the Yoruba town of Ilorin, traveling also to Lagos, Nigeria, for study and later twice visiting the Middle East. In 1955 he founded the Center for Arabic Education at Agege, near Lagos, an institution designed to provide an Islamic education to young men through the medium of Arabic. Later he installed a printing press, which published his own writings and materials generated by the center. The graduates of his center have become important advocates of Arabic education in southern Nigeria.

Al-Ilori authored more than sixty works in Arabic, including a history of the Yoruba, a biographical dictionary of Yoruba scholars, and a history of Nigeria, as well as reformist works such as *Al-Islam wataqalid al-jahiliyya* (*Islam and Pre-Islamic Customs*). Ever forward looking, in his latter years he wrote *Islam and Human Rights* and *Islam and the Challenges of the Fifteenth Islamic Century.*

See also **Education, School; Islam.**

BIBLIOGRAPHY

Hunwick, John, and R. S. O'Fahey. *Arabic Literature of Africa*, Vol. 4: *The Writings of Central Sudanic Africa*. Boston: Brill, 2003.

JOHN HUNWICK

IMMIGRATION AND IMMIGRANT GROUPS

This entry includes the following articles:
AFRICAN AMERICAN
ARAB
CHINESE
EUROPEAN
INDIAN
LEBANESE

AFRICAN AMERICAN

During the eighteenth and nineteenth centuries African Americans from Brazil, the Caribbean, and the United States immigrated to various parts of Africa for different reasons. The major wave of migrants went to West Africa, though there is evidence that other parts of Africa also received immigrants. The perception that oppressive conditions within their societies did not allow them to live in racist-free nations precipitated emigration sentiments. There were other reasons for migration. One, frequently cited, was that as descendants of Africa, African Americans had a duty to help uplift and regenerate the continent of their ancestors. The desire and determination of black Americans to establish separate nations, which would be self-governing, was also cited as a reason for migration. The settlement of Liberia by blacks from the United States is perhaps the most well-known migration movement. Other migrations included Brazilians who settled in port cities in West Africa, and blacks from the United States and the Caribbean who settled in Sierra Leone. Like Sierra Leone, Libreville was settled by freed slaves from the French Caribbean.

During the late eighteenth and nineteenth centuries, blacks in the United States faced many challenges. As slavery hardened in the South, greater restrictions were put on African Americans, slave and free, while discrimination made conditions for northern blacks more oppressive. The American Revolution's ideals of liberty and equality strengthened the divisions between the races as Americans confronted their ideas about freedom and democracy. With the end of the revolution came an intense racism among whites, making life difficult for African Americans. Some African Americans began to question white rhetoric of liberty and justice for all. The need to maintain racial subordination in a slave society ensured that blacks would be restricted economically, politically, and socially. Increasingly, the expansion of democratic rights for whites was accompanied by diminution of black rights. Throughout the nineteenth century African Americans struggled to fit into American society. By the end of the nineteenth century blacks were virtually disenfranchised and discriminatory laws continued to impede their progress.

Though most African Americans fought against racial discrimination and oppression, struggling to better their situation, some believed they would never gain equality on American soil and sought other solutions. One such alternative was emigration and small groups of African Americans championed the cause of colonization. The controversial American Colonization Society (ACS) helped them in this endeavor. Established in 1816 the aim of the society was to colonize free blacks, preferably in Africa. Though lacking widespread support among African Americans, who saw it as deportation scheme, in 1821 the first African Americans settled in Liberia. By 1847 when Liberia became independent it was characterized by a largely Christian population of free and freed blacks.

Sierra Leone's origins were closely tied to the British antislavery movement. Its immigrant population included blacks loyal to the British in the American Revolution, Maroons (runaway slaves) from Jamaica, African Americans and West Indians who came to the colony for various reasons, and freed slaves settled by antislavery squadrons. In 1816 the black New England merchant, Paul Cuffe, brought thirty-eight settlers to Sierra Leone. Individual blacks from the United States and the Caribbean continued to make their way to the British colony over the course of the nineteenth century. The immigrant community evolved into a society largely made up of merchants and traders, who considered themselves different from to the indigenous people.

West Africa also received immigrants from Brazil. Beginning in the eighteenth century small numbers of blacks settled in Ouidah taking up trade as an occupation. Perhaps the most famous Brazilian settler was Francisco de Souza, who became a slave trader in Bénin. This small group would form the core of a larger community that was established later. After an 1835 slave revolt in Bahia, restrictions on the black population forced many blacks to emigrate. A small Brazilian community was established in Accra in 1836, and migration continued in small numbers. In the wake of Brazil's abolition of slavery in 1888 many ex-slaves migrated to Africa. They settled in Ouidah, Lagos, Badagry, Porto Novo and other West African cities, taking up various occupations.

The communities formed by all these immigrant groups were shaped and influenced by their experience in the Americas. Consequently, these immigrant communities did not always fare well. Cultural, economic, and political tensions often existed between black colonists and the indigenous African populations they encountered, resulting in skirmishes and all out conflicts. The identities the migrants created for themselves were often at odds with the African context and way of life. Though some settlers tried to strike a balance between their Eurocentric worldview and that of their African neighbors, friction often persisted. The immigrants believed they had brought much to Africa—Christianity, civilization as they defined it, and exposure to Western ways. Coming with these ideas, and the belief that their sojourn in the Americas had exposed them to these concepts, they felt duty-bound to share their values with their African brothers and sisters. This ethnic and cultural chauvinism and missionary mentality often served to devalue the rights, aspirations and culture of the indigenous population.

The immigrants helped to promote capitalist, Christian missionary, and Western cultural penetration of Africa. They introduced political ideas, trade practices, foods, and ideas about land ownership. For the most part, immigrant communities were hybrid societies and African cultural influences played a significant role. Furthermore, migration often served to raise consciousness and create nationalism among African Americans, even those who chose not to leave the Americas. Though they often faced many hardships in Africa immigrants had the opportunity to start new lives in freedom, unfettered by the discrimination and oppression they had faced in the Americas. Although some migrants did not find Africa to be the Promised Land they had hoped for, and returned, there were just as many migrants who, despite the hardship, expressed the idea that they would rather live free in hardship, than under a yoke of oppression in the Americas.

See also **Accra; Lagos; Liberia; Ouidah; Porto Novo; Refugees; Slave Trades.**

BIBLIOGRAPHY

Harris, Joseph E., ed. *Global Dimensions of the African Diaspora.* Washington, DC: Howard University Press, 1993.

Miller, Floyd. *The Search for a Black Nationality: Black Emigration and Colonization, 1787–1863.* Urbana: University of Illinois Press, 1975.

Ralston, Richard D. "The Return of Brazilian Freedmen to West Africa in the Eighteenth and Nineteenth Centuries." *Canadian Journal of African Studies* 3, no. 3 (Autumn 1969): 577–593.

Sanneh, Lamin O. *Abolitionists Abroad: American Blacks and the Making of Modern West Africa.* Cambridge, MA: Harvard University Press, 1999.

Shick, Tom. *Behold the Promised Land: A History of Afro-American Settler Society in Nineteenth Century Liberia.* Baltimore, MD: Johns Hopkins University Press, 1980.

NEMATA A. BLYDEN

ARAB

Arabs, meaning the various Arabic-speaking peoples of Arabia, may have been present as camel drivers in Egypt between the Nile and the Red Sea in Ptolemaic times. But large-scale entry of these peoples into Africa began with the Arab conquest of Egypt in 640–642, and developed in two main waves. The first, consisting of the tribal armies of Islam, conquered the former territories of the Roman empire in Africa as far as northern Morocco between 640 and 710. These armies established a series of camps on or near existing sites that rapidly grew into cities: Fustat (later Cairo); Barqa in Cyrenaica; Tripoli; Qayrawan (Kairouan) and Tunis in Tunisia; Tlemcen in Algeria; and Tangier in Morocco. As these cities developed, and others such as Alexandria and Fez were either occupied or founded, a civilian population that considered itself Arab by descent, language, religion and history grew out of the original garrisons in the course of the eighth and ninth centuries.

Ibn Khaldun, the fourteenth-century North African historian who belonged to this population, contrasted it with the Christian Copts of Egypt and the tribal Berbers of North Africa, but also with what he called the Arabs of the fourth generation. These were the tribesmen from whom the armies of the conquest had been drawn, but who had been left in the desert to carry on their nomadic way of life. Having followed or dropped out of the armies of the conquest in Egypt, these bedouin formed the second wave of Arab immigration into Africa. Establishing themselves in the Egyptian desert in the eighth and ninth centuries, they moved slowly southwards up the Nile into Nubia, and from the end of the tenth century onwards more rapidly westwards across the Sahara, to begin a further process of Arabization.

Implanted by invasion and settlement, the Arab element in the population of Egypt and North Africa thrived on the establishment of the Arab empire and the formation of Islam as a worldwide civilization. After the initial immigration of the Arabs in the seventh and eighth centuries, its numbers increased by recruitment and reproduction, and its share of the population as a whole by a combination of replacement and assimilation. Through the acquisition of clients, slaves, and women, the armies of the conquest became the nucleus of a growing population of mixed origin but Arab identity, which survived the replacement of the Arabs by troops of other nationalities in the armies of the Arab empire and its successors, and the consequent disappearance of what Ibn Khaldun

Detention camp in Tripoli. Illegal immigrants wait to be deported at a detention camp in Tripoli, October 2005. A large share of African traffic to Europe passes through Libya, which has over 1.2 million illegal immigrants representing every African nationality among its 5.6 million residents. OSAMA IBRAHIM/AFP/GETTY IMAGES

called the Arabs of the third generation into the mass of subjects of the Islamic state they had created.

In Egypt, in the confines of the Nile Valley and Delta, the expansion of that population into the countryside combined with the settlement of Arab bedouin from the desert to begin the establishment of Islam as the religion of the great majority of Egyptians, and Arabic as the language of them all. The process was slow: the indigenous Coptic Christian population may have remained in the majority down to the eleventh century. It was nevertheless continuous, partly as a result of conversion but more as a consequence of a higher rate of reproduction, which over the generations replaced the one population by the other, until Christians were in a small minority, and their Coptic language had been lost.

In Egypt Arabization outstripped Islamization. To the west of Egypt, in North Africa from Libya to Morocco, it lagged far behind, despite the arrival of Arab merchants and princes in the wake of the invading armies, and the multiplication of military and commercial foundations along the route of the conquest from Egypt into Spain. As in Egypt, the growth of the Arab population of the garrison cities out of the original immigrants was at the expense of the (Latin) Christian minority of the native population, which had disappeared by the twelfth century; except in Tunisia there was no Arab colonisation

of the countryside, where the great Berber majority of the native population was at least nominally Muslim from the time of the Arab conquest. Arab inroads into that population did not begin until the eleventh century, when the bedouin Arab tribes of the Banu Hilal moved westwards from Egypt in the second wave of Arab immigration into Africa. These were warriors whose victory at the battle of Haydaran in 1052 forced the Zirid sultan of (modern) Tunisia to abandon the old garrison city of Qayrawan. They were not, however, conquerors; instead they became the indispensable tribal allies of successive Berber dynasties as far west as Morocco. As nomads they occupied the lowlands and level uplands, while the mountains and hills were left to the Berbers. The population of the open countryside that they dominated became a mixture of peasants and nomads excluded from the warrior elite, for whom the Arabic of the bedouin, as distinct from the Arabic of the cities, became the dialect.

By the time of Ibn Khaldun towards the end of the fourteenth century the pattern was well established, and continued to develop down to the French conquest and occupation in the nineteenth and twentieth centuries. The warrior Arab nomad then disappeared, and nomadism itself was marginalized; but vernacular Arabic became established as the language of the majority of North Africans. The attempt since independence to complete this Arabization by the imposition of modern literary Arabic as the national language of each country, however, has proved difficult and divisive.

The spread of the Banu Hilal followed by the Banu Sulaym extended across the northern into the western Sahara. From Cyrenaica through to the Algeria Sahara, nomadic Berber peoples were either replaced or assimilated. In southern Morocco to the south of the High Atlas, immigrant Hilalians regrouped in the thirteenth century to form the Banu Ma'qil, from whom the tribes of the Banu Hassan moved southwards into the desert. By the end of the seventeenth century, traditionally after the war of Shurr Bubba, they had taken over from the Berber Sanhaja as the warriors of the western Sahara, above the existing Zwaya or "clerical" tribes, and introduced their Arabic dialect under the name of Hassaniya as the language of the region. The south-central Sahara remained in possession of their Berber counterparts, the Tuareg, but to the east the bedouin tribes grouped around Aswan moved up the Nile and across the desert from the end of the thirteenth century on to eliminate the two Christian kingdoms of Nubia and occupy the savanna as far south as Khartoum by the end of the fifteenth.

In the Nile valley itself a mixed Arab and Nubian population, the Ja'ali, came into existence. To either side of the river "Juhayna" is the comprehensive term for a population of Arab nomads, some of whom may have come from the Yemen. To the west of the Nile, through Kordofan and Darfur, these nomads are named after their animals: Kababish (shepherds) and Baggara (cattlemen). Toward Lake Chad they have met up with the bedouin of Libya to join the two migrations out of Egypt and form a continuous Arab population in the eastern Sahara.

In East Africa, a third wave of Arab immigration from the ninth century onwards was of a different kind, far less extensive but highly influential. It consisted of merchants from the Hadramawt in southern Arabia and the Gulf, who combined with the population of the coast of Kenya and Tanzania to create a series of Muslim city-states, most notably Kilwa in the thirteenth century. The most obvious product of the combination was the Swahili language, with its Bantu syntax and Arabic vocabulary, which, as a result of the opening up of the interior in the nineteenth century, has become the *lingua franca* of East Africa. In this a major part was played by the creation of the Arab Sultanate of Zanzibar by Omani Arabs from the Gulf in the first half of the century.

Such secondary waves of Arab immigration have occurred at intervals over the past thousand years. Arabs like the family of Ibn Khaldun, priding themselves on their descent from the conquerors, entered North Africa from Muslim Spain as their homeland fell to the Christian kingdoms of the peninsula from the middle of the thirteenth century to the conquest of Granada in 1492. From the thirteenth century onwards there appeared in North Africa and the Nilotic Sudan families of *ashraf* or *shurafa*, "nobles" who laid claim to descent from the Prophet and may have been immigrants from Arabia. Meanwhile the Nilotic Sudan was Islamized by an influx of scholars and saints from Arabia from the sixteenth century on. In the nineteenth and

twentieth centuries, Lebanese merchants took advantage of the European presence to establish themselves in West and East Africa.

From the beginning to the end of this long history of immigration, the question "who and what is an Arab" has been problematic. Defined by language, the modern Arabic-speaking population of northern Africa is divided by dialect, religion, nationality and ethnicity, and only partially unified by a common literary language, the media, and the cult of Arab nationalism. The importance of an Arab identity varies in consequence according to circumstance, among which immigration has given way to the emigration of Arabs out of Africa into Europe, a trend that seems set to continue.

See also **Alexandria; Cairo; Fez; Ibn Khaldun, Abd al-Rahman; Islam; Refugees; Tangier; Tripoli; Tunis; Zanzibar Sultanate.**

BIBLIOGRAPHY

Brett, Michael. *Ibn Khaldun and the Medieval Maghrib.* Aldershot, U.K.: Ashgate/Variorum, 1999.

Brett, Michael. "Population and Conversion to Islam in Egypt in the Mediaeval Period." In *Egypt and Syria in the Fatimid, Ayyubid and Mamluk Eras,* ed. U. Vermeulen and J. Van Steenbergen. Leuven: Uitgeverij Peeters, 2005.

Brett, Michael, and Elizabeth Fentress. *The Berbers.* Oxford: Blackwell, 1996.

Hasan, Yusuf Fadl. *The Arabs and the Sudan.* Edinburgh: Edinburgh University Press, 1967.

Horton, Mark, and John Middleton. *The Swahili.* Oxford: Blackwell, 2000.

Lane-Poole, Stanley. *The Story of Cairo.* London: J. M. Dent, 1902.

MacMichael, Harold A. *A History of the Arabs in the Sudan* [1922], 2 vols. London: Frank Cass, 1967.

Norris, Harry Thirlwall. *The Arab Conquest of the Western Sahara.* Harlow, Essex, U.K.: Longman, 1986.

MICHAEL BRETT

CHINESE

The first Chinese to immigrate to Africa arrived in the seventeenth century. Mainly merchants and artisans from Canton and Fujian, they settled along the Dutch-controlled coast of South Africa and in Mauritius, which served as a gateway to Madagascar,

Réunion Island, Cape Colony, and Natal. By the middle of the nineteenth century, there were more than 1,160 Chinese merchants in Mauritius, as well as a number of craftsmen and agricultural workers. Chinese shopkeepers were operating in Madagascar by 1862, and Chinese services such as laundries grew common in the larger towns. Indentured workers from China were recruited to work in the sugar fields (1844) and tea plantations (1901) of Réunion, and in construction in Madagascar (1896). Chinese laborers were imported for a railway project in the French Congo and to work in the goldmines in the Gold Coast (present-day Ghana) and South Africa. Immigration of Chinese women in the late nineteenth century expanded the Chinese communities in areas such as Mauritius and Réunion.

By the 1940s, South Africa, Mauritius, Réunion Island, and Madagascar each had some 4,000 Chinese residents, and Rhodesia, Tanganyika, and Kenya hosted smaller settlements. Immigration to Africa slowed after the Communist victory in 1949 in China, and began to reverse after African independence in the 1960s. Natural increases, however, had expanded the size of the Chinese communities. By the end of the twentieth century, the largest Chinese communities were still those in Madagascar (18,000), Mauritius (25,000), Réunion (20,000–25,000), and South Africa (20,000–25,000).

Chinese immigrants in countries with larger Chinese populations tended to preserve their identities, establishing Chinese schools, temples, and business associations, and celebrating Chinese New Year. The early male settlers often formed relationships with local African women, and frequently taught their offspring to speak Chinese. In the early twenty-first century, the Chinese language and culture remain fairly strong in Mauritius (which has three Chinese-language newspapers) and in parts of South Africa (Johannesburg has two Chinese-language newspapers).

After 1978, as China began its Open Door policy, increased trade and an expanded aid program led to a renewal of interest in African settlement. A number of Chinese were sent by their provinces to establish aid projects and trade outlets, while Chinese business networks sparked industrial development in Mauritius and parts of Nigeria and Lesotho.

China's voracious demand for resources, and the "go global" policy enunciated in 2001, sharply accelerated trade, investment, and aid across the sub-continent. South African officials have accused local Chinese criminal gangs or 'triads' of organized sex trafficking, abalone poaching, and the import of counterfeit goods. By 2007, from 80,000 to 100,000 Chinese immigrant workers were employed in African factories, infrastructure projects, and private Chinese shops.

See also **Madagascar and Western Indian Ocean, History of; Refugees; Réunion; Travel and Exploration: Chinese.**

BIBLIOGRAPHY

Eisenman, Joshua, and Joshua Kurlantzick, "China's Africa Strategy." *Current History* May 2006: 219–224.

Pan, Lynn, ed. *The Encyclopedia of the Chinese Overseas.* Cambridge, MA: Harvard University Press, 1999.

Snow, Philip. *The Star Raft: China's Encounter with Africa.* Ithaca, New York: Cornell University Press, 1989.

DEBORAH A. BRAUTIGAM
REVISED BY JAMIE MONSON

EUROPEAN

During the fifteenth century, Europeans, stimulated by the early interest in spices and other riches, explored the African coast. When the Portuguese, in 1482, built a fortress, São Jorge da Mina (present-day Elmina in Ghana), on the Gold Coast, they established a new presence in tropical Africa. In time the Danes (1642) the Swedes (1647), and the Brandenburgers (1682) came, all building forts to support trading posts. By the seventeenth century the Portuguese had completed the outline of the African coast, and traders (and slavers) had become a common presence. Subsequently explorers, starting with James Bruce in 1769, moved into the interior to explore and map, what was for them, the dark continent.

Two regions, the Gold Coast and its immediate environs and the Cape of Good Hope, experienced the bulk of this early European concentration. In the Gold Coast region, Portuguese remained the language of trade even after the Dutch replaced the Portuguese. From 1594 the Dutch East India Company, under a board of directors, was responsible for settlements in western Africa. It established control of the Gold Coast in 1637 and the Cape in 1652. Both locations were initially marked by castle or fortress occupation, dependence on locals for food products, and sexual relations with local African women resulting in a hybrid population group.

In the meantime, during the 1530s and 1550s, respectively, the English and French had explored and settled traders in West Africa. Three centuries later, a French and British presence along the western African coast was firmly established and permanent European traders were resident in coastal towns. The interior of much of Africa was discouraging to European settlers due not only to inhospitable peoples but also to diseases such as malaria, blackwater fever, and sleeping sickness. Only after 1850, with the discovery of the prophylactic actions of quinine, was it possible for European settler groups to gain a degree of immunity from at least one of these tropical diseases, namely malaria. Between the first and second halves of the century there was a 75 percent drop in the death rate among Europeans in Africa.

Germany was a latecomer to the West African trade. In 1849 a large Hamburg company started trading in western Africa, and by 1880 German traders were present in much of Gabon, Togo, the Cameroons, and Southwest Africa. In the early 1880s France moved to protect its trading priorities, thus straining relations with the Germans. The Berlin Conference (1884–1885) was convened to bring order to the scramble for African territories, and European powers partitioned Africa. The colonial era formally began.

Before the seventh century northwest Africa was occupied by the indigenous Berber peoples. Following the death of Mohammed, Muslim Arabs spread along the north rim of Africa establishing what would become Morocco, Algeria, and Tunisia. In 1830 Algeria was occupied by French forces establishing the region as a military colony. After 1870 French settlers gradually moved into Algeria as the French government centralized its empire, setting up French style government institutions and incorporating the colonies as parts of France Outre-Mer. The latter part of the nineteenth century saw an influx of European settlers but simultaneously large numbers of young Algerians, mostly men, settling in France.

.Southern and East Africa formed part of the British Empire. Expanding its land holdings, Britain reached beyond South Africa to claim the trans-Limpopo territory. In the mid-1800s missionaries were established in Matabeleland and Barotseland. By 1889, Cecil John Rhodes had established the Chartered Company and in 1891 the lands north of the Zambezi were formally placed under the Charter thus becoming a Protectorate under the British South Africa Company. What emerged were Southern Rhodesia (present-day Zimbabwe), Nyasaland (Malawi), and Northern Rhodesia (Zambia). This was part of Rhodes' dream of British territory "from Cape to Cairo." In 1953 these three territories were administratively linked as the Central African Federation. There were approximately 7 million Africans and 213,000 whites, mostly from the British Isles and South Africa. While the Federation was fragmenting, Southern Rhodesia changed to Rhodesia in 1964 and Premier Ian Smith issued a Unilateral Declaration of Independence the following year.

In the meantime Britain had established a presence in east Africa by creating the protectorate of Uganda in 1894. The whole area to the east coast was administered by the Imperial British East Africa Company. In July 1895 this area became a British Protectorate. Ten years later the East African Protectorate was transferred from Britain's Foreign Office to the Colonial Office. As responsible government was extended by Britain, Uganda and Kenya emerged. Kenya has some of the best and some of the worst climates in central Africa and its local affairs were administered from Nairobi. Soon white settlers from the British Isles found the highlands desirable. Negotiations had also been carried on between the administration and Boers following the Anglo-Boer War in South Africa. Between 1904 and 1914 a sizable number of Boers settled in Kenya coining the term "the White highlands."

At this point it is essential to differentiate national philosophies concerning the colonies because they influenced settlement policy. The egalitarian doctrines expressed so strongly in the French Revolution were at the basis of the French assimilationist theories. Colonies were seen as parts of the mother country, colonial peoples were to be assimilated as French, and population mobility was not restricted. As large new regions in western Africa were added assimilation made way for association which recognized and valued native institutions. By contrast, British policy from the beginning was aimed at retaining traditional culture (indirect rule) while encouraging settlement by Europeans. Portugal in theory aimed at producing assimilados but in fact kept the population as an indigena class while Europeans settlers performed much of the skilled work. The Belgian Congo, in certain respects like the Portuguese territories, was run by a small group of interlocking companies and the Roman Catholic Church. German policies were essentially aimed at extracting wealth from the colonies while permitting settlement essentially by company and business representatives.

DISTRIBUTION

By 1900, people in coastal towns in western Africa had lived with Europeans among them for three centuries, and in other regions for shorter periods. In South Africa the Great Trek had resulted in a population expansion into the interior and the establishment of independent republics. In East Africa, European rule resulted in a German-controlled region (later called Tanganyika, after Ruanda and Urundi were excised), a British-controlled protectorate (later called Kenya), and Uganda Protectorate. European settlers moved into the higher elevations, where a milder climate was more hospitable. The largest number of European settlers, however, made their homes in central Africa (the Rhodesias and Nyasaland) and in South Africa.

In most of Africa the majority of European settlers came to work or farm the colonial regions administered by their home governments. The majority retained their citizenship and thus could return if matters did not suit them or if conditions deteriorated. Children were frequently sent away to school, even to the mother country, and aging settlers usually returned home upon retirement.

The Federation of French West Africa stretched from coastal settlements (such as Senegal, French Guinea, Côte d'Ivoire and Dahomey) all the way to Algeria in the north, but European settlers were sparse. Further south, Portuguese settlers were of two kinds: in Angola there were essentially poor peasants who could make a better living than they did in Portugal; Mozambique, because of growing

industrialization, required skilled workers. Permanent European settlers in South Africa had created a firm economic infrastructure, and universities produced professionals while technical colleges were training workers. Due in part to the mild climate as well as the permanence and numbers that marked the European presence in South Africa, settlers continued to arrive from many European and African countries.

A number of internal European migrations contributed to population distribution and linkages. Various treks, marked by the Great Trek of 1838, took place between 1836 and 1846 as Afrikaners moved into the interior, even north of the Limpopo River. In 1875 (and again in 1905) disgruntled Afrikaners, mostly from the South African Republic (Transvaal), left South Africa and trekked into Angola, the main group settling at Humpata while others went to Bihe. Most of these people were repatriated to Southwest Africa (which South Africa administered under the League of Nations Mandate) in 1928. By 1960 there were still eighty-five families of Afrikaner extraction living in the Huila and Benguela districts.

Following the Anglo-Boer War, in 1902 more than 1,300 Afrikaners—mostly from Transvaal and the Orange Free State—settled in eastern Africa, first at Meru in Tanganyika and finally at Eldoret in Kenya. In time this community functioned like a colony; its members formed a congregation of the Dutch Reformed Church; a pastor was sent from South Africa; settlers sent their children to school in South Africa; and they retained their ethnic and linguistic identity. When Kenya gained independence in 1963 there were about 55,000 non-Africans, predominantly persons of European descent (as well as Arabs and Asians). Currently this category comprises less than one percent of the population.

In a less organized way, but producing many of the same consequences, there was a continuous movement of South Africans of European descent north into what became the Central African Federation. The largest influx of settlers (about 180,000) occurred after World War II, with the majority of immigrants coming from South Africa (31%) and the British Isles (28%). Africanization policies were introduced during the immediate postindependence years, producing less security for Europeans. The result was a reverse migration as large numbers of European settlers moved to

South Africa from Zaire, Zambia, and Kenya (in the 1960s), and more than a decade later also from Angola, Mozambique, and Zimbabwe.

POPULATION FIGURES

Statistics for population tend to show a gradual increase of European settlers under colonial administration and then a significant decline immediately following independence. Thus between June and November 1975, 275,600 *retornados* (returning migrants) arrived in Portugal from Angola. In some African countries, such as Côte d'Ivoire, there is again an increased European presence, though Africanization has discouraged a large presence of expatriates.

By 1950 about 1 million Europeans (only half of whom were French) lived in Algeria. They were almost exclusively urban dwellers—Europeans owned about 26,000 farms—performed professional and skilled work and served as traders. In 1959 there was a non-Arab population of 1,025,000 (85% European and 15% Jewish). But struggles for independence had started. A peak of European settlement was reached in 1956 before hostilities caused rapid emigration of the *pied noirs* (or "black feet" as the European descendants of long-term settlers were called) and Jews as well as capital. At independence in 1962 all European land holdings (about 40% of the total cultivated area) were nationalized and the European population dropped to 50,000.

Most white Rhodesians were town-dwellers. Most of the country was owned by whites who constituted less than five percent of the population. The two major cities, which contained the largest white populations as well as the majority of African wage-earners, were Salisbury (present-day Harare) and Bulawayo. Under Ian Smith Rhodesia experienced Unilateral Declaration of Independence in 1965, became a Republic in 1970, and in 1978 (after years of guerrilla hostilities) negotiated an accord with three black leaders. In 1980 the first democratic elections took place. Less than one percent of the population was white yet they owned 70 percent of the arable land. In 1999 there has been a major policy of land redistribution. Under the Robert Mugabe government Europeans and other non-Africans (Arab and Asian) have left in large numbers. The total population is over 9 million and less than 1 percent

is white and the numbers are dwindling due to administrative pressure.

Population data for Africa are notoriously suspect, owing in part to difficulties in counting, incomplete censuses, and population displacement. The figures presented here have been gleaned from official sources, but no official census figures exist for most of Africa. One should also remember that Europeans in Africa were predominantly urban dwellers. Even in Rhodesia (before it became Zimbabwe) only 15 percent of the European settlers lived in rural areas, and close to 62 percent of the total lived in Salisbury and Bulawayo.

In most countries European settler presence has declined—in some instances quite dramatically—particularly in the farming sector. Yet the French have increased their presence in Gabon and Côte d'Ivoire, where there are currently about 50,000 in each country, and also in the People's Republic of the Congo. The figures for South Africa are misleading. Immediately preceding and following that country's move to majority rule in 1994, large numbers of professional and skilled persons of European descent emigrated. Most of them went to Australia, Canada, the United States, and European countries.

OCCUPATIONS

Europeans who came to Africa did so essentially in three phases. The first were traders and missionaries, followed by (colonial) administrators, and finally by skilled workers, technicians, and farmers. The third category of settler was particularly sensitive to improvements in protective medicine, hygiene, and sanitation as well as developments in communication and transportation. Each category of settler had a definite influence on the African scene.

Towns and cities frequently grew as a result of European settlements; cities such as Salisbury, Bulawayo, Dakar, Leopoldville, and Nairobi were conspicuous for their large numbers of European residents. Areas such as the Copperbelt and Katanga (later Shaba) drew miners, technicians, and engineers.

Farming in Africa presented new challenges. Europeans tended to locate in the milder uplands: the High Veld (South Africa), Benguela Highlands (Angola), Kivu Highlands (Congo), or the Great Rift Valley (Kenya and Tanganyika). These regions were free of tsetse fly, with the result that imported beef and dairy breeds were viable and could be crossbred with native cattle for a hardy stock. Poor soils and prolonged drought periods militated against large-scale agricultural undertakings except in South Africa. What plantation farming there was (sisal, cotton, coffee, tea) could not long compete on the world markets. In the years before independence the Office de la Recherche Scientifique et Technique d'Outre-Mer (in French colonies), the Institut National pour l'Étude Agronomique du Congo Belge, the Junta das Missoes Geograficas e de Investigacoes do Ultramar (in Portuguese colonies), and a number of research institutes in British colonies and many others, some under U.S. Agency for International Development (USAID) or United Nations (UN) direction, aimed at improving the scientific basis of farming. Higher-yielding, disease-resistant strains of field and tree crops were introduced, and livestock were better adapted as a consequence of research.

Throughout the colonial period, Europeans were awarded skilled jobs and opportunities to train and qualify for these jobs. This was also true on state-owned railways (e.g., in Rhodesia), in factories, and in mines. The result was that Europeans enjoyed a favored status and a pay differential that made it profitable for many to live in the colonies.

CULTURAL FEATURES

During the colonial and early postcolonial years social interaction was highly selective. As a result of financial conditions and ethnic preferences, Europeans tended to form residential and cultural enclaves. The solid brick homes in segregated neighborhoods, all-white schools, and restricted country clubs marked colonial cities. So, too, did the Saturday afternoon cricket, rugby, or tennis matches and the leisurely golf games. A glass of sherry as the sun set or an evening playing bridge and enjoying a cognac or two always involved only fellow Europeans. It is said that even as the French turned over parts of western Africa to independent rule, most of the departing officials had never entertained an African in their home. That is equally true for most of Africa.

Persons of European extraction who live in Africa today include essentially two categories: those who for financial and other reasons cannot leave, and those who live there by choice. In each case appropriate interaction patterns and cultural

expressions have emerged. The former continue a neocolonial social network, whereas the second have increasingly integrated their lives and cultures with modern Africa and its peoples.

See also **Bulawayo; Colonial Policies and Practices; Dakar; Harare; Islam; Mugabe, Robert; Nairobi; Refugees; Rhodes, Cecil John; Travel and Exploration: European.**

BIBLIOGRAPHY

Abshire, David M., and Michael A. Samuels, eds. *Portuguese Africa: A Handbook.* London: Pall Mall Press, 1969.

Blake, John W. *Europeans in West Africa, 1450–1560.* London: Hakluyt Society, 1942.

Brelsford, W. V., ed. *Handbook of the Federation of Rhodesia and Nyasaland.* London: Cassell and Co., 1960.

Crowder, Michael. *West Africa under Colonial Rule.* Evanston, IL: Northwestern University Press, 1968.

Gann, Lewis H., and Peter Duigan. *White Settlers in Tropical Africa.* Baltimore, MD: Johns Hopkins University Press, 1962.

Hailey, Lord. *An African Survey.* London: Oxford University Press, 1938.

Hibbert, Christopher. *Africa Explored: Europeans in the Dark Continent, 1769–1889.* London: Cooper Square Publishers, 2002.

Nelson, Harold D., et. al. *Area Handbook for Southern Rhodesia.* Washington, DC: U.S. Government Printing Office, 1975.

Oliver, Roland, and Michael Crowder. *The Cambridge Encyclopedia of Africa.* London: Cambridge University Press, 1981.

BRIAN M. DU TOIT

INDIAN

While the people of the Indian subcontinent had contact with Africa as early as the first millennium BCE their substantial settlements there began only in the second half of the nineteenth century. Indian merchants served the Sultan in Zanzibar from the 1830s. In the 1840s, there were 3,000 Indians in Zanzibar and Pemba, and an equal number on the mainland. British imperial rule in India and the expansion of colonial rule in eastern, central, and southern Africa from the 1890s provided both the incentive and the structures for Indian settlement and dispersal in those areas. Together with the Lebanese and Chinese, Indians make up the largest non-African diasporic communities.

By 1904 British rulers imported 32,000 indentured Indians to help build railways in East Africa in order to consolidate imperial hold over the region. Some 7,000 Indians remained behind. They encouraged other Indians to exploit commercial opportunities. Sir John Kirk, then the British agent at Zanzibar, hoped that eastern Africa would become "India's America," and indeed some Indians aspired to the creation of Greater India in this region. Two thousand Indians helped to manage and run the railways. British colonial rulers similarly used Parsi clerks, Punjabi soldiers and policemen, and Gujarati traders. Indians, however, contributed in the growth of the manufacturing sector. They numbered about 34,000 in 1914, and increased to 105,000 by 1939. About the time that the eastern African countries (Kenya, Uganda, and Tanzania) achieved independence in the 1960s, the total Asian population had reached 366,000.

South Africa received two categories of immigrants from India. The first was state-sponsored indentured Indians who began arriving in 1860 on five-year contracts to work on sugar plantations in Natal, over one-third of whom elected to remain in South Africa. In the 1870s a second, much smaller group of Indians began arriving from western parts of India or from Mauritius in the Indian Ocean, to engage in trade. By 1910, when the Union of South Africa was established, the South African Indian population was 150,000, and increased to 477,000 by 1960.

Small numbers of South Africa's Indians migrated to neighboring countries such as Botswana, Lesotho, Malawi, Swaziland, Zambia, and Zimbabwe. The Indian population in Mozambique came mainly from Portuguese-held enclaves in India, most notably Goa. Immigration of indentured Indians to Mauritius swelled their numbers to 450,000 by 1909, most of whom remained on the island.

The Indian immigrants who settled in these parts of Africa were widely divergent in their cultural and religious backgrounds. Coming from western and northeastern areas of India, the immigrants in eastern Africa were predominantly Hindus and Muslims, with sprinklings of Jains, Sikhs, Ismailis, Goans, and Parsis, who spoke Gujarati, Kutchi, Hindi, Marathi, or Urdu. In South Africa, south

India and the Ganges plains introduced Telegu-, Tamil-, and Bhojpuri-speakers.

The immigrants' long contact with formal Western education in Africa helped them to acquire new identities with proficiency in a European language, most notably English. They also attained varying degrees of facility in regional indigenous tongues such as Swahili and Zulu. While the Indians gained some familiarity with the indigenous peoples, official colonial policies and convention combined to keep them in separate ethnic groups creating social distances between themselves and the indigenous populations. In their new environments, Indians largely experienced a rise in social, educational, and economic status. They engaged in retail and wholesale trade, and many entered the professions. In South Africa, a significant proportion of Indians became industrial workers and teachers. Indians were concentrated in urban centers like Dar es Salaam, Durban, Johannesburg, and Nairobi, mainly because of their exclusion from the agricultural sector.

Indian political developments have been unique in each setting, but it is nevertheless possible to divide them into three broad categories. First, in the colonial setting, the earlier official view of the Indians' usefulness in consolidating imperial interests gave way to intransigent white-settler opposition to unrestricted immigration and equality. In South Africa, this policy gave rise to the Indian nationalist leader Mohandas K. Gandhi (1869–1948), who launched his famous *satyagraha* (passive resistance) campaign in 1906. Second, in the pre-independence period Indians had the option of accepting modest communal rights or aligning themselves with the African liberation movements. Even when they opted for communal representation, as in East Africa where some considered them "junior partners" in colonial administration, significant Indian leadership supported independence and, as in South Africa, made common cause with the liberation organizations.

Third, in the period since independence, Indians have had to adjust to the realities of African majority rule. Upwardly mobile Africans saw Indian middle-level entrepreneurs as obstacles to their improvement. Indians generally remained socially separate from African communities. The resulting tensions have resulted in friction and their

Mohandas K. Gandhi, surrounded by workers in his law office in Johannesburg, South Africa, in 1902. With Gandhi are his clerk, H. S. L. Polak (left), and Miss Schlesin (right), a Russian woman; behind them are two office clerks. Gandhi, the country's first person of color to be admitted to the bar, spent most of his twenty years in South Africa protesting the treatment of Indians by the British. © AP IMAGES

gradual re-migration to non-African countries or, as in the case of Uganda, in the expulsion of 74,000 Indians by Idi Amin Dada in 1972. Some 300,000 Asians left eastern and central Africa since 1970, over two-thirds of whom have settled in the United Kingdom. In South Africa, the introduction of apartheid after 1948 heightened racially based inequities. With democratic rule in place since 1994, Indian and whites are adjusting to the pressures of the redistributive reconstruction process. In Mauritius, Indians, who make up a majority, have helped to create democratic rule.

The distribution of Indians in Africa has shifted dramatically since the 1980s, with large numbers only in South Africa and Mauritius, where they number 1.2 million (2.6%) and 800,000 (68%) respectively in 2004. New immigrants from South Asian nations have settled in eastern, central, and southern parts in the wake of their closer economic ties with Africa. Uganda has encouraged émigré Indians to return. The estimated numbers of Indians in the rest of Africa are as follows: Botswana 9,000 (2000); Kenya, 70,000 (2000); Malawi, 5,700 (1991); Mozambique 15,000 (2004); Uganda 10,000 (1989); Réunion 240,000 (2000); Swaziland 220 (1990); Tanzania, 40,000 (2000); Zambia, 10,000 (1970); and Zimbabwe, 12,000 (2004). On the reverse side, 250,000 descendants of Africans living in India came from places along the east African coast between the Sudan and Mozambique.

See also **Amin Dada, Idi; Apartheid; Colonial Policies and Practices; Dar es Salaam; Johannesburg; Nairobi; Refugees.**

BIBLIOGRAPHY

Beachy, R. W. *A History of East Africa, 1592–1902.* New York: Tauris Academic Studies, 1996.

Bhana, Surendra, and J. B. Brain. *Setting Down Roots: Indian Migrants in South Africa, 1860–1911.* Johannesburg, South Africa: Witwatersrand University Press, 1990.

Ghai, Dharam, P., and Yash P. Ghai, eds. *Portrait of a Minority: Asians in East Africa.* Nairobi, East Africa: Oxford University Press, 1970.

Gregory, Robert G. *South Asians in East Africa: An Economic and Social History, 1890–1980.* Boulder, CO: Westview Press, 1993.

Indian Diaspora. Available from http://www.ahtg.net/TpA/indiasp.html.

Mamdani, Mahmood. *From Citizen to Refugee: Ugandan Asians Come to Britain.* London: Frances Pinter Ltd., 1973.

Mangat, J. S. *A History of the Asians in East Africa, c. 1886 to 1945.* Oxford Studies in African Affairs. Oxford: Clarendon Press, 1969.

Non-Residents Indians. Available from http://www.indiaatbest.com/nriindex.htm.

Ogot, B. A., and W. R. Ochieng. *Decolonization and Independence in Kenya 1940–1993.* Athens: Ohio University Press, 1995.

SURENDRA BHANA

LEBANESE

Arabic-speaking peoples of the Levant (Jordan, Syria, and Lebanon) have been dwelling in West Africa since the late nineteenth century. Locally called Lebanese, these early migrants, mostly Maronite Christians, settled in rural centers and initially made an inconspicuous living as petty traders. In the wake of the expanding colonial cash-crop economy during the interwar period, many of them became intermediaries between European companies exporting agricultural commodities and African peasant farmers. After independence, Lebanese traders started concentrating in urban centers where some ventured into textile and hardware trade, whereas others set up grocery shops, warehouses, and supermarkets. Their numbers gradually increased throughout the 1970s, and the outbreak of the 1975 Lebanese civil war marked an intensified influx of migrants, mainly Shia and Sunni Muslims. In addition to expanding their trading activities, some of them diversified around this time into running restaurants, managing hotels, and operating small manufacturing industries.

The Lebanese presence in contemporary West Africa is closely related to the new markets that emerged alongside the widespread adoption of economic liberalization policies by African governments since the 1980s. For instance, Lebanese businessmen, some descendants of the early traders, others without previous acquaintance with Africa, came to play a prominent role in the burgeoning (international) money transfer system, secondhand car trade, and travel business. By drawing on an extensive migration network, these Lebanese businessmen developed an advanced form of vertical business integration that linked West African economies to the wider world. Their consequent control of crucial aspects of new forms of economic activity reiterated the stereotype of Lebanese businessmen as successful entrepreneurs. Yet in reality Lebanese enterprise can go through a rapid succession of different economic activities with diverging outcomes, resulting in financial losses and periodic outmigration of bankrupt businessmen.

In early-twenty-first-century West Africa, Lebanese are organized into distinct migrant communities that are open social entities: Members maintain contacts with other migrant communities and with the African societies wherein they reside. As a consequence, although Lebanese businessmen depend on close family members at the beginning of their careers, later on their business network may include contacts with Lebanese peers and Africans. Contacts with colleagues often originate in bars, clubs, and other places of entertainment, and they are subsequently reproduced at markets, ports, and similar centers of economic activity.

Lebanese car trader with Nigerian employee on West Africa's main second-hand car market in Cotonou, Bénin. Lebanese businessmen are closely associated with the emergence of new product markets in late-twentieth-century Africa. For instance, in the fast-growing second-hand car business from Europe to West Africa, Lebanese control the sourcing and transportation. PHOTOGRAPH BY J. P. BRUGGEMAN

Lebanese-African relations stem chiefly from a shared profession or trade. Common examples are the recruitment of labor or the issuing of credit to former employees, but it may also include more balanced forms of collaboration, such as joint ventures with African entrepreneurs. Relationships between Lebanese men and African women present a more contested form of social contact; although such liaisons are widespread, they rarely result in formal marriage. In sum, Lebanese-African relations are extensive, yet in the popular imagination Lebanese feature as a special social grouping. Although that appears consistent with the expulsion of the Lebanese in the recent past (for instance, Lebanese were expelled from Ghana in 1969–1970, and from Côte d'Ivoire in 2003–2004) and with violence against them in the present, Lebanese communities remain firmly embedded in West African society through a network of informal and personal contacts.

See also **Refugees.**

BIBLIOGRAPHY

Beuving, Joost. "Lebanese Traders in Cotonou: A Socio-cultural Analysis of Economic Mobility and Capital Accumulation." *Africa: Journal of the International African Institute* no. 76 (2006): 324–351.

Boone, Catherine. "Trade, Taxes, and Tribute: Market Liberalizations and the New Importers in West Africa." *World Development* no. 22 (1994): 453–467.

Rais, Marina. *The Lebanese of West Africa: An Example of a Trading Diaspora.* Berlin: Das Arabische Buch, 1988.

Van der Laan, Laurens. "Migration, Mobility, and Settlement of the Lebanese in West Africa." In *The Lebanese in the World: a Century of Emigration*, ed. Albert Hourani and Nadim Shedani. London: Tauris, 1992.

J. JOOST BEUVING

IMPERIALISM. *See* Colonialism and Imperialism.

INCOME DISTRIBUTION. *See* Stratification, Social.

INDEPENDENCE AND FREEDOM, EARLY AFRICAN WRITERS.

The original wave of interest in early African writers focused on celebrating the writers' presence using the written word to defend Africa against racist imperial denigration. Africans writing before about 1940, for example, were typically presented as precursors to the nationalist movements that swept the continent in the mid-twentieth century because they imagined more noble pasts and more promising futures for Africa than did most Europeans.

A generation or more since these movements won independence, however, the nationalist movement is widely recognized as only a troubled phase in a longer and more complex struggle by Africans to define their place in the world while seeking justice, order, and security in the face of both external and internal challenges. This development, in turn, has encouraged scholars to develop new perspectives on early African writers. Although the latter clearly helped establish the ideological content and political forums for independence movements, early African writers had far more complex concerns—and left much richer legacies—than initial appreciations made apparent. They engaged many of the issues that endure in contemporary African intellectual life and not only confronted colonial domination, but also sought out the knowledge that might provide the foundation for truly independent and viable modern African states and societies. They needed to understand the qualities of African societies in order to not just preserve but also remake them, to ask how Africans' pasts and futures connect to narratives beyond the continent, to criticize ongoing social change, and to define and protect Africans' identity in the modern world.

In appreciating these complex concerns scholars writing since about 1990 have also freed African writers from the binary constructions typical of the nationalist era. Whereas early African writers often pitted themselves as Africans against the outside world, some also joined organizations and found common cause with non-Africans. If African writers regularly spoke as Africans defending their race or continent against its detractors, they also spoke with many voices about the relations between Africa and its diaspora, and among Africans on the continent.

Precolonial writers pursued many of these concerns in different contexts. One informative example is the early nineteenth century Swahili poetry by Muyaka bin Haji (1776–1840) and Zahidi Mngumi debating the impact of Omani imperial expansion along the Kenyan coast. This poetic tradition of social commentary and criticism continued into the European colonial period with such notable Swahili writers as Shaaban Robert (1909–1962), and lives on in the culture of popular Swahili poetry and song. The Sudanic region provides many other examples, much enlarged by the collection of manuscripts in and around Tombouctou. Mahmoud Kati's (d. 1593) *Tarikh at-fattash* and 'Abd al-Rahman al-Sadi's (c. 1569–1655) *Tarikh al-Sudan* both completed in the seventeenth century, locate and acclaim the Songhay Empire within the narrative of Islamic history. Islamic reformers from the late eighteenth century and especially the nineteenth century, driven by crises arising from slave trading and other economic changes and shaped by wider Islamic intellectual movements, wrote on pressing social, political, and religious issues. Notable here is among these was 'Uthman dan Fodio, founder of the Sokoto Caliphate.

As Europe's impact on Africa pressed deeper after the seventeenth century, new problems arose, not least from the slave trade's effects. This contact also generated small communities of Africans literate in European languages. As Europeans came to interfere more broadly in Africa, so African writings in European languages became an increasingly important forum of African response. From its inception, this writing in European form also engaged the content of European thinking about Africa. A constant theme of African writing from the eighteenth century forward is the defense of Africans against the negative ideas associated with the Atlantic slave trade, and later the racism that underpinned colonial rule. But ideas about Africa in the Atlantic world were never monolithic, and Africans of all eras could find voices more sympathetic—or at least useful—outside the mainstream: abolitionists were key early on, select educators, missionaries, and activists later. African writers constantly adopted or adapted such ideas to their case, as they also made use of the wider traditions of European political and social thought.

Two notable early works are attacks on the slave trade by former victims of it: *Thoughts and Sentiments on the Evil and Wicked Traffic of the Slavery and Commerce of the Human Species* (1787) by Ottobah Cuguano (b. c. 1757), and *The Interesting Narrative of the Life of Olaudah Equiano or Gustavus Vassa, the African* (1789). Both illustrated the humanity of their natal societies (Fante and Igbo respectively) against slavers' presumptions of depravity, and combined economic, biblical, and moral arguments to push the case for abolition sharply forward. Over time clear traditions of thought developed between generations of African writers, but these traditions always intersected with contemporary thought in the wider world.

Significant communities of African writers appeared along the west coast from the early nineteenth century where, within the context of abolition and growing commodity trade, mission education, commercial exchange, and new port cities generated growing numbers of male clerics, clerks, teachers, entrepreneurs, and professionals. From these groups writers soon emerged, using newspapers to discuss issues of concern to them. Women, however, would only appear in force

within the educated community and as writers from the middle of the twentieth century. The earliest papers run by Europeans came out early in the nineteenth century; African-run papers proliferated from the middle of that century in Sierra Leone, Ghana, and Nigeria. Initially with a largely diasporan staff, they were increasingly in West African hands as the century closed.

The *Sierra Leone Weekly News* was one of the longest lasting, running from 1884 to 1951. Diasporan Africans, attracted to Sierra Leone and Liberia and often spreading along coastal trade routes, dominated the early scene. Addressing the need to lead Africa's recovery from the slave trade, they adapted ideas from the African American race tradition and from the international abolitionist agenda. The African American reverend Alexander Crummell (1819–1898) delineated his vision from Liberia in *The Future of Africa* (1862), hoping that returnees could help Africans realize their full potential by exposing them to Christianity and Anglo-American culture. Similar ideas about the need for external Christian inspiration were espoused in Senegal by the mulatto cleric Pierre Boilat (1814–1901) in his *Esquisses sénégalaises* (1853). Africanus Horton is another exemplar of this age. Educated in Britain with the support of the Anglican Church and the army, he became a medical officer in British service. His *West African Countries and Peoples* (1868) and *Letters on the Political Condition of the Gold Coast* (1870) simultaneously defended African abilities against racist denigration and assessed different West African polities in light of European political history to describe how African governments might evolve into more modern forms.

As the era of so-called legitimate commerce gave way to imperial conquest from the 1880s, Africa's autonomous futures were foregone, and Africans had to rethink their immediate future within the confines of colonial rule. This required political organizing to make West African interests heard by policy makers. Leadership and political writing went hand in hand, as defending African rights required defining them. John Mensah Sarbah's *Fanti Customary Laws* (1897) and J. E. Casely-Hayford's *Gold Coast Native Institutions* (1903) both researched and outlined Fante land tenure and other legal traditions to establish grounds on which to counter colonial legislation. These lawyers' efforts were echoed by many later studies. Both were also key figures in the Gold Coast Aborigines Rights Protection Society, founded in 1897 in alliance with colonial chiefs to protest a proposed land bill.

A similar pattern unfolded in South Africa in response to deepening African subordination under white settlers. Mission-educated Africans formed organizations such as the *Imbumba Yama Afrika* in Transkei in 1882, and newspapers such as John Tengo Jabavu's (1859–1921) *Imvo Zabantsundu* (*Native Opinion*) in the eastern Cape Colony in 1884. As settler power was consolidated under the Union of South Africa in 1910, numerous regional elite organizations united their voices of protest in the South African Native National Congress in 1912 (renamed the African National Congress in 1923). One Congress leader, the journalist Solomon Plaatje, composed *Native Life in South Africa* (1916), a lengthy polemic against the emergent order detailing the effects of British policy on rural life and appealing to British justice as a solution.

Racism, now applied directly by colonial governments, had to be resisted because of its material effects on lives and careers. The ideas of Caribbean-born Edward Wilmot Blyden were attractive in this struggle. Pursuing an influential career as scholar, educator, and diplomat in Liberia and Sierra Leone, Blyden's mid-nineteenth-century writings resembled Crummell's. But over time and in the face of ever more virulent racism, Blyden came to appreciate how African cultures themselves, including Islamic ones, might use their own essential virtues to define their futures. His *Christianity, Islam, and the Negro Race* (1887) and *African Life and Customs* (1908) accepted the idea of racial difference but denied grounds for racial hierarchy, arguing that Africans as a race possessed a unique spirituality that they could bring to the world. This resonated with early colonial writers because it helped make the case that Africans needed to lead fellow Africans along their own path, even as they accepted that European rule was necessary to provide an impetus forward. In Lagos, Mojola Agbebi (1860–1917) applied these ideas in developing a church African in membership and values, as explained in his *Africa and the Gospel* (1889). Casely Hayford, in his 1911 autobiographical novel

Ethiopia Unbound, celebrated Blyden's African genius. In South Africa, the American-educated Congress leader Pixley ka Isaka Seme (c. 1881–1951) voiced sympathetic ideas in his 1906 appeal for the regeneration of Africa.

Alongside this defense of Africans as a race, a new generation of writers in the early twentieth century began to write about the history and culture of their natal societies with insiders' perspectives. It is in this generation that writing in other parts of sub-Saharan Africa got in step, as more recently established literate communities began addressing issues common to colonial situations. In part augmenting the ongoing defense of Africans as a race, they were also intent on describing how specific communities worked, and the relations that existed between these communities' relations to both the colonial order and other African communities. These additional interests began to separate their work from much diasporan writing.

Historical foundations became important as a step toward imagining how these relations should unfold. Thus C. C. Reindorf's (1834–1917) *History of the Gold Coast and Asante* (1895) tried to gather much of the colonial territory within a single account, feeling its way toward a joint future that would be inspired by British rule but shaped by African agents. The historical legal studies by Sarbah and Casely-Hayford figure here, identifying the principles animating Fante society partly to prove such existed, but also to enter the complex politics of alliance and rivalry between colonial chiefs, the educated elite, and the colonial state that marked Gold Coast (present-day Ghana) politics.

The Yoruba missionary Samuel Johnson undertook research on oral and written stories to produce his enduring *History of the Yoruba* (1921), which delineated a linked past and joint future for the Yoruba of Nigeria while also mounting a case for the centrality of Oyo over Ife within Yoruba history. In Uganda, the influential Bugandan politician Apolo Kagwa composed *The Customs of the Baganda* (1934) to celebrate the richness of an African culture and simultaneously address political issues important both within the social hierarchy of Buganda and in Buganda's relations with the British colony of Uganda that enclosed it. As before, writers of this generation continued the well-established tradition of speaking to contemporary ideas among Africanists in general while also deploying sympathetic ideas and deflecting harmful ones. Anthropology attracted a number of young student writers. The Kenyan politician Jomo Kenyatta studied social anthropology in London before writing *Facing Mount Kenya* (1938), which attacked British denigration of Gikuyu society but also intervened in internal Gikuyu political questions about authority, land, and female initiation.

Ethiopia, having avoided colonial conquest, produced a prolific group of young intellectuals who wrestled with the problems of reform and modernization within and outside the state. The most industrious was Heruy Walda-Sellase (1878–1939). In North Africa a rising movement of reform within the Ottoman Islamic world advocated the need to jointly modernize Islam and confront European imperialism. The emancipation of women was a notable concern, along with the question of balancing fidelity to Islam, Arab identity, and more local loyalties. Ideas of the influential Iranian thinker Jamal al-Din al-Afghani (1838–1897) were picked up in Egypt in the late nineteenth century by, among others, Muhammad Abduh (1849–1905), and were used to shape Egyptian independence from British rule in 1922. These ideas were in turn deployed in Algeria by Abd al-Hamid Ben Badis (d. 1940) in the early twentieth century. The tradition inspired by al-Afghani developed in tension with various others looking for more secular or more purely Islamic futures.

French African writing emerged in these years intertwining two traditions: the French republican and socialist assertions of equal rights exemplified by Lamine Guèye (1891–1968), and the Négritude tradition that emerged among African and Black Caribbean students in Paris in the 1930s. Négritude played off African American celebrations of African culture, and found support in the celebrations of Africa's cultural riches by European Africanists such as Maurice Delafosse (1870–1926) and Leo Frobenius (1873–1938). The Négritude writers' elaborate assertion of the special qualities of African humanity (most evident in the writings of Martiniquan Aimé Césaire and Senegal's Léopold Senghor) parallel in many ways Blyden's earlier assertion of an African personality. These ideas clearly buttressed emergent claims that no theory of racial difference could sustain a case for African inferiority.

The interwar period was a moment of strong Pan-African connection, highlighted by a series of Pan-African Congresses between 1919 and 1927 in Europe and the Jamaican Marcus Garvey's (1887–1940) Universal Negro Improvement Association. Africans joined this largely diasporan movement to add weight to their campaign to have the rights of Africans recognized within the new world order promised under the League of Nations; they aimed for the most part at the reform, rather than removal, of colonial control.

The National Congress of British West Africa organized in 1920 by Casely-Hayford similarly advocated reforms that would protect both elite interests in the region and the dignity of African cultures. Africans in London organized groups such as the West African Students Union in 1925 to jointly lobby at the imperial center, forge Pan-African links, and facilitate the study of Africa. These themes, connected to an appeal for political commitment among the rising generation, are evident in Ladipo Solanke's (1884–1958) *United West Africa (or Africa) at the Bar of the Family of Nations* (1927) and J. W. de Graft Johnson's (b. 1893) *Towards Nationhood in West Africa* (1928).

There were numerous organizations of students and politicians, usually combining West African and diasporan Africans, such as Tovalou Houénou's (1887–1936) *Ligue universelle pour la défense de la race noire* and the *Comité de la défense de la race nègre* that was led by Lamine Senghor. It was especially in these metropolitan settings that writers were exposed to diverse political parties and reform movements espousing international currents of thought about political and social progress and planned economic development, finding there obviously attractive material in their quest to imagine Africa's future. Students from other colonies also shared ideas. The Labour Party and Fabian Society were important in Britain, as were the communist and socialist movements important in France. At the 1945 Pan-African Congress in Manchester, continental Africans dominated, and moved the Pan-African tradition toward the fight for self-government.

By the eve of World War II, especially in West and South Africa but ever thicker elsewhere, communities had been established to define, debate and celebrate African concerns in books, pamphlets, and newspapers. Explicitly political associations of diverse sorts had existed in most colonial and metropolitan capitals for decades, even in Portuguese Africa and the Belgian Congo, with their still restricted Western-educated community. The same is true of the other types of organizations—literary societies, professional unions, churches, and welfare unions—which provided forums for intellectual exchange on diverse issues, from politics to theology to marriage practices. Generational changes had been marked as African-born writers replaced diasporan writers. Casely-Hayford's *Ethiopia Unbound* entailed a critique of African American claims to lead Africans on the basis of race, asserting that Africans knew their own context best. A generation later, Nnamdi Azikiwe's (1904–1996) *Renascent Africa* (1937) attacked Casely-Hayford's generation for their quietist Victorian notions of progress and Christian faith, adding fuel to the youth movements rising in British West African colonies impatient for more African influence and better access to education. As African demands for change rose in the face of proliferating social problems, African writers expressed more clearly their positions on what could be done.

World War II redirected African intellectual life as circumstances rapidly changed. Wartime crises weakened imperial power; wartime propaganda undermined the imperialists' own case for continued racial domination and colonial exploitation. Africans, abused afresh by imperial demands, seized upon these changes. The diverse inquiries of the interwar period quickly focused on the central problem of colonial rule itself, and stark oppositions were now drawn between loyalty to Africa and loyalty to empire. Redeploying Allied war propaganda against itself easily made the case for African freedom.

Within Nigeria these ranged from the impatient (Kingsley Mbadiwe's 1942 *British and Axis Aims in Africa*) to the cautious (Obafemi Awolowo's 1947 *Path to Nigerian Freedom*). But across the spectrum, Kwame Nkrumah's call from Ghana moved the continent: "Seek ye first the political kingdom." Whatever social problems or developmental blockages Africans might have identified, the first step to solving them was by putting Africans in charge of their own house. The various organizations of the interwar years merged into mass movements—*rassemblements* and unions in French colonial Africa, conventions and congresses in British—focused on achieving this first crucial step toward Africa's future. And as writers moved into the era of decolonization, the new and urgent problems of constitution writing, economic development, and educational reform consumed many. Colonial regimes slow to foster communities of educated Africans, or forceful in suppressing them—such as settler states—could not resist these calls to a new future.

The urgent questions opened by decolonization have certainly not been solved as of the early twenty-first century. But as perspectives lengthen on Africa's modern history, the library left by Africa's early writers—concerning, not least, how African values and institutions could be integrated into a modern state—warrant and garner the attention of contemporary writers afresh.

See also **Blyden, Edward Wilmot; Casely-Hayford, Joseph Ephraim; Césaire, Aimé; Crowther, Samuel Ajayi; Equiano, Olaudah; Garvey, Marcus Mosiah; Historiography; History and the Study of Africa; Horton, James Africanus Beale; Johnson, Samuel; Kagwa, Apolo; Kenyatta, Jomo; Mondlane, Eduardo Chivambo; Nationalism; Nkrumah, Francis Nwia Kofi; Plaatje, Sol; Political Systems; Postcolonialism; Sarbah, John Mensah; Senghor, Léopold Sédar; 'Uthman dan Fodio; World War II.**

BIBLIOGRAPHY

Desai, Gaurav. *Subject to Colonialism: African Self-Fashioning and the Colonial Library.* Durham, North Carolina: Duke University, 2001.

Falola, Toyin. *Nationalism and African Intellectuals.* Rochester, New York: University of Rochester, 2001.

July, Robert W. *The Origins of Modern African Thought.* New York: Faber, 1967.

McDougall, James. *History and the Culture of Nationalism in Algeria.* Cambridge and New York: Cambridge University Press, 2006.

Newell, Stephanie. *Literary Culture in Colonial Ghana.* Manchester, U.K.: Manchester University, 2002.

Van Hensbroek, Pieter Boele. *Political Discourses in African Thought 1860 to the Present.* London: Praeger, 1999.

Walshe, Peter. *The Rise of African Nationalism in South Africa: The African National Congress 1912–1952.* Berkeley and Los Angeles: University of California Press, 1971.

Zachernuk, Philip. *Colonial Subjects: An African Intelligentsia and Atlantic Ideas.* Charlottesville: University Press of Virginia, 2000.

Zewde, Bahru. *Pioneers of Change in Ethiopia.* Oxford: James Currey, 2002.

PHILIP S. ZACHERNUK

INDEPENDENCE ERA. *See* **Government; History of Africa; Political Science and the Study of Africa.**

INDIAN OCEAN, AFRICA, HISTORY OF (1000 BCE TO 600 CE).

While the population of the western Indian Ocean is quite well known from the eighth century CE onward, this region, a meeting point for important cultures (Cushitic, Bantu, Perso-Arabian and Austronesian), nonetheless presents a number of difficulties for the period from 1000 BCE until its partial Islamization in 600 CE.

Cushitic pastoralism predominated in the area from 2000 to 1000 BCE, although a form of agriculture may have also developed. It was also during this period that contact with the Early Iron Age Bantu occurred. Between 200 and 600 CE, Cushitic pastoralists from the north of Kenya (who had settled in the Tana basin) mixed with Bantu agriculturists and became the progenitors of the Swahili. It was during this period (of so-called Tana Ware from the northern Swahili region) that coastal settlements were established.

Contrasting views exist about this initial settlement: one position posits that an ancient people developed agriculture, metallurgy and livestock farming in situ. A contrasting position attributes these developments to immigrants. Another assigns an earlier role to the Bantu. Early Iron Ware originating from the Urewe in the Taita hills then took hold in southeast Kenya and northeast Tanzania (Kwale pottery). Around the fifth century, this extended to Mozambique. Several phases followed

this: Limbo (second century BCE) until the third century, Kwale (third through fifth centuries) with chevrons, triangles and zigzags, and grooves). Triangular Incised Ware (TIW) began around 500 or a little earlier (fourth through seventh centuries, according to one scholar).

Some believe that it was during these periods that Swahili culture originated but they do not agree on the period or region in which it spread. Felix Chami, for example, attributes the establishment of Swahili civilization to the Bantu culture on the African coast at the start of the Christian era, that was already trading in the well-developed milieu on the coast of the Indian Ocean.

The other active parties around the Indian Ocean were also present in the region. The possibility that there was an ancient trading system, distinct from the Arab group, which joined Madagascar, the Comoros and the south-east coast of Africa should not be ruled out. Nevertheless, the Austronesian elements found on the African coast are, in some scholars' opinions, borrowings from the ocean environment rather than adaptations to the locale, as Chami holds for the outrigger canoe. They argue that there would not be the same term all around the ocean: *gala-gala* (Indonesia)/*galawat* (Gudjerat)/*ngalawa* (throughout the Comoros in Swahili) unless there were such oceanic borrowings. In addition Blood Group O, a genetic feature of Austronesians, has not been found in Mozambique, making direct Austronesian penetration improbable.

The study of Arabic texts and the use of relative dating (the persistence of the same redundant information under different names, where the latter may be dated and this, in turn places the redundant information noted in an earlier time) allows scholars to fix the presence of the Oceanian coconut palm, the large Asian bamboo, in the western Indian Ocean from a very early date. Arab writers portray coconuts as young women (the *wakwak* tree), the giant flightless elephant bird of Madagascar (*Aepyornis*) as the rokh bird and call the island of *Gezirat al-Komr* the island of Komr, that is the island of white clouds, the Clouds of Magellan, along with their representation of the nut *nardil* from the bamboo, which emerged from the feathers of the great mythical bird.

Information such as this leads to the conclusion that there were contacts with East Asia from very early times. A closer examination of works by classical authors reveals their interest in tortoise shell. The Greeks referred to the ocean using the term *Prasode* to indicate "sea plant" (eaten by tortoises) and Pliny talking about *Regio Amithoscutta* simply denotes the region that provides tortoise shell (*skutta*).

Diogenes referred to the so-called *Lunae Montes* (Mountains of the Moon), and it may be the case that the island of Iambulos in Diodorus Siculus has features that are borrowed from Madagascar. Ptolemy talks about Menuthias, which Horton identifies as Madagascar. Sinclair Miller is more controversial, but his theory which has cinnamon being brought through Grande Ile Madagascar has been accepted by some Malagasy scholars.

A coin of Constantine (used in Yemen at that time) has been found at Majunga in Madagascar. Ptolemaic, Parthian, Sassenid, Greek, and Roman coins have been found on the African coast, often with no location or stratigraphic date.

Dyen thinks that the Maanyan and Malagasy languages, which Otto Christian Dahl has indicated are related, separated around 1,900 years ago, but a direct link for pottery between Borneo, Sumatra, and Madagascar cannot be made. Besides how certain is it that this vegetal civilization may have had pottery? Several Sulawesi pottery pieces (of interlaced design) have nonetheless been found on Madagascar. Adelaar agrees with Dahl but observes the wider contribution to Malagasy of Austronesian languages.

Transformation of the natural vegetation, the growth in grasses, the increased scarcity of forest species, and coal deposits in the sediment are probable indicators of population settlement. Palynological research in Lake Kavitaha reveals the presence of hemp from 500 CE and perhaps the presence of human beings from that period.

Andavakoera, in the north of the island, was occupied from 400 CE. A good quantity of pottery in arca style, very rare on the African coast, is present and this becomes increasingly common from the Comoros to Madagascar. A thigh bone from a dwarf female hippopotamus bearing a groove made with a knife has been found at Ambolisatra (on the southwest coast) dating from the Christian era.

There is a gap between the beginning of the Christian era and 700 CE. The link may be in the Comoros, where the oldest known site Mayotte, Kungu, has TIW pottery along with arca style pottery (often attributed to Proto-Malagasy). It could mean a meeting of two groups, one African, the other Austronesian. The site has two almost identical datings (from the beginning of the eighth century).

Recent genetic data confirms an Austronesian substratum in the Comoros, early Bantu influences in Madagascar, and the absence of the Indian genome in Madagascar (although the southeast part of the island has not been examined). Finally, DNA analysis points to the arrival of men and women from southeast Asia at the same time.

See also **'Abd al-Qādir; Ceramics.**

BIBLIOGRAPHY

Adelaar, S. "Borneo or a Crossroads." In *The Austronesians: Historical and Comparative Perspectives*, ed. Peter Bellwood, James J. Fox, and Darrell Tryon. Camberra: Department of Anthropology in association with the Comparative Austronesian Project, Research School of Pacific Studies, Australian National University, 1995.

Adelaar, S. "Une perspective linguistique sur les origines asiatiques des Malgaches." In *Cultures of Madagascar: Flux et reflux des influences*, ed. S. Evers and M. Spindler. Working Papers Series 2. Leiden: International Institute for Asian Studies, 1995.

Adelaar, S. "Malagasy Culture History: Some Linguistic Evidence." In *The Indian Ocean in Antiquity*, ed. Julian Reade. New York: Keagan Paul, 1996.

Allibert, C. "Wakwak: végétal, minéral ou humain? Reconsidération du problème." *Etudes Océan Indien* 12 (1991): 171–189.

Allibert, C. "The Archaeology of Knowledge: Austronesian Influences in the Western Indian Ocean." In *Archaeology and Language*, Vol. 3: *Artefacts, Language, and Texts*, ed. Roger Blench and Matthew Spriggs. New York: Routledge, 1999.

Chami, F. A. "Graeco-Roman Trade Link and the Bantu Migration Theory." *Anthropos* (1994): 205–215.

Chami, F. A., and P. I. Msemwa. "A New Look at Culture Trade on the Azanian Coast." *Current Anthropology* 38, no. 4 (1997): 673–677.

Dahl, O. Ch. *Malgache et Maanyan, une comparaison linguistique*. Oslo: Egede Instituttet, 1951.

Dahl, O. Ch. *Migration from Kalimantan to Madagascar*. Oslo: Institute for Comparative Research in Human Culture, Norwegian University Press, 1991.

Dewar, R. E., and H. T. Wright. "The Culture History of Madagascar." *Journal of World Prehistory* 7, no. 4 (1993): 417–466.

Hurles, M. E., et al. "The Dual Origin of the Malagasy in Island Southeast Asia and East Africa: Evidence from Maternal and Paternal Lineages." *American Journal of Human Genetics* 76 (2005): 894–901.

Macpheer, D. E., and D. A. Burney. "Dating of Modified Femora of Extinct Dwarf Hippopotamus from Southern Madagascar: Implications for Constraining Human Colonization and Vertebrate Extinction Events." *Journal of Archaeological Science* 18 (1991): 695–706.

Soodyall, H., et al. "The Peopling of Madagascar." In *Molecular Biology and Human Diversity*, ed. A. J. Boyce and C. G. N. Mascie-Taylor. Cambridge, U.K.: Cambridge University Press, 1996.

CLAUDE ALLIBERT

INDIRECT RULE. *See* **Colonial Policies and Practices.**

INFERTILITY. *See* **Demography: Fertility and Infertility.**

INFIBULATION. *See* **Initiation: Clitoridectomy and Infibulation.**

INFORMAL ECONOMIES. *See* **Capitalism and Commercialization; Economic Systems; Trade, National and International Systems.**

INITIATION

This entry includes the following articles:
OVERVIEW
CLITORIDECTOMY AND INFIBULATION

OVERVIEW

Initiation ceremonies are means through which people are incorporated into a new status, an association, or an office. In various parts of Africa, such changes may include initiation into adulthood, into secret societies, into healing associations, or into political office. As with other transition rites, initiation involves making and marking social or physical transformations. In different African societies, however, different occasions and changes may be recognized as culturally important through ritual performance. Cultural definitions and understandings of those changes also vary widely in different places and at different times. Nonetheless, initiation and other transition rites manifest some broad structural similarities and have certain symbolic types in common.

THE CATEGORY OF TRANSITION RITES

Arnold van Gennep (1873–1957), a German-born folklorist educated mainly in France, developed the category of rites of passage in the early 1900s. Rites of passage also came to be called transition rites. Whereas most scholars of his day did comparative analyses of religion by using fragments of ritual, van Gennep compared entire ceremonies, seeking patterns in their sequential orders. He found that a diverse group of rites that all had to do with some change of state had a broadly similar three-phase structure. These rites of transition included ceremonies performed at marriages, funerals, initiations, calendrical and seasonal rites (e.g., to mark the new year), and some territorial passages.

According to van Gennep, the ceremonies proceeded through three structural phases: separation (symbolically and ritually marking the starting point of the transition), liminality (an in-between phase creating conceptual and symbolic separation as part of the transition), and reaggregation (marking the ending point of the transition). Van Gennep saw this ritual structure as part of the renewal and regeneration needed in every society, and noted symbolic patterns commonly associated with each of the three phases. In any particular time and place, however, the themes and understandings incorporated into a transition rite include more than the broad structural pattern van Gennep identified.

First published in 1909, van Gennep's *The Rites of Passage* was translated into English in 1960. Later in the 1960s, anthropologist Victor Turner (1920–1983) published several influential essays focused on one of van Gennep's stages: the liminal. Turner explored the ambiguous nature of ritual liminality as falling between cultural categories: betwixt and between. He proposed that such moments in and out of time symbolize and produce a sense of equality and united community (that he called communitas); they sometimes invert or seem outside the usual structures of society. Both van Gennep's book and Turner's essays have been influential for ritual analysis, perhaps especially so in anthropology and comparative religion.

INITIATION IN AFRICA

Initiation into adulthood is probably the most widespread kind of initiation in Africa. In many places, people tell stories or myths about the history of their initiation. They may explain how people in their society began the practice, whether they adopted it from neighboring peoples, whether they modified their ceremonies at various times, and whether some people stopped practicing them. Numerous societies have a history of both male and female initiation, including the Kaguru in Tanzania, the Lovedu in Southern Africa, the Ndembu in Democratic Republic of the Congo, and the Kuranko in Sierra Leone. Others practice male initiation only (e.g., the Nuer in Sudan and the Wagenia in Democratic Republic of the Congo), but initiation for women alone is rare. In all cases, initiation into adulthood is related fundamentally to notions of personhood and ethnic identity; it has an educational role and often a political role, as well. Initiation marks social maturity and the end of childhood, but people in different societies see adulthood as beginning at different ages and stages of biological maturation. In Kenya, for example, the Gusii people initiate their children at around eight years old (younger than in precolonial times), whereas the Maasai people initiate children into adulthood at between fifteen and eighteen years of age.

For both girls and boys, initiation into adulthood usually includes physical trials, although the trials vary. Circumcision is the major trial in many societies, but other physical signs characterize initiation in others. For instance, Luo initiation in western Kenya includes the removal of certain teeth, whereas Poro initiation in western Africa involves scarification.

Although they produce a permanent physical sign of initiation, such trials are only one part of more elaborate ceremonies that may last for days or months. Ceremonies often include diverse ritual events and objects, special ways of speaking, songs, dances, distinctive costumes and places, and many other symbolic aspects. In the initiation ceremonies of different regions and different African societies, these diverse media are organized in particular dramatic configurations, incorporating distinctive meanings and references to specific social environments, histories, and cultural philosophies. A large number of people are usually involved, whether in ritual events themselves or in the feasting and celebration normally included in the ceremonies.

For example, the Bemba people in Zambia call their female initiation *chisungu*; several other ethnic groups in Central Africa practice similar ceremonies. Anthropologist Audrey Richards (1899–1984) attended Bemba chisungu ceremonies at Chinsali in 1931 and later described them in detail. The ceremonies continued for about a month and included a series of ritual events at woodland locations and in an initiation house, dramatic episodes, secret words, special songs and dances, and many other distinctive aspects. The girls' parents hired an older woman experienced in chisungu to organize them, as mistress of the ceremony (*nachimbusa*). Wall paintings and a wide assortment of special pottery emblems that represented animals, historical characters, domestic objects and activities of daily Bemba life were also used in the rites. These objects were used to teach initiates about adult social obligations and accepted norms and attitudes toward gender relations, marriage, sexuality, and motherhood. The pottery emblems, their names, associated songs and interpretations brought important elements and values of daily life into the ceremonies. They were also a kind of secret knowledge that initiates were shown and could gradually master.

Although people throughout Africa often consider their initiation ceremonies to be central to their cultural tradition, history, and ethnic identity, the ceremonies are not unchanging. As historical and social circumstances change over time, people may change aspects and interpretations of their ceremonies. For instance, some Bemba told Richards of modifications in *chisungu* ceremonies that related to their shifting circumstances in the late 1920s. Although missionaries forbade *chisungu* in the late 1800s, people continued to celebrate the ceremonies. By 1930, the Bemba had shortened the rituals from over six months to about one month, were making ceremonial payments in cash instead of with objects such as bark cloth, had incorporated modern dances reminiscent of school drills along with older, more familiar dances, and had omitted some events. Bemba labor migration to Southern African mines also influenced the participants and the interpretations of some symbols and acts. Most aspects of the ceremonies were still meaningful then and remain so into the early twenty-first century. The Bemba continue to regard *chisungu* as central to young women's maturation and marriage. Contrary to Richards' prediction that they would abandon the ceremonies, they have continued to perform *chisungu*, with some further condensation and adaptations (such as efforts in the 1990s and 2000s to incorporate AIDS education into them, an adaptation made in initiation ceremonies in a number of other cases, as well).

The pottery emblems of *chisungu* exemplify another aspect common to initiations of all kinds: revealing secrets and esoteric knowledge to those initiated. Concealing special knowledge is one way to maintain differences between the initiated and the uninitiated. Secret knowledge is often associated with differences of power, authority, or other privileges. Paradoxically, these social differences are created and maintained in part by displaying the existence of secrets, though the actual secrets are closely guarded. In many parts of western Africa, initiation into adulthood simultaneously incorporates individuals into secret societies. Masquerades with elaborate dances, songs, masks, and costumes are among the most prominent and dramatic kinds of secret knowledge displayed by these societies.

Sande societies for women and Poro societies for men are widespread and well-documented examples of secret societies, each with distinctive masquerades in most places. For at least four centuries in Sierra Leone, Liberia, Guinea, and parts of Côte d'Ivoire, these societies have been integrally involved with political and economic organization. Initiation into the first grade of the society (which is all most members achieve) occurs at puberty; those who have been through initiation are regarded as adults. However, Poro and Sande each have a hierarchy of grades into which members may advance through further instruction and payment of fees. Members of higher Poro grades are involved in decisions concerning judicial matters, agriculture, and trade, and were formerly arbitrators of war. Often they are also members of high-ranking families.

Poro has had continuing influence on political affairs, as illustrated by its important role in mobilizing people in the widespread Mende Rising of 1898 (a revolt against colonial taxes in Sierra Leone), in antigovernment demonstrations in the 1950s (sometimes known as the Protectorate Disturbances), and by its central role in local government in Liberia and in Guinea (where it was outlawed after independence because of that political role). During the decade of war in Liberia and Sierra Leone in the 1990s, Poro initiation was the basis for some of the practices and meanings associated with joining militias. In postwar Sierra Leone, girls' initiation ceremonies have served as occasions through which people may re-establish social relations and community.

Establishing relations with spirits and controlling powerful medicines are important aspects of Poro and Sande associations. Whereas different kinds of initiation may be distinguished analytically, some aspects of puberty rites, secret societies, healing associations, and spirit-possession cults may be combined in some societies and periods. Possession cults, for instance, often include healing capacities, though healing associations do not necessarily involve spirit possession. In other situations, only some of these practices exist and they are treated separately.

Whereas initiation into adulthood is most clearly related to processes of socialization, all kinds of initiation are concerned with questions of personhood (e.g., how persons are socially defined, and how people experience and achieve those definitions), as well as with related ideas about social values, morality, rights, and responsibilities. Initiation into adulthood is likely to focus on notions of childhood, adulthood, gender, and ethnic identity. These concepts are entwined throughout the initiation ceremonies of the Okiek people of Kenya, but they are emphasized differentially in the ritual events that make up the ceremonies. In Swazi royal installation rites, by contrast, key categories of personhood relate to hierarchies of rank as well as to gender, ethnic identity, and kingship.

With notions of personhood and social difference so central, most transition rites have political implications. Often the social transformations accomplished through the ceremonies simultaneously help to create and legitimize differences of status, power, and authority that pervade daily community life. These differences may be based on gender, age, wealth, ethnicity, lineage status, or other criteria. Similarly, the ceremonies often represent as ideal certain values that favor some interests and segments of the population over others. At times, initiation ceremonies may also be settings in which those differences and values are questioned or challenged.

In addition to these local political aspects, some initiation rites have figured in wider political arenas, as with the Poro society examples mentioned. In Madagascar, Merina initiation for boys has been appropriated for various political purposes since the late 1700s. At different times it has been a local rite, a royal state ritual, a means of labor recruitment, or a self-consciously anti-Christian act. In Kenya in the 1920s and 1930s, several Christian missions attempted to ban Gikuyu female initiation and clitoridectomy. The rites became an important cause among Kenyan nationalists; the ensuing struggle was part of the impetus to establish independent schools in Kenya. Many other examples exist, in each case related to particular cultural understandings of ceremonies and their social and historical circumstances. Initiation and other rites of transition are occasions that involve and represent central social relations and fundamental cultural concepts. When incorporated into other political enterprises, they may help mobilize powerful experiences, emotions, and allegiances for other goals and interests.

See also **Age and Age Organization; Gender; Religion and Ritual; Secret Societies; Spirit Possession.**

BIBLIOGRAPHY

Ahmadu, Fuambai. "Rites and Wrongs: An Insider/Outsider Reflects on Power and Excision." In *Female "Circumcision" in Africa: Culture, Controversy, and Change*, ed. Bettina Shell-Duncan and Yvla Hernlund. Boulder, CO: Lynne Rienner, 2000.

Beidelman, Thomas, O. "Swazi Royal Ritual." *Africa: Journal of the International African Institute* 36, no. 4 (1966): 373–405.

Beidelman, Thomas, O. *The Cool Knife: Imagery of Gender, Sexuality, and Moral Education in Kaguru Initiation Ritual.* Washington, DC: Smithsonian Institution Press, 1997.

Bellman, Beryl. *The Language of Secrecy: Symbols and Metaphors in Poro Ritual.* New Brunswick, NJ: Rutgers University Press, 1984.

Bloch, Maurice. *From Blessing to Violence: History and Ideology in the Circumcision Ritual of the Merina.* Cambridge, U.K.: Cambridge University Press, 1986.

Coulter, Chris. "Reflections from the Field: A Girl's Initiation Ceremony in Northern Sierra Leone." *Anthropological Quarterly* 78, no. 2 (2005): 431–441.

Ellis, Stephen. "Young Soldiers and the Significance of Initiation: Some Notes from Liberia." Paper presented at conference on Youth and the Politics of Generational Conflict in Africa, 24–25 April 2003, at the Afrika-Studiecentrum, Leiden, The Netherlands.

Kratz, Corinne. *Affecting Performance: Meaning, Movement and Experience in Okiek Women's Initiation.* Washington, DC: Smithsonian Institution Press, 1994.

Nooter, Mary H. *Secrecy: African Art That Conceals and Reveals.* New York: Museum for African Art, 1993.

Richards, Audrey. *Chisungu: A Girl's Initiation Ceremony Among the Bemba.* London: Routledge, 1982.

Turner, Victor. *The Ritual Process: Structure and Anti-Structure.* Reprint edition. Chicago: Aldine Transaction, 1995.

Van Damme, Annemieke. *Spectacular Display: The Art of Nkanu Initiation Rituals.* London: Philip Wilson Publishers, 2003.

Van Gennep, Arnold. *The Rites of Passage.* Trans. Monika B. Vizedom and Gabrielle L. Caffee. Chicago: University of Chicago Press, 1961.

CORINNE A. KRATZ

CLITORIDECTOMY AND INFIBULATION

Rites that include some form of female genital cutting are performed in numerous African cultures in northeastern, eastern, central, and western Africa. The types of cutting performed vary tremendously, although all forms are frequently referred to by the general terms female circumcision, female genital mutilation (FGM), or female genital cutting (FGC). Clitoridectomy is the removal of all or part of the clitoris and usually the clitoral prepuce (or hood). Intermediate forms referred to as excision include removal of the clitoris, clitoral prepuce, and some or all of the labia minora (inner lips) and often some or all of the labia majora (outer lips). In some areas, especially in northern Sudan, Somalia, Eritrea, Djibouti, and, to some extent, Mali, the removal of tissues is followed by infibulation, or closing, by joining the raw tissue on the two sides so that scar tissue forms across the vaginal opening. A straw or other thin object is used during healing to preserve a single tiny aperture for urination and menstrual flow. First intercourse is extremely difficult after infibulation, resulting in tissue damage or the necessity of cutting a bride open at marriage (usually by a midwife).

The World Health Organization uses a typology to label the variant forms. Partial or complete clitoridectomy is Type I, intermediate excision is Type II, and infibulation is Type III. Other miscellaneous changes to the female genitalia are labeled Type IV. In societies where infibulation is culturally practiced, reinfibulation (also called recircumcision) is ordinarily performed following each childbirth and may be performed at other times if a woman wants to have herself tightened.

Various forms of female genital cutting are practiced in about twenty-eight countries of Africa, including all the countries of coastal West Africa (Mauritania to Cameroon) across the continent to the east coast from Tanzania to Egypt. The highest incidence of the severe forms is found in Djibouti, Somalia, some areas of Eritrea and Ethiopia, and central and northern Sudan. It is estimated that only very small percentages of women are circumcised in Zaire, Uganda, and Tanzania (5–10%); less than half (20–30%) in Mauritania, Senegal, Ghana, and Niger; and one-half or more in the remaining countries of the delineated area.

CULTURAL MEANINGS AND REASONS VARY

An indication of the ideological support or presumed origin of these practices is reflected in the terminologies used. In Sudan and Egypt the surgeries, of whatever type, have been commonly referred to by the Arabic word for purification (*tahur* or *tahara*) and is thought to render the girl clean and pure. When clitoridectomy is combined with infibulation—the most common practice in Sudan, Somalia, and Eritrea—people call it

pharaonic purification (*tahur faroniya* in Sudanese Arabic), reflecting the belief that it dates back to the ancient civilizations of the pharaohs in the Nile Valley. The term sunna purification (*tahur as-sunna*) has been popularly used for the less severe forms of the surgeries, that is, partial or total clitoridectomy or prepuce removal. By using the term for the traditional practices associated with the prophet Muhammad (*sunna*), practitioners invoke the contested idea that the prophet approved removal of the prepuce or even partial or total clitoridectomy. This interpretation is disputed by many Muslim scholars, who assert that any sort of circumcision of females is against the teachings of Islam. Nevertheless, many Muslims continue to use the term sunna for whatever form of the surgeries they practice, including excision of all external genitalia.

There is great cultural variation in the purpose of the surgeries. Although often assumed to have religious meanings, female genital cutting has been practiced by members of all the major religions in Africa, including Islam, Christianity, and Judaism, as well as by followers of other African indigenous religious belief systems. In some cultural groups, such as the Gikuyu and Maasai of Kenya, excision traditionally has marked a girl's transition to womanhood, usually performed between the ages of eight and thirteen. The Maasai did excisions just weeks prior to marriage and the Gikuyu prior to first menstruation. In these cases, the surgeries are commonly accompanied by symbolic rituals (such as the shaving of heads among the Maasai) and communal celebrations; the girls are expected to adopt changes in behavior or clothing. Young women experience the transition individually among the Maasai, collectively among the Gikuyu. Where such transitions are ritualized collectively, the circumcision experience may form the basis of an age-set, as among the Gikuyu. In addition, being circumcised according to traditions has often been interpreted as necessary for affiliation with one's ethnic group.

In many societies, however, the age at which the circumcisions are performed is so young that it is clearly not intended to mark the onset of womanhood. In Sudan, girls are most commonly infibulated between the ages of five and seven, though in recent research some have begun performing clitoridectomies on babies; in western

Africa, circumcision seems to be not uncommon as young as age three. Instead, it seems to mark the end of early childhood, to be accomplished before a girl enters school or begins to be significantly involved in family labor that takes her outside the home, long before she approaches sexual maturity. The reasons for this in some cultures are explicitly related to the goal of attenuating sexual desire in preadolescent girls and women, and, in the case of infibulation, preventing illicit intercourse by constructing a barrier of scar tissue. Among Arab Sudanese of many ethnic groups, for example, failure to preserve a daughter's virginity in this socially marked way would dishonor the entire family. Additional reasons given include cleanliness, femininity and the removal of "masculine" parts, and an aesthetic preference for smoothness. During the colonial period opposition by European missionaries, medical workers, and administrators led to efforts to suppress female circumcision. Nationalist reaction, most notably in Kenya, led to political defense of the practices. In the early twenty-first century the topic elicits strong resentment among many Africans toward outsiders who condemn the practices.

PROCESS OF CHANGE

Change has been occurring over the last several decades. Young Gikuyu women and urban Kenyans have largely given up circumcision, and many urban and rural Sudanese have shifted to the less severe sunna or stopped doing any form. However there has also been persistence or even expansion of the practices in situations where migrants or displaced persons seek to assimilate to the practices of higher-status ethnic groups with more severe forms. Hygienic conditions have improved in many areas. Well-trained circumcisers with access to modern equipment and supplies perform clitoridectomy and infibulation with sterile razors, needles, and sutures, and utilize antibiotic powder, but for many areas unhygienic circumstances are still a concern. However, there has been growing consensus among reformers that medicalization or reduced severity of the cutting should be rejected and only complete abandonment of the practices should be advocated.

Concerns with psychological and sexual impairment have begun to be researched in a few places. Because of the many health risks associated

with these surgeries (including hemorrhage, septicemia, shock, infections, urine retention, and obstructed labor), both international and African criticism has grown in recent years. Numerous public health education efforts and programs are being promoted by international organizations (e.g., UNICEF, World Health Organization), national governments, and international and local nongovernmental organizations (e.g., the Inter-African Committee Against Harmful Traditional Practices [IAC], CARE) in each of the affected countries.

Because the surgeries are usually performed on children, with or without their consent, a human rights concern for the right to bodily integrity motivates change efforts, some of which are aimed at educating people about their rights as encouragement to protect themselves and their children despite cultural pressures. Also, as theological discussions have led some religious leaders to question and even condemn some or all types of the practices, religious leaders have increased their involvement, most notably Islamic teachers who are speaking out against the idea that sunna circumcision is permissible. However, there continue to be some Muslim leaders who defend the less severe form.

In addition to basic work to promote women's literacy and empowerment, change efforts employ many creative ideas. In some countries, change agents have successfully promoted alternate rituals without cutting. Governments and organizations have cooperated on projects to raise awareness in neighborhoods and rural communities, combining religious messages, health messages, songs, and skits. The IAC has sponsored boys' soccer tournaments (the FGM Cup, for example) to promote male awareness. Posters, videos, radio programs, and religious songs with anti-circumcision messages are being utilized.

Several factors contribute to the resistance to change efforts. First, people are concerned that their daughters will not be accepted for marriage, both because of the social expectations that circumcision is important to virginity as well as beliefs about the greater sexual satisfaction for males afforded by a tightly infibulated vaginal opening. The preservation of ethnic and/or religious traditions and identity serves as the other major barrier to acceptance of change.

See also **Gender; Human Rights; Sexual Behavior.**

BIBLIOGRAPHY

Abusharaf, Rogaia Mustafa, ed. *Female Circumcision: Multicultural Perspectives.* Philadelphia: University of Pennsylvania Press, 2006.

Gruenbaum, Ellen. *The Female Circumcision Controversy: An Anthropological Perspective.* Philadelphia: University of Pennsylvania Press, 2001.

Shell-Duncan, Bettina, and Ylva Hernlund, eds. *Female "Circumcision" in Africa: Culture, Controversy, and Change.* Boulder, CO: Lynne Reinner, 2001.

UNICEF. *Changing a Harmful Social Convention: Female Genital Mutilation/Cutting.* Florence, Italy: UNICEF Innocenti Research Centre, 2005. Available from http://www.unicef.org/irc.

ELLEN GRUENBAUM

INSANITY. *See* Disease.

INTERLACUSTRINE REGION, HISTORY OF (1000 BCE TO 1500 CE).

The Great Lakes of Victoria, Kivu, Mwitanzige, and Tanganyika are surrounded by a stunning array of environments. People living there before 1500 CE developed equally diverse livelihoods that blurred and, later, highlighted distinctions between farmer, herder, and forager, and complex arts of living that in turn blurred and later highlighted distinctions between insider and outsider, first-comer and newcomer, leader and follower. This complex tapestry of social forms underlay the growth of numerous different state forms after circa 1500 CE. Environmental diversity lies at the heart of these earliest experiments in livelihood. Social diversity lies at the heart of their later embracing of hierarchy.

AGRICULTURE

Agricultural communities speaking four distinct languages had settled the region by 500 BCE. Each group practiced a slightly different system of food production, suited to a specific environment. The earliest farmers and herders spoke Central Sudanic and Eastern Sahelian languages. They grew

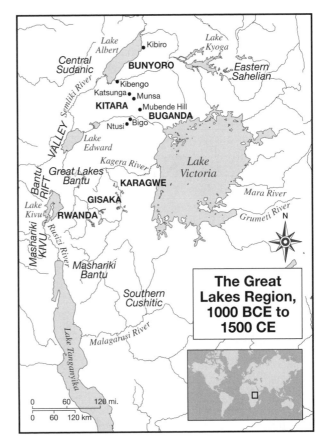

COURTESY OF TOM O'CONNELL, DIGITAL MEDIA SERVICES, NORTHWESTERN UNIVERSITY

cereal crops, such as sorghum, and herded livestock, such as cattle. They lived in the lower and drier lands in the northern and eastern parts of the region. Their neighbors spoke Southern Cushitic and Mashariki Bantu languages. The southern Cushites emphasized cattle raising over their grain crops and settled thinly across the driest grasslands in the south of the region. Mashariki Bantu speakers settled amidst the other three groups. They grew root crops such as yams, kept goats, and fished. All four groups almost certainly hunted as well. Central Sudanic and Eastern Sahelian speakers, together with their Bantu-speaking neighbors, smelted iron and forged tools, weapons, and jewelry from the raw metal. It is possible that the earliest settlers grew bananas as well. All of these communities changed their physical environments by clearing forests for new fields, for lumber, and for wood to make charcoal for their furnaces. These distinct but neighboring communities characterized most of the last millennium BCE populations.

AN ECLECTIC AGRICULTURAL SYNTHESIS

This mosaic of different food systems gave way to communities who practiced mixed food systems as farmers and herders settled entirely new lands, as their numbers grew in their ancestral lands, and as a period of increased aridity set in during the last centuries before the common era. The blurring of the correspondence between environmental zone and agricultural system simultaneously involved the replacement of an older set of linguistic identities by a powerful set of communities who came to speak one set of related languages, called Great Lakes Bantu, descended from Mashariki Bantu.

Words in Great Lakes Bantu for cattle and grains come from Cushitic, Eastern Sahelian, and Central Sudanic languages. This reflects the fact that Great Lakes Bantu-speaking people learned of these important sources of food and wealth from their neighbors. The process probably also involved some Central Sudanic, Eastern Sahelian, and Southern Cushitic speakers learning Great Lakes Bantu speech. Over a period of generations, as they married Bantu-speaking women who then raised their children to speak their mother's language, the cluster of dialects that constituted Great Lakes Bantu became a common tongue across the region. Great Lakes Bantu speakers may also have displaced some Central Sudanic, Eastern Sahelian, and Southern Cushitic communities from their pastures and fields. After 500 BCE, people speaking Great Lakes Bantu possessed the agricultural expertise necessary to settle anywhere in the region. By 800 CE, the entire Great Lakes region was largely Bantu-speaking. This Great Lakes Bantu synthesis included new forms of political and healing institutions tied to both mixed and specialized forms of agropastoral production.

SPECIALIZATIONS AND PROSPERITY

Between 800 and 1500, new forms of political, religious, and economic life stamped the region with a set of cultural–geographic contours that differed widely from the world of the first millennium CE. Specialized pastoralism, cereal agriculture, and intensive banana farming marked clear boundaries between the drier interior and the wetter lands near the Great Lakes. Cattle and cereals, on the one hand, and bananas, on the other hand, insured these communities against the environmental stresses and strains placed on their lands during the first millennium CE.

Pastoralists sought to reverse a trend of falling yields of yams by breeding cattle and tending large herds and growing more drought-resistant grains such as *eleusine* (a kind of millet) and sorghum. They sharpened their skills in the drier central grasslands around archaeological sites such as Ntusi. Other communities embraced banana farming as their answer to the problem of environmental stress. Banana gardens yield steady, perennial supplies of that starchy staple which can then be roasted, dried to make flower, or brewed as a savory beer. The best lands for this crop occur discontinuously in high rainfall areas in the Kivu Rift and near the northern and western shores of Lake Victoria. Families who tended these banana gardens built villages clustered around their rich lands. Families who raised herds of cattle and grew cereals in the central grasslands established seasonal patterns of movement in search of water and pasture while staying in close contact with large farming settlements like Bigo, Ntusi, and Munsa.

Successful herders, cereal farmers, and banana growers built many new settlements of large size and used a new style of pottery throughout the region. Changes in climate shaped these developments, with alternating drier and wetter periods favoring different combinations of farming and herding. In these changing contexts, people invented new ways for their communities to grow in size and complexity. Among the most important were social ties that bound land owners and cattle owners to people who wanted these two precious things. Innovations in healing practices designed to ensure prosperity and to address the challenges to fertility enjoined by agricultural specializations also created new social bonds.

NETWORKS AND POWER

After about 1200, herder-farmers invented a new form of clientship that cut across older networks of obligation based on matrimonial alliance and on the inheritance of land. The new forms assigned use rights in cattle to the client, regardless of their status as kin. In the western portion of the Great Lakes region, where this occurred, cattle formed an entirely new source for generating large numbers of followers. Parties to this sort of clientship could now reconfigure ties of kinship as they saw fit.

Though probably never on the scale boasted about in the royal dynastic traditions, herders and farmers built alliances with their neighbors. Groups rich in cattle loaned some animals to a neighboring group to create a patron-client tie. A group representative might begin by making a loan between two lineages; the client hoped to make a new start or to improve his or her local standing, the patron hoped to do the same. Responsibilities for loans were corporate, they bound together not only the individuals but their lineages as well. Leaders of richer and more numerous groups together might threaten or initiate military action against a weaker neighbor. If successful, the booty in animals and women would have added to the attackers' strength by attracting still more followers to their fold because of their ability to distribute their increased holdings to yet more clients. Neighbors of equal strength in wealth and numbers, or living in a ritually powerful area could also enter into a tribute relationship with expansionist neighbors. Clientship relations may have helped as well to reduce the risk to cattle of disease epidemics by dispersing animals and settlements more evenly and thereby transforming wilderness into homesteads, fields, and pastures.

These economic innovations led to the emergence of new centers of political and religious power in Kitara (Munsa, Ntusi, Bigo, and Kisengwe), Karagwe, and the highlands. Parts of this historical experience have been conserved in the oral traditions from Bunyoro-Kitara and Rwanda. For example, historical traditions about the kings of Rwanda recall that the first king, Gihanga, received his cattle from Kazigaaba, the eponymous head of one of the three clans that all elements of Rwandan society agree were already in Rwanda before the emergence of the kingship. These stories tell us that the association of royal power with cattle owes a great debt to the preexisting mixed farmers.

Women, as mothers, sisters, and wives, played a central role in these changes. They developed agricultural expertise and stimulated demand at local markets for iron hoes. They embodied alliances between lineages. A woman who married into a lineage would bear children for that lineage, but she would maintain social ties to her natal lineage. As the main providers of socialization to children, women reproduced Lakes Bantu societies materially, biologically, and ideologically. Women commonly possessed encyclopedic control over genealogies and were therefore routinely consulted in matters of succession to kin offices. In societies speaking languages ancestral to Rundi, Rwanda, and Ha, a mother with many healthy children possessed a diadem of motherhood that signified her standing and power as a source of life.

GROWTH AND SUFFERING ANCESTORS

Political and economic patronage expanded settlement and concentrated wealth. However, it invited new forms of conflict and suffering as the possibility of cattle raids, epidemic cattle diseases (in Bunyoro, Karagwe, or Gisaka) and conflicts over access to fields rich enough to support perennial crops like bananas and coffee (in Rwanda, Buhaya, and Buganda) increased. New responsibilities for healers and chiefs emerged to address these challenges. People speak of these inventions most clearly in their oral traditions about the founding and dissolution of royal dynasties. The more widespread and well understood of these stories tell of ancient persons known as Cwezi, or of great leadership figures like Ryángombe and Kiranga and Nyabingi.

These figures began to appear in the oral histories both of homesteads and the royal court, probably as early as the fifteenth century. They were important parts of the ways in which growing communities understood their options for meeting the challenges posed to fertility by expanding populations and by the growing scale of military conflict. The Cwezi, Ryángombe, Kiranga, and Nyabingi addressed issues that had formerly been the province of ancestral and territorial spirits. All of the stories about these figures raised tough questions about the scope of royal power, and they did so by attributing to these persons special power over matters of fertility and fecundity. The Cwezi figures best exemplify these themes.

People who told stories about the Cwezi and their mediums often highlighted their authority over people's fertility and prosperity. Nineteenth-century descriptions of Cwezi mediums often represent them as moving about the countryside, bringing communities into contact with the particular Cwezi spirit to whom they were consecrated. It is unclear how old the practice of itinerating is but these spirits and their mediums displaced the authority of the older, local spirits in two ways. Ancestral and territorial spirits served their own descendants or the residents of a particular territory, but the Cwezi spirits addressed the tensions surrounding the quest for fertility of people who had no kinship ties with them. Ancestral and territorial spirits had mediums and propitiators who had been central to founding new settlements in the central grasslands. They were located at specific shrines that may have made it difficult to compete with Cwezi mediums whose mobility brought their healing powers to communities at the margins of centralizing kingdoms.

Though Cwezi figures came to be associated with particular places, their healing powers were not tied down there. The chiefdoms at sites such as Mubende Hill and Kasunga were associated in oral traditions with Cwezi figures. And archaeologists have unearthed evidence of ritual activity—such as burying people in pits formerly used to store grain— associated cereal agriculture. If making offerings to Cwezi figures helped secure the prosperity of these chiefdoms, it is not hard to see how the appeal of that activity could travel.

This new form of spirit mediumship—based on the Cwezi and told of in traditions and recoverable in the meanings of ancient words for spirit possession and types of spirits—came together from the threads of political and economic struggle that resulted from agricultural specializations. These specializations required communities either to settle altogether unfamiliar lands (before 1400 at the drier Ntusi, and after 1300 at the wetter sites of Mubende Hill, and Kasunga, between Lake Victoria and the Kivu Rift) or to commit to intensified landuse strategies (as banana farmers did in the wetter zones near the lakes and in the highlands of the Rift massif and Mount Elgon). An intensified agropastoralism also developed during a transitional period from relatively high rainfall, in the fifteenth and sixteenth centuries, to a period of low rainfall, from the 1500s to the later eighteenth century (coinciding with the "Little Ice Age" of the northern latitudes). This is perhaps visible in the larger settlements of Bigo, Munsa, and Kibengo, which were surrounded by earthen ditches. At these locations, old local spirits were less able to meet the needs of people who, in addition to the far older concerns

with human fertility and well-being, also required protection from cattle raids and who worried about the fertility and well-being of livestock and the prosperity of fields planted in cereals. Cwezi mediums created new nodes of authority that helped newcomers meet the challenges they now faced in the central grasslands.

However expansionist the new chiefdoms were, after the fifteenth century, local healers still played an important role in formulating criticisms of royal power and they continued to shape the court's ability to extend its rule. Contractual relations around land and cattle, and control over a small but significant flow of luxury items like glass beads, ivory and copper jewelry, also still integrated outsiders into royal systems of patronage and clientship. Reciprocal relations and social hierarchy between the Great Lakes rested on the region's exceedingly fertile agricultural base. And this in turn meant then (as it does now) that rich and regular surpluses of food and cattle could be managed to support specializations in trade, industry, and statecraft. Before the sixteenth century, Great Lakes leaders and followers, patrons and clients, healers and chiefs designed rich political, social, and philosophical innovations as they negotiated the challenges and opportunities of a fecund but changing physical environment with extraordinary cognitive virtuosity.

See also **Agriculture: Beginnings and Development; Death, Mourning, and Ancestors; Desertification, Reactions to, History of (c. 5000 to 1000 BCE).**

BIBLIOGRAPHY

Chrétien, Jean-Pierre. *The Great Lakes of Africa: Two Thousand Years of History.* New York: Zone Books, 2004.

Cohen, David William. *Womunafu's Bunafu: A Study of Authority in a Nineteenth-Century African Community.* Princeton, NJ: Princeton University Press, 1977.

Ehret, Christopher. *An African Classical Age: Eastern and Southern Africa in World History, 1000 B.C. to A.D. 400.* Charlottesville: University Press of Virginia, 1998.

Feierman, Steven. "Political Economy and Political Culture in Early East Africa." In *African History,* ed. Philip Curtin, et al., 3rd edition. London: Longmans, 1995.

Kiwanuka, M.S.M. *A History of the Kingdom of Buganda.* London: Longmans, 1971.

Lejju, J.S.; Peter Robertshaw; and David Taylor. "Africa's Earliest Bananas?" *Journal of Archaeological Science* 33 (2006): 102–113.

Reid, Andrew. "Early Settlement and Social Organization in the Interlacustrine Region," *Azania* 29–30 (1994–1995): 303–313.

Robertshaw, Peter, and David Taylor. "Climate Change and the Rise of Political Complexity in Western Uganda." *Journal of African History* 41, no. 1 (2000): 1–28.

Schmidt, Peter R. *Iron Production in East Africa: Symbolism, Science, and Archaeology.* Bloomington: Indiana University Press, 1997.

Schoenbrun, David L. *A Green Place, A Good Place: Agrarian Change, Gender, and Social Organization Between the Great Lakes to the Fifteenth Century.* Portsmouth, NH: Heinemann Publishers, 1998.

Tantala, Renee. "Early History of Kitara in Western Uganda: Process Models of Religious and Political Change." Ph.D. diss., University of Wisconsin—Madison, 1989.

Vansina, Jan. *The Antecedents to Modern Rwanda: The Nyiginya Kingdom.* Madison: University of Wisconsin Press, 2005.

Wrigley, Christopher. *Kingship and State: The Buganda Dynasty.* Cambridge, U.K.: Cambridge University Press, 1996.

DAVID LEE SCHOENBRUN

INTERLACUSTRINE REGION, HISTORY OF (1500 TO 1900).

The interlacustrine region of East Africa encompasses central and southern Uganda, Rwanda, Burundi, and northern Tanzania, a historically integrated zone characterized during the period under examination by population movement, economic diversification, and political complexity. In terms of physical geography, the vast plateau of central East Africa has as its highest point the Ruwenzori Mountains, sometimes described as the spine of Africa; the plateau is peppered with a number of lakes, the largest being Tanganyika and Victoria, followed by Albert, Kyoga, Kivu, Edward, and George. Although much of the land is hot and dry, the interlacustrine region is an important exception; in particular, the region between lakes Victoria, Kyoga, Kivu, and the northern part of Tanganyika has abundant rainfall and the resultant fertility has made it a natural center of civilization.

EARLY HISTORY

Between the eleventh and fifteenth centuries, the increased incidence of cattle-keeping and changes in pottery style suggest a series of migrations into the area, and the new arrivals appear to have influenced the growth of a series of commercially and politically interconnected chiefdoms. Archaeological sites at Bigo, Ntusi, and Kibiro indicate an increasingly complex economic system based on pastoralism by the fifteenth century. The most important of these by the middle of the fifteenth century was Kitara, in southwest Uganda, initially ruled by a dynasty known as the Chwezi from their capital at Bigo. Between the fifteenth and seventeenth centuries, a wave of Nilotic migrations took place, so called because of the migrants' original use of Nilo-Saharan languages from the area of southern Sudan and Ethiopia.

These resettlements had a major impact on state building and the creation of new societies and cultures in the region, and the migrants usually interacted with extant Bantu speakers and adopted Bantu languages. The western Nilotes, the most important for the region under study, carved the new state of Bunyoro from the former Kitara, and appear to have been instrumental in the foundation of the kingdom of Buganda on the northern shore of Lake Victoria. They also probably originated the pastoralist groups of Ankole—where they were known as Hima—and Rwanda and Burundi, where they were known as Tutsi. Other related states in the region included Toro, located in western Uganda and situated south of the Kagera River. All these polities were amalgamations of clans, and they shared much in the way of custom, political structures, symbolism, and semi-mythical narratives of origin; but the smaller states were vulnerable to the larger political ambitions of Bunyoro and Buganda.

In the sixteenth century, Bunyoro was the most powerful state in the area, but it was increasingly troubled by the rise of Buganda to the south, and in the course of the seventeenth and eighteenth centuries, Buganda replaced Bunyoro as the dominant state in the interlacustrine region. With economic stability provided in large part by banana plantain cultivation, the Ganda developed an effective and hierarchical administrative system; they also articulated a powerful sense of identity, expressed most effectively in the military context. Buganda had expanded to control, directly or indirectly, a large swathe of southern, western and central Uganda by the beginning of the nineteenth century.

Further south, also highly fertile, were the states of Rwanda and Burundi, where the agricultural majority—the Bantu-speaking Hutu—came increasingly to be dominated by a pastoral minority. The Tutsi, who adopted local language and much local custom, had nonetheless become well established as ruling elites by the eighteenth century. At first they traded cattle for food with the Hutu; in time, however, the Tutsi clans developed the commercial relationship into a position of domination, lending cattle to farmers who offered herding services in return. Political leadership in both Rwanda and Burundi thus came to be associated with ownership of cattle; livestock owners became an aristocratic warrior elite, offering protection to their subjects from raids by rival clans.

POLITICAL AND ECONOMIC CHANGE IN THE NINETEENTH CENTURY

In the course of the nineteenth century, the interlacustrine region became engaged in long-distance trade, centered on the island of Zanzibar at the coast, where the Omani sultan Seyyid Said had moved his capital in the 1830s. Zanzibari trading caravans had reached the Great Lakes region by the end of the 1840s, by which time several states and peoples had already begun to respond to external commercial stimuli. Omani-Swahili merchants, initially following existing trade routes across the interior, established permanent trading posts at Unyanyembe in northern central Tanzania, and at Ujiji on Lake Tanganyika. These these functioned as entrepots, drawing the region into an extensive trading network.

The first coastal traders had reached Buganda by 1844, traveling to the west of Lake Victoria, and an Arab community was more or less permanently established there by the end of the 1850s. These aggressive adventurers sought to take advantage of decentralized societies, and also became influential in a number of chiefdoms. In Unyanyembe they wielded considerable influence over the political establishment from the late 1850s, and also in Karagwe, west of Lake Victoria, where the commercial settlement at Kafuro became one of the most important such centers in the region. Further north, however, Buganda kept coastal traders under control, notwithstanding the growing influence of Islam within the kingdom. Traders singularly failed to penetrate either Rwanda or Burundi.

Elsewhere, commercial impulses at least in part explained the rise of new and aggressive states, most famously the one Mirambo created in northwest Tanzania in the 1870s. It was highly militaristic and aimed at breaking Arab domination of interior commerce and controlling Lake Victoria trade routes. Lake Victoria had become a key arena of commercial competition and military ambition by the 1860s and 1870s. Slaves were the main export from the region, although ivory was also important.

The overall impact on the interlacustrine region was a rise in violence, the increasing militarization of African society, and the dislocation of people. Lake Victoria and the broad arc from Unyanyembe to Buganda and Bunyoro had become a corridor of conflict. Buganda responded aggressively to commercial opportunities. It became the largest exporter of slaves in the northern lacustrine region and sought to dominate Lake Victoria: to this end, the Ganda developed a fleet of canoes that extended their influence considerably at a time when their armies were becoming less effective on land.

Meanwhile, the Nyamwezi became famous as porters, and later as highly successful traders, adventurers, and entrepreneurs. Indeed, the term Nyamwezi—meaning people of the moon—was largely invented in the nineteenth century to describe the commercial people of northwest Tanzania. In fact, however, nineteenth-century commerce was inimical to the region's long-term economic development. The slave trade was doomed, particularly with growing European influence in the area. Commerce in ivory was also headed for disaster, as the elephant population was either decimated or moved deeper into the Central African interior. Both trades were based fundamentally on war and violence, and only colonial occupation changed this pattern, establishing cash crops for export as the basis of the East African economy.

THE ADVENT OF COLONIAL RULE

The presence of missionaries (notably in Buganda and at the south of Lake Victoria), explorers, and consular officials preceded the advent of colonial rule. By the 1880s, Britain and Germany, by mutual agreement, had divided central eastern Africa. Britain took Kenya and Uganda and surrendered its traditional sphere of influence over the Zanzibari coast to Germany, which acquired Tanganyika, Rwanda, and Burundi. Responses to European invasion varied from society to society. Resistance was more or less immediate in some areas: the Germans were confronted with stiff resistance in central Tanzania from the mid-1880s, and Bunyoro fought against the British almost as soon as the latter had established a permanent presence north of Lake Victoria. Other societies sought to turn the European presence to their advantage. Perhaps the most dramatic example of such collaboration was Buganda, which acted as the agent of British imperialism in southern and central Uganda through much of the 1890s, and later gave a version of its name to the territory. Buganda secured an advantageous position in the British protectorate through the 1900 Uganda Agreement.

Interlacustrine Africa, and swathes of eastern Africa more generally, experienced cumulative environmental crises in the late nineteenth century. Through the nineteenth century, large areas had witnessed changing patterns of human settlement as a result of the slave trade, leading to a sleeping sickness epidemic at the north end of Lake Victoria by the end of the 1890s; this coincided with the rinderpest epidemic that swept through the area from the beginning of the 1890s and left pastoral communities in particular vulnerable and destitute at a time of aggressive foreign incursion. In 1900, as colonial states consolidated politically and looked toward the creation of viable cash crop systems, the region was on the cusp of major socioeconomic change.

See also **Ceramics; Ecosystems; Interlacustrine Region, History of (1000 BCE to 1500 CE); Languages: Nilo-Saharan.**

BIBLIOGRAPHY

Beattie, John. *The Nyoro State*. Oxford: Clarendon Press, 1971.

Chretien, Jean-Pierre. *The Great Lakes of Africa: Two Thousand Years of History*, trans. Scott Straus. Rev. edition. New York: Zone Books, 2006.

Karugire, Samwiri R. *A History of the Kingdom of Nkore in Western Uganda to 1896*. Oxford: Clarendon Press, 1971.

Katoke, Israel. *The Karagwe Kingdom: A History of the Abanyambo of North Western Tanzania c. 1400–1915*. Nairobi, Kenya: East African Publishing House, 1975.

Nyakatura, John. *Anatomy of an African Kingdom: A History of Bunyoro-Kitara*. New York: Anchor Press, 1973.

Ogot, B.A., and J.A. Kieran, eds. *Zamani: A Survey of East African History*. Nairobi, Kenya: East African Publishing House, 1968.

Oliver, Roland Mathew, and Gervase Mathew, eds. *History of East Africa*, Vol. I. Oxford: Clarendon Press, 1963.

Reid, Richard J. *Political Power Pre Colonial Buganda: Economy Society and Warfare*. Athens: Ohio University Press, 2003.

Steinhart, Edward I. *Conflict and Collaboration: The Kingdoms of Western Uganda 1890–1907*. Princeton, NJ: Princeton University Press, 1977.

Sutton, J. "The Antecedents of the Interlacustrine Kingdoms." *Journal of African History* 34 (1993): 33–64.

Vansina, Jan. *L'evolution du royaume rwanda des origins a 1900*. Brussels, Belgium: Academie Royale des Sciences d'Outre-Mer, 1962.

RICHARD REID

INTERNATIONAL MONETARY FUND.

The International Monetary Fund (IMF) is an international organization of 184 member countries based in Washington, D.C. It was established to promote international monetary cooperation, exchange stability, and orderly exchange arrangements; to foster economic growth and high levels of employment; and to provide temporary financial assistance to countries to help ease balance of payments adjustments. Since its founding in 1945 (together with the World Bank), the IMF's general purposes have remained unchanged but its operations—which involve economic surveillance, financial assistance, and technical assistance—have evolved constantly, reflecting shifts in development thinking. The IMF and the World Bank are sister institutions in the United Nations system. Their stated goal of raising living standards in their member countries is the same. But their approaches to this goal are different, with the IMF focusing on ensuring the short-term stability of the international financial system, whereas the World Bank concentrates on long-term economic development and poverty reduction.

SURVEILLANCE

IMF economists visit each member country on a regular basis to gather information and hold discussions with government and central bank officials, and sometimes business executives, labor representatives, members of parliament, and civil society organizations. The mission then submits a report to the IMF's Executive Board for discussion. The board's views are subsequently summarized and transmitted to the country's authorities for action. The objectives of surveillance are to detect vulnerabilities and risks at an early stage, to help member countries strengthen their policy frameworks and institutions, and to improve transparency and accountability. It covers a wide range of economic policies, with the emphasis varying in accordance with a country's individual circumstances:

- Exchange rate, monetary, and fiscal policies are at the core of the process; the IMF provides advice on issues ranging from the choice of exchange rate regime to ensuring consistency between the regime and fiscal and monetary policies.

- Financial sector issues have received greater emphasis in recent years, following the crises of the late 1990s.

- Assessment of risks and vulnerabilities stemming from large and sometimes volatile capital flows has also become more central to IMF surveillance in recent years.

- Institutional and structural issues have also gained importance in the wake of financial crises and in the context of some countries' transition from planned to market economies. Working closely with the World Bank, the IMF has played an influential role in developing, implementing, and assessing internationally recognized standards and codes in areas crucial to the efficient functioning of a modern economy such as central bank independence, financial sector regulation, and policy transparency and accountability.

FINANCIAL ASSISTANCE

A core responsibility of the IMF is to provide loans to countries experiencing balance of payments problems, that is, those that cannot find sufficient financing on affordable terms to meet their net international payments. This financial assistance enables countries to rebuild their international reserves, stabilize their currencies, continue paying for imports, and restore conditions for strong economic growth. Unlike some other development institutions such as the World Bank, the IMF does not lend for specific projects.

An IMF loan is usually provided under an arrangement that stipulates the specific policies and measures a country has agreed to implement to resolve its balance of payments problem. The economic program underlying the arrangement is formulated by the country in consultation with the IMF, and is presented to the Fund's Board in a Letter of Intent. Once an arrangement is approved by the Board, the loan is released in phased installments as the program is carried out.

Over the years, the IMF has developed various loan instruments, or facilities, that are tailored to address the specific circumstances of its diverse membership. Almost all African countries borrowing from the IMF do so through a particular credit line called the Poverty Reduction and Growth Facility (PRGF). The interest rate levied on PRGF loans is 0.5 percent, and loans are to be repaid over a period of 5½–10 years. Nonconcessional loans are provided mostly to middle-income countries, mainly through Stand-By Arrangements (SBA), and occasionally using the Extended Fund Facility (EFF), the Supplemental Reserve Facility (SRF), or the Compensatory Financing Facility (CFF). The IMF also provides emergency assistance to support recovery from natural disasters and conflicts, in some cases at concessional interest rates.

TECHNICAL ASSISTANCE

The main objective of IMF technical assistance is to help countries build up their human and institutional capacity to design and implement effective macroeconomic and structural policies. Normally provided free of charge to any requesting member country, about three quarters of IMF technical assistance goes to low and lower-middle income countries, particularly in sub-Saharan Africa and Asia. Postconflict countries are also major beneficiaries, with Democratic Republic of the Congo being the top African recipient in recent years. The IMF provides technical assistance in its main areas of expertise: macroeconomic policy, tax policy and revenue administration, expenditure management, monetary policy, the exchange rate system, financial sector sustainability, and macroeconomic and financial statistics.

CONTROVERSIAL EFFECTS OF IMF POLICIES

Over the years, IMF policies have come to symbolize what is wrong with globalization, and quite a few African intellectuals and policymakers have publicly referred to IMF policies as the main impediments to economic and social progress in their countries. The IMF approach to economic stabilization and its conditionality (requirement for borrowing countries to commit to specific economic and financial policies) have been subject to many criticisms. Chief among these are the claims that IMF programs in African countries tend to impose a difficult fiscal retrenchment of approximately the same size and composition that relies heavily on regressive tax rate hikes and undue compression of public investment; that they often require a large exchange rate devaluation that worsen the situation of the poor; and that these programs seldom pay attention to corrupt managerial practices by unaccountable government officials.

The IMF has attempted to respond to its critics by improving transparency in its operations and committing itself to the protection of social programs in government budgets. But much remains to be done to substantially change its heavy reliance on traditional, mechanical economic models derived from neoclassical thinking, and to change the distribution of power on its Executive Board where sub-Saharan African countries still represent less than 1 percent of total voting rights.

See also **Aid and Development; Money; World Bank.**

BIBLIOGRAPHY

Fischer, Stanley. "Applied Economics in Action: IMF Programs." *The American Economic Review* 87, no. 2 (1997): 23–27.

International Monetary Fund. Available from http://www.imf.org.

Killick, Tony. *IMF Programmes in Developing Countries: Design and Impact.* London: Routledge, 1995.

Mohamed, Elsaudi. "Sub-Saharan African Debt and IMF Programs: A Critical. Evaluation." Ph.D. diss. Colorado State University, 1994.

Mussa, Michael, and Miguel Savastano. *The IMF Approach to Economic Stabilization.* Working paper no. 99/104. Washington DC: International Monetary Fund, 1999.

Tchundjang Pouémi, Joseph. *Monnaie, servitude et liberté: la repression monétaire de l'Afrique.* Paris: Editions Jeune Afrique, 1980.

CÉLESTIN MONGA

INTERNATIONAL RELATIONS. *See* **Cold War; Economic Community of West African States (ECOWAS); United Nations.**

ISLAM

This entry includes the following articles:
OVERVIEW
NORTHERN AFRICA
WESTERN AFRICA
EASTERN AND CENTRAL AFRICA
SOUTHERN AFRICA
SUFI ORDERS
ISLAMISM
MODERNISM

OVERVIEW

When the word "Islam" is mentioned or written, the general audience or reader in the West tends to think of the Arabs and/or the Middle East. Yet there are more Muslims in Africa than in the Middle East, while the country with the largest Muslim population outside East Asia is not Arab or Middle Eastern but African. It is Nigeria. The earliest Muslims who fled persecution in Mecca took refuge with King Negus of Ethiopia in 615 CE. This connection later produced the first *mu'azzin*, or caller for prayer, in the person of Bilal, an ex-slave of Ethiopian origin. When Muslim armies embarked on their spectacular conquests outside Arabia shortly after the death of Prophet Mohammed in 632, North Africa was added to Islam almost simultaneously with Syria and Palestine. Africa gave sanctuary to Muslim "heretics" from the east, the Shi'a and the Kharijites, where they were able to establish their first independent states (the Fatimids in Tunisia and later in Egypt, the Idrisids in Morocco, and the Ibadi Kharijites in Tehert and other oases in the Sahara.

During the nineteenth and early twentieth centuries imperial Europe met formidable challenges from numerous jihads in Africa but hardly any in the Middle East proper. Except for Indonesia and perhaps Malaysia, African countries individually continue to send more pilgrims to the holy land in Saudi Arabia than most other countries. So

African Muslims can legitimately claim that, from the days of Islam's infancy, they were full participants in what came to be known as the Islamic empire and civilization.

There are over 300 million Africans who profess Islam as their religion, or about one-fourth of the Muslim world population. Put differently, one in every three Africans is a Muslim, but adherence to Islamic dogma and precepts has varied considerably over time and place and Islam remains a crucial force that has helped shape the cultural, ethical, legal, political, literary and aesthetic milieu of many African communities where it has established roots. Only the more recent European industrial revolution and the colonialism associated with it could be said to have had as great or even greater influence on the lives and the thinking of Africans.

EXPANSION INTO SOUTHERN MEDITERRANEAN

Historians identify the five following phases of the Islamic expansion in Africa north and south of the Sahara: an early phase of conquest (640–1050 CE), during which Islam became dominant politically and increasingly culturally in Egypt and in North Africa; a long intervening phase (1050–1750), which witnessed the slow spread of the faith across the Sahara; a third and relatively short phase (1750–1901) characterized by militant Islamic reform movements in tropical Africa; a fourth one coterminous with colonialism; and a postcolonial phase that continues to this day.

Islam established itself in Africa either through conquest or by peaceful means. It accompanied Arab warriors into Egypt and North Africa from where it spread peacefully into the savanna region of tropical Africa in the west, and along the Nile in the east. Similarly, it also reached the coastal area of East Africa. Muslim traders, itinerant clerics, Sufi leaders and, later, pilgrims were the main agents of diffusion.

Led by Amr ibn al-Aas, Arab armies easily captured the richest Byzantine province of Egypt in 641 CE, long weakened by religious differences between the Egyptian Copts, who were determined to defend their Monophysite creed against the ambition and interference of an overbearing Byzantine Emperor

and a dogmatic Eastern Church. Egypt secured, Muslim armies, eventually strengthened by new committed Berber converts, marched westward along the southern Mediterranean coast to conquer the remaining domains of the ailing Byzantine empire in North Africa; Tunisia, Algeria, and Morocco.

However, conquering North Africa was easer than keeping it under the firm control of Damascus, since 660 CE, the capital of the Umayyad Caliphate. The stiff and protracted resistance, which lasted till the end of the century, proved as difficult to the new invaders as it was to the Byzantines and to the Romans before them. In the end, however, Islam prevailed but only because of the predominance of Muslim Berbers who soon managed to govern themselves independent of the Umayyads in Damascus and later of the Abbasids in Baghdad (750–1258). It was these committed converts to Islam who in 710 crossed the straights of Gibraltar to add yet another territory, Spain, to the Muslim empire.

ISLAMIZATION AND ARABIZATION

Each of the five phases of Islamic expansion in Africa has its own distinguishing features, though the beginning and end of each phase may not have been as precise as stated above. The first phase of conquest and penetration was accompanied by two important developments, conversion and Arabization. In Egypt and in North Africa both processes occurred, though not necessarily concurrently. Conversion to Islam was relatively faster than Arabization, even as Arab rulers discouraged conversion to prevent the disappearance of a large base of paying *dhimmi*s or non-Muslims.

Arabization, on the other hand, took much longer, especially in North Africa, and would not at any rate have achieved the degree of thoroughness and permanency it eventually did had it not been for the massive migration into the region of the Banu Hilal Arab tribes. In the second half of the eleventh century the Fatimid caliph in Cairo unleashed these marauding tribesmen to punish his rebellious North African subjects.

While the different states in this part of Africa separately maintained their independence from the east, their citizens lost their tongue to Arabic. In time the two processes of Islamization and Arabization facilitated a fundamental linguistic, religious, cultural and social transformation of the entire region and wove them into an insoluble relationship with the Arabs and Arabized Muslims of the Middle East.

ECONOMIC GROWTH

During the three to four centuries following conquest, North Africa, including Egypt, experienced an unprecedented economic growth, thanks to the presence of numerous trade and agricultural centers, the expansion of irrigation, the relative stability of administration, population growth, diversification of produce, and the voluminous and profitable trade within the Mediterranean world and across the Sahara in gold and slaves. The Fatimids in Egypt excelled in grand public buildings for religious, educational, and medical purposes. The opulence of the Caliph's palaces in Cairo, the extravagance of viziers' residences, the elegance of glassware, wood carving and arabesque, and the magnificence of the Fatimids' architectural style still displayed in surviving mausoleums are clear testimony of unprecedented prosperity and wealth. The same could be said of the important political and commercial centers in North Africa; Marrakesh, Fez, Tlemcen, and Kairawan.

THE FIRST PURITANICAL MOVEMENTS

Perhaps as a reaction to this ostentatious style of living among Muslims, North Africa experienced two major puritanical religious movements in the eleventh and twelfth centuries. It also witnessed the appearance and spread of religious orders and fraternities led by mystics or Sufi shaykhs. The first revivalist movement to challenge the status quo was al-Murabitun (Almoravids), circa 1070–1147, a Sanhaja Berber-based jihadist insurrection from southern Morocco. The Almoravids quickly controlled the Maghrib or western North Africa. From their newly build capital of Marrakesh, they enforced a rigid adherence to Islamic law interpreted in accordance with the conservative Maliki *madhhab* or school of Islamic jurisprudence. It was the Almoravids, according to Ibn Khaldun, the fourteenth century North African historian, who destroyed the Sudanic kingdom of Ghana in the south in the eleventh century, and invaded Spain in support of its disunited Muslim rulers beleaguered as they were by their Christian enemies.

Shortly thereafter the Almoravid rulers themselves became victims of the same urban vices for which they so ruthlessly condemned their predecessors. Their enemies and successors, the Almohids (Unitarians; 1128–1269), were quick to capitalize on the Almoravids' highhandedness and incompetence and waged a determined jihad against them. Supported mainly by the agriculturalist Masmuda tribesmen of the Atlas Mountains, the Almohids fought against the rigorous legalism of the Almoravids in favor of a more personal and esoteric Sufi Islam. By 1160 they united the Maghrib as a whole under one government, which was to last till 1269.

Three important legacies survived the Islamic revivalism of this period: Sufism, conservative Malikism, and militant Islam. These three elements were to have a great impact on Islam at both ends of the Sahara, as will be seen in the case of the militant Islamic reformism of the eighteenth century in tropical Africa, and the vocal and violent Islam of the nineteenth in Algeria, Nigeria, Egypt, and the Sudan.

DIFFUSION SOUTHWARD

Islam reached tropical Africa at different places and times during the second phase of expansion. It came to the southern edge of the great Sahara sometime after the middle of the tenth century, carried there by Berber traders, Kharijite preachers, Sufi sheikhs or Sunni itinerant *faqih*s or clerics. Migrating Arab nomads, traders and Muslim mystics and clerics brought Islam to the Nile valley as well as along the coast of East Africa, though with greater difficulty and, with the exception of Northern Sudan, with much less impact. It is generally understood that the many termini of trade at the southern end of the Sahara or along the Nile valley and the mini maritime states on the East Africa coast were the staging points of Islam's spread deeper into tropical Africa.

It is believed that by the middle of the eleventh century many kings and their immediate entourages in West Africa became Muslims, at least nominally. The ruler of the kingdom of Mali on the Niger Bend, the Sarakin or chiefs of the Hausa state in what is now northern Nigeria and the king of Kanem to the north east of Lake Chad all embraced Islam during or shortly after this period. However, thanks to the long and fierce Nubian resistance, it took much longer for Islam to supplant Christianity in Nubia, while its propagation beyond the coastal area of East Africa was slowed considerably by the eastward migration of the Bantu-speaking peoples.

For many reasons African monarchs found it efficacious to profess Islam while keeping to their traditional beliefs and customs. The benefits of literacy, mathematics, weights and measures, commerce, credit, medicine, architecture, clerics' arbitration in inter-state disputes and relations with a comparatively advanced Muslim world were clear to them. Nevertheless, such advantages could not substitute for the political legitimacy derived from local cults and rituals to which the majority of the population still adhered. The result was religious pluralism and syncretism or the mixing of Islamic precepts and practices with local belief and rituals.

As a minority dependent on the goodwill of their royal hosts, Muslim traders and clerics were not much concerned about the strict observance of Islamic ordinances and restrictions among the new converts. For one thing, being followers of one or the other of the many Sufi *tariqa*s or orders emanating from North Africa, they themselves were not strict practitioners of orthodox Islam. The brand of Islam that was thus transmitted to sub-Saharan Africa was tolerant and adaptable as it was essentially Sufi in ritual and conviction and only secondly Maliki in jurisprudence and adjudication. It was precisely this tolerant and accommodating attitude of the Muslim scholars, clerics and Sufi sheiks that enabled them to develop and profitable working relations with their non-Muslim hosts. In time many towns in tropical Africa, Timbuktu, Jenné, Gao, Kano, Katsina, Sennar, and others, developed into reputable centers of Islamic education with standards and quality that rivaled any the Middle East.

REVOLUTIONARY ISLAM

By the second half of the eighteenth century the generally tolerant attitude of Sufism toward traditional beliefs and practices seemed to have reached its limits in many parts of tropical Africa. This was the start of the third phase of the Islamic expansion (1750–1901), during which militant Muslim leaders from Guinea and Senegal in the West to Somalia in the East had the destiny of numerous Muslim and non-Muslim communities in their hands. Many factors contributed to this outcome;. Internally, West Africa had been suffering from increased desertification since the fifteenth century, and many camel-herding Tuareg and cattle-raising Fulbe and other nomads pushed south and eastward looking for better pastures and water sources. Much reminiscent of the widely publicized intertribal conflict in Dar Fur of the early twenty-first century, the Tuareg and Fulbe pastoralists squeezed their reluctant host farming communities for more pasture land, especially in Northern Nigeria. Many Hausa kings and others responded by taxing nomads more than farmers; an infraction in Islamic law publicly condemned by the reformers.

Additionally, as Islam gradually spread beyond the confines of royal residence and town, Muslims in many instances became no longer the hapless minorities they once were. Because of increased contact with the Middle East through trade, pilgrimage or in the pursuit of further education, Muslims in West Africa became increasingly aware of major developments in the other parts of Dar al-Islam. They were apprehensive of the creeping annexation of Muslim lands by Christian Europe: the British occupied India in 1784 and Bonaparte conquered Egypt in 1799. Muslim intellectuals and reformers attributed the Muslim world's inability to rebel aggression to religious laxity and indifference. Many clerics began openly to condemn customs and rituals they deemed incompatible with the orthodox Islam they had experienced in their travels or identified in available Muslim classical works.

More importantly, the eighteenth century puritanical Wahhabi revolution in the Arabian Peninsula, which condemned *bid'a* or unorthodox beliefs and practices, put Muslim communities around the world on notice that they must forcibly cleanse Islam of innovation and pollutants. Many militant Muslim leaders in tropical Africa set out to eradicate syncretism by force of arms, if necessary. Such a meritorious enterprise was made even more urgent because the widespread millenarian expectations among Muslims in north and south of the Sahara, as elsewhere, of the impending end of time and the subsequent appearance of the Mahdi or the messiah. The expected Mahdi was to restore order and bring about justice and tranquility where oppression and injustice had prevailed. The eschatological and apocalyptic chaos and disbelief associated with the end of time made it easy for religious leaders like 'Uthman dan Fodio of Northern Nigeria, Seku Ahmadu of Masina on the middle Delta of the Niger, 'Umar Tal of Mali, Muhammed Ahmad al-Mahdi of the Sudan, and others to rally behind them disenchanted Muslims in search of an ideal Islamic dominion.

During the nineteenth century these committed clerics led successful jihads against lax Muslims as well as non-Muslims and subsequently established shari'a-based states in their respective territories. The reformists believed that the theocratic states they created were informed by laws and principles of governance earlier implemented by the Prophet Mohammad in Medina early in the seventh century. Most of these states survived to the end of the century and offered the advancing European armies stiff though unsuccessful resistance and challenge.

NONMILITANT TRADITION

Not all religious leaders in tropical Africa in this time period were bent on bringing about change by militant means. Al-Hajj Salim Suwari was a sixteenth century quietest scholar in southern Mali who left behind a strong tradition of Muslim tolerance and forbearance. He taught that conversion to Islam is the decision of Allah, not man, and forcing unbelievers to profess Islam was interference with Allah's will, hence jihad against them was legally indefensible. The Suwarian tradition is very strong among the Dyula and other communities active in the savanna-forest trade. The quietist and collaborative tradition among the Tijaniyya Murids of colonial Senegal is well known. In the Sudan to the east, both the Khatmiyya and the Hindiya *tariqa*s actively opposed the jihad of al-Mahdi. The former even collaborated with the British to bring an end to the Mahdiyya, a betrayal for which the followers of the Mahdi never forgave their fellow Sudanese.

In contemporary Sudan, the Muslim Republicans are known for their teachings of an Islam that is inclusive, liberal and egalitarian. They also preach a break away from the shari'a as currently understood and applied, and call of a fresh and unconventional interpretation of the Qur'an in light of modern reality. This is also the case of a small but productive group of Muslim intellectuals in South Africa, a country where Muslims constitute about 3 percent of the population.

THE AFTERMATH OF JIHAD

The impact of the Islamic revivalist movements on Muslims in tropical Africa was profound. Two processes went hand in hand: Islam's territorial expansion and the concomitant addition, occasionally forceful, of new converts; and the intensification and purification of belief among people who were already Muslims. However, unlike the situation in North Africa and in Northern Sudan, Islamization here was not accompanied by Arabization. Along the Swahili coast of East Africa, settlers form the Arabian Peninsula even lost their Arabic, which they replaced by Kiswahili.

With their comparatively effective administration and central control, attendant cultural assimilation, growth of long distant trade and the flourishing of an educational system focused exclusively on the Islamic heritage, the caliphates established by jihads became an important factor that fostered emerging identities in this part of Africa, identities that were largely Islamic and, in theory at least, self sufficient. It is common knowledge that these Islamic or Arab-informed identities played a major, often catastrophic role in the postindependence period of many nation states carved out of or around these caliphates.

A case in point is Nigeria and the Sudan where ethnic and geographic cleavages often coincide with religious fault lines. There were other developments beside the emerging separate identities. Raiding neighboring "pagan" communities in the name of Islam produced a good supply of captives most of whom were sold into slavery and joined the millions of Africans forcefully deported to the New World. When exporting slaves became increasingly impossible after the 1807 ban, slaves in Northern Nigeria ended up manning the growing and prosperous plantations in the Sokoto caliphate. They thus helped provide their masters with the necessary economic resources and free time to pursue careers other than farming. Many became scholars, a fact that explains why Northern Nigeria experienced a period of unprecedented intellectual and literary growth during the nineteenth century. As the caliphate was governed by the shari'a, and the legacy this legal system left behind haunts contemporary Nigerians. It pits Northerners who are mainly Muslims against the southerners who are largely Christians over the controversial question of the shari'a federal court.

ISLAM'S UNEXPECTED ALLY

The fourth phase, the colonial period, is the shortest, though by no means unimportant. The atmosphere of general peace and order that eventually prevailed under colonial rule and the easy and more efficient means of travel provided opportunities hitherto unavailable to Muslim traders and proselytizers. These men ventured widely in areas and among peoples who in the past opposed them and hindered their progress. The result was that Islam spread both geographically and demographically, especially in West Africa. Again, governing African societies on the cheap obliged the financially starved colonial administrators to rely in many instances on indigenous leadership, often Muslim traditional rulers, as the British did in Nigeria and in the Sudan, and the French in Mali and in Senegal. Urban populations grew gradually, weakening in the process tribal links, obligations and traditional beliefs. Islam, with its universal fraternity and acumen became thus an attractive alternative. Even among the Bambara of Mali, once a formidable enemy of the jihadists, Islam made not inconsequential gains under French rule. Though the imperial powers managed to crush Islam as a political power, they unknowingly and unintentionally helped it spread fast, and in time it regained its political posture, especially in the postcolonial period.

MOVING FORWARD OR GOING BACK

The postindependence period in sub-Saharan Africa has witnessed an Islam that has so far proven to be potentially as explosive as the jihad phase of the nineteenth century. To be sure, Islam was an indispensable vehicle of resistance to colonialism. After World War II, nationalists in countries with a Muslim majority or sizeable Muslim minority were largely the product of western and not traditional Islamic education. They, nevertheless, used Islamic symbols, language and rituals to bring an anticolonial, though not necessarily anti-West or anti-modernist message to Muslim audiences that were predisposed to such powerful and emotive communication. The liberation struggle these secular-minded western-educated Muslim intellectuals led was nationalist, liberal, communitarian, and solidly modernist. They harked back to the jihads of 'Uthman dan Fodio in Nigeria, the Mahdi in the Sudan, Abdul-Qadir in Algeria or the Sanusi in Libya as well as to others for the sake of unity, liberation and nation building. To them, these Islamic reformers of early decades were first and foremost national heroes, admired for their love of freedom and independence, not for their piety or fidelity to Islam.

After independence in the 1950s and early 1960s, Islamic heritage lost its appeal among the political leadership in Muslim Africa and was thus on the defensive. As a religious, political, and social force, Islam was considered intransigent and hence incompatible with modernity, while its followers, particularly the Sufi, were seen as conservative and reactionary. The standoff continued for awhile between the Muslim secularists holding the reins of power as presidents or army generals and the Muslim scholars, Sufi shaykhs and their large body of followers. Since the 1980s, however, Islam reemerged to play a significant and growing role. Secularists everywhere in Africa failed to deliver on the promises of the liberation struggle. Corruption was rampant, economic stagnation and poverty replaced the growth and prosperity of the early sixties, interethnic strife and warfare became common, lawlessness was the order of the day in many urban centers, even the very survival of the nation-state became questionable. Africa was facing its toughest challenge for survival.

THE CHALLENGE OF ASSERTIVE ISLAM

A new breed of Muslim activists has stepped in the fill up the vacuum in social and political leadership. These young, exuberant, articulate, disciplined, and well-educated Islamists are committed to a new-old Islamic political, economic, and social vision, a vision that is bolder, more assertive, more complex and far reaching than any entertained by the early reformers. They find guidance and inspiration in the voluminous writings of many Muslim thinkers and revolutionaries; Sayyid Qutb of Egypt (1906–1964), al-Mawdudi of Pakistan (d. 1979), al-Ghannuchi of Tunisia (b. 1942), Abbasi Madani of Algeria (b. 1940), Turabi of the Sudan (b. 1932), Abu Bakar Gummi of Nigeria (d. 1992), and others. Though these Muslim intellectuals may differ in their diagnosis of the problems facing Islam in general and their respective communities in particular, they all agree that "Islam is the solution." This slogan is current in every Muslim society where Islamic activism or "fundamentalism" prevails.

The purposeful new call of Islam is unapologetic in its condemnation of many customs, attitudes and behaviors believed to be Western. In this Islam-centered discourse, western civilization, with its materialistic determinism, free market capitalism, insatiable consumerism, and institutionalized liberal individualism, has been found wanting. The new order these Islamists are struggling to create is a political, legal, economic and social system informed mainly by the shari'a, and accountable to human beings in so far as they remain obedient vicegerents of God on earth. In this worldview the physical and metaphysical are perceived to be inseparable; the sacred and the profane are eternally intertwined.

The banner bearers of assertive and often militant Islam in Africa are generally young men and women who are anti-mystic, well educated, and motivated usually recent immigrants to the blustering and congested urban centers. They form an wide spectrum that includes student associations like the vociferous Muslim Student Society in Northern Nigeria, the Muslim Brotherhood Youth Organization in the Sudan, the Yan Izala of Nigeria bent, as the name in the Hausa language indicates, on eradicating all innovations in Islam, and politico-religious organizations like the Muslim Brothers in Egypt and the Sudan, the Nahda or renaissance in Tunisia, and the Islamic Salvation Front (Front Islamique du Salut, or FIS) in Algeria. There are, in addition, militant splinter groups that targets not only non-Muslims but also Muslims they consider apostates because of their actual or perceived support for current secular governments in many countries.

Representatives of these are the Egyptian Jama'at Islamiya (Muslim Community) of Shaykh Omar Abdel-Rahan, the Islamic Jihad Community of Mohammed Faraj, and the al-Takfir wal Hijra, and the Algerian faction within the Islamic Salvation Front led by the charismatic young mosque preacher, Ali Belhadj which was blamed for murdering thousands of Algerians in the 1990s. They differ from the mainstream Islamist organizations on the means of achieving the goal, but not the goal itself. The organizations in the first group

have reluctantly accepted the status quo and are working within the political system, flawed and corrupt as it is, because they believe society and even its secular rulers are redeemable. The militant groups, on the other hand, see no possibility of redeeming a society so steeped in *Jahiliyya* or ignorance; and certainly not its pro-Western rulers. The conflict between Islamists and the secularists in Africa and among the Islamists themselves, and between these and the rising Christian evangelism will be in existence for some time to come.

See also **Barghash Ibn Sa'id; Egypt, Early; Fez; Gao; History of Africa; Ibn Khaldun, Abd al-Rahman; Jenné and Jenné-jeno; Kano; Marrakesh; Nubia; Timbuktu; 'Uthman dan Fodio.**

BIBLIOGRAPHY

Abdo, Geneive. 2000. *No God but God: Egypt and the Triumph of Islam.* New York: Oxford University Press.

Abun-Nasr, Jamal. *The Tijaniyya: A Sufi Order in the Modern World.* New York: Oxford University Press, 1965.

El-Affendi, Abdelwahab. *Turabi's Revolution: Islam and Power in the Sudan.* London: Grey Seal, 1991.

Entelis, John, ed. *Islam, Democracy, and the State in North Africa.* Bloomington: Indiana University Press, 1997.

Hiskett, Mervyn. *The Development of Islam in West Africa.* New York: Longman, 1984.

Horton, Mark. *Shanga: The Archeology of a Muslim Trading Community on the Coast of East Africa.* London: British Institute of in Eastern Africa, 1996.

Hunwick, John, ed. *The Sharia in Songhay.* New York: Oxford University Press, 1985.

Last, Murray. *The Sokoto Caliphate.* London: Longman, 1967.

Levtzion, Nehemia, and Randall L. Pouwels, eds. *The History of Islam in Africa.* Athens: Ohio University Press, 2000.

Lewis, I. M., ed. *Islam in Tropical Africa.* Bloomington: Indiana University Press, 1980.

Martin, G. B. *Muslim Brotherhoods in Nineteenth-Century Africa.* Cambridge, U.K.: Cambridge University Press, 1976.

McHugh, Neil. *Holymen of the Blue Nile: The Making of an Arab-Islamic Community in the Nilotic Sudan, 1500–1850.* Evanston, IL: Northwestern University Press, 1994.

Pouwels, Randall. *Horn and Crescent: Cultural Change and Traditional Islam on the East African Coast (800–1900).* Cambridge, U.K.: Cambridge University Press, 1987.

Robinson, David. *Muslim Societies in African History.* Cambridge, U.K.: Cambridge University Press, 2004.

Robinson, David. *The Holy War of Umar Tal.* Oxford: Clarendon Press, 1985.

ISMAIL H. ABDALLA

NORTHERN AFRICA

There is a tendency in literature on Islam in North Africa to reproduce the political duality of the *bilad as-siba* (the lands of dissidence) and the *bilad al-makhzan* (the lands under the sultan's authority, mainly towns and their surroundings) in the context of religion. This distinction has often been used to imply an unorthodox Islam in the countryside with veneration of saints and shrines versus a learned, scripturalized, and orthodox Islam in the towns. This dichotomy distorts complex traditions and relations.

After the Arab conquest in the eighth century, North Africa rapidly Islamized, in contrast to countries such as Egypt, but it did not become totally Arabized. In the thirteenth century, Christianity disappeared from the region, although Jewish communities remain in Morocco and Tunisia in the twenty-first century.

ISLAMIZATION THROUGH HETERODOX TRADITIONS

Islamization came through heterodox traditions, it seems. The Berbers mostly embraced Islam after the Arab conquests but chose religious-doctrinal forms of resistance against the Arab conquest. Although Muslim, Arabs nonetheless discriminated against Berbers and exploited them, and Berbers saw this discrimination as un-Islamic. Until the tenth century, the heterodox *Khariji* form of Islam was a kind of Berber "national religion" (H. Halm). A core *Khariji* doctrine was the possibility for the Muslim community (the *umma*) to choose its *imam* (leader) and to destitute him in case of unworthiness, abuses of power, or evident incompetence. This doctrine allowed Berbers to resist rule by an Arab governor in Kairouan and to select an Arab or Berber *imam* on its own. There are still *Khariji*, or Ibadi, Muslims found in northwestern Libya (Jabal Nafusa), on the island Jerba in southern Tunisia, and in the small towns of the Mzab around Ghardaya in southern and in Tahert in western Algeria.

The Idris dynasty in Morocco (789–926) and the Fatimid Caliphate (909–1171, in North Africa until 1049) were Shi'i at the outset. Shi'ism did not last in the region, despite of the continued significance of descendants of the Prophet in the Maghrib.

The Almohads (1130–1269) created a cultural, political, and economic unity in Islamic Spain and North Africa. Natural sciences and medicine made enormous progress, and philosophy and theology flourished, with scholars like Ibn Tufayl, Ibn Rushd (Averroës), and Ibn Zuhr. In 1230 the region firmly adopted the Maliki school (*madhhab*) of law, first introduced by the Almoravid dynasty (1056–1147).

BECOMING "ORTHODOX" SUNNI

The Marinid dynasty (1196–1549), unlike the Almoravid and Almohad dynasties, had no distinctive interpretation of Islam of its own, so the Marinids legitimized themselves as fighters for orthodox Sunnism. Marinid rulers took the unusual title of *amir al-muslimin* (prince of the Muslims) and founded *madrasa*s (mosque schools) throughout the Maghrib to train theologians and jurists. Thus, a majority of North Africans became and remained Sunni Muslims of the Maliki school, with exceptions in the regions where the Ottomans introduced their official Hanafi *madhhab*. Centers of learning included the university-mosques of Zaituna in Tunis, the Qarawiyin in Fez, and the Yusufiya in Marrakesh.

SUFISM AS A POLITICAL AND SOCIAL FORCE

Perhaps the most North African feature of Islam is the phenomenon of holy men, living or dead, the *salihun* (the pious ones, singular *salih*), the *wali*s (friends of God), or marabouts (from the Arabic *murabit*). Quite often linked to mystical orders (*turuq*), the *salihun* live—or are buried—in *zawiya*s, a sort of lodge or cloister, which were and are spiritual—and also economic—centers of a region or even beyond. A marabout has a specific *baraka*, a charismatic supernatural blessing power, mostly as a descendant of the Prophet Muhammad (*sharif*, pl. *shurafa'*). A *salih* is an intermediary between God and humans, between the ruler and the ruled, or between tribes. From the fourteenth century on, local *zawiya*s and Sufi orders, such as the Qadiriya,

Shrine of a *marabout* in the valley of Drâa, Morocco.
Marabouts are unknown saints. *Marabouts* and the veneration
of their shrines play an important role in North African Islam.
Shrines are found nearly everywhere in the region. COURTESY OF
SANDRA PETERMANN, MAINZ

Shadhiliya, and the Darqawa, became an important
factor of social and political life, especially in the
countryside. New orders were founded until the
nineteenth century. Marabouts mobilized their followers to resist the Portuguese and Spaniards, but
became by the late nineteenth and twentieth centuries accused of collaboration with the colonial
French.

Sufi practices can range from meditative recitation of the Qur'an to spectacular ecstatic rituals
involving music, dance, and healing practices. The
ulama (the learned men) sometimes fiercely opposed
the practices, but they too were often Sufis. Until the
nineteenth century, nearly every male Maghribi was
member of one or more Sufi orders. Thus, Sufism

was the cement of society, crossing social and ethnic
frontiers. Some orders were only locally active; others,
like the Tijaniyya and Sanusiyya, built transnational
networks that reached far into sub-Saharan Africa and
sometimes played major political roles. The leader of
the Sanusiyya order, for example, eventually became
the Libyan king.

After independence, the influence of Sufi orders
disappeared to a large extent. In the twenty-first
century, however, North African governments use
Sufism as a tool against Islamism and terrorism and
encourage and support the orders, an attitude that
has led to their revival.

REFORM AND REFORMERS

Mulay Sulaiman, the Alawite sultan of Morocco
from 1793 to 1822, under the influence of
Muhammad ibn 'Abd al-Wahhab, the founder of
Wahhabism, started fighting against what he considered un-Islamic practices, namely the veneration
of saints and other aspects of popular religion. His
overall goal, however, was to control the influential
Sufi orders.

In the middle of the nineteenth century, Khayr
ad-Din (1822–1883)—reformer, minister, and
from 1873 until 1877 prime minister—tried institutional and legal reforms in Tunisia, introducing a
constitution and a parliament.

Salafi thinking, meaning a reform program
intended to reintroduce the Golden Age of Islam and
the pious lifestyle of the early Muslims, came to North
Africa from the East. Its aim was to revitalize Islamic
culture and civilization, fight against unquestioned
tradition and popular and mystic forms of Islam, and
preach an educated urban Islam. Reformists considered maraboutism as *shirk* (associationism), the greatest sin in Islam. In 1903 the Egyptian reformer
Muhammad 'Abduh visited Tunis and Algiers, instigating local reform activities, carried on by the Algerian
Shaykh Abdelhamid Ben Badis (1889–1940). In
Morocco in the 1930s, urban merchants influenced
by the Qarawiyin university-mosque in Fez spread
reformist thinking in the countryside.

In the late 1980s, the Algerian Islamist move-
ment, the Front Islamique de Salut (Islamic
Salvation Front), articulated the popular political
protest against the state-party National Liberation
Front (Front de Libération Nationale, or FLN).
Successful in the national elections of 1991, the

Eickelman, Dale F. *Moroccan Islam: Tradition and Society in a Pilgrimage Center.* Austin: University of Texas Press, 1976.

Eickelman, Dale F. *Knowledge and Power in Morocco: The Education of a Twentieth-Century Notable.* Princeton, NJ: Princeton University Press, 1985.

Ferrié, Jean-Noël. *La religion de la vie quotidienne chez les Marocains musulman.* Paris: Karthala, 2004.

Geertz, Clifford. *Islam Observed: Religious Development in Morocco and Indonesia.* New Haven, CT: Yale University Press, 1968.

Geertz, Clifford. "Suq: the Bazaar Economy in Sefrou." In *Meaning and Order in Moroccan Society: Three Essays in Cultural Analysis,* ed. Clifford Geertz, Hildred Geertz, and Lawrence Rosen. Cambridge, U.K.: Cambridge University Press, 1979.

Joffé, George. "Maghribi Islam and Islam in the Maghrib." In *African Islam and Islam in Africa: Encounters between Sufis and Islamists,* ed. Eva Evers Rosander and David Westerlund. London: Hurst, 1997.

JÖRN THIELMANN

Courtyard and minaret of the Great Mosque in Kairouan, the *Jami Sidi Uqba*. The minaret, named after the celebrated Muslim conqueror of North Africa, is the oldest in North Africa. Built in the 3rd century AH/9th century CE, its style greatly influenced Islamic architecture in the Maghreb and al-Andalus. STEVE OUTRAM/MIRA.COM/DRR.NET

military banned the party in a coup d'état with a resulting civil war. In Morocco, the main Islamist movement *al-ʿadl wa-l-ihsan* (Justice and Charity) of Shaykh Abdassalam Yassine acts in half legality. The Tunisian Rachid Ghannouchi, head of the Islamic movement Renaissance, lives in London in exile. Popular Islamic opposition movements are opposed to military-bureaucratic elites.

See also **Fez; Judaism in Africa; Marrakesh; Morocco; Religion and Ritual; Tunis; Tunisia.**

BIBLIOGRAPHY

Andezian, Sossie. *Expériences du divin dans l'Algérie contemporaine: Adeptes des saints de la region de Tlemcen.* Paris: CNRS Editions, 2001.

WESTERN AFRICA

No definite date can be established for the introduction of Islam in western Africa. The kingdom of Kanem to the east of Lake Chad had the earliest known contact with Islam, beginning around 800 CE, and by 1085 Hume Jilme had become the first ruler of Kanem to proclaim Islam as a state religion. According to the Arab geographer Ibn Hawqal (f. 973), Muslim traders were present as early as 884 in Tadmakkat, an influential city situated along the Saharan caravan routes that is said to have maintained commercial connections with Qayrwan, Ghadames, and Tripoli in the north and with Gao in the south.

In the middle of the tenth century, Arab historian Ali al-Masudi (d. 965) wrote that the Ibadi Muslims of Morocco were in control of the gold trade with a center on the river Senegal. The Arab historian Abu Ubayd al-Bakri (d. 1094), who recorded the existence of Muslim communities in different parts of western Africa, stated that Warjabi b. Rabis (d. 1040) was the first Muslim ruler of the kingdom of Takrur on the Senegal River, and claimed that only Muslims could be entrusted to rule in Kaw Kaw, the state on the Niger Bend better known as Gao. Though no ruler of the ancient empire of Ghana accepted Islam, Muslims were employed there as scribes and ministers, and a mosque was built near the palace of Tunka Manin, who ruled from 1063 to 1068. The collapse of the empire of Ghana was brought about in part by the Almoravid movement (1050–1147), started by 'Abdallah b. Yasin (d. 1059) to revive Islam among the nomadic Sanhaja of the western Sahara. The Almoravids signaled the rise of Islam as a militant political force in western Africa.

The subsequent political history of Islam in the region has been linked to two related themes: trade, and the rise and fall of kingdoms and empires. There seems to be a consensus among historians that the trade in gold, slaves, salt, cloth, and horses between northern and western Africa brought Muslim merchants (Arabs and Berbers) into western Africa, where some of them settled in commercial centers such as Tadmakkat and Awdaghust. The desire for taxes and control over trade led chieftains of local polities to conquer towns and villages along the trade routes, resulting in the emergence of multiethnic kingdoms that were in due course transformed into multinational empires such as Mali (c. 1235–1390), Songhay (c. 1464–1591), and Kanem-Bornu (c. 1386–c. 1800). In such situations the particularistic religions of the diverse nationalities became anachronistic, making it easy for empire builders to impose the universalism of Islam to unify the disparate peoples within their empires. An added push for Islam might have come from the Muslim merchants, whose settler communities became influential political constituencies because of their trading connections to the outside world. Where rulers recognized Islam as a source of power, they sought to keep the influence of Islam within their courts and main cities, and away from rivals and subordinates.

RELIGIOUS DIMENSIONS

The theory that attempts to control trade led to the transformation of local polities into empires that adopted Islam as their unifying ideology explains the role of Islam in the political history of western Africa, but the theory is silent on a rather important point: the religious dimensions of Islam in the region. In fact, there have been few studies of the religious aspect since Joseph Trimingham (1959) drew attention to Islam introducing new beliefs, rituals, and ceremonies in addition to social and political changes. In al-Bakri's account of the advent of Islam into the Malinke kingdom of

Mali, the introduction of monotheism and prophethood appears, as represented in the basic Islamic creed: there is no god but Allah and Muhammad is his messenger.

The concept of a supreme deity was not new to western African religions, but the Islamic characterization of the supreme deity was novel. Allah, believed in Islam to be a unity unique in essence, attribute, power, and deed, was introduced as the only deity worthy of devotion and to whom all prayers should be addressed for favorable intervention in human affairs. Belief in the efficacy of Muslim prayers and charms, including magical use of the Qur'an became widespread even among western Africans who did convert to Islam. The function of Muhammad as the messenger of the supreme deity may have resembled the role of the diviner in the indigenous religions, but there were important doctrinal differences. Among other religious practices introduced by Islam, pilgrimages to Mecca must have been instrumental in exposing western Africa and the wider world of Islam to each other, as the famous pilgrimage of Mansa Musa (d. 1337) indicates. Muslim prayers at five appointed times daily and the religious festivals in the Islamic calendar may have introduced a consciousness of lineal, in contrast to circular, time.

POLITICAL AND SOCIAL DIMENSIONS

Islamic influences on civic institutions and processes have often generated tensions in the political sphere. Rulers of most western African polities had also been the custodians of the indigenous religions of their respective communities. Once a ruler became a Muslim, problems arose: acceptance of Islam entailed abandoning certain aspects of the indigenous religions, but failure to patronize the indigenous religions compromised the legitimacy of the ruler. Many rulers faced contending with pressures from Muslim scholars and the indigenous priests, as well as from the non-Muslim majority within their kingdoms.

Conflict between Islam and indigenous religions in western Africa was not confined to politics, it produced social tensions as well. Ibn Battuta noted many inconsistencies during his 1352 to 1353 tour of the region. Particularly interesting is his account of gender roles, in which he found many Muslims not observing the strict female-male segregation emphasized in classical Islamic legal texts. There has been a general tendency over the centuries to invoke Islam to justify subordinating women to male authority, yet Islamic influences on gender roles have varied from one area to another, with pre-Islamic gender ideas and practices still active even long after Islamization. Thus, among the Hausa of northern Nigeria, women of childbearing age are usually excluded from public life and often kept in *purdah* (the practice of keeping women hidden, either physically or by their clothing, from men), in contrast to the largely unrestricted public life of Yoruba Muslim women of southwestern Nigeria.

Women's studies began in the 1970s to unravel the complexities of Islam and gender relations in western Africa, and also the gradual changes in gender roles that are becoming more discernible, especially with the spread of Western education in Muslim communities. An excellent example of this trend is Jean Boyd's *Caliph's Sister* (1989), which highlights the influential roles of Nana Asma'u (1793–1865) as a female Islamic scholar, poet, and leader not only in the Sokoto Caliphate (1804–1903), but also in contemporary northern Nigeria.

It must be emphasized that conflict has not been the only relationship between Islam and western African religions. Complexities abound, especially regarding conversion, syncretism, and reform. Conversion to Islam in western Africa has been characterized by a gradual process of peaceful adoption, unlike northern Africa where conversion came more swiftly through military conquest. Although radical religious reform may be directly linked to conversion and syncretism, these were not the only factors. Among the important reasons for the eventual rise of Islamic reform movements in western Africa was the growth of Islamic learning, resulting in the increased number of radical clerics who championed the reforms and provided leadership for the reform movements.

ISLAMIC SCHOLARSHIP

The fame of Ibrahim al-Kanemi (d. 1211), a poet and man of letters who taught Arabic grammar and literature in northern Africa, indicates that Islamic learning in Kanem must have developed in the previous centuries to produce such an accomplished literary figure. The Syrian encyclopedist al-'Umari (d. 1349) recorded that students from the kingdom of Kanem attended the famous al-Azhar University in Cairo.

Timbuktu, Jenné, Takedda, Katsina, and Gazargamu were among the centers of Islamic learning from where Islamic scholars emerged during the fourteenth to sixteenth centuries as influential leaders serving as ministers, scribes, envoys, and peacemakers. From around 1500 CE onward, Islamic scholars debated whether they should work within the political establishment or keep their distance, especially from Muslim rulers who had not completely jettisoned indigenous religions. In the end many scholars decided they had to carry out armed struggle (jihad) to wrest power from those rulers in order to reform their societies on more strictly Islamic patterns.

THE JIHAD ERA: EIGHTEENTH TO NINETEENTH CENTURIES

The leaders of the jihads belonged to Sufi orders, and some of them were regarded by other Muslims as saints who performed miracles. The Sufi doctrine dictating absolute obedience and loyalty of disciples to their spiritual mentors provided charismatic models of political leadership. The jihad leaders invoked the Sufi doctrine of seeing God in mystical visions to proclaim religious authority for their political projects. Sufi orders helped in mass mobilization and in the construction of collective identities for the communities and states that resulted from the jihads. Some of the jihad leaders were also erudite scholars who produced extensive bodies of literature, thus underscoring the link between Islamic scholarship and militant religious reform during the jihad era.

Malik Sy's jihad, which started around 1690 on the Senegal River, was followed by several others during the next two centuries. 'Uthman dan Fodio (d. 1817) led a jihad that united for the first time the Hausa city-states into the Sokoto Caliphate, the largest and most enduring of all the Islamic states that resulted from the jihads; its legacy is still a live political issue in Nigeria. In the Manding region of modern Mali, al-Hajj 'Umar Tal, a Tukolor from Futa Toro in Senegal, launched his jihad in 1852 among the largely non-Muslim Bambara. He had to contend with the French forces who eventually ended all the jihad movements in western Africa around 1900.

ISLAM AND COLONIALISM

The relationship between Islam and European colonialism from the 1880s to the 1960s continues being debated, often with polemical undercurrents. Where Muslims, especially the influential Islamic scholars, cooperated with colonial authorities, Islam is portrayed in colonial reports and studies as a civilization higher than African paganism. But where Islam was invoked to mobilize opposition to colonialism, the negative portrayal of Islam as a superstitious religion militating against the civilizing mission of colonialism is emphasized.

Furthermore, to the extent that Islamic scholars were influential leaders of public opinion, they became contenders with African nationalists for power and prestige. For this reason some African nationalists reechoed the colonialists' negative attitudes toward Islam. Additionally, African nationalists often charged Islamic leaders with the capital sin of collaborating with colonialism, of adopting an Arab religion foreign to Africa, and of leading the conservative opposition to modernization. However, long before African nationalists became active in the midcolonial period, Muslim leaders such as Mamadu Lamine (d. 1887) and Samori Touré (d. 1900) had led armed resistances against the colonial powers; hence Muslim leaders are sometimes counted among the heroes of African nationalism.

Finally, western African Muslims quite naturally object to all these negative portrayals. Instead, they emphasize the negative impact of colonialism on Islamic institutions, especially Islamic law and education, both replaced by largely secular European models. Muslims' responses to colonialism in western Africa have been complex and divergent and cannot be fitted neatly into models of collaboration or resistance.

ISLAM IN THE POSTCOLONIAL ERA

The conflicting perspectives on Islam and colonialism are easily discernible, but harder to see are the more subtle aspects of the symbiosis that has evolved between the two into the postcolonial era. For example, the challenge from European secular education has led to the modernization of the old system of Islamic learning, whereas Islamic organizations have sought to influence governmental policies otherwise dominated by European secular ideas. French colonial policies of assimilation devastated Islamic political institutions, but the Tijaniyya and Mouridiyya Sufi orders (the Tijani and the Mourides) provided an Islamic public order as an alternative to the colonial one. As one-party regimes sought to monopolize power in the postcolonial era, Sufi orders have emerged as veritable political parties and economic cooperatives challenging the hegemony, efficiency, and legitimacy of the one-party regimes that have now become widely discredited. This trend had been particularly evident in Senegal, where the various Sufi orders and their leaders (*marabouts*) have been influential in the political, economic, and social domains.

The economic changes resulting from colonialism have intensified the historical link between the spread of Islam and long distance trade, as noted earlier. The colonialists introduced trains and automobiles that increased the mobility of Muslim traders and merchants into regions hitherto not easily accessible. Dyula and Hausa trading diasporas (*zango*) helped the spread of Islam during the colonial period. Affiliation with Sufi orders and participation in their congregational devotion cemented the trust and creditworthiness that undergirded the financial and commercial networks connecting the trading diasporas all over western Africa. Islamic scholars served as notaries public, accountants, legal advisers, and as the ritual experts who officiated in the Islamic religious life of the trading diasporas. The Tijaniyya Sufi order had been the more active in linking these diasporas and spreading Islam, especially through its Senegalese leader, Shaikh Ibrahim Niasse, who composed Arabic poems on his extensive travels throughout western Africa from the 1940s to his death in 1975. On the other hand, the Mouridiyya order has been famous for organizing its members into a sort of an agricultural collective that helped boost the production of peanuts, a major export of the Senegalese economy since the colonial period.

European secular legal systems bequeathed by colonialism are still predominant among Muslim communities in western Africa. However, Islamic law, sometimes influenced by local customs, is still applied in family cases. In Nigeria, Muslims' demand for expanding the jurisdiction of Islamic law had often led to intense political and constitutional controversies in the 1970s and 1980s. The adoption of *shari'a* law in nearly a third of Nigeria's northern states in 2000 makes it the only western African nation to do so, and resulted in violence between Muslims and Christians. As was the case during the jihad era, the years since the mid-1980s have witnessed the emergence of Islam as a contending political force against the one-party regimes that have ruled Muslim communities in western Africa since independence from colonialism in the 1960s. There are some exceptions. In Senegal, Islam functions as a constructive political force mostly in support of the modernizing, secular state.

A related development is the emergence of movements opposed to the Sufi orders, despite their contributions to Islam in western Africa over the centuries. These anti-Sufi movements, ideologically informed by Saudi Arabian Wahhabism, resulted from increased contacts with the wider Islamic world, especially through studies in Saudi Islamic universities and pilgrimage to Mecca, made easier and more frequent by commercial air travel. In response, Shaikh Ibrahim Niasse employed print and electronic media to popularize and expand the activities of the Sufi orders not only in his native Senegal but also in nearly all the Muslim communities of western Africa. Still, conflict between Sufis and their opponents has increased since the 1980s.

It is estimated that there are over 140 million Muslims living in western Africa in the early twenty-first century. Christian missionaries, many of whom arrived in western Africa along with colonialism, have often defined their mission in opposition to both Islam and African religions. Over the last century, Christianity has gained millions of adherents but has neither supplanted Islam nor erased the African religions. The overall winner in the earnest competition between Islam and Christianity for the souls of Africans remains to be seen. Despite the millions of new converts claimed for both Islam and Christianity, the indigenous religions remain the overarching cosmology within which Islam, Christianity, and Westernization are received, sifted, and responded to accordingly.

See also **Asma'u, Nana; Colonial Policies and Practices; Gao; Gender; Ibn Battuta, Muhammad ibn Abdullah; Jenné and Jenné-jeno; Mansa Musa; Prophetic Movements: Western Africa; Timbuktu; Touré, Amadou Toumani; Touré, Samori; 'Uthman dan**

Fodio; Women: Women and Islam in Sub-Saharan Africa.

BIBLIOGRAPHY

Badru, Pade. *The Spread of Islam in West Africa: Colonization, Globalization, and the Emergence of Fundamentalism.* Lewiston, New York: Edwin Mellen, 2006.

Bangura, Ahmed S. *Islam and the West African Novel: The Politics of Representation.* Boulder, CO: Lynne Rienner Publishers, 2000.

Brenner, Louis. *West African Sufi: The Religious Heritage and Spiritual Search of Cerno Bokar Saalif Taal.* Berkeley: University of California Press, 1984.

Brenner, Louis. *Controlling Knowledge: Religion, Power, and Schooling in a West African Muslim Society.* Bloomington: Indiana University Press, 2001.

Callaway, Barbara J. *Muslim Hausa Women in Nigeria: Tradition and Change.* Syracuse, New York: Syracuse University Press, 1987.

Callaway, Barbara J., and Lucy Creevey. *The Heritage of Islam: Women, Religion, and Politics in West Africa.* Boulder, CO: Lynne Rienner, 1994.

Clarke, Peter B. *West Africa and Islam: A Study of Religious Development from the Eighth to the Twentieth Century.* London: E. Arnold, 1982.

Falola, Toyin, and Biodun Adediran. *Islam and Christianity in West Africa.* Ile-Ife, Nigeria: University of Ife Press, 1983.

Harrow, Kenneth W., ed. *Faces of Islam in African Literature.* Portsmouth, NH: Heinemann, 1991.

Hiskett, M. *The Sword of Truth: The Life and Times of Shehu Usuman dan Fodio.* New York: Oxford University Press, 1973.

Hiskett, M. *The Development of Islam in West Africa.* New York: Longman, 1984.

Hunwick, John O. *Arabic Literature of Africa,* volume 2. *The Writings of Central Sudanic Africa.* Leiden, The Netherlands: Brill, 1995.

Hunwick, John O. *Arabic Literature of Africa,* volume 4. *The Writings of Western Sudanic Africa.* Boston: Brill, 2003.

Hunwick, John O., ed. and trans. *Shari'a in Songhay: The Replies of al-Maghili to the Questions of Askia al-Hajj Muhammad.* New York: Oxford University Press, 1985.

Kenny, Joseph. *The Spread of Islam through North to West Africa, 7th to 19th Centuries: A Historical Survey with Relevant Arab Documents.* Lagos, Nigeria: Dominican Publications, 2000.

Levtzion, Nehemia. *Islam in West Africa: Religion, Society and Politics to 1800.* Brookfield, VT: Variorum, 1994.

Levtzion, Nehemia, and Humphrey J. Fisher, eds. *Rural and Urban Islam in West Africa*. Boulder, CO: Lynne Rienner Publishers, 1987.

Levtzion, Nehemia, ed., and J. F. P. Hopkins, ed. and trans. *Corpus of Early Arabic Sources for West African History*. New York: Cambridge University Press, 1981.

Lewis, M., ed. *Islam in Tropical Africa*, 2d edition. Bloomington: Indiana University Press, 1980.

O'Fahey, R. S. *Arabic Literature of Africa*, volume 1. *The Writings of Eastern Sudanic Africa to c. 1900*. Leiden, The Netherlands: Brill, 1994.

O'Fahey, R. S. *Arabic Literature of Africa*, volume 3. *The Writings of the Muslim Peoples of Northeastern Africa*. Leiden, The Netherlands: Brill, 1999.

Robinson, David. *The Holy War of Umar Tal: The Western Sudan in the Mid-Nineteenth Century*. Oxford: Clarendon, 1985.

Sanneh, Lamin O. *Piety and Power: Muslims and Christians in West Africa*. Maryknoll, NY: Orbis Books, 1996.

Sanneh, Lamin O. *The Crown and the Turban: Muslims and West African Pluralism*, Boulder, CO: Westview Press, 1997.

Trimingham, John Spencer. *Islam in West Africa*. Oxford: Clarendon, 1959.

Trimingham, John Spencer. *History of Islam in West Africa*. New York: Oxford University Press, 1963.

Willis, John R., ed. *Studies in West African Islamic History*, volume 1. *The Cultivators of Islam*. London: F. Cass, 1979.

MUHAMMAD SANI UMAR
REVISED BY MATTHEW KUSTENBAUDER

EASTERN AND CENTRAL AFRICA

Islamic communities represent a significant minority, and in some case a large majority of the nations of eastern and Central Africa. Accurate figures are hard to obtain, but it is generally maintained that about 35 percent of the population of eastern Africa and 15 percent of Central Africa are Muslims. These figures hide large variations. Somalia and Djibouti are close to 100 percent Islamic, Ethiopia and Eritrea around 50 percent, Tanzania 35 percent and Kenya 18 percent, Uganda and Rwanda 15 percent. In terms of population there are around 13 million Muslims living in Central Africa, and 66 million in eastern Africa.

A particular feature of Islam in this region is the diversity of practice and religious observance, as well as membership of different sects and branches of Islam and a widespread popular adherence to Sufism. This reflects the history of Islam in the region, and its complex spread through Africa during the last 1,200 years, especially in the last 150 years as a result of European colonial policies. There is no single Islamic authority in the region, instead there are often a myriad of different organizations in each nation state representing local Muslim interests. Most countries recognize the limited practice of Islamic law and Islamic courts that can operate alongside European-based legal systems for civil matters. Indeed, Islam in the region is a mosaic of communities and faiths that have developed largely through a complex history of conversion and trade with the Islamic world to the north and east.

EARLY HISTORY

The early history of Islam in eastern Africa is often based, somewhat uncritically, on traditions and chronicles written many years after the event, and which often do not bear up to modern scholarly scrutiny. Islam may have reached eastern Africa in the earliest years of the spread of the new faith, but evidence to support this is lacking. For example, an important Islamic tradition tells of Christian Aksum as place of refuge for Muslim exiles from Mecca in 615 CE, although they later returned to Medina. There were certainly close trading connections either side of the Red Sea, as well as architectural links, and it has been reasonably deduced that the Ka'ba in Mecca, with its alternate courses of stone and wood, derive from Aksumite architectural traditions. Early ports on the African side of the Red Sea with Muslim populations may include Badi (Sudan) and the Dahlak archipelago (Eritrea) that by the ninth century came largely under Muslim control. Both places have impressive inscriptions dating from the tenth century. Little is known about the early Islamic history of the ports of northern Somalia—ports that have their origins in the pre-Islamic trade of the Indian Ocean—but that became important again with the expansion of Abbasid monsoon-based trade during the early ninth century.

Some traditions tell of an invasion of Muslim soldiers from Damascus during the seventh century in the towns of the northern Kenyan coast, but although often repeated they should be seen as mythological accounts, fashioned in the African-Arab politics of the nineteenth century. Archaeological evidence from Shanga (Kenya) provided definitive proof of a community of converted Africans in about 780 CE, who built timber mosques and minted their own silver coins. The Arab geographer al-Masudi (c. 896–956), who visited East Africa in 916 CE, recorded a Muslim community at the island of Qanbalu (probably Pemba), and recorded that it had been established around the changeover between the Umayyad and Abbasid dynasty (approximately 750 CE). It is likely that these early Muslims were either Shia or Ibadi (two early Ibadi mosques have recently been found on Pemba), and that Islam reached East Africa through trade, although the possibility of refugees seeking out East Africa during the various waves of religious conflict in the Persian Gulf should not be discounted. Swahili traditions of the establishment of seven towns by brothers from Shiraz (Fars, Iran) should be seen as foundation myths, although the earliest dated inscription and mihrab at Kizimkazi (Zanzibar) of 500 H (1107 CE) is stylistically close to the products of stone workshops operating at Siraf. This is a major Iranian port and close to Shiraz, and seems to have enjoyed particular close commercial links with East Africa during the Abbasid period.

The Swahili towns (and associated rural settlements) appear to have been exclusively Muslim from the eleventh century and have left an impressive number of surviving monuments, including mosques, houses, and tombs, that represent an African Muslim civilization. These towns extended from region of Mogadishu to Mozambique and included areas of northern Madagascar, the Comoros, Zanzibar, Pemba, and Mafia. The religious affiliation of the Swahili seems to have been initially mixed (Ibadi, Shia, and Sunni), although by the fourteenth century was exclusively Sunni-Shafi, as was recorded by Ibn Battuta (1304–c. 1368) in his visit in 1332. This change seems to have been the result of the migration of sharifs from the Hadhramaut, a process that began in the thirteenth century and continued into the nineteenth.

Remarkably, the Swahili Muslims made little attempt to allow the spread of Islam into Africa's interior through caravan routes and contact with contiguous coastal populations such as the Mijikenda and Pokomo until the nineteenth century. Indeed, the Swahili towns remained stable and religiously conservative, and even the Portuguese attempts in the sixteenth and seventeenth centuries to colonize and convert the coast had little impact on either trade or religion. Religious leadership was in the hands of 'ulama— those respected in Islamic law or scholarship, whose advice was sought by the myriad of local rulers and sultans (or in the case of towns such as Barawa, Siyu, and Lamu by councils of elders drawn from the leading clans).

NORTHEAST AFRICA

In northeast Africa, the situation was rather different. Islam spread inland from the coast from around the tenth century. Early sultanates inland included Shewa (sometimes written Shoa, supposedly founded in 896 CE) and Ifat in Ethiopia. Recently, ruins from three towns have been discovered that may form the heart of the Shewa kingdom. These communities derived their wealth in trade (mostly ivory, gold, and slaves) with Christian Ethiopia, and for the first few centuries lived in peaceful coexistence with their Christian neighbors to the north. Ifat absorbed the Shewa state in about 1295, and was ruled by the Walashma dynasty until 1415 until taken over by the Adal state (also ruled by a branch of the Walashma). Another major center of Islamic culture developed around the walled city of Harar in the fifteenth century and flourished as a center of learning and literature in the sixteenth and seventeenth centuries. The city still contains over 100 mosques, and numerous shrines and religious places. The landscape around Harar, and between Harar and the coast, is filled with ruined settlements that belonged to a Muslim-controlled trade between highland Ethiopia and the coast of the Gulf of Aden.

From these urban (or semiurban) centers, Islam spread into the tribal nomadic groups of northeast Africa. The exact chronology remains obscure, but is generally thought to have taken place in the thirteenth century onward, and to have included the Afar (or Danakal), some of the Beja, and the Somali. The degree of Islamization also remains debatable, with few monuments (such as mosques and tombs) that can be attributed to this early date. However, the presence of a large number of armed and warlike tribes who professed at least a fairly nominal Muslim faith, allowed the Muslim sultanates to wage a long running jihad against Christian Ethiopia between the fifteenth and seventeenth centuries (which itself was largely a response to Ethiopian expansion under the Solomonic dynasty in the fourteenth century) that established a tradition of Ethiopian-Somali conflict and bitterness that continues into the early twenty-first century. The war weakened both sides, created widespread misery, and disrupted trade, learning, and scholarship. One consequence of the jihad was the migration of the pastoralist and non-Muslim Oromo around 1600 into highland Ethiopia, a country left ravaged by the fighting, as well as into Somali, northern Kenya and as far south as River Tana. It seems that this migration forced the Somali into the hinterland of the northern Swahili coast, spreading Islam into more southerly areas of the interior and into contact with the ancient Swahili Muslim cultures. Many of the Oromo became Muslim themselves in the eighteenth century, and a major center of Islamic learning was established at Welo under Oromo protection.

THE NINETEENTH CENTURY

During the nineteenth century several new factors affected the practice of Islam in the region. The Omani Arabs took control of Mombasa from the Portuguese in 1698, and by the early nineteenth century, the Swahili coast became commercially important for the supply of slaves and ivory, as well as for plantations of spices, cobras, and copal (a type of resin). The Busaidi dynasty under Said bin Sultan established Zanzibar as their capital in 1832 and rapidly developed the island as the hub of their commercial empire, linking the Indian Ocean (and indeed Atlantic worlds) with caravan routes into the interior. The increasing wealth from this trade resulted in a revival of Islam through the rebuilding and founding of mosques (many of the coastal mosques still in use date from this time) and an interest in Islamic scholarship and learning in the traditional centers, such as Lamu, Mombasa, and the Comoros, but increasingly in Zanzibar itself, where many of the 'ulama were attracted.

The Busaidi (and most of the Arab colonists that came with them) were Ibadi, and the period also saw the construction of significant numbers of Ibadi mosques. Most of the Swahili, however, remained Sunni, and were allowed to continue to worship in their own mosques, run their own

religious affairs, and operate waqf, or Islamic trusts that came to own extensive property. The Busaidi rulers made more formal arrangements than had been the case previously when the Swahili looked after their own affairs, with appointed qadis (one Ibadi, one Shafi'i) in Zanzibar and Mombasa. Under Sultan Barghash (1870–1888) a network of Islamic courts was established extending to Lamu, Mombasa, Bagamoyo, Lindi, and Kilwa with the qadis directly appointed by the sultan. Under British protection and colonial rule, the qadi courts lost much of their jurisdiction, deciding only on domestic and family law, whereas secular courts considered criminal and civil matters, although with an appeal court that contained both Muslim and British judges.

The commercial prosperity of Zanzibar also attracted traders and merchants from India, who acted as shopkeepers and moneylenders, often rising to positions of great power and wealth. Of particular importance were the Khoja families (represented by the Ismaili, Hanafi, and Ithnasheri) that numbered over 500 families in the 1870s, and the Dawoodi Bohoras with about 250 families. By 1910, the census recorded 8,757 Asians on Zanzibar. They each retained distinctive communities, with their own mosques and madrasas, and rarely married outside their own group. Although most lived in Zanzibar, some families moved to the other coastal towns (Kilwa Kivinje, Chake Chake, Mombasa, and Lamu), and during the twentieth century many moved up-country to Nairobi and Uganda and came to play a vital role in the development of industry and commerce in the colonial economy.

In the nineteenth century the Muslims of northeast Africa increasingly turned to Sufism. Although Sufism may have been present earlier in Harar, its widespread introduction—or—probably dates to the eighteenth century. There are three main brotherhoods: Qadiriyya, the oldest and most conservative, centered in the Adal sultanate and Harar; the Idrisiyah, based on the teachings of Ahmad ibn Idris (1785–1837) and introduced by sheikh Ali Maye Durogba in the nineteenth century; and Salihiyah, the most radical founded by Muhammad ibn Salih in 1887. Dervishes were particularly associated with these Sufi practices, and wandered from place to place as experts in rhythmic chanting and dancing. Sufism stressed devotional activities, abstinence from stimulants and the rejection of *tawassul*—the idea that holy men or saints could intercede with God. The influence of the Sufis was to cleanse many of the Islamic practices that had retained elements of non-Islamic and traditional religions and to put an end to ritual feuds between tribal groups.

Sufism took particular hold in the Oromo areas, especially at Welo, and was seen as anti-Western and anti-Ethiopian. Welo itself was subject to devastating attacks between 1855 and the late 1880s by the Ethiopian emperors. In western and southern Somali, the more radical form of Sufism, the Salihiyya, took root during the late nineteenth century, and saw expression in a jihad led by Sayyid Muhammed Abdalla Hasan (1856–1920). Between 1898 and 1920, Sayyid Muhammed's dervishes successfully opposed Ethiopian and British forces in the Ogaden until 1919, rejecting colonial authorities and what he and his followers considered impure forms of Islam.

The nineteenth century also saw the spread of Islam into the interior of Africa and this too was influenced by the spread of Sufism. Coastal groups had lived alongside the Muslim Swahili for centuries, often enjoying complex trading and social relations, but never adopting Islam. For reasons that still remain unclear, many of these groups—from the Mrima coast of Tanzania to the River Tana—choose to adopt Islam, albeit in a loose fashion. Toward the end of the nineteenth century Sufism (in particular the Shadhiliyya) took particular hold on second generation converts and encouraged both the purification of ritual practices and resistance to colonial expansion, as well as a buffer to colonial missionary activity.

The other mechanism for the spread of Islam was the activity of long distance traders, who were almost entirely Muslim. Although there was little scope along the routes themselves, with low population density, at the termini, such as Tabora and Ujiji, substantial Muslim communities developed, through intermarriage and conversion. The most remarkable such community was in the kingdom of Buganda, a centralized kingdom where a Muslim trader, Ahmed bin Ibrahim engaged Kabaka Suna (c. 1832–1856) in lengthy theological discussions, and was allowed to convert a number of court officials to Islam. Kabaka Mutesa (r. 1856–1884) was initially even more enthusiastic about Islam, building a mosque in his court and encouraging the conversion of his subjects, but toward the end of his reign he largely repudiated Islam. The significant numbers of African Muslims (known as Baganda Muslims) in modern Uganda are the result of this encounter.

COLONIAL AND POSTCOLONIAL POLICIES TOWARD ISLAM

Colonial policy toward Islam remained ambivalent and *ad hoc*. British policy was to respect other world religions, so institutions such as the courts that they inherited were retained, and this was broadly followed by the other colonial powers. The office of Chief Qadi remains in postcolonial Tanzania, Kenya, and Uganda, although the Islamic courts have little authority beyond community and family disputes.

Pressure from missionaries to convert Africans to Christianity could create deep conflict, and these missionaries had initially little success in the coastal regions where Islam had been longer established. Ironically, many of the freed slaves, working on the coastal plantations, chose the religion of their former agricultural, rather than colonial, masters. Colonial policies to open up the interior provided opportunities for Muslim settlement and expansion, and employment for literate clerks and administrators. The use of Muslim soldiers in colonial armies provided other routes for settlement, of which the most notable are the descendants of Nubians still living around Aringa in West Nile District of Uganda, where Maliki law is uniquely followed in the region.

In the long run, Muslims have fared less well. After World War I, Christian missionaries were able to consolidate their position and, with the support of the colonial authorities, set up mission schools that provided many Africans with literacy and a Western education that was denied to Muslims. These literate Africans were more useful to the colonial authorities, and the Muslims became marginalized. The widespread system of state-run primary education from the 1950s has equalized the situation to some extent, but many Muslims still feel disadvantaged in Christian-led national and regional administrations and remain poorly represented in the economy, parliament, or government. It is feared that this situation is a breeding ground for fundamentalism and terrorism, and the heavy-handed security operations in late 2006 and into 2007, in Mombasa, and along the Kenya and Somali coast cannot have helped the cause of Muslim integration.

The East African Asians have been able to exploit their community and family ties, as well as devoting community resources to private education and health care, to retain an important part in the economy of the region, especially in Tanzania and Kenya. Many of their charitable foundations (most notably those linked to the Aga Khan) help other Muslims as well as non-Muslims. The success the Asians has led to some envy, and there have been political campaigns against them, such as during the Zanzibar revolution in 1964, in Kenya in the late 1960s and the mass expulsion in 1972 of 50,000 Asians from Uganda.

In northeast Africa, Somalia remains chaotic; any vision of a socialist Islamic state has been lost in twenty years of civil war. Several of the ideas behind the jihadist activities of the Sufi brotherhoods of the early twentieth century reemerged in the Islamic Courts Union, only to be defeated by a U.S.-backed Ethiopian invasion in late 2006. In Ethiopia, the significant Muslim minority lives in the south and east, and Sufism remains strongly embedded.

Islam in the region remains fragmented—either through civil war—or because it is a minority faith in Christian-led nations. Expressions of national Islamic identity are rare, although the massive new National Mosque on Old Kampala Hill, funded by the Libyan Government in Uganda may be a significant development. Islam remains strong at a community level however, centered on the mosque and its *madrasa*. Many mosques are wealthy, with the charitable foundations (*waqt khayri*) to support them. It is likely that Islam will continue to draw its strengths at local and domestic level in the years to come.

See also **Barghash Ibn Sa'id; Comoro Islands; Harar; Hasan, Muhammad 'Abdallah; Ibn Battuta, Muhammad ibn Abdullah; Ivory; Law: Islamic; Mombasa; Mutesa I; Nubia; Slave Trades; Travel and Exploration.**

BIBLIOGRAPHY

Gregory, Robert G. *India and East Africa. A History of Race Relations within the British Empire 1890–1939.* Oxford: Clarendon Press, 1971.

Horton, Mark, and John Middleton. *The Swahili: The Social Landscape of a Mercantile Society.* Oxford: Blackwell Publishers, 2000.

Levtzion, Nehemia, and Randall Pouwels, eds. *The History of Islam in Africa.* Athens: Ohio University Press, 2000.

Lewis, I. M. *The Modern History of Somaliland, from Nation to State.* New York: F. A. Praeger, 1965.

Nimtz, August H. *Islam and Politics in East Africa. The Sufi Order in Tanzania.* Minneapolis: University of Minnesota Press, 1980.

Pouwels, Randall L. *Horn and Crescent. Cultural Change and Traditional Islam on the East African Coast, 800–1900.* Cambridge, U.K.: Cambridge University Press, 1987.

Seidenberg, Dana April. *Mercantile Adventurers: The World of East African Asians 1750–1985.* New Delhi, India: New Age International, 1996.

Trimingham John Spencer. *Islam in Ethiopia.* London: Oxford University Press, 1952.

MARK HORTON

SOUTHERN AFRICA

Muslims comprise around 10–15 percent of Southern Africa's population of approximately 140 million, with a presence in nearly every country in Southern Africa, even those in the center and southwest that were relatively untouched by the precolonial advance of Muslim traders, slave raiders, and scholars. There are substantial numbers (in millions) of Muslims in Angola (1.5), Malawi (3–4), Mozambique (2.3), Tanzania (16), South Africa (1), Zambia (2.5), Madagascar (1.2), and the Democratic Republic of the Congo (5.6), and lesser numbers (not in millions) in Botswana (1,000), Lesotho (700), Mauritius (200,000), Namibia (34,000), Swaziland (12,000), and Zimbabwe (13,000). Islam coexists with African traditional religion, which is predominant in Botswana, Mozambique, and Madagascar, and with Christianity, which is dominant in Angola, Kenya, Lesotho, Malawi, Namibia, Mauritius, South Africa, Swaziland, Uganda, and Zimbabwe. It is only in Tanzania that no single belief system has more than 50 percent of the population as adherents. Islam is not the primary public identity of most Muslims; rather it is their race, ethnicity, class, or national group.

Islam came to root along the East African coast during the eighth century as part of ongoing trade exchanges between inhabitants on the east coast and traders from the Persian Gulf and Oman. Marriages between women of Africa and men of the Middle East forged a rich Swahili culture from Mogadishu (Somalia) in the north to Ruvuma River (Mozambique) in the south. Islam remained an urban littoral phenomenon until the nineteenth century, when many inland chiefs in Tanzania, Uganda, and Kenya converted to Islam and cooperated with coastal Muslims as trade in slaves and ivory increased as part of the Indian Ocean commerce with Arabia and India. Asian migrants have been instrumental in establishing Islam in many parts of Southern Africa.

Most Muslims in South Africa are descendents of the involuntary migration of slaves from Southeast Asia or indentured immigrants from India. Migrants from the Indian subcontinent also established Islam in Zimbabwe, Botswana, and Swaziland. The Bombay-based Isma'ili branch, the second largest community after the in Iran, was prominent in Kenya, Uganda, and Tanzania from the late nineteenth century. Most adherents were forced to flee after the Zanzibar Revolution of 1964 and Idi Amin's (c. 1924–2003) decision to expel Asians from Uganda in 1972. The Aga Khan IV (b. 1936) facilitated the resettlement of Isma'ilis in Europe and North America. The presence of Indian Muslims remains a source of tension in the early twenty-first century. There is a perception among African Muslims in Botswana, Zimbabwe, and South Africa that Islam is an Asian religion that perpetuates racism, oppresses women, and is confined to the rich. In these countries, African Muslims are trying to forge what they have termed an indigenous Islam rather than accept historically imported versions of Islam.

One cannot speak of a Southern African Islam or homogeneous Muslim community. Although Muslims refer to the same written religious source, the Qur'an, understanding of Islamic doctrine is mediated through race, ethnicity, continuing connections with African culture, and, in the case of Asians, with India. Muslim communities are consequently pluralistic with competing doctrinal interpretations.

Immigration, legal and illegal, is transforming Islam in important ways. Angola's Muslim population, for example, has grown almost sixfold from a quarter of a million from 1996–2006. Many Angolans have embraced Islam through the influence of Muslim traders and merchants from West Africa who have settled there. During this time, there has been an upsurge in the construction of mosques, Islamic centers, and Qur'anic schools in many Angolan cities. South Africa has witnessed large-scale migration from other African countries as well as from India, Pakistan, and Bangladesh. Refugees, mainly political exiles from the DRC, Burundi, Rwanda, and Malawi have augmented the African Muslim population in South Africa and may help spread Islam in townships in the future.

International hostility following the September 11, 2001, attacks on the United States has also impacted on Islam and Muslims in the region. The reaction against Muslims in Southern Africa has been ambiguous. Many Africans opposed to globalization and neocolonialism are not openly antagonistic toward Islam. But the 1998 bombings of U.S. embassies in Dar es Salaam, Tanzania, and Nairobi, Kenya, have alarmed many, as it seems that the region will not escape the conflict. There is some security cooperation with the United States because of perceptions that Islam is intrinsically linked to terrorism. In South Africa, the rise of the vigilante group People Against Gangsterism and Drugs (PAGAD) during the late 1990s gave Islam a violent public face; Christian-Muslim violence in Malawi included the torching of numerous mosques and churches; the proposed Anti-Terrorism Bill in Kenya led to violent public protest, and there is increasing tension between Arabs and Africans in Tanzania. It remains to be seen how this conflict will pan out.

Social and political changes in the early twenty-first century have transformed the contours of Muslim society and triggered important behavior modification. The most striking is the growth of personal piety. There are increases, for example, in the growth in Islamic radio stations, the rise of Muslim schools, and the numbers of women who veil. Another conspicuous feature of the new Islam is self-reformation. Growing numbers of Muslims are becoming attached to shaikhs (spiritual mentors) in their search for personal stability and guidance. Traditional Islamic scholars are becoming bearers of new forms of Islam, and employing power and knowledge to influence the actions of others. The influence of the Tablighi Jamaat movement that originated in early twentieth-century India and first took hold among Indian Muslims in South Africa is gradually spreading throughout many Southern African countries. The way that Muslims in Southern Africa understand Islam and how they present and represent themselves has been constantly transforming and will continue to do so.

See also **Amin Dada, Idi; Dar es Salaam; Immigration and Immigrant Groups; Slave Trades; Women: Women and Islam in Sub-Saharan Africa.**

BIBLIOGRAPHY

Brenner, Louis. "Introduction: Muslim Representations of Unity and Difference in the African Discourse." In *Muslim Identity and Social Change in Sub-Saharan Africa*, ed. Louis Brenner. Bloomington: Indiana University Press, 1994.

Caplan, Pat, and Farouk Topan, eds. *Swahili Modernities: Culture, Politics, and Identity on the East Coast of Africa*. Trenton, New Jersey: Africa World Press, 2006.

Esack, Farid. *On Being a Muslim*. Oxford: OneWorld Publications, 1999.

Jumbe, Aboud. *The Partnership: Tanganyika-Zanzibar Union: 30 Turbulent Years*. Dar es Salaam: Amana Publishers, 1994.

Mamdani, Mahmood. *Good Muslim, Bad Muslim: America, the Cold War, and the Roots of Terror*. Reprint edition. New York: Three Leaves: 2005.

Nyozi, H. *Muslims and the State in Tanzania*. Dar es Salaam: Dumt, 2003.

Jeppie, Shamil, and Goolam Vahed. "Multiple Communities: Muslims in Post-apartheid South Africa." In *The State of the Nation: South Africa 2003-2004*, ed. John Daniel, Roger Southall, and Adam Habib. Cape Town: Human Sciences Research Council, 2004.

GOOLAM VAHED

SUFI ORDERS

Sufism, the mystical tradition of Islam, is almost as old as Islam itself in Africa. Developing in Egypt from Islam's early periods, it grew in the Maghreb in the Middle Ages. Important figures such as Abu Madyan (d. 1198) gave rise to Sufi piety, and when organized Sufism grew from the fourteenth century, it was the Shadhiliyya *tariqa*, or way, associated with Abu 'l-Hasan al-Shadhili (d. 1258) that

became the most widespread. An important popularizer of Shadhili piety was the Moroccan Muhammad ibn 'Abd al-Rahman al-Jazuli (d. 1465). The great philosopher of Sufism, the Andalusian Muhyi 'l-Din ibn al-'Arabi (d. 1140), spent part of his life in North Africa and his teachings influenced African Islam profoundly.

In Egypt, Sufism came to be dominated by such wide Pan-Islamic tariqas as the Qadiriyya (associated with 'Abd al-Qādir al-Jilani of Baghdad, d. 1166) and the Rifa'iyya (from Ahmad ibn al-Rifa'i, d. 1182), as well as orders of Egyptian origin such as the Badawiyya (from Ahmad al-Badawi of Tanta, d. 1276) and the Dassuqiyya (from Ibrahim al-Dassuqi, d. 1288). In the nineteenth century, the Sufi institution in Egypt came under closer public control with the institution of the *shaykh al-sajjada*, the overall head of the Sufi orders.

Sufism was an integral part of Islam throughout sub-Saharan Africa, propagated by locally based holy lineages that increasingly linked themselves to the larger international intellectual traditions of the Sufi brotherhoods. Many of the beliefs and practices of so-called popular Islam throughout Muslim Africa have their origin in Sufism.

The various tariqas differ from each other in their rituals and methods, but share the overall aim of achieving a direct experience of the divine presence through the performance of prayers, communal rituals, and similar. Some tariqas perform their prayers silently in a group, others use vocal prayers, often accompanied by rhythmical motion, music, clapping of hands, and other elements, sometimes approaching ecstasy, that may be frowned upon by more sober Sufis and non-Sufis alike. Unlike Christian monasticism, membership in a Sufi order does generally not mean relocation to a convent or a change of daily life, although some orders do have agricultural communities where brethren work either for their own livelihood or for the good of the order.

Mostly, however, membership entails participation in weekly rituals, *dhikrs*, where they perform the prayers prescribed by their spiritual leader, *shaykh* or *murshid*. Each tariqa has a particular prayer formula (*hizb*) that distinguishes it from the others, but will also draw from a larger literature of prayers at various levels of complexity. The way is divided hierarchically into ranks in spiritual awareness that an adherent wants to ascend, always under the indispensable guidance of his murshid. The highest level, awarded by God only, is that of friend of God (*wali*, or saint), or at its pinnacle a *qutb*, or axis, with the ability to perform miraculous acts. This power is known as *baraka*, grace from God.

In a number of orders, initiation may also include a period of seclusion, *khalwa*, from the external world for one or two months, focused on prayer and asceticism. The Khalwatiyya order takes its name from such seclusion, but many other orders also practice it.

The central element of the order is the local shaykh, whose house will often also function as the center, *zawiya*, or lodge, of the village branch. Not all shaykhs are members of a larger order, and in many orders adherence to the larger structure means little more than sharing a hizb prayer, a ritual, and acknowledging a spiritual paternity to the medieval founder. Other orders, however, have a stronger organization, with real national or international leadership with varying degrees of influence over the local branches.

In either case, both initiated brethren and local villagers who identify with the order of their shaykh and lodge may gather to large regional and national festivities, *mawlids*, marking the birthday or death of the founding fathers of their order.

Women also play a role in Sufism, either as initiates, often either in separate orders or branches of the order, but also as saints and focuses of veneration. Many also pray at the graves of past saints, male or female. This latter aspect of Sufism has come under particular criticism from scripturalist Muslims. While God may, in their view, award living saints the power to perform miracles, grave veneration give dead saints a status that belongs only to God. Many reformists, even within Sufi circles, have thus focused on combating the idolatry of visiting graves.

In French-speaking Africa, Sufism has also often been linked to maraboutism, which is criticized as superstition. Some consider the two to be identical, while others see a clear distinction between the literary and intellectual Sufism of such renowned scholars as al-Ghazali and Ibn al-'Arabi on the one hand, and the illiterate marabouts of the villages on the other. A more nuanced view is

probably one of a continuum of scholarly awareness from the advanced philosophers to the popular rituals among the uninitiated, without any clear dichotomy. The scholarly history of such west African centers of learning as Shinqit (Chinguetti) and Timbuktu show Sufis to have not only a high awareness of the literary traditions, but also to actively create works of great complexity within Sufi scholarship.

The various orders accept each other mutually, and a scholarly shaykh may take many tariqas in addition to his main affiliation. This will normally mean a spiritual initiation into the new way from an accepted master of that order, with the right to disseminate its hizb to others. The shaykh will, however, maintain one tariqa as his primary order.

The transition from local and lineage-based Sufism to larger and more organized orders took place at the beginning of the nineteenth century in West Africa, in particular from the time of al-Mukhtar al-Kunti of Mali (d. 1811). The Fulani jihads of the same period were influenced by their leaders' adherence to the Qadiriyya, although the movements were not directly based on Sufi organization.

In Sudan, holy families had attached themselves to the Qadiriyya for centuries, whereas the Somali experience was linked to the establishment of agricultural communities (*jama'as*) in particular in the nineteenth century. Along the East African coast, Sufism was largely a matter of the immigrant trading communities until the Shadhiliyya, as well as the Qadiriyya, started to spread into the mainland at the end of the nineteenth century.

Thus, in many ways the nineteenth century was Africa's Sufi century. It was characterized by the spread across Sudanic Africa of newer orders. The most expansive of these was the Tijaniyya, founded by the Moroccan Ahmad al-Tijani (d. 1815). Originating in Fez, it established its center in the desert oasis of 'Ayn Madi, in present-day Algeria. Important for the Maghreb was also the Darqawiyya offshoot of the Shadhiliyya order, founded by al-'Arabi al-Darqawi (d. 1823), who combined asceticism with political activity. The Madaniyya branch of the Darqawiyya spread to Tripolitania, Palestine, and to East Africa, where it was known only as the Shadhiliyya.

The Tijani tariqa was taken up by the jihad leader *al-hajj* 'Umar Tal (d. 1864), who became its *khalifa*, leader, in West Africa. In addition to his political work, he also wrote some of the most important contributions to Tijani scholarship after those of the founder. The order survived the fall of his jihad state and flourished as a pacific and pious organization, partly under his descendants, partly under the Sy family. The Niassiyya branch of the Tijaniyya under Ibrahim Niasse (d. 1975) of Kaolack spread to Nigeria, where it became the largest Sufi order with several million adherents, and further east to Sudan and beyond.

Of great importance were also the various orders stemming from the teachings of Ahmad ibn Idris (d. 1837), a Moroccan. Among these are the Sanusiyya, established in Cyrenaica and the Sahara by Muhammad ibn 'Ali al-Sanusi (d. 1859); the Khatmiyya, which was taken to the Sudanese Nile Valley by Muhammad 'Uthman al-Mirghani (d. 1852); and the Rashidiyya and Salihiyya, founded by Ibrahim al-Rashid (d. 1874), a Sudanese, that spread in Sudan, Egypt, Lebanon and Somalia, and later to Southeast Asia. The coming of these new orders forced the older affiliations to redefine themselves. An example is the revived Qadiriyya way of Uways al-Barawi (d. 1906) of Brava in southern Somalia that had great impact throughout East Africa.

The new orders that appeared in the nineteenth century differentiated from the older decentralized Sufi traditions in both organization and doctrine. They were supratribal, hierarchical organizations led by the families of their founders. The most elaborately organized was the Sanusiyya, based in a series of zawiyas that controlled both education and trade in the eastern and central Sahara. The zawiyas of the Salihiyya in Somalia brought agricultural innovations and often recruited their members from marginal social groups such as ex-slaves.

Doctrinally, the orders brought a new awareness of Islam and often pioneered the teaching of Islam in local languages. Popular hymns and simple works of piety were produced in Hausa, Fulfulde, Swahili, and Somali, and emphasis was laid on a stricter adherence to the formal requirements of scriptural Islam and devotion to the Prophet.

At the onset of colonialism, Sufi orders and leaders sometimes became focuses of resistance. In the Maghreb, 'Abd al-Qādir of Algeria based some of the legitimacy of his campaign on his, and his father Muhyi al-Din's, status as local leaders of the Qadiriyya order. Later Algerian resistance was founded on other Sufi orders. Further east, the Sanusiyya brotherhood of the central and eastern Sahara became involved in the resistance to French advances in Chad from approximately 1900, and when the Italians invaded Libya in 1911, the Sanusis took on the leadership of the most effective resistance. Under 'Umar al-Mukhtar, guerrilla warfare kept the Italians at bay until 1931 when al-Mukhtar was captured and killed. After independence in 1951, the Sanusi leader Muhammad Idris became the king of Libya and revived the order under royal protection and control. After his fall in 1969, the order was banned in Libya.

Other examples of Sufi-led anticolonial resistance are the movements of the Fadili shaykh Ma' al-'Aynayn (d. 1911) in Western Sahara and the Salihi *sayyid* Muhammad ibn 'Abd Allah Hasan, the Mad Mullah of Somalia (d. 1922). Other Sufi orders such as the Muridiyya (French, *mouride*) in Senegal and the Khatmiyya in Sudan, cautiously collaborated with the colonial authorities, but were suspiciously watched by them. Some, such as the Hamalliyya branch of the Tijaniyya in Mali, were regarded as oppositional even when not politically active.

In Sudan, the Mahdist movement took on many features of Sufi-style organization. It and the Khatmiyya order each formed a political party that became the two main protagonists of political life in the independence process and in civilian political life in Sudan throughout the twentieth century. Other characteristics of the Sufi brotherhoods in the colonial period were increasing urbanization, expansion of business opportunities and the ease with which Sufi elites took to Western education—a striking proportion of the Sudanese educated elite comes from Sufi families.

Since independence, the Sufi orders have been increasingly challenged by Salafi reformist or Wahhabi-inspired movements—such as the Wahhabis in Mali and Côte d'Ivoire and the Yan Izala movement in northern Nigeria—that attack the Sufis as doctrinally unorthodox sectarians and as morally corrupt. With ever increasing urbanization and new forms of communication, the classical Sufi organizations appear to be giving way to new forms led by charismatics operating at the local or national level. The Tijaniyya, at least the Niassiyya branch, and the revived Sammaniyya order of Hasan al-Fatih Qarib Allah in Omdurman (Sudan), are exceptions.

See also 'Abd al-Qādir; Fez; Hamallah of Nioro; Hasan, Muhammad 'Abdallah; Idris, Ahmad ibn; Initiation; Mukhtar, Sidi al-; Religion and Ritual; 'Umar ibn Sa'id Tal (al-Hajj).

BIBLIOGRAPHY

Abun Nasr, Jamil M. *The Tijaniyya: A Sufi Order in the Modern World.* London: Oxford University Press, 1965.

Cornell, Vincent J. *Realm of the Saint: Power and Authority in Moroccan Sufism.* Austin: University of Texas Press, 1998.

Hunwick, John O., and R. S. O'Fahey, eds. *Arabic Literature of Africa.* Leiden, The Netherlands: Brill, 1994–.

Karrar, Ali Salih. *The Sufi Brotherhoods in the Sudan.* London: Hurst, 1992.

Knysh, Alexander. *Islamic Mysticism: A Short History.* Leiden, The Netherlands: Brill, 2000.

Martin, Bradford G. *Muslim Brotherhoods in Nineteenth-Century Africa.* Cambridge, U.K.: Cambridge University Press, 1976.

O'Fahey, R. S. *Enigmatic Saint: Ahmad ibn Idris and the Idrisi Tradition.* Evanston, Illinois: Northwestern University Press, 1990.

Robinson, David, and Jean-Louis Triaud, eds. *Le Temps des marabouts: Itinéraires et stratégies islamiques en Afrique Occidentale Française v. 1880–1960.* Paris: Karthala, 1997.

Vikør, Knut S. *Sufi and Scholar on the Desert Edge: Muhammad b. 'Ali al-Sanusi and His Brotherhood.* London: Hurst, 1995.

Villalón, Leonardo A. *Islamic Society and State Power in Senegal: Disciples and Citizens in Fatick.* Cambridge, U.K.: Cambridge University Press, 1995.

R. S. O'FAHEY
REVISED BY KNUT S. VIKØR

ISLAMISM

Islamism has become a strong and internally diverse political and ideological movement in all parts of Muslim Africa. Its project is to redefine Muslim identity in order to found society, law, and politics on Islamic principles. In particular, Islamists strive to implement the shari'a law, as well as Islamize and Arabize the educational curricula in opposition to the predominance of local dialects or European languages. In countries with dominant Muslim majorities, the central project is to establish or to strengthen an Islamic state, but the movements differ on the means of attaining such a goal. Some prefer to Islamize society first, thinking that the polity will necessarily follow, while others want either to participate in the political process in order to take over the government legally or to destroy the existing regimes through the use of violence.

LOCAL DIVERSITY AND URBAN SOCIAL BASES

Islamist trends in Africa manifest themselves in different ways: in North Africa, the movement has been politically strong and popular since the 1970s, because of the religious homogeneity of this region. The ideology of the Egyptian Muslim Brotherhood (founded in 1928) has influenced the *Nahda* movement in Tunisia, the Islamic Salvation Front in Algeria and the Justice and Development Party in Morocco. Powerful movements exist in Nigeria with the Izala of Abubakar Gumi (d. 1924–1992), or in Sudan with the Muslim Brotherhood. In West Africa, Wahhabism and the literature authored by medieval scholar Ibn Taymiyya (1263–1328) has had an important influence from the 1980s on. However, in Senegal, Sufi brotherhoods have been an obstacle to the development of Islamist trends. In countries where Muslims do not form the dominant majorities, movements that revive and politicize Islam are important, but appear less relevant and powerful politically, even if they reinforce interreligious strife, as in Ethiopia, Nigeria, Tanzania, or Chad.

Most Islamist movements have emerged within modern universities, with student-led political activism, and displaced the leftist movements in the 1970s and 1980s. Their members are young, educated, and recently urbanized. Rather than being "traditionalists," they use modern technologies and redefine their societies in new ways. Islamists insist on reading Muslim sacred texts without the help of the '*ulama*, who are part of the national official religious institutions. Islamists are, therefore, the heirs of early reformists, whom they have politicized and somewhat de-intellectualized in order to emphasize political ideology over theology. However, recent studies have also shown that Islamist ideologies have also taken roots among the '*ulama*'s circles and institutions.

TENSIONS AND CONFLICTS: SUFISM AND ISLAMISM

In most of Muslim Africa, Sufism has remained a potent religious and political force that has evoked an Islamist critique, and led to political tensions. Sufism may also, but more rarely, be politicized and become the basis of a political project; the sufi leader Abdessalam Yassine of Morocco, for example, defines his project in Islamist terms and questions the legitimacy of the Moroccan monarchy. In the rest of the Maghrib, however, Islamist movements use reformist and puritanical interpretations of Islam. While the critique of Sufi projects is part of their aims, it is not central to their ideology. Sufi brotherhoods have also transformed, urbanized and emphasized a strict adherence to shariʿa in order to respond to competition from the Islamists.

RADICAL MOVEMENTS

Islamist movements developed violent tactics in North Africa and Egypt in the 1970s against states and societies that they consider "impious." Their main influence, Sayyid Qutb, had radicalized the Muslim Brotherhood's ideology in the 1950s. From the assassination of Egyptian president Anwar al-Sadat in 1981 by the Jihad group, or violent attacks on secularist Muslim intellectuals or non-Muslim minorities, to the September 11, 2001, terrorist attacks, radical groups have metamorphized under state repression from nationally based sectarian movements to elusive transnational networks. In particular, members of radical groups from North Africa have been well represented in Al Qaeda or Al Qaeda–inspired networks of violence, as demonstrated in the Casablanca attacks in March 2003, the Madrid attacks in 2004, or the attacks of Djerba in April 2002. But radical Islamism has receded in national contexts since the height of violence in the 1990s.

EXPLAINING ISLAMIST MOVEMENTS

The emergence and success of Islamist movements is usually explained by the socioeconomic and political failures of African independent states. Islamist movements respond to developmental problems and provide well-organized and efficient socioeconomic services when the welfare state has become too weak, and offer avenues of political participation to their members. They often radicalize under repression, but can also become more flexible when given

chances to participate in the political process. Regimes often outlaw Islamist parties, which then must operate in new settings in order to circumvent state repression. In 1979 Ahmad Khalifa Nyass formed a party of God (Hisboulahi), in Senegal, which was outlawed. In Tanzania, educational Islamist movements, such as the Islamic Writers' workshop, founded in the 1970s, continues to function in the early twenty-first century by publishing Islamic literature in spite of repression.

But in the end of the twentieth century, some states, such as Algeria, Morocco, or Egypt, became less reluctant to allow Islamists to participate—although not continuously—in the electoral process. Hence, Islamists have become crucial political actors in the twenty-first century, yet they have transformed their ideology into a less comprehensive application of Islamism in order to be accepted within the political establishment and to deepen their electoral successes. They have defined Muslim identity more in national than transnational terms in spite of their identification to a universal Muslim community (*umma*), and tried to participate in elections wherever and whenever possible. Some movements have integrated the vocabulary of religious and political pluralism, such as some of the ideologues of the Egyptian Muslim Brothers or the Moroccan Party of Justice and Development.

Transnational trends, founded upon a fast and wide circulation of ideas made possible by new media and migrations, also provide an important explanation for the emergence of Islamist movements in Africa. Islamic world institutions, such as the Saudi Arabian Muslim World League, or the Organization of Islamic Conference and more informal networks of influence, have played an important role in Africa through the subsidizing of mosques, Islamic and educative centers, built alongside or integrated within traditional madrasa systems.

If state failures and transnational influences are important factors, historical continuities are also relevant. While scholars of Islamism analyze Islamist trends as recent, because they have developed in the second half of the twentieth century, Islamists also identify strongly with early movements of Islamic reform and nationalism. In this regard, Islamist movements are linked to the modernization of African societies. They are the products of profound transformations: the building of new nation-states, the introduction of market economies, urbanization, the democratization of access to education, and the growing access to new media.

In alliance or opposition to the state, Islamist movements have emerged as contenders to define the cultural foundations of their societies, hence fragmenting the sphere of religious authority. But in those countries where they have taken over, as in Sudan under Umar Hassan al-Bashir, or northern Nigeria, they have strived to homogenize culture and politics in authoritarian ways. Scholars debate if these movements are declining. However, Islamist movements are polarized between radical sectarian groups unable to take over the nation-states and more flexible movements that have been integrated in society and state and deeply transformed them, sometimes peacefully, and at other times through violent confrontations.

See also **Education, School: Muslim Africa; Literatures in African Languages: Islamic; Political Systems: Islamic; Sadat, Anwar al-.**

BIBLIOGRAPHY

Brenner, Louis. *Controlling Knowledge. Religion, Power and Schooling in a West African Muslim Society,* Bloomington: Indiana University Press, 2001.

Burgat, François. *The Islamic Movement in North Africa.* Austin: Center for Middle Eastern Studies, University of Texas at Austin, 1993.

Eickelman, Dale F., and James Piscatori, *Muslim Politics.* Princeton, NJ: Princeton University Press, 1996.

Kane, Ousmane. *Muslim Modernity in Post-colonial Nigeria: A Study of the Society for the Removal of Innovation and Reinstatement of Tradition.* Boston: Brill, 2003.

Gilles Kepel. *Jihad. The Trail of Political Islam.* Cambridge, MA: Harvard University Press, 2002.

Loimeier, Roman. *Islamic Reform and Political Change in Northern Nigeria.* Evanston, IL: Northwestern University Press, 1997.

Soares, Benjamin. *Islam and the Prayer Economy: History and Authority in a Malian Town.* Ann Arbor: University of Michigan Press, 2005.

Tozy, Mohamed. *Monarchie et Islam politique au Maroc.* Paris: Presses de Sciences Po, 1999.

Westerlund, David, and Eva Evers Rosander, eds. *African Islam and Islam in Africa. Encounters between Sufis and Islamists.* Athens: Ohio University Press, 1997.

Zeghal, Malika. *Gardiens de l'Islam: Les oulémas d'al-Azhar dans l'Egypte contemporaine.* Paris: Presses de Sciences Po, 1996.

Zeghal, Malika. *Les islamistes marocains. Le défi à la monarchie.* Paris: La Découverte, 2005.

MALIKA ZEGHAL

MODERNISM

As Western imperialism, colonization, and cultures influenced the African continent in the nineteenth century, Muslim societies responded in different ways, including modernism. The term "modernism" in Islam can be defined as a complex configuration of projects of reinterpretation and/or reform in which the religious tradition interacts with new ideas and institutions from the West. However, it is not entirely clear if these transformations of Islam were a direct response to "Westernization" or if they had started earlier. Therefore, Muslim modernism can also refer to the ability of Muslim reformers to mediate social change. Movements of Islamic reform and renovation had been taking place in Africa since the eighteenth century. This entry examines the internal processes of modernization of Islam that seem to have taken place in the late eighteenth century, as well as modernism as a set of ideological and theological trends that have been evolving in two opposing directions since the nineteenth century, both toward conservatism and, on the other hand, toward more liberal interpretations of Islam.

NEO-SUFISM AND MODERNITY: THE EIGHTEENTH CENTURY

Before Muslim areas of Africa came under European control during the nineteenth century, Islam was internally transforming. Historians have described late-eighteenth-century northern and sub-Saharan Africa organizational and intellectual trends toward innovation under the name of "neo-Sufism." Sufi *tarîqas* were organized around the veneration of a living or dead saint and were defined by a relation between the Sufi master and his disciples, whom he initiated and led in "the way" (*tarîqa*). At the end of the eighteenth century, new *tarîqa*s took a more active role in society as a force for centralization and stability that provided a basis for their political activity, notably in Morocco and Algeria, as well as in sub-Saharan Africa and the Sudan.

In Morocco, the early Salafiyya movement of the eighteenth and nineteenth centuries, under the influence of Wahhabism, was radically opposed to Sufi *tarîqa* popular practices. Similar to the rest of Muslim Africa, however, a blend of reform and revival emerged within Sufi practices through neo-Sufi movements eager to reinforce but also rationalize Sufi organizations. Neo-Sufi Moroccan Ahmad ibn Idris (d. 1837) had a deep influence in Africa and beyond. The regeneration of Sufi tarîqas also had an influence on the African East Coast: the Shadhiliyya led by Shaykh Muhammad Ma'rûf (1853–1905) consolidated rigorous forms of Islam in this region. The founder of the Sanusiyya, North African Ibn 'Ali al-Sanusi (1787–1859) also built a transnational neo-Sufi network whose aim was to reform local religious practices. In Sudan, Western and Central Africa, neo-Sufi interpretations developed, emphasizing the rejection of *taqlîd* (imitation of the elders, or tradition) and of ecstatic popular practices. Some historians argue that they also moved from theocentric to anthropocentric worldviews that envisioned Islam as a resource for social organization and/or political resistance.

Intellectually, however, these organizational changes were accompanied by an emphasis on study of *hadîth* (the prophetic traditions) and on the union with the person of the prophet. Historians debate if these transformations have to be interpreted as "modern" and compared with Western "Enlightenment." While Africa has always been defined as a "peripheral" part of Islam, it is interesting to note that the question of modernity in Islam is being researched in most original ways around late eighteenth century Sufi *tarîqa*s in Africa.

MOVEMENTS OF MODERNIST REFORM

Islamic modernism also manifested itself in theological reform and later in nationalist ideologies, which built an ambiguous relationship with Islam. In nineteenth-century Tunisia, Morocco, and Egypt, political and intellectual elites, faced with European technological and military challenges, became concerned with the construction of a modern state and military. Reform of society and Western influence introduced intellectual reform into new systems of education as well as the intellectual and theological perspectives on Islam. Influenced by modernization theories in the 1960s, historians have interpreted these movements as modern because they appear to converge with Western modern thought. Tunisia

and Egypt engaged in a process of reform in education and law, two domains wherein the role of religion was redefined. One common feature of these new projects and policies was the critique of *taqlîd*, in order to recover the "original" meaning of the faith without relying on historicized and "outdated" interpretations. Folk practices related to Sufi brotherhoods involving superstitions and human intercession came under sharp critique.

The best known among these figures of modern reforms, Mohamed 'Abduh in nineteenth century Egypt, Khayr al-Din Pasha in nineteenth century Tunisia, and Allal al-Fassi (1910–1974) in Morocco, proposed reinterpretations of Islam that underlined the compatibility between scientific reason and Islam; they proposed to reorganize Muslim society along more rational lines, while continuing to be faithful to an orthodox Islam. Algerian Shaykh 'Abd-al-Hamid ibn Bâdîs (1889–1940) was a prominent influence upon sub-Saharan reformers. In East Africa, Shaykh al-Amin b. 'Ali Mazrui (1890–1947) was a reformer who disseminated scriptural Islam and education in connection with Middle Eastern reform movements. West African "Wahhabis"—certainly a misnomer—were influenced by the reformist early Salafiyya, and created a network of schools where religious studies and Arabic language were an important part of a curriculum that countered the influence of French education. This movement became the template for the Union Culturelle Musulmane, created in Senegal by Sheikh Touré in 1953 with the aim of fighting the colonial system as well as Sufi brotherhoods. The Union developed branches in Western Africa, in Upper Volta, and had influences in Guinea.

Another type of modernist reinterpretation insisted on the necessity of separation of state and Islam in the writings of Egyptian 'Ali 'Abd al-Raziq (1888–1966). This reinterpretation gave birth to secularist and liberal interpretations without removing Islam from individuals' spiritual life. It has remained an isolated trend developed by reformist intellectuals against fundamentalist Islam.

MODERNISM AND ISLAM IN NATIONALIST MOVEMENTS AND STATES

Before independence, nationalist movements participated in these debates, and elements of Islam were integrated into the discourses of anticolonial nationalism. After independence, this interaction continued to transform definitions of Islam, particularly in countries with dominant Muslim majorities where states devised reformist and authoritarian agendas vis-à-vis Islam. Nation building used or opposed references to Islam to bolster ideologies of progress, socialism or simply economic development. Islam played an ambiguous role in the definition of the juridical systems or the modernization of Islamic institutions of learning.

The early independent government of Northern Nigeria adopted a new system of criminal justice: the personal status code related to family matters was based on Islamic law, while the rest of the legal system was to universally apply to the Nigerian population, a step similar to those taken in other independent states. However, after independence in 1958, the Parti Démocratique de Guinée under the authority of Sékou Touré and the influence of the Union of Soviet Socialist Republics, waged campaigns against *shari'a* and custom law. In the field of education, modernist reformers criticized educational systems based on a dichotomy between Western secular and religious education.

Modernist ideology—especially if blended with socialist ideas—was often criticized by conservative 'ulama and intellectuals as "anti-Muslim." Nevertheless, the dichotomy between modernism and Islam is the product of political rivalries to define the nation, rather than reflect historical realities. These agendas were modernist, but not in the sense of a separation of state and Islam. States appropriated, nationalized and redefined Islam in accordance with a reformist agenda, whose aim was to rationalize Islam and to use it to legitimize political power.

These state appropriations of Islam became contentious in the 1970s. Grounded in their relationship to early reform movements, Islamist movements have put into question the use of Islam in political discourse by states and have called for the founding of Islamic states and the establishment of *shari'a* law in order to recover an "Islamic" identity. In opposition to these projects, some Muslim intellectuals have proposed new interpretations of Islam that eschew the question of identity and deepen a hermeneutic of the Qur'an and the hadith introduced by the early reformers. What distinguishes these new Muslim intellectuals is that they want to go beyond the question of adapting Islam to modernity. 'Abdullahi Ahmed An-Na'im in Sudan, Mohamed Talbi in Tunisia, and Mohamed 'Abid al-Jabri in

Morocco, developed their hermeneutics independently, without being obsessed by the West or the myth of being modern.

See also **Allal al-Fassi; Education, School: Muslim Africa; Modernity and Modernization: Antimodernism and Postmodernism Movements; Touré, Sékou; Women: Women and Islam in Sub-Saharan Africa.**

BIBLIOGRAPHY

Brenner, Louis. *Controlling Knowledge: Religion, Power, and Schooling in a West African Muslim Society.* Bloomington: Indiana University Press, 2001.

Hofheinz, Albrecht. "Internalizing Islam: Shaykh Muhammad Majdhub, Scriptural Islam and Local Context in the Early Nineteenth Century Sudan." Ph.D. diss., Universitetet i Bergen, Norway, 1996.

Hourani, Albert. *Arabic Thought in the Liberal Age, 1798–1939.* Cambridge, U.K.: Cambridge University Press, 1983.

Kaba, Lansine. *The Wahabiyya: Islamic Reform and Politics in French West Africa.* Evanston, IL: Northwestern University Press, 1974.

Kane, Ousmane. *Muslim Modernity in Postcolonial Nigeria.* Boston: Brill, 2003.

Loimeier, Roman. *Islamic Reform and Political Change in Northern Nigeria.* Evanston, IL: Northwestern University Press, 1997.

Martin, Bradford J. *Muslim Brotherhoods in Nineteenth-Century Africa.* New York: Cambridge University Press, 1976.

Merad, Ali. *Le réformisme musulman en Algérie de 1925 à 1940: Essai d'histoire religieuse et sociale.* Paris: Mouton, 1967.

Monteil, Vincent. *L'Islam noir.* Paris: Seuil, 1971.

O'Fahey, Rex S. *Enigmatic Saint: Ahmad Ibn Idris and the Idrisi Tradition.* Evanston, IL: Northwestern University Press, 1990.

Rahman, Fazlur. *Islam.* Garden City, NY: Doubleday, 1968.

Trimingham, J. Spencer. *The Sufi Orders in Islam.* New York: Oxford University Press, 1971.

Voll, John. *Islam: Continuity and Change in the Modern World.* Boulder, CO: Westview Press, 1982.

Zeghal, Malika. *Gardiens de l'Islam: Les oulémas d'al-Azhar dans l'Egypte contemporaine.* Paris: Presses de Sciences-Po, 1996.

MALIKA ZEGHAL

ISLAM: LAW. *See* **Law: Islamic.**

ITALIAN COLONIES. *See* **Colonial Policies and Practices: Italian.**

IVORY. African elephant ivory has long been among the most sought-after luxury items from the continent. Hunting elephants and trading ivory have provided African men with an important source of prestige and disposable wealth.

The earliest records of ivory trade in Africa date to the Sixth Dynasty of ancient Egypt (2420–2258 BCE), and later records, including royal burials, make it clear that ivory was among the most prized possessions of its rulers. Most of the ivory supplied to dynastic Egypt came from eastern and central Sudan, elephants having disappeared from the Sahara during the third millennium BCE. The ivory trade again flourished during the heyday of the Roman Empire, which harvested its ivory from the upper reaches of the Nile Basin and eastern Africa.

Following the collapse of the Roman Empire, India and China emerged as the main markets for ivory from both northeastern and eastern Africa by the tenth century. The most compelling evidence of the significance of ivory trading for the peoples of the interior comes from archaeological sites at Ingombe Ilede, on the north bank of the Zambezi River, and Mapungubwe, in the Limpopo Valley, and dates to the fourteenth and fifteenth centuries. In northeastern Africa, the consolidation of Christian Abyssinia under the Solomonid dynasty in the fourteenth century greatly expanded the area for elephant hunting and ivory exports to the Indian Ocean network.

Reinvigoration of the demand for ivory in the Mediterranean dates from the later tenth century, and from the twelfth century the Crusades gave further impetus to the European demand. Although eastern Africa remained the major source of ivory for medieval Europe, this renewed demand reached well into central and western Africa, where the earliest evidence of ivory trading dates to finds at Jenné (c. 800), in Burkina Faso, and Begho (c. 965–1125), in northern Ghana. Ivory trading reached its peak in the western Sudan under the empire of Mali, especially during the fourteenth century.

The intervention of the Portuguese in Africa at the turn of the fifteenth century provided a new opening for ivory exports from the forest regions of western and west-central Africa. Although ivory was never the main product from these regions, it was very actively traded from the late sixteenth well into the mid-eighteenth century, from the upper Guinea coast to the mouth of the Congo River.

In eastern Africa, there was no such slackening. Sustained by Indian merchant capitalists operating from Gujarat, in western India, and based regionally at Zanzibar, Mozambique Island, and other eastern African ports, the ivory trade enjoyed a period of great vigor after 1500. By the late eighteenth century the demand for ivory exports in eastern Africa had produced a vast procurement network that reached deep into the continent, as far as the Congo Basin.

Leading African peoples who specialized in hunting elephants for their ivory and transporting it to the coast included the Kamba of the coastal hinterland of what is today Kenya, the Nyamwezi of central Tanzania, the Yao of northern Mozambique, and the Bisa of eastern Zambia. By the time Zanzibar emerged in the middle of the nineteenth century as the principal ivory marketplace in the world, the steady Eastern demand was supplemented importantly by new European and American requirements for ivory. Rising prices for ivory stimulated elephant hunting to such an extent that many herds across the continent were decimated. One model suggests an annual decline of 2 percent in the elephant population throughout Africa during the nineteenth century.

The imposition of European colonial rule in Africa—accompanied by colonial policies that inadvertently protected game by restricting African hunting as a means to force men into the labor market—and changes in the world economy inhibited this frenetic search for ivory. By the 1930s, however, ivory exports from eastern Africa were steadily increasing, driven by colonial policies that promoted sport hunting through tourism and turned indigenous African hunters into poachers and criminals. From 1950 to 1987, Africa's elephant population seems to have declined at an increasing rate. In the 1970s, rising prosperity in the Far East, political instability caused by wars of liberation in Angola and Mozambique, and widespread availability of automatic weapons produced a major new scramble to hunt elephants and profit from the ivory trade. World wildlife conservation forces decried

Kenyan president shows opposition to ivory trafficking. Kenyan president Moi sets fire to twelve tons of ivory tusks worth US$2.5, demonstrating his opposition to ivory trafficking at Nairobi National Park, July 18, 1989. Elephant ivory is a source of prestige and income for many locals. The issue of poaching in ivory trading, however, has fueled a century-long debate over whether or not the industry should be banned. ALEXANDER JOE/AFP/GETTY IMAGES

the looming extermination of the African elephant to such an xtent that in October 1989 an international agreement—the Convention on International Trade in Endangered Species of Wild Fauna and Flora (CITES)—placed the African elephant on the endangered species list, although Botswana and Zimbabwe (and later Namibia) insisted on a provision to allow their well-managed elephant herds to be excluded from the international ban on ivory trading.

According to various estimates, by 1996 the continent's population of elephants had been reduced from about 1.2 to 1.3 million to below 580,000. In Southern Africa, however, elephant populations have grown significantly in recent years, seriously outstripping the carrying capacity of the environment and causing major habitat destruction. When in September 2005 the South African Government announced a plan to cull up to 10,000 elephants in Kruger National Park, it caused a national and international uproar. Sport hunting and poaching remain significant issues as sources of revenue, both legal and illegal, but the main problem facing these countries is how to manage both expanding elephant and human

populations. At the beginning of the twenty-first century, the greatest external demand for ivory came from China's rapidly expanding middle class, while African ivory carvers constituted an important internal market for ivory. Meanwhile, the debate between those who support maintaining the international ban on ivory trading and those who favor state management of elephant populations and legalizing the trade remains unresolved.

See also **Colonial Policies and Practices; Wildlife.**

BIBLIOGRAPHY

Alpers, Edward A. *Ivory and Slaves in East Central Africa.* Berkeley: University of California Press, 1975.

Alpers, Edward A. "The Ivory Trade in Africa: An Historical Overview." In *Elephant: The Animal and Its Ivory in African Culture,* ed. Doran H. Ross. Los Angeles: UCLA Fowler Museum of Cultural History, 1992.

Bulte, Erwin H., and G. Cornelis van Kooten. "Economics of Antipoaching Enforcement and the Ivory Trade Ban." *American Journal of Agricultural Economics* 81 (1999): 453–466.

Harms, Robert. *River of Wealth, River of Sorrow: The Central Zaire Basin in the Era of the Slave and Ivory Trade, 1500–1891.* New Haven, CT: Yale University Press, 1981.

Milner-Gulland, E. J., and J. R. Beddington. "The Exploitation of Elephants for the Ivory Trade: An Historical Perspective." *Proceedings of the Royal Society of London: Biological Sciences* 252, no. 1333 (1993): 29–37.

Sheriff, Abdul. *Slaves, Spices, and Ivory in Zanzibar.* London: James Currey, 1987.

Steinhart, Edward I. *Black Poachers, White Hunters: A Social History of Hunting in Colonial Kenya.* Athens: Ohio University Press, 2006.

Thornbahn, Peter Frederic. "The Precolonial Ivory Trade of East Africa: Reconstruction of a Human-Elephant Ecosystem." Ph.D. diss. University of Massachusetts, 1979.

EDWARD A. ALPERS

IVORY COAST. *See* Côte d'Ivoire.

J

JA JA, KING (1821–1891). Ja Ja rose from slavery to become one of the foremost traditional rulers of the nineteenth-century Niger Delta. Of Igbo descent, he was sold as a slave in the 1830s at the age of twelve to a trader from the Okolo-Ama city-state (called "Bonny" by Europeans). At that time he was given the name Jubo Juboga. Later he was sold again, this time to the ruling Anna Pepple House in Bonny. There he used his skills as merchant and politician to expand Bonny's territory and influence and became head of the house. Rivals opposed his rise to power, however, and a civil war ensued. Ja Ja and his followers broke away from Bonny and, in 1870, he established the state of Opobo. Over the next few years he transformed Opobo into one of the richest of all the Niger Delta city-states. He cultivated trade and political relations with the British, and during the Asante war he supplied the British with a contingent of his soldiers. In appreciation, he was awarded a sword by Queen Victoria in 1875.

Conflict with the British began with the proclamation of a British protectorate over Opobo in 1885. Ja Ja's opposition to increasing British influence in the area led to his deportation to Accra, where he was tried in 1887 and sentenced to exile in the West Indies. The British action against Ja Ja excited much popular protest in Opobo. He was consequently invited home to be reinstated. He died during his return trip, on July 7, 1891. His body was brought home to Opobo, where it was buried.

See also **Colonial Policies and Practices.**

JA-JA, THE DEPOSED AND EXILED KING OF OPOBO, WEST AFRICA

King Ja Ja of Opobo (1821–1891). Former slave Ja Ja earned his way out of slavery to become a leader in the palm oil trade. His monopoly on the product ended after he was arrested by the British for refusing to stop taxing their traders. © HULTON-DEUTSCH COLLECTION/CORBIS

BIBLIOGRAPHY

Alagoa, Ebiegberi Joe. *Uses of Hindsight as Foresight: Reflections on Niger Delta and Nigerian History.*

Port Harcourt, Nigeria: Onyoma Research Publications, 2004.

Dike, Kenneth Onwuka. *Trade and Politics in the Niger Delta, 1830–1885: An Introduction to the Economic and Political History of Nigeria.* Westport, CT: Greenwood Press, 1981.

Ejituwu, Nkparom C. *A History of Obolo (Andoni) in the Niger Delta.* Oron, Nigeria: Manson, 1991.

C. OGBOGBO

JENNÉ AND JENNÉ-JENO.

Jenné and Jenné-jeno (ancient Jenné) are successive *tell* (manmade occupation mounds in a floodplain) settlements in the upper Inland Niger Delta of Mali, which together span over two millennia of continuous occupation on the floodplain. Both have been designated World Heritage sites by UNESCO. The 111-acre *tell* of Jenné is inhabited today by approximately 10,000 people. Historical sources detail the central role that Jenné played in the commercial activities of the Western Sudan during the last 500 years. In the famous Golden Trade of the Moors, gold from mines far to the south was transported overland to Jenné, then transshipped on broadbottom canoes (pirogues) to Timbuktu, and thence by camel to markets in North Africa and Europe. Leo Africanus reported in 1512 that the extensive boat trade on the Middle Niger involved massive amounts of cereals and dried fish shipped from Jenné to provision arid Timbuktu. The stunning mud architecture of Jenné, in distinctive Sudanic style, is a legacy of its early trade ties with North Africa. Archaeological research has revealed over 19.5 feet of cultural deposits that began accumulating in the early second millennium CE.

Roughly two miles to the southeast is the 82-acre mound of Jenné-jeno. Scientific excavations in the 1970s and 1980s penetrated nearly 20 feet of deposits to reveal that Jenné-jeno was founded around 250 BCE by iron-using peoples who cultivated rice, millet, and sorghum, and who herded stock, fished, and hunted. Other excavations and surface investigations documented the rapid growth of Jenné-jeno from an original settlement of under 10 acres to 82 acres by 850 CE, as well as the majority of the sixty-nine *tells* within a 2.5 mile radius. This created a remarkable population concentration (10,000–27,000 people) within the Jenné-jeno Urban Complex, an integrated multisite system. The appearance of exotic trade goods, such as copper and stone, suggests that growth accompanied an increased participation in trade. These discoveries marked the end of assumptions that urban settlements and long-distance trade in West Africa were secondary to the development of trans-Saharan trade by North African Arabs after the ninth century.

The population of Jenné-jeno declined after 1200 until the settlement was definitively abandoned by 1400. Most of the nearby mounds followed the same pattern. Their demise was coeval with the period of early settlement documented at Jenné, but the reasons for this shift in settlement location are not yet understood.

See also **Archaeology and Prehistory; History of Africa; Niger River; Sahara Desert; Urbanism and Urbanization.**

BIBLIOGRAPHY

Bovill, Edward W. *The Golden Trade of the Moors: West African Kingdoms in the Fourteenth Century*, 2nd edition, revised. Princeton, NJ: M. Weiner, 1995.

Caillié, Réné. *Travels through Central Africa to Timbuctoo, and Across the Great Desert, to Morocco, Performed in the Years 1824–1828*, 1st edition. London: Cass, 1968.

Leo Africanus. *The History and Description of Africa and of the Notable Things Therein Contained*, trans. John Pory, ed. Robert Brown. New York: Burt Franklin, 1963.

Levtzion, Nehemia. *Ancient Ghana and Mali.* London: Methuen, 1973.

McIntosh, Roderick, et al. "Exploratory Archaeology at Jenné and Jenné-jeno, Mali." *Sahara* 8 (1996): 19–28.

McIntosh, Susan Keech, ed. *Excavations at Jenné-Jeno, Hambarketolo, and Kaniana (Inland Niger Delta, Mali): The 1981 Season.* Berkeley: University of California Press, 1994.

McIntosh, Susan Keech, and Roderick J. McIntosh. *Prehistoric Investigations in the Region of Jenne, Mali: A Study in the Development of Urbanism in the Sahel.* Oxford: British Archaeological Reports, 1980.

SUSAN K. MCINTOSH

JEWELRY. *See* **Arts: Beads; Body Adornment and Clothing.**

JINGA. *See* **Njinga Mbandi Ana de Sousa.**

JOHANNESBURG. Johannesburg is situated inland (26 degrees south longitude, 28 degrees east latitude, altitude 5,942 feet) on grasslands of the so-called highveld in the Republic of South Africa. Although not located on an ocean or major waterway, a remarkable degree of economic activity has always distinguished the city. The former Central Business District (CBD)—now called the inner city—straddles a series of rocky hills, the east-west water divide called the Witwatersrand, meaning ridge of white waters. This ridge previously gave its name, generically, to the gold-bearing reefs south of it and to the region as a whole.

The present municipality of the City of Johannesburg (henceforth Johannesburg) was elected in 2006. The city center is called the City of Johannesburg Metro (Johannesburg Metro). Jozi and iGoli are popular nicknames, but the brand name Johannesburg (often shortened to Joburg), seemingly rebuts a name change, unlike Tshwane, formerly Pretoria.

SIZE AND EXTENT

The city, a jagged, elongated geographical expanse, roughly fifty by nineteen miles, extends northwards from Orange Farm through Johannesburg Metro to Midrand, and in a west-east line from Roodepoort to Edenvale. The area, approximately 928 square miles, with approximately 3.2 million people (2005), has the highest average population density in South Africa.

Johannesburg encompasses the municipality that existed before the 1994 political dispensation that gave equality and independence to all South African people, bringing an end to apartheid, the system in which whites were racially separate and all-dominant. It comprises a CBD ringed by 427 suburbs, almost exclusively white though some inner-city residential areas were decasualized. What became Greater Johannesburg in 1995 included the suburbs, plus additional north and northwestern municipalities (Sandton, Randburg, and Roodepoort); the townships, (notably South Western Townships—Soweto, for Africans) where so-called nonwhites—Africans, Indians, and Coloureds (persons of mixed descent)—had been legally and ethnically segregated since the 1920s and especially during the apartheid era; and the shack-and-shanty informal settlements that spread in the 1990s. Most of the informal settlements—approximately 100—are near Soweto, the largest being Orange Farm with around 164,000 persons and comprising roughly 19 percent of Johannesburg's black population. In 2000, a northern arch of sizable towns, including most of Midrand, the latter halfway between the city centers of Johannesburg and Tshwane, was added to Johannesburg's boundaries.

Although 53 percent of Johannesburg's population is concentrated in Soweto and Orange Farm, many former township residents have moved to the traditionally less affluent western suburbs; others have inclined to the predominantly white suburbs of the north that are moneyed and leafy, containing more than 5,000,000 exotic residential trees. Yet Soweto's improved infrastructure, affordability, and cultural appeal have created a residential steadiness in this historically African suburb.

PAST AND PRESENT-DAY FUNCTIONS

Stone Age and Iron Age sites predate Johannesburg, as well as large settled Sotho and Tswana communities dating from the sixteenth and seventeenth centuries. But in 1886, when Johannesburg was founded following the gold discoveries, the highveld, then part of the Afrikaner South African Republic, was sparsely inhabited by Africans.

Johannesburg's transition from digger camp to town to city (in 1928) was rapid. In 1899, when the Witwatersrand was already the world's top gold producer, Johannesburg was the financial, commercial, and industrial hub of South Africa. Despite the virtual disappearance of its original enterprises (gold mining, service industries for the mines, and the later manufacturing industries), Johannesburg still holds the premier economic position in the country that derives mainly from service sectors and small-scale manufactures. It houses Africa's largest stock exchange (the Johannesburg Securities Exchange), most head offices of national financial, commercial, and business corporations, including major and minor enterprises, leading professional and technical services, plus high-tech and information, communications, and logistics industries.

The legislative capital of Gauteng (Sotho for place of gold), the smallest but richest of South Africa's nine provinces, contributes approximately 35 percent of the country's gross domestic product (GDP). Johannesburg's share of this is about 16 percent, with women constituting 41 percent of the city's African employees. The average annual income per Johannesburg household (of an estimated 1,006,030 households) is R31,948. This figure is higher than those of South Africa and Gauteng by 57 and 9 percent, respectively. Although Gauteng's economic growth has been the nation's highest since 1995 (3.9%), poverty levels have risen with an unemployment rate of 62 percent (2005). Of the unemployed, 91 percent are Africans, among whom nominal disposable incomes have risen most sharply (169%), but among whom the widest income gap between rich and poor is also registered.

Johannesburg is adjacent to the largest international airport in the country (recently renamed OR Tambo International airport, after a founder member of the African National Congress [ANC], now the country's ruling party), and an excellent system of roads and highways provides access to all parts of the country. Since 1994 there has been a burgeoning number of vehicles on the roads. Indeed, in 2006, country-wide, new car-sales rose to a record 714,340 with at least 8 percent increases expected in the following years. The daily advent by 2006 of 2,000 new cars on the roads has been stimulated by a number of economic factors, not least being the increased buying power of formerly disadvantaged people who were not white.

Nowhere are the resultant overcrowded roads and highways more marked than on the freeways between Johannesburg and Tshwane, which record vehicle loads of up to 160,000 per day. This prompted the Gauteng Provincial Government to collaborate with the City of Johannesburg in building a railway, the Gautrain Rapid Rail, running north to south between the two cities, and east to west between Sandton and OR Tambo International airport. Its construction, which began in January 2007, will comprise a number of underground stations in the built-up areas, and a few above ground in the more rural regions. Apart from its limited daily capacity, high commuter fares, substantial running costs, and huge construction expenses that have escalated from six to seventeen billion rands, the project's opponents doubt that it will alleviate the freeway congestion. Its protagonists, in contrast, not only believe it will be a success but foresee its completion by 2010 in time for the FIFA World Cup to be held in South Africa where Johannesburg will be a major host.

The parastatal, Wits Metrorail (responsible for all train services in Gauteng), runs the cheapest form of local public transport in Johannesburg and so caters in a big way, though not solely, for the economically poor; more than 50 percent of the commuters' incomes are estimated at being less than R2,500 per month, only double the legal minimum wage. A major disadvantage of the metro railway system is its two axial city routes: One connects the older parts of Johannesburg's southern areas, including Soweto, northwards to Park Station, the largest station in South Africa, situated in the heart of the city's former CBD; the other traverses the historic Witwatersrand outcrop mines, also through Park Station, along its west-east axis adjacent to the Main Reef Road, from where it veers north to Tshwane. There is, accordingly, no rail connection both to the older northern suburbs and to the newer northern areas, such as Sandton, Randburg, and Midrand—and their satellites—with their important business, shopping, service and residential sectors. Although railway travel is the city's cheapest mode of transport, fares nevertheless for many passengers constitute a high item of expense. Nor does the commute necessarily end at the terminal station of choice: another stage of travel is often necessary before the journey ends, by mini-buses or buses whose ranks are located at all the stations.

Metrobus, a privatized corporation owned by the Johannesburg municipality, possesses a fleet of 600 single- and double-decker buses, of which about only one-third are modern. They negotiate roughly 84 city routes and carry approximately one and a half million passengers per month.

Because of their historic connections with low-income residential areas, both the trains (heavily guarded by security officials) and the buses are handicapped by their limited routes. This transport gap has been filled by the more expensive mini-buses, known also as kombi-taxis, which are privately operated by African-owned companies. Many residents use them because of their flexibility. Without either

Old Fort on Constitution Hill. The Old Fort on Johannesburg's Constitution Hill, now a museum and landmark, was formerly a prison. Both Mohandas K. Gandhi and Nelson Mandela were held there. © ROGER DE LA HARPE/CORBIS

timetables or formal starting-and stopping-points, the mini-buses criss-cross the entire city and manage to reach even the shack-and-shanty informal settlements. The city government's response to the lack of an affordable public transport system has seen the start, in 2007, at an estimated cost of two billion rand, of the "Rea Vaya Bus Rapid Transit" project, consisting of dedicated bus lanes.

The city is a significant media center, and has a higher-education and cultural focus: It produces five daily newspapers and accommodates the national broadcasting and television center. Johannesburg houses two universities, many diverse theatres, art galleries, and heritage sites, and cultivates three botanic gardens, which are extraordinarily well patronized by all racial groups especially when they serve as venues for jazz and classical concerts, which are often free.

There are at least eight museums, including the renowned Apartheid Museum, as well as smaller

ones located in traditionally African areas. One such museum is in Kliptown (in Soweto) where the Freedom Charter was presented in 1955. (It was later the basis for the ANC's Bill of Rights and the new South African constitution.) Another similar museum in Soweto is that of Hector Pieterson in Orlando West. This commemorates the Students' Revolt of 16 June 1976, the day on which the police tragically shot the eponymous schoolboy.

Two major festivals are held in Johannesburg. In February the First National Bank (FNB) Dance Umbrella, launched in 1998, presents works ranging from community-based dance troupes to international companies, and is the showcase in southern Africa for the full range of contemporary dance. The singularity of the festival (hosted by the Wits Theatre attached to the University of the Witwatersrand) is twofold: it permits the performance of only new and indigenous choreography; and no prior dance or choreographic experience is required. In September the four-day Arts Alive festival, held at various venues in the inner city, gives an opportunity to approximately 600 artists to present a variety of poetry, music, visual arts, and dance. It culminates in the main concert held at the Johannesburg Stadium, at which international superstars perform, and on the final day, at the Zoo Lake, there is a free open-air jazz concert which is usually jam-packed.

Since 2005, a less formal festival has emerged and has been likened to Rio de Janeiro's annual carnival: the Afro-inspired New Year's Day Parade. Under the auspices of the City Council and the South African Police Force, thousands of revellers celebrate on foot for five miles. The procession encompasses historic and celebrated sights such as Constitution Hill, the Nelson Mandela Bridge, the former military Drill Hall, and the old CBD. It ends at Newtown, at the Mary Fitzgerald Square, where an all-style jazz concert takes place. Although various forms of dance and music are significant in the parade, the costumes, flags, and floats are the highlights. In 2007 the carnival, called "*Nyakza*—Joburg on the move," aimed to emphasize the development of the inner city and its adjacent suburbs (Hillbrow, Joubert Park, and Newtown) and to involve their residents in a community occasion. A uniquely South African feature of the procession was the marching *vuvuzela* orchestra with "musicians," thoroughly rehearsed, playing their long, colored, plastic, hollow horns, and producing in chorus a whooping noise more usually associated with soccer matches. There are also one-off or occasional festivals in which local communities, destroyed by apartheid, have reclaimed their heritage, such as the forced removals from Sophiatown, and the closing of businesses, belonging particularly to Indians, in Fordsburg (or Fietas).

The current CBD has moved just north of the old one to Sandton (and areas north of it), though everywhere fortress homes, palisaded suburbs, and barbed-wired, electric-fenced complexes visually testify that the whole of Johannesburg is the world's most crime-ridden city. Such levels of crime can be ascribed, amongst other things, to poverty, income disparities, unemployment, and the decades of privation and conflict that underpinned apartheid. Yet less is spent on the national police force than on private security. Working class people and those even economically poorer, who are greatly affected by crime and what appears to be

the emergence of a culture of violence cannot, however, subscribe to private security companies or afford other forms of property protection, as this would exceed household incomes. Instead, they are obliged to resort to more rudimentary methods of defending themselves, including the formation of vigilante groups and police fora and, increasingly, where there is an absence of community organization, to mob justice.

Notwithstanding some decentralization in the mid-twentieth century, most corporations, graded hotels, professionals, and prestigious retailers fled the city center for the north in the 1990s because of increased violence and pollution. Most of the old CBD's substantial office buildings have deteriorated; many have been closed or have degenerated into overcrowded residential slums often filled with squatters. Even so, a few corporations remain, several occupying self-contained villages alongside heavily barricaded retail shops lining the pavements. Closed-circuit TV cameras, operated by police, help curtail crime in limited areas.

Despite the construction of some twenty-one prodigious shopping malls in the north since 1990, Johannesburg Metro, the shopping hub for Sowetans, still constitutes the nation's largest formal trading area with putatively the biggest annual retail turnover (R50,000,000). Roughly 860,000 persons daily traverse it as a destination or transit point and patronize some 10,000 street vendors, mostly Africans, half probably women. These patterns may, however, change on the completion in Soweto of two outsize shopping malls.

Even before 1994, the city planners implemented city-center renewal schemes. Such was Newtown, in the west, in the early twenty-first century an important cultural precinct for theatre, arts, crafts and museums, and linked to Braamfontein by the 2003 Mandela Bridge, a province-funded project, as was the new Constitutional Court. Other municipal schemes include facilitating black-owned production units and boosting the fashion district, upgrading the fresh produce market, and building two taxi service centers. With the aid of modest private funding, but at substantial government cost, the council has restored or converted to residences fifty of the approximately three hundred office blocks and has constructed a handful of new apartment buildings designed for middle- to lower-income earners; the most recent, at a cost of R89,000,000, is the 600-apartment establishment in Brickfields, adjacent to Newtown, comprising one-, two-, and three-room flats. Such housing strategies, however, including improvements to Soweto, are localized and patchy.

A major ambition of the city planners (and the provinces) is the reclassification by 2030 of Johannesburg as a world class city; an intangible concept but, as is claimed, a place where foremost people visit, live, work, and are entertained. An alternative goal, which some consider to be patronizing, is also often punted: Johannesburg—a world class African city. Although Johannesburg is characterized by vibrancy, energy, and entrepreneurship, common identified obstacles to this goal are: too much emphasis on recreating the old central business district without an overall plan; the continuation of violent crime and petty theft, a deterrent to investment; the lack of transport; and the shortage of management, professional, and technical skills.

The adverse impact of the rising HIV/AIDS epidemic is also a major deterrent to foreign long-term capital investment. The overall infection rate for Johannesburg of 26 percent is greater than the 24 percent average for Gauteng with Johannesburg Hospital statistics indicating that here—at a major institution—30 percent of pregnant mothers and 40 percent of admitted children are HIV positive, while 75 percent of children's deaths are AIDS related. This has morbid consequences not only for Johannesburg but its immediate environs, namely, a low fertility and demographic rate, and an increasingly prevalence of children orphaned by AIDS, caused by the premature mortality of men and women (often semi-skilled and skilled) in their prime.

ETHNIC COMPOSITION

About 73 percent of the city's population consists of Africans, including migrant laborers (roughly 86,000), but excluding the huge contingent of foreign African immigrants, whose numbers are unknown. The rest of the population comprises whites (approximately 16 percent), Coloureds (approximately 6%), and Asians (approximately 4%).

Speakers of all eleven official languages in South Africa reside in Johannesburg. The major 112 home languages are Nguni (34%), Sotho (26%), English (19%), and Afrikaans (8%). The city remains cosmopolitan—most speak English plus their mother tongue—with communities of varying sizes from all of Europe, Africa, and Asia, the last mostly Indian.

Christians (53%) include most whites, 67 percent of Africans (mainstream and African Traditional), many Coloureds, and a tiny group of Indians and other Asians. Muslims (3%) include Coloureds and Indians. Hindus (1%) are predominantly Indian. The Jewish community (1%) is the largest in South Africa.

LOCAL GOVERNMENT

Since 2000, Johannesburg has had a single-tier system of local government for the city's eleven administrative regions, each consisting of approximately 300,000 people. In the municipal elections of March 2006, 1,384,327 Johannesburg residents voted out of a possible 1,739,292 in the 107 wards. Of the 17 political parties which contested the election the ANC won an outright victory of 62 percent. Its ward seats plus those granted on the basis of the 108 proportional representation offices give the ANC 136 seats out of a possible 217. The opposition party is the Democratic Alliance (DA), which with 27 percent of the votes has 59 seats. Behind are the Inkatha Freedom Party (with 3 percent of the votes and seven seats) and the Independent Democrats (with 2 percent of the votes and four seats). The African Christian Democratic Party and the Pan Africanist Congress of Azania (the PAC) each have two seats and the following seven each have one: the Independent Party, the Azanian People's Organisation (Azapo), the Vryheidsfront Plus, the Christian Democratic Party, the United Democratic Movement, the Christian Front, and the Operation Khanyisa Movement. As in Johannesburg, the predominance of the ANC at local council level is the norm. The one exception is Cape Town where the DA, with a majority of three, governs on a coalition footing. Throughout the country the increased importance of women is notable: On average, in the Johannesburg municipal council, they constitute 35 percent.

The council is headed by a portfolio-driven mayoral committee, selected by the executive mayor, a political nominee, to whom the appointed city manager is accountable. In each region, now reduced from eleven to six and alphabetically labeled instead of numbered, a director and management team operate a people's center, the functions of which have been pared to dealing almost solely with municipal payments and enquiries. In the interests of "efficiency" most of their former functions have been nominally regionalized but in practice centralized, for instance, the running of libraries and sports facilities. Many previous regional activities are also centrally controlled, such as Housing, Human Resources, Social Development, and Health, which includes providing primary, public and environmental health, managing clinics, imparting pharmaceutical knowledge, and supplying education concerning HIV/AIDS.

Many core utilities and amenities have been commercialized and corporatized. Despite their manifold problems in dealing with aged infrastructures designed to cope with far smaller populations, official municipal statistics state that 96 percent of households have piped water (or have a nearby tap), 84 percent have toilets, 88 percent have refuse removal, and 85 percent have access to electricity. These figures, however, do not include that estimated third of Johannesburg households that are situated in the informal shack-and-shanty settlements. Thus the provision of utilities, amenities, and other structures, including housing, continues to remain a central municipal obligation.

See also **Apartheid; Archaeology and Prehistory; Cape Town; Disease: HIV/AIDS, Social Aspects; Ethnicity: Southern Africa; Popular Culture: Southern Africa; Pretoria; South Africa, Republic of; Urbanism and Urbanization: Housing.**

BIBLIOGRAPHY

Beavon, Keith. *Johannesburg: The Making and Shaping of the City.* Pretoria: University of South Africa Press, 2004.

Bremner, Lindsay. *Johannesburg: One City; Colliding Worlds.* Johannesburg, South Africa: STE Publications, 2004.

Burger, Delien, ed. *South Africa Year Book 2003/04.* Johannesburg, South Africa: Government Communication and Information System, 2004.

Centre for Development and Enterprise. *Johannesburg Africa's World City: A Challenge to Action,* ed. Anne Bernstein. Johannesburg, South Africa: Centre for Development and Enterprise, 2002.

De Villiers, Susan, ed. *Johannesburg: An African City in Change.* Cape Town, South Africa: Zebra Press, 2001.

Maud, John Primatt Radcliffe. *City Government: The Johannesburg Experience.* Oxford: Clarendon, 1938.

Maylam, Paul. *A History of the African People of South Africa: From the Early Iron Age to the 1970s.* New York: St. Martin's Press, 1986.

Parsons, Neil. "'The Time of Troubles': Difaqane in the Interior." In *The Mfecane Aftermath: Reconstructive Debates in Southern African History,* ed. Carolyn Hamilton. Johannesburg, South Africa: Witwatersrand University Press, 1995.

ELAINE NATALIE KATZ

JOHNSON, SAMUEL (1846–1901).

The Anglican pastor and historian of the Yoruba Samuel Johnson was born on June 24, 1846, in Hastings (an outlying village of Freetown, Sierra Leone) to Henry Johnson, a liberated slave and descendant of Abiodun, the last great king of Old Oyo. In 1857 Samuel Johnson accompanied his father (and three brothers) back to Yorubaland, where his father was appointed an agent at one of the Christian Missionary Society (CMS) mission stations. Samuel was educated during 1858–1863 at the CMS school at Kudeti, run by Anna Hinderer (wife of the mission head at Ibadan). During 1863–1865 Johnson studied at the CMS Training Institution in Abeokuta. He was appointed schoolmaster of the Kudeti and Aremo CMS schools in Ibadan, 1866–1875, and catechist at the Aremo church, 1875–1886. He was ordained deacon in 1886 and appointed pastor of the CMS church in Oyo in 1887.

From about 1879 on, Johnson became the principal intermediary between the Alafin and the Ibadan war chiefs and the British in an effort to end the Sixteen Years' War among the Yoruba (1877–1893). In the process, he influenced the installation of the British protectorate. He collected oral traditions mostly from elders at Ibadan and official court historians at Oyo and in 1897 produced a manuscript of nearly 1,000 pages titled *The History of the Yorubas: From the Earliest Times to the Beginning of the British Protectorate.* CMS authorities advised that it be shortened and translated into Yoruba for use in the mission schools. When Johnson resisted this suggestion, the manuscript was passed to a commercial publisher, who lost it. It was Johnson's medical doctor brother Obadiah who, after Samuel's death in 1901, rewrote the work from notes and drafts. It was eventually published in 1921, and remains the single most important source on Yoruba history.

See also **Historiography; History and the Study of Africa; Liberia.**

BIBLIOGRAPHY

DeMaria, Robert. *The Life of Samuel Johnson: A Critical Biography.* Cambridge, MA: Blackwell, 1993.

Doortmont, M. R. "Samuel Johnson (1846–1901): Missionary, Diplomat, and Historian." In *Yoruba Historiography*, ed. Toyin Falola. Madison: University of Wisconsin, 1991.

Falola, Toyin. *Pioneer, Patriot, and Patriarch: Samuel Johnson and the Yoruba People.* Madison: University of Wisconsin, 1993.

J. F. ADE. AJAYI

Ellen Johnson-Sirleaf (1938–). On January 16, 2006, Johnson-Sirleaf was sworn in as Liberia's president during an inauguration ceremony at the Capitol Building in Monrovia. Johnson-Sirleaf is Africa's first female to be elected head of state. JIM WATSON/AFP/GETTY IMAGES

JOHNSON-SIRLEAF, ELLEN (1938–).
Ellen Johnson was born on October 29, 1938, in the Liberian capital of Monrovia, of Americo-Liberian descent. She was educated in Monrovia until, at the age of 17, she married James Sirleaf. The couple moved in 1961 to Wisconsin in the United States, where she studied accounting at Madison Business College. She graduated in 1964. In 1969 she attended Harvard University's Kennedy School, earning her masters degree in public administration in 1971. After Harvard, she returned to Liberia to serve in then-President William Tolbert's (1913–1980) government as minister of finance (1972–1973). She left the administration because of policy disputes.

In Liberia, the two most deeply opposed factions are the Americo-Liberians (of repatriated slave descent) and the Krahn, who are the largest of Liberia's indigenous ethnic groups. In the early 1980s, the Krahn faction staged a coup, executed Tolbert, and installed Samuel Doe (c. 1950–1990) as president. Johnson-Sirleaf found it wisest to escape to Kenya. In 1983 she became the director of Citibank, Kenya, but returned to Liberia two years later when new presidential elections were held. She campaigned against the Doe regime, which earned her a ten-year prison term. She was offered

early release if she would leave the country, so she returned to Kenya, then moved to Washington, D.C., to work at the Equator Bank. From there she took a position with the United Nations. A lifelong campaigner for women's rights, Johnson-Sirleaf was a founding member of the International Women's Institute in Political Leadership. In 1988 she won the Franklin D. Roosevelt Freedom of Speech Award.

In 1990, rebel forces led by Charles Taylor (b. 1948) killed President Doe, thus clearing the way for Johnson-Sirleaf to safely return to Liberia. She again became politically active, supporting Charles Taylor's assumption of the presidency. During the elections of 1997, however, she chose to run against him. Her candidacy was unsuccessful, but Taylor still chose to punish her, charging her with treason.

In 1999, Liberia erupted into civil war. By 2003, international pressures forced Taylor out, and Johnson-Sirleaf served on the Government Reform Commission that organized new elections. In 2005, Johnson-Sirleaf ran for president on the Unity Party ticket. Her closest rival was George Weah (b. 1966), a soccer star who was popular with young voters. Johnson-Sirleaf won the most votes, but Weah's showing in the election forced a runoff in November 2005. Johnson-Sirleaf won and was sworn in as Liberia's president on January 16, 2006. Her first act in office was to open her assets to public scrutiny, in an attempt to overcome the public impression that all politicians were corrupt.

See also **Liberia; Taylor, Charles Gahnhay.**

BIBLIOGRAPHY

Johnson, Ellen Sirleaf, and Francis Nyirjesy. *The Outlook for Commercial Bank Lending to Sub-Saharan Africa.* Washington DC: World Bank, 1991.

NANCY E. GRATTON

JOSEPH, HELEN (1905–1992). Helen

Joseph (née Fennell) was one of seven leaders of the famous march of 20,000 women against the pass laws to the Union Buildings in Pretoria on August 9, 1956. Born in Midhurst, Sussex, in the United Kingdom, Joseph was educated at a convent and at King's College, University of London. She came to South Africa in 1931 after teaching for three years in India. Married to a Durban dentist, for a few years Joseph lived a privileged white middle-class life. World War II changed her life. She joined the Women's Auxiliary Air Force as a welfare and information officer and learned of the realities of racial oppression and discrimination in South Africa. Later, she worked in community health among the Coloured communities in Elsies River on the Cape Flats. In 1952 in Johannesburg she became secretary-director of the Medical Aid Society of the Garment Workers' Union. There she met Solly Sachs (1900–1964) who was general secretary of the Union and whose influence on her both intimately and politically was profound. In December 1956 she and 155 others were arrested for treason and stood trial until March 1961. She was Accused No. 2 after Nelson Mandela. She was detained, banned for fifteen years, house arrested (confined to home after 5 PM), listed (which meant she could not be quoted), harassed, and threatened by police. She remained a committed democrat until her death in 1992.

See also **Apartheid; Mandela, Nelson; Mandela, Winnie; South Africa, Republic of; World War II.**

BIBLIOGRAPHY

Joseph, Helen. *If This be Treason.* London: Andre Deutsch, 1963.

Joseph, Helen. *Side by Side: The Autobiography of Helen Joseph.* London: Zed Press, 1986.

SHEILA MEINTJES

JOURNALISM. *See* **Media: Journalism.**

JUDAISM IN AFRICA. Judaism and

Jews in Africa can be divided into several categories. For hundreds of years, large, culturally vibrant Jewish communities existed in North Africa, particularly Morocco, Egypt, Tunisia, and Libya. North Africa was one of the great centers of Jewish learning and culture for centuries. Following the establishment of the State of Israel in 1948, most of the Jews in these countries emigrated. In 2002 slightly more than 5,000 Jews resided in Morocco and an additional 1,500 were found in Tunisia. Farther south there are Jews of European or Middle Eastern descent who have settled in various African countries. By far the largest population in this category in the early twenty-first century is found in South Africa, where over 80,000 Jews reside. Substantial Jewish emigration from South Africa since the 1970s (over 40,000) has been partially compensated for by Jewish immigration, especially from Israel (10,000). About 500 (down from a peak of 8,500) Jews live in Zimbabwe, and a slightly smaller population (400) is found in Kenya. No other African countries have Jewish populations of European or Middle Eastern heritage of over 100.

A second category consists of local African populations who claim to be of Jewish or Israelite descent, often tracing themselves to the mythical Ten Lost Tribes or other early Jewish groups. In the past, scholars adopting a diffusionist approach that imagines coherent tribal movements over long distances often accepted such claims at face value. From the late 1990s and beyond, however, most consider these groups to have local roots and to have independently adopted Judaism and a Jewish identity. The groups appear to have had little direct contact with other

Jews prior to the second half of the twentieth century but absorbed biblical and Hebraic elements through contacts with Christians or Muslims. These include the Lemba of South Africa and the Bayudiya of Uganda.

Another category includes the Beta Israel (Falasha) of Ethiopia. Although they have long been viewed as descendants of Jewish immigrants who reached the Horn of Africa at the beginning of the Christian era, since the 1980s scholarship has indicated that this ethnic group originated in Ethiopia between the fourteenth and sixteenth centuries. They have, however, been recognized as Jews by the State of Israel, and between 1977 and 2006 over 70,000 Beta Israel emigrated to that country. Only a small number now remain in Ethiopia. Their emigration has spurred many descendants of Beta Israel who had accepted Christianity in the past (their numbers are estimated at between 30,000 and 100,000) to claim or reclaim their Jewish identity in the hope of also being allowed to emigrate to Israel. Other groups and individuals in southern Ethiopia, Somalia, Nigeria, and Ghana desiring to settle in Israel in recent years have put forward similar claims.

In addition to the aforementioned groups, many Africans, particularly members of independent churches, have incorporated Jewish-biblical ritual and symbols into their religious systems. Often they strongly identity with the narratives of the Hebrew Bible (Old Testament) and the ritual practices of the Israelite tribes. Noteworthy among these ritual elements are Sabbath observances, ritual purification, and circumcision. In some cases, biblical customs are cited in justification of African practices such as polygamy, levirate marriage, divination, and sacrifice, which Western missionaries frowned upon.

Finally, there are African peoples whose indigenous customs display a certain affinity with practices described in the Bible and in Jewish literature. Some scholars have cited these similarities as evidence of Israelite influence in Africa, whereas others have viewed them as of value only for the sake of phenomenological comparison.

See also **Christianity; Immigration and Immigrant Groups; Islam; Morocco; South Africa, Republic of.**

BIBLIOGRAPHY

Della Pergola, Sergio. "World Jewish Population 2002." *American Jewish Year Book*. New York: American Jewish Committee, 2002.

Parfitt, Tudor. *The Lost Tribes of Israel: The History of a Myth*. London: Phoenix Press, 2003.

Parfitt, Tudor, and Emanuela Trevisan Semi. *Judaising Movements: Studies in the Margins of Judaism in Modern Times*. London: Curzon Press, 2002.

STEVEN KAPLAN

JUNGLE. *See* **Ecosystems: Tropical and Humid Forests; Forestry.**

KABAREGA (1859–1923). Kabarega's father was Kyebambe IV Kamurasi, who ruled Bunyoro from 1852 until his death in 1869. Nyoro traditions indicate that Kamurasi, under siege by the rebellious Chope princes, took temporary refuge with his son in Bulega (in present-day eastern Congo Republic). On returning, the Banyoro called the child Akaana k'Abalega (child of the Balega).

A war of succession between Kabarega and his elder brother Kabigumire followed Kamurasi's death. Kabigumire was favored by the nobility and chiefs; Kabarega was supported by the army and the commoners. The war was won by Kabarega, who had by 1870 been crowned King Chwa II Kabarega.

Kabarega sought to create a strong and stable state and to restore the ancient Kitara Empire, which had been broken up in the 1600s by an invasion by the Luo people. To this end he created a standing army known as the Abarusura, which he used for defensive purposes as well as for extending Kabarega's sphere of influence and conducting raids against neighboring territories to obtain wealth and slaves. The Abarusura waged campaigns against the neighboring people of Busoga, Nkore, Bulega, and northern Uganda. Kabarega reintegrated Bugungu and Chope into his kingdom and by 1876 he had reconquered Toro. Kabarega's representatives also controlled Bulega, Busongora, Bukonjo, Bwamba, Bubira, and Mboga, and he had influence over Nkore, Rwanda, Karagwa, Teso, Acholi, Alurland, and Lango.

Kabarega's control over these considerable areas was not, however, uniform. Chiefs far from the Bunyoro capital remained more or less autonomous, and the existence in outlying areas of officials put in place by Kabarega did not guarantee the support of the populace. Kabarega had no way to monitor all these areas to keep them under his control. Some scholars have seen Kabarega as a nation builder who succeeded in creating a broad-based government and who encouraged intermarriages between various groups and clans.

Though Kabarega was successful in spreading his rule over a large area and in creating loyalty to himself through the institution of common ceremonies, he was unable to promote unity among the people of the various countries under his control. Even at the time of colonial intrusion, no national awareness linked the many peoples under Kabarega's direct and indirect rule. Some scholars have asserted that Kabarega contributed greatly to the reduction of famine and disease in his kingdom. He encouraged public works (*oruharo*) such as the building of roads, and he built granaries for the storage of surplus food for use during times of shortage.

It should be noted, however, that Kabarega's public works were not intended to serve only the interests of the people. Bunyoro was to some extent a feudal state, and Kabarega obtained much wealth from the exploitation of peasant labor. He also presided over the sacrifice of many of his subjects to the Omukewo tree, which was cut periodically in accordance with Nyoro traditions.

Kabarega is best known for his resistance to European imperialism. The conflicts between Kabarega and the Europeans started when Samuel Baker, the British administrator in Sudan under the Egyptian government, entered Bunyoro in 1872 and announced the annexation of Kitara to Egypt. The relations between Kabarega and Baker worsened when Baker attacked Kabarega's palace after Baker's soldiers had been disoriented by the beer sent by Kabarega. The British soldiers burned the Banyoro houses in Kihande and retreated.

During the 1890s the British again tried to establish their influence over Uganda. An agent of the Imperial British East Africa Company, Captain Frederick Lugard, first encountered Kabarega's forces in 1891 in Toro. After defeating Ireta's division and recruiting Selim Bey's troops into his army, Lugard constructed forts along the Toro-Bunyoro border from which to strike Kabarega's forces and disrupt the flow of arms into Bunyoro.

Lugard had restored King Kasagama, who had signed a treaty of protection with Lugard, to the Toro throne. He was determined to keep Kabarega out of Toro. In November 1893 Kabarega sent Ireta and Rwabudongo to attack Toro, which resulted in the removal of King Kasagama from the Toro throne.

After a meeting with the Ganda chiefs on December 4, 1893, the new British commissioner, Col. Colville, declared war on Kabarega. The British-Baganda soldiers crossed the Kafu River on December 27, 1893, and by January 2, 1894, captured Kabarega's capital, Mparo. Kabarega retreated into the Budongo forest (in present-day Masindi district). At the end of January 1894 the Buganda forces, led by General Kakungulu, attacked Kabarega's camps in Budongo forest. This forced Kabarega into Lango, which became the base of operations for a subsequent guerrilla war led by Kabarega.

Although Kabarega failed to rally much support from the masses to fight the British-led forces, he at times impressed his enemies. On March 2, 1895, Kabarega was attacked in Kijunjubwa near Masindi, but his army managed to defeat the enemy forces. The British then withdrew to Hoima for reorganization, and more forces were called from Buganda. The attack on the Banyoro, in which the British were victorious, began on April 22, 1895. Kabarega's mother and children were captured during the siege.

Kabarega had been joined by King Mwanga of Buganda in July 1898. They were captured together in Lango by the British forces on April 9, 1899, and were later exiled to the Seychelles Islands. Kabarega was allowed to return home in 1923 but died in Busoga en route.

Scholars have taken differing views on this African leader. Afrocentrist historians have depicted Kabarega as a hero and a proto-African nationalist, while Eurocentrist historians have seen him as a barbaric tyrant and a murderer. Adding to the lack of objectivity with which Kabarega has been approached, much of the information about him was obtained through oral tradition and from the writings of Kabarega's relatives. What is certain, however, is that Kabarega staged a fierce resistance to European imperialism for more than twenty years.

See also **Kagwa, Apolo; Kakungulu, Semei Lwakirenzi; Lugard, Frederick John Dealtry; Uganda: History and Politics.**

BIBLIOGRAPHY

Nyakatura, J. W. *Anatomy of an African Kingdom: A History of Bunyoro-Kitara*, trans. Teopista Muganwa and ed. Godfrey N. Uzoigwe. Garden City, NY: NOK Publishers, 1973.

Steinhart, Edward I. *Conflict and Collaboration: The Kingdoms of Western Uganda, 1890–1907*. Princeton, NJ: Princeton University Press, 1977.

Uzoigwe, G. N. "Kabalega and the Making of a New Kitara." *Tarikh* 3, no. 2 (1970): 12–29.

GODFREY OKOTH

KABILA, LAURENT DESIRÉ AND JOSEPH

(1939–2001; 1971–). President since May 1997 of Democratic Republic of the Congo (DRC) when he overthrew Mobutu Sese Seko, Laurent Desiré Kabila was born on November 17, 1939, in Jadotville (present-day Likasi) in what was then the Katanga province of the Belgian Congo. When the region achieved independence in 1960, Kabila *père* was a supporter of Patrice Lumumba, who led the Congolese independence and took over rule of the DRC. After Joseph Mobutu's successful coup a few months later, the elder Kabila fled to Zaire to plan a countercoup. He received assistance from Che Guevara there in 1965, when Guevara was a revolutionary presence in Africa. However, Guevara thought Kabila was inconsequential, more interested in women and strong drink than in achieving revolution.

In 1967, with the help of Chinese patrons, Kabila formed the People's Revolutionary Party, espousing communist goals. He gained followers in South Kivu province (on the western shore of Lake Tanganyika), which he led in secession from Mobutu's Congo. His new state collapsed in 1988, and was reabsorbed into DRC. Kabila himself disappeared and was presumed dead. He was only hiding, however, and regathering his forces. In 1996 he returned to Democratic Republic of the Congo, leading ethnic Tutsis in revolt against Mobutu, engaging the first Congo War. By 1997 he had enlisted support from Burundi, Rwanda, and Uganda in the so-called Alliance of Democratic Forces, and by May of that year he had captured Kinshasa, forcing Mobutu to flee. He took over the government in May of 1997, creating what he called the Public Salvation Government of Democratic Republic of the Congo.

No longer a Marxist, Kabila introduced a combination of capitalism and collectivism to the country. Nonetheless, he faced charges of corruption and human rights abuses. His former allies in Rwanda and Uganda broke with him, supporting a new uprising called the Congolese Rally for Democracy. Kabila found new support in Zimbabwe, Namibia, and Angola, and put down uprisings in the south and west of the country, leaving the north and east in violent contestation. In 2001 an assassin's bullet ended Laurent Desire's life.

While he ruled the state of South Kivu, Laurent Desiré Kabila and his wife, Sifa Mahanya, had a son, Joseph (on June 4, 1971). Joseph Kabila Kabange was educated there, and in Dar es Salaam and Mbeya, both in Tanzania. He became a soldier in his father's army in 1996, and served as operations commander during the First Congo War (1996–1998). Once his father took control of DRC, Joseph went to China for training at the National Defense University in Beijing. He returned home with the rank of major general, and became chairman of his father's joint chiefs of staff in 1998, then army chief of staff in 2000. Upon his father's assassination, he took charge and ordered a retaliatory strike. A total of 135 people were arrested on suspicion of complicity in the assassination attempt and brought to trial. Forty of these

Laurent Desiré Kabila (1939–2001). Kabila was president of the Democratic Republic of the Congo from May 1997, after overthrowing dictator Mobutu Sese Seko, until his assassination by Rashidi Kasereka, a member of his own party, in January 2001. He was succeeded by his son Joseph. ODD ANDERSEN/AFP/GETTY IMAGES

were later acquitted, sixty-nine were imprisoned, and the other twenty-six were executed.

Since assuming the presidency in 2001, Joseph Kabila has attempted to negotiate a peace in the ongoing civil war. He established an interim government that included his political rivals, but unrest continued. In March 2004, former Mobutu supporters attempted a coup attempted near Kinshasa, and another attempt followed three months later. Both failed, and in December 2005 a referendum approved a new constitution, calling for elections on July 30, 2006. Kabila has registered as the candidate for the People's Party for Reconstruction and Democracy, just one in a field of thirty-three

Joseph Kabila (1971–). The Democratic Republic of Congo president waits for the start of the UN-sponsored conference concerning the Great Lakes Region, December 14, 2006. Eleven African presidents were invited to the Kenyan capital for the international conference aimed at stabilizing the region. MARCO LONGARI/AFP/GETTY IMAGES

presidential candidates. Continued violence threatens the prospect of an orderly vote, but as of this writing, the elections are going forward.

See also **Congo, Democratic Republic of; Mobutu Sese Seko; Warfare: Civil Wars.**

BIBLIOGRAPHY

Nzongola-Ntalaga, Georges. *The Congo, from Leopold to Kabila: A People's History.* London: Zed Books, 2002.

NANCY E. GRATTON

KADALIE, CLEMENTS (1896–1951).
Born near Blantyre, Nyasaland (present-day Malawi), Clements Kadalie finished school in 1912, taught for one year, and then traveled south through Mozambique, Southern Rhodesia, and South Africa, arriving in Cape Town in 1918. Later that same year Kadalie founded the Industrial and Commercial Workers Union of Africa, popularly known as the Industrial and Commercial Union (ICU). The union, known for challenging white rule, was also known to Africans as ICU *Mlungu*: "I see you, white man."

The union was very effective. In its first strike (1919), Kadalie led four hundred Cape Town dockworkers to win wage increases. In 1919 and 1920 the ICU led successful strikes among gold miners on the Rand (Johannesburg, Transvaal) and in other parts of the country. At one point Kadalie got wage concessions for other Cape Town dockworkers simply by threatening to strike. The ICU grew quickly, with Kadalie as national secretary. By 1923 the union had seventeen regional branches in South Africa and peaked in the 1920s at 100,000 members, making it the largest non-white union in the country, and thus a threat to the white minority government. The ICU did not align with any white unions or with the mostly white Communist Party of South Africa (CPSA).

After the government of Jan Smuts passed the Urban Areas Act in 1923, which further segregated towns, and the Industrial Conciliation Act in 1924, which granted all groups save blacks the right to collective bargaining in the workplace, Kadalie encouraged Africans to give their support to a coalition between the National party and the Labor party against Smuts. The coalition won the election in 1924 but did not prove to be any more agreeable to African rights than Smuts: they instituted a policy of "civilized labor," which reserved certain jobs for whites.

In 1929, after A. W. G. Champion and his ICU members in Natal broke with the national union, Kadalie resigned his secretaryship and formed the independent ICU. The new union carried off a general strike in the industrial East London area, and Kadalie spent two months in jail for his role. Kadalie's autobiography, *My Life and the ICU: The Autobiography of a Black Trade Unionist in South Africa*, was published in 1970, almost twenty years after his death.

See also **Labor: Trades Unions and Associations; South Africa, Republic of: Geography and Economy.**

BIBLIOGRAPHY

Bunting, Brian. *Moses Kotane, South African Revolutionary: A Political Biography.* Beltville, South Africa: Maylbuye Books, 1998.

Phiri, Desmond Dudwa. *I See You: Life of Clements Kadalie, the Man South Africa, Malawi, Zimbabwe, and Namibia Should Not Forget.* Lantyre, Malawi: College Pub. Co., 2000.

Roux, Edward. *Time Longer Than Rope: A History of the Black Man's Struggle for Freedom in South Africa,* 2nd edition. Madison: University of Wisconsin, 1964.

THOMAS F. MCDOW

KAGAME, ALEXIS (1912–1981).

A Tutsi born in Buriza Province (northern Rwanda), the Rwandan scholar and writer Alexis Kagame was ordained in 1941 as a Roman Catholic priest and received a Ph.D. in philosophy in 1955. He was subsequently a journalist, a teacher, and a professor at the national university of Rwanda (1963). He played a major political role in the 1950s, as confidential adviser to King Mutara of Rwanda, and as kingmaker in the 1959 coup that triggered the Rwandese revolution. He published more than 150 articles and a score of books in French and Kinyarwanda; they cover Rwanda's history, philosophy, and language and include didactic materials and a huge epic, *La divine pastorale*, which attempts to place Christianity in a Rwandan setting. An ardent nationalism runs through all his works.

Kagame was totally convinced both of the moral superiority of Rwandan ethics over Western practices and of the Christian revelation. His crowning works are *La philosophie bantu comparée* (Paris, 1976) and *Un abrégé de l'ethnohistoire du Rwanda* (Butare, Rwanda, 1972–1975). His corpus of oral traditions, gathered from 1935 onward, is his major legacy to scholarship.

See also **Rwanda.**

BIBLIOGRAPHY

Coupez, A., and Thomas Komanzi. *Littérature de cour au Rwanda*. Oxford, U.K.: Clarendon Press, 1970.

Kagame, Alexis. *La divine pastorale*. Bruxelles: Marais, 1952.

JAN VANSINA

KAGWA, APOLO (1868–1827).

Apolo Kagwa was a Christian military and religious leader in present-day Uganda. He rose to prominence in the 1880s during the religious wars fueled by the European scramble for control of territory in eastern Africa. Henry Nyonyintono, a Catholic military commander, controlled the Christian Party that fled to Nkore. When Nyonyintono died in 1890, Kagwa, a Protestant, succeeded him as head of the party. He supported the Church Missionary Society and later the British East Africa Company, two external allies that ensured the triumph of Protestants over Catholics and Muslims. Kagwa organized the deposition of King Mwanga of Buganda and enthroned Chwa, a minor, who presumably would be easier to control. He was *katikiro* (prime minister) from 1889 to 1926 and leader of the three regents who ruled Buganda during the years that Chwa was too young to rule in his own right (1900–1914).

Kagwa was the chief negotiator of the 1900 agreement between the British and the Ganda, which established freehold land tenure independent of the king's grants and reduced the power of the monarchy. He was instrumental in creating key educational institutions such as King's College in Budo and Gayaza High School, and he authored two works on the history and culture of Buganda: *Basekabaka be Buganda* (London, 1912) and *Ekitabo kye mpisa za Baganda* (New York, 1934). Kagwa realized the futility of fighting invaders who possessed superior technology and collaborated with them in such a manner that he preserved a measure of autonomy for Buganda. His insight largely explains why Uganda was accorded protectorate status, while other conquered African countries were treated as colonies. Kagwa was knighted by the British in 1905.

See also **Colonial Policies and Practices; Land: Tenure.**

BIBLIOGRAPHY

Kiwanuka, M. S. M. Semakula. *A History of Buganda from Foundation of the Kingdom to 1900*. New York: Africana Pub. Corp., 1972.

Roscoe, John. *The Baganda: An Account of Their Native Customs and Beliefs*, 2nd edition. New York: Barnes & Noble, 1966.

Twaddle, Michael. *Kakungulu and the Creation of Uganda, 1868–1928*. Athens: Ohio University Press, 1993.

APOLO R. NSIBAMBI

KAHENA.

Kahena, which means priestess or prophetess, was born in the Aures Mountains in Algeria sometime in the 600s CE. During her lifetime, Arab generals began to lead armies into North Africa, preparing to conquer the area and introduce Islam to the local peoples. Kahena directed the most determined resistance to the seventh century Arab invasions of North Africa. About 690, Kahena assumed personal command of the African forces and, under her aggressive leadership, briefly forced the Arabs to retreat.

The Berbers of the seventh century were not religiously homogenous. Christian, Jewish, and pagan Berbers were spread through the region that is in the early twenty-first century Morocco, Tunisia, Algeria, and Libya. Kahena emerged as a war leader who could rally the people during this tense period, and proved amazingly successful at leading the different tribes to join together against their invaders. Her reputation as a strategist and sorceress spread, and she managed to briefly unite the tribes of Ifrikya, the Berber name for North Africa, ruling them and leading them in battle for five years before her final defeat. Kahena took her own life to avoid capture by the enemy, and sent her sons to the Arab camp with instructions that they adopt Islam. Ultimately, Kahena's sons participated in invading Europe and in the subjugation of Spain and Portugal. Kahena's speeches and poems were all destroyed after her death. Only a four-line poem by her under the title *My Berber Horse* survived and is still sung in Algeria by young militant Berbers.

See also **Literature: Women Writers, Northern Africa; Literatures in European Languages: Francophone Northern Africa.**

BIBLIOGRAPHY

Ibn Khaldun. *The Muqaddimah, An Introduction to History*, 2nd edition, trans. Franz Rosenthal. Princeton, NJ: Princeton University Press, 1967.

Sadiqi, Fatima; Moha Ennaji; and Amira Nowaira; eds. *Women Writing Africa: The Northern Region.* New York: The Feminist Press at The City University of New York, forthcoming.

FATIMA SADIQI

KAKUNGULU, SEMEI LWAKIRENZI (1868–1928).
The Ugandan political leader Semei Lwakirenzi Kakungulu was born in the tiny kingdom of Koki in modern-day Uganda. By the late 1880s he was a chief in the neighboring state of Buganda, where by the 1890s he also had become second minister. With the approval of incoming British administrators, he carved out a kingdom for himself to the north and east of Buganda among a very wide range of politically decentralized peoples. In 1906 he was persuaded by British administrators to become president of the Busoga chiefly council to the east, a position with more prestige than power. He held it until 1913, when he returned to live among the peoples he and his Ganda followers had conquered before coming to Busoga.

Unfortunately for Kakungulu, most of these peoples were by then administered directly by other Ganda agents, most of them originally his own followers. His political kingdom effectively over, Kakungulu attempted to create a religious one. In 1914 he supported Malaki Musajakawa, an Anglican evangelist from Buganda, in establishing a new denomination throughout eastern and northern Uganda opposed to the hospitals and vaccinations sponsored by European Christian missionaries. A few years later, Kakungulu broke with Malaki and formed another denomination opposed to Western medical practices, this time based upon Judaism as well as Christianity. He died in 1928, and was buried in the western foothills of Mount Elgon in the far eastern corner of the colony according to rites he himself had devised after reading the Bible, which had been translated into Luganda by Christian missionaries during the 1890s. His time on Mount Elgon is still recalled in the common local greeting *Mulembe!* (Peace) that he initiated.

See also **Christianity: Overview; Kabarega; Uganda: History and Politics.**

BIBLIOGRAPHY

Roberts, A. D. "The Sub-imperialism of the Baganda." *Journal of African History* 3, no. 3 (1962): 435–450.

Twaddle, Michael. *Kakungulu and the Creation of Uganda, 1868–1928.* Athens: Ohio University Press, 1993.

MICHAEL TWADDLE

KALAHARI DESERT.
Although geographically much larger, culturally the Kalahari Desert is generally understood to encompass only the western two-thirds of Botswana plus adjacent parts of Namibia and Angola; there it is grass-tree savanna rather than desert. Some ethnographers

stress its hot arid summer to paint a picture of severe desert conditions where isolated San speakers survive as remnants of prehistoric foragers. Other anthropologists and most historians focus on the Bantu peoples of the region, stressing their agropastoral economy in an ecology with cycles of drought and labor migration. This disjunction in the depiction of a single region has engendered debate over the ethnographic status of San peoples and their historical relation to Bantu speakers. This author argues that all Kalahari peoples have been actively engaged with their neighbors throughout history and that, therefore, San speakers are not primal hunter-gatherers but poor rural people who forage when denied other economic means.

KALAHARI PEOPLES

Originally, only Khoesan peoples lived throughout southern Africa, where they developed mixed economies based on hunting, fishing, and gathering that were adapted to highly diverse local ecologies. The term "Khoesan" is composed of two words, *khoe* (people) and *san* (aborigines or foragers). This distinction came to be solidified as marking a real difference between Khoe herders (called Hottentot in the past) and San hunter-gatherers (Bushmen). In the early twenty-first century, Kalahari San peoples speak three mutually unintelligible languages plus a number of dialects. There are three divisions of this language family—!Kung (five dialects, including Zhucoasi), Khoe (the largest group), and Twi—each with a distinct grammar and vocabulary. There may be 100,000 Khoesan-speakers living in and around the Kalahari as of 2007; about 50,000 are ethnographically classified as San. Although described as foragers, they have long engaged in a range of economies, including pastoralism and wage labor.

The Kalahari speakers of the widespread Bantu language family include Tswana and Kalanga in the east, Kgalagadi in the center, Herero and Ambo in the west, and Mbukushu and Yeyi on the Okavango Delta, plus several others in small numbers. Their languages belong to four major branches of Bantu, and most are mutually unintelligible. All of these peoples are herders to varying degrees, and all prefer cattle as their primary animal; but with a few exceptions, only Tswana and Herero are able to maintain large herds. Ambo and Mbukushu are principally farmers, Yeyi are fishers,

and Kgalagadi are goat keepers. There are about 1.5 million Bantu speakers in the (ethnographic) Kalahari today; perhaps half are Tswana. The ancestors of all these Bantu peoples once lived in a broad belt across the center of the continent.

SOCIAL HISTORY

This diversity of languages and economies indicates a complex history for the Kalahari. About two thousand years ago, cattle and sheep were introduced from sources in the north and incorporated into foraging. Historians are confident that Khoe speakers played an important role in this transfer, because the basic pastoral vocabulary of most southern African herders—including Bantu—is Khoe in origin. Bantu peoples began moving down from central Africa shortly after this, bringing sorghum, millet, cowpeas, melons, and goats as well as iron and copper metallurgy with them. Relations between groups must have involved considerable mutual exchange.

Most peoples who speak Khoe languages in the Kalahari in the early twenty-first century are genetically and physically indistinguishable from their Bantu neighbors, and until the late twentieth century Khoe social forms were predominant. This is strong evidence that Bantu were drawn into Khoe social networks through marriage and other alliances. Yeyi, a Bantu language, incorporates a large click inventory, implying that Yeyi people have a long history of intimate association with Khoesan speakers. Herero and Kgalagadi came into the Kalahari at the latest by 1600 CE; since then they have maintained close economic and social ties, including marriage, with San. Around 1750, Tswana peoples began moving up from the south; at that time they were not very different economically or politically from the Khoe and Kgalagadi, whom they met in the Kalahari.

This relative social equality came to an end early in the nineteenth century. European goods were then filtering in, and the Kalahari became a major source of ivory and ostrich feathers. Tswana were ideally situated to exploit the trade; as a result their polities grew, largely by incorporating other Bantu as well as Khoesan peoples, to include 30,000 people under one leader. The indigenous social landscape was severely disrupted; San and Kgalagari hunters produced almost all goods for trade, and cattle were consigned to them under conditions of patronage.

The Hoodia, a cactus-like plant in the Kalahari Desert.
San Bushmen hunters traditionally ate this cactus shrub to
cut their appetite and thirst while on long hunts in the desert.
© LOUISE GUBB/CORBIS

Tswana gained thereby a degree of control over these peoples' economic lives, which was translated into political control. Tswana class structure was strengthened, and by the mid-nineteenth century a serf class had arisen, composed almost entirely of San, Kgalagadi, and Yeyi peoples. Those whose labor was not needed were not incorporated; these people necessarily relied more heavily on foraging than did others. When the economic vitality of trade collapsed in the mid-1880s, labor lost further value, thereby deepening rural poverty, reducing some San to subsistence foraging while kinship inequalities facilitated the slipping of some impoverished Tswana individuals and families into servitude. When trade collapsed, however, gold and diamonds were discovered in South Africa; the Kalahari rapidly became a labor reserve. The absence of Tswana men, who were responding to the money wages paid by the mines, left a labor vacuum on cattle posts and farms. This vacuum was filled mainly by San and Kgalagadi men who were paid little or nothing and who were barred from employment in the mines until the 1950s.

RURAL POVERTY IN THE LATE TWENTIETH CENTURY

A common pattern of cattle ownership has emerged: about one-third of the families in a language group own cattle, and fewer than 10 percent of these families own over one-half of all animals held by their group. In 1980, with an adjusted income of $180 (compared with $600 for Botswana as a whole), San families with wage earners (roughly 14%) were in the lowest 10 percent of the population in terms of income level, far short of the $250 considered necessary for the bare essentials of life. Those without animals or fields foraged and scavenged and had no disposable income at all; many of these people left their homes to seek employment on the fringes of towns. These inequities in the overall political economy are shared by all the rural poor of Botswana, regardless of group identification. They reproduce the structural deprivation of a rural underclass divested of a market for its labor. These inequities are the modern legacy of progressive deprivation shared by all peoples of the region whose coordinated history has been scanned in the last two millennia. Thus, in the political economy of the Kalahari one cannot speak of social relations particular to San or Tswana or any other separate cultural entity; the peoples' histories are too interlocked.

See also **Agriculture: Beginnings and Development; Ecosystems: Deserts and Semi-Deserts; Ethnicity; Languages; Production Strategies.**

BIBLIOGRAPHY

Barnard, Alan. *Hunters and Herders of Southern Africa: A Comparative Ethnography of the Khoisan Peoples.* Cambridge, U.K.: Cambridge University Press, 1992.

Thomas, David, and Paul Shaw. *The Kalahari Environment.* Cambridge, U.K.: Cambridge University Press, 1991.

Wilmsen, Edwin. *Land Filled with Flies: A Political Economy of the Kalahari.* Chicago: University of Chicago Press, 1989.

Wylie, Diana. *A Little God: The Twilight of Patriarchy in a Southern African Chiefdom.* Middletown, CT: Wesleyan University Press, 1990.

EDWIN N. WILMSEN

KAMPALA. Kampala is the capital city of Uganda. Its population is about 1.2 million according to the official census (2002), but it may be as high as 2 million if unofficial residents are counted. Marked by seven hills, it was the site of the Kabaka of Baganda's hunting grounds in precolonial times. In 1890 Captain Fredrick Lugard established his camp adjacent to the palace at an area reserved for grazing the Kabaka's antelopes. Soon after that, the colonial offices and residences were moved to Nakasero Hill and the hills continued to mark racial and religious residential segregation. Europeans worked and lived on Nakasero and Kololo hills, while Old Kampala Hill was occupied by primarily Arab and Asian traders until they were expelled by President Idi Amin in 1972. A Muslim prince donated land for a mosque on Kibuli Hill. The Kabaka granted Namirembe and Rubaga to the Protestants of the Church Missionary Society and the Catholic White Fathers, respectively. Makerere Hill became the site of Makerere University, and Mulago was home to a major hospital. Primary industries in the early twenty-first century include trade related to the railhead and lake port and government business, including the hosting of many international conferences.

See also **Amin Dada, Idi; Lugard, Frederick John Dealtry; Uganda.**

BIBLIOGRAPHY

Kampala City Council. *The City of Kampala: One Hundred Years.* Kampala, Uganda: Crane Publishers, 1991.

Kirwan, Brian; Norman Hart; and Kenneth Roberts. *The Hills of Kampala.* Kampala: Uganda Urgus, 1964.

Nuwagaba, A. "Urban Poverty and Environmental Health: The Case of Kampala City, Uganda." In *Human Impact on Environment and Sustainable Development in Africa,* ed. M. B. Kwesi Darkoh and Apollo Rwomire. Burlington, VT: Ashgate, 2003.

Wallman, Sandra. *Kampala Women Getting By: Wellbeing in the Time of AIDS.* Athens: Ohio University Press, 1996.

CHRISTINE OBBO SOUTHALL

KANEMI, MUHAMMAD AL-AMIN AL- (c. 1775–c. 1837).

Born in Fezzan (in southwest Libya) to a Kanembu scholar from the Lake Chad area (Bornu) and an Arab mother, al-Kanemi received his education in Fezzan, Bornu, Tripolitania, and finally in Hejaz (in Arabia). Around 1799 he left Hejaz and, after sojourns south of the Sahara in Fezzan, Kanem, Wadai, and Bagirmi, settled in Ngala in Bornu. His erudition and deep knowledge of developments in the Muslim world soon attracted a community of scholars, mainly his Kanembu and Shuwa Arab kin. It was thus not mere coincidence when *Mai* (ruler) Ahmad (r. 1791–1808) of Bornu called upon al-Kanemi for help in containing the military and ideological aggression of the Fulani jihadists in Hausa areas to the west.

Al-Kanemi mobilized his followers and successfully defended metropolitan Bornu, though he failed to recover the western provinces. He opened up a written debate from around 1808 to 1812 with the Fulani leaders who had consolidated their victories in the devoutly Islamic Sokoto caliphate over the justification of the jihad on Muslim Bornu, a feat that enhanced his prestige and somehow contributed to the cessation of hostilities. Al-Kanemi also succeeded in putting up an effective administrative machinery that saved the state from total disintegration. The people of Bornu, who regarded al-Kanemi as the savior of the nation, believed that he was divinely guided. Although by 1819–1820 al-Kanemi, as *shehu*, was the de facto king of Bornu, it was his son and successor, Shehu Umar ibn al-Kanemi (r. 1837–1881), who abolished the dynasty of the *mais* and consolidated power in the house of the Kanemi *shehus*.

See also **Lake Chad Societies.**

BIBLIOGRAPHY

Barkindo, Bawuro Mubi. *The Sultanate of Mandara to 1902: The Evolution, Development, and Collapse of a Sudanese Kingdom.* Stuttgart: F. Steiner, 1989.

Brenner, Louis, and Ronald Cohen. "Borno in the Nineteenth Century." In *History of West Africa,* Vol. 2, ed. J. F. Ade Ajayi and Michael Crowder. Harlow, U.K.: Longman, 1987.

BAWURO M. BARKINDO

KANO.

Kano is the largest city in northern Nigeria, the administrative center of colonial Kano Province, and the capital of the present Kano State. As of 2004 its population approached 300,000 in the municipal area alone. It is situated on the Jakara River 442 kilometers north of Abuja, Nigeria's federal capital, and 1,175 kilometers northeast of Lagos, with which it is connected by rail, road, and air. Indigenous inhabitants are mostly Hausa peoples and of the Islamic faith. The city is becoming increasingly cosmopolitan.

The historic city-state of Kano was one of the seven principal Hausa states that were founded by Bayajidda Abuyazid, reputedly a refugee prince from Baghdad. The city reached the height of its glory under the rule of Mohammad Rumfa (1463–1499), who established a strong Islamic tradition. Kano became an important entrepôt of the trans-Saharan caravan trade, and its indigo-dyeing pits, as well as its cotton textiles and other products were famous throughout the western and central Sudan. It was captured by the British in 1903.

Kano is in the early twenty-first century a prosperous commercial and industrial center. It exports chiefly peanuts, cotton, hides, and skins. Local industries include cotton textile spinning, weaving, and dyeing, and the production of leather goods and metalware. Kano has a modern teaching hospital, a university, an imposing mosque, an Islamic school of law, and several Qur'anic and conventional schools. An international airport, named after one of Nigeria's foremost politicians, the late Mallam Aminu Kano, is located in the city and is served by major international airlines.

See also **Lagos; Nigeria: History and Politics, Northern Nigeria.**

BIBLIOGRAPHY

Hogben, Sidney John, and Anthony Hamilton Millard Kirk-Greene. *The Emirates of Northern Nigeria: A Preliminary Survey of Their Historical Traditions.* Brookfield, VT: Gregg Revivals, 1993.

Shaw, Flora L. *A Tropical Dependency: An Outline of the Ancient History of the Western Sudan with an Account of the Modern Settlement of Northern Nigeria.* Baltimore: Black Classic Press, 1997.

Usman, Y. B., et al. "Cities of the Savannah: A History of Some Towns and Cities of the Nigerian Savannah." *Nigeria Magazine* special publication, Cultural Division, Federal Ministry of Information. Lagos, n.d.

S. ADEMOLA AJAYI

KANO, ALHAJI AMINU (1920–1983).

The Nigerian Arabic scholar and radical politician Alhaji Aminu Kano was born into a Hausa-speaking family of Arabic scholars in the Sokoto Caliphate in colonial northern Nigeria, heirs to the radical traditions of the Tijaniyya Islamic brotherhood,

as opposed to the Qadiriyya school prevalent in the region. His mother initiated him to the study of the Qur'an at an early age, and he was educated in Arabic, Hausa, and English in Kano. After training at Kaduna College from 1937 to 1942 and the University of London Institute of Education from 1946 to 1948, Kano worked as a teacher in Bauchi and Sokoto. He was the founder and secretary-general of the Northern Teachers Association from 1948 to 1953.

In 1949 Kano helped to found the Northern Peoples Congress, the primary political party in Northern Nigeria during the preparations for independence, but withdrew when he saw its conservative and autocratic tendencies. In 1950 he founded and became president-general of the Northern Elements Progressive Union (NEPU), which usually allied with the National Council of Nigeria and the Cameroons (NCNC) and other progressive southern parties in the elections of the 1950s. During the First Republic he was elected to the Nigerian House of Representatives (1959) as a radical pan-Africanist socialist. He held political office only during the first military regime, which seized power in 1966, as federal commissioner for communications during the civil war (1967–1971), and then as commissioner of health (1971–1974) during reconstruction. In the Second Republic (1979–1983) Kano was leader of the People's Redemption Party (PRP), successor to NEPU, which won notable electoral victories, including governorships of Kano and Kaduna states in the north. A monogamist by conviction and a religious reformer, he held public expositions of the Qur'an during the month of Ramadan (Muslim fast) to show that his radicalism and people-oriented politics were well grounded in Islam. He led a simple life among the people in Kano and opened out his house, with its fabulous library, as a center of inspiration and education for radical youth. He wrote *Politics and Administration in Post War Nigeria* in English and several plays and collections of songs and poetry in Hausa.

See also **Nigeria: History and Politics, Northern Nigeria.**

BIBLIOGRAPHY

Ogbonnia, Chiedozie Alex. *Nigerian Peoples and Politics: An Overview.* Emene, Enugu, Nigeria: Institute of Ecumenical Education, 2003.

Sklar, Richard L. *Nigerian Political Parties: Power in an Emergent African Nation.* Princeton, NJ: Princeton University Press, 1963.

J. F. ADE AJAYI

KATEB, YACINE (1929–1989).

Yacine Kateb was born in Constantine on August 6, 1929, and died in Grenoble in 1989. Along with Mohammed Dib, he is the most important Algerian author working in French, even if his output has been rather modest. He published an initial collection of poems, *Soliloques* [*Soliloquies*], at his own expense in 1946, as well as numerous poems and newspaper articles. His key work, the novel *Nedjma* (1956), the series of plays *Le cercle des représailles* [*The Circle of Reprisals*] (1959), and the novel *Le polygone étoilé* [*The Starry Polygon*] (1966), are works in which the same characters and the same collection of themes can often be found: the broken Identity, the Necessity of inventing a national Identity, not only through Ideas or War, but by creating a new literary Language.

Nedjma is particularly noteworthy for its subversive form, marking a break with the standard French novel. It is a fascinating work on myth and a verbal dramatization that makes it a kind of foundation text for Algerian and Maghreb literature written in French. Kateb's later dramas (published in French in 1999 under the title *Boucherie de l'espérance* [*Butchery of Hope*]), starting with *Mohammed, prends ta valise* (*Mohammed, Pack your Bags*), in 1971, performed in an Arabic dialect in an improvised style by the cast, were often written in French. The majority of his works were published by Editions du Seuil (Paris).

See also **Literature.**

BIBLIOGRAPHY

Aresu, Bernard. *Counterhegemonic Discourse from the Maghreb. The Poetics of Kateb's Fiction.* Tübingen, Güntter Narr Verlag, 1993.

Arnaud, Jacqueline. *Recherches sur la littérature maghrébine de langue française. Le cas de Kateb Yacine.* Paris: L'Harmattan, 1982.

Bonn, Charles. *Le roman algérien de langue française.* Paris: L'Harmattan, 1984.

Chaulet-Achour, Christiane. *Anthologie de la littérature algérienne.* Paris: Bordas francophonie, 1990.

Gontard, Marc. *Nedjma de Kateb Yacine. Essai sur la structure formelle du roman.* Paris: L'Harmattan, 1985.

Kateb, Yacine. *Nedjma,* trans. Richard Howard. Charlottesville: University Press of Virginia, 1991. This translation contains a good introduction in English by Bernard Aresu.

CHARLES BONN

KAUNDA, KENNETH (1924–).

Born of Malawian parents in Lubwa, northern Rhodesia (present-day Zambia), Kenneth David Kaunda was Zambia's founding father and a statesman prominent throughout Africa. Trained as a teacher, he

President of Zambia Kenneth Kaunda (1924–). Kaunda was an outspoken supporter of the anti-apartheid movement in South Africa. He also allowed several African liberation fronts to set up in Africa. AP IMAGES

became active in politics in the 1950s as a local organizer and later secretary-general of the African National Congress, the colony's first national political party. He broke with African National Congress leader Harry Nkumbula in 1958, citing the latter's cautious style. Following a stint in colonial detention in 1960, Kaunda formed the United National Independence Party (UNIP) to vigorously oppose the white settler-dominated Central African Federation, of which northern Rhodesia was a dependent part.

Kaunda led Zambia to independence on October 24, 1964, under a republican constitution and became the first president. Kaunda was subsequently reelected six times—after 1973, in one-party elections. Intolerant of opposition, he preferred to build consensus and distribute rewards within a single ruling party. Internationally, Kaunda used the chairmanship of the Organization of African Unity (1970–1971, 1987–1988), the Non-Aligned Movement (1970–1973), and the Front Line States (1985) to try to broker moderate solutions to decolonization conflicts in southern Africa. Within Zambia in the 1980s, a combination of falling commodity prices (for Zambian copper) and economic mismanagement (the result of Kaunda's particular creed of "Zambian humanism") led to mass protests over declining living standards. Kaunda lost power in competitive elections on October 31, 1991, the first independence-generation leader in Africa to do so. Characteristically, he accepted defeat with dignity.

In 1991 Kaunda established a peace foundation that bears his name. He has devoted his energies to conflict resolution in Africa and to combating the ravages of poverty and HIV/AIDS.

See also **Disease: HIV/AIDS, Social and Political Aspects; Organization of African Unity; Postcolonialism; Zambia: History and Politics.**

BIBLIOGRAPHY

Brownrigg, Philip. *Kenneth Kaunda.* Lusaka, Zambia: Kenneth Kaunda Foundation, 1989.

Kaunda, Kenneth D. *Zambia Shall Be Free: An Autobiography.* New York: Praeger, 1962.

Kaunda, Kenneth D. *Humanism in Zambia and a Guide to Its Implementation.* Lusaka, Zambia: Zambia Information Services, 1967.

Macpherson, Fergus. *Kenneth Kaunda of Zambia: The Times and the Man.* New York: Oxford University Press, 1974.

Nasong'o, Shadrack Wanjala. *Contending Political Paradigms in Africa: Rationality and the Politics of Democratization in Kenya and Zambia.* New York: Routledge, 2005.

MICHAEL BRATTON

KEITA, FODEBA (1921–c. 1969). Fodeba Keita was a Guinean poet, civil servant, choreographer, and founder of the first major international African ballet. Born and raised in the Maninka heartland in upper Guinea, Keita absorbed local traditions in music and dance as a child. He attended the École William Ponty in Senegal, learning about French culture, including staging techniques. After teaching for several years, he moved to Paris in the late 1940s to pursue his university education. His *Poèmes Africains*, published in 1950, was a pioneering effort in valorizing local African culture in print and foreshadowed his efforts at moving it onto the stage. Its revolutionary political potential was cited at length by Frantz Fanon in his *Wretched of the Earth* (1961).

Keita organized a dance troupe with Africans living in Paris, formally debuting in Paris in 1952 as *Les Ballets Africains de Keita Fodeba*. The first of its kind to stage African dances and stories for an international audience, the dance company toured the world and released several recordings in the 1950s. Exploiting the power of culture as a propaganda tool, President Sékou Touré named them the National Ballet of Guinea upon independence. Keita was appointed Minister of National Defense and Security in the new Touré government and ultimately became a victim of Touré's ruthless autocracy, being imprisoned in 1969. Conflicting sources date his death to either 1969 or 1971.

See also **Guinea: History and Politics; Literature; Touré, Sékou.**

BIBLIOGRAPHY

Kaba, Lansiné. "The Cultural Revolution, Artistic Creativity, and Freedom of Expression in Guinea." *Journal of Modern African Studies* 14, no. 2 (1976): 201–218.

Members of the Fodeba Keita African Dancers perform a war dance on stage, 1956.
Keita founded the first international African ballet when he organized *Les Ballets Africains de Keita Fodeba* in Paris in 1952. © HULTON-DEUTSCH COLLECTION/CORBIS

Keita, Fodeba. *Poèmes africains.* Paris: Pierre Seghers, 1950. Reprinted with other material as *Aube africaine et autres poèmes africains.* Paris and Dakar: Présence Africaine, 1994.

ERIC CHARRY

KEITA, SALIF (1945–).
Salif Keita is a Malian singer, composer, and bandleader. Born and raised in Djoliba, Mali, Keita moved to Bamako around 1967 and began playing in local bars. In 1970 he joined the Rail Band as lead vocalist and in 1973 he switched to Les Ambassadeurs, which relocated to Abidjan around 1978 and broke up a few years later when Keita moved to Paris. Keita gained a major recording contract with Mango Records and with the debut of *Soro* in 1987 released his first of six solo recordings with them.

Already well known in Francophone West Africa in the 1970s, Keita became an important spokesperson through his music for African immigrants in France in the 1980s. In the late 1980s Keita's career as an international solo artist in the newly conceived world music market took off. He was nominated for a Grammy Award in the first year of its world music category in 1991 (with his CD *Amen*), as well as in 2000 (*Papa*) and 2003 (*Moffou*). Keita's early career was marked by two obstacles: he was born into a social class that forbade professional musical performance and he is albino. Keita was a pioneer in the new high-technology synthesized sound of the 1980s, combining in his lyrics a deep concern about contemporary issues confronting Malians and other Africans with a fresh outlook on international popular music styles.

See also **Music.**

BIBLIOGRAPHY

Durán, Lucy. "Monsieur Ambassadeur." *Folk Roots* (November 1995): 42–47.

Keita, Cheick M. Chérif. *Salif Keita: L'oiseau sur le fromager.* Bamako, Mali: Le Figuier, 2001.

ERIC CHARRY

KENYA

This entry includes the following articles:
GEOGRAPHY AND ECONOMY
SOCIETY AND CULTURES
HISTORY AND POLITICS

GEOGRAPHY AND ECONOMY

Geographically Kenya is one of the most diverse countries in the world. Its features range from coral reefs to plains to alpine tundra, alpine glaciers to humid, wet tropics to arid savannas. There is little relation between Kenya's national borders and the regional geography; for example, Kenya includes just a small part of Lake Victoria. There is also little relation between the borders and Kenya's ethnic communities, with many spilling over into other countries. Nevertheless—and despite its geographical diversity—Kenya maintains a national identity, especially compared to neighbors Ethiopia, Somalia, and Sudan. Similarly Kenya has been relatively stable since independence, at times even economically prosperous, although it has suffered from what is locally labeled "political tribalism."

TOPOGRAPHY AND CLIMATE

Five major regions define Kenya's landscape: the coastal plain bordering the Indian Ocean; central highlands; the Great Rift Valley, which divides the country from north to south; western highlands, which descend to the shores of Lake Victoria; and semiarid plateaus and mountains in the north and northeast. Mount Kenya (17,058 feet), the highest point in Kenya, is near the center of the country in the central highlands. Mount Elgon (14,178 feet), the highest point in the western highlands, is located north of Lake Victoria on Kenya's northwest border

with Uganda. Kenya's longest river, the Tana (500 miles), has its headwaters on Mount Kenya and flows first northeast and east, then south toward the coast.

The coast, with an extensive coral reef offshore, is a mixture of mangrove swamps, river inlets, and sandy beaches. Close to the southern coast lies the island of Mombasa, where Mombasa the city is the country's chief port. Moving west, the coastal plain gives way to drier savanna that rises and flattens onto a plateau. The heart of Kenya is the central highlands, and the western highlands, once green with forests and other vegetation due to rich volcanic soils. With only 14 percent, or approximately 50,000 square miles, of Kenya's land well suited for agriculture or ranching, there is heavy competition for Kenya's scarcest resource, farmland. Densely populated, these regions are the sites of both the country's large plantations and numerous small holdings, with tea and coffee grown on the upper slopes; and maize, beans, vegetables, and cut flowers on the lower. At higher elevations in the highlands the forest reserves are under tremendous pressure for farmland. The Great Rift Valley, a semiarid region of latent volcanic activity, divides the central and western highlands. A string of lakes runs through the valley including Turkana and Naivasha, both a source of drinking water and fish; Bogoria and Nakuru, which form important wildlife habitats; and Magadi, a valuable source of soda ash.

Kenya's climate is highly varied and changes dramatically across the country's range of elevations. Altitude particularly affects temperatures; Mount Kenya, for example, situated near the equator, has a tropical climate around its base but glacial formations on its upper reaches. Generally the coastal belt is hot, humid, and thickly vegetated while the coastal hinterland is hot, dry, and sparsely vegetated. In fact, most of the country receives less than the 29.5 inches of rainfall per year that ordinarily are necessary for subsistence farming. The eastern plateau (between the central highlands and the coast), the northern plains, and the southern border region are quite dry, with an average annual rainfall of less than 20 inches. Average rainfall in the central and western highlands, however, is 30 inches per year, or more, and at times even exceeds 79 inches.

Most of the country has generally experienced two rainy seasons: March–May and October–

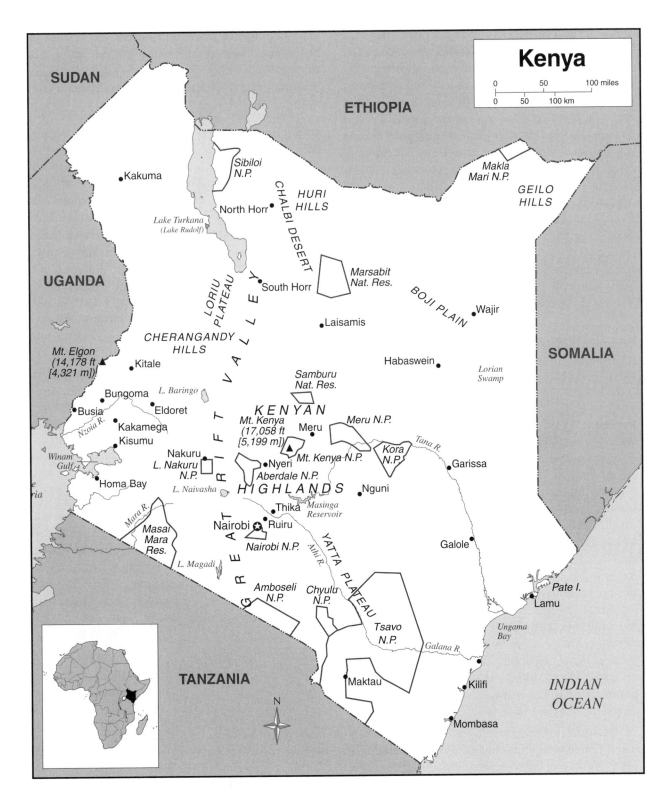

Kenya

0   50   100 miles
0 50 100 km

SUDAN

ETHIOPIA

Kakuma

Sibiloi
N.P.

HURI
HILLS

Makla
Mari N.P.

GEILO
HILLS

North Horr

Lake Turkana
(Lake Rudolf)

CHALBI DESERT

UGANDA

LORIU
PLATEAU

South Horr

Marsabit
Nat. Res.

BOJI PLAIN

Wajir

CHERANGANDY
HILLS

Laisamis

Habaswein

Lorian
Swamp

SOMALIA

Mt. Elgon
(14,178 ft
[4,321 m])!

Kitale

L. Baringo

Samburu
Nat. Res.

Bungoma

K E N Y A N

Busia

Eldoret

Meru N.P.

Nzoia R.

Kakamega

Mt. Kenya
(17,058 ft
[5,199 m])

Meru

Kora
N.P.

Tana R.

Kisumu

Winam
Gulf

Nakuru
L. Nakuru
N.P.

Nyeri

Mt. Kenya N.P.

Garissa

Homa Bay

L. Naivasha

Aberdale N.P.

HIGHLANDS

Nguni

Mara R.

Thika

Masinga
Reservoir

Masai
Mara
Res.

Nairobi

Ruiru

Galole

Nairobi N.P.

Athi R.

L. Magadi

YATTA PLATEAU

G R E A T   R I F T   V A L L E Y

Amboseli
N.P.

Chyulu
N.P.

Pate I.

Lamu

Ungama
Bay

Tsavo
N.P.

Galana R.

INDIAN
OCEAN

TANZANIA

Maktau

Kilifi

N

Mombasa

December, although climate averages are increasingly difficult to count on. The exception is the western highlands, which are subject to rainfall throughout the year. Areas with two rainy seasons usually result in two cropping seasons each year, but rainfall in Kenya can be highly erratic, with consequences not only for agriculture and pastoralism but also for industries dependent on hydroelectric power. Droughts are common in Kenya. Particularly devastating episodes occurred in

1984, again from 1991 to 1993, with another that began in 2003 and as of 2006 had not ended. The drought of 1984, said by many to have been the worst in Kenya in fifty years, was widespread throughout the country and affected all major food crops. As much as 80 percent of the livestock is said to have died in certain regions. Widespread famine was avoided, because the government responded relatively quickly—and the rains returned in 1985. The droughts that began in 1991 and 2003 affected the north and northeastern part of Kenya. In 1991 government failed to respond until two years into the crisis, with the result that many people in the north suffered starvation and a substantial number died. In the current crisis government is heavily dependent on international donors and nongovernmental organizations for aid.

KEY SECTORS OF THE ECONOMY

The major resource in Kenya is land, but less than 8 percent of it is cropped. Nevertheless agriculture accounts for almost 30 percent of gross domestic product (GDP) and engages about 75 percent of the labor force, with more than half subsistence farming. European and Asian investors established large-scale commercial plantations (initially with forced African labor) during the colonial period, but land reforms after independence created a substantial number of African smallholders. Most smallholders own plots of less than 5 acres. Tea, which can be picked every fourteen days year-round, is the crop of choice on both large and small farms and is the country's principal export crop. In the early twenty-first century cut flowers have surpassed coffee and tourism to become the second most important source of foreign exchange. Other export earnings come from horticultural products such as fruit, especially pineapple, nuts such as cashews, wheat, corn, and sugarcane. Maize, sorghum, cassava, and bananas are the principal staple crops.

Manufacturing constitutes the third largest sector of the economy, producing about 20 percent of GDP. It has been stimulated by a relatively free market and, until the late 1990s, a nearly continuous flow of foreign investment since the country achieved independence. Manufacturing in Kenya includes the production of plastics, furniture, soap, cement, textiles, and clothing; trucks and passenger vehicles; tires; chemicals; and petroleum products (based entirely on imported crude oil). Kenya has a diverse range of other industries, too, including publishing, steel rolling, and a limited amount of mining. All told, 25 percent of the total labor force is employed in industry and the service sectors.

The service sector—restaurants, hotels, government services, and trade—constitutes more than half of Kenya's economy. There is a host of other economic activities, primarily of local or regional significance. Pastoralism is the principal livelihood in northern Kenya, especially in the northern part of the Great Rift Valley: two-thirds of Kenya is classified as grazing land. Pastoralists raise cattle, camels, goats, and sheep; farmers keep cattle, sheep, goats, chickens, and pigs for domestic use; some also raise cattle and pigs for export products—among them, milk, cheese, butter, and bacon. Fishing is important to local economies along the coast and around lakes Victoria and Turkana, and increasingly for export. Another key sector of the economy is made up of economic activities that go unrecorded as part of GDP. Many households are sustained by the small-scale manufacture of products such as baskets, handicrafts, or charcoal stoves, and the selling of "street" foods (snacks, meals, and beverages), and second-hand goods, especially clothing and shoes, from small market stalls in both urban and rural areas.

In the last two decades of the twentieth century, tourism emerged as Kenya's principal source of foreign revenues. Visitors were, and continue to be, drawn to the Kenyan coast as well as the country's game reserves and national parks, especially Masai Mara, Amboseli, and Tsavo, along the border with Tanzania, those around Mount Kenya, and further north such as Samburu. The tourist industry has promoted resource and wildlife conservation, but parks and wildlife conservation remains a contentious issue. Disputes over land, grazing, and wildlife illustrate that most local people receive little direct benefit from wildlife conservation, although this is beginning to change with local involvement in both wildlife management and partnerships in tourist camps. The decline in elephant and rhinoceros populations, primarily due to poaching since the 1970s, has now been generally brought under control. However, those declines, combined with occasional but well-publicized attacks on tourists and other security problems derived from local political tensions and international terrorism, have seriously undermined the tourist economy.

In the first years of the twenty-first century, Kenya is nowhere near returning to the sense of economic well being that marked the years immediately following independence. The collapse of international agreements between coffee-producing and consuming nations, cheaper lower-quality Asian coffees, and mismanagement of local cooperatives have led farmers to replace their coffee trees with subsistence crops or abandon them totally. Tea and horticultural products have replaced some of these losses, but the new demands of an increasingly urbanized population for products such as bread, instead of beans and corn, need to be balanced with the higher value that can be obtained from exporting wheat compared to corn. Substantial trade deficits, aggravated by higher oil prices that began in the mid-1980s, and a growing national debt have caused serious economic strain. When coupled with corruption, acknowledged by Kenyans as one of the major problems facing their country, and with foreign donors periodically suspending aid in an effort to effect reform, Kenya is experiencing enormous difficulty meeting the challenges of the new century. Even with the declining population growth from 3.6 percent in the 1980s to 2.6 percent between 1995 and 2000, Kenya's fertility rate of 4.9 percent is one of the highest in the world. This does not bode well for a population where the median age is 18.2 years and only 4.2 percent of the population is over 65 years of age. Without a government safety net to fall back on, the majority of Kenyans are desperate to eke out a living for themselves and their families and the resulting decisions they make impact issues of health, environment, and societal relationships, all of which will continue to present ongoing challenges.

See also **Aid and Development; Climate; Ecology; Ecosystems.**

BIBLIOGRAPHY

Downing, Thomas E.; Kangethe W. Gitu; and Crispin M. Kimau. *Coping with Drought in Kenya: National and Local Strategies.* Boulder, CO: Lynne Rienner, 1989.

The Economist Pocket World Figures 2002. London: Profile, 2001.

Nelson, Harold D., ed. *Kenya: A Country Study.* Foreign Area Studies, the American University. Washington, DC: Headquarters, Department of the Army, U.S. Government Printing Office, 1984.

Ojany, Francis F., and Reuben B. Ogendo. *Kenya: A Study in Physical and Human Geography.* Nairobi: Longman, 1973.

Sobania, Neal. *Culture and Customs of Kenya.* Westport, CT: Greenwood, 2003.

Tiffen, Mary; Michael Mortimore; and Francis Gichuki. *More People, Less Erosion: Environmental Recovery in Kenya.* Chichester, NY: J. Wiley, 1994.

Waters, Grahame H. C., and John Odero. *Geography of Kenya and the East African Region.* London: Macmillan, 1986.

THOMAS E. DOWNING
REVISED BY NEAL SOBANIA

SOCIETY AND CULTURES

Kenya is a land of 37 million people and over forty ethnic communities. The Kikuyu group, which makes up 22 percent of the population, is the largest; the Elmolo, who number under three hundred individuals, is the smallest. Other ethnic groups of significant size include the Kalenjin (12%), Luo (13%), Luyha (14%), Kamba (11%), Kisii (6%), and Meru (6%). None of the other groups, sometimes better known, such as the Maasai, Samburu, Somali, Swahili, and Turkana, makes up more than 2 percent of the country's total population; non-Africans (Arab, Asian, and European) together account for 1 percent. Ethnically then, Kenya is not one Kenya but many Kenyas. Spread across a diverse range of environments, speaking languages from three different major families (Bantu, Nilotic, and Cushitic) that are not intelligible to each other, ethnic groups are composed of believers from many faiths who practice a broad range of customs.

What scholars call ethnicity, Kenyans talk about tribalism. Largely formations of the recent precolonial era, they are all too often depicted as having existed forever and with fixed boundaries. A legend of the coast suggests that an ancient migration of peoples from a place called Singwaya brought all the people who now live there and in the adjacent hills, including the Mijikenda, Swahili, Taita, and Pokomo. Yet this tradition conveniently leaves out other movements of other peoples and the merging of these new arrivals with communities that already existed in the region. Similarly, the Maasai, or Maa-speaking peoples who epitomize the herding peoples of Africa, also include agriculturalists and hunter-gatherers, and the pastoralists among them came to dominate the plains of East Africa only in the eighteenth century. Traditions from across the north of Kenya tell the same tale with the agro-pastoral Dasanech, for example, an amalgam of peoples. Some already lived along the northern reaches of Lake Turkana, and they were joined by others who migrated from both the east and the west, and still others who arrived as identifiable Samburu and Rendille groups, at the end of the nineteenth century.

Ethnic boundaries have always been rather permeable and became especially so at times of ecological crises and civil disorder. Well understood was the principle that in times of peril an individual, family, or even larger group could find refuge and ultimately permanent residency in a neighboring society, leading quickly to adoption of a new ethnic identity. The succession of droughts, famines, and diseases of the 1880s and 1890s provides some of the best documentation for these shifts in ethnicity, with groups of Samburu and Rendille becoming Dasanech, and individual Samburu and Turkana in the dry north becoming Elmolo. However, the relationships and ties that made these population shifts possible in bad times had been previously established in good times as aspects of everyday life. Networks of trading partners existed for the exchange of foodstuffs, livestock, and material goods. For example, Giriama traders from the Tana River valley had partners among the coastal Swahili, upland Kamba, and Oromo pastoralists. The Kamba had partners all around Mount Kenya and with herders to the north. Other relationships were formed around marriageable women. The Luo and Gusii, the Kalenjin and Luhya, all in the western Kenya highlands, and the Kikuyu and Maasai, among others, were known for marrying each other's women. People also loaned needed labor, pawned children, and acknowledged a relationship that they phrased as a shared clan name, and therefore an assumed history. Even when there was discord, when for example warriors of these same societies were raiding each other, established customs, including among the Kikuyu and Maasai, and Kikuyu and Samburu, allowed women to continue trading peacefully with each other.

Despite this history of cooperation and coming together, ethnicity has had profound consequences for peoples' lives, and more often than not togetherness represents separateness from others. This sense of division and competition is in large measure a product of the colonial period, when rigid Western notions of tribe were imposed by colonial administrators, who labeled individuals and communities as belonging to one and only one ethnic group, and defining hard-and-fast artificial boundaries between neighbors. The British assumed deeply rooted antagonisms between ethnic groups, and in their mission to enlighten and civilize the groups, fixated on the need to eliminate the raiding that upset the peaceful balance the colonizers sought to impose. Although the results of raids were obvious—animals missing, people injured and killed—the colonizers ignored the less visible relationships that had promoted peaceful interaction. Without trade, exchange, and intermarriage, people, by being identified with belonging to a particular tribe, were left with few proven means to lessen interethnic strains, and as a result, ethnic rivalries were aggravated.

Where historically there existed a wide variety of forms of political leadership, the colonial authorities appointed chiefs according to a one-size-fits-all model. The Luhya, for example, had a hereditary ruler, a *Nabongo*, who ruled through appointed chiefs. The Gusii and Kuria also had hereditary chiefs, but a council of elders could remove a chief who proved incompetent. In the precolonial period, councils of elders were probably the most widespread form of political leadership. Responsible for dispelling discord and maintaining and promoting harmony within and among social groups, these councils worked at the community or clan level to build consensus. Among the Luo, the *ruoth* was the leading elder in a council of his peers who advised him. Councils of elders, called *kiama*, also governed the Meru, and there, as in most elder councils, the ability to speak well and offer sound advice was regarded highly. The Meru called this quality *ugambe*, and depending on the nature of the relationship one elder might have with another—for example, if he owed livestock from a bridewealth payment, or loaned livestock in times of ecological disaster—one elder in a traditional council could have significantly more *ugambe*. Although the voices of elders were not entirely silenced, the ones to whom British colonial officials listened primarily were the ones the British appointed chiefs, and later to Local Native Councils at the larger level of the administrative districts they created.

Some proved to be voices that raised concern over low wages, scarcity of employment, the need for better health services, and lack of agricultural extension education. A particular point of continuing tension was over the erosion of the customs that people felt made them who they were by the imposition of Western ways. These sensitivities were particularly strong when women were involved. Colonial and customary paternalisms might have found common ground, except for the constraint of Western legal definitions of marriage, which included no legal status for polygamous arrangements, and the opening of space for women to seek education and ultimately wage employment in colonial institutions. Bridewealth was about forming a relationship between the two families of the groom and bride, and the formal recognition of giving a bride to the groom's family and replacing loss of the bride's labor to her own family. Where bridewealth was once negotiated, or followed a culturally prescribed transfer of livestock, as for example heads of cattle or camels among peoples such as the Maasai, Rendille, Samburu, and Turkana, the modern practice increasingly has a Kenyan shilling equivalent, or demand for certain material goods.

In the early twenty-first century, among the Kikuyu and others, it was not unusual for bridewealth to include requests for new cars, appliances, and large sums of cash. However, the negotiation that occurs over food and drink is also about the bride's family signaling the groom's that the bride, when she is incorporated into that family, is to be treated well and looked after properly. When later an envelope of money is actually handed over, it is rarely examined, as that would be insulting, and that is the last that is heard of the large amount originally requested. A Somali bride's family sends a wedding basket filled with spices, dates, butter, and meat, covered in leather, sewn shut, and decorated with cowries to the groom's family, who must untie the elaborate stitching without spilling or spoiling the food. Again, the invitation is to demonstrate the kind of care the bride's family expects the groom's to take with their daughter and new family member. Betrothals and weddings are always about acknowledging the new relationship

being made. The Pokot and others recognize that, if the father of a girl agrees to a male's request to marry her, he will drink beer with him. The Turkana and other herders recognize the marriage by the roasting and eating of an ox by the males of both families. And the Swahili formally present the bride and groom each to the other's family in traditional chairs with ivory and bone inlay following their taking of vows.

The run-up to independence in 1963 brought a return to sustained cooperation across ethnic lines but was largely limited to an elite of intellectuals, activists, and labor organizers working in the sphere of colony-level politics. Following independence, however, regional rivalries and tensions grew, and there soon emerged ethnically based political parties. The cooperation that had led to British concessions, and ultimately independence, dissipated. The main contenders were the two largest ethnic groups, the Kikuyu of the central province (and location of the national capital, Nairobi), under the leadership of Jomo Kenyatta, a Kikuyu who soon thereafter became president (1964–1978), and the Luo of western Kenya under Oginga Odinga (c. 1911–1994), who was vice president. The falling-out that soon characterized their relationship, and the ethnic patronage of presidential politics, was mirrored in the infighting among the other leaders of the independence struggle. As Kenyatta consolidated power and increasingly shifted authority to himself and the civil service he appointed, and away from the nationally elected parliament, an outcry grew for fairer distribution of the country's land and wealth. As opposition voices were pushed to the sidelines, and the power and influence of labor unions was curbed, public fear spread and critics were generally silenced. Daniel arap Moi, a Kalenjin, succeeded Kenyatta as Kenya's second president (1978–2002) and shifted the ethnic favoritism to the western groups from which he had come.

At the turn of the twenty-first century, urban communities in Nairobi were increasingly multiethnic. Yet there too, the stresses and hardships that characterize the life of urban dwellers, who regularly face low wages or joblessness, shortages of food, limited community services, and inadequate access to education and health care, result in people reverting to what is sometimes called

Republic of Kenya

Population:	36,913,721 (2007 est.)
Area:	582,646 sq. km (224,960 sq. mi.)
Official languages:	English
Languages:	English, Kiswahili, Kikuyu, Nandi, Kamba, Lukuya, Luo
National currency:	Kenyan shilling
Principal religions:	indigenous beliefs 10%, Protestant 45%, Roman Catholic 33%, Muslim 12%
Capital:	Nairobi (est. pop. 2,100,000 in 2006)
Other major urban centers:	Mombasa, Nakuru, Kitale, Eldoret, Nyeri, Kisumu, Thika, Malindi, Kericho, Nanyuki
Annual rainfall:	762 mm (30 in.) in highlands and coastal belt to 508 mm (20 in.) for most of the country
Principal geographical features:	*Mountains:* Chyulu Range, Taita Hills, Mount Kulal, Mount Marsabit, Mount Kenya, Mount Niandarawa, Mount Elgon, the Aberdare and Mau Ranges, Elgeyo Escarpment, Cherangani Hills, Kericho Highlands, Gwasi and Homa Mountains *Lakes:* Naivasha, Elementeita, Nakuru, Magadi, Hannington (now Bogoria), Baringo, Victoria Nyanza, Turkana *Rivers:* Tana, Athi-Galana, Goshi, Nzoia, Yala, Mara *Islands:* the Lamu Archipelago (Lamu, Manda, and Patta)
Economy:	*GDP per capita:* US$1,260 (2006)
Principal products and exports:	*Agricultural:* tea, coffee, corn, wheat, sugarcane, fruit, vegetables, dairy products, beef, pork, poultry, eggs *Manufacturing:* small-scale consumer goods (plastic, furniture, batteries, textiles, soap, cigarettes, flour), agricultural products, aluminum, cement, commercial ship repair *Mining:* salt, iron ore, lead, silver, zinc, copper, ruby, nickel, gold *Tourism:* Important to the Kenyan economy. Principal attractions are the nature preserves, including Tsavo National Park.
Government:	Independence from Great Britain, 1963. Constitution enacted in 1963, amended in 1964, 1966, 1975, 1991, 1992. Multiparty democracy (single-party until 1991). President elected to 5-year term by direct universal suffrage. 210-member unicameral National Assembly, 198 elected, 12 appointed by the president, plus the attorney general and the speaker. President appoints cabinet. For purposes of local government there are 7 provinces and 1 area, headed by provincial (or area) commissioners. The provinces are further broken down into districts, headed by district commissioners; divisions, headed by division officers; and locations and sublocations, headed by chiefs and subchiefs.
Heads of state since independence:	1963–1964: Prime Minister Jomo Kenyatta 1964–1978: President Jomo Kenyatta 1978–2002: President Daniel arap Moi 2002–: President Mwai Kibaki
Armed forces:	President is commander in chief. Minister of Defense runs the Defense Council. Voluntary enlistment. *Army:* 20,500 *Air force:* 2,500 *Navy:* 1,200 *Paramilitary:* 5,000
Transportation:	*Rail:* 2,778 km (1,726 mi.). The parastatal Kenya Railways Corporation runs 1,937 km (1,201 mi.) of the rail, including the main line from Mombasa to Uganda. *Port:* Mombasa *Roads:* 63,265 km (39,311 mi.), 14% paved *National airline:* Kenya Airways *Airports:* Major international airports at Nairobi and Mombasa. Smaller international airports at Malindi, Kisumu, Embasaki. More than 200 airstrips throughout country.
Media:	5 daily newspapers, including the *Daily Nation, The Standard, Kenya Times, Taifa Leo.* The latter 2 are owned by the governing party, KANU. 12 weeklies, more than 40 monthlies. There are 20 major publishers, including the East African Publishing House and East African Literature Bureau. The Kenya Broadcasting Corporation (state-controlled) broadcasts both radio and television service.
Literacy and education:	*Total literacy rate:* 73.6% (2006). Education is free but not universal and compulsory. 8 technical and vocational schools. Postsecondary educational facilities: Kenya Polytechnic (at Nairobi), Mombasa Polytechnic Institute, Village Polytechnic Council (run by the National Christian Council of Kenya), University of Nairobi, Kenyatta University, Moi University (at Eldoret), Jomo Kenyatta College of Agriculture and Technology, Kenya Medical Training College.

political tribalism in order to survive. People coming from the rural areas, where ethnic homogeneity is still the norm, and where ethnic clashes seem to be increasing (these are the outbreaks of tribalism that make headlines in Kenya and abroad), are populating these ever-expanding urban centers. These outbreaks, characterized in the postcolonial era by armed gangs with spears or aging rifles, were typically over issues of land usage or preferential treatment, perceived or actual, by local officials to members of a competing community. In the early twenty-first century, however, these encounters were increasingly carried out with military assault rifles, making the driving of people from their grazing or farmlands ever more deadly.

Even with Kiswahili as a common national language to potentially unite Kenyans, the use of ethnic mother-tongue languages, especially in social activities and among those newly arrived in the urban areas, leaves non-Kiswahili speakers as outsiders. When people identify through their ethnic affiliations and language usage, interethnic tension lies just below the surface and can easily be manipulated. Indeed, accusations of the government's exploiting these tensions, even instigating them, were particularly prominent in the last decade of the twentieth century and the years immediately before the first genuinely contested election in nearly four decades, in December 2002. The government's challenge as of 2007 remained one of how to allow for the expression of ethnicity, without it being to the detriment of many others, while sharing power, ending financial corruption, and improving the economy. As populations burgeon (and in this area, Kenya, with 44 percent of its population under the age of fifteen, and a median age of 17.9 years, is—similar to so many other African nations—one of the fastest-growing populations in the world), pressures for land and the demands made on the environment cannot but continue to have corrosive effects on the ecosystem, water, and the sustainability of agriculture and grazing. Building a nation from such a diverse base has never been easy, even in the best of times, or accomplished in short order, and Kenya is not yet fifty years old.

See also **Bantu, Eastern, Southern, and Western, History of (1000 BCE to 1500 CE); Colonial Policies and Practices; Ethnicity; Kenyatta, Jomo; Languages; Moi, Daniel arap; Zanzibar.**

BIBLIOGRAPHY

Ambler, Charles A. *Kenyan Communities in the Age of Imperialism.* New Haven, CT: Yale University Press, 1988.

Kanogo, Tabitha. *African Womanhood in Colonial Kenya, 1900–50.* Athens: Ohio University Press, 2005.

Lonsdale, John. "When Did the Gusii (or Any Other Group) Become a 'Tribe'?" *Kenya Historical Review* 5, no. 1 (1977): 123–133.

Sobania, Neal. "Fisherman Herders: Subsistence, Survival and Cultural Change in Northern Kenya." *Journal of African History* 29, no. 1 (1988): 41–56.

Sobania, Neal. *Culture and Customs of Kenya.* Westport, CT: Greenwood, 2003.

Spear, Thomas, and Richard Waller, eds. *Being Maasai: Ethnicity and Identity in East Africa.* Athens: Ohio University Press, 1993.

Waller, Richard, and Neal W. Sobania. "Pastoralism in Historical Perspective." In *African Pastoralist Systems: an Integrated Approach*, eds. Elliot Fratkin, Kathleen A. Galvin, and Erica Arbella Roth. Boulder, CO: Lynne Rienner, 1994.

NEAL W. SOBANIA

HISTORY AND POLITICS

BRITISH COLONIAL RULE

Britain's initial interests in East Africa in the 1870s and 1880s focused on Uganda and Zanzibar, not Kenya. Its interest in Uganda was strategic, because the Nile River was presumed to begin there, and Britain's interests in Egypt and the Suez Canal would be in jeopardy without control of the upper Nile. Its focus on the island of Zanzibar was similarly related, because sea traffic into and out of the canal passed through the Indian Ocean. Putting an end to Arab slaving was an additional consideration, and the adjacent mainland linked these interests.

Britain's first formal involvement in the region came in the wake of the Berlin Conference in 1885, when it granted a royal charter to the Imperial British East Africa Company (IBEAC), indicating to the other European powers that Britain claimed this region as part of her sphere of influence. Britain's first direct colonial involvement came in 1895. With the IBEAC near bankruptcy and ineffective at controlling the area, Britain established the East Africa Protectorate, a colony in all but name. Then to ensure its claims on Uganda, to ease communication with the interior region, and to eliminate any remnants of the slave trade, it built the Uganda Railway from the coast to Lake Victoria. Not long after completion of the railroad in 1901, the railhead workshops and offices located halfway along the route became the foundations for the city of Nairobi, the country's capital in the early twenty-first century.

Construction of the railway brought a growing population of people from British India—nearly 32,000 laborers, skilled and unskilled. As these workers had done in British India, they built and then ran the railroad. Other workers came as indentured laborers to grow cotton, tobacco, sugar, and other cash crops on the coast, and generated income for Arab traders and Indian financiers. Still other skilled workers, including masons and carpenters, built provincial and district colonial headquarters and then staffed them as clerks and bookkeepers, as the British spread their administration into the interior. Settlers from Britain, from elsewhere in Europe, and from South Africa followed the railway into the now-accessible central highlands and Rift Valley. Supported by cheap land and the promise of cheap labor, white settlers were seen as the best means to make both the railway and the colony self-sufficient. They established farms and never asked after the owners of the land, but then as Sir Charles Elliot (1862–1931), who arrived as governor in 1901, noted, "The sooner [the African] disappears and is unknown, except in books of anthropology, the better" (Sir Charles Elliot to Lord Lansdowne, 9 April 1904, FO2/835, Public Records Office).

These Africans were, of course, not all the same, but divided into different cultural communities, derived through dynamic processes of individuals and groups interacting with each other. Sometimes such relationships were harmonious, other times discordant. Out of changing circumstances, from cataclysmic events such as drought and disease to more common practices including marriage and trade, there emerged the distinctive culturals of Kenya's forty-plus ethnic groups. The Kikuyu, for example, traded with the Maasai and married each other's girls. The Mijikenda settled on different hilltops near the coast grew into nine distinct communities. The herding peoples of the Rift Valley and the north raided each other's animals, but they also intermarried, lent labor, and formed alliances that enabled individuals and family units to take refuge among neighbors in times of disaster. In other locations people were absorbed and incorporated through wars of expansion. The Luo and Luhya realized their dominant position by the controlling of cattle, which as stored wealth they used to acquire brides, and then children. Ethnic boundaries were not impermeable, but culturally porous.

With the expansion of colonial administration, many Africans were driven from their land, including from some tracts acquired by conquest or through military pacification campaigns. Then, with no one living there, the colonial administration declared the land the property of the Crown and sold it to the white settlers for small sums. From only thirteen settlers in 1901, in 1904 Europeans soon controlled 220,000 acres of land and nearly five million acres by 1915. The significance of these extensive land transfers to Europeans is particularly poignant when one recognizes that only 14 percent of Kenya's land area is well suited for farming or intensive ranching.

By the 1920s nearly half the men of Kenya's two largest ethnic groups, the Kikuyu and Luo, worked as laborers on these white-owned farms, often on the very land they had themselves once farmed as their own. Government tax schemes that required each adult male to pay a poll or head tax, or a hut tax on every house occupied by a member of his family pushed men into the wage economy, most commonly to work on European farms or ranches. The women were then left to carry the burden of providing the family's subsistence. Herding peoples in the Rift Valley or in the far north too had to pay these taxes, but because they often moved their settlements, they were better able to avoid tax collectors.

Because taxes did not generate enough income to pay for the administration, the British imposed forced labor for infrastructure projects such as roads and introduced cash crops: tea, coffee and sisal. It was the international reputation of Kenyan maize, however, and increased internal demand from growing populations upon which the Kenyan economy was based. Exported, these crops generated income for white farmers but often left Africans, even if they had poor patches of land on which to grow them, without time to tend their own food crops and with too little income to buy provisions. Women in particular suffered as they worked to provide for their family, and increasingly had to work on settler farms and government projects. Protests occurred, but those making the demands were Africans educated in the schools of the colonized simply seeking rights within the colonial system for themselves.

Education, however, was not widely available, and only those communities where the government built its administrative centers, or where missions were established, had access to schools. Pivotal to where these centers were built was the Uganda Railway's route, which cut across the temperate plains below the Central Highlands. The Maasai and Kikuyu were among those most directly impacted. The Maasai, preferring to avoid colonial involvement, moved their settlements and herds south of the tracks and for a time lived on the margins of government interest. The Kikuyu had no similar option. Displaced by white settlers who now farmed and ranched on their land, their labor was critical to the fortunes of the white settler farmers. The early beneficiaries of modern mission education—including the Kamba, Kikuyu, Luhya, and Luo, even if only at an elementary level—were able to move to the urban areas and take up wage labor as clerks, artisans, traders, and teachers.

With missions also came strains on traditional cultural practices. Protestant missionaries sought to eliminate the practices that they found morally reprehensible, ranging from dress, dancing, and burial practices to polygamy and ancestor beliefs. Especially repugnant was female genital mutilation (FGM), against which they mounted ongoing campaigns from the mid-1920s. When in 1929 the missionaries among the Kikuyu tried to get the Kikuyu Central Association (KCA) to support a ban on FGM, its leaders opposed the ban, and used their opposition to garner increased political support. The ensuing circumcision crisis split African churches with those Christians who were expelled for not signing a pledge against FGM.

Other points of tension arose over practices of governance, which varied widely across the region. For example, the Kikuyu brought governing councils of elders and lineage heads into the early colonial era, Luo arranged their clans in alliances, the head of which had a council of elders, and the few, usually smaller, communities who had hereditary chiefs, such as the Gusia and Kuria, also had councils of elders who could replace an incompetent chief. Thus, when colonial officials appointed local chiefs, who soon wielded dominating power in the name of the government, they were seen as wholly illegitimate by their subjects. Increasingly, discontent with the local chiefs grew. Grievances focused on confiscation of land, payment of taxes, and the introduction of a registration system for all Africans, the *kipande* system, which required every African to carry an identity document, designed to control their movement and compel labor in the interest of the government and the settlers.

The desire of the European settlers was to rule Kenya as a white man's country. As the settler population expanded, so too had the Asian community, along with the practice of customs and cultural traditions it brought from India. More importantly, they came to dominate the commercial sector of the economy. Their strong presence was contrary to the settler view of a white man's country that would reflect British patterns and cultural traditions and ultimately become politically independent of the London Foreign Office. The Colonial Office's 1923 Devonshire White Paper reminded both immigrant populations—the Europeans, who numbered only about 9,000, and Asians, who were themselves from another colony—that primarily, Kenya was an African territory, and that African interests were therefore paramount.

FROM PROTEST TO INDEPENDENCE

An attempt in 1921 to cut Africans' wages led to protests by some mission-educated workers. One of these, Harry Thuku, emerged as leader of the East African Association (EAA), a multiethnic, urban-based political association of African Christians and Muslims. When in 1922 he was arrested and deported to the coast, rioting erupted in Nairobi and a number of protesters were shot dead, including Mary Muthoni Nyanjiru. A leader of these demonstrations, her challenge was directed not only at the colonial authorities, but also at Kenyan men for their inability to make their voices heard. This initial multiethnic approach to political assertion soon gave way to ethnically based organizations, including the Young Kavirondo Association (YKA) in the west, and KCA in the central highlands. Among the founders of the latter was another young mission-educated man, Johnstone Kamau (1893–1978). Later he took the name Jomo Kenyatta. The important role that missions played in the early thinking of such groups is evident in the KCA's slogan, Pray and Work. In 1925, the government introduced

Local National Councils (LNCs) to counter the influence of the urban, educated groups. Chaired by the local district commissioner and made up of rural elders and chiefs, whose own power was threatened by organizations of educated Africans such as the KCA and the YKA, the LNCs advised colonial district officers and raised and distributed local revenues. The LNCs essentially co-opted local African leaders and implemented an effective policy of divide and rule among the African population.

Increasingly, growing numbers of the urban political nationalists were unhappy with these LNCs and wanted Africans to be elected directly to the Kenya Legislative Council, a central body with real policy-making powers. The KCA sent Jomo Kenyatta to England in 1929 to make its case about land administration directly, but the Colonial office turned down his repeated requests to be heard. Two years later he returned to Britain, this time as a student of anthropology, and wrote a dissertation published later as *Facing Mount Kenya*, which in many ways presented the values of Kikuyu culture as a nationalist response to attempts to make Africans wholly European. When Kenyatta returned to Kenya from England in 1946, the leadership of the Kenya African Union (KAU) stepped aside so he could be elected its president. After the government banned it, the KAU emerged in 1944 as a principal African voice for independence.

In post–World War II Kenya, with African unemployment high, pressure for farm land unmet, and nationalist demands for a greater say in policy formation rebuffed, African leaders realized that change would not occur merely by their asking for it. Also new to the agitated political equation were the returned veterans who fought in Europe. Unlike their fathers' generation, who had served only in the Carrier Corps in World War I, these veterans were trained to fight with guns. As their impatience for jobs and land grew, so too did their dissatisfaction. Localized and sporadic opposition to land displacement and the condition of squatters on settler farms finally erupted in 1951 in the Mau Mau, a well-organized guerrilla rebellion dominated by the Kikuyu. This Land and Freedom Army based itself in the forests around Mt. Kenya, where they targeted white farmers. Thirty-two Europeans were killed, and 1,800 Africans killed—including many of the profiteering rural chiefs who were seen as collaborators with the government. The British declared a State of Emergency, arrested Kenyatta as the leader of the rebellion, and imprisoned him for nine years.

The succeeding war, which the British prosecuted ruthlessly, in an extensive government campaign to eradicate Mau Mau, lasted until 1960, and resulted in the deaths of more than eleven hundred of the Mau Mau fighters. Women were combatants and played critical roles in providing supplies and information, and were called upon to spread ideas of freedom. Still debated is whether the Mau Mau revolt significantly moved the British toward the eventual granting of independence in 1963. Clear, however, are the fear and rumors of savagery that government propaganda generated across the country, with the authorities eventually making a series of concessions that in 1957 included the election of Africans to the Legislative Council, followed in 1959 by repealing the laws that had prevented Africans from living in the White Highlands. With Ghana's independence in 1957, it was apparent that the tide toward African independence had irreversibly turned, and Kenyans would soon regain the political independence they had lost eighty years earlier.

INDEPENDENCE

Uhuru, independence, came to Kenya at midnight on December 12, 1963, along with unrealistic expectations for economic progress that the new government could never meet. Even such programs as the Million Acre Scheme, in which the government purchased land from the white settlers to subdivide into plots and sell to peasants to farm, could not satisfy the need for land. Increasingly, a growing and wealthy African elite chose to keep most of the benefits of independence for themselves and leave the rural peasants and urban workers—many of them scarred veterans of the Mau Mau revolt—at the margins. The problems of unemployment and poverty proved just as insurmountable to these new national leaders as they had to the British at the end of colonial rule.

Instead, the politicians in charge of the new nation focused on the consolidation of their own power. As leader of the majority party, the Kenya African National Union (KANU), seventy-year-old Kenyatta became prime minister of the country. A year after independence he consolidated his personal rule when members of two opposition parties joined with KANU to amend the constitution to make Kenyatta the president of what for all practical purposes had become a one-party state. He progressively shifted the control of power and authority from KANU to himself and to his political clients in the civil service. In large measure he was able to become the single dominating figure in Kenya's politics because others who had struggled for independence began to fight among themselves.

When the nationalist leaders had focused on achieving independence, they had generally been able to ignore their differences. Following *uhuru* this unity gave way to factionalism. The opposition parties in parliament came to be identified with the vice-president, Oginga Odinga (c. 1911–1994), a Luo from western Kenya. He was increasingly vocal about pressuring the government to speed up Africanization of jobs, to nationalize business and industry, and to achieve a fairer distribution of the country's land and wealth, and so the government swiftly moved to silence Odinga. At a special meeting of KANU in 1966, they forced him from office.

Other opposition leaders suffered a worse fate. Tom Mboya (1930–1969), who had been a major strategist in the run-up to independence and subsequently a major player in KANU, was widely considered to be Kenyatta's successor. When he was assassinated in 1969 on a street in Nairobi, many believed he had been eliminated because he had simply become too powerful. In 1975 the same fate met another opposition leader and member of parliament, Josiah M. Kariuki (b. 1929). A populist, self-styled man of the people, J.M., as he was widely known, had emerged as the principal critic of the government. He faulted it for its inability to forge a single nation from the country's many and increasingly divided ethnic groups. Although his grisly death on the edge of Nairobi did not silence all opposition to Kenyatta's government, it did cause widespread public fear, for a time limited the dissent of its critics, and eliminated a potential successor to Kenyatta. It did not resolve concern over Kenyatta's age and who would succeed him.

When President Kenyatta died in 1978, he was succeeded by his handpicked vice president, Daniel arap Moi (b. 1924). Moi, from a small group among the Kalenjin peoples of northwestern Kenya, moved quickly to consolidate his position by calling for the people to follow in Kenyatta's footsteps (*Nyayo*). During the first years of Moi's rule the opposition remained relatively quiet. There were even signs that the widespread corruption that characterized Kenyatta's last years was subsiding, but the optimism did not last. Soon the same factors that had typified Kenyatta's rule also characterized Moi's—single-party rule, government corruption, and economic mismanagement. Students at the university struck, but the most serious threat came in August 1982 with a bloody coup attempt led by young air force officers. With the coup attempt turned back, Moi went on to promote a cult of personality. He also moved to broaden the base of KANU's membership in support of his one party state. In 1987, for example, KANU brought Maendeleo ya Wanawake, a rural-based nationwide women's membership organization, into its fold. However, many responded with increased calls for a multiparty system.

With unemployment at 25 percent, state-owned enterprises being sold to Moi's political allies, and donor nations all but cutting Kenya off from further credit and refusing to provide debt relief, the opposition remained divided. Among those demanding multiparty elections and an end to political corruption was Wangari Maathai (b. 1940), the 2004 Nobel Peace Prize recipient. First imprisoned for her politics in 1992, she later ran as a presidential candidate in 1997, using her notoriety as founder of the grassroots environmental Green Belt Movement to bring rural women in particular more actively into the electoral process and the formulation of public policy.

Finally, in the lead-up to the December 2002 election, and the constitution requiring Moi step down after twenty-four years in office, the opposition parties set aside their bickering and formed a common cause to defeat a son of the former president and Moi's hand-picked successor, Uhuru Kenyatta (b. 1961). Fifty-six percent of voters who cast ballots gave the opposition National Rainbow Coalition (NARC), led by a septuagenarian economist, Mwai Kibaki, 125 seats in the parliament, including Maathai, to KANU's sixty-four seats. This set up a heightened sense of optimism and renewed, but unrealistic, expectations for change that had not been met even as campaigning began for the next election in December 2007.

See also Colonial Policies and Practices: British East Africa; Initiation: Clitoridectomy and Infibulation; Kenyatta, Jomo; Maathai, Wangari; Moi, Daniel arap; Postcolonialism; Thuku, Harry; Uganda; Zanzibar.

BIBLIOGRAPHY

Ambler, Charles. *Kenyan Communities in the Age of Imperialism.* New Haven, CT: Yale University Press, 1988.

Kanogo, Tabitha. *African Womanhood in Colonial Kenya, 1900–50.* Athens: Ohio University Press, 2005.

Kenyatta, Jomo. *Facing Mount Kenya.* New York: Vintage, 1962.

Kershaw, Greet, and John Lonsdale. *Mau Mau from Below.* Athens: Ohio University Press, 1997.

Lonsdale, John. "Mau Maus of the Mind: Making Mau Mau and Remaking Kenya." *Journal of African History* 31 (1990): 393–421.

Ochieng, William, ed. *A Modern History of Kenya, 1895–1980.* Nairobi, Kenya: Evans Brothers, 1989.

Presley, Coa Anne. *Kikuyu Women, the Mau Mau Rebellions and Social Change in Kenya.* Boulder, Colorado: Westview, 1992.

Tignor, Robert. *The Colonial Transformation of Kenya: The Kamba, Kikuyu and Maasai from 1900–1939.* Princeton, NJ: Princeton University Press, 1976.

NEAL W. SOBANIA

Jomo Kenyatta (c. 1888–1978), founding father of Kenya. When Kenya became a republic on December 12, 1964, Kenyatta became its executive president. He brought Kenya into the United Nations and followed pro-Western, anti-Communist foreign policies. CORBIS

KENYATTA, JOMO (c. 1888–1978).
Born Kamauwa Muigai in Ngenda, central Kenya, Jomo Kenyatta attended Thogoto Scottish Mission school from 1909 to 1914, joining a small but eventually crucial group of the emerging African elite. Baptized Johnstone in 1914, he dropped this and other names to become Jomo Kenyatta upon leaving school. In 1928 he became the general secretary of the Kikuyu Central Association (KCA), a regional political organization established in 1924. He was also editor of *Muiguithania* (The Reconciler), a journal that articulated African grievances.

In 1929 Kenyatta was appointed by the KCA to present Kenyan grievances stemming from British colonial policies in London. The issues included stolen African lands, lack of political representation, taxation, forced labor, low wages, and lack of—or provision of inadequate—social amenities such as schools and housing. But Kenyatta never received an official audience. He wrote articles in British newspapers about the atrocities of colonialism in Kenya and cultivated the support of various members of the British Labour Party. He also enrolled at the University of London and completed his thesis in anthropology, writing *Facing Mount Kenya* (1938), an anthropological study of the Gikuyu culture in which he had grown up.

While in Britain, Kenyatta was an official of various international organizations concerned with the political and civil rights of colonized people, African Americans, and black people in Britain. He was honorary secretary to the International African Friends of Abyssinia, assistant secretary to the International-African Service Bureau (IASB), and a member of the executive board of the *Journal of International African Opinion*, established in 1938. In 1944

Kenyatta, Kwame Nkrumah, and George Padmore, among others, were cofounders of the Pan-African Federation when IASB and the journal merged. With other founders of the federation, Kenyatta participated in the organization of the fifth Pan-African Congress held at Manchester, England, in 1945.

In 1946, Kenyatta returned to Kenya to find a very politicized, militant, and impatient scene. Widespread squatter impoverishment, land shortages, unpopular conservation plans, and poor living and working conditions created widespread agitation. In 1947 he became head of the Kenya Africa Union (KAU), a multiethnic party formed in 1944.

Kenyatta's return from Britain coincided with the simultaneous radicalization of the KAU and the KCA. In the KAU the ascendancy of younger, militant activists resulted in the creation of the Central Committee, a secret leadership that excluded Kenyatta, the KAU's president. Both parties used intensive mass oathing ceremonies for mobilizing Gikuyu unity against the colonial state. By 1951 political militants in the KAU were administering the Batuni "platoon" oath that anticipated and swore its partakers to an armed revolt against the colonial government, a development that, in exaggerated form, the alarmed British interpreted as "Mau Mau," a peasant guerrilla liberation movement which the government equated with savage regression into a dark past. Under government duress, Kenyatta denounced Mau Mau in August 1952. He was ambiguous in his statements, and the government mistrusted his denunciation.

On October 19, 1952, Kenyatta and more than 150 other nationalist leaders were arrested; the government saw Kenyatta as the unquestionable Mau Mau "leader unto darkness," its evil genius. The government linked Kenyatta, the official leader of the KAU, with the KCA, the Gikuyu Karing'a Educational Association, the trade-union movement, World War II veterans, and other groups associated with the spread of Mau Mau. Yet Kenyatta was not privy to key centers of political radicalization or violence. At his eventual trial at Kapenguria in remote northern Kenya, Kenyatta denounced Mau Mau but was convicted and detained at Maralal, one of many internment camps. This served to lionize Kenyatta and propel him to national popularity.

The Mau Mau guerrilla war of 1952–1956 left about twelve thousand Africans and one hundred Europeans dead by 1956. As a result Britain was forced to reconsider its policies in Kenya. Kenyatta was released in August 1961 and two months later assumed the presidency of the Kenya African National Union (KANU) political party, newly formed to head the negotiations that would lead Kenya to political independence. He became the first prime minister of federal Kenya in June 1962 and of independent Kenya in December 1963. In 1964 Kenya became a republic and Kenyatta its president. After 1965 Kenyatta concentrated on nation building, employing his political slogan "Harambee," which evoked unity and hard work. In 1969 he outlawed the Kenya People's Party, the main political opposition, thus steering Kenya into a one-party state. He died in office on August 22, 1978.

See also **Colonial Policies and Practices; Kenya; Nkrumah, Francis Nwia Kofi.**

BIBLIOGRAPHY

Aseka, Eric M. *Jomo Kenyatta: A Biography.* Nairobi, Kenya: East African Educational Publishers, 1992.

Enwezor, Okwui, ed. *The Short Century: Independence and Liberation Movements in Africa, 1945–1994.* New York: Prestel, 2001.

Kenyatta, Jomo. *Suffering without Bitterness: The Founding of the Kenyan Nation.* Nairobi: East African Publishing House, 1968.

Kenyatta, Jomo. *Facing Mount Kenya: The Tribal Life of the Gikuyu* [1938]. New York: AMS Press, 1978.

Murray-Brown, Jeremy. *Kenyatta*, 2nd edition. London: Allen and Unwin, 1979.

Slater, Montagu. *The Trial of Jomo Kenyatta.* London: Heinemann, 1975.

TABITHA KANOGO

KERMA. Kerma, or Karmah, is a town and archaeological site in northern Sudan on the Nile. The ancient kingdom of Kerma was founded about 2300 BCE and was known as Yam or Kush, the oldest kingdom south of Egypt. It had non-Egyptian styles for burial, architecture, and pottery, and it also practiced complex trade, military, and political articulation with Egypt and the Nubian "C-Group," a contemporary cattle culture located between Kush and Egypt. With no local written sources, Kerma is known from archaeological excavations of its cemeteries and towns, which held remains of humans and animals as well as products of wood, metal, pottery, brick, stone, and minerals. Egyptian texts also refer to Kerma.

Kerma's wealth derived from Egyptian trade for slaves, gold, incense, and animal products. Excavations have shown that Kerma had marked social stratification, shown in royal grave mounds (reaching 290 feet across) with cattle and human sacrifice (up to 322 retainers) and in two large mud-brick buildings called *defuffa* (a Nubian word for ancient ruins). One *defuffa* is 170 feet long and is linked to a palace and reception complex. Craftsmen and royal guards lived inside the royal quarter; others resided beyond the defensive walls. The streets of Kerma wandered through domestic housing units, comprised of one to three rooms, with provisions for domestic animals and grain storage. Another eastern *defuffa* is located at a royal cemetery.

Kerma had fine red and black "tulip beakers," pottery typically showing a white horizontal band. Some funerary rituals included spouted flasks. Kerma grew during Egypt's Middle Kingdom (2050–1786 BCE) and after 1786 BCE achieved its Classical phase. There was some mummification and the existence of funeral chapels, both suggesting an Egyptian influence, but Kerma bed burials have parallels with modern Nubians. Some bodies were preserved by natural desiccation.

When the Asiatic Hyksos conquered northern Egypt they allied with Kerma, trapping Egyptians between the two regions. Some Kerma grave sites show bodies with violent injuries and burials with various weapons. Kerma was a military and commercial threat to the Egyptians, who built a defensive military network of massive mud-brick forts between the first and second cataracts on the Nile downstream of Kerma. In the sixteenth century BCE, the Egyptian pharaoh Ahmose attacked Kerma and returned to Egypt with a dead Kerma king. Traces of Kerma vanish under the Egyptian New Kingdom (1567–1090 BCE).

The religion of Kerma centered on a divine king with his religious workers and an idea of an afterlife. Stellar and animal images in tomb wall tiles suggest that animal deities of Nubia were included in the religious system. Traces of Egyptian religion can be found in Kerma's religion: statues, certain deities, and a solar disk icon reflect an Egyptian influence. The tenacious fly was used a symbol on Kerma's military badges.

See also **Archaeology and Prehistory; Ceramics; Nubia.**

BIBLIOGRAPHY

Adams, William Y. *Nubia: Corridor to Africa.* Princeton, NJ: Princeton University Press, 1977.

Bonnet, Charles. "Kerma, an African Kingdom of the Second and Third Millennium BC." *Archaeology* 36 (1983): 38–45.

Dunham, Dows. *Excavations at Kerma, Part 6.* Boston: Museum of Fine Arts: 1982.

Kendall, Timothy. *Kerma and the Kingdom of Kush, 2500–1500 BC.* Washington, DC: Smithsonian Institution, 1996.

Lobban, Richard A. *Historical Dictionary of Ancient and Medieval Nubia.* Lanham, MD: Scarecrow Press, 2004.

Reisner, George A. "Excavations at Kerma, I–V." *Harvard African Studies* 5– 6 (1923–1924).

RICHARD LOBBAN

KHAMA, SERETSE (1921–1980).

Seretse Khama, the first president of Botswana, was the grandson of Khama III. He became the extremely popular uncrowned chief of the Ngwato following his highly controversial marriage to a white Englishwoman, Ruth Williams, in 1949. This marriage offended the apartheid government in South Africa and forced the British Imperial government to exile Seretse to England from 1949 to 1956. In 1962, Seretse formed the Botswana Democratic Party (BDP), which won the country's first democratic elections in 1965 and formed the post-independence government. Unlike most African leaders, who sooner or later declared their countries one-party states, persecuted political opponents, and ruined economies, Seretse was a staunch promoter of the multi-party democracy and accountable leadership that has made Botswana the oldest democracy in Africa.

Sir Seretse Khama (1921–1980). As Botswana's first president, Khama tried to encourage the poor country's export businesses, including those selling beef, diamonds, and copper. As a result, between 1966 and 1988 Botswana had the fastest-growing economy in the world. EVENING STANDARD/ GETTY IMAGES

Khama's open and responsible style of leadership laid a firm foundation for national unity and economic prosperity for the post-colony. He was a founder member of the Frontline States, which sought to replace white minority regimes in Southern Africa with majority governments. The Southern African Development Coordination Conference (SADCC), later renamed Southern African Development Community (SADC), was his brainchild. Seretse died in 1980 leaving behind a legacy of government accountability that endures in the early twenty-first century and greatly helps the ruling BDP win elections in the conservative section of the society.

See also **Botswana: History and Politics; Kenya; Khama, Tshekedi; Khama III.**

BIBLIOGRAPHY

Carter, Gwendolen M., and E. Philip Morgan, eds. *From the Frontline: Speeches of Sir Seretse Khama.* London: Rex Collins, 1980.

Crowder, Michael. "Botswana and the Survival of Liberal Democracy in Africa." In *Decolonization and African Independence: The Transfer of Power, 1960–1980,* ed. Prossard Gifford and William Roger Louis. New Haven, CT: Yale University Press, 1988.

Dingake, Michael. *My Fight against Apartheid.* London: Kliptown Books, 1987.

Dutfield, Michael. *Marriage of Inconvenience: The Persecution of Seretse and Ruth Khama.* Oxford: Routledge, 1987.

Henderson, Willie. "Seretse Khama: A Personal Appreciation." *African Affairs* 89, no. 354 (1990): 27–56.

Hyam, Ronald. "The Political Consequences of Seretse Khama: Britain, the Bangwato and South Africa, 1948–52." *The Historical Journal* 29, no. 4 (1986): 921–947.

Mbanga, Wilf, and Trish Mbanga. *Seretse and Ruth: Botswana's Love Story.* Cape Town, South Africa: Tafelberg Publishers, 2005.

Parsons, Neil. "The Central District: The Bangwato Crisis 1949–1956." In *The Birth of Botswana: A History of the Bechuanaland Protectorate, 1910–1966,* ed. Jeff Ramsay and Fred Morton. London: Longman Group United Kingdom, 1990.

Parsons, Neil; Thomas Tlou; and Willie Henderson. *Seretse Khama, 1921–1980.* London: Macmillan, 1995.

CHRISTIAN JOHN MAKGALA

KHAMA, TSHEKEDI (1905–1959). Tshekedi Khama, regent of the Ngwato Tswana subgroup for his nephew Seretse Khama for twenty-four years, was a leading and contentious defender of Tswana sovereignty in the Bechuanaland Protectorate (present-day Botswana). From 1925 he, as regent, joined with Bathoen II of the Ngwaketse to resist British colonial efforts to restrict chiefs' authority and to prevent the incorporation of the Bechuanaland Protectorate into the neighboring settler-controlled Union of South Africa. He also spoke out against South Africa's attempts to annex Southwest Africa (present-day Namibia). Less successful were his attempts to keep Bechuanaland from being transformed into a labor reserve for South Africa.

Tshekedi actively supported the monopoly of the London Missionary Society over education and other religiously linked programs among the

Ngwato, and advocated temperance, among other church-influenced policies. However, he never challenged the slave conditions of the San (Kalahari desert hunters and gatherers), and meted out harsh treatment to the minority Kalanga, opponents of his autocratic rule. Factional conflicts within the Ngwato elite, common in Tswana polities, led to an assassination attempt in 1926 by the Ratshosa brothers, leaders of a faction that favored a significant role for "tribal councils" drawn from the educated elite and opposed the LMS monopoly. Doubting the loyalty of many members of the Ngwato elite, Tshekedi exiled and imprisoned many of them. He pursued an autocratic style of governing and came into frequent conflict with Charles Rey (1877–1968), Resident Commissioner from 1930 to 1937.

In 1933 Tshekedi ordered the flogging of a white man, and Rey used the occasion to suspend Tshekedi's regency. Official opinion in Britain and South Africa pushed Rey to reinstate him, and Tshekedi led the chiefs' successful resistance to full implementation of Rey's Native Proclamations, which would have forced chiefs to include local headmen in governance and strengthened the authority of the Resident Commissioner over chiefs. Tshekedi opposed the 1948 marriage of his nephew Seretse to a white Englishwoman on the grounds of Ngwato custom and refused to give up his regency, resulting in his temporary exile. He renounced his claim to chiefship in 1956, reconciled with Seretse, and continued as an active force in Bechuanaland politics until his death in 1959.

See also **Colonial Policies and Practices; Khama, Seretse.**

BIBLIOGRAPHY

Crowder, Michael. *The Flogging of Phinehas McIntosh: A Tale of Colonial Folly and Injustice: Bechuanaland 1933, 1934–1988.* New Haven, CT: Yale University Press, 1988.

Parson, Jack, ed. *Succession to High Office in Botswana.* Athens: Ohio University Center for International Studies, 1990.

Vaughan, Olufemi. *Chiefs, Power, and Social Change: Chiefship and Modern Politics in Botswana, 1880s–1990s.* Trenton, NJ: Africa World Press, 2003.

Wylie, Diana. *A Little God: The Twilight of Patriarchy in a Southern African Chiefdom.* Middletown, CT: Wesleyan

University Press; Hanover, NH: University Press of New England, 1990.

JUDITH IMEL VAN ALLEN

KHAMA III (c. 1836–1923). Khama III was a shrewd ruler of the Ngwato ethnic group in Botswana. He was baptized into Christianity in 1860 and became a fundamentalist while his father, Sekgoma (1815–1883), remained a traditional religious conservative hard-liner and incurred the detestation of both the European missionaries and traders. Consequently, a civil war broke out in 1866 in which the traders and missionaries supported Khama against Sekgoma. However, Sekgoma triumphed and forgave his son.

In 1875, Khama assumed chieftainship and replaced many Ngwato laws and customs with Christian practices. He expelled from his domain European traders who disobeyed his stringent anti-alcohol regulations. He brought under his control numerous hitherto independent or semi-independent tribal groups in his region, and built an empire.

Khama readily accepted the British colonization of Botswana in 1885. His cooperation made him unique, and the British considered him the most respected African, calling him Khama the Great. He was one of the first local rulers to successfully localize the crucial post of Tribal Secretary in the early 1890s, hitherto held by missionaries. So successful was Khama that his Tswana contemporaries tried to emulate his clever manipulation of the British colonial officials and missionaries. He died in 1923, leaving behind an enduring legacy of statesmanship.

See also **Botswana; Kenya; Khama, Seretse; Political Systems: Chieftainships.**

BIBLIOGRAPHY

Chirenje, Jack Mutero. *Chief Kgama and His Times c. 1835–1923: The Story of a Southern African Ruler.* London: Rex Collings, 1978.

Harris, John Charles. *Khama: The Great African Chief.* London: The Livingstone Press, 1922.

Landau, Paul Stuart. *The Realm of the Word: Language, Gender, and Christianity in a Southern African Kingdom.* Portsmouth, NH: Heinemann, 1995.

Long, Unah. *The Journals of Elizabeth Lees Price, Written in Bechuanaland, Southern Africa 1854–1883.* London: Edward Arnold, 1956.

Parsons, N. Q. "Khama III, the Bamangwato, and the British: With Special Reference to 1895–1923." Ph.D. diss., University of Edinburgh, 1973.

Schapera, Isaac. "The Political Organisation of the Ngwato of Bechuanaland Protectorate." In *African Political Systems*, ed. Meyer Fortes and Edward Evans-Pritchard. London: Routledge, 1987.

Tlou, Thomas; Neil Parsons; and Willie Henderson. *Seretse Khama, 1921–80.* Gaborone, Botswana: Macmillan, 1995.

CHRISTIAN JOHN MAKGALA

KHARTOUM. The capital of Sudan, Khartoum is situated at the historic confluence of the White Nile and the Blue Nile. The conurbation of Khartoum, Omdurman, and Khartoum North is the largest urban area and the political, Islamic, and industrial center of the country.

Founded on the site of the clay-built town of Halfaya, Khartoum's strategic location brought it early prosperity as a slave-trading center. In 1821 it was an Ottoman-Egyptian army camp, and three years later the Ottomans moved their outpost from Omdurman across the river to Khartoum. The name of the capital came from the Arabic word for an elephant's trunk, because the long promontory between the rivers was reminiscent of a pachydermal proboscis. Khartoum, astride the main caravan route to Cairo, grew quickly to a population of about 30,000 and became a marketplace for a wide array of Eastern and European goods. By 1850 some 3,000 houses had replaced many of the mud buildings, and the Ottoman-Egyptian governor-general had built an opulent palace for himself in the city.

After a long siege, Mahdist forces destroyed Khartoum and killed many of its residents, including the British governor-general, Major General Charles Gordon, in 1885. The Mahdists believed their Ottoman-Egyptian overlords had abandoned Islam and sold out to the British. They also believed that their leader, the Mahdi, was the successor to the prophet Muhammad and had come to earth to bring justice and equity. The Mahdi and his followers abandoned the ruined Khartoum and established their capital across the river at Omdurman. The Mahdist theocratic state ruled from the Red Sea to central Africa for twenty years, until a British force under Lord Horatio Kitchener captured Omdurman in 1898. Kitchener rebuilt Khartoum and made it the capital of the Anglo-Egyptian condominium in Sudan that lasted until 1956.

Khartoum retains some of its colonial atmosphere, with banyan tree-lined boulevards and British colonial architecture. The city produces textiles, gums, and glass and is at the center of many trading networks. Railroads link Khartoum to Egypt, al-Ubayyid, and Port Sudan on the Red Sea, and a pipeline completed in 1977 brings oil from the Red Sea.

Bridges connect Khartoum with Omdurman, the country's Islamic cultural center and largest *souk* (market), and with Khartoum North, the primary industrial area of the nation. The city is hot and dry, with a peak annual temperature of 117 degrees Fahrenheit and less than seven inches of rain per year. An estimated 1,036,600 people lived in Khartoum proper in 1998 (the last year for which reliable figures are available), and the combined population of the Three Town area was more than 3 million. These numbers are so great because of the ongoing civil war with the southern-based Sudan People's Liberation Movement, which has led to a massive exodus from the violent rural areas. The war caused hardships in the city, including shortages of gasoline, energy, and other necessary resources in the mid-1990s.

See also **Gordon, Charles George; Nile River; Sudan: History and Politics.**

BIBLIOGRAPHY

Moorehead, Alan. *The Blue Nile.* New York: Harper and Row, 1980.

Warburg, Gabriel. *Egypt and the Sudan: Studies in History and Politics.* London: Frank Cass, 1985.

THOMAS F. MCDOW

KHOISAN LANGUAGES. *See* **Languages: Khoesan and Click.**

KIBAKI, MWAI (1931–). Born in Gatuyaini, Kenya, Mwai Kibaki was the son of a prosperous farmer. He went to Makerere University in Uganda, receiving a bachelor's degree in economics in 1955. Having graduated first in his class, he won a scholarship to attend the London School of Economics where he graduated with a bachelor's degree in public finance. From 1958 to 1960 he taught economics at Makerere University. In March 1960 Kibaki helped found the Kenya African National Union (KANU), which ruled the nation, initially under President Jomo Kenyatta, from independence in 1963 to 2002. The following December he became the party's chief executive officer. In 1963 Kibaki was elected to a seat in Parliament. From 1966 to 1991 he held a variety of cabinet posts, including minister of finance (1970–1981). When Daniel arap Moi succeeded Jomo Kenyatta as president in 1978, he appointed Kibaki as vice president. In 1988, Moi demoted Kibaki, removing him as vice president and shifting him from minister of home affairs to minister of health.

Mwai Kibaki (1931–). Kenyan president Kibaki makes a speech after the signing of an accord by various Somali factions and leaders, in Nairobi on January 29, 2004. In 2006, Kibaki set up a new political party, Narc-Kenya, which won three out of five parliamentary seats. © PATRICK OLUM/REUTERS/CORBIS

In 1982 the Parliament, at Moi's behest, amended the constitution to make KANU Kenya's only legal party. Nine years later Parliament removed the single-party provision. A few days after that, Kibaki formed the opposition Democratic Party, although he had played no role in the single-party removal campaign. In 2002 he was elected president on his third try after allying his party with several others to establish the National Alliance Party of Kenya (NAK), which then joined with the Liberal Democratic Party to form the National Rainbow Coalition (NARC).

Although elected on a platform of fighting the vast corruption of the Moi years, Kibaki's own government was also extensively corrupt. With a number of his cabinet ministers suspected of graft, early in 2005 four senior cabinet members severely attacked the government they were part of and called for the firing of those ministers. John Githongo, the top adviser to Kibaki on fighting corruption, resigned over the lack of progress. The United States and Germany cut off funds for Kenya's anti-corruption agencies, with the European Union and Japan threatening to follow. Ostensibly to fight corruption, Kibaki later in 2005 proposed a constitutional amendment that would greatly increase his powers. However, Kenyans voted it down in a November 21 referendum. Two days later he took the highly unusual move of firing his entire cabinet as another means of strengthening his control of the government.

See also **Kenya; Kenyatta, Jomo; Moi, Daniel arap.**

BIBLIOGRAPHY

Mbugua, Ng'ang'a. *Mwai Kibaki: Economist for Kenya.* Nairobi, Kenya: Sasa Sema Publications, 2003.

Ngunjiri, Njuguna, and William Okoth Ong'aro. *President Mwai Kibaki: The Long and Bumpy Road to State House*, ed. Mburu wa Mucoki. Nairobi, Kenya: Immediate Media Services, 2003.

MICHAEL LEVINE

KIGALI. The Rwandan capital, Kigali covers four hills near the center of the small, densely populated, landlocked country. Before the civil war of the 1990s, the colonial-era city was lined with beautiful flowering trees, the outlying countryside was heavily cultivated, and the terraced hills could be seen from Kigali. Like the rest of Rwanda, the population of Kigali is a mix of Hutu and Tutsi; the competition between the two groups for political power in the civil war led to the death and dislocation of nearly one-third of the country's population.

In the nineteenth century Kigali was part of the Tutsi-ruled kingdom of Ruanda (present-day Rwanda). The area became a trade center after 1895, when the Germans made the kingdoms of Ruanda and Urundi part of German East Africa. White Father missionaries established missions in Ruanda around 1900 and set up the first schools. When the Germans were defeated in World War I, the League of Nations assigned Ruanda-Urundi as a mandated territory to Belgium. Under Belgian rule many workers left for the mines in the neighboring Belgian Congo, and the wages they sent back or brought home provided a substantial economic boost to the colony. Upon independence in 1962 the colony of Ruanda-Urundi was divided into the nations of Rwanda and Burundi, and Kigali was made the capital of Rwanda. Kigali, the only major town in a country in which 96 percent of the population was rural, was more than ten times as populous as the next largest town before the civil war.

After Rwandan president Juvenal Habyarimana, who had served for twenty years, was assassinated in 1994, a series of mass killings took place in Kigali. Political groups, most notably the Coalition for the Defense of the Republic (CDR)—Hutu who did not want to negotiate with the Tutsi—and the Rwandan Patriotic Front (RPF)—a military faction cum political party founded by Tutsi refugees who had grown up in Uganda—tried to consolidate power. More than 20,000 people were killed in Kigali within three weeks. As the killing spread to the countryside an estimated 500,000 people, mostly Tutsi, were killed. Many Rwandans fled to neighboring countries. Almost as many people died in the aftermath of the massacres—from wounds, cholera, dysentery, famine, and conditions in refugee camps—as had died during the fighting.

When the RPF captured Kigali in July 1994 hundreds of thousands of Hutu fled the country, most of them into Tanzania and Zaire. At the end of July nearly one-third of Rwanda's entire population was outside its boundaries. By the beginning of 1996, refugees were beginning to return, but hundreds of thousands remained in camps abroad.

Although there was massive population displacement during the war years, by 2004 the population of Kigali had finally recovered to its prewar level of 300,000.

Before the fighting broke out, many expatriates, international organizations, and a mining company had been based in Kigali. The industrial area to the southeast of the city produced paint and varnish, assembled radios, and manufactured shoes, but the war largely destroyed the country's industry, services, and infrastructure. During the postwar years, the country has moved slowly but with some real success toward restoring services and rebuilding damaged properties in the city. Ongoing tensions in the region, including a still-active Hutu insurgency, made recovery a difficult process.

See also **Colonial Policies and Practices: Belgian; Colonial Policies and Practices: German; Ethnicity: Central Africa; Rwanda; Warfare: Civil Wars.**

BIBLIOGRAPHY

Africa Today, 3rd edition. London: Africa Books, 1996.

Fisanick, Christina, ed. *The Rwanda Genocide*. San Diego, CA: Greenhaven Press, 2004.

THOMAS F. MCDOW

KIMBANGU, SIMON (c. 1887–1951).

The Congolese religious charismatic Simon Kimbangu was born at Nkamba in the Lower Congo and brought up within the ethos of the British Baptist mission. He was baptized with his wife in 1915 and was accepted as a lay preacher in 1918. Later that year, having experienced a series of dreams and visions, he set off to work in Léopoldville (present-day Kinshasa), apparently to escape them. Unsuccessful in this endeavor, Kimbangu returned to Nkamba in 1921, with the conviction that he had been appointed "an apostle." In March of that year, he began his healing ministry. Huge crowds converged on Nkamba, convinced of his miraculous powers, and a movement of mass conversion and the destruction of the "fetishes" of traditional religion followed. A considerable group of Baptist deacons accepted his ministry as "the work of God" and set about organizing it, but the missionaries were more skeptical, especially when a wave of other prophets with a variety of doctrines began to appear.

The Belgian authorities attempted to arrest Kimbangu in June 1921 but failed. They succeeded in September; he was tried and, in an extraordinary perversion of justice since he had committed no obvious crime, condemned to death. He was reprieved on the petition of the Baptist Missionary Society to King Albert I of Belgium. Many of his followers were exiled to the Upper Congo, but Kimbangu was kept in prison in Elizabethville (present-day Lubumbashi) until his death. The movement he had begun continued surreptitiously until the Kimbanguist Church was formally established by his sons in the late 1950s, shortly before Congo gained political independence. The Kimbanguist Church has since been admitted to the World Council of Churches.

See also **Fetish and Fetishism.**

BIBLIOGRAPHY

Chome, Jules. *La passion de Simon Kimbangu, 1921–1951.* Bruxelles: Les Amis de Présence Africaine, 1959.

Martin, Marie-Louise. *Kimbangu: An African Prophet and His Church*, trans. D. M. Moore. Grand Rapids, MI: Eerdmans, 1976.

ADRIAN HASTINGS

KIMPA VITA, DONA BEATRIZ

(c. 1684–1706). Dona Beatriz Kimpa Vita was a religious leader in the area that is present-day Angola. She was a member of a noble Kongo family, and, following a severe illness, she claimed that she had died and been resurrected as Saint Anthony, as his spirit possessed her. Under the persona of that Catholic saint, she preached for the restoration of the Kongolese monarchy, which had suffered from three decades of civil war. Her message of peace and reconciliation appealed to many followers, who called themselves Antonians. She also attracted the displeasure of the local Catholic hierarchy, as she claimed that Jesus Christ was Kongolese and she petitioned for the recognition of black saints. A coalition between two aristocratic households adhering to orthodox Catholic beliefs brought Dona Beatriz to trial for heresy, and she was burned at the stake in 1706. Her movement continued until

1709 when her followers were decisively defeated by Pedro IV's (1798–1834) army.

See also **Christianity.**

BIBLIOGRAPHY

Thornton, John. *The Kongolese Saint Anthony: Dona Beatriz Kimpa Vita and the Antonian Movement, 1684–1706.* Cambridge, U.K.: Cambridge University Press, 1998.

KATHLEEN SHELDON

KING LISTS AND CHRONOLOGIES.

Throughout history, societies everywhere have made efforts to recall and reconstruct their pasts. Royal genealogies and lists of officeholders have been popular means to achieve this. Such lists are the focus of perceived origins, but may also be used to measure the passing of time, though seldom by the societies themselves. In Africa, the practice has been typically widespread in both oral and literate societies, and these data have been used by modern historians to construct political chronologies.

Despite their usefulness, genealogies and king lists labor under several handicaps. In origin and in construction they are primarily legitimizing tools and have been frequently manipulated to serve changing political and social objectives. The problems in interpreting these sources are necessarily more acute in oral societies, where evidence of change is likely to be more elusive. Among the more common defects in such genealogies are the inclusion of spurious names, especially in their earlier parts, simply to establish a greater antiquity as seen in Bunyoro and Rwanda; the inclusion of collateral rulers, or rulers later deemed to have been usurpers, as found in the Akan states and Munhumutapa; implausible claims of long father-to-son sequences; and the co-optation of data from written sources as evident in the Fante and Hausa states.

It is impossible to predict where and whether these distortions will occur in any particular genealogy or king list, or to assume that all oral lists of this kind are less accurate than any written ones. Some orally preserved lists of rulers from Senegambia seem to correlate well with the available external evidence, whereas written genealogies along the Swahili coast, designed to demonstrate Arabic origins for their ruling lines, are palpably in error.

At first, modern academic historians were naturally eager to use the data incorporated into African genealogies, some originating as far back as the eighteenth century, most recorded during colonial rule, and still others collected in the field by modern scholars. A special issue of the *Journal of African History* in 1970 represented the acme of this enthusiasm. Shortly thereafter, application of a wider comparative perspective, drawing on cases from both inside and outside Africa, began to demonstrate that African genealogies were no more immune to distortion than were their counterparts elsewhere.

The case of Rwanda reflects the most extreme example of royal genealogies that was wielded for unabashedly political purposes, yet survives. Royally sponsored research in the 1930s generated a father-to-son royal line extending back, by generational reckoning, to the tenth century. This interpretation is, in the early twenty-first century, still widely accepted and promulgated in Rwanda. In an even more extreme case, a Belgian ethnographer was persuaded early in the twentieth century that the succession of Kuba rulers in Democratic Republic of the Congo extended unbroken back to the second century CE.

The numerous tiny Akan statelets of Ghana are yet another example of the tendency to assert early origins by producing royal genealogies to support claims of paramountcy. In these matrilineal societies it is difficult to use genealogies for dating purposes, but the chronic jurisdictional disputes in the colonial period (a phenomenon observed elsewhere as well) produced scores of contradictory king lists to be unraveled. Problems with the Akan lists were aggravated by constant recourse to sources printed by various proponents who were intent on producing lists and genealogies that would seem to have the support of external documentation.

The several states of the Great Lakes area of eastern Africa provide a convenient microcosm of the procedural methods of both indigenous and Western historians with respect to genealogies. Subjected to indirect rule by the British and the Belgians, in that unqualified political leaders were either foisted upon local communities, or locally approved leaders were allowed to take or remain in office only with colonial approval, these states found it expedient to resist or exploit their overlords and their competitors, partly through mobilizing competing and expanding king lists. Educated indigenous historians were able to produce work in the coherent narrative style that appealed to the colonial rulers; royal names were suitably multiplied to create the necessary clusters of new generations; and the colonial administration rewarded the enterprise by accepting the new data.

The advent of professional historians only added to the confusion because, rather than questioning the bona fides of the existing genealogies, they tended only to collect more lists and to use these to establish baseline chronologies. By the early 1970s, historians widely believed that they had been able to impose a firm, if inexact, chronological schema that extended back as far as the twelfth or thirteenth century for the whole Great Lakes region. Since then, there has been a reversal of fortune, and most historians would now be reluctant to posit any exactitude for dating before about the middle of the eighteenth century.

If Africans used genealogies and king lists to legitimize present politics, modern scholars have found in them precious opportunities to mark the chronology of various African societies. Leaving aside the question of these genealogies' validity, such efforts have included devising average lengths of reigns and generations, establishing apparent synchronisms with neighboring societies or with the recorded activities of Europeans, and searching out possible references to datable occurrences, such as solar eclipses and droughts. Each of these procedures has proved vulnerable to criticism, and this, combined with the unlikelihood that many of the genealogies and other lists are accurate in the first place—and none can be proved to be—has already rendered most of this work obsolete.

Nevertheless, much can be done to refine the existing knowledge and to explore the contexts in which African king lists came into being. The thrust of the work carried out more recently has been to untie African genealogies and king lists from African chronology, and at the same time to bring the interpretation of these sources closer to work in better attested areas. As a result, most datings for oral Africa before the beginning of the eighteenth century will need either to be cross-checked with archaeological data or based in some fashion on whatever written evidence exists from the earlier period.

See also **Kingship; Kinship and Descent.**

BIBLIOGRAPHY

Henige, David. "The Problem of Feedback in Oral Tradition: Four Examples from the Fante Coastlands." *Journal of African History* 14 (1973): 223–235.

Henige, David. *The Chronology of Oral Tradition: Quest for a Chimera.* Oxford: Oxford University Press, 1974.

Perrot, Claude-Hélène, ed. *Le passé de l'Afrique par l'oralité/African History from Oral Sources.* Paris: La documentation francaise, 1993.

Vansina, Jan. *Antecedents to Modern Rwanda: The Nyiginya Kingdom.* Madison: University of Wisconsin Press, 2004.

DAVID HENIGE

KINGS AND KINGDOMS.

The understanding of monarchy has a deep and enduring tie to African studies. In large part this is due to Sir James Frazer, who in *The Golden Bough* (12 vols., 1890–1915) repeatedly cited African material to support his arguments, especially accounts of sacred kingship and ritual king-killing among the Shilluk of the southern Sudan. For Frazer, sub-Saharan African societies provided striking contemporary links between the ancient, classical Greek and Latin materials, which first inspired him to seek origins of religion in kingship, and the complex kingships of civilizations in Europe, Asia, and Egypt. African kingships, being supposedly less complex polities than these others, were assumed to provide crucial insights into how the institutions of monarchy evolved. While Frazer's views were simplistic, his insights inspired a large number of brilliant studies of kingship in Africa that have had a profound impact on the understanding of monarchies everywhere, and indeed of how beliefs and symbols support polities.

Royal rule in Africa usually involved men as kings, though in a few cases, such as the Lovedu of southern Africa, women ruled in their own right. Even where men ruled, considerable authority and power were wielded by women as queen mothers, as queenly wives of kings, and at times as regents for young kings. In all these cases, African kings' authority was modeled on more basic patriarchal authority, as typified by heads of kin groups and households. A king was a patriarch in two senses: he was a father to a land and nation, and he was the head of a royal house or congeries of royal kin groups and aristocrats, including a royal household and court. At times such kings ruled over large polities containing more than a million people, as in the kingdoms of the Yoruba and the kingdom of Bénin of Nigeria; the Asante kingdom of Ghana; the interlacustrine kingdoms of eastern Africa; and the Zulu, Sotho, and Swazi kingdoms of southern Africa. Yet some accounts of those rulers termed "kings" describe polities of only a few thousand people; thus, some might term such rulers "chiefs" rather than kings. The key factor behind the application of the term "king" to such a wide range of rulers in Africa is not so much the size of the polity ruled as the fact that the ruler embodies the nation, the people, their land, and their history in his sacred person and that this institution of kingship is envisioned as undying. As with kingships elsewhere, individual African rulers may die but the monarchy that governs and sustains a nation endures.

KINGSHIP AS A POLITICAL INSTITUTION

Kingship in Africa is a political institution deeply embedded in manifold and complex beliefs and sentiments. Royal rule incorporates the key symbols that define a society. Without such symbols, African kingships would lack the powerful and persistent support of their subjects. It is through such symbols, drawn from the surrounding environment and society, that African kings are able to epitomize their people and ways of life. Besides being fathers to their nations, kings are variously described as herdsmen to their national flock, or as fierce lions, leopards, or elephants powerfully dominating and intimidating, but also defending, a throne and people. Kings are sometimes epitomized as descendants of mysterious or divine outsiders, not readily subsumable into local kin and ethnic groups, and sometimes are associated with alien conquerors; such imagery is especially powerful among some of the East African interlacustrine kingdoms and among the northern Nigerian emirates. Kings are providers of rain; sources of fertility and health to the land, people, and livestock; and, as such, masters of supernatural powers.

In part, these powers are inherent in a king's being, but powerful magical medicines and rituals are frequently employed to maintain and enhance them. Mystical powers are sometimes conferred upon a king as part of his installation when he takes office. At other times these medicines and rituals are periodically reapplied, often at annual rites associated with the seasons, most particularly planting or harvest times. Kings' powers may also be enhanced by their reputations as procreators of myriad offspring or by their leadership in warfare and conquest, especially through the humiliation and execution of enemy rulers and people. Kings' powers are often especially enforced through the supernatural powers of their ancestors.

Many kingdoms—for example, Buganda in eastern Africa; Lozi of Zambia; Sakalava of Madagascar; and Asante, Yoruba, and Bénin in western Africa—have important shrines to the royal dead or require periodic visits and sacrifices by kings at the sanctuaries and tombs of earlier rulers. Such shrines may have their own properties, courts, caretakers, and sometimes even spirit-mediums who speak for the dead rulers. All these work to sustain a sense of the undying character of the kingship.

SYMBOLS OF KINGSHIP
Through royal ancestral shrines, tombs, and, above all, royal regalia, African kingships maintain their immortality. Such regalia may be relatively simple objects such as spears, bead necklaces, and wooden stools, as in the case of the Anuak of southern Sudan. Or regalia may consist of a vast treasury of sacred, ancestral objects such as the famous golden stool of Asante, sacred jewelry, weapons, staffs, fans and fly whisks, and statues of former rulers. Sometimes, as among the Yoruba, ornate beaded crowns obscure the sacred visage of a ruler. The great treasury of the kingdom of Bénin in Nigeria consisted of thousands of valuable brass plaques, heads, statues, and jewelry, and ivory and wood carvings, which were looted by the British when they conquered the Bénin capital. In the early twenty-first century, many of the most prized royal objects of Bénin are among the most famous treasures of African art in European and American museums. These works were fashioned over many centuries, some made as early as the fifteenth century. The Edo people of Bénin therefore viewed such objects as embodying the ancient continuity of the Bénin royal state. Today, many Africans seek the repatriation of such treasured patrimony because they see such objects as the epitome of their ethnic identities and histories. Such demands are especially strong where such works are associated with actual polities such as kingdoms.

The symbols of kingship, since they embrace the totality of the social and physical environment, are both positive and negative. In cosmological terms the king manifests forces of destruction and danger as well as of creativity, the dangers of lightning as well as the plenitude of rain, the fierceness of animal predators as well as the sustenance of livestock and crops. In social terms he is a source of punishment and judgment as well as of rewards and generosity. The king links the natural or cosmological spheres with the social; he also links disparate social groups—diverse clans and lineages, extensive land areas, royal kin and commoners, the living and the ancestral dead, the free and the enslaved.

To fill these many roles, a king embodies attributes from all these groups and categories while necessarily standing above and beyond any and all of them. For example, a king is paramount among all his royal kin, yet at the same time he stands as a defender of commoners against the abuses and incursions of his royal relatives. A king embodies and defends the rights and privileges of royals and aristocrats yet necessarily also undermines these same people's powers to some degree, so that they cannot usurp his and other royals' authority. Kings are consequently everyone's friends, yet also everyone's enemies. They embrace everyone yet stand uniquely alone and apart. African kingship, like monarchy everywhere, is founded upon a synthesis of contradictions that make it a unique office. These qualities account for a king's power, but they also make kingship socially fragile, prone to incursions of witchcraft by dissatisfied subjects, to plotting by royal relatives, and to physical attacks by enemies from both within and outside the kingdom. The violent histories of many African kingdoms, such as Zulu, Bénin, and Buganda, attest to the precarious and dangerous situation of royal office.

The symbolism of kingship also depends on mystification, a presentation of the royal self that repeatedly affirms the complex supernatural groundings of the institution of royal, divine rule. African kings rely upon a combination of symbolic display and concealment. Sacred rulers are repeatedly presented as living icons at public rituals—in processions, in national rites of purification and fertility, in rituals before and after warfare, during installation of themselves and members of their courts, and through their holding of audiences and judgments. In the more complex kingdoms, such as Buganda, Yoruba, Bénin, Dahomey, Zulu, and Luba of Zaire, kings established royal settlements where the magnificence and scale of the edifices proclaimed the potency and wealth of royal rule. Royal residences often included multiple dwellings for wives, children, servants, artisans, guards, and soldiery, and structures to hold stores of regalia, foodstuffs, and wealth. They became spatial symbols of the royal power to command labor, as well as of the royal power to attract and distribute wealth.

Mystification of royal power also required concealment. Some royal rites and their associated regalia were shrouded in secrecy. They were inaccessible to ordinary subjects, though for this secrecy to be symbolically affective, this concealment had to be popularly expressed and recognized. Every subject was made aware that secret, dangerous, sacred rites were practiced by kings, even while at the same time subjects were repeatedly impressed with their own unworthiness to know what these powerful rites and supernaturally endowed objects actually entailed. Arcane lore always accompanies kings.

PRACTICAL ASPECTS OF KINGSHIP

The sacred attributes of kings as sources of power and wealth were further supported by kings' more practical roles as collectors and distributors of wealth. A king was not only a supernatural source of fertility and well-being but also, in fact, a real source of material prosperity. Kings collected resources in the forms of goods and labor through levies upon their subjects. They also gathered a large body of servants, slaves, and artisans, as well as numerous wives and offspring. Kings and their officials collected payments of food, livestock, and raw materials and commissioned luxury goods. Rulers of large kingdoms employed numerous craftsmen who produced luxury goods in metal, ivory, textiles, beadwork, and carved wood. Kings supported praise singers and orators to recite the genealogies and epic exploits of royal kin as well as the national history. They also encouraged musicians and dancers who enacted and glorified the royal being and his world.

Investigating the sources and meanings of much African art requires an understanding of royal patronage and the need for public display of royal largesse and splendor. Such art proclaimed royal power and could be distributed to subjects as signs of royal favor or of the delegation of royal authority. Kings often greatly augmented their powers by dominating and initiating trade, both within their kingdoms and with foreign peoples. In the eighteenth and nineteenth centuries, African kings often acquired arms and luxury goods, and disposed of enemies and criminals, through trade—exchanging people, ivory, and gold for European and Asian goods.

Kings were the sources of power and authority delegated to subordinate princes and chiefs. They were often elected and supported by the chiefs and princes under them; they also often held powers to support and promote, or to remove, such followers. Consequently, kings were seen as the sources of local political power as well as of material wealth, the bestowers and distributors of honors, titles, and offices that constituted important social resources for those beneath them. Kings often were the spokesmen for the national or ethnic welfare and consciousness.

KINSHIP, MARRIAGE, AND SUCCESSION

These special features of kingship resemble broader features of patriarchy in general, in that elder kinsmen serve as sources of wealth and entitlement to their younger kin yet depend for their powers upon the loyalty and subservience of their wives and offspring. This parallel is significant because African kingship, like monarchy elsewhere, is deeply enmeshed in kinship. It has already been noted that African kings were heads of royal kin groups and leaders of a congeries of aristocrats or privileged kin groups. They modeled much of their royal ritual and pageantry upon the activities of a patriarchal, polygynous family, on the perquisites of fatherhood and husbandhood, with all their manifold associations with knowledge, eloquence, leadership, fertility, and strength. African kings tended to base their powers on ties to important lineages and clans situated strategically throughout their kingdoms. Marriage to women of such powerful lineages or clans, associated with different ritual and political prerogatives, bolstered kingship. Polygyny allowed kings to spread such ties over diverse sectors of their realms. In such ways kings often drew diverse and scattered groups into the orbit of royal politics. A king's in-laws could hope that one of their women would become the mother of a future king.

For these reasons royal marriage, kinship, and succession have always been crucial and problematical aspects of kingship in Africa. Broadly speaking, two options for such royal kin strategies were available. Kings could try to regulate and normalize succession by naming their heirs or by trying to institute a form of regular inheritance, such as succession by an eldest son or by the first-born son of the paramount and most privileged wife. This option might have prevented massive conflict over inheritance to a throne, but it automatically cut off many affiliated groups from their expectations of future access to the kingship. The alternative strategy was to declare no heir, and let the leaders of the key commoner lineages and clans elect a successor from the many contending royal heirs. This kept all the competing groups divided but continually absorbed in ongoing court affairs. It also led to periods of considerable conflict and disorder following the death of a king, until a successor was finally able to achieve power. Fratricide was a common feature of such turbulent royal politics.

Students of kingship around the world know that one of the main dangers to any king is his own royal relatives who seek to replace him. African kings, like kings elsewhere, depended on royal relatives yet also needed to subdue and weaken them because they were the chief intriguers against the kings' rule. One way that especially successful African kings in patrilineal societies, such as those among the Ganda of eastern Africa and the Zulu of southern Africa, sought to solve this political puzzle was to depend heavily on their mother's kin. Maternal kin would remain in power only so long as their kingly son ruled. Hence, royal maternal kin made loyal, dependable deputies.

Another way to secure loyal underlings was to commission royal servants (or even royal slaves) to form a protobureaucracy entirely dependent for its authority and even safety upon the king's favor. Such royal servants could not ordinarily aspire to rule on their own because they lacked the royal or aristocratic connections of kin to support them. Their inherently lowly status constituted their reliability. Such delegatory means were found to be particularly effective by the rulers of the interlacustrine kingdoms of eastern

Africa and the kingdom of Bénin, as well as by some of the kings of southern Africa and the Muslim emirs of western Africa. The creation of these incipient royal bureaucracies in some parts of Africa parallels similar processes in kingdoms elsewhere. For example, royal bureaucracies in Egypt, the ancient Near East, and China had their origins in similar royal strategies for solving the difficult search for loyal officials.

RULING VERSUS REIGNING

Finally, kings may rule or they may merely reign. Some African kings, such as those of Bénin, Buganda, and Asante, often ruled with great, even tyrannical power. Some rulers managed to undermine local privileged clans and kin groups whose traditional influence had initially supported them, but whose support now set limits to royal rule. As already noted, some ambitious kings augmented their powers by expanding the duties and authority of appointed royal officials and by correspondingly diminishing the traditional rights of privileged clans and aristocrats who expected to hold office by automatic rights of inheritance and tradition.

Another major means for augmenting kingly power was through warfare. As war leaders, kings gained powers to distribute newly acquired booty, slaves, and administrative offices governing those who had been conquered. Such benefits, being new to the kingdom, did not fall under any traditional rights of inheritance and might therefore be assigned however a king wished. It was hoped that those who received such bounty would be loyal to the generous king rather than to any elders of the traditional social order.

Kings were also held in respect and awe on account of the sheer inexplicability and fearsome nature of their judgments. Early accounts of some African kings are rife with anecdotes of mass killings and capricious punishments and rewards. Such terrifying and at times inscrutable behavior often enhanced the awe that subjects felt toward their king, just as it was thought that similar behavior by ancestral spirits or other supernatural beings merited awe from mortals. In contrast to such despotic rulers, other kings, such as those among the Shilluk and Anuak of the southern Sudan and the Jukun of Nigeria, look more like living icons who provided a ritual and spatial focus through whom diverse and struggling groups were able to articulate and compete for social statuses, but who held little actual political power. Such weak, more priestly rulers may be said to have reigned rather than ruled.

ORIGINS AND DIFFUSION OF KINGSHIP

Some scholars have sought to describe African kingship in terms of broader cultural-historical theories with wider political and ideological implications. The most persistent and popular such theory is one relating kingship in sub-Saharan Africa to kingship in Egypt and the Near East. Charles G. Seligman was one of the first anthropologists to promote such speculation. Such arguments have taken forms deeply implicated in both racist and political agendas. One theory is that notions of kingship in sub-Saharan Africa had their origins in ancient Egypt, spreading slowly by contact down the Nile watershed into eastern Africa and eventually all the way to southern Africa, or else across the Sahara into western Africa. Another theory holds that kingship was a sub-Saharan African concept that spread into Egypt and eventually the Near East.

Two points are clear. First, there has been a considerable flow of ideas and material culture not only up and down the Nile watershed but also in both directions across the Sahara. Second, it is demeaning to any people and culture, including those of sub-Saharan Africa, to think that any cultural concept, including that of monarchy, could not be repeatedly invented independently by many peoples all over the world. African kingships exhibit many common features, but this is because kingship involves similar structural and symbolic features everywhere from Africa to Meso-America and the Andes, and from Europe through Asia to the Pacific. There is no reason to believe African kingship has a single geographical source or that it is unique. Independent invention is a more attractive and plausible theory than cultural diffusion in accounting for such similarities. Human beings are capable of inventing similar social arrangements time and time again over much of the world. Kingship is not likely to be the invention of only one people in one place and at one time.

Two further, more contemporary issues remain to be considered. First, what are the key studies of kingship in Africa and why are they significant for the understanding of social life? Second, what are the present state and significance of kingships in Africa?

KEY STUDIES OF KINGSHIP

The works of E. E. Evans-Pritchard and Hilda Kuper were the pioneer accounts of kingship in Africa that renewed sociological interest after Frazer's earlier writings. In 1940 Evans-Pritchard published his monograph on the Anuak of the southern Sudan. The Anuak are a people with a relatively simple economic and social system that might lead researchers not to expect kingship. Evans-Pritchard describes Anuak kingship as functioning essentially as a prestigious ritual office that various Anuak kin groups struggled to occupy perhaps more for its prestige than for actual political power. This study reaffirmed a Frazerian view of kinship as primarily a priestly and ritual institution leading only later to more secular forms of authority as it gradually developed. After World War II, Evans-Pritchard's views were reiterated even more clearly and forcefully in his Frazer Lecture of 1948. There he reasserted a picture of African kings as ritual leaders precariously integrating an incipient, centralizing African polity. His points were especially influential on account of the prestige of the Frazer Lectures and because he illustrated his arguments by using the Shilluk of the southern Sudan, the very people on whom Frazer had first developed his theories.

In 1947 Hilda Kuper published the first masterful monograph on an African kingship, describing how it worked in a complex polity, that of the Swazi in southern Africa. Her study remains a classic, emphasizing the socioeconomic and political as much as the ritual aspects of kingship. Her study continues to prompt comment and re-analyses. The most famous of these was Max Gluckman's Frazer Lecture of 1952, in which he attempted to demonstrate how such rituals worked to support social order. His analysis has been repeatedly criticized (e.g., by T. O. Beidelman). It was followed by Monica Wilson's Frazer Lecture of 1959, which contrasted divine kingship among the Nyakyusa and Ngonde of southern Tanzania in terms of sacred versus secular functions of rule. By that time such writing had established kingship as a major and recurrent theme in political and religious studies in Africa, serving as a useful theme linking and contrasting "actual" and "symbolic" aspects of social motivation and organization.

Subsequently, an immense literature has described monarchical institutions over a wide part of Africa. Some of the most distinguished of these studies are by Alfred Adler (1982), Luc de Heusch (1982), Godfrey Lienhardt (1954, 1955), Audrey I. Richards (1961, 1969), and Michael Young (1966). Three other ethnographies merit special mention. Randall Packard (1981) examines the symbols and practices linking lower-level authority, such as that of chiefs, with more complex kingship; Simon Simonse (1992) describes actual ritual king killing of senile, ailing, or inept kings in the southern Sudan, a custom long thought to be only metaphorical and not actually ever done, even though Frazer assumed that it was; and John Pemberton and Funso Afolayan's study of Yoruba ritual kingship (1996), to date probably the single most detailed and sophisticated analysis of the rituals of African kingship yet published. It is, however, not possible to provide proper description here of the vast range of social studies now available on kingship in Africa. Gillian Feeley-Harnik (1985) has provided a thoughtful and detailed survey. Her article is especially valuable because, although it emphasizes African materials, it persuasively relates these writings to kingship elsewhere in the world and provocatively suggests how all these findings illuminate more fundamental social issues regarding the nature of and interrelations between authority, power, social organization, ritual, and belief.

PRESENT KINGSHIPS IN AFRICA

Aside from the constitutional monarchies of Lesotho and Swaziland in southern Africa, no autonomous kingdoms remain in Africa in the early twenty-first century. The ancient Christian kingdom of Ethiopia is no more, and the famous Tutsi kingdoms of Rwanda and Burundi have vanished. While only two kings rule, many still reign. The traditional kings of the Asante, Yoruba, and Bénin kingdoms, the emirs of northern Nigeria, and many other monarchs are still venerated and honored by their former subjects. While such rulers have lost most or all of their political powers, they remain as social icons embodying their peoples' history and cultural integrity. They are still rallying points for their people, who view them as sacred, living vehicles for continuing to express their regional and cultural identity despite the efforts of African national states that threaten to engulf and efface such local ethnicity. René Lemarchand provides a somewhat dated but useful survey of these threatened kingships. In the persistence of African monarchical values one can see that the ideas surrounding kingship continue to offer many Africans intensely valued symbols and rituals that the amorphous modern nation-state has often failed to provide.

See also **Ethnicity; Gender; Kinship and Affinity; Kinship and Descent; Queens and Queen Mothers; Religion and Ritual; Secret Societies; Symbols and Symbolism.**

BIBLIOGRAPHY

Adler, Alfred. *La mort est le masque du roi: La royauté sacrée des Moundang du Tchad*. Paris: Payot, 1982.

Beidelman, T. O. "Swazi Royal Ritual." *Africa* 36, no. 42 (1966): 373–405.

Evans-Pritchard, E. E. *The Political System of the Anuak of the Anglo-Egyptian Sudan*. Monographs on Social Anthropology No. 4. London: P. Lund Humphries & Co. Ltd., 1940.

Evans-Pritchard, E. E. "The Divine King among the Shilluk of the Nilotic Sudan." In *Social Anthropology and Other Essays*. New York: Free Press of Glencoe, 1962.

Feeley-Harnik, Gillian. "Issues in Divine Kingship." *Annual Review of Anthropology* 14 (1985): 273–313.

Fortes, Meyer. "Of Installation Ceremonies." *Proceedings of the Royal Anthropological Institute for 1967* (1968): 5–20.

Gluckman, Max. "ituals of Rebellion in South-East Africa." In *Order and Rebellion in Tribal Africa*. New York: Free Press of Glencoe, 1963.

Heusch, Luc de. *The Drunken King; or, The Origin of the State*, trans. Roy Willis. Bloomington: Indiana University Press, 1982.

Krige, Eileen Jensen, and J. D. Krige. *The Realm of a Rain-Queen: A Study of the Pattern of Lovedu Society*. New York: AMS Press, 1978.

Kuper, Hilda. *An African Aristocracy: Rank among the Swazi of Bechuanaland*. New York: Oxford University Press, 1947.

Lemarchand, René, ed. *African Kingships in Perspective: Political Change and Modernization in Monarchical Settings*. London: Cass, 1977.

Lienhardt, Godfrey. "The Shilluk of the Upper Nile." In *African Worlds: Studies in the Cosmological Ideas and Social Values of African Peoples*, ed. Daryll Forde. New York: Oxford University Press, 1954.

Lienhardt, Godfrey. "Nilotic Kings and Their Mothers' Kin." *Africa* 25, no. 1 (1955): 29–42.

Packard, Randall. *Chiefship and Cosmology: An Historical Study of Political Competition.* Bloomington: Indiana University Press, 1981.

Pemberton, John, III, and Funso S. Afolayan. *Yoruba Sacred Kingship: "A Power Like That of the Gods."* Washington, DC: Smithsonian Institution Press, 1996.

Richards, Audrey I. "African Kings and Their Royal Relatives." *Man: Journal of the Royal Anthropological Institute* 91 (1961): 135–150.

Richards, Audrey I. "Keeping the King Divine." *Proceedings of the Royal Anthropological Institute for 1968* (1969): 23–35. The Henry Myers Lecture of 1968.

Seligman, Charles Gabriel. *Egypt and Negro Africa: A Study in Divine Kingship.* New York: AMS Press, 1978.

Simonse, Simon. *Kings of Disaster: Dualism, Centralism, and the Scapegoat King in Southeastern Sudan.* New York: Brill, 1992.

Wilson, Monica. *Divine Kings and the "Breath of Men."* Cambridge, U.K.: Cambridge University Press, 1959.

Young, Michael W. "The Divine Kingship of the Jukun: A Re-evaluation of Some Theories." *Africa* 36, no. 1 (1966): 135–152.

T. O. BEIDELMAN

KINGSHIP. For African scholars, political anthropology began in 1940 with the publication of *African Political Systems* by E. E. Evans-Pritchard (1902–1973) and Meyer Fortes (1906–1943). In their preface, they contrast acephalous segmental societies, based upon lineage, with complex societies that have central institutions. The latter generally consist of kingdoms that the authors regarded as states or as state-like. This distinction produced a gray area of societies that reject the power, though not the social order, of the numerous chiefdoms whose size and institutions mean that they cannot be regarded as kingdoms.

Kingdom states are generally founded as a result of military conquest. Emmanuel Terray (b. 1935) believed the majority of states that emerged south of Middle Niger were created by soldiers of fortune who had broken away from the framework of lineage-based societies. There is a distinction between African states that are simply warlike and those that, although they intervene militarily in neighboring states' affairs if necessary (to carry off women, slaves, or wealth),

have as a central concern an ideology of Divine Kingship, though it is preferable to describe this as sacred kingship. Among the most important kingships is the Central African Republic Bandia. The legitimacy of the king is not based upon his ritual functions, as with other African monarchies. War is a requirement for prosperity. The ruling clan retains power by setting itself up as the provider of women, in order to establish client relationships. It is the practice of razzia, not exchange, that introduces these human and material commodities into the social system. The king, the absolute master of goods and people, personally directs military operations.

Sacred kingship does not have a common historical origin, although some authors claim to see the remote influence of ancient Egyptian civilization, or the presence of a prehistoric basis shared by the founders of these and the ancestors of the many other African sacred kingships that have survived into the twentieth century. It may be noted that there the military function was generally delegated to a substitute for the king, to the extent that the latter, who is ritually responsible for prosperity and general fertility—life forces—could not see a corpse nor shed a victim's blood. The king, although he did not personally take part in battle, benefited from the plunder. According to an oral tradition in the ancient empire of Ghana (now the name of a republic in West Africa), the king may not bear arms, nor go to war. At the beginning of the twentieth century, throughout Mali there were "strange kings without weapons or warriors, lacking the means of imposing anything by force, they possessed the power of veto on appeal" (Bazin, 375). Bazin believes that these arbitrators of disputes are descendants of the sultans, who were vassals in the kingdom of Mali in the seventeenth century and had the same title: *mansa.*

Sacred kingship appears under a wide range of guises that all may be reduced to the same structure that is outside the order of kinship. If a dynastic lineage exists, a magical transcendent power is thought to be present in it. This power is found at the center of the social organization and outside it, in nature, whose rhythms the sacred king controls. This position fascinates, enjoins respect and fear, and allows an understanding of the specific prohibitions that his somewhat lengthy initiation imposes upon the future king. There is a recurring trait in the initiations: the king's premature, quasi-sacrificial, killing. Rather than consider the African king invested with a sacred function to be a god the kingship can be seen as a kind of living fetish—a repository of spiritual power—condemned to die when his powers wane or after a certain number of years have elapsed.

THE KING AS HUNTER, TWIN, BLACKSMITH

Frequently, myth presents the dynastic founder as a hunter-hero who came from elsewhere, crossed a vast wilderness, and lingered in a place that is not domestic, but is the source of fertility. Many traditions are found in the forest or uncultivated land, where wild animals and spirits live. Whether he is filthy and hairy (the Moundang of Chad), or a highly civilized prince (a tale of the Luba-Lunda from the Democratic Republic of the Congo), the hunter-hero, the dynasty's ancestor, astounds the people who welcome him with his generous gifts of meat. The people offer in exchange one or two native wives (or that he should marry the leading female in the host group, as in the Lunda myth). He also receives supreme power, and it is either his warrior son or his distant descendant (Rwanda) who founds a state amid the native people. The hunter-hero precedes the arrival of the warrior king, providing a prosperity that had been lacking, or introducing a superior civilization. The initial gift by the stranger metaphorically represents the benefits that are expected from him and his successors.

The theme of the king-twin that sometimes appears alongside the hunter-king (Moundang), or on its own (Swazi), demonstrates the fertility of the ancestor who crossed and tamed the wilderness. He is linked with the fertility of animals that are multiparous, such as the parents of twins. The sacred king of the Kuba invites twins to his court; on his death he is regarded as a nature spirit. In mythology, the figure of the blacksmith-king also appears, possessing analogous attributes: the forge is associated with fertility, and iron-working artisans are central to the African cultural order. In many cases the initiation of a king contains an element that places the candidate for the sacred kingship outside of society (incest, anthropophagy, or some other transgression that symbolically frees the king from being subject to the laws of society). This aspect indicates his negative transcendence and transforms him into a sacred monster: hence the kinship is sometimes compared with evil

sorcery (Tio, Kuba). The sacred kingship meanwhile guarantees prosperity and fertility, as well as hierarchical order within the kingdom, while externally it ensures control of the forces of nature.

RITUAL REGICIDE

The quasi-sacrificial killing of the supreme leader is a recurring theme. The spiritual status of the sacred king, hemmed in by taboos, condemns him to death prematurely, unless a substitute victim (human or animal) can be found in his place.

The Swazi, peasant cattle breeders, are a homogenous ethnic group. They accept the authority of a king imposed by force. The mythical powers of the sacred king are thought to weaken every year at the time of the summer solstice. A great ritual is performed before the people and his army with alternating antiphons: in turn they praise the weakening of the king, then his strength. A ritual sacrifice brings about his renewal: a black ox is slaughtered in place of the king.

In many of the Nilotic societies in southern Sudan, chiefs considered responsible for rainfall are put to death in the event of drought. The status of rainmaker has been interpreted as having a positive ritual aspect, the negative side of which is prolonged drought. If drought occurs, the role of scapegoat (driving away the drought by killing the king) comes to the fore.

SACRED KINGSHIP AND SOCIOPOLITICAL STRUCTURE

Sacred ritual function already appears, albeit in embryonic form, in some small societies that lack central political institutions. The Samo (Burkina Faso) do not have a state, nor a chiefdom of any significance. Yet in every village, alongside the land chief is a mysterious figure: the *tyiri*, or rain chief. The first does nothing without the second, who is the more remarkable of the two. The tyiri is chosen by divination from a predetermined lineage and is the guarantor of village and inter-village peace, an idea linked to the common good—a notion related to both peace and rain—with the latter coming from his head. He is an ambivalent figure, like the sacred kings in centralized states. This ritualistic figurehead, who maintains peace and prosperity, is regarded as caught or bound, and is given dirty jobs. He must accept the harshness of his role, having no authority at his command. As peace-maker, the tyiri does not take part in war.

In the large Mongo linguistic group that inhabits the southwest of the great forest (Democratic Republic of the Congo), the word *ekopo* denotes the particular power accorded by the leopard skin. Closely related to sacred kingship, it is found in small village communities. The ekopo belongs to the *kumu* following due initiation, after he has generously distributed his wealth. In exchange, he is given magical religious powers over nature. Henceforth he controls the fate of a small group and is entitled to receive a hunting tribute. He is considered an outsider in the order of kinship. The status of kumu was introduced to the southern Ntomba by a cultural hero, half-man, half-beast. This myth originated further south, from south of the Kuba kingdom to north of the Kasai.

In the small village chiefdoms of the Rukuba of Nigeria, the future sacred chief, chosen from a specific patrilineage, is a prisoner of the group that has chosen him. When he is selected for the role, he flees and seeks refuge with his maternal uncle. During the ritual that he is forced to undergo, he unknowingly eats a piece of human flesh from a baby belonging to his own clan. He has thus broken one of the fundamental rules of the social fabric that he is supposed to maintain. He is symbolically cast out of the social system and becomes a scapegoat. Among the Rukuba, he is not responsible for agricultural success, but he is stripped of his functions in the event of a natural or social disaster. Although the Rukuba chief commits alimentary incest during his investiture ritual, actual incest is symbolically committed by the future king in a large number of central African kingdoms.

Among the Nilotic peoples, the different forms of power lie within a continuum that could be described as a transformation system. The sacred kingship exists among the Shilluk, who belong to the same linguistic group and pastoralist culture as the Nuer, and the Shilluk king was long held up as the model of sacred kingship in black Africa. Yet Nuer society, which is lineage-based and acephalous, with no individual having legislative, judicial, or executive powers, also exhibits the magical religious principles that underlie the Shilluk kingship, albeit in the embryonic form of the leopard-skin chief.

WAR AND PEACE

Although initiation made the king sacred in black Africa, it rarely made him a god, unlike in Egypt and in the majority of historical instances where the state of which the king became leader was confirmed via sacred scripture. The nature of the Ashanti king (Ghana) has been regarded as an exception, as he represented the sun on Earth, yet he was not considered a sun god like the pharaoh. Covered with gold jewelry, in the image of the sun, his body was even coated with gold dust. A golden throne contained the soul of the nation. The state in which the king was the center was based upon trade and military power. It was, however, clearly a sacred kingship and not a divine kingship. The king did not take part in war; in fact he was not allowed to have contact with death. His body had to be perfect, his soul, the source of life and prosperity, was purified every week. It rejoined the sun on his death, while his bodily soul became a spirit.

Several small states lie around the powerful Akan kingdom. The king of Akuapem, one of these states, strengthens his links to his human matrilineal ancestors via an initiation that profoundly alters his status. This takes place in a house containing six thrones (the symbols of the power of former kings) that have been blackened with sacrificial blood. Blindfolded, the future king chooses the throne upon which his fate depends. If a prince chooses a throne that belonged to a dead king who was linked with war, he will himself become a warrior-king. If the opposite is the case, he will become a peaceful king, concerned mainly with the well-being of his subjects, although the thrones were carried to the battlefield regardless.

The dynastic cycle that was formerly established for the kings of Rwanda also involved a choice between war and peace. The reigns of Mutara and of Yuhi were peaceful, both those being shepherd-kings who were symbolically concerned with the economic function of magic, the main source of wealth being livestock. The two intervening kings who succeeded Mutara, Kigeli and Mibambwe, were warrior kings. Here too, royal power was linked to the possession of fetish objects: some large drums served as palladia. In this instance however, the order of kings devoted to prosperity via magic/religion and warrior kings was carefully set out by tradition, whereas it was a matter of chance in the kingdom of Akuapem. The two main functions of sacred kingship (war and prosperity) were reunited in an important annual ceremony that brought together the king (as he grew weaker) and his army in order to reinvigorate the whole nation.

THE ROLE OF WOMEN IN SACRED KINGSHIP

The phallocratic nature of the male sex does not serve to explain completely why women do not take pride of place, as their nature would seem to require in a certain sense, in the exercise of the ritual of sacred kingship: the guarantee of fertility. The position of the queen of the Lovedu in southern Africa, who is responsible for rain, is an exception. Even here, it should be noted that actual power is exercised by her brothers in her place. This general disqualification of women is connected with the banishment of women in Africa to a special hut while they are menstruating. As an example, the menstruation of the autochthonous queen in Lunda mythology renders everything infertile, and the kingdom can only be restored to life with the arrival of a foreign hunter whom she will marry. This is a way for men to gain control of the reproductive power that they do not possess naturally.

In Ghana, the Ashanti king is not allowed to come into contact with a menstruating woman for any reason at all. According to a (mythical) Kuba oral tradition, at the dawn of time two queens were brought up to assume the royal throne. In order to conceal that the second was having her monthly menses, a court official had a fence built around the palace; one day when the queen was holding court, the officials present saw traces of menstrual blood and decided that never again should a woman have supreme power. In the interlacustrine region, such as in Swaziland, the mother of the king ruled alongside her son. This is not a sign of a former matrilineal regime there. The queen mother is encouraged not to have children while she holds this position, which allows her son to be unique, the one and only. He is chosen from his father's youngest sons.

In Rwanda there is a royal myth that is similar to the Oedipus legend. The king looked after the son who had been chosen, and separated from the rest of the court from an early age, as he grew up. Once he reached adulthood, the king committed suicide and his son succeeded him alongside his own mother. Such dramatic circumstances serve to stress the continuous, and yet discontinuous, nature of the patrilineal dynasty and its magical character. The mother-son link was symbolically emphasized in Swaziland, where the king and his mother were regarded as twins. A sociological fact may be added here: The selection of the queen mother allows several clans to be linked with royal power, because their male members are in effect the king's uncles on his mother's side. The Rwandans allowed three clans, reportedly of divine origin, to give birth to the heir to the throne. This has not stopped the history of Rwanda from being as troubled as one of Shakespeare's family plays.

AROUND THE SACRED KING

Participation in power by princes, members of the royal family, represents a difficult question. They are sometimes excluded, sometimes included. In societies where kinship and the kingship are governed by matrilineal rules, a large number of the polygamous king's children are ineligible to reign. They play an important part among both the Akan of Akuapem in Ghana and the Kuba in the Democratic Republic of the Congo. In the first case, the sons and grandsons of the king are his closest advisers; they form one of his councils, the other being made up of chiefs from seven non-royal matrilineages. In the case of the Kuba, the sons and grandsons of the king, who are normally wealthy because of their father or grandfather, constitute a privileged nobility with the same rank as the closest members of the ruling matrilineage. The most distantly related members of this lineage enjoy a privileged legal status (they are generally polygamous in a society where monogamy is the norm), but they are ineligible to hold one of the many political roles that are accessible to all free men.

The Kuba kingship is not dictatorial. Nine senior officials, with an official legal status, are collectively responsible for the sacred basket. Yet royal power is limited by various councils. The first is the coronation council that is permitted to reprimand the king if necessary. The second deals with current affairs that are reassessed by a third. The king attends these councils, and includes a large number of officials. Finally, there is a national council that includes the whole body of officials to deal with important subjects. The populace as a whole attends this council.

Among the patrilineal Mossi in the kingdom of Yatenga (Burkina Faso), the aristocratic lineage, consisting of all the descendants of the conquering warriors, the people of the spear, have complete control of political power. (They leave the native people the people of the earth, to carry on the cult that is related to the latter.) However, the sons of the owner of a village are the only ones who hold such positions and a number of aristocrats are thus permanently excluded from power. The sacred king, the supreme head of the most important aristocratic lineage, makes an alliance with the people of the earth at his investiture and becomes sacred. Although he is the master of force the king takes no part in war. A war chief replaces that role for him.

The physiognomy of power is different among the Bamum of Cameroon. At the end of the nineteenth century, shortly before the Europeans arrived, King Njoya converted to Islam. This religion is widespread throughout modern sub-Saharan Africa where it guarantees social advancement. At that time, however, it advocated the military role of the king. It is evident that the magical and religious powers of the king of the Bamum were reduced, limited to sacrifices to royal ancestors. The king led his armies in person. His authority stemmed directly from war. He engaged in continuous warfare to acquire more women and he distributed a large number with whom he had children, thus increasing his political alliances. He also captured an impressive number of male slaves, who swelled the ranks of his servants and played an essential part in the administration of the state. This relied entirely upon the existence of patrilineages. A certain number of these were founded by the principal servants of the kingdom. The lineage chiefs had direct access to the king. The number of lineages increased without becoming segmented: they were all linked to the royal line. The state therefore formed a vast lineage of the maximum possible size. Apart from the king's advisers (who were generally lineage chiefs), various hierarchical secret societies played an important political role. They were of two kinds: one of princes who were allowed to vote; the other consisting exclusively of principal servants and those descended from lesser nobility. A similar structure exists in many kingdoms in this region.

CASTES AND CLANS: KINSHIP AND CLIENT LINKS

In the interlacustrine civilization, in the east of Central Africa, there were a variety of kingdoms of differing importance. Livestock breeders and farmers were opposed to one another on the highest levels. The pastoralists were of higher rank than the farmers in Rwanda. The absolute ruler of two million people at the end of the nineteenth century, the king of Rwanda relied upon a standing army. He handed out positions as he pleased to high-ranking members of the pastoralist Tutsi nobility, who owned the majority of the cattle. Client links held the political structure together. The important nobles in the Tutsi aristocracy were, in a personal capacity, clients of the king, from whom he received vast herds as usufruct. In some parts of the country, this client system also created links of dependency between rich Tutsi (though they were not all rich) and Hutu peasants.

The same sociopolitical division existed between the largely nomadic Hima livestock breeders and the Iru farmers among the northern neighbors of Rwanda, and the Nkole of Uganda, although the numbers were much fewer. Their hierarchy was distinct and they formed a separate castes. Not only did they not marry each other, but only the Hima could own livestock. The pastoralists were the armed clients of the sacred king, who received individual oaths of loyalty. The landed chiefs, all clients of the king, had those collecting Iru taxes under their command.

The Rwandan and Nkole systems reduced the number and importance of patrilineal clans considerably (including the Tutsi/Hima and the Hutu/Iru). On the other hand, the petty kings who ruled over the Haya in the far northeast of Tanzania took into account the clan, the ancient institution based upon fictive kinship, while preserving the hierarchy of breeders and farmers. The sovereigns reserved the right to ennoble certain Iru clans for services rendered and demote Hima clans. The princes who were members of the royal clan held hereditary client fiefdoms, which may explain the slight influence of these small kingdoms. The fiefdoms became independent eventually.

The royal clan of Bunyoro arrived at another solution: the abolition of all stratification between the pastoralists (Huma) and Iru farmers. This was a medium-sized state (around 100,000 inhabitants). The clans, and there were many of them, were often part Huma, part Iru. This distinction played no political role, however. It was "now hardly visible" when Beattie stayed there from 1951 to 1953. The sacred king made use of the social mobility of individuals, whatever their origin. In Bunyoro, the landed chiefs, who were appointed and dismissed at-will by the king, were his direct clients. In sociological terms, however, the sacred king was connected to the whole of the population; he was linked by marriage to most of the clans. The primary socioeconomic groups were not in castes or pseudo-castes on the basis of how much livestock they owned, like in Ankole and Rwanda; they were likely to be merged together in mixed clans. Their representatives at court undertook a variety of duties.

None of the structures in the interlacustrine region can be likened to European feudalism, although all of them are based upon a client system. In another traditional Ugandan kingdom, the patrilineal clan was the backbone of political organization, the formerly powerful Buganda. No social or cultural stratification between pastoralists and farmers occurred here. There were a large number of diverse clans (around forty) and each one had its own territory. In addition, they had a direct relationship with the court, for which they had to undertake particular duties.

Among the Ganda, just as among the Moundang of Chad, the appearance of kingship has produced only a minimal social hierarchy. In these two instances, the developing state has not destroyed the existing clan system. Among the Moundang, royal children are themselves integrated in a clan with the same rights as the others. The same applies to princes who are the descendents of dead kings: they have their own clan and are not a privileged aristocracy.

SACRED KINGSHIP AND ECONOMY

The method of domestic production has hardly changed at all, if one examines the thriving Kuba kingdom and their neighbors, the Lele of Kasai. The Lele are a lineage society unlike Kuba; they possess a failed or degenerate, or in any event, impotent, kingship. The principal change is the intensity of the exchanges. The Kuba are more hardworking than the Lele, and this change in behavior is connected with a number of significant political factors. The sacred kingship is located at the center of a network of internal and intertribal exchanges, characterized by numerous markets. The role of kinship is conspicuously changed; in particular, the role of matrilineal lineage has become solely economic. Although it remains pivotal in the social structures of the Lele, for the Kuba it has become purely economic. Every lineage, whose other functions are in every respect nonexistent, used the income they gained to establish mutual insurance funds for the benefit of their members. They try hard to attain one of the many positions that are available within the main Bushong chiefdom. The conclusion of Marshall Salhins is striking: "In the course of primitive evolution, main control over the domestic production seems to pass from the formal solidarity of the kingship structure to its political aspects. As the structure is politicized especially as it is centralized in ruling chiefs, the household economy is mobilized in a larger social cause" (1972).

Sacred kingship, as an illusory mechanism of production, must have played a decisive role in this process. Nonetheless, interpretations have attempted to explain the growth of the institution on the basis of economic factors. Thus, some think that it is possible to explain the appearance of the kingdom of Kongo before the fifteenth century via the presence of its center of influence on the crossroads of two ancient trading routes. The position of kumu was achieved by means of large payments and Vansina links the development of this institution, which predates the sacred kingship on the Congolese coast, to economic factors: the leader gains support if he is located on an arterial trading route.

The forms of African sacred kingship can be separated according to a historical typology that takes into account the level of development of certain features, particularly trade and markets, but also other factors strictly related to the system of political organization. Economic factors also contributed to the development of the states of West Africa. For example, the prosperity of the old empire in Ghana relied on the gold trade. In general, states that are based on oral tradition are fragile. Politically they are weak, however ritually strong they may be at their center. Few of the ancient kingdoms have managed to establish themselves within the borders of the new independent states, the majority of which were created after colonization.

See also **Initiation; King Lists and Chronologies; Kings and Kingdoms; Kinship and Descent; Queens and Queen Mothers; Women.**

BIBLIOGRAPHY

Adler, Alfred. *La mort est le masque du roi.* Paris: Payot, 1982.

Adler, Alfred. *Le pouvoir et l'interdit: Royauté et religion en Afrique noire.* Paris: Albin Michel, 2000.

Bazin, J. "Princes désarmés, corps dangereux: les rois-femmes de la région de Segu." *Cahiers d'études africaines* 28 (1988): 375–441.

Claessen, Henri. "Specific Features of the African Early State." In *The Study of the State*, ed. Henri Claessen and Peter Skalnik. The Hague: Mouton de Gruyter, 1981.

Dampierre, Eric de. *Un ancien royaume Bandia du Haut-Oubangui.* Paris: Plon, 1967.

Dieterlen, Germaine, and Diarra Sylla. *L'Empire de Ghana: Le Wagadou et les Traditions de Yéréré.* Paris: Karthala, 2000.

Evans-Pritchard, Edward. *The Divine Kingship of the Shilluk of the Nilotic Sudan.* Cambridge, U.K.: Cambridge University Press, 1948.

Evans-Pritchard, Edward, and Meyer Fortes, ed. *African Political Systems*, Reissue edition. London: Trubner, 2005.

Heusch, Luc de. *Du pouvoir. anthropologie politique des sociétes d'afrique centrale.* Nanterre: Société d'Ethnologie, 2002.

Izard, Michel. *Gens du pouvoir, gens de la terre. Les institutions politiques de l'ancien royaume du Yatenga (Bassin de la Volta Blanche).* Paris: Maison des Sciences de l'Homme, 1995.

Jensen Krige, Eileen. *The Realm of a Rain-Queen: A Study of the Pattern of the Lovedu Society.* London: Publisher for the International African Institute by the Oxford University Press, 1943.

Kuper, Hilda. *An African Aristocracy. Rank among the Swazi.* Teaneck, N.J.: Holmes and Meier, 1980.

Maquet, J. *Le système des relations sociales dans le Ruanda traditionnel.* Tervuren: Musée royal du Congo belge, 1954.

Meyerowitz, Eva. *The Sacred State of the Akan.* London: Faber, 1951.

Muller, Jean-Claude. *Le roi bouc émissaire: Pouvoir et rituel chez les Rukuba du Nigeria Central.* Québec: Serge Fleury

Salhins, Marshall. *Stone Age Economics.* Somerset, N.J.: Aldine Transaction, 1972.

Simonse, Simon. *Kings of Disaster: Dualism, Centralism and the Scapegoat King in Southeastern Sudan.* Leiden, the Netherlands: Brill Academic Publishers, 1992.

Tardits, Claude, ed. *Princes et serviteurs du royaume: Cinq études de monarchies africaines.* Paris: Société d'Ethnologie, 1987.

Vansina, Jan. *Le royaume kuba.* Tervuren, Belgium: Musée Royal de l'Afrique Centrale, 1964.

LUC DE HEUSCH

KINJIKITILE (c. 1870–1905). Kinjikitile Ngwale of Ngarambe was born about 1870, an Ngindo-speaker of the northern Ikemba descent group, in present-day Tanzania. He was executed by hanging on August 4, 1905. He rose to prominence as one of three spirit mediums who provided the ideology for the Maji Maji revolt of 1905 to 1907 against the administration of what was then German East Africa. In 1904 concerns about agricultural vulnerabilities began to emerge from local shrines; these apprehensions quickly grew into a millenarian assertion that God would return to earth to destroy the Germans with floods and wild animals. Kinjikitile and the other spirit mediums administered a liquid medicine (in Swahili, *maji* means "water") to local people, tying them to the movement while conferring invulnerability against bullets.

Kinjikitile was not a military leader as such, or even the most senior medium in the region. But the military conflict began in his area, and his execution at the outset of the rebellion, marked by a defiant speech from the gallows, attracted contemporary observers. His activities also made him a fitting nationalist icon for post-independence Tanzanians, a position which was reinforced when Gilbert Gwassa, the first Tanzanian doctoral student in history at the University of Dar es Salaam, wrote about him. On the centennial of his death in 2005 his role was still important, but in a much more balanced way than it had been five decades earlier.

See also **Colonial Policies and Practices; Prophetic Movements; Tanzania.**

BIBLIOGRAPHY

Gwassa, Gilbert. "Kinjikitile and the Ideology of Maji Maji." In *The Historical Study of African Religion*, ed. Terence O. Ranger and Isaria N. Kimambo. Berkeley: University of California Press, 1972.

Wright, Marcia. "Maji-Maji." In *Revealing Prophets: Prophecy in Eastern African History*, ed. David M. Anderson and Douglas M. Johnson. London: James Currey, 1995.

LORNE LARSON

KINSHASA. Kinshasa originated as a small trade station, established by the Belgian King Leopold II's (1835–1909) envoy Henry Morton Stanley upon his arrival on December 1, 1881, between authochtonous Teke in Ngaliema Bay along the Congo River. Renamed in 1966 from Léopoldville, it became the Belgian Congo's main urban center between 1908 and 1960. In 1940, Léopoldville was home to approximately 50,000 inhabitants. At the end of World War II, the number of residents had doubled, increasing further to 200,000 in 1950 and reaching 400,000 in 1960. In the early twenty-first century, the capital of the Democratic Republic of the Congo has developed into the second largest city south of the Sahara, inhabited by at least 6 million people.

In the early decades of the twentieth century, Léopoldville developed along the axis Kintambo-Kalina. Kintambo consisted of the city's first main industrial sites. Kalina, present-day Gombe, became the capital's administrative area and housed offices, residential villas, and the headquarters of

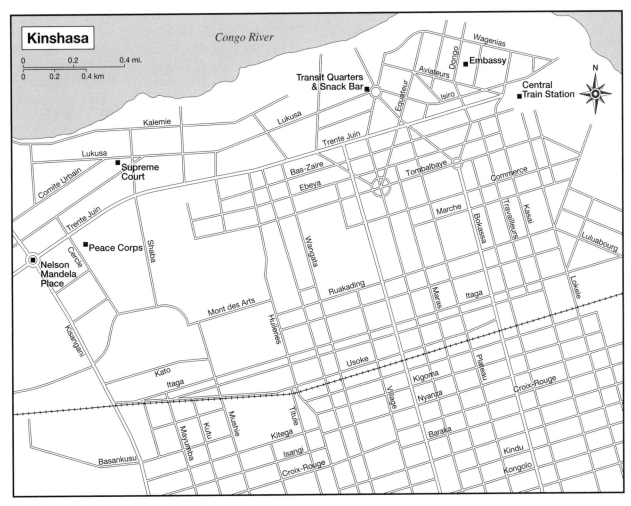

U.S. DEPARTMENT OF STATE (1983); ARCHIVES AT THE PERRY-CASTANEDA LIBRARY MAP COLLECTION, UNIVERSITY OF TEXAS AT AUSTIN

several Catholic congregations such as the Jesuits and Scheut. Gombe has retained that function to the present day. Kintambo and Kalina were soon connected by a railroad. Around this axis gradually developed commercial centers and several native quarters and settlements, as well as a number of strategically located garrisons occupied by the soldiers of the *Force Publique*, the colonial power's military arm. Mostly recruited among Bangala from the distant Equateur Province, these soldiers became the motor behind the development of Lingala as the city's major lingua franca.

From the beginning, Léopoldville emerged as a racially segregated city with a strict demarcation line between a central white Ville and a peripheral African city, the polyethnic *cité indigène* (of which Kinshasa, Barumbu, and Lingwala form the oldest neighborhoods). The colonial economic necessities also occasioned a demographic, strongly gendered, segregation. Before 1930, the male-female ratio in Léopoldville's indigenous neighborhoods was three to one. At the end of World War II men still outnumbered women two to one. This imbalance reflected not only the colonial endeavor to control the city's growth rate but also the simple fact that these indigenous quarters mainly functioned as depots of cheap African labor, in which there was room for neither women nor the unemployed. In the indigenous *cités* a new urban musical culture and associational life emerged, in new spaces of leisure—the bars or *nganda*. These meeting places also generated a local political awareness that eventually led to the end of the colonial rule in 1960.

After independence the state gradually abandoned all efforts at formal urban planning. Since then, Kinshasa has expanded into an endless and continually growing sprawl of informal peripheral urban zones.

See also **Congo, Democratic Republic of the; Stanley, Henry Morton.**

BIBLIOGRAPHY

De Boeck, Filip, and Marie-Françoise Plissart. *Kinshasa: Tales of the Invisible City.* Gent, Belgium: Ludion, 2004.

Lafontaine, Jean S. *City Politics. A Study of Léopoldville 1962–63.* Cambridge, U.K.: Cambridge University Press, 1970.

Trefon, Theodore, ed. *Reinventing Order in the Congo: How People Respond to State Failure in Kinshasa.* London: Zed Books, 2004.

FILIP DE BOECK

KINSHIP AND AFFINITY. The main contribution to the study of traditional kinship and marriage in Africa has been Alfred Radcliffe-Brown's (1881–1955) introduction to *African Systems of Kinship and Marriage* (1950), which in the early twenty-first century remains a brilliant essay on kinship in preindustrial societies, with most of the examples taken from that continent. Lucy Mair's (1901–1986) *African Marriage and Social Change* (1969) is a comparable survey devoted to marriage alone. Given the diversity of marriage and kinship systems, and given rapidly changing conditions, it is difficult to make general statements about Africa.

The societies of Africa in the early twentieth century (here described as traditional) were characterized by the dominance of unilineal descent groups (clans and lineages tracing descent through only a single parent, either the mother—matrilineal—or the father—patrilineal), mainly of a patrilineal kind. However, in western and Central Africa, matrilineal clans were the rule in some large areas (the Asante of Ghana and the Bemba of Zambia were type cases); in some parts, generally situated between the two, clans of both kinds were to be found in the same society (the Yakö of Nigeria and the LoDagaa of Ghana). Other societies, both among hunters such as the !Kung and in states such as the Lozi of Zambia and the Gonja of Ghana, were marked by the absence of lineages and by the consequent stress on cognatic kinship (wherein descent is traced through both parents) resembling, in some limited respects, the kind of descent known in Western Europe as bilateral.

In his analysis, Radcliffe-Brown examined Africa from a general theoretical point of view and was concerned to point to structural principles, such as those of descent (cognatic and the unilineal); the (external) unity of the sibling groups; the solidarity and unity of the family; the classificatory systems of terminology; the generation principle, involving the inequality between proximate generations and the merging of alternate generations; and the principle of the unity of the lineage group. One of his major contributions is insistence upon the social (rather than the biological sense emphasized in North America and Europe) nature of kinship that leads to a discussion of the female father (a woman who marries another woman and who will have children on her behalf), of ghost unions (whereby a woman has children on behalf of a dead man), and of the more general breaking down of concepts such as marriage into a range of possible rights and duties. Such an analysis clarifies the nature of bridewealth and parenthood and makes it possible to compare different systems.

Radcliffe-Brown also touched upon what Meyer Fortes (1906–1983) referred to as the developmental cycle of domestic groups; Fortes discussed the gradual dissolution of the parental family following the death of parents and the weakening of the household by the departure of children (where that takes place). These analyses point to two types of domestic groups: kinship (the family) and residential (the household), though the indigenous terms are often the same. Extended households occur when children of one sex stay and their spouses arrive; similar extensions may be based on cognatic or uterine ties.

Under shifting agriculture, there is a need for generous access to reserves of fallow land, and its provision was one important role of the lineage that asserts claims for its members over an area within which they may move their farms. If the population was sparse, there was no need for much control. If the population was dense, land tended to be attached to smaller units, or, individualized.

With easy access to resources, families would not be expected to try to limit the number of children. Daughters did not share in the property of their fathers and were not differentially endowed at marriage. In fact, they attracted the bridewealth from other families necessary to pay out later to other groups for the women to marry their brothers. Girls were as necessary as boys, and there is no evidence of any fertility stopping rule, or indeed of any tendency to prefer children of one sex.

In Africa, sons received no specific endowment at marriage—they simply moved onto what land was available. This meant that people were concerned with having too few children, regardless of gender, rather than too many. Bridewealth was standardized for the community rather than individual and variable amounts, as was the case with the dowry elsewhere in the world. Ancestor worship and support for the elderly, whether of men or women, continued whether there were few offspring or a surplus. There was no need to calculate the downward transmission of resources, especially the basic means of production, either to maintain family status externally in a differentiated system (and Africa because of the limited productivity of how technology was not differentiated with regard to landholding) or internally with regard to the siblings; it makes no sense to think of primogeniture when there is little to conserve—even political offices tended to be transmitted laterally through a mass dynastic group rather than linearly from father to son. There was effectively no inheritance between spouses. That is, husbands and wives were not brought together by a conjugal fund (that may take many forms) and therefore were not separated from their kin in the same way as in the classic Chinese or Indian patterns. The latter in Europe and Asia led in general to somewhat smaller households and farm units.

Lineages (though often overplayed in the literature, to the detriment of families and households) are a widespread feature of African society, their importance being related to the need for reserves of land for pastoralism or for swidden (shifting) agriculture, over which a group exercises control, as well as to defense, to offense, to local solidarity, to marriage, and to religious practice. These lineages were groups of unilineally defined kinfolk, with access to land and sometimes to political or other sorts of office. The most extensive were in effect clans (the members of which technically do not have precise genealogical links), and the smallest (or minimal) were lineages linked to the structure of the household. In the last analysis, land was often viewed as collectively owned by a lineage, although smaller groups within it, especially the domestic unit, engaged in production and possessed primary rights of access. In acephalous societies, without institutionalized rulers, lineages were critical to sociopolitical organization, providing the candidates for specific (largely ritual) roles.

The importance of the lineage has been questioned by anthropologists who have worked in societies where cognatic links through both parents have been of greater importance. In Africa, the changing conditions of work and ideology are undoubtedly eroding the significance of descent groups, but observers attest to their importance in much of earlier Africa. In every society, extended kinship ties continue to play a large part in people's lives.

More recent studies introduce an element of agency and negotiation into kinship studies, arguing that the Radcliffe-Brown model was too static in dealing with social structure. Anthropologists in the 1930s had virtually no historical material to go on, as they were dealing with oral societies and therefore could not deal with historical agency in recent history. Nevertheless, the actual situation also led to change. In any case, even changing situations display some kind of structure for one to negotiate, some habitus to inhabit. The elements of choice created by Christian and globalized influence rather than earlier local ones is important not so much in introducing a measure of flexibility into earlier structures (though this doubtless needs to be done) as in attempting to delineate the present changes in the situation, also an imperative. However, one must differentiate between the current rural and more structured context and the market-oriented individualistic behavior of city dwellers. One problem of fieldwork is that observations take place at different times, so that the modern is never simply a comment on the past, just as observers in the colonial period often neglected the district commissioner and the mission.

Kinship in sub-Saharan Africa was never limited to lineage ties. Lineages were largely exogamous (encouraging marriage outside the group), in contrast to lineages in the Near East and North Africa that encouraged endogamy (marriage within the group, in Muslim societies to the father's brother's daughter). Thus every individual had significant ties not only through his or her father (in patrilineal societies) but also through his or her mother and her lineage (in matrilineal societies). Hence the mother's brother was significant in many life-cycle rituals, providing support for his sister's children, a situation that is enacted in various rites. Such ties often led outside the locality and were therefore especially valuable in providing a haven when the local community was affected by drought, war, pestilence, or other calamities.

The traditional system in Africa required a high degree of cooperation between members of the same household (family) and lineage (or other wider grouping of kin or community). Given the absence of government services and of centralized welfare institutions, there was considerable dependence upon kith and kin. Orphanhood, widowhood, and divorce, although always personal tragedies (despite the assumptions of some European family historians and demographers), were not faced alone. Although in certain regions chiefs had an obligation to supervise those suspected of witchcraft or other dangerous individuals such as identical twins, government traditionally played a radically different role than it began to do, at least in small measure, following the division of Africa among colonial powers beginning in the 1880s, and especially with postindependence moves toward social development. Neither ecclesiastical nor secular charity played any great part until the advent of Christian missions.

Although Muslims made some provision for the deprived in the form of the Friday *saddaqq* (alms) and other institutionalized gift-giving, there was not the sustained surplus to set up trusts or foundations of the kind widely found throughout Europe and Asia. The difference is profound and long standing. As early as the Sumerian code of Ur-Nammu (late third millennium BCE), provision was made for state protection of orphans, widows, and the poor from ill-treatment and abuse. Over time such provisions expanded. In the virtual absence of such arrangements in Africa, the kin group was of correspondingly greater importance, as it continues to be in the early twenty-first century, although often on a reduced scale, especially because it is clear that the current economies have difficulty supporting the average citizen, let alone the weak.

It is this continuing interdependence, although less strong than before, that often supports women and their children in rural areas while their husbands are away working in cities or industrial complexes; that contributes to the return fares of these migrants in distress; and that helps with the expenses of relatives' schooling—all of which, in the short term at least, reinforce interaction and mutual dependencies. In this sense extended ties of kinship (or extended families) are critical aspects of contemporary Africa. And although in Tunisia in the twenty-first century, as in China and India earlier in the twentieth century, such dependencies may be rejected by the very modernizing young who have so often benefited from them, they are essential to situations in which the community can neither supply nor afford other forms of welfare. In other words, such ties need to be preserved (or, better, left alone), even though agricultural and other experts feel that they are frustrated in their attempts at development by the absence of the kind of individualized tenurial systems that exist in Europe and North America. One cannot easily have the one with the other, and a too-heavy dose of individualizing could reduce a community to a moral desert populated by people in distress. No growth will compensate for such an outcome; morality and welfare are intrinsic components of all development, of all economic activity.

The presence of lineages in no way excludes a lower level of organization, based on domestic groups. Nor yet a more inclusive one based on the state. The wider lineages engage in political and ritual activities at the local level; it is the households (or other domestic units) that provide the groups for farming, for consumption, and for much of everyday life. Compared with populations in Eurasia, population in Africa was relatively sparse, kin ties were often widely dispersed, the associated kinship rights and duties were complex, and the opportunities for full-time specialization were restricted by available technology and by demand. Most domestic groups, even of craftsmen, engaged in agriculture, usually forming farming groups of limited size. In the 1950s, the average farming group among the LoWiili of northern Ghana was one of the largest reported (11.1 persons); in the 1958 aggregate United Nations census the average size of household (or perhaps houseful) for African countries varied between 3.5 and 5.0, rural Tanzania averaging 3.9 and urban Zaire 4.0.

In most societies, the core of the domestic group is a family, either a conjugal pair and their children, or a man and two (occasionally more) wives and children, or a lineal extended family (parents, sons and their wives, and their children), or a laterally expanded family that includes brothers and their wives. However, in some matrilineal societies (and some cognatic ones) more emphasis may be placed upon the mother-daughter tie, with husbands joining their wives only for a period. In these societies, even when the husband does gain the right of bride removal, the children and the wife are likely to return to her kin, leading to a kind of divorce that has been referred to as terminal separation. As an institution, divorce is widespread in Africa, though it appears to have been less common

among some patrilineal groups that incorporate wives into the husband's lineage. However, it is not clear that this term provides an adequate description, because wives (as distinct from slaves) always retain some complementary filiation ties with their natal families and lineages, which remain important for the children.

The appearance of incorporation is provided by the prevalence of bridewealth transactions (though these are substantially less pervasive in matrilineal societies). Most marriages involve the transfer of substantial amounts of goods or cattle from the kin of the groom to the kin of the bride. Such transfers cannot be satisfactorily interpreted as the purchase of brides; what they accomplish is the transfer of rights in the woman: her sexuality, her fertility, and her domestic services. From now on, her adultery incurs a debt to the husband's lineage to which any children will belong. At the same time, she acquires some rights in the husband. Divorce requires a return of some part of the bridewealth transfers, and although young children may originally accompany the mother, they will be expected to return to the husband's home upon maturation.

Marriage is generally out rather than in, except when the Islamic preference exists for marriage to the father's brother's daughter (thus between members of the same patrilineal lineage). Otherwise cousin marriage is rare, certainly in a prescribed form. Marriage with the mother's brother's daughter was important among the Lovedu (northern South Africa) and father's-sister-daughter marriage brought back what had been dispersed at a previous generation. But these existed in preferential rather than prescriptive form. However, widow inheritance (or the levirate—marriage of a widow by the brother of her deceased husband) was practiced everywhere as a way of looking after widows of guarding marital investment and of providing children for dead members.

Dowry, as distinct from bridewealth, is rare in Africa; except under Islam, women do not usually inherit part of their father's property, but only that of their mother. As mentioned, there effectively is no conjugal fund. When a woman enters marriage, she may be given kitchen utensils, but she does not normally acquire other types of property. Access to land comes through her husband, not her parents.

The average age at which women marry varies regionally from below seventeen to about twenty-two. The lowest ages are in western Africa and the highest in eastern Africa; the figures seem to have remained stable over time, with the possible exception of a shift in Kenya to a later age. The age at which men marry varies more radically but is considerably later than for women. The differential marriage ages for men and women relate to the rates of polygyny and of widow remarriage, as younger men must not be allowed to marry in order to provide multiple wives for even a small portion of older men, and widows are at a premium as marriage partners for widowers or other unmarried older males.

One of the most striking features of African domestic life, even compared with the Muslim states of the Mediterranean littoral (where up to four wives are permitted by law), is the high rate of plural marriage. Polyandry, the marriage of one woman to more than one man, was rare if nonexistent earlier in Africa, although there are cases of a younger brother (especially a twin) being allowed conjugal rights, in particular in the case of the original couple's childlessness. There were occasions where one woman took a plurality of partners in a situation of polycoity that resembled prostitution, an institution that has increased rapidly with the growth of towns and the physical separation of the partners in a marriage recognized in a rural community.

Polygyny, the marriage of one man to more than one woman, was common. Whereas in Islamic societies the rate rarely was more than 4 percent of marriages, in Africa it reached a third. In a survey of polygyny in Africa, the mean percentage of married men who were polygynists was 24.7 percent in East Africa, 33.8 percent in western Sudan, and 43 percent on the Guinea coast, with a mean for sub-Saharan Africa of 35 percent. A 1997 survey based upon the Demographic and Health Surveys is limited to women in contemporary plural marriages that showed 30–50 percent in West Africa and 20–35 percent in East. The survey adopted a categorical distinction between polygyny and monogamy, but it should be remembered that most marriages are monogamous at any specific moment, whereas most also have periods of polygyny.

Polygyny, marriage age, and household size: east-west differences		
	West Africa	East Africa
Polygyny	more	less
Marriage of women	earlier	later
Marriage of men	later	earlier
Household size	larger	smaller

Table 1.

The rate of polygyny is related to household size, which tends to be larger in West Africa than in East Africa. Size is affected by the degree of polygyny not only because of the larger number of wives and children per married man (not per woman), but also because the greater extent of plural marriage means that men's marriages are delayed. Men continue to work with their fathers for a longer period of time because they cannot afford to set off on their own without a wife. Family fission is thus postponed. In addition, if the women marry earlier, the men may be married to more wives for a shorter space of time than in monogamous situations. The East African–West African differences are summarized in Table 1.

Later marriage for women is, by and large, connected with simpler households, whereas earlier unions are associated with more complex ones. The reasons are obvious. Given the young age of marriage of most women in contemporary Africa, as in northern India, they are hardly in a position to set up separate households, even if their husbands are considerably older. Rather, they may set up separate cooking units (hearths) within a more complex dwelling group, in which other tasks are carried out cooperatively. Such is the situation, for example, among the LoDagaa of northern Ghana.

Two conditions under which a separate residence becomes possible for the young wife are when the husband's mother is a widow and when domestic servants are available. In rural Africa, there was no institution of domestic service by slaves, who, if they were women (as most were), tended to become co-wives. One aspect of the widespread practice of the noncrisis (that is, not orphans) fostering of children lay in their provision of domestic services, but this was rarely the major feature of a custom that took the form of care of kin by older women rather than by the employment of unrelated servants. The role of grandparents as caretakers is particularly important in some migrant situations, where the wife is working or where the family have been disrupted by AIDS. This has proved a basic focus for recent research.

Polygyny, of course, is widely practiced in many regions of the world. But in Africa it displayed a different pattern from that in Asia (at least in the major societies of that continent) in terms of rates. In Asia, fewer than 5 percent of marriages are polygynous, even in Islamic areas. This contrasts to Africa's much higher rate of one-third. The large majority of these were duogynous, a factor that, especially when combined with divorce, meant that most couples in Africa (and their children) lived for part of their lives in such unions.

The results of polygyny for household structure are significant. Widespread polygyny is possible because of a great difference in marriage age, not because of differential sex ratios (these were more evenly balanced at birth than in Eurasian populations). For instance, in extreme cases (e.g., the Konkomba of northern Ghana) men married at between thirty-five and forty, preempting mates by infant betrothal. The difference was also partly made up by the greater longevity of women, who were rarely unmarried even as elderly widows where widow inheritance prevailed. Indeed, the competition is such that there has recently been a tendency among the Konkomba to preempt the unborn child of a pregnant woman (that is, claim it in the event that it turns out to be a girl, for future marriage), further increasing the differential betrothal age. At the same time, the opportunities to escape from such arrangements have become greater (albeit fewer for women than for men), mainly by leaving the neo-traditional rural sector for work in urban areas.

Although increased migration to towns since the 1960s has meant that initially a man is often separated from his wife, this has not substantially lowered polygyny rates. A survey of Accra, the capital of Ghana, carried out in 1971–1972 showed that, of 100 married males, 39 were married polygynously; this figure is higher than for some African cities (for example, Abidjan, 15). At the same time it is higher than the overall rate for Ghana, which, according to the 1960 census postenumeration survey was 26, which in turn is low in comparison with

Guinea (38) and Dahomey (31). Polygyny in the urban setting seems to have increased rather than declined, but it takes a different form, as René Clignet showed for Côte d'Ivoire. Each of the several wives of one man may have a different home, rather than living in parts of a single compound, as is the case in rural areas (Only in crowded slums and in planned resettlement villages may two wives be observed living in the same room.).

The effects of widespread polygyny are radical. Women marry early, soon after menstruation (and may be betrothed even earlier), and their fertility is less than in monogamous unions. If they are childless (or otherwise unsatisfactory from the man's point of view), they are supplemented, often supplanted, rather than divorced; if they are widowed early (as is likely to happen with later marriages for men), they tend to become the wives of other men, by the levirate, or widow inheritance; in the first case, the children they bear are considered to be fathered by their dead husband—that is, claimed by his surviving relatives as a legacy. In Ghana, the university-educated group displays the lowest rate of polygyny, with 19 percent of marriages, according to a survey published in 1978. But the effect of education was nonlinear; for those with no education the polygyny rate was 28 percent, whereas for those with secondary and primary education it was 48 percent and 65 percent, respectively. The same evident disadvantage of the least qualified, combined with monogamy among the most so, occurred when marriage was measured by wealth (using areas of residence as the index). According to Andrews F. Aryee, "In the high status area, 26 percent of male marriages were polygynous, in the poorest area about the same, but in the middle area the figure rises to 49 percent" (1978). The nonlinearity of this distribution makes trends difficult to predict, especially because norms of monogamous marriage, incorporated in the teachings of most Christian churches and in the expectations of most modernizers, are accepted by women more readily than by men, for obvious reasons. Men resist the change, which leads to the substitution of polycoity for polygyny, or to the establishment of partners in separate households.

A number of factors, apart from size, affect the structure of coresidential farming groups. In earlier Africa, the location of the marital home was associated with the type of descent group. In patrilineal societies, that was the husband's home. In matrilineal societies the location varied, although virilocal residence (residence determined by the man) was often practiced, but usually for a shorter period of a woman's life, after which she returned to her natal group. Urbanization appears to increase the tendency for the marital home to be defined by the husband and his work, as is the case in Europe.

Although one of the simplest variables from which to obtain information is mean household size, that forms a constant of most census records, the results are frequently difficult to use because they are usually based on the concept of the hearth (cooking unit) that may be embedded in wider groupings (the farming group), or on the idea of the houseful or dwelling group. Indeed, the activities of consumption and production may well extend beyond any boundary-maintaining units through the exchange of food, of labor, and of other services. Wider kinship relations continue to be important in many contexts, including the exchange of children. The existence of these relations makes calculations based on the value of children difficult to assess, because one's own children are not the only relevant ones. Particularly in matrilineal societies, maternal uncles assist in putting their sister's children through school. Although in many contexts there is an increasing concentration upon the conjugal family, this is not the case with the inheritance of property in matrilineal societies (such as Asante cocoa farms), where the reduction of oral custom to written law has had the effect of conserving the model of uterine transmission and, to a large extent its practice.

The average size of the domestic group in contemporary developed countries is three persons, and in developing societies around five. Households are generally smaller in towns than in the country. Nelson O. Addo's 1974 survey of southeastern Ghana showed an average size of 3.5 in towns and 4.8 in the villages. In the towns, 27 percent of households were female-headed, and these units were larger than the male-headed ones (4.1 versus 3.3), a fact related to the predominant matrilineal system. Many migrants are single, and even the married, especially those who are illiterate, come without wives and children; indeed, among the employed,

the formalities and responsibilities of marriage are increasingly avoided by women as well as men. Average households in towns grew in size between 1960 and 1966, whereas those in the villages shrank. This may be partly due to migration, but it is also the case that the richer and better educated have larger households, not only because of servants but also because of resident kin and the responsibilities for their education. Social mobility has a halo effect. Such extended households, or even the more inclusive set of relatives living close together, provide the support needed for work or having children, partly through the child care offered by nonchildbearing women, either grandmothers or daughters.

The problems concerning the number of children are several; under present conditions (that seem likely to change only slowly, especially with the recurrence of malaria) one cannot predict how many children will survive, nor what sex they will be. Both questions are partly responsive to medical science, which affects the number of children conceived and born and can predict identify the sex of the unborn child. Parental strategies are also complicated by the likelihood that children who have attended school will leave and hence deplete the local working group.

Except among the employed, there has been little of the early retirement characteristic of some European regions. That is, in rural households, most elderly people continue to live as heads, not as dependents; that was the case with 87 percent of men aged sixty-five and over in the Ghanaian census of 1970. Even 46 percent of elderly women were heads of their own households. This is not to say that control is vested exclusively in the senior generation; even in neotraditional rural areas, the role of those who have been to school and who participate in or are able to manipulate the modern sector is acknowledged. Nevertheless, the idea of handing over control of resources during one's lifetime finds little favor, except in some pastoral communities such as the Fulani, in which cattle have long been passed on *inter vivos.*

There is one aspect of the influence of education on family behavior that is of some relevance to recent family patterns. Because the languages of instruction and of political action are basically English, French, and Portuguese, individuals constantly have to translate or employ European terms to explain words for family relationships in their mother tongues. In this way the local word for brother becomes differentiated into brother and cousin (or sometimes cousin-brother); the terms for father and mother are treated in similar ways. In other words, every schoolchild learns an individualizing, rather than a classificatory, terminology in the context of a high-status family. Such usages emphasize the nuclear family (or, rather, the direct line of filiation) rather than the wider ties of lineage or kindred, and therefore tend to stress limits to the obligations of relatives to one another.

In the early twenty-first century, towns are particularly affected by such individualizing or conjugal family oriented pressures; especially in work. But all neotraditional village families feel the erosive effects of the migration of men and women to the towns, the imposition of taxes, and the fluctuating prices of foodstuffs that result from the changing nutritional demands of towns, of some nonfarming rural workers, and of secondary boarding schools. However, the differences in the traditional kinship and marriage structures and the differential impact of vectors of change also need to be taken into account.

As has been seen, some African societies had matrilineal groups with consistent systems of inheritance (of property), succession (to office), and descent (to social groups); others had patrilineal groups; some had both concurrently (double-descent); and yet others displayed an absence of descent groups (that is, they were bilateral) but transmitted property and offices from parents to children. Systems of all of these types have changed, but each society retains certain earlier characteristics, the strength of which depends upon an individual's position in the new hierarchy and the impact of external factors.

Matrilineal inheritance and succession, for example, persist under a great variety of changing circumstances. Although such systems may have initially developed under conditions of early hoe-farming—the woman's harvesting role in hunting-and-gathering societies may have led to her assumption of farming tasks—they are today found under a variety of socioeconomic conditions, by no means the least complex, as the example of the Asante of western Africa shows. The Asante, who, with rich forest and mineral resources formed an important military state, became early cash-crop farmers when they adopted cocoa at the end of the nineteenth century. Although Christian missionaries and politicians made efforts to instigate a change to a European mode of reckoning inheritance with transmission from husband to wife to children, the Asante persist in passing down office, land, and property through the uterine line. Matrilineal family farms are the typical units of much cocoa production. Some observers report an increasing tendency to transmit property to the wife and son, that is, within the conjugal family. But this may not signify a major shift; early records and standardized myths suggest that some transmission to sons, often in secret, was a frequent feature of matrilineal systems.

Yet, whereas in the past in matrilineal societies men inherited from men, and women from women, in the early 2000, there appears to be an increasing emphasis on the passage of gifts from husband to wife, reflecting a strengthening of conjugal ties and a corresponding narrowing of lineage ones. The transmission of property to wife and sons (that was insisted upon by the early missionaries as a way of eliminating matriliny, instilling the idea of a Christian marriage, and providing for widows and orphans) meant that even brothers would now be excluded; hence the sibling group was likely to split economically before this event occurred. The traditional system came under early pressure from European legal ordinances, as well. Although the critics had some limited success, the matrilineal family has displayed great powers of persistence even under the new circumstances of cash-crop production, and this mode of social organization has even been incorporated into the written laws of Ghana, thus giving it further renewed life.

It was not only in traditional matrilineal systems that no property was transmitted between husband and wife. Universally, it was members of the lineage, whether matrilineal or patrilineal, rather than husband and wife (members of different lineages by exogamy), who inherited a man's property, brothers first (uterine or agnatic), then either sons or sister's, depending upon the dominant mode of reckoning. In the case of women, daughters (and sometimes sons) inherited from their mothers. This maintained the widespread system in which men inherited from men, and women from women, even in bilateral societies.

The development of conjugality and its problems among civil servants in Ghana in the 1970s has become a trend of this kind among the new salariat. Indeed, it was always the case that, even among the matrilineal Asante, conjugal ties were closer when couples were physically separated from their kin; once again this trend represents a new application of an existing tendency. Nevertheless, property continues to be mainly held by the spouses separately, which clearly needs to be the case where the rate of polygyny remains as high as it does in African societies. In this respect, conjugality seems likely to remain qualified in the foreseeable future because demographic and economic pressures do not appear to directly affect the situation. It is the older, established men who have more wives.

However, the Caribbean model of a high percentage of female-headed households has always had some presence in Africa. Asante was well endowed with female-headed households and visiting husbands, and some earlier, and even later, views of the matrifocal family in North America and the Caribbean saw the matrifocal family as deriving from African roots. Competing and more powerful theories have associated the American matrifocal family with the earlier slave economy and with the marginal domestic role the man plays in other lower-class strata. Apart from the matrilineal Asante, western Africa has been noted for its powerful market ladies (mammies)—that is, women traders—who are generally past the age of marriage. (Some award a scholarship to a younger man to keep them company.) Moreover, the predominantly male migration into towns leaves many married women to cope at home (in Botswana with the plough), whereas unmarried women in town cope with their men otherwise alone there. In addition, there are some educated women who live independently, by choice or by force of circumstance, some of them bringing up children on their own and supporting themselves. But this is a long way from the Caribbean pattern. In some respects, that phenomenon is much less marked in Africa than in contemporary England, France, or the United States, where one-parent families are not uncommon, especially in cities.

In a sense, the Caribbean system of matrifocality remains a possibility for part of the African population, simply because there is no conjugal fund to bind husband and wife together. Still, the matrifocal family remains characteristic of socioeconomically lower groups, not higher ones. In Europe, too, it was and is part of the culture of poverty, an expected aspect of each union. In contrast, in Africa it was associated with strong, successful women, and has little relation to stratification. It is associated with wage labor or with the separate economic activity of each sex. It is not easy to survive in a single-sex household in rural Africa, at least in the savanna zones.

What accounts for these contemporary changes? Traditional systems were built around a mode of livelihood that depended mainly upon hoe agriculture with comparatively low levels of population growth. Africa, the continent that saw the emergence of modern human beings (*Homo sapiens*), as well as their hominid predecessors, remained a continent that was underpopulated by Eurasian and recent North American standards. Births and deaths were roughly in balance.

However, the twentieth century saw devastatingly rapid population growth. One factor contributing to the growing numbers has been the better food supply brought about by improved crop varieties, by imports, and generally by more peaceful conditions and the abandonment of slavery, sparing in particular the lives of women and young children. Another has been better public health, personal hygiene, and recent medicine; and a third, the impact of cheap iron farming tools from abroad that have greatly increased productivity. A fourth, more difficult to assess, is the decrease in polygyny and the possible decay of the (probably unintentional but long-standing) constraints on births, such as the widespread postpartum taboo on intercourse, a taboo easier to ignore under urban conditions and with supplies of milk and infant food available for purchase. Population growth has also been attributed to the role of the lineage; but non-lineage societies held equally favorable attitudes toward producing children.

Demographers are looking for the onset of a transition from the recently high to the low birthrates characteristic of more prosperous societies. There is some evidence of such a shift. Until recently, more children survived, but the goal of continuous reproduction remained. The positive gains of large families overshadow the negative costs, for individuals have been somewhat protected from the full impact of high dependency ratios by partly free services—schooling, medicine, and some supplementary food supplied by national governments, by outside aid and development, and by missionary societies. But the economic base can no longer support such inputs. So, formally or informally, hospitals charge, schools require fees, and foreign aid does not keep pace with demand. Everywhere there is some evidence of a demographic transition, but one responding to poverty, not prosperity.

Kinship and family systems have in some areas been devastatingly affected by the epidemic of AIDS. It has been argued that the high rates of polygyny in Africa may have accelerated the spread of the disease. Rather, it is high rates of polycoity and of prostitution in towns that increase the danger. These, as has been seen, may occur with monogamous marriage or, more readily, with delayed marriage. Conditions conducive to polycoity—rural-urban relocation of women and men, prostitution, increase in single travelers, of outside wives (as they are known locally)—arise in towns, but increasingly in rural areas, as well.

See also **Childbearing; Demography: Fertility and Infertility; Family; Gender; Household and Domestic Groups; Kinship and Descent; Law; Marriage Systems; Prostitution; Sexual Behavior; Urbanism and Urbanization.**

BIBLIOGRAPHY

Addo, Nelson O. "Household Patterns among Urban and Rural Communities in South-Eastern Ghana." In *Domestic Rights and Duties in Southern Ghana*, ed. Christine Oppong. Legon: Institute of African Studies, University of Ghana, 1974.

Aryee, Andrews Frederick. "Urbanization and the Incidence of Plural Marriage: Some Theoretical Perspectives." In *Marriage, Fertility, and Parenthood in West Africa*, ed. Christine Oppong, et al. Canberra: Australian National University, 1978.

Bledsoe, Caroline, and Pison, Gilles. *Nuptuality in Sub-Saharan Africa: Contemporary Anthropological and Demographic Perspectives.* Oxford: Oxford University Press, 1994.

Bourdieu, Pierre. *The Logic of Practice.* Stanford, CA: Stanford University Press, 1990.

Brass, William, et al., eds. *The Demography of Tropical Africa.* Princeton, NJ: Princeton University Press, 1968.

Clark, Gracia. "Negotiating Asante Family Survival in Kumasi, Ghana." *Africa* 69 (1999): 66–86.

Clignet, René. *Many Wives, Many Powers.* Evanston, IL: Northwestern University Press, 1970.

De Graft-Johnson, Kwan Esiboa. "Succession and Inheritance among the Fante and Ewe." In *Domestic Rights and Duties in Southern Ghana*, ed. Christine Oppong. Legon: Institute of African Studies, University of Ghana, 1974.

Dorjahn, Vernon R. "The Factor of Polygamy in African Demography." In *Continuity and Change in African Cultures*, ed. William R. Bascom and Melville Herskovits. Chicago: University of Chicago Press, 1959.

Fortes, Meyer. "Kinship and Marriage among the Ashanti." In *African Systems of Kinship and Marriage*, ed. Alfred Reginald Radcliffe-Brown and Daryll Forde. London: Oxford University Press, 1950.

Goody, Esther N. *Parenthood and Social Reproduction: Fostering Occupational Roles in West Africa.* Cambridge, U.K.: Cambridge University Press, 1982.

Goody, Esther N. *Contexts of Kinship: An Essay in the Family Sociology of the Gonja of Northern Ghana.* Cambridge, U.K.: Cambridge University Press, 2005.

Goody, Jack. "The Evolution of the Family." In *Household and Family in Past Time*, ed. Peter Laslett. Cambridge, U.K.: Cambridge University Press, 1972.

Goody, Jack. *Production and Reproduction: A Comparative Study of the Domestic Domain.* Cambridge, U.K.: Cambridge University Press, 1976.

Hayase, Yasuko, and Kao-Lee Liaw. "Factors on Polygamy in Sub-Saharan Africa: Findings Based on the Demographic and Health Surveys." *The Developing Economies* 35, no. 3 (1997): 293–327.

Hill, Polly. *The Migrant Cocoa-Farmers of Southern Ghana: A Study in Rural Capitalism.* Cambridge, U.K.: Cambridge University Press, 1963.

Isiugo-Abanihe, Uche C. "Child Fosterage in West Africa." *Population and Development Review* 11, no. 1 (1985): 53–73.

Kuper, Adam. "Lineage Theory: A Critical Retrospect." *Annual Review of Anthropology* 11 (1982): 71–95.

Kuper, Adam. *African Marriage in an Impinging World: The Case of Southern Africa.* Leiden, The Netherlands: Afrika Studiecentrum, 1985.

Lesthaeghe, Ron J., ed. *Reproduction and Social Organization in Sub-Saharan Africa.* Berkeley: University of California Press, 1989.

Mair, Lucy. *African Marriage and Social Change.* London: Cass, 1969.

Oppong, Christine. *Marriage among a Matrilineal Elite.* London: Cambridge University Press, 1974.

Radcliffe-Brown, Alfred Reginald, and Daryll Forde, eds. *African Systems of Kinship and Marriage.* London: Oxford University Press, 1950.

Smith, Raymond Thomas. *The Negro Family in British Guiana: Family Structure and Social Status of the Villages.* London: Routledge and Paul, 1956.

Verdon, Michel. "Kinship, Marriage, and the Family: An Operational Approach." *American Journal of Sociology* 86 (1981): 796–818.

Ware, Helen. "Female and Male Life-Cycles." In *Female and Male in West Africa*, ed. Christine Oppong. London: Allen and Unwin, 1983.

JACK GOODY

KINSHIP AND DESCENT.

Kinship includes relations between people created through blood, reproduction, marriage, adoption, and sometimes simply a belief in common ancestry. The ways in which the resulting groups define themselves through common ancestry, whether through a single line or through a variety of kinship links, constitute their respective systems of descent.

Sub-Saharan Africa has a great diversity of such kinship and descent systems. These reflect differences in the past political organization of ethnic groups, as well as differences in the way land is used and subsistence is maintained both in traditional and in modern contexts. Many of the classic anthropological examples of patrilineal descent come from Africa, but the other major forms of descent (matrilineal, double, and bilateral or cognatic) are also represented on the continent.

DESCENT AND DESCENT GROUPS

Anthropologists distinguish four kinds of descent systems. Patrilineal descent involves tracing relationships from father to child through the generations. Matrilineal descent is that in which relationship is traced exclusively from mother to child. Double descent, a rare type, characterizes societies in which both patrilineal and matrilineal connections are traced, generating both kinds of kin groups, and each person belongs to one of each kind of descent group. Bilateral, or cognatic, descent is the relationship between the generations, or among individual kin, where unilineal descent (patrilineal or matrilineal) does not occur or is relatively unimportant. In a sense, all kinship systems have a cognatic quality, in that all peoples recognize kinship not only with clan or lineage members, but also with relatives who belong to other kin groups (see Figure 1).

Anthropologists commonly distinguish two kinds of descent group by their sizes or spans: lineages and clans. Lineages are patrilineal or matrilineal descent groups in which members define their exact relationships to all others within the group. Clans are much larger such units. Individuals recognize their common membership in the

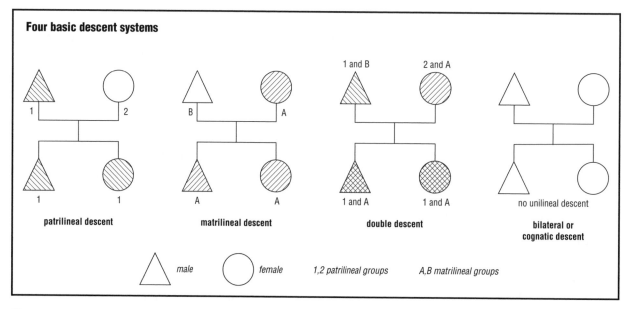

Four basic descent systems

patrilineal descent

matrilineal descent

double descent

bilateral or cognatic descent

1 and B   2 and A

1 and A   1 and A

no unilineal descent

male   female   *1,2 patrilineal groups*   *A,B matrilineal groups*

Figure 1.

group but do not know exactly how they are all related to one another. They may, for example, all believe themselves to be descended from a common ancestor, but not be able to trace all the links from their own respective lineages of known kin to their early ancestor.

Pastoral societies tend to organize themselves around patrilineal principles. Clans and lineages may compete for land and may be involved in disputes, including blood feuds, that pit all members of one group against the entire membership of another. Sometimes this form of descent-group organization coexists with strong political organization, as among the South African Zulu and the Swazi. Sometimes it, in a sense, replaces political organization itself, as has been argued for the Nuer of Sudan prior to World War II.

Societies that practice extensive agriculture, especially where cattle are relatively rare, as in Central Africa, often have matrilineal group structures. The Bemba of Zambia, for instance, have matrilineal kin groups, and women of these groups own the fields they work and pass them on to their daughters. The difficulty matrilineal societies often have, however, is how to trace descent through women while giving men political authority within the group. One way this may be done is through avunculocal residence, a system in which a male youth moves at adulthood to live with his mother's brothers, whereas a young woman moves to her husband's village upon marriage or shortly afterward. This form of residence, practiced by some Bemba and other Zambian peoples, such as the Ndembu in the far western plains, keeps men of the matrilineal groups together and disperses the women through whom they trace their descent. Uxorilocal residence, wherein a man comes to live in his wife's village, keeps women of such groups living together.

Double descent, a fairly rare form, occurs in western and southern Africa. The best-known examples are found among the Yakö of Nigeria, and the Herero and closely related Himba of Namibia. In true double-descent systems, each person belongs to one patrilineal group (that of his or her father) and one matrilineal group (that of his or her mother). Residence will be according to one line of descent or the other, and other rights and obligations, and even inheritance, will be split between the two

groups. Often religious or symbolic associations differ according to the kind of lineage. For example, among the pastoralist Herero and Himba, ordinary cattle are inherited through the matrilineages, whereas those cattle that are considered sacred are inherited patrilineally. Sometimes, historical influences create elements of double descent. For example, the Tuareg of Mali and Niger were once a matrilineal people, and this is still reflected in the matrilineal inheritance of symbolically important "milk cattle," whereas through Qur'anic influence most inheritance in the early twenty-first century passes patrilineally (two third to sons and one third to daughters).

Bilateral or cognatic descent, in contrast, involves the complete absence of significant unilineal descent groups. A person is considered equally related to kin as individuals on both the father's and the mother's sides. These systems are common in many parts of the world, including Europe, but are relatively rare as the sole form of descent in African societies where unilineal descent is the norm. However, in Africa, cognatic kin groups are found among current and former hunter-gatherers. Such bands and band clusters are the basis of flexible group organization that allows individuals to claim membership in either their mothers' or their fathers' local groups, or in the similarly loose groupings of other kin and affines (relatives by marriage). This kind of flexibility has enabled groups like San, Hadza and Pygmies to survive outside threats into the twenty-first century.

OTHER ASPECTS OF AFRICAN KINSHIP

The concern with the study of descent groups is called descent theory, in contrast to alliance theory, an alternative perspective on the groups created that instead emphasizes relations among groups or families linked through marriage. Apart from descent-group structure itself, other aspects of descent theory include institutions such as the avunculate, complementary filiation, and the developmental cycle, whereas such institutions as dowry, bridewealth, and bride service are topics of interest in both descent and alliance theory.

The avunculate is the close relationship between a mother's brother and his sister's son. This relationship is frequently an indulgent one, that is, personal and voluntary rather than structurally obligatory, with the mother's brother required to give his best cattle to, or to submit to teasing by, his young sister's son. Often in Southern Africa, the mother's brother is called male mother, a term that reflects this is a similarly affective relationship. In some societies, the opposite relationship, with the father's sister, is found; she becomes an authority figure and is termed the female father. The Tsonga (Thonga) of Mozambique and the Nama of Namibia provide examples of this avunculate, though the custom is dying out and they no longer practice all its aspects to the degree they once did.

Another of the key concepts of kinship in Africa is that of complementary filiation. The idea is that, whereas one has special obligations within one's own descent group, one will have a different set of obligations toward the side of the family, or indeed the descent group, of the parent through whom one does not trace descent. For example, in a patrilineal society, complementary filiation represents the relationship a person has with his or her mother's side of the family. In a matrilineal society, it represents the relationship he or she has with the father's side of the family.

Residence can be an important aspect of kinship and is often related to rules of descent. In some rural African societies, these residential group structures change through time, as homesteads expand with the arrival of spouses and the births of children, and decrease in population as elders die out, young men or women move away in marriage, or groups of siblings split apart to form separate homesteads of their own. These dynamic aspects of kin-group residential structure, characterized as the developmental cycle of domestic groups, have been prominent in studies of the matrilineal Asante and the patrilineal Tallensi peoples, both of Ghana.

The developmental cycle is important among bilateral hunter-gatherers too, but societies as these often add a broadly integrative twist. Kinship may be extended throughout the whole of society. Thus, there is no such thing as non-kin, because everyone is classified as belonging to some specific category of kin. Among the Juc'hoansi (also known as Ju/'hoansi or !Kung, of Botswana and Namibia), children are usually named for their grandparents. The Juc'hoansi believe that anyone with the identical name as someone else is descended from the same original namesake ancestor. Thus all namesakes are kin, and one's sister's namesake, for

example, is one's sister. This mechanism not only relates everyone in their society to everyone else, but the classification of kin also defines how one behaves toward specific members of that society. Classificatory brothers and sisters are expected to behave as if real brothers and sisters; they must sit apart from one another, for example, and they may not have sexual relations with each other or even tell sexual jokes in each other's company. Of course they know who is a real brother or sister and who is not, but it is important both to them as individuals and to their social system to extend kinship beyond close kin. Even outsiders can be incorporated into "kinship" with Juc'hoansi, simply by giving them appropriate names to fit them into the system. A converse situation occurs in parts of West Africa, where former slaves are excluded from the recognition of kinship with their surrounding neighbors, even though they may be biologically related. These examples illustrate well the fact that kinship in every society is a symbolic construction, and more than simply a matter of biological relationship.

KINSHIP TERMINOLOGIES

Juc'hoansi classify kin differently from English-speakers. However, they are similar in that both groups make a distinction between siblings and cousins, and do not distinguish among different kinds of cousins. Such a system is, in fact, unusual in Africa, where there is usually a distinction made between parallel cousins and cross-cousins. Parallel cousins are those related through a same-sex sibling link (either a father's brother's children or a mother's sister's children), and cross-cousins are those related through an opposite-sex sibling link (either a father's sister's children or a mother's brother's children; see Figure 2). This kind of classification is, in fact, the most common in the world's languages; the system found in Europe and North America (all cousins being the same) is rarer worldwide.

There are three main reasons for making such distinctions. First, these categories identify close (parallel) and more distant (cross) cousins on the basis that a same-sex sibling link is an especially close one; in fact, it establishes kinship itself. A person is thus equated with his or her same-sex generational mate as a sibling in a way that he or she is not equated with an opposite-sex sibling counterpart of the same generation. Second, these categories often define

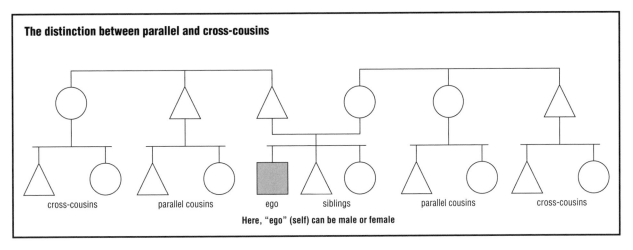

The distinction between parallel and cross-cousins

cross-cousins   parallel cousins   ego   siblings   parallel cousins   cross-cousins

Here, "ego" (self) can be male or female

Figure 2.

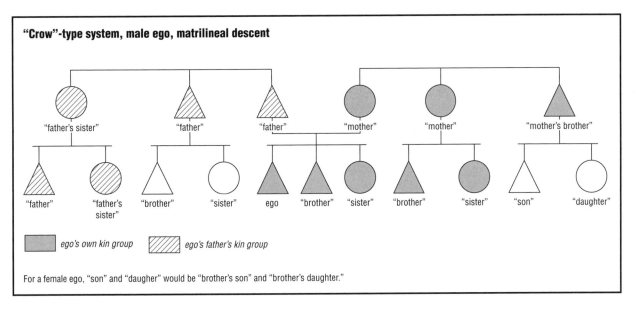

"Crow"-type system, male ego, matrilineal descent

"father's sister"   "father"   "father"   "mother"   "mother"   "mother's brother"

"father"   "father's sister"   "brother"   "sister"   ego   "brother"   "sister"   "brother"   "sister"   "son"   "daughter"

ego's own kin group   ego's father's kin group

For a female ego, "son" and "daugher" would be "brother's son" and "brother's daughter."

Figure 3.

whether a person is marriageable or not. Thus, in many African societies, cross-cousins are marriageable, whereas parallel cousins are classified and treated as brothers and sisters, and are therefore unmarriageable. Third, in unilineal societies, parallel cousins on the side of the family through which descent is traced will be members of the same descent group, whereas cross-cousins will not be.

Some African societies have separate terms for each of the four possible types of cousin: father's sister's children, father's brother's children, mother's sister's children, and mother's brother's children. This classification is common in societies with strong patrilineal ties, such as the peoples of the

southern Sudan. There, descent-group membership and place of residence are both important. Exact kinship status is defined, but there are no broad categories, such as marriageable cross-cousin, to group the specific genealogical relationships of individuals. In yet other African societies, including some of those in Nigeria, the opposite principle holds: the different types of cousin within a lineage are not distinguished either from each other, or from brothers and sisters. All members of one's own generation are termed as if they were one's brothers or sisters. This form of classification obviously denies the importance of both genealogical distance and precise individual relationships to create a single, inclusive category of close affiliation.

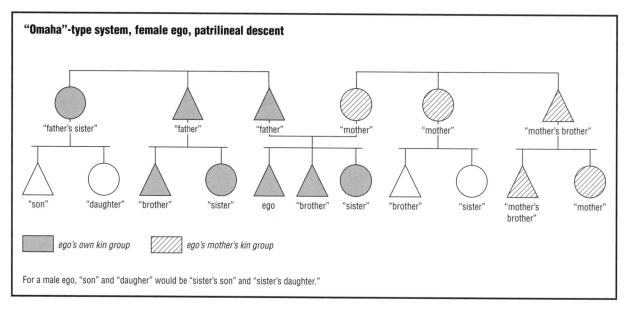

"Omaha"-type system, female ego, patrilineal descent

"father's sister" "father" "father" "mother" "mother" "mother's brother"

"son" "daughter" "brother" "sister" ego "brother" "sister" "brother" "sister" "mother's brother" "mother"

☐ ego's own kin group   ▨ ego's mother's kin group

For a male ego, "son" and "daugher" would be "sister's son" and "sister's daughter."

Figure 4.

Yet other types of classification are found in those societies in which lineage membership overrides generation, rather than generation overriding the divisions of lineage. In the matrilineal version shown in Figure 3 (known as Crow, after the Native American people whose terminology has this structure), one's father's sister's daughter is classified by the same term as one's father's sister. Likewise, one's father's sister's son is classified by the same term as one's father's brother and one's father—all these individuals belonging to the same father's matrilineal group. Thus, a single term classes together all the female members of an entire descent group, and another term groups all the male members. Similarly, for example, one's mother's father's entire matrilineal group, or everyone in one's father's father's matrilineal group, may each be classified by a single pair of terms—one for the females and one for the males. In all these cases, individuals of different generations are classified by the same, generationally ambiguous, term. However, members of one's own matrilineal group will be distinguished by a variety of more specific terms that do reflect which generation they belong to.

In the patrilineal version shown in Figure 4 (known as Omaha, after another Native American people), one classifies the mother's brother's son as a mother's brother, the mother's brother's daughter and the mother's sister as a mother, and so on. This results in the mirror image of the Crow system, in the sense that it accomplishes the same

collapsing of generational time but proceeds patrilineally rather than matrilineally. In an Omaha system, one's mother's brother's daughter's children (a generation below one's own children) are classified as brother and sister, as if they were in one's own generation, because they are the children of one's own mother's patrilineal group.

These systems seem complicated to those who are unfamiliar with them, but to people growing up in such societies, they seem perfectly natural and accomplish, often elegantly, social goals. Children grow up not only knowing how to categorize their specific kinsmen but also knowing intuitively the structural rules behind such categorization, namely that kin-group membership is a more important principle of classification than either generation or actual proximity of biological generation relationship.

African examples of Crow systems are rare, but the type is found sporadically, especially among the Mongo peoples of the Democratic Republic of the Congo. Omaha systems are much more common. Well-known examples in Africa include the Igbo (Ibo) of Nigeria, the Tsonga of Mozambique, the Shona of Zimbabwe, and the Nyoro of Uganda.

DOMAINS OF KINSHIP AND RELATIONS BETWEEN GROUPS

Whereas the nuclear family may be the root of kinship in all societies, African kinship organizations are created to generally extend connections through concrete personal relationships well beyond the confines of the nuclear family, both within and outside the descent group. Often families and descent groups thus have complementary roles. Nuclear and extended biological families are the domains in that people feel moral obligations to visit frequently, to share the produce of their land, or to support each other in other ways. In contrast to this moral domain, the abstract jural domain is defined by membership in a classificatory descent group. In West Africa especially, an individual has obligations toward his or her own descent group and toward the descent groups of specific close relatives. Thus, a man may have special obligations at the funerals of members of the patrilineal descent group of his mother—for example to perform ritually dangerous activities—that he is forbidden to perform for members of his own patrilineal descent group.

Where systems such as the preceding ones do not erase the divisiveness that lineality otherwise introduces, descent groups establish formal relationships among themselves through structured marital alliances. Of concern here, though, are particularly those aspects that involve the transfer of property within and between kin groups. Dowry (a set of marriage gifts from a bride's family to her groom's, or an endowment of the marriage) is rare in sub-Saharan Africa, but bridewealth is common, especially among pastoralists and even in urban contexts among former pastoralists and horticultural peoples. Bridewealth involves the gift, often of livestock in the case of pastoralists, from a groom or his family to the family of his bride. The act of giving is seen in African societies as a means to confirm the marriage and to legitimize—and, in patrilineal societies such as these, also to claim—the children born to it. Bride service, an alternative, is rarer and occurs where families have little investment in transferable wealth. Mainly found in hunter-gatherer societies, bride service involves the groom moving to his wife's local group and hunting for, or doing other work on behalf of, his parents-in-law.

ANTHROPOLOGICAL VIEWS OF AFRICAN KINSHIP

Anthropological approaches to kinship have emphasized diverse aspects, depending on both the location of the field research conducted by the anthropologist and his or her national tradition. British anthropologists have been particularly prominent, and they have tended to emphasize descent-group structure and factors related to descent, such as complementary filiation and the developmental cycle of domestic groups. French interests in kinship studies have emphasized the rules and politics of marriage, and to some extent kinship terminologies. American cultural anthropologists as a group have had a much greater interest in the study of kinship terminologies, but they have made few detailed analyses of kinship terminologies in Africa. Among African anthropologists and sociologists, all these approaches are represented, as are concerns with the family and with the economic and political aspects of marriage.

In the 1970s and 1980s, traditional anthropological approaches, especially descent theory, were called into question as scholars began to realize that African kinship systems were not as simple as Europeans and North Americans had previously represented them. Many judged the work of earlier theorists such as Edward Evans-Pritchard and Meyer Fortes to be too idealized in its representations of the relation of abstractions such as descent groups to real residential units. Studies of kinship in Europe, North America, and Asia have come to emphasize the symbolism of kinship (for example, the idea of being related by blood) and other aspects of participants' own understandings of what it means to be kin.

These developments are beginning to be represented in African kinship studies too, as the cultural, as well as the social, nature of kinship gains prominence. For example, a recent study of Xhosa migrants in Cape Town emphasizes the cultural values of common clanship as well as the ways clanship is used to form new social networks in an urban context. Other studies are focusing on how individuals interpret bridewealth transaction, kin networks and the idea of the family or the household, in light of changes in demographic structures due to urbanization and social development. Still other studies are considering aspects of generational conflict, ever-present even in traditional contexts, but now also of concern due to rapid cultural changes and social problems such as those associated with the spread of HIV/AIDS.

See also **Household and Domestic Groups; Kinship and Affinity; Marriage Systems.**

BIBLIOGRAPHY

Barnard, Alan, and Anthony Good. *Research Practices in the Study of Kinship*, new edition. London: Academic Press, 1987.

Carsten, Janet, ed. *Cultures of Relatedness: New Approaches to the Study of Kinship*. Cambridge, U.K.: Cambridge University Press, 2000.

Crandall, David P. *The Place of Stunted Ironwood Trees: A Year in the Lives of the Cattle-Herding Himba of Namibia*. New York: Continuum, 2000.

Ephirim-Donkor, Anthony. *The Making of an African King: Patrilineal and Matrilineal Struggle among the Effutu of Ghana*. Trenton, NJ: Africa World Press, 2000.

Evans-Pritchard, Edward. *Kinship and Marriage among the Nuer*, reprint edition. New York: Oxford University Press, 1990.

Fortes, Meyer. *The Dynamics of Clanship among the Tallensi, Being the First Part of an Analysis of the Social Structure of a Trans-Volta Tribe*. Oxford: Oxford University Press, 1967.

Fortes, Meyer. *Time and Social Structure, and Other Essays*. London: Oxford University Press, 1970.

Goody, Jack R., ed. *The Developmental Cycle in Domestic Groups*. Cambridge, U.K.: Cambridge University Press, 1969

Goody, Jack R. *Comparative Studies in Kinship*, reprint edition. New York: Routledge, 2005.

Kuper, Adam. "Lineage Theory: A Critical Retrospect." *Annual Review of Anthropology* 11 (1982).

Marshall, Lorna. *The !Kung of Nyae Nyae*. Cambridge, MA: Harvard University Press, 1976.

Radcliffe-Brown, Alfred R. *Structure and Function in Primitive Society*. New York: Free Press, 2002.

Radcliffe-Brown, Alfred R., and Daryll Forde, eds. *African Systems of Kinship and Marriage*. Reprint. London: Trubner & Company, 2005.

Spiegel, Andrew D. "Using Clanship, Making Kinship: The Dynamics of Reciprocity in Khayelitsha, Cape Town." *African Anthropology* 4, no. 2 (1997): 37–76.

ALAN BARNARD

KISANGANI. Kisangani, formerly Stanleyville, is a city on the Congo River in the northeast of Democratic Republic of the Congo. At Kisangani, the Congo River descends Boyoma Falls (formerly Stanley Falls), and turns to the west on its way to Kinshasa and the Atlantic Ocean.

Kisangani has been a provincial or district capital since the dawn of the colonial era. The city is known as a place where many ethnic groups cohabit. That reputation was enhanced in 1959–60, when Stanleyville became the domain of the Congolese National Movement (MNC-Lumumba) of Patrice Lumumba, although his Tetela community was not strongly represented in the local population.

After Lumumba had been overthrown in 1960, his deputy premier Antoine Gizenga (b. 1925) attempted to revive the nationalist government at Stanleyville. In 1964, Lumumbist insurgents established their People's Republic of the Congo at Stanleyville. The People's Republic was decapitated at the end of 1964 when Belgian paratroopers dropped on Stanleyville from American aircraft. American-backed Joseph Mobutu seized power in Congo and changed the name Stanleyville to Kisangani.

When foreign armies invaded Congo in 1996 and 1998, Kisangani's importance was confirmed. The Ugandan and Rwandan armies clashed repeatedly for control of the city, which had become a major center of the diamond trade. In 2006, when free elections were held, incumbent president Joseph Kabila received strong support in Kisangani, as he did throughout the Swahili-speaking eastern provinces.

See also **Congo, Democratic Republic of; Congo River; Lumumba, Patrice.**

BIBLIOGRAPHY

Democratic Republic of Congo. *War Crimes in Kisangani. The Response of Rwandan-Backed Rebels to the May 2002 Mutiny*. New York, Human Rights Watch, 2002.

MacGaffey, Janet. *Entrepreneurs and Parasites, the Struggle for Indigenous Capitalism in Zaire*. Cambridge, U.K.: Cambridge University Press, 1987.

Pons, Valdo G. *Stanleyville: An African Urban Community under Belgian Administration*. London: Oxford University Press for the International African Institute, 1969.

Verhaegen, Benoît. *Femmes zaïroises de Kisangani. Combats pour la survie*. Paris: L'Harmattan, 1990.

THOMAS TURNER

KIWANUKA, JOSEPH (c. 1896–1966).

Joseph Kiwanuka, an outstanding Catholic leader in Uganda, was educated at Katigondo Seminary and ordained a priest in 1929. After studying in Rome and becoming the first African doctor of canon law, he joined the White Fathers missionary society and made his novitiate in North Africa. In 1939 he was chosen as first vicar apostolic of Masaka, Uganda, and consecrated bishop by Pope Pius XII in Rome. Twenty years later Kiwanuka became archbishop of Kampala, and he attended the Second Vatican Council (1962–1965). He died at Rubaga.

Kiwanuka's importance lies in his having been the first black diocesan bishop in any mainline church since the Nigerian Samuel Crowther died in 1891. For more than twelve years, he remained the sole African bishop in the Catholic Church (outside Ethiopia and Madagascar). The diocese of Masaka, wholly staffed by local priests, was seen as an experiment. Kiwanuka's achievement was outstanding. His clergy multiplied and he sent several overseas for further training, but his development of elected lay parish councils and parents' associations for church schools was no less significant and quite out of line with contemporary missionary practice. His political influence was considerable. In a colonial age and under considerable missionary suspicion, Kiwanuka pioneered the way for the hundreds of African bishops of the next generation.

See also **Christianity; Crowther, Samuel Ajay; Uganda.**

BIBLIOGRAPHY

Waliggo, John Mary. *A History of African Priests: Katigondo Major Seminary, 1911–1986.* Masaka, Uganda: Katigondo National Major Seminary, 1988.

ADRIAN HASTINGS

KNOTTING. *See* Arts.

KNOWLEDGE

This entry includes the following articles:
OVERVIEW
TRADITIONAL

OVERVIEW

If the classic philosophical definition of the term *knowledge* as justified belief should generally apply, it rings true in African contexts just as anywhere else. Yet extending this standard to Africa largely depends upon the degree to which the determinants of the concepts of truth, justification, and belief are known in their social contexts, and much research remains in these areas. This cultural integrity of knowledge points researchers to the need to investigate related fields underpinning and informing ways of knowing and forms of knowledge insofar as they are historically grown and socially embedded. This relativity, or contextual embeddedness, again directs one to the fundamentally circular character of human understanding. For what is identified as knowledge is always already the outcome of prior processes that have shaped the understandings of those who claim to know. Keeping this hermeneutic principle in mind when thinking about knowledge in Africa (or anywhere else) draws attention to the constitutive role of the relationship between the knower—and the multiplicity of factors influencing him or her—and what is claimed as known.

Recognition of this epistemological complexity is important on two levels. First, it relates to the social constitution of knowledge within groups, through historical processes and within cultural and linguistic paradigms that provide a certain coherence in the collective constitution of meaning. In other words, it concerns one's ideas about Yoruba knowledge, Swahili knowledge, and the like; what is commonly accepted as knowledge (of specialists and of ordinary people) in everyday life within distinct sociocultural contexts. Second, it makes one aware that diverse approaches (and their inherent conceptions and criteria) predetermine or at least shape what is then identified and presented as knowledge. This multiplicity of knowledge is important to note, as the body of literature focusing explicitly on knowledge in African societies is limited but growing. Studies may not always be compatible or easily comparable, due to scholars' differing research interests and theoretical paradigms.

This overview addresses both cultural contextualization and the resulting multiplicity of knowledge by referring to selected descriptive *and* analytical sources in the wider field of African studies (including African philosophy). Knowledge in social contexts is not static but situated within dynamic processes, shifts, and transformations, and thus it is also important to consider the social negotiation and contestation of creating knowledge. This contested quality relates to what the philosopher Paulin Hountondji called in 1996 an "internal pluralism" at work within African societies, a phenomenon that itself provides a starting point for the investigation of intellectual and philosophical traditions.

The negotiation of epistemologies in social settings draws on religion and cosmologies (which are in turn influenced by the lived-in-environment) and expressed through language. People's conceptualizations and experiences of the world are in part determined also by accepted social rules, norms, and limits of the conceivable and the real, with a sphere of divination, prophecy, or possession mediating between the two. Some anthropological research has sought to identify wider regional clusters of intellectual traditions and schools of knowledge and practice that have developed historically. These regional patterns continue to influence the basic parameters of what it means to know in particular instances. They are expressed within regionally specific genres that may be either discursive (like proverbs or poetry) or performative (like healing practices), or both (like praise poetry or ritual invocations). All of these aspects are being researched in different regions, but to very variable degrees.

Considering the vast range of the topic to be covered, and its infinite local and momentary manifestations, what can be presented and discussed here is limited. For instance, this entry refers largely to English-language sources, thus neglecting other academic traditions and a wide scope of African-language sources. Within these limitations, this entry seeks to present a useful summary of research on knowledge in Africa and its relations to social practice, and thus to provide basic orientation to African thought.

Africanist research shows that interdisciplinary or trans-disciplinary approaches are fruitful for taking African conceptions of knowledge seriously in their own right; the use of conventional conceptual boxes of the social sciences, differentiating between presumed subfields like religion, art, politics, and economy (developed out of, and also to describe, modern Western societies), produces misleading representations of African realities and their internal theoretical conceptualizations. Much effort has been put into investigating conceptual frameworks at work within African societies, focusing on the internal dimensions of knowledge in discourse and practice, thereby reviewing, reframing, or solidifying pathways laid out in earlier anthropological research.

Before general statements can be made with confidence, however, empirical and historical research has to take on the challenge of working through the languages and cultural traditions of all of Africa's regions. So far, some regionally distinct political cultures have been identified through long-term historical research on changing social cosmologies, ritual practices, key concepts, and their relations to forms of expression and social hierarchy. In some cases, these specific local systems of thought may be linked to broader traditions of knowledge, for instance the Central African rainforest or western Bantu region, the central and southeastern Bantu region, and the southern African region—three regional examples which themselves also interlink and overlap. Further, some bodies of regional scholarship, due to high densities of research and publication (e.g. on the Yoruba, Akan, and Swahili contexts), allow a closer look than others at the interconnecting layers and dimensions of knowledge within social practice.

The idea that distinguishable, relatively homogenous subunits of Africa exist, or even a unitary idea of Africa itself, as proposed first by Eurocentric and later Afrocentric perspectives, has long been severely problematized. This shift toward multiplicity is reflected in a decreasing use of overarching singular labels like "the African mind" and "Bantu philosophy" in titles, topics, and key words. The plural "African worlds" and "African systems of thought" can also be observed; the latter expression came to characterize an ongoing series of monographs. A problematically singular yet widely used expression for knowledges in Africa was "African traditional knowledge," related to "African traditional religion" (known as ATR in Anglophone West Africa). Introduced by British anthropologists during colonial times, it was conceptually refined by Robin Horton in his article "African Traditional Knowledge and Western Science" (1967), yet scholarly commitment to the idea remained ambivalent.

On the one hand, Horton argued for the existence of theoretical, generalizing interests and frameworks within African societies (linked to cosmology and religion), yet on the other he denied them the possibility of science, of the development of completely logical, empirically based explanations, thus contrasting them as a set with a similarly homogenized rational/empirical thought. This latter he connected to "open" and thus potentially (or *de facto*) modern societies, following Karl Popper. In contrast, he described African societies as "closed," embedded in an array of unchanging folk-conceptions of the world. Such a line of argument had long been used for casting them as traditional societies *per se*, that is, as static and backward-looking, impermeable to external changes, including modernity. This stereotype of "traditional Africa" has been influential until the early twenty-first century, particularly in Western popular discourse. In contrast, a range of studies has shown that African traditions and conceptions are flexible and highly adaptable to the (modern or postcolonial) conditions of the contemporary world, as this entry develops in detail.

African philosophers such as Kwasi Wiredu (1980) have criticized Horton's contrastive typology for its uneven levels of comparison, stating that it compared the incomparable—Western science and African folk thought—while one should rather compare Western and African folk thought, and explore the possibilities of developing and applying science in and for Africa as part of a sensible modernization strategy. Scientific knowledge, not exclusive to the West, was an achievement based on long historical processes, and as such open to all of humanity. Paulin Hountondji also rejected the adjective *traditional* as a general qualifier for African knowledge or religions, as it casts them as "static, cold and ageless" (Hountondji 1997, 16). At the same time, he makes the case for "a re-discovery of African *traditions* of thought" and religious practices. Instead of "traditional knowledge" Hountondji suggested the use of "endogenous knowledge," qualifying "an internal product drawn from a given cultural background" (1997, 17). Unlike "indigenous knowledge," Hountonjdi's phrase did not continue to spread derogatory connotations of Africa as primitive and exotic, or as conceptually confined and restricted to local points of view. All of this restates the point that reason and tradition are neither opposed nor incompatible.

At the same time, African philosophical discourse has continued to draw from the conventional opposition of tradition and modernity, while also starting to make analytical use of the notion of postcolonial.

Across disciplines, the postcolonial dimensions of political realities and everyday scenarios have been addressed, in general terms as well as in their relation to knowledge and the conception of self and other. Further case studies have been provided by anthropological research, for instance on the modernity of witchcraft and the contemporaneity of social phenomena such as prophecy, divination, healing, and spirit possession that had conventionally been dismissed or suppressed as traditionalist.

Along the lines of Michel Foucault's archaeology of knowledge and somewhat parallel to Edward Said's critique of Orientalism, in their emphasis on the historical constructedness of knowledge, particularly about "others," V. Y. Mudimbe made the point that all research on knowledge in Africa—by Africans and outsiders—was dependent "on a Western epistemological order" (1988, x). This emphasis refers to the negative forces limiting understandings of Africans' knowledges: the discourse that invented Africa and determined its connotations was Western, shaped by missionary and colonizing epistemologies, and construed within a scientific model, a Western episteme that saw Africa as an Other inferior to Europe. According to Mudimbe, discourses of Africanism produced a distorted image that became both central and obstructive to the study of African knowledges ever since. This image was taken up by Africans themselves (academics and others), thus complicating further attempts to distinguish between abstract scholarly perspectives and authentic insights on knowledge in and from Africa.

That a fundamental colonization of thought about Africa needed to be addressed and overcome was as a primary concern for African intellectual endeavors also within African philosophy and literature. Understanding internal categories "requires asking how people put their thoughts together" (Cooper 2005, 11), including a view on the social processes of how knowledge is constituted. Indeed, knowledge has been used as a conceptual entry point and analytic tool for the study of society and its internal dynamics: Michael Lambek's ethnography of a village in the Muslim Comoro Islands shows how a focus on the qualifications, contestations and constant renegotiations of knowledge (with its various links to practice) provides one with an overarching perspective of a social universe that is in flux alternative to the abstractions of modern social science.

KNOWLEDGE FRAMEWORKS AND EPISTEMOLOGIES

Seeing knowledge systems as forming coherent, but always selective, paradigms can provide basic orientation about epistemology as well as about the social structures and social practices that they express. Reviewing the internal transformations of knowledge and education in Mali (historically dominated by Sufism), Louis Brenner (2001) described the erosion of an "esoteric paradigm" of knowledge through a "rationalist paradigm" of public Western secularism and Islamic modernism over the twentieth century. The esoteric paradigm, or "esoteric episteme," is associated with a hierarchically structured community of experts and their favored initiates, in which secrecy and privileged spirituality dominate the acquisition, transmission and performance of knowledge. In contrast, the rationalist paradigm is characterized by explicitly defined and openly accessible criteria for knowledge, empirically external to the knowers. Such typification is a useful general analytical device, applied flexibly across regions, ethnicities, and religions. As a general characterization, for instance, it applies to many networks of diviners or other ritual experts more generally throughout Africa, as much as to Sufi brotherhoods.

No systematic surveys of epistemologies in Africa exist, so scholars rely largely upon regional studies which highlight epistemological aspects of other primary interests, and from diverse methodological angles. One fieldwork-based study of the Yoruba context by the analytic philosophers Barry Hallen and J. Olubi Sodipo investigated the distinction in Yoruba ordinary language use between the terms *knowledge* and *belief* (1997). They found Yoruba expressions *mo* and *gbagbo* to differ significantly from their closest English-language counterparts, *knowing* and *believing*. The Yoruba epistemological system was found to be stricter than the English, as it demanded first-hand experience or a process of verification derived from first-hand experience before accepting something as *imo*

(knowledge). Reversing common Western prejudice, the English-language epistemological system was shown to be less critical and more naïve, and thus closer to the established "model for traditional thought systems" than the Yoruba one (1997, 81). In a subsequent study on Yoruba morality and aesthetics, Hallen confirmed this critical "bias against tradition" in the Yoruba system (2001, 19). Considering the relationship between epistemology and morality, he described the epistemic as "a kind of master key (...) to the value system" (2001, 65). The Yoruba context is one where a whole host of studies provides scholars with many insights about various aspects of knowledge to be found in aesthetics, divination, proverbs, poetry, history and religion. Similar regional examples can be played through, to name just a few, for the Akan, Swahili, or Kongo contexts.

KNOWLEDGE AND PRACTICE: HEALING

Healing is a good example of a wide-ranging systematic field of knowledge-oriented practices that are performed in everyday life but also derive from coherent epistemologies, which in turn are linked to regional cosmologies and religions. Not only are they socially rooted and reflect historical intellectual traditions in practice, they are often linked to mediating spiritual forces or powers that are believed to facilitate, conduct, or assist the healing processes of the afflicted. This mediatory role for the practitioner is a common feature for many African regions, whether in Muslim, Christian, or endogenous religious settings.

KNOWLEDGE AS VISION: DIVINATION AND PROPHECY (POLITICS AND LEADERSHIP)

Divination and prophecy are two types of visionary knowledge that often overlap with healing, also in terms of practitioners. With reference to the Kongo context, Wyatt MacGaffey suggested they are related to social science in the constant empirical testing of practices. Concerned with personal and social aspirations and hope for a good life and a better future in times of strife and hardship, they partly venture over into the political realm. Indeed, for several regions cases of socially acknowledged prophetic figures have been well documented where the (male or female) prophet became a political *and* religious leading figure.

KNOWLEDGE AND WISDOM

While diviners and prophets can be seen as two kinds of inspired sages, the Kenyan philosopher H. Odera Oruka sought to investigate the knowledge of wise elders. He created a research project called sage philosophy in response to denials of the existence of philosophy in Africa. He met with sages, elders who were acknowledged as wise within their communities, discussed philosophical topics with them, and studied the documented interviews with a view to identifying their original thinking and critical reasoning. While this approach provoked both critical and positive reactions, few have attempted to apply it to other regions or further topics.

It remains to point out examples of empirically based research that is explicitly engaged with notions of morality and moral knowledge and to note that the relation between knowledge and power has been investigated in biographical portrayals, in ethnographies of apprenticeship, and for other forms of knowledge transmission. Mediating genres and internal contestations of knowledge should also be kept in mind. Poetry (oral and written) is often used for the mediation of knowledge and values and for enacting communal memories. Performed in ritual-like settings, it may fulfill religious or political functions and reemphasize history as a strand of common identity, depicting and restating norms and common beliefs, and casting models of social behavior. These features apply to Islamic didactic poetry too, of which there are long-standing traditions in West and East Africa. In Muslim (predominantly Sufi-oriented) communities internal contestations of knowledge and power have often, over the twentieth century, given way to external challenges, by Western frameworks and Islamic reformist ones. This erosion of inherited value systems led to colonial and postcolonial transformations in the social order. Similar effects of such challenges to established paradigms of knowledge and power can also be observed in non-Muslim contexts, as old convictions were replaced by new uncertainties. Such constellations provide leeway for political powers to dominate and demand strict conformity and compliance without public recourse to knowledge, thus creating situations which lead to subversive forms of protest and rejection, and the cultivation of counter-discourses of knowledge from below.

This selective overview has tried to shed light on selected key areas of the study of knowledge in Africa, placing issues of conceptualization and contextualization at the forefront, in order to underline the task of studying knowledge, as much as possible, on its own terms and in its practical situatedness.

See also **Divination and Oracles; Healing and Health Care; Islam: Sufi Orders; Person, Concepts of; Philosophy; Prophetic Movements; Research.**

BIBLIOGRAPHY

Appiah, Kwame A. 1992. *In My Father's House: Africa in the Philosophy of Culture.* Oxford: Oxford University Press, 1992.

Brenner, Louis. *Controlling Knowledge: Religion, Power, and Schooling in a West African Muslim Society.* Bloomington: Indiana University Press, 2001.

Cooper, Frederick. *Colonialism in Question: Theory, Knowledge, History.* Berkeley: University of California Press, 2005.

Dilley, Roy. "Ways of Knowing, Forms of Power." *Cultural Dynamics* 11, no. 1 (1991): 33–55.

Eickelman, Dale. *Knowledge and Power in Morocco: The Education of a Twentieth-Century Notable.* Princeton, NJ: Princeton University Press, 1985.

Evans-Pritchard, E. E. 1937. *Witchcraft, Oracles and Magic among the Azande.* London: Oxford University Press, 1937.

Hallen, Barry. *The Good, the Bad, and the Beautiful: Discourse about Values in Yoruba Culture.* Bloomington: Indiana University Press, 2001.

Hallen, Barry, and J. Olubi Sodipo. *Knowledge, Belief, and Witchcraft: Analytic Experiments in African Philosophy.* Stanford, CA: Stanford University Press, 1986, 1997.

Horton, Robin. "African Traditional Thought and Western Science." *Africa* 37, nos. 1 and 2 (1967). Reprinted Horton's *Patterns of Thought in Africa and the West: Essays on Magic, Religion and Science.* Cambridge, U.K.: Cambridge University Press, 1993.

Hountondji, Paulin J. *African Philosophy: Myth and Reality.* Bloomington: Indiana University Press, 1976, 1996.

Hountondji, Paulin J., ed. *Endogenous Knowledge: Research Trails.* Dakar: CODESRIA, 1997.

Kresse, Kai. *Philosophising in Mombasa: Knowledge, Islam, and Intellectual Practice on the Swahili Coast.* Edinburgh: Edinburgh University Press, 2007.

Lambek, Michael. *Knowledge and Practice in Mayotte.* Toronto: Toronto University Press, 1993.

MacGaffey, Wyatt. *Modern Kongo Prophets: Religion in a Plural Society.* Bloomington: Indiana University Press, 1983.

MacGaffey, Wyatt. *Religion and Society in Central Africa: The BaKongo of Lower Zaire.* Chicago: University of Chicago Press, 1986.

MacGaffey, Wyatt. *Kongo Political Culture: The Conceptual Challenge of the Particular.* Bloomington: Indiana University Press, 2000.

Mudimbe, V. Y. *The Invention of Africa.* Bloomington: Indiana University Press, 1988.

Mudimbe, V. Y. *The Idea of Africa.* Bloomington: Indiana University Press, 1994.

Mudimbe, V. Y., ed. *The Surreptitious Speech: Présence Africaine and the Politics of Otherness, 1947–1987.* Chicago: University of Chicago Press, 1992.

Oruka, H. O. *Sage Philosophy. Indigenous Thinkers and Modern Debate on African Philosophy.* Leiden: Brill, 1990.

Wiredu, Kwasi. *Philosophy and an African Culture.* Cambridge, U.K.: Cambridge University Press, 1980.

Wiredu, Kwasi. *Cultural Universals and Particulars: An African Perspective.* Bloomington: Indiana University Press, 1996.

KAI KRESSE

TRADITIONAL

Construed in its broadest sense, the term *knowledge* may include the entirety of people's worldview, some parts of which they speak about explicitly whereas other parts remain implicit for various reasons. Implicit knowledge may be taken for granted so that it is unnecessary to state it—other than to an outsider. Or, implicit knowledge may involve knowing how to do something, rather than how to talk about doing it. The term may also be used for presuppositions about the nature of the world that remain unchallenged, and almost unrecognized, for long periods because they provide the foundations for explicit claims to knowledge. Finally, people know some things that are difficult to put into words, however strongly they are felt. Thus, knowledge in its broadest sense may be explicit, taken for granted, practical, or unstatable. Accounts of what knowledge was in indigenous African societies, of how it was made and how it was transmitted, are not descriptive in a simple sense but also rely on quasi-philosophical assumptions a writer makes about the kinds of knowledge that are to be reported and analyzed.

This entry is concerned predominantly with explicit claims to knowledge made in African societies—that is, with knowledge understood narrowly as an approximate translation for a similar term in an African language. Such claims and counterclaims are made against the background of broader notions of what is to qualify as knowledge in this marked sense, who is authorized to claim it, how such knowledge is made and transmitted, and how the distribution of knowledge relates to issues of relative power within society. Anthropologists attempting to write accounts of indigenous definitions and evaluations of knowledge during the twentieth century have had to abstract the locally mediated influences of Islam and Christianity, and of European society and culture more generally. But the accounts they have written are themselves evidence of such influences, which need to be read not as plain records of African notions of knowledge but with an eye both to their definition of knowledge and to the ways in which they have sought to distinguish indigenous from locally mediated (indigenized) notions. Both the assumptions made to define African knowledge and the methods used to distinguish indigenous from indigenized knowledge are open to charges of ideological bias.

EARLY TWENTIETH-CENTURY APPROACHES
Between the two world wars, British and French anthropologists brought different emphases to their study of African conceptions of knowledge. Although not representative of all French work during this period, the writings of the French ethnographers Marcel Griaule (1898–1956), Germaine Dieterlen (1903–1999), and their collaborators have become reference points for the study of African cosmologies. Predominantly writing about the Dogon and Bambara peoples of Mali (then French Soudan), Griaule and Dieterlen sought to demonstrate that African cosmologies produced conceptual correspondences between, for instance, the body or domestic dwelling and the principles attributed to the cosmos, as particularly revealed in accounts of the origin of the world. A short book by Griaule (1965) reports what the Dogon elder of its title told Griaule about the creation of the world. These conversations took place when Dogon elders collectively decided that Griaule was to be allowed access to deep learning. The record of his continuing initiation into Dogon knowledge was published posthumously and took its title from Yourougou, the fallen brother of Nommo the

creator, who, in the form of the pale fox, advises Dogon diviners through his paw prints left overnight in sand on which has been traced a grid of lines with markers to represent some pressing problem. The works of Griaule and his team suggested that deep African knowledge was gained only from elderly men after prolonged fieldwork. This knowledge was arcane and constituted a philosophy known in detail only to initiates.

Much of the controversy that still surrounds Griaule's work concerns his working method that relied particularly on interviewing key informants through translators over a period of years. Were the views of these informants idiosyncratic or indicative of notions shared by Dogon? And if shared, then how widely? A later researcher, Walter E.A. van Beek (b. 1943), found himself unable to replicate Griaule's findings. Obviously, Griaule's writings result, among other things, from the interviews he conducted, but how far and in what sense did the system of ideas he describes exist outside his questioning and writing? How far should the ideas of the Dogon be taken as representative of a regional or even African culture? Two waves of reception of Griaule's work—initially by his contemporaries of the British school and more recently in the light of a general questioning of the authority of ethnographic accounts—have highlighted these questions. But all accounts of African knowledge raise similar issues, none of which are easily resolved.

To their contemporary counterparts of the British social anthropological persuasion, French ethnographers of Africa appeared to be concerned with ideas to the relative neglect of their social contexts. Ethnographers of the British school emphasized participant observation in the lives of the peoples they studied and focused their descriptions on the organization of societies. Claims and counterclaims to knowledge were to be interpreted as an aspect of social process. These claims would therefore vary according to the characteristics of the society in which they were made, although gender and age were significant everywhere.

Meyer Fortes (1906–1983), writing of the Talensi—a relatively uncentralized people prior to their colonial incorporation into what is now northern Ghana—stressed the many ways in which access to ancestral power supported hierarchical relations between elders and juniors and, in this strongly patrilineal society, especially the relations of authority and respect between a father and his eldest son. Edward E. Evans-Pritchard (1902–1973), elucidating the logic of beliefs in witchcraft and sorcery among the Azande (Zande) of Sudan, argued that allocation of responsibility for the misfortunes that befall people had to be understood in terms of broad suppositions about the nature of their world that become manifest in their particular explanations of cases of illness or accident. Both Azande suppositions about the nature of witchcraft and sorcery, for example, and the technology they had for exploring particular accusations, for instance through various forms of divination (oracles) controlled ultimately by Azande princes, had to be taken into account in order to understand why Azande beliefs made sense to them, why these beliefs were not subject to refutation, and how their beliefs reinforced the authority of their princely class.

Both Evans-Pritchard and Fortes based their writings on research carried out before World War II. Later writers extended their insights to show how claims to knowledge and power may correspond not only to the maintenance of stable hierarchical relations but also to regular processes by which these relations changed over time. John Middleton (b. 1921), writing of the Lugbara of Uganda and Zaire, another relatively uncentralized society, showed how power struggles between different family heads, and between family heads and their descendants, were contested in terms of their beliefs in witchcraft and sorcery, in their ancestors, and in their oracles. The argument of these books that is common to a generation of British ethnographies of sub-Saharan Africa is that African beliefs cannot be understood by attending only to their logical interrelations as ideas. They must also be sought in the ways that these ideas are used in the everyday practices of maintaining or changing relations of authority and power between people—that is to say, in their practical social logics. These writings have been termed functional to the extent that they focused on the effects of given characters and distributions of knowledge, and structural-functional because they located these effects predominantly in their impact on social structure. Thus, for instance, it may be argued that a pattern of witchcraft accusations by men predominantly against women expressed tension between men and women.

Alternatively, accusations between male elders facilitated the fissioning of local communities, which was a routine structural feature of some central African societies. The rationality of belief had, in short, to be assessed in the context of a form of life.

KNOWLEDGE AND DIFFERENCE

Although the interwar differences between French and British schools of anthropology have become less polarized, and most studies benefit from both perspectives as well as from more recent thought, some tension between sociological and philosophical approaches to the making and transmission of knowledge in indigenous African societies remains. The two approaches need not be antipathetic, once it is recognized that the sociologically defined differences between people (for instance, men and women, old and young) are everywhere understood in terms of the broader philosophical presuppositions (about gender, age, and so on) that constitute these differences and make them intelligible. Part of the differences among people in African societies concerns what they should or may legitimately know. Thus, the capacity for knowledge tends to be defined as an aspect of the sort of person someone is, and that different sorts of people lay claim to differing types and degrees of knowledge reinforces the sense that they are different. Explicit claims to knowledge rest on implicit acceptance of these differences among people, and knowledge is made by and transmitted among social agents, construed according to social and cultural criteria.

Although elaborated more in some places than in others, social distinctions on the basis of gender and age were stressed in all African societies. This categorization meant that some kinds of knowledge were the prerogative of men and not women, and some the prerogative of women and not men. One sex either should not know what was the prerogative of the other, or else had to dissemble such knowledge.

As a generalization, most African peoples—unlike most contemporary North Americans and Europeans—held to theories of procreation and conception that strongly differentiated the contributions made by men and women to their children; for instance, men may be thought to donate bone and women flesh. Conception itself was frequently

represented in terms of thermodynamic conditions—the generation of heat was a widely believed prerequisite. Given that large numbers of dependents were prestigious for both men and women in most African societies, it follows that gender was strongly characterized in terms of reproductive capabilities, and human conception and reproduction were common metaphors for other generative activities (such as agriculture or iron smelting). Knowledge about the specific natures of men and women was partly propositional, but also to a high degree embedded in both their everyday roles and in particular rituals that recognized or produced gender difference.

Suzette Heald (b. 1943) has sensitively described how the experience of circumcision for Gisu (Uganda) youths between eighteen and twenty-four years old allows them to achieve manhood, displaying their capacity for *lirima*, an essentially masculine emotion of power, courage, and anger, that is required to withstand the pain of circumcision but also legitimated by entry to manhood. Audrey Richards's (1889–1984) classic study of girls' initiation among the matrilineal Bemba of Zambia shows how they are also changed by the experience they undergo during the monthlong *chisungu* series of ceremonies. The girls learn how to become women as they are also taught the values of marriage, authority, and relations between men, women, and children.

Both these exemplary studies deal with, among other things, gender and age. Indeed, in African societies these dimensions cannot be separated neatly as a rule: because of the centrality of human reproduction as a metaphor of generation, men and women are most strongly differentiated during women's years of fertility. Children and the aged are less polarized in gender terms: postmenopausal women may behave in ways typical of men but forbidden to younger women; male children may be associated symbolically with some qualities of femaleness that they lose as they age. Explicit knowledge is construed as appropriate to men or women and occasionally in more nuanced ways with gender attributes that are male and female. But gender also is a subject of knowledge so that the gendering of knowledge has to be understood in a double sense—it is in terms of their knowledge of gender that African people associate knowledge in a marked sense with the capacities of men and women.

As elsewhere, children were expected to learn from their kin and neighbors—as much from their example as through formal teaching. African storytelling for the Koranko of Sierra Leone, as the anthropologist Michael Jackson (b. 1940) has shown convincingly, is not just a diversion but also a way of exploring moral precepts through exemplars. Elders of both sexes were generally reckoned more knowledgeable than their juniors, and the right to attain elements of this knowledge particular to seniors could be tied to procedures of continuing initiation. In some, especially eastern African societies, age was particularly stressed as a criterion of social organization.

KNOWLEDGE AND DIFFERENCE: SPECIALISTS

Specialists in technique (restricted knowledge that was embodied and applied) were recognized in all African societies—although there were more of them in some societies than others. Smiths and smelters and their wives, who were often potters, were denied some degree of commensality in most African societies and were attributed specialist knowledge that was maintained within families by apprenticeship. Refusal of some degree of commensality was one aspect of complexly ambivalent attitudes toward their special knowledge or power and toward their practical indispensability to nonsmiths. Such specialists were at once admired, feared, and deprecated. Similar, sometimes less obvious, ambivalence characterizes people's feelings toward specialist esoteric abilities more generally.

Sub-Saharan Africa had only a few specialized gathering and hunting societies in recent centuries; however, village farmers commonly tried their hand at hunting and some amongst them were recognized as true hunters, possessing specialized hunting lore and techniques, and perhaps inherent capacity. Hunters are frequently portrayed in legends as pioneers of new settlements who are endowed with extraordinary powers that allow them to flourish at the margin between the realms of the human and the wild. These ambivalent powers have again become prominent in the late twentieth century because of the role played by hunting associations as local defense militias in

some of West Africa's civil wars, as Thomas Bassett (b. 1953) has shown for Côte d'Ivoire.

Diviners in African societies use numerous differing techniques to produce knowledge about the circumstances of illness and misfortune or to recommend courses of future action. In doing this, diviners may also discover the operations of witchcraft—in some African societies interpreted as an innate propensity of a sort of person but in others seen as a type of knowledge acquired by people who enter into blood debts. In yet other African societies, both forms are recognized and distinguished. Because diviners draw upon a counterknowledge to witchcraft, they commonly find themselves under suspicion of witchcraft.

Possession, which involves an outside personality and intelligence taking over a person's body, may also be considered a specialist knowledge of a particular type. The degree of control or recollection exercised by the possessed person varies widely, but possession is documented both for men and women in Africa. The half-hour film *Les maîtres fous* (The mad masters), shot in Ghana (then the Gold Coast) by the French ethnographer Jean Rouch (1917–2004) in 1954, remains a powerful and controversial record of the *hauka* spirits that possessed male migrants from Niger. Janice Boddy wrote an account of women's possession among Arabic-speaking Muslim women of northern Sudan, arguing that untoward and anomalous experience challenging the conventional terms of women's selfhood is converted into a narrative of possession by foreign *zar* spirits. Possession has ambiguous consequences: although it characterizes foreignness, thus throwing northern Sudanese identity into relief, it also makes exotic elements familiar and everyday. Similarly, possession highlights expected female behavior by contrast with the behavior of the possessed, while also allowing an oblique questioning of the constraints that govern women's lives.

In more stratified forms of African society, the number of recognized and distinguished proprietors of specialist forms of knowledge multiplied. The societies of Mande, Wolof, and Tukulor speakers in western Africa fall into this more complex category. Not only smiths, smelters, and woodcarvers but also weavers, leatherworkers, and griots (praise singers) were distinguished within a system of social classification of a rigidity described by some writers as caste-like. Griots were oral artists charged with preservation of the past in the form of sung recitations that might be adapted to the service of their current patrons. The position of griots and their art have been studied in detail and their recitations recorded in close translation by, for example, John William Johnson (b. 1942) and Fa-Digi Sisòkò.

Where priests and chiefs were recognized, they also were credited with specialist knowledge. Yoruba *babalawo*, or priests of Ife divination, underwent extended apprenticeships, in the course of which they traveled widely to learn the *odu* (verses) that corresponded to configurations of their divination equipments. Chiefs may be inducted into secret knowledge at their accession. Aidan Southall argued in the case of the Alur, that access to such knowledge may explain the willingness of people to be incorporated into expanding states. For Bantu-speakers south of the Congo forest, Luc de Heusch has demonstrated how variations on a common mythological system came into being with the foundation of chiefdoms.

KNOWLEDGE AND SECRECY

Proprietorship over restricted knowledge is a facet of power; contrarily, exclusion indicates relative powerlessness; paradoxically, secrecy publicizes and dramatizes these relations rather than concealing them. In many parts of Africa, there existed and still exist institutions within which initiated members came into proper proprietorship of forms of knowledge not disclosed to other members of society. The tendency in African societies for specialized knowledge to be envisaged as a restricted possession has been widely remarked. Pervasively, an office, individual, or group of people own ritually effective modes of action and the knowledge needed to carry them through. Often this ownership is most marked in its infringement, which is sanctioned either automatically or by reaction on the part of the owners that is generally conceded to be justified. The restrictive sense of knowledge in English, which usually refers either to ideas or to the practical capacity to do or explain something, may become an impediment to understanding these cases. African initiates often are shown and see things, or touch and hold them, or hear and experience them, and each of these may be subsumed under what is being translated as knowledge. Thus, the taboos that protect special

knowledge from the uninitiated may be breached if they inadvertently see, touch, or hear some aspect of what is restricted.

Sanctioning becomes particularly prominent in relation to more elaborated forms of the general tendency to ownership of ritual technique. In numerous societies (Tiv of central Nigeria and Chamba of Nigeria and Cameroon are examples) there exist groups of initiates who control complexes of paraphernalia, knowledge, and ritual technique that are held to be effective in controlling particular misfortunes. Frequently, these techniques and their apparatuses have to be purchased, and initiation into proper knowledge about them requires further payment. It seems likely that these techniques went in and out of fashion, spreading to different societies in which they were appropriated and understood according to local style as techniques related to cult groups, rituals, deities, or otherwise. The knowledge attributed to members of such groups has its counterpart in the prohibitions placed upon nonmembers. In these cases, the idiom of secrecy (or the series of injunctions against witnessing or revelation of what is guarded) may be as, or more, important than the details of what is protected from outsiders. Here the idiom of knowledge as a vehicle of power achieves a high degree of autonomy from the necessarily concealed qualities of whatever is hidden.

Phenomena described by some people, or in some places, simply as the effects of cult technique might elsewhere be explained as the actions of divinities, or as combined effects of cultic and divine powers. Given the difficulties human beings face in gaining knowledge of phenomena conceived as extraordinary, understandings of exceptional powers are typically fluid. Yoruba *orisa* and Ewe *vodún* are examples of divinities that have shrines, priests, and followers, and receive particular offerings. Each cult has its rituals, music, oral literature, dances, and divination techniques, and each potentially brings not only benefits to its followers but also misfortunes if it is neglected or its rules of conduct broken. These institutions create multiple fields of knowledge, mastered unequally by initiates.

In some societies (notably those of the western African forest belt, such as Gola, Kpelle, Mende, Soso, Temne, Vai), secret societies are virtually coextensive with the entire adult male and female population. *Poro* for men and *sande* for women are societies entered by initiation that enjoin their members not to reveal what they learn there. However, the association of claims to knowledge with secrecy found in these societies should not be envisaged as anomalous, but rather as an extreme of an indigenous tendency to associate powerful knowledge with occlusion.

RECENT THEORETICAL APPROACHES

In contemporary studies of African knowledge (that would usually take account of Islam and Christianity, among other nonindigenous influences omitted here, particularly secular science), investigators expect to study both the overall system of thought and the ways in that knowledge was distributed and allocated to particular statuses.

Since the 1960s, Robin Horton has argued that African religions be envisaged as an extension of the field of social relations among human beings to nonhuman entities (the dead, forces of the wild, divinities). Relations with nonhuman entities are somewhat similar to relations between occupants of highly disparately ranked statuses, so that there is much in common in the relationships between commoner and king and between supplicant and divinity. African traditional knowledge, Horton argues, should be treated as akin to Western science in its concern to explain, predict, and control the course of events. With respect to the transmission of knowledge, Horton would contend that indigenous African ideas of the way the world worked were subject to constant empirical testing against the outcomes of attempting to put these ideas into practice. However, in common with Evans-Pritchard earlier, he would accept that African traditional thought was constrained by its foundational presuppositions and in this respect may be characterized as a relatively closed system by comparison with the openness of Western science.

Stereotypes of the transmission of a timeless African knowledge between generations are wrong empirically. Pejorative preconceptions have played a large role in making static depictions of African knowledge credible, but these derive also from the necessity of reconstructing much of the African past only from noncontemporary evidence. Comparative studies of variations between neighboring peoples, and within peoples known by a single ethnic name,

may go some way toward redressing an impression of the absence of change in precolonial times when direct evidence is lacking.

Recent scholarship has shifted attention away from knowledge as a body of verbal propositions that may be elicited from informants. Regional comparisons have been facilitated by widespread adoption of the methods, if not theories, of structuralist anthropology, that is, the wide provenance of myths, ritual, and institutions in sub-Saharan Africa that may be analyzed as systems of transformation, in that the positions and values of their elements are rearranged. Such patterning has suggested historical relations between African peoples previously described as culturally distinct "tribes." Local African informants' accounts of this distribution are restricted because they are concerned with those parts of broader regions that are adjacent to themselves. It is within this broader regions that historians may discern patterns of transformation. Hence, regional scholarship attempts to transcend local studies in order to characterize more widely distributed features of African systems of knowledge.

Although regional scholarship has addressed the underlying logic of African knowledge on a broad scale, another trend in recent scholarship has accentuated attention to highly localized knowledge. This scholarship has been concerned with experience and with the embodiment of complex knowledge that is difficult to put into words. Godfrey Lienhardt's (1921–1993) phenomenological study of the religion of Dinka pastoralists in Sudan that stressed how important Dinka experience of their world was to understanding their religious thought and practice has been claimed as an early example of this approach. Lienhardt's phenomenological orientation has been combined with an appreciation of the Dinka's relatively powerless position in Wendy James's (b. 1940) innovative and sensitive study of the marginalized Uduk of Sudan. Although in many respects consistent with British, post–World War II anthropological scholarship, Victor W. Turner's (1920–1983) studies of the multivalent symbols used in Ndembu rituals, and his emphasis upon ritual as experience, have had a profound influence on later scholars, who have emphasized the full range of human sensory experience in the attempt to move beyond accounts of knowledge constrained by over-reliance on verbalized exegesis.

Contemporary scholarship of African indigenous knowledge continues to develop numerous strands initiated by previous writers, and U.S. writings are particularly pluralist in this respect. Structural, phenomenological, symbolic, and dialogic approaches (the latter continuing the tradition of Griaule in some respects) are all to be found in recent works on African knowledge. However, their multiplicity contributes to the sense to be given to indigenous knowledge becoming increasingly problematic.

POSTCOLONIAL WRITERS AND THE IDEA OF AFRICAN KNOWLEDGE

If the phrase "indigenous African knowledge" means knowledge that was antecedent to outside influence, then there are problems in deciding whether African—or any other—societies were ever isolated in the sense that this formulation begs, and if so, when. Supposing that such isolation had occurred—but long ago—then what would be the evidence for the knowledge that then prevailed? Studying people's knowledge involves difficult methodological questions, even given access to living informants and copious textual sources; in the absence of either, these questions become more pressing but harder to resolve satisfactorily.

If indigenous knowledge is understood as knowledge currently claimed not to derive from the outside, then it is important to ask how this local category of knowledge considered indigenous is itself made and transmitted, and what interests it serves. Whether it is possible for insiders or outsiders to delimit indigenous African knowledge as a topic for study is itself a complex and politically charged question.

Several postcolonial writers, including V. Y. Mudimbe (b. 1947) and Kwame Anthony Appiah (b. 1954), have subjected representations of African indigenous knowledge to philosophical scrutiny. Strongly influenced by Michel Foucault (1926–1984), the French historian of ideas, Mudimbe's effort to write a history of ideas of Africa has sought to reveal ways in that discourses about Africa have necessarily relied upon Western categories and conceptual systems. For his part, Appiah has been particularly critical of attempts to present Africa as culturally uniform or possessed of a unitary essence. These two astute writers delineate a similar and

fundamental dilemma: in some degree Africa's future depends on a reckoning to be made with forms of knowledge and identity that predate imperialism and colonization (and perhaps also the trans-Atlantic slave trade), but there is no neutral point from which such indigenous resources may be addressed. All commentators (whether African, diasporic, or non-African) contemplate these matters from the different, complex subject positions that have resulted in the course of the history they attempt to understand—the same history that has also given rise to claims to knowledge about Africa.

See also **Anthropology, Social, and the Study of Africa; Divination and Oracles; Gender; Philosophy and the Study of Africa; Research; Rouch, Jean; Secret Societies.**

BIBLIOGRAPHY

Appiah, Kwame Anthony. *In My Father's House: Africa in the Philosophy of Culture.* London: Methuen, 1992.

Bassett, Thomas. "Dangerous Pursuits: Hunter Associations (*donzo ton*) and National Politics in Côte d'Ivoire." *Africa* 73, no. 1 (2003): 1–30.

Bellman, Beryl Larry. *The Language of Secrecy: Symbols and Metaphors in Poro Ritual.* New Brunswick, NJ: Rutgers University Press, 1984.

Boddy, Janice. *Wombs and Alien Spirits: Women, Men, and the Zar Cult in Northern Sudan.* Madison: University of Wisconsin Press, 1989.

Evans-Pritchard, Edward E. *Witchcraft, Oracles, and Magic among the Azande.* Oxford: Clarendon Press, 1965.

Fardon, Richard. *Between God, the Dead, and the Wild: Chamba Interpretations of Religion and Ritual.* Edinburgh: Edinburgh University Press for the International African Institute; Washington, DC: Smithsonian, 1991.

Fortes, Meyer. *Religion, Morality, and the Person: Essays on Tallensi Religion,* ed. Jack Goody. Cambridge, U.K.: Cambridge University Press, 1987.

Griaule, Marcel. *Conversation with Ogotemmêli.* London: Oxford University Press, 1965.

Griaule, Marcel. *The Pale Fox,* trans. Mary Beach. Chino Valley, AZ: Continuum Foundation, 1986.

Heald, Suzette. *Controlling Anger: The Anthropology of Gisu Violence,* 2nd edition. Oxford: James Currey, 1998.

Herbert, Eugenia. *Iron, Gender, and Power: Rituals of Transformation in African Societies.* Bloomington: Indiana University Press, 1993.

Heusch, Luc de. *The Drunken King; or, The Origin of the State,* trans. Roy Willis. Bloomington: Indiana University Press, 1982.

Horton, Robin. *Patterns of Thought in Africa and the West: Essays on Magic, Religion, and Science.* Cambridge, U.K.: Cambridge University Press, 1993.

Jackson, Michael. *Allegories of the Wilderness: Ethics and Ambiguity in Kuranko Narratives.* Bloomington: Indiana University Press, 1982.

James, Wendy. *The Listening Ebony: Moral Knowledge, Religion, and Power among the Uduk of Sudan.* Oxford: Clarendon, 1988.

Johnson, John William, and Fa-Digi Sisòkò. *The Epic of Son-Jara: A West African Tradition.* Bloomington: Indiana University Press, 1992.

Lienhardt, R. Godfrey. *Divinity and Experience: The Religion of the Dinka.* Oxford: Clarendon, 1961.

Middleton, John. *Lugbara Religion: Ritual and Authority among an East African People.* Oxford: James Currey, 1999.

Mudimbe, V. Y. *The Invention of Africa: Gnosis, Philosophy, and the Order of Knowledge.* Bloomington: Indiana University Press, 1988.

Richards, Audrey. *Chisungu: A Girls' Initiation Ceremony among the Bemba of Zambia,* 2nd edition. London: Tavistock, 1988.

Southall, Aidan. *Alur Society: A Study in Processes and Types of Domination,* 2nd revised edition. Münster, Germany: Lit Verlag, 2004.

Turner, Victor Wittor. *The Forest of Symbols: Aspects of Ndembu Ritual.* Ithaca, NY: Cornell University Press, 1967.

van Beek, Walter E. A. "Dogon Restudied: A Field Evaluation of the Work of Marcel Griaule." *Current Anthropology* 32, no. 2 (1991): 139–167.

RICHARD FARDON

KOK, ADAM, III

(1811–1875). Adam Kok III was the nineteenth-century leader of the Phillippolis Griquas, an Afrikaans-speaking group of mixed, predominantly Khoe, descent. Kok was born in 1811, the son of Adam Kok II, whom he succeeded as captain of the Philippolis Griquas on the latter's death. These people had settled along and to the north of the Orange River during the eighteenth century under the leadership of the Kok and Barends families. After 1800, in part under the influence of the missionaries, they coalesced into small polities, first in Griquatown, just north of the middle Orange River, and then, beginning in 1826, at Philippolis, in what was to become the

southern Orange Free State. While other Griquas were important raiders on the highveld, the community under Adam Kok III was more settled, tried to maintain good relations with the Cape Colony, and grew rich on merino sheep farming. However, conflict with Afrikaner Voortrekkers spreading throughout the region after 1835, and particularly after the independence of the Orange Free State in 1854, made their position untenable. Therefore, in 1859–1860, Kok led a migration of the Philippolis Griquas eastward over the Drakensberg Mountains to Nomansland, later Griqualand East, where he founded a new captaincy centered on Kokstad, which dominated the neighboring African communities along the Indian Ocean Coast. In its turn, though, Griqualand East was annexed by the Cape Colony in 1874, shortly before Kok's death.

See also **Cape Colony and Hinterland, History of (1600 to 1910).**

BIBLIOGRAPHY

Ross, Robert. *Adam Kok's Griquas: A Study in the Development of Stratification in South Africa.* New York: Cambridge University Press, 1976.

Shephard, John Brownlow. *In the Shadow of the Drakensberg.* Durban, South Africa: Griggs, 1976.

ROBERT ROSS

KONGO, ANGOLA, AND WESTERN FORESTS, HISTORY OF (1500 TO 1880).

At the beginning of the sixteenth century, West-Central Africans carried out lifestyles similar to most populations around the globe. Agriculture, hunting, and fishing were the primary means of subsistence, and occupational specializations provided a basis for local trade and social stratification. Where an abundance of natural resources was to be found (such as iron-ore deposits, salt pans, and raffia palms), specialized production led to the development of long-distance trade and surplus wealth. With the exception of Ubangian speakers along the northernmost edge of the rain forest, all of the people within the region spoke Bantu languages. As such, they shared important cultural traits and similar conceptions regarding earthly and supernatural sources of political legitimacy, the role of territorial and ancestral spirits in religious ritual, and the negative effects of antisocial behavior (witchcraft) wrought by human jealousy, avarice, or hate.

Within the western rain forests, where population densities were low, the basic political unit was the village, organized around a specific lineage or clan. At its head was an individual who claimed direct descent from the original founder, effectively managed resources (trade goods, land, and people), and above all, was able to influence earthly events through access to supernatural powers. As in many areas of the world, political legitimacy was intimately linked with having been the first to occupy the land. The Central African twist to this logic, however, was the belief that the buried ancestors of such first-comers played a role in assuring the well-being of latter occupants, especially as pertained to the fertility of people and land. In the rain forest, Batwa populations (Pygmies) had long been posited as original inhabitants, but the rise of Bantu hegemony precluded any substantive political role for the Batwa. Instead, Batwa served as forest-specialists, carriers of forest goods across vast expanses of land. Their ancestors, however, came to be associated with the spirits of the land. It was thus the headman's responsibility to appeal to both kinds of spirits—those of the lineage ancestors and those of the territory/ancient Batwa—in order to ensure continuity of the clan.

South of the rain forest are savanna-forest mosaics. Bantu populations had long settled into the river valleys of this region (such as Niari and Zaire) in order to exploit the great variety of natural resources. The abundance of people, wealth, and trade allowed new forms of political centralization to appear, whereby effective leaders could claim a multiplicity of villages (a district) as their political domain, and eventually a multiplicity of districts (a principality), as well. Reigning over a principality was the lord of the land (*kitome* in Kongo), an enhanced version of the village headman. This individual served as a supreme earth priest, interceding with territorial spirits on behalf of his followers. All territorial lords claimed descent from a founding Bantu lineage, and in most cases a mythical Batwa figure as well. Their effectiveness as political and religious leaders was judged by their capacity to bring forth rain and large harvests,

ensure the fecundity of women, attract a large numbers of followers, and lead in times of war.

By the sixteenth century a number of these southern principalities had fused, creating small kingdoms on both sides of the Zaire River (Loango, Kongo, Tio). Oral traditions relate that the founders of these states were conquering outsiders with impressive supernatural and military skills. In keeping with earlier traditions, however, these states recognized two bodies of titleholders: those associated with the royal court, and those recognized as indigenous lords of the land. This system was beneficial in that it honored first-comer status and prevented despotic tendencies within the royal clan. It was detrimental, however, in that it limited the degree of political and economic centralization a monarch could undertake, because disgruntled territorial lords could challenge the legitimacy of royal lineage itself.

To the south in the middle Kwango River valley, arable lands and rich iron deposits led to the formation of Ndongo, an incipient state composed of Mbundu-speaking people. Large farming communities were also located on the central highland plateau, where the Ovimbundu speech community took shape. In these southern regions, political formations were greatly affected by shortages of rainfall. Droughts generally occurred in each decade, and at least once in each of the last four centuries a drought reached catastrophic proportions (lasting five to ten years). During these periods, agriculturalists descended from the northern and western flanks of the central highlands, as well as the northern tributary valleys of the Kwanza, to raid for cattle and crops. The violence that ensued led populations to gather in isolated areas where geographic features provided for defense (such as rock outcrops and mountain redoubts). Warlords arose to organize such populations, creating a form of political centralization in which title-holders were chosen by personal appointment, rather than lineage politics or first-comer claims. The kingdom of Ndongo developed along this model; its political center was located in isolated stands of granite boulders at Pungo Andongo in the middle Kwanza, where a permanent refugee center was established.

The Portuguese arrived in Kongo in 1483. At that time Kongo was a loose confederation of small states with a monarch who was elected by regional constituents (territorial lords) but held little political sway beyond the central province. All resources, however, were channeled through the capital Mbanza Kongo, allowing for effective centralization in the economic sphere. During the first few decades of contact, the Portuguese sought to establish religious and political alliances much as they did with other sovereign nations around the globe.

The Kongolese aristocracy accepted Christianity, making it the official religion of the state. In doing so they essentially added it to the existing retinue of religious beliefs and practices, focusing on elements of the new cult that held concordance with Kongolese cosmological views. In return, the Portuguese sent priests, craftsmen, traders, and luxury goods, aiding the aristocracy in its attempt to modernize and centralize the state. These transformations had a profound impact. The royals monopolized the new resources and religious cult, allowing power to become highly centralized in the figure of the king. Under King Afonso I (1509–1543) many elites converted, gained literacy skills, and adopted European fashions and names. From the royal perspective, partnership with the Portuguese was beneficial in its earliest stages, for it allowed greater control over the provinces and provoked new alliances with interior tribute-paying states.

Problems arose, however, as the demand for African slaves began to mount. In the late fifteenth century Kongo had supplied a small number of slaves to Portuguese settlers on the nearby island of São Tomé, where sugar plantations were established. By 1510 the Portuguese were buying captives for sale at various points along the West African coast. In order to meet the growing demand, the Kongolese carried out border wars to the Northeast and the South. Havoc began to reign within the kingdom as well, because Portuguese priests, traders, and local elites were lured by the large profits to be made. In 1526 Affonso I complained to King John of Portugal that slaving activities were destroying his kingdom. By this point, however, the Portuguese had established their own contacts at the large inland market at Malebo Pool. The slave trade continued unabated.

Seeking access to greater markets, the Portuguese crown attempted to forge an alliance with the kings of Ndongo in the 1520s. Due to protests by the Kongolese monarch, the alliance was thwarted. Instead, Euro-African traders from São Tomé moved in. With their help, Ndongo kings began raiding for slaves along the southern borders of Kongo, the middle Kwango, and south of the Kwanza (1520–1560s). These activities helped to solidify Ndongo, but also provoked the rise of refugee warrior bands that eventually undermined the state. Most notorious of these were the Imbangala, or Jaga, who ravaged the lower valleys and coasts south of the Kwanza. Capitalizing on a long series of droughts in the last third of the sixteenth century, the Imbangala were renowned for indiscriminate, ruthless killing and were unbeatable by Portuguese and African armies alike. Much of their power derived from their disregard for cultural elements that defined humanness in the central African world: they disdained agriculture, practiced cannibalism and human sacrifice, and as Thornton has noted, "abandoned the cult of territorial deities in favor of strict propitiation of their own ancestors, who were [represented as] wicked people like themselves ... " (Thornton 2002).

The Imbangala invaded Kongo in 1569 and occupied the capital for six years. After being ousted by Kongolese military and six hundred Portuguese troops, a number of Imbangala settled around the upper Kwango River to establish the Kasanje kingdom (in the early seventeenth century). Meanwhile, the Portuguese took advantage of Kongo's weakness by seizing Luanda Island to the south and establishing a military post on the mainland just opposite. Over the next thirty years they used diplomatic channels to gain power within the Ndongo royal court while employing Imbangala mercenaries to harass the kingdom from outside. These actions, along with a prolonged drought, led to the demise of Ndongo by 1620. This episode presaged a pattern of political development that would become common in Central Africa. The initial entry into Atlantic economies allowed for African political and economic gains and even the creation of new states. The violence and treachery associated with slaving, however, eventually undermined the stability of such states, provoking crises of security and political legitimacy that were impossible to overcome.

In the north, a Dutch demand for ivory and slaves led to contacts with the Vili peoples of the Loango kingdom. The Vili had long been intrepid traders, traveling inland on overland routes to the Teke Plateau where they exchanged salt for iron. Independent Batwa communities supplied much of the ivory during this period, paying it as tribute to local territorial lords. The Vili tapped into these rain forest networks and, when the Dutch demand for slaves increased (1630s), expanded their overland routes to reach the major slave markets at Malebo Pool and in the Kasanje kingdom to the southeast. With British and French entry into the slave trade at Loango (1640s), Vili networks began to overshadow those of Kongo, leading to the latter's economic decline. Kongo also suffered from the increasing power of its maritime province Nsongo, which had stopped paying tribute to the monarchy and established independent trade routes to Malebo Pool. Increased European competition led Portugal to abandon any pretense of diplomacy with Kongo. The Portuguese military, aided by Imbangala troops, ousted the Kongolese king in 1665 in the Battle of Mbwila. Thereafter, rival royal factions battled to regain Kongolese power, resulting in a forty-year civil war and the eventual demise of the state.

During the seventeenth century, the impact of the slave trade began to be felt deep within the continent. Within the rain forest new hierarchies of power developed, as communities located at strategic locations became traders in the ever-expanding network. The Bobangi, for example, were originally fishing peoples occupying the confluence of the Ubangi and Zaire Rivers. By the end of the seventeenth century they had become major carriers of trade between there and Malebo Pool, extracting people and ivory from the heart of the African continent. Traders such as the Bobangi guarded their trade connections jealously, established new institutions to maintain them (blood-brotherhood), and, as guns increasingly entered the continent, used violence to force neighbors into highly exploitative systems of patron-client relations. This was especially the case for Batwa peoples, whose skills as ivory hunters remained essential to the wealth of local big men well into the early nineteenth century, when European demand for slaves began to wane.

By the early nineteenth century, West-Central Africans had undergone more than three hundred years of violence, dislocation, and political breakdown. They found themselves in a profoundly altered social, political, and spiritual milieu. Leadership had become rooted in the ability to accumulate material wealth, and followers were gained through coercion or purchase. Although the populace still maintained the view that worldly success was made possible through possession of superior supernatural skills, the ravages of the slave trade convinced them that such skills had been turned to individualistic gains at the expense of the community. Local popular religious associations such as Kimpassi (Kongo), that focused on beneficent territorial spirits and communal well-being arose in response to the perception that witchcraft (evil self-interest) had pervaded Central African life. New group identities had also been created and hardened, making ethnic lines much harder to cross. Most destructive over the long term was that Central African economies became entirely dependent on the Atlantic trade, inaugurating a system of extractive economies that continue to cause African poverty into the early twenty-first century. All of these factors impaired Central Africans' ability to resist the divide-and-conquer tactics employed by Europeans as the Europeans moved into the continent after 1880 to establish imperial rule.

See also **Christianity; Colonial Policies and Practices; Congo Independent State; Ivory; Kimpa Vita, Dona Beatriz; Njinga Mbandi Ana de Sousa.**

BIBLIOGRAPHY

Harms, Robert. *River of Wealth, River of Sorrow: The Central Zaire Basin in the Era of the Slave and Ivory Trade, 1500–1891.* New Haven, CT: Yale University Press, 1981.

Klieman, Kairn. *"The Pygmies Were Our Compass": Bantu and Batwa in the History of West Central Africa, Early Times to c. 1900 CE.* Portsmouth, NH: Heinemann, 2003.

Miller, Joseph C. "The Paradoxes of Impoverishment in the Atlantic Zone." In *History of Central Africa,* Vol. 1. ed. David Birmingham and Phyllis Martin. London: Longman Group, 1983.

Miller, Joseph C. "Central Africa during the Era of the Slave Trade, c. 1490s–1850s." In *Central Africans* and *Cultural Transformations in the American Diaspora*, ed. Linda M. Heywood. Cambridge, U.K.: Cambridge University Press, 2002.

Thornton, John. "Religious and Ceremonial Life in the Kongo and Mbundu Areas, 1500–1700." In *Central Africans and Cultural Transformations in the American Diaspora*, ed. Linda M. Heywood. Cambridge, U.K.: Cambridge University Press, 2002.

Vansina, Jan. *Paths in the Rainforest: Toward a History of Political Tradition in Equatorial Africa.* Madison: University of Wisconsin Press, 1990.

KAIRN A. KLIEMAN

KONGO CHRISTIANITY. *See* Christianity.

KOUMBI-SALEH.

The 100-acre urban site of Koumbi-Saleh is located in the eastern Hodh, several miles from Mauritania's southeastern border with Mali. It comprises more than sixty mounds, delimited by large streets, of debris from collapsed buildings constructed with plaques of locally available schist. In 1914 Albert Bonnel de Mezières suggested that the site was the capital of the empire of Ghana described by al-Bakri in 1068. Various excavation programs (by Bonnel de Mezières, Robert Mauny, and Sophie Berthier) have subsequently sought to confirm this identification epigraphically, without success. Most of these excavations have been published summarily, with the exception of Berthier's work from the late 1970s, which focused on architectural change in the stone-built ruins. Digging twenty feet down through the deposits within a single large building, Berthier identified a distinctive architectural style belonging to the period of "grande urbanization" at the site, radiocarbon-dated to the eleventh through fourteenth centuries, after which the house was abandoned. The extensive areas of Koumbi-Saleh that lack stone ruins still remain to be investigated. If the site is indeed the ancient capital, these may be the remains of the indigenous town in which the pagan king (*ghana*) lived, described by al-Bakri as separate from the stone-built town inhabited by Muslims and northern traders.

See also **Archaeology and Prehistory; Mauritania.**

BIBLIOGRAPHY

Berthier, Sophie. *Recherches archéologiques sur la capitale de l'Empire de Ghana.* BAR International Series 680. Oxford: British Archaeological Reports, 1997.

Bonnel de Mezières, Albert "Recherche sur l'emplacement de Ghana (fouilles à Koumbi Saleh et Settah)." *Comptes Rendus de l'Académie des Inscriptions et Belles Lettres* 12 (1920): 227–273.

Mauny, Robert, and P. Thomassey. "Campagne de fouilles à Koumbi Saleh (Ghana?)." *Bulletin de l'Institut Français de l'Afrique Noire* 13 (1951): 438–462.

Mauny, Robert, and P. Thomassey. "Campagne de fouilles de 1950 à Koumbi Saleh (Ghana?)." *Bulletin de l'Institut Français de l'Afrique Noire* 18 (1956): 117–140.

McIntosh, S. K., and R. J. McIntosh. "The Early City in West Africa: Towards an Understanding." *African Archaeological Review* 2 (1984): 73–98.

Robert, D., and S. Robert "Douze années de recherches archéologiques en République islamique de Mauritanie." *Annales de la Faculté des Lettres* 2 (1972): 195–233.

SUSAN K. MCINTOSH

KOUROUMA, AHMADOU

(1927–2003). Author Ahmadou Kourouma was born on November 24, 1927, and received his early education in Bamako, Mali. He served in the French army from 1950 to 1954, then studied accounting in Lyons from 1955 to 1959. During the colonial upheavals of the 1960s, he was forced into exile in 1963 and subsequently worked in banking and insurance in Algeria, Cameroon, and Togo. During this period he also wrote his first two novels: *The Suns of Independence*, published in 1968, and *Monnew*, published in 1990.

In 1993 Kourouma returned to Abidjan to work for United Nations Education, Scientific, and Cultural Organization (UNESCO) and to complete his third novel, *Waiting for the Vote of the Wild Animals*, a satire of Cold War dictatorships in Africa. In that same year, he also published a children's novel titled *Yacouba, chasseur africain*. His final novel, published in 2000, was *Allah n'est pas obligé*. Kourouma died on December 11, 2003.

Kourouma's first novel relates the picaresque misadventures of Fama Doumbouya in the newly independent "Ebony Coast." It was one of the first novels to present what have since become staple themes in Francophone literature: satire of the postcolony, critique of the one-party state, a shift from programmatic polemic to massive skepticism and uncertainty. Rather than renewal, independence is here a moment of supreme disillusionment and disorientation. The quixotic Fama is an appropriately complex vehicle for the impossible situation Kourouma describes: honorable but inept, determined but impulsive, he is a mass of misplaced loyalties, the last of a literally dying breed. Heirless, "sterile," and illiterate, Fama has no place in the new society he so eloquently despises. His wife, Salimata, "a woman of infinite goodwill," confronts rape and violent abuse. Fama's empty existence ends when the death of a cousin propels him into the puppet chiefdom of a desperately poor, border village, Togobala. However, depressed by his inability to restore the old order, he is arrested soon afterward on trumped-up charges and condemned to a "camp without name." By the time he returns to Togobala, "death had become his only companion," and a final confrontation with petty border officials—"the bastard sons of bitches and slaves"—leads to an end somewhere between pathetic delusion and honorable suicide.

Kourouma's second novel presents the catastrophic life of Djigui, king of Soba, whose reign begins just before the French conquest and ends with independence. Like Fama, Djigui is unable to adapt to the new order and remains a largely passive spectator, witness to the introduction of forced labor, conscription, taxes, and cash crops, as well as to two world wars and the hypocrisy of successive French regimes. He eventually loses his position to his scheming son Béma, in anticipation of "the single party, the charismatic man, the Father of the Nation" and "the struggle for national unity, for development, for socialism, tribalism, nepotism," an endless litany of broken promises and empty slogans that leave the people "skeptical, skinned, half-deaf, half-blind, voiceless." Unlike Fama, however, Djigui lives in partial collaboration with the French, seduced by the promise of a train and manipulated by his ubiquitous interpreter. If Kourouma's precolonial Soba stagnates in the self-proclaimed certainties asserted by a mob of "fetishists, marabouts, soothsayers, and griots," the interpreter (like the writer) mediates a situation defined by uncertainty, duplicity, and complicity—as by literary innovation. Kourouma's work remains an open experiment in the search for new kinds of interlinguistic "adequation" (or, the rendering or telling of an experience adequate to the peculiar features of that experience) in a style as "proverbial" as it is experimental. In the midst of massive displacement, his writing helps to restore *la parole*, at least, to a newly possible place.

See also **Literature.**

BIBLIOGRAPHY

Kourouma, Ahmadou. *Les soleils des indépendances.* Paris, 1968. Translated by Adrian Adams as *The Suns of Independence.* New York: Africana Press, 1981.

Kourouma, Ahmadou. *Monnè, outrages et défis.* Paris, 1990. Translated by Nidra Poller as *Monnew: A Novel.* San Francisco: Mercury House, 1993.

Kourouma, Ahmadou. *Waiting for the Vote of the Wild Animals.* Charlottesville: University of Virginia Press, 2001.

PETER HALLWARD

KRUGER, PAUL (1825–1904).

Paul Kruger was born in Bulhoek in the Steynsberg district, South Africa, in the eastern Cape Colony on October 10, 1825. He was largely uneducated as all schooling ceased for him when his family joined the Voortrekkers heading north to escape growing British influence in 1836. The family settled in Rustenberg, Transvaal, in 1838. In 1841, when Kruger turned sixteen, he was granted his own land at the base of the Magaliesberg Mountains. The following year he married Maria du Plessis, and within another year they had a son. However, both the young wife and infant died the following season, reputedly of malaria. Kruger married his wife's sister, Gezina du Plessis (d. 1901), and together they had seven daughters and nine sons, not all of whom lived to adulthood.

Kruger joined the Transvaal military, earning regular promotions until he attained the rank of Commandant-General of the South African Republic (the then-Transvaal). Politically adept, he became a member of the *Volksraad* (legislative assembly) and helped draw up a constitution for the renamed Transvaal. In

Paul Kruger (1825–1904). Kruger was elected president of Transvaal in December 1880. In 1891, when gold was discovered in his homeland, the leader was forced to fight off British outsiders eager to take control of the valuable resource and topple his government. He held out until his defeat in 1900. MANSELL/TIME & LIFE PICTURES/GETTY IMAGES

of them British, into Transvaal who were seeking their fortune. Conflicts soon erupted between the Boer settlers and the uitlanders. In 1895, Leander Starr Jameson (1853–1917), a collaborator of the Cape Prime Minister (and director of the British South Africa Company) Cecil Rhodes (1853–1902), led forces into Transvaal, hoping to inspire an uitlander revolt and topple the Kruger government. Jameson's raid failed, but it triggered the chain of events that led to the second Boer war, 1899–1902.

In 1898, Kruger was reelected for the last time. Hostilities between uitlanders and Boers erupted into open war in October 1899. This time, the British faction won. On May 7, 1900, Kruger was forced to leave Pretoria, and in October of that year he left the country for good. Kruger traveled to France and the Netherlands before settling in the Swiss town of Clarens, where he died on July 14, 1904. His body was returned to Pretoria for burial.

See also **Rhodes, Cecil John; South Africa, Republic of.**

BIBLIOGRAPHY

Cloete, Stuart. *African Portraits: A Biography of Paul Kruger, Cecil Rhodes, and Lobengula, Last King of the Matabele.* Capetown, South Africa: Constantia Publishers, 1969.

SARAH VALDEZ

1873 he resigned his military commission and was elected to the Transvaal executive council.

When the British annexed Transvaal in 1877, Kruger led deputations to the United Kingdom to press the case for independence. Rebuffed by the British, Kruger took up arms during the first Boer war (1880–1881). He was elected president of Transvaal in December 1880 (he would be reelected three more times). In 1891, the Boer forces defeated the British, and Transvaal was formally granted its independence.

The discovery of gold in Transvaal in the early 1890s sparked a flood of outsiders (*uitlanders*), many

KUFUOR, JOHN (1938–). Born into an influential and distinguished family in the Ashanti region, John Kufuor had his early education in Ghana before proceeding to London in 1959 to study law at Lincolns Inn. In the middle of his legal studies, he enrolled in Oxford University to earn a degree in philosophy, politics, and economics. He took and passed the English Bar exam in 1962, the same year he married his wife Theresa, with whom he had five children. The Kufuors returned to Ghana in 1965.

Kufuor's induction into Ghanaian politics came in 1967 with his appointment as town clerk (city manager) of Kumasi. With the return to civilian rule and the commencement of the Second Republic, he was elected to represent the Atwima-Nwabagya constituency in the national assembly and subsequently appointed deputy foreign minister in the Busia government. After the government's overthrow in 1972, he was put under protective custody for over

Ghanaian president John Agyekum Kufuor with South Korean President Roh Moo-Hyun, Seoul, 2006. Kufuor (1938–) was appointed deputy foreign minister of the Busia government in 1969. Three years later, the government was overthrown and Kufuor transitioned into private business. He served again in parliament from 1979 to 1981. He became president in 2001. JEON HEON-KYUN-POOL/GETTY IMAGES

a year; upon his release he went into private business. Constitutional rule was restored in 1979, and he once again won his parliamentary seat. After the military takeover of 1981, Kufuor was briefly detained but later accepted to serve as secretary for local government in the new Provisional National Defense Council (PNDC) regime. Although he resigned after only seven months, he continues to be criticized for working with a military regime.

From the mid-1980s through the early 1990s, Kufuor was one of the leading voices in the opposition to the Rawlings regime. With the introduction of the Fourth Republican constitution, his party, the New Patriotic Party (NPP), emerged as the leading opposition group. In his first attempt to be elected president in 1996, he lost to the incumbent, Jerry Rawlings. Four years later, his party was successful in

unseating the National Democratic Congress (NDC) and Kufuor became president. He was elected for a second term in 2004.

Although Kufuor is perhaps the most unglamorous and uncharismatic head of state Ghana has ever had, he has succeeded in turning his country into the most stable in a highly volatile region of Africa. The excessive use of state power that characterized the preceding regime was considerably curtailed, the economy redirected, and the nation, it would appear, given a new sense of purpose.

See also **Ghana: History and Politics; Rawlings, Jerry.**

BIBLIOGRAPHY

Agyeman Dua, Ivor. *Between Faith and History: A Biography of J. A. Kufuor.* London: Africa World Press, 2003.

Ayee, Joseph R. A. "A Decade of Political Leadership in Ghana, 1993–2003." Paper presented at the Council for the Development of Social Science Research in Africa Workshop, University of Ghana, April 2004.

YAKUBU SAAKA

BIBLIOGRAPHY

Adarkwa, Ghana Kwafo, and Johan Post. *Fate of the Tree: Planning and Managing the Development of Kumasi.* Amsterdam: Thela Thesis, 2001.

Wilks, Ivor. *Asante in the Nineteenth Century.* Cambridge, U.K.: Cambridge University Press, 1975.

DONNA J. MAIER

KUMASI. With a population of 1,517,000 (2005), Kumasi is the second-largest city in Ghana and the capital of the Ashanti region. It is located 155 miles northwest of Accra in the forest zone of West Africa.

Kumasi is of great historical importance, founded around 1690 by the *Asantehene* (king) Osei Tutu as capital of the expanding Asante state. The town's population grew to 20,000 by the early 1800s, developing as a nucleus of Asante's commercial networks and royal seat of government. The Asantehene's palace (Manhiya), court, mausoleum, and the townhouses of provincial authorities were located there. Kumasi was burned but not occupied by the British in 1874, and gradually recovered until formal British occupation occurred in 1896.

The city's administrative importance continued under British rule, but significant urban growth did not occur until after Ghana's independence in 1957. Since then, Kumasi has prospered as a key center for the timber, cocoa, and gold mining industries, and has also been an educational center because of the Kwame Nkrumah University of Science and Technology. The population now includes multiple ethnic groups besides Ashanti. The modern state has superseded the role of the Asantehene, but he still holds court in Kumasi, arbitrating customary disputes.

Some features of the city include Ghana's largest open-air market (Kumasi Central Market), a zoo, the British Fort (1896), and the National Cultural Centre where various Asante royal memorabilia can be viewed, as well as exhibitions of traditional dance and weaving. The largest stadium in Ghana (seating for 100,000) is home of the city's successful football (soccer) team, the Asante Kotoko.

See also **Accra; Colonial Policies and Practices; Ghana; Osei Tutu; Postcolonialism.**

KUNTI, AL-. *See* **Mukhtar, Sidi al-.**

KUSH. *See* **Nubia.**

KUTI, FELA (1938–1997). Fela Kuti was a Nigerian musician and political dissident. The son of activist parents and the grandson of a well-known composer of Christian religious music, Kuti was educated in music at London's Trinity College before returning to Nigeria in 1963 and becoming a well-known musician playing the locally popular "highlife" music. He began composing political music after a trip to the United States in 1969 that exposed him to African-American political activists. From 1970 he became one of Nigeria's most popular musicians, creating a mixture of highlife, jazz, and funk music that he called "Afrobeat." His popularity also enabled him to become an outspoken public figure, using his music to ridicule and castigate Nigeria's ruling classes, clergy, and military rulers. Fela also led a very unconventional lifestyle, openly espousing marijuana smoking and sexual promiscuity. His politics and lifestyle made him the target of harassment from Nigeria's authorities. His compound was attacked on several occasions by police and soldiers of the Nigerian army. Despite his turbulent life, Fela was one of Africa's greatest composers of popular music. He was also very popular outside of Africa, particularly in Europe. Fela changed his surname to Anikulapo-Kuti in 1976.

See also **Music, Modern Popular: Western Africa.**

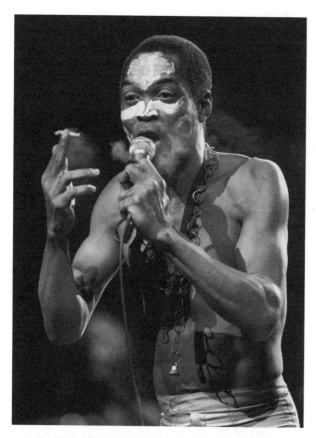

Kuti, Fela (1938–1997). From 1970 he became one of Nigeria's most popular musicians, combining highlife, jazz, and funk music into a style he called "Afrobeat." He was also an outspoken public figure and a critic of Nigeria's ruling classes, religious clergy, and military rulers. AP IMAGES

BIBLIOGRAPHY

Moore, Carlos. *Fela, Fela: This Bitch of a Life.* London: Alison & Busby, 1982.

Olaniyan, Tejumola. *Arrest the Music!: Fela and His Rebel Art and Politics.* Bloomington: Indiana University Press, 2004.

Schoonmaker, Trevor. *Black President: The Art and Legacy of Fela Anikulapo-Kuti.* New York: New Museum of Contemporary Art, 2003.

Veal, Michael. *Fela: The Life and Times of an African Musical Icon.* Philadelphia: Temple University Press, 2000.

MICHAEL VEAL

LA GUMA, ALEX

LA GUMA, ALEX (1925–1985). The black South African writer and political activist Alex La Guma, the son of a prominent left-wing activist, was born and educated in Cape Town in the Depression years. From a young age he was associated with the communist and workers' movements. He joined the Young Communist League in 1947, and in 1954 he became an organizer for the South African Coloured People's Organization (SACPO). In 1955 he was elected chairman of this organization; a year later the Nationalist party government arrested him and charged him with treason. Defying a state order prohibiting him from engaging in further political activity, he was confined in 1962 to a five-year house arrest. His writings were not permitted to circulate in South Africa. Having been subjected to an attempt on his life in 1958, another arrest, and a four-month detention without trial, La Guma was forced into exile in 1966. He went with his family to London, where he continued to write and work for the international antiapartheid movement. In 1969 he was awarded the Lotus Prize for Literature by the Afro-Asian Writers Association, and in 1975 he was elected deputy secretary-general of this association. He maintained his engagement in politics, visiting Chile, Vietnam, and the Soviet Union. In 1978 the African National Congress appointed him their chief Caribbean representative, with residence in Cuba. He served in this position until his death of a heart attack in Havana in 1985.

La Guma began his writing career as a journalist and short story writer. His story "Etude," published in *New Age* in 1957, is generally cited as the first short story of wide publication, though in October 1956 he published "The Machine" in the journal *Fighting Talk*

and a few months later "A Christmas Story," also in the same journal. He is the author of the novels *A Walk in the Night* (1962), *And a Threefold Cord* (1964), *The Stone Country* (1967), *In the Fog of the Seasons' End* (1972), *Time of the Butcherbird* (1979), the travelogue *A Soviet Journey* (1978), as well as political essays, cartoons, articles, short stories, book reviews, commentaries, radio programs, and detective dramas. La Guma, in common with other writers of the "Drum generation" (named after the famous magazine of that name) of South Africa–based writers in the 1950s and 1960s, used the dialogues and images of the streets of South Africa to speak of hardship and persecution. His novels present the animated and eccentric voices as well as the bitter realities of black South African experience.

See also **Apartheid; Literature; Popular Culture: Southern Africa; South Africa, Republic of: Society and Cultures.**

BIBLIOGRAPHY

Abrahams, Cecil A. *Alex La Guma.* Boston: Twayne, 1985.

Odendaal, André, and Roger Field, eds. *Liberation Chabalala: The World of Alex La Guma.* Belleville, South Africa: Mayibuye Books, 1993.

Yousaf, Nahem. *Alex La Guma: Politics and Resistance.* Portsmouth, NH: Heinemann, 2001.

SUSANNA LEE

LABOR

This entry includes the following articles:
CHILD
CONSCRIPT AND FORCED
DOMESTIC

CHILD

The term "child labor" is usually defined as harmful work performed by children, but it is frequently extended to include to any illegitimate employment, whether or not it is harmful. The term implies that childhood is a time for leisure and school, when strenuous work is inappropriate. Many African societies, however, see children as gaining rights and taking on responsibilities, including work, as they grow. In this view, the labor of children is something positive for the children and for their families and communities.

Over half of Africans are under the age of eighteen (as opposed to less than one-fifth of the population in the developed world) and few adults have access to substantial incomes to support these young people. Children necessarily take some responsibility for their livelihood, especially when supporting adults who are dying of AIDS. International attempts to keep children out of economic activities sometimes inhibit children from exercising this responsibility, which can damage the livelihoods of the poor.

In most African societies, children take on various tasks, including economic activities, and acquire standing in their families through their ability to contribute. Their work includes simple household chores, including caring for younger siblings, termed "child-minding," which frees adults for other work; caring for the sick; fetching provisions such as fuel, water, and purchased goods; helping in gardens and fields; and caring for domestic animals. Where family livelihood depends on commercial activities such as craftwork, trading, or contract employment, children may help their parents as far as their years and competence allow. Some work, such as minding young children or herding, can be combined with play. Other work combines with education in the broad sense of training for adult life. Since much family work requires resources, the work of children relates only weakly to poverty at the household level.

In many African societies, children spend time away from their parental home, usually in homes of extended family, where they exchange services for maintenance. This work provides a means of learning extra skills, appreciating responsibilities toward kin, and acquiring security against household disasters. Children from needy families sometimes benefit by performing household chores for families that are better off, in exchange for wages or other forms of support.

Many children earn money for schooling through employment, which can therefore benefit education under appropriate conditions. The experience of work may be as valuable for children's future lives as the schooling available to them. In the 1980s, many African countries adopted policies of combining education with production: such policies have fallen away in an international climate hostile to child labor.

Children's work can be hazardous and sometimes leaves inadequate time for leisure, for socializing with peers, and particularly for schoolwork. Certain children may be required to satisfy the demands of a number of adults in an extended family. Where adults are incapacitated, or where there are no adults present, children may have heavy responsibilities of providing for their families. Where children and adolescents live under the

Pupils at a secondary school in Zimbabwe picking tea. These children contract to work on the estate that runs the school to cover expenses and earn extra income. Many African societies view child labor in a positive light, encouraging members to take on various tasks, from domestic duties to economic activities. PHOTOGRAPH BY M. F. C. BOURDILLON

guardianship of extended family or stepparents, they may be expected to provide for their keep. Traditional tasks, such as herding animals or agricultural work in peak seasons, sometimes conflict with schooling. Other economic activities can also interfere with the children's schooling and deprive them of basic training in literacy and numeracy. It is rare for educational systems to adapt to such external demands on the time of children.

Girls are particularly vulnerable. Like their adult counterparts, girls are expected to perform time-consuming household chores, such as cooking and cleaning, fetching water, caring for the sick, and minding infants. There is often discrimination against girls in utilizing scarce resources for education, resulting in girls sometimes working at home instead of going to school. On the other hand, their contribution to family welfare can sometimes give status to girls, and particularly a degree of independence against pressures to marry young.

Children providing domestic services away from their parental home are often denied the normal rights of employees, and are expected to be on call at all hours for low rewards. In some cases, children are abused physically and emotionally by their employers.

In situations where marginalized people are exploited by employers, or are forced to earn their livelihoods in low-profit, informal employment, children are particularly vulnerable. In small-scale agriculture, children's workloads increased with increasing demands for cash for taxes or purchases. In plantation agriculture, children can provide cheap labor in peak seasons or throughout the year: the exploitation of children in cocoa farming in Côte d'Ivoire received international attention in the early 2000s. Some employers in plantation agriculture demand that employees provide family labor, and children are consequently forced to work. In the urban informal sector, children frequently work long hours for low pay in dangerous jobs. Children are sometimes involved in small-scale mining, for example, working in extremely uncomfortable and hazardous conditions.

Marginalized children, such as street children, are easily incorporated into prostitution: especially girls, but also boys. In the context of HIV and AIDS, this practice is not only abusive but also endangers life. Particularly in West Africa, children have been taken into virtual slavery and moved across international boundaries for poorly paid work, and sometimes for sex. Such trafficking may have the connivance of poor parents who are persuaded that the child will have greater opportunities away from home. There is also considerable economic migration, often illegal, by young people to countries more wealthy than their own.

In several instances, children have become involved in armed conflict, ranging from voluntarily taking part in resistance to oppression (as against apartheid in South Africa) to being coerced into joining armies. When children are pressed to join fighting groups, there may be continuities between the roles they take on in these groups and cultural conceptions of childhood involving work and learning away from home through initiation and apprenticeships.

Children involved in the worst forms of child labor—slavery, war, and prostitution— comprise a small minority of working children in Africa, most of whom work on family farms. In 2005, the International Labor Organization (ILO) estimated that around 29 percent of children aged five to fourteen in sub-Saharan Africa are involved in child labor, but it is not clear how reliable this figure is or whether the children concerned are necessarily involved in harmful work. Surveys have usually focused on simply on economic activities of children and rarely take account of varying workloads in different agricultural seasons.

By 1990, only ten African countries had ratified Convention 138 (1976) on the minimum age of employment. This number had increased to fifty-four by 2005; moreover, one-third of these countries had raised the minimum age of employment to fifteen or sixteen years old, often without considering light work that may be allowed for children younger than this age. Ratification may on occasion be in response to external pressure. It is not clear that families in need of contributions from children, or the children themselves, benefit from such legislation, which fails to control the hours and conditions of work and instead makes all children's work illegal and clandestine. The ILO International Program for the Elimination of Child Labor was operative in twenty-nine African countries by 2005.

The African Movement of Working Children and Youth started in West Africa in the early 1990s and by 2005 claimed associations in fifty-seven towns and eighteen countries. Led by children and youth, the movement works to strengthen children's rights, including the right to light and limited work as well as the right to appropriate education. While it cooperates with programs against exploitation and harmful work, it has pointed out that a campaign against child labor opposes the children's means of subsistence.

See also **Children and Childhood; Economic Systems; Education, School; Family: Economics; Prostitution; Slavery and Servile Institutions.**

BIBLIOGRAPHY

Bass, Loretta E. *Child Labor in Sub-Saharan Africa.* Boulder, CO: Lynne Reiner, 2004.

Bhalotra, Sonia. *Child Labor in Africa.* Paris: Organization for Economic Cooperation and Development, 2003.

Bourdillon, Michael, ed. *Earning a Life: Working Children in Zimbabwe.* Harare, Zimbabwe: Weaver Press, 2000.

Shepler, Susan. *The Social and Cultural Context of Child Soldiering in Sierra Leone.* PRIO Workshop on Techniques of Violence in Civil War, Oslo, 2004.

Sommerfelt, Tone, ed. *Domestic Child Labour in Morocco: An Analysis of the Parties Involved in Relationships to "Petites Bonnes."* Fafo Report 370. Oslo: Fafo Institute for Applied Social Science, 2003.

M.F.C. BOURDILLON

CONSCRIPT AND FORCED

The abolition of slavery and effects of emancipation in the New World, the industrial revolution, and the politics of class in Europe all contributed to the substance of colonial labor policies and ideologies in Africa. Colonial officials and settlers quickly discovered that they could not rely on market forces to satisfy their vast labor needs. Mines, farms, and cash crop plantations, as well as the construction of railways, roads, ports, urban water pipes, and state buildings required a large, steady supply of manpower in contexts where one did not exist. Africans were noncompliant about growing compulsory cash crops on their land or selling their labor for private enterprise. Moreover, they often demanded higher wages than prospective colonial employers were willing to pay. Colonial authorities took recourse in the institution of forced labor, defending against international criticism with moral justification. Rather than attributing their labor shortages to inequitable relations of power, Europeans blamed Africans for their allegedly inherent laziness. Compulsory and forced labor, it was argued, would reform the savage and indolent African character to accord with the demands of a free labor, capitalist economy.

PRESSURES LEADING TO FORCED LABOR

The scramble for Africa in the late nineteenth century left each European empire competing with its rivals to develop robust colonial economies. Africa contained primary products, such as cocoa, palm oil, rubber, hardwoods, coffee, grains, copra, sisal, cotton, wool, and groundnuts, as well as minerals of all kinds. Colonial powers sought to extract and export these raw materials to Europe to satisfy expanding manufactory needs there. Fledgling colonial industries, such as the gold mines in the Transvaal and the Gold Coast, copper mines in the Rhodesias, and cash crop plantations of East Africa and French West Africa, depended on the steady supply of cheap labor. This could only come about by alienating Africans from the means of production—the land. Authorities believed that if wage work became a necessity rather than a convenience for African peasants, then a viable labor market would emerge.

In general, Africans' eschewal of wage labor and regular employment bolstered Europeans' racist interpretations of the African character. From Africans' point of view, however, wage labor offered little incentive to abandon horticulture, pastoralism, or trade. Such livelihoods allowed individuals to set their own work pace, which was typically oriented around seasonal tasks rather than hourly output. When the need for cash arose, people could seek out casual labor on docks, and in plantations and timber concessions. In African societies, work not only structured time and social reproduction but also constituted cultural and moral dimensions of people's lives. The commoditization and coercion of African labor affronted African values as much as they dislocated rural areas.

Colonial authorities sought to convert customary land tenure systems, generally based on communal and individual usufruct rights, into a system of private property as a way to secure land titles for colonial settlers and increase commodity production. Private property, it was thought, would also provide incentive

Miners at Republic Gold Mining Company, De Kaap, South Africa, 1888. Gold has been an important aspect of the South African economy since its discovery by European prospectors in the mid-nineteenth century. Gold mining industries depend upon cheap labor to supply a constant flow of the valuable resource to Europe. © BETTMANN/CORBIS

to African landowners to cultivate cash crops. The goal of land reform ultimately failed, and authorities instead recruited the assistance of African chiefs and notables in creating aggressive labor recruitment organizations.

METHODS OF COERCION

Belgian, German (prior to World War I), French, British, and Portuguese authorities employed a variety of methods to capture African labor. In East and Southern Africa in the late nineteenth century, the British assigned fertile land to whites and removed Africans to reserves with poor quality land. Officials argued that restricting the land available to Africans would create a population of wage seekers who would supply labor to the gold mines and sugar plantations.

Instances of explicit slavery also lingered in the colonies, often camouflaged by formal labor policy. German colonial policy sanctioned the ransom of

slaves by German planters, who in purchasing slaves' freedom could exploit their labor until the ransom debt was worked off. Strong-arm methods of exacting labor were used throughout the continent. King Leopold II of the Belgians (1835–1909) notoriously ordered his agents to kidnap, brutalize, and torture African males, often holding females hostage as collateral, and forced them to work as porters and rubber tappers in the Congo Free State. The practice of corporal punishment of workers in African colonies belied official attempts to portray labor recruitment as voluntary.

In French West Africa, *corvée* laborers were rounded up by recruiting agents and soldiers in order to build the Congo-Océan Railway. Workers lived in miserable work camps stationed along the rail line. *Corvée* denoted a limited term of unremunerated labor for public works, including the tillage of administrative fields and the construction of roads. Prestation, virtually synonymous with *corvée*, represented a labor tax exacted by the state.

Sometimes, labor shortages were so severe that colonial states instituted indentured labor systems with workers from outside Africa, such as Indian workers on the sugar plantations of Mauritius or Chinese coolies in Madagascar. Coercive contract labor was typically used in the mines and on plantations in East and Southern Africa. Prospective workers signed contracts of engagement under threat of enslavement or land confiscation. In Portuguese colonies, the contractual term lasted several years and employers, similar to slave owners, possessed the legal right to mistreat workers.

Although from the onset of colonial rule France drafted its African subjects into the French military (the Senegalese riflemen of World War I were renowned), other European powers gradually followed suit. During the interwar years, France instituted military-style labor recruitment in such programs as the Service de la Main-d'Oeuvre de Travaux d'Interêt Général of Madagascar and the Service Temporaire des Travaux d'Irrigation du Niger of French West Africa. Men deemed unfit for soldiering were siphoned into work camps, where for a period of two to three years they performed public works. During World War II, the British instituted similar practices in the Rhodesias to build new aerodromes. The preferred method for officials to fill the ranks of the so-called Labour Corps involved calling on traditional African authority figures to fill the requisite quotas.

SOCIAL AND POLITICAL EFFECTS OF FORCED LABOR

Colonial labor regimes destabilized African households and altered the gendered division of labor. As African men necessarily migrated or were forcibly removed to mines, plantations, and work camps along road and railway lines, they left women, children, the old, and the infirm to tend to rural households and subsistence agriculture. Over time, cash and commodities infiltrated life in the colonies. The rising cost of living burdened poor households, and a growing number of able-bodied African men and women sought out wage work in burgeoning urban centers.

As colonial states intensified their efforts to capture labor after World War II to increase production

levels, Africans' strategies of resistance escalated. Over time, colonial authorities found themselves contending with the reality of a politicized African working class and nascent trade union movement. Workers staged protests and organized unions to the point where, by the 1940s, French and British authorities could no longer neglect the social needs of the African proletariat. Officials sought to contain the more radical elements of the working classes by co-opting African labor leaders and nurturing a labor aristocracy that could identify culturally with colonizers. The concept of economic development arose from the crucible of sustained and sometimes violent resistance led by urbanized African workers.

See also **Children and Childhood: Soldiers; Colonial Policies and Practices; Slave Trades; Slavery and Servile Institutions.**

BIBLIOGRAPHY

Arrighi, Giovanni, and Saul, John S. *Essays on the Political Economy of Africa.* New York: Monthly Review Press, 1973.

Cooper, Frederick. *Decolonization and African Society: The Labor Question in French and British Africa.* Cambridge, U.K.: Cambridge University Press, 1996.

Cooper, Frederick. "Conditions Analogous to Slavery. Imperialism and Free Labor Ideology in Africa." In *Beyond Slavery: Explorations of Race, Labor, and Citizenship in Postemancipation Societies,* ed. Frederick Cooper, Rebecca J. Scott, and Thomas C. Holt. Chapel Hill: University of North Carolina Press, 2000.

Echenberg, Myron. *Colonial Conscripts: The Tirailleurs Senegalais in French West Africa, 1857–1960.* Portsmouth, NH: Heinemann, 1991.

Eschenberg, Myron, and Jean Filipovich. "African Military Labour and the Building of the Office du Niger Installations, 1925–1950." *Journal of African History* 27 (1986): 533–551.

Fall, Babacar. *Le travail forcé en Afrique-Occidentale française, 1900–1946.* Paris: Karthala, 1993.

Hochschild, Adam. *King Leopold's Ghost: A Story of Green Terror, and Heroism in Colonial Africa.* Boston: Mariner Books, 1999.

Isaacman, Allen, and Richard Roberts, eds. *Cotton, Colonialism, and Social History in Sub-Saharan Africa.* Portsmouth, NH: Heinemann, 1995.

Paulin, Christopher M. *White Men's Dreams, Black Men's Blood: African Labor and British Expansionism in Southern Africa, 1877–1895.* Trenton, NJ: Africa World Press, 2001.

Phillips, Anne. *The Enigma of Colonialism.* Bloomington: Indiana University Press, 1989.

Sunseri, Thaddeus. *Vilimani: Labor Migration and Rural Change in Early Colonial Tanzania.* Portsmouth, NH: Heinemann, 2001.

Valensky, Chantal. *Le soldat occulté: Les malgaches de l'armée française, 1884–1920.* Paris: l'Harmattan, 1995.

Van Onselen, Charles. *Chibaro: African Mine Labour in Southern Rhodesia, 1900–1933.* London: Pluto Press, 1980.

Vickery, Kenneth P. "The Second World War Revival of Forced Labor in the Rhodesias." *The International Journal of Africa Historical Studies* 22, no 3 (1989): 423–437.

GENESE SODIKOFF

DOMESTIC

When Jacklyn Cock's *Maids and Madams: A Study in the Politics of Exploitation* appeared in 1980, it was the first major study of domestic labor in South Africa. Before then, only a handful of studies had been published on late nineteenth-century shifts from pawnship, debt service, and other forms of dependent work to wage labor in the wake of colonization. Only in southern Africa had scholarship on race relations attended specifically to paid domestic labor.

Cock's work inspired a wave of publications. She described the feminization of domestic service in the Eastern Cape as the ultra exploitation of women, resulting from the convergence of gender, race, and class within this occupation. Subsequent research has shown that these factors do not converge in a tidy way, but are affected by complex interactions of cultural, political, and economic factors that differ regionally and over time.

THE LABOR PROCESS IN DOMESTIC SERVICE

Domestic labor is, first and foremost, a relationship between employer and worker. The labor process that developed in colonial domestic service had little in common with slavery, servitude, or dependent labor as practiced in many precolonial African societies. Domestic employment did not exclude dependent workers from social interaction with members of the groups for whom they worked. With the spread of the cash economy, notions of loyalty and mutual obligations between servants and masters gave way to individuated relationships structured by the need for labor in exchange for wages.

Domestic work was one of the earliest forms of labor relationships in which Africans were socialized into wage labor, and it formed an important entry point for their unequal incorporation into the colonial economy, first for men, then for women. Although labor legislation and ordinances on migration, housing, and work structured the master-servant relationship, most decisions were at the employer's discretion. The diffuse nature of domestic labor, its locus within the private household, and the isolation of the worker from other workers make domestic labor different from industrial labor. These features affect the duties and routines in domestic service, its wages and benefits, distinctions between inside and outside workers, and the relations between servant and employer.

Studies on domestic service in Africa pertain almost exclusively to the former settler colonies, especially in southern and eastern Africa. After the abolition of slavery in South Africa in 1834, poor Afrikaner and British women brought over from Europe worked as domestics in white households. As members of household staffs consisting mainly of black African men, these white women's presence proved problematic, and they were replaced by black African men soon after the turn of the century. African men persisted in domestic service on the Witwatersrand until the late 1930s but were replaced by Coloured (mixed race) and black African women in the Cape much earlier. In the early twenty-first century in South Africa, domestic service is considered a black African woman's job; it remains a lifelong occupation through which married and unmarried women, as well as single mothers, pursue a series of dead-end jobs.

The proliferation of domestic service studies after 1980 have explored, among other subjects, how domestic service came to be taken for granted; how race and sex structured the labor process in domestic service during the colonial period; and how these categories are being replaced by class and sex in the postcolonial period. In societies where men outnumber women in paid domestic service, scholars have clarified the interplay of factors (demographic, economic, political, as well as cultural and ideological) that over time have shaped the division of labor in domestic service. This in effect construes black African women's gender role in such a way that they were excluded from most urban wage labor, and particularly domestic service.

There is little research on domestic service outside of southern and eastern Africa. The exception is work on young girls performing household work without pay, commonly referred to in West Africa as fostering. Growing international concerns about child labor has revealed the exploitative nature of such household work across the African continent. A recent research focus is on African women's work in household service in Europe and North America.

In pamphlets, photo novellas, feature articles, letters to the editor, and cartoons ("Madam and Eve," syndicated in South Africa, about a household worker and her boss), the popular print media discuss matters pertaining to domestic service—such as problems of wages and housing, work exploitation, interpersonal tensions between women servants and their female employers, and sexual interaction between female servants and their male bosses. Both feature films and documentaries (for instance, *La noire de; Maids and madams; Chocolat*) have turned to domestic service for a depiction of these complex issues.

Creative writers have used the figure of the servant to highlight intimate power relationships, to represent the African oppressed, or to serve as a measure of the health or sickness of postcolonial African society. Doris Lessing and Nadine Gordimer, writing on Southern Rhodesia and South Africa respectively, have offered sensitive if not shocking descriptions of the domestic service institution. But few writers have surpassed Ezekiel Mphahlele's *Mrs. Plum* (1967). This story gives voice to the black African woman servant, depicts the economic and interpersonal situation in the servant-keeping context, and suggests that servants, despite all odds, retain some power in the relationship.

RECENT DEVELOPMENTS

Black Africans constitute the largest segment of the servant-keeping population in many countries on the continent. This is prompting redefinitions of the employment relationship and the labor process itself. It is also changing the experiences of servants who no longer differ from their employers by race. Tight household budgets and the need to earn money have increased the demand for childcare among urban mothers, who increasingly employ nannies, some of whom receive poor, if any, pay.

In Africa's crisis-ridden economies, domestic service continues to be an important entry-level occupation for people with few marketable skills, and for migrants from the countryside. Inflation, unemployment, and lack of political interest in the domestic work sector contributed to the reappearance of many conditions resembling those of the colonial era in household work. Even then, trade unions for servants have been established in some countries in Africa; South Africa had a number of local domestic servants' associations which, in 1986, were combined as a registered labor union under the Congress of South African Trade Unions.

In spite of legislation concerning wages, leaves, and housing, and in spite of the formation of unions in some countries, the previous era's specialized household servants are giving way to general workers, except at the top level of society. As household work has become more diffuse, it is executed in return for low wages and under asymmetrical labor arrangements. Where pension funds exist for domestic workers, such as in Zambia and South Africa, employers rarely contribute to them. Domestic workers who have had employment choices have gladly left this job to those who have not: men to women; and women of better means to women of lesser means, whose conditions often are worse because of their youth, lack of education, and rural backgrounds. That domestic service remains an important source of employment for large numbers of adult women and men, and for youth of both sexes, in most sub-Saharan African countries is a vexing indication of the lack of opportunity in African society at large.

See also **Children and Childhood: Status and Roles; Gender; Gordimer, Nadine; Household and Domestic Groups.**

BIBLIOGRAPHY

Andall, Jacqueline. *Gender, Migration and Domestic Service: The Politics of Black Women in Italy.* Aldershot, Hampshire: Ashgate, 2000.

Bujra, Janet. *Serving Class: Masculinity and the Feminisation of Domestic Service in Tanzania.* Edinburgh: Edinburgh University Press, 2000.

Chocolat. Directed by Claire Denis. New York: Orion Films, 1988.

Clarke, Duncan. *Domestic Workers in Rhodesia: The Economics of Masters and Servants.* Gwelo, Southern Rhodesia: Mambo Press, 1974.

Cock, Jacklyn. *Maids and Madams: A Study in the Politics of Exploitation.* Johannesburg: Ravan Press, 1980.

Fapohunda, Eleanor. "The Child-Care Dilemma of Working Mothers in African Cities: The Case of Lagos, Nigeria." In *Women and Work in Africa*, ed. Edna G. Bay. Boulder, CO: Westview Press, 1982.

Goody, Esther N. *Parenthood and Social Reproduction: Fostering and Occupational Roles in West Africa.* Cambridge, U.K.: Cambridge University Press, 1982.

Gordimer, Nadine. *July's People.* New York, 1981.

Hansen, Karen Tranberg. *Distant Companions: Servants and Employers in Zambia, 1900–1985.* Ithaca, NY: Cornell University Press, 1989.

La noire de (Black Girl). Directed by Ousmane Sembène. Films Domirer, 1965.

Lessing, Doris. *The Grass Is Singing.* London: M. Joseph, 1950.

Maids and Madams. Directed by Mira Hamermesh. South Africa: Associates Film Production/Sered Films, 1985.

Momsen, Janet F., ed. *Gender, Migration and Domestic Service.* New York: Routledge, 1999.

Mphahlele, Ezekiel. "Mrs. Plum." In *In Corner B and Other Stories.* Nairobi, Kenya: East Africa Publishing House, 1967.

Preston-Whyte, Eleanor. "Race Attitudes and Behavior: The Case of Domestic Employment in White South African Homes." *African Studies* 35 (1976): 71–89.

Sanjek, Roger. "Maid Servants and Market Women's Apprentices in Adabraka." In *At Work in Homes: Household Workers in World Perspective*, ed. Roger Sanjek and Shellee Colen. Washington, DC: American Ethnological Society, Monograph Series 3, 1990.

Van Onselen, Charles. "The Witches of Suburbia: Domestic Service on the Witwatersrand, 1890–1914." In *Studies in the Social and Economic History of the Witwatersrand, 1886–1914.* Vol. 2, *New Nineveh*, ed. C. van Onselen. London: Longman, 1982.

KAREN TRANBERG HANSEN

INDUSTRIAL AND MINING

That Africans had been active in mining long before the arrival of European colonizers in the nineteenth century is universally accepted. Iron and copper ores and gold digging, for instance, long predated the advent of Europeans in the southern African region. Before the development of modern mining, African societies used family labor and other traditional forms of labor for this and other industrial activities. Because precolonial African mining was done mainly by individual families and on a comparatively small scale, the labor requirements for it were equally as limited. Where family labor was inadequate, individual households of African miners and smelters resorted to the employment of outside specialists. Such industries included gold and copper digging, diamond mining, and iron-smelting, as well as other less specialized activities, such as salt-digging and the production of red ochre and other ointments in Lesotho in Southern Africa. Africans also manufactured hunting weapons and agricultural tools. Many African societies in South, East, and West Africa used work parties for agricultural activities such as land clearing, cultivation, and harvests. The hosts usually served food and beer to the workers and sometimes offered them part of the proceeds as compensation. For more community-oriented work projects, however, the organization of labor lay in the hands of the political leadership. European conquest in the late nineteenth century disrupted these community-based labor policies and practices.

DIAMONDS AND GOLD

In Southern Africa prior to the mineral discoveries in the second half of the nineteenth century, no significant industries required supplies of labor beyond the scale of the productive communities. With the beginning of diamond mining in Kimberley from the 1860s, and large-scale gold diggings on the Rand from the 1880s, however, a large wage-labor force came into existence. Once the demand emerged, it became necessary for the government and the mine owners to work out a labor policy that would both control the workers and ensure a constant and adequate supply of them. As the first major mining site in Southern Africa, the diamond fields set the framework for future similar labor relations and policy on the other mining complexes in the region. Initially, the diamond mines relied on unskilled, occasional workers from the immediately surrounding areas. These laborers included the local Tswana, Sotho, and Coloureds, who flocked to the fields to earn enough money to buy a gun for their own protection. Soon the mines began to recruit from other regions of South Africa, such as the Transkei and Ciskei (present Eastern Cape). Up to that point, the labor supply was generally restricted to the area south of the Limpopo River. By the close of the nineteenth century, however, these sources had also become inadequate. Consequently, the mine owners decided to enlarge their catchment area and recruited African workers from as far as Mozambique, Basutoland, Bechuanaland, Swaziland, and the Rhodesias. These laborers were employed on short contracts lasting from three to twelve months.

The government's objective in restricting the terms of employment was to ensure a constant turnover of African labor that they expected to remain perpetually unskilled and therefore unable to challenge the white employees' superior pay and skilled positions. Even when Africans withdrew their labor in the face of the economic hardships arising from the South African War (1899–1902), the government's response was to bring in cheap similarly indentured Chinese laborers to take their place rather than to pay a living wage. Even the policy of Asian contract workers came into force only after an agreement between the government and the mine owners that neither Chinese nor African workers were to touch any of the skilled or semiskilled jobs, in order to minimize threats to the white workers' positions.

According to this arrangement, the Chinese would remain "a discreet, returnable, harmless source of muscular energy" bound to be repatriated after a specific contract period (Denoon 1973, 146). It effectively established the industrial color bar on the South African gold mines. Meanwhile, the first-generation white immigrants, who saw themselves as temporary rather than permanent residents of South Africa, carried out the more specialized work requiring skilled labor. This racial allocation of work became the entrenched policy and practice in the mining industry throughout southern Africa. The Mines and Works Act of 1911 officially permitted racial discrimination in the mining industry. The Mines and Works Amendment Act of 1926 further reinforced the provisions of the old act and decreed in very clear terms the color bar in certain specified jobs in the mining industry. The consequences were disastrous for African workers in several ways. They had no protection as workers; they were no longer the indispensable base of the industrial labor pyramid that they had been at the start of mining; they had no organized trade union worth the name. In fact, it was illegal for them to form such a union, and

therefore all their strikes were spontaneous and not organized affairs.

COPPER

During the interwar years, large copper deposits were developed in the Katanga region of the Belgian Congo (subsequently Zaire and presently the Democratic Republic of the Congo). The area became yet another center of major industrial mining, requiring an enormous supply of labor. A Belgian company, Union Minière du Haut-Katanga (UMHK), owned the Katanga mines. They were, however, confronted immediately with a labor shortage, as the area was thinly populated and not well endowed with a dependable water supply. At first, the company's policy was to recruit labor by force. As had happened at Kimberley and on the Rand, the mining company was soon obliged to expand its recruitment sources to the most distant corners of Katanga itself first, then to Ruanda-Urundi (Rwanda and Burundi, also Belgian colonies), and later to the Rhodesias (Zambia and Zimbabwe), Nyasaland (Malawi), and Angola, competing there with British and Portuguese local needs for labor.

In the 1920s and early 1930s, additional copper deposits in large quantities were located across the border in Northern Rhodesia (Zambia). By the end of the 1930s, copper production was well established within the Northern Rhodesian copper belt. Two mining companies, the Rhodesian branch of the Anglo-American Corporation and the Rhodesian Selection Trust, had established four large mines. Exploitation of the Northern Rhodesian copper belt created a new labor market and thus prompted significant changes in the mining companies' labor recruiting policies. First, instead of going across to Katanga, Northern Rhodesian labor stayed at home. For many years, as Andrew Roberts pointed out in his 1978 work, the mine owners had operated their African labor policies on the basis of short contracts, inadequate housing for their employees, and generally very strict regulations. Working conditions in the mines had not taken into consideration the family situations of the African laborers. The mine owners expected that the laborers' families would survive on subsistence cultivation, even in the absence of men from the local labor pools. Most employers of both mining and industrial labor in southern, central, and east Africa had treated the

African workers as if they were all single men. Both their wages and housing arrangements were tailored to individuals rather than families.

All this changed, however, in the early 1930s with the adoption of a new policy of "labor stabilization." The Northern Rhodesian mining companies and the UMHK provided better wages for their workers and housed their families in separate compounds and townships that were normally much better serviced than the surrounding areas. In addition, the mining companies provided for their workers' health and spiritual welfare by constructing clinics on the compounds and introducing clergy. They also provided educational facilities for the workers' children. Furthermore, the new policy granted longer contracts for married men, even though the mine management still discouraged permanent African settlement on the compounds. The mine owners also began to allow Africans to move into skilled positions previously reserved for Europeans. The reasoning behind labor stabilization was entirely in the companies' own interests: African workers were likely to perform more efficiently if they brought their families to the mining compounds. This policy continued well into the postindependence period in Zambia in the 1970s and 1980s.

LABOR IN COLONIAL AFRICA

Throughout Africa, the governments, mine owners, and industrial companies pursued labor policies intended to accomplish two objectives: minimize costs by employing labor presumed to be "cheap and abundant"—even though in reality it was difficult to obtain workers readily except by coercion—and maximize profits. This general picture can best be illustrated by examining what happened in the major regions of the continent from the late nineteenth century up till independence in the early and mid-1960s, where sizeable proportions of the economies depended on mining and industrial development. Basically similar colonial policies were employed to obtain labor on the Southern African mines, the tin-fields of Nigeria in West Africa, the commercial industries of Kenya in East Africa, and the large industrial companies of colonial Algeria in North Africa. Africans underwent forced "proletarianization": the process of being transformed from semi-independent peasant agriculturalists into laborers entirely dependent

on wages, mainly as a result of extensive expropriation of the lands that sustained them. As the Africans lost ownership of their land to white settlers, they became unable to live off of subsistence farming. The introduction of colonial taxation increased rural farmers' need for cash and hastened their entry into wage employment on their employers' terms. In settler-dominated Kenya and Algeria, this strategy was used to coerce the Africans into wage labor on the commercial farms; in Nigeria, the colonial administration, mine owners and local government officials known as the "Native Authorities" usually collaborated to redirect the flow of labor to the mines. In Kenya, Rhodesia, and South Africa, the Africans were forcibly removed from fertile lands and placed in barren reserves to guarantee their availability as wage laborers. In Kenya, as in South Africa, the introduction of the *kipande* (pass book, similar to its South African equivalent) restricted the movements of Africans outside the reserves.

COLONIAL LABOR POLICIES AND DECOLONIZATION

The central role of labor in the colonial history of Africa cannot be overemphasized. In his 1996 study of this phenomenon, Frederick Cooper showed that both French and British colonial labor policies from the 1930s to the 1950s provoked the emergence of worker militancy and trade union organization, closely linked to the almost contemporaneous African anticolonial political struggle of the 1950s. For much of the colonial period, Cooper argued, the British and French had viewed the Africans in their colonies as simple "tribesmen" who provided "seasonal" or occasional labor, not as people permanently committed to and dependent on the wage-labor market. Africans questioned this attitude, however, as they demanded to be treated as workers in their own right and asserted themselves through strikes and other forms of resistance. Furthermore, the two European colonial powers came under immense pressure from the emerging educated nationalist political elites who, in Cooper's view, took advantage of the labor struggles to demand rapid political transformation toward independence. Industrial relations in the European countries themselves were undergoing change, whereas the International Labor Organization (ILO) had also by the 1950s stepped up its campaign against forced labor.

At the same time, Cooper maintained, the colonial state also wanted to build institutions that would permit the creation of a "detribalized" and urban-based permanent working class, as opposed to allowing the majority of the Africans to continue to live in the rural areas. All these factors combined to lead the colonial powers into rethinking not only their colonial labor policies, but also the very ideas of decolonization and independence.

AFRICAN STRATEGIES: COLONIAL AND POSTCOLONIAL

Clearly, the African population was not helpless or passive in the face of the labor control strategies of the powerful colonial forces. If the African workers were unable to organize themselves into trade unions or to initiate official work stoppages, they resisted by striking illegally, by refusing to be recruited, or by simply deserting their jobs. In addition to these strategies, as Charles van Onselen showed in his 1980 work, many miners in Southern Rhodesia protested their working conditions individually and informally. Africans also resisted by finding alternative ways of raising cash; for example, by selling farm animals or agricultural produce. Finally, during the late 1970s and early 1980s the strategy of "industrial sabotage," which sometimes involved deliberately vandalizing company-owned equipment, became quite common, as did walkouts.

In Southern Africa, therefore, the absence of an African trade movement until the formation of the Industrial and Commercial Workers' Union (ICU) in 1919 did not mean the absence of African resistance in earlier years. The various protests that broke out in South Africa's mines at the end of the nineteenth century and again before the 1920s illustrate the capacity of workers there to stand up for their own interests. They also show that the employees were already beginning to have a sense of "worker consciousness" described so eloquently by van Onselen in the case of Southern Rhodesia, outlined by Charles Perrings for the Katanga and Northern Rhodesian copper belt, and captured so strikingly by Cooper for both French and British colonial Africa more generally.

While the contribution of the labor movement to the anti-colonial struggle in Zimbabwe, for instance, has received increasing attention and recognition, the post-liberation period has seen much less clearly delineated contests between labor and the independent governments of Africa. Indeed, Zimbabwe's experience, like that of neighboring Zambia under former president Frederick Chiluba (r. 1991–2001), who was himself a former trade unionist, would seem to validate Cooper's argument that nationalism left workers in postindependence Africa with even fewer alternatives to the wage-labor market, and put them in an awkward position, in which the African political leadership expected them to subsume their interests within the ideal of "state-building."

See also **Colonial Policies and Practices; Decolonization; Metals and Minerals; Rhodes, John Cecil.**

BIBLIOGRAPHY

Cooper, Frederick. *Decolonization and African Society: The Labor Question in French and British Africa.* African Studies Series 89. Cambridge, U.K.: Cambridge University Press, 1996.

Cooper, Frederick. *Africa since 1940: The Past of the Present.* Cambridge, U.K.: Cambridge University Press, 2002.

Denoon, Donald. *A Grand Illusion: The Failure of Imperial Policy in the Transvaal Colony during the Period of Reconstruction 1900–05.* London: Longman, 1973.

Denoon, Donald, and Balam Nyeko. *Southern Africa since 1800.* London and New York: Longman, 1984.

Eldredge, Elizabeth A. *A South African Kingdom: The Pursuit of Security in Nineteenth-Century Lesotho.* African Studies Series 78. Cambridge, U.K.: Cambridge University Press, 1993.

Freund, Bill. *The Making of Contemporary Africa: The Development of an African Society since 1800.* London and Basingstoke: Macmillan, 1984.

Mothibe, T. H. "Organized African Labor and Nationalism in Colonial Zimbabwe, 1945–1971." Ph.D. diss. University of Wisconsin, 1993.

Penvenne, Jean Marie. *African Workers and Colonial Racism: Mozambican Strategies and Struggles in Lourenco Marques, 1877–1962.* Portsmouth, NH: Heinemann, 1995.

Perrings, Charles. *Black Mineworkers in Central Africa: Industrial Strategies and the Evolution of an African Proletariat in the Copperbelt 1911–41.* London: Heinemann, 1979.

Raftopoulos, Brian, and Ian Phimister, eds. *Keep on Knocking: A History of the Labor Movement in Zimbabwe, 1900–1997.* Harare, Zimbabwe: Baobab Books, 1997.

Roberts, Andrew D. *A History of Zambia.* London: Heinemann, 1976.

van Onselen, Charles. *Chibaro: African Mine Labor in Southern Rhodesia, 1900–1930.* Johannesburg, South Africa: Ravan Press, 1980.

van Zwanenberg, R. M. A. *Colonial Capitalism and Labor in Kenya, 1919–1939.* Nairobi, Kenya: East African Literature Bureau, 1975.

Webster, Eddie, ed. *Essays in Southern African Labor History.* Johannesburg, South Africa: Ravan Press, 1978.

BALAM NYEKO

MIGRATION

Labor migration, the movement of people to work, was a defining feature of colonial Africa and remains a central feature of African society in the postcolonial era. In the early twenty-first century, there are distinctive migrations to Europe and the United States, as well as significant flows within and between African countries. Historically, men have predominated as migrant laborers, but women are undertaking independent migration in increasing numbers. Theoretically, studies of African labor migration have shifted from privileging structures to privileging agency, and the challenge remains as to how to synthesize both.

TYPOLOGIES

Distinguishing the movement of people to work from other migrant types (such as refugees, asylum seekers, and exiles) is not always easy, because political and economic factors are invariably intertwined. Typologies of labor migration commonly distinguish between forced and voluntary, permanent and temporary, speculative and pre-arranged, documented and undocumented, skilled and unskilled, seasonal/circular and one-way, rural-rural and rural-urban, and intra- and international. However, migrant processes are rarely amenable to straightforward classification. Indeed, it is argued that labor migration is more than an empirical category, and the more recent focus on the experiences and subjectivities of migrants allies with a concern for the production of meaning, the discursive and the imaginary.

THE MIGRANT-LABOR SYSTEM

Studies of labor migration in the colonial era revolve around the so-called migrant-labor system that wrested a cheap, plentiful, and temporary supply of African labor for the mines and plantations established with European capitals. Working conditions were poor, varying degrees of coercion were deployed, families were divided, and women and children were typically confined to distant labor reserves. Whereas the gold mines of South Africa relied on male labor from as far as Angola, Tanzania, Zambia, and Malawi, as well as the neighboring countries of Lesotho, Botswana, Zimbabwe, and Namibia, Ghana's forestry and construction industry recruited men from Togo, Nigeria, Liberia, Guinea, and Côte d'Ivoire, and the plantations of Tanzania took female and male labor from Rwanda, Burundi, and Mozambique. Once their contracts were complete, these laborers returned, for a while at least, to the rural areas from whence they came.

Detailed historiography in the 1980s and 1990s has complicated any narrative of a migrant-labor system designed in the abstract and imposed on the African population, presenting instead a process of contingencies, defeats, and compromises. First, the interests of the white settlers, entrepreneurs, and administrators were not necessarily unified, and migratory practices varied within and between countries. Second, (potential) migrants sought to maintain leverage, avoiding wage labor where possible, preferring independent employment to agency recruitment, trading information about wages and working conditions so that the worst employers could be avoided, and organizing collectively to pursue grievances. Third, gender norms and inequalities both shaped and were shaped by migration. From Tanzania to Lesotho and from Botswana to Kenya, a complex collusion of interests between the African elite and the white administration served to restrict women's mobility, as male migrants appropriated female labor to retain their rural livelihoods.

As the twentieth century progressed, the migrant-labor system gradually gave way to labor stabilization on the mines and plantations, a process that accelerated with independence. However, South Africa's mines are a notable exception. Whereas Tanzania, Zambia, and Malawi withdrew access to their labor in the 1970s and 1980s, migrants from the satellite states of Lesotho and Swaziland remain pivotal to the industry, notwithstanding assumptions that a post-apartheid government would end contract labor.

POSTCOLONIAL MIGRATIONS

Intra-African Labor Migration.

Migration within Africa, arguably neglected in contemporary literature, varies enormously, from the rural-rural movements of seasonal migrants to the rural–urban movements of those seeking to escape poverty, and the multifarious movements of women traders across the continent. Statistical data are limited, but such movements are generally seen as the norm, rather than the exception. Within particular regions there are distinct patterns: in West Africa, overall labor migration is southwards to Côte d'Ivoire from Burkino Faso, Guinea, Mali, and Togo. The Sahel region is particularly noted for out-migration, with up to one-third of Malians estimated to be working abroad. Côte d'Ivoire and South Africa are the two most important destinations for labor migrants within Africa, with the thriving economies of Botswana and Namibia making those countries also attractive.

International Labor Migration.

On the one hand, Africa's share of international labor migrants may be decreasing, 9 percent in 2000 compared with 12 percent in 1970, although the underenumeration of undocumented migrants raises issues of data reliability. On the other hand, there is a diversification of destinations and having a migrant laborer in the diaspora, sending regular remittances, has come to be regarded as a common survival strategy for many African families. Globalization's new world order may drive international labor migration. For example, structural adjustment programs have resulted in rising unemployment and high inflation, increasing the economic migration of the impoverished majority and professional minority alike, some of whom have sought work in Europe and the United States. Economic liberalization in Morocco that was intended to boost economic growth and opportunity has served only to destabilize the economy and increase international relocation. At the same time, networks of migrants in diaspora may seek to mould globalization to their own ends, as Diouf (2000) argues in the case of Murid traders from Senegal now living in North America, Europe, and Asia.

International labor migration is typically structured around both colonial links—thus Malians and Algerians are particularly likely to seek work in France; Angolans and Cape Verdeans in Portugal; Nigerians and Zimbabweans in the U.K.—and geographical proximity—hence Moroccans are particularly likely to seek work in Spain. Social networks are pivotal; established migrants pave the way for others from their family/community/nation to follow. Whereas nonprofessional migrants to Europe have historically worked in manufacturing and agriculture, increasing numbers are now employed in the service industries or are self-employed, and labor migrants are thus becoming commercial migrants.

From the 1970s onward most European countries increased immigration controls, earning the title "Fortress Europe." This fuelled increasingly risky attempts from North Africans in particular to enter Europe clandestinely, and also fed a migration industry that profited from control over access routes that often failed. Notwithstanding the major contribution to the economy being made by African labor migrants, the climate in Europe is often hostile to outsiders. A new xenophobia has also been noted in the more prosperous African economies that attract labor migrants, such as South Africa and Botswana.

WHO MOVES?

Whether or not labor migrants share socioeconomic characteristics remains contested, although it is generally agreed that the poorest lack the capital to migrate. Less contested is that more and more African women are migrating in pursuit of employment or other income-generating opportunities, often independently from men. Moreover, there is some evidence that female labor migrants are more reliable remitters than male. The majority of women migrate voluntarily through legal routes, but there is evidence of trafficking, such as the trading of women from Edo State in Nigeria to work in the Italian sex industry.

EFFECTS OF LABOR MIGRATION

Rural studies of labor-producing areas have traditionally focused on the agricultural labor shortages caused by out-migration and the women left behind to cope. Yet remittances, the proportion of migrants' earnings that are sent back to their families, may well be used to reinvigorate agriculture. Data are scarce, but contemporary remittances are clearly important to the local and national economy, as well as the migrant's own family. For example, between 1980 and 1999, official remittances in Bénin averaged 4.5 percent of the gross domestic product (GDP), 5.8 percent in Burkino Faso, and 13.5 percent in Cape Verde. Moreover, women's de facto empowerment in men's absence may be one factor behind their increasing propensity to migrate themselves. Labor migration often divides families and communities, but easy assumptions that this would spell social disintegration have ceded to consideration of the ways in which social relations are reconstituted in both source and origin. Long-term circulations of economic capital (money and goods), human capital (new migrants, including children), and social capital (visits, telephone and e-mail communication) are common between absent migrants and their home communities.

Labor migration also has more detrimental consequences. Conjugal conflict is not uncommon between divided spouses, and population mobility is contributing to HIV/AIDS transmission. Rural–urban migration is fuelling the growth of African "megacities," such as Addis Ababa, Lagos, Cairo, and Nairobi, which are characterized by slum housing, poverty, ungovernability, and corruption. Migrant remittance levels can be volatile, and the loss of human capital is significant—the so-called brain drain. The World Bank estimates that 25 percent of Ghanaians with tertiary education work outside Ghana. Meanwhile, Zimbabwe loses 20 percent of its health-care professionals annually to the U.K., mostly female nurses.

Chikanda's study (2005) of the independent migration of Zimbabwean nurses to the U.K. was illustrative of several features of contemporary labor migration in Africa: its increasing feminization; the difficulty of separating economically motivated migration from politically motivated migration; the extent to which international migration patterns are often based on colonial links; and the need to privilege agency in the conceptualization of labor migration. It also marked the welcome contribution that African academics are making to the labor migration literature, following a lengthy monopolization by European scholars.

See also **Addis Ababa; Agriculture; Cairo; Colonial Policies and Practices; Disease: HIV/AIDS, Social and Political Aspects; Economic History; Gender; Globalization; Lagos; Metals and Minerals; Nairobi; Production Strategies; Slavery and Servile Institutions; World Bank.**

BIBLIOGRAPHY

Akyeampong, Emmanuel. "Africans in the Diaspora: The Diaspora and Africa." *African Affairs* 99, no. 395 (2000): 183–215.

Bilger, Veronika, and Albert Kraler. *African Migrations. Historical Perspectives and Contemporary Dynamics.* Special issue of *Vienna Journal of African Studies* 8 (2005).

Chikanda, Abel. "Nurse Migration from Zimbabwe: Analysis of Recent Trends and Impacts." *Nursing Inquiry* 12, no. 3 (2005): 162–174.

Crush, Jonathan; Alan Jeeves; and David Yudelman. *South Africa's Labor Empire: A History of Black Migrancy to the Gold Mines.* Oxford: Westview, 1991.

Davis, Mike. *Planet of Slums.* London: Verso, 2006.

Diouf, Mamadou. "The Senegalese Murid Trade Diaspora and the Making of a Vernacular Cosmopolitanism." *Public Culture* 12, no. 3 (2000): 679–702.

Ifekwunigwe, Jayne O. "Recasting 'Black Venus' in the New African Diaspora." *Women's Studies International Forum* 27, no. 4 (2004): 397–412.

International Organization for Migration. *World Migration 2003: Managing Migration—Challenges and Responses for People on the Move.* Geneva, Switzerland: International Organization for Migration, 2003.

White, Gregory. "Encouraging Unwanted Immigration: A Political Economy of Europe's Efforts to Discourage North African Immigration." *Third World Quarterly* 20, no. 4 (1999): 839–854.

Wright, Caroline. "Gender Awareness in Migration Theory: Synthesizing Actor and Structure in Southern Africa." *Development and Change* 26 (1995): 771–791.

CAROLINE WRIGHT

PLANTATION

Unlike the Americas, plantation labor in Africa has attracted less attention, except for a few seminal works, such as Frederick Cooper's *From Slaves to Squatters* (1980). Yet this paucity obscures the effects of plantations on the lives of men, women, and children in many parts of Africa, both historically and in the twenty-first century.

From the early nineteenth century the end of the Atlantic slave trade, shifts in regional and international trade networks, and growing demands for commodities gave rise to plantations drawing on slave, indentured, and forced labor. Relying on a mix of socioreligious institutions and direct force, state agents siphoned labor to plantations by distributing captives, servants, and ethnically marginal

I am a cutter, too. The single male migrant plantation worker predominates in popular and official discourse as the prevailing figure of plantation labor. Katrina, from Kigoma, a sisal cutter from Songea in the southwest working on plantations in the northeast of Tanzania, is a reminder of the predominant yet invisible presence of women and children as plantation workers. HANAN SABEA

groups, and enforcing regulations regarding mobility, vagrancy, land access, inheritance, marriage, and manumission. The violence of enslavement and forced labor not only ravaged communities, but also reinforced the marginality of certain ethnic groups and regions within a transforming politico-economic and social landscape. For those laboring on plantations, asserting their humanity ranged from negotiating family, land access, working times, payments for tasks, ownership of property, to using socioreligious idioms to challenge the power of planters, to litigation, theft, murder, and running away.

The institution of formal colonial rule occasioned a boom in plantation agriculture and the consolidation of the labor and race nexus that would mark plantation labor until independence. Given the resistance of indigenous communities to plantation work, planters and colonial state agents resorted to taxation, labor for food, conscription, limiting access to land and markets, crop restrictions, and the reliance on criminal and customary laws to increase the flow of labor. Local authorities were called upon to supply workers and trace deserters, while private recruiters, medical tests, and tax tickets regulated the movement of Africans.

The outcome was a mix of recruited and voluntary migrant labor on contracts, local labor on seasonal or casual basis, and squatter and tenancy arrangements. Although men tended to predominate in numbers and in official discourse, women and children provided a regular supply of dependents, local, and migrant workers. Along with age and gender, ethnicity was a key principle for procuring, organizing, and controlling labor. The failure to control plantation labor, however, contributed to new policies by the late 1940s geared toward stable working families, the introduction of social welfare, and labor unions.

Plantation labor for workers and communities meant a continuous struggle to retain control over labor use and time, mobility, social reproduction, and access to land. Workers resorted to absenteeism and desertion to work on own plots of land, go home during planting season and for family events, or seek other employers. They negotiated the length of the working day, standards of tasks, payments, land to grow own food, types of unions between men and women, and use of leisure time. Litigation, strikes, and blacklisting of plantations were powerful reminders of the limits of planters' control. Many migrant workers renewed their contracts or settled in plantation areas, reconstituting kin and ethnic relations, but their presence also contributed to tensions over power, land, and resources. Skills, networks, and cash accumulated from plantation work allowed some men and women alternative forms of productive labor and access to property. Negotiating divisions of labor within households enabled many to combine wage and non-wage labor and limited their dependence on plantations; yet this also pushed the cost of social reproduction of labor onto local communities. In some labor reserve areas economies and ecological management practices were disrupted resulting in their increased vulnerability. Although plantation labor collapsed the social distance between regions, it also heightened economic disparities and contributed to struggles over authority and resources, and new definitions of gender, hierarchy, and ethnicity.

The close association between plantations and colonialism partially shaped the trajectory of plantation labor after independence. Nationalist ideologies, alternative economic opportunities, and the stigmatization of migrant labor dampened labor migration and shifted its terms to monthly work. Many limited their engagement to casual labor, combining it with social benefits distributed by the state, especially on nationalized plantations. The 1970s economic crises, the collapse of state subsidies, and limited access to cash, land, and markets drew men and women to plantations, as monthly migrant workers, casual laborers, and tenants. Structural adjustment policies, the privatization of plantations, and the influx of private investors revived the demand for plantation labor. Communities formerly outside of plantation labor networks were pulled in by increased poverty, droughts and failed crops, HIV/AIDS pandemic, regional economic disparities, and drop in commodity markets. Wars further disrupted local and national economies and increased the pool of labor from displaced persons. Liberalizing land, labor, and trade union laws, coupled with cost-reduction and increased-production schemes and layoffs on plantations, forced many men and women to intensify the use of their labor power and limited their ability to negotiate terms of employment. For many plantation workers and local communities the gains they were able to wrestle from colonial regimes in controlling their

productive and reproductive powers were fading in the twenty-first century.

See also **Plantation Economies and Societies; Slave Trades; Slavery and Servile Institutions.**

BIBLIOGRAPHY

Cooper, Frederick. "African Workers and Imperial Design." In *Black Experience and the Empire*, ed. Philip D. Morgan and Sean Hawkins. New York: Oxford University Press, 2004.

Lovejoy, Paul E. "The Characteristics of Plantations in the Nineteenth-Century Sokoto Caliphate (Islamic West Africa)." *American Historical Review* 84, no. 5 (1979): 1267–1292.

Mbilinyi, Marjorie, and A. Maria Semakafu. *Gender and Employment on Sugar Cane: Plantations in Tanzania.* Geneva: International Labor Office, 1995.

Vail, Leroy, and Landeg White. *Capitalism and Colonialism in Mozambique: A Study of Quelimane District.* London: Heinemann, 1980.

HANAN SABEA

TRADES UNIONS AND ASSOCIATIONS

With the exception of South Africa, organized labor did not play a significant role in Africa until the period of World War II. During the early decades of European colonial rule, colonial powers did not recognize the existence of an African working class and made little efforts to address workers' demands. Moreover, the majority of African workers were casual laborers who moved between the cities and the rural areas. The legalization of trade unions was part of the response of colonial governments to the wave of strikes and labor unrest that took place in different parts of Africa. Strikes occurred in such colonies as Kenya, Senegal, Nigeria, Ghana, and Rhodesia. These protests were prompted by declining living conditions including low wages, inflation, and poor housing and social services. However, these protests were built on a long tradition resistance and organization that began since the establishment of European colonial rule. Despite the fact that colonial powers did not allow the development of trade unions in early years, African workers engaged in various forms of resistance and collective actions in response to low wages and poor working conditions. They also established voluntary and mutual aid associations, artisan groups, workers' clubs, and regional organizations. In some African countries such as Nigeria and Sierra Leone, these informal organizations existed as early as the late nineteenth century.

Colonial powers began to take steps to legalize trade unions in Kenya and Nigeria in the late 1930s and early 1940s. However, it was in South Africa that a powerful trade union movement emerged earlier. The mineral discoveries in the nineteenth century laid the foundation for large-scale industrialization and led to the development of an industrial working class. Trade unions were introduced in South Africa in the nineteenth century by immigrant artisans, most of whom came from Europe. But it was the system of racial segregation that evolved in South Africa that had a great impact on the trade unionism as labor organizations fragmented along racial lines. Although legalized labor unions were dominated mainly by white workers, one of the most important unions that attempted to organize black workers was the Industrial and Commercial Workers Union (ICU), which was founded in 1919. In the 1920s, the membership of the ICU reached 100,000 workers. The ICU forged close relations with the South African Communist Party and tried to create an effective trade union movement.

However, state repression, internal conflicts, and failure to bring tangible benefits to workers led to the collapse of the ICU in the late 1920s. It was succeeded by the Congress of Non-European Trade Unions (CNETU), which expanded its membership among black workers during World War II, but was dissolved in 1946. In the 1950s the South African Congress of Trade Unions (SACTU) was formed and established close links with the African National Congress (ANC) as well as the South African Communist Party. However, the banning of the ANC in the 1960s had crippled SACTU. Several unions emerged in the 1970s, but the continuous repression by the apartheid regime rendered them ineffective. With the reduction of restrictions for nonracial trade unions in the 1980s, the number of unions expanded and their membership grew rapidly. In 1985 these new trade unions formed a federation known as the Congress of South African Trade Unions (COSATU), with a membership of 565,000 workers. Other unions included, the Council of Unions of South Africa (CUS), which advocated a more militant nationalist position and focused mainly on black workers. Despite government repression trade unions played a major role in the resistance against the apartheid system. It was the alliance between the African National Congress, South African Communist Party, and the labor movement that formed the core of the anti-apartheid movement and paved the way for the political transformation of South Africa in the early 1990s.

In other parts of Africa, trade unionism was spearheaded by transportation workers such as railway and dock workers. The high level of militancy of transport workers can be attributed to their sheer size, their strategic position in the colonial economy, and their strong sense of community and corporate identity. The period of World War II witnessed a series of strikes by railway and dock workers in such colonies as Senegal, Nigeria, Ghana, Kenya, and Sudan, just to name a few. Labor unrests also occurred among mine and plantation workers as well as white-collar workers. These protests forced colonial governments to rethink their labor policies and develop new strategies to contain the militancy of African workers. The new strategies included the provision of family wages, decent housing, and social services, and the legalization of trade unions and collective bargaining. However, by introducing trade unions, colonial powers intended to create a nonpolitical, more malleable, and docile working class, and to keep labor disputes within legal boundaries.

Moreover, one of the primary concerns of colonial powers was to curb communist influences on African trade unions. For instance, the British Trade Unions Congress sent delegations to many African colonies to help build non-communist trade union movement. Despite these efforts, African workers increased their militancy and used trade unions to demand more entitlements and engage a wide range of social and political activities. In some colonies such as the Sudan and Egypt, the labor trade unions became closely associated with radical communist parties. Moreover, in many parts of Africa labor unions became highly politicized. This was particularly the case during the period of the nationalist struggle for independence in the late 1940s and 1950s, when the labor movement allied itself with the nationalist movement, which was dominated by the small educated class. In other words, labor protests provided the social base for the nationalist struggle and played a pivotal role in the achievement of independence.

In the postcolonial period, African trade unions continued to struggle for better working conditions, but they were faced with hostile governments. Both conservative and leftist regimes in Africa made relentless efforts to control and limit the influence of trade unions. Virtually all postcolonial governments in Africa did not allow the development of autonomous institutions that could threaten their power base. They also considered themselves the patron of the working class. From their perspective, the most important and urgent task that was facing the newly independent nations was economic development. Hence, workers' demand for better wages and living conditions were not welcomed.

In Ghana for instance, the Convention People's Party Kwame Nkrumah, which came to power after independence, became increasingly authoritarian and tried to bring the labor movement under its control. This period witnessed major confrontations between workers and government, which led to the erosion of workers' support for Nkrumah's government. Increased repression led to the decline of the Ghanaian labor movement. Although the successive regimes that followed Nkrumah in the late 1960s adopted more liberal policies toward trade unions, the deterioration economic conditions led to unprecedented labor unrest in the 1970s.

As in Ghana, the postcolonial government in Nigeria tried to patronize trade unions and to bring them under its control. However, the government efforts to impose national wage rates, led to a wave of strikes, the most important of which was the 1964 general strikes. Nevertheless, the powerful trade union movement faced severe repression under the successive military regimes that dominated Nigerian politics for most of the postcolonial period.

In the Sudan from the beginning, the labor movement was closely associated with radical, leftist organizations such as the Sudanese Communist Party. Despite the hostility of the postcolonial Sudanese governments, trade unions remained militant and engaged in fierce battles for better working conditions. Sudanese trade unions formed the core of a popular movement that included professional associations, students, and peasant organizations. These groups advocated progressive social and political change and played a pivotal role in the modern history of the Sudan. On two occasions, these associations led popular uprisings that brought down military regimes—those of Ibrahim 'Abboud in 1964 and Ja'far Nimeiri in 1985.

The power and influence of trade unions in Africa declined in the 1970s and 1980s as a result of the deteriorating economic conditions, the policies of structural adjustment, and the proliferation of authoritarian regimes in the continent. Nonetheless, with the recent trends of democratization, African trade unions have become the cornerstone of civil society movements and began to regain some of the political clout they had once enjoyed.

See also **Apartheid; Civil Society; Colonial Policies and Practices; Nationalism; Nkrumah, Francis Nwia Kofi; Postcolonialism; World War II.**

BIBLIOGRAPHY

Atkins, Keletso. *The Moon Is Dead! Give Us Our Money! Cultural Origins of an African Work Ethics, Natal, South Africa, 1843–1900.* Portsmouth, NH: Heinemann, 1993.

Cooper, Frederick. *Decolonization and African Society: The Labor Question in French and British Africa.* Cambridge, U.K: Cambridge University Press, 1996.

Crisp, Jeff. *The Story of an African Working Class: Ghanaian Miners' Struggles, 1870–1980.* London: Zed Books, 1984.

Freund, Bill. *The African Worker.* Cambridge, U.K.: Cambridge University Press, 1988.

Gutkind, P.R. Cohen, et al. *African Labor History.* Beverly Hills and London: Sage Publications, 1978.

Oberst, Timothy. "Transport Workers, Strikes and the Imperial Response: Africa and the Post–World War II Conjuncture." *African Studies Review* 31, no. 1 (1988): 117–134.

Sandbrook, Richard, and Robin Cohen, eds. *The Development of an African Working Class: Studies in Class Formation and Action.* London: Longman, 1975.

AHMAD ALAWAD SIKAINGA

TRANSPORT

The development of mechanical transport was one of the major accompaniments of European colonial rule in Africa. Although river and road transport infrastructure was founded on existing rudimentary structures, sea and rail transport facilities were innovations. Beginning in South Africa and Egypt from the nineteenth century, the provision of modern transport facilities necessitated the employment of labor, both for constructing and for running the transport services. In many colonies and postindependence African states, the transport sector was a major employer of labor. In order of importance, the railway, dock, road, and urban transport workers took the lead in organizing themselves into labor unions, which engaged in struggles over a wide variety of issues during the colonial period and after.

Railway construction was a major project of all the European colonizers of Africa. The Dutch at the Cape, the French, Germans, British, and Belgians embarked on various schemes that invariably linked the hinterland with seaports. On a continental scale, hundreds of thousands of workers were engaged in massive rail construction works. However, forced labor was exploited in French, Belgian, and Portuguese colonies in executing public works, including the laying of railway tracks. After the lines had been completed, African labor was required to operate the railways in the various sections of what was a major colonial enterprise. The trend outlived the colonial period, as the railway was the largest employer of wage labor in the public sector. The ports and the motor transport business too employed substantial numbers of Africans. Throughout the transport sector, wages were generally low, often a deliberate policy of the colonial and postindependence governments, and conditions of service generated discontent and labor militancy. The colonial-era tradition of general strikes were led by railway workers. In Nigeria, the Michael Imoudu-led railway workers union spearheaded a major general strike in 1945, which was replicated in the postindependence era with another major strike in 1964. However, government strikebreaking, including the use of force, and the ideological polarization of union leadership had done much to undermine workers' solidarity and the potency of their agitations.

Working conditions on the railway, in the ports, and in urban motor parks engendered a working-class consciousness that was forged in the peculiar context of colonialism. Low wages, discriminatory service conditions (including job insecurity and inadequate compensation for loss of jobs and injury), and bleak career prospects (exemplified by casualization) initially fuelled labor unrest. A higher level of consciousness developed with the involvement of the unions in nationalist politics. However, both tendencies coalesced in the militant independence movements in which union leaders also emerged as nationalist leaders in their own right.

The 1930s and 1940s witnessed a rash of strikes by transport labor. Notable ones were the Mombassa dockworkers' strike of 1934, 1939, and 1942; the Nigerian General Strike of 1945 that was led by railway workers; a railway strike in Southern Rhodesia in 1945; and the strike of 1947–1948 that paralyzed the entire railway system in French Africa. Worth noting is that the tendency for trade union strikes to dovetail or snowball into general strikes as in Tanganyika, Nigeria, the Gold Coast, Senegal, Southern and Northern Rhodesia, and South Africa. Some of these general strikes were so effective that they had to be brutally suppressed. The reason for the conflation of union and general strikes is that, except for miners' strikes, African labor activism was an urban phenomenon. Working-class solidarity and shared economic plights and social relationships transformed local strikes into national and general strikes.

Such mass protests involved unionized and nonunionized workers, especially market women associations. The strikes may have become mass actions because the work forces were little differentiated. The colonial urban milieu and shared workplace experiences had fostered trans-ethnic working class solidarity in the increasingly overpopulated urban centers. The rural-urban drift had been induced by a combination of factors—the quest for wage earnings to pay tax in rural communities or to fulfill certain social obligations, and young men's desire to escape to urban centers to evade rural patriarchy. A striking feature of transport labor was the overwhelming preponderance of male workers and the ethnic diversity and high mobility of that workforce. Women's roles in the transport labor force were essentially secondary or supportive, in the sense of provisioning and entertaining the male workers.

Labor militancy on the railways and at the ports, in particular, was potent essentially because these sites were the arteries of the colonial economy. It was impossible to replace the striking workers without huge costs, and the toll of a protracted strike—as exemplified by the twelve-day shutdown of Mombasa port in 1947 and the five-month railway strike in French Africa in 1947–1948—proved unsustainable. Hence, workers' wages improved, especially as the colonial governments resorted to the policy of stabilization: paying African men wages that could support their families within a pay structure that included wage increase increments and incentives. Evidence from the life histories of Nigerian railway workers suggests that regular wages and increments enhanced the social status and ensured the stability (and longevity) of the marriages of the male workers, though the male breadwinners were subject to periodic transfers.

Much of the pattern of colonial-era labor politics was replicated in the postindependence period. A major difference in most parts of Africa was that labor agitation was essentially devoted to improving workers' standards of living rather than seeking to effect a change of government. Where Labor was overtly involved in politics, even to the point of forming labor parties, its rare success, as in post-Kaunda Zambia, was contingent upon mass discontent and the collaboration of various opposition groups. However, the economic crises of the 1970s and 1980s, which necessitated various schemes of structural adjustment, compounded relations between labor on the one hand, and the state and capital on the other. With the devaluation of national currencies, the collapse of produce export markets, official corruption, the closure of industries, and massive retrenchment of workers, the stage was set for protracted strikes and other acts of labor militancy. Labor activism on the railways and at the ports was fuelled by the commercialization or privatization of state-owned enterprises, notably, the railways, ports, and light manufacturing industries. In South Africa and Nigeria, the privatization of the railways and ports generated much controversy and the process was stalled because of workers' apprehension about job losses. Pressure from Labor forced governments to make arrangements for ameliorating the impact of mass retrenchment, which underscores

the continuing strategic importance of transport labor in African economies.

See also **Colonial Policies and Practices; Kaunda, Kenneth; Mambasa; Marriage Systems; Transportation.**

BIBLIOGRAPHY

Cooper, Frederick. *Decolonization and African Society: The Labour Question in French and British Africa.* Cambridge, U.K.: Cambridge University Press, 1996.

Cooper, Frederick. *Africa since 1940.* Cambridge, U.K.: Cambridge University Press, 2002.

Gutkind, Peter C.W.; Robin Cohen; and Jean Copans; eds. *African Labor History.* New York: SAGE, 1978.

Lindsay, Lisa A., and Stephan F. Miescher, eds. *Men and Masculinities in Modern Africa.* Portsmouth, NH: Heinemann, 2003.

AYODEJI OLUKOJU

LABOR: SEX WORK. *See* **Prostitution; Sexual Behavior.**

LADYSMITH BLACK MAMBAZO.

Ladysmith Black Mambazo (mambazo is Zulu for "axe") is an all-male South African choral group. Founded by Bhekizizwe Joseph Shabalala in the early 1960s, Ladysmith Black Mambazo is the premier choir performing in the isicathamiya tradition. Isicathmiya dates back to the 1920s and originated among Zulu-speaking migrant laborers. Performed mainly in all-night competitions in major urban centers, isicathamiya blends rural vocal traditions with more Westernized choral practices.

The group rose to prominence on the South African music scene in the 1970s, amidst a state-run media campaign aimed at promoting the ideology of separate development or apartheid. After distancing themselves from politics and having collaborated on Paul Simon's seminal album *Graceland* (1986), Ladysmith Black Mambazo became among the first African musicians to attract worldwide attention. Since then, the group has teamed up with numerous international stars including Stevie Wonder, Dolly Parton, the Winans, George Clinton, and Michael Jackson.

South African singing group Ladysmith Black Mambazo. Founder Joseph Shabalala (1941–) leads the other band members at the microphone, April 2005, Town Hall, New York. Ladysmith Black Mambaza is a Grammy Award–winning South African a cappella group formed by Shabalala in 1960. © AP IMAGES

The group has recorded more than two dozen albums, the most popular being their first album *Amabutho* (1972), *Phansi Emgodini* (1981), and *Shaka Zulu* (1987), which won a Grammy Award, and *Two Worlds One Heart* (1990). Written primarily in Zulu (and also in English since 1990), many of the songs sung by the group carry a strong religious or spiritual message. Joseph Shabalala and his musicians have perfected a musical sound that, unlike that of rival isicathamiya groups, features velvet sonorities and smoothly blended vocal parts over a rolling, riff-like bass section.

See also **Music, Modern Popular: Southern Africa.**

BIBLIOGRAPHY

Erlmann, Veit. *Nightsong: Performance, Power, and Practice in South Africa.* Chicago: University of Chicago Press, 1996.

Thembela Alex J., and Edmund P. M. Radebe. *The Life and Works of Joseph Shabalala and the Ladysmith Black Mambazo.* Pietermaritzburg, South Africa: Reach Out Publishers, 1993.

VEIT ERLMANN

LAGOS. The city of Lagos is located in the southwestern corner of Nigeria. It fronts West Africa's coastline along the Gulf of Guinea where it occupies several islands and the adjacent mainland. As one of the largest cities in sub-Saharan Africa, its growth has been dramatic. The first census, taken in 1866, counted 25,083 people. A century later the population had grown more than tenfold to 267,083. The most significant increases took place after World War II, such that by 2000 the number had reached some 13 million, and the United Nations estimated that it would be 20 million by 2010.

There was virtually no activity in the Lagos area when it was observed by a Portuguese trader in the late fifteenth century. By the second half of the sixteenth century, however, it was functioning as a regional military and trading center on behalf of, and as a colonial outpost for, the powerful kingdom of Bénin. Direct trade with Europeans was light until the late eighteenth century, when Lagos became a significant port in the Atlantic trade, and, as such, diverse ethnic and linguistic groups congregated there from all directions, populating the area.

Missionaries came in the mid-nineteenth century and were joined by slaves liberated by the British antislavery squadron returning from Sierra Leone, Cuba, and Brazil; by refugees fleeing warfare in the north; and by increasing numbers of Europeans who were seeking trade opportunities. To this end, the British imposed a colonial regime in Lagos in 1861. In 1906 it became the capital of a vastly expanded Nigeria, and its center of commerce, transportation, and communications.

Colonial Lagos attracted a highly educated, creative, and articulate populace. Lagos continued to be the capital when independence was achieved in 1960, and it remained the center of the nation's political activity for the next three decades. When the capital was officially transferred away from Lagos to Abuja at the end of 1991, Lagos retained its preeminence in cultural and economic affairs. Cultural life centers on numerous institutions, including museums, galleries, the National Theater, filmmakers, libraries, and institutions of higher learning. Artists of all types congregate in the city, including a large literary community.

The metropolitan area of Lagos houses about half the country's indigenous and foreign banks, commercial and merchant; the head offices of 68 percent of the nation's insurance firms; and the nation's stock exchange. It has a quarter of the country's industries, more than half of its manufacturing employees, and 45 percent of the nation's skilled and unskilled workforce. Nevertheless, employment has two sectors. The formal sector consists of most wage-paid occupations, especially in industrial or civil service positions. The informal sector, the main one, includes casual labor, fishing, domestic service, and petty trade. Between 50 and 70 percent of the workforce relies on informal undertakings for its income.

The metropolitan area has eight local government authorities administered by the Lagos State Government. Each has elected chairmen and councilors who are vested with overseeing affairs of the civil servant staff and local services. The government plays its greatest role in providing social support through education and health.

Continuing growth is expected to make the city one of the largest metropolitan areas of the world. Rapid urbanization has led to unplanned and uncontrolled urban expansion, and therefore a paucity of services necessary to a large population. The greatest hardship falls on the poorest residents, who constitute the largest challenge to local leadership.

See also **Colonial Policies and Practices; Nigeria; Slave Trades.**

BIBLIOGRAPHY

Abiodun, Josephine Olu. "The Challenges of Growth and Development in Metropolitan Lagos." In *The Urban Challenge in Africa: Growth and Management of Its Large Cities,* ed. Carole Rakodi. Tokyo, New York, Paris: United Nations University Press, 1996.

Barnes, Sandra T. *Patrons and Power: Creating a Political Community in Metropolitan Lagos.* Bloomington: Indiana University Press, 1986.

Cole, Patrick. *Modern and Traditional Elites in the Politics of Lagos.* Cambridge, U.K.: Cambridge University Press, 1975.

Lagos State Government. "Lagos State Centre of Excellence." Available from http://www.lagosstate.gov.ng/.

Olowu, Dele. *Lagos State: Governance, Society and Economy.* Ikeja, Lagos: Malthouse Press, 1990.

SANDRA T. BARNES

LAKE CHAD SOCIETIES.

Lake Chad is one of the largest natural water reservoirs of the Central Sudan. The lake provides water to more than 20 million people living in the surrounding four countries: Nigeria, Niger, Chad, and Cameroon. For immigrants from all over West and Central Africa, the lake serves as a migration center, crossroads, and political hinterland.

In precolonial times the Buduma (Yedina and Kuri group) were the predominant inhabitants of the islands located east of Lake Chad. Economically, they concentrated on cow-husbandry and trading natron. They formed a society loosely connected through clans and lineages, with chiefs having only little authority. With the decline of the Borno Empire in the eighteenth century, cattle and slave raids became part of Buduma's economy, contributing to their reputation as "pirates of the papyrus." In consequence, the politically dominant groups—Kanuri and Shuwa Arabs—had to stay away from the Lake Chad area and could not survey its population by collecting taxes and tributes. Whereas the transhumant Shuwa-Arabs, and the nomadic living Wodaabe, Tuareg, and Tubu approached the lake mainly from

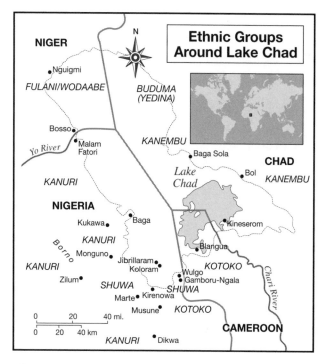

Ethnic Groups Around Lake Chad

NIGER

Nguigmi

FULANI/WODAABE

BUDUMA (YEDINA)

Bosso

Malam Fatori

Yo River

KANEMBU

Baga Sola

Lake Chad

CHAD

Bol

KANEMBU

KANURI

NIGERIA

Kukawa

Baga

Kineserom

Borno

KANURI

Monguno

Jibrillaram

Koloram

Wulgo

Gamboru-Ngala

Blangua

KOTOKO

Chari River

KANURI

Zilum

SHUWA

Marte

Kirenowa

SHUWA

Musune

KOTOKO

0   20   40 mi.

0   20   40 km

KANURI

Dikwa

CAMEROON

© PLATTE/FROBENIUS-INSTITUT

the west and the north in order to look for green pasture, the agriculturalists Kanuri, Kotoko, Kanembu, and part of the Kuri cultivated the land predominantly west, south, and east of the lake. Both pastoralists and agriculturalists share the same religion, Islam. The agriculturalists, including the Buduma, share common ancestry, all being partly descended from the So. These people were said to be the initiators of many of the so-called little-kingdoms and city-states that were established before the empire of Kanem-Borno expanded its power west and south of Lake Chad.

Since 1920 colonial powers established their control over the Chad Basin and consolidated the borders of Nigeria, Niger, Chad, and Cameroon. Colonial presence stopped the raiding activities of the Buduma and people from the mainland (Kanuri and Shuwa), and people from more distant places (Jukun, Igbo, and Hausa) moved into and close to Lake Chad. This immigration and the subsequent introduction of a market economy led to technological advances, including the manufacturing of iron fishing hooks and nylon nets, and new marketplace activities, such as the smoking of fish. With the drying up of the lake during the Sahelian droughts of the 1970s and 1980s, wide areas of formerly overflooded land opened up and gave space for a

new generation of dwellers to inhabit. People of the mainland (Kanuri, Shuwa, Kanembu, and Kotoko) as well as newcomers (Hausa), assumed political and administrative power. The pastoralists (Shuwa, Wodaabe) periodically passed through the former lake floor; temporary fishery camps were occupied by Hausa, Jukun, and Bozo; people arrived to earn money on the expanding beans and maize fields; and permanent settlements have developed into multiethnic towns with populations of over 5,000.

See also **Water and Irrigation.**

BIBLIOGRAPHY

Baroin, Catherine. "What Do We Know about the Buduma? A Brief Survey." *Man and the Lake: Proceedings of the 12th Mega Chad Conference, Maiduguri, December 2–9, 2003.* Maiduguri, Chad: Center for Trans-Saharan Studies, 2005.

Bouquet, Christian. *Insulaires et Riverains du Lac Chad.* 2 vols. Paris: Èditions L'Harmattan (1990): 199–217.

Konrad, Walter. "Neue Beiträge zur Kenntnis der Buduma." Braunschweig: Limbach. *Zeitschrift für Ethnologie* 88 (1963): 332–336.

Krings, Matthias, and Editha Platte, eds. "Living with the Lake: Perspectives on History, Culture and Economy of Lake Chad." *Studien zur Kulturkunde* 121 (2004).

Nachtigal, Gustav. "Das Becken des Tsade und seine Bewohner." *Zeitschrift der Gesellschaft für Erdkunde zu Berlin* (1877): 30–88.

EDITHA PLATTE

LAKES REGION. *See* **Interlacustrine Region, History of (1000 BCE to 1500 CE).**

LAKWENA, ALICE (1956–2007). Alice Lakwena, born in northern Uganda, became the medium of a Christian spirit named Lakwena, meaning "messenger" and "apostle" in the Acholi language, during Uganda's civil war (1981–1986). In opposition to local pagan spirit mediums, she established a Christian cult of affliction, treating primarily barren women and injured soldiers. In 1986, when the government army (NRA) had conquered and occupied Acholi, she founded the Holy Spirit Mobile Forces (HSMF), entered the public sphere as a Christian prophetess, and started to wage a "holy war" not only against the NRA, but also against internal enemies, including impure soldiers, witches, and "pagan" healers. She recruited mainly former soldiers from other more secular guerrilla movements. After the first military successes, peasants, students, teachers, a few businessmen, a former government minister, and a number of girls and women also joined her army.

Under the titles "Chairman" and "Commander in Chief," Lakwena invented a complex ritual of initiation, thereby cleansing her soldiers of evil and making them "holy." She taught her troops Holy Spirit Tactics, a form of warfare that combined modern military techniques with ritual practices, and she tried to establish a new moral order by instituting a number of prohibitions, called Holy Spirit Safety Precautions. Through them, she succeeded in controlling her soldiers and gaining the support of large portions of the population, not only in Acholi but also in Lango and Teso.

Between seven and ten thousand men and women of the HSMF marched from Kitgum to Lira, Soroti, Kumi, Mbale, Tororo, and beyond. They were defeated near Jinja at the end of October 1987. Lakwena fled to Kenya, where she was granted political asylum and as of 2006 continued to live in a refugee camp. After her defeat, the discourse and practices she invented were taken over, with variations, by her father Severino Lukoya, who fought between 1987 and 1989, and then by Joseph Kony, whose Lord's Resistance Army (LRA) was still waging war in northern Uganda in the early twenty-first century.

Alice Lakwena died in a refugee camp at Garissa in Kenya in January 2007; she was fifty-one years old.

See also **Uganda: History and Politics.**

BIBLIOGRAPHY

Allen, Tim. "Understanding Alice: Uganda's Holy Spirit Movement in Context." *Africa* 61 (1991): 370–399.

Behrend, Heike. "Is Alice Lakwena a Witch? The Holy Spirit Movement and Its Fight against Evil in the North of Uganda." In *Changing Uganda*, ed. Holger Bernt Hansen and Michael Twaddle. Athens: Ohio University Press, 1991.

Behrend, Heike. *Alice Lakwena and the Holy Spirits: War in Northern Uganda.* Athens: Ohio University Press, 1999.

HEIKE BEHREND

LALIBÄLA. Lalibäla (or Lalibela) is the name of a saintly Ethiopian king and of his capital where eleven rock-hewn churches, whose construction is ascribed to him, are concentrated. Largely because of these churches and his compassion for the poor, Lalibäla is the most famous king of the Zagwe dynasty and a highly revered native saint of the Ethiopian Orthodox Church. His wife Mäsqäl Kəbra was also a saint in her own right. Lalibäla was also a priest and celebrated Mass at his palace church.

Although uncertain, there is some consensus that King Lalibäla ruled from 1185 to 1225 CE. During his reign, his capital was called Roha, the Arabic name of Edessa in Syria; it was later renamed after the saint. In the early twenty-first century, the monastic town of Lalibäla, in the province of Lasta in north-central Ethiopia, remains an annual pilgrimage center for the faithful.

Archaeologists, historians, and others often list the monolithic churches of Lalibäla among the wonders of the world. Some, like the Church of Saint George, stand free on all sides, while others are attached, on one or two sides, to the rock from which they are excavated. The hagiographical history of Saint Lalibäla states that the king received the architectural plans for the churches from heaven. However, the tradition that all eleven churches were built by, or during the reign of, Lalibäla has not received much acceptance; some might have been built before him.

See also **Architecture; Kings and Kingdoms.**

BIBLIOGRAPHY

Gerster, George. *Churches in Rock, Early Christian Art in Ethiopia*, trans. Richard Hosking. London: Phaidon Press, 1970.

Jäger, Otto A., and Ivy Pearce. *Antiquities of North Ethiopia: A Guide.* London: Paul, Trench, Trubner and Co., 1974.

Perruchon, Jules. *Vie de Lalibala, roi d'Éthiopie.* Paris: Ernest Leroux, Paris, 1892.

Sellassie, Sergew Hable. *Ancient and Medieval Ethiopian History to 1270.* Addis Ababa: United Printers, 1972.

Van Donzel, Emeri. "Ethiopia's Lalibäla and the fall of Jerusalem 1187." *Aethiopica International Journal of Ethiopian Studies* 1 (1998): 27–49.

GETATCHEW HAILE

LALIBELA. *See* Lalibäla.

LAND

This entry includes the following articles:
TENURE
REFORM

TENURE

At the beginning of the twenty-first century, Africa is experiencing a crisis that has economic, cultural, political, and moral dimensions.

In such a context, the question of land tenure moves increasingly to the fore. Land tenure is behind the ethnic and tribal conflicts that have bloodied so many countries—Rwanda, Liberia, and Somalia, for example. It is also part of the pacification of South Africa, which emerged from apartheid in the early 1990s. Land tenure remains an ongoing issue in Zimbabwe, despite the Lancaster House agreements of 1980 guaranteeing the rights of the white minority. It is equally important in Mauritania, where it was the cause of a conflict with neighboring Senegal in 1989. Finally, it remains potentially explosive in other countries from Côte d'Ivoire to Uganda, including Niger, Chad, Nigeria, and Ghana. In fact, the list could include every country in sub-Saharan Africa. Clearly, then, at the beginning of the twenty-first century, Africa has not worked out a satisfactory land tenure system that will permit what the international community considers sustainable development: lasting, reproducible, and equitable enough to be accepted by the majority of people.

The failure is all the more vexing because neither the countries nor their foreign aid donors have directed their efforts toward financial or agro-financial reforms (in the case of the aid-receiving countries) or have insisted upon structural adjustment programs as a condition of intervention (in the case of foreign assistance donors). It need not, however, be inevitable that solutions to make land ownership more secure will not be found.

If there was a failure, it was the imitative model of development. This model, drawn from an evolutionist and ethnocentric perspective, led people to suppose that the solutions used by developed countries—Western capitalist economies or socialist planned economies—would be appropriate to apply to the problems of developing countries.

In the 1990s, approaches to land tenure took a new turn under the influence of the World Bank, whose policy is directed toward expansion of private ownership. Nonetheless, the capitalist and socialist development models have retained their influence.

Given the failure of development efforts since the mid-1960s, and of first-generation land tenure policies, it is useful to devise new approaches for the future. Only by analyzing the whole can one identify what new factors are at stake in the area of land tenure at the beginning of the twenty-first century. In doing so, one must adopt a pragmatic philosophy that is more concerned with bringing security to existing situations than with, so to speak, playing sorcerer's apprentice to development.

EXOGENOUS MODELS, CONFUSED MANAGEMENT, AND POORLY DEFINED GOALS

When invoking the language of medicine to treat the "sick" body that is Africa, one must remember that the term "diagnostic" is widely used in the operations of research and development. Making an assessment does not guarantee recovery, but it can allow the adaptation of the operation to the present condition of the subject.

Problematic Extroversion. In Africa, approaches to land tenure systems reflect the social and political characteristics exhibited during the slave trade, during colonialization, and most recently in unequal economic exchange. In particular, research shows the persistence of an ethnocentrism that claims to address the confrontation between two worldviews—the one animist, communitarian, and sometimes Muslim; the other, Judeo-Christian and individualist—as the meeting of tradition and modernity under the aegis of the state and the market.

During the first three decades of the twentieth century, this type of approach gave rise to a specialized French-language literature that elaborated the legitimization of colonial land improvements and land tenure policies, making it possible to appropriate land without indemnifying its African occupants. A 1982 analysis by Émile Le Bris,

Étienne Le Roy, and François Leimdorfer labeled these models "precolonial referent" for two reasons. On the one hand, the label encompassed every model developed prior to the modernization period. Such models were based on the assumption of "ideal types" (in Max Weber's sense), which were thought to adequately represent all the organizational forms of every society, whether sedentary or nomadic, acephalous or with a centralized chiefdom. The "precolonial referent" also expresses the sense that the comparison is not between two situations in different periods—before and after the colonial conquest—but between the culture considered to be superior—the "civilization" of the colonizer—and the "state of nature" in which Africans were seen to be imprisoned before colonization enabled them to profit from the supposed benefits of modernity, particularly property rights.

One of the first authors to identify the trap of this ethnocentrism was the anthropologist Paul Bohannan:

> In the past, Westerners have approached the study of African land customs by searching for "rules of tenure" based on three *a priori* judgments regarding these factors:
>
> (1) that the Western type "map" must be initiated in the area, or else more naively that it is already present but unknown to the people;
> (2) that property concepts provided an adequate means for expressing all types of man-thing unit; and
> (3) that contract and law of succession are the basic mode for dealing with social relationships in a spatial context (pp. 103–104)

Since the end of the 1980s, many of these naive representations have been corrected and replaced with new propositions based on research in post-independence Africa.

Two approaches to the representation of space and land tenure relationships have confronted one another since the beginning of the colonial period. They are called "spatiotemporal matrices." According to works devoted to this topic, a spatiotemporal matrix is "a conceptual framework permitting one to read the space where social relations are projected. It is a 'machine,' an active principle, a transformer of social relations and spatial categories" (Crousse, Le Bris, and Le Roy, 21).

Interpretations of space that have been made according to anthropological and geographical processes have brought the two representations to light. On the one hand, one can identify a "topocentric" (Greek *topoi*, locations) representation of space, which is so ancient that it originated in the Neolithic revolution and formed the basis of the "archaic" African spatiotemporal matrix.

The topocentric model postulates a number of coexistent centers of differentiated powers (religious, political, agrarian, lineage-based, commercial) superimposed upon each other. This occurred within the framework of an animist worldview that gave value to the movement of forces and the organization of the life in society according to the principle of multiple, specialized, and interdependent authorities. Each of these authorities was defined by its associated center of power (*topos*), which particularized and defined it. Corresponding to these different centers of power—which are represented, for instance, by the political "heads," land chiefs, or priest of the shrine—are the physical spaces. Thus the land itself supports several spaces over which a number of rights can be exercised. Writing about the Barotse, Max Gluckman tried to express this superposition of spaces and rights, so foreign to the colonial conception, when he spoke, improperly, of a "hierarchy of estates." This topocentric conception remains poorly understood because of the modern conception of land tenure introduced by colonization.

By contrast, the "modern" Western conception of land tenure is considered exclusive, a would-be substitute for ancient African land tenure formulas. Its origin maybe as early as the African ones, possibly associated with the urban checkerboards of the Ionian cities of the seventh century BCE; systematized during the great voyages of discovery in the fifteenth and sixteenth centuries CE, it constitutes such a rupture that one can speak of a "revolution of space." Again it is Bohannan who revealed the ways it appeared (thanks to marine measurement instruments) and was applied (with the new cartography):

> Westerners divide the earth's surface by use of an imaginary grid, itself subject to manipulations and redefinitions. We then plot the grid on paper or on a sphere and the problem becomes one of correlating this grid to the physical features of land and sea.... We have...perfected a system of measurement which allows us to repeat

precisely operations that have been carried out in the past; thus we are able to locate and measure pieces of the earth's surface and to record our computations on maps. These measured pieces become, for some purposes at least, identifiable "things." (pp. 101–102)

This possibility of measuring the globe gave rise to a "geometric" conception (from the Greek *geo*, earth; and *metron*, measure). Through this, a new conception of the land tenure relation, based on a relation between an "author" and a thing through the mediation of a right—the right of ownership—came to be generalizable. To the extent that this generalization is realized within the context of a globalized capitalist economy, it is a *capitalist* spatiotemporal matrix which has been put in concrete form. Since the beginnings of market capitalism, the notion of ownership has been linked to the functioning of the generalized market, but it is equally inseparable from the territorial sovereignty of the modern state. Market, ownership, and sovereignty are central and complementary concepts of institutional modernity. With colonization, these concepts were transferred to Africa, and their effects were viewed as positive, independent of their implementation and regardless of their possible failure. Indeed, one must consider the possibility of a failure, especially regarding the generalization of private ownership.

Two concepts, then, of land tenure continue to exist side by side in Africa: that based on the traditional African communitarian model and that based on Western individualistic and written law. In communitarian societies, "traditional" appropriation, in which the means of exchange are not usually determined by the market and the land is "not transmittable" outside the group that exploits it or occupies it, can be defined as the allocation of area to customary uses. The question of ownership, whether private or supposedly collective, therefore does not arise. Land tenure rights are understood as the exercise of specific controls over the land or its resources. The nature of these rights can be identified by three characteristics:

1. The statuses of the representatives of the occupying groups and those who manage its resources

2. Categories distinguishing appropriate land use, such as agricultural, residential, ritual, hunting, or gathering (see Daniel Biebuyck on the division of space among the Nyanga of Zaire)

3. The specific places and localities like family estates, particular plots of land, fallow land, sacred woods, forest reserves, and so on.

Corresponding to each of these characteristics is a mode of control, identified by status, and a mode of use (e.g., agricultural, pastoral, or forest)—and thus a specific right.

In the traditional model, the land tenure system is the totality of actual and potential land tenure controls exercised by individual members of a community concerned with land uses designed to assure food production and group reproduction. Although it has the halo of sacrality and is inscribed in societies' cosmological concepts, the land tenure system of traditional societies is the expression of juridical techniques belonging to oral, communitarian, and pragmatic law. It is neither more nor less "secular" than the law introduced by the colonizer.

By contrast, appropriation in the Western sense, is the reservation of a space to a user who can exercise a perpetual, exclusive, and absolute right. In this regard, English juridical terminology distinguishes—in contrast to the French Civil Code—between property rights and ownership. According to Edella Schlager and Elinor Ostrom, property rights confer the right to exclude outsiders but not to dispose of the land. Ownership, conversely, establishes the right of discretionary transfer, and thus corresponds to the definition in article 544 of the Civil Code of 1804: "the act of using and disposing of things in the most absolute manner."

The legal concepts of England and France differ according to their legal traditions. England accords importance to common law, which is more sensitive to specific local usages, and thus to African customary concepts; the Francophone tradition emphasizes codified law, which gives rise to the compilation of customs and modern legal codes.

Finally, in order to understand the different places given to indigenous and exogenous concepts, one must consider the role given to territories considered to be "settlement" colonies, such as Rhodesia and "white" parts of Kenya, as opposed to the colonies of exploitation. In the "settlement" colonies, land tenure concepts of the colonizing power were introduced on a sustainable basis and appeared as unusual examples of the relative generalization of land ownership. In this context, appropriation, understood to be the allocation of land to usages, continues to prevail. Only the uses and the modes of allocation have changed profoundly.

The base model of land tenure relations in Africa cannot be found in legal texts, in contractual relations, or in rules of succession (in Bohannan's sense). Rather, it is found in the observation of land tenure practices that are "polymorphous, polysemous, and polyvalent." Land tenure practices are expressed in such adages as "The land belongs to the one who works it," "The state is the master of the soil," and "The land belongs to the one who values it." These adages correspond to a "pragmatic law" which emerges from the encounter between traditional and contemporary experiences, in order to bring about contemporary solutions in a context of land tenure transition. The issues are no longer clearly identifiable, even though countries and their financial backers have chosen modernizing reforms. Each group is inclined to develop its own law. As a result, the practices are quite diverse, giving numerous possibilities from which to choose (a phenomenon that Keebet von Benda-Beckmann identified as "forum shopping") and providing the opportunity for reinterpretation and manipulation.

This "law of practice" has been ignored by legislation and little understood by magistrates. At the local level, it serves as a regulating framework, stabilizing land tenure relations, but it is not in itself sufficient to guarantee the stability of land tenure in the case of strong demographic pressures, such as the result of migration and conflict between indigenous peoples and outsiders, or from the implementation of development projects. In these situations, as Jean-Luc Piermay has observed in Zaire, uncertainty about land tenure turns to outright confusion.

In such circumstances, in addition to the social crisis, land tenure is insecure, which prevents sustainable investment in the land, which in turn precludes the accumulation of capital and the beginning of the process of endogenous economic development.

Ineffective Land Tenure Policies. Among the causes of ineffective land tenure policy are the shortcomings of the objectives and interests pursued. At

times, legislation has worked to achieve the colonial goal of making private ownership more widespread. More often, however, this policy has been accompanied or replaced by state intervention that creates a monopoly over land tenure. These policies, justified by requirements of political structures or by the constraints of development, and often used by authoritarian regimes to see that the interests of the classes who support them will prevail, began to be seriously questioned when the winds of democracy blew into Africa at the beginning of the 1990s.

It was excessive to propose that Africa, in the course of a few decades and in the framework of authoritarian models, should achieve what Europe had practiced with over several centuries through the process of increasing democratization. Although it was necessary to consider the economic examples of Asia, particularly Japan, in order to understand the conditions upon which modernization and the domestication of capitalism are based, planners preferred to blindly apply exogenous models, insisting that peoples adapt not only their techniques and ways of living but also their worldviews to fit them. Obviously, such a task of reappropriation and internalization could not be achieved so quickly, nor could it succeed when it was begun on the foundation of the simple development practiced under colonial exploitation. It was also a show of intellectual conceit to underestimate the coherence and effectiveness of endogenous mechanisms—what has been called, in an oversimplified way, customary law. Thus it is understandable that African populations responded to attempts to "domesticate" the innovations with avoidance—indeed, with strategies designed to divert objectives or manipulate foreign interests to serve their own immediate needs.

Faced with such a mess, how can one approach the future and contribute to the development of beneficial land tenure policies that will attract support in the twenty-first century?

LAND TENURE AT THE END OF THE TWENTIETH CENTURY

What follows below constitutes an original approach to the land tenure question. This approach is possible both because the world has changed and because scholars' knowledge of the issues and the conditions of intervention permit them to conceive of innovative responses.

Land Tenure: A Transnational Issue. The first document to cover the issue well comes from the context of present-day Africa. A 1994 internal memo by Émile Le Bris for the Association for the Promotion of Research and Land Tenure Studies of Africa noted that, since the 1970s, Africa has passed from a policy of "extrovert modernization," characterized by a strong demand for raw materials and a reaffirmed importance of the role of the individual state, to a conception advocating "a transnational neomodernization." As a result, while the key focus in the 1980s was "the state and land tenure," ten years later the key focus is "the World Bank and land tenure."

> During the 1980s, debt became the North's instrument for imposing a new means of force on the South. Unfortunately, the successive discourses about adjustment constituted the official and hegemonic discourse about development... where the international controlled the national; the norms of private enterprise controlled the state; the private sector controlled the public sector. The vision remains universalist but, whereas in the preceding phase a global order was sought, today it is postulated that such an order exists, and that it is economic. (Le Bris)

According to Le Bris, citing Peemans, in the rural sector, this shift in perspective became concrete through a

> consolidation of one pole of private accumulation in the hands of a more or less successful minority, and the exclusion of large masses of the peasantry. In this evolution, the land tenure question is absolutely crucial. For the developing capitalist sector, the security of land ownership is vital, and it thus favors an accelerated evolution toward the privatization of land. This evolution is facilitated... by the destabilizing effects that agricultural modernization policies and the agrarian crisis have had on rural structures.... At the level of ideas as well, this evolution is encouraged by several observers, from World Bank experts to certain authors.... The former think that a market economy requires the establishment of an institutional framework based on private property; the latter claim that Africa, like Europe, must necessarily pass through the phase of primitive accumulation. The two trends converge toward an entirely instrumental view of the peasantry, all in the service of accelerating modernization, which consequently seems to be a simple figurehead for the incredibly brutal reality of accumulation.... The trends demonstrate the distance separating the logic of accumulati on and the rationality of development, while

the concept of modernization has tended to confuse the two. (Le Bris)

The picture is bleak for the cities as well. Le Bris stated that

> social disaggregation is achieved through the general spread of poverty. Conflicts arise regarding access to the property of marginalized strata, and urban violence stems from the absence of a plan for social mobility... and thus of an alternative plan for urban management. On the other hand, in a context of megapolization, the hegemonic claim of liberal ideology runs into the restoration or widening of market mechanisms. This evolution affects all sectors of land tenure and real estate, as well as machinery and services. As a result, problems of access to urban land and housing, and the phenomena of exclusion worsen. The massive exclusion witnessed in the megapoles blurs the identification between the categories of poverty and exclusion. (Le Bris)

Consequently, one is faced with a paradoxical situation in which, as the formulas for organizing societies are globalized, the social fabric is simultaneously being shredded and partial and local solutions have come to predominate. While the relevant questions are being posed solely at the global level, the only answers relevant to "sustainable development" appear at the local level. Thus, there is an oscillation between universalization and the rise of particularisms and the consideration of only local, specific features.

How can one reconcile these paradoxes while working to give producers greater security?

Innovations That Will Give Security to Rural and Urban Producers. Reconciling global and local concerns, the universal and the particular, the global market and indigenous forms of production and reproduction (which are improperly called the informal sector) has become a necessity for contemporary research. In the context of land tenure systems, this involves learning to reflect, in a coherent way, in a single summarizing attempt, upon the experiences and solutions that were earlier identified as different, indeed contradictory.

This approach poses apparent logical difficulties. Nevertheless, the experience of participant observers with African peasants and city dwellers teaches that the so-called frontiers, the contradictions or limits, are not necessarily where Cartesian thought places them.

Consider some examples that show that the explanations thought to be stabilized at the end of the 1980s are in the process of being transformed.

First, sometimes to their cost, Africans have learned to reconcile the two paradigms of land tenure (indigenous and colonially imposed)—at times by superimposing them, at other times by creatively manipulating them. Since the beginning of the 1900s, in the central districts of Lomé, the capital of Togo, "capitalist" land tenure practices have been progressively reinterpreted by endogenous logic. Plots of land, at first treated as market goods, became "family houses," then lineage-based inheritances that could be transmitted to outsiders. As a result, market exchanges now affect only a tiny minority of plots, which are highly sought after by the banking and commercial sector.

Second, Africans have adapted their conception of appropriation as the allocation of the land and its resources to the modern definition of ownership. Land tenure law of the exclusive type, benefiting individuals or their immediate families, is becoming more widespread. Under certain limited conditions, it creates the possibility of exercising the right of disposal, and thus of passing from "property right" to "ownership."

Third, the problem is one of the juridical framing of these changes, in both a historical and a legal sense. Contracts and wills have come into general use, but without regard for the norms of land tenure codes or civil codes. In addition, transactions are implemented in a way that deviates from traditional law, adding legal insecurity to policy confusion when, as often happens, the governments affected either no longer possess the human and financial resources for enforcing their regulations or have already diverted them for their own or their clients' gain. As a result, the practices remain confused and "polymorphous or polysemic." In a sense, though, they are less "polyvalent"—issues are exacerbated, and the objective of achieving security becomes indefinable.

As a result, the need for the legal security of investments made in or on the land is urgent. Despite the means implemented by the World Bank to test innovative solutions (for example, the Land Tenure Plan in Côte d'Ivoire), such approaches may remain too influenced by the precedents of colonial and postcolonial policies, with scarcely any effect on the juridical and cultural hybrids that are taking shape.

In 1992, I proposed an alternative approach, the relevance and effectiveness of which have been tested. It is based on the theory of land tenure matrices. Using my fieldwork and American research on the management of communal resources (Schlager and Ostrom, 1992), I identified five different modes of appropriating land and resources, each based on the exercise of a specific law: undifferentiated control of land linked to the right of access; priority control allowing the extraction of resources; specialized control associated with the right to manage the land according to recognized uses; exclusive control barring outsiders; absolute control, where the discretionary right to convey property is recognized.

In a similar way, I identified five modes of management while introducing, between the so-called public and private modes of modern law, three modes characteristic of traditional societies: external, internal-external, internal. The succession of management modes is as follows: what is shared by all is public; what is shared by several groups is external; what is shared by two groups is internal-external; what is shared by one group is internal; what belongs to a legal person is private.

By combining the five modes of appropriation and the five modes of management in a double-entry table, one can form a twenty-five-cell land tenure matrix (see Table 1).

Although one of these forms corresponds to the Western conception of individual private ownership, as reflected in the civil code, others can be used to establish juridical frameworks that are not yet subject to an exclusive and absolute law.

Land tenure systems

Controls/ Management	Undiff.	Priority	Spec.	Excl.	Absol.
Public	X	X	X		
External	X	X	X		
Int.–Ext.			X	X	X
Internal				X	
Private				X	Civil code ownership

Table 1.

To test this model, consider how it could be used to guarantee that producers will gain greater security. As an illustration, take pastoralism. One would have to combine ten of these modes (marked with an X in Table 1) in order to assure the security of herders; this takes into account processes ranging from access to wells and pasturage, to salt curing of meat in the northern Sahel, transhumance, and the sale of animals in the urban markets.

This type of approach provides a possible solution to Africa's most delicate problem; making investments secure in order to ensure the primitive accumulation of capital at the lowest possible cost.

See also **Agriculture; Colonial Policies and Practices; Ecology; Food; Forestry; Kinship and Descent; Law; Peasants; Production Strategies.**

BIBLIOGRAPHY

Benda-Beckmann, Keebet von. "Forum Shopping and Shopping Forums: Dispute Processing in a Minangkabau Village in West Sumatra." *Journal of Legal Pluralism and Unofficial Law* no. 19 (1981): 117–159.

Bennet, John W.; Steven W. Lawry; and James C. Riddell. *Land Tenure and Livestock Development in Sub-Saharan Africa.* Washington, DC: Agency for International Development, 1986.

Biebuyck, Daniel. "Introduction." In *African Agrarian Systems,* ed. Daniel Biebuyck. London: Oxford University Press, 1963.

Bohannan, Paul. "'Land,' 'Tenure' and 'Land Tenure.'" In *African Agrarian Systems,* ed. Daniel Biebuyck. London: Oxford University Press, 1963.

Choquet, Catherine; Olivier Dollfus; Étienne Le Roy; and Michel Vernières; eds. *État des savoirs sur le développement.* Paris: Karthala, 1993.

Crousse, Bernard; Émile Le Bris; and Étienne Le Roy; eds. *Espaces disputés en Afrique noire: Pratiques foncières locales.* Paris: Karthala, 1986.

Falloux, François, and Aleki Mukendi, eds. *Desertification Control and Renewable Resource Management in the Sahelian and Sudanian Zones of West Africa.* Washington, DC, 1988.

Gluckman, Max, ed. *Ideas and Procedures in African Customary Law.* London: Oxford University Press, 1969.

Hesseling, Gerti, and Étienne Le Roy. "Le droit et ses pratiques." *Politique africaine* no. 40 (1990): 1–7.

International Association of Legal Science. *Le droit de la terre en Afrique (au sud du Sahara).* Paris, 1971.

Land Tenure Center Library, University of Wisconsin, Madison, comp. *Land Tenure and Agrarian Reform in Africa and the Near East: An Annotated Bibliography.* Boston: G. K. Hall, 1976.

Le Bris, Émile. "Contribution au débat." *Journées de réflexion de l'APREFA* (May 9–10, 1994).

Le Bris, Émile; Étienne Le Roy; and François Leimdorfer. *Enjeux fonciers en Afrique noire.* Paris: Karthala, 1982.

Le Roy, Étienne. "The Peasant and Land Law: Issues of Integrated Rural Development in Africa by the Year 2000." *Land Reform, Land Settlement and Cooperatives* no. 1–2 (1985): 13–42.

Le Roy, Étienne. "La sécurité fonciére dans un contexte africain de marchandisation imparfaite de la terre." In *Terre, terroir, territoire, les tensions foncières,* ed. C. Blanc-Pamard and L. Cambrezy. Paris, 1995.

Noronha, Raymond. *Traditional Land Tenures and Land Uses Systems in the Design of Agricultural Projects.* Washington, DC, 1983.

Piermay, Jean-Luc. "Le détournement d'espace." *Politique africaine* 21 (1986): 22–36.

Piermay, Jean-Luc. "'Espace, un enjeu nouveau." In *Espaces disputés en Afrique noire,* ed. Bernard Crousse, Émile Le Bris, and Étienne Le Roy. Paris: Karthala, 1986.

Piermay, Jean-Luc. ed. "All'ombra della legge e della consuetudine: Sistemi fondiari in trasformazione nelle citta dell'Africa nera." *Storia urbana* 63 (1993).

Riddell, James C., and Carol Dickerman, eds. *Country Profiles of Land Tenure: Africa 1986.* Madison: University of Wisconsin-Madison, 1986.

Schlager, Edella, and Elinor Ostrom. "Property Rights Regimes and Natural Resources: A Conceptual Analysis." *Land Economics* 68, no. 3 (1992): 49–62.

Snyder, Francis G. *Capitalism and Legal Change: An African Transformation.* New York: Academic Press, 1981.

ÉTIENNE LE ROY

REFORM

Land reform policies aim to transform the distribution of land and the terms under which people hold land. The history of land reform in Africa reflects the influence of colonial administrations and international donors, the limits of African states, and the resilience and adaptability of indigenous tenure institutions.

Since the 1990s, land reform has taken place in a neoliberal policy context. Structural adjustment has limited the capacity of African states to intervene in rural land affairs, and given the World Bank considerable influence in land policy. Viewing tenure insecurity as an obstacle to the conversion of land to capital and collateral, and a disincentive to investment, reform policies have emphasized land titling and other tenure reform measures as a means to strengthen or create land markets, often with an explicit aim of facilitating foreign investment.

These new policies have shared a critical feature with previous land reforms: Throughout Africa's modern history, underfunded and partially implemented reforms have sowed confusion, created competing sources of authority over land, and aroused unsatisfied popular discontent. As a result, they have tended to disrupt rather than transform indigenous systems of land tenure, which have proven resilient and able to adapt to or bypass new policies. In some cases, land reform has been a vehicle for both African and foreign elites to accumulate land, contradicting its ostensible aims.

LAND REDISTRIBUTION AND RESTITUTION

Large-scale redistribution of land and the restitution of land that was lost under colonialism have been relatively uncommon in Africa. The most significant redistribution program underway in the early twenty-first century is in South Africa. From 1995 to 1999, the state issued grants to enable groups of poor people to purchase land; since 2001, however, the program has been controversially reoriented to focus on black commercial farmers, targeting beneficiaries who can bring skills and capital to redistributed land. The program relies on a market-based approach to identify land for redistribution, but critics have noted that land offered for sale is often of poor quality, and have decried purchases of land from white farmers who had benefited from apartheid. The redistribution program has also incorporated nonstate land reform in the form of farm equity schemes. Under these schemes, farm owners have entered into financial partnerships with groups of workers who are funded through state grants.

South Africa is also the site of the only significant contemporary land restitution program, underway since 1995. When the program stopped accepting claims in December 1998, more than 63,000 claims had been filed. Initially slow and cumbersome, the program has accelerated from 1999 due to administrative changes and a focus on urban claims, which are often resolved with cash payments rather than actual transfers of land.

South Africa's redistribution policies echo prior programs in the settler colonies of Anglophone Africa. Conflicts over colonial appropriation of land underlay the Mau Mau revolt in Kenya in the 1950s. Preceding Kenya's independence at the end of 1962, the British government financed a plan to transfer a million acres of white-owned land to some 25,000 African families, providing an outlet for whites who wanted to sell prior to independence. Likewise, in the negotiations over Zimbabwe's independence, the British government agreed to underwrite half the costs of the program to resettle Africans on land purchased from whites on a willing buyer–willing seller basis.

More recently, the slow pace of redistribution in Zimbabwe has contributed to the government's policies of expropriation and *de facto* support of land invasions, which have paralyzed the commercial farming sector. The 2000 Land Acquisition Act effectively removed the requirement that land redistribution take place through the market, enabling the state to seize land for fast-track resettlement. By April 2003, approximately 600 white owners of the formerly more than 4,000 remained, and more than a quarter of Zimbabwe's territory had been seized.

Socialist regimes in Ethiopia and Mozambique also undertook radical redistribution policies. The Mengistu regime in Ethiopia (1974–1991) based its agrarian policies on Soviet models; it saw Ethiopia's peasant agriculture as backward and attempted to eliminate traditional landowning elites and emerging capitalist farmers. Initially, policies called for redistributing up to twenty-five acres of land to every household; later measures created marketing cooperatives and large-scale, mechanized, and capital-intensive state farms. In Mozambique, after gaining power in 1975, the Liberation Front of Mozambique (FRELIMO) government aimed to reduce smallholder agriculture in favor of socialist-styled production and farms, and state- controlled trading networks, oriented toward export crops. With changes in political regimes and the end of the Cold War, however, both states have abandoned these policies. The post-1991 regime in Ethiopia has sold some state farms, restored some to their former owners, and liberalized agricultural marketing. Likewise, since the mid-1990s the Mozambican government has aimed to dispose of state farms and allow for community registration of landholdings.

LAND TENURE REFORM

Land tenure reform has been the most widespread type of land reform in Africa since the 1980s, as policy-makers have resurrected longstanding critiques of indigenous tenure, seeing it as an obstacle to the conversion of land to capital and collateral, and a disincentive to investment. Although most African countries have had laws allowing some kind of private ownership since the colonial period, this was mostly limited to colonial expatriates and African elites. This situation created a distinction between property-owning citizens, and subjects who held land under indigenous (often misnamed as customary or communal) tenure, loosely administered and regulated by the state, but dependent on local communities and indigenous institutions for day-to-day administration. Individual titling is decidedly exceptional; in the 1990s in Zambia, for example, only 6 percent of land was held as private tenure.

Early tenure reforms focused on the creation of individually held private property on a European model. Throughout the continent, colonial officials and missionaries alike had praised the alleged virtues of private property, which was said to provide security and promote investment in agriculture. Kenya's Swynnerton Plan, initiated in the 1950s but continued after independence, is probably the most widely studied individual titling program in Africa.

A substantial literature on the plan's effects has shown that the new system only added another legal framework, rather than eliminating customary tenure. Titles were seldom updated and transfers generally went unrecorded, leading to considerable discrepancies between legal records and situations on the ground; in some cases, land was reallocated and administered as if it were still under indigenous tenure. Moreover, the expected benefits of agricultural investment did not materialize.

The Kenyan experience and others have led critics to argue that the costs of individual titling frequently outweigh any potential benefits. Critics have also noted that tenure cannot be assumed to be the primary obstacle to agricultural intensification, given the importance of labor shortages, lack of inputs, access to markets, and other constraints, and have pointed to cases where intensification and *de facto* increases in

tenure security under indigenous tenure have taken place despite the absence of formal title.

The Swynnerton Plan and other titling programs have also been criticized for ignoring gender. In much of Africa, women are responsible for farming, but titling programs generally registered land in men's names, increasing women's dependence on male kin. Likewise, under indigenous tenures, women often rely upon seasonal access to resources such as thatching grass and medicinal plants; when land is titled, rights to these resources are typically not acknowledged, and may be eliminated.

In the early 1980s, when the World Bank began requiring African governments to submit to Structural Adjustment Programs as a condition for granting credit, it advocated tenure reform based on individual titling and the creation of markets. By the mid-1990s, however, researchers within the Bank were acknowledging the shortcomings of titling. In an important Bank-sponsored work, Bruce and Migot-Adholla (1993) summarized the literature on communal tenure, concluding that the security offered by indigenous landholding institutions is relatively strong, while a more recent policy statement has acknowledged the limits and adverse effects of past individual titling programs, and the need for greater attention to strengthening policy implementation (Deininger 2003). Recent reforms have focused on working with indigenous tenure, which has appeared able to accommodate competition over land and market-like transactions in many settings, and providing non-mandatory registration procedures.

Since the early 1990s, new land tenure laws have come into force in Tanzania, Uganda, Namibia, Malawi, Eritrea, Mozambique, Zambia, and Côte d'Ivoire, among others. These laws generally aim to facilitate registration of land under indigenous tenure and create forms of property that can allow for outside investment. In West African contexts of intra-rural migration and smallholder cash cropping, they have also aimed to reduce conflict over land.

The practical effects of these new laws largely remain unstudied, but in an important work, Zambia's controversial 1995 land tenure law has been examined in relation to its goal of increasing tenure security (Brown 2005). The law has made it easier for outside investors and Zambians to acquire private title to customary land if the proposed use is deemed to be of community or national interest, thereby taking land out of customary tenure permanently. In practice, the law appears to be exacerbating economic inequality. Titling has concentrated around cities and in areas with high agricultural and/or tourism potential. Smallholders have seldom applied for titles because of a lack of publicity and the high costs of registration and surveying. Nearly all title recipients have been Zambian elites and foreigners. Foreign investors have also used the registration process to speculate in land, making exorbitant profits from the difference between the market value of titled land and the low cost of acquiring it. Moreover, once land has been titled, existing occupiers have been legally reclassified as squatters and subjected to evictions. Ironically, a law ostensibly designed to create more secure forms of land tenure is leading to unprecedented forms of dispossession.

The new wave of land laws has also been criticized for its reliance on indigenous institutions. South Africa's 2004 Communal Land Tenure Act currently faces constitutional challenges, in part because it would transfer land ownership in the former African homelands to the same unelected Tribal Authorities who administered land under the apartheid government. Similarly, in an important critique, African feminist lawyers have argued that the turn to customary tenure will not promote justice for women with regard to land access, given men's domination of customary institutions.

See also **Agriculture; Cold War; Labor; World Bank.**

BIBLIOGRAPHY

Abate, Teferi. "Government Intervention and Socioeconomic Change in a Northeast Ethiopian Community: An Anthropological Study." Ph.D. diss. Boston University, 2000.

Bassett, Thomas, and Donald Crummey. *Land in African Agrarian Systems.* Madison: University of Wisconsin Press, 1993.

Brown, Taylor. "Contestation, Confusion and Corruption: Market-based Land Reform in Zambia." In *Competing Jurisdictions: Settling Land Claims in Africa,* ed. Sandra Evers, Marja Spierenburg, and Harry Wels. Leiden, The Netherlands: Brill, 2005.

Bruce, John, and Shem Migot-Adholla, eds. *Searching for Land Tenure Security in Africa.* Dubuque, IA: Kendall/Hunt, 1994.

Davison, Jean. *Agriculture, Women and Land: The African Experience.* Boulder, CO: Westview Press, 1988.

Deininger, Klaus. *Land Policies for Growth and Poverty Reduction: A World Bank Policy Research Report.* Oxford: Oxford University Press; and Washington, DC: The International Bank for Reconstruction and Development, 2003.

Fitzpatrick, Daniel. "'Best Practice' Options for the Legal Recognition of Customary Tenure." *Development and Change* 36, no. 3 (2005): 449–475.

Goebel, Allison. "Is Zimbabwe the Future of South Africa? The Implications for Land Reform in Southern Africa." *Journal of Contemporary African Studies* 23, no. 3 (2005): 345–370.

Harbeson, John W. "Land Reforms and Politics in Kenya, 1954–70." *Journal of Modern African Studies* 9, no. 2 (1971): 231–251

Mamdani, Mahmood. *Citizen and Subject: Contemporary Africa and the Legacy of Late Colonialism.* Princeton, NJ: Princeton University Press, 1996.

Manji, Ambreena. "Land Reform in the Shadow of the State: The Implementation of New Land Laws in Sub-Saharan Africa." *Third World Quarterly* 22, no. 3 (2001): 327–342.

McAuslan, Patrick. *Bringing the Law Back In: Essays in Land, Law and Development.* Aldershot, U.K.: Ashgate, 2003.

Moore, Donald. *Suffering for Territory: Race, Place, and Power in Zimbabwe.* Durham, NC: Duke University Press, 2005.

Palmer, Robin. "Land Reform in Zimbabwe, 1980–1990." *African Affairs* 89, no. 355 (1990): 163–181.

Palmer, Robin. *Contested Lands in Southern and Eastern Africa: A Literature Survey.* Herndon, VA: Stylus Pub., 1997.

Pitcher, M. Anne. "Disruption without Transformation: Agrarian Relations and Livelihoods in Nampula Province, Mozambique, 1975–1995." *Journal of Southern African Studies* 24, no. 1 (1998): 115–140.

Platteau, Jean-Philippe. "The Evolutionary Theory of Land Rights as Applied to Sub-Saharan Africa: A Critical Assessment." *Development and Change* 27 (1996): 29–86.

Reyna Stephen P., and Richard E. Downs. *Land and Society in Contemporary Africa.* Hanover, NH: University Press of New England, 1988.

Shipton, Parker. "Land and Culture in Tropical Africa: Soils, Symbols, and the Metaphysics of the Mundane." *Annual Review of Anthropology* 23 (1994): 347–377.

Whitehead, Ann, and Dzodzi Tsikata. "Policy Discourses on Women's Land Rights in Sub-Saharan Africa: The Implications of the Return to the Customary." *Journal of Agrarian Change* 3, nos. 1 and 2 (2003): 67–112.

Alden Wily, Liz. *Governance and Land Relations: A Review of Decentralisation of Land Administration and*

Management in Africa. London: International Institute for Environment and Development, 2003.

DERICK FAY

LANGUAGE

This entry includes the following articles:
CHOICE IN WRITING
GOVERNMENT AND MISSION POLICIES
SLANG
SOCIOLINGUISTICS

CHOICE IN WRITING

One consequence of the history of literature in Africa has been the problematization of the concept of African literature. The reason is that, unlike other literatures around the world whose qualifiers indicate the languages (and therefore cultures) they express, the word African in African literatures is misleading, for what it commonly designates is literature written in English, French, or Portuguese. The European powers that colonized virtually the entire continent effectively established their own languages as the preferred ones for official and most other purposes, literary among them, in the respective territories they controlled. Scholars have lately adopted the practice of including in their discussion of African literature a section devoted to literatures in African languages, but the attention accorded them always seems grudging.

Although African cultures developed and maintained texts of various descriptions that served functions similar to those of the written texts of literate cultures, many African versions were unwritten but preserved in memory, maintained by regular repetition, and passed orally from one generation to the next. Some African languages, most notably Swahili and Hausa, were written in Arabic script, and Ethiopic languages were written in the ancient Ge'ez script. There are extensive literatures with long histories in these and some additional African languages, but literacy came initially in most African languages at the behest of missionaries who faced the task of spreading the gospel among people who had no knowledge of European languages and therefore had to be reached in their indigenous languages. For that purpose they needed African

helpers, for whose preparation they established mission schools. The products of these schools were also expected to help in producing literature in applicable local languages suitable for proselytization and instruction.

The French policy of assimilation aimed from the start to produce educated Africans (*évolues*) fluent only in French, but in those areas under British influence the missionaries initially favored indigenous languages. Here too, though, the onset of colonialism imposed a change. The colonial administration's need for messengers, clerks, civil servants, court interpreters, and the like took precedence over the missionaries' need for missionizing agents; consequently, the missionaries were easily induced by the colonial administration, with the aid of subventions, to change their linguistic preferences. School instruction began, then, in African languages but quickly switched to European languages with the intention of getting pupils to begin using the colonial languages as quickly as possible. The product of the colonial education system was thus fluent in the language of the colonizer and practically incapable of functioning effectively in his or her native tongue.

The end of the colonial period has not brought an end to the preference for European languages on the continent or their attraction for Africans. What was true during colonialism remains true in the postcolonial era: the surest guarantee for success in the new economy is a good command of the language of the colonizers, no matter if one's career is in politics or literature. The explanations are multiple. One has to do with the multiethnic composition of the new African states, whose different ethnic groups speak languages that are mutually unintelligible and whose citizens can communicate among themselves only in the languages of their colonizers. As the South African writer Ezekiel (Es'kia) Mphahlele once put it, even after the end of colonialism on the continent, European languages still serve as a unifying force. In eastern Africa, Swahili has served this unifying function. Not surprisingly, champions of national cohesion even argue for the permanent substitution of European languages for African ones, arguing that the latter perpetuate what they regard as the evil of tribalism.

With regard to literature, as a product of the assimilated elite its language was always a settled matter, because the elite formation process privileged European languages and inculcated some disdain for African languages in the minds of the elite, or at least a conviction that they are defective instruments for any serious purposes.

The choice of language is also an indicator of the audience African writers have chosen to address. For writers in European languages that audience is decidedly outside the confines of the continent. Chinua Achebe, for example, believes that the serious writer must be engaged in international exchange (1975). Such a writer has something to say to the world and must say it in European or so-called world languages. He describes writers who opt for African languages as nondescript. That view reflects the conviction of many writers who, similar to him, assume an obligation to interpret and justify Africa to the world, to prove that Africa had a past and a culture of dignity and human complexity. An analogy that has considerable attraction for exponents of the view is that of Caliban and his appropriation of his master Prospero's language. Although Caliban (Achebe) does not revel in the language Prospero (the colonizers) bequeathed him, seeing it rather as an emblem of his colonized state, the African writer proudly celebrates this colonial bequest, sometimes asserting his or her right to it when the native speakers of the language in question suggest that the African is a linguistic poacher or interloper. In one instance, an offended African suggested that the name of the language English be changed because it had become a universal language belonging to all.

The antagonism that developed between rulers and writers soon after independence spawned a tradition of dissidence according to which militant or oppositional writers found it necessary to appeal to world opinion against the regimes that victimized them. This was true of South Africa during the period of apartheid. Another factor in the South African situation, though, was the writers' perception that the white authorities were encouraging Africans to stick to their mother tongues as a means of thwarting any tendencies toward mass political activism, and their determination, therefore, to frustrate the authorities' wishes.

The writers' need to reach enough readers to make a decent living from their writing has also been a major factor in their choice of language. As Ousmane Sembène once pointed out, for the African writer, writing is a job as any other. Using himself as an example he pointed out that to be able to support himself with his job he had to write in French rather than his native Wolof. If he wrote in the latter language, he said, he would reach only a few readers, and added pointedly that, in any case, 85 percent of the population of Senegal was illiterate, and those who could read and write did not read African authors. It was for this reason that Sembène turned to filmmaking and made films in Wolof. The same argument could be generalized for the entire continent, as Achebe has in fact done. After making the same point that educated Africans did not read African writers, he added that African intellectuals read (if they read anything at all) history, economics, mathematics, and the like, hardly ever fiction or poetry, not having developed the habit of reading such things for pleasure as their European counterparts had.

Furthermore, by writing in European languages the writers guarantee for themselves international attention that often translates to invitations to deliver speeches at international forums or to take up temporary or even permanent professorships at foreign universities. That may also bring such coveted honors as the Nobel Prize, which the Nigerian Wole Soyinka became the first African writer to win in 1986. Until the Egyptian Naguib Mahfouz won the Nobel Prize in 1988 for his Arabic-language works, African writers were convinced that only European-language writing out of Africa could win a major prize administered in Europe or any of the Western countries (or the Asian ones for that matter), because that had been the fact up until that point.

One would be wrong to imagine that the sole beneficiaries of the African writers' choice of language are the writers themselves. The discipline of African literary studies would suffer a major loss of personnel were these writers to convert to African languages. African studies in general is unique among area studies in that many scholars involved in it do not regard a working command of any African language necessary. One would think that scholars of African literatures would be an exception, but they are not. Non-African scholars have expressed the view that the choice of European languages by African writers is a boon to foreign readers and scholars who would otherwise be excluded from their writing unless they learned African languages. It is also true that France, for example, actively encourages the use of French in all the countries of the French community, because France measures its international stature in terms of how many people around the world use French, which is the central pillar of *la francophonie*.

In his Nobel acceptance speech, Soyinka justified his adherence to a European language by arguing that if the writers turned their sights inward (by using African languages) they "could not so easily understand the enemy on our doorstep, nor understand how to obtain the means to disarm it. ... When we borrow an alien language to sculpt and paint in," he continued, "we ... begin by coopting the entire properties of that language as correspondencies to represent our matrix of thought and expression" (quoted in Henry Louis Gates, Jr., "On the Rhetoric of Racism in the Profession," *ALA Bulletin*, 21).

Yet their preference for European languages has forced the writers to seek some other means of placing an African stamp on their works. One such device is the copious use Achebe makes of proverbs, which were so profuse in his earlier works such as *Things Fall Apart* (1958) and *No Longer at Ease* (1960) as to call attention to themselves. In these novels he also resorted to the practice of cushioning, or of using African words together with their English translations, as in "*agadi-nwayi*, or old woman or of attaching usually brief (but sometimes extended) explanatory diversions to English terms when he wished to indicate that they signified things different from what they normally would. Others' stratagems produced more pleasing results, the boldest and most interesting example of which is the experiment Gabriel Okara carried out in *The Voice* (1964). In that novel he combined the syntax of his Ijo language with English vocabulary.

Although the argument for retaining European languages for African literatures has not weakened significantly, some of its ardent proponents now make tentative moves in the direction of rehabilitating African languages. Thus, the African Literature Association has in recent years paid more attention to work in African languages and has even adopted a resolution encouraging African-language panels at its annual meetings. Few members believe in the practicality of its implementation, though. Other developments, perhaps more important, involve writers' gradual conversion to the desirability of returning to African languages. Accordingly, Chinua Achebe has lately revised his earlier opinion, saying that "the fatalistic logic of the unassailable position of English in our literature" now leaves him colder than it earlier did (*Morning Yet on Creation Day: Essays*, xiv). More dramatic is Ngũgĩ's turn away from English. Having wondered in amazement why Africans were so assertive in their claim to other peoples' languages and so indifferent to the fate of their own, he announced in 1986 that he was giving up English in preference for Gikuyu and Swahili. In 2000 Ngũgĩ, Nawal el Saadawy, Mbulelo Mzamane, and Ama Ata Aidoo organized a conference in Asmara, Eritrea, to celebrate writing in African languages. Nonetheless, the dominance European languages enjoy on the African scene seems assured for the foreseeable future.

See also **Achebe, Chinua; Apartheid; Languages; Literature; Mahfouz, Naguib; Media: Book Publishing; Ngũgĩ wa Thiong'o; Popular Culture; Sembène, Ousmane; Soyinka, Wole.**

BIBLIOGRAPHY

Achebe, Chinua. *Morning Yet on Creation Day: Essays.* London: Heinemann Educational: 1975.

Barber, Karin, and Graham Furniss. "African Language Writing." *Research in African Literatures* 37, no. 3 (2006): 1–14.

Dathorne, O. R. "Amos Tutuola: The Nightmare of the Tribe." In *Introduction to Nigerian Literature*, ed. Bruce King. New York: Africana Publishing Corporation, 1971.

Gates, Henry Louis, Jr. "On the Rhetoric of Racism in the Profession." *ALA Bulletin* (African Literature Association) 15, no. 1 (1989): 11–21.

Mitterand, François. *Réflexions sur la politique extérieure de la France: Introduction à vingt-cinq discours, 1981–1985.* Paris: Fayard, 1986.

Mphahlele, Ezekiel. "Polemics: The Dead End of African Literature." *Transition* 3, no. 11 (1963): 7–9.

Ngũgĩ wa Thiong'o. *Decolonising the Mind: The Politics of Language in African Literature.* London: Heinemann, 1986.

Ngũgĩ wa Thiong'o. "Europhonism, Universities, and the Magic Fountain: The Future of African Literature and Scholarship," *Research in African Literature* 31, no. 1 (2000): 1–11.

OYEKAN OWOMOYELA

GOVERNMENT AND MISSION POLICIES

Language policy in Africa has always been more than a linguistic matter. Colonial administrators strictly limited Africans' opportunities to learn European languages. They thereby channeled African political thought into a parochial, contained field, limiting Africans' ability to speak as citizens of the metropole. Postcolonial African governments likewise sought to channel political discourse through language policy. They used language as a vehicle for nation-building, manufacturing large-scale imagined communities by inviting citizens to read from the same page. But official language policies were always challenged from below, as Africans took hold over languages both old and new. Where colonial governments sought to freeze Africans in place, African subjects moved into their rulers' world, learning English and French so as to participate in metropolitan civic discourse. And where postcolonial governments sought to promote the purity and integrity of national languages, African speakers borrowed creatively from foreign tongues. Language policy in colonial and postcolonial Africa is and has been a field of argument.

Africa's language history has been deeply shaped by its environmental history. Eastern Africa's broken terrain, its shallow rivers, and its disease-bearing insects have for centuries inhibited long-distance commerce. Political leaders found it hard to command obedience, and human communities tended to be small in scale. Eastern Africa is in consequence a remarkably polyglot place: The country of Tanzania, with a population of 36 million people, is reckoned to be home to more than 120 languages. By contrast, western Africa's comparatively even topography and its slow-moving rivers made political consolidation relatively easier to accomplish. From the tenth century CE onward, a series of empires—Ghana, Mali, and Songhay in the west, and Kanem-Borno and the Hausa states to the east—facilitated the growth of interregional trade and promoted the development of larger-scale languages. Hausa, Mandinka, and Soninke, used widely in earlier times as vehicles of commerce, are spoken in several different western African states in the early twenty-first century. Particularly in western and northern Africa, Islamic influence has from the thirteenth century onward promoted the use of Arabic as a platform for large-scale intellectual and economic exchange.

The diversity of African languages was reinforced in the nineteenth century when Christian missionaries began systematically to translate the scriptures into African vernaculars. Missionaries were very often the first to create orthographies and grammar books for African languages, most of which (except for Amharic in Ethiopia and Bamum in present-day Cameroon) had not previously been written. Missionary linguists were aided in their work by texts such as A. C. Madan's 1905 *An Outline Dictionary Intended as an Aid in the Study of the Languages of the Bantu and Other Uncivilized Races*, which listed English terms on an overleaf and left the opposite page blank for amateur linguists to fill in. Madan gave missionaries the words they needed to preach the gospel, words such as belief, sin, king, and law. Where such words were not immediately available, missionaries conjured them up. In central Kenya, for example, Gikuyu people had not in the nineteenth century recognized political authorities outside their own homesteads. Presbyterian and Anglican linguists had therefore to adopt a novel Gikuyu word, *muthamaki*, as king. The word meant spokesman in Gikuyu thought, not an absolute authority. By this and other acts of linguistic appropriation, missionaries created the vocabularic and theological grounds for comparative conversations about religion.

With vocabularies and grammar books in hand, missionaries set out to publish. The first texts published in African vernaculars were almost always excerpts from the New Testament. *The Pilgrim's Progress*, an emblematic work of English nonconformism, was published in more than eighty African languages (Hofmeyr 2004). Missionary presses also churned out dozens of collections of proverbs, folktales, and historical texts in the late nineteenth and early twentieth centuries, many of them authored by Christian converts. These texts played a pivotal role in the consolidation of Yoruba, Shona, and other political communities. Through the historical and ethnographic work they did in mission stations, early African intellectuals came to see themselves as sharers of wider ethnic or national identities.

COLONIAL LANGUAGE POLICY

Colonial policymakers entered into a field where missionaries and African converts were already standardizing vernaculars, studying cultures, and imagining ethnicities. European rulers sought to herd Africans into predictable, containable spheres of discourse. In language policy as in governmental structure, they emphasized the distance between rulers and ruled, limiting Africans' opportunities to participate as citizens in metropolitan governance. African thinkers most often practiced a strategy of equivalence. They sought to lay hold of their rulers' language, so better to exercise agency in the colonial world.

In British Africa, the illiberal thrust of colonial-era language policy belies the humanist, improving ethos of an earlier time. The earliest educational institutions in Sierra Leone and in the Cape Colony were conceived as missions to people who could, by virtue of education, be made into equals. The recaptives whom the Royal Navy settled in Freetown were drawn from all over West Africa, though the majority were speakers of Yoruba. Recaptives were taught English language and took on European names, dress, and habits. In 1827 the Church Missionary Society established Fourah Bay College east of Freetown. In 1876 the college affiliated with Durham University, and conferred British degrees on graduates. Recaptives occupied high positions in English church and government: Samuel Ajayi Crowther was bishop of the Church of England and head of the Anglican mission to Niger peoples. African elites in the Cape Colony likewise enjoyed access to English-language higher education. The Lovedale Institution, opened in 1841 on the eastern Cape, educated more than 2,000 Africans over the first fifty years of its existence.

But by the later nineteenth century, British ideas about Africans' mental and moral capacity were changing. With the rise of scientific racism, and with the evidence of the India Mutiny of 1857 before them, British thinkers began to doubt whether Africans could be made into obedient, civilized, Christian citizens. By the time of the scramble for Africa in the last decades of the nineteenth century, a new ideology drove Britain's enthusiasm for empire. If the African empire of the earlier nineteenth century had been a commercial and evangelical mission to potential equals, it had now become a mandate to develop and protect an inferior race. The British policy of Indirect Rule preserved traditional political and cultural institutions, and blocked Africans from participating in the institutions of modern, liberal government. In western Africa, Africans were in the later nineteenth century effectively barred from positions of control within the Anglican church. When Bishop Crowther died in 1893, he was replaced by an English cleric. Crowther was the only African to be appointed diocesan bishop in West Africa until the 1950s.

Indirect Rule shaped British language and education policy by locking Africans' intellectual and political life into the pattern of tribe. In politics, colonial officials reinforced the supposedly traditional prerogatives of African rulers in order to facilitate the work of the native authority. In law, administrators and anthropologists identified or created customary legal codes that native tribunals could use. And in language, colonial linguists standardized vernacular grammar and orthography for use in government business. In 1927, the London-based International Institute of African Languages and Cultures (IIALC) published its *Practical Orthography*, which laid out a phonetic alphabet for writers of African vernaculars to use. Early in 1927, the government of the Gold Coast mandated that all publications in Twi, Fante, Ga, and Ewe should use the new orthography. In 1929, the colonies of Nigeria and Sierra Leone accepted the IIALC's recommendations for several major languages, including Hausa, Yoruba, and Ibo. By 1933, the IIALC's phonetic alphabet was being used to write many of Africa's major languages, including Acholi, Dinka, Luganda, Mende, Kpelle, Shona, Sosso, Malinke, Zande, Xhosa, and Zulu.

By this sweeping act of language standardization, European linguists sought to create a continent-wide empire of letters. The phonetic alphabet imposed an order on disparate African languages, taking its place alongside customary law, pass laws, chiefly authority, and tribal reserves as means by which European officials froze Africans into the manageable containers of Indirect Rule.

But African thinkers would not stay in place. In intellectual life and in politics, they challenged colonial officials' efforts to wall them into a linguistic ghetto. In 1940s Buganda, activists of the populist Bataka Party argued that even the youngest students should be taught to read and speak English. "Make an effort to learn [the English] language which will help you greatly," advised the 1945 Luganda language pamphlet *Buganda Nyafe* (Buganda our Mother). African entrepreneurs in Kenya similarly sought to take hold of the English language. African-run schools mushroomed during the 1930s, teaching English language to first year students. Independent school leader Johanna Kunyiha explained their pedagogical strategy in a 1936 letter to the governor, saying "I am one of the subjects of the [British] Noble King, and I am bound to teach his tongue in our schools" (Peterson 2004, 147–148). Their command over the English language made Africans into citizens of the British empire, entitled to recognition and rights. When in the early 1950s the Beecher Report set strict limits on the number of African children who could learn English in the Kenyan government's schools, Gikuyu men and women took oaths promising never to send their children to a Beecher school.

Political entrepreneurs in southern Africa likewise used the English language to defend their rights. Writing to the Lovedale mission newspaper in 1882, the Xhosa poet Citashe reminded his readers that "your cattle are gone, my countrymen! Go and rescue them! Leave the breechloader alone and turn to the pen. Take pen and ink, for that is your shield." (Mzamane 184). Anglophone African thinkers were using English to claim a place in their rulers' world. They worked to position themselves as confreres of English people, as inhabitants of their rulers' linguistic and political world.

Language policy in French West Africa was likewise an arena where colonial officials' strategy of governance conflicted with Africans' political ambitions. In four trading towns along the Senegalese coast of western Africa, African residents had since the eighteenth century enjoyed rights as French citizens. In the late nineteenth century, however, French armies conquered much of western Africa, and the inhabitants were classed not as citizens but as subjects. French government held out to them the possibility of assimilation, by which Africans could, by virtue of their education, earn the rights of French citizenship.

But the hurdles were so high that by the 1930s only 500 Africans had successfully assimilated. The vast majority of the inhabitants of France's West African empire, some fifteen million people, were governed under a punitive legal system designed to elicit obedience, not to protect rights. In language policy as in political life, colonial government sought

to channel Africans' political discourse. Rural schools taught even the youngest pupils to speak and read the French language, while also emphasizing agricultural skills appropriate for an economy where Africans' opportunities were sharply limited. French West African intellectuals felt themselves straddling an African inheritance and a cosmopolitan French culture that would not grant them admittance. "I am not a distinct country…facing a distinct Occident, and appreciating with a cool head what I must take from it and what I must leave with it by way of counterbalance," wrote Senegalese intellectual Cheikh Hamidou Kane (b. 1928) in his 1961 novel *L'aventure ambiguë*. "I have become two."

In French Africa, as in Anglophone Africa, postwar African entrepreneurs worked to carve out a larger space for themselves in their rulers' world. In 1946, the Lamine Guèye law abolished the distinction between citizen and subject. African labor unions proved particularly adept at putting the promises of French citizenship to their own purposes. In a massive railway strike in late 1947 and early 1948, workers demanded that they, as the French railwaymen did, should earn family benefits and enjoy housing provided by their employers. Union leader Ibrahima Sarr called in October 1947 for the "abolition of antiquated colonial methods condemned even by the new and true France which wishes that all its children, at whatever latitude they may live, be equal in duties and rights" (Cooper, 219–220). Sarr and other unionists were not implacably opposed to all things French. Theirs was not a politics of nativism. They were molding postwar French rhetoric into a language of claim-making. Unionists' strategy reached its fruition in November 1952 with the passage of a workers' code. It gave Africans workers a forty hour work week, the right to organize, the right to strike, and other benefits.

In the Belgian Congo, as in French Africa, colonial government sought to constrain Africans' political ambitions by limiting their education. Catholic and Protestant missionaries conducted primary education in vernacular languages, and standardized the major lingua franca—Chiluba, Lingala, Kikongo, and Kingwana—as vehicles of teaching. Belgian administrators were encouraged to study Kingwana as a language of command: official grammar books were always cast in the imperative. Africans' opportunities for education beyond the elementary level were sharply curtailed. Government grants for education were restricted to lowest levels only; there was no higher education for Africans, apart from those training as Catholic priests. Not until 1952 was a black man from the Congo authorized to attend a Belgian university. Until the late 1950s, there was no African representation on the colonial legislative council, nor was there an independently owned African newspaper until 1957.

The Congo's dismal history of education reflects a larger reality in colonial Africa. The ruling fictions of government differed: British officials sought to convince Africans of the authority of tradition, and emphasized vernacular language teaching; French authorities promised that Africans could, by virtue of their educational attainment, become French citizens; Belgian planners limited education funding, and locked Africans into a parochial political world. All colonial powers thought that Africans who spoke European languages were potentially subversive of colonial authority. They erected pedagogical and political barriers that limited Africans' linguistic attainments, and channeled students' ambitions toward a carefully delimited field. African thinkers, for their part, sought to lay hold of colonial languages, so better to exercise agency in a world they shared with their rulers. Language policy in colonial Africa stood at the crossroads of African thinkers' and European officials' contending projects.

LANGUAGE POLICIES AFTER INDEPENDENCE

Official and National Languages. Postcolonial African leaders needed to transform the polyglot assortment of unions, cooperatives, peasants' organizations, and political parties that had opposed colonial government into a patriotic citizenry. Language policy was one means by which governments sought to create a cohesive national culture.

Ghana was the first of Britain's colonies to achieve independence. But its people did not naturally think themselves citizens of a national polity. Kwame Nkrumah's Congress People's Party shared the political stage with a variety of regional organizations, including the Asante-based National Liberation Movement, the Northern People's Party, and the Togoland Congress. After independence in 1957, President Nkrumah's government inaugurated a cultural program meant to sap regional loyalties of their

power. The cultural exhibitions laid on to celebrate independence included Asafo drumming, the installation of an Akan chief, and a pageant display featuring a Ghana market scene, the birth of highlife, Agbekor dance, and the days of the old District Commissioner. The National Museum established after independence had as its first exhibit a hall full of Asante stools, at the head of which was a portrait of Nkrumah. Nkrumah's cultural officers were co-opting the symbols of Asante sovereignty and mixing up elements from Ghana's diverse cultures into a syncretic whole.

Ghana's language policy reflected this effort to create grounds for national unification. There were more than seventy languages in use in Nkrumah's Ghana. But English was chosen to be the official language of governance. In language as in culture, Nkrumah was consolidating citizens' loyalties around a nation. The radio and television stations created after independence broadcast largely in English. "Radio," explained Nkrumah in 1959, "is a great unifying agency in our country. Through it, people all over Ghana can appreciate that we are all of the same nation with the same ideas and aspirations" (Hess, 69). The Avoidance of Discrimination Act of 1957 forbade the existence of parties on a regional, tribal, or religious basis. Nkrumah was working to consolidate citizens' political loyalties and their languages.

Ghana's political strategy was duplicated in the great number of African states that adopted European languages after independence. In the Gambia, Ghana, Kenya, Liberia, Malawi, Mauritius, Nigeria, Seychelles, Swaziland, Zambia, and Zimbabwe, English was chosen to be the official language, whereas in Bénin, Burkina Faso, the Central African Republic, Chad, Republic of the Congo, Côte d'Ivoire, Gabon, Guinea, Mali, Niger, Senegal, Togo, and Democratic Republic of the Congo, the official language was French. Angola, Cape Verde, Guinea-Bissau, Mozambique, and São Tomé e Príncipe retained Portuguese as their official language, and Equatorial Guinea chose Spanish. Mauritania, a predominantly Muslim country, chose Arabic as its official language, as did Sudan.

Although the majority of postcolonial states identified European languages as the official medium of government discourse, a few polities, gifted with a relatively homogenous language situation, adopted

African languages. Lesotho chose English and Sesotho as its official languages, whereas Botswana adopted Setswana and English. Similarly, Burundi, Rwanda, and Madagascar adopted Kirundi, Kinyarwanda, and Malagasy alongside French.

In socialist Tanzania, as in Nkrumah's Ghana, leaders sought to sap parochial loyalties by promoting a unitary national culture. But in Tanzania, unlike Ghana, the vehicle of national discourse was an African language, Swahili. During eastern Africa's nineteenth century trading boom, Swahili was used as a lingua franca along the caravan routes that crisscrossed the region. African nationalists seized on Swahili as a vehicle of political unification. Tanzanian President Julius Nyerere mandated that Swahili would be used as the medium of instruction at the primary school level, and as the sole mode of political discourse. At his Republic Day speech in 1962, Nyerere argued that "a country which lacks its own culture is no more than a collection of people without the spirit which makes them a nation . . . I want it to seek out the best of the traditions and customs of all the tribes and make them part of our national culture" (Askew, 171). Similar to his West African contemporary Nkrumah, Nyerere sought to knit together Tanzania's diverse cultures and languages into an integral whole. This culture-building exercise was necessarily a selective process: government-sponsored dance troupes performing a traditional Swahili repertoire still performed on stage, in a manner very different than their nineteenth century forebears. Nyerere and his successors were creating something new, asking citizens to subordinate their particular cultures, and languages, to a national archetype.

But in Tanzania as in other venues, the high politics of nation building was always contested by citizens who would not agree to confirm their cultures, or their tongues, to policymakers' archetypes. In urban Nairobi and in Dar es Salaam, youth have for the past several decades been speaking *Sheng*, a hybrid language mixing English, Gikuyu, Luo, and other words with Swahili grammar. Speakers of Sheng borrow shamelessly from English: to chill out, for example, has become the verb *ku-chili*; money has become *do*, headmaster has become *hedii*, and to eat has become *ku-hog*. By these phrases Sheng speakers shade English vocabulary into the auditory and grammatical structure of Swahili, making their language both cosmopolitan and cool.

Linguists in Tanzania and elsewhere regard Sheng as an aspect of the young people's slavish imitation of the West. But more than a cultural corruption, Sheng illuminates official language policy for what it is: an effort to impose an order on human communities that are, in reality, too heterodox to be conformed to a predetermined mold.

Language Policy in Education. At independence, Francophone and Lusophone countries inherited school systems in which French and Portuguese were used throughout a child's tenure in education. In most Francophone countries the early twenty-first century, children learn French from their first years in school. Some Francophone countries, such as Senegal and Bénin, have attempted to introduce vernacular language instruction, but have had limited success. In Mozambique, Liberation Front of Mozambique (FRELIMO) continues to mandate the use of Portuguese in schools and in mass literacy campaigns.

In Anglophone countries, schools generally utilize vernacular languages for the first several years of education, then switch to English sometime between the third and the sixth years. There are exceptions to this rule: In the Gambia, English is the medium of instruction for all education, as major languages such as Mandinka lack a published literature. In Sierra Leone, English was adopted at independence for use in all schools. Recent projects to introduce Mende, Temne, and Limba have had some success.

Some countries do not fall neatly into either the Anglophone or Francophone pattern. Cameroon, a federation of two former colonies, initially carried forward the language policies of its colonial predecessors: in the Anglophone west, primary education was given in primary languages, whereas in the Francophone east, French was utilized. After the establishment of the United Republic of Cameroon in 1972, all education was transferred to central government control, and an ambitious policy aimed at achieving French-English bilingualism through education was drawn up. After 1978, education policy was modified to allow time for instruction in a Cameroonian language. Parents, who consider French and English to be of more value to their children, have not enthusiastically endorsed this policy.

South Africa's history of education illuminates the problems of postcolonial language policymaking more generally. The Bantu Education Act was promulgated by South Africa's National Party regime in 1953. Fueled by a Herderian view of folk identity, the Act stipulated that black students would be educated in their vernacular languages from the first through the eighth grades. The Act also gave English and Afrikaans an equal basis as media of learning in black schools. South Africa's black students saw their educational opportunities foreclosed. In 1976, schoolchildren's indignation fueled the Soweto Uprising, a series of protests that culminated in the shooting of several children by police. In apartheid South Africa as in Anglophone Africa more generally, African students refused to be walled into a linguistic ghetto. They looked for leverage and opportunity through their education, and resisted governmental efforts to curtail their access to English.

The Bantu Education Department was abolished with the fall of apartheid in 1994. South Africa recognizes eleven languages in the early twenty-first century: English, Afrikaans, Zulu, Sotho, Xhosa, Pedi, Venda, Tswana, Tsonga, Ndebele, and Swati. By law, official documents must be made available in the vernacular languages that most South Africans speak. In most schools, African languages are offered as media of learning from the first through the fourth grades. English becomes the instructional medium in the fifth grade, and is utilized up to the university level. Children of wealthy parents often attend English-language schools. Opportunities for African students to learn other African languages in a formal manner are minimal.

Contemporary thinkers such as the Kenyan novelist Ngũgĩ wa Thiong'o have celebrated vernaculars as repositories of authentic African culture, and as bastions of cultural integrity in a world increasingly dominated by the languages of the old colonial powers. African leaders in Tanzania and South Africa have sought to promote vernacular languages as vehicles for nation building. But vernacular languages have not always been seen as a means of advancing Africans' agency. For colonial governments, vernacular language education was a means of limiting Africans' political opportunities. For students in colonial schools, vernacular-language education was experienced as a kind of intellectual enclosure. African pupils actively appropriated their rulers' languages, utilizing French and English as vehicles of claim-making. Language policy stands at the center of Africa's long-running arguments over nationalism and cosmopolitanism.

See also **Christianity: Missionary Enterprise; Colonial Policies and Practices; Crowther, Samuel Ajayi; Dar es Salaam; Education, School; Government; Independence and Freedom, Early African Writers; Islam; Languages; Literacy; Nairobi; Ngũgĩ wa Thiong'o; Nkrumah, Francis Nwia Kofi; Nyerere, Julius Kambarage; Socialism and Postsocialisms.**

BIBLIOGRAPHY

Askew, Kelly. *Performing the Nation: Swahili Music and Cultural Politics in Tanzania.* Chicago: University of Chicago Press, 2002.

Bamgbose, Ayo. *Language and the Nation: The Language Question in Sub-Saharan Africa.* Edinburgh: Edinburgh University Press for the International African Institute, 1991.

Bickford-Smith, Vivian. "The Betrayal of Creole Elites." In *Black Experience and the Empire,* ed. Philip Morgan and Christopher Brown. Oxford: Oxford University Press, 2004.

"Buganda Nyafe." In Public Records Office FCO 24/1393.

Cooper, Frederick. *Decolonization and African Society: The Labor Question in French and British Africa.* Cambridge, U.K.: Cambridge University Press, 1996.

Fabian, Johannes. *Language and Colonial Power.* Cambridge, U.K.: Cambridge University Press, 1986.

Fardon, Richard, and Graham Furniss, eds. *African Languages, Development and the State.* London: Routledge, 1994.

Hess, Janet. "Exhibiting Ghana: Display, Documentary, and 'National Art' in the Nkrumah Era." *African Studies Review* 44, no. 1 (2001): 59–77.

Hofmeyr, Isabel. *The Portable Bunyan: A Transnational History of* The Pilgrim's Progress. Princeton, NJ: Princeton University Press, 2004.

International Institute of African Languages and Cultures. *Practical Orthography for African Languages.* London: Oxford University Press, 1930.

Kallaway, Peter, ed. *Apartheid and Education: The Education of Black South Africans.* Johannesburg, South Africa: Ravan Press, 1984.

Kane, Cheikh Hamidou. *Ambiguous Adventure.* New York: Walker, 1963.

Landau, Paul. "Religion and Christian Conversion in Africa: A New Model." *Journal of Religious History* 23, no. 1 (1999): 8–30.

Madan, Arthur Cornwallis. *An Outline Dictionary Intended as an Aid in the Study of the Languages of the Bantu and Other Uncivilized Races.* London: Henry Frowde, 1905.

Moga, Jacko. *Sheng Dictionary*, 2nd edition. Nairobi, Kenya: Ginseng Publishers, 1993.

Mzamane, Mbulelo. "Colonial and Imperial Themes in South African Literature." *Yearbook of English Studies* 13 (1983): 181–195.

Ngugi wa Thiong'o. *Decolonising the Mind: The Politics of Language in African Literature.* London: J. Currey, 1986.

Peel, John. *Religious Encounter and the Making of the Yoruba.* Bloomington: Indiana University Press, 2000.

Peterson, Derek. *Creative Writing: Translation, Bookkeeping, and the Work of Imagination in Colonial Kenya.* Portsmouth, New Hampshire: Heinemann, 2004.

Peterson, Derek. "Language Work and Colonial Politics in Eastern Africa: The Making of Standard Swahili and 'School Kikuyu'." In *The Study of Language and the Politics of Community in Global Context*, ed. David Hoyt and Karen Oslund. Lanham, Maryland: Lexington Books, 2006.

Ranger, Terence. "Missionaries, Migrants, and the Manyika: The Invention of Ethnicity in Zimbabwe." In *The Creation of Tribalism in Southern Africa*, ed. Leroy Vail. Berkeley: University of California Press, 1989.

DEREK R. PETERSON
REVISED BY SANDRA SANNEH

SLANG

Slang is usually regarded as unconventional style of speech where the norms of "standard" language are either suspended or deliberately ignored. It involves borrowing and the creation of new linguistic forms or creative adaptations of old forms. It is fast paced, syncretic, occasionally vulgar and coarse, and associated with lower body parts. Slang is used as an in-group resource that holds the group's speakers together, creating a sense of identity among them. Due to its association with informal situations and a subculture, it is considered by some people as imperfect and even ungrammatical. It is different from jargon.

Slang expressions are more robust, especially at the lexical level, than is usually assumed because expressions may spread from the in-group to other groups. The Swahili word "poa" ("cool") is in wide usage in East and Central Africa. In addition, due to frequency of use, slang words may be adopted by the standard language. For instance, "tapeli" (to defraud), from French *taper* (to beat), has become a part of standard Swahili; this is credited to a Tanzanian band that carried the word from their music tour of the French-speaking country of Congo (Mensah 1995).

In most cases, archaic expressions are modified through morpho-phonological treatment such as syllable clippings, or back pronunciation, lengthening (as in pig Latin), and even metathesis. Slang is not a language per se, but a code which involves insertions of nonmainstream words into the normal utterances for humorous or expressive effect.

Since slang expressions are derived from the existing languages, multilingualism in Africa provides a conducive linguistic environment for its creation. In South Africa for instance, the slang will come from languages such as Afrikaans, Zulu, English, Sotho, Xhosa. A good example is *Tsotsitaal* or *Tlaaitaal*, which roughly translates as "gangster language," derived from *tsotsi* ("thug" in Zulu) and *taal* ("language" in Afrikaans). In East Africa, on the other hand, Swahili and English dominate youth slang, though some expressions might be borrowed from other languages in use. The influence of Swahili, aided by the burgeoning popular culture and mediated by hip-hop music, has resulted in cases of cross-border diffusion of slang. A good example is the word *keroro* ("to be too drunk"), which originated from Kenya but has entered the Tanzanian slang. Kenyan slang also appears in the hip-hop lyrics of Joseph Mayanja "Chameleon" (Uganda) and Godfrey Tumaini "Dudu Baya/Zuri" (Tanzania).

In Kenya, *sheng*, a mixed code spoken in the urban areas is normally regarded as slang. In fact, the word "sheng" itself is a derivation and is believed to be an acronym of Swahili-English slang. In Cameroon, the language mixing between French and local languages has resulted in the invention of *Camflaglais*, a local code which may also be regarded as slang. If one broadens the definition of slang as the nonstandard, one can also regard the various West African Creoles (e.g., Sierra Leonean *Krio*, Cape Verdian Creole), and pidgins (Nigerian pidgin, Ghanaian pidgin, etc.) along these lines, though care must be taken since some of these have a long history as well as unique origins. A more typical slang may be what Francis Moto (2001) calls Malawi's "new language," which is attributed to the university students at Chancellor College in Malawi. While Moto does not call this new language slang, it is clear from the word creation process and topics of interaction that it is slang. Slang is mainly associated with urban areas that are rich in popular culture derived from local and global sources.

See also **Languages; Literature: Modern Poetry; Literatures in African Languages; Literatures in European Languages; Media: Language.**

BIBLIOGRAPHY

Makhundu, K. D. P. "An Introduction to Flaaitaal." In *Language and Social History: Studies in South African Sociolinguistics*, ed. R. Mesthrie, 298–305. Cape Town: David Philip, 1995.

Mensah, J. K. "Swahili Journalistic Language: A Linguistic Study (view)." *Nordic Journal of African Studies* 4, no. 2 (1995): 93–102.

Moto, Francis. "Language and Society Attitudes: A Study of Malawi's "New Language." *Nordic Journal of African Studies* 10, no. 3 (2001): 320–343.

Ntshangase, D. K. "Idaba Yami I-straight: Language and Language Practices in Soweto." In *Language and Social History: Studies in South African Sociolinguistics*, ed. R. Mesthrie, 291–297. Cape Town: David Philip, 1995.

Spyropoulos, M. "Sheng: Some Preliminary Investigation into a Recently Emerged Nairobi Street Language." *Journal of the Anthropological Society of Oxford* 18, no. 1 (1987): 125–136.

KIMANI NJOGU

SOCIOLINGUISTICS

Sociolinguistics deals with the study of language use as a function of social factors. It examines language and how it operates in society. As a discipline, linguistics is studied within the context of a speech community, which is its analytical tool. Within the Chomskyan School of Thought, the speech community is an idealized construct with three major components: social linkage, constant interaction, and similarity of speech. The Chomskyan approach generalizes the speech habits of people as if they were homogeneous, paying little attention to the particularities of language use in ordinary speech events. People, even those who share a common language, have a wide repertoire of styles that are manipulated to serve the needs of their interactions.

There may also be external constraints and variations that dictate the linguistic styles of the interlocutors. These variations may be in the form of in-group codes or vernaculars, accents, idiolects, dialects, and intonations, and they betray certain elements of the speaker's social location, associations, and personality. They may be guided by age, gender, ethnicity, social status, and educational background. Consequently, the way we speak points to our orientations as well as our attitudes.

Any discussion of sociolinguistics in Africa must begin with the recognition of the intense multilingualism that defines most of the continent. There are over 2,000 languages on the continent, although about 300 of these are in danger of disappearing. These languages are found in four broad families: Afro-Asiatic, Nilo-Saharan, Khoesan (Click), and Niger-Congo. The dynamics of multilingualism demands that speakers engage in acts of negotiation in their daily interactions. Interlocutors may reap maximum benefits from certain linguistic choices or incur loss by the choice others. Hence, they have to make decisions when it comes to code choice. Certain linguistic codes are marked, but although communication favors the use of the unmarked codes, it is sometimes important to use the marked codes in order to satisfy certain interaction demands. In many African countries there are lingua franca or national languages that unite the different ethnic groups, and these may be stipulated in the national constitution. During cross-ethnic interactions, use of ethnic language is normally marked, but in some situations, this marked code might be favored if the intention is to deliberately exclude outsiders who do not share a salient ethnic identity.

The complexity of the sociolinguistic environment in Africa has its genesis in the colonial era when colonial modes of production resulted in the incorporation of Africans into the colonial system. Foreign languages were imposed and these were regarded as the languages of power and privilege. Africans were taught only to the extent that they facilitated interaction between the colonial administration and the subjects or met the needs of assimilation in Francophone Africa. At the onset of independence, the colonial languages had become entrenched and were taken up by independent governments as languages for education, international commerce, and diplomacy. Consequently, French is dominant in West and Central Africa where there were French colonies, and English dominates most interactions in East and Southern Africa and in former British colonies in West Africa such as Nigeria and Ghana. Similarly, Portuguese remains of importance in Mozambique, Angola, and Guinea-Bissau. Spanish, Italian, and German are still spoken, but are more marginal.

In the early twenty-first century, African countries are faced with the dilemma of promoting their national languages as markers of national pride and identity, while also promoting national cohesion, and the continued use of foreign languages in educational institutions for pragmatic reasons. Regional languages such as Kiswahili (East Africa) and Hausa (West Africa) are promoted as viable alternatives to European languages. The linguist Neville Alexander has been championing the harmonization of South African languages and the Kenyan writer Ngũgĩ wa Thiong'o has been urging creative writers to write in their mother tongue. There are many efforts to preserve indigenous languages in Africa that are endangered due to language shift and language death, a consequence of nonuse, urbanization, and the power dynamics between languages. These struggles have been accelerated in the context of globalization and the dominance of English. Within the educational system, many countries have opted for colonial languages as the medium of instruction, whereas African languages have been excluded from pedagogic functions except in adult literacy classes. In spite of the recognition of the intellectual benefits of teaching using the language that students are very comfortable with, little has been done to promote the use of African languages in education.

Urban areas in Africa, as points of convergence, are characterized by widespread language contact. Two scenarios are expected from these convergences. Ethnic languages may be abandoned in favor of more neutral languages in line with the ideal of a cultural-linguistic melting pot. It is also possible to come up with pidgins and creoles or new codes that pick up the fragments of ethnic languages and the emergence of a new language for expressing the new identity. Although the first scenario is not so common in Africa, the second has been attested in a number of countries, especially in West Africa. The urbanites continue to use their ethnic languages that contradict claims to total integration. Accounting for the urban speech communities in Africa would have to take into account that people are heterogeneous rather that homogeneous.

The emergent urban varieties have not solved the heterogeneity problem because they are, themselves, characterized by internal variations which are functions of the dominant ethnic community in a certain locality or the age, gender, status, and locality of the speakers. An often cited case of an urban youth slang is *sheng*, spoken in Kenyan urban centers. Sheng spoken in affluent neighborhoods is markedly different from that spoken in poor neighborhoods. In addition, the sheng spoken by people identified with a certain profession, such as taxi touts or sex workers, is also different from that spoken by members of other professions. The most prominent variation, however, can be seen in the sheng spoken by different age groups. Whereas older people speak the more outdated sheng, the young people speak the more recent kind. For instance, "buda" has been replaced by "mbuyu" and "zaks" in reference to "father," "mose" has been replaced by "mathee" and "masa" in reference to "mother," and "karua" has been replaced by "popo" and " triga" in reference to police officer.

The sociolinguistic situation in Africa is vibrant because of its multilingual nature. Moreover, the tension resulting from multilingualism in Africa does not diminish with the presence of colonial language but is, in fact, accentuated. Furthermore, even the so-called neutral languages display social hierarchies that further complicate the power dynamics between languages.

See also **Globalization; Languages; Linguistics, Historical; Linguistics and the Study of Africa; Ngũgĩ wa Thiong'o.**

BIBLIOGRAPHY

Githinji, Peter. "Sheng and Variation: The Negotiation and Construction of Layered Identities in Nairobi." PhD diss. Michigan State University, 2006.

Halliday, Michael A. K. *Language as Social Semiotic: The Social Interpretation of Language and Meaning.* Baltimore: University Park Press, 1978.

Labov, William. *The Social Stratification of English in New York City.* Washington DC: Center for Applied Linguistics, 1966.

Myers-Scotton, Carol. *Social Motivations for Codeswitching: Evidence from Africa.* Oxford: Clarendon Press, 1993.

Njogu, Kimani. "Language Policy in Kenya: The Opportunities and the Challenges." In *Linguistic Typology and Representation of African Languages*, ed. John Mugane. Trenton, New Jersey: Africa World Press, 2003.

Ricento, Thomas, ed. *An Introduction to Language Policy: Theory and Method.* Oxford: Blackwell Publishing, 2006.

Wright, Sue. *Language Policy and Language Planning: From Nationalism to Globalization.* New York: Palgrave Macmillan, 2004.

KIMANI NJOGU

LANGUAGES

This entry includes the following articles:

OVERVIEW

There are more than 2,000 African languages, an estimated one-third of the world's total, spoken by some 800 million speakers in 54 countries, though the European "Scramble for Africa" has meant that existing ethno-linguistic and national boundaries are rarely coterminous (approximations of total numbers of speakers and languages are based mainly on Raymond Gordon's *Ethnologue* [2005]). Some, for example, Amharic, Fula(ni), Hausa, and Swahili, are major transnational languages that function as lingua francas (with creolized varieties)—multilingualism is extensive throughout the continent—and Arabic is a world language. Others are on the brink of extinction. (Ill-informed remarks such as "Africa has hundreds of *dialects*" tend to reflect the misguided notion that they are somehow inferior forms of language, despite the (universal) difficulty of distinguishing "languages" from "dialects.") Important ex-colonial languages in widespread use in the early twenty-first century include English, French, and Portuguese.

Given the conventional "single-origin" view within evolutionary science that the ancestors of modern humans originated in Africa between 100,000 and 200,000 years ago, eventually migrating to and colonizing the rest of the world, then language as a unique human innovation must have been used on the African continent longer than anywhere else. The massive time-depth involved and resulting linguistic diversity, however, have meant that the phylogenetic classification of African languages has at times been extremely controversial, and a plausible and comprehensive classification was not in fact achieved until the second half of the twentieth century. The matter is further complicated by the lack of reliable documentation compared, for example, with many European and Asian languages. Despite these complications, African languages have made a major contribution to phonological theory in particular, especially in the domains of tone and vowel harmony.

Following the generally recognized classification proposed by the American linguist Joseph Greenberg in 1963, African languages group into four distinct phyla or super-families—Afroasiatic, Niger-Congo, Nilo-Saharan and Khoesan.

AFROASIATIC

The Afroasiatic super-family (sometimes incorrectly referred to as "Hamito-Semitic") contains close to 350 distinct languages, spoken by more than 300 million people in North and East Africa, the Lake Chad area of West Africa, and southwest Asia (see Diakonoff 1988; Hayward 2000; Crass 2006). There are six constituent families—Ancient Egyptian (its direct descendant survived as Egyptian Coptic until the eleventh and twelfth centuries CE), Semitic (77 languages), Berber (26), Chadic (150), Cushitic (47), and Omotic (28). The diverse nature of the numerous languages in these families suggests that the source proto-language was spoken up to 15,000 years ago, perhaps more, probably in northeast Africa. Speakers of formerly important but now extinct Afroasiatic languages achieved some of the earliest breakthroughs in developing writing systems, for example, Ancient Egyptian hieroglyphs (fourth millennium BCE), Akkadian using Sumerian-based cuneiform (third millennium BCE), and the Semitic "consonantory/*abjab*" system used for Phoenician (eleventh century BCE) and Aramaic from the ninth century BCE (varieties of Aramaic are still to be found).

Principal Semitic languages include the many regional varieties of Arabic, spoken by well over 200 million speakers within north Africa and the Middle East (southwest Asia), and widespread in parts of Africa as a second language, Hebrew (5 million,

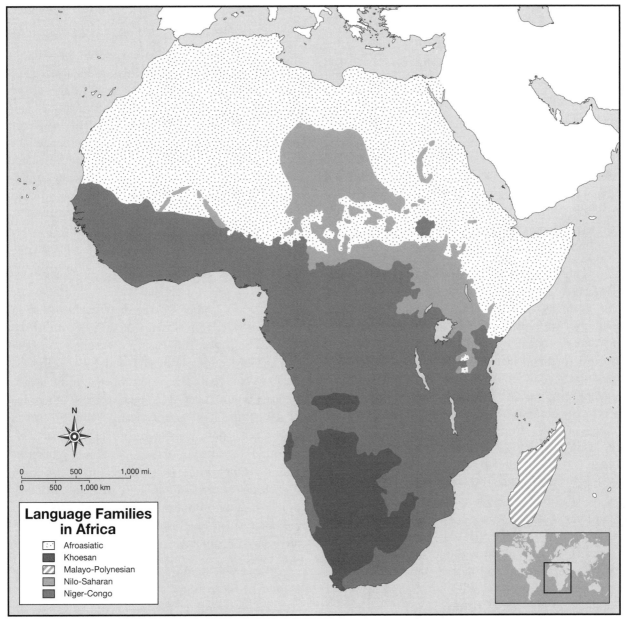

Israel), and the South (Ethiopian) Semitic languages Amharic (15 million [18 million], Ethiopia), and Tigrinya (5 million, Ethiopia, Eritrea). (Numeric figures in square brackets denote estimated numbers of second-language users.) Amharic and Tigrinya are written in the ancient (Ge'ez) Ethiopic script which dates from the third or fourth century CE.

Berber languages, for example Kabyle (3 million), and Tamazight (3.5 million), are spoken mainly in Morocco, Algeria, Tunisia, and Libya, in addition

to the west Sahel region, for example, Tamajaq/ Tuareg (640,000, Niger, Mali), and Berber-speakers colonized the Canary Islands historically. Some Berber languages are written in the traditional Arabic-based *tifinagh* script.

Chadic languages are found to the east, south and west of Lake Chad in West Africa. By far the most prominent and widespread is Hausa, spoken by close to 30 million [40 million] people, mainly in northern Nigeria and southern Niger (the largest number of first-language speakers for any indigenous sub-Saharan language). Hausa was first written using a system (*ajami*) based on the Arabic script. Some smaller Chadic languages have less than a thousand speakers, and many are under threat from the ever-expanding Hausa.

The Cushitic family includes languages spoken in east Africa and the Horn of Africa, for example, Oromo (17 million, Ethiopia, Kenya), Somali (13 million, Somalia, Djibouti, Ethiopia, Kenya), and Afar (1.5 million, Ethiopia). Omotic languages, for example, Wolaytta (1 million), are spoken in southwestern Ethiopia. It is worth noting that the inclusion of Omotic within Afroasiatic is contested by some.

Inherited morphological properties of Afroasiatic languages include: shared personal pronoun sets, for example, second person pronouns beginning with *k- and ending in *-N in the feminine form (* = reconstructed hypothetical form), cf. Ancient Egyptian čn and Hausa kin; an *n/t/n masculine/feminine/plural marking pattern; agential, instrumental and locative nouns formed with a prefix *mV- (where V = vowel); shared noun plural suffixes, for example, *-Vt, *-n-, cf. Hausa rìigaa/rìigunàa "gown/gowns" (grave accent = low tone, otherwise high tone) and Berber axxam/ixxamən "house/houses", and (possibly) internal *-a-; and pharyngealized/glottalized etc. consonants. Chadic, Omotic, and many Cushitic languages have grammatical and lexical tone. A subject-verb-object (SVO) basic word order is widespread throughout the Chadic family, SOV is common in Ethiopian Semitic, Cushitic and Omotic languages, and VSO is prevalent in Berber languages and Central Chadic.

NIGER-CONGO

The massive Niger-Congo phylum comprises roughly 1,500 languages, more than any other phylum in the world, with around 400 million speakers. Niger-Congo subdivides into a number of highly dense families and sub-families covering most of sub-Saharan Africa, for example, Atlantic (60), Mande (70), Gur (100), Kru (40), Kwa (80), Ijoid (10), Adamawa-Ubangi (160), and Benue-Congo (960). It also includes Kordofanian, a more distantly related family of 20 or so languages (some under threat), spoken in the Nuba mountains of the Kordofan area in central/western Sudan. (See also Williamson and Blench 2000 and Bendor-Samuel 2006.)

Atlantic languages extend along the Atlantic coastline of west Africa and include Fula(ni) = Fulfulde (10 million [15 million], mainly Sahel areas), and Wolof (3 million [7 million], Senegal). Fulani, together with, *inter alia*, Swahili, was originally written in Arabic script. The Mande language family is spread over western areas of west Africa and includes Bambara (3 million, Mali, Senegal), and Mende (1.5 million, Sierra Leone, Liberia), though its inclusion within Niger-Congo is an unresolved question. Kwa languages are found along the coast between Côte d'Ivoire and Nigeria, and include Akan = Twi/Fanti (8 million, Ghana) and Ewe (3 million, Ghana, Togo).

The vast Benue-Congo family extends from southern Nigeria/Bénin into the rest of sub-Saharan Africa. The largest languages are Yoruba (20 million [22 million], Nigeria, Bénin), and Igbo = Ibo (17 million, Nigeria). The extensive Bantu branch of Benue-Congo ranges over much of the southern half of Africa (the term *bantu* means "(the) people" in many of the constituent languages). This spread is the historical consequence of the expansion of agricultural Bantu peoples from west Africa (mainly southern Cameroon/Nigeria) about 3,000 years ago, facilitated by the use of iron from around 500 BCE. This migration led to the displacement and absorption of pre-existing Central African Pygmy languages.

The genetic unity of the Bantu branch of Benue-Congo has been firmly established for more than a century, and some of the better known Bantu languages are Bemba (3/4 million, Zambia), (Lu)ganda (3 million, Uganda), Kikuyu = Gikuyu (5 million, Kenya), (Kinya)rwanda (6/7 million, Rwanda), Lingala (2 million [7 million], Democratic Republic of the Congo, Zaire Republic of the Congo), Shona (10 million, Zimbabwe), Swahili (5 million [30 million], mainly Tanzania, also Kenya, Burundi, Democratic Republic of the Congo, Uganda, Somalia), Xhosa and Zulu (7 million, 10 million [16 million], South Africa). A variety of Swahili (Comorian) is also spoken on the islands of Madagascar and Comoros; otherwise the major (genetically non-African) language spoken there, Malagasy (6 million), is a member of the Malayo-Polynesian branch of Austronesian.

Niger-Congo languages (especially Bantu) are well known for their elaborate system of noun classification which uses affixes to signal singular/plural pairs (so-called noun class systems), with agreement on other sentence elements. The semantic classification and marking typically distinguish humans, (domestic) animals, plants, mass nouns, and liquids, and some languages have as many as 20 or so classes. In Swahili, for example, the ki-prefix denotes languages, *inter alia*, for example, Ki-Swahili, Ki-Kuyu, and m-/wa- are the singular/plural prefixes for humans, cf. m-tu/wa-tu "person/people." Niger-Congo languages are also predominantly tonal, word-initial nasal clusters are common, for example, /nd/, /mb/, together with vowel harmony, where all the vowels in a word share the same features, for example, [± advanced tongue root/ATR]. SVO neutral word order is common throughout Niger-Congo (with SOV prevalent in some groups). So-called serial verbs are also common, where two verbs with the same subject function like a single predicate, for example, (Yoruba) mo rà ọ̀ gẹ̀ dẹ̀ jẹ̀ (I buy banana eat) "I bought and ate bananas."

NILO-SAHARAN

The internally diverse Nilo-Saharan phylum contains around 200 languages with an estimated 70 million speakers, most of them located near the southern reaches of the Nile and Chari (central Africa) rivers, extending west to east from Mali, Niger, Nigeria, and Chad, across to Sudan, Ethiopia, Democratic Republic of the Congo, Kenya, and Uganda (see Bender 2000; Dimmendaal 2006). Nilo-Saharan languages are so structurally dissimilar, however, that their genetic unity and internal composition are in dispute; attempts to collapse Nilo-Saharan and Niger-Congo into a higher macro-phylum have also to gain wide acceptance. Proposed families within Nilo-Saharan include, *inter alia*, Saharan (5 million), Songhay (3 million), Central Sudanic (6 million), and Eastern Sudanic (16 million, including the extensive Nilotic subfamily). The Saharan family includes Kanuri, spoken by 3/4 million speakers in northeast Nigeria, Niger, Cameroon and Chad. Songhay (3 million, Mali, Niger), the westernmost language, is considered an isolate with no obvious relatives, with some linguists linking it to the Mande group of Niger-Congo.

Prominent Nilotic languages are Dinka (2/3 million, Sudan), Kalenjin (2/3 million, Kenya), Luo (3/4 million, Kenya, Tanzania), Maasai (1 million, Kenya, Tanzania), and Nuer (1 million, Sudan, Ethiopia); Lugbara (1 million, Uganda) belongs to the Central Sudanic branch. Nubian, an Eastern Sudanic language (1 million, Sudan, southern Egypt) was written in an alphabet largely based on Coptic and Greek, probably used by Christian communities from the eighth to tenth centuries CE, and Kanuri was traditionally written in Arabic script. (The Meroitic script dates back to the third century BCE and Meroitic (Sudan) was possibly a Nilo-Saharan language related to Nubian.)

Nilo-Saharan languages are largely tonal and ATR-vowel harmony is common. They typically mark pronominal subjects (and sometimes objects) on the verb, for example, (Maasai, acute = high tone) kí-dɔ́l nínyɛ (3sg>2sg-see (s)he) "(s)he sees you," and many languages use case-marking on nouns to signal grammatical relations and semantic functions, for example, dative, instrumental—cf. (Kanuri) agógó shí-<u>ro</u> cóko (watch 3msg-dative past.give.1sg) "I gave him a watch." There is a widespread distinction between perfective and imperfective tense-aspects, and a common word order in the phylum is SVO and SOV, with VSO attested in Eastern and Southern Sudanic.

KHOESAN

Khoesan languages (considered by some linguists to be the oldest phylum in Africa) are spoken by small populations, located mainly in the Kalahari Desert areas of Namibia and Botswana. The Khoesan languages encompass what earlier linguists referred to as "Hottentot" and "Bushmen" languages, and the cover-term "Khoesan" is a composite of the Khoekhoe (formerly Hottentot) words *khoe* ("person") and *san* ("foragers"). Historically, most of southern Africa was probably inhabited by aboriginal Khoesan-speakers, and the Khoe ("Hottentot") and San ("Bushmen") were pastro-foragers and hunter-gatherers respectively. However, due to the expansion of Bantu-speaking peoples from the north and the European occupation of the area from the mid-seventeenth century, many Khoesan languages have either died off (especially in the Southern group), or are seriously endangered, and only 20 to 30 remain, totaling not many more than 350,000 or so speakers, used in communities that are generally marginalized and stigmatized (see Güldemann and Vossen 2000; Haacke 2006).

The genetic status and internal relationships of the putative Khoesan phylum are a matter of debate, partly because of the paucity of reliable descriptions. Most approaches, however, set up three families for the languages spoken in southern Africa—Central (also = Khoe), Northern and Southern (also = non-Khoe). Central Khoesan languages are spoken in Namibia as well as Angola, Botswana, South Africa, and Zambia, and the largest is Nama/Damara (230,000, Namibia). Other Khoesan languages are spoken by no more than a few hundred speakers, for example, Ts'ixa (Central), or a few thousand, for example, Kxoe (Central), Juǀ'hoan (Northern). There are also two isolates—Hadza (800) and Sandawe (40,000)—linguistically and geographically remote remnant languages spoken in Tanzania, where they are surrounded by Bantu languages.

The sound systems of Khoesan languages are elaborate and include the so-called clicks (unique consonants that have found their way into neighboring Bantu languages such as Xhosa and Zulu). Clicks are produced by varying the position of the tongue, and sucking air into the mouth cavity to produce the click burst, and the various types are sometimes represented in the orthography with such special symbols as | (dental), ‖ (lateral), and ! (alveolar)—cf. the language names |Xam, ‖Ani, and !Ora. A bilabial ("kiss") click ⊙ is also present in the Southern branch. Khoesan languages are tonal and the Central family typically uses a complex system of suffixes to mark person, number and gender on nouns, for example, (Naro) hàúgù-m dì(-s) ǀʼóán-sà (dog-msg poss(-fsg) bone-fsg) "dog's bone." SVO word order is common in the Northern and Southern branches, and SOV predominates in Central languages.

See also **History of Africa; Language; Linguistics and the Study of Africa; Literature; Writing Systems.**

BIBLIOGRAPHY

Bender, M. Lionel. "Nilo-Saharan." In *African Languages: An Introduction*, ed. Bernd Heine and Derek Nurse. Cambridge, U.K.: Cambridge University Press, 2000.

Bendor-Samuel, J. "Niger-Congo Languages." In *Encyclopedia of Languages and Linguistics*, ed. Keith Brown. 2nd edition. Amsterdam and Oxford: Elsevier, 2006.

Brown, Keith, ed. *Encyclopedia of Languages and Linguistics*, 2nd edition. Amsterdam and Oxford: Elsevier, 2006.

Crass, J. "Afroasiatic Languages." In *Encyclopedia of Languages and Linguistics*, ed. Keith Brown. 2nd edition. Amsterdam and Oxford: Elsevier, 2006.

Diakonoff, Igor M. *Afrasian Languages*, trans. A. A. Korolevana and Victor Porkhomovsky. Moscow: Nauka, 1988.

Dimmendaal, G. J. "Nilo-Saharan Languages." In *Encyclopedia of Languages and Linguistics*, ed. Keith Brown. 2nd edition. Amsterdam and Oxford: Elsevier, 2006.

Gordon, Raymond G., Jr., ed. *Ethnologue: Languages of the World*, 15th edition. Dallas, TX: SIL International, 2005.

Greenberg, Joseph H. *The Languages of Africa*. Bloomington: Indiana University Center in Anthropology, Folklore and Linguistics, and The Hague: Mouton, 1963.

Güldemann, Tom, and Rainer Vossen. "Khoesan." In *African Languages: An Introduction*, ed. Bernd Heine and Derek Nurse. Cambridge, U.K.: Cambridge University Press, 2000.

Haacke, W.H.G. "Khoesaan Languages." In *Encyclopedia of Languages and Linguistics*, ed. Keith Brown. 2nd edition. Amsterdam and Oxford: Elsevier, 2006.

Hayward, Richard J. "Afroasiatic." In *African Languages: An Introduction*, ed. Bernd Heine and Derek Nurse. Cambridge, U.K.: Cambridge University Press, 2000.

Heine, Bernd, and Derek Nurse, eds. *African Languages: An Introduction*. Cambridge, U.K.: Cambridge University Press, 2000.

Jaggar, Philip J. "History of African Language Classification." *Encyclopedia of African History*, Vol. 2, ed. Kevin Shillington. New York and London: Fitzroy Dearborn, 2005.

Williamson, Kay, and Roger Blench. "Niger-Congo." In *African Languages: An Introduction*, ed. Bernd Heine and Derek Nurse. Cambridge, U.K.: Cambridge University Press, 2000.

PHILIP J. JAGGAR

AFRO-ASIATIC

The Afro-Asiatic (Afroasiatic, Afrasian, Hamitosemitic, Hamito-Semitic, Semito-Hamitic) languages comprise some 300 modern and a dozen dead languages. The speakers of the living ones may be estimated at approximately 300 million, spread across northern, central, and eastern Africa as well as western Asia. The Afro-Asiatic languages are genetically related and form a linguistic phylum that consists of six branches, each having the status of a linguistic family: Ancient Egyptian, Berber, Semitic, Chadic, Cushitic, and Omotic. The first branch is represented only by dead languages; Berber and Semitic include both dead and living; and the latter three are known only from living languages. The number of speakers of the individual languages within these branches ranges between a few hundred and millions.

The term "Afro-Asiatic" was introduced by Joseph Greenberg in the 1950s to replace the connotation of a linguistic opposition between Semitic and the remaining languages of the phylum suggested by "Semito-Hamitic" and similar terms. The Ancient Egyptian branch is represented by the language of pharaonic Egypt from the third millennium BCE and its subsequent stages of development, including Coptic, which was spoken until the sixteenth century CE.

The numerous Berber languages and dialects are spoken mostly in North Africa between Morocco and Egypt as well as in the Sahara and Sahel (southwestern Mauritania [Zenaga], Niger, and Mali [Tuareg]). The name Berber comes via Arabic from the Greek *bárbaros*, originally meaning a person speaking a language other than Greek. This branch is also known as Berber-Libyan due to the inclusion of the Old Libyan (Numidian) language (attested by inscriptions only). Some scholars classify the extinct Guanche languages of the Canary Islands in this branch, labeling it Libyan-Guanche.

The Semitic branch, named after Shem, a son of Noah (Genesis 9:18), includes dead languages—Akkadian (with Babylonian and Assyrian dialects), Ugaritic, Phoenician, Aramaic, Hebrew, Geʿez—as well as living ones: Arabic, Modern Hebrew (Israel), Neo-Aramaic (Syria, Iraq, Iran, Turkey), Modern South Arabian (southern part of the Arabian Peninsula and Socotra Island), and the Ethio-Semitic languages—Amharic, Tigrinya, Tigre—spoken mainly in Ethiopia and Eritrea. Among the latter, Amharic is a first or second language for about 19 million people. Of all the Afro-Asiatic languages, Modern Standard Arabic and its dialects in the whole of North Africa, Western Sahara, Nigeria, Chad, Sudan, and Southwest Asia are the most widespread, with probably more than 160 million speakers.

With its 160 languages the Chadic family, named after Lake Chad, is the most numerous Afro-Asiatic branch. The Chadic-speaking peoples are spread throughout northern Nigeria, Chad, and northern Cameroon. Hausa is used widely as a means of interethnic communication in western Africa; for more than 40 million speakers in Nigeria, Niger, Cameroon, Chad, Togo, Bénin, Ghana, Burkina Faso, and in Sudan it is a first or second language.

The Cushitic languages, named after Cush, a grandson of Noah (Genesis 10:6–8), are spoken in Ethiopia, Somalia, the Sudan, Kenya, and Tanzania. Oromo (mainly in Ethiopia) and Somali (mainly in Somalia) are spoken by 10 million and 5.6 million people, respectively. In the 1970s a group of languages spoken in southwestern Ethiopia, and previously classified as West Cushitic, was separated by some scholars to form a new Omotic branch (named after the Omo River).

Comparative study of Afro-Asiatic languages faces the problem of differing knowledge of the time depth of the individual languages: on the one hand, almost five thousand years of Ancient Egyptian written language history; on the other hand, newly discovered languages from the Chadic, Cushitic, and Omotic branches whose description is still in progress. In this context, with the formation of nation-states and the development of modern means of communication, minority languages have been given up or are in the process of extinction. Comparative and reconstruction research within each Afro-Asiatic branch is needed, and is being carried out. More attention is being paid to the specific geolinguistic situation, mainly in the Sahara and Sahel, which has resulted in a multiplicity of contacts among the languages in question as well as with other nonrelated linguistic groups. Thus, for instance, Cushitic languages are spoken in areas where Ethio-Semitic-, Nilotic-, or Bantu-speaking peoples also live; many Chadic languages have been in long-standing contact with speakers of Nilo-Saharan and Niger-Congo languages. In addition, with the spread of Islam, Arabic has affected the languages of the whole region. Also indisputable is the impact of lingua francas in all multiethnic societies. The question of keeping linguistic substrata, adstrata, and superstrata apart is a must for understanding the history of Afro-Asiatic languages.

The degree of differentiation within the families varies strongly: Members of the Berber and Semitic families are much closer to one another than are those of the Chadic and Cushitic branches. Tonal languages are found within Chadic, Omotic, and Cushitic. Among the common linguistic features shared by all branches are a consonantal phonological trichotomy: voiceless:voiced:glottalized/emphatic; a feminine *t* marker in the nominal and verbal systems; a perfective:imperfective verbal dichotomy (the latter marked by an *a(a)* infix and/or by reduplication of the second or third root consonant); an internal plural formation (broken plurals) with an *a(a)* infix. The attempts to reconstruct proto-Afro-Asiatic have led to the conclusion that its speakers might have settled in the southeastern Sahara and eastern Africa in the tenth or ninth millennium BCE. The hypothesis for an Asian origin of the Afro-Asiatic speakers cannot be confirmed by the contemporary linguistic evidence.

The writing systems of the Afro-Asiatic languages belong to the earliest scripts in the world: the hieroglyphic of Ancient Egyptian (forth-third millennium BCE); the cuneiform system of Akkadian (mid-third millennium BCE); the cuneiform quasialphabetic script of Ugaritic (mid-third millennium BCE); and the Phoenician alphabet (mid-second millennium BCE), from which emerged (consequently or independently) the Aramaic, Hebrew, Arabic, Amharic, Tuareg (called Tifinagh), Greek, and Latin scripts. The modern Afro-Asiatic languages without a tradition of writing use mainly the Latin script.

See also **Language; Linguistics and the Study of Africa; Writing Systems.**

BIBLIOGRAPHY

Bender, Lionel M., ed. *The Non-Semitic Languages of Ethiopia*. East Lansing: African Studies Center, Michigan State University, 1976.

Diakonoff, Igor M. *Afrasian Languages*. Moscow: Nauka, 1988.

Galand, Lionel. "Le Berbére." In *Les langues dans le monde ancien et moderne*, ed. Jean Perrot. 2 vols. Paris: Éditions du CNRS, 1988.

Greenberg, Joseph. *The Languages of Africa*. Bloomington: Indiana University, 1963.

Hayward, Richard J., ed. *Omotic Language Studies*. London: School of Oriental and African Studies, 1990.

Hayward, Richard J. "Afroasiatic." In *African Languages: An Introduction*, ed. Bernd Heine and Derek Nurse. Cambridge, U.K.: Cambridge University Press, 2000.

Jungraithmayr, Herrmann, and Dymitr Ibriszimow. *Chadic Lexical Roots*. 2 vols. Berlin: Dietrich Reimer, 1994.

Kossmann, Maarten. *Essai sur la phonologie du proto-berbère*. Köln, Germany: Rüdiger Köppe, 1999.

Lipinski, Edward. *Semitic Languages: Outline of a Comparative Grammar*. Leuven, Belgium: Peeters, 1997.

Moscati, Sabatino; Anton Spitaler; Edward Ullendorff; and Wolfram von Soden. *An Introduction to the Comparative Grammar of the Semitic Languages*. Wiesbaden, Germany: Otto Harrassowitz, 1964.

Vycichl, Werner. *Dictionnaire étymologique de la langue copte*. Leuven, Belgium: Peeters, 1983.

DYMITR IBRISZIMOW

ARABIC

Arabic belongs to the Semitic branch of the Afro-Asiatic languages. Together with the other Semitic languages, Arabic shares a number of structural properties, in particular the tendency to organize its lexicon on the basis of triliteral roots with a common semantic basis and the assignment of morphological functions to these roots by means of internal reorganization in different patterns. In syntax, classical Arabic has preserved the original proto-Semitic declension of nouns, and a distinction between a prefix- and a suffix-conjugation of the verb. In phonology, Arabic has a relatively poor vowel inventory, just as most other Semitic languages, and a rich consonantal inventory, including uvular and pharyngeal consonants, plus a series of so-called emphatic (velarized) consonants.

There is no consensus about the exact classification of Arabic within the Semitic languages. The language has important common links with the South Semitic languages, such as South Arabian and Ethiopian, but it is also connected by a number of isoglosses with the Northwest Semitic languages, such as Hebrew and Aramaic.

Bedouin speakers of Arabic may have been present in the Sinai Peninsula as early as the first century CE, but the actual spread of the language in Africa took place during the Arab conquests in the seventh century CE. During the initial stage of the conquests, between 640 when Egypt was conquered and 711 when the Arab armies crossed the Straits of Gibraltar to conquer Spain, garrison cities such as al-Fustat in Egypt and Kairouan in Tunisia were established. In these urbanized areas, the indigenous population came in direct contact with the Arab invaders and most of them took over the Arabic language and religion. The rural areas remained outside the sphere of influence of Arabic and Islam until Bedouin groups such as the Banu Sulaym and the Banu Hilal started to migrate from the Arabian Peninsula in large numbers in the ninth century, first to Egypt and then to North Africa, where they reached Mauritania in the twelfth century. In the course of this second invasion, the process of Arabization was completed in the rural areas of Upper Egypt and all of North Africa. Eventually, Arabic became the language of the majority of the population. Those dialects that originated in this second stage represent a more Bedouin-type of dialect, whose hallmark is a voiced realization of the phoneme /q/ as /g/, as against voiceless /q/ or /'/ in the sedentary dialects.

The indigenous languages in the conquered areas did not disappear entirely. In Egypt, Arabic gradually replaced the Coptic language in a matter of centuries. But in North Africa, a sizeable minority retained the original Berber languages. Nonetheless, Modern Standard Arabic has become the official language in all political, cultural, literary, and religious domains throughout the North African countries. In countries such as Morocco and Egypt, an urban *koine* has emerged that may be regarded as a kind of national language.

From Egypt and the Maghreb, Arab migrants and traders brought Arabic and Islam to the sub-Saharan regions. From Egypt, they went south and brought the Sudan and other sub-Saharan African regions within the sphere of influence of the Arabophone world. From there, nomadic tribes travelled westward along the so-called bagara belt, settling in northern Chad, Niger and eventually in northern Nigeria, where the province of Bornu still harbors a large group of speakers of Arabic (Owens 1993).

From the Maghreb, traders went south along the coast and by caravan routes through the Sahara, reaching Mali and Senegal in the ninth century. These countries never became Arabophone, but they did convert to Islam and used Arabic, at first as a trade language and then as the language of scholarship and religion in centers of learning such

as Timbuktu. The various kingdoms came to employ Arabic in official correspondence. On the East African coast, seafarers established trade relations, first from Shiraz, and then from South Arabia and Oman. The language of the traders did not replace the existing lingua franca, Swahili, but the contacts led to an influx of Arabic words in this language, and may even have contributed to the emergence of simplified varieties of Swahili.

Currently, more than 140 million people speak Arabic in Africa as their first language. Virtually all inhabitants of Mauritania (2.5 million), Tunisia (9 million), Libya (4.2 million), and Egypt (71.4 million) are Arabophone. In Morocco (18.9 million speakers of Arabic) and Algeria (20.5 million speakers of Arabic), Arabic is the only official language, but there are large minorities of Berber (Tamazight) speakers—between 25 and 40 percent of the population—according to some estimates. Some of them may be monolingual speakers, but for the vast majority of Berber speakers, Arabic is the second language, in which they communicate outside their homes.

In the Sudan (population 15 million), Arabic is the official language, but the inhabitants of the south speak a multitude of Nilo-Saharan and Afro-Asiatic languages. In Chad, about 800,000 people in the northern part of the country speak Chad Arabic as their mother tongue; more than one hundred local languages are spoken but only Arabic and French have both been recognized as official languages. Smaller groups of speakers of Arabic live as a minority in Nigeria (100,000), Cameroon (63,000), and the Central African Republic (63,000). The variety of Arabic spoken in Mali (106,000), Senegal (6,000), and Niger (30,000) is that of Mauritanian Arabic (Hassaniyya). Native speakers in East Africa, as in Tanzania (195,000), are usually immigrants from the Arabian Peninsula, in particular from Oman.

Arabic has also become an official language in Djibouti and Eritrea, where some people are native speakers of varieties of Saudi or Yemeni Arabic (in Djibouti around 52,000). In Somalia, Arabic has remained the main language of instruction and politics. Elsewhere, Arabic is a trading or vehicular language, usually in a pidginized form. In the southern Sudan, pidginized Arabic is used as a lingua franca by 20,000 people, with some emergent creolization (Juba Arabic); this pidgin arose in the wake of the Anglo-Egyptian campaigns in the Sudan in the nineteenth century. At the end of the nineteenth century, it was transported to Uganda and Kenya, where it became the creolized language (Ki-)Nubi, spoken by approximately 10,000 speakers in Kenya and 15,000 in Uganda (Wellens 2005).

Even in those Islamic countries where Arabic is not used as a mother tongue or a trade language, it has always played an important role as the language of the Qur'an. Most Islamic people acquire at least a smattering of knowledge of the language in Qur'anic schools. In modern times, Islamic reformist movements have set up *madrasas* (Islamic schools), which have become popular.

In the course of Islamization, Arabic became the language of learning and reading. In addition, some African languages were at one time written with Arabic script, and languages like Fulfulde, Kanuri, Songhay, and Wolof contain many Arabic loanwords, especially in the domains of religion and learning. Hausa has a long history of contact with Arabic, which has led to the introduction of a great many loanwords; in the eastern Sudan, Hausa speakers are usually bilingual in Hausa and Arabic, which leads to extensive code switching. In East Africa, the contribution of Arabic to Swahili is clearly visible in the lexicon: up to 40 percent of the lexical items is reputedly of Arabic origin. In present-day Uganda, Tanzania, and Kenya, the use of Arabic in education has greatly diminished after the colonial period, but nonetheless, the intimate connection of Arabic with the literary history of Swahili has persisted and is clearly visible in the 40 percent of the lexicon that is of Arabic origin.

See also **History of Africa; Islam; Linguistics and the Study of Africa.**

BIBLIOGRAPHY

Abu-Manga, Al-Amin. *Hausa in the Sudan: Process of Adaptation to Arabic.* Cologne, Germany: R. Köppe, 1999.

Badawi, Elsaid; Michael G. Carter; and Adrian Gully. *Modern Written Arabic: A Comprehensive Grammar.* London: Routledge, 2004.

Baldi, Sergio. *A First Ethnolinguistic Comparison of Arabic Loanwords Common to Hausa and Swahili.* Naples, Italy: Istituto Orientale di Napoli, 1988.

Brenner, Louis. *Controlling Knowledge: Religion, Power and Schooling in a West-African Muslim Society.* Bloomington: Indiana University Press, 2000.

Caubet, Dominique. *L'arabe marocain.* Paris: Louvain: Peeters, 1993.

Da Costa, Yusuf and Achmat Davids. *Pages from Cape Muslim History.* Pietermaritzburg, South Africa: Shuter and Shooter, 1994.

Fischer, Wolfdietrich. *A Grammar of Classical Arabic.* 3rd edition. New Haven, Connecticut: Yale University Press, 2001.

Hetzron, Robert. *The Semitic Languages.* London: Routledge, 2006.

Holes, Clive. *Modern Arabic: Structures, Functions and Varieties.* 2nd edition. Washington, DC: Georgetown University Press, 2004.

Owens, Jonathan. *A Grammar of Nigerian Arabic.* Wiesbaden, Germany: O. Harrassowitz, 1993.

Versteegh, Kees. *The Arabic Language* 2nd edition. Edinburgh: Edinburgh University Press, 2002.

Wellens, Ineke. *The Nubi Language of Uganda: An Arabic Creole in Africa.* Leiden, The Netherlands: E. J. Brill, 2005.

KEES VERSTEEGH

CREOLES AND PIDGINS

Creoles and pidgins are language varieties that developed during the seventeenth through the nineteenth centuries out of contacts of colonial nonstandard European dialects with non-European languages on the islands and coasts of the Atlantic, Indian, and Pacific Oceans. Examples include Saramaccan and Sranan (Suriname), Papiamentu (the Netherlands Antilles), Gullah (United States), Jamaican, Haitian, Guadeloupean, and, in Africa, Cape Verdian, Kriyol (Guinea-Bissau and Senegal), Krio (Sierra Leone), Nigerian Pidgin, Cameroonian Pidgin, Mauritian, and Seychellois. The terms have also been extended to varieties that developed during the same period out of contacts of primarily non-European languages; examples of these include Kikongo-Kituba and Lingala (Democratic Republic of the Congo and the Republic of the Congo), Kinubi (southern Sudan and western Uganda), Sango (Central African Republic), and Fanagalo (also known as Fanakalo, South Africa). While common, the inclusion of lingua francas such as Swahili, Hausa, Songhay, and the like in this category is controversial. Although there are no universal structural features that define creoles and pidgins, these latter lingua francas do not share many structural features attested in the "classic creoles" of the Caribbean and the Indian Ocean, which are based on Western European languages. Their structures have not diverged as extensively from those of their "lexifiers" (the original varieties from which they have evolved) as have, putatively, true creoles and pidgins. The main reason for the extension of the terms is the association of their emergence and/or geographical expansion with European colonization, especially their adoption as major non-elite vernaculars or lingua francas during and after that period.

Since the early twentieth century, pidgins have been distinguished from creoles in that they are said to have no native speakers, have limited communicative functions—restricted typically to trade—and have less complex structures than creoles. However, Nigerian Pidgin and Cameroonian Pidgin show as much structural complexity and communicative breadth as Krio, a creole, and they also have significant proportions of native speakers. It is thus necessary to distinguish between *pidgin*, used strictly for reduced lingua franca varieties spoken in sporadic contacts such as of trade, and *expanded pidgin*, which shows structural complexification resulting from its more frequent uses as a vernacular in more diversified domains of interaction, such as in urban centers.

It has also been claimed that creoles are former pidgins which were vernacularized by children, but historical facts dispute this view. The term "creole" was originally coined in the Iberian colonies, apparently in the sixteenth century, for descendants of Iberians and Africans born in American colonies. Having been borrowed into other European languages by the early seventeenth century, it was extended later to descendants of Africans and Europeans born in other colonies. The term was apparently not applied to language in English until 1825. It seems to have had an isolated use earlier in French, in the late seventeenth century. The extension of the term "creole" to language variety may have been initiated by metropolitan Europeans to disfranchise particular ways in which their languages were spoken in the plantation settlement colonies, especially among non-Europeans. Ironically, no language varieties have been identified as creoles in Iberian New World colonies, where the term was coined.

Papiamentu emerged in Dutch colonies, and Palenquero among the Maroons of Colombia. Both are Portuguese-based and represent isolated developments in territories where the dominant colonial languages were Dutch and Spanish, respectively.

The term "pidgin" was first introduced in English in 1807, in reference to the English adopted as the lingua franca of the British trade colony in Canton. Nothing in the history of this Chinese Pidgin English suggests that it developed into a creole. The social histories of the western Atlantic and Indian Oceans suggest that their creoles developed directly from varieties closer to those spoken by European colonists and diverged only gradually into their *basilects* (the varieties most different from their "lexifiers"), probably during the eighteenth century, when infant mortality was high on the plantations, life expectancy short, the labor-force populations increased more by importation than by birth, and the proportion of fluent or native speakers of the earlier colonial varieties kept decreasing.

One of the most central questions in studying creoles regards the mechanics of their development. The most current hypotheses today invoke the substrate, superstrate, and language bioprogram, as explained below.

According to substratists, creoles in the strict sense owe most, or several, of their structural features to the languages previously spoken by the Africans enslaved in the New World and the Indian Ocean. Originally, substratists reacted in part to dialectologists (the superstrate hypothesis), according to whom the primary, if not the exclusive, sources of creoles' structures are the nonstandard varieties of their "lexifiers" to which the Africans were exposed. They have also been challenged by the language bioprogram hypothesis, which argues that creoles were invented by children from the syntaxless pidgins spoken by their parents and according to default principles and parametric settings specified in the bioprogram (another term for the Chomskyan Universal Grammar).

Few creolists interested in creole genesis still subscribe to one exclusive explanation. The complementary hypothesis seems to be an adequate alternative, provided one can articulate the linguistic and nonlinguistic conditions under which the competing influences (between the substrate and

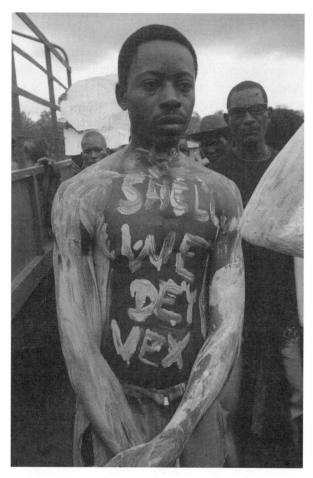

Protest against Shell. A youth wears a painted message in pidgin, "Shell, we dey vex" ("Shell, we are angry"), during a march to protest Shell Petroleum's unfulfilled promise to build the 38-kilometer Otuegila-Nembe road in their community, Otuegila, Nigeria, May 2005. PIUS UTOMI EKPEI/AFP/GETTY IMAGES

superstrate languages, and within each group) may have converged or prevailed upon each other.

Still, the future of research on the development of creoles has some problems to overcome. So far, information on the nonstandard varieties of the "lexifiers" spoken by the European colonists remains limited. There are still few comprehensive descriptions of creoles' systems, which makes it difficult to determine globally how the competing influences interacted among them and to assess whether the uniform cross-creole restructuring plan suggested by some hypotheses is justified. Very few structural facts have been correlated with the conclusions suggested by the sociohistorical backgrounds of individual creoles.

African language varieties identified as creoles or pidgins (Kikongo-Kituba, Lingala, Fanagalo, Sango, and Kinubi, for example) are, as previously noted, very much associated with the exploitation colonization of the continent, although the Africans themselves have developed them. The colonial agents provided the contact settings, the colonial posts and factories, to which people of different ethnolinguistic backgrounds migrated, and where they needed a common lingua franca to communicate with each other. Typically, they developed these new language varieties from an ethnic language that had already served as a lingua franca in interethnic trade before European colonization (Kituba from Kikongo-Kimanyanga, Lingala from Bobangi, Sango from Ngbandi) or from an important language spoken around the colonial post or factory (Fanagalo from Zulu). Kinubi is the only one based on Arabic and is associated with Arabized blacks in Sudan, Kenya, and Uganda who descend from the nineteenth-century Turco-Egyptian army in present-day southern Sudan. The varieties developed through structural changes that the "lexifiers" underwent while being appropriated by the non-native speakers.

See also **Creoles; Language; Linguistics and the Study of Africa.**

BIBLIOGRAPHY

Alleyne, Mervyn C. *Comparative Afro-American*. Ann Arbor, MI: Karoma, 1980.

Heine, Bernd. *Status and Use of African Lingua Francas*. Munich: Weltforum Verlag, 1970.

Mufwene, Salikoko S., ed. *Africanisms in Afro-American Language Varieties*. Athens: University of Georgia Press, 1993.

Mufwene, Salikoko S. *The Ecology of Language Evolution*. Cambridge, U.K.: Cambridge University Press, 2001.

Sylvain, Suzanne. *Le créole haïtien*. Wetteren, Belgium: Imprimerie de Meester, 1936.

Turner, Lorenzo D. *Africanisms in the Gullah Dialect*. Chicago: University of Chicago Press, 1949.

SALIKOKO S. MUFWENE

KHOESAN AND CLICK

The Khoesan (formerly spelled Khoisan) languages are non-Bantu, non-Cushitic African languages, characterized notably by the original and extensive use of click consonants. Clicks are found in a number of Bantu languages, but these have arisen through assimilation from the Khoesan languages during periods of contact. Clicks also occur in Dahalo, a Cushitic language, where they appear to be part of a pre-Cushitic substratum. The term "click language" is therefore a purely typological one referring only to languages in which click consonants are an integral part of the phonology. In this sense, click languages are restricted to Africa.

Linguist Joseph Greenberg (1915–2001) claimed that the Khoesan languages are members of one family with varying degrees of relationship to one another, but this view is no longer supported by Khoesanist linguists who regard Khoesan as representing three to six unrelated families. The greatest concentration of these languages is in southern Africa from Angola through Zimbabwe to Swaziland, but in the early twenty-first century, almost all speakers are found in Namibia and Botswana. The referential term Khoesan includes two unrelated Tanzanian languages, Hadza and Sandawe.

In southern Africa, there are three main groups. These are the Juu (or Northern), the Khoe (or Central), and the Tuu (or !Ui and Taa, or Southern) groups. The Juu and Taa languages are frequently referred to as San languages, but this is misleading linguistically because they do not form a distinct group of related languages, and because some Khoe languages are also called San. An extinct language of southwestern Angola, Kwadi, may be distantly related to the Khoe family. An endangered language of central Botswana, ǂHuan (Eastern ǂHoan), appears to be distantly related to the Juu family.

Greenberg's attempt to demonstrate relatedness between the Khoesan languages failed to use the Comparative Method. This system is the gold standard in historical linguistics wherein words in different languages are cognate, or related to a reconstructed original proto form for a word, from which the observed differences between languages may be derived by rules of sound change. The large number of similarities seen across Khoesan families is the result of borrowing and convergence that has taken place across centuries, if not millennia.

The vitality of the southern African Khoesan languages has been influenced in historical times by the dominant European (largely Dutch and Afrikaans)

and Bantu (largely Nguni) cultures. This led to a dramatic language shift and ultimately to the near-death of all the Khoesan languages of South Africa. Negative attitudes toward the surviving Khoesan languages and their speakers persist into the early twenty-first century. Nevertheless, children are still learning a number of southern African Khoesan languages, such as the Khoe languages Khoekhoegowab (Namibia), with more than 100,000 speakers; Naro (Botswana), with about 12,000 speakers; Kxoe with around 8,000 speakers; Juǀ'hoansi (Namibia and Botswana), with approximately 11,000 speakers; and !Xoon (Botswana), with fewer than 3,000 speakers. In Tanzania there are roughly 800 Hadza and 40,000 Sandawe speakers.

There is no mutual intelligibility between the languages of the Khoesan families, yet it is not uncommon for a speaker of one language to be fluent in another, unrelated Khoesan language. In addition, many southern African Khoesan speakers are bilingual to some degree in a Bantu language (Herero in Namibia; Mbukushu, Tswana, or Kgalagadi in Botswana). There is also restricted bilingualism in Afrikaans, particularly in Namibia.

Internal language change in the Khoe group involves the replacement in some dialects of certain click consonants with acoustically similar non-clicks; a voicing contrast between stops (for example, d vs. t, or g vs. k) has been reinterpreted in Khoekhoegowab as a tonal contrast. In some Khoe varieties, the masculine, feminine, and common gender suffixes found on Khoekhoegowab nouns are incomplete and may even be omitted. In the Tuu group, !Xoon has developed a unique noun class and concordial system in which various words in a sentence must bear a suffix that shows agreement with the class of governing noun.

Historically, some Khoesan languages have had a considerable impact on the phonologies and lexicons of certain Bantu languages. The most dramatic and best documented case involves the South African language Xhosa, the phonology and lexicon of which were extended under the influence of Khoe languages some 500–700 years ago. Other Bantu languages showing varying degrees of Khoesan linguistic influence are Zulu (South Africa), Sotho (Lesotho), Gciriku and Yeyi (Botswana), and Mbukushu, Kwangali, Fwe and Mbalan'we (Namibia).

See also **Language; Linguistics and the Study of Africa; Linguistics, Historical.**

BIBLIOGRAPHY

Batibo, Herman M., and Joseph Tsonope, eds. *The State of Khoesan Languages in Botswana.* Gaborone, Botswana: Tasalls Publishing and Books for the Basarwa Languages Project, 2000.

Greenberg, Joseph H. *The Languages of Africa.* Bloomington: Indiana University Press, 1963.

Güldemann, Tom. "Reconstruction through 'De-construction': The Marking of Person, Gender, and Number in the Khoe Family and Kwadi." *Diachronica* 21, no. 2 (2004): 251–306.

Hastings, Rachel. "Evidence for the Genetic Unity of Southern Khoesan. Khoisan: Syntax, Phonetics, Phonology, and Contact." *Cornell Working Papers in Linguistics* 18 (2001): 225–246.

Miller-Ockhuizen, Amanda, and Bonny Sands. "!Kung as a Linguistic Construct." *Language and Communication* 19, no. 4 (1999): 401–413.

Traill, Anthony. *Khoesan Languages. Language in South Africa*, ed. Raj Mesthrie. Cambridge, U.K.: Cambridge University Press, 2002.

Traill, Anthony, and Hirosi Nakagawa. *A Historical !Xóõ-G|ui Contact Zone: Linguistic and Other Relations. The State of Khoesan Languages in Botswana*, ed. H. Batibo and J. Tsonope. Gaborone, Botswana: Tasalls Publishing and Books for the Basarwa Languages Project, 2000.

Vossen, Rainer. *Die Khoe-Sprachen. Ein Beitrag zur Erforschung der Sprachgeschichte Afrikas.* Cologne, Germany: Köppe, Rüdiger, Verlag, 1997.

ANTHONY TRAILL
REVISED BY BONNY SANDS

MALAYO-POLYNESIAN

The term "Malayo-Polynesian" refers to one of the main subgroups of the Austronesian family of languages. The other subgroups are Atayalic, Bunun, East Formosan, and Formosan. Malayo-Polynesian was earlier used to refer to all languages in the Austronesian family of languages. The Malayo-Polynesian subgroup includes 1,000 to 1,250 languages spoken on a wide range of Indian Ocean and Pacific Ocean from Madagascar in the west to Easter Island in the east. In terms of number of languages it is second only to the Niger-Congo group of languages. Following the work of R. A. Blust, in 1993 Andrew Pawley and Malcolm Ross

indicated that the Malayo-Polynesian subgroup consists of two main groups of languages: western Malayo-Polynesian and central/eastern Malayo-Polynesian. *Ethnologue* distinguishes a much larger number of groups including Bali-Sasak, Barito, and central/eastern Malayo-Polynesian.

In both classifications western Malayo-Polynesian languages/Barito languages include the languages of the Philippines, Malaysia, western Indonesia, and the Malagasy languages of Madagascar, the only African languages in the subgroup. According to Blust, Pawley, and Ross, central Malayo-Polynesian includes the languages of eastern Indonesia except Halmahera. The eastern Malayo-Polynesian languages include two further subgroups: Halmahera and the languages of western New Guinea and Oceanic languages (the eastern Malayo-Polynesian languages of the Pacific islands). Because of the diversity of the Malayo-Polynesian languages spoken in the Philippines, it is often assumed that this was the dispersal center for the languages of the group, although it is more frequently suggested that the original immigrants to Madagascar came from Indonesia. In addition to Malagasy languages other well-known languages of the Malayo-Polynesian subgroup include Tagalog, as well as Indonesian, Hawaiian, and Fijian languages.

There has been considerable study of word order and of quantification in Malayo-Polynesian languages. The word orders: subject/verb/object, verb/subject/object and verb/object/subject are found among languages in this group. In the verb/object/subject languages of Malayo-Polynesian when the object is definite, the verb is generally passive.

Linguistic and archeological evidence indicates that speakers of what became Malagasy languages migrated from Southeast Asia between the seventh and thirteenth centuries. Unlike other Malayo-Polynesian languages, Malagasy languages include borrowings from Bantu languages as well as from French.

See also **Language; Linguistics and the Study of Africa.**

BIBLIOGRAPHY

Adelaar, K. A. "Malay Influence on Malagasy: Linguistic and Culture-Historical Implications." *Oceanic Linguistics* 28, no. 1 (1989): 1–46.

Pawley, Andrew, and Malcolm Ross. "Austronesian Historical Linguistics and Culture History." *Annual Review of Anthropology* 22 (1993): 425–459.

Randriamasimanana, Charles. "The Malayo-Polynesian Origins of Malagasy." In *From Neanderthal to Easter Island: A Tribute to and Celebration of the work of W. Wildried Schuhmacher Presented on the Occasion of His 60th Birthday*, ed. Neile A. Kirk and Paul J. Sidwell, pp. 26–43. Melbourne, Australia: Association for the History of Language, 1999.

Ross, Malcolm. "On the Origin of the Term 'Malayo-Polynesian.'" *Oceanic Linguistics* 35, no. 1 (1996): 143–145.

ANN BIERSTEKER

NIGER-CONGO

The Niger-Congo (or Niger-Kordofanian) language family contains an estimated 1,500 languages—about one-fifth of the world's languages—making it the largest language family in the world. There are about 400 million speakers of Niger-Congo languages. The name Niger-Congo is derived from the two major rivers in the region.

The Niger-Congo languages cover most of sub-Saharan Africa. The northern border of the family stretches along a line between Senegal in the west and Kenya in the east. In the extreme southern part of the continent, Niger-Congo languages are intermingled with languages from the Khoesan family. The large Bantu subgroup of Niger-Congo covers most of Africa south of the equator.

Niger-Congo languages with at least five million speakers each include Fufulde (found in western and Central Africa), Moore (Burkina Faso), Akan (Ghana), Igbo and Yoruba (Nigeria), Lingala and Luba (Democratic Republic of the Congo), Gikuyu (Kenya), Swahili (Kenya, Tanzania, and elsewhere), Nyanja (Malawi), Rwanda-Rundi (Rwanda and Burundi), Shona (Zimbabwe), and Xhosa and Zulu (South Africa).

LANGUAGE CLASSIFICATION

In *The Languages of Africa* (1963), Joseph H. Greenberg introduced the name Niger-Congo for a language family that included what had earlier been known as the Western Sudanic and Bantu language families. For the internal classification of Niger-Congo, he generally followed Diedrich Westermann (1927) in dividing his family into six branches. A comparison of the two classifications appears in Table 1.

Branches of Niger-Congo compared with Western Sudanic

Greenberg (1963)	Westermann (1927)
West Atlantic	West Atlantic Group
Mande	Mandingo Languages
Gur	Gur Languages
Kwa (including Togo Remnant)	Kwa Languages
Benue-Congo	Togo Remnant Languages
Adamawa-Eastern	Benue-Cross Group (not included)

Table 1.

Greenberg made four major changes to Westermann's classification. He added Fufulde (Fula, Peul) to the West Atlantic branch, grouped specifically with Wolof and Serer. He included Westermann's Togo Remnant languages with Kwa and included the whole of Bantu within Benue-Congo; the change of name from Benue-Cross was intended to emphasize the southward extension of Niger-Congo that results from the change. Finally, Greenberg added the Adamawa-Eastern (=Adamawa-Ubangi) branch that had not been considered by Westermann. After some initial controversy over the position of Bantu, these changes were all generally accepted by the 1980s.

Greenberg originally classified Kordofanian as a separate language family. In 1963, he treated it as a coordinate branch to Niger-Congo and named the resultant grouping Niger-Kordofanian.

Some major modifications of Greenberg's classification, and many corrections of detail, have been made in the light of the discussion aroused by his work and the greatly increased knowledge of African languages. An influential study by Patrick R. Bennett and Jan P. Sterk (1977), together with proposals by John Stewart (1976), resulted in a working consensus used in *The Niger-Congo Languages* (1989), edited by John Bendor-Samuel and Rhonda L. Hartell and summarized in Figure 1. Most of the changes in classification were proposed by Bennett and Sterk, but the terminology follows a pattern initiated by Stewart and developed in the Bendor-Samuel and Hartell work.

This classification differs from Greenberg's in several ways. Bennett and Sterk proposed an initial three-way branching of Mande, Kordofanian, and the remaining languages grouped together as

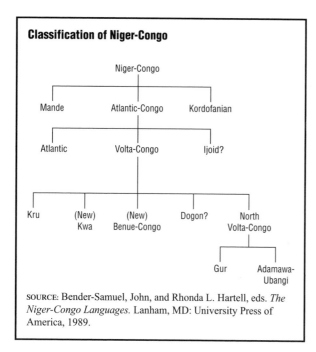

Classification of Niger-Congo

SOURCE: Bender-Samuel, John, and Rhonda L. Hartell, eds. *The Niger-Congo Languages.* Lanham, MD: University Press of America, 1989.

Figure 1.

Atlantic-Congo. The Bendor-Samuel and Hartell work further proposed a second, tentative three-way branching between Atlantic (=West Atlantic), Ijoid (=Ijo, included by Greenberg within Kwa, and Defaka), and the remaining languages, named Volta-Congo by Stewart. It is possible that Ijoid branches off at a lower point than Atlantic.

Within Volta-Congo, the Bendor-Samuel and Hartell volume proposed multiple branching:

a) Kru (included by Greenberg within Kwa, and suggested by Bennett and Sterk as part of North Volta-Congo);

b) (New) Kwa, differing from Greenberg's Kwa by the removal, proposed by Bennett and Sterk, of Ijo, Kru, and Eastern Kwa (essentially the languages of Nigeria that were classified by Greenberg as Kwa);

c) (New) Benue-Congo, differing from the Benue-Congo of Greenberg by the addition, proposed by Bennett and Sterk, of Eastern Kwa to the original Benue-Congo;

d) the removal of Dogon from Gur; and

e) the grouping of Gur and Adamawa-Ubangi (=Adamawa-Eastern) as North Volta-Congo.

More recent assessments of Niger-Congo have essentially retained the Bendor-Samuel and Hartell classification, with some minor speculative changes.

It has occasionally been suggested that Niger-Congo could be combined with Greenberg's Nilo-Saharan to form a larger grouping. This would correspond roughly to Westermann's Sudanic family, comprising Western Sudanic (=Niger-Congo) and Eastern Sudanic (=Nilo-Saharan). However, this larger unit has not been widely accepted.

DISPERSION

Most branches of Niger-Congo are found in western Africa, which has therefore generally been considered to be its homeland. In this region, the older branchings tend to be in the north and the younger ones in the south; presumably the drying up of the Sahara was one cause forcing southward movements of sections of speakers. The speakers of Ubangi have spread back toward the east through Central Africa, whereas the dramatic expansion of Bantu speakers from the Nigeria-Cameroon borderland into Central, eastern, and southern Africa has been extensively discussed by historians. This is thought to have occurred within the past 3,000 years or so.

BORROWINGS AND MODIFICATIONS

The most dramatic case of phonological borrowing is the borrowing of clicks from Khoesan by some of the Southern Bantu languages. Robert K. Herbert (1990) has suggested that Khoesan wives of Bantu speakers, culturally required to avoid words that resembled names of the dead, replaced the tabooed terms with words from their first language, where clicks were common. Their children grew up speaking the Bantu language of their fathers but replaced certain words with words of Khoesan origin that contained clicks. Another case of phonological borrowing is the labiodental flap. This sound likely originated in the Adamawa-Ubangi branch of Niger-Congo and was borrowed extensively into Chadic and Central Sudanic.

Studies of lexical borrowings between Niger-Congo languages and their neighbors, including Songhay and Chadic, have often been inconclusive because cultural words in particular tend to have a crosslinguistic distribution within a geographical area, so that it is frequently impossible to determine which is the donor and which is the recipient language.

A few Niger-Congo languages have been simplified in structure as the result of being adopted as a lingua franca. Examples include the Bantu language Swahili spoken in East Africa that has lost its tones; Tuba (Kituba), a Kongo-based Creole spoken in the Democratic Republic of the Congo; Fanagolo, a Xhosa-based pidgin spoken in South Africa; and the Ubangi language Sango, a Ngbandi-based Creole spoken in central Africa.

NOTABLE LINGUISTIC FEATURES

Widespread phonological features of Niger-Congo include the common use of labialvelar stops and vowel harmony systems based on the expansion or contraction of the pharynx, often referred to as Advanced Tongue Root (ATR). Somewhat less common are implosive stops, the labiodental flap, and nasalized vowels.

Most Niger-Congo languages have tone systems, in which distinctions between lexical items (or grammatical constructions) are made solely by differences in pitch. Systems with two or three level tones are most common. The feature of downstep is common, in which the pitch of a high tone is lower than a previous high tone because of an intervening low tone. The pitch of a high tone may also be lowered by a preceding depressor consonant, usually a voiced obstruent. The tone system of many eastern Bantu languages has evolved into a pitch-accent system, which has a single high tone per word.

The most outstanding morphological feature of Niger-Congo is the occurrence of a noun class system with concord. Bantu languages provide the clearest examples. Typically, the nouns are divided into a number of classes, each of which is marked by a prefix. The prefix changes to mark the plural of the noun: e.g., in Swahili *ki-tabu* (book), *vi-tabu* (books). Other words in the sentence that agree with the noun show a concord prefix: e.g., *ki-tabu ki-zuri* (a good book), *vi-tabu vi-zuri* (good books). Almost all branches of Niger-Congo either have such a system or show signs of having had one previously. Some branches, including Mande, Ijoid, Kru, and North Volta-Congo have suffixes rather than prefixes. Verbs often show a system of verbal extensions that occur as suffixes to the verbs and modify the meaning and often the number of arguments (such as subject, direct object) of the verb root; typical verb forms expressed by extensions convey causative, reciprocal, separative, and benefactive notions.

In syntax, most Niger-Congo languages have subject-verb-object word order, though Ijoid and Mande languages show full and partial subject-object-verb order, respectively. The occurrence of a series of verbs in a single clause, sharing a common subject and tense, and not linked by the word "and," is extremely widespread.

See also **Linguistics, Historical; Linguistics and the Study of Africa.**

BIBLIOGRAPHY

Bendor-Samuel, John, and Rhonda L. Hartell, eds. *The Niger-Congo Languages.* Lanham, MD: University Press of America, 1989.

Bennett, Patrick R., and Jan P. Sterk. "South Central Niger-Congo: A Reclassification." *Studies in African Linguistics* 8 (1977): 241–273.

Gordon, Raymond G., ed. *Ethnologue: Languages of the World*, fifteenth edition. Dallas, TX: SIL International, 2005.

Greenberg, Joseph H. *The Languages of Africa.* Bloomington: Indiana University Press, 1963.

Gregersen, Edgar A. "Kongo-Saharan." *Journal of African Linguistics* 4 (1972): 46–56.

Herbert, Robert K. "The Sociohistory of Clicks in Southern Bantu." *Anthropological Linguistics* 32 (1990): 295–315.

Olson, Kenneth S. "On Niger-Congo Classification." In *The Bill Question*, ed. Howard I. Aronson, et al, 153–190. Bloomington, IN: Slavica, 2006.

Stewart, John M. *Towards Volta-Congo Reconstruction (Inaugural Lecture).* Leiden, the Netherlands: University Press, 1976.

Stewart, John M. "The Potential of Proto-Potou-Akanic-Bantu as a Pilot Proto-Niger-Congo, and the Reconstructions Updated." *Journal of African Languages and Linguistics* 23 (2002): 197–224.

Westermann, Diedrich. *Die westlichen Sudansprachen und ihre Beziehungen zum Bantu.* Berlin: de Gruyter, 1927.

Williamson, Kay, and Roger Blench. "Niger-Congo." In *African Languages: An Introduction*, ed. Bernd Heine and Derek Nurse. Cambridge, U.K.: Cambridge University Press, 2000.

KAY WILLIAMSON
REVISED BY KENNETH S. OLSON

NILO-SAHARAN

Nilo-Saharan is one of the four generally accepted language phyla in Africa. Besides Niger-Kordofanian, Khoesan, and Afro-Asiatic, Nilo-Saharan is the most recent—and least widely accepted—of the established groupings. Joseph Greenberg proposed the new unit in 1963. Earlier, the languages concerned were considered to consist of twenty-two individual families, clusters, or isolated units without being grouped under a larger unit. Before Greenberg arrived at a Nilo-Saharan phylum, he had proposed three linguistic units: Eastern Sudanic, Central Sudanic, and Koma. In a second step Eastern and Central Sudanic were joined together with Temein, Teuso, Berta, and Kunama in a Macro-Sudanic branch that he renamed later as Chari-Nile. To this he joined Songhay, Saharan, Maba, For, and Koma.

The Nilo-Saharan languages extend from the shores of the Niger River in Mali (Songhay) eastward to the Lake Chad area (Saharan), to Dar Fur (e.g., Maba, For), and to the Nile River in Sudan, and southward to Lake Victoria (Nilotic).

In addition to lexical agreement, Greenberg's criteria for the coherence of the Nilo-Saharan languages included similar personal pronouns, plural formatives, verbal extensions, and locative markers. A predominant feature is the nominal formative (Greenberg referred to it as "article") k, for example, Kanuri âm (people), kâm (person). Though Greenberg noted assumed lexical cognates, it should be admitted that the common lexical coherence within Nilo-Saharan is very limited and often not based on valid criteria, while lexical agreement in subgroups is apparent.

Greenberg's method was based on "mass comparison" (i.e., the comparison of surface forms in as many as possible languages of an assumed linguistic unit) and not the more reliable linguistic reconstruction. Though the latter might have revealed more accurate data, this would have hardly been possible at Greenberg's time of classification (1940s–1960s). Many then-existing linguistic analyses were too scanty to allow in-depth analyses. The branches of Nilo-Saharan according to Greenberg's 1963 classification are shown in Figure 1. The defunct Meroitic was also proposed to be a member of Nilo-Saharan though reliable data may not be sufficient to reach a conclusive decision.

There exists some controversy about the validity of the Nilo-Saharan phylum. Attempts to remove languages or language groups from Nilo-Saharan and link them with Afro-Asiatic or Niger-Kordofanian also continue.

In the past decades the Nilo-Saharan issue has been discussed at conferences. This has increased considerably the knowledge of individual languages and linguistic affiliations within the phylum. Influenced by the data presented and the discussions held at the conferences, M. Lionel Bender presented a proposal of Nilo-Saharan subclassification in 1995. Bender's classification differs from that of Greenberg in a decisive point. His model of linguistic relationship (see Figure 2) is not based on a straight hierarchic and genetic tree. By setting up a "core" and a "satellite" group as well as three outliers, Bender shows that areal features or contact

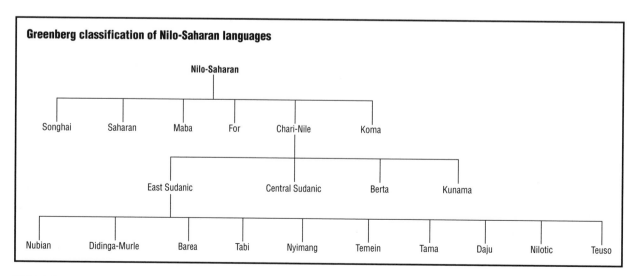

Greenberg classification of Nilo-Saharan languages

Figure 1.

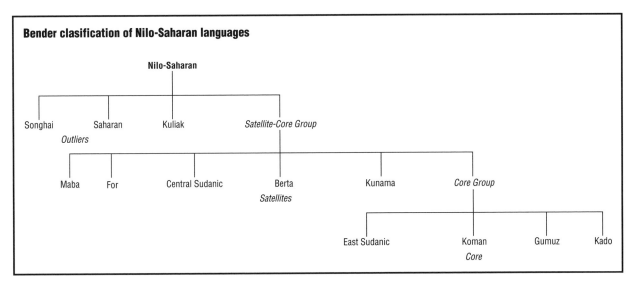

Bender clasification of Nilo-Saharan languages

Figure 2.

phenomena are also included in order to obtain a clearer picture of the Nilo-Saharan complex.

In 1993 Christopher Ehret proposed another Nilo-Saharan model (see Figure 3): Ehret proposed for Proto-Nilo-Saharan an age of more than ten thousand years by relating linguistic and archaeological data. Whether this tentative chronological placement will prove to be accurate is not easy to confirm. The relatively poor lexical agreement between Nilo-Saharan subunits suggests that many of the languages have had intensive linguistic contact with members of other linguistic affiliations. Areal typological features also had their impact on the phylum. On the other hand, structural features in Nilo-Saharan and its subgroups were more resistant than lexical similarity. Therefore, a classification attempt primarily based on lexical comparison may not, in the Nilo-Saharan context, reflect the actual age of linguistic groupings and separations.

The most controversial member of Nilo-Saharan is Songhay, being the westernmost language of the phylum. The language was also connected with Niger-Kordofanian and Afro-Asiatic. Around the turn of the twenty-first century, it was proposed that Songhay shares Nilo-Saharan Mande (Niger-Kordofanian) and Berber (Afro-Asiatic) features, thus being a creolized language.

The Saharan languages, too, have sometimes been connected with Afro-Asiatic, and even Niger-Kordofanian. However, scholars do not generally accept this view. One may rather assume that areal features have influenced the respective languages, so that the few existing similarities are a result of linguistic contact rather than genetic influence.

The total number of Nilo-Saharan languages comes to about 150. Only four of them are spoken by more than 1 million people: Songhay (1.2 million speakers in Niger, Mali, Burkina Faso, and Nigeria); Kanuri (Kanembu) (4 million; Saharan, Nigeria, Niger, Chad); Luo (1.7 million; Nilotic, Kenya, Tanzania); and Dinka (1.2 million; Nilotic, Sudan). The documentation of Nilo-Saharan languages varies. Nilotic, Saharan languages (especially Kanuri) and Songhay have a longer research tradition. For other languages research has increased since thet late twentieth century—for example, in the cases of Maba and For—while for a greater number of languages a good documentation is still lacking.

Robert Nicolai maintains a general Nilo-Saharan concept. However, he distances himself from a predominantly genetic concept. In his 2003 work he proposed a loose unit, in which contact phenomena play a greater part.

The concept of Nilo-Saharan is still vague and sometimes diffuse. However, the discussion of the subject after Greenberg's proposal in 1963 led to an intensified consideration of the issue. Extensive research in Nilo-Saharan linguistics since the mid-twentieth century provided a clearer picture on the structure of individual languages in specific and on the

Ehret classification of Nilo-Saharan languages

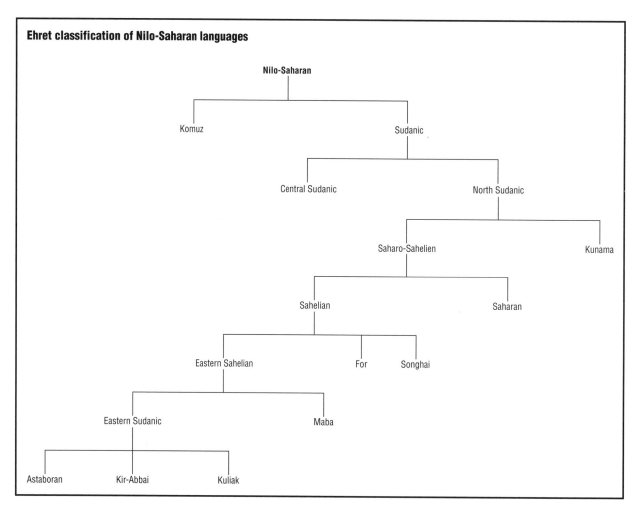

Figure 3.

status and validity of Nilo-Saharan in general. The initial criticism of Greenberg's new phylum receded continuously as evidence in favor of Nilo-Saharan became greater. While many believed Nilo-Saharan to be a remnant group which could not be affiliated with the other, more established, phyla, it became over the past years increasingly a reality, though the internal classification may still be puzzling.

One of the problems in tackling the Nilo-Saharan phenomenon was a methodological one. It has become evident that historical reconstruction may not be the only approach to understand the Nilo-Saharan complex. Many of the languages were exposed to speakers of languages with different linguistic affiliations (Afro-Asiatic, Niger-Kordofanian). Mutual linguistic influence may have taken place over a long period of time. This has led to a large amount of diversity, on the one hand, and on the

other to a considerable amount of structural and conceptual retention of linguistic features over the long period of common membership.

See also **Language; Linguistics and the Study of Africa.**

BIBLIOGRAPHY

Bender, M. Lionel. "Nilo-Saharsn." In *African Languages: An Introduction*, ed. Bernd Heine and Derek Nurse. Cambridge, U.K.: Cambridge University Press, 2000.

Ehret, Christopher. "Nilo-Saharans and the Saharo-Sudanese Neolithic." In *The Archaeology of Africa: Food, Metals, and Towns*, ed. Thurstan Shaw, Paul Sinclair, Bassey Andah, and Alex Okpoko. London: Taylor and Francis, 1993.

Ehret, Christoper. *A Historical-Comparative Reconstruction of Nilo-Saharan.* Köln, Germany: Rüdiger Köppe, 2001.

Greenberg, Joseph H. "The Languages of Africa." *International Journal of American Linguistics* 29, no. 1 (1963).

Nicolai, Robert. *La force des choses ou l'épreuve 'nilo-saharienne.'* Cologne, Germany: Rüdiger Köppe, 2003.

Tucker, Archibald N., and M. A. Bryan. *The Non-Bantu Languages of North-Eastern Africa.* New York: Oxford University Press, 1956.

NORBERT CYFFER

SURROGATES

For ages talking instruments were used in large areas of western and central Africa to transfer messages in surrogate languages based on verbal utterances in spoken languages. Different from drum signalling restricted to convey coded messages, drum languages, similar to other aural surrogate languages, can beat out messages that cover almost any situation in social life.

Surrogate languages are generally intended to stimulate or guide social action or social behavior by the transmission of messages and announcements (warnings, alarms). In African surrogate languages there is an emphasis on names as well as on kinship affiliations due to their function as media for the announcement of funerals and other social events. Technically speaking a chief function of surrogate languages is to supplement oral reporting in situations where the voice would be too feeble or where information is better conveyed by instrumental sounds than by normal speech.

While any sound-producing instrument may be used for communicating messages, only a few types of instruments have been actually used for that purposes: aerophones (flutes, trumpets, whistles), double bells, membranophones (drums), and idiophones (slit drums or telephone drum). Among these drums, slit drums have been the most popular and the most widely used talking instruments in Africa.

From a technical point of view, the latter message-sending logs are not drums at all, since they do not have a thin skin or membrane that vibrates when they are beaten. Instead, the entire log vibrates like a big cylindrical gong, so musicologists call this type of instrument a slit gong.

Communicating messages by means of drums and gongs was so effective that in many places colonial administrators engaged drummers for their own communicative purposes, in particular when they wanted to get the immediate attention of many listeners. Most members of linguistic groups had at least some comprehensive competence whereas the production of messages by drumming or whistling was normally carried out by specialists. The tonal quality of most African languages is of great assistance in this regard; that is, the talking instruments usually imitate and transmit the tones, phonemic stresses, and number of syllables in the utterance. Ambiguities due to shared tone figurations of spoken texts constitute a common limit of surrogate languages.

With the advent of modern mass media, radio, television, and telephone, talking drums lost their function as the main media of mass communication, in particular in urban areas. In some regions, however, they still play an important role in rural communities. In Ghana, for example, they are still used during annual festivals and funeral ceremonies of important people in the community. They are also used to broadcast the praises of chiefs, to send messages of condolence, and to entertain.

While aural surrogate languages are almost completely replaced by modern media, courses for playing talking drums are increasingly offered all over the Western world. The wide distribution of such courses indicates that drum language is a highly attractive subject. Given that talking by means of drums or gongs requires a high competence in the underlying spoken language, it is hardly conceivable that students can acquire a "speaking" competence that would allow for the communication of more complex content than signals. In fact, talking drums and gongs now serve as musical instruments.

See also **Media; Musical Instruments.**

BIBLIOGRAPHY

Nketia, J. H. Kwabena. "Surrogate Languages of Africa." In *Current Trends in Linguistics,* Vol. 7: *Linguistics in Sub-Saharan Africa,* ed. Jack Berry et al. The Hague: Mouton, 1971.

Sebeok, Thomas A., and Donna Jean Umiker-Sebeok, eds. *Speech Surrogates: Drum and Whistle Systems.* The Hague: Mouton, 1976.

HELMA PASCH

LANGUAGES: BANTU. *See* **Languages: Niger-Congo.**

LAW

This entry includes the following articles:

OVERVIEW

African law consists of a complex set of institutions, documents, and practices, some of them modern, some old and of long standing. A guide to African law online with multinational references can be found on the Web under the title Law Library of Congress (http://www.loc.gov/index.html). There are many other Web sources, among them the Law of Africa Collection (http://www.up.ac.za/), providing law reports and legislation, and the Journal of African Law (http://journals.cambridge.org), published by Cambridge University Press.

A sketch of the general structure of African law follows here. To begin with the modern sector at the highest level: the general principles of international law apply, but particularly pertinent to Africa, there are the rules of the African Union, an organization established in 2001 to which all the states of Africa belong. It is pledged to promoting peace and economic development, while simultaneously being committed to the principles of domestic sovereignty and non-intervention. The African Union outlined ambitious projects at its inception, but its effectiveness has, along with other problems, been plagued by a lack of funds.

There are many multilateral organizations, treaties, conventions, and declarations pertaining to Africa. A comprehensive list can be found on the Web, but some of them will be named here. For example, there are the treaty establishing the African Economic Community; the African Development Bank; and the West African Economic and Monetary Union. All of these are legally binding on the signatories.

Leaving the international level, there are, at the national level, many formal sources of law. Each of the more than fifty African states has a constitution. These constitutions tend to use the law of the ex-colonial power as a model. In addition, all the countries have national legislation, decisions of the courts, local ordinances, religious law (mostly Islamic law), and, particularly pertinent to rural areas, so-called customary law. In most countries there is legislation pertaining to everything from banking law to labor law, from family law to business law, from legislation on national resources to human rights. Much of this modern law is analogous in form to that found in the ex-colonial countries. However, its application is uneven.

It should also be acknowledged here that there are a few areas of Africa in which there is so much collective violence that it would be difficult to conceive of these places as governed by law at all (parts of the Congo, and the Western Sudan). There are also several countries in which the judiciary has no independence, and the heads of state control the courts and the parliament.

The formal system of African courts that exists in each polity is one location where legal rules are stated and enforced, and disputes are settled. However, there are other sites of official enforcement: the domains of government officials, administrative bureaus, police, and, in some areas, of military personnel. Generally those in urban areas resort to the national official system. In rural areas there are local authorities, some designated by the central government, and some others who owe their positions to the customs of the communities in which they serve.

To understand the bi-modal content of African law in the early twenty-first century, modern and customary, one needs to know something of African history. All African states were once ruled by colonial governments and generally achieved their independence in the 1960s. Colonial law tended to be modeled on the domestic law of the ruling country, with significant emendations adapted to local exigencies. Some of this body of law has been continued in the law of the independent states. Also, during the colonial period, the existence of local customary law was usually officially recognized by the government, and in postcolonial rural areas, it remains in force whether officially recognized or not.

Customary refers to indigenous African legal rules, procedures, institutions, and ideas. Although the label is sometimes applied retrospectively to pre-colonial customs, the importance of the idea of an African customary law came into its own during the colonial period and continues to have significance in post-independence legal systems. Thus, since the nineteenth century, administrative policy concerns have led governments to recognize the existence of local, ethnic-group legal practices. These, though often alluded to as traditional, are generally deeply transformed versions of earlier arrangements.

The conception of an indigenous, culturally specific local law draws a sharp line between the official system of the central state, its laws and ordinances (including, for example, elements of English common law introduced into Anglophone countries; of Roman, Dutch, and English law into South Africa; of French codes into Francophone countries), and those enforceable practices that supposedly had their source in African cultural tradition. Distinctions drawn according to source did not, however, result in the total separation of state from customary systems. Such local systems were both recognized and partially incorporated into national ones in Anglophone and Francophone countries. In various ways, the governments in both allowed customary law to be invoked in and enforced by courts set up by the central government. Legal tradition was radically transformed in this process of accommodation.

By no means were all local customs allowed to continue. For example, the practice of slavery and trials for witchcraft were forbidden. Moreover, the extensive precolonial jurisdiction of chiefs and other local political authorities over the persons, labor, and resources of their subjects, was severely curtailed. In Anglophone countries, the legal theory that selected what was to be preserved and what was to be eliminated held that customary practices were allowed to continue as law (in both colonial and postcolonial periods), as long as they were not repugnant to natural justice, morality, or incompatible with written law. The wording of this repugnancy clause varied only slightly among Anglophone countries.

In Francophone countries, local practice was not as directly made official because it was not codified and hence did not qualify as law in the official system. However, oral *droit coutumier* (customary law) was

nevertheless recognized to exist and also was applied to native affairs in officially recognized tribunals. Thus there is a marked distinction of formal theory between Francophone and Anglophone countries in the official treatment of customary law. This is revealed partly in the extent and style of official recognition of customary laws, and partly in the effect of special legal doctrines, such as legal theories regarding the domain of the state and its regulatory and property interests in land and other resources, postulates about the nature of village and community organization, and the like.

Despite the considerable changes wrought by the establishment of central states, colonial and then independent, a kind of fiction continued that local rules and institutions, to the extent that they were not European in form, were ancient traditional arrangements that had endured unchanged. Both African peoples and central governments had a stake in maintaining this static-traditionalist conception. Local communities made such claims in order to legitimize their monopoly of control over certain matters in and out of local courts. National governments often affirmed those claims to exclusivity that were founded on tradition for different reasons. Colonial and successor governments were often forced to recognize that large areas of social activity were not within their effective administrative reach. Thus, it has often been expedient for governments to decide that, where local practice does not impinge negatively on state interests, local controls should prevail. Consequently, there has been a frequent convergence of local and state attitudes about affirming the modern validity and utility of tradition.

Contrary to what was once imagined about the static quality of so-called traditional systems, there is strong evidence that local juridical ideas and practices were, and are, continuously in the process of change. The dearth of written records and the immense amount of local cultural, political, and economic variation in Africa have meant that the specific tracing of many of these transformations has often been difficult. However, wherever the history is known, it is clear that the context and often the content and meaning of local practice have changed considerably, whatever the local claims that tradition is being upheld.

In the Anglophone and Francophone settings, it was one thing to officialize customary law procedurally by allowing some of it to seep into court practice. It was another to ascertain what the content of local custom may in fact be. Periodically, in colonial Francophone Africa, there were plans to record on paper the essence of local custom, to transpose the principles of custom into code-like lists of rules—rendered, of course, in French. One notion that impelled some of this work was that ultimately, by comparing the customary laws of many peoples and abstracting their common features, a uniform code of customary law might be devised, one that would be simplified and somewhat tailored to fit the assimilationist aims of the colonial state.

The magnitude of the fact-gathering task; its contradictory methods and objectives that included paying attention to particular variations in order to produce standardization; and the difficulty of reducing active, nuanced processes into simplified lists of rules ultimately defeated most of these projects. However, the process did produce a huge collection of documents. Meanwhile, colonial courts in the Francophone areas had decisions to make. They were conscious of the existence of local custom but, where they saw fit, tended to produce judgments and rulings consonant with their own notion of the direction of progress. Thus, the effort to ascertain and conform to local ideas did not always have the first priority.

After independence, the goal of codifying customary rules was abandoned in the Francophone countries. In general, Francophone African countries have considered the adoption of variants of French codes to be the most desirable course for state legal systems. The abrogation of local custom was and is seen as progressive. This notion that progress and juridical Frenchification are identical has been strong, probably because the formal system in which the African jurists of these countries have been trained is the French one. Nevertheless, the reality is that some elements of local customary practice persist almost everywhere in rural Francophone Africa. These dominant local customary practices are clearly distinguishable from state law, but they are not necessarily traditional in the historical sense, though they are often legitimized by claims to that effect.

In Anglophone countries, local custom was ascertained through a variety of techniques similar to those used in the Francophone lands. Colonial officers were regularly exhorted to write down the rules of customary law in their districts, and some did so. Some anthropologists made similar compendiums. Intermittently, there was talk about recording all native laws. This (unrealized) ambition continued for some years after independence (see, for example, the *Restatement of African Law* monograph series). In this interpretation, law is equated with lists of rules. It was well known to those supporting this strategy that the procedures, the principles, the ideas, and the subtleties of the social-political milieu were going to be lost in the process of producing rule lists. No matter; rules were what courts were accustomed to applying. Converting indigenous systems into rules would modernize those systems and make them more usable in the courts. Handbooks and monographs were produced to this end.

Where no statements of the local rule system were encapsulated in written form, there were more modest techniques for ascertaining what the relevant native law was in relation to a particular case. It became a standard practice in Anglophone and Francophone countries—indeed, a prescribed one in customary law cases—for the court to engage two local laymen, called assessors, to sit with the judge and advise him on matters of customary or Islamic law.

What has been said thus far should be understood to apply only to civil law. In African countries, criminal law is normally in the exclusive jurisdiction of the state, and there is generally no officially recognized criminal customary law. Nevertheless, there have been many instances in which customary ideas about crime have had to be taken into account in the courts.

Though neither colonial law nor colonial juridical systems persisted intact after independence, there were, at least for a time, substantial continuities in many matters. This was particularly true of the attitude toward customary law and the prevailing tendency to try to domesticate it to contemporary ends. In Tanzania, for example, the idea of distilling a standardized statutory version of family customary law from the practices of many peoples was brought to fruition. A standardized customary law for patrilineal peoples and another for matrilineal peoples were drafted and adopted as models.

Instead of directly being made national law, these were offered to the various regions of the country for local adoption and implementation. Needless to say, in content this law was not simply an essence of local practices, officializing the lowest common denominator. It was also shaped by government policy regarding what was deemed to be desirable. Moreover, in Tanzania all land was nationalized, and special land courts were established to deal with conflicts over the possession and beneficial use of land. These courts were enjoined to follow socialist principles in making their decisions. The practical bearing of these principles on land court cases, and on transactions entered into under customary law, raises questions about local practice that have not, as of the early twenty-first century, been fully studied. Other Anglophone countries did not follow the Tanzanian model, but made other legislative changes that deeply affected local communities and altered the ambience within which customary law operated. Kenya, for example, adopted a system of land registration.

Thus, major differences of legal policy exist from period to period and from country to country. As a result, any attempt to understand the nature of formal law and customary law in a particular African setting is no small undertaking. It requires considerable attention to historical change, not just in the official system, but also in the cultural, economic, and political contexts in which local transactions, understandings, and commitments are and have been generated.

See also **Colonial Policies and Practices; Slavery and Servile Institutions; Witchcraft; Women: Women and the Law.**

BIBLIOGRAPHY

Aderinwale, Ayodele, ed. *Corruption, Democracy and Human Rights in East and Central Africa*. Entebbe, Uganda: Africa Leadership Forum. 1994.

An-Naim, Abdullahi A., ed. *Cultural Transformation and Human Rights in Africa*. London: Zed Books, 2002.

Anderson, James. *Islamic Law in Africa*. London: Frank Cass, 1970.

Chanock, Martin. *Law, Custom, and Social Order: The Colonial Experience in Malawi and Zambia*. New ed. edition. Portsmouth, NH: Heinemann, 1998.

Cohen, David William, and E. S. Atieno Odhiambo. *Burying SM: The Politics of Knowledge and the Sociology of Power in Africa*. Portsmouth, NH, 1992.

Cohen, Stanley. "Bandits, Rebels, or Criminals: African History and Western Criminology." *Africa: Journal of the International African Institute* 56, no. 4 (1986): 468–483.

Journal of African Law 28, nos. 1–2 (1984). Special number, *The Construction and Transformation of African Customary Law*.

Le Roy, Étienne, and Mamadou Wane. "A formation des droits non étatiques." In *Encyclopédie juridique de l'Afrique*. Volume 1, *L'état et le droit*. Dakar, Senegal, and Abidjan, Côte d'Ivoire, 1982.

Moore, Sally Falk. *Social Facts and Fabrications: "Customary" Law on Kilimanjaro, 1880–1980*. Cambridge, U.K.: Cambridge University Press, 1986.

Mwalimu, Charles. "A Bibliographic Essay of Selected Secondary Sources on the Common Law and Customary Law of English-Speaking Sub-Saharan Africa." *Law Library Journal* 80, no. 2 (1988): 241–289.

Restatement of African Law. Monograph series. London, 1968–1973.

Vanderlinden, Jacques. *Bibliographie de droit africain, 1947–1966*. Brussels, 1972. *Supplement, 1977–1980*. Brussels, 1981.

Vanderlinden, Jacques. *Les systèmes juridiques africains*. Paris: Presses Universitaires de France, 1983.

Vanderlinden, Jacques. *Bibliographies internationales de la doctrine juridique africaine*. Moncton, NB: Editions du Centre international de la common law en français, 1992.

Wilson, Richard *The Politics of Truth and Reconciliation in South Africa*. Cambridge, U.K.: Cambridge University Press, 2001.

Zoethout, Carla; M. E. Pietermaat-Kros; and P. W. C. Akkermans; eds. *Constitutionalism in Africa*. Rotterdam, the Netherlands: Sanders Institut, 1996.

SALLY FALK MOORE

ANGLOPHONE CENTRAL AFRICA

An ideal and appropriate evaluation of a country's legal system is expected to take into account the historical, political and socioeconomic contexts underpinning the legal system. Such an analysis, it should be emphasized, must examine also factors that contribute to the validation and efficacy of the legal norms and processes in that society. In Central Africa, as in many other geographical regions, there are strong reasons for paying closer attention to such jurisprudential issues. Dualist legal traditions, drawing on legal norms from indigenous African customary law on the one hand, and the English common law on the other, characterize the legal systems of many Anglophone countries in Central Africa.

DUALISM OF THE LEGAL SYSTEM

Generally, dualism of legal systems in many Central African countries has resulted in part from the legacy of colonialism that, in turn, saw the introduction of the English common law in the former colonies. By contrast, African customary law focuses mainly on such areas as customary marriages, farming, general land use, and inheritance issues. These indigenous African laws have their roots in various tribal customs that pass from one generation to another. Conversely, much of the common law in the Anglo-Saxon world is influenced by English jurisprudence.

In spite of the circumstances under which the common law was introduced in Central Africa, whether by settlement, conquest, or cession, the change of sovereignty did not result in the disappearance of African customary laws. Customary law was being enforced by courts established by the British Administration as long as it was not repugnant to natural justice, equity, and good conscience, or was not incompatible, directly or by implication, with any piece of legislation in force at the time.

Some countries, such as Cameroon, have a convoluted system of legal traditions because of its complicated colonial past. Cameroon has two divergent foreign legal traditions that have historically struggled for supremacy over the each other. Prior to Cameroon attaining political independence, the country was under British and French colonial rule. As such, the country inherited a dual legal system, including parts of the Napoleonic Code and the English common law that was introduced in southern Cameroon. Even though common law and statutory law are generally recognized as the main sources of law in Cameroon, the majority of people, particularly in rural areas, still look to African traditional, local customs and norms when adjudicating or settling disputes.

The system did not change after the country's independence in 1960. Almost all legal institutions and administrative units in the English common law jurisdiction of Cameroon play host to customary law. The courts dealing with matters of African customary law rank at the level of the magistrate courts and are staffed with members who adjudicate disputes

according to local customs and traditions. A litigant who intends to appeal a decision of the customary court can apply to the High Court of Appeal. And, generally, the common law and statutory law will prevail over norms of African customary law in the event that there is a conflict between them.

TENURE DUALISM

During the rapid expansion of British influence in the first half of the twentieth century the colonial administration had little alternative but to work at local level with the powers in existence. Although Indirect Rule was presented as a virtue, it arose out of necessity. The official position of the British was that customary land rights should be respected, including the traditional land administration responsibilities of local leaders. At the end of 1950s, the nationalist movements and world opinion pressed for self-determination. This brought about political independence in many British colonies and protectorates.

Several studies on customary land tenure reveal important variations in tenure arrangements between the different territories, reflecting the ethnic origin of the population and the prevailing system(s) of land use. One common characteristic is the importance of community control over the means of subsistence. The basic issue is that colonial powers imported systems of common law and statute law for their own purposes, and operated them alongside the existing system(s) of customary law.

After independence, different countries in Central Africa have pursued different policies with regard to legal dualism. The colonial relegation of customary law to second-class status has usually been maintained. Constitutional developments in a number of countries have sought to create a domestic unitary system of laws in which statute and imported common law are paramount. Only recently have some countries formally recognized the integral role and equivalent status of customary law within such overarching legal frameworks.

The role of traditional chiefs in land administration has been a recurring issue. This has its roots in the colonial past. In his classic study, *The African Husbandman* (1965), William Allan (b. 1904) describes land tenure arrangements prevailing in customary areas of Zambia in the first half of the last century. The customary rules he describes are unexceptional. In Zambia, the country still provides the basic framework of customary land law for the majority of farmers. Allan's explanation draws on the work of Max Gluckman (1911–1975) among the Bantu-speaking peoples of Central Africa who explained that chiefs did not allot the land directly to their subjects who used it. Rather, land was allocated to subchiefs who in turn allotted shares to village headmen. At the village level, the headman allotted land to heads of subsections or heads of families, and they distributed land to their dependants.

Gluckman refers to this aspect of the land tenure system as estates of administration. Shared estates of cultivation belonged to a particular tribe. The same principle applied to traditional grazing. These rights were not held at the discretion of the chief or headman. The chief or headman was required to provide residential, arable, and grazing land for all his subjects. A tribesman was entitled to land without giving anything for it, but he had a duty to protect and conserve it. Although the concept of individual absolute ownership was unknown, the rights to residential land were exclusive and permanent. The holder could protect his rights by civil action against any person, even against the chief, except when the land needed to be acquired in the public interest. In this case the chief would allocate an equivalent piece of land in compensation.

On attaining independence, Central African governments have found it convenient to hold on to this legacy of the colonial system. Even in Botswana, which has a reputation for being more enlightened in these matters, it was not until 1992 that the government recognized that compensation for customary land acquired for public purposes must be based on market-related value if comparable alternative land were not available:

> The low compensation for Tribal land is the result of policy, influenced by the mode of acquiring such land as well as the fact that the land is not held in absolute ownership. But this has now led us to the crisis that we find ourselves in, where excessive artificial intervention in the operation of market forces led to a collapse of tribal land administration....
> The Government has considered the long term corrupting effects of excessive artificial suppression of Tribal land values and has decided in principle that Tribal land should be covered by both the Constitution and the Acquisition of

Property Act to enable landholders to receive compensation commensurate with the value of the land as dictated by market forces.

Any description of customary tenure arrangements, however brief, would be incomplete without reference to the rights of women in African traditional societies. The basic rule in patrilineal societies was that, whereas men gained rights to land through their lineage or clan, women gained access only through their husbands, or, in the case of women without husbands, fathers or brothers. Men would allocate some land to their wives at their own discretion. As women were usually responsible for providing food for the household, they tended to use the land received from their husbands or fathers for subsistence purpose and that prevented them from growing crops for sale. This principle has survived in many parts of rural Africa into the early twenty-first century. Land policies have been typically blind to the gendered nature of property and its consequences. For example, in the Zimbabwean case of *Magaya v. Magaya*, the Zimbabwean Supreme Court ruled that, because under customary law women are juveniles, a woman could not inherit her father's property even though she was named in his will. The Supreme Court ruled that customary law had precedence over the Constitution.

At independence, most African governments emphasized state control over land and other resources as an important tool to assert their power over local chiefs and to enable the governments to acquire land for development purposes. The idea was to disarm local chiefs of excessive powers which they have when dealing with land matters. Thus, policies of nationalization and the conversion of freehold to leasehold were rampantly and hurriedly introduced. But customary law regarding land tenure remained tenacious, despite the reforms to strengthen state control over customary land. Over time, governments have recognized that customary laws are often best placed to manage land directly, and that formal legal codes do not fit the diverse settings and associated customary systems.

More recently, land-related policies and legislation in Central Africa have embraced land tenure dualism in a more proactive and imaginative way. New laws have sought evolutionary approaches that allow customary law and practice to continue in land tenure and management, but provide clear and secure paths to more modern modes as people identify the need for them. Whereas land tenure and administration are integrated in single statutes, tenure dualism may be recognized as a resource rather than an obstacle in the changing livelihoods of the poor. That said, land reform is required to regularize land tenure that exists outside the legislative framework, especially in urban and periurban areas.

In Uganda, the Uganda Land Act of 1998 vested land in the citizens of Uganda, rather than the state, as it had previously done. It defined the different types of rights in land that may be held. It decreed that rights of customary ownership and lawful, bona fide occupancy would be recognized, even if not supported by a certificate of title. It set out the procedures that must be pursued in order to formalize both customary ownership rights on former public land and rights of occupancy on *mailo* land, through the acquisition of certificates of title. It also specified the procedures that must be followed in order to transform these rights into freehold tenure. Under that statute, the procedures for the acquisition of land title and the resolution of land disputes in Uganda are not obligatory. In other words, no one is compelled to acquire a land title in order to enjoy legitimate possession of the land.

ACCESS TO JUSTICE

As far as Central African countries are concerned, the legal and judiciary systems are still grappling with serious issues of public accessibility and institutional effectiveness. A number of these problems are related to ethical, political, socioeconomic, and cultural factors. Many Central African legal systems face challenges, rendering access to justice pervasive for the majority.

Historically, external systems of values have been imposed and juxtaposed on the existing system, leading to changing patterns and approaches as regards the understanding of justice services delivery and access to justice. The adoption of common law has been packaged as a positive evolution that required the progressive adaptation of native institutions to modern conditions. The problem with this process is that it was never a result of consultation with the citizens, but rather an outcome of so-called institutions modernization imposed on Africa at independence.

CONCLUSIONS

In the late twentieth century, most countries in Central Africa experienced rapid population growth, slow economic development, and accelerated environmental degradation. Unresolved conflicts over land issues and other natural resources increasingly undermined the capacity of poor people to produce food. In the early twenty-first century, the poor and vulnerable are rarely able to defend themselves against the strong-arm tactics of powerful land grabbers. In some cases, customary land administration arrangements have fallen away but have not been replaced by satisfactory statutory arrangements. Rapidly growing urban populations are particularly vulnerable to the inefficiency of land tenure systems that still reflect tenure dualism introduced by colonial regimes and adopted by independent African states.

Recent years have seen an increased interest in the variety of cultures coexisting within a particular jurisdiction and a growing acknowledgement of the values found in pluralistic social structures. It becomes essential to examine the manner in which indigenous people can function in modern states, preserve their traditional customs, and simultaneously adapt aspects of their culture to the challenges posed by twenty-first century life. Whereas it was formerly assumed that these tribal frameworks were doomed to extinction, there has been a revival in their vitality, linked to recognition of their rights through the legal system.

See also **Kinship and Descent; Land: Tenure; Peasants; Urbanism and Urbanization; Women: Women and the Law.**

BIBLIOGRAPHY

Allan, William. *African Husbandman*. Westport, Connecticut: Greenwood Press, 1965.

Breitinger, Eckhard, ed. *African and Western Legal Systems in Contact*. Bayreuth, Germany: Bayreuth University, 1989.

Daniels, William C. Ekow *The Common Law in West Africa*. London: Butterworths, 1964.

Gluckman, Max. *Order and Rebellion in Tribal Africa*. London: Cohen & West, 1963.

Hutchison, Thomas W., ed. *Africa and Law*. Madison: University of Wisconsin Press, 1968.

Menski, Werner. *Comparative Law in a Global Context: The Legal Systems of Asia and Africa*. New York: Cambridge University Press, 2006.

Sheleff, Leon. *The Future of Tradition: Customary Law, Common Law, and Legal Pluralism.* London: F. Cass, 2000.

Woodman, Gordon R., and Obilade A.O., eds. *African Law and Legal Theory.* New York: New York University Press, 1995.

PATRICE TALLA TAKOUKAM

ANGLOPHONE EASTERN AFRICA

The contemporary laws of Anglophone eastern Africa are the products of three historical periods: precolonial, colonial, and postcolonial, each of which has made a distinctive contribution.

THE PRECOLONIAL PERIOD

In the long history of human settlement in the varied environments of eastern Africa, many different communities emerged with diverse sociopolitical and legal systems. Characteristic over much of the area were small-scale, egalitarian, stateless (chiefless) communities (such as the Gikuyu, Luo, and Langi), which maintained order without rulers, courts, or other formal legal apparatus and with minimal resort to organized force. Economic and social relations were regulated by flexible customs of land use and family relationships, upheld by social pressure, family heads, and elders. Extreme cases of intolerable antisocial conduct like dangerous witchcraft provoked ad hoc mechanisms of community response to expel or execute offenders. Distinctive patterns of custom characterised cattle-keeping societies like the Maasai, with intricate generational networks distributing authority by age ranking. Among the small bands of hunter-gatherers like the Hadza or Ik, the absence of any formalized authority showed that small-scale societies could exist apparently without law. In striking contrast, the ancient kingdoms of the interlacustrine area (such as Karagwe, Ankole, Bunyoro, and Buganda) evolved into highly organized bureaucratic states in which the power of the monarchs was balanced by that of queen-mothers, other senior functionaries, clan heads, and hierarchies of subordinate chiefs, all of whom held courts which settled disputes and enforced obedience to customary and enacted laws.

The religion and law of Islam was introduced at the coast and inland by Arabs who dominated trade in goods and slaves from the pre-Christian era.

From the tenth century CE, Persian settlers established an empire along the coast; inter-marriage with the indigenous communities resulted in the distinctive Swahili culture and language. Portuguese conquest of the coast was intermittent in the sixteenth and seventeenth centuries and did not endure north of Mozambique. Arab dominance was consolidated in the eighteenth century under the sultans of Oman (the Mazrui Arab rulers of Mombasa were not subdued until 1840). In 1832 the sultan moved his capital to Zanzibar, the center for international trade; diplomatic relations were established with, and extraterritorial jurisdiction granted to, the United States in 1833, Britain in 1839, and France in 1844.

THE COLONIAL PERIOD

Eastern Africa was under European colonial rule for a little more than the first sixty years of the twentieth century. European dominance of the mainland was foreshadowed when Germany and Britain defined their respective spheres of influence by the Berlin Agreement of 1886; despite his extensive territorial claims over the mainland, the sultan (who had not been consulted) was left with sovereignty over the islands of Zanzibar, Pemba, Lamu, and Mafia and over a coastal strip only ten miles wide.

Zanzibar was formally placed under British "protection" in 1890 and was administered as a protectorate by a British resident. From 1926 the resident was advised by appointed executive and legislative councils.

On the mainland rudimentary administration by the Imperial British East Africa Company preceded the establishment of the British East Africa Protectorate in 1895. In 1920 it was annexed to the dominions of the British Crown as Kenya Colony, although the narrow coastal strip remained under the sultan's sovereignty as the Kenya Protectorate.

The Uganda Protectorate was established in 1894 under an agreement between British representatives and chiefs representing the infant *kabaka* (king) of Buganda. The territory was gradually extended to include neighboring kingdoms and other areas. A further ill-considered agreement of 1900 introduced into Buganda a distorted form of registered freehold land tenure (*mailo* land), which caused great social and economic dislocation and legal confusion.

The German East Africa Protectorate was established in 1891, and German colonial law was introduced. During World War I British forces seized control from Germany, and in 1920 Britain accepted the League of Nations Mandate to administer what was renamed Tanganyika Territory. In 1946 it became a Trusteeship Territory, with Britain responsible to the United Nations for its administration.

Colonial rule had a decisive impact in establishing these territorial units, defining their boundaries, and creating their legal systems and laws. Within the overarching system of colonial government directed from the Colonial Office in London, which prescribed the basic laws, there was much diversity in the policies of local colonial governments, dominated by their respective governors.

The law of England—defined as "the common law, doctrines of equity, and statutes of general application"—was introduced as the basic law, although defined as it existed at different times for different territories: for Zanzibar (where the laws of Bombay, including English law, had been applied since 1884) and Kenya in 1897; Uganda in 1902; and Tanganyika in 1920. Judicial systems of the English type were set up and a unified legal profession of advocates was introduced; lawyers (immigrant Europeans or Asians) qualified overseas (in England or India), there being no local law school until the eve of independence; the first African lawyers qualified only in the final years of colonial rule. Under the "dual jurisdiction" in Zanzibar, Islamic law of the Ibathi and Shafi'i schools was the fundamental law, applied in Muslim courts; English law was applied by the British court.

For many subjects, the celebrated nineteenth-century "Indian" codes of law were adopted instead of uncodified English law. The Indian Penal Code 1860 was applied in Zanzibar (1867), the East Africa Protectorate (1897), Uganda (1902), and Tanganyika (1920). Many other "Indian" laws were introduced, including the Contract Act 1872, the Evidence Act 1872, the Codes of Civil and Criminal Procedure 1882, and the Succession Act 1865. These codes, broadly based on English legal principles, were comprehensive and had been designed for application in imperial India by colonial magistrates

and other officers who were not necessarily fully trained lawyers. Although it became official policy to replace these codes by legislation drafted to meet local needs and circumstances, the precedent of codification was generally followed. New Penal Codes, modeled on the Criminal Code of Nigeria and thus versions of the celebrated Queensland Criminal Code 1899, replaced the Indian Penal Code throughout East Africa in the 1930s; with few amendments, they continue in force. The other Indian codes have been replaced by enactments mainly based on the Indian models, although the Contract Act was replaced by the uncodified English common law of contract in Kenya (1960) and Uganda (1962).

English law was imposed only so far as it was applicable and subject to modification according to local circumstances. Thus, trial by jury, fundamental to English criminal trials, was omitted, except for the trial of Europeans in Kenya, in favour of trial by a judge advised by local assessors. The colonial governments routinely invoked powers of executive detention and deportation denied under peacetime laws of England. Colonial laws adopted some English legislation reforming the common law but mainly implemented the socioeconomic policies of the local colonial administration: local enactments imposing taxes, regulating access to land and liquor, and controlling labour were critical elements in colonial policy.

British colonial governments, following policies of indirect rule, relied upon traditional political authorities, especially chiefs, to conduct local administration under supervision. In formerly stateless societies chieftaincies—which had not previously existed—were constructed. A significant element of such policies was the recognition and application of African customary law, originally termed "native law and custom." Such law was mainly applied by the local native courts, later renamed "African" (in Tanganyika, "local") courts, exercising jurisdiction over Africans only. These courts were supervised by the district officers of the colonial administration, who could alter judgments on appeal or revision. The integration of these courts in unified judicial systems became official policy before independence, although for much of the colonial period African courts in Kenya and Tanzania formed separate systems, with final appeal to special courts that included administrative officers.

Customary laws were not applied where they were inconsistent with written laws or "repugnant to justice or morality," a doctrine that was seldom formally invoked. Customary laws were pliable and dynamic, evolving to reflect socioeconomic and political changes. Colonial rule brought many such changes: new administrative structures; economic innovations (new crops, the cash economy, and new urban centers); new types of education and religion; and others. Such factors propelled continuing changes in values, lifestyles, and customs. It has been questioned whether African customary law was truly either African or customary, or whether it was a colonial invention, molded by British administrators and their local collaborators as a convenient instrument of social control. In East Africa customary laws changed substantially under colonial rule but, in the largely untraceable processes of incremental adaptation, African responses to changing circumstances were probably more determinative than colonial policies.

It was partly because of the fluidity of customary law that, during the British colonial period, there were only occasional, individual attempts to compile and publish records of it, mainly by anthropologists or administrative officers. In German East Africa the administration supported a systematic inquiry into customary laws that was continued in Tanganyika under British rule. Islamic law, the fundamental law of Zanzibar, applied elsewhere as the personal law of Muslims (including immigrant Muslims from Asia) on such matters as marriage, divorce, and inheritance. Hindu family law was also recognized.

In Kenya land law was characterized by the expropriation of many indigenous communities to facilitate the alienation of large estates to European settlers, establishing the extensive upland areas known as the White Highlands. Resulting African land grievances fuelled the so-called Mau Mau rebellion of the 1950s, which provoked a vigorous military response and repressive emergency laws, including the extensive imposition of capital punishment for a variety of offences and mass detentions without trial. The effect was to accelerate decolonization.

The control of these contiguous territories by the same colonial power prompted efforts to coordinate the administrations and provide common services. Of special legal significance was the Court of Appeal for Eastern Africa, a regional institution dating from 1902. Cooperation was facilitated by the Conference of Governors from 1926 and the East African High Commission (1948–1961). Common services provided included railways, ports, harbors, postal services, currency, and income tax collection.

THE ERA OF INDEPENDENCE

East Africa gained independence from colonial rule in the early 1960s: Tanganyika in 1961; Uganda in 1962; and Zanzibar and Kenya in 1963. Zanzibar retained its own sovereign, the sultan; the other countries, following the Commonwealth pattern, became independent as monarchies under the British Crown but substituted local heads of state after one year. The elaborate independence constitutions, constructed through negotiation with nationalist leaders, proved ephemeral.

Tanganyika became a republic with an executive president in 1962. More significant change came when, following the revolution in Zanzibar that overthrew the sultan and constitution within weeks of independence, Tanganyika and Zanzibar merged by agreement in 1964 to form the United Republic of Tanzania (as it was named later in the year). Zanzibar retained considerable autonomy under the Articles of Union, which effectively established a quasi-federation. In 1965 Tanzania became a one-party state under a new constitution, albeit with two ruling parties, the Tanganyika African National Union (TANU) in Tanganyika and the Afro-Shirazi Party (ASP) in Zanzibar, until their union to form Chama Cha Mapinduzi (CCM) (Revolutionary Party) in 1977. A new constitution enacted then in the national language, Swahili, continues in force, much amended. The innovative electoral system gave voters a choice between party candidates, but the parliament—in which appointed members outnumbered elected members and Zanzibar was overrepresented—was weak, with party organs dominant.

Controversial emergency-type laws enacted to counter economic problems in the early 1980s provoked a vigorous reassertion of the rule of law, led by the judiciary. In 1984, with effect from 1988, a comprehensive constitutional bill of rights was adopted; the courts have applied it in many cases to invalidate legislation, government action, and rules of customary law. The Commission on Human Rights and Good Governance was established by constitutional amendment in 2000, replacing the less powerful Permanent Commission of Enquiry established in 1965 to investigate complaints of maladministration.

The most important constitutional amendment, in 1992, ended one-party rule in favor of a multiparty system. However, in three subsequent elections CCM candidates have won the presidency (each limited to two five-year terms) and, as the majority in the National Assembly, continued to form the government. The constitutions have thus given mainland Tanzania more than forty years of political continuity, initially under the respected leader Mwalimu (teacher) Julius Nyerere (president 1962–1985). Zanzibar participates in the government and parliament of Tanzania in respect of specified union matters, while retaining its own president, government, legislature, and judiciary, with authority over all other matters. The Zanzibar Constitution (1984) includes a comprehensive bill of rights but important amendments in 2002, expressly adopting the separation of powers, also require the government to take account of international human rights laws.

The unique quasi-federal relationship between mainland Tanzania and Zanzibar, with two governments and legislatures, gives rise to legal and political issues and has provoked continuing public debate, for example, concerning the scope of Zanzibar's autonomy and the proposal for a third government for the mainland; even the very continuance of the union had been questioned.

Uganda adopted a unique constitutional form in 1963, installing a ceremonial president elected by parliament for a five-year term from among the kings and other traditional or elected heads of the various districts. The independence constitution established a unique quasi-federation, granting a significant measure of autonomy to the kingdom of Buganda and minor powers to the three other southern kingdoms (Ankole, Bunyoro, and Toro). The inevitable election of the powerful *kabaka* of Buganda as the first president foreshadowed political conflict between him and the government led by the northerner Milton Obote as prime minister; the latter became executive president in 1966, after driving the *kabaka* into exile by attacking the royal palace, and continued in office under a new unitary constitution in 1967. Obote was ousted in turn by

military coup, and Idi Amin Dada became president in 1971; he was driven into exile in 1979 by military defeat following an invasion by Ugandan exiles with Tanzanian support.

Obote returned as president following elections in 1980, but continuing political and economic problems prompted his second overthrow in 1985 by the army, which in turn was defeated in the field by the National Resistance Movement (NRM) army led by Yoweri Museveni, who has been president since 1986. Under NRM leadership Uganda has been preoccupied with attempts to rebuild a shattered economy, infrastructure, and administration; to promote reconciliation (for example, by restoring three of the kings); and to design and implement a new Constitution, adopted in 1995. In a referendum in 2000 88 percent rejected multiparty democracy, voting to retain the no-party form of government. The NRM led by Museveni has remained dominant through successive elections.

The independence constitution of Kenya, hastily constructed to reassure minorities fearing domination by the veteran nationalist leader Jomo Kenyatta, as prime minister, his party, the Kenya African National Union (KANU), and his Gikuyu people, introduced a complex, quasi-federal *majimbo* system, which distributed power among the various regions. On the first anniversary of independence in 1964, constitutional amendments predictably abandoned the *majimbo* system, centralizing power around Kenyatta as executive president. The constitution, further amended subsequently, gave Kenya continuity of government under the dominance of KANU, with only two presidents in almost forty years: Kenyatta (1964–1978) was succeeded on his death by Daniel arap Moi (1978–2002). Kenya was a one-party state, de facto from 1969 and de jure by constitutional amendment in 1982. Although a multiparty system was restored for the 1992 and 1997 elections, KANU remained victorious; only in 2002, when President Moi retired, did KANU suffer defeat in elections for president and National Assembly. Fundamental constitutional reform proposed by an official commission awaits implementation.

The cooperation between these territories under colonial rule prompted proposals for federation between them as independence approached. The East African Common Services Organization

(1961–1967) continued the common services during negotiations for federation, which floundered on the rocks of independent sovereignties, internal problems, and political diversity; instead, the first East African Community was established by treaty in 1967 as a promising basis for economic integration. However, disagreements between the respective governments, especially after Amin seized power in Uganda, caused the collapse of the community and its institutions, including the shared East African Court of Appeal, by the mid-1970s. In deciding appeals from the East African territories for over seventy years, this court helped to assimilate their laws; its judgments are still valuable precedents that are regularly cited.

Under a new treaty between the three countries signed in 1999, the new East African Community was inaugurated in 2001, to promote co-operation in political, economic, cultural, social, security, and legal affairs. A customs union, common market, and monetary union are seen as steps toward the long-term aim of federation. Organs of the Community include the Summit of Heads of State or Government, the Council of Ministers, the Legislative Assembly and the East African Court of Justice, with initial jurisdiction to interpret the treaty, which may be extended later by agreement.

The current laws of Kenya, Tanzania, and Uganda reflect their richly textured sources. Each country continues the basic laws inherited from colonial rule, with the common law of English origin overlain by local legislation, some dating from the colonial period (such as their similar penal codes). Each country now has its own final appellate court (the Supreme Court of Uganda, courts of appeal in Kenya and Tanzania). Much legislation enacted since independence (in Tanzania, increasingly in Swahili) reflects the varied economic and other policies of the respective national governments. In the late 1960s, Tanzania nationalized major industrial and commercial undertakings, including banks and even trade unions, in accordance with a TANU policy commitment in the Arusha Declaration of 1967; in the 1990s the policy was partly reversed by selective privatisation and the restoration of free trade unions.

Land law reforms in Tanzania increased state control by eliminating freehold title and government leaseholds in favour of rights of occupancy, a

colonial innovation, granted for fixed (renewable) periods and revocable for failure to comply with specified conditions of development. Most Tanzanians hold land under customary law, with deemed rights of occupancy. This policy was largely continued by the Land Act of 1999. In contrast, to encourage private enterprise, Kenya continued a late colonial policy of converting customary land rights into individual freehold titles. In Uganda the abolition of 'mailo' land titles in 1975 was reversed by the Land Act of 1998 which, however, severely restricts the powers of mailo, freehold and leasehold owners, while providing for certificates of customary ownership to be issued to individuals, families or communal associations incorporated for this purpose.

Islamic law applies as the basic law of Zanzibar, as a local law at the coast and as the personal family law for Muslims in each country. Local customary laws are applied in recognized though unofficial dispute-settlement processes and in the lower courts of the unified judicial systems (and on appeal therefrom). Official projects to compile and publish records of customary law resulted in statutory "declarations" of local customary laws in Tanzania (1963) and "restatements" of customary laws in Kenya (1968–1969); these are regularly cited in the courts as authoritative (although nonbinding) sources.

The scope of customary (or Islamic) laws, still the basic personal law for most citizens, has been reduced. In Kenya and Uganda, legislation of 1972 replaced the plural systems of inheritance law with unified modern succession laws, favoring spouses and children over more remote customary heirs. Tanzania alone in Commonwealth Africa has legislated (in the Law of Marriage Act of 1971) to regulate the different forms of marriage and divorce law (customary, Islamic, Christian, and others) within a common framework, while preserving many of their respective features (for example, recognising both monogamous and polygamous forms of marriage). Although diminishing in scope, customary laws have preserved a measure of local autonomy and identity as power was increasingly concentrated in national governments and their attendant bureaucracies. The vigor of customary law was affirmed when the Kenya courts, in a celebrated 1987 case, awarded the right to bury the body of a deceased lawyer to his traditional clan, rather than his widow; no written law applied, so customary law held sway.

The laws and legal systems of eastern Africa still await fundamental reform; legislation is needed to reform outdated laws and resolve internal conflicts of law (such as marriage and child law). The machinery of the law is hampered by lack of resources. Criminal justice is impeded because police, prosecutors, magistrates, and prisons are overstretched, lacking basic resources and training. Some courts with logjams of untried cases lack adequate buildings, libraries, staff, and training. Publication of law reports, essential in common-law systems that rely upon judicial precedents, has been irregular in recent years. Legal education, provided by the universities (with postgraduate professional law schools in Kenya and Uganda), is under pressure. The independence of the judiciary from executive interference, a principle established by the constitutions, requires constant reinforcement.

See also **Amin Dada, Idi; Colonial Policies and Practices; Education, University and College: Western Africa; Government; Islam; Kenyatta, Jomo; Marriage Systems; Moi, Daniel arap; Mombasa; Museveni, Yoweri; Nyerere, Julius Kambarage; Obote, Milton; Postcolonialism; Women: Widows; Women: Women and the Law; World War I; Zanzibar.**

BIBLIOGRAPHY

Anderson, David. *Histories of the Hanged: Britain's Dirty War in Kenya and the End of Empire.* London: Weidenfeld and Nicolson, 2005.

Cotran, Eugene. *Restatement of African Law*, Vol. 1: *The Law of Marriage and Divorce: Kenya I.* London: Sweet and Maxwell, 1968.

Cotran, Eugene. *Restatement of African Law*, Vol. 2: *The Law of Succession: Kenya II.* London: Sweet and Maxwell, 1969.

Cotran, Eugene. *A Casebook of Kenya Customary Law.* Abingdon, U.K.: Professional Books Ltd., 1987; reprinted 1995 Nairobi University Press.

Elkins, Caroline. *Britain's Gulag: The Brutal End of Empire in Kenya.* London: Jonathan Cape, 2005.

Ghai, Yash P., and J. P. W. B. McAuslan. *Public Law and Political Change in Kenya.* New York: Oxford University Press, 1970.

James, R. W. *Land Tenure and Policy in Tanzania.* Toronto: University of Toronto Press, 1971.

Moore, Sally Falk. *Social Facts and Fabrications: "Customary" Law on Kilimanjaro, 1880–1980.* Cambridge, U.K.: Cambridge University Press, 1986.

Morris, Henry F., and James S. Read. *Uganda: The Development of Its Laws and Constitution.* London: Stevens, 1966.

Morris, Henry F., and James S. Read. *Indirect Rule and the Search for Justice: Essays in East African Legal History.* Oxford: Clarendon Press, 1972.

Peter, Chris Maina. *Human Rights in Africa: A Comparative Study of the African Human and People's Rights Charter and the New Tanzanian Bill of Rights.* New York: Greenwood Press, 1990.

Peter, Chris Maina, and Ibrahim Hamisi Juma, eds. *Fundamental Rights and Freedoms in Tanzania.* Dar es Salaam: Mkuki na Nyota Publishers, 1998.

Shivji, Issa G. *Law, State and the Working Class in Tanzania, c. 1920–1964.* London: J. Currey, 1986.

Shivji, Issa G. *The Legal Foundations of the Union in Tanzania's Union and Zanzibar Constitutions.* Dar es Salaam: Dar es Salaam University Press, 1990.

Vaughan, J. H. *The Dual Jurisdiction in Zanzibar.* Zanzibar: Government Printer, 1935.

Widner, Jennifer A. *Building the Rule of Law.* New York: W.W. Norton, 2001.

JAMES S. READ

ANGLOPHONE WESTERN AFRICA

Anglophone West Africa includes Nigeria, Ghana, Sierra Leone, and the Gambia (former British dependencies) and Liberia (after Ethiopia, the oldest independent state in sub-Saharan Africa). It also includes the western part of Cameroon which, after German control was ended in 1916, was administered by Britain as a League of Nations mandate and later a United Nations Trust Territory. Within the Anglophone area national legal systems are based on English (in Liberia, Anglo-American) common law, which was superimposed upon the pre-existing indigenous laws.

INDIGENOUS LAWS

Indigenous African societies developed their own laws and legal systems over many centuries. West Africa had a particularly rich and varied political history: through migrations, wars, and conquests, kingdoms and empires rose and flourished over past millennia, many prospering through the lucrative international trade northward across the Sahara.

Indigenous laws have more than historical interest: vital elements of contemporary legal systems have their roots in precolonial laws.

Modern Ghana does not encompass any of the territory of the ancient empire from which it takes its name, but includes the Ashanti kingdom and the Fanti states, which originated in early centuries of the second millennium CE. In Nigeria the Yoruba and Bénin kingdoms also have an ancient history. Such indigenous states had well-established systems of government, laws, and machinery for their enforcement and for dispute settlement. But so too did the "stateless" communities, such as the Igbo and Tiv of Nigeria and the Tallensi and neighboring peoples of northern Ghana, who developed republican forms of controlled leadership exercising power by consent, without kings or chiefs. These included the city-states of the Niger Delta, some of them (the Old Calabar towns) ruled by the Ekpe or Leopard associations of merchants.

In some of the diverse Igbo-speaking communities elders reinforced their status through "title societies" entered by the payment of fees, while others practiced village democracy, adult men (and sometimes women) participating in communal decision making. The Glebo, settled for centuries in coastal towns of present-day Liberia, were described in 1842 as having "the purest of democracies" (Rev. John Payne, quote in Moran, 39). To considerable swathes of inland West Africa the expansion of Islam brought its own law, courts, and judges, literacy and learning, although Muslim authorities also recognized the strength and vitality of local customs.

Most indigenous societies did not differentiate laws or the legal system from all the processes, integrated in social and political life, which defined norms of behavior and resolved disputes. Most laws sprung from the routines and regularities of daily life, were maintained by common assent and evolved as customs and habits changed; rules were generally manipulatable, because effective dispute settlement rested upon negotiation and popular acceptance. Supernatural beliefs and attendant practices were significant in dispute settlement (trial by oath or ordeal or resort to oracles) and sanctions (e.g., cursing). Legislation by rulers or elders was a supplementary source of law.

Even in centralized states tyranny was rare: the power of most rulers was restrained by evolving political structures, typically imposed upon older social formations. Extended family relationships in the form of descent lines, lineages, or clans were prominent and fundamental aspects of the social structure, with significant legal implications. The Yoruba kingdoms were described as larger versions of families and the country as a collection of kingdoms whose rulers regarded each other as relations. Their walled cities, linked in a loose confederation, were each made up of compounds occupied by extended families. The Fanti towns were divided into "companies," small independent republics, each with its own hereditary chief, laws, and customs symbolized by its own flag and anthem.

Decentralization of government to local chiefs was common. Conciliar forms of government were typical; rulers relied upon councils of senior chiefs to proffer advice and share responsibility for decisions. In some states such chiefs were also kingmakers, like the Oyo Mesi nobles of the Yoruba kingdom of Oyo, who not only elected the *alafin* but could even remove him by demanding his suicide (notoriously symbolized by sending him parrots' eggs), although this decision could be vetoed by another group of chiefs. Such ideas influenced the neighboring kingdom of Bénin, where nobles elected the new *oba* (ruler) until a sixteenth-century *oba* substituted a rule of succession by the deceased *oba*'s eldest son.

Most indigenous laws recognized the significant role of the family. Patrilineal systems were most common, identifying the family through descent in the male line. However, some societies such as the Akan of Ghana were matrilineal, constructing the family through the female line, and a few recognized dual descent, affirming relationships in both male and female lines (such as the Afikpo and Ohaffia Igbo and Yako of Nigeria). Land, the basis of life, was generally not subject to individual ownership but regarded as belonging to the whole community. Some societies recognized systems of family property in which land was held by families and allocated to individual members by the head of the family, advised by a council of senior members. Such a system, based on a complex web of rights and duties, was fundamental to the structure of Yoruba society and to maintaining the residential family compounds, the basis of both vibrant city life and successful farming enterprise. The matrilineal Akan also regarded land as the property of the family, which included the ancestors, the living and generations yet unborn. Such systems provided a basis and incentive for rules and practices respecting and protecting the environment.

Indigenous laws recognized marriage as a matter for private contractual arrangement between the respective families and women's rights were generally restricted: whether as wives, widows, daughters, or other dependants they were expected to be adequately provided for by continuing dependence upon men. Polygamy was generally recognized and parenthood was vital in attaining full adult status. However, economic and social developments enabled some women to take active, even dominant, roles in trade and to enjoy enhanced rights, for example, to own and control their own separate property and to share in the enjoyment of family property, as in Yoruba law.

Indigenous laws, within their cultural contexts, protected some of the human rights universally recognized in the twenty-first century, including the right to life, expressed in terms of access to land as the means of subsistence and cooperation and sharing of resources in times of need. The right of access to justice was recognized by processes of public litigation, characteristic of indigenous laws. Without a specialized judiciary, public attendance and participation in such hearings encouraged fairness in the decisions made by the chiefs or elders who presided. Public participation was also common in political decision making at local levels: searching for consensus has come to be regarded as characteristic of the African political method.

Trade and conquest contributed to the expansion of Islam in West Africa, including in the fourteenth century the Hausa states of Gobir, Kano, Katsina, and Zaria. As the termini of the central Saharan trade routes, these grew in importance from the seventeenth century. 'Uthman dan Fodio's general jihad in 1804 replaced all the Hausa rulers by Fulani emirs who, largely isolated from the outside world, sought to impose the strict letter of Islamic law, according to the Maliki school. However, many existing local customs survived and modified the application of Islamic law.

COLONIAL LAWS

Colonial rule in West Africa was preceded by centuries during which the international Atlantic slave trade, dominated by the British, had a traumatic effect upon indigenous societies and cultures, including their legal systems. Some communities like the Ashanti prospered by collaborating in the trade, other victim societies were undermined or even destroyed.

The relatively short period of formal colonial rule in West Africa had a formative effect in defining the modern states, their territories, and basic national legal systems. In Anglophone states this includes the structure and role of the courts, the judiciary and the legal profession, the use of decided cases as authoritative precedents, and the form of legislation. It also extends to fundamental divisions and principles of the common law. However, colonial claims to have introduced the rule of law misrepresent the nature of indigenous societies, the character of colonial rule, and the weakness of the foundations it laid to maintain the rule of law in the independent states it created.

Promoting commerce prompted initial British interest in the West African coast, through ports administered at first by trading companies chartered by the Crown. Castles built by the European powers along the coast to protect their merchants and interests also served to detain slaves awaiting transportation and provided bases for the extension of colonial rule. British consular officials adjudicated in disputes between British and foreign merchants and by agreement with local rulers informal "courts of equity," composed of British officers and local chiefs, heard disputes between traders and locals.

Formal British jurisdiction arose with the settlement at Freetown in 1787 to provide a home for freed slaves, the origin of the colony of Sierra Leone. Official "Instructions" of 1791 for the administration of justice there gave members of the governing council the powers and functions of lay justices of the peace in England, requiring them to apply the law of England and summon local juries to try civil and criminal cases. In 1861 King Docemo was forced to sign a treaty under which Britain acquired the port and town of Lagos as a colony. Britain also claimed title to the castles of the Gold Coast, around which British officials exercised informal jurisdiction over local inhabitants. In 1865 a formal notice asserted exclusive authority over territory within five miles (a cannon-shot distance) of each castle, within which area "none but British laws can be recognized, or enforced ... respecting, however, as far as practicable, native laws and usages."

Each British West African dependency consisted of the original colony at the coast and the much more extensive interior, later added as a protectorate, strictly foreign territory retaining its own rulers (if any) but under British overrule. British rule was generally extended with the consent of local rulers, expressed in treaties of dubious validity and legal effect, although in some areas by military conquest. Britain exercised powers over protectorates as extensive as over colonies.

In each territory the whole body of English law was purportedly introduced as the general law, by the formula "the common law, doctrines of equity and statutes of general application" in force in England at a specified date. This reception date varied from one territory to another, being a relevant date in the formalization of local colonial administration: for the Gold Coast, 1874; for Sierra Leone, 1880; for the Gambia, 1888; for Nigeria, 1900. English law applied only so far as it was applicable and subject to modification or adaptation to fit local circumstances. Furthermore, the colonial authorities were required, as far as practicable, to respect indigenous laws, termed "native laws and custom" or, later, "African (local) customary laws," so far as they were applicable and insofar as they were not deemed to be "repugnant to natural justice, equity and good conscience," a test only rarely expressly invoked. In relevant areas, such as northern Nigeria, the indigenous law enforced under this rubric was Islamic law.

This multilayered legal system was applied by dual systems of courts, reflecting the British colonial policy of indirect rule. English law and local legislation was administered by colonial judges in the High Courts (some misleadingly titled Supreme Courts) and by Magistrates' Courts presided over in a few urban areas by legally qualified magistrates but elsewhere by colonial administrative officers; native courts, presided over by approved local chiefs or other indigenous authorities but supervised by administrative officers, were authorised to apply mainly native law and cus-

tom, and some local legislation, including minor criminal laws. Appeals from native courts, later retitled Customary Courts, lay via native appeal courts to the High Courts. In Northern Nigeria, native courts were conducted by qualified *alkalis* or *qadis* (judges) with wide jurisdiction over civil and criminal cases, including homicide trials. Under colonial rule appeals from the High Courts lay to the regional West African Court of Appeal; a small number of appeals taken further to the Judicial Committee of the Privy Council in London, the final court of appeal for the empire, prompted some significant judgments. Beyond this official judicial system, in some areas in reaction against it, indigenous processes of adjudication continued unofficially and were often preferred by litigants, at least as the first stage in dispute settlement, because they more closely applied the established customs of the community. Although sometimes seen as unwelcome rivals to the colonial courts, such processes came to be accepted as forms of customary arbitration.

Although Liberia was not an American colony, the community of freed slaves and freeborns remained under the authority of the American Colonization Society from 1821 until the settlers declared their independence in 1847 and adopted a Constitution closely modelled on that of the United States. As European powers engaged in the scramble for Africa intensified their pressures around, and even upon, it, Liberia also extended its territory into the hinterland, mainly by agreement with local rulers, and established a form of colonial administration in which the Americo-Liberian minority dominated the diverse indigenous peoples of the interior, who were not admitted to citizenship until 1904.

The adoption of the common law left room for considerable variation, even among colonial governments, in its practical implementation. Significant legal differences arose between different parts of the same dependency: the Colony of Lagos and the Protectorates of Southern and Northern Nigeria were amalgamated in 1914, but a fundamentally different regime of land law was applied in the North, imposing centrally regulated tenure while recognising local customary "rights of occupancy," a pattern repeated in the Northern Territories of the Gold Coast. In Sierra Leone, customary land law applied in the protectorate but there was no provision for the application of any customary law in the colony.

Trial by jury, a characteristic feature of Anglo-American law, had only limited application in West Africa: only Liberia retained the full panoply of grand juries to indict defendants and trial juries; in Nigeria and Sierra Leone juries sat only in the colony areas, to try capital and other serious offences; in Ghana only the most serious offences were tried by juries of seven members, other offences by a judge sitting with three assessors.

The outcome of these arrangements was the creation of plural legal systems and difficult questions of internal conflicts of laws, particularly in the realm of family law, including marriage and succession laws. Such questions have to be resolved on a case-by-case basis in decisions of the superior courts.

THE ERA OF INDEPENDENCE

In Liberia the Constitution of 1847 remained in force until the military coup of 1980, but for more than one hundred years from 1877 Liberia under the True Whig party provided the first African model of a single-party state. Although the laws and Supreme Court judgments were not compiled and published until the 1960s, the Constitution and the common law, with its dual American and English parentage, have been vigorously asserted and examined in the courts.

European decolonization in sub-Saharan Africa came first to the Gold Coast, which at independence in 1957 adopted the name of the ancient empire of Ghana; independence for Nigeria (1960), Sierra Leone (1961), and the Gambia (1965) followed. At independence each new state had a constitution, drafted on principles agreed by local elected political leaders, which established parliamentary government on the Westminster model, paradoxically with the British monarch (Queen Elizabeth) as head of state; the constitution of Nigeria established a federation of three regions. Each state later adopted a republican form of government with an executive president. Following referenda in 1961, Northern Cameroon became part of Nigeria while Southern Cameroon opted to join the Francophone state of Cameroon, while retaining English law and language.

However, colonial rule had established no enduring foundation for constitutional government, which was interrupted by military coups in Ghana (1966, 1972, and 1981), Nigeria (1966 and 1983), and the Gambia (1994). Sierra Leone experienced a one-party state (1978), successive military coups (1992, 1996, 1997) and a brutal civil war, before international intervention restored constitutional government (2000). In 1979 Ghana and Nigeria adopted new constitutions that abandoned the Westminster model in favor of the Washington model, with separation of powers and directly elected executive presidents appointing ministers from outside the legislature, a pattern repeated in later constitutions (Ghana in 1993, Nigeria in 1999). In the Gambia the 1994 coup leader was elected president under the new constitution of 1996.

Military governments have ruled Nigeria, Africa's most populous state, for more than half of the years of independence; they have also presided over constitutional reform and the restoration of civilian governments in 1979 and 1999. Nigeria, at independence an unstable federation of three regions, is in the early twenty-first century a federation of thirty-six states with an executive president and state governors, all directly elected for four-year terms, renewable once. The Constitution of 1999 prescribes the federal structures and also the single constitution applicable to every state. It provides for the recall of elected members of all legislatures, although impracticably requiring for this purpose a petition signed by half the registered voters. Traditional authorities unrecognized by the constitution, including the sultans and emirs of the northern states and the rulers of the Yoruba states, continue to dominate social hierarchies and to exercise great influence and patronage.

Entrenched, justiciable guarantees of fundamental rights, modeled on the European Convention on Human Rights (1950), first introduced in Nigeria in 1959, have been retained in subsequent constitutions there and adopted in the other Anglophone states in West Africa and elsewhere.

English law still provides the basis of these national legal systems, although in Ghana references to common law have replaced explicit references to English law and in Ghana and western states of Nigeria old English statutes are no longer applied, those required having been adopted by local legislation. Judgments of the English courts, no longer of binding authority, are still cited by the courts, as are judgments from other common-law countries. Except in Sierra Leone, criminal law in these states is in different codified versions of English law, of colonial origin.

The basic dual structure of courts has generally been retained. Although Ghana abolished customary courts, tribunals established in the 1980s with extensive criminal jurisdiction (later reduced) reflected public pressure for accessible machinery of people's justice.

The colonial governments made no provision for local legal education. A few self-taught attorneys were admitted to practice in the courts in the nineteenth century (from 1821 in Sierra Leone, 1853 in the Gold Coast, and 1865 in Lagos). For several decades they served private clients, the wider community, and even the colonial governments and courts (as registrar, prosecutors, and magistrates). To qualify as lawyers Africans had to study overseas, normally in London for call to the Bar at one of the Inns of Court. The first African barrister returned from London and enrolled at the Lagos Supreme Court in 1880 and practiced also in the Gold Coast; thirty years later there were only twenty-five lawyers practising in southern Nigeria, half of them from Sierra Leone. At that time the colonial authorities adopted a new system of courts to exclude lawyers from appearing outside Lagos and other specified towns, curtailing the jurisdiction of the Supreme Court in favor of courts in which administrative officers presided and lawyers had no right to appear. Public opposition continued for twenty years until this judicial system was reformed.

Official suspicion of lawyers was also reflected in the reluctance to appoint African lawyers to official posts in the colonial administration or judiciary. The first African magistrate in Nigeria was appointed only in 1931; he became the first African Supreme Court judge in 1944. University law faculties and professional law schools established soon after independence have created substantial, unified legal professions (without the English distinction between barristers and solicitors).

The problems of plural legal systems and resulting internal conflicts of law continue. Customary laws, distorted by colonial rule and molded by economic, social, educational, and other forces that accompanied it, continue in force and, with Islamic law, provide the basic legal regimes and the substance of the rule of law for the substantial rural majorities of these populations. Land law reform in Nigeria (the Land Use Act of 1978) extended to Southern Nigeria the state control applied in Northern Nigeria under colonial rule.

The movement for Islamicisation in Northern Nigerian states prompted legislation from 2000 reinstating the Qur'anic penal provisions of the *shari'a* law for Muslims, including the hadd punishments for adultery (unlawful sexual intercourse outside marriage) and drinking alcohol (both already offences for Muslims under the Penal Code), theft, robbery, and false accusations of adultery. The laws also apply the *shari'a* law of homicide, allowing the victim's next of kin to remit the death sentence for intentional homicide, accepting payment of *diya* (blood money), and prescribe the death penalty or life imprisonment for witchcraft offences. These states replaced the former Area (*alkalis'*) Courts, which applied the *shari'a* in civil cases and the Penal Code of 1960 in criminal cases, with *shari'a* Courts, in most places with the same judges. These changes, supported by popular Muslim opinion, although arguably unconstitutional, provoked reactions by Christians (to whom they do not apply).

See also **Age and Age Organization; Colonial Policies and Practices; Death, Mourning, and Ancestors; Family; Freetown; Government; Human Rights; Islam; Kinship and Affinity; Kinship and Descent; Lagos; Land: Tenure; Marriage Systems; Political Systems: Chieftainships; Slave Trades; 'Uthman dan Fodio; Women: Widows; Woman: Woman and the Law.**

BIBLIOGRAPHY

Adewoye, Omoniyi. *The Judicial System in Southern Nigeria, 1854–1954.* Atlantic Highlands, NJ: Humanities Press, 1977.

Aguda, T. Akinola, ed. *The Challenge of the Nigerian Nation: An Examination of Its Legal Development 1960–1985.* Ibadan: Published for Nigerian Institute of Advanced Legal Studies by Heinemann Educational Books (Nigeria) Ltd., 1985.

Ajomo, M. Ayo, ed. *Fundamentals of Nigerian Law.* Lagos: Nigerian Institute of Advanced Legal Studies, 1989.

Allott, Antony N. *New Essays in African Law.* London: Butterworths, 1970.

Asante, Samuel K. B. *Property Law and Social Goals in Ghana, 1844–1966.* Accra: Ghana Universities Press, 1975.

Daniels, W. C. Ekow. *The Common Law in West Africa*. London: Butterworths, 1964.

Derrett, J. Duncan M., ed. *Studies in the Laws of Succession in Nigeria: Essays*. London: Published for the Nigerian Institute of Social and Economic Research by the Oxford University Press, 1965.

Elias, Taslim O. *Groundwork of Nigerian Law*. London: Routledge and Paul, 1954.

Elias, Taslim O. *Ghana and Sierra Leone: The Development of Their Laws and Constitution*. London: Stevens, 1962.

Elias, Taslim O. *Nigeria: The Development of its Laws and Constitution*. London: Stevens, 1967.

Harvey, William B. *Law and Social Change in Ghana*. Princeton, NJ: Princeton University Press, 1966.

Moran, Mary H. *Liberia, the Violence of Democracy*. Philadelphia: University of Pennsylvania Press, 2006.

Nwabueze, B. O. *Nigeria's Presidential Constitution 1979–1983: The Second Experiment in Constitutional Democracy*. London: Longman, 1985.

Ogbu, O. N. *Modern Nigerian Legal System*. Enugu: 2002.

Okonkwo, Cyprian O. *Introduction to Nigerian Law*. London: Sweet and Maxwell, 1980.

Ollennu, Nii Amaa. *The Law of Succession in Ghana*. Accra: Presbyterian Book Depot Ltd., 1960.

Peters, Ruud. *Islamic Criminal Law in Nigeria*. Ibadan: Spectrum Books Ltd., 2003.

Sarbah, John M. *Fanti Customary Laws*, 3rd edition. London: Cass, 1968.

Smart, H. M. Joko. *Sierra Leone Customary Family Law*. Freetown, Sierra Leone: Fourah Bay College Bookshop, 1983.

JAMES S. READ

BURUNDI, CONGO, AND RWANDA

A discussion of the laws of Burundi, Democratic Republic of the Congo, and Rwanda has been particularly difficult in the 1990s and early 2000s, given the complete state of lawlessness prevailing there during that period. The worst has come with constant bloody disturbances in Burundi, a civil war in some parts of the Democratic Republic of the Congo (also known as Congo-Kinshasa) and, last but not least, a genocide in Rwanda. But starting in the early twenty-first century, some signs of a legal stabilization appeared, especially in the constitutional field. These elements will enable the scholar to allocate less space to the historical developments that took place in these three legal systems of Central Africa during the twentieth century.

PRECOLONIAL PERIOD

At the time of the so-called Scramble for Africa, in the last quarter of the nineteenth century, Belgium, France, Great Britain, and Portugal partitioned most of Africa into colonial dependencies, and the legal systems of what are now Burundi, Democratic Republic of the Congo, and Rwanda were, at least in some respects, different from one another. Rwanda and Burundi existed roughly within their present confines in a state—such as political structure, whereas Congo-Kinshasa, which spanned the basin of what was then known as the Zaire River, encompassed within its limits a wide variety of sociopolitical entities. From acephalous lineage-based societies to kingdoms such as the Kuba, or empires such as the Lunda, what early twenty-first century lawyers would call constitutional structures were, in each case, adapted to the local cultural, economic, geographical, and social conditions of the region.

In spite of this, one may say that legal systems throughout the three countries were prevalently customary, in the sense that the essentials of everyday law were derived from accepted and enforceable patterns of social conduct and restraint. The dictates of sociopolitical authorities (legislation), the decisions of dispute-solvers (case law), and advice from those deemed to know the law (legal science), were operative in each society but tended to be subordinate to the shared behavior of the group—that is, to custom. A clear separation, therefore, between law-producing bodies and the society at large rarely, if ever, existed.

COLONIAL PERIOD

When Belgium took over the Congo Free State from Léopold II (1835–1909) and transformed it into the colony of the Belgian Congo, it immediately established a centralized administrative and constitutional system through a special law known as the *charte coloniale*. Although the ultimate power rested with the Belgian Parliament in Brussels, the Belgian king's Minister for Colonies was made, for all practical purposes, the ordinary legislator for the colony in name of the king. Consent of the *conseil colonial* was required on any piece of royal legislation (*décrets*) meant to be enforced in the colony. That primary delegation of legislative powers was accompanied by a more limited one to the governor general, who represented the king in the colony.

In Brussels and in Léopoldville (modern-day Kinshasa), consultative councils (*conseil du government*) were appointed. In Africa, the *conseil du government* expressed the wishes of the European community in Africa to the governor general once a year. Europeans, among whom missionaries played a prominent role, represented Africans in the council. Yet fundamentally, Belgian rule in the Congo was hegemonic; at the higher level, there was never any serious conflict between the three main components of colonial power: the administration, the capital, and the missions. Yet locally, in the field, diverging interests often led to tensions.

The size of the country, combined with the low level of budgetary resources and the scarcity of European personnel, forced the Belgians into a system of indirect rule. Throughout the Congo, the lower administrative units presided over by European civil servants were divided into successive African administrative subunits (the *chefferie* or *secteur*, the *groupement*, and the village). This organization was coupled with the consolidation of an African judicial system (*juridictions indigènes*, or native courts) in which the native authorities recognized under the indirect-rule principles were given judicial duties. Thus, a limited field, covering essentially private law (family relations, property, inheritance, contracts, and torts) but also some criminal and procedural law, was left to precolonial custom.

That customary production of law was carefully controlled by colonial authorities. First, a general provision in the *décret* on native courts provided for the nonrepugnancy (compatibility) of African custom, not only to legislation but also to universal public order that was rapidly equated to Belgian public order. Second, the enforcement of this blank provision was entrusted to the European administrator of each *territoire*, who had permanent control of the activity of native courts, and to a member of the public prosecutor's office (*parquet*). Both were allowed an extensive appeal and revision jurisdiction.

The powers entrusted to the European administrative and judicial authorities were coupled with a considerable effort to ensure a knowledge of existing customs. The *Revue juridique du Congo belge* and the *Bulletin des juridictions indigènes et du droit coutumier congolais* were published in the Congo from the 1920s onward. But the way in which Belgian civil servants and judges approached precolonial legal systems and their main source was heavily tainted with their own legal background. Thus, frequent and sometimes heavy distortions occurred in their presentation of custom in what was then called customary law (*droit coutumier*), considered in the early twenty-first century as European-fabricated African law. A somewhat adapted Belgian law was applicable to Europeans in the Congo, and also to Africans who decided to subject any of their legal acts to that imported exogenous system.

In the early 1920s, Belgium accepted the mandate on Burundi and Rwanda (the far western part of German East Africa) from the League of Nations. After having envisaged the establishment of a protectorate in the two countries, it decided in the early 1930s to transfer the model adopted in the Congo to Burundi and Rwanda. The three countries were administratively united, and Ruanda-Urundi, as it was then known, became a governorate under the governor-general of the Belgian Congo and Ruanda-Urundi. Constitutionally and administratively speaking, Ruanda-Urundi was governed in generally the same way as the Congo was, although its international status was different, as it was a mandated territory and not a colony; this implied regular reports to the Mandates Commission of the League of Nations and some limitations deriving from the Mandates system.

Finally, although this was not expressly defined in the law until much later—in the course of World War II—the jurisdiction of Ruanda-Urundi precolonial political and judicial authorities, in spite of their kingly status, was limited in administrative and judicial matters exclusively to their African subjects. This system was similar to the one adopted in the Congo, but it somewhat took into account precolonial political structures.

POSTCOLONIAL DEVELOPMENTS

Burundi, Democratic Republic of the Congo (or Zaire, as it was known for some thirty years), and

Rwanda have, the first two in 2005 and the third in 2003, completely renewed their constitutions. This state of affairs was preceded by many ups and downs on some fundamental issues.

The first issue involved the balance between unitarism and federalism in Congo-Kinshasa. When confronted with the economic, social, and political diversity of the Congo, Belgian authorities advocated a unitary constitutional frame (hence the slogan, "a united Congo means a strong Congo"). Yet some people advocated taking into account that diversity in order to achieve a federal model. As a result, Congo-Kinshasa's first constitution (the Loi Fondamentale, or Fundamental Law, of May 19, 1960) provided for an uneasy compromise between unitarism and federalism with a clear dominance of the former. The constitution of August 1, 1964 (the so-called Luluabourg Constitution) was definitely federalist. That of June 24, 1967, and all its numerous amendments and consolidations, provided for a completely centralized state, and the constitution adopted in 2006, is a unitary one although there are detailed lists of matters falling either in the exclusive jurisdiction of the "central" power, or in that of the provinces or, finally, which come under the joint jurisdiction of both the "central power" and the provinces. It clearly appears that the constituent tried to find a compromise between unitarism and federalism as it did in the 1960 Loi fondamentale. The newly created Constitutional Court will decide in case of conflicts.

In the three countries there was also a struggle between parliamentarianism and presidentialism. In a parliamentary system, parliament is sovereign and the head of state is a purely representative figure. Belgium had tried to introduce such regime in its colonies, inspired by the Belgian constitution and the Westminster model. This was most easily achieved at least on paper in Burundi, a traditional kingdom, but encountered difficulties in Rwanda, where the Hutu majority strongly rejected any idea of reestablishing a monarchy. Yet in Rwanda, the constitution of November 24, 1962, and in Democratic Republic of the Congo, the Loi Fondamentale, provided for a parliamentarian republic.

The first country to move away from constitutional scheme was Democratic Republic of the Congo, which introduced presidentialism along with federalism in the 1964 constitution and maintained it

in the 1967 document, although the adopted regime would best be described as semi-presidentialism, as practiced by the French. The 2006 draft of the transitional Congolese constitution goes mostly back to the 1960 parliamentarian model. As for Burundi, after the demise of the parliamentary monarchy through a military coup in 1966, the ensuing republican regime was clearly presidential and even went to the extreme of abolishing any popular representation in the 1974 constitution. The constitution of 2005 provides for semi-presidentialism. In Rwanda, the second republican constitution, dated December 20, 1978, also moved away from parliamentarism and toward the French model of presidentialism. The constitution, established in 2003 after the invasion of the country by Tutsi émigrés in 1990, established the same kind of regime, but with many features of its own reflecting the ambiguities of the factual situation.

Finally, there is the balance between multipartism and monopartism. After all three countries moved away from the multiparty system advocated by their Belgian rulers and followed the monoparty model that became the hallmark of African constitutions until the 1990s, the winds of change brought back multipartism in all three countries. But, as in Rwanda, it is one thing is to proclaim multipartism and another to have a state of affairs where one party is effectively ruling the country.

As for the administration of justice, especially in Congo-Kinshasa from roughly 1985 onward, it has met with a general collapse of the judiciary that accompanied state control of the populations; this was felt in rural areas and in midsize cities. This does not mean, however, that the country was in a state of lawlessness. The population turned itself to various—in many cases already existing—social structures, such as foreign missions, trade unions, neighborhood organizations, local churches, elders, or traditional authorities. In short, whatever or whomever they trusted to solve their legal problems. The state of law in Congo-Kinshasa may thus be assessed as being one of legal pluralism in its most radical sense.

In the field of private law, the most noticeable feature is the incapacity of the governments of Burundi, Democratic Republic of the Congo, and Rwanda to completely obliterate the precolonial legal systems from the books. In spite of an extensive work of codification that has, in principle, virtually eliminated custom as the dominant source of law in private relations between citizens, it still proves difficult to remove the precolonial systems. These new codes are at best distorted on some of their most important modernizing provisions and at worst completely ignored by the masses. This heavily contributed to the disaffection from the state judicial organization in a country such as Congo-Kinshasa.

Finally—and this is perhaps the most important legal challenge that Burundi and Rwanda face—comes the problem of legally solving the aftermath of ethnic tensions that still exist in the two countries and that led, in the first one, to regular massacres of one or the other ethnic group on a local scale, and, in the second one, to the 1994 genocide. In Burundi, this is reflected in the 2005 constitution, which provides for the Council of Bashingantahe for Unity and Reconciliation. The Council's organization, composition, and procedures are, as of 2006, yet to be determined. Finally, in Rwanda, besides a repeated reference to national unity and the rejection of ethnic categories and divisiveness, the main problem is a judicial solution of the 1994 genocide. Thousands of people have been waiting for years in overcrowded jails for an appearance in court. The decision to entrust the solution to popular local justice through the traditional *gaçaça* seems to work, but at a very slow pace. What is more, the penal questions raised before these courts are not traditional in their nature and magnitude. On the other hand, an end had to be brought to the delays in the unbearable prison situation.

See also **Colonial Policies and Practices; Kinshasa; Postcolonialism; Sudan: Wars; Warfare; Women: Women and the Law; World War II.**

BIBLIOGRAPHY

Reyntjens, Filip. "Les nouveaux habits de l'empereur: analyse juridico-politique de la constitution rwandaise de 2003." In *L'Afrique des Grands Lacs, 2002–2003.* Paris: L'Harmattan, 71–87.

Vanderlinden, Jacques. *Congo, in Introduction bibliographique à l'histoire du droit et à l'ethnologie juridique.* Brussels, Belgium: Institut de Sociologie, 1969.

Vanderlinden, Jacques. *Burundi et Rwanda, Introduction bibliographique à l'histoire du droit et à l'ethnologie juridique.* Brussels, Belgium: Institut de Sociologie, 1974.

Vanderlinden, Jacques, ed. *Bibliographies internationales de la doctrine juridique africaine.* Moncton, New Brunswick, Centre internationale de la common law en français, 1993–1994.

Vanderlinden, Jacques. *L'ordre juridique colonial belge en Afrique centrale. Eléments d'histoire.* Brussels, Belgium: Académie royale des sciences d'outre-mer, 2004.

JACQUES VANDERLINDEN

FRANCOPHONE WESTERN, EQUATORIAL, AND INDIAN OCEAN AFRICA

Any analysis of legal systems in Francophone and Equatorial Africa and in the Indian Ocean should start with a review of the main schools of jurisprudence and theories of law that have shaped them throughout history. It should then highlight the sociopolitical context in which the existing legal systems emerged (mostly during the colonial period and the struggle for freedom) and briefly discuss the complexity and effectiveness of judicial systems and procedures. Such an analysis reveals the enormous challenges of the legal systems in most of the formerly French territories and their difficulty to perform some key social functions.

TAXONOMY OF LEGAL THEORIES IN FRANCOPHONE AFRICA

Law has always been defined in many different ways throughout history, but three general types of concept have predominated. The first concept focuses on the relationship between law and moral justice. This approach tends to see "both the ultimate origin of law and the ultimate sanction of law in the 'right reason'" (Berman-Greiner 1980, 18). The second type of concept stresses the links between law and political power, thus defining law primarily in terms of the will of the state. The third approach emphasizes the relationship between law and the total historical development of the community, and tends to see the purpose and legitimacy of law in traditions, customs, or even the national character.

Historians have often identified some of these traditional concepts of law in their study of African civilizations. It has been argued, for instance, that in precolonial times during the formative era of the development of West African legal systems, most concepts of law tended to focus on its relationship to moral justice. Legal systems operated in other ways than through the formulation of written rules.

"It was rather a system of keeping the balance, of arriving at satisfactory results: it was geared not to intellectual persuasion but to emotional approval, not to decisions imposed but to acceptable solutions" (Nekam 1966, 3). Building on Aristotle's view of law as reason unaffected by desire or by the subjective passions of individuals, some late-nineteenth-century theologians argued that African law should be based on divine law. The same idea was often expressed during the period of 1945 to 1960 by many nationalist leaders who opposed French colonial rule in French and Equatorial Africa and who considered law to be a theory of right and wrong, or as an art of the good and the equitable as Byzantine Emperor Justinian once defined it.

These natural law theories were based on the assumption that law gets its meaning from the nature of humans as moral and rational creatures. They were challenged by the positivist approach taken by first French colonial rulers, who believed that the law has its origin and its sanction in the will of officials and ultimately the state. In contrast with the previous conception, the new dominant legal philosophy was based on French Jacobinism that favored a dominant state and gave much weight to the political authoritativeness of legal rules. This view of law was subsequently adopted by African rulers after independence, most of who sought and followed the advice of a group of Paris-based French jurists for the drafting of the constitutions of their newly independent territories.

Taking issue with both natural and positivist theories of law in Francophone Africa, which they considered to be judicial mimetism, some legal scholars such as Tchoungang and Wabnitz offered a third type of theory of law that finds its origin and its sanction neither in reason and morals, nor in political power, but in the culture, traditions, and customs of the community. Adding a historical dimension to the concept of law, they suggested that law should have an organic connection with the character and spirit of the people of the newly independent French territories. Law should then be seen as reflecting popular faith and the common consciousness of a people at a given time and place. This philosophical stance is reminiscent of that of the so-called historical jurisprudence school developed in the late nineteenth century by German jurist Friedrich Karl von Savigny.

With the wave of democratization that occurred in the early 1990s, a new concept of law has emerged in Francophone and Equatorial Africa. Much closer to what is usually referred to in the philosophy of law as legal realism, adherents of this school tend to challenge not only the philosophical assumptions of natural law theorists, but also the analytical rigidity of positivism, and the open-endedness of the definition of law by historical jurisprudence. Natural-law theory is seen as focusing too much on the elements of Western-centered reason and morality, thus ignoring the presence of unreasonable or unjust laws in African legal systems. The positivist theory tends to focus excessively on the political element in law and to exclude from consideration important areas such as international law and customary law (especially in Equatorial Africa where the state did not exist and political authority was more diffuse). Also, they justify military law, which became dominant and led many former French territories to become *de jure* and *de facto* dictatorships after independence (Cameroon under Ahmadou Ahidjo and Paul Biya; Gabon under Léon Mba and Omar Bongo; Republic of the Congo under Marien Ngouabi and Denis Sassou-Nguesso; Central African Republic under David Dacko, Jean-Bédel Bokassa, and André Kolingba; Chad under Hissein Habre; Côte d'Ivoire under Félix Houphouët-Boigny; Zaire/Democratic Republic of the Congo under Mobutu Sese Seko, Laurent-Désiré, and Joseph Kabila; Comoros under Ahmed Abdallah; and Djibouti under Hassan Gouled Aptidon).

Finally, as noted by Berman and Greiner (1980, 25), "theories which derive law from the national character or common consciousness of a people, or see it as a product of historical evolution, tend to make the area of the legal so wide that it becomes impossible to encompass it, or indeed to know where to begin to analyze it." Therefore, there is a danger that the distinctive elements of a legal system will be lost in this approach, which fuses law with social history.

Moving from conceptual definitions to everyday practice, it is important to keep in mind all these various theories of law and their limitations. Clearly, given the complex political histories of these societies, it would be inappropriate to validate one particular theory of law to the exclusion of the others. Rather, the prevailing legal systems in most of contemporary Francophone and Equatorial Africa and in former French territories of the Indian Ocean area appear to be syntheses of all of them.

POLITICAL GENESIS OF CURRENT CONSTITUTIONAL ARRANGEMENTS

After World War II, a new class of African elites in West and Equatorial Africa resented more strongly French colonial authoritarianism. The war effort had prevented any industrialization of the colonies and alienated the peasant masses that tended to respond enthusiastically to the ideal of the liberation of peoples the Allies had propagated during their campaign against Nazi Germany. As the end of hostilities seemed obvious, it appeared that large segments of population in colonial territories—especially the so-called *évolués* (educated, business community)—would not accept the political status quo. Moreover, there was strong international pressure for a new legal framework for decolonization. In fact, the United States and the USSR took an extremely strong stance against colonialism at the United Nations, focusing especially on North Africa and Indochina.

Trying to anticipate some of these pressures, the Free French authorities held the Brazzaville Conference in January and February 1944 in Brazzaville. As Person pointed out, the real objective of General de Gaulle and most of the participants (the great many of whom were high-ranking colonial officials) was "to consolidate the colonial system definitively by renovating it" (144). To this end, they felt that the adoption of an entire new constitutional and legal framework was needed in French West Africa—a country comprising seven colonies: Mauritania, Senegal, Guinea, Sudan (Mali), Côte d'Ivoire, Niger, and Dahomey. The termination of forced labor and of the native code (*indigénat*), a limited participation in elections, and extension of the voice of Africans in public affairs were recommended. A similar political and legal evolution took place in French Equatorial Africa (Gabon, Middle-Congo, Ubangui-Shari, and Chad), albeit at a slower pace. French authorities decided to adopt a legal framework for a partial transfer of power from the colonial administration to the traditional chiefs. Despite such proclamation for reform, there was actually little change. Mbokolo observed that

> French policy, which consisted in granting power without jeopardizing fundamental interests, succeeded the more easily because the African elites

in French Equatorial Africa—surprised by the swift pace of events, cut off from the mass of the people, and won over to the idea of collaboration—conceived of independence as merely obtaining powerful positions, without there being any change in the structure of society or in the nature of their relations with the former tutelary power. (210)

It is in that political context that the formal legal systems in all the former French territories, except Guinea, emerged. Not surprisingly, these former French territories became independent under constitutions that drew heavily from the 1958 French constitution, of which they were initially virtual copies. Among the countries formerly under Belgian rule, Zaire (present-day Democratic Republic of the Congo) was the only one to gain independence under a 1960 *Loi Fondamentale* that was actually an Act of the Belgian parliament. Just as Burundi's 1962 autochthonous constitution was, Zaire's constitution was strongly influenced by the Belgian constitution.

Although a few countries—Chad, Madagascar, and Mali—and the former Belgian territories—Burundi, Rwanda, and Zaire—held on to a parliamentary system during the 1960s and 1970s, most newly independent countries quickly replaced their parliamentary system from the colonial period with a presidential regime, which allowed for the concentration of power in the president. It was then argued that the complex mechanics of a stable parliamentary system were difficult to understand by the people, and unsuited for unscrupulous politicians in highly fragmented societies. Constitutional arrangements in most of Francophone Africa had the following features: The president was generally elected by direct universal suffrage—with the notable exception of the Central African Republic. He had wide-ranging power to regulate by decree. He dominated the legislative process through his right to initiate, promulgate, or veto laws passed by parliament. He was also granted special, sweeping powers under exceptional circumstances, which he himself could determine.

In this so-called *état d'exception*, almost all rights and freedom were suspended. The domain of the law remained limited, because the president held most of the normative power. Although the relationships between the branches of government was intended to be respectful of the separation of powers, they actually gave rise to a functional cooperation between the constitutional powers. This evolved to the benefit of the president thanks to the opportunities it offered him to exercise pressure on the assembly. This type of regime has been labeled Negro-African presidentialism.

POSTCOLONIAL TRANSFORMATIONS AND CHALLENGES

Though the organization of the judicial system may vary from one country to another, justice is usually organized on several levels. The trial courts are the lowest level of the system. The Ministry of Justice supervises their operations. There are four groups of trial courts: Courts of First Instance hear juvenile cases, minor criminal cases, and general civil cases; the Courts of Assize hear major criminal cases; the Courts of First Degree hear cases involving customary law; and the Justice of the Peace Courts hear petty civil and petty criminal cases. Labor courts (*tribunaux de travail*) often exist, having jurisdiction over labor disputes. The president of the Republic fixes by decree the number of appellate courts, the number of appellate judges, and the number and functions of different chambers within each appellate court. By statute, these courts are competent to hear civil, criminal, commercial, and administrative appeals.

The constitution provides for a Supreme Court with several units, called chambers. It is the highest level of the judicial system, though the president is also the head of the Superior Council of the Judiciary, which often makes some of the major decisions about the judicial system. In many countries, there is a Court of State Security or a Military Court that operates outside of the legal framework and tries political cases. Some countries have a High Court of Justice, which is a special tribunal for trying government officers of all levels (including the president of the republic) who have committed criminal offenses. Unlike the members of the Supreme Court, the judges on the High Court are not full-time justices. Rather, they are elected on occasion among deputies from the National Assembly who then convene as High Court judges when an impeachment proceeding becomes necessary. Needless to say, procedures in place for initiating such proceeding generally give so much veto power to the president himself that there is no precedent of a head of state having been submitted to the High Court of Justice.

In most Francophone countries, the constitution guarantees two rights with respect to criminal proceedings: a) All persons arrested are presumed innocent until proven guilty, and; b) no one may be arbitrarily detained, except under exceptional and specific circumstances provided by statutes. Yet almost no government in Francophone and Equatorial Africa actually practices these provisions. Every year, human rights organizations such as Amnesty International document a large number of detentions without trial and ill treatment of detainees. For civil and criminal cases that do not involve political acts, trials are public. Although legal counsel is often provided for indigent defendant accused of felonies or major offenses under certain conditions, the reality of limited budget allocations to the judicial system and the poor organization make this provision almost impossible to implement. In general, magistrates who are independent (in theory) and sometimes assisted by juries representing the population exercise the judicial power.

But among the many issues facing legal systems in Francophone Africa in the early twenty-first century, legal pluralism—that is, the fact that peoples of different cultural groups live within the same nation-states under different systems of law—is perhaps the most challenging. As a sign of respect and recognition of historical and cultural differences within countries that were arbitrarily designed, most African governments made the decision after independence to offer to all citizens, at least in theory, the option of jurisdiction (the possibility of choosing which legal system to use). As a result, modern legal systems derived from the colonial experience operate side by side with numerous systems of customary (indigenous) African law.

In Cameroon, which was never formally a French colony but rather a territory placed by a Society of Nations/United Nations mandate under French and British administration, there have always been two different modern legal systems: one inherited from the French and another derived from British common law. Each has imprinted its character on national life—especially in urban areas. In Democratic Republic of the Congo (DRC), Burundi, and Rwanda, account must also be taken of the significant role played in the past, and still being played, by Belgian law. Even within customary systems there are many variations. In countries such as Gabon and Congo, matrilineal systems coexist with and differ significantly from patrilineal ones. And within each of these systems, in turn, there are notable regional variations. An additional layer of complication arises in those countries and areas where Islam has established itself as a major source of law (Senegal, Mali, Burkina Faso, Niger, Chad, and northern Cameroon).

Some authors claim that legal pluralism was managed more or less effectively during the colonial period. Morris-Hugues has argued that in the colonial past, some broad categorizations and assumptions were made: a) political rights and activity were regarded as falling within the domain of constitutional law; b) commercial activity was regarded as falling within the domain of statutory law; c) civil law, especially those issues relating to property rights, land tenure, inheritance and succession, and family relations in general were covered by customary law.

> In a [postcolonial] context characterized by government desire to promote an *état de droit* (state based on laws) founded on the supremacy of written law over customary laws and practices, such neat categorization is no longer realistic. Land tenure is often the basis of commercial activity. Ownership of land provides collateral, and collateral translates into access to credit for further commercial activity. Inheritance is a means of wealth acquisition and the basis of generating further wealth. If women are constrained under customary law in their inheritance rights and in the ownership of land, they are likely to be marginalized from the process of directly generating and directly benefiting from further wealth. (1999, 1)

Although legal pluralism is neither a new phenomenon, nor a uniquely African problem, it raises at least one challenging question to Francophone countries: Is it an impediment to the emergence of a uniform legal system and the modernization of the small, poor economies of these countries? If so, to what extent should it be allowed to continue? Should African rulers follow the example of Turkey's Kemal Ataturk, who abruptly imposed in 1926 the radical substitution of a modern law of Swiss origin for the prevailing multiplicity of personal religious laws in the Ottoman Empire? Clearly, "some branches of law are more deeply and more emotionally involved with the life and culture of a people than others and hence more resistant to sudden and radical change by legislative fiat" (Cowen 1963, 17). This is probably the case,

for example, with family law and the law of succession, by opposition to, say, the law of international financial transactions. For this reason, radical legislative reform may not be effective in family law.

Judicial procedure is generally similar throughout most of Francophone Africa today. Most Francophone African countries devote on average only about 0.7 percent of their gross domestic product to the judiciary. Such meager budget allocation is generally insufficient to address the enormous challenges (lack of infrastructure, material, and human capacity) confronting the judicial system. As a consequence, corruption is often high and survey results indicate that few people believe in the fairness of the system. In certain areas such as business law, major initiatives aiming at the harmonization of procedures and the reduction of transaction costs are ongoing.

UNFULFILLED SOCIAL FUNCTIONS OF LAW

The evolving meanings and scope of law in Francophone Africa reflect the evolving legal theories upon which it is conceived. Ultimately, the nature of law in these countries is more fully understood not only in terms of its origins and sanctions or in terms of the organization and functioning of the judicial system, but in its functions.

Legal scholars tend to focus on three of such functions: the first is the ability to resolve disputes in society, that is, to restore equilibrium to the social order when that equilibrium has been seriously disrupted. According to Berman and Greiner, "law arises in the first instance from claims made in the name of the social order" (31). That criminal cases (in which the state prosecutes) and civil cases (in which one private party claims remedy) differ does not change each judicial case being both a private conflict and a social disequilibrium. A well-functioning legal apparatus (whether judicial, legislative, administrative, contractual, or other) offers a process of resolution of disputes that serves as an alternative to private vengeance, settlement, or brutal force. Clearly, the large number of unresolved violent crimes (Côte d'Ivoire), social conflicts (Bénin, Togo), political upheavals and military coups (Burkina Faso, Niger), civil wars (Chad), and unstable governments (Comoros) that have marked the history of Francophone and Equatorial Africa and countries in the Indian Ocean area over recent decades seem to indicate that law has not been well designed and well implemented to perform its very first social functions.

The second major function of law in any society is to enable citizens to act with reasonable expectations about the behavior of others. Someone who deposits savings in an account at the bank does so with confidence that the money will be available when needed. Such confidence is largely based upon the legal obligation imposed upon financial institutions to ensure that the funds will be made available within the agreed contractual arrangement. Law then becomes necessary as a means of helping citizens made rational, calculable financial decisions. It has the function of regulating social action. Yet again, the postcolonial history of many countries in Francophone and Equatorial Africa provides countless examples of legal systems not being capable of performing adequately this function. Many years after the major banking crisis that occurred in Cameroon in the early 1990s, thousands of clients still could not access their savings from collapsing state-owned financial institutions, despite guarantees offered by their contracts. This was also the case in other Francophone countries such as the Central African Republic, Republic of the Congo, and the Democratic Republic of Congo.

The third function of law is to instill people with the correct attitude and behavior, to mold the moral beliefs of a society. Although the willingness to act in accordance with generally accepted standards is usually taught in the first instance by families, communities, churches, schools, and other social organizations, lessons from history and from human experience also suggest that law is often required to rationalize social interaction and transmit (new) social values from one generation to another Yet again, it appears that Francophone African countries have struggled ensuring that this function of the law is performed satisfactorily. Indeed, between 1960 and 1985 there were 43 constitutions in 18 French-speaking countries, an average of 2.4 constitutions per country. That pace has been maintained in the past two decades, thanks to the major political changes that occurred throughout the continent in 1990 and 1991 following Nelson Mandela's release from prison and Bénin's national conference (February 1990). Such high levels of instability of Francophone legal systems since independence and the inflation of statutes and rules (often mockingly referred to as textual harassment of the citizenry by popular opinion) is evidence that law has not yet been able to educate the moral conceptions of those who are subject to it.

The views expressed in this article do not necessarily represent the views of the World Bank.

See also **Age and Age Organization; Ahidjo, El Hajj Ahmadou; Bokassa, Jean-Bédel; Brazzaville; Colonial Policies and Practices; Houphouët-Boigny, Félix; Kabila, Laurent Desiré, and Joseph; Mandela, Nelson; Mobutu Sese Seko; Postcolonialism; Sassou-Nguesso, Denis; Warfare; Women: Women and the Law.**

BIBLIOGRAPHY

Berman, Harold J., and William R. Greiner. *The Nature and Functions of Law* 4th edition. Mineola, New York: The Foundation Press, 1980.

Buchmann, Jean. *L'Afrique noire indépendante.* Paris: Librairie générale de Droit et de Jurisprudence, 1962.

Conac, Gérard. "L'évolution constitutionnelle des Etats francophones d'Afrique noire et de la République démocratique malgache." In *Les institutions constitutionnelles des Etats d'Afrique francophone et de la République malgache.* Paris: Economica, 1979.

Cowen, Denis V. "African Legal Studies—A Survey of the Field and the Role of the United States." Quoted in "African Law: New Law for New Nations." The *American Journal of Comparative* Law 12, no. 4 (1963): 609–611.

Diop, Cheikh Anta. *L'Afrique noire précoloniale: étude comparée des systèmes politiques et sociaux de l'Europe et de l'Afrique noire de l'Antiquite à la formation des Etats modernes.* Paris: Présence africaine, 1987.

Iye, Ali Moussa. *Le verdict de l'arbre: le Xeer Issa, étude d'une démocratie pastorale.* Dubaï, United Arab Emirates: International Printing Press, 1991.

Ki-Zerbo, Joseph. *Histoire générale de l'Afrique.* Paris: Jeune Afrique, 1980.

Mbokolo, Elikia. "French Colonial Policy in Equatorial Africa in the 1940s and 1950s." In *The Transfer of Power in Africa: Decolonization, 1940–1960,* eds. Prosser Gifford and Wm. Roger Lewis. New Haven, Connecticut: Yale University Press, 1982.

Monga, Célestin. *Measuring Democracy: A Comparative Theory of Political Well-Being,* 2 volumes. Boston: Boston University, African Studies Center Working Papers, 1996.

Monga, Célestin. "Is African Civil Society Civilized?" In *Regionalisation in Africa: Integration and Disintegration,* ed. D. Bach. Bloomington: Indiana University Press, 1999.

Morris-Hughes, Elizabeth. "Gender and Law in Francophone Sub-Saharan Africa: The Role of the World Bank." *Findings*, no 148, on Gender and Law Initiatives in Francophone Sub-Saharan Africa, Washington, DC: World Bank, December, 1999.

Nekam, Alexander. *Experiences in African Customary Law*, Third Melville J. Herskovits Memorial Lecture, The University of Edinburgh, Centre of African Studies, February 28, 1966.

Person, Yves. "French West Africa and Decolonization." In *The Transfer of Power in Africa: Decolonization, 1940–1960*, eds. Prosser Gifford and Wm. Roger Lewis. New Haven, Connecticut: Yale University Press, 1982.

Redden, Kenneth Robert. *Modern Legal Systems Cyclopedia, Africa*, vol. 6 revised. Buffalo, New York: William S. Hein & Co., 1990.

Reyntjens, Filip. "Recent Developments in the Public Law of Francophone African States." *Journal of African Law* 30, no. 2 (1986): 75–90.

Tchoungang, Charles. "Le cadre juridique des sociétés commerciales au Cameroun." *Revue Camerounaise de Management* no. 3–4, (1986): 247–256.

Wabnitz, Hans-Werner. *Provision of Justice and Equity in Francophone Africa by Changing the Law and the Courts*. Washington, DC: World Bank, 2004.

CÉLESTIN MONGA

ISLAMIC

Islamic law is based on God's revealed law, the *shari'a*, as written down in the Qur'an and the *sunna*, the traditions (*hadith*s), or doings and sayings, of the prophet Muhammad. The *shari'a* is both a juridical corpus and an ethic. However, *shari'a* does not mean a legal corpus, and the Qur'an is not a legal code. Instead, the Arabic term *shari'a* is used for any system of laws and the totality of the message of a particular prophet.

The *shari'a* (the path to a spring) is the just order of the world as given by God. It covers not only the relationships between human beings—called *mu'amalat* in Arabic—but also the relationship between man and God—the *'ibadat*. Instead of Islamic law, one can speak of an Islamic normativity. The relatively few legal prescriptions in the Qur'an, mainly stipulations for inheritance, marriage, contracts, and the so-called *hudud* (singular *hadd*)—the Qur'anic punishments for robbery, stealing, drinking of wine, adultery, and false

accusation of adultery—are interpreted and applied to concrete cases in *fiqh* (knowledge) and Islamic jurisprudence by the *fuqaha'*, the Islamic jurists. Islamic law, then, is the product of the interpretative activity of the *fuqaha'*. *Fiqh* and *shari'a* are often used synonymously. Nevertheless, *fiqh* is considered human and *shari'a* divine in origin.

SCHOOLS AND PROFESSIONALS

A differentiated legal system, influenced by laws and customs of the conquered peoples and developed its own complex methodology, emerged out of local circles of people interested in legal issues during the eighth century. By the late ninth century, schools of law (*madhhab*, plural *madhahib*) were formed around eponymous scholars who stand for a certain use of the sources and for a specific methodological approach. Before that time, the main split among legal scholars had been between the *ahl al-hadith*, scholars who based their judicial expertise on the traditions (*hadith*s) of the Prophet, his companions and successors, and the *ahl ar-ra'y*, the adherents of reasonable opinion who tried to figure out suitable and pious solutions by reasoning. The *ahl al-hadith* followed different traditions: sometimes regional, for example Iraqi, sometimes of a specific town, such as Medina. Out of the various schools known in Islamic history, four Sunni schools of law and one Shi'i school survived. After long clashes, the schools decided to accept each other as orthodox, even in cases of contradictory opinions.

The oldest school is the *Hanafiyya*, named after Abu Hanifa (d. 767), a jurist from Kufa in Iraq. Abu Hanifa did not leave a written work, but his disciples al-Shaybani (d. 805) and Abu Yusuf (d. 798) spread his teachings. Here, the legal practice of Iraq was collected with its emphasis on the opinion (*ra'y*) of the competent jurist, and the use of *istihsan* (approval), a discretionary opinion in breach of a strict analogy. The Hanafi school also made use of the technique of *hiyal* (singular *hila*, meaning legal devices) to circumvent undesired prescriptions and results.

Malik ibn Anas (d. 179/795), the eponymous founder of the *Malikiyya* school, was charged by the second 'Abbasid caliph to establish a unified judicial system integrating the various systems and practices of the Islamic lands. Malik presented his

Courtyard of the famous madrasa al-Yusufiya in Marrakesh, Morocco, 10th century AH/16th century CE. This madrasa, or college, was the most important in southern Morocco. It was the last Muslim educational institution to be "conquered" by Western imperialism. PHOTOGRAPH BY GERHARD ENDRESS, BOCHUM

legal doctrine and the practice of Medina, where he lived and worked, in his book *al-Muwatta*', the oldest surviving legal book in Islam. Particular stress was laid on the Medinan traditions of the Prophet, his companions and successors.

Beyond the Medinan practice, the *Malikiyya* takes the overall interest (*maslaha*) of the Muslim community (*umma*) into account. Al-Shafi'i (d. 820), founder of the *Shafi'iyya*, studied with Malik in Medina and with Hanafi scholars in Iraq. He died in Egypt. With his masterpiece, the *Risala*, ash-Shafi'i systematized the Islamic jurisprudence, balancing between the schools and trying to limit arbitrary decisions, thus rejecting the Hanafi *istihsan* and the Maliki *maslaha*. He also limited the use of traditions to the traditions (*sunna*) of the

prophet Muhammad himself. The smallest Sunni school of law is the *Hanabila*, named after Ahmad ibn Hanbal (d. 855), who studied with al-Shafi'i. Sometimes ibn Hanbal is considered more a traditionalist than a jurist, and his major work, the *Musnad*, is a collection of traditions. He became famous through his fierce opposition to the doctrine of the createdness of the Qur'an, proposed by the rationalistic Mu'tazili. The *Hanabila* is rigorous in questions of cult and dogma, but liberal concerning commerce and contracts.

Fiqh, meaning knowledge in Arabic, is the Islamic science par excellence, far more important than theology. The jurists work as judges (*qadi*s) or jurisconsults (*mufti*s), and have played an important role of developing Islamic law. Where *qadi*s are always appointed and salaried by the rulers, and often limited in time, space, or subject matter, *mufti*s can be officially installed, but also act in complete independence and freedom. Here, recognition by the Muslim public was and still is important. Mostly, the *qadi* is in charge of civil and personal law. Penal and administrative law lay in the hand of the ruler or of his deputies. Traditionally, the *qadi* pronounces his verdict, the *hukm*, as a single judge with no possibility for appeal, hence, the dictum of *Kadijustiz*, meaning absolute discretionary power. He is assisted by the *katib* (scribe), the clerk of the court. The verdict aims at assessing the legal validity or invalidity of acts and possesses executive power. This concerns the inner worldly realm of this life.

The *mufti* on the other hand, on request of the faithful, a *qadi*, or a ruler, gives a legal opinion on a concrete issue, a *fatwa*. This *fatwa* should help to lead a pious and moral life; its realm is the hereafter. A *fatwa* is not enforceable and not binding for the questioner. Each case should be concentrated in a question, which can be answered by yes or no.

A further legal figure is the *muhtasib*, the supervisor of the markets and public places, guardian also of morality and the observance of religious duties. He should be a *faqih*. The *muhtasib* was not found in sub-Saharan Africa, but the underlying Qur'anic principle *amr bil-ma'ruf wa-nahy 'an al-munkar* (commanding the right and forbidding the wrong; Sura 3, verse 104) was, of course, known and sometimes practiced. The present-day

Religious Police in Northern Nigeria is based on this principle.

SOURCES AND PRINCIPLES (*USUL*)

The term *usul*, roots, covers the complex of legal theory in Islamic law. Here, the sources of the law are fixed and principles of legal reasoning and interpretation developed. There is general agreement among the schools of law on the main sources and principles, but differences concerning the legitimacy of some legal methods and sources.

The first source of Islamic law is the Qur'an. Being in modern times presented by Islamists as something close to a legal code, the Qur'an, however, contains only a few verses related to legal issues, mainly in the field of family law and inheritance, and also concerning the ritual, such as prayers, fasting, or pilgrimage.

The second source is the tradition of the prophet Muhammad, the *sunna*, as collected in the reports of sayings and doings of the prophet, the *hadith*s. There exist several canonical collections; the most respected are the *Sahih*s of al-Bukhari (d. 870) and Muslim (d. 875). A *hadith* consists of a chain of transmitters, the *isnad*, going back to the prophet, and the textual report itself, the *matn*. Islamic scholarship developed criteria for the authenticity and trustworthiness of *hadith*s and labeled them accordingly as sound (*sahih*), good (*hasan*), weak (*da'if*), or false (*mawdu'*). Since the late nineteenth century, North American and European scholarship has considered all these *hadith*s fabricated and inauthentic. Recent studies, however, show that this does not hold true, at least for some *hadith*s.

The third source is the consensus of scholars, the *consensus sapientium*, *ijma'*, with regard to particular issues. It is not always clear if this consensus covers all legal scholars, all scholars of a particular law school, a town, region, or country, and if there are limits in time. However, a consensus is normally reached after a dispute (or also without a dispute, if an opinion does not meet contradiction), and is influenced by the opinions of previous scholars. These agreements are liable to change when there are new insights.

The fourth source is the use of analogy, *qiyas*, to find solutions for legal problems. That means that the legal scholar looks for cases with similarities

Inscription from a madrasa in Marrakesh. The basis of Islamic jurisprudence is the Qur'an, used also as decoration in mosques and madrasas. This inscription reads *ar-rahman ar-rahim* ("the Merciful the Compassionate"). COURTESY OF SANDRA PETERMANN, MAINZ

to the actual case he is trying to solve, if there is no precedence to be found in the Qur'an, the *sunna*, or the legal literature. Here, general principles—governing the goals and intents of the law and being different according to the various legal schools—such as the orientation at the overall interest of the community of believers (*umma*), the *maslaha*, or the giving preference to a specific opinion (*istihsan*, approval), are used to widen the scope of possible legal solutions, even in breaking with strict analogy (*qiyas*) and without a textual source. The use of legal devices (*hiyal*) also help to circumvent legal rules.

After the fourth/tenth century, many Muslim scholars considered the interpretation of the Qur'an and the Prophetic traditions (*sunna*) as completed.

Acceptance and transmission of authoritative texts of previous scholars deemed them necessary. This is called *taqlid*, reliance on the teaching of a master. The independent and individual intellectual effort, the *ijtihad*, of a legal scholar, qualified as a *mujtahid*, seemed no longer possible, as the door of *ijtihad* closed. For a long time, European and North American scholarship took this for granted, but now it is acknowledged that, throughout Islamic history, at least some Muslim jurists practiced *ijtihad*.

The original Qur'anic classifying categories for beings and things are taboo/forbidden (*haram*), and not forbidden (*halal*). Then, the Islamic jurists developed a scale of five norms (*al-ahkam al-khamsa*, the five legal qualifications) to categorize applicable legal rulings: (1) the obligatory (*wajib*), (2) the recommended (*mandub*), (3) the indifferent or permissible (*mubah*), (4) the forbidden (*haram*), and (5) the repugnant (*makruh*). This scale aims at an

Islamic ethic, and is not simply a matter of legal technique. The performance of an obligatory act entails reward, its omission punishment. The five daily prayers are obligatory, for example, but each is of limited obligation, which means that it is bound to a specific daytime and has to be performed during the appropriate time to be valid. An obligation can be individual (*fard al-'ain*) or collective (*fard al-kifaya*). The collective obligation is fulfilled if the necessary number of individuals fulfils it. Recommended acts are rewarded when performed, but do not entail punishment. Concerning the legal effects—as stated in a verdict (*hukm*)—of religious observances (*'ibadat*) and transactions (*mu'amalat*), another scale of qualifications was developed: (1) valid (*sahih*), (2) allowed (*ja'iz*), (3) operative (*nafidh*), (4) binding (*lazim*), (5) defective, voidable (*fasid*), and (6) void (*batil*). This scale follows other guiding principles than the five legal qualifications

The legendary Jemaa el-Fna in Marrakesh, Morocco. Every evening, acrobats, storytellers, and healers gather in this place, surrounded by crowds. Music, magic practices, and other expressions of popular culture and religion are condemned by Muslim jurists as un-Islamic. PHOTOGRAPH BY GERHARD ENDRESS, BOCHUM, 1972

above: During the obligatory Friday Prayer (*salat al-jum'a*) commerce is forbidden, but a sales contract concluded during this time is valid and binding.

Written evidences played no role in legal procedures. Instead, *qadi*s based their considerations on oral testimonies. In North Africa professional witnesses working at the courts often gave them. In colonial and postcolonial Africa, this has changed, due also to new technical possibilities of archiving documents.

FIELDS AND ISSUES OF POSITIVE LAW (*FURU*)

Islamic law has, until the nineteenth century, never been codified in a Western sense. Instead, it was a jurists' law, based on interpretations of religious doctrine and transmitted both orally and by written texts, such as handbooks and commentaries of handbooks and collections of legal opinions. Verdicts by *qadi*s played no role nor did the executive, the rulers, and the administrations.

The *furu'*, the branches, delineate legal and moral obligations, from religious to worldly, covering rituals, contracts, sales, personal status, and penal law, among other things. They differentiate between religious observances (*'ibadat*) and inter-human transactions (*mu'amalat*), and also between the rights of persons (*huquq al-'ibad, huquq al-ada-miyyin*)—for example contracts, obligations, and personal status, aiming at balance and justice between parties—and the rights of God (*huquq Allah*), covering the general interests of the public and the Islamic community (*umma*) and being absolute and indivisible. The benefits of the rights of God are for all human beings, and not for particular women or men. In some cases, both rights of persons and rights of God are touched, but one or the other prevails; sometimes they coexist such as in the case of theft, where the owner of the stolen property has the right to get it back (a right of persons), but where the thief also has to be punished with having his right hand cut off, a Qur'anic punishment that belongs to the rights of God.

THE HISTORY AND CURRENT PLACE OF ISLAMIC LAW IN AFRICA

Until the nineteenth century, Islamic law dominated the life of nearly all Muslims due to its centrality for a pious and good life. Islamic law, however, coexisted and competed in most places with other legal systems, such as tribal and customary law. Muslim people normally considered their own local practice as Islamic and as a true expression of *shari'a*.

Under European influence, codification attempts following European examples started in the nineteenth century. The most famous case is the Ottoman *Mejelle* of 1876, a civil law book based on *shari'a*. Sometimes, European, mainly French, codes were simply translated and promulgated. Radical changes in world economy and the colonial penetration in North and sub-Saharan Africa by France and Great Britain changed the situation completely. Both the British and French imported their own legal system and codes. Furthermore, the French developed and applied in their colonial law courts in North Africa, Mauritania, and Senegal their *droit musulman algérien* (Algerian Muslim Law).

To Africa, Islamic law brought a new concept of status and rights based on religion rather than membership in a kinship or territorial community. Islamic law also emphasizes more the rights and obligations of individuals. However, concerning real property rights, Islamic law and jurisprudence is able to accommodate various customary practices. Three types of legal processes and institutions can be distinguished. One is an informal legal sector, where people seek advice and counseling by a local imam, teacher or pious man, especially on rituals and social comportment. Another is a formal legal sector with *qadi*s and *mufti*s, a clear set of rules and with judicial authority delegated or, sometimes, assumed by the ruler. The *qadi* has a difficult position insofar as he is the point where political authority interferes directly in the daily life of people. However, until the introduction of modern colonial administration in Africa, the judiciary was not centralized or hierarchically structured. The third institution includes nationwide bureaucratic systems that emerged, no longer involved in local political haggling, but far more under central control. In most cases, this meant the reduction of Islamic law to the domain of family law only, whereas European codes were applied in all other matters and a European centralized court system was established.

Between the fourteenth and nineteenth centuries, Islamic legal traditions were elaborated in the urban centers of the Arabic-speaking lands and vigorously adapted in the Sudanic lands and East Africa. This process was related to the revival of Christian military power in the Iberian Peninsula, leading to Portuguese settlements all along the African coastline. In North and West Africa, Sufi orders (*tariqa*s) facilitated the often difficult relationship between the urban centers and rural areas. In the Sudanic lands and East Africa, Muslims were challenged not only by persistent traditional religions, but also by political and economic patterns that were different from Arabic and North African traditions, and they had to adapt their religion to these circumstances. Therefore, there are no religious endowments (*waqf*s) in western Sudan, because a *waqf* requires private property and this was unknown there, where royal power was founded on the role as ultimate arbiter in matters of real property. However, the Muslims in Africa are no less Islamic than their Arab counterparts.

Islamic law was crucial in disputes on the legitimacy of rulers. It also helped setting up a status system by defining criteria for being a Muslim or not, important for slave raiding and imposing heavy taxes, because Muslims could not be enslaved or subjected to non-Islamic taxes.

Northern Africa. In all North African countries, Islamic law has been widely applied since at least the third/ninth century. The Maliki school of law is prevalent, but in the former Ottoman provinces the Hanafi school—as the official *madhhab* of the Sublime Porte—is present, too. In Algeria and Tunisia, the heterodox 'Ibadites are a tiny minority with their own legal tradition. Maliki legal scholarship is mostly associated with a wealthy urban elite. Islamic law governed all aspects of religious, social, and economic life, and also the shape of the cities.

The French constructed an artificial divide between Arabs and Berbers with regard to customs and law and, in 1930, enacted the so-called *dahir berbère*, the Berber Decree, intended to codify Berber customary laws that were considered different from Islamic law. The Berbers protested violently against it because they considered their customs as absolutely Islamic, and the French withdrew its application.

In the early twenty-first century, in Morocco, Algeria, Tunisia, and Libya, Islamic law is restricted to family law covering marriage, divorce, adoption, and inheritance. European-inspired codes rule all other legal domains. Beside these two legal systems, customary laws play an important role in the daily life of people with regard to rituals and social comportment. In Tunisia, Algeria, and Morocco, Islamic law is not mentioned in the constitutions as a source of legislation, but in Mauritania it is.

In Libya, some of the Qur'anic prescribed punishments have been integrated in 1975 in the penal code, for example the amputation of the right hand for theft, but not stoning for illicit sexual relations by a person who has ever had a valid marriage.

In Tunisia, *qadi* courts were abolished in 1956, as well as public religious endowments. Polygamy—Islamic law allows for a man to marry up to four women—was forbidden by the new family law in 1957 and made a criminal offence. Divorce cannot be pronounced by initiative of the husband (*talaq*, repudiation), but by a court only. Man and woman are equal before the law. Concerning the law of succession, the Tunisian code adheres in general to Islamic prescriptions, but introduced important changes in favor of the daughter and the son's daughter. In traditional Islamic law, women inherit only half of the share of male relatives. Contrary to Islamic law, adoption of children is allowed. However, the Tunisian lawmaker carefully avoided the impression of abolishing Islamic law.

In colonial Algeria, renouncing the application of Islamic law in matters of personal status was a prerequisite to acquire French citizenship. Thus, everything related to Islam and Algerian Islamicness was important in the struggle for independence. The first codification of comprehensive family law, always perceived by Muslims as the kernel of Islamic law in their lives, was, however, enacted only in 1984. In a process of intense debate and fighting between the state and religious scholars and Islamist activities, Islamic law and Algerian customs are integrated into the otherwise secular legal systems. It seems nevertheless more appropriate to speak of a sacralization of a certain family model than sacralization of the legal system.

The Moroccan *Mudawwana*, the code of personal status and inheritance, was enacted 1957 and 1958. In the late 1990s and early 2000s it was the object of several reforms that aimed at strengthening women's rights, and these reforms encountered fierce opposition by Islamists.

The *qadi*, Hajj Abd al-Rahman al-Mansouri (1912–1995). This photograph was taken shortly after he finished his studies at the famous al-Yusufiyya mosque-university in Marrakesh in the 1930s. Eickelman, *Knowledge and Power in Morocco* (1985), portrays his life and the role of Islamic law and learning in Moroccan society. © 1976, DALE F. EICKELMAN

West Africa. From the seventh/thirteenth century on, Muslims in West Africa were of the Sunni Maliki *madhhab*. However, Islam and Islamic law coexisted with previous legal and religious traditions and practices, such as animism. Rulers applied various laws as it suited them. An early and continuing exception in this regard is the city of Timbuktu in Mali with its strict Islamic observance. Islamic law and its commercial rules fostered sub-Saharan trade and instigated conversions to Islam among the trading classes. By the end of the twelfth/eighteenth century, several *jihad* movements tried to impose a stricter observance of the *shari'a* and to fight against unlawful innovations (*bida'*, singular *bid'a*). The most famous is the *jihad* of the Hausa Shehu 'Uthman dan Fodio leading to the establishment of the Sokoto Caliphate in present-day Northern Nigeria. Here, Islamic law was applied more or less consistently. The British introduced their legal system, but gave under indirect rule Northern Nigeria a large degree of autonomy in legal matters, thus preserving

Islamic law with the exception of so-called inhumane punishments, such as amputation or stoning. The French introduced their *droit musulman algérien* also in the so-called Four Communes (four cities), in Senegal, and in Mauritania.

Muslims are, in some West African states such as Senegal, the majority. However, in no state but the states of Northern Nigeria is Islamic law part of the official legal system. Islam is mostly considered a personal belief system. In Northern Nigeria, the situation is different: Islamic law is applied there without interruption. After World War II, a process of Islamization started, leading to massive conversion to Islam and to a wider adoption of Islamic dress and Islamic names. The legal system in Northern Nigeria is a dual one: secular British-inspired law and Islamic law. The law of the federal state, however, is secular and the Christian Southern Nigeria is eager to maintain this situation against heavy pressure from Islamists and the Northern states. Thus, they blocked the creation of a *shari'a* Court of Appeal on the federal level. On appeal, federal courts have annulled all of the spectacular decisions of Islamic courts (amputation of the right hand for theft or stoning for illicit sexual relations). However, 90 percent of civil law cases in the Northern region are brought to *shari'a* courts. This is also due to the fact that Islamic courts are accessible and not so costly.

Southern Africa. In South Africa, the Dutch East India Company brought in the first Muslims from Southeast Asia. A tiny minority, they played nevertheless an important role in the anti-apartheid struggle. Muslims used to practice Islamic personal status law informally and outside of state structures, administered by the Muslim scholars (*'ulama*) in the mosques. After apartheid, some Muslim groups pressed for recognition of Islamic personal status law inside the legal system of the state, and the state installed a commission in charge of this issue. The new constitution of 1997 provides for the introduction of some aspects of Islamic law, if not in contradiction with the Bill of Rights. The debate about what parts of Islamic law are to implement and how is still ongoing.

In Malawi, the Asian Muslims are all Sunni Hanafi. The other Muslims are of east coast origins and are of the Shafi'i school of law. The great majority of them are still greatly influenced by traditional customs and beliefs. Muslims from the matrilineal Yao or Chewa people follow Islamic law only if it does not contradict their customs. They accept more easily a Muslim woman marrying a Christian man than a Muslim man marrying a Christian woman, in absolute contrast to Islamic law. Concerning divorce and succession, they also follow their customary law rather than Islamic law.

EAST AFRICA AND THE HORN OF AFRICA

Most Muslims in East Africa live in the long-Islamized coastal strip. They are mainly Sunni Shafi'i, even if their rulers in the past were 'Ibadi from Oman, governing in Zanzibar. The British recognized Muslims courts in these areas, but in the interior English law and African traditions were applied. The Muslims, however, lost their political power—especially after the unification of Tanganyika with Zanzibar to Tanzania—so that, after independence, secular legal systems were installed in East Africa without any reference to Islamic law. Islamic law is practiced only informally, such as in West Africa.

In Somalia, the socialist regime of Muhammad Siad Barré (1919–1995) who reigned from 1969 until 1991, considered Islam a personal faith and ignored all Islamic institutions such as the *shari'a*. Its modernizing policies and especially the Family Law Edict of 1975 that broke with Somali traditions, together with the imprisonment of leading Muslim figures, led to civil war which lasted more or less until the present.

See also **Apartheid; Education, School: Muslim Africa; Family; Islam; Marriage Syatems; Postcolonialism; Socialism and Postsocialisms; Taboo and Sin; Timbuktu; 'Uthman dan Fodio; Warfare: World Wars; Youth: Youth and Islam.**

BIBLIOGRAPHY

Anderson, James Norman Dalrymple. *Islamic Law in the Modern World*. New York: New York University Press, 1959.

Coulson, Noel James. *A History of Islamic Law*. Edinburgh: University Press, 1964.

Eickelman, Dale F. *Knowledge and Power in Morocco. The Education of a Twentieth-Century Notable*. Princeton, New Jersey: Princeton University Press, 1985.

Evers Rosander, Eva, and David Westerlund, eds. *African Islam and Islam in Africa. Encounters Between Sufis and Islamists*. Athens: Ohio University Press, 1997.

Hallaq, Wael B. *Authority, Continuity and Change in Islamic Law*. Cambridge, U.K.: Cambridge University Press, 2005.

Johansen, Baber. *Contingency in a Sacred Law. Legal and Ethical Norms in the Muslim Fiqh*. Leiden, The Netherlands: Brill, 1999.

Levtzion, Nehemia, and Randall L. Pouwels, eds. *The History of Islam in Africa*. Athens: Ohio University Press, 2000.

Rosen, Lawrence. *The Justice of Islam: Comparative Perspectives on Islamic Law and Society*. New York: Oxford University Press, 1999.

Schacht, Joseph. *The Origins of Muhammadan Jurisprudence*. Oxford: Clarendon Press, 1950.

Schacht, Joseph. *An Introduction to Islamic Law*. Oxford: Clarendon Press, 1964.

JÖRN THIELMANN

LUSOPHONE AFRICA

Lusophone Africa comprises the former Portuguese mainland colonies of Angola, Mozambique, and Guinea-Bissau and the island territories of Cape Verde and São Tomé e Príncipe. Much of Portugal's African colonies were not brought under full Portuguese military and administrative control until the early 1930s, when the Estado Novo (New State) dictatorship was established and the enactment and enforcement of harsh colonial laws began. In the early 1960s, armed liberation struggles were launched in the mainland colonies. After more than a decade, the fighting culminated in the proclamation by the Partido Africano da Independência de Guiné e Cabo Verde (PAIGC) of the independence of Guinea-Bissau (September 24, 1973). As a result, all the remaining territories became independent in 1975, following the collapse of the Lisbon dictatorship caused by the military coup of April 25, 1974.

In Angola the three main nationalist movements, the Movimento Popular de Libertação de Angola (MPLA), the União Nacional para a Independência Total de Angola (UNITA), and the Frente Nacional de Libertação de Angola (FNLA), contested the legitimacy of any single party to assume total power. This resulted in the Alvor Accord of January 1975, establishing a transitional government that collapsed within a month and provoking a twenty-seven-year civil war that ended with the battlefield death of UNITA leader Jonas Savimbi in February 2002. In Mozambique, the legitimacy of the new government of the Frente de Libertação de Moçambique (FRELIMO) was immediately challenged by the Resistência Nacional Moçambicana (RENAMO) rebel movement, plunging the country into a sixteen-year destructive civil war ended by a peace settlement mediated by the Vatican in October 1992. These costly conflicts ravaged the political and social institutions of both countries, and both have yet to fully recover from the devastations of prolonged war.

ONE-PARTY STATE AND POPULAR JUSTICE

Unlike the majority of former European colonies in Africa, the newly independent Lusophone nations all immediately adopted single-party political models and socialist policies. Article four of all the new party-promulgated constitutions enshrined the supremacy of the ruling parties, promised social and economic justice to all citizens, and established the new judicial and legal frameworks that incorporated Portuguese civil code and largely shunned customary law and practices—generally viewed as incapable of promoting equality for women. Furthermore, enacted laws quickly nationalized land, major enterprises, and many social institutions, and by 1977 the vanguard parties in Angola and Mozambique had declared their respective countries Marxist-Leninist states.

In Angola, Mozambique, and Guinea-Bissau, the new judicial systems were founded on military law (*lei da justiça militar*) promulgated during the wars of liberation. The systems dealt with both military and civilian justice in the liberated areas, and were characterized by popularly elected courts known as *tribunais do povo*. Generally, these justice systems took some aspect of customary law into account for minor offenses. Above these village-level courts were the higher courts at the regional level, and above that was the highest court, the *tribunal de guerra* (war tribunal), with powers to pass longer jail sentences and the death penalty. With independence, the inherited Portuguese civil code was grafted onto this system of popular justice. As a result of war, political instability, state fragility, and inadequate physical infrastructure, the code had limited impact on most rural dwellers. These people remained subjected to their traditional laws that were tolerated by the government

when they did not contradict the basic principles of the formal justice systems.

COLONIAL ANTECEDENTS

During the colonial period a dual legal system was established in Portugal's African colonies, with the notable exception of Cape Verde, whose inhabitants were all considered civilized. On the one hand, the metropolitan Portuguese civil code was applied to the tiny urban-based civilized population; on the other, the *indigenato* (native) code was rigorously imposed on the largely rural-based uncivilized majority.

The indigenato code was based on well-defined legal texts, including the *Political, Civil, and Criminal Statute of the Natives* (1929), the *Colonial Act* (1930), the *Organic Charter of the Portuguese Colonial Empire* (1933), and the *Overseas Administrative Reform* (1933). It selectively recognized customary law in order to regulate traditional practices pertaining to the family, property, and succession rights, but the Portuguese criminal code was applied to crimes and the administration of justice. Colonial administrators assisted by native assessors—invariably local Portuguese-appointed chiefs known as *regulos* in Guinea-Bissau and Mozambique and *sobas* in Angola—presided over the established native courts. The incorporation of these pliable native authorities (officially regarded as government agents) was aimed at entrenching Portuguese sovereignty and facilitating colonial exploitation.

The indigenato reinforced the inequality of women in both matrilineal and patrilineal societies by recognizing the authority only of the male-dominated native authorities that adjudicated all kinds of local disputes, including marriage and bridewealth issues, control over children, the right to own and inherit land, and control of other socially valuable resources. In general, traditional customs and practices in the mainland colonies left women disadvantaged and discriminated against. Especially in patrilineal societies, customary law generally treated women as minors under the guardianship of their husbands, if married, or under the guardianship of their fathers, if unmarried. Generally, a woman did not have rights or access to land without the endorsement of a husband or male relatives. Customary laws usually did not recognize such human rights violations as physical abuse and marital rape by husbands, whereas in cases of adultery the woman would bear the greater responsibility and therefore heavier sanction. Furthermore, the practice of compulsory wife inheritance by the brother-in-law of a widow was a widely recognized custom.

The Portuguese colonial legal tradition, concerned more with effective domination than the prevalence of justice, continues to be influential in independent Lusophone Africa. Although in the mainland countries codified law coexists with customary authority, the two legal systems have yet to be fully reconciled. Notwithstanding constitutional guarantees and the legal reforms brought about by the post–Cold War democratization exigencies, national legislation, especially in Angola, Guinea-Bissau, and Mozambique, continues to restrict such fundamental liberties as the freedom of expression, association, assembly, and demonstration. Freedom of speech and the press is restricted by the criminalization of defamation; freedom of association is limited by the stringent requirements for government recognition; and the right of assembly and demonstration is controlled by the requirement for advance notification and the identification of the organizers.

CHALLENGED DEMOCRATIC LEGAL SYSTEMS

After almost two decades of one-party rule, major legislative and judicial reforms began to be implemented in Lusophone Africa as in the rest of the continent. By the mid-1990s, in response to both internal and external pressure for economic and political liberalization, the original constitutions of the mid-1970s were amended or replaced, allowing for political pluralism; freedom of expression, association, and assembly; the right to strike; and, among other things, an independent press and private radio broadcast. Legislation to establish free-market economies with incentives for private investment resulted in privatization of state enterprises and marked reduction of the government's role in economic activities. Laws to facilitate the democratization process created relatively vibrant civil societies and culminated in the realization of multiparty elections in Cape Verde (1991), São Tomé e Príncipe (1991), Angola (1992), Guinea-Bissau (1994), and Mozambique (1994). The constitutional changes for political pluralism resulted in the defeat of the hitherto formidable ruling parties in the two island nations of Cape Verde and São and Príncipe, whereas their counterparts in the mainland managed to retain power. All the Lusophone countries became signatories of numerous international treaties that guaranteed the right to fundamental freedoms, including the International Covenant on Civil and Political Rights, the African Charter on Human and People's Rights, and the Convention on the Elimination of All Forms of Discrimination Against Women.

It is in Cape Verde that the implementation of constitutional reforms has unfolded most peacefully and most effectively. The country has regular presidential, legislative, and local elections, a high degree of transparency and accountability of public office-holders, and sufficient independence of the judiciary to enforce legal provisions that guarantee basic freedoms and enable judicial review of legislative and executive action. The statutory system has undergone a profound restructuring, and the prevalence of an efficacious rule of law has facilitated the transformation of the archipelago from least developed country status to a middle-income developing nation with a deepening democratic culture.

In the rest of Lusophone Africa, notwithstanding the notable progress made in institution-building to consolidate the democratization process, such as the establishment of independent electoral commissions, the inauguration of multiparty national parliaments, the proliferation of civil society organizations, the appearance of vociferous independent media, and the creation of auditor-general offices and anticorruption agencies, a salient feature remains the lack of independence and the weakness of the respective judiciaries. The absence of these undermines the implementation of the critical laws passed. This has been clearly demonstrated in the three civil war–affected mainland nations where, despite the duration of the bloody conflicts and the urgent postconflict reconstruction needs, law and legality have been particularly challenging issues.

In Angola and Mozambique, constitutional reforms were integral parts of peace processes (respectively, the 1991 Bicese Peace Accords and the 1992 Rome General Peace Agreement), with peace consolidated in the latter and war resumed in the former (until it finally ended a decade later). Whereas Mozambique has consolidated its transition to peace and political pluralism (during the 2004 presidential elections,

Joaquim Chissano [b. 1939], the country's long-serving president, declined to run for another term and instead supported his party's candidate, Armando Guebuza [b. 1943], who won with 64 percent of the votes), Angola has yet to organize multiparty presidential and legislative elections since the first ill-fated attempt in 1992 (realization of the scheduled 2006 elections remains uncertain, not least because further revision of the constitution is still ongoing). Nevertheless, in both countries there have been recurrent reports by national and international human rights organizations of police use of lethal force, arbitrary arrests and prolonged pretrial detentions in overcrowded life-threatening cells, and persistent impunity for the perpetrators.

Unlike Mozambique, Guinea-Bissau failed appallingly to consolidate the democratization process, largely as a result of incessant political instability (with numerous alleged attempted military coups), culminating in a destructive eleven-month civil war in 1998–1999, followed by a postconflict period characterized by the most flagrant attacks on the constitutional order in Lusophone Africa—which included President Kumba Yala's (b. 1953) ordering the dismissal, arrest, and imprisonment, without formal charge, of the president, vice president, and two judges of the country's Supreme Court, for ruling against his unlawful expulsion of a foreign religious group. During the period 2001 to 2005, the Guinean judicial system was effectively dysfunctional, totally lacking independence from an executive branch that manipulated politically appointed judges to legitimize its rule; most criminal cases that reached the few functioning courts stalled in the preliminary hearing stage, never going to trial. A strong culture of impunity characterized the failed justice system that has yet to be revitalized.

Although São Tomé e Príncipe has not endured violent civil strife, the island nation has nevertheless experienced recurrent assaults on the constitutional order. The bloodless military coups of August 1995 and July 2003, persistent high levels of fraud and graft, and an endemic culture of impunity in the context of growing expectations of a huge windfall from imminent exploitation of the substantial oil reserves discovered within territorial waters epitomize these attacks.

A fundamental challenge still facing Lusophone Africa, with the possible exception of Cape Verde, remains the thorough overhauling of the judicial systems and their effective independence—urgent tasks requiring strong commitment from the highest level of government.

See also **Colonial Policies and Practices; Government; Kinship and Descent; Labor: Trades Unions and Associations; Political Systems; Postcolonialism; Savimbi, Jonas; Socialism and Postsocialisms; Warfare: Civil Wars; Women: Widows; Women: Women and the Law.**

BIBLIOGRAPHY

Birmingham, David. *Empire in Africa: Angola and Its Neighbors.* Athens: Ohio University Press, 2006.

Chabal, Patrick, et al., eds. *A History of Post Colonial Lusophone Africa.* Bloomington: Indiana University Press, 2002.

Davidson, Basil. *The Fortunate Isles: A Study in African Transformation.* Trenton, NJ: African World Press, 1989.

Gundersen, Aase. "Popular Justice in Mozambique: Between State Law and Folk Law." *Social and Legal Studies* 1, no. 2 (1992): 257–282.

Hodges, Tony. *Angola from Afro-Stalinism to Petro-Diamond Capitalism.* Oxford: James Curry, 2001.

Isaacman, Barbara, and Allen Isaacman. "A Socialist Legal System in the Making: Mozambique Before and After Independence." In *The Politics of Informal Justice*, vol. 2, ed. Richard L. Abel. New York: Academic Press, 1982.

Lobban, Richard. *Cape Verde: Crioulo Colony to Independent Nation.* Boulder, CO: Westview Press, 1995.

Rudebeck, Lars. *Guinea-Bissau: A Study of Political Mobilization.* Uppsala: Nordiska Afrikainstitutet, 1974.

Sachs, Albie, and Gita Welch. *Liberating the Law: Creating Popular Justice in Mozambique.* London: Zed Books, 1990.

Seibert, Gerhard. *Comrades, Clients, and Cousins: Colonialism, Socialism, and Democratization in São Tomé and Príncipe*, 2nd edition. Leiden, the Netherlands: Brill, 2006.

PETER KARIBE MENDY

SOUTHERN AFRICA

The transformation of the Republic of South Africa in the last decades of the twentieth century required the transformation in particular of the legal system, which had been the foundation of the oppressive and divisive system of apartheid. After the repeal of the legislative foundations of apartheid, the process of transformation required the adaptation and integration of other South

African laws, the diverse sources of which present a rich and unique heritage, shared by neighboring states in southern Africa.

INDIGENOUS LAW

The indigenous African societies of southern Africa in the precolonial period were mainly centralized, chiefly communities ordered by unwritten "customary" laws supplemented by legislation in the form of chiefly orders; dispute settlement processes included conciliation and arbitration and adjudication by chiefs' courts. Such structured legal systems and stable communities supported strong governments able to wage war on neighboring communities, to migrate to colonise new areas, and, in places and at times, to resist European colonial penetration even by defeating imperial armies in battle. The Zulu kingdom became the most powerful in the area in the nineteenth century. The capacity for evolving new constitutional orders was shown in the forging of the Basuto nation, from diverse elements, under the leadership of Moshoeshoe I in the early nineteenth century. Basuto law reflects the basic principle of consensual chieftaincy in the doctrine that "a chief is a chief by the people."

However, the oldest indigenous communities in southern Africa, the San, show the ability of small-scale societies to eschew law in favor of other forms of social control more effective for them. The small, nomadic family bands of San Bushmen lack formal legal apparatus, effectively maintaining order by social processes based on mutual sharing.

COMMON LAW

Dutch settlers at the Cape from 1652 introduced Roman-Dutch law, which is the basis for the common law of southern Africa and a system unique not only in this continent but worldwide. This law was retained under British rule of Cape Colony from 1806 and applied to Natal (1845), the Transvaal and Orange Free State Republics, Basutoland (present-day Lesotho), Bechuanaland (present-day Botswana), and Swaziland, as well as to Southern Rhodesia (present-day Zimbabwe), and South-West Africa (present-day Namibia).

Roman-Dutch law is based on the principles of Roman law, supplemented by customary laws followed in Holland; the highest authority is given to several seventeenth- and eighteenth-century treatises by Dutch jurists including Grotius, Voet, Van der Linden, and Van Leeuwen. Custom remains a valid source of law, although most customs have been superseded by legislation or recognition in judicial decisions.

Although Roman-Dutch law has continued as the basis of the South African legal system, under British rule throughout the nineteenth century English law became a supplementary but pervasive source, as British judges and lawyers in the colonial courts tended to follow English practice, precedents and textbooks. The early introduction of the English principle of *stare decisis*, giving judgments effect as binding precedents, was definitive. English rules of evidence and procedure in both civil and criminal cases were adopted. In the Cape Colony and Natal some English legislation was applied, either by local enactments in similar terms or by direct application, including much English commercial law. Colonial forms of "responsible government" introduced some English principles of constitutional law.

The common law and local legislation continue to provide the basic general law, although scholars disagree in estimating the relative contributions of Roman-Dutch and English law to its content.

INDIGENOUS LAW UNDER COLONIAL RULE AND APARTHEID

In the nineteenth century colonial governments tried to co-opt indigenous authorities and customary laws as instruments in the control of African communities. "Native commissioners" were colonial administrative officers and magistrates who presided over special courts with original jurisdiction in civil and criminal cases involving Africans and appellate jurisdiction to hear appeals from chiefs' courts. In Natal a Code of Native Law was enacted in 1886. By such means, systems of customary law were curtailed and modified, even partially reinvented, to accommodate the needs of the colonial administration and economy and to reflect other influences, such as those of Christian missions and new forms of education. The vitality of African society in resisting such pressures contributed to the survival of laws supporting basic social structures such as the extended family, but industrialization and urbanization, with enforced migrant labour, wrought profound changes in the social foundations of such laws.

CONSTITUTIONAL DEVELOPMENT

The Union of South Africa as a self-governing dominion of the Crown, uniting the Cape Colony, Natal, the Orange Free State, and the Transvaal as four provinces, was created in 1910 by the (British) South Africa Act of 1909, which established a parliamentary form of government entirely dominated by the minority white population. A Supreme Court was established, with a local division in each of the four provinces and a national Appellate Division. Formally independent from 1931, South Africa maintained a colonial style administration of its majority population, systematized by the Native (later retitled Bantu, then Black) Administration Act of 1927, which provided for the administration of African affairs through native commissioners and recognised the Governor-General as the "Supreme Chief." As later amended, this provided the foundation for the apartheid state. With the adoption of a republican form of government in 1961 South Africa relinquished membership of the Commonwealth.

APARTHEID AND THE LEGAL SYSTEM

Apartheid was imposed through the instrumentality of the law. For nearly four decades from 1950, South African law was dominated by legislation seeking to enforce racial segregation, including the Mixed Marriages Act of 1949, the Population Registration Act of 1950, the Group Areas Act of 1950, the Immorality Act of 1951 (which broadened earlier legislation penalizing interracial sexual relationships), the Separate Amenities Act of 1953, the Bantu Education Act of 1954, and many other provisions. The widespread opposition provoked was vigorously countered by such measures as the Unlawful Organizations Act of 1960 and the Terrorism Act of 1967.

Apartheid came to its purported fruition in the establishment, under the Black States Constitution Act of 1971, of the ten rural "homeland" states, designated respectively for different sections of the African population. Of these states, Transkei, Bophuthatswana, Venda, and Ciskei were granted "independence" (which received no international recognition) at the cost of the South African citizenship of their peoples. Customary laws continued as essential parts of the respective legal systems of these states.

Yet, in the context of a system based upon the principle of legality and the rule of law, the law also offered a significant weapon which, albeit invoked by only a minority of lawyers, against many obstacles and despite repeated failures, often before an unresponsive judiciary, made a significant contribution to the struggle against apartheid. Examples of the use of the law in this way were the defense of accused persons and the protection of communities threatened with forced removal.

THE TRANSFORMATION OF THE REPUBLIC OF SOUTH AFRICA

A small step toward constitutional development was taken in 1984 with the introduction of a tricameral parliament, from which, however, Africans were still excluded. As the implementation of apartheid had relied strongly upon legal instruments, its abandonment required not merely the repeal of those instruments but far-reaching innovations in the constitutional and legal system to redress the iniquities of the past. First steps were taken, during the process of constitutional negotiation in the Convention for a Democratic South Africa (CODESA), by the repeal of the basic apartheid legislation in 1991–1992. South African citizenship was restored to the peoples of the "independent" homelands on January 1, 1994.

The Transitional Constitution of 1993 (in operation from April 24, 1994, until early 1997) acknowledged the need "to create a new order in which all South Africans will be entitled to a common South African citizenship in a sovereign and democratic constitutional state in which there is equality between men and women and people of all races." The constitution went on to proclaim itself "a historic bridge between the past of a deeply divided society characterised by strife, conflict, untold suffering and injustice, and a future founded on the recognition of human rights, democracy and peaceful co-existence and development opportunities for all South Africans, irrespective of colour, race, class, belief or sex."

This statement represented a completely fresh start for South Africa, a massive transformation represented by free elections and universal adult suffrage, multiracial politics, and the successful candidacy for election as president of the leader of the long-banned African National Congress Nelson Mandela. The impact upon the legal system was profound and far reaching. The constitution established a bicameral parliament with a National Assembly of four hundred members directly elected by proportional representation and a senate, from 1997 renamed the Council of Provincial Assemblies, in which each of the nine provinces is now represented by ten members, led by the provincial premier.

The constitution added nine African languages to the former two official languages, Afrikaans and English; all eleven official languages must be treated equally. The constitution, as supreme law, provides comprehensive and detailed guarantees of fundamental rights—a bill of rights—with a new Constitutional Court of eleven judges with final power to interpret and enforce the constitution, including fundamental rights and the constitutionality of any law, bill or executive or administrative act. The constitution also established the public protector, an independent officer empowered to investigate alleged maladministration, abuse of power, improper enrichment etc., the Human Rights Commission to promote awareness and observance of fundamental rights, and the Commission on Gender Equality.

As required by the transitional constitution, parliament, sitting as the constituent assembly, in 1996 enacted the permanent constitution, which came into force early in 1997 after certification by the Constitutional Court that it complied with the constitutional principles. South African judges responded vigorously in applying the new constitution, showing intellectual and moral authority especially in applying the bill of rights in the context of a legal system still bearing residual imprints of apartheid. The courts are required to develop the common law to promote the spirit and objects of the bill of rights. The most notable decisions have come from the Constitutional Court. In landmark judgments given soon after its inauguration in 1995 this court abolished the death penalty and the corporal punishment of juveniles, as infringing the constitutional guarantees against cruel, inhuman or degrading punishment or treatment. The court has upheld the right of prisoners to vote in elections and applied the innovative constitutional protection of socioeconomic rights, including the

rights to housing and health care services. Judgments on the right to equality have had a special resonance in the post-apartheid context. In 2006 legislation provided for same-sex marriage, implementing the guaranteed freedom from discrimination on the ground of sexual orientation.

An important element of transitional justice was the Truth and Reconciliation Commission, which was empowered to grant amnesty in return for confessions of past offences. The application of customary laws was transformed by the abolition of the former special courts for Africans (1986); since 1988 every court can apply "indigenous law" and irrespective of whether either or both parties to a suit are African. An element of the former system continues in the provision that a court may take judicial notice of indigenous law provided that it is not "opposed to the principles of public policy or natural justice." Customary law therefore continues to provide the personal law, including family and succession law, for the overwhelming majority of South Africans, and is also a source of laws of delict and contract in appropriate situations. Nevertheless the precise role of customary law in the evolving legal system remains to be determined in the course of future litigation and legislation. For example, customary laws discriminating against women must be adjusted to conform with the constitutional guarantee against gender discrimination: the Constitutional Court held invalid a statutory provision enacted in 1927 which applied customary laws, including the rule of male primogeniture, to intestate succession to African estates.

BOTSWANA, LESOTHO, NAMIBIA, SWAZILAND, AND ZIMBABWE

In Botswana, Nambia, Swaziland, and Zimbabwe, which adjoin South Africa, and Lesotho, which is landlocked within it, South African law was introduced during the colonial period. Since becoming independent (Botswana and Lesotho in 1966, Swaziland in 1968, Zimbabwe in 1980, and Namibia, through a unique process of decolonization involving the United Nations, in 1990) these five states retain national legal systems based on the same blend of Roman-Dutch and English law. However, customary laws provide a vibrant source of law for the majority of their populations, so that the received common law has only a limited application. The constitutional monarchy of Lesotho and the more traditional monarchy of Swaziland preserve national systems of customary law and the associated chiefdoms of Botswana apply many common principles of customary law.

See also **Apartheid; Botswana; Human Rights; Mandela, Nelson; Marriage Systems; Namibia; South Africa, Republic of; Women: Women and the Law; Swaziland; Zimbabwe.**

BIBLIOGRAPHY

Abel, Richard L. *Politics by Other Means, Law in the Struggle against Apartheid 1980–1994.* New York: Routledge, 1995.

Bekker, J. C., and J. J. J. Coetzee. *Seymour's Customary law in Southern Africa,* 4th edition. Cape Town: Juta, 1982.

Bennett, T. W. *A Source Book of African Customary Law for Southern Africa.* Cape Town: Juta, 1991.

Chanock, Martin. *The Making of South African Legal Culture 1902–1936: Fear, Favour and Prejudice.* Cambridge, U.K.: Cambridge University Press, 2001.

Corder, Hugh. *Judges at Work: The Role and Attitudes of the South African Appellate Judiciary 1910–1950.* Cape Town: Juta, 1984.

Devenish, G. E. *The South African Constitution.* Durban: LexisNexis Butterworths, 2005.

Dyzenhaus, David. *Hard Cases in Wicked Legal Systems: South African Law in the Perspective of Legal Philosophy.* New York: Oxford University Press, 1991.

Forsyth, C. F. *In Danger for Their Talents: A Study of the Appellate Division of the Supreme Court of South Africa from 1950–1980.* Cape Town: Juta, 1985.

Gibson, J. T. R. *Wille's Principles of South African Law,* 7th edition. Cape Town: Juta, 1977.

Hahlo, H. R., and Ellison Kahn. *The Union of South Africa: The Development of Its Laws and Constitution.* London: Stevens; Cape Town, Juta, 1960.

Hinz, Manfred O., ed. *The Shade of New Leaves: Governance in Traditional Authority, A Southern African Perspective.* Berlin: Lit, 2006.

Joubert, W. A., ed. *The Law of South Africa.* 35 vols. Durban: LexisNexis Butterworths, 2003–.

Schapera, Isaac. *A Handbook of Tswana Law and Custom,* 2nd edition. New York: Oxford University Press, 1959.

Van Leeuwen, Simon. *Commentaries on the Roman-Dutch Law.* London: J. Butterwoth and Son, 1820.

Zimmermann, Reinhard, and Daniel Visser. *Southern Cross: Civil Law and Common Law in South Africa.* New York: Oxford University Press, 1996.

JAMES S. READ

LAYE, CAMARA. *See* **Camara Laye.**

LEAKEY, LOUIS AND MARY

LEAKEY, LOUIS AND MARY (1903–1972); (1913–1996). The husband-and-wife team of Louis and Mary Leakey were paleoanthropologists preeminently responsible for demonstrating that sub-Saharan Africa is the location of the origin and early development of humankind. Louis Seymour Bazett Leakey was born in Kenya, the son of a missionary, Canon Harry Leakey, who was the first to translate the Bible into Gikuyu. Louis grew up with the Gikuyu and was initiated as a Gikuyu adult. After education at Cambridge he led several archaeological expeditions to eastern Africa before ultimately returning to live permanently in Kenya. In addition to his famed work in paleoanthropology at Olduvai Gorge (Tanzania), Louis Leakey promoted behavioral work on the contemporary great apes of Africa and Asia. He was an expert on African string figures and also published an extensive ethnography of the Gikuyu people.

Mary Douglas Nicol married Louis Leakey in 1936. Prior to this, the couple had begun work together at Olduvai Gorge in northern Tanzania. Mary Leakey had an unconventional upbringing and education, spending much of her time traveling in southern Europe with her father, a professional artist. She introduced to sub-Saharan Africa archaeological procedures developed in Europe, and insisted on a greater degree of precision and rigor than had been customary. She discovered and documented the oldest known tool-making industry, the Oldowan, and her excavations at Olduvai and elsewhere established the basis of the archaeological succession for the Early Stone Age in Africa.

It was Mary who found many of the important fossils which brought the Leakeys academic and popular fame, such as the skull of *Proconsul heseloni* from Rusinga in 1948 and the cranium of *Paranthropus boisei* from Olduvai in 1959. The latter demonstrated the great antiquity of humankind. It was the first hominid specimen to be dated by radiometric means at 1.75 million years. After Louis's death in 1972, Mary began work at the site of Laetoli, Tanzania, which they had first visited together in 1935. It was here that she discovered

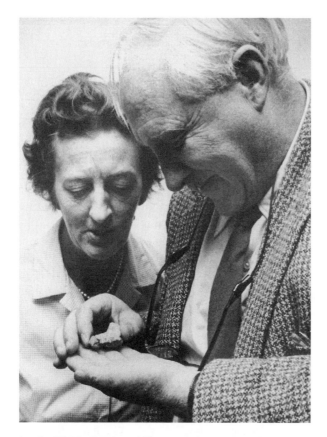

Louis (1903–1972) and Mary (1913–1996) Leakey. The Leakeys worked to uncover tools and fossils in Olduvai Gorge. Their work established human evolutionary development in Africa. AP IMAGES

Leakey, Louis S. B. *White African*. London: Hodder and Stoughton, Ltd., 1937.

Leakey, Louis S. B. *By the Evidence: Memoirs (1932–1951)*. New York: Harcourt Brace Jovanovich, 1974.

Leakey, Mary Douglas. *Disclosing the Past*. Garden City, NY: Doubleday, 1984.

Leakey, Richard E. *One Life: An Autobiography*. Salem, NH: Salem House, 1984.

Morell, Virginia. *Ancestral Passions: The Leakey Family and the Quest for Humankind's Beginnings*. New York: Simon & Schuster, 1995.

Roe, Derek. *The Year of the Ghost: An Olduvai Diary*. Bristol: Beagle Books, 2002.

ANDREW HILL

even older hominids, belonging to the species *Australopithecus afarensis*, and a spectacular trail of their fossilized footprints dating back more than 3.5 million years. Mary and Louis's son, Richard Erskine Frere Leakey (b. 1944), also embarked upon paleoanthropological research while director of the National Museums of Kenya. Along with his wife, Meave Gillian Leakey (b. 1942), he led expeditions around Lake Turkana in northern Kenya from the late 1960s onward. The many hominid fossils they unearthed there greatly augmented the discoveries of his parents, resulting in a much more detailed and refined account of human ancestry.

See also **Anthropology and the Study of Africa; Human Evolution.**

BIBLIOGRAPHY

Helligman, Deborah. *Mary Leakey: In Search of Human Beginnings*. New York: W.H. Freeman and Company, 1995.

LENSHINA, ALICE (c. 1930–1978).

Alice Lenshina Mulenga was a Zambian religious leader and prophet. The founder and leader of the Lumpa Church, she was born around 1920 in Chinsali District in northern Zambia. Since the early 1900s Chinsali, the district administrative headquarters, had been a center of Presbyterian mission activity. In 1905 David Kaunda and his wife, Helen Nyirenda, were sent from Livingstonia Mission in Malawi to found a school and open a mission station known as Lubwa. Over the years, Lubwa trained Bemba and northern Zambia African elites who became founders of and leaders in political and religious movements, including the United National Independence Party (UNIP) led by Dr. Kenneth Kaunda, the first president of Zambia, and the Lumpa Church.

Alice's father, Lubusha Kasaka, the son of a minor Bemba chief, served as a soldier in World War I and as a messenger of the local native administration. Although employed, Lubusha was a poor man, with several wives. Alice was the daughter of one of his junior wives. As a young woman she received training to become a member of the mission church at Lubwa but failed to complete her course of religious studies. Although illiterate, she was familiar with biblical texts.

In 1953 Alice lived in Kasomo, a village some five miles from Chinsali. She was the mother of five children, and her husband, Petros Chintankwa Mulenga, had worked at Lubwa as a carpenter. After experiencing serious bouts of illness, probably malaria, Alice visited Lubwa, where she met with the Reverend Fergus Macpherson. She claimed to have died four times and to have met with Jesus and risen from the dead. She said that Jesus had taught her hymns, shown her special religious texts she called the Book of Life, and given her spiritual powers.

Though she was baptized and renewed her religious training after this experience, she soon left the Presbyterian Church and founded her own, the Lumpa Church. She became known as Alice Lenshina, the Bemba pronunciation of the Latin *regina* (queen). Her fame as a healer and religious leader spread rapidly. The Lumpa Church, basically a prophetic movement, swept through northern and eastern Zambia and along the line of rail into the Copperbelt. By 1959 it had about 148 congregations, of which 132 were in the northern and eastern provinces and sixteen in the urban centers. The membership was estimated at between 50,000 and 100,000, and an untold number of people from Central and southern Africa visited Alice's church at Kasomo.

As Zambia moved toward independence under UNIP, Alice instructed her followers to withdraw from all secular activities, antagonizing the colonial government, the chiefs, and UNIP. In the months prior to the declaration of Zambian independence in 1964, Lumpa and non-Lumpa engaged in fierce battles, resulting in the death of more than seven hundred Zambians. Troops were sent in to quell the disturbances. The defeated Lumpa were detained in prison camps or sought refuge in government rehabilitation centers to avoid reprisals from the relatives of those who had been killed. Many fled to Zaire and Angola. In August 1964 Alice and her husband were arrested. She was detained, escaped twice, and was recaptured. She was released in 1975 and placed under house arrest in Lusaka, where she died in 1978. By 2002 in the northeastern region of Zambia, many adults, who as children and adolescents had been detained in prison camps, were now fully integrated into local life. They no longer held allegiance to Alice. They accepted government authority and had joined established independent Christian churches.

See also **Christianity; Kaunda, Kenneth; Prophetic Movements.**

BIBLIOGRAPHY

Bond, George C. "A Prophecy That Failed." In *African Christianity*, ed. George Bond et al. New York: Academic Press, 1979.

Hinfelaar, Hugo. "Women's Revolt: The Lumpa Church of Lenshina Mulenga in the 1950s." *Journal of Religion in Africa* 21, no. 2 (1991): 99–129.

Hudson, John A. *Time to Mourn*. Lusaka: Bookworld Publishers, 1999.

Roberts, Andrew. "The Lumpa Church of Alice Lenshina." In *Protest and Power in Black Africa*, ed. Robert I. Rotberg and Ali A. Mazrui. New York: Oxford University Press, 1970.

van Binsbergen, Wim M. J. *Religious Change in Zambia*. London: Kegan Paul International, 1981.

GEORGE CLEMENT BOND

LEO AFRICANUS (c. 1486–c. 1532).

Known in Europe as Leo Africanus, al-Hasan ibn Muhammad ibn Ahmad al-Wazzan al-Gharnati al-Fasi was born in Granada a few years before that city fell to Spain in 1492 and was brought up in Fez, where his family moved to escape forced conversion to Christianity. Educated in the madrassas (Islamic religious schools) of Fez, he was trained by his uncle in the arts of diplomacy and became an ambassador for the Wattasid sultan of Fez. In that capacity, he traveled throughout the region now called Morocco; crossed the Sahara to visit the Songhay empire, including stops at Timbuktu and Gao, and the kingdoms of Aïr and Bornu; and spent time at the courts of the sultans of Tlemcen and Tunis in the Maghreb and the Mediterranean coastal camp of the pirate-prince 'Aruj Barbarossa. Cairo he visited at least twice, once in 1513 during the rule of the Mamluk sultan Qansuh al-Ghawri (d. 1516) and then again in 1517 when he witnessed the conquest of that Mamluk kingdom by the Ottoman Selim I (1465–1520), whose court al-Wazzan had seen the year before. Throughout his travels, al-Wazzan inspected sites, libraries, and inscriptions, and took side trips, including sailing up the Nile to Aswan and crossing the Red Sea for pilgrimage to Mecca and Medina.

In the summer of 1518, the boat on which he was returning from Cairo to Fez was seized by Spanish Christian pirates and al-Wazzan was captured and turned over to Pope Leo X (1475–1521). After fifteen months in the papal prison at the Castel Sant'Angelo, al-Wazzan converted to Christianity, being baptized in January 1520 by the pope's own hand and given the pope's names Giovanni Leone (or, as he called himself in Arabic, Yuhanna al-Asad). For the next seven years, he lived in Italy. He taught Arabic to Cardinal Egidio da Viterbo (c. 1469–1532), who hoped for a crusade against the Turk and the conversion of all Muslims to Christianity, and corrected a Latin translation of the Qur'an for him.

For other patrons, he transcribed Arabic Christian texts. With Jacob Mantino (d. 1549), a learned Jewish physician and translator of Averroës (Ibn Rushd) from the Hebrew, he collaborated on an Arabic-Hebrew-Latin dictionary. Mainly, he became an author of books in European languages about the world he had known. His Italian *Cosmography and Geography of Africa*, completed in 1526, was the most important: a geography, travel account, ethnography, and history. Circulating for years in manuscript, it was revised and published by Giovanni Battista Ramusio in 1550 as *La Descrizione dell'Africa*, with several subsequent editions and translations that added anti-Muslim sentiments. He also composed in Latin a short biographical dictionary of learned Arabs and Jews, and a treatise on Arab prosody, and two lost manuscripts in Italian: an epitome of Muslim chronicles, and a treatise on Islamic faith and Malikite law. He seems to have returned to North Africa and to Islam in 1527. According to the last mention of him, he was living in Tunis in 1532.

See also **Geography and the Study of Africa; Travel and Exploration.**

BIBLIOGRAPHY

Africanus, Leo. "La descrizione dell'Africa di Giovan Lioni Africano." In *Navigazioni e Viaggi*, ed. Marica Milanesi. Turin: Giulio Einaudi, 1978.

Leo, Johannes. *A Geographical Historie of Africa*. Trans. John Pory. Amsterdam: Theatrum Orbis Terrarum, 1969.

Oumelbanine Zhiri. *L'Afrique au miroir de l'Europe: Fortunes de Jean Léon l'Africain à la Renaissance*. Geneva: Librairie Droz, 1991.

Rauchenberger, Dietrich. *Johannes Leo der Afrikaner. Seine Beschreibung ds Raumes zwischen Nil und Niger nach dem Urtext*. Wiesbaden: Harrasowitz Verlag, 1999.

Zemon Davis, Natalie. *Trickster Travels. A Sixteenth-Century Muslim between Worlds*. London: Faber and Faber, 2007.

NATALIE ZEMON DAVIS

LEOPOLD'S CONGO. *See* **Congo Independent State.**

LEPROSY. *See* **Disease.**

LESOTHO

This entry includes the following articles:
GEOGRAPHY AND ECONOMY
SOCIETY AND CULTURES
HISTORY AND POLITICS

GEOGRAPHY AND ECONOMY

Lesotho is a small land-locked country of 11,720 square miles that is totally surrounded by South Africa. Situated at the highest part of the Drakensberg mountains, all of Lesotho's land is more than 1,000 meters above sea level. Thabana-Ntlenyana, at 3,481 meters, is the highest mountain in southern Africa. The eastern two-thirds of the country is mountainous and slightly populated, while the western one-third is lowlands and home to 70 percent of the country's population of about 2.1 million.

Lesotho's modern economy was shaped by two developments in the nineteenth century: the conquest of much of the Basotho kingdom's most fertile land and the development of diamond and gold mining in South Africa. In 1865–1866 the Basotho fought a war with the Orange Free State in which the Afrikaners seized about one-third of the Basotho kingdom's land. In 1868 diamonds were discovered near modern-day Kimberley, setting off a rush by tens of thousands of prospectors and laborers. Basotho farmers profited by selling grain to the diamond fields, while young men found employment for short periods at the mines to earn money to start homesteads, to buy plows,

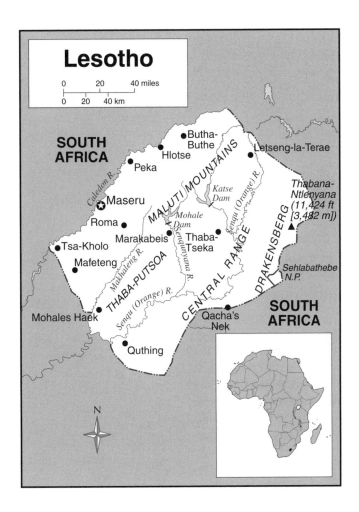

and to purchase guns for self-defense against white settlers.

During the 1870s the Basotho kingdom exported so much grain that it was known as the grain basket of the region. However, after the British resumed colonial rule in 1884, its officials viewed Basutoland not as a territory worth developing, but as an economic appendage to South Africa. As Basotho grain production declined, the migrant labor economy became entrenched as 15,000 Basotho workers sought employment on Afrikaners farms, on rail projects, and in the diamond mines. Once the Witwatersrand gold mines opened up after 1885, even more Basotho adult males flocked there for jobs. For much of the colonial period, between 65,000 and 100,000 Basotho migrant laborers annually found jobs in South Africa largely in the mines and on white farms. By the 1930s, as Basutoland's farmland eroded, Basotho farmers produced more for their family's subsistence, and wool eclipsed grain as Lesotho's primary export.

Lesotho's status as a migrant labor economy did not change with its independence in 1966. By 1976 some 27,500 Basotho were employed within Lesotho, while 200,000 found employment in South Africa. Approximately 85,000 were gold miners who annually sent back a total of $17 million to their families, who increasingly relied on the remittances for survival. With the decline in the international price of gold in the 1980s, mining companies began to favor South Africans over foreign workers and the number of Basotho mineworkers has steadily declined ever since. In 2003 some 61,000 Lesotho citizens found work in the gold mines, remitting about $40 million to their families.

Basotho find it difficult to secure wage employment in Lesotho since few new jobs have been created since the mid-twentieth century. Diamond mines at Letseng-la-Terae in the mountains have generated some employment, but the greatest expansion has been in the textile industry. The U.S. government's African Growth and Opportunity Act of 2000 gave a number of African countries, including Lesotho, access to the American market by abolishing duties on selected exports. Textile companies from Taiwan, China, and Malaysia took advantage of the legislation in Lesotho with large-scale investments and opened more than a dozen factories that primarily employed women. The number of workers in the textile industry jumped dramatically from 20,000 in 2002 to 56,000 in 2004. However, with the strengthening of the South African rand (the Lesotho currency is tied to the rand) vis-à-vis the U.S. dollar in the 2000s and the ending of the worldwide Multi-Fiber Agreement that protected textile industries in developing countries, more than 6,000 of these workers lost their jobs in 2005.

Because tax revenues from citizens are so small, the Lesotho government's revenue relies on other sources such as the Southern African Customs Union, which includes South Africa, Swaziland, Botswana, Namibia, and Lesotho. South Africa collects customs on all goods imported into the region and allocates a percentage of the revenue to the other countries based on the value of goods brought into that country. Since the early 1990s Lesotho's share has varied from 17.5 percent to 22.5 percent. In 1994–1995 that share generated about $153 million and accounted for 58 percent of government revenues.

Lesotho's government has also generated revenue from the sale of water to South Africa through the Highlands Water Project, a cooperative project between Lesotho and South Africa that was launched in 1988. The project's primary objectives are to divert water from Lesotho's mountains to South Africa and to generate hydroelectric power for Lesotho. Phase one of the project was completed in 1998 with the construction of the Katse Dam. Because of concerns over exorbitant construction costs, labor disputes, and the displacement of families, international lending agencies were reluctant to fund all of the other phases of the project, but Phase 1B was completed with the construction of the Mohale Dam in 2002. The project generated much controversy when it was revealed that some international firms had bribed a senior Lesotho civil servant to secure construction contracts. Four companies were found guilty of bribery and paid large fines.

See also **Labor: Industrial and Mining.**

BIBLIOGRAPHY

Gill, Stephen. *A Short History of Lesotho, from the Late Stone Age until the 1993 Elections.* Morija, Lesotho: Morija Museum and Archives, 1993.

Pule, Neville, and Motlatse Thabane, eds. *Essays on Aspects of the Political Economy of Lesotho, 1500–2000.* Roma, Lesotho: National University of Lesotho, 2002.

Rosenberg, Scott, and Richard Weisfelder. *Historical Dictionary of Lesotho.* Lanham, MD: Scarecrow Press, 2004.

ROBERT EDGAR

SOCIETY AND CULTURES

The dominant ethnic group in Lesotho is the Basotho. It was formed from a variety of tribes and clans in the 1820s and 1830s. At that time one of the clan leaders, Moshoeshoe, brought them together for self-defense when the mountainous region came under attack by Shaka, the Zulu leader, and others. At the turn of the twenty-first century, the Basotho constitute 99.7 percent of the population. The remaining few thousand include Europeans and Asians. The official languages are Sesotho, the language of the Basotho, and English. Sesotho is spoken almost universally, while English is widely known in the urban centers and surrounding areas. Zulu and Xhosa are also used.

With the urban population of Lesotho only about 25 percent of the whole, the heart of Lesotho society remains the rural village. It is organized around kraals, every kraal a collection of buildings belonging to an extended family—a husband, his wife (or wives), unmarried daughters, sons with their wives and children, and other dependents. The lands around the village are divided up by a village chief, who is accountable to an area chief. Cattle raising, performed by males, is central not only to the economy but to the culture. Crop raising is the domain of women. The authority of the chiefs is strongest in the more remote regions. These are high in the mountains, where the pony is the major form of transportation and there is relatively little contact with the outside world. Adherence to traditional beliefs and practices follows a similar pattern.

The indigenous religion of the Basotho has been described as "particularistic." There was no common god among the Basotho. Rather, each extended family had its own ancestor spirits.

Kingdom of Lesotho

Population:	2,125,262 (2007 est.)
Area:	30,355 sq. km (11,720 sq. mi.)
Official languages:	English, Sesotho
Languages:	English, Sesotho, Zulu, Xhosa
National currency:	loti
Principal religions:	Christian 80%, including Roman Catholic (majority), Lesotho Evangelical, Anglican, other denominations; other religions include Islam, Hindu, indigenous
Capital:	Maseru (est. pop. 173,700 in 2006)
Other urban centers:	Teyateyaneng, Leribe, Mafeteng, Mohale's Hoek
Average annual rainfall:	635 mm (25 in.)
Principal geographical features:	*Mountains:* Maluti Mountains, Cave (Stormberg) Sandstone foothills *Rivers:* Orange, Singunyane, Singu, Makhaleng (Kornetspruit), Maubamatso, Caledon (along the northwest border)
Economy:	*GDP per capita:* US$2,600 (2006)
Principal products and exports:	*Agricultural:* corn, wheat, pulses, sorghum, barley, livestock *Industries:* food, beverages, textiles, apparel assembly, handicrafts, construction *Mining:* diamonds *Tourism:* Tourism is also important to the economy.
Government:	Independence from Great Britian, 1966. Independence constitution, 1966, suspended in 1970. New constitution approved in 1991, enacted in 1993. Constitutional monarchy with a bicameral parliament consisting of a 33-member Senate (11 appointees of the king and 22 hereditary members) and a 120-member elected National Assembly. There is a prime minister and an appointed 16-member cabinet. For purposes of local government there are 10 districts headed by district administrators.
Heads of state since independence:	*Kings:* 1966–1990: King Moshoeshoe II 1990–: King Letsie III (formerly Prince Mohato) *Heads of government:* 1966–1986: Prime Minister Leabua Jonathan 1986–1991: Military Council chief Major-General Justin Lekhanya 1991–1993: Colonel Elias P. Ramaema 1993–1998: Prime Minister Ntsu Mokhehle 1998–: Prime Minister Pakalitha Mosisili
Armed forces:	The Lesotho Defense Force consists of an army, an air wing, and a paramilitary and comprises about 4,000 personnel. There are an additional 3,000 to 4,000 members of the Lesotho Mounted Police Service.
Transportation:	Linked by rail and roadway to South Africa. *Rail:* 2 km (1 mi.) *Roads:* 5,940 km (3,691 mi.), 18% paved *National airline:* Lesotho Airways *Airports:* International facility at Thoteng-za-Moli near Maseru. 27 additional airstrips throughout the country.
Media:	Main periodicals: *Mochochonono, Lesotho Today, Lentsoe la Basotho, Moeletsi oa Basotho, Leselinyane la Lesotho, Mphatlatsane, Lesotho Weekly, Molepe, The Mirror.* Lesotho National Broadcasting Service controls Radio Lesotho as well as the television station. The Catholic School Secretariat also controls a radio station. Publishing is limited.
Education and literacy:	*Total literacy rate:* 84.8% (2003). Schooling is free for grades 1 through 7 but not compulsory. There are 7 teacher-training institutes, 9 vocational institutes and 1 university, National University of Lesotho.

Apparently, the spirit of the oldest-remembered ancestor, the *molimo*, was the supreme one. The family members appealed to more recent ancestors to intervene with the *molimo* for good harvests, good health, success in war, and so on.

Western missionaries arrived during the 1830s and came in growing numbers later in the century under British rule. Christianity is the religion of 80 percent of the population, and more than half of all Christians are Catholic. Protestants include

significant numbers of Lesotho Evangelicals and Anglicans. There are smaller numbers of Muslims, Hindus, and practitioners of the indigenous religion.

Free primary school education for ages six to thirteen was introduced in January 2000. There are also secondary and vocational schools. The National University of Lesotho in Roma, founded in 1966, had an enrollment of about six thousand in 2003, compared to just fourteen hundred in 1996. Most of its students receive scholarships from the ministry of finance. Some children still attend traditional initiation schools, at which customary knowledge and practices are passed on.

The adult literacy rate of Lesotho, estimated by UNICEF at 83 percent in the year 2000, is one of the highest in sub-Saharan Africa. Unusually, it is higher for women than for men. That is partly because 32 percent of the boys between the ages of five and nineteen are cattle herders and do not get formal schooling—cattle herding is an essential part of male identity, representing a step to manhood.

Most primary and secondary schools are operated, as they have been since the late nineteenth century, by Christian missions, and these church-controlled schools have resisted curriculum modernization. Two major attempts at reform by post-independence governments produced little change. A third effort began in the year 2000.

Lesotho is a very poor country, with a per capita annual income of $415 in 1999. It is ranked 120 out of 162 countries on the United Nations Development Program's Human Development Index. It has low levels of economic growth and the future does not look bright. Many of Lesotho's men have for decades found employment in South Africa's mines, but layoffs in recent years have sent thousands of them back home, where they find themselves without work. In addition to growing unemployment, increasing alcoholism and crime and the breakdown of the traditional family are among the consequences. Meanwhile, the agricultural sector is declining, partly as a result of poor farming practices, a result being an influx of population to the cities, further eroding the traditional family.

Major twentieth-century gains in health have been reversed by the high rate of HIV/AIDS. The prevalence rate is about 31 percent overall and more than 40 percent in Maseru. Some 14 percent of the nation's children have been orphaned by AIDS. Practices such as widow inheritance (a custom by which a man marries the widow of his late brother), polygamy, promiscuity, and the reluctance of men to use condoms are major causes. Lesotho Planned Parenthood and other organizations are working to educate people—especially boys—about HIV/AIDS, but a significant downturn in average life expectancy because of the

disease is anticipated for the first decade of the twenty-first century.

Customary Basotho law of marriage and inheritance subordinates women to men, with women being considered minors. Nevertheless, with many men working out of the country, women constitute 72 percent of small business owners. Also, some women are exercising their right under Lesotho's dual legal system to place themselves under common law, which gives them more rights. Women are present, but vastly underrepresented, in government offices, the civil service, and large business organizations, especially at the higher levels.

See also **Disease: HIV/AIDS, Social and Political Aspects.**

BIBLIOGRAPHY

Ashton, E. H. *The Basuto: A Social Study of Traditional and Modern Lesotho.* London: Oxford University Press, 1967.

Ayisi, Ruth Ansah. *Lesotho: A Country in Transition.* Maseru, Lesotho: UNICEF, 2004.

Gill, Debby, ed. and comp. *The Situation of Women and Children in Lesotho.* Maseru, Lesotho: UNICEF, 1994.

Gill, Stephen J., et al. *Lesotho: Kingdom in the Sky.* Berg en Dal, Netherlands: Netherlands-Lesotho Foundation, 1993.

MICHAEL L. LEVINE

HISTORY AND POLITICS

The modern nation of Lesotho traces its origins to the early nineteenth century when Moshoeshoe (c. 1786–1870) began a process of nation building during the midst of the Difaqane, the conflicts that swept southern Africa between 1820 and 1850. Moshoeshoe brought together bands of Sotho-speakers and refugees fleeing wars and forged the Basotho kingdom. By the 1830s the kingdom's boundaries encompassed present-day Lesotho and about one-third of the Free State province of South Africa.

The greatest threat to the kingdom in the following decades came from the Afrikaner Voortrekkers who began migrating into the interior of southern Africa in the mid-1830s. Although Moshoeshoe loaned Afrikaner farmers pasture for their cattle, the Boers eventually laid claim to the land and established a rival state, the Orange River Sovereignty (later renamed the Orange Free State).

Moshoeshoe was adept at diplomacy and exploiting the rivalry between the British and Afrikaners and using it to his nation's advantage, but disputes over land and cattle led to two wars between the Free State and Basotho in 1858 and 1865. During the second war, the Afrikaners conquered much of the Basotho kingdom's most fertile land. Desperate to protect his kingdom's sovereignty, Moshoeshoe successfully appealed to the British for protection in 1868. Basutoland (as the British called it) was administered initially by the Cape Colony, but after the Basotho rebelled against Cape officials in the Gun War of 1880–1881, the British reassumed control of the colony in 1884.

The British administered Basutoland as a High Commission Territory. The British regarded Basutoland as little more than a labor reservoir serving the South African economy and thus put few resources into developing the territory. Following the British policy of indirect rule, colonial officials cooperated with chiefs and headmen to carry out administrative duties and collect taxes. In 1903 the British established an advisory body, the Basutoland National Council, which was dominated by chiefs. Commoner organizations expressed their anticolonial views through such groups as the Progressive Association and *Lekhotla la Bafo* (Council of Commoners).

Modern African political activity emerged in the post–World War II era with the formation of two political parties that dominated Lesotho for the rest of the century. Founded in 1952, the Basutoland Congress Party (BCP) was led by Ntsu Mokhehle and drew its main support from those educated in Protestant mission schools. The BCP opposed traditional chiefs and the South Africa regime and its apartheid system and supported freedom movements throughout Africa. Its main rival was the Basutoland National Party (BNP), established in 1957 and headed by a great-grandson of Moshoeshoe, Chief Leabua Jonathan. Backed by chiefs and the Roman Catholic Church, the BNP was staunchly anti-communist and favored accommodating the South African government.

When the British set up a directly elected council in 1960 the BCP won a majority of seats, but in the next election in 1965, the BNP scored a victory. Hence, when the British granted Lesotho its independence in 1966 Jonathan became prime minister. However, when it became obvious that the BCP was going to win a majority of seats in the 1970 election, Jonathan declared a state of emergency, voided the election, and suspended the constitution. Following a failed coup attempt by the BCP in 1974, Mokhehle and other BCP leaders fled the country and settled in countries such as Zambia and Botswana. Because Jonathan's government lacked legitimacy in Lesotho and internationally, he attempted to accommodate other Basotho politicians and he publicly condemned the apartheid regime in international forums such as the United Nations. This won Jonathan's government recognition and donor assistance from Western countries, but also the enmity of the South African regime, which was alarmed at Jonathan's budding friendship with the African National Congress (ANC) of South Africa.

In the late 1970s and 1980s the South African government waged a campaign of destabilization against the Lesotho government, closing borders periodically to slow traffic and interrupt the flow of migrant workers, withholding customs payments, giving aid to the BCP's guerrilla wing, the Lesotho Liberation Army, and raiding Lesotho on two occasions to attack ANC members. On January 1, 1986, the South African government imposed an economic blockade on Lesotho, shutting down its borders. On January 20, Lesotho's military, under the command of Major-General Justin Lekhanya, overthrew Jonathan's government, instituted a military council, and deported ANC members.

The military council ruled the country until 1993. It allowed Mokhehle to return from exile in May 1988 and, in March 1990, after waging a dispute with King Moshoeshoe II over his constitutional role, it stripped the king of his powers and forced him into exile. The king was subsequently deposed and his son, Letsie III, was crowned in his place. After military officers overthrew Lekhanya in 1991, his successor, Major-General Pitsoane Ramaema, agreed to step aside in favor of civilian politicians.

Lesotho was returned to democracy in March 1993 with elections in which Mokhehle's BCP won a landslide victory, garnering all 65 seats in the National Assembly. However, this did not insure stability. In late 1993 an army mutiny nearly toppled the government, and in mid-1994, King Letsie II, still angered by the manner in which his father had been dethroned, dismissed the Mokhehle government and suspended the constitution. After pressure from regional states and the British Commonwealth, Letsie agreed to reinstate Mokhehle's government.

Following a split within his own party, Mokhehle formed the Lesotho Congress of Democrats (LCD) which kept a majority of seats in the National Assembly. The ailing Mokhehle (he died in 1999) retired from public life, and his deputy Pakalitha Mosisili succeeded him as prime minister. In elections in May 1998 the LCD won 78 of the 80 seats in an expanded National Assembly. In September 1998 the Lesotho military moved to oust Mosisili who successfully appealed to South Africa and Botswana to send troops to restore him to power.

Because of the continuing instability Lesotho adopted a new constitution that provided for 80 seats in the National Assembly contested in constituencies and 40 elected by proportional representation. In 2002 elections the LCD won almost all of the constituency seats and most of the proportional seats. However, the fact that the opposition had representation gave them a voice in deliberations and has reduced tensions.

See also **Cape Colony and Hinterland, History of (1600 to 1910); Colonial Policies and Practices; Moshoeshoe I; South Africa, Republic of.**

BIBLIOGRAPHY

Gill, Stephen. *A Short History of Lesotho, from the Late Stone Age until the 1993 Elections.* Morija, Lesotho: Morija Museum and Archives, 1993.

Pule, Neville, and Motlatse Thabane, eds. *Essays on Aspects of the Political Economy of Lesotho, 1500–2000.* Roma, Lesotho: National University of Lesotho, 2002.

Rosenberg, Scott, and Richard Weisfelder. *Historical Dictionary of Lesotho.* Lanham, MD: Scarecrow Press, 2004.

Weisfelder, Richard. *Political Contention in Lesotho, 1952–1965.* Roma, Lesotho: Institute of Southern African Studies, 1999.

ROBERT EDGAR

LEWIS, SAMUEL (1843–1903). The Sierra Leonean lawyer and patriot Samuel Lewis was born into a family of slaves (*aku*) of Egba (Nigerian) origin freed as "recaptives" in Freetown by the British West Africa Squadron under missionary tutelage. His father, William, became a successful merchant and shipowner and was a leader in both the *aku* community and the Wesleyan Methodist Church. Under Wesleyan patronage, Lewis went to England in 1866 and qualified in 1871 as a barrister. On returning to Freetown in 1872, he built a successful legal practice in which he combined skill in detecting fine legal distinctions with an eye for broader principle.

Lewis returned equipped for civic leadership at a critical period in the development of the Krio (Sierra Leonean creole) community in Freetown. He was a leader of its religious and cultural life; he experimented with agricultural innovation; on two occasions he was appointed to act as chief justice of the colony. As an "unofficial" (nongovernment) member of the Legislative Council (1882–1903), Lewis was primarily concerned with protecting British constitutional principles and the civil rights of the Krio as British subjects and with encouraging the expansion of his community within the British Empire. Though always ready to criticize imperialist excesses, Lewis believed that Sierra Leoneans had a "manifest destiny" to participate in the modernization and development of Africa.

Much more aggressive and exclusionary methods and spirit of British expansion during the 1890s frustrated these hopes. In 1895, Lewis became the first elected mayor of Freetown, and in 1896, the first African to be knighted. However, Governor Frederic Cardew (who recommended that honor) found Lewis unwilling to acquiesce to his authoritarian methods in the newly proclaimed protectorate. Lewis' last efforts were therefore in defense of the status and civil rights of an embattled Krio community.

See also **Colonial Policies and Practices: British West Africa; Creoles.**

BIBLIOGRAPHY

Cole, Gibril Raschid. "Embracing Islam and African Traditions in a British Colony: The Muslim Krio of Sierra Leone, 1787–1910." Ph.D. diss., University of California at Los Angeles, 2000.

Hargreaves, John. *A Life of Sir Samuel Lewis.* London: Oxford University Press, 1958.

Wyse, Akintola. *The Krio of Sierra Leone: An Interpretive History.* London: Hurst, in association with the International African Institute, 1989.

JOHN D. HARGREAVES

LIBERIA

This entry includes the following articles:

GEOGRAPHY AND ECONOMY

The Republic of Liberia became the first independent republic in Africa in 1847. Liberia lies on the West African coast between 6 degrees and 30 degrees north longitude, and 9 degrees and 30 degrees west latitude. It is bordered by Sierra Leone, Guinea, and Côte d'Ivoire. It has a total area of 43,000 square miles and a population of 3.2 million made up of seventeen ethnolinguistic groups that have long been interconnected. Monrovia is the capital.

PHYSICAL GEOGRAPHY

Liberia's terrain rises from a coastal plain of savanna, mangrove swamps, and beaches to wooded rolling hills, then to an interior plateau and mountains dominated by dense tropical forests. None of the six principal rivers are navigable. Temperatures are high throughout the year with an annual mean of 77.5 degrees Fahrenheit, ranging from extremes of 48 degrees Fahrenheit to 111 degrees Fahrenheit. There are two rainy seasons in the south and one in the north, with intermediate rainfall regimes in between. Annual rainfall ranges from 200 inches per year on the coast to 80 inches per year in the interior. Most of Liberia is underlain by ancient Precambrian gneiss and granite, with elevations made up of harder volcanic diabase. Lateritic soils

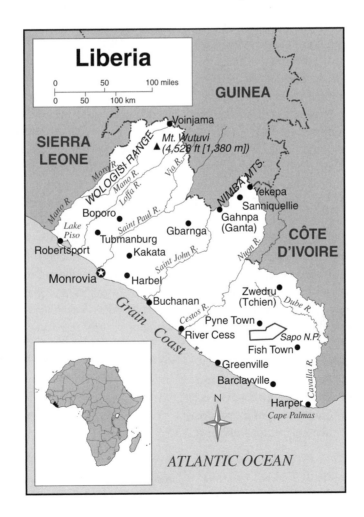

cover much of the interior and sandy and swamp soils cover the coast.

ECONOMY

According to the International Monetary Fund, Liberia's gross domestic product in 2005 was $548.4 million. Much of Liberia's infrastructure was destroyed in the civil wars of 1980 to 2003. The economy is dominated by rubber exports, followed by cacao and coffee. Timber and iron ore are expected to be important exports in the twenty-first century with the reconstruction of the economy. International sanctions against Liberian diamonds are still in place due to their role in funding regional conflicts. Liberia is also known for its large foreign-owned "flag of convenience" shipping fleet, which flourishes due to low taxes and lenient inspection policies. Liberia is heavily indebted, with an approximate debt of $3.5 billion.

Liberia has long been a part of world and regional economies. Before the settlement of repatriated free people of color from the United States in 1822, indigenous African communities practiced subsistence agriculture and participated in commodity and slave trades. In the nineteenth century, a coastal settler elite dominated Liberia's economy. Much of the indigenous-dominated interior was not integrated into the economy until the twentieth century. After independence in 1847, Liberia experienced two decades of prosperity based on trade in coffee, ivory, and other commodities. The economy declined in the 1870s when European-owned steamship fleets gained control of trade and new industrial products replaced key Liberian-produced commodities. Lacking capital, economic infrastructure, and the backing of a colonial power, Liberia was not able to compete with French and British colonies. With the collapse of trade, government service became the principal economic enterprise of the settlers. Exploitation of indigenous labor was also crucial to the economy until the most severe practices were exposed and eliminated in the 1920s. In 1872 a disadvantageous loan from British financiers began a cycle of indebtedness and dependence on foreign aid and investment.

The development of an industrial extractive economy in the twentieth century led to a period of relative prosperity. American influence replaced British in 1926 when the U.S.-based Firestone Rubber and Tire Company was granted a concession of 1 million acres and the Liberian government was forced to accept a $5 million loan. In 1934 rubber became Liberia's major export. Indigenous African communities in the interior combined low-wage labor, cash cropping, and subsistence agriculture in new livelihood patterns. President William Tubman's (1944–1971) "open door policy" toward foreign investment led to increasing integration of the interior and the exploitation of iron-rich ores. In the 1960s Liberia became the largest African exporter of iron ore, and a total of 25 percent of Liberia's land area was given over to concessions. However, these enclaves of industrialization did not lead to long-term development, and most economic benefits remained with a settler-descended elite.

Liberia was deeply affected by high oil prices and the slump in steel prices of the 1970s. Despite a sharp increase in American military and economic aid following the overthrow of the settler-dominated government by Samuel Doe (1980–1990), economic development was neglected, and the ensuing civil war led to destruction of economic infrastructure and economic collapse. Charles Taylor, the leader of one of the armed factions and later president (1997–2003), and other armed leaders plundered Liberia's natural resources, especially timber, each accruing millions of dollars annually. Taylor's involvement in conflicts throughout the region, including gunrunning and the smuggling of Sierra Leone diamonds, led to the imposition of international sanctions in 2001. More than half the Liberian population was displaced by violence, and unemployment reached 85 percent in 2003. Taylor was forced into exile in 2003, and reconstruction and reform continues under the leadership of President Ellen Johnson-Sirleaf (who took office in 2006) with the support of international organizations.

See also **Debt and Credit; Ecosystems; International Monetary Fund; Monrovia; Production Strategies: Agriculture; Slave Trades; Taylor, Charles Gahnhay; Transportation: Shipping and Ports; Tubman, William Vacanarat Shadrach.**

BIBLIOGRAPHY

Liebenow, J. Gus. *Liberia: The Quest for Democracy.* Bloomington: Indiana University Press, 1987.

Sawyer, Amos. *The Emergence of Autocracy in Liberia: Tragedy and Challenge*. San Francisco: Institute for Contemporary Studies Press, 1992.

Schulze, Willi. *A New Geography of Liberia*. London: Longman, 1973.

CATHERINE GUIMOND

SOCIETY AND CULTURES

Liberia, located on the great bulge of the west African coast, is a country with a unique history and relationship to the United States. Many journalistic and even scholarly accounts begin with the assertion that freed American slaves founded the country. The name "Liberia" refers to the liberty that these settlers were seeking; the name of the capital, Monrovia, refers to James Monroe, the American president at the time of colonization. For several reasons, however, the statements above are misleading. The true founders of Liberia were a group of wealthy white Americans who, in 1816, formed the American Colonization Society (ACS). This organization sought to mobilize and apply private funds to the removal and resettlement not of slaves but of Free People of Color; those who by their presence in the United States challenged the moral and constitutional possibility of slavery.

The earliest American immigrants, arriving in 1822, were mostly freeborn; many were literate, and they came from a range of occupations including professionals and small business owners. It was this group, rather than the manumitted field slaves who came after them, who shaped Liberia's political culture. Declaring independence from the ACS in 1847, they claimed sovereignty over the approximately one million indigenous people who already occupied the area, and led the nation to its status as the oldest black republic in Africa.

There was only sporadic central control over the territory beyond the coastline and a long history of local resistance, as well as various forms of cooptation and alliance with indigenous authorities. Descendants of the settlers monopolized the formal structure of national government and the domestic market economy from the mid-nineteenth century until the overthrow of the First Republic by military coup in 1980. From late 1989 to the late 1990s, Liberia was wracked by civil war, bloody factional fighting, and the collapse of the central state. Under a regional West African peace plan, new elections and a return to civilian rule took place in July 1997, but incomplete demobilization of troops and the election of Charles Taylor, the most notorious warlord of the 1990s, almost guaranteed that peace would not hold. Fighting broke out again in 1999-2000 and ended only with Taylor's exile to Nigeria in August of 2003. An interim government was selected to lead the country to new elections in October of 2005.

GEOGRAPHY

Liberia lies between the eighth and fourth parallels on the tropical coast of West Africa, in the region known as the Upper Guinea Coast. The underlying rock formations are estimated to be among the oldest parts of the earth's crust. The land surface consists of laterite and lateritic soils typical of a moist equatorial environment. Annual rainfall averages 190 inches, and there are distinct rainy and dry seasons. The annual mean temperature is 77.5 degrees Fahrenheit, with average humidity of 85 to 95 percent. About 58 percent of the country is covered with tropical forest, of which about 37 percent is characterized as primary high forest. This combination of factors accounts for the importance to the national economy of such export commodities as rubber and forest hardwoods.

Liberia is bounded by the Atlantic Ocean along a 353 mile-long coast. To the northwest, the Mano River forms the international border with Sierra Leone and to the southeast, the Cavalla River is the frontier with Côte d'Ivoire. Numerous creeks and rivers cut the coast. The action of the heavy surf has resulted in a series of sand bars, narrow barrier beaches, and salt and freshwater lagoons. A few high promontories, such as Cape Mount, Cape Montserrado, and Cape Palmas, add drama to an otherwise low and swampy coastline. There are no natural deep-water harbors, a feature that discouraged the presence of permanent European trading posts along this part of the west African coast in the seventeenth and eighteenth centuries.

Although monsoon tropical forests probably extended almost to the sea several hundred years ago, the recent concentration of human occupation along the coast has resulted in a park-like savanna environment on the broad plain immediately to the interior of the beaches. This plain extends about fifteen to twenty-five miles in width as one moves away from the coast, giving way to rolling hills, increasing forest, and eventually the plateaus and mountain ranges of the northern highlands. The highest elevations are in the northern part of the country in the Nimba Range, around the towns of Saniquillie and Yekepa, up to a height of 4,540 feet. Along with the Wologisi Range in Lofa County, this area has been the source of major deposits of iron ore, on which Liberia's greatest period of economic growth was founded.

Other natural resources, in addition to iron ore, rubber, and timber, are diamonds and gold. These have been mined in small, unmechanized diggings and have become more important in the early twenty-first century as a source of income for the various armed factions contesting civil wars in Liberia, Sierra Leone, and Côte d'Ivoire. Deposits of barite, manganese, and bauxite have been identified during geological surveys, but have not yet been commercially exploited.

The present geographical boundaries of Liberia are a result of several distinct purchases of land from the indigenous people by the American Colonization Society or its state chapters in the United States, combined with the claims extended by the new republic after independence in 1847. Claims to territory in the west and north were ignored by the British and French, who were establishing colonies in what is now Sierra Leone, Guinea, and Côte d'Ivoire. With an underequipped military and a lack of international recognition, Liberia found itself unable to either establish full control over the territory it claimed or to compete with its colonial neighbors. When the European nations met in Berlin in 1884 to divide Africa among themselves, Liberia, the only independent state on the continent, was not invited to the conference. The threat of absorption into either the French or British colonial empire was real until well into the twentieth century.

ECONOMY

As in most African countries, the Liberian economy consists of two loosely integrated systems. A subsistence agricultural and gathering-hunting sector coexists with a market economy, and extensive participation in the two characterizes the economic lives of most individuals. Both sectors have been severely disrupted by the civil war that began in 1989, and, as of 2005, 85 percent of Liberians are unemployed, and most appear to be dependent on international aid for survival. In contrast, as little as forty years prior to that, Liberia registered the second highest rate of economic growth in the world, after Japan.

The subsistence economy is dominated by the production of dry, upland rice, Liberians' staple food. Rice is produced by the method of extensive shifting cultivation, in which an area of forest vegetation is cut down, the brush is left to dry for several weeks, and the field is then burned. The system is timed to the alternating pattern of wet and dry weather. Rice seed is planted, either by broadcasting into hoed soil or by drilling with a dibble stick, toward the end of March, when the first rains are anticipated. Partially burned tree trunks are left on the ground to help control erosion when the fragile topsoil is exposed to driving rains. Fallowing cycles average between seven to twelve years; if the field is used too soon, the soil is exhausted. Cassava, maize, eggplant, peppers, okra, and other vegetables are intercropped with the rice, and weeding and bird driving are major tasks while the crop matures. Between August and November the harvest takes place. The rice must then be left to dry in the sun, separated from the stalk, and pounded with a mortar and pestle to remove the tough outer bran.

With the exception of felling the largest trees, burning the field, and sometimes constructing fences to keep out forest animals, all of this labor is done primarily by women and children. Indeed, women define themselves as farmers in Liberia, and the act of providing food (not just cooking it) for the family is an essential aspect of the cultural construction of femininity. A U.S. Agency for International Development report concluded that, culturally, "a man cannot make a rice farm without a wife, but a woman can make a rice farm without a husband" (Carter and Mends-Cole 1982). Cassava fills the gap between the previous year's supply and the new harvest, but rice remains the most psychologically and culturally important food. The subsistence technology described above has never been capable of generating a surplus large enough to meet market demand, and urban populations depend on imported rice, mostly from the United States. Compounding this, the long years of war caused extensive disruption to the indigenous subsistence system, with large numbers of rural people displaced internally to coastal cities or as refugees in neighboring countries.

Even the most isolated farming households before the war required cash to purchase cloth, cooking pots, tools, salt, and other necessities, as well as to pay taxes to the central government. Cassava, vegetables, and palm oil are produced for sale as well as for household consumption, and citrus fruits, bananas, plantains, sugarcane, and rubber are also important cash crops. Cane and rubber are generally seen as men's crops; the proceeds from their sale is not considered part of the family budget.

In the cities, the import-export and retail sectors have, for at least the last fifty years, been controlled by the immigrant Lebanese community. Because citizenship is limited by the constitution to those of African descent and only citizens can own land and other real estate property, these Lebanese businesses have Liberian shadow partners in order to operate legally. The Mandingo and other Islamic ethnic groups are also associated with the retail sector. As elsewhere in Africa, the marketing of fresh produce and other foodstuffs is largely in the hands of women.

In the 1920s, the Firestone Corporation opened a rubber plantation outside of Monrovia. The concession agreement with the Liberian government, signed in 1927, granted Firestone one million acres of land at annual rent of six cents an acre for a period of ninety-nine years. In addition, the company received numerous tax incentives and required Liberia to accept a U.S. 5 million dollar loan. Indigenous workers were sometimes forcibly provided to the company by the state, resulting in an international labor scandal in the 1930s that almost cost Liberia its sovereignty. At its peak, Firestone's Liberia installation was the largest rubber plantation in the world, producing 200,000 pounds of dried rubber each day and employing about 8,000 people in 1989.

The policy of developing the national economy via foreign-owned concessions continued through the twentieth century. Iron mining, initiated by Swedish and American investors, began in the early 1950s and helped produce an average annual growth rate of 5.7 percent between 1964 and

1974. In 1975, iron ore alone contributed almost 75 percent of the value of all exports; rubber and iron ore combined equaled 81 percent of all exports between 1973 and 1976. Yet a team of American economists concluded in 1966 that Liberia was a classic case of growth without development. Most of the profits from Liberia's natural resources left the country with the foreign investors, and what remained went largely into the purchase of imported goods, rather than being invested in local enterprises. Except in the concession areas, the foreign operators contributed little to infrastructure, leading to the classic enclave pattern of uneven development. For example, the Firestone plantation had its own system of roads, a hydroelectric plant, schools, and worker housing, but none of these amenities continued off the plant. A railroad system designed to transport iron ore from the Nimba mountains to the port of Buchanan was never extended to facilitate the movement of passengers or goods for the domestic market. Reduced tariffs on the importation of capital equipment into the country succeeded in luring investors but resulted in almost no domestic spin-off industries that might have grown up to service the concessions.

By centering its economy on a few major exports, Liberia was left vulnerable to the world economic downturn of the 1970s. With almost no domestic manufacturing sector, both educated and low-skilled workers were dependent upon the concessions or on government service for employment. As energy costs rose, the concessions cut back on employment. At the same time, international demand for Liberia's rubber and iron ore was in decline. Between 1976 and 1980, there was literally no growth in the annual value of all domestic goods and services. Worker unrest in the mining industry, along with high urban unemployment, a stagnant agricultural sector, and growing political opposition to the American-identified elite were all important factors leading to the military coup of 1980.

Economic projections for postwar Liberia are not encouraging. Massive amounts of foreign aid will be needed to rebuild infrastructure, retrain the thousands of young people who spent years fighting rather than in school, and create a climate of stability that may once again attract foreign investment. During the long years of the civil war, leaders of the various armed factions entered into private contracts with European firms to provide forest timber, diamonds, and other resources in exchange for military hardware and personal enrichment. The extent of the damage done to Liberia's fragile and nonrenewable tropical forest during this period is, as of the early twenty-first century, still unknown.

HISTORY

The nineteenth-century American settlers were not the first to bring European culture and commodities to Liberia. Portuguese, Spanish, Dutch, French, and British ships were trading along the coast by the mid-sixteenth century, disrupting long-established patterns that had directed products such as pepper, gold, ivory, and dyewoods north to the trans-Saharan routes. Liberia's long coastline was hotly contested as indigenous groups sought to reorient themselves to the new source of demand. As the Atlantic slave trade grew from the sixteenth through the nineteenth centuries, local populations adapted in a variety of ways. The Mande- and Mel-speaking peoples of the north, organized into stratified chiefdoms, formed several large and predatory confederacies that controlled trade and provided slaves for export. In the south and east, the less centralized Kruan-speaking peoples participated as hired longshoremen, deck hands, and migrant laborers, usually under two-year contracts to European ships.

The American settlers were intent upon eliminating the slave trade and wished to insert themselves into the intermediary position in the coastal economy. The struggle over trade characterized the relationship between the settlers and indigenous Africans during the nineteenth century. Incorporation of both coastal and interior groups was accomplished not only by military intervention but also by a series of trade agreements, treaties, and even politically astute marriages between rural indigenous elites and their national counterparts in Monrovia.

Many standard sources on Liberia have emphasized the cultural gulf separating the settler elite from the indigenous masses. Carl Patrick Burrowes has demonstrated that the older accounts of Liberian history read like a morality play in which evil, Americanized former slaves imposed the same oppression they were escaping upon helpless natives.

The actual situation, not surprisingly, was far more complex and the exchange of cultures more mutual than many have supposed. Yet, it is undeniable that self-identified natives, or people of tribal origin, were discriminated against in schools, businesses, churches, and the civil service. Unlike other colonial societies in Africa, the lack of a color bar between the colonizers and the colonized made it possible for significant numbers of educated indigenous people to pass into the elite. The practice of informal polygyny by settler men and the incorporation of indigenous wards, servants, and adopted children also augmented the settler group. In spite of these additions, the so-called Americo-Liberians continue, in the early twenty-first century, to total less than 3 percent of the population. The concentration of political and economic power in the hands of such a small and foreign-identified group was, until 1980, the most salient force driving Liberian national history.

The man most associated with the modern nation state was President William V. S. Tubman, who served from 1944 to 1971. His election in 1943 represented a break with the traditional dominance of a small group of Monrovia families through the True Whig Party (TWP) that had effectively controlled Liberian polities since 1877. Although he was of American settler descent, Tubman came not from Monrovia but from Maryland County, 200 miles south of the capital and considered something of a backwater. He proved himself a TWP loyalist, however, while also building a base of support among the indigenous people.

During his long administration, Tubman was responsible for several major initiatives that sought to maintain the delicate balance of minority rule while heading off challenges from the indigenous majority. The Open Door Policy, announced in his first term, sought to increase the attractiveness of Liberia to foreign capital. The elite had long been worried that too much contact between outsiders and the indigenous masses could be destabilizing. Tubman argued that such isolationist policies would ultimately backfire; anticolonialist movements were already stirring in Liberia's neighbors in the early post–World War II period. It was hoped that by opening up more economic opportunities for the indigenous people, calls for increased political power could be forestalled. Tubman extended suffrage to people of tribal origin, lowered the property requirement to vote, and enfranchised women, but all within the context of a one-party state.

In the field of foreign relations, Tubman was the first Liberian president to be received at the White House, and Liberia was the first African state to be seated on the United Nations Security Council. The Kennedy administration made Liberia the centerpiece of its Peace Corps program and contributed large amounts of aid for the construction of schools and hospitals. In the early years of decolonization, Tubman tried to position Liberia as a continental leader of the new states just emerging from European control. Liberian conservatism exerted an important influence on the formation of the Organization of African Unity and countered the Pan-Africanist ambitions of Kwame Nkrumah of Ghana. By the time he died in office in 1971, Tubman was the only president a significant number of Liberians had ever known.

The vice president, William Tolbert (1913–1980), succeeded him. Tolbert was a member of a prominent Monrovia family and TWP stalwart. Although Tolbert benefited from the consolidation of power in the executive branch that Tubman had achieved, he also wished to be perceived as more open to dissent and to dialogue with emerging student, worker, and poor peoples' organizations than his predecessor. It has been argued that neither Tubman nor Tolbert actually intended to share power with the indigenous people, only to create the illusion of doing so in order to buy more time for the settler-identified elite.

By 1979, that time seemed to be running out. The economy had been in serious decline since the mid-1970s and the TWP was being challenged politically on a number of fronts. When Tolbert announced the lifting of price controls on rice in the spring of 1979, the Progressive Alliance of Liberians (PAL), led by Gabriel Baccus Matthews (b. 1948), organized mass protests. Along with the Movement for Justice in Africa (MOJA), associated with Dr. Amos Sawyer (b. 1945) and other academics at the University of Liberia, the PAL had been working to organize workers, students, the urban unemployed, and a variety of other constituencies. On April 14, 1979, police and army units responded to 2,000 unarmed protestors. The situation escalated when the police began firing into the crowd, killing

an unknown number of people. Not trusting his own military, Tolbert called on neighboring Guinea to send troops to restore order. The Rice Riots are seen as the prelude to the coup of 1980 and the first ominous sign of the future role of the Liberian army.

Almost exactly one year to the day of the Rice Riots, on April 12, 1980, a small group of seventeen enlisted men gained access to the Executive Mansion, assassinated Tolbert, and announced themselves as the People's Redemption Council (PRC). Their leader, Samuel Kanyon Doe (c. 1951–1990), was a twenty-seven-year-old master sergeant from Grand Gedeh County. The initial PRC government was formed from the coup leaders, prominent civilians who had been jailed by Tolbert at the time of the coup, and some holdovers from the previous administration. Doe appointed a committee to draft a new constitution, headed by Amos Sawyer, and promised elections in 1985. During those five years, however, he consolidated his own power base, purged the PRC leadership of competitors, and filled governmental appointments with his own supporters. Doe imbued both the elite military forces and the civil service with a tribal character that had not been an aspect of Liberian politics up to that time. His ethnolinguistic group, the Krahn, thus came to be seen as the successors of the Americo-Liberians in controlling state power.

The elections of 1985, which Doe claimed to win with 50.9 percent of the vote, were widely believed to have been stolen. Exit polls and independent observers agree that the Liberian Action Party, led by Jackson Doe (1934–1990; no relation to Samuel K. Doe) was ahead by 60 to 70 percent when the counting of ballots was halted. One month after the election, former PRC member General Thomas Quiwonkpa (d. c. 1985) led a coup attempt that almost succeeded in ousting Doe. Quiwonkpa, who was killed in the attempt, was, like Jackson Doe, a member of the Gio or Dan ethnolinguistic group from Nimba County. Samuel Doe sent troops into the Gio homeland, where they went on a rampage of killing, looting, and burning villages. In Monrovia, civilians from Nimba were harassed or detained, and many simply disappeared. What observers have called the new tribalism in Liberia was becoming manifest.

On Christmas Eve 1989, Charles Taylor (b. 1941), a former official in the Doe regime, entered

Nimba County from Côte d'Ivoire with a small group of armed men. Doe immediately sent the military into the area, and the local people, who had been brutalized four years earlier, responded by joining Taylor's movement. Although from settler descent, Taylor's National Patriotic Front for Liberia (NPFL) took on the ethnic character of the Gio and Mano recruits. The Liberian military was by now largely Krahn in make-up and identification. Although these blocs have emerged only since the late 1980s, the Western media insisted on reporting that the ensuing civil war was motivated by ancient tribal hatreds.

By the summer of 1990, the Economic Community of West African States (ECOWAS) intervened, citing the spillover of refugees and fighters into neighboring countries. An international military force led by Nigeria prevented Taylor from taking Monrovia, but Doe was captured and killed by a rival faction. ECOWAS formed and installed an interim government of prominent civilians, headed by Amos Sawyer, but Taylor continued to control most of the countryside. Regionally and ethnically based armed factions multiplied, and a number of peace agreements were quickly violated. Taylor discovered that he could market Liberia's valuable resources without the formal legitimacy of the state, and so had little incentive to agree to any plan that would end the conflict. After one last violent looting of Monrovia in April of 1996, a disarmament program was instituted and at least partially completed in time for the 1997 elections.

It was widely believe that many weapons were cached in the countryside, rather than turned in to United Nations peacekeepers. Taylor, who ran on the platform that, because he had destroyed Liberia, he should be the one to rebuild it, had considerably more resources than any of the other candidates. He personally owned the most powerful radio station in the country and had his own newspaper and transportation to all parts of the country. Taylor also let it be known that he was fully capably of restarting the war if he was not elected. It was therefore not surprising when he was declared the winner with 75 percent of the vote.

The five years of Taylor's government were marked by little recovery or relief for most Liberians. Taylor harassed the press, eliminated or terrorized critics, and continued to run the country the way he

had his armed faction. New rebel groups, reconstituted from the armed groups of the first phase of the war, soon arrived on the scene. Liberians United for Reconciliation and Democracy (LURD), with apparent financial support from Guinea, harassed Taylor's troops but seemed incapable of a sustained assault on Monrovia. Movement for Democracy and Elections in Liberia (MODEL) pressed Taylor from the south. The United Nations restricted travel abroad for Taylor and members of his government. The UN also imposed sanctions on Liberian diamonds and considered a ban on Liberian timber.

Under pressure on several fronts, Taylor ventured abroad to peace talks in June of 2003 but hurried home when the United Nations court in Sierra Leone unsealed a war crimes indictment against him for supporting the carnage in that country. By August, he had departed for exile in Nigeria. Liberia then became the location for the largest peacekeeping operation in United Nations history: 15,000 troops were deployed to secure the country, disarm the fighters, and prepare for a new round of elections in late 2005. Ellen Johnson-Sirleaf (b. 1938), the first woman to be elected head of state in Africa, took office in January 2006 after winning in the second round over soccer star George Weah (b. 1966).

GOVERNMENT

The constitution of the First Republic was modeled on the American constitution, providing for executive and judiciary branches, and a bicameral legislature. In the early years of the First Republic, constitutional government applied only to the five settler-dominated counties along the coast. The hinterland and its indigenous occupants were governed by a modified version of indirect rule, with local chiefs incorporated into a hierarchy of administrative units under district commissioners. Tubman's reforms in the 1960s created four new counties, thus allowing interior populations to elect representatives to the legislature for the first time. At the time of the 1985 election, Doe had also created new counties by carving up the more populated coastal units to produce a total of thirteen.

The basic structure of the 1847 constitution was retained by the 1984 constitution of the Second Republic, but it differed from the 1847 constitution in significant ways. The 1984 constitution strengthened civil rights protections and included a clause that separated church and state. In spite of the checks and balances built into both constitutions, the Liberian government has long been plagued by the dominance of the executive branch and the subordination of all other structures, at both the federal and local level, to presidential power. Under the 1847 constitution, county superintendents, the equivalent of state governors, were appointed by the president; this system was retained by the 1984 document but with the provision that candidates for the position be put forward by local officials. The immense power over local administration vested in the president had served to consolidate one-party rule in Liberia for almost one hundred years and contributed to the cult of the presidency that had reached its pinnacle with Tubman.

During the war years, and especially since 2000, a number of informal governance groups concerned with constitutional have been established, both in the Liberian exile communities of the United States and in the country. Some argued that a thorough review of the 1984 constitution should have preceded elections in 2005, but this has been countered by a desire to reinstitute democratic processes and allow a new government to go forward with a true electoral mandate. Calls for a decentralized administrative structure with more local control and autonomy have been incorporated into some of the planning documents, and there is hope of revitalizing some of the more democratic forms of decision-making that characterized local politics in the prewar period.

PEOPLES AND CULTURES

The indigenous populations of Liberia are categorized, somewhat arbitrarily, into sixteen different ethnolinguistic groups. These units fall into three major language groups of the Niger-Congo stock: Mande, Mel (or West Atlantic), and Kruan (or Kwa). The Mel languages of Gola and Kissi appear to be the surviving remnants of the autochthonous inhabitants of Liberia; Mande speakers began arriving in the forest belt from the northern savannas about the fifteenth century, whereas the Kruan speakers are linguistically related to peoples living to the east in the Niger Delta. The Mande group consists of the Mandingo, Vai, Gbandi, Kpelle, Loma, Mende, Gio, and Mano peoples, and makes up the largest group in terms of population. The

Kruan speakers include the Bassa, Dei (Dey), Grebo, Kru, Belle (Kuwaa), Krahn, and Gbee. The largest of the sixteen groups is the Kpelle, with 20 percent of the total national population. Many Liberians share ethnic identity with populations living across the international borders in Sierra Leone, Guinea, and Côte d'Ivoire.

The Saint John River constitutes a cultural and linguistic boundary roughly dividing the Mande and Mel speakers from the Kruan populations to the south and east. The Mande and Mel are characterized by hierarchical chiefdoms based on ranked patrilineages, and by the presence of universal secret initiatory societies; Poro for men and Sande (or Bundu) for women. Historically, the societies operated across ethnic and language lines, allowing for a measure of regional integration in the absence of centralized states. Some have suggested that Poro and Sande were a means of adaptation to the complex multiethnic political context created in the Liberian forests by the movement of peoples away from the collapsing empires of the western savannas in the fifteenth and sixteenth centuries. Others have argued that they function to secure the dominance of high-ranking lineages. Kruan peoples to the southeast are far less stratified and may have adopted agriculture much later than their northern neighbors.

Liberia has conducted only two censuses in the modern era: in 1962 and 1974. All contemporary figures are based on projections from the 1974 census, and both censuses have been criticized for lack of accuracy and comparability. Average population density is low, although the period of the civil war saw a greater concentration of people into coastal cities, and some rural areas were effectively depopulated. Total national population at the beginning of the war was estimated to be 2.5 million, although the seven years of war may have claimed about 200,000 lives.

Religion has been, and continues to be, important for Liberians of both settler and indigenous descent. Local religious practices focused on ancestor veneration and the various secret societies; through the impact of Western missionaries, many indigenous Liberians are members of Christian churches, as well. The settlers brought with them a number of Protestant American denominations, as well as Masonic organizations. Islam, expanding south from the Sahel since the fifteenth century, has become a major force in the early twenty-first century with the prominence of faction leader Al Haji Kromah (b. 1953), who ran for president in the 1997 and 2005 elections. Although Liberia's national leaders used to characterize it as a Christian nation in the pre-coup era, it is clear that a great deal of syncretism between Western, Islamic, and local religious practices has existed for many years.

The growth of ethnic hostility in the past few years has been treated above. Although it is difficult to imagine Liberians coming together to rebuild the nation and a national identity after such devastating upheaval, it is important to keep in mind the contingent and strategic nature of these tribal identities. Most Liberians before the war found it possible to maintain multiple and even contradictory affiliations: to be Christian and Muslim (although not at the same moment); civilized and native; or Liberian and Vai, Gola, or Grebo depending on

---

Republic of Liberia

Population:	3,195,931 (2007 est.)
Area:	111,370 sq. km (43,000 sq. mi.)
Official language:	English
Languages:	English, 16 indigenous languages
National currency:	Liberian dollar
Principal religions:	animist 40%, Muslim 20%, Christian 40%
Capital:	Monrovia (est. pop. 1,000,000 in 2006)
Other urban centers:	Buchanan, Ganta, Gbarnga, Kakata, Harbel
Annual rainfall:	ranges from 5,210 mm (203 in.) on northwestern coast to 2,540 mm (100 in.) at southeastern tip of country to 1,780 mm (70 in.) on central plateau
Principal geographical features:	*Mountains:* Nimba Range, Wologisi Range *Rivers:* Mano, Moro, Lofa, St. Paul, St. John, Cess (Cestos), Cavalla, Duobe (Douobé)
Economy:	*GDP per capita:* US$1,000 (2006)
Principal products and exports:	*Agricultural:* rubber, coffee, cocoa, rice, cassava (tapioca), palm oil, sugarcane, bananas, sheep, goats, timber *Manufacturing:* rubber processing, palm oil processing *Mining:* iron ore, diamonds, gold
Government:	Independence from the American Colonization Society, 1847. Constitution, 1847. New constitution approved in 1984 and 1986. Republic. Bicameral National Assembly consists of Senate and House of Representatives. Rebellion in 1989 led to periodic civil war; transitional government in place after war ended in 2003. Democratic elections held in 2005. For purposes of local government there are 15 counties.
Rulers since World War II:	1944–1971: President William Tubman 1971–1980: President William Richard Tolbert 1980–1986: Master Sergeant (later General) Samuel K. Doe, Chairman of People's Redemption Council 1986–1990: President Samuel K. Doe 1990–1994: Interim President Amos Sawyer 1994–1995: David Kpormakor, chairman of Council of State 1995–1996: Wilton Sankawulo, chairman of Council of State 1996–1997: Ruth Sando Perry, chairman of Council of State 1997–2003: President Charles Taylor 2003–2006: Gyude Bryant (transitional government) 2006–: President Ellen Johnson-Sirleaf
Armed forces:	President is commander in chief. The Armed Forces of Liberia consists of an army, navy, and air force. Voluntary enlistment with no conscription.
Transportation:	*Rail:* 483 km (300 mi.), no passenger railway *Ports:* Monrovia, Buchanan *Roads:* 10,600 km (6,587 mi.), 9% paved *National airlines:* Air Liberia, Air Taxi Company of Liberia *Airports:* Roberts International Airport, James Spriggs Payne Airfield. 50 other small airports.
Media:	*Newspapers: The Liberian Times, The Liberian Analyst Corporation, The Daily Observer.* Book publishing is a recent development. Liberian Broadcasting Corporation provides both radio and television service.
Literacy and education:	*Total literacy rate:* 20% (2003). Education is free, universal, and compulsory for ages 6–16. Universities include University of Liberia at Monrovia, Cuttington University College.

---

social context. That Liberians seem to view these categories as, in some sense, flexible and contextual is a hopeful sign for the ultimate delimination of a new inclusive national identity.

See also **Decolonization; Economic Community of West African States (ECOWAS); Ecosystems; Ethnicity: Western Africa; Forestry: Western Africa; Nkrumah, Francis Nwia Kofi; Organization of African Unity; Production Strategies; Slave Trades: Atlantic, Central Africa; Soils; Taylor, Charles Gahnhay; Transportation: Railways; Tubman, William Vacanarat Shadrach; Warfare: Civil Wars.**

BIBLIOGRAPHY

Anderson, Benjamin. *Narrative of the Expedition Dispatched to Musardu by the Liberian Government in 1874.* London: Cass, 1971.

Bellman, Beryl L. *Village of Curers and Assassins: On the Production of Fala Kpelle Cosmological Categories.* The Hague: Mouton, 1975.

Bledsoe, Caroline H. *Women and Marriage in Kpelle Society.* Stanford, CA: Stanford University Press, 1980.

Burrowes, Carl Patrick. "The Americo-Liberian Ruling Class and Other Myths: A Critique of Political Science in the Liberian Context." Temple University Occasional Papers no. 3. Philadelphia: Temple University 1989.

Carter, Jeanette, and Joyce Mends-Cole. *Liberian Women: Their Role in Food Production and Their Educational and Legal Status.* Monrovia: USAID/University of Liberia, 1982.

Clower, Robert W.; George Dalton; Mitchell Harwitz; and A. A. Walters. *Growth Without Development: An Economic Survey of Liberia.* Evanston, IL: Northwestern University Press, 1966.

D'Azevedo, Warren L. "Some Historical Problems in the Delineation of a Central West Atlantic Region." *Annals of the New York Academy of Science* 96 (1962): 512–538.

Dunn, D. Elwood, and S. Byron Tarr. *Liberia: A National Policy in Transition.* Metuchen, NJ: Scarecrow Press, 1988.

Ellis, Stephen. *The Mask of Anarchy: The Destruction of Liberia and the Religious Dimension of an African Civil War.* New York: New York University Press, 1999.

Ellis, Stephen, and Gerrie Ter Haar. *Worlds of Power: Religious Thought and Political Practice in Africa.* New York: Oxford University Press, 2004.

Fraenkel, Merran. *Tribe and Class in Monrovia.* London: Oxford University Press, 1964.

Gershoni, Yekutiel. *Black Colonialism: The Americo-Liberian Scramble for the Hinterland.* Boulder, CO: Westview Press, 1985.

Harris, David. "From 'Warlord' to 'Democratic' President: How Charles Taylor Won the 1997 Liberian Elections." *Journal of Modern African Studies* 37 (1999): 431–455.

Hasselman, Karl H. *Liberia: Geographical Mosaics of the Land and the People.* Monrovia: Ministry of Information, Cultural Affairs, and Tourism, Government of Liberia, 1979.

Hlophe, Stephen. *Class, Ethnicity, and Politics in Liberia.* Washington, DC: University Press of America, 1987.

Holloway, Joseph E. *Liberian Diplomacy in Africa: A Study of Inter-African Relations.* Washington, DC: University Press of America, 1981.

Huberich, C. H. *The Political and Legislative History of Liberia.* New York: Central Book Co., 1947.

Liebenow, J. Gus. *Liberia: The Quest for Democracy.* Bloomington: Indiana University Press, 1987.

McDaniel, Antonio. *Swing Low, Sweet Chariot: The Mortality Cost of Colonizing Liberia in the Nineteenth Century.* Chicago: University of Chicago Press, 1995.

Moran, Mary H. *Civilized Women: Gender and Prestige in Southeastern Liberia.* Ithaca, NY: Cornell University Press, 1990.

Moran, Mary H. *Liberia: The Violence of Democracy.* Philadelphia: University of Pennsylvania Press, 2006.

Sawyer, Amos. *The Emergence of Autocracy in Liberia: Tragedy and Challenge.* San Francisco: Institute for Contemporary Studies, 1992.

Shick, Tom. *Behold the Promised Land: A History of Afro American Settler Society in Nineteenth-Century Liberia.* Baltimore: Johns Hopkins University Press, 1984.

Staudenraus, P. J. *The African Colonization Movement, 1816–1865.* New York: Columbia University Press, 1961.

Sundiata, I. K. *Black Scandal: America and the Liberian Labor Crisis, 1929–36.* Philadelphia: Institute for the Study of Human Issues, 1980.

Utas, Mats. "Sweet Battlefields: Youth and the Liberian Civil War." Ph.D. diss. Uppsala University, Sweden, 2003.

Wiley, Bell I., ed. *Slaves No More: Letters from Liberia, 1833–1869.* Lexington: University of Kentucky Press, 1980.

Wonkeryor, Edward L., Ella Forbes, James S. Guseh, and George Klay Kieh Jr. *American Democracy in Africa in the Twenty-First Century?* Cherry Hill, NJ: Africana Homestead Legacy Publishers, 2000.

MARY H. MORAN

HISTORY AND POLITICS

Liberia is an African nation located on the west coast of the continent. Officially known as the Republic of Liberia, it is bordered by Côte d'Ivoire in the east and northeast, Guinea in the north, and Sierra Leone in the west. It was founded in 1822 as a colony for free blacks who elected to emigrate from the United States to Africa. Its foundation and early development was under the tutelage of the Society for the Colonization of Free People of Color of America (popularly known as the American Colonization Society or ACS). The society was established in 1816 to colonize American free blacks in Africa.

The intersection of the politics of abolition and colonization in the early nineteenth century was an important element in the foundation of Liberia. As slaves increasingly gained their freedom, the prospect of a large population of free blacks in America was unwelcome to many whites. The slave-holding class in particular feared the presence of many free blacks who could encourage slave conspiracies and insurrections. Colonization was thus seen as a way to rid America of what many whites considered undesirable elements. At the same time, some whites believed that colonization offered blacks the best opportunity to live a truly free life unencumbered by American racism. Then too, in the evangelical community there was the hope that black colonization would serve the course of American missionary endeavor in Africa in which African Americans were expected to play a leading role.

The twin concept of emigration and colonization was embraced by some free blacks who agreed that black people would never find freedom, equality, and social justice in America. They saw a territory of their own in Africa as the only remedy to racial oppression in America. However, colonization was never popular in the black community and was, indeed, rejected by a number of prominent black leaders including the abolitionist Frederick Douglass. Many argued that the long sojourn of black people in America and their contributions to its development called for their continued struggle there until the attainment of full legal rights of citizenship.

In 1821 the ACS purchased land at Cape Mesurado on the west coast of Africa to establish the first colony. The first settlers arrived the following year, and more followed subsequently leading to the establishment of other colonies. But the ACS never succeeded in sending a large number of blacks to Liberia. By 1867, the émigrés numbered just about 13,000, although this number was augmented by a few thousand "recaptives," that is, America-bound slaves rescued aboard slave ships off the coast of West Africa.

For much of its early history Liberia occupied an ambiguous status in the international community. In 1838 the hitherto independent colonies, namely Monrovia, New Georgia, Caldwell, Millsburg, Marshall, Bexley, Bassa Cove, and Edina, united to form the Commonwealth of Liberia, and adopted a constitution in 1839. But the commonwealth was neither an independent state nor a formal American colony. In that precarious state, European colonial powers, particularly Britain, threatened to annex parts of its territory. The commonwealth was also confronted with incessant hostility from indigenous peoples of the hinterland. These problems, compounded by financial troubles, persuaded the ACS to relinquish authority over the colony.

The formal declaration of independence was made on July 26, 1847, and Liberia became a sovereign state. The new state adopted a constitution strikingly similar to that of the United States and made Monrovia, named for the fifth president of the United States, James Monroe, its political capital. However, the United States' official recognition of Liberia's independence did not come until 1862 under President Abraham Lincoln. By the late 1920s the United States had begun to exercise informal economic and political influence over the republic beyond its traditional preoccupation with missionary activities. Firestone Rubber Plantation, a giant U.S. company that dominated Liberia's rubber industry, was the major instrument of American hegemony.

American interest in Liberia grew significantly during World War II when the country assumed a strategic importance in United States and allied war effort in West Africa. A 1942 bilateral defense agreement militarized Liberia, and provided for American construction of strategic roads, ports, and air bases in the country. Roberts Field and other bases served as military depots and way stations for America's war supplies, which were ferried across West Africa destined for the North African theatre. The United States also stationed troops in

Liberia, an all-black contingent to man its military facilities. At the request of the United States, Liberia entered the war in 1944 and declared war on Germany. Liberia's importance in America's war effort in the southern Atlantic was underscored by President Franklin D. Roosevelt's visit to the country in late January 1943 while returning from the Allied Casablanca Conference in Morocco. America's wartime presence in Liberia yielded for the African nation economic growth and transportation modernization.

On the domestic front, the political and economic life of Liberia was for almost two hundred years dominated by the descendants of the black American émigrés, the Americo-Liberians. Considerably influenced by American culture, they formed a distinct, privileged group distanced from the majority Liberian population, composed of indigenous people. Until the bloody coup d'etat of April 12, 1980, that brought the military into power, the Americo-Liberians, under their party, the True Whig Party, exclusively monopolized political power at the expense of indigenous Liberians.

The 1980 coup was executed by a group of dissident noncommissioned officers led by a master-sergeant, Samuel Kayon Doe. This coup is significant in that it transferred political power to the indigenous Liberians for the first time. The new leader, Doe, became the first indigenous Liberian to hold power since the foundation of the republic. His immediate predecessor, William Tolbert, Jr., was killed in the coup, and many of his government functionaries were subsequently executed, effectively bringing about an end to Americo-Liberian political dominance.

With the overthrow of Americo-Liberian power, Doe formed and headed a new ruling body, the People's Redemption Council (PRC). The coup was initially welcomed by many Liberians happy to see the overthrow of the corrupt Tolbert regime. Doe's staunch pro-West stance in the early 1980s also earned him American support, and Liberia became a recipient of generous U.S. foreign aid. Doe's popularity, however, soon began to wane as the government became increasingly corrupt and authoritarian. He outlawed opposition political parties, curtailed press freedom, and increasingly favored his own ethnic group, the Krahn. In a stage-managed presidential election held in October 1985 in which he was declared winner,

Doe transformed himself into a civilian president. With the waning of the Cold War, and as the regime became more autocratic, Washington's support for Doe began to slip.

A civil war broke out in December 1989, orchestrated by an invasion of the country from Côte d'Ivoire by a rebel group, the National Patriotic Front of Liberia (NPFL) led by Charles Taylor, a former ally of Doe. Taylor's aim to topple the Doe regime culminated in a full-scale civil war in which other competing warring factions were involved. By 1990 much of Liberia including Monrovia was under the control of rebel factions. Doe himself was captured on September 9 and was subsequently brutally executed by the rebel forces of another faction leader, Prince Yormie Johnson.

A 1996 peace agreement that brokered a cease-fire brought a temporary end to the Liberian conflict. Following a transitional period, a newly elected government was inaugurated in 1997 with the former rebel leader Charles Taylor installed as president, following his victory in the presidential election. Taylor's regime was not only autocratic and intolerant of opposition, it was characterized by corruption and ineptitude. Moreover, the government was unable to stem the tide of economic downturn as well as bring about political stability and lasting peace. Taylor himself was also accused of fuelling the civil war in neighboring Sierra Leone by aiding a rebel faction, the Revolutionary United Front (RUF), in its brutal campaign against the government and perpetration of untold atrocities against the people.

Liberia's fragile peace collapsed when the war resumed in 1999. By mid-2003 the renewed violence had considerably escalated, becoming a major threat to Monrovia. American intervention in the conflict, widely expected by Liberians, did not materialize. However, the United States backed with logistical and financial support the peacekeeping force called ECOWAS Monitoring Group (ECOMOG), which had been deployed to Liberia by the West African regional organization, the Economic Community of West African States (ECOWAS), to contain the violence. Meanwhile, international pressure, particularly from the United States, forced Taylor to resign from office in August 2003 whereupon he departed to exile in

Nigeria, where he had been granted asylum. Taylor left behind a country in economic shambles, near total infrastructural collapse, and a populace greatly impoverished.

Post–civil war Liberia is faced with the formidable task of political and economic reconstruction. A transitional government instituted after Taylor's flight to exile succeeded in organizing and holding a free and fair election on October 11 and a run-off on November 8, 2005, which was won by Ellen Johnson-Sirleaf, a Harvard-trained economist, who had been active in Liberia's public life and had emerged second to Taylor in the July 1997 election. Johnson-Sirleaf was inaugurated the twenty-fourth president of Liberia on January 16, 2006, becoming also Africa's first female president. In March President Johnson-Sirleaf formally requested from the Nigerian government the extradition of ex-president Taylor who had in June 2003 been indicted by a United Nations tribunal for war crimes for his role in the brutal militarized civil conflict in Sierra Leone. Taylor was extradited on March 29, 2006, initially to Sierra Leone, and subsequently to the Hague to face the charges against him.

See also **Cold War; Economic Community of West African States (ECOWAS); Johnson-Sirleaf, Ellen; Taylor, Charles Gahnhay; Tubman, William Vacanart Shadrach; Warfare: Civil Wars.**

BIBLIOGRAPHY

Levitt, Jeremy I. *The Evolution of Deadly Conflict in Liberia: From "Paternaltarianism" to State Collapse.* Durham, NC: Carolina Academic Press, 2005.

Moran, Mary H. *Liberia: The Violence of Democracy.* Philadelphia: University of Pennsylvania Press, 2006.

Nelson, Harold D., ed. *Liberia: A Country Study.* Washington DC: U.S. Government Printing Office, 1985.

Sawyer, Amos. *Beyond Plunder: Toward Democratic Governance in Liberia.* Boulder, CO: Lynne Rienner Publishers, 2005.

Smith, James Wesley. *Sojourners in Search of Freedom: The Settlement of Liberia of Black Americans.* Lanham, MD: University Press of America, 1987.

Smith, John David, ed. *The American Colonization Society and Emigration: Solutions to "The Negro Problem."* New York: Garland Publishers, 1993.

ADEBAYO OYEBADE

LIBRARIES.

Libraries in Africa have deep historical roots. The great library at Alexandria, built in 295 BCE during the reign of Ptolemy I, is in the early 2000s the site of a research library sponsored by the United Nations Educational, Scientific, and Cultural Organization (UNESCO) collecting the cultural heritage of Egypt, the Mediterranean region, Africa, and the Arab world. The spread of Islam and Arabic writing through Africa beginning in the eighth century led to the production and collection of manuscripts on religious and cultural subjects in Arabic or local languages written in Arabic script. The most famous of these were in Timbuktu, brought to wide public attention by *Wonders of the African World*, the television documentary directed by Henry Louis Gates. Manuscript libraries were common throughout the Sahel. Collections from Mali and Mauritania are being digitized for preservation and dissemination by the Library of Congress, Northwestern University, Cultural Survival, and other universities, organizations, and scholars. Similar manuscript collections in Ge'ez and Amharic can be found in Ethiopian monastic libraries and the Institute of Ethiopian Studies in Addis Ababa.

The first public library opened in Liberia in 1826, followed in 1896 by a public library in Bulawayo, Southern Rhodesia (present-day Zimbabwe). Public libraries spread throughout Africa in the twentieth century, filling a vital educational role by providing space and reading materials for people studying for degrees or certification exams. In 1975 the Nigerian author Chinua Achebe noted that Nigerians in Lagos libraries read for exams, whereas foreigners read for recreation.

In rural areas, public libraries are an essential component of literacy education, providing newspapers, how-to manuals, and recreational reading to new readers. Bookmobiles—sometimes using camels and donkeys for delivery—bring books to far-flung villages. These library services also deliver vital health, agricultural, and political information. The collections offered by public libraries are limited, however, by shortages of funds and lack of publications in local languages on topics of interest to readers.

The first academic library in sub-Saharan Africa was at Fourah Bay College in Sierra Leone, founded in 1827. The Bibliothèque du Centre de Recherche et de Documentation du Sénégal, at Saint-Louis, followed in 1837. In 1862 the University of Liberia established a library. University development surged in the twentieth century, with Makerere University in Uganda in 1922, the University of Ibadan in Nigeria in 1947, and the University College at Dar es Salaam in 1961. The move toward independence in the mid-twentieth century saw substantial growth in academic libraries as more universities were founded.

National libraries in Africa serve as repositories for books deposited for copyright, promote library services, and produce national bibliographies. As the permanent record of books published in a given country, national bibliographies make the intellectual and cultural product of a nation accessible to its own citizens and to the rest of the world. Not all African nations can afford libraries, but most nations do establish national archives to preserve essential documents. Both national libraries and archives are important resources for researchers.

Research institutes, whether a part of universities, government agencies, or international organizations, often have specialized libraries and documentation centers supplying researchers with the information necessary for their work and disseminating the results of research. Centers such as the International Livestock Research Institute (ILRI) in Addis Ababa, Ethiopia, the International Institute of Tropical Agriculture (IITA) in Ibadan, Nigeria, and others are in the vanguard of information technology, including computerized databases and electronic document delivery. The Pan African Development Information System (PADIS), formed by the United Nations Economic Commission for Africa (UNECA) in Addis Ababa, is a major force in making development information available throughout Africa.

Trained librarians are essential for library services in Africa. The first African library school was the Institute of Librarianship at the University of Ibadan, established in 1961. In 1967 a school was established for Francophone Africa at the University of Dakar, and in 1963 the East African School of Librarianship began classes at Makerere University in Kampala, Uganda. Graduate programs in library science are offered at many universities, supplemented by undergraduate degrees and diplomas at polytechnic colleges and training schools.

After the period of optimistic development in the 1960s and 1970s, the economies and stability of many African countries declined, and all categories of libraries suffered severe setbacks. During the 1980s books were in short supply due to the general state of national economies, restrictions on imports, and lack of sufficient infrastructure in the local publishing and book trade. Numerous philanthropic organizations undertook measures to remedy the "book famine" in Africa through donations of books and journals to academic, public, and school libraries. Some projects sent container loads of poor quality or inappropriate materials, but most were better targeted to the real needs of recipients. Although print materials will always be needed, many libraries in Africa are attempting to use advances in information technology to overcome shortages.

CD-ROMs, capable of providing hundreds of pages on a single disk, seemed to be the ideal way of providing information and research to Africa's readers. The rapid change in technology, however, meant that choices made by African libraries or donors could quickly become obsolete. Information and scholarship readily available on the Web to researchers in developed nations is out of reach to African students and scholars because of limited equipment and bandwidth. Nevertheless, projects such as the Association of African Universities' Database of African Dissertations and Theses (DATAD) and the Digital Imaging Project of South Africa (DISA), combined with donor projects such as WIDERnet, which provides open source resources on hard drives for local area networks within universities, are flourishing.

African librarians are addressing the problems of their libraries through regional associations such as the Standing Conference of Eastern, Central, and Southern African Library and Information Associations (SCECSAL) and the Standing Conference of African University Libraries–Western Area (SCAULWA). Librarians worldwide cooperate with African libraries through organizations such as the Africana Librarians Council of the African Studies Association, the Cooperative Africana Microforms Project, and AEGIS (Africa-Europe Group for Interdisciplinary Studies).

See also **Achebe, Chinua; Education, School; Education, University and College; Islam; Literacy; Research; Writing Systems.**

BIBLIOGRAPHY

Aman, Mohamed M. *The New Biblioteca Alexandrina: A Link in the Historical Chain of Cultural Continuity.* Milwaukee, WI: University of Wisconsin-Milwaukee, School of Library and Information Science, 1991.

Libraries of Timbuktu for the Preservation and Promotion of African Literary Heritage. Available from http://www.sum.uio.no/research/mali/timbuktu.

Olden, Anthony. *Libraries in Africa: Pioneers, Policies, Problems.* Lanham, MD: Scarecrow Press, 1995.

Rosenberg, Diana. *University Libraries in Africa: A Review of Their Current State and Future.* London: International African Institute, 1997.

Sitzman, Glenn L. *African Libraries.* Metuchen, NJ: Scarecrow Press, 1988.

Sturges, R. P., and Richard Neill. *The Quiet Struggle: Libraries and Information for Africa.* London: Mansell, 1998.

Wise, Michael, ed. *Aspects of African Librarianship: A Collection of Writings.* London: Mansell, 1985.

Wise, Michael, and Anthony Olden, eds. "Information and Libraries in the Developing World." In *Sub-Saharan Africa*, Vol. 1. London: Library Association, 1990.

GRETCHEN WALSH

LIBREVILLE. The capital of Gabon, Libreville lies on the northern side of the mouth of the Gabon Estuary as the river enters the Gulf of Guinea. The area was originally inhabited by Fang-speaking peoples. In 1843–1844 the French established a fort, trading post, and Roman Catholic mission there. It became a settlement for slaves freed by the French naval forces suppressing the Atlantic trade in captives after 1849, when it became known as Libreville. During the "Scramble" among the colonial powers for territory in Africa, Libreville became the main launching pad for French expansion into Gabon.

Among the main features of the town is the deepwater port in Owendo, which was opened in 1964. Libreville is also a flourishing commercial center, with logging, sawmilling, fishing, and paper pulp processing industries. It is the Gabon headquarters of major crude oil, uranium, and manganese mining companies. Libreville has an international airport and a university. In 2007 its population was 604,200.

See also **Colonial Policies and Practices: French North Africa; Freetown; Gabon: History and Politics; Slave Trades.**

BIBLIOGRAPHY

Ajayi, J. F. Ade., ed. *General History of Africa*, Vol. 6: *Africa in the Nineteenth Century until the 1880s.* Paris: UNESCO, 1989.

Gray, Christopher J. *Colonial Rule and Crisis in Equatorial Africa: Southern Gabon, c. 1850–1940.* Rochester, NY: University of Rochester Press, 2002.

C. OGBOGBO

LIBYA

This entry includes the following articles:
GEOGRAPHY AND ECONOMY
SOCIETY AND CULTURES
HISTORY AND POLITICS

GEOGRAPHY AND ECONOMY

When Libya gained independence in 1951 it was one of the poorest countries in the world, ravaged by its struggle against Italian colonization (1911–1931) and World War II.

Reconstruction of the Kingdom of Libya began in 1951 and gained pace after the first discoveries of oil in 1956, but the economy only benefited from this newly found wealth after Muammar Qadhdhafi came to power in 1969, transforming the Kingdom into the Great Socialist People's Libyan Arab Jamahiriya. His first objective was to free the country from what he characterized as Libya's foreign economic stranglehold. Qadhdhafi then used the 1973 oil shock to accelerate the nationalization of energy resources. Thus independent Libya had exceptional resources with which to develop itself but remained dependent on the fluctuating price of oil (95% of exports), foreign labor (representing one-half of workers) and the importation of food, materials, and technology.

From 1969 until the mid-1980s, the increasing power of the state accompanied the implementation of a socialist economy with control over entire sectors of production, and the massive employment of Libyans in the public sector. However, the

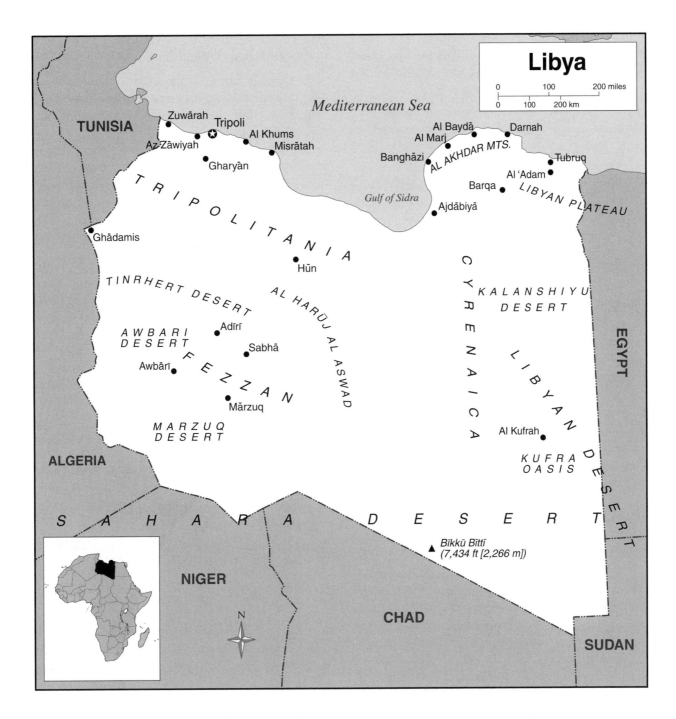

Libya

Mediterranean Sea

0   100   200 miles
0 100   200 km

TUNISIA

Zuwārah
Tripoli ☆
Az-Zāwiyah
Al Khums
Misrātah
Gharyān

Al Baydā   Darnah
Al Marj
Banghāzi   AL AKHDAR MTS.
Tubruq
Al 'Adam
Barqa   LIBYAN PLATEAU

Gulf of Sidra

Ajdābiyā

T R I P O L I T A N I A

Ghādamis

Hūn

C Y R E N A I C A

K A L A N S H I Y U
D E S E R T

T I N R H E R T   D E S E R T

AL HARŪJ AL ASWAD

A W B A R I
D E S E R T

Adīrī

Sabhā

F E Z Z A N

Awbārī

Mārzuq

L I B Y A N   D E S E R T

EGYPT

M A R Z U Q
D E S E R T

Al Kufrah

K U F R A
O A S I S

ALGERIA

S A H A R A   D E S E R T

NIGER

Bīkkū Bīttī
(7,434 ft [2,266 m])

N

CHAD

SUDAN

economy's fragility was revealed during the oil counter-shock of the mid-1980s that subjected the regime to a drop in its revenues, 75 percent of which came from oil. In 1987, a limited economic liberalization, the *infitah* ("opening" in Arabic) began and continued despite UN sanctions (1992–1999). Living conditions deteriorated and the GNP per person dropped from $8,520 in 1984 to $4,300 in 1997, but in 2003 increased to $6,400 due to the increase in oil prices.

With over 1 million square miles, Libya is the fourth largest country on the African continent and a real crossroads, bordering six countries: Tunisia and Algeria in the Maghrib; Egypt in the Mashriq; and Niger, Chad, and the Sudan in sub-Saharan Africa. Its 1,242 miles of Mediterranean coastline are in sharp contrast to this arid country of which 95 percent is desert. Consequently, only 7 percent of Libya possesses a Mediterranean climate whereas in the rest of the country the average annual rainfall does not exceed 1 inch and temperatures vary in extremes: Ghadames is the hottest (106 degrees Fahrenheit), as well as the coldest (38 degrees Fahrenheit), town.

These physical constraints are overcome by a strong regional master planning policy based on urbanization and water self-sufficiency, financed through oil revenues.

As of the 1960s, the three geographical regions of Tripolitania (northwest), Fezzan (southwest), and Cyrenaica (northeast) were linked by road to each other. At the end of the 1970s, the asphalted Libyan road system was 2,500 miles long; it multiplied sixfold in the ensuing fifteen years until the oil counter-shock. By 1985 asphalted roads linked all populated areas.

Eighty percent of Libyans live along the coast and the population density is only 2.6 people per square mile (compared to 31 per square mile in the United States). Consequently, the Libyan regime attempts to balance the different parts of its territory to benefit regions in the interior of the country by creating administrative cities and by diversifying the economies of medium-sized cities already possessing basic infrastructure in health, education, and housing. Thus Libyans are no longer Bedouin or farmers but mainly city dwellers (88%), half of whom live in one of the two largest cities, Tripoli (1.3 million inhabitants) and Benghazi (660,000 inhabitants).

Faced with critically needed groundwater resources, a limited average annual rainfall of 2.2 inches, and the absence of permanent water tables, Libya's Great Man Made River Project has become the most important fossil water extraction and transfer program in the world. This project will be completed by 2010, enabling the pumping of 2 billion cubic meters of water per year at a cost of $30 billion. Its life expectancy will probably not exceed fifty years, but will give Libya a delay during which other, more long-term options will be developed.

The modernization of Libya since its independence is undeniable: population has grown fivefold to about 6 million (6,036,914 in 2007) and up to 7 million including foreigners; school attendance has gone from 20 percent to 100 percent; the number of farm workers (7%) has been divided by a factor of 10; since the early 1980s the child-birth rate per woman has fallen from 7.5 to 3.2,

and the Human Development Index is the highest in Africa (64th in 2000).

Although Libya has found an original path to development, the various projects begun in the mid-twentieth century have yet to be completed. In the coming decades less economic dependency on oil revenues (that make up 30% of gross national product), a more diversified list of foreign trading partners (60% of imports are from the European Union, Libya's primary trading partner resulting from U.S. sanctions taken against Libya in 1982), a better balance between regions, and surmounting its need for water are all on Libya's horizon.

See also **Qadhdhafi, Muammar; Socialism and Postsocialisms.**

BIBLIOGRAPHY

Allan, J. A., K. S. McLachlan, and M. M. Buru, eds. *Libya, State and Region: A Study of Regional Evolution.* London: SOAS Center of Near and Middle Eastern Studies in association with Al Fateh University, Tripoli and the Society for Libyan Studies, 1989.

Burgat, F., and A. Laronde. *La Libye.* Paris: PUF, 2003.

Niblock, Tim. *"Pariah States" and Sanctions in the Middle East: Iraq, Libya, and Soudan.* Boulder, CO: Lynne Rienner, 2001.

Pliez, Oliver. *La nouvelle Libye, espaces, sociétés et géopolitique,* Paris: Karthala, 2004.

Vandewalle, Dirk. *A History of Modern Libya.* New York: Cambridge University Press, 2005.

OLIVER PLIEZ

SOCIETY AND CULTURES

Libya became independent in 1951 and consists of three geographical provinces: Tripolitania, Cyrenaica, and Fezzan. In 1963 King Idris I combined the three provinces, inhabited by Arabs, Berber and Tuareg, into a centrally administrated united state. This was a difficult task because the three provinces had different tribes, interests and goals, contrasting ethnic compositions, and different geographical conditions and histories. The inhabitants of the Fezzan, the Tuareg, were conscious of prior autonomy and dissociated themselves from the north. Characteristic for the Sanusi-led monarchy was the integration of tribal elements with the political role of a few influential families who dominated Libya between 1951 and 1969. With the beginning of the oil exploration in 1959, the political elite began to enrich itself enormously, exacerbating the social tensions between them and the rest of the population, living on a subsistence level. Socioeconomic problems multiplied, including depletion of resources, migration from the countryside, increasing urbanization, missing education, and insufficient health services. After 1969, Muammar Qadhdhafi tried to unite the three provinces not only politically and economically but also on an ideological level, creating a Libyan national identity beyond tribal, ethnic or religious differences. Nevertheless local conceptions of affiliation are integrated into the supralocal construction of the national identity.

NATIONAL IDENTITY AND LOCAL IMPLICATIONS

Qadhdhafi's revolution on September 1, 1969, set in motion major political and social change. Qadhdhafi sought to establish an ethnically homogenous national state with four characteristics:

1. In prerevolutionary Libya, the country's Arab tribes, the majority of the population, held political power. Qadhdhafi sought to place the ethnic minorities on an equal footing: Berber (Imazighen) in Tripolitania and few in Cyrenaica, and the Tuareg (Imuhagh/ Imajeghen) and Tubu (Teda) in Fezzan. On a religious level, he also placed the Ibadi Muslim minority on an equal footing with the Sunni majority.

Great Socialist People's Libyan Arab Jamahiriya (Libya)

Population:	6,036,914 (2007 est.)
Area:	1,759,540 sq. km (1,093,327 sq. mi.)
Official language:	Arabic
Languages:	English, French, Italian, Arabic
National currency:	Libyan dinar
Principal religions:	Sunni Muslim 97%, other 3%
Capital:	Tripoli (est. pop. 1,300,000 in 2006)
Other urban centers:	Benghazi
Annual rainfall:	Around 100 mm (4 in.) on the coast to less than 25 mm (1 in.) further inland
Principal geographical features:	*Mountains:* Tibesti Mountains (range), Djebel Al Awaynat, Bikku Bitti, Haruj *Other:* Libyan Desert, Arkenu craters
Economy:	*GDP per capita:* US$12,300 (2006)
Principal products and exports:	*Agricultural:* wheat, barley, olives, dates, citrus, vegetables, peanuts, soybeans, cattle *Manufacturing:* iron and steel, food processing, textiles, handicrafts, cement *Mining:* petroleum
Government:	Independence from U.N. trusteeship, 1951. Constitution, 1969, amended in 1977. First operated as a constitutional and hereditary monarchy. Changed to military dictatorship after coup d'etat in 1969 by the Revolutionary Command Council. Unicameral General People's Congress (GPC; members elected indirectly through a hierarchy of people's committees). Head of government elected by GPC. For purposes of local government, there are 31 municipalities.
Heads of state since independence:	1951–1966: King Idris 1969–: Colonel Muammar Abu-Minyar al-Qadhdhafi (de facto)
Armed forces:	Service is conscript and voluntary. *Army:* 45,000 *Air force:* 22,000 *Navy:* 8,000
Transportation:	*Rail:* Libya is in the process of building a railway system. *Ports:* As Sidrah, Az Zuwaytinah, Marsa al Burayqah, Ra's Lanuf, Tripoli, Zawiyah *Roads:* 83,200 km (51,698 mi.), 57% paved *National airline:* Libyan Arab Airlines *Airports:* International facilities at Tripoli and Benghazi. There are more than 100 smaller airports throughout the country. Libya has 2 heliports.
Media:	*Al Jamahiria* is the national newspaper, published in Arabic. The Libyan Jamahariya Broadcasting Corporation provides radio and television service. 19 radio stations, 12 television stations.
Literacy and education:	*Total literacy rate:* 82.6% (2006). Education is free and compulsory for 9 years. Postsecondary education is provided by 12 universities, including Al Fateh University in Tripoli and Garyounis University in Benghazi, and more than 80 technical and vocational institutes.

2. Although Qadhdhafi sought to promote socio-economic equality, language differences remained. Arabic is the Libyan national language, and the Berber languages are considered dialects. Qadhdhafi considers Libya a part of the Arab nation, so the Berber languages, like the spoken Hausa of the southern Fezzan, continue to be spoken but have never been officially recognized.

3. Qadhdhafi's Libyan national idea was followed by a decrease of the tribal influence. Qadhdhafi rejects tribes as political units, since he considers them, like political parties and classes, as inimical to the sense of Libyan nation. Tribal structures nevertheless still plays a major role in Libya. Nonetheless, in the 1990s Libya experienced a "phase of retribalization" that manifested in a formal recognition of leading tribal personalities and their institutionalization in the form of the People's Social Leadership Committees, consisting of tribal chiefs and heads of families. These committees function as local authorities and mediate local disputes as long as they do not conflict with national regulations.

4. Qadhdhafi has declared that the "family" is the basis of Libyan society. This statement is embodied in the "Green Book," Qadhdhafi's manifestation of his political, economic, and social ideas. The family offers social protection to the individual, embodies and roots it in the supraordinate national system, and indoctrinates the Muslim and tribal conceptions of society, the moral basis of the nation.

INDICATIONS OF LOCAL CONCEPTIONS
In spite of Qadhdhafi's efforts to create a national society of equals, major differences remain important. Despite the sedentarization of nomads, a commitment to universal education, and increasing urbanization, social and tribal stratification persists. Urbanization has increasingly ended the spatial separation of social classes, so that families with free or noble origin and descendants of former slaves now can live door at door and nomads find themselves in close proximity with townspeople. Children from different social strata are put together in schools, and Arabs from the north find themselves pulled to the south since the state promoted intra-Libyan migration for employment reasons. Tuareg and Berber now work side by side

with Arabs, women enter the job market, craftsmen participate in local administration, and descendants of former slaves can attain leading positions. The spatial as well as the social aspects of the prior system of social stratification is rapidly breaking down. This process is not without problems and is the reason for increasing tribal tensions and disputes, especially as traditional ideas of hierarchy continue to play a major role in marriages.

See also **Ethnicity; Family: Organization; Languages: Arabic; Qadhdhafi, Muammar.**

BIBLIOGRAPHY

Anderson, Lisa. "Tribe and State: Libyan Anomalies." In *Tribes and State Formation in the Middle East*, ed. Philip Khoury and Joseph Kostiner. Berkeley: University of California Press, 1990.

Anderson, Lisa. "A Last Resort, an Expedient and an Experiment: Statehood and Sovereignty in Libya." *The Journal of Libyan Studies* 2, no. 2 (Winter 2001): 14–25.

Davis, John. *Libyan Politics: Tribe and Revolution*. London: Tauris, 2001.

Kohl, Ines. "Nationale Identität, tribale Zugehörigkeit und lokale Konzeptionen im Fezzan, Libyen. Eine Farbenlehre." In *Veränderung und Stabilität: Normen und Werte in islamischen Gesellschaften*, ed. Johann Heiss. Wien: Akademie der Wissenschaften, 2005.

Kohl, Ines. Tuareg in Libyen. *Identitäten zwischen Grenzen*. Berlin: Reimer, 2006.

INES KOHL

HISTORY AND POLITICS

The Libyan Arab Popular and Socialist Jamahiriyya, the official name of the state of Libya, is a self-declared revolutionary state governed by an organization of popular committees and congresses with a rich oil-based economy. This regime is the creation of what most Libyans call the First of September revolution. It originated on September 1, 1969, with a group of young pan-Arab officers in the Libyan Royal Army, led by a twenty-seven-year-old charismatic officer named Mu'ammar Abu-Minyar al-Qadhdhafi. Inspired by the earlier example of Egypt's Gamal Abdel Nasser, Qadhdhafi overthrew the monarchy of King Muhammad Idris al-Sanusi in a bloodless coup d'état. The twelve junior officers were the central committee of a secret organization within the Libyan army called the Libyan Free Unionist Officers Movement. Renaming itself the

Revolutionary Command Council (R.C.C.), the committee of twelve officers declared the creation of the Libyan Arab Republic.

The R.C.C. assumed all executive, legislative, and judicial powers and began to refer to its political and social policies as a revolution. Although advocating Arab nationalism, Islam, anticolonialism, anticommunism, and anticorruption, the R.C.C did not have a clearly delineated program, although Libyan society experienced major social, political, and economic transformations after 1969. The new government initially enacted social, economic, and political policies from above without significant popular participation from below. After consolidating power in 1975, Qadhdhafi began to experiment with creating a precapitalist socialist society using the luxury of oil revenues and employing many non-Libyan workers.

MODERN HISTORY AND CULTURE

Libya between 1650 and 1911, known as Tarabulus al-Gharb, was a poor and peripheral province of the Ottoman Empire. In 1911 Italy invaded the country, waging one of the most brutal colonial wars in modern Africa, but could not control the interior until 1932. Libyan anticolonial resistance was based in regional and kinship organizations and on the Islamic ideology of the Sanusi brotherhood. The Sanusi resistance in Barqa, led by ʿUmar al-Mukhtar, fought the Fascist armies of Italy until 1931 when al-Mukhtar was captured and executed. The following year the colonial government managed to conquer the entire country. Members of the R.C.C., and particularly Qadhdhafi, saw themselves as heirs to the anticolonial resistance of ʿUmar al-Mukhtar.

PROCESS AND POLITICS UNDER THE MONARCHY, 1952–1969

After Italy's defeat in World War II, the British assumed responsibility for administering Libya. The country's independence in 1951 was brought about by Britain in alliance with the exiled Sanusi and some Tripolitanian leaders in Egypt. Britain wanted to use Libya as a key asset to protect Britain's security in the Middle East and to hold back the waves of Arab nationalism by supporting the Sanusiyya in eastern Libya over the Tripolitania urban nationalist movement. The exiled leader of the Sanusiyya, Muhammad Idris al-Sanusi (1889–1983), grandson of the founder of Sanusiyya order,

agreed to support British interests in return for political independence. On December 24, 1951, Idris was crowned King Idris I of the United Libyan Kingdom, a constitutional federal monarchy with two capitals and three provincial governments in the country's main regions of Tripolitania, Barqa, and Fezzan. Upper-class urban families and tribal leaders, mainly from Barqa, the home base for King Idris, and the Sanusiyya dominated the government. The new state was extremely poor, with per capita income of US$35. It rented military base rights to Britain and the United States, and also received economic aid as payment. Young Libyan activists and Qadhdhafi in the late 1960s criticized the monarchy and the old elite for betraying Libya's long anticolonial national struggle for independence by giving military bases to Western countries.

After the discovery and the exportation of oil in 1961, the monarchy initiated modernization programs in education, health, transportation, and housing. A new Libyan university with two campuses in Benghazi and Tripoli provided expanded educational opportunities. New educational policies led to the rise of new salaried middle class, a student movement, a small working class, trade unions, and modern intellectuals by the late 1960s. Many young Libyans became involved in Arab nationalist politics. The crisis of the monarchy was aggravated because the king was socially detached, living in Tubruq near the main British military base at al-ʿAdam. This made it appear that he preferred the company and protection of the British. Worsening the situation for the king's regime, corruption was widespread among the elite. Despite the country's oil revenues, many ordinary Libyans remained poor in rural areas. The monarchy became the victim of its own modernization programs when it did not also modernize politically to provide participation to its growing middle class. The military faction of an emerging middle class was the most organized of all the antimonarchist groups, and, in the absence of political parties, was the only force able to effectively challenge the old elite. On September 1, the Free Officers Union, led by Qadhdhafi, used the Libyan army to overthrow the monarchy.

PROCESS AND POLITICS UNDER THE REVOLUTION: 1969 ONWARD

The ideology of the central committee of the Free Officers Union, which renamed itself the Revolutionary

Command Council or R.C.C., stressed Arab nationalism, Islam, self- determination, social justice, and denounced the corruption of the old regime. The officers were also anti-Communist, which brought them support from the U.S. Nixon administration. The new regime continued the modernization polices of the monarchy. It developed the country's infrastructure on a larger scale, building new hospitals, roads, and schools. Most Libyans began to benefit from the expanded welfare state thanks to increased oil revenues. The regime benefited from increased popular support after it successfully negotiated the departure of British and U.S. forces from Libya. Asserting Libyan control over its oil resources, the revolutionary government raised prices and achieved state participation in oil production in 1973. This policy differed from that of the old regime, which had left the entire oil sector under the control of multinational corporations.

The R.C.C., similar to the monarchy, banned political parties and independent trade unions in 1970. The council adopted the Egyptian one party system in 1971. This was called the Arab Socialist Union. But this form of government was abandoned two years later because it failed to inspire and mobilize the majority of the Libyan people. Faced with opposition from the traditional elite and the failure of the Arab Socialist Union, Qadhdhafi declared his own popular revolution against the old bureaucracy in a famous speech in Zuwara in July 15, 1973. He asked the people to replace the ineffective bureaucracy with popular committees of employees in their places of work. Qadhdhafi's innovation led to a division within the R.C.C. over the role and authority of the new popular committees. The split over these issues reflected major ideological differences inside the R.C.C. over the direction of the revolution. The inability to resolve the internal conflict led to a coup attempt against Qadhdhafi by some members of the R.C.C. The coup failed, and Qadhdhafi then consolidated his power, also dissolving the R.C.C.

Qadhdhafi then began to apply the ideas, which were presented in his *Green Book*. It advocated what he called the Third Universal Theory, a third way between capitalism and Marxism based on direct democracy through popular participation in congresses and committees. This involved an effort to undermine other social and political organizations,

including independent trade unions, student organizations, and even the army itself. In March 1977, the People's General Congress met in the southern city of Sabha and, proclaiming people's power, renamed Libya The Libyan Arab Popular and Socialist Jamahiriyya. Qadhdhafi became impatient with opposition within the popular committees and the People's General Congress, and called for the formation of a new organization, the Revolutionary Committees, that would instruct and mobilize the popular committees. In reality, the new committees were made of Qadhdhafi loyalists indoctrinated to protect the security of the regime. Still, many Libyans continued to enjoy the benefits of the welfare state and supported the government during most of the 1970s.

At this stage, an estimated 100,000 of the best-educated Libyans lived outside the country. In 1988, Qadhdhafi blamed the Revolutionary Committees for being too zealous and for abusing their power. He released political prisoners and abandoned many of his experiments with collective markets and bartering. This signified the decline of Jamahiriyya populist experiment. Instead, Libya became an authoritarian national security state. Since then Libyan politics have formal and informal institutions. The formal structure of the popular committees and congresses was dominated by the informal role of Qadhdhafi, revolutionary committees, and the security apparatus.

By the early 1980s, the regime faced new challenges, and a hostile regional and international environment. It severed relations with Sadat's Egypt over that country's agreements with Israel and the United States, and it faced a series of confrontations in the Gulf of Syrte with the Reagan administration that accused Qadhdhafi of supporting terrorist groups. Worst of all the challenges was the Libyan military defeat in the war with Chad in 1981. Many soldiers were captured, along with their weapons and military bases. The regime became isolated in the Arab world and was targeted for overthrow by the U.S. government. A number of opposition groups were formed in exile, and then oil prices declined drastically in 1986, significantly reducing Libya's international export earnings. Also in 1986, the United States, blaming Libya for a Berlin, Germany bombing attack on U.S. soldiers, launched an air raid on Libya in which a number of people were killed. The United States in 1992 also blamed

Libyan agents for planting the bomb that destroyed a Pan American airliner in December 1988 over Lockerbie, Scotland, and the United Nations placed new economic sanctions on Libya in response. In January 2001, a Scottish court for the airliner bombing convicted one Libyan agent. Libya agreed to pay reparations to families of the victims and most sanctions were lifted in 2004.

Libyan foreign policies toward Africa went through three stages since the 1969 revolution. Until 1980, Libya supported liberation movements. The period from 1980 to 1994 was characterized by isolation and confrontation with the United States, a policy that led to internal struggle in Libya and the disastrous defeat in Chad, along with American and UN Sanctions in 1986 and 1992. In this period Libya's foreign policies supported repressive regimes in Uganda, Liberia, and the Central African Republic.

Libyan policies toward Africa became more realistic and positive after 1994. The regime accepted the International Court of Justice's 1994 ruling on the Aouzou Strip dispute with Chad, despite the fact Libya lost the case. It accepted responsibility for the Lockerbie bombing. Libya also led the effort to revitalize the Organization of African Unity (OAU) and to create the African Union in 2001. It mediated many African disputes and has invested millions of dollars in other African states—more than any other country with the exception of South Africa. In short, twenty-first century Libya seeks to play a constructive and positive role in African conflicts.

See also **Colonial Policies and Practices; Nasser, Gamal Abdel; Nationalism; Qadhdhafi, Muammar.**

BIBLIOGRAPHY

Ahmida, Ali Abdullatif. *The Making of Modern Libya: State Formation, Colonialization, and Resistance, 1830–1932.* Albany: State University of New York Press, 1994.

Ahmida, Ali Abdulaltif. *Forgotten Voices: Power and Agency in Colonial and Postcolonial Libya.* New York: Routledge, 2005.

Anderson, Lisa S. *The State and Social Transformation in Tunisia and Libya, 1830–1980.* Princeton, New Jersey: Princeton University Press, 1986.

Davis, John. *Libyan Politics: Tribe and Revolution.* Berkeley: University of California Press, 1987.

Obeidi, Amal. *Political Culture In Libya.* London: Routledge Curzon, 2001.

ALI ABDULLATIF AHMIDA

LILONGWE. The town of Lilongwe was founded in 1902 as a British colonial administrative post in the central highlands of its central African colony of Nyasaland, fifty miles southwest of Lake Malawi at the intersection of a major north-south and east-west trade route. Lilongwe, named for a nearby river, had a population of 130 people in 1910. The leading agricultural center of Malawi, Lilongwe was selected to be the future capital of Malawi in 1964, shortly after independence, as part of a development plan by President Hastings Kamuzu Banda. Until it was more fully developed, however, the capital stood at Zomba. The expansion of the city did not begin until the 1970s, a period in which Banda alienated his African neighbors by making claims to Tanzanian territory and establishing full diplomatic relations with the apartheid state of South Africa. Loans provided by South Africa went toward infrastructure development in Lilongwe and for a rail link to Nacala on Mozambique's Indian Ocean coast.

The town grew rapidly in the decade after independence: from 19,425 in 1966 to 102,924 in 1977. Lilongwe replaced Zomba as the capital in 1975 after the construction of Capital Hill, three miles from the old city center. Capital Hill houses government buildings and embassies, while the old city is the service and distribution center and location of the country's largest market. In the late 1970s and early 1980s the town continued to expand, with the addition of an international airport and industrial area. In 2004, with an estimated population 234,000 people, Lilongwe was the largest city in Malawi after Blantyre, the main commercial and industrial center.

See also **Banda, Ngwazi Hastings Kamuzu; Malawi: History and Politics.**

BIBLIOGRAPHY

Oliver, Roland, and Michael Crowder, eds. *The Cambridge Encyclopedia of Africa.* Cambridge, U.K.: Cambridge University Press, 1980.

THOMAS F. McDOW

LINGUISTICS, HISTORICAL.

For regions south of the Sahara, and to a lesser extent for northern Africa, older written records are relatively scarce and often do not date back more than a few centuries. Consequently, the scholar interested in the culture history of a specific area may want to consider other potentially relevant sources, such as oral traditions or language studies. In what ways could the historical and comparative study of African languages enhance an understanding of the history of the continent? There appear to be three possibilities: genetic classification, reconstruction, and contact phenomena. These methods, their strengths, and some of their potential intricacies as ancillary disciplines, are discussed herein.

THE COMPARATIVE METHOD AND OTHER CLASSIFICATION TECHNIQUES

Although scholars from the Middle East appear to have been aware of a Semitic language family as early as the tenth century, the historical-comparative study of languages developed in particular in the nineteenth century. With this method, one compares the lexicon and grammar of individual languages and tries to find out whether there are systematic sound-meaning correspondences between them, taking into account in particular basic vocabulary (because items to this latter domain are not easily borrowed). Languages are assumed to be genetically related when they descend from a common ancestor or proto-language. Since the mid-nineteenth century, the approximately two thousand languages on the African continent have also been subject to genetic classification.

According to Joseph Greenberg's overall comparison and classification, made in 1963, there are four major phyla or macro-families on the continent: Nilo-Saharan, sandwiched between Afroasiatic (mainly in the north), and Niger-Congo, the latter mainly to its south and situated in a region ranging from Senegal in the west toward Kenya in the east as well as south of this region, and, finally, the Khoesan phylum in southern Africa. Greenberg's hypotheses, based on a judicious evaluation of lexical and grammatical evidence, reflect brilliant intuitions whose validity, however, has not been demonstrated yet by means of the comparative method in all cases.

Moreover, Khoesan may be an areal grouping, in fact consisting of three different families (North, Central, and South Khoesan). Also, apart from the phyla or macro-families proposed by Greenberg there appear to be several linguistic isolates, in other words, last representatives of otherwise obsolescent language families (like Basque in Europe), namely Biraile (or Ongota) and Shabo (or Mekeyir), both in Ethiopia, Laal (in Chad), and possibly others.

Attempts have been made by different authors for subgroups within each of these proposed genetic units to statistically measure how closely the members of these subgroups are related, through a method known as lexicostatistics. With this method, one tries to assess the number of shared or similar words in languages that are assumed to be genetically related by way of a comparison of 100- or 200-word lists containing basic vocabulary (e.g. words for body parts, or "eat," "drink," because these are assumed not to be easily borrowed between languages). The method is based on the premise that the rate of retention for basic vocabulary over a certain period of time (say 1,000 years) is approximately the same cross-linguistically; this latter assumption in turn is based on the historical study of languages with a long written tradition. However, research since the 1960s has shown that languages differ widely in the rate of retention (or replacement) in their lexicon and grammatical systems, for example, as a result of contact with other languages; see Derek Nurse's 1997 work for a critical assessment, also for a discussion of of its subset, glottochronology, which aims at dating language development in absolute terms, estimating the time since genetically-related languages began to diverge out of their common ancestor.

With the comparative method on the other hand, subgrouping within genetic units is defined on the basis of so-called shared innovations; these are phonological, lexical, and grammatical changes, shared by two or more genetically related languages, which are assumed to have taken place before they split up as separate languages from a common ancestor.

THE SPREADING OF LANGUAGES AND POPULATION MOVEMENTS

Language families are usually represented by way of family trees as static models, with language groups sharing specific lexical and/or grammatical innovations being represented as separate branches. It is important not to misinterpret this arboreal representation as being isomorphic with the physical movement of peoples from one point in space (and time) away from one another. The divergence of a proto-language into daughter languages indeed reflects the divergence of a speech community into new and separate communities. Geographical separation, for example, as a result of social conflicts or migrations, usually leads to linguistic differentiation over time; population growth and subsequent moving into new territories is another factor. But language shift is another common and widespread phenomenon as part of a social adaptation process, often resulting in the spreading of certain languages (and thereby of specific language families) and obsolescence for others. Such expanding languages may be dominant languages of the region, or lingua francas, often associated traditionally with centralized states, as with Ashante (Twi), Hausa, Kanuri-Kanembu, Songai, and Yoruba in West Africa; as a result, such languages are sometimes spoken by millions of people.

Linguists in the nineteenth and early twentieth centuries commonly associated languages with self-contained ethnolinguistic groups, which were seen as relatively discrete and little changing. But a probably more realistic picture is one characterized by permanent processes of ethnic fusion and fission. One outcome of such historical dynamics is the attestation of identical clan names in communities speaking different languages; compare, for example, Günther Schlee's 1989 work showing blood relationship through shared clan names as being spread over communities in eastern Africa speaking different languages. Contrary to some other parts of the world, for example, with respect to the Austronesian family in southeast Asia, there appear to be very few cases showing interesting correlations between gene flow, the spreading of language families, and population movements in Africa. (For some preliminary observations see Cavalli-Sforza et al. 1994.) The complex language mosaic and historical dynamics of language spreading in an African context may be illustrated through the following three examples.

Although in the early twenty-first century Fulani is spoken in an area ranging from Senegal all the way toward Sudan and Ethiopia, the language must have originated in the former area, because all other members of the Atlantic family, the branch within Niger-Congo to which Fulani belongs, are spoken in Senegal and neighbouring countries. The spreading of Fulani over the past one thousand years or so probably resulted from migrations mainly of pastoral Fulani, but also from language shift; that is, the absorbing of speakers of different languages into their speech community. Moreover, ethnic Fulani themselves occasionally gave up their language, as the history of the Hausa states of northern Nigeria in the nineteenth century shows.

Climatological changes also need to be taken into account when trying to link the spreading of languages or language families to the movement of people. The skewed distribution of the Nilo-Saharan phylum may serve as a case in point. Whereas several subgroups are situated in an area ranging from the eastern Sahel towards Ethiopia and Eritrea as well as south of this zone, there are major regions in northern Sudan not covered by this phylum. Possibly, the disappearance in about 1000 BCE of the Wadi Howar (also known as the Yellow Nile), a former tributary of the Nile flowing eastwards from eastern Chad through northern Sudan and entering the Nile between the third and fourth cataracts, forced out speakers of Nilo-Saharan (and possibly other) languages.

The question of how and why the Bantu branch within Niger-Congo (the larger phylum of which it is part) spread over major areas between Cameroon in the west and Kenya in the east and south of this area has also fascinated scholars. The most probable location of their common ancestor may be inferred from the modern-day geography of Bantu languages by way of the so-called principle of least effort. According to this principle, the area with the greatest genetic distance within a family usually constitutes the original homeland. In the case of Bantu, this would be the northwestern corner (Cameroon and surrounding regions), which is also the area where the closest relatives of the Bantu languages are spoken. A probably realistic scenario of the Bantu expansion, as argued by, for example, Jan Vansina (a historian who also applied historical-linguistic methodologies) in 1990, involves a wave of advance of subsistence farmers and shifting cultivators with knowledge of iron working, combined with frequent shorter or longer distance movements, hopping across ecological barriers not suitable for agriculture, combined with local dispersals; speakers of Bantu languages probably also assimilated preceding populations, for example pygmoid groups and other communities.

It is sometimes claimed that agriculture is the primary agent in language dispersals. Though no doubt true for Bantu, it would not necessarily hold as a general trigger for the spreading of other language families, such as Nilotic. For this branch within Nilo-Saharan various lexical roots related to pastoral culture can be reconstructed, thus pointing toward ancient nomadic traditions.

THE "WORDS-AND-THINGS" METHOD

The comparative method allows scholars, by working one's way backward from forms occurring in today's languages, to reconstruct lexical and grammatical properties of the ancestral or proto-language; the relative success of course depends on the historical level and the genetic distances involved. With the so-called words-and-things technique one aims at the reconstruction of lexicon related to the material culture or the mental world of the community associated with the reconstructed proto-language. Compare the set of proto-Bantu forms as reconstructed by Malcolm Guthrie (1967–1971); from his list it may be deduced, for example, that the earliest speakers of Bantu languages were agricultural specialists who lived in villages, and who occasionally went hunting (e.g., by catching birds with limesticks).

Forms whose meaning have not or have hardly changed over time attest to long-term cultural continuities. But due to a number of reasons, vocabularies may undergo changes in the daughter languages, not only in form but also in meaning, as shown by Claire Gregoire (1976) in an interesting case study on a widespread Bantu etymon. The Proto-Bantu stem *-bánjá, meaning "land prepared for building," has reflexes with a variety of different meanings in modern Bantu languages ranging from "chief's court" or "trial" to "town" and other meanings all resulting from a sequential chain of changes in the referential meaning of this stem.

BORROWING

Lexical data as the artifacts of the past may be of interest for at least one other reason, the spreading of cultural innovations Bilingualism or multilingualism

is and presumably has been an important property of daily life in Africa. Transfer of cultural activities (e.g., of iron working and other new technologies) through contact often involves a transfer of lexicon from one speech community associated with these innovations to another community. For a case study on agricultural innovations and their linguistic reflexes, see the 1998 study by Gerda Rossel, who investigated the origin and spread of plantain cultivars as an important staple food in Africa as well as their vernacular names across the continent.

Historians may feel that more recent periods are better covered by written accounts (or oral traditions). But the study of loanwords can make potentially interesting contributions as well. As shown by Joseph Greenberg in his 1960 contribution, where he also explains the methodology involved in establishing the direction of borrowing, the study of loanwords may also shed new light on history. According to the Kano Chronicle, Islam was introduced into Hausa society from the empire of Mali. But linguistic evidence suggests that the cultural-historical significance of the Kanuri-speaking neighbors (to the east) in this respect should not be underestimated.

The spreading of Swahili is another example. Although probably more of a major lingua franca in eastern Africa than ever, Swahili also used to be spoken as far south as Moçambique until the European colonial expansion resulted in the dissolvement of a maritime network in which Swahili had served as the contact language. The former presence of Swahili speakers and their cultural heritage along the southeast African coast is attested, not only by archaeological findings, but is also reflected in the extensive lexical borrowing from Swahili into southern Bantu languages (even though the modern speakers of these languages no longer speak Swahili).

Linguists studying African languages have become increasingly interested in the different types of language change resulting from social interaction between communities speaking different languages; compare the influential 1988 study by Sarah Grey Thomason and Terrence Kaufman for a survey of the different outcomes of language contact in Africa and other parts of the world. Moreover, testing hypotheses on genetic affiliations as formulated by Greenberg (who used a method known as "mass comparison," thereby comparing lexicon and grammar from a large range of languages to ascertain distant genetic relationships, as a preliminary to the comparative method) still has high priority. For a more extensive discussion of the methods as well as the achievements of historical-comparative linguistics of potential interest to other disciplines, see Nurse (1997).

See also **Language; Languages; Linguistics and the Study of Africa.**

BIBLIOGRAPHY

Cavalli-Sforza, L. Luca; Paolo Menozzi; and Alberto Piazza. *The History and Geography of Human Genes.* Princeton, NJ: Princeton University Press, 1994.

Greenberg, Joseph H. "Linguistic Evidence for the Influence of the Kanuri on the Hausa." *Journal of African History* 1 (1960): 205–212.

Greenberg, Joseph H. "The Languages of Africa." Bloomington, Indiana University Research Center in Anthropology, Folklore, and Linguistics, Publication 25. *International Journal of American Linguistics* 29, no. 1 (1963): Part 2.

Gregoire, Claire. "Le champ sémantique du thème Bantou *-bánjá. *African Languages* 2 (1976): 1–13.

Guthrie, Malcolm. *Comparative Bantu: An Introduction to the Comparative Linguistics and Prehistory of Bantu Languages.* 4 vols. Farnborough, U.K.: Gregg Press, 1967–1971.

Nurse, Derek. "The Contributions of Linguistics to the Study of History in Africa." *Journal of African History* 38 (1997): 359–391.

Rossel, Gerda. *Taxonomic-linguistic Study of Plantain in Africa.* Leiden: School of Asian, African and Amerindian Studies, 1998.

Schlee, Günther. *Identities on the Move: Clanship and Pastoralism in Northern Kenya.* Manchester: Manchester University Press, 1989.

Thomason, Sarah Grey, and Terrence Kaufman. *Language Contact, Creolization, and Genetic Linguistics.* Berkeley: University of California Press, 1988.

Vansina, Jan. *Paths in the Rainforest: Toward a History of Political Tradition in Equatorial Africa.* London: James Currey, 1990.

GERRIT J. DIMMENDAAL

LINGUISTICS AND THE STUDY OF AFRICA.

The languages of Africa have had a significant impact on the development of modern linguistic theory, due to certain converging factors.

The main goal of linguistics is developing a theory of the nature of all human languages, and of the nearly 7,000 languages of the world more than 2,000 are spoken in Africa. Since this is nearly one-third of all human languages, one would expect the problems posed by African languages to feature prominently in linguistic theory, but the fact that the languages are not very widely studied has skewed their impact on linguistics. Very few African languages have a long history of documentation and study, compared to Western languages or major Asian languages. The median speaker population for European languages is around five times larger than that of Africa, and only a handful of African languages, including Hausa, Yoruba, Amharic, and Swahili, are reasonably well studied. Much of scholars' knowledge of African language structures is the result of research undertaken since the mid-twentieth century: what this means is that the foundation of modern linguistics was laid and reasonably well tested without the benefit of considering facts from African languages. Once scholars learned more about African languages, it became evident that research models had to be revised to take these discoveries into account.

One of the most significant areas of impact arising from African languages is in phonology, the study of sound systems. African languages employ a number of sound types that are unknown or very rare outside of Africa, and their discovery forced an expansion of the concept "possible language sound," so that these too could be explained by research models. An example of sound-exotica from Africa would be click consonants, produced by closing off the vocal tract at two locations then creating a vacuum inside the mouth by lowering the tongue. Clicks are found primarily in Bantu and Khoesan languages of southern Africa, and in a few languages of East Africa. Sample words from various southern African languages can be heard at David Odden's link through the Ohio State University Web site. Linguistic theory claims that language sounds are built from simple recurrent properties, so the puzzle is how to explain clicks given existing theories of how language sounds are composed.

Another sound-type discovered in African languages are the labial-velars, which require simultaneous closures at the lips and back of the mouth, as in the Eggon word *kpu* "to die" (examples from

Idoma can be heard at the Ohio State University Web site). Significant modifications to the theory of sound-representation were necessary in order to explain these and related issues, and one of the most influential contemporary works on sound structure, written by Elizabeth Sagey in 1986, is predominantly occupied with accounting for these African sounds. Researchers have discovered a number of other novel sounds in African languages, and later found to exist elsewhere, including pre-nasalized consonants and Advanced Tongue Root vowels.

The most significant contribution of African languages to linguistics has been in the study of tone. Tone is classically associated with Asian languages like Chinese, but the vast majority of Africa's languages use tone, so understanding tone especially demands investigation of African languages. Tone is a difficult aspect of language for Western ears, and descriptions of African languages usually omitted data on tone. As more tone-marked material from Africa became available and scholars were better able to integrate that information into theories of language sound, it became evident that African tone could not be explained within existing theories, and a new model of phonology, autosegmental phonology, was born in the attempt describe the function of tone in African languages such as Igbo, Tiv, and Mende, as described in the works of Will Leben (1980) and John A. Goldsmith (1979).

This model holds that tones are not a tightly bound feature of particular vowels, each vowel having one tone; rather, tones are seen as partially independent segments, which can be synchronized with vowels in complex ways. Thus the Shona word *hóvé* (meaning "fish"), which appears to have two high-toned vowels, actually has one high tone synchronized with both vowels; the Lomongo word *básà* (meaning "they search"), which seems to have a falling tone on the first vowel and a low tone on the second, actually has both a high tone and a low tone synchronized to the first vowel, and the low tone also synchronizes with the second vowel. Autosegmental theory elegantly explains the fundamental properties of tone in African languages (as reviewed in Odden 1995, 2005). This theory solved numerous analytical problems regarding tone, not only in African languages, but throughout the world. The basic idea of the model was so successful that it resulted in an extension of the idea to areas other than tone (the representation of clicks, for example), and this model now constitutes the standard theory of representation for language sound.

The theory of sentence structure (syntax) has also been heavily influenced by properties of African languages, especially the relationship between sentence and word structure in Bantu languages. Words in Bantu languages can have a complex structure, with a single word expressing what requires many words in other languages. For instance, the Shona verb *pavakandobikisirana* translates as "when they went and made cook for each other," and is built from the root verb *bik*, meaning "cook." Traditional theories of syntax are designed to explain how words are put together in a sentence to convey notions such as subject, object, and indirect object, how these relate to clause-types such as "when" clauses, and where the words go (does the object go before the verb or after?). Bantu languages especially challenge the notion that syntax should give primacy to arrangements of words as atomic units and should not be concerned with the internal structure of words; a rich line of research into the interaction between sentence and word structure engendering is found in the works of Mark Baker.

See also **Christianity; Language; Languages; Linguistics, Historical.**

BIBLIOGRAPHY

Baker, Mark. "The Mirror Principle and Morphosyntactic Explanation." *Linguistic Inquiry* 16 (1985): 373–415.

Baker, Mark. *The Polysynthesis Parameter.* New York: Oxford University Press, 1996.

Goldsmith, John A. *Autosegmental Phonology.* New York: Garland Publishing, 1979.

Ladefoged, Peter. Collection of Clicks in African Languages. Available at http://ling.osu.edu/~odden/lada.html.

Ladefoged, Peter. Examples of Labiovelar Consonants in Idoma. Available at http://ling.osu.edu/~odden/ladb.html.

Leben, Will. *Suprasegmental Phonology.* New York: Garland Publishing, 1980.

Odden, David. "Tone: African Languages." In *The Handbook of Phonological Theory*, ed. John Goldsmith. Oxford: Blackwells, 1995.

Odden, David. *Introducing Phonology.* Cambridge, U.K.: Cambridge University Press, 2005.

Sagey, Elizabeth. *The Representation of Features in Non-Linear Phonology: The Articulator Node Hierarchy.* New York: Garland, 1990.

DAVID ODDEN

LITERACY. Literacy in Africa has a long and diverse history prior to the introduction of European languages. Perhaps the earliest known example of literacy in indigenous African languages dates back to 3000 BCE, when hieroglyphics were invented in Egypt. Evidence exists of literacy in the Kush kingdom capital city Meroe during the last five centuries of the first millennium. In the fourth century CE in ancient Axum (present-day Ethiopia), the classical language, Geʿez, facilitated the rise of a literate class. These languages had their own specialized writing styles.

Mediterranean cultures along the northern shores of the continent brought Greek and Latin literacy into the region during the classical period. After the seventh century, Arabic literacy became an integral part of the rapid spread of Islam initially along the northern and eastern coasts of Africa, and then from the Maghreb into the Sahel region. Between the ninth and fifteenth centuries, trans-Saharan trade routes between Tripoli and Tunis in the north and the ancient sub-Saharan city of Kano spread Arab culture and Arabic literacy into sub-Saharan Africa along the Sudanic belt.

The fifteenth-century expulsion of Jews and Muslims from Andalusia resulted in their resettlement in nearby Morocco; cross-fertilization of scholarly endeavors connected literate Arabic speaking scholars in a rich network of established centers of learning from the Maghreb to the sub-Saharan region, in the cities of Fez, Timbuktu, and Jenné. In Fez, the tenth century founding of the Karaouine mosque and medresa established the city's reputation as a center of learning. At the same time Timbuktu and Jenne were on the rise, reaching their zenith as scholarly centers during the fifteenth and sixteenth centuries.

Twentieth-century scholarship underlines the complexity of scholarly networks between the sub-Saharan region and the Maghreb. In subsequent years, the inclination of devout African Muslims to make the pilgrimage to Makkah resulted in a path of settlement along the west-east route from Senegal to Sudan, spreading Arabic literacy in populated areas throughout the savanna region at the edge of the Sahara. Meanwhile, on the east coast of Africa, north-south trade routes plied by Arab merchants carried Arabic literacy and Islamic scholarship from Somalia in the north as far south along the coast as South Africa.

Literacy in European languages began tentatively to influence African cultures in the fifteenth century, as the Portuguese explored and made contact with indigenes along Africa's western coast. At the southern tip of the continent, the arrival of the Dutch at the Cape of Good Hope in 1652 signaled a new approach to literacy, as the Dutch language merged with indigenous languages, resulting in literacy in a new lingua franca called Afrikaans, which was to become the language of white supremacy during the modern, apartheid era in South Africa. During the seventeenth and eighteenth centuries the Belgians, British, French, and Germans joined the Portuguese and the Dutch in exploring and exploiting Africa; forms of literacy were a direct result of these incursions, to a small extent as merchants in direct contact with Europeans learned the newcomers' languages and became literate in them for business purposes.

It was not until the nineteenth century, the full-blown period of colonialism in Africa, that the forms of literacy most familiar to the continent came about. Each European colonial power—the Belgians, British, French, and Germans—sought to exploit the people power, as well as natural resources of their African colonies. To do this required a degree of literacy among the masses. In Nigeria the British promoted literacy in English through writing contests rewarded with the publication of stories and poems in volumes produced in newly established English-language publishing houses. They built schools and enlisted missionaries to teach English to colonized peoples. Providing for minimal literacy in populations facilitated government activities that benefited colonists, such as census-taking, taxation, and preparation of personnel for administrative duties. In the early twentieth century African men were conscripted to serve in Europe during World War I and in both the European and Pacific theaters during World War II. Minimal literacy was necessary to a systematic enlistment of African troops.

The British policy of indirect rule had a long-term effect on the conditions of literacy in Nigeria. Absence of colonial intervention in the Muslim north left indigenous Islamic rule intact (albeit with Emirs hand-picked for the accommodation of British policy), and with very few government-sponsored schools, as the British deferred to a network of traditional Islamic schools already in place. Furthermore, reflecting Victorian gender sensibilities, colonial policy initially did not include the education of Muslim girls, although eventually a few girls' schools were established. This lopsided education policy in Nigeria had tragic consequences in the postcolonial era: It left literate southerners at an advantage in qualifying for administrative positions throughout the country, especially in the Muslim north, where banks, post offices, and other public agency jobs were filled by southerners while northerners—albeit perhaps literate in Hausa and Arabic—remained unemployed. It is speculated that the ethnic unrest engendered by this disequilibrium in the north fueled the flames of the Biafra conflict. Riots and bloodletting in the city of Kano in the 1960s were a direct, long-term result of an unbalanced promotion of literacy in early-twentieth-century British colonial Nigeria.

Meanwhile, throughout West Africa promising young men who had grown up during colonial rule were selected to benefit from higher education programs in England and the United States. Rising political stars and intellectuals like Ghanaian Kwame Nkrumah returned to their countries positioned to guide them into independence on the strength of their individual academic achievement. In the absence of a literate population at home, the men who relied on their education for success found little to prevent their own slide into political and economic corruption. Attempts in countries like Nigeria and Ghana to promote government sponsored programs of universal primary education met with some success in the 1970s, but found themselves burdened by the economic cost of such programs.

In South Africa the promotion of literacy proved to be at the root of political conflict. Early Dutch incursions into the region in the seventeenth century resulted in the evolution of Afrikaans, a mixture of Dutch and local Bantu languages. During the next two centuries Afrikaans became the language of an increasingly controlling white minority. British colonial intervention in the region during the nineteenth century was reflected in the establishment of English as the language of a competing power. However, it was the establishment of apartheid in 1948, with its attention to the use of Afrikaans in the schools, which became the catalyst for resistance in the latter part of the twentieth century. The tragic 1976 Soweto uprising was a direct rejection of white South African government policy that half of all school subjects be taught in Afrikaans, the language of the white minority. Clearly, literacy for the masses was not the aim of this political decision. In this case, literacy was the privilege of the white minority, whose policies aimed to keep literacy skills away from the average South African.

In the late twentieth century international development agencies like the World Bank and U.S. Agency for International Development sought to redress gender and ethnic disadvantage in a multiplicity of African countries by facilitating education for women. Studies indicated that birth rates were in converse relation to the level of a mother's education, and lower birth rates corresponded directly to a higher quality of life for the family. Thus investing in education was seen to be the most cost-effective approach to improving a country's standard of living. But many well-funded African education projects in the late twentieth century were inadequate in both structure and curriculum, as the Western models on which they were based failed to meet the needs of a local population. As a result, at the start of the twenty-first century there exist reports on the dire state of literacy in Western languages for nearly every African country. Furthermore, it is problematic to assess the effects of indigenous education systems, as few studies exist that address these programs.

This raises the issue of orality in relation to education. Historically, education has been transmitted in indigenous languages, both orally and in written form. To ignore these means of transmitting knowledge is to fail to recognize African literacy in its own context. The assumption that most African populations were illiterate prior to the introduction of a written European language is misleading. Literacy among ancient civilizations, like those in ancient Egypt, Kush, and Ethiopia, was enjoyed by those in an elite class. Literacy spread more widely among the masses when it was transmitted in Arabic, in the context of Islam, but even in these cases, orality was key to the transmission of Islam, and much of the education process in this context did not necessarily include literacy. While the elite may enjoy literacy, this fact does not preclude the education of the masses by oral transmission of information. Numerous examples exist of general education conveyed through oral poetry and narrative. Nigerian Nana Asma'u's training of itinerant teachers of rural women in the Sokoto Caliphate during the nineteenth century is a case in point. Traditional education programs can be complex and extend to exalted levels of understanding without including literacy. In fact, among certain contemporary Sufi groups education based on memorization and oral transmission is preferred as a higher form of education than that which relies on the written word. The latter can be destroyed, it is argued, while what is internalized cannot be eliminated.

Nevertheless, literacy in European languages is central to African nations' economic and political welfare. Almost half a century after independence, the legacy of inadequate colonial intervention continues to plague African countries where literacy levels in European languages still fall below what is necessary for successful economic competition in international markets. As these examples demonstrate, inequitable access to literacy is directly linked to failing economic and political welfare. Withholding access to literacy is a means of concentrating power in the hands of educated elites, and facilitating their abuse of illiterate masses. Conversely, an illiterate populace is insufficiently skilled to benefit its society.

See also **Asma'u, Nana; Education, School; Fez; Jenné and Jenné-jeno; Libraries; Timbuktu; World Bank.**

BIBLIOGRAPHY

Agnaou, Fatima. *Gender, Literacy, and Empowerment in Morocco.* New York: Routledge, 2004.

Boyle, Helen N. *Qur'anic Schools: Agents of Preservation and Change.* New York: Routledge, 2004.

Brown, Geoffrey, and Mervyn Hiskett. *Conflict and Harmony in Education in Tropical Africa.* London: George Allen and Unwin, 1975.

Fafunwa, A. Babs. *History of Education in Nigeria.* London: Allan Unwin, 1974.

Hanna, Nelly. *In Praise of Books: A Cultural History of Cairo's Middle Class, Sixteenth to the Eighteenth Century.* Syracuse, NY: Syracuse University Press, 2003.

Lulat, Y.G.-M. *A History of African Higher Education from Antiquity to the Present: A Critical Synthesis.* Westport, CT: Praeger, 2005.

Motala, Enver, and John Pampallis, eds. *The State, Education and Equity in Post-Apartheid South Africa: The Impact of State Policies.* Burlington, VT: Ashgate, 2002.

Reese, Scott Steven, ed. *The Transmission of Learning in Islamic Africa.* Leiden: Brill, 2004.

Sehoole, Molatlhegi Trevor Chika. *Democratizing Higher Education Policy: Constraints of Reform in Post-Apartheid South Africa.* New York: Routledge, 2005.

Sunal, Cynthia Szymanski, ed. *Schooling in Sub-Saharan Africa: Contemporary Issues and Future Concerns.* New York: Garland, 1998.

Uruch, George E. F. *Education in Sub-Saharan Africa.* New York: Garland, 1992.

BEVERLY B. MACK

LITERATURE

This entry includes the following articles:
OVERVIEW
EPICS AND EPIC POETRY
ISLAMIC
MODERN POETRY
ORAL
POPULAR LITERATURE
PROVERBS AND RIDDLES
TRANSLATION
WOMEN WRITERS, NORTHERN AFRICA
WOMEN WRITERS, SUB-SAHARAN AFRICA

OVERVIEW

It would be tempting to present an overview on African literature in the last ten centuries by providing a simple chronological account. This kind of account would show how African literature has developed in distinctive periods and phases, all connected to key political and cultural moments in the history of the continent. It would provide a trajectory of African literature moving from its foundational moments in oral forms—closely associated with preliterate societies and cultures—and eventually evolving, over a span of time, into written modes of expression. Such a trajectory could be conceived both as a reaction to local events, such as internal migrations, and to the encounter with foreign cultural and political states and institutions, beginning with Asian Christianity in the first few centuries and Islam in the eighth century to modern European colonialism. If oral literature is the form through which Africans have asserted their identity and autonomy since time immemorial, as many scholars have argued, Orthodox Christianity and Islam constitute the dominant centers of African writing until the end of the fifteenth century. Some of the earliest institutions for the production of written literature in Africa were associated with these religions. Literature in Ge'ez, for example, was closely linked with the consolidation of Orthodox Christianity in Ethiopia; the depository of African literature at Timbuktu was part of Islamic culture in West Africa.

From a literary historian's perspective, however, the defining moment of a modern African literary culture is the colonial encounter that, beginning in earnest in the nineteenth century and ending after World War II, radically transformed African cultural institutions. It is within the culture of colonialism, represented by both governmental institutions and Christian missions, that writing came to surpass, if not substitute, orality as the primary factor in the imaginary institutions of society. Nevertheless, the easily recognizable and globally celebrated forms of African writing, associated with the works of Nobel Prize winners such as Wole Soyinka (b. 1934), Nadine Gordimer (b. 1923), Naguib Mahfouz (b. 1911), and J. M. Coetzee (b. 1940), emerged only after decolonization. It is a notable fact that the canon of modern African literature appeared in the period after World War II when African cultures sought to both assert their autonomy from the institutions of colonialism and to engage with global cultural movements. Whether viewed from its beginnings in orality or in its more recent manifestation in European languages, African literature has always been engaged with its particular localities and the world at large.

LITERATURE AND THE IDEA OF AFRICA

A simple chronological account of the emergence and development of African literature often fails to account for the continent's complex history and human geography. The development of literary culture on the continent is caught up in the multiplicity of African temporalities. What may appear in one part of the continent to be located in a distant Islamic medieval period may, in another place, be part of contemporary social experience. Neither African cultural history nor its literature can fit into a simple chronological frame. In fact, because of the complex nature of the African timeline, writing an overview of African literatures presents challenges and complexities that are rarely found in other geographic regions of the world. Time, or chronology, is compounded by an assortment of other cultural factors.

There is, in addition, the obvious challenge presented by the idea of Africa itself: The ostensible uniformity of the continent's cultural spaces reflects an external view of Africa; it was outsiders, beginning with ancient Greeks to modern European colonizers, who tended to see the continent's blackness as a sign of uniformity and thus to miss the complex diversity of its human geography. The challenge, then, is how to provide an overview of a cultural landscape where similarities between traditions and practices conceal powerful differences even within one region. Given this complexity, a linear history of African literature is inadequate: periods and periodizing depends on region and genres. Furthermore, however definitive they may initially appear, key moments in the history of Africa, even those that are taken up as key themes in the continent's literature, need to be examined in relation to the institutions that enable cultural expression itself and the set of theoretical problems that have preoccupied African writers and critics, from debates about the idea of literature itself, to continuing conflict over the language of African literature and its audiences.

ON LITERARY HISTORY

For literary scholars, the situation is confounded by the existence of thousands of languages on the continent, almost all laying claim to one form of literature or other, either oral or written. And yet this linguistic diversity is not reflected in dominant histories of African literature, which are often organized around the literatures of major linguistic groups, or those with a long tradition of writing. The situation is further complicated by the existence of regional languages, such as Arabic, Hausa, and Swahili, whose long and remarkable histories have either enabled or retarded the growth of literatures in other languages in contiguous areas. Moreover, African writing has often been produced in the languages of its European colonizers, and there is a sense in which the terms that have now come to define African literature—Anglophone and Francophone, for example—reflect the political dominance of Britain and France in colonial Africa. African literature has been produced in other colonial languages, including Portuguese, Spanish, and Italian, but the power of English and French in creating a canon of letters in Africa is evident in the ways in which even writers working in traditions with long histories of writing, such as Amharic writers in Ethiopia or Wolof writers in Senegal, have turned to English and French.

Generalizations present an obstacle to understanding African literature and its role in the making of African cultures; still, no literary historian of the continent can escape them. One such generalization is that the modern idea of Africa, one that literature has helped cultivate and popularize, is bound up with the process of colonization and resistance against it. Indeed, it may be said that it is colonialism that has created the central paradigms and institutions that enable us to compare literary and cultural traditions across ethnic and linguistic boundaries and regions. Produced within the institutional and political practices of European colonizers, African literature has developed in two ostensibly opposed directions: one connecting writers to the canons of their respective European traditions and reflecting an intertextual engagement with it; the other trying to find a detour around colonialism and its cultural institutions and establish a link with oral traditions. In both cases, however, African literature both affirms and questions the dominant idea of what literature is, what work it does, and its modes of interpretation.

ORALITY AND WRITING

Sometimes even the categories that African scholars have invented to account for the existence of a literature outside the written—terms such as *orality*, *orature*, or the *imagination of the preliterate*—present their own set of problems. Consider, for example, what Dan Izevbaye (2004) has called the preliterate period in African literature. The term *preliterate* is used to refer to forms of cultural expression that do not depend on writing for their

existence; it also signals a moment in time when oral literatures seemed to occupy the center of African cultural life. The problem with the category of preliterate is that it cannot be fixed in time and space, nor can a moment of preliteracy be identified in which a written literature is also not a marked feature of African literary production. The ubiquity of oral literature in Africa suggests that the category of a literary culture before writing cannot be confined to any specific period. As a space of cultural expression, orality is as old as African communities; it has been described aptly as a vector for the production of social life, enabling the organization of social categories such as time, work, and play.

Similarly, orality marks the diversity of African cultures themselves. This diversity is evident in the preponderance or dominance of certain genres of oral literature in specific regions and traditions. Praise poetry, for example, is a marked feature of Southern African oral cultures, whereas oral epics are dominant in West and Central Africa; in both cases, there is a structural connection between the work of genre and the foundational politics of kingdoms and moieties. But orality is not always related to state power or foundational historical moments. There are forms of poetic and dramatic expression, such as the dervish poetry of Somalia, the Gikuyu Gicaandi, the Yoruba Ijala, or Ijaw festival theater, that have functioned as the conduit through which African cultures in the colonial period have sought to secure their independence and autonomy in reaction to the cultural projects of colonialism.

In all these situations, the dominance of orality does not signify the unmodern or what has come to be known as tradition; indeed, a marked feature of oral literature in Africa is its keen sense of the challenges and possibilities provided by modernization and technological transformations. New technologies, such as radio and television, have provided a powerful medium for oral poets. It has been through radio that oral forms have expanded their reach in terms of audience and region. Through radio, for example, Taarabu music, once confined to the East African Swahili coast, has traveled inland. The emergence of video and television may appear to have destroyed the classic Yoruba traveling theater, or even Ghanaian party concert drama, but it is through video that those traditions have been transported to continental and global audiences. Nigerian and Ghanaian soap operas, popular all over sub-Saharan Africa, have drawn their poetics, as it were, from older forms of popular drama.

THE GENESIS OF WRITING

It is when one turns to writing that African relations with the outside world become most apparent. Except in North Africa and isolated areas of the Horn of Africa, written literature in Africa is closely associated with European colonialism. But the consolidation of a culture of letters on the continent points to the significance of cultural encounters in the making of the African imagination before colonialism. Two points are worth underscoring here: the first is that Egyptian, Nubian, and Ethiopic writing represents a notable scriptural moment in African literature, one in which the work of writing is intimately connected to the metaphysics of culture. The second point is that writing registers the important transformations that take place on the African landscape from the tenth century to the advent of European colonialism in the eighteenth and nineteenth centuries. African language literatures represent a powerful example of the relation between language and power. Ge'ez, the language of Old Ethiopia, was nurtured by its association with the royal court; its demise was assured when it was replaced by Amharic as the language of power in the fourteenth century. Arabic literature, originating on the continent from the tenth century, is another example of the relationship between power and writing. Arabic was the language of Islam and thus tended to favor genres such as poetry that reinforced, rather than challenged, its central doctrines.

More important, it was religious expansionism that enabled the language and its literature to spread from North Africa to West and eastern Africa. By the thirteenth century, Arabic scholarship had been established in northern Nigeria and the Yoruba heartland and across the Sahel. A surge of writing in Arabic is evident in the wake of the Hausa revival of the late nineteenth century, which produced writers and scholars such as 'Uthman dan Fodio and Mohammed Bello. Although Arabic writing was often seen as an extension of religious belief and piety, one of the most remarkable aspects

of the spread of Arabic into West and East Africa was its capacity to generate forms of literature that were not tied to Islamization. African writers such as Gonja Muslims in northern Ghana and the Wolof of Senegal had come to writing through Islam; but at the same time they were able to create new forms of literature on the margins of Arabic. The two most prominent examples of this kind of literature were the Ajami tradition in West Africa and Swahili on the East African coast, both influenced by Islam and Arabic, but not colonized by either.

WRITING AND THE CHRISTIAN MISSION

Another linguistic factor to consider is that the transformation of the idea and category of literature in Africa was part of the revolution generated by the consolidation of colonial rule on the continent in the nineteenth century. The effect of colonialism is most obvious in its well-known impact on the structure of African societies and its effect on psychologies. Colonialism challenged or disrupted all the major categories of social life on the continent, from religion and metaphysics to the institutions of socialization such as education, work, and marriage. The encounter between Europeans and Africans has been a major theme of African literature, but it is at the institutional level that the transformation of the idea and practice of literature engendered by colonial culture was most palpable and irreversible. After colonialism was established, the meaning of literature and its role in society changed. Where oral literature had been the foundation of the imagination, colonialism privileged print and the book.

The most important agents of the emergence of print as the center of literary culture were colonial missionaries, who were the first to set up printing presses on the continent. Missionaries also founded the schools that trained two or three generations of African writers and readers. It was at the mission and school that written literature in the modern period emerged. Yoruba literature has its roots in the Church Missionary Society at Abeokuta, where, beginning in the late 1840s, repatriated slaves led by Bishop Samuel Ajayi Crowther embarked on the production of Yoruba texts and the translation of the Bible. In southern Africa, the elite that was to produce Xhosa literature was congregated around the Scottish Mission at Lovedale; Sotho written literature, exemplified by the works of Thomas Mofolo (1876–1948), was first produced at the French mission at Morija. The pattern was repeated in East Africa, where the Church of Scotland enabled the first writers and readers in Gikuyu, and the Anglican Church created the institutions for the production of Buganda literature.

Missionaries were actively involved in the reduction of African languages into writing, producing orthographies, dictionaries, and primers. They were also heavily invested in the work of translation. They translated the Bible into hundreds of African languages. They also translated John Bunyan's *Pilgrim's Progress* (1675), a book that they valued for its morality, but one that was to become, for colonial subjects, an invaluable model of how a Christian ethos could be enhanced by the process of storytelling. It is hard to think of a pioneering African writer in the African languages who did not pass through a Christian mission: Mofolo at Morija and writers produced at Lovedale, including pioneers such as Tiyo Soga (1829–1871), William Wellington Gqoba (1840–1888) and, later, A. C. Jordan (1906–1968). In West Africa, Daniel Fagunwa (1903–1963), the prominent Yoruba novelist, was a product of the Anglican Church in western Nigeria.

LITERATURE AND THE COLONIAL BUREAUS

Surprisingly, colonial governments did not seem to have any interest in the growth of African literature; or when they did, their primary goal was to harness African creativity to the mandate of colonial rule. In the late 1800s and early 1900s, German colonial officials collected both oral and written literature in what was German East Africa, including Swahili poetry that documented the German conquest. French colonial administrators were keen to encourage the collection and dissemination of African oral literatures as early as the 1920s, and an African theater thrived at the Ecole Normale William Ponty in Senegal in the 1930s. These were often works that were intended to fulfill, rather than challenge, the colonial mandate. After World War II, the British colonial government founded or funded literary bureaus in East Africa and southern Rhodesia, and although these were primarily intended to produce materials for supporting adult literary classes, they were to become important conduits for writers in African languages in the 1950s. For example, Solomon

Mutswairo's Shona novel, *Feso*, was first published by the Rhodesian Literature Bureau in 1957.

One notable aspect of African literature is that writing in European languages was not produced in the institutions sponsored by either missionaries or the colonial governments. Indeed, pioneering works of African literature in the European languages were produced outside or in opposition to those institutions. Rene Maran's *Bataoula* (1921) and Sol Plaatje's *Mhudi* (1930) are examples of the literature that emerged when the colonial elite turned to writing to resist the colonialist ideology. Instead of being driven by the ecumenical spirit, African literature after 1945 was closely aligned with the secular project of decolonization. Significantly, this elite turned to European languages as the most potent medium of anticolonial resistance. In French West Africa, for example, beginning as early as the 1930s, resistance to French colonial policies were expressed by writers, such as the Négritude poets, who were masters of the French language and its forms. Leading African poets in French, most notably Léopold Sédar Senghor, produced their works in Paris.

Ultimately, it was when the colonial ideology had been weakened and colonialism was no longer seen as the horizon of expectation that a secular African literature emerged out of the shadows of the colonial library. The classic novels of African literature in the European languages were produced in the aftermath of what was called a dying colonialism. Examples of such works are Chinua Achebe's *Things Fall Apart* (1958), Camara Laye's *The Dark Child* (1954), Yacine Kateb's *Nedjama* (1956), and Assia Djebar's *La soif* (1957). With decolonization, the form and terms of African literature seemed to have changed. At the universities established in the last decades of colonialism—institutions such as Ibadan in Nigeria and Makerere in Uganda—a new generation schooled in modern literature self-consciously sought to inscribe an African world and project outside the ideologies of colonial rule. Those institutions, and their counterparts in North Africa, produced the majority of the continent's pioneering modern writers.

POSTCOLONIAL CULTURE

There were significant regional and linguistic variations in the literature that developed in the age of decolonization, but the African writers who emerged in the late 1950s and 1960s tied the form and function of their works to the project of decolonization. The work of literature was associated with two projects, both articulated clearly and powerfully by Chinua Achebe in "The Role of the Writer in a New Nation" (1973). The first one was to counter the colonial slander that Africa was, in cultural terms, a blank slate at best and a barbaric space at worst; the second was to educate the African out of the colonial complex. In this context, the theme of cultural rehabilitation became perhaps the dominant theme of African literature in the first decade of independence; but African writers were also engaged with topical themes such as the migration to the city, the status of women, and the challenges of decolonization, including the crisis of politics and the collapse of institutions.

Indeed, a significant and discernible transformation in the tenor and form of African writing in the postcolonial period is connected to the changing fortunes of the narrative of decolonization itself, with the celebratory and redemptive narratives that acted as the handmaidens of independence giving way to a literature of disillusionment in the late 1960s and 1970s. It was within this context, too, that leading women writers such as Flora Nwapa and Buchi Emecheta (Nigeria), Aminata Sow (b. 1941) and Mariama Bâ (1929–1981, Senegal), Grace Ogot (Kenya), Assia Djebar (Algeria), Nawal el-Saadawi (Egypt), and Yvonne Vera (d. 2005) and Tsitsi Dangarembga (b. 1959, Zimbabwe) established their international reputations. Finally, an obvious consequence of the failure of democracy and the collapse of institutions in the 1980s and afterward was the dispersal of African writers to Europe and North America. Increasingly, African writers are to be found in the former centers of colonial power, such as Britain and France, and in North America as part of a new diaspora of African people and letters.

See also **Achebe, Chinua; Bâ, Mariama; Bello, Muhammad; Camara Laye; Coetzee, J. M.; Colonial Policies and Practices; Crowther, Samuel Ajayi; Djebar, Assia; Emecheta, Buchi; Gordimer, Nadine; Kateb, Yacine; Language; Languages; Literature and the Study of Africa; Mahfouz, Naguib; Media: Book Publishing; Nubia; Nwapa, Flora; Ogot, Grace; Plaatje, Sol; Saadawi, Nawal el-; Senghor, Léopold Sédar; Soyinka, Wole; Timbuktu; 'Uthman dan Fodio; Writing Systems.**

BIBLIOGRAPHY

Achebe, Chinua. "The Role of the Writer in a New Nation." In *African Writers on African Writing*, ed. Gordon Douglas Killam. London: Heinemann, 1973.

Andrzejewski, Bogumil W.; Stanislaw Piłaszewicz; and Witold Tyloch; eds. *Literatures in African Languages: Theoretical Issues and Sample Surveys*. Cambridge, U.K.: Cambridge University Press, 1985.

Ge'rard, Albert S. *African Language Literatures: An Introduction to the Literary History of Sub-Saharan Africa*. Washington, DC: Three Continents, 1981.

Gikandi, Simon, ed. *Encyclopedia of African Literature*. London: Routledge, 2003.

Gunner, Liz. "Africa and Orality." In *The Cambridge History of African and Caribbean Literature*, vol. 1, ed. F. Abiola Irele and Simon Gikandi. Cambridge, U.K.: Cambridge University Press, 2004.

Irele, F. Abiola, and Simon Gikandi, eds. *The Cambridge History of African and Caribbean Literature*, 2 vols. Cambridge, U.K.: Cambridge University Press, 2004.

Izevbaye, Dan. "West African Literature in English: Beginnings to the Mid-Seventies." In *The Cambridge History of African and Caribbean Literature*, vol. 2, ed. F. Abiola Irele and Simon Gikandi. Cambridge, U.K.: Cambridge University Press, 2004.

Mortimer, Mildred. "African Literature in French: Sub-Saharan Africa During the Colonial Period." In *The Cambridge History of African and Caribbean Literature*, vol. 2, ed. F. Abiola Irele and Simon Gikandi. Cambridge, U.K.: Cambridge University Press, 2004.

SIMON GIKANDI

EPICS AND EPIC POETRY

Since the 1960s, following a long period of controversy, there has been a near consensus regarding the existence of the epic in Africa, even though scholarship on epics and epic poetry continues to suffer from what has been called the imperialism of writing. Concepts stemming from European literate culture are used in discussing African epics and epic poetry. The challenge is to overhaul the standard concepts and terminology so as to dwell and operate entirely within the realm of oral tradition, studying African verbal arts using African categories, nomenclature, and aesthetic principles.

The epic is a genre revolving around the distant past, with securely established characteristics, unlike the novel, which is a developing genre. This emphasis on the past appears in Karl Marx's observations on the Greek epic. He wondered why those epics exert an eternal charm on us, even though they arose from an epoch representing the childhood of the human race. Epics are closely bound to religious beliefs as well as to national or ethnic identity, consciousness and destiny. These criteria, Eurocentric as they may sound, apply to the African primary epics, such as those of Abu Zayd, Sundiata, Kambili, Gassire's Lute, Liongo Fumo, and Ibonia. Equally applicable are Mikhail Bakhtin's observations about the special nature, and even the sacred aura, of epic discourse and values.

As G. W. F. Hegel noted, behind the epic lies an epic spirit or an epic consciousness, which gives rise to and is expressed by the discourse that we define as epic. Not all societies, however, have the epic spirit or consciousness to the same degree. This spirit can materialize in many ways and forms, such as poetry, narrative, ritual observances, and dance. In some societies, certain songs, folktales, or other forms embody the epic in a rudimentary or germinal form. In other societies, the epic appears as fully elaborated. Some epics exist in the form of poetry and deserve to be called epic poetry, but poetry is not an ultimate or defining characteristic of the epic.

Epics deal with heroes and heroism; they present heroes and project and investigate the concept of heroism. The bestowing and acquisition of names are central to this process. Heroes are such not only because of their deeds, qualities, or character, but also because of the names and praises they acquire as based on those deeds, qualities, or character. Heroes desire to have their names established for posterity. This quest is the foundation of praise poetry, heroic poetry, epic poetry, and epics as such. The name is the kernel or the primary building block of the epic; epics are centered on creating a name for the hero. The praise poetry and heroic poetry of Southern Africa such as the *dithoko* of the Sotho or the *izibongo* of the Zulu exemplify these characteristics and dynamics. The Mande epics of West Africa, it appears, developed from a base of the heroic songs of the hunters. Epic poetry is often embedded in the larger totality of the epic and is the core around which the epic is built. Although the name is a central preoccupation of the epic, this is not always a positive name. Negative characteristics of the hero are also acknowledged and incorporated

into the composition and epic is centered on creating a name for the hero's performance.

The process of diffusion is central in the existence of epic, as is the process of recomposition. A typical African epic is dispersed across a wide territory, appearing in some areas as a substantial narrative and in other areas as perhaps a folktale, a song, or an anecdote. Such is the case with epics such as Ibonia, Mwindo, and Sundiata. The transformations can go to the extent that the characters celebrated as heroes in some versions of the story can appear as villains in other versions.

The Banu Hilal tradition spread from the Arabian Peninsula to North Africa. The Arabian Peninsula is also the original home of some epics found on the East African coast. The diffusion of the African epics across wide territory and the proliferation of modes of their dissemination, from word of mouth to cassette and video, raise key questions, such as what meanings and functions the epics acquire in their new and ever-changing contexts.

The research tradition shapes the understanding of African epics. Scholars' knowledge of the African epic traditions reflects the interests and biases of scholars. Scholars have assumed, for example, that the Sundiata tradition is a Mande phenomenon. That assumption has shaped their research and theorizing and established conventional thinking about the Sundiata tradition. If they had started their research in areas where characters other than Sundiata are celebrated, the view of the Sundiata tradition would have been different. Similarly, the scholars have established the Liongo epic as a tradition centered on the Swahili. Yet the epic exists among other people as well, such as the Pokomo. If the scholars had started and persisted in studying the Pokomo tradition, then the Liongo epic might be viewed as a Pokomo tradition.

It must be asked how the Sundiata story is told in areas outside the Mande and how it functions in those areas. What is the place of the story of Ibonia in areas outside Merina? Is it appropriate to assume that the Sundiata epic evolved and consolidated itself among the Mande before anywhere else? Could it have started elsewhere, only to be appropriated by the Mande?

Whether epic traditions are considered centered in a particular area, it may not always have been that way; the center of the tradition maybe have shifted from one place to another. The Bani Hilal tradition is now firmly entrenched in North Africa and the Maghreb, but it spread to those areas from the Arabian Peninsula. Research needs to focus on such processes in order to illuminate the nature of them and their implications for the tradition itself. It is currently not known how much an epic retains, gains, or loses in the process of such diffusion.

Scholars and researchers of African epics have often come across what they call epic fragments and have striven to look for and record what they call the complete epic. Guided by these notions, some researchers have made epic performers strain themselves and produce lengthy performances to incorporate a totality that does not accord with the way the epic is normally performed. This is to satisfy scholars' literate bias about the nature of epic, a bias that has been entrenched largely because of the existence of texts such as the *Iliad* and the *Odyssey*. These are false notions, a product and evidence of the imperialism of writing. What appear as fragments in an oral tradition might be meaningful and complete in themselves within the context of a performance.

This fixation on texts continues to hamper scholars' understanding of such natural features of oral epics as narrative inconsistencies and linguistic obscurities. Scholars talk, for example, about lines in a given epic. There are no lines in an oral performance. Scholars talk about an epic or an epic poem being long or short. These are problematical notions, based on written texts, but certainly at variance with the reality and dynamics of oral performance. The discourse on epic tends to rely on the written text as the yardstick and reference point. In discussions and in scholarship, the epic ought to be seen in its natural mode as performance. The orality of the epics and epic poetry must be kept in mind, and there must be different concepts and terms for discussing them.

The African epics are not identical in their artistic features, concepts of heroism, array of characters, or performance styles, but the epic spirit and consciousness underlies and informs them all. There are striking similarities among these epics, which invite further investigation of the possibility and dynamics of diffusion. The buffalo motif, for

example, exists in the Sundiata epic, the epic of Ng'wanamalundi of northern Tanzania, and the Liongo epic on the East African coast. *Abu Zayd* bears striking resemblances to *Liongo Fumo*.

One of the most important recent developments in the study of African epic is the recognition of the role of women in the epics: their influence on the course of the events, their influence on the heroes, and their role as heroes. As Charles Bird notes, "Although the hero Kambili plays an important role, the storyteller goes to great pains to show the debt he owes to the women in his life. Through his mother's supernatural powers he becomes a great hunter, and through his wife's magical powers he is able to kill the lion-man of Jimini" (1979). This is one of the major unexplored areas, which has the potential to change the way African epics are understood.

See also **Communications: Oral; Dance; Religion and Ritual.**

BIBLIOGRAPHY

Bakhtin, Mikhail. *The Dialogic Imagination*, ed. Michael Holquist, trans. Caryl Emerson and Michael Holquist. Austin: University of Texas Press, 1983.

Bird, Charles. "Heroic Songs of the Mande Hunters." In *African Folklore*, ed. Richard M. Dorson. Bloomington: Indiana University Press, 1979.

Hegel, G. W. F. *Hegel: On the Arts*, trans. Henry Paolucci. New York: Frederick Ungar, 1979.

Lukács, Georg. *The Theory of the Novel*, trans. Anna Bostock. Cambridge, Massachusetts: MIT Press, 1971.

Marx, Karl. "Introduction to a Critique of Political Economy." In *The German Ideology*, ed. Christopher J. Arthur. New York: International Publishers, 1978.

Nagy, Gregory. "An Evolutionary Model for the Making of Homeric Poetry: Comparative Perspectives." In *The Ages of Homer: A Tribute to Emily Townsend Vermeule*, ed. Jane B. Carter and Sarah P. Morris. Austin: University of Texas Press, 1995.

Ong, Walter. *Orality and Literacy: The Technologizing of the Word*. London: Methuen, 1982.

JOSEPH L. MBELE

ISLAMIC

For more than a millennium Islam and Islamic literature have been significant in Africa, spread through commerce and scholarship. The pursuit of knowledge is central to Islam, beginning with

God's message to humankind through the Angel Gabriel's first words to the Prophet Muhammad in the seventh century: "Read! Recite!" This dual mandate of devotion and intellectual development has continued wherever Islam has been established.

Foremost in Islamic literature is the Qur'an, the "recitation of the word of God," revealed to the Prophet Muhammad over a period of twenty-three years, beginning in 620 CE. In the case of the Qur'an, scripture is also literature. Among Muslims universally, the Qur'an is the basis for literacy, grammar, theology, and worldview. Thus, through attention to the Qur'an, African Muslims share a fundamental understanding of their faith with those far removed in distance and culture. The Qur'an is known as a multivalent source, available on as many levels of understanding as there are readers or listeners. Furthermore, as the foundation of Islam, the Qur'an is as accessible in its spoken, audible form as in its written form.

From as early an age as three or four, children hear and internalize the Arabic poetic form of Qur'anic verse, even if their first language is linguistically far removed from Arabic. Familiarity with this source instills a keen aesthetic appreciation of its rhyme, meter, and symbolic language. The Qur'an's opening Sura, the *Fatiha*, is considered a microcosm of the entire Qur'an, containing all that is essential. Its first line, the formulaic *basmallah* (*"Bismillahi arahamani arahim"* "[Begin] in the name of God, the Compassionate, the Merciful"), is the line that may be most familiar to the average Muslim in his or her lifetime, as it is used to begin any action or endeavor in one's life. Poets in Muslim northern Nigeria regularly begin performances with the *basmallah*. This opening prayer is the basis of a child's first encounters with the Qur'an, and constitutes one's first writing lesson. Thus, it is also the basis for literacy. Whether or not one continues to memorize the rest of the Qur'an—a common practice among the devout—Muslims universally begin religious study with the same Arabic words. This leads to the prospect of being united through their literature—its sound, its form, and its meaning—regardless of the language they speak in daily conversation.

As is the case throughout the world, classical forms of Arabic Islamic literature in Africa reflect major historical and cultural influences on the faith. The short-lived Umayyad Dynasty (seventh to eighth century) centered in Damascus was overtaken by Abbasid control centered in Baghdad. The initial aim of Abbasid caliphs was to strengthen piety, but this "Golden Age" is arguably best remembered for its florid love of poetry, heavily influenced by Persian literary style. Although the Abbasid dynasty devolved and fell to Shi'ite, Fatimid control during the tenth through twelfth centuries, the literary styles that marked the Umayyad and Abbasid periods remain some of the most influential styles in Islamic literature wherever it appears.

From these origins, classical Islamic literature came to include a wide range of styles, most of which are evident in the Islamic literature indigenous to Africa. Oral poetry and narrative, *sira* (biography of the Prophet), *qasidah* (ode, praise, eulogy), *qitah* (jokes, satire), *ghazal* (love song), *mathnawi* (story in rhymed couplet), *roba'i* (poetic quatrain), and *maqamah* (rhymed prose). In addition to these classic forms, literary works in Islamic Africa also include treatises on the political and historical conditions of the place and time. Arabic Islamic literature in North Africa, influenced by regional nomadic cultures, Hausa literature in West Africa, and Swahili literature in East Africa commonly include examples of all these types of Islamic literature in both poetic and narrative forms, conveyed both orally and in written works.

Islam spread rapidly in Africa, and Islamic literature along with it. By the mid-tenth century, Cairo had become an established center of learning, with the Al-Azhar mosque and madrasa (now university) established as a focus of authority for Sunni Muslims. From Egypt, Islam moved westward along Africa's northern coast, where scholars in Tunisia, Algeria, and Morocco embraced it, and communities of Islamic scholars developed. Islam moved down through the Maghreb along Africa's westernmost coast to Senegal, and then, by the fourteenth to seventeenth centuries, moved inland, eastward into what is now Nigeria and Chad. Along this sudanic belt great centers of Islamic learning evolved, like Timbuktu in Mali. Meanwhile, on the eastern side of Africa, Islam had moved down past the Horn of Africa, and along the coast, transforming societies in Somalia, Kenya, and Tanzania. Although not as evident as in urban centers, Islam was also embraced by rural communities and desert nomads like the Touareg and Berbers.

Between the tenth and fifteenth centuries Islam had spread widely throughout Africa. Conversion carried with it a focus on the spoken and written word: a reverence for Arabic language, and the promotion of literacy. North Africans in the Maghreb and Mediterranean coastal regions were likely to use Arabic as a lingua franca, while Arabic fluency and literacy in sub-Saharan Africa remained restricted to the scholarly elite. The average convert to Islam was nevertheless conversant with Arabic for basic prayers, and was privy to literary entertainments from the Islamic canon, translated into the indigenous language. Therefore, Arabic had its place in the daily religious practices of new converts, regardless of the local language of their ethnic groups, and became part of major regional languages like Hausa in the West and Swahili in the East early in the process of the establishment of Islam in sub-Saharan Africa.

Islam began with the oral transmission of knowledge, and many Islamic literary forms exist in performed, oral forms as well as in written documents. Regardless of the level of literacy of the region, Islamic oral literature was a part of the socio-religious influence on the communities that embraced Islam. While Muslim scholars focused on reading and writing scripts, the masses enjoyed oral performances of Islamic literatures as they were adopted by indigenous Muslim African performers and poets. In certain contexts the oral transmission of knowledge is preferred over a written form. This is the case among Sufi study groups in Morocco and Nigeria, particularly women, who meet on a regular basis to teach one another and analyze religious perspectives on political and social problems. Indeed, most written works are meant to be performed orally; when the method of checking them for accuracy is to judge by a "reading"—the smooth recitation of a work by a credible scholar.

Although Islam fostered the use of Arabic language and literacy throughout Africa, it did not replace indigenous languages. Instead, indigenous African languages in newly Islamic areas began to be written in Arabic script, a merging of grammars and scripts described by the term *ajami*. This was common in both Hausa and Swahili speaking areas. These *ajami* forms of writing were the norm until the early twentieth century when British and French colonial intervention actively promoted the use of Latin script in state-sponsored schools. During the late twentieth century many Islamic regions—northern Nigeria is a prime example—made political statements in their decision to return to the use of *ajami* and Arabic script for publications like newspapers, alongside Latinate forms.

At the beginning of the twenty-first century, scholarly discovery and preservation of historical documents indicates there is a long history of extensive Islamic literary productivity in African Muslim communities. Certainly the documents of the Sankore mosque and medrasa in Timbuktu attest to this, as do the materials produced in the nineteenth century by the Fodiyo family in what is now known as Sokoto, Nigeria. The Fodiyo clan was known for its intellectual activism; the Shehu himself wrote more than one hundred treatises in Arabic on government, military tactics, and religion. Others in the family—the Shehu's brother Abdullahi, son Bello, and daughter Asma'u—wrote in a range of languages and literary styles, making their works accessible to local populations. Their works in Arabic, Fulfulde, and Hausa were all written in Arabic script; these are examples of *ajami*. Continued scholarly attention to the preservation of Islamic literary works in Africa, like that of the multivolume Arabic Literature in Africa project, promises an increasingly rich collection of historical testimony about Islamic influence on the continent.

Estimates from the early 2000s indicate that of the 800 million people in Africa, half are Muslim; they are distributed fairly evenly throughout the continent, with the exception of southern Africa, were their numbers are smallest. Islamic literature is an integral part of these contemporary Muslim cultures and ethnic groups throughout Africa, modified through the influence of local languages and literary styles. While each society speaks its own distinct indigenous language, Arabic is familiar to African Muslims as the language of Islam, beginning with the Qur'an, its founding literary and oral guide. Islam's mandate that the individual amass knowledge as a means of advancing on the path toward God is often the motivating factor for the production of Islamic literature. Indeed the search for knowledge may be Islam's most significant obligation.

See also **Cairo; Camara Laye; Islam; Sembène, Ousmane; Timbuktu; 'Uthman dan Fodio.**

BIBLIOGRAPHY

Boyd, Jean, and Beverly Mack. *The Collected Works of Nana Asma'u, Daughter of Usman 'dan Fodiyo (1793–1864).* East Lansing: Michigan State University Press, 1997.

Hiskett, Mervyn. *A History of Hausa Islamic Verse.* London: School of Oriental and African Studies, 1975.

Hunwick, John, and Sean O'Fahey. *Arabic Literature of Africa.* 6 vols. Leiden: Brill, 1994–2003.

Knappert, Jan. *Swahili Islamic Poetry.* Leiden: Brill, 1971.

Mack, Beverly. *Muslim Women Sing: Hausa Popular Song.* Bloomington: Indiana University Press, 2004.

Sperl, Stefan, and C. Shackle. *Qasida Poetry in Islamic Asia and Africa.* Leiden: Brill, 1996.

BEVERLY B. MACK

MODERN POETRY

Modern African poetry has long been studied as the outcome of twentieth-century European colonialism and modernism. But this narrow Eurocentric perspective is rapidly giving way to a broader canon. More and more, scholars are recognizing the centrality of verse written in indigenous African languages, as well as in Arabic and other African languages. These neglected currents of the triple heritage of African verbal arts are inheritors of much older traditions of verse-making that are associated with nearly two millennia of Christian and Islamic intermeshing with indigenous African traditions.

MODERN POETRY IN AFRICAN LANGUAGES
There are two main streams of poetry in African languages. The roots of the older stream go back to the apogee of the development of Ge'ez as a literary language of Ethiopia under Ezana (fourth century, reigned ca. 320–340 CE), an accomplished poet and the first Christian king of Aksum. By the seventeenth century, the Ethiopian bible and other Christian texts had been translated into Ge'ez. An offshoot of these developments was a virile tradition of hymnody that produced countless hymns (mostly in praise of Mary), attributed to such hymnodists as Abba Salama (1348–1387) and Abba Giyorgis of Gasecha (fifth century). Out of these hymn-making efforts emerged various hybrids between Christian hymnody and traditional song, notably *dəggua* (antiphony), *malkə* (likenesses), and *qene* (hymns). These forms ultimately evolved into a wide assortment of sophisticated poetic genres. *Qene* later established itself as the mother of modern Ethiopian poetry in Ge'ez and the progenitor of such forms as *k'inē* and *git'im* in Amharic and other Ethiopian languages. Composed as *qene* of two to eleven lines in accordance with age-old prosodic rules of subtle juxtaposition of images known as *siminna werk'* (wax-and-gold, by analogy to the lost-wax method of metal-casting), *k'inē* sparkles with double entendres and other forms of verbal subtleties akin those found in the modernist lyric. Perfected by Hiruy Welde Sillase (d. 1938), modern transformation of *k'inē* and *git'im* have continued to flourish in Ethiopia and Eritrea into the twenty-first century.

In the nineteenth and early twentieth centuries, this tradition of modern verse-making in Ethiopian languages merged with the second stream of African language poesy, one created by European Christian missionaries. This second stream was part of the so-called linguistic labors whereby the missionaries collected vocabularies, wrote grammars, and recorded unwritten literature as models for translating the scriptures, hymns, and other Christian literature into African languages. The skills gained from these labors were then employed in the production of school primers, usually including translations from European folktales (such as Grimm's fairy tales) and classics (for example, Bunyan's *Pilgrims Progress* and Lamb's *Tales from Shakespeare*). Throughout the late nineteenth and early twentieth centuries, primers of this kind served as templates for modern poetry and other writing in African languages. Outside Ethiopia, the earliest poetic outcome of this process is the Great Hymn of Ntsikana kaGabba (c. 1780–1820) and three other hymns in which the visionary convert from a Xhosa traditional religion invokes his newfound Christian God in what is essentially a Xhosa praise poem to the Creator of the Heavens who "whirls the stars around in the sky,/ We call on him in his dwelling-place,/That he may be our mighty leader" (Brownlee, 1827).

Subsequently, in the nineteenth and early twentieth centuries, poetry in African languages in South Africa, composed by such Xhosa pioneers as Tiyo Soga (1829–1871), Krune Edward Mqhayi (1875–1945), H. M. Ndawo (1883–1949), G. B. Sinxo (1902–1962), and J. J. R. Jolobe (1902–1976) followed the conventional hymnodist and evangelical formulae of Nsikana's Hymn. Similar trends are evident in poetry in other South African languages (Zulu, Sotho, and Tswana) as in the major languages of East, Central, and West Africa—Shona, Mande and neighboring languages, Akan, Twi, Yoruba, Hausa, Fula, Somali, Amharic, Malagasy languages, Swahili, and San and related languages. But modernist departures began to appear as early as the 1920s, exemplified by the works of South African poets such as Nontsizi Elizabeth Mgqwetho or Mgqwetto (Xhosa, flourished 1920s), S. E. K. Mqhayi (Xhosa, 1875–1945), and Benedict Vilakazi (Zulu, 1906–1945).

Mgqwetho (nicknamed the literate *imbongi*, or praise-poet laureate) was a woman poet who wrote in masculine idiom of the praise poem, *izibongo*. Although she called herself a she-python, rousing men to war against racial oppression, she also proudly maintained her feminine identity. Mqhayi (nicknamed Poet of our race), celebrated as the praise-poet laureate (*imbongi*) of the Xhosa nation, is notable for the ironic and paradoxical fervor of his satiric assaults against British colonialist perfidy, as in his famous poem ostensibly celebrating the visit of the Prince of Wales to South Africa: "O, Roaring Britain! Which must we embrace?/You sent us the truth, denied us the truth;/You sent us the life, deprived us of life,/You sent us the light, we sit in the dark,/Shivering benighted in the bright noonday sun" (trans. A. C. Jordan). Similar trends are observable in West, East, and Central Africa, as well as in the horn of Africa. Several of the verse passages of *Feso* (1956) by Solomon Mutswairo (b. 1924), routinely recited publicly under the unsuspecting watch of the white racist oligarchy of Southern Rhodesia (present-day Zimbabwe), are nationalist laments for a vanquished Shona nation sprung from the ancient civilization of Mwenemutapa: "Today all the wealth of the land has been taken/.../And we are lean as diseased dogs/...gagged, strangled with bindings."

Beyond the nationalist rhetoric and ideological preoccupations of these early twentieth century poets in African languages, the postindependence era has witnessed the birth of modernist poetry in African languages by avant-garde African writers such as Okot p'Bitek (Acholi, 1930–1982), Mazisi Kunene (Zulu, 1930–2006), Chinua Achebe (Igbo, b. 1930), Said A. Mohamed (Swahili), Alamin Mazrui (Swahili), and Christopher Okigbo (Igbo, 1932–1967).

Okot p'Bitek's dramatic monologues—*Song of Lawino*, *Song of Ocol*, and *Song of the Prisoner*—all composed in Acholi and rendered by the author into English have long been admired for the poignancy of their deployment of traditional idioms and poetic tropes within the construction of a modernist satire against the postcolonial elite. Thus, as Ramazani (2006) observes, "Though often seen as nativist, Okot p'Bitek employed brisk, modernist free verse and defamiliarizingly literal translation to satirize the hypocrisy and pomposity of African missionaries and politicians."

Achebe's Igbo poems, recently reprinted in English translations, offer a remarkable experiment in what may be described as aesthetic deschooling or the detachment of African poetry from formal Euromodernist aesthetics. A radical (but by no means nativistic) search for indigenous aesthetics, these two poems on contemporary themes—*Uno Onwu Okigbo*, "Okigbo's Funeral House," a memorial tribute to the poet, Christopher Okigbo, and *Akuko Kpulu Uwa Iru*, "The Story That Turned the World Upside-down," an allegorical image of the moral chaos and eclipse represented by the postindependence politics and civil war in Nigeria in which Okigbo was killed—are created on the bases of formal-thematic templates derived from well-known Igbo folksongs.

Current trends in the theme and style of poetry in African languages across Africa are indeed a vindication of Ngũgĩ wa Thiong'o's (1986) contention that it is only by writing in African languages that African writers can best represent authentic African memories without the strictures of colonial mentality and colonialist mythology. But these developments, though impressive, remain stunted and peripheral in the absence of top-rated, pan-African journals, anthologies, translations, and prizes devoted to their promotion.

AFRICAN ISLAMIC POETRY IN ARABIC, AJAMI, AND SWAHILI

Several generations of African poets schooled in the Islamic sciences, law, grammar, and poetics, have created poetry in a wide diversity of genres such as *quasida* and *takhmis*, among others. These styles have continued to evolve into an even more complex variety of modern forms since the twentieth century, as can be gleaned from the hundreds of poets in the major languages of the Islamic regions of Sudanic, Eastern, and the Horn of Africa.

In Somalia (which is famous as a nation of poets) and related Cushitic nations in the Horn of Africa, poetry has from time immemorial played a central role in crucial historical moments and as a primary means of social interaction in everyday life. During the early colonial period, especially under the grip of the Dervish insurrection, verse passed through a phase of radical nationalism in this highland enclave. Much of this modern nationalist poetry continues to be orally composed and memorized for reproduction with minimal improvisation in the appropriate political and social settings, as in the case of the provocative lyrics of the nationalist Dervish leader, Maxamed Cabdile Xasan (c. 1860–1921): "Grevious times are now upon us, times of death and woe/The sky has turned to smoke/There is uproar and shrieking, columns of dust—/in truth this world is smouldering with strife/And with forebodings of war.../Loyalty to one's kind, and respect for the parents of one's spouse/Are ways of life which are now dead" (in Andrezjewki and Andrezjewski 1993, 42).

POETRY IN EUROPEAN LANGUAGES

Against the foregoing background, modern African poetry in European languages (including their vernaculars, pidgins, patois; and Creoles, including Afrikaans) takes it proper place in the canon, not as the whole, but as one of the currents of a vast triple heritage. Parallel in origins and motivation as modern European poetry, its antecedents are a few eighteenth- to twentieth-century verses composed in the staid metrical rhymes and poetic diction of European neoclassicism, romanticism, and nineteenth century Victorianism, against which modernism was a necessary rebellion. Taught in colonial schools as works representing the great tradition, poems of this order were produced by the first African poets and poetasters—the rhymers of nineteenth century Lagos, colonial metropolitan anthologists, and early nationalist poets in European languages such as R. E. G. Armattoe (1913–1953), Gladys May Casely-Hayford (also known as Aquah Laluah, 1904–1950), Nnamdi Azikiwe (1904–1996), and Dennis Osadebay (1911–1995). These authors were apparently oblivious of the emergent modernist voices around them and wrote in hackneyed cadences such as the following: "Pray give me none of your airs/..../Being black and old, I need none;/No smart black silk, nor false airs" (Armattoe, "Forensic Airs"); "Let me play with the whiteman's ways/Let me work with the black man's ways" (Osadebay, "Young Africa's Plea"); "I who am black now face the belching fire/Where bullets spurt, to quench another's ire" (Casely-Hayford, "Wings").

Nevertheless, their antiracist, pan-African, cultural nationalist sentiments were coterminous with, and rooted in, the same postcolonial angst as that out of which stemmed the thematic preoccupations of avant-garde modernist poets of the twentieth century, beginning with the poets of the Négritude movement whose *agent provocateur* was the French colonialist assimilation policy.

In the meantime, European settler communities, mostly in East, Central, and Southern Africa, continued to dominate the African literary scene with arcane sonnets going back to Edward Heath Crouch's 1911 *Sonnets of South Africa*. In the South African Cape, the best poetry was for long dominated by the escapist preoccupation with the figure of Adamastor (from Greek for imitative rival of Adam), a mythical beast created by the Portuguese poet Luís de Camões (c. 1524–1580) in his epic poem *Os Lusíadas* (*The Lusiads*, first printed in 1572), as a symbol of the forces of nature Portuguese navigators had to overcome when trying to round the Cape of Storms, henceforth called Cape of Good Hope. The place of this poetry in the canon of modern African poetry will continue to remain ambiguous and debatable. Suffused with memories of Europe, alienated from African traditions, powered by colonialist mythology, this poetry, by *Voorslag* writers such as Roy Campbell (1901–1957) and William Plomer (1903–1973), was at best paternalistic and for the most part alienated from various expressions of cultural nationalism which energized most postcolonial African poetry.

By and large, Anglophone modernist poets rejected what they saw as the spuriousness of the Négritude cant. Thus Soyinka's famous dictum, "The tiger does not proclaim its own tigritude" is matched by Okigbo's ripostes on the fruitless ("barren") worship of the black mystique: "DOLLS.../ Forms/ Of memory,/ To be worshiped/ Adored/ By innocence:/ Creatures of the mind's eye/Barren—/ Of memory/ Remembrance of things past"

(*Four Canzones* IV, 1961). But what the Anglophones rejected was the thematic preoccupations, rather than the stylistic accomplishments, of the Négritude poets. Obumselu (2005) has persuasively traced the provenance of the stylistic triumphs of Okigbo's later chants to his reading of Senghor; and there is a tacit acknowledgement of Okigbo's own admiration for Tchikaya U'Tamsi in some jottings in his previously unpublished papers. By and large, it is evident that, despite differences in tone, Francophone African Négritude poets not only share but also may have strongly influenced the fusion of what has been described as describes as modernist bricolage and postcolonial hybridity in modern African Anglophonic poetics.

These are not the hallmark of only the style of Okigbo and his West African Anglophone contemporaries from the great Mbari Renaissance of the late 1950s and early 1960s (J. P. Clark, Gabriel Okara, Wole Soyinka, Lenrie Peters, Kofi Awoonor, Michael J. C. Echeruo, and Atukwei Okai); the same tendency is clearly evident in anti-apartheid South Africa poetry by Dennis Brutus (b. 1924); Mazisi Kunene (b. 1930), Richard Rive (1931–1989), Keorapeste [William] Kgositsile (b. 1938), and Oswald Mtshali (b. 1940), and in the robust anticolonial modernism of David Rubadiri, Okello Oculi, Taban lo Liyong, and other East African poets. Thus, commenting on the English-Swahili heteroglossia of Rubadiri's oft-anthologized lines ("*Mtu mweupe karibu*"/White man you are welcome,/The gate of reeds closes behind them/And the west is let in; Gikandi (2006) notes that these lines "have come to signal the doubleness of the postcolonial literary project, namely the imperative to mark a space of local identity in the language of the other and to reroute the signifiers of colonialism."

But it is Okigbo who embodies the quintessence of modernist bricolage and postcolonial hybridity in modern African poetry: Any sequence of Okigbo's verse can be cited to illustrate these strategies. At the same time, it is also Okigbo who demonstrates a self-critical reassessment of the pitfalls of this same aesthetic. In the second part of his *Silences* ("Lament of the Drums")—a poem lamenting the imprisonment of Awolowo and the death of his eldest son—Okigbo creates a dynamic verbal equivalent to Akan talking drums: "Long-drums, we awake/Like a shriek of

incense,/The unheard sullen shriek/Of the funerary ram://Liquid messengers of blood,/Like urgent telegrams,/We have never been deployed/For feast of antelopes" (section II) but in the process rejects his own Euromodernism as "a dead letter unanswered"—a "rococo/Choir of insects" and as "null/Cacophony/..void as a debt summons served/On a bankrupt" (section IV). Later, in *Distances*, this obscurantist modernism ('my scattered cry") is destroyed "Death herself" as god of creation, leading to the poet's aesthetic and psychic "homecoming," the promise of which is seen in his late occasional poems, especially "Lament of the Masks" and "Path of Thunder."

The Lusophone poets of Angola, Mozambique, Guinea-Bissau, and Equatorial Guinea—Agostinho Neto (1922–1979), Amílcar Cabral (1924–1973), and others such as Joahim Dias Cordeiro da Matta, Alda do Espírito Santo, Jorge Barbosa (1902–1971), Francisco José Tenreiro (1921–1963), José Craveirinha (1922–2003), Antonio Jacinto [do Amaral Martins], pseud. Tavora Orlando (1924–1991), Costa Alegre, Viriato da Cruz (Angola), Noemia de Sousa, Rui de Noronha, Geraldo Bessa Victor, Alfredo Margarido, Ovidio Martins, and Almada Negreiros—were faced from the beginning with the menace of malignant and unyielding Spanish and Portuguese colonialism. The aestheticist embellishments of modernism that is so evident in Anglophone modern verse are noticeably intermingled with hard-nosed realism. These trappings yield ground to robust, direct, and often colloquial fireworks whereby the words of the poem on the page can be experienced as dynamic verbal correlatives to the bullets, grenades, bombs, and bayonets for which there was constant demand in the long years of the people's wars of independence. But often the underlying anger, disappointment, and bitterness is paradoxically mediated by hope and humane faith in the possibility of a world without barriers, as seen in the lines of Alda do Espirito Santo: "The blood of those fallen/In the forest of death/The innocent blood/The soaks the earth/In a shuddering silence/Will fertilize the earth/And claim justice//The flame of humanity/Songs of hope/For a world without barriers/Where freedom becomes the banner/Of all human beings."

Similar poetry has emerged from other wars, be they revolutionary wars of independence (Namibia, Zimbabwe), wars of resistance against repressive or genocidal regimes (South Africa, Sudan, or Rwanda), or the civil wars that have arisen from other faces of the endemic postcolonial moral chaos and sectarian and religious strife in Africa's numerous failed states (Nigeria/Biafra, Congo, Ethiopia/Eritrea, Somalia, Liberia, and Sierra Leone). Exemplified by the poetry of the Nigerian civil war, the imagery of violence and bloodshed that have been fused from the experience of the postcolonial wars of Africa are often rooted in the angst of the postcolonial crises that have found their way into the literature. The authors (for example, Okigbo, Soyinka, and Ayi Kwei Armah) adopt a tone of disillusionment with the postindependence situation.

The same disillusionment can be seen at the base of the feminist voices (such as Daniele Amrane, Leila Djabali, Anna Greki, Malika O'Lahsen, Andree Chedid, Malak' Abd al-Aziz, Joyce Monsour, Rachida Madani, Amina Said, Irene Assiba d'Almeida, Ifi Amadiume, Molara Ogundipe-Leslie, Micere Githae Mugo, and many others in such anthologies as Busby's *Daughters of Africa*, 1992, and Chipasula's *African Women's Poetry*, 1995). In "To Be a Woman," Sjakuntala Hawoldar offers a powerful fusion of personal and collective, as well as private and public feminist/feminine angst in her portrayal of the once powerful African womankind as "a shadow without form/extinguished by sunlight,/Wombing meaningless men/in the endless chain of need;/...worn on rainy days,/like colorless old shoes/groping between pots and pans."

In many respects, Soyinka is right in describing the generation of poets who began writing after the publication of the landmark anthology, *Modern Poetry from Africa* (Moore and Beier 1964), as The Wasted Generation. Working in the wasteland of Africa's postindependence moral and spiritual nullity, laid to waste physically and psychologically by endemic warfare, political crises, and negations of the ideals of the open society, and deprived by political repression, arrests, imprisonment, and exile from making positive contributions in their prime to the orderly growth of their home states, the tone of the poetry of this generation of African poets is one of unrelieved pessimism. At best it could be described as a revolutionary vision ranging from a pragmatic prescription for decolonizing the mind to radical political alternatives covering the entire range of the leftist political spectrum.

Apart from the poets of the Nsukka school, to be discussed below, leading poets of the wasted generation include Funso Aiyejena, Jared Angira, Kofi Anyidoho, Sly Cheney-Coker, Steve Chimombo, Shimmer Chinodya, Frank Chipasula, Tahar Djaout, Kobina Eyi, Harry Garuba, Chenjarai Hove, Kojo Liang, Jack Mapanje (b. 1944), Dambudzo, Marechera, Felix Mnthali, Charles Mungoshi, Mukhtar Mustapha, Richard Ntiru, Odia Ofeimum, Tanure Ojaide, Atukwei Okai, Niyi Osundare, Sony Labou Tansi, and Ken Saro-Wiwa. Not only have these authors published at least one volume of poetry or been featured in leading new poetry anthologies, several have won national prizes such as the annual Association of Nigerian Authors/Cadbury Poetry Prize, or continent-wide prizes such as the Noma Award and the Christopher Okigbo prize, or global prizes such as the Commonwealth Poetry Prize.

The Nsukka is particularly vibrant and unified by a coherent network of aesthetic-thematic linkages resulted in the new series, Nsibidi Library of Nsukka Poets, edited by Chukwuma Azuonye. As noted in the Introduction to the first anthology of the works of this school, *Nsukka Harvest* (Azuonye, ed. 1972), "By 1965, most of the students writing at Nsukka—Wonodi, Clem Abaziem Okafor, Pol Ndu, Egudu, Bona Onyejeji, Edward Okwu, and Sam Nwaojigba—had featured in important anthologies and literary magazines, and their poetry had become sufficiently engaging to suggest an anthology. Ulli Beier has readily supplied this in a volume titled *Nsukka*, long awaited from Heinemann. If, and when, Ulli Beier's anthology appears, it will be the first harvest of Nsukka poetry and this 'gathering' will then take its proper place as the second harvest anticipated by Kevin Echeruo." It is against this background that Obiechina (1992) later observes that "Okigbo has influenced not one but two generations of poets, both of which has made Nsukka their habitat, the generation of Wonodi and Ndu, and the civil war/ post-civil war generation of Obiora Udechukwu, Kevin Echeruo, Chukwuma Azuonye), Onuora Enekwe, Akomaye Oko, and others." Chief among the others are Dubem Okafor, Esiaba Irobi (b. 1950), Kalu Uka, Olu Oguibe, and Chimalum Nwankwo. Beyond the physical geographical and psychological space of the Nsukka environment, reverberations of the stylistic preoccupation of the Nsukka school with "the figure of the Nigerian Muse as Watermaid or Dancer," as noted by Peter Thomas (1972), can be gleaned in the works of poets from other regions of Africa, among them Richard Ntiru (b. 1946) whose only collection, *Tensions* (1971), has been described as "rich in imagery reminiscent of the poetry of Christopher Okigbo and Pol Ndu."

Repression, imprisonment and exile remains a unifying force between other poets of the Wasted Generation, as can be seen from the poetry of Bernard Binlin Dadié (b. 1916), Ken Saro-Wiwa (1941–1995), Steve Chimombo (b. c. 1945), Felix Mnthali (b. c. 1944), Jack Mapanje, Charles Mungoshi (b. 1947), Mutuzeli Matshoba (b. 1950), Dambudzo Marechera (1952–1967), Tahar Djaout (b. 1954), Chenjarai Hove (b. 1956), Shimmer Chinodya (b. 1957), Frank Chipasula, and several others. These poets were featured in Jack Mapanje's anthology, *Gathering Seaweed: African Prison Writing* (2002) and his earlier personal collection, *Chattering Wagtails of Mikuyu Prison* (1993).

NEW BEARINGS IN MODERN AFRICAN POETRY

Since the 1990s, there has been a continued deterioration and uniform failure of the postcolonial states of Africa, and a massive emigration of African writers and intellectuals to Europe and the Americas under pressure from decadent and repressive regimes. As a result, the traditional division of African poetry into Arabic, African, and European language traditions, or within the European language tradition into Anglophone, Lusophone, and Francophone, is rapidly giving way to a new global consciousness characterized in part by a decolonizing poetics and in part by a universalism that urges the poet to be seen as a purveyor of universal humane values. Thus, Nnamdi Azuonye (1982–2001), who left behind four books of poetry before his premature death in a car crash, envisioned a paradigm city far beyond "where the homeless/ are sheltered with an endearing caress" (Paradigm City 2002, 3). Exile and globalism poetics not only

deigns the emergent universalist generation of African poets to sing songs of themselves in abjuration of strictures to personal freedom and a yearning for a free world, it has also ignited debates on the relevance of writing in any language other than indigenous African languages, not including Arabic. Universalist poetics, on the other hand, is in itself an expression of freedom from the narrow straights of the still narrowing African aesthetic space. But such freedom has, in some cases, lured some poets, especially of the new African diaspora—born and raised or flourishing for most of their adult lives in Europe and north America—into the decadent forms of modernist and postmodernist poetry for the sake of poetry. The directions of these new trends in modern African poetics are yet to be fully understood as the third millennium unfolds.

See also **Achebe, Chinua; Armah, Ayi Kwei; Azikiwe, Benjamin Nnamdi; Cabral, Amílcar Lopes; Christianity: Missionary Enterprise; Creoles; Literature: Epics and Epic Poetry; Literatures in African Languages; Literatures in European Languages; Neto, Agostinho; Ngũgĩ wa Thiong'o; Saro-Wiwa, Ken; Sony Labou Tansi; Soyinka, Wole.**

BIBLIOGRAPHY

Andrzejewski, B. W., and Sheila Andrzejewski. *An Anthology of Somali Poetry.* Bloomington: Indiana University Press, 1993.

Andrzejewski, B. W.; Sheila Pilaszewicz; and W. Tyloch; eds. *Literatures in African Languages: Theoretical Issues and Sample Surveys.* Cambridge, U.K.: Cambridge University Press, 1985.

Azuonye, Chukwuma. "Christopher Okigbo at Work: A Preliminary Survey of the Unpublished Papers of His Previously Unpublished Papers." Presented at the African Literature Association Conference, Accra, Ghana, May 20-24, 2006.

Azuonye, Chukwuma, and Steven Serafin, eds. *Columbia Anthology of African Literature.* New York: Columbia University Press, 2007.

Bivar, A. D. H., and Melville Hiskett. "The Arabic Literature of Nigeria: A Provisional Account." *Bulletin of the School of Oriental and African Studies* 25, no. 1 (1962): 104–148.

Cantalupo, Charles, and Ghirmai Negash. *Who Needs a Story? Contemporary Eritrean Poetry in Tigrinya, Tigre and Arabic.* Asmara, Eritrea: Hdri Publishers, 2005.

Chinweizu, Onwuchekwa Jemie, and Ihechukwu Madubuike. *Toward the Decolonization of African Literature.* Enugu, Nigeria: Fourth Dimension Publishers, 1980.

Dathorne, Oscar R. *The Black Mind: A History of African Literature.* Minneapolis: University of Minnesota Press, 1974.

Furniss, Graham. *Ideology in Practice.* Cologne, Germany: Rüdiger Köppe, 1995.

Gérard, Albert. *African Language Literatures: An Introduction to the Literary History of Sub-Saharan Africa.* Essex, U.K.: Longman, 1981.

Gikandi, Simon. "Preface: Modernism in the World." *Modernism/Modernity* 13, no. 3 (2006): 419–424.

Harries, Lyndon. *Swahili Poetry.* Oxford: Clarendon Press, 1962.

Hunwick, J. O., and R. S. O'Fahey, eds. *Arabic Literature of Africa.* Leiden, The Netherlands: E. J. Brill, 1994.

Knappert, Jan. *Four Centuries of Swahili Verse: A Literary History and Anthology.* London: Heinemann Educational, 1979.

Mazrui, Ali A. *The Africans: A Triple Heritage.* Boston: Little, Brown, 1986.

Menkiti, Ifeanyi, trans. "Uno Onwu Okigbo." In *Collected Poems,* ed. Chinua Achebe. New York: Anchor Books, 2004.

Moore, Gerald, and Ulli Beier, eds. *Modern Poetry from Africa.* Harmondsworth, U.K.: Penguin, 1966.

Nazombe, Anthony, comp. *Operations and Tears: A New Anthology of Malawian Poetry.* Zomba, Malawi: Kachere Series, 2003.

Ntuli, Deuteronomy B. Z., and Chris F. Swanepoel. *Southern African Literature in African Languages: A Concise Historical Perspective.* Pretoria, South Africa: Thorold's Africana Books, 1993.

Ngũgĩ wa Thiong'o. *Decolonising the Mind: The Politics of Language in African Literature.* London: James Currey, 1986.

Obumselu, Ben. "Christopher Okigbo: A Poet's Identity." In: *The Responsible Critic: Essays on African Literature in Honor of Professor Ben Obumselu,* ed. Isidore Diala. Trenton, New Jersey: Africa World Press, 2006.

Opland, Jeff. *Xhosa Poets and Poetry.* Cape Town, South Africa: David Philip Publishers, 1998

Ramazani, Jahan. "Modernist Bricolage, Postcolonial Hybridity." *Modernism/Modernity* 13, no. 3 (2006): 445–463.

CHUKWUMA AZUONYE

ORAL

The remarkable narratives, songs, declamations, and other oral performances in Africa have played a significant part in challenging the traditional view of "literature" as confined to written forms. Once dismissed or marginalized as "folklore," "primitive tales," "oral tradition," or, at best, as only a qualified form of "full" literature, the oral performances of Africa are reaching their proper international recognition within the mainstream of comparative literature.

The oral literature of the great, diverse, and changing continent of Africa is too varied to allow for easy generalizations (tempting though these have sometimes proved to be). The main points to emphasize are African oral literature's diversity, versatility, and performance qualities.

MAJOR FORMS

African oral literature comes in many forms: stories, praises, laments, epics, lyrics, oratory, drama, songs, and poetry. It ranges from the high panegyric utterances associated with royal courts to the electronically mediated singing groups, radio performances, and popular culture of the twenty-first century, and it is often interfused with music and with dance.

Stories are everywhere and have been much collected. Some describe animal characters as a subtle commentary on the actions and experiences of humans. The trickster spider (a counterpart of the Caribbean Anansi) is portrayed in many tales as a crafty, arrogant, and asocial character, often heading for some ludicrous downfall. There are fictional stories about human heroes, too, named and unnamed: the young man in search of a wife, the willful young girl, the dangers of power, the antics of fools, fantastic journeys through unknown places, fabulous monsters, or the dilemmas of everyday living. The origin of creation also features in these fables, often overlapping in theme or protagonists with tales of animals and humans. Narrative is not confined solely to traditional or uncontentious subjects, however; marginal peoples or special-interest groups can use a story to convey political messages, assert their identities, and express their viewpoints.

Praise poetry is another notable and often highly elaborate form of literature dating from at least the nineteenth century, with especially famous examples from western and southern Africa. Such poems are sometimes composed for rulers in a grand and esoteric style, full of praise epithets, but they also may be composed for a host of other

The Lugufu Band, formerly known as Mwenge d'Uvira, before arriving as refugees in Tanzania. Here they are shown playing with instruments and an amplifier that they made themselves, October 1, 1999, Lugufu, Kigoma, Tanzania. © GRIGGS MATT/ CORBIS SYGMA

designees, such as cattle, spirits, political parties, and inanimate objects—even for Nelson Mandela and the South African football team.

Epic poems have been much collected and studied: these lengthy narratives relate the miraculous lives and deeds of heroes such as Sunjata, famous throughout the Mande region as the legendary founder of the Mali empire. Although "epic" has admittedly been a controversial description (one example of the problems of importing European genre terms with their sometimes emotive baggage), critical reassessments of the special features of these African forms together with copious collecting have given epics an established place within the African corpus. Commonly performed through declaimed, sung, or emotionally heightened delivery and often with instrumental accompaniment, epic narratives are presented in person in traditional settings as well as on radio, cassette, disc, and film.

In addition to epics, oral literature in Africa includes the ubiquitous lyrics—relatively short series of words clothed in song. These lyrics relate to almost every imaginable subject and setting: mourning songs, religious and ceremonial songs, songs for special groups (such as hunters or sports teams), children's verse, personal songs, political taunts, and songs inserted into stories or accompanying work. They are often sung in conjunction with dances following a leader-chorus structure, a traditional style now emulated by contemporary pop groups.

Many other forms of literature thrive within and among the many regions and generations of Africa, including oratory; theatrical performances (past and present); and proverbs, riddles, or praise names that contain literary elements. Moreover, Africa hosts other established and emergent local genres that are too subtle, diverse, or fluid to be fully encapsulated within the previous categories.

David Yali-Manisi (1926–1999) at the University of Fort Hare, South Africa, 1974. Yali-Manisi was South Africa'a noted praise poet. His oral and written work in Xhosa thrived during apartheid rule. PHOTOGRAPH BY JEFF OPLAND

Teenaged Xhosa storyteller during a contemplative moment. Every new generation of Xhosains in South Africa develops within the context of the stories of the past. Members of these generations then develop their own traditional stories to be passed along, never memorizing them, always working them into the tradition. PHOTOGRAPH BY HAROLD SCHEUB

ORAL ARTISTS AND THEIR ROLES

African literary forms are not rooted in the distant past, nor are they the products of "the tribe" or "community" (as scholars once assumed); in fact, they are developed by individual men and women who impart their own personality and creativity to accepted styles and topics. Their art is sometimes learned informally. Everyone in a particular community may have some ability to tell stories, for example, or to sing (or at least join in choruses). Other individuals work at acquiring expertise in specific genres, perhaps as self-taught students or through a more formal arrangement, such as the expert women performers of specific song genres, the praise singers attached to rulers' courts, or the hereditary griots in the West African Sahel region.

Similar to literature in other regions of the world, some African oral literary genres are gender-, status-, or age-specific, and some practitioners are more marginalized than others. Overall, however, African oral artists come from every kind of background, and they are not confined to a few functions or settings. They perform in homes and villages as well as in more formal settings such as courts, theaters, street enactments, radio programs, and films. And just as literary artists everywhere accomplish a range of purposes with their art, so too do the oral performers and composers of Africa: they entertain, propagandize, beguile, satirize, rebel, subvert, preach, show off, enlighten, obfuscate, innovate, delight with the beauty of word and voice, and more. They can uphold authority, but they can also challenge it (praise poets, for example, offer criticism as well as praise). Here again, diversity reigns instead of the blanket generalizations offered by scholars in previous generations.

In contrast to the continuity of some traditions, oral literature in Africa is also notable for its change and versatility. Older genres are often revived or adapted to suit contemporary concerns or new ones are created, such as the Zulu Nazarite hymns or the popular *balwo* lyric form started by a Somali lorry driver in the 1950s. The oral literature forms from the past are being extended by poetry on video or on the Web; by rap bands; by praise singers on television; and by trade union songs, contemporary life stories, songs about AIDS, and the intersection of writing, voice, and broadcast media in a plethora of contexts. Forms that might once have been designated "hybrid" or "non-African" are becoming accepted as the creative products of innovative practitioners working in a global arena, such as the northern Nigerian performers who combine Islamic vocabulary with a performance style recalling both praise singing and Indian film song, film representations of the epic hero Sunjata, or a South African praise poet's compact disc (CD) in a mixture of Xhosa and English set to hip-hop music.

PERFORMANCE AND COMPOSITION

Oral literature depends on performance; that is how it becomes literature. Its essence lies not just in the text of a story or song, but also in the dynamics of the occasion, in the art of the performers' delivery, in the participation of the audience, and in the mix of verbal and nonverbal media. The dramatic guttural declamation and posture of the Xhosa praise poet; the emotion-laden tones, sobs, facial expressions, and movements of Akan dirge singers; the soaring voice, musicality, and choreography of lyric delivery by a leader echoed by a following chorus—these dimensions are all crucial to the literary experience. Storytellers use both voice and body to convey the narrative, deploying gesture, ideophones (mini-images in sound), and mimicry, as well as artful use of songs with audience chorus, enactment of their characters' speech, and variations in tempo, pitch, stress, volume, and atmosphere. Interaction with their co-participants is part of the performance, too—the term "audience" is perhaps too passive a term for observers who also act as co-creators.

Mid-twentieth century and later scholars have challenged the assumption that African oral literary forms have remained essentially unchanged from their traditional past. The cross-cultural "oral-formulaic" analyses of the 1960s and later demonstrated that, rather than being fixed, oral forms are commonly modified during performance: the composer-performer draws on formulaic phrases and themes to put together a unique creation for a specific occasion. There are many African cases of this widespread form of oral composition. Thus, in storytelling, the same story or set of motifs is often developed differently by different narrators or even by the same narrator on different occasions, as the performer responds to the demands and inspiration of the moment. Similarly, lamenters and praise singers may draw on conventional themes and imageries to produce unique performances to fit specific personalities or occasions. Other genres, however, in Africa and elsewhere, depend on separating composition from performance. Women's personal *impango* songs in mid-twentieth-century Zambia, for example, were thought out first by one woman who elaborated on them with her friends; next, the songs were worked over for days by an expert composer; and finally they were rehearsed and memorized before their final performance. Somali poets spend hours, sometimes days, composing certain forms of poetry; the author's name is acknowledged when the poem is recited and deviations from the memorized text are noted by the audience.

Writing often enters the oral literature canon as well, perhaps as script or performance notes, or sometimes as an alternative channel for forms that are also performed orally (South African praise poets, for example, have for generations published written versions of their poems). Audio, video, film, and the Web also make their own important contribution to the composition, performance, and dissemination of oral literature.

FROM PERFORMANCE TO TEXT

Oral performances have long been represented as written texts. But capturing the work as a written document—that is, dictating, recording, transcribing, translating, publishing, and somehow communicating the elements of the performance—is very difficult to accomplish. The written word cannot adequately describe the full characterization, emotion, irony, or dialogue conveyed during a performance, nor can it display the gestures, movements, tone, music, or interplay of overlapping performers. The single-voice verbal text—the outcome of a series of decisions by those who have processed and controlled its final shape—gives only a thin and misleading impression of the creative and subtle artistry of oral literature.

The increasing availability of audio, video, and new information technologies has improved the situation, however. Although these new media also involve comparable questions of choice, selectivity, and control, they afford a more dynamic and multi-modal framework for representing oral performances and, especially through the global reach of the Web, for disseminating them to wider audiences in ways that partly break through the traditional constraints of print.

That there are problems in transforming performance into other media does not mean, however, that authentic African oral literature exists only in some original untouched state before being processed by foreign collectors and rewriters. Just as modern scholars now acknowledge that accurate translation must involve not only "faithfulness" but also "recreation," so too the presentations of African oral performances, whether written, recorded, or Web-based, have their own existence and influences—part of the continuing unfolding of literary and cultural forms within and beyond Africa.

ISSUES AND DEBATES

Despite the fact that contemporary scholars use the term "oral literature" in comparative study, it still causes arguments. Some scholars consider it a contradiction, because the Latin etymology of the word "literature" derives from "letters" (and thus writing). Moreover, the term "literature" tends to invoke a spatially defined, one-line text centered on the verbal, thus sidelining the realities of dynamic, multidimensional performance. Use of the word can also lead to classifying African forms under genres from the traditional Western canon, which are shaped by outsiders' definitions rather than local culture. Some researchers therefore prefer terms like "orature," "auriture," "oraliture," or the recently coined "technauriture." These new words attempt to describe the voiced and auditory qualities of performance. Other scholars, however, argue for retaining the phrase "oral literature" in order to challenge the narrow identification of

literature with writing and also to avoid the potentially "othering" connotations of special terminology (as if African forms lay outside the established cross-cultural concepts and needed their own descriptions). The term "literature" highlights the artistry and the verbal elements and their exegesis—as important for oral as for written forms—and it draws the study of African oral forms into the terminology and debates of international scholarship, mutually benefiting scholars within and outside of Africa.

A few researchers contend that oral and literary modes are independent of each other or even that they are mutually incompatible. In fact, there are many past and present examples of interaction and overlap between oral and written forms. In Africa, as throughout most of the world, such interplay has long been a normal part of human communication and expression. Oral and written media interpenetrate and flow into each other, in the complex influences of oral genres on written literary works. And literary artists in Africa and elsewhere continue to move readily across the permeable oral-written boundary, combining songs, spoken word, manuscripts, audio recordings, films, written scores, and live performances.

See also **Camara Laye; Communications: Electronic; Dance; Language; Literature and the Study of Africa; Mandela, Nelson; Media: Book Publishing; Music; Myth and Cosmology; Ngũgĩ wa Thiong'o; Popular Culture; Senghor, Léopold Sédar; Theater.**

BIBLIOGRAPHY

Barber, Karin, ed. *Audiences in Africa*. Special issue of *Africa* 67, no. 3 (1997): 347–499.

Finnegan, Ruth. *Oral Literature in Africa*. Oxford: Clarendon Press, 1970.

Finnegan, Ruth. *The "Oral" and Beyond: Doing Things with Words in Africa*. Oxford: James Currey; Chicago: University of Chicago Press; and Scottsville, South Africa: University of KwaZulu-Natal Press, 2007.

Furniss, Graham, and Liz Gunner, eds. *Power, Marginality and Oral Literature in Africa*. Cambridge, U.K.: Cambridge University Press, 1995.

Gerstle, C. Andrew; Stephanie Jones; and Rosalind Thomas; eds. *Performance Literature*. Spec. issue, *Oral Tradition* 20, nos. 1–2 (2005).

Görög-Karady, Veronika. *Bibliographie annotée: littérature orale d'Afrique noire*. Paris: Conseil International de la Langue Française, 1992.

Irele, Abiola F., and Simon Gikandi, eds. *The Cambridge History of African and Caribbean Literature.* Vol. 1. Cambridge, U.K.: Cambridge University Press, 2004.

Kaschula, Russell H., ed. *African Oral Literature: Functions in Contemporary Contexts.* Claremont, South Africa: New Africa Books, 2001.

Okpewho, Isidore. *African Oral Literature. Backgrounds, Character and Continuity.* Bloomington: Indiana University Press, 1992.

Ricard, Alain, and C. F. Swanepoel, eds. *The Oral-Written Interface.* Spec. issue, *Research in African Literatures* 28, no. 1 (1997): 1–199.

RUTH FINNEGAN

POPULAR LITERATURE

Popular literature, in its African model, denotes an urban-based form of literature with a strong, multifaceted, but often troubled attachment to the locality of its ascendance. Well known is the Onitsha market literature, locally produced and distributed booklets about how to make Igbo smartness a vehicle for personal (male) success and material acquisition. In the 1950 and 1960s, this literature initiated a revolution in literary entrepreneurship with wide regional and thematic repercussions for the rest of the continent. The pamphlets were, at the outset, primarily written by young men, graduates, secondary school students, and journalists, many of whom acquired more advanced writing skill with time; their audiences, however, remained low-level office workers, taxi drivers, and, when the pamphlets found their way into English literacy programs in schools, school teachers and their students. There was no clear socioethnic link between the authors (if they may be identified at all) and their audiences; neither was there any clear affiliation between author and publisher except monetary as the traders or bookseller-publishers normally bought the manuscript and then did what they wanted with it (even rewriting it).

The Onitsha chapbook industry had its boom in the late 1960s, when some forty separate booksellers competed for space and the *naira* (Nigerian currency) on New Market Road in the city. Titles such as *Veronica My Daughter* would be reprinted and appropriated in many and various editions, resulting in over one hundred thousand copies being sold. The industry was an inspiring model for other initiatives in local book making and

marketing ability (also in film and the comics) across a book-hungry Africa. A parallel phenomenon, also with roots in the colonial times, is Hausa popular fiction that had its roots in conservative Muslim societies and cities such as Zariya, Kaduna, Katsina, Sokota, and Kano. From 1984 onwards, Kano market literature has been one of the most uncompromising and innovative text productions on the continent. Young Muslim youths started at this time to transform locally produced television melodramas into full-length novels or novellas, struggling not only against unwilling publishers but also a conservative public in their takes on forced marriage and the interplay between womanhood, culture, and religion.

Local entrepreneurship and indigenous creativity with literary aspirations have operated from the beginning in an interface with the global, where the two are enmeshed with each other to the extent that the conventional dichotomy of center/periphery becomes an inadequate term to describe the African book market. The global, whether it represents this literature's penchant for the North American or European romance, thriller, detective story, and the Indian film or the competitive and extended activity of multinational publishers of, say, Heinemann, Macmillan, and Longman, is deflected and refracted by local interpretation and resonances. So the romance form, when appropriated in the Longman *Drumbeat* series, provides space for indigenous women writers to debate questions of social transformation, careers, education, and marriage; Macmillan's *Pacesetter* series and Heinemann's *Heartbeat* recast and reacculturate their models in a similar disrupting manner in order to intersect with the desires of their readers for accountability. The Nairobi thriller of the 1980s Spear Books series (East African Educational Publishers; former Heinemann) indigenizes New York street texts into topical urban dramas about a disintegrating Kenyan masculinity and nationality.

African small fiction is multimedial, producing separate texts that comment on, amplify, and quote one another, however foreign in conventional terms they may be to each other. Hausa popular literature is inspired by Hollywood and Bollywood cinema; the life-skills comics of South African (Johannesburg) Storyteller's Group's *Heart to Heart* (from 1994) and the Soul City project's

Body and Soul (1997) are equally media rich, both local and trans-African in content and theme. In these text formations, global homogenizing structures merge with indigenizing, excluding ones. The outcome is a polyphonic ensemble that mimics and transliterates the parts of which it is made. Its discursive feature is repetition, imitation, and hybridization. Academia's overall rejection (by silencing, reduction, and scorn) of African popular literature is based on ignorance of how the principles of intertextuality and intermediality work.

For many, another disturbing feature of popular literature is its unabashed will to both entertain and educate simultaneously, mixing moral or political standpoints with the fantasy world of the comic, the ebullient, and the exciting. The most amazing literary enterprises have developed where the authors-as-storytellers preach the virtues of education and healthy lifestyle through proverb-speaking errant heroes and heroines, in love stories, short fiction, and comics. The comics of *Joe* (Kenya, 1973–1979), for instance, focused on the ordinary as the utopia through educating, far beyond the relative short period of its existence, a middle-class urban population how to cope with life in the city via acts of self-derision and laughter at the other. The romance formula and the urban thriller arena are two other modes for education and entertainment in the broad sense with a wide appeal across the continent. To turn the romance or the thriller into a radical, socially transformative text requires both skill and audacity. The Hausa women's self-reflective novellas of the 1980s and onwards interrogate gender and space relations and break cultural taboos. The Spear Books thrillers (Kenya) of the same period also adopted the autobiographical approach to discuss sociopolitical realities of the urban poor. Repentant ex-criminals and degenerate police officers masculinize African short fiction that still manages, directly or indirectly, to debate social amendments.

State bureaus have been agents of much destruction, but also an inspiration for popular fiction writing in Africa. The South African *Drum* magazine and its urban stories of the 1950s and those of the *Staffrider* magazine, produced two decades later, had their offspring in township community defiance. The intersection of the printed and the spoken word in Africa is deeply implicated by communal and collective desires. It is no wonder that authorities of all kinds (religious, patriarchal, political, and ethnic) react, often violently, when their interests are questioned by popular words and gestures. Polygamy, marriages of coercion, *purdah* (the Islamic tradition of seclusion), and education of women, are issues that Kano market literature grapples with, and as a consequence, it is constantly threatened by censorship and banning orders.

Women writers such as Zaynab Alkali (b. 1950), Nandi D'lovu (b. 1919), and Helen Aiyeohusa Ovbiagele (b. 1944) (in Macmillan's *Pacesetters* series) defy masculine ideological registers and experimentally search for new gender identities and non-affiliated kinship structures. If male popular literature is waging an ongoing battle against the state bureau, feeding on it, and also occasionally collapsing under it, women's popular literature has opted to write back to a traditional authority composed not only of patriarchal regulations but also of rigid storytelling conventions and generic stereotyping. Women's rewriting becomes an act of subversion without turnabouts. Newell writes: "Positioned thus, they [women writers] might problematise the figures of the ideal wife, the rural mother or the good-time girl, but they do not necessarily reject these popular constructions of femininity" (2002, 8).

One of popular literature's grand signifiers is hybridity, and nowhere is this phenomenon more prevalent than in its lingual text worlds. Hausa literature, for instance, interacts with the video market as much as it transfers its texts between English and Hausa, also mixing the two (Engausa). English here, as in the Onitsha chapbooks, is associated with self-promoting, individualism, and the rich world; it is prestigious and iconic to the point of effacing intelligibility and proficiency. English is remarkably not read for what it says but for what it shows. It is synonymous with modernity and access to material and symbolic capital, thus it is also a sore postcolonial problem. Most African writers of popular fiction shuffle between languages and translate, transliterate, and retranslate them and themselves in the process of writing. "No rules, no syntax," is how Saro-Wiwa describes the rotten English spoken by Sozaboy (of the novel of the same name). The in-between, disparate, unsettled character of the language of this novel could be seen as an attempt at enacting an alternative national self-reflection based on plurality.

This is not to say that African popular literature is all in English. There is an abundance of small fiction and popular novels in Swahili, Pidgin, Hausa, Igbo, Yoruba, and many other languages that are read for their poignant comments on everyday life. For instance, the Swahili popular novel of Tanzania has for decades been preoccupied with the *Ujamaa* treatise (African socialism), speaking vehemently for and against it; in more recent times this focus has splintered in its attempts to confront the disillusion and dire social conditions that weigh down the region (Kenya and Tanzania). African language-centered popular fiction has long been part of a mythologizing of the nation that is more conservative than revolutionary. Furthering an African language is always a political act, but so is the opposite move. The Tanzanian novelist Muhammed Said Abdulla's (b. 1918) detective hero Bwana Msa (an African Sherlock Holmes) may be seen as a linguistic and nationalistic propagandist (Swahili and Tanzania). However, despite the politics of purity versus impurity that may be inferred from their different language practices, Bwana Msa and Saro-Wiwa's Sozaboy are equally likeable heroes, each mesmerized and appalled by the spectacle of power that surrounds them.

See also **Globalization; Kano; Marriage Systems; Popular Culture; Saro-Wiwa, Ken; Women; Youth.**

BIBLIOGRAPHY

Barber, Karin, ed. *Readings in African Popular Culture.* Bloomington: Indiana University Press, 1997.

Chapman, Michael, ed. *The Drum Decade. Stories from the 1950s.* Pietermaritzburg: University of Natal Press, 2001.

Granqvist, Raoul J. *The Bulldozer and the Word: Culture at Work in Postcolonial Nairobi.* Berlin: Peter Lang, 2004.

Lindfors, Bernth. *Popular Literatures in Africa.* Trenton, NJ: Africa World Press, 1991.

Newell, Stephanie, ed. *Readings in African Popular Fiction.* Bloomington: Indiana University Press, 2002.

Obiechina, Emmanuel. *An African Popular Literature: A Study of Onitsha Market Pamphlets.* Cambridge, U.K.: Cambridge University Press, 1973.

RAOUL J. GRANQVIST

PROVERBS AND RIDDLES

Proverbs and riddles are among the poetic verbal art forms of most African societies. Compared to other poetic forms, and indeed to all other forms of verbal art, they are extremely short—in the case of riddles sometimes as brief as a word or a sound. Of the two, proverbs, by far the more important, have attracted the attention of more collectors and scholars. They are ubiquitous in African societies, with the possible exception of the Khoesan of southern Africa, and the Nilotic and Hamitic groups residing in a stretch from the area of the Horn north and west along the Mediterranean coast.

Their appeal to collectors and scholars reflects their popularity in traditional discourse. The Igbo (Ibo) of eastern Nigeria describe them as the palm oil with which words are eaten, while the Yoruba, their compatriots to the west, say proverbially that proverbs are the vehicles of speech; when communication goes awry, proverbs come to the rescue.

Proverbs are incisive in their propositions and terse in their formulation. They are deduced from close observations of life, the characteristics and habits of life forms, and the environment and natural phenomena, and from sober reflections on these. Because they are held to express unexceptionable truths, resort to them in a discussion or argument is tantamount to appeal to incontrovertible authority. This is one reason they are virtually indispensable in formal and informal verbal interactions; their absence in speech reduces its impact, while their apt use significantly enhances it. They even pervade all other (major) forms of verbal art, in which their use confers greater effectiveness. Archer Taylor must have had the general acceptance of their sagacity and veracity in mind when he described proverbs as "the wisdom of many and the wit of one": the artistry involved in their formulation is one person's (usually anonymous), but their truth is accepted by all ("The Wisdom of Many and the Wit of One," *Swarthmore College Bulletin* 54 [1962]: 4). Yet no society's proverbs speak with one voice, a society's repertoire being a record of the plurality of views, opinions, and attitudes that society has known. For every proverb that makes a judgmental assertion, one would most probably find others expressing a contradictory view. This eclectic quality makes them invaluable

PEOPLE AND CULTURES

Marking the summer solstice at Aswan. At Elephantine Island, near the Nile's First Cataract, Eratosthenes once took astronomical measurements of the summer solstice. Many regimes have governed the region through the intervening millennia. Here the same measurements are commemorated in modern Egypt. © BOB SACHA/CORBIS

TOP RIGHT: Chief dancing at festival. Traditional textiles and insignia derived from the British crown mix in the regalia of this contemporary official in Nigeria. Africans have always incorporated their current experiences with the heritage of their pasts. © TIM GRAHAM/CORBIS

MIDDLE RIGHT: Nairobi bombing anniversary. The 1998 terrorist bombing of the U.S. embassies in Kenya and Tanzania emphasized Africa's involvement in world affairs. Africa's modern diversity is no less than its historical complexity. Here clergy of different faiths and races join in the first anniversary commemoration of the bombing. AP IMAGES

BOTTOM RIGHT: A new chief in Botswana. Mosadi Seboko receives the traditional leopard skin in 2003 to signify her authority as the first Botswana woman paramount chief of the Balete (or Bamalete) people. In 2005, Ellen Johnson-Sirleaf, of Liberia, became Africa's first female head of state. AP IMAGES

TOP LEFT: Muslim women in Egypt. Africans have excelled at soccer, running, and other sports, often competing on the world stage. Islamic fundamentalists have raised concerns about women's public exposure, but local dress and values have generally not constrained African interests in global sport. AP IMAGES

MIDDLE LEFT: Herero women. These Herero women of Namibia have mixed the dress styles of early-twentieth-century German missionary women with headdresses expressive of their own culture. Herero communities raise livestock on the northern fringes of the Kalahari Desert, where their ancestors were victims of a massive German military assault in 1904. © MICHAEL MARTIN

BOTTOM LEFT: Venda potter. Women of the Venda people of South Africa and Zanzibar continue to practice their arts of wall painting and pottery. Artists like this South African woman perform tasks of everyday utility that provide both artistic enrichment and tourist-economy income. © KERSTIN GEIER; GALLO IMAGES/CORBIS

Karo man painted like cheetah, Ethiopia. Body painting, tattooing, and scarification are among the diverse ways in which Africans have historically expressed themselves; this festival adornment may reflect skills of the hunt. Today Africans use cosmetics and other means of adornment no less than any other people in the world. © KAZUYOSHI NOMACHI/CORBIS

TOP RIGHT: Berber nomad wedding preparations. In the High Atlas region of Morocco, Berbers take pride in holding onto a traditional culture now largely abandoned by their urban kin. ALEXANDRA BOULAT/VII/AP IMAGES

BELOW: Initiation ceremony, Uganda. The marking of life-stage transitions is emblematic not only of age and gender, as formerly, but today also of social differences and professional status, as in graduation ceremonies from schools and rituals of baptism in Christian churches. © MICHAEL MARTIN

TOP LEFT: On the trans-African highway, Uganda. Modern roads have been created in many parts of Africa by both colonial and national regimes, but not all Africans have been able to benefit from them. The challenges of maintaining vehicles and infrastructure have stimulated recycling and other creative solutions throughout the continent. © MICHAEL MARTIN

BOTTOM LEFT: Salt caravan in the Ténéré Desert, Niger. Caravans once bore gold, slaves, and minerals across one of the most desolate regions on earth. Today the Tuareg salt trade remains essential to the region's pastoral economy. © MICHAEL MARTIN

TOP RIGHT: Tea harvest in South Africa. Commercial crops, grown on large plantations like this tea estate on the Indian Ocean coast of South Africa, have employed large numbers of African workers, often under varying degrees of compulsion during colonial times. In other cases, African entrepreneurship has generated significant exports of cacao, peanuts, maize, and other commodities. © ROGER DE LA HARPE/CORBIS

BELOW: Tuareg mosque in Agadez. This famous mosque, in the Sudanese clay style, is a noted monument in Niger. Saharan Tuareg herders have been Muslim for centuries, and Islam in many forms continues to attract believers throughout the northern half of the continent. © MICHAEL MARTIN

Ponta da Sol fishing village, Cape Verde. Africa's thousands of miles of coastline, including several island nations, ensure the continuing importance of maritime cultures. © Riccardo Spila/Grand Tour/Corbis

archives of the intellectual and ideational history of the community.

Proverbs not only lend rhetorical effectiveness to speech but also perform important social functions. They may indicate the sort of behavior society considers appropriate, as does, for example, the Jabo (Liberia) proverb, "a grown-up who emulates children is a fool," or they may comment on an occurrence, as with the Zulu saying, "the beast has fallen on its horns," referring to a person's prostration by misfortune. The Fulani of Nigeria say "before the old woman made soapsuds the tick bird was clean," a rebuke to a person who erroneously believes that he or she is indispensable to another's well-being. Perhaps most importantly, proverbs' cryptic and indirect manner of expression make them most useful in African societies which, being close-knit in general, place great stock in relational delicacy and tact.

Riddles are closely related to proverbs in that they are also brief and based on close observation of nature. Some riddles are a mere word or sound long, for example the Kamba (Kenya) riddle "seh!" whose answer is "A needle stabbed the sand," "seh" being the sound the needle supposedly made on entry. Essentially they are metaphorical; they pose questions (implicit or explicit) to be solved by identifying a thing whose characteristics match those indicated in the question. The analogy might be of sound, rhythm, tone, or appearance (for example the Yoruba "a thin staff touches earth and sky" whose answer is rain), and it might be simply metaphorical, as in the Sotho riddle from South Africa, "a tree on which all birds sit"—a chief.

Proverbs are usually not associated with special occasions but occur virtually anytime people speak; riddles, by contrast, are confined to a few special instances of verbal gaming and are for that reason less popular. Some scholars have dismissed them as being of minor and childish interest, meant for mere entertainment rather than education. That judgment is only partially correct, however. Among the Yoruba, for example, riddling is typically a preliminary to evening storytelling. The riddles exercise the intellect and bring it to a state of heightened alertness before the telling of the tales from which the listeners must extract important morals. Riddles are thus kin to dilemma tales,

which also demand the application of intelligence to solving difficult problems. As for the relegation of riddles to childish interest, it can be rebutted with the fact that in Nigerian circles riddles are often an item on the entertainment program for adult birthday parties and wedding receptions.

The closeness between proverbs and riddles is evident in the following Yoruba proverb-riddle: "The elephant died and Mangudu ate it; the buffalo died and Mangudu ate it; Mangudu died but found no creature to eat it." As a proverb it could refer to a person who always came to the aid of those in need, but found no succor in his or her own time of need. As a riddle its answer is the grave.

See also **Language; Languages; Literatures in African Languages; Literatures in European Languages.**

BIBLIOGRAPHY

Finnegan, Ruth. *Oral Literature in Africa*. Oxford: Clarendon Press, 1970.

Harries, Lyndon. "The Riddle in Africa." *Journal of American Folklore* 84 (1971): 377–393.

Okpewho, Isidore. *African Oral Literature: Backgrounds, Character, and Continuity*. Bloomington: Indiana University Press, 1992.

Owomoyela, Oyekan. *Yoruba Proverbs*. Lincoln: University of Nebraska Press, 2005.

Seitel, Peter. "Proverbs: The Social Use of Metaphor." In *Folklore Genres*, ed. Dan Ben-Amos. Austin: University of Texas Press, 1976.

OYEKAN OWOMOYELA

TRANSLATION

Translation and lack of translation affect the daily lives of African people no less than political, economic, social, and cultural activities in African countries. Over 2,000 languages are spoken in Africa. Historically, translation and multilingualism have been essential to intercultural communication, and this remains the case. Many, perhaps most, people in Africa are multilingual and often are adept at practical translation. In most African countries, the language of the former colonial country remains the language of government, business, and education, even though only a minority of the population may speak it. Colonial governments and postcolonial dictatorships seldom made efforts to translate legal documents or government policy statements into the languages understood by most African subjects. In addition, the provision of education, health care, and social services has often been constrained by limited translation and interpretation capability. In post-apartheid South Africa and since the 1990s in countries with strong democratization movements, there has been considerable effort devoted to translation of medical, legal, and policy documents into various vernaculars. Translation is of particular importance in countries where tourism is significant to the economy. Language and translation training are provided by government-sponsored and private schools.

There has been little study of translation in Africa, and most of the few available studies of translation focus on literary translation into English or French. The works most widely translated into African languages have been the Bible, the Qur'an, John Bunyan's *The Pilgrim's Progress*, and Shakespeare's plays. Bible translation work has been extensive and is ongoing, both in translation of the Bible into additional languages and in the revision of existing translations. *The Pilgrim's Progress* has been translated into eighty African languages. There have been sixty translations of Shakespeare's plays into languages of South Africa. A few works by major African authors have also been translated into African languages. Works by authors such as Chinua Achebe, Ngũgĩ wa Thiong'o, and Wole Soyinka have been translated into Swahili. In South Africa, there has been extensive translation between English and Afrikaans.

During the colonial era, missionaries and colonial officials translated a variety of additional texts into African languages and also collected and translated examples of African-language literatures. Although many of these translations are based on handwritten transcriptions of spoken words and are only of historical interest, a few translations from this period, such as William E. Taylor's (1856–1927) *Saws from Swahililand* and Robert S. Rattray's (1881–1938) *Akan-Ashanti Tales*, are of enduring value. Another example, recently translated into English, is the collection of Swahili historical poems by German colonial officials now available in the volume *Kala Shairi*.

Anthropologists and historians have also collected, transcribed, and translated a wide range of African language texts. Notable translations by anthropologists have included those in Melville J. (1895–1963) and Frances S. Herskovit's (b. 1897) *Dahomean Narrative*, Karin Barber and Báyò Ògúndijo's *Yoruba Popular Theater*, Peter Seitel's *See So That We May See*, and Kelly Askew's *Performing the Nation*. Johannes Fabian (b. 1937) and Vincent de Rooij (b. 1962) provide English translations for most of the texts in their *Archives of Popular Swahili* on their Internet site "Language and Popular Culture in Africa" (http://www2.fmg.uva.nl/lpca/).

Historians who have translated major works or other texts in African languages into English have included John Hunwick (*Sharia in Songhay* and *Timbuktu and the Songhay Empire*), Mustapha Kane and David Robinson (*The Islamic Regime of Fuuta Tooro*), Sarah Mirza and Margaret Strobel (*Three Swahili Women*), Rex S. O'Fahey (b. 1940; *Land in Dar Fur*), Randall L. Pouwels (*The Shaf'i Ulama of East Africa*), Leroy Vail and Landeg White (b. 1940; *Power and the Praise Poem: Southern African Voices in History*), and Charles Van Onselen (*The Seed Is Mine*).

The majority of English translations of African literary works were published from the 1960s to the 1990s in the Heinemann African Writers Series. Significant translations from French in this series included Léopold Sédar Senghor's *Nocturnes*, Tchicaya U. Tamsi's *Selected Poems*, Mongo Beti's *Mission to Kala*, Ferdinand Oyono's *Houseboy*, and Ousmane Sembène's *God's Bits of Wood*. Works originally written in Portuguese that were published in the series included Luis Bernardo Honwana's *We Killed Mangy Dog and Other Mozambique Stories*, Lília Momplé's *Neighbors*, José Luandino Vieira's *Luuanda: Short Stories of Angola*, *The Real Life of Domingos Xavier*, and *Poems from Angola*. Works translated from Arabic in the series included Naguib Mafhouz's *Miramar*, Tayeb Salih's *Wedding of Zein*, *Season of Migration to the North*, and *An Egyptian Childhood: The Autobiography of Taha Hussein*. Translations of works in other African languages published in the series included Ngũgĩ wa Thiong'o's novels *Devil on the Cross and Matigari*, Ngũgĩ wa Thiong'o and Ngugi wa Mirii's *I Will Marry When I Want*, *Amadu's Bundle: Fulani Tales of Love and Djinns*, *Igbo Traditional Verse*, and Thomas Mofolo's *Chaka*. During the same period, Oxford University Press published translations of oral literatures in the *Oxford Library of African Literature* series.

More recently, American University in Cairo Press has published numerous English translations of works in Arabic, as has the University of Texas Press in its *Modern Middle Eastern Literature in Translation Series*. The University Press of Virginia has published English translations of works in French by African authors, including a bilingual collection of the poetry of Léopold Sédar Senghor. Other publishers that have produced English translations of works by African authors have included Zed Press, Michigan State University Press, and Red Sea Press/Africa World Press. English translations of African language epics have included *The Mwindo Epic* and *The Epic of El Hadj Umar Taal of Fuuta*. Excerpts from translations of twenty-five West, North, and Central African epics are included in *Oral Epics from Africa*.

Translators and editors have used a variety of strategies to resolve the difficulties of translating poetry. For example, two translators, one of whom was a poet, translated each of the poems in *Modern Arabic Poetry*. Similarly, the poet Charles Cantalupo collaborated with the author Reesom Haile to translate the latter's poetry in Tigrinya, and Red Sea Press published bilingual editions of the poems with the Tigrinya text written in Ge'ez. The publisher also produced CDs that included the poems and the translations.

See also **Achebe, Chinua; Apartheid; Beti, Mongo; Languages; Literatures in African Languages; Literatures in European Languages; Mahfouz, Naguib; Ngũgĩ wa Thiong'o; Postcolonialism; Salih, Tayeb; Sembène, Ousmane; Senghor, Léopold Sédar; Soyinka, Wole.**

BIBLIOGRAPHY

Amadu, Malum. *Amadu's Bundle: Fulani Tales of Love and Djinns*. Collected by Gulla Kell. Trans. Ronald Moody. London: Heinemann Educational, 1972.

Askew, Kelly. *Performing the Nation: Swahili Music and Cultural Politics in Tanzania*. Chicago: University of Chicago Press, 2002.

Barber, Karin, and Báyò Ògúndijo, ed. and trans. *Yoruba Popular Theater: Three Plays by the Oyin Adéjobi Company*. Atlanta, Georgia: African Studies Association, 1994.

Beti, Mongo. *Mission to Kala*, trans. Peter Green. London: Heinemann Educational, 1964.

Caam, Birahim. *The Epic of El Hadj Umar Taal of Fuuta*, trans. Samba Diop. Madison: African Studies Program, University of Wisconsin-Madison, 2000.

Egudu, Romanus N., and Donatus Nwoga. *Igbo Traditional Verse*. London: Heinemann, 1973.

Farsy, Shaykh Abdallah Salih. *The Shafʿi Ulama of East Africa, ca. 1830–1970. A Hagiographic Account*, trans. Randall L. Pouwels. Madison: African Studies Program, University of Wisconsin-Madison, 1989.

Haile, Reesom. *We Have Our Voice*, trans. Charles Cantulupo. Lawrenceville, NJ: Red Sea Press, 2000.

Herskovits, Melville J., and Frances S. Herskovits. *Dahomean Narrative*. Evanston, IL: Northwestern University Press, 1958.

Hofmeyr, Isabel. "How Bunyan Became English: Missions, Translation and the Discipline of English Literature," *Journal of British Studies* 11 (2002): 84–119.

Jayyusi, Salma. *Modern Arabic Poetry: An Anthology*. New York: Columbia University Press, 1987.

Johnson, John William; Thomas Hale; and Stephen Belcher, eds. *Oral Epics from Africa: Vibrant Voices from a Vast Continent*. Bloomington: Indiana University Press, 1997.

Kala, Shairi. *German East Africa in Swahili Poems*, eds. Gudrun Miehe, Katrin Bromber, Said Khamis, and Rolf Grosserhode. Koln, Germany: Rudiger Koppe Verlag, 2002.

Kane, Mustapha, and David Robinson, et al. *The Islamic Regime of Fuuta Tooro*. East Lansing: African Studies Center, Michigan State University, 1984.

Mafhouz, Naguib. *Miramar*, trans. Fatma Moussa. London: Heinemann, 1978.

Mirza, Sarah, and Margaret Strobel. *Three Swahili Women*. Bloomington: Indiana University Press, 1989.

Mofolo, Thomas. *Chaka*, trans. Daniel Kunene. London: Heinemann, 1981.

Ngũgĩ wa Thiong'o. *Devil on the Cross*. London: Heinemann, 1982.

Ngũgĩ wa Thiong'o. *Matigari*, trans. Wangui wa Goro. London: Heinemann, 1987.

O'Fahey, Rex Sean, trans. *Land in Dar Fur: Charters and documents from the Dar Fur Sultanate*. Cambridge, U.K.: Cambridge University Press, 1983.

Oyono, Ferdinand. *Houseboy*, trans. John Reed. London: Heinemann Educational, 1966.

Rattrey, Robert Sutherland. *Akan-Ashanti Folk-tales*. Oxford: The Clarendon Press, 1930.

Ṣālih, al-Ṭayyib. *The Wedding of Zein and Other Stories*, trans. Denys Johnson-Davies. Washington, DC: Three Continents Press, 1985.

Ṣāliḥ, al-Ṭayyib. *Season of Migration to the North*, trans. Denys Johnson-Davies. London: Penguin, 2003.

Seitel, Peter. *See So That We May See: Performances and Interpretations of Traditional Tales from Tanzania*. Bloomington: Indiana University Press, 1980.

Sembène, Ousmane. *God's Bits of Wood*, trans. Francis Price. London: Heinemann Educational, 1969.

Senghor, Léopold Sédar. *Nocturnes*, trans. John Reed and Clive Wake. London: Heinemann Educational, 1969.

Senghor, Léopold Sédar. *Collected Poetry*, trans. Melvin Dixon. Charlottesville: University of Virginia Press, 1991.

She-karisi Rureke. *The Mwindo Epic*, trans. Daniel Biebuyck and Kahombo C. Mateene. Berkeley: University of California Press, 1971.

Taha Hussein. *An Egyptian Childhood: The Autobiography of Taha Hussein*, trans. Evelyn Henry Paxton. London: Heinemann, 1981.

Tamsi, Tchicaya U. *Selected Poems*, trans. Gerald Moore. London: Heinemann Educational, 1970.

Taylor, William Ernest. *African Aphorisms or Saws from Swahililand*. London: Sheldon Press, 1924.

Vail, Leroy, and Landeg White. *Power and the Praise Poem: Southern African Voices in History*. Charlottesville: University of Virginia Press, 1991.

Van Onselen, Charles. *"The Seed in Mine": The Life of Kas Maine, a South African Sharecropper, 1894–1985*. New York: Hill and Wang, 1996.

Wolfers, Michael. *Poems from Angola*. London: Heinemann, 1979.

Wright, Laurence. "Shakespeare in South Africa: Alpha and 'Omega.'" *Postcolonial Studies* 7, no. 1 (2004): 63–81.

ANN BIERSTEKER

WOMEN WRITERS, NORTHERN AFRICA

Maghrebi women writers are well known for postcolonial literary productions and autobiographical writings. These writings are rooted in social realities and seek to challenge institutional discourses, (re)define the architecture of the public and private spaces, and promote change. This literature is mainly couched in French and Arabic. Francophone literature started in the late 1960s and beginning of the 1970s, more than a decade after the independence of Maghrebian countries (1956 for Morocco and Algeria, and 1962 for Algeria). The pioneer Francophone Maghrebi women writers, such as Fatema Mernissi (Morocco) and Assia Djebar (Algeria) were urban, educated, and belonged to the elite. In her writings, Mernissi

addresses the male exploitation of the Arab-Islamic political system. She describes the painful relationship between women and political Islam, maintaining that men have always used religion to obtain and maintain power and exclude women. Djebar has written extensively about Algeria and its struggle from colonial powers. She depicts the suffering of Algerian women and their contributions to the war of independence. Tunisia's Azza Filali (2003), from a younger generation, depicts middle-class and well-educated women; her female characters have university degrees and professions that allow them economic independence. Filali's heroines are active both at home and at work. In contrast, men come home to eat, read the newspapers, and watch television.

From the early 1970s onward, Maghrebi women's Francophone literature was accompanied by women's literature in Arabic. Leila Abouzeid and Khnata Bennouna (1967) of Morocco are two examples. Whether in French or Arabic, Maghrebi women's writings tackle the same topics: women's oppression and struggle for self-expression. In the early twenty-first century, Maghrebi women's writings are multilingual and versatile. The main axes around which reflection is organized reside at the crossroads between social structures, political institutions and their agendas, cultural values and norms, and economic constraints. Imagination in the Maghrebi women's writings is often shaped by the stories told by mothers in childhood. Leila Abouzeid (2000) is one example.

A significant aspect these writings is that they are so rooted in oral cultures and traditions. The emerging vibrant literature, female cinema industry, and other media are using the best of orature to retrace and relocate women's history in Morocco, Algeria, Tunisia, and Mauritania.

In contrast to written literature, orature is orally composed and transmitted, and often created to be verbally and communally performed. Central to this creation is language. Language is the primary means of learning and transmitting one's culture, and it is used to help define and distinguish different ethnic groups and cultures. Maghrebi women's voices are multilingual and multiethnic. However, of all women's oral tongues, Berber is the most female of all. Thanks to women, Berber survived for more than 3,000 years despite that it has never been the official language of a central government (even under Berber dynasties), and despite that it has always had to compete with strong, often religion-backed languages such as Phoenician, Latin, and Arabic.

Oral texts comprise poems, songs, folktales, and testimonies. In addition to their aesthetic beauty, the oral texts show that, by detaining religious and sacred healing power, as well as leadership skills and nationalistic fervor, women were not only prominent in their family, community, and country, but they also held the creative power to express their deep personal concerns in an environment that has been hostile to such an expression. Many of the texts show that women reacted orally to diverse matters relating to family, culture, society, community, leadership, nationalistic drives, language loyalty, and the inner self.

Spiritual and political guidance sometimes constitute a natural mix in Maghrebi women's orature. Such female leadership relies more on recognized personal power than on institutionalized authority. Kahena was a notorious Berber queen and army leader who was born and lived in the Aures Mountains in Algeria some time in the 600s CE. She is depicted in Ibn Khaldun's Al-Muqaddimah as the woman who dared defy the Arabs. The myths and legends of Kahena are used in the literature.

Orature was also used by North African women to express strong rebellion and anger against the European colonizers. Although their voices were not recorded in the official historical accounts of nationalist movements, many of them were so strong that they have been transmitted throughout the decades that followed the independence of the North African countries and immortalized in popular songs and testimonies. Also, old women have kept alive many poems, songs, and oral testimonies. In Morocco, the poems of Tawgrat Walt Issa N'ait Sokhman, a Berber illiterate and semi blind professional poet who lived at the end of the nineteenth and beginning of the twentieth centuries, are an example of such orally transmitted works. Tawgrat's poems are crucial for highlighting the Middle Atlas armed resistance. In addition to urban areas, Moroccan armed resistance took place in the Rif Mountains in the north, the Middle Atlas in the center, and the High Atlas in the south.

See also **Abouzeid, Leila; Djebar, Assia; Ibn Khaldun, Abd al-Rahman; Kahena; Literatures in African Languages; Mernissi, Fatima; Women.**

BIBLIOGRAPHY

Djebar, Assia. *Fantasia, An Algerian Cavalcade*, trans. Dorothy S. Blair. Portsmouth, NH: Heinemann, 1993.

Ibn Khaldun, A. *The Muqaddimah, An Introduction to History*, abridged version. trans. Franz Rosenthal. Princeton, NJ: Princeton University Press, 2004.

Sadiqi, Fatima. *Women, Gender and Language in Morocco.* Leiden, The Netherlands: Brill, 2002.

FATIMA SADIQI

WOMEN WRITERS, SUB-SAHARAN AFRICA

In Africa one could safely say that women's writing came on the wings of freedom. With the exception of South Africa and the Portuguese colonies, most African countries had liberated themselves from colonialism by the late 1950s or early 1960s. A decade later, women writers started to appear all over the continent, bringing the African woman's point of view into the public sphere for the first time, thus breaking the ancestral custom which barred women from public speaking. For African women, writing came as a double liberation, first from the oppression of colonialism and second from the patriarchal imposition of silence.

As writers in European languages, African women belong to a relatively new literary tradition, born for the most part of colonialism and engaged in the reaction against it after World War II. The late 1950s was a watershed period for African letters, with the appearance of such young male novelists as Mongo Beti, Camara Laye, Cheikh H. Kane, Chinua Achebe, Ngũgĩ wa Thiong'o and Wole Soyinka. Brought up under colonialism, these young writers came of age with independence and thus simultaneously became the witnesses of their liberation and the creators of a new African literature.

As for women writers, very few wrote during the colonial period, and those who did were Anglophone. These include Adelaide Casely-Hayford (1868–1959) from Sierra Leone and her daughter Gladys May Casely-Hayford or Aquah Laluah (1904–1959); Mabel Dove-Danquah (b. 1910) from the Gold Coast (Ghana); and Caroline Ntseliseng Klaketla (b. 1918), who was the first woman from

Lesotho to be published. African women's writing became formally and globally recognized with the Nigerian novelist Flora Nwapa's first novel, *Efuru*, published in 1966 by Heinemann in London. Thirty years later, African women writers constituted an ever-increasing literary presence on the continent. In sub-Saharan Africa at the close of the twentieth century, women's writing was entering its second generation. Although a fair amount of poetry, songs, and plays are written in various African vernaculars, the bulk of the corpus is in European languages and more precisely in French and English.

This essay considers female novelists writing in French and English who are of African descent. The rationale behind inclusion is not a question of race but rather of history and analytical coherence. Black African women writers, regardless of their specific cultures and languages, share a major historical experience: the trauma of a colonial past. However, an exception will be made in the case of the Nobel Prize–winner Nadine Gordimer. Her work will be discussed briefly in the section on South Africa. Furthermore, they are linked by a commonality of traditions and customs that can be found in many African societies, such as polygamy; the importance of motherhood; gender-defined field and household tasks, which are basically the same all over the continent; as well as the major role women have always played in commerce and storytelling. To these common experiences one must add the joint heritage of oral literature, or "orature," defined by the Ugandan literacy critic Pio Zirimu as any unwritten creativity. Although these unwritten texts vary with each African culture, epic and initiation poems, songs, folktales, and proverbs are found all over the continent. The oral literature of Africa represents an enormous literary corpus that is as much an integral part of the contemporary African writer's inspiration and influence as the Western literary canon learned in European schools. This rich and diverse common background gives to the African woman's writing a remarkable coherence of vision in spite of the cultural differences.

In contemporary African societies, plagued by economic and social difficulties, women and the family constitute the cornerstone of the social stability upon which the future of the continent will be built. Keenly aware of this fact, African women writers cast a cold eye on their respective societies and use their fictional worlds to denounce ancestral misogyny and the many injustices that are and have always been inflicted against women. In their criticisms of certain traditional mores such as polygamy, forced marriages, genital mutilation, and limited access to education, they exhibit what the West would interpret as a feminist attitude. And yet, most female novelists refuse the label "feminist" as another Western ideological frame into which they must fit. They distance themselves from an ideology that was elaborated for a world that bears very little resemblance to their own. African women's demands for equality and the abandonment of certain traditions no longer valid are not to be viewed as strictly gender related, but rather as comprising their participation in the larger goal of nation building. For example, as a rule African women have the right to vote; many have occupied ministerial posts, and in 2006 Ellen Johnson-Sirleaf was elected president of Liberia. But in many instances girls still do not have access to education. In contemporary Africa, the state came into existence before the nation, and African women writers envision their liberation in the context of a nation in the making, which implies deep social change as well as political will.

THE WRITERS AND THEIR AUDIENCE

But who are these women who, going against the traditional grain, feel that the time has come for them to speak up? Are they the modern avatar of the griots so prominent in traditional West Africa, or that of the ancestral storytellers? This filiation, proposed by many critics, is in fact quite problematic. For if it holds, the female griots or praise singers, in contrast to their present or past male counterparts, never sing the history of the group or the royal genealogy. As praise singers, they can be at the disposal of a single, notable individual. They often perform traditional songs at weddings or festivities. In fact, their role is defined by centuries of practice, and the range of their creativity remains in their performance and vocal quality.

The same can be said of the storyteller, whose role is to teach her audience, mostly women and children, the wisdom of the clan, the tales being as a rule didactic in intent. If, according to Chinua Achebe, the modern writer is to be the teacher of his or her people, the message of the written text differs radically from the oral one. Contemporary African writers in general, but female writers in particular, do not praise the tradition, nor do they wish to maintain the status quo—quite to the contrary. The written word of women weaves subversive tales: texts that are no longer the new performance of an old story but a creation born of the writer's imaginary world, a private universe spun from the experiences and emotions of an individual often in conflict with her own culture. It may be that the solitude essential to writing—especially writing in a foreign language-inevitably distances the writer from her social context.

So who are these women writers? They are, for the most part, Western educated and the product of some of the best French and British schools. They write in a language that is not theirs, the language of the former colonialist. This plight of the African writers sentenced to create a whole literature in an imposed language was the object of passionate discussion among the male writers of the first generation. The debate is still open and is revisited periodically. Interestingly, women writers show very little anguish in regard to the language question. They see French or English as a tool which gives them access to self-expression, a means "to break the silence," to quote Calixthe Beyala. This desire to be heard publicly, to be present, to have a voice and to give a voice to the silent majority of women, is an end in itself. Like the Senegalese writer Nafissatou Diallo (b. 1941), who feels that she did not write just to tell a story but to break the taboos that prevent women from publicly lifting the veil from their private thoughts, the African woman writer, willingly or not, speaks not only for herself but often serves as the spokesperson for the women of her society. Conscious of this grave responsibility, the Nigerian critic and poet Molara Ogundipe-Leslie (b. 1949) considers that the African woman writer has a triple obligation: as a woman, as a writer, and as a third-world citizen. Not all women writers espouse this ontology, but as a rule they agree, even if they feel burdened by it, that when they speak their voice is plural.

But for whom do they write? For the Western public, which has easy access to the books that are mostly published in Europe, although publishing houses are present here and there in Africa. In an interview given to the *New York Times*, the Nigerian novelist Buchi Emecheta (b. 1944) said that it was time for Africa to tell its own story in its own terms. Tsitsi Dangarembga (b. 1959), a poet, playwright, novelist and filmmaker from Zimbabwe, said she wanted to write because she realized that she was absent from the books that she read. As for the African public, only the educated segment of the population is literate, and this means fewer women than men read. And yet, Africans show an ever-increasing interest in their literature and, according to the Senegalese novelist Aminata Sow Fall, those who are unable to read manage to have books read to them.

The immense success of Mariama Bâ's first novel, *Une si longue lettre* (1979; published in English as *So Long a Letter* in 1981), underscores this point. This novel marks a turning point in the history of the African novel in that for the first time, the narrative voice is that of the female protagonist telling her own story. The emergence of this first-person narration, the overwhelming presence of this fictional "I," was revolutionary in the literary context of the time. In contrast to the autobiographical first person much in favor in Western women's writing, which represents only the narrator-author, the fictional "I" of Mariama Bâ's heroine is collective. It represents the voice of the Senegalese woman, telling her society and the world that she exists as an individual, that she is suffering from societal injustices, and that from now on she will decide how to live her life. The novel became a best seller whose success is yet to be equaled, thus indicating the need that women had to read their own story: for the first time they had a voice.

WRITING ABOUT THEMSELVES

What do African women write about? Before answering this question, it must be noted that in spite of the enormous cultural diversity that characterizes the African continent, the cohesiveness of women writers' preoccupations comes as a remarkable yet not so surprising finding. After all, most African states are experiencing the same postcolonial socioeconomic difficulties, which greatly affect the welfare of women and children, particularly in the urban areas. Furthermore, the status of women, which stems from traditional rural customs in effect all over the continent since time immemorial, is confronted everywhere with the forces of change brought on by women's access to education and their newly established rights as citizens.

Women write about themselves; from the 1970s onward, a fair amount of autobiographies were published in conjunction with the appearance of the feminine novel. In Francophone Africa, Nafissatou Diallo led the way with her autobiography, *De Tilène au plateau: Une enfance dakaroise* (1975; published in English as *A Dakar Childhood* in 1982), followed in 1983 by the remarkable *Le baobab fou* (*The Abandoned Baobab: The Autobiography of a Senegalese Woman*, 1991) by Ken Bugul (Marietou M'Baye) and by Andrée Blouin's *My Country, Africa: Autobiography of the Black Pasionaria*, which, oddly enough, was written in English with the help of an American woman. According to the Bénin critic Irène Assiba d'Almeida, these three texts share a common goal, that of autobiography as a means for self-discovery. A similar claim could be made for the works of Anglophone writers such as Charity Waciuma's *Daughter of Mumbi* (1969), Noni (Nontando) Jabavu's autobiographical novel *Drawn in Color: African Contrasts* (1960), Sekai Nzenza's *Zimbabwean Woman: My Own Story* (1988) and the Kenyan Marjorie Oludhe Macgoye's *Coming to Birth* (1986). These autobiographies read as a personal rendition of their authors' lives, but they also weave themselves with the history of a nation thus stand as feminine and political testimonies, valuable for the Western and African reader alike.

Women also write about themselves in their fiction, which represents the main corpus of their literary production. The fictional writing of African women can be analyzed along three main axes or thematic fields of creative inquiry: the world of women; women in the world; and the world according to women.

The world of women refers to the gendered psychic space into which women are born and in which they find themselves locked, fulfilling the role that society has allocated them in the name of biology. Consequently, in female fiction the first role to be revisited is that of motherhood. The maternal image so prominently explored by male writers of the first generation, and particularly in Francophone fiction, in which the mother often symbolizes Africa in its ancestral glory, is

demystified in women's fiction. Here, mothers and mothers-in-law usually occupy secondary roles. Their rigid attitudes anchored in the past are seen as a negative force burdening the young generation, which they often beat into compliance through emotional blackmail.

In traditional thinking, maternity and sterility, like a Janus mask, represent the two faces of the African woman's destiny. Women writers reject this concept, which reduces woman to her biology and promotes motherhood to the rank of an institution. Rather, they portray motherhood as a choice and not an obligation; they insist that being a mother is not tantamount to being a woman. Buchi Emecheta, in her famous novel *The Joys of Motherhood* (1979), whose title is borrowed from Flora Nwapa's *Efuru*, enlarges the doubt expressed by Nwapa as to the validity of a woman's wanting children above all else, even though motherhood does not always lead to fulfillment. Emecheta, with the piercing irony reflected in her novel's title, denounces vigorously what the American poet Adrienne Rich calls "the institutionalization of motherhood."

This is not to imply that women writers are opposed to motherhood. Simply, they view the act of bearing children as a reality and not a fatality—a reality which in contemporary Africa is not without tragic overtones in view of the economic difficulties affecting many rural areas. In today's world, children are no longer automatically a blessing. Calixthe Beyala in her novel *Tu t'appelleras Tanga* (1988; published in English as *Your Name Shall Be Tanga* in 1996) denounces the plight of children who populate the streets of big-city slums, often abused by their parents who brought them into a world where they are no longer a gift or a sign of wealth. Similarly, Mariama Barry in *La Petite peule* (2001; The young peul girl) portrays the selfishness of the parents who disregard their children's basic needs for understanding and love.

As for sterility, it is still regarded among many in today's Africa as a woman's ultimate tragedy. Women writers de-dramatize this subject in pointing out that contrary to traditional thinking, a barren woman is still a woman. Sterility must not be lived as a humiliation and an existential crisis. Barren women do not deserve the disdain of society. In many novels, the sterile heroine is persecuted by her husband's family as well as her own. In order to conceive, she is portrayed as willing to go to any extreme, consulting local medicine men and ingesting any available potions, driving herself to the edge of despair and even madness, as in Flora Nwapa's short story "The Child Thief," Aminata Maiga Ka's novel *La voie du salut, suivi de le miroir de la vie*, Ntyugwetondo Rawiri's novel *Fureurs et cris de femmes* (1989; Women's furies and cries of women), and the aforementioned *Joys of Motherhood*.

ON MEN

So what are women writers' views of marriage and of husbands? As a rule they are very negative. Polygamy, the customary matrimonial regime of Africa, is not viewed kindly in African letters. Male writers have unanimously denounced it as an injustice toward women as well as an economic disaster in the world economy. Women writers, while agreeing with these arguments, add to their criticism of polygamy another dimension that reflects their priorities. They consider polygamy as an obstacle to the well-being of the couple, since it prevents closeness and trust. They affirm the desirability of monogamy, not as a panacea against the difficulties of marriage and as the promise of instant happiness, but as a mark of respect. Women want to enter the matrimonial bond as equal partners and not as one of many. Furthermore, women writers equate polygamy with a reactionary male mentality detrimental to a healthy interaction between the sexes. To them it is a deterrent to the progress of modern society.

It is in fact male mentality that is at the forefront of the novelists' preoccupation and the subject of their most virulent criticism. Heroes are a scarce commodity in women's writing. Rather, the contemporary African male is put on trial as the source of the majority of African women's problems. This negative portrait of the male, who strives to maintain the social status quo because it is to his advantage, highlights the malaise of a contemporary Africa torn between two worlds. The depiction goes beyond the usual dichotomy of tradition versus modernity so often analyzed by the critics. Rather, it is a question of social power and of generation. The mores of the past corresponded to the reality of agrarian patriarchal societies, where time and wealth had different meaning from that of

the modern world and where women were for the most part a commodity belonging to the group.

Throughout their fictional work, women writers delineate clearly the profound differences which exist among women according to their generation. Older women reject change because somehow it devalues their lives and their suffering. Many African males cling to the patriarchal order because it gives them a sense of power and an identity no longer easily found in their changing society. Younger heroines, often the author's spokesperson, entertain the belief that the future of the continent will not be realized without its women, whose survival lies in the death of the old masculine mentality.

This metaphorical execution is at the core of Tsitsi Dangarembga's novel *Nervous Conditions* (1989), whose heroine begins her narrative by stating, "I was not sorry when my brother died." The death of the brother symbolizes the end of male domination, the end of the patriarchal order. His demise was her only opportunity to further her education in that she was able to take his place. Had he lived, she would have had to stay in the village and the story would never have been told: a story of escape as she calls it; escape from woman's ancestral fate.

In *C'est le soleil qui m'a brûlée* (1987; published in English as *The Sun Hath Looked Upon Me*, 1996), Calixthe Beyala also equates the liberation of woman with the symbolic death of the traditional male. Another provocative example of feminine affirmation in opposition to the patriarchal order is Werewere Liking's *Elle sera de jaspe et de corail* (1983; It shall be of jasper and coral, 1983) subtitled *Journal of a Misovire*. "Misovire" is a neologism invented by the author to offset the word "misogyny," but with a positive twist—the word refers not to a man hater but to a woman who has not yet found a man worthy of her admiration. Contrary to the categorical flat semantic of the word "misogyny," "misovire" connotes many possible interpretations, even a hopeful one (after all, the man may exist), but more importantly offers an opening on the future of gender relationships. This hope for a better understanding between the sexes, not only at the private level but as fundamental to a new social order, is the raison d'être of women writers' criticism of patriarchy.

DEFINING THE NEW AFRICAN WOMAN

Entertaining the dream of a better future for themselves and their societies, women writers are creating the blueprint of the new African woman. Women's writing counts many heroines who, confronted with the difficulties of life, are forced to reconsider their lives and resolve to escape their predicament entirely by themselves. In so doing, they achieve a new consciousness of who they are and more importantly who they want to be. This redefinition of the self, more common in an urban context, does not mean a simple refusal to conform to societal norms but the difficult task of discovering one's own specificity and the strength to move forward.

The paradigm for this newly found self-awareness is Mariama Bâ's protagonist, Ramatoulaye, heroine of *Une si longue lettre*. In this epistolary novel, dedicated to all women and men of good will, the recently widowed Ramatoulaye writes a long letter to her childhood friend Aïssatou, who is now living in the United States. Ramatoulaye's writing starts as a therapeutic exercise in which she pours her heart out, telling her friend of her husband's betrayal after twenty years of marriage, his taking of a second wife the age of their oldest daughter, and his subsequent death, leaving her with nothing but debts to care for their twelve children. Ramatoulaye, who is a teacher, came of age with independence. Free, educated, idealistic, and young, she and her husband participated in the genesis of a nation. Because they shared the same enthusiasm and the same ideals, her husband's betrayal is more than the failing of the flesh, but a breach of faith. A devout Muslim, Ramatoulaye accepted the second wife, even though her children wanted her to divorce. Aïssatou herself had left her husband when, intimidated by his mother, he took a second wife. Ramatoulaye, however, looking at herself in the mirror, realizes that at her age and in her circumstances she has no option but to stay married. Forced to fend for herself because of her husband's death, she slowly emerges as an "I" instead of a "we." The power of words leads her toward a new equilibrium and a discovery of her true self. Through the act of writing she discovers her voice and finds the courage to speak up "after thirty years of silence."

Ramatoulaye's life story resonated with many women, which explains the novel's extraordinary reception in Senegal and the fact that it is now a classic of African letters. But the great appeal of the text resides not in its reflection of the life drama lived by so many but in the vitality of Ramatoulaye, a woman among many who became a heroine and a role model in spite of herself. Becoming aware of who she is, she refuses to slip back into what she must be in order to conform to societal and family expectations. She no longer exists only to please others but also to please herself. She has learned to say no; she has become an individual, a creator of her own destiny. She is also a writer, telling her own story from her point of view, in her own words. Ramatoulaye's story could easily have been a third-person narrative, but through her heroine's writing Bâ introduces the important theme of women's self-generated creativity.

Many African women novelists equate the creative act of writing to maternity. A novel is like a child, "a brain-child" to quote Buchi Emecheta's heroine, Adah, protagonist of *Second-Class Citizen* (1974), who feels that a book is a special offspring because it involves only one progenitor; it is a totally free endeavor, therefore it is the supreme creation. This metaphor of the book as a child seems a natural concept for women whose cultures value them primarily as mothers. To bear a child or write a book constitutes a social act, a contribution to society. Writing, like children, guarantees the immortality of the group, but for women it is also the gateway to equality. The written word implies education; the thirst for knowledge is an overwhelming theme of African female fiction. Very few fictional heroines have second thoughts about the fact that going to school means a Western education. As already mentioned, women writers are a product of Western education, even if they did their schooling in Africa, and in their work they equate education with liberation. They do not subscribe to the cultural angst which tormented some male writers, as evidenced in such works as Mongo Beti's *Mission terminée* (1957; published in English as *Mission to Kala*, 1969), Okot p'Bitek's *Song of Lawino* (1966), Cheikh H. Kane's *L'aventure ambiguë* (1961; published in English as *The Ambiguous Adventure*), and others who saw Western education as what Ngũgĩ wa Thiong'o called another form of colonization. Although they may agree that Western schools constitute a threat to indigenous cultures and traditional mores, as far as they are concerned the benefit outweighs the risk.

Tsitsi Dangarembga's *Nervous Conditions* presents a particular interest in this subject, since the cultural alienation of its protagonist, Nyasha, leads this character to self-destruction. Nyasha's rejection of the West is antithetical to her cousin Tambu's embracing of Western education, although the latter knows full well that there is a price to be paid for her actions. The difference between the two girls stems from their socioeconomic backgrounds. Nyasha comes from the well-to-do branch of the family; Tambu is a poor relation from the bush where she was raised in poverty. She cannot afford to have an existential crisis; but once educated she will empathize with her cousin's plight and write about it, to pay homage to her suffering and their differences. In this text, the author reexamines a common theme of African literature, the city versus the country, and it is evident that her heroine entertains no nostalgia about life in the bush. For her the village is not a lost childhood paradise as it is sometimes portrayed in male fiction, but a harsh place where harsh demands are made of women. Tambu's sentiments echo those of many young African women, fictional or otherwise. The city, in spite of its many pitfalls, provides the hope of a better life, but most of all the possibility of education.

ATTACKING SOCIAL AND POLITICAL ILLS

The vision that women writers have of their world is that it must change to accommodate their aspirations to live as equal partners with men, to be educated, and to control their own bodies. As artists and as women, they are most eager to be instrumental in bringing on that change.

As citizens of free states, African women writers, like their male counterparts, denounce the social and political abuses of their respective countries. African literature being a literature "engagée," women novelists no doubt echo Liking's "misovire," asking herself "will my writing be useful?" Almost twenty years later, Ken Bugul answers this question stating in an essay on writing "il faut écrire l'espoir" (hope must be written). Consequently, in their work they address some of the most problematic issues plaguing African societies today. Among the societal issues they engage are witchcraft, infanticide, the corrupting power of money, prostitution, AIDS, and the increasing violence plaguing many African societies.

It will suffice in this essay to give an overview of women writers' viewpoints on the power of money

and the social and political ills that it generates in African societies. This troubling reality is a major theme of the postcolonial novel. It is worth noting that female novelists in their denunciation of the overall immorality of their respective societies do not only accuse the elite in power but point out that the average citizen, man or woman, bears some responsibility for the moral decay of the state. In putting their compatriots on trial, it would seem that women writers are trying to energize the silent majority into a more active role in redressing of the moral drift.

For example, in *La grève des bàttu* (1979; published in English as *The Beggars' Strike, or, The Dregs of Society*, 1986) Aminata Sow Fall revisits the theme of corruption already explored in Ousmane Sembène's novel *Xala* (1973). Although both authors denounce the same problem in the same context—corruption in the city of Dakar—they view the situation quite differently. Sembène condemns corruption in the name of a Marxist orthodoxy, while Fall deplores it in the name of failing moral convictions. This ethical preoccupation has been at the forefront of women's writing from the beginning. In Senegal, Fall has been a constant critic of the unconditional valorization of money, a subject that she explores once again in her latest novel *Festins de la détresse* (2005; Feasts of anguish). In Nigeria and Ghana, respectively, Nwapa and Ama Ata Aidoo deplore throughout their work the nefarious influence of money. The second generation of writers, among them Beyala, Ntyugwentondo Rawiri, Liking, Veronique Tadjo, Tanella Boni, and Emecheta denounce such corruption even more aggressively.

The most troubling manifestation of the corrupting power of money remains female prostitution, rampant in late-twentieth-century African urban centers. The character of the young prostitute occupies an important place in African letters in general. For the male novelists, she is often a positive protagonist, examples being the heroine, Penda, in Sembène's *Les bouts de bois de Dieu* (1960; published in English as *God's Bits of Wood*, 1962), the eponymous Jagua Nana of Ekwensi, and Wanda in Ngũgĩ's *Petals of Blood* (1977). The image of the prostitute with the heart of gold and the right political convictions remains a masculine myth. In women's writing, the character of the prostitute is never romanticized, and prostitution is viewed as a totally negative activity provoked and maintained by a disastrous socioeconomic climate. In women's fiction, prostitution mirrors a pathetic and sordid reality: the young woman who sells herself to a rich man, or "big man," as he is often ironically labeled by the novelists, for an easier life, a good job, or a diploma. The young woman who exercises what Nigerian women call "bottom power" is in the process of becoming a banality. The obsession of the writers with this deplorable state of affairs manifests itself in the brutality of their denunciation. Their verdict is clear; appalling poverty often caused by political corruption and mismanagement gives birth to moral decay.

Among the numerous examples of the moral tragedy of prostitution to be found in women's writing, some situations recur like haunting leitmotivs. One of them describes the mother as a procurer of johns for her own daughter, as in Ntyugwentondon Rawiri's *G'amérakano—Au carrefour* (1988), Nwapa's short story "The Delinquent Adults," Beyala's *Tu t'appelleras Tanga*, and others. The other situation that recurs in stories about prostitution involves the young woman as a willing participant. Often characters are shown as becoming the mistress of a rich man in order to better their material condition, as in Ata Aidoo's short story "Two Sisters." In this narrative, Mercy is a typist who lives with her sister Connie, who is married and expecting a child. Mercy wants more than what she can afford with her salary and she finds "a big man" willing to satisfy her needs. Her sister, who disapproves, will end up accepting gifts from the man and justifying her moral abdication. Here again, the writer levels an ironic and chilling gaze on the complacency of the protagonists, who represent all levels of society and who participate in destroying its moral fiber. Sometimes the desired outcome of prostitution is other than money—in Emecheta's *Double Yoke* (1990), a young student sells herself to an important professor in order to get a good grade.

As for political and ideological conflicts, the fictional universe of women writers closely reflects the malaise of a continent where the political structure is still in the making and neocolonialism is a major but often anonymous player. As for the underprivileged women and children, they are cast adrift in political turmoil over which they have no control: they must submit in order to survive. Their struggle, usually absent from history books, is immortalized in the fictional universe of female novelists.

One of the most dramatic postcolonial conflicts was that of Nigeria: the secession of the eastern region of Biafra and the civil war that followed. This war, which lasted from 1967 to 1970, could not but mark the psyche of Nigerian novelists. Nwapa and Emecheta, the two most famous women writers of the country, bore witness in their fiction, in very different ways, to the violence and senselessness of the conflict. Nwapa, in a collection of short stories *Wives at War* (1980) and a novel *Women Are Different* (1986), depicts the ordeal for the average woman and family trying to survive. Neither ideology nor political arguments are held by the protagonists, who are indifferent to the political circumstances of the conflict gripping their homeland. In fact, in the novel, in order to feed her five children the heroine opens a bakery, an opportunity offered by the war, and manages to get rich. After the war her success is attributed by others to wrongdoing. No negative judgment is passed on the protagonist by the author, but rather an admiring homage is paid to her courage and ingenuity. We feel the author's sympathy for this woman, who in the midst of a situation she does not understand, does what women have done since time immemorial—takes care of her own as best she can.

Emecheta, in her historical novel *Destination Biafra* (1982), differs greatly from Nwapa in the portrait that she gives of the conflict. She was not in Nigeria during the war but being an Igbo (Ibo), she felt the urgency to testify for the women and children who were killed mercilessly during the conflict. She dedicates her book to them. In contrast to Nwapa's heroine, Emecheta's heroine is a young educated woman who belongs to the Nigerian elite. Like Nwapa, she empathizes with the ordinary folk who are helpless victims of a conflict they do not understand; however, her heroine understands very well the political interests and the corruption of those in power, which keep the conflict alive. This awareness gives to the text an urgency, a moral outrage, and an accusative tone absent from Nwapa's text.

After so many years, Biafra still haunts the creative imagination of the younger generation of

Nigerian women, and the very fine novel *Half a Yellow Sun* (2006) by Chimamanda Ngozi Adichie attests to the ongoing anguish and questioning of the past. In 1994, the Rwanda genocide and its moral scandal shook the world. The Tchadian writer Nocky Djedanoum initiated a collective work called *Rwanda: Writing as a Duty to Memory*. Many women writers responded to the challenge and Véronique Tadjo's text *L'ombre d'Imana* (2000; The shadow of Imana: travels in the heart of Rwanda) is a remarkable testimony of inhumanity and the suffering of women. Tadjo brings no answer as to the reason for Rwanda's senseless massacre, but by refusing to forget she keeps the question alive and her work stands as a warning.

The struggle against apartheid and the government that sustained it since 1948 constitutes the major theme of black South African literature. As is often the case, women have played an important though overlooked role in the struggle: their weapons were patience and silence, their struggle quiet and without glory, keeping as best as possible the family together and the dream of freedom alive. For years women waited for their men to come back: from the mine, from jail, from forced labor, while facing alone the brutality and chicanery of the police. South African women writers such as Lauretta Ngcobo and Miriam Tlali have drawn a very fine portrait of the African woman's ordeal and survival against all odds. Tlali, first woman writer of Soweto, in such works as *Muriel at Metropolitan* (1975) and *Amandla* (1980)—both novels were censured by the government—and her collections of short stories, *Mittloti* (1985) and *Soweto Stories* (1989), exposes every facet of women's lives: not only their difficulties with the apartheid regime but the sexism they must face from their own communities. The author provides insight into the daily lives of the common people, their failures and small victories. In her fiction she takes a strong stand against injustice, regardless of who is inflicting it, and refuses to be silent about the brutality of men toward women or the sexual attraction between the races, which occurred in spite of the anti-miscegenation law. Her fictional characters are infused with the energy drawn from moral courage and the clarity of vision of those who have little to lose.

An other aspect of South African women's lives can be found in a collection of short stories titled *You Can't Get Lost in Cape Town* by Zoê Wicomb (1987). In her narratives, she poignantly explores the ambiguous situation of the "colored woman" during the apartheid period, a plight not often examined in South African fiction.

Finally, it seems fitting to mention the work of Nadine Gordimer who stood up against apartheid through her writing and her political actions. She won the Nobel Prize for literature in 1991 for a considerable body of work comprising thirteen novels, around two hundred short stories and several volumes of essays. According to most critics, her most important novels are *Burger's Daughter* (1979), *July's People* (1981), and *My Son's Story* (1990), which deals with post-apartheid South Africa. Nadine Gordimer shares with black South African women writers her struggle against apartheid which she fought relentlessly with great moral courage. As a member of the ANC she lost no opportunities to protest against the cruelty and immorality of the regime.

ALIENATION

As mentioned earlier, women's writing reflects the moral anomie besieging African societies. The alienation of the protagonists underlines the disintegration of the social and moral fiber particularly evident in the large urban centers. Metaphorically, this malaise is often equated with madness, and the alienated character is portrayed as suffering from a mental breakdown. There are many mad women in women's fiction, and the cause of their illness is always man-made, which constitutes a breach with traditional thinking, in which madness is as a rule linked with the other world, the world of spirits off limits to ordinary human intervention. But in the imaginary universe of women novelists, human responsibility is at the core of the madness or depression of the heroine and can therefore be redressed. It is a question of societal will, thus highlighting the moral dimension of women's writing. The multiple causes of the protagonist's mental alienation, be they political, social, or affective, are directly connected to their environment.

With the exception of the South African novelist Bessie Head, political alienation appears mostly in the fiction of the second generation of women writers. Their protagonists express their anger and frustration through uncommon behavior, which is interpreted as provocation by the political power, itself the cause of the characters' subversive behavior. In *Tu t'appelleras Tanga*, Beyala depicts the social and political alienation of two women who, refusing to accept the intolerable behavior of the state, find themselves in prison, subjected to a terrible repression. Their protestation will not be heard except by the reader, so the text itself, written in a lapidary and provocative style, vindicates the ordeal of the protagonists. The writer in her function as witness enshrines for posterity the futile and gallant gestures of the unsung heroine.

This impassioned and useless refusal to submit characterizes Tsitsi Dangarembga's heroine, Nyasha, in *Nervous Conditions*. Her cousin, narrator of the text and helpless witness to Nyasha's descent into madness, which in her case takes the form of anorexia, records the ordeal. Nyasha suffers from an acute identity crisis due in part to the fact that she spent a great part of her childhood in England; upon her return she felt like a foreigner in her own land. But what makes her suffering even more unbearable is the colonized attitude of her father. Unaware of his lost identity, since he is more Westernized than the British masters of his land, he cannot comprehend his daughter's drama. Unable to accept the unfairness of history which has made her into a cultural hybrid, Nyasha lashes out at herself in a self-destructive rage.

As for the social and affective reasons that cause the heroine's profound alienation, they often stem from deeply rooted social mores, such as the importance of ethnicity in traditional society, still operative, or from the opposite, the disintegration of traditional values. Interestingly, Senegalese women writers, critics and witnesses of their society, have throughout their work underlined the disastrous consequences of these issues. For example, in many novels, the fate of the foreign wife takes on a tragic cast. She finds herself totally isolated and rejected by her in-laws, who often condone the misbehavior of the husband at the expense of common decency. In Mariama Bâ's *Une si longue lettre* (So long a letter) and *Un chant écarlate* (1981; published in English as *Scarlet Song*, 1986), the foreign wives, respectively from Côte d'Ivoire and from France, become ill with unhappiness and grief. In fact, in the second novel, the French wife sinks into total madness and kills her child, who was never accepted by the

Senegalese family because of his mixed parentage. Bâ's novel is not a warning against mixed marriages but rather an accusation against her society of being closed-minded and keeping alive traditional mores that no longer have any meaning.

Even more dramatic is the problem of infanticide, once fairly common in African urban centers. To kill one's child in a culture where maternity is an end in itself can be seen as a form of madness, as it can only be the result of total despair and complete alienation from one's society. Senegalese novelists concerned by this new social drama have, through their fiction, attracted the attention of the public to the fact that these young women are not monsters but desperate young country girls working as maids in the city, who because of their loneliness and naiveté are easily seduced and abandoned by irresponsible young men. These young males are themselves drifting alone in the city, accountable to no one. When the girls realize that they are pregnant and alone, they do not know where and to whom to turn. Shame prevents them from returning to the village, and the indifference and callousness of their employers prevent them from asking for help.

Aminata Maiga Ka in *Le miroir de la vie* (The mirror of life), Aminata Sow Fall in *L'appel des arènes* (1982), Mariama Ndoye in her short story "Yadikône or the Second Birth" from her collection *De vous àmoi* (1990), Ken Bugul's *La folie et la mort* (Madness and death, 2000), Isabelle Boni-Claverie's *La grande dévoreuse* (2000; The great devouring city) depict the ordeal of these girls, and in doing so put African societies on trial, particularly the members of the upper class, who treat the poor as if they were born only to serve. This traditional attitude stems in part from the caste system still in place as well as the loss of values, which in many instances has been replaced by a systemic corruption. It is evident that women novelists, like their male counterparts, see themselves as teachers of their people and hope to serve as catalysts for social change.

This questioning of the world in which all women writers live results in what could be labeled a historical self-consciousness, and since the 1990s many women writers have written interesting essays on a variety of subjects. For example, in Cameroon, Axelle Kabou in *Et si l'Afrique refusait le développement?* (1991; What if Africa refuses development?)

accuses African societies of being mostly responsible for the economic and social chaos besieging their societies. But in Mali, Aminata Traoré, former Minister of Culture, in three successive essays—*L'etau* (1999; The Vise), *Le viol de l'imaginaire* (2002; The rape of imagination), and *Lettre au Président des Français à propos de la Côte d'Ivoire et de l'Afrique en general* (2005; Open letter to the French President on the subject of the Ivory Coast and the African continent)—denounces the mystification of global economics and its negative effects on African development.

In *L'ombre d'Imana* (2000; The shadow of Imana) Véronique Tadjo reflects upon the Rwanda genocide. It is evident that the essay is a new forum for sub-Saharan women writers, a public space in which the writer writes in her own voice, and therefore takes full responsibility for the opinions expressed, no longer hiding behind the mask of a fictional character. This accountability gives the writer's voice a tangible presence since it allows her to claim authority on social and political subjects, not only as a writer but as a citizen, thus politicizing the role of the woman artist.

So what is the world according to women writers? It is neither a utopia nor an unattainable dream, but a tangible world where the pursuit of happiness is a legitimate endeavor. Let it be remembered that happiness as a social concept is a relatively new idea. It appears in Europe in the eighteenth century at a time of great sociopolitical upheaval. It coincides with the desire of people to become citizens, to be in charge of their destiny in a democratic world, not without parallel in modern Africa. In the context of African letters, happiness in women's writing is associated with the hope and dream of a better future at both the social and personal levels.

In other words, happiness is a projection, not yet a reality, but sometimes it can act as a buffer against the harsh demands of big-city slums so forcefully described in Beyala's novels. In *Tu t'appelleras Tanga*, the heroine dreams of the perfect man and a "little house in the meadow" like the ones she has seen in Hollywood movies. Meanwhile, she decides to alter the terrible present and "kidnap happiness" in order to give it to an abandoned street kid by acting as his caring mother, the one he never had. In Zaynab Alkali's *The Stillborn*

(1984), the female protagonist, Li, concludes that even though some dreams are stillborn, others will come to life and succeed if the dreamer is strong enough. She goes back to the city to find her husband, with whom she will share her dream. Finally, Ramatoulaye, the heroine of Bâ's *Une si longue lettre*, ends her long letter with the word "happiness." She says that she will keep on looking for it, and that it will have the face of a man.

See also **Achebe, Chinua; Aidoo, Ama Ata; Apartheid; Bâ, Mariama; Beti, Mongo; Camara Laye; Emecheta, Buchi; Gender; Gordimer, Nadine; Head, Bessie Emery; Johnson-Sirleaf, Ellen; Language: Choice in Writing; Marriage Systems; Ngũgĩ wa Thiong'o; Nwapa, Flora; Sembène, Ousmane; Soyinka, Wole; Women.**

BIBLIOGRAPHY

Andrade, Susan Z. "Rewriting History, Motherhood, and Rebellion: Naming an African Woman's Literary Tradition." *Research in African Literatures* 21, no. 1 (1990): 91–110.

Borgomano, Madeleine. *Voix et visages des femmes dans les livres écrits par les femmes en Afrique francophone.* Abidjan: CEDA, 1989.

Brire, Éloise; Beatrice Rangira-Gallimore; and Marie-Noelle Vibert; eds. "Nouvelles écritures féminines." *Notre librairie*, nos. 117–118 (1994).

Bruner, Charlotte H., ed. *Unwinding Threads: Writing by Women in Africa.* London: Heinemann, 1983.

Busby, Margaret, ed. *Daughters of Africa: An International Anthology of Words and Writings by Women of African Descent from the Ancient Egyptian to the Present.* New York: Pantheon Books, 1992.

Cazenave, Odile. *Femmes rebelles: Naissance d'un nouveau roman africain au feminine.* Paris, L'Harmattan, 1996. Translated as *Rebellious Women: The New Generation of Female African Novelists.* Boulder, CO: Lynne Rienner, 1999.

D'Almeida, Irene Assiba. *Francophone African Women Writers: Destroying the Emptiness of Silence.* Gainesville: University Press of Florida, 1994.

Davies, Carole B., and Anne A. Graves, eds. *Ngambika: Studies of Women in African Literature.* Trenton, NJ: Africa World Press, Inc. 1986.

Guyonneau, Christine H. "Francophone Women Writers from Sub-Saharan Africa." *Callaloo* 24 (1985): 453–478.

Lee, Sonia. *Les romancires du continent noir.* Paris: Hatier, 1994.

Lee, Sonia. "The Emergence of the Essayistic Voice in Francophone African Women Writers: Véronique

Tadjo's *L'Ombre d'Imana*." In *The Modern Essay in French*, ed. Charles Forsdick and Andrew Stafford. Bern, Switzerland: Peter Lang AG, European Academic Publishers, 2005.

Minh-Ha, Trinh. *Woman, Native, Other: Writing Postcoloniality and Feminism*. Indianapolis, Indiana University Press, 1989.

Mortimer, Mildred. *Journeys through the French African Novel*. Portsmouth, NH: Heinemann, 1990.

Mudimbe-Boyi, Elizabeth, ed. "Anglophone and Francophone Women's Writing." *Callaloo* 16, no. 1 (1993).

Mudimbe-Boyi, Elizabeth, ed. "Post-colonial Women's Writing." *L'esprit créateur* 33, no. 2 (1993).

Thiam, Awa. *La parole aux négresses*. Paris: Denoël-Gonthier, 1978.

SONIA LEE

Painting of the African storyteller //Kabbo by W. H. Schroeder. Storytelling, both written and oral, has long been a part of African tradition. Narratives, songs, and ancient written tales have helped to shape the culture of its inhabitants by gaining a more profound signifance with each new generation.

LITERATURE AND THE STUDY OF AFRICA

ORAL TRADITIONS: THE MYTHIC MODEL

It is the task of the storyteller to fashion a connection between two domains, a real world and a mythic realm. Bringing those spheres into alignment establishes the working metaphor in the stories of Lydia umkaSethemba, a Zulu storyteller who performed in 1868. In one of her tales, she limned a complex mythic being, a mountain containing the manifold possibilities of nature. This figure becomes a mirror of the real-life character who is undergoing an identity transformation. One of the myths told in the nineteenth century by a San mythmaker, //Kabbo, occurs at the beginning of the age of creation: from God's dreams emerges San civilization. The mythic center of the San world is created as God subsequently puts all beings and things into their proper places; humans must now learn to make appropriate use of what God has given them.

Nongenile Masithathu Zenani, a Xhosa storyteller, mythically mirrored ostensibly unlike images, crafting complex allusive connections. She performed a prodigious epic, forging a model composed of God, an ancestral mother, and a chimerical ox. Out of this rhythmic combination comes the contemporary Xhosa nation. As Mwindo, in Candi Rureke's version of the Nyanga epic of the Congo, struggles with the various manifestations of his father, his own destructive side is shadowed, at odds with his aunt, Iyangura, who is linked to the positive side of the hero and to the gods, establishing thereby a mythic center. In the griot Bamba Suso's Mandinka version of *Sunjata*, the hero is tested and reveals his stature before he moves to battle with Sumanguru, a supernatural character who attempts to destroy him. The mythic core of this story includes the greatness of the Mandinka past, embodied in the griots who play prominent roles in the epic.

WRITTEN TRADITIONS: SUSTAINING THE MYTHIC MODEL

The rich oral traditions of Africa give rise to an equally resonant written tradition. Naguib Mahfouz's novel, *al-Liss wa-l-kilab*, is a story of a bungling avenger. Just out of prison, he sets about to destroy

Nongenile Masithathu Zenani during a 1972 perform-ance, Nkanga (Gatyana), Transkei, South Africa. The storyteller takes images from the past and links them to images of the present. In that way, there is a regular interaction between the contemporary world and history. PHOTOGRAPH BY HAROLD SCHEUB

those who were responsible for his incarceration: his mentor, his wife, her lover. They are, in his eyes, dogs. But, in his frenzied effort to kill them, he destroys himself. There are mythic centers, Nur and the sheikh, but he does not comprehend the words of the sheikh and he comes to understand his love for Nur too late. In the end, the thief is destroyed by the very dogs that he himself would have killed.

THE MYTHIC PAST

In Yacine Kateb's *Nedjma*, history becomes myth, as the black man of the Arabian Nights ties the real-life Nedjma to history. Now she merges with myth, taken by an ancient man, perhaps her father, and

her lover Rachid, perhaps her brother, into the venerable mythic origins of the Keblout people. She no longer belongs to the two pilgrims who brought her here: she is in effect their religion, their history, their myth; she is subsumed into myth, nature, history, by a black man who may or may not be real, who by his own interpretation is mythic, sent by a jinn.

In *Maru*, by Bessie Head, Margaret Cadmore, the mythic center, has touched Moleka, the heir apparent to the throne, as no one else has been able to do, and in that sense what she has done is important to schemes of the king, Maru. She unlocks Moleka's passion, as she re-creates the world of Dilepe, simultaneously and ironically cre-ating her own future—but partnered with Maru, the political philosopher, rather than with Moleka, the man she loves. She paints a final statement of her affection for Moleka, but he is not to be her destiny. By means of the mythic past, she revitalizes Dilepe through her art, touching its universal and eternal elements.

In J. M. Coetzee's *Life and Times of Michael K*, Michael K is a survivor, a creator, walking the earth as if for the first time, planting the seeds of the future in his mother's ashes, the mythic past. There is an unbroken generational linkage, with the mother before him, and her mother before her, and so back in time; he is eternal, among the survivors: they live close to the earth, in the earth.

CHARACTER AND MYTH

What is at stake in A. C. Jordan's Xhosa novel, *Ingqumbo Yeminyanya*, is the possible shattering of the ancient mythic model that has held Xhosa soci-ety together for so long. But the hero Zwelinzima's fate is far more complicated than that of a man crushed between competing worlds. His fate also springs from his own character, and if he is caught up in the currents of change, it is only because his human concerns and ideals have led him to attempt to harness those currents. Jordan evolves his charac-ter within a broader mythic context.

In Chinua Achebe's *Things Fall Apart*, the *chi* is mythic: "At the most one could say that his *chi* or personal god was good. But the Igbo people have a proverb that when a man says yes his *chi* says yes also. Okonkwo said yes very strongly; so his *chi* agreed." The *chi* and Okonkwo: fate versus free will.

Xhosa storyteller creating a story, Nkanga (Gatyana), Transkei, South Africa, 1967. With her body and her voice, the performer gives resonance to the words that she employs. Dance and music are integral ingredients of storytelling. PHOTOGRAPH BY HAROLD SCHEUB

His father, Unoka, "...had a bad *chi*..., and evil fortune followed him to the grave...." Okonkwo, absent from his Umuofian community because of a seven year exile, returns and considers himself a messiah: "Perhaps I have been away too long."

In written stories as in oral tales, the storyteller uses mirroring images to move the audience into the central character's mind. This is evident in *Efuru*, by Flora Nwapa, in which a cursed doctor and the goddess, Uhamiri, represent the two possibilities of Efuru. One represents her fate if she is moved by her society to its boundaries because of her inability to bear children; the other represents her fate if the society is sufficiently tolerant to allow her to develop her innate talents without reference to her biological state. Efuru questions this mythic connection: Uhamiri is eternal, and she therefore needs no offspring to carry on her greatness; Efuru,

however, is mortal, and her greatness will die with her if she has no progeny.

In Thomas Mofolo's *Chaka*, the hero will control nature, the wind and the storms; the ancestral dead send him their blessings. Chaka bestrides the earth, or so it seems; his very immensity, coupled with and aided by his magical powers, makes him a difficult character with whom to identify, as his callousness cuts off all threads of sympathetic rapport. Supernatural beings reflect Chaka's vision, mirror his frustrations, and become mythic manifestations of his gradual deterioration.

The mythic model in Ben Okri's *Stars of the New Curfew* is Arthur's nightmare: reality and nightmare, reality and myth, are the same. The stars of the new curfew, the human stars of the new dispensation, are a part of Arthur's phantasma. "The earliest storytellers," Okri said, "...wrestled with the mysteries and transformed them into myths which coded the world and helped the community to live through one more darkness, with eyes wide open, and with hearts more set alight."

MYTHIC WOMEN

Buchi Emecheta's novel, *The Slave Girl*, traces the history of Ojebeta, an *ogbanje* child. Her status as an *ogbanje* child becomes the story's mythic center, a child who is born, dies, then is reborn to the same mother repeatedly. Ojebeta, sold into slavery by her brother, Okolie, becomes at seven a slave for Ma Palagada in Onitsha, experiencing the agony of bondage. This occurs against the background of British colonialism in Nigeria. In the end, she is freed, returns to her home, forgives her brother, is married, and like her mother begins to lose her babies. "Slave, obey your master. Wife, honor your husband, who is your father, your head, your heart." The mythic *ogbanje* child becomes the wretched core of a story that has to do with the plight of women.

In Nawal El Saadawi's *Imra'ah 'inda nuqtat al-sifr*, Firdaus, whose name ironically means "paradise," is a woman experiencing a rebarbative experience of gender colonialism, a woman at point zero, living in a male-dominated world. Her mythic center consists of a remembered early childhood relationship with a boy and her close ties to her mother. These propel her during her ultimately futile quest.

Tahar ben Jelloun's *L'enfant de sable* tells of a woman disguised as a man; it is a story shadowed

Zulu storyteller Asilita Philisiwe Khumalo sculpting a story, Nongoma, kwaZulu, South Africa, 1972. The oral performer uses images, usually ancient, to evoke emotional responses from members of the audience. In that way, the audience is worked into the form of the story. PHOTOGRAPH BY HAROLD SCHEUB

by the hero, Antar, the epic providing an ironic blueprint for the development of this modern retelling of that storied prince; the masculine ideal of heroism is undercut or strengthened by the fact that the ideal is but a mask. It is also a mirror: a child is created, or re-created, but the substance of creation is sand, a girl in the process of being reformed into a boy, the slow fabrication of a frail mask that covers the face but not the mind and the spirit of the central character. As the veil is being crafted, the sand-child being formed, another story is developing, within the narrator's tale, about the person beneath the mask. Two stories, the creation of an illusion and the material being made into that illusion, will reach the stage at which illusion and reality inevitably collide.

The basic movement of Tsitsi Dangarembga's novel, *Nervous Conditions* is constructed on Tambu's rite of passage, a ritual that blends themes of gender and race, making the one a metaphor for the other, as the horrors of racism become metaphors for sexism. During her passage to womanhood, Tambu is confronted with alternatives, Nhamo and Nyasha, the one seduced by "Englishness," the other suspicious of "Englishness"; the one cutting herself off from her African past, the other reassessing the African past; the one wondering about gender roles, the other with a decided idea about those roles. Looming over all is the shadow of the mythic Babamukuru, always influencing, insistent, the organizer, the planner, the connection. And over Babamukuru lurk the British and "Englishness," and decided ideas about the behavior of women, about the behavior of those men and women who are beneath him in class. In the end, in Africa and the West, is the woman not similarly bound and a slave?

Assia Djebar's *L'amour, la fantasia* is a novel of an artist who creates her reality out of the fragments of memory that are found in the form of chronicles, of oral tradition. Never complete, these are glimpses, memories. What kind of history can be constructed from such shards? She takes her little girl's hand in hers, and moves the tale along parallel lines: the stories of Cherifa growing up and of Algeria moving from colonized to freedom, of Algerian Moslem women moving tentatively out of the veil, stories of liberation and also of the word, the art of the storyteller.

Ousmane Sembène's novel, *Les bouts de bois de Dieu*, is the story of "god's bits of wood," the workers on the railroad who are involved in a strike; it is also the story of women and their breaking of former molds. Among them is Maimouna, a blind market woman; she is the eternal woman, giver of life, from whom life is taken, at home wherever she is put, unable physically to see where she is going, but with a quiet force of her own. As

the women break the shackles of African tradition and European racism, so in an even more dramatic way does Maimouna: in the end, she will remain behind in Dakar, nursing an orphaned child whose name is Strike.

MYTHIC AFRICA AND EUROPE

The hero of Cheikh Hamidou Kane's novel, *L'aventure ambiguë*, is Samba Diallo, a boy growing into manhood; the story also deals with the historical meeting of Africa and the West, with the boy growing into a man standing at the crossroads between them. Samba Diallo's mythic Africa is a world that eschews all material things. His Europe is a world in which the dominant symbol is streets that are not owned by humans but by mechanical devices, a world in which a human seems divested of humanity. His is an integrated world, a harmonious world. This is lost in the West.

The movement in Camara Laye's *Le regard du roi* is from earthly to transcendental king, from earth to sky, from uncertainty to certainty, from the nadir to the sublime. It is a rebirth, a renewal of the European Clarence as he sloughs off his animal parts and moves to the mythic radiance of the African king. The key to this rigorous assault on Joseph Conrad's *Heart of Darkness* is to be found in the process of Clarence's rhythmic odyssey.

Tayeb Salih's *Mawsim al-hijrah ilá al-Shamāl* sets up extremes—South and North, Sudan and England—with Mustafa Sa'eed moving between them, migrating to the North where he establishes a mythical Africa, becoming an invader, destroying those whom he encounters. But it is a dangerous game, like colonialism, for the victimizer becomes the victim. The game is a part of him from the beginning, a part of his destiny, his character. Behind these extremes, the historical experience of colonialism is linked to the love affairs of Mustafa Sa'eed.

In Nadine Gordimer's *July's People*, the Smales family escapes from a Johannesburg suburb (seven rooms, swimming pool), with the help of their African servant, July. They go north, to his people, and hide there while a war goes on. Maureen's apolitical role in pre-revolutionary Johannesburg is as the wife of a liberal architect. She sees herself and her family as largely untainted by the grotesque prejudices of the white master-race norm, the mythic center of this novel. This belief collapses in her final confrontation with July.

In Ngũgĩ wa Thiong'o's *A Grain of Wheat*, the people stand on the eve of independence uneasy and afraid, crippled by their past, suspicious of each other. The British have gone, but colonialism has been replaced by an oppression of the spirit, by indiscretions and crimes of the past. The stage is set for a messiah, ironically Mugo, a traitor who was once thought of as heroic, who fashions himself in his dreams and hopes as a Moses who would lead his people out of bondage.

THE MYTHIC FUTURE

In Wole Soyinka's *The Interpreters*, Kola seeks escape in his paintings. The other interpreters, who cannot express themselves through art, find ways to associate themselves with Kola's mythic pantheon, since it expresses their desires and enables them to attain an understanding of their social situation and their destinies, to become reconciled to their human limitations. The work promises to organize the experiences of the interpreters, giving them a better understanding of themselves. Both gods and men are portrayed; Kola seeks in his art a bridge between heaven and earth to link the two sets of beings. Art and reality: Soyinka has asked, "When is playacting rebuked by reality? When is fictionalizing presumptuous? What happens after playacting?" Where *is* the mythic center?

See also **Achebe, Chinua; Camara Laye; Coetzee, J. M; Djebar, Assia; Emecheta, Buchi; Gordimer, Nadine; Head, Bessie Emery; Kateb, Yacine; Literature; Mahfouz, Naguib; Ngũgĩ wa Thiong'o; Nwapa, Flora; Saadawi, Nawal el-; Salih, Tayeb; Sembène; Ousmane; Soyinka, Wole.**

BIBLIOGRAPHY

Bleek, Wilhelm H. I., and Lucy C. Lloyd. *Specimens of Bushman Folklore*. London: George Allen, 1911.

Callaway, Henry. *Nursery Tales, Traditions, and Histories of the Zulus*. Springvale, Natal: John A. Blair, 1868.

Okri, Ben. "The Joys of Storytelling I." In *A Way of Being Free*. London: Phoenix House, 1997.

Zenani, Nongenile Masithathu. *The World and the Word*, ed. Harold Scheub. Madison: University of Wisconsin Press, 1992.

HAROLD SCHEUB

LITERATURES IN AFRICAN LANGUAGES

This entry includes the following articles:

ARABIC

Literary writing in Arabic in the Maghrib—as distinct from popular oral poetic forms and the longstanding excellence of North Africans in the Islamic sciences, theology, law, and geography—began in fiction with the adoption of the Western genres the novel and the short story. It was part of the Arab *Nahda* (Renaissance), a result of contacts with the West, in the nineteenth century. Classical Arabic poetry, on the other hand, continued to be a popular genre, perpetuating a tradition that dates back to the fifth century CE. Strong calls for renovation in both content and form came from Arab poets, specifically Iraqi poets.

A shared colonial experience of French rule in the three Maghribi countries, Algeria, Tunisia, and Morocco, created a common denominator that explains some of the cultural similarities in their modern literatures. France maintained its control over Algeria for 130 years, from 1830 to 1962; its presence in Tunisia was slightly shorter beginning in 1888 and ending in 1956. The French did not conquer Morocco until 1912 and left the country in 1956. In Algeria, France applied itself through its "bureaux arabes" to dismantle the Sufi brotherhoods, the sources of a strong support system that served to rally the population against European occupation. The *zawiyas* (communities centered around Sufi holy men) and the *talebs* (teachers in Qur'anic traditional schools) became the targets of the colonial repression, and the Qur'anic schools were replaced by French *lycées*. Arabic language was gradually displaced by French, which became the language of officialdom.

Morocco and Tunisia did not face a similarly intense onslaught on their national cultures. The efforts made to Westernize the population were balanced by the existence of a strong Arabic cultural tradition kept alive, in Morocco, through the efforts of the Qarawiyyin mosque in Fez. In Tunisia, al-Zaytuna mosque was a center of learning where Arabic language and Islamic studies found the support they needed to survive and thrive.

Libya, under Italian rule, endured even less pressure to abandon its Arabic traditions, received its independence early, in 1951, and benefited from its proximity to Egypt and from the Arabic cultural revival that began at the end of the nineteenth century.

The most distant Maghribi country, Mauritania, was the last to acquire its independence, in 1960. Its cultural ties with the Arab world were weak, leaving the country no choice but to center its cultural activities on religious texts and revive old Arabic literary genres; that is, rhymed verse in the tradition of the Jahiliyya (pre-Islamic) period. The tradition continued to dominate exclusively the literary scene, undeterred by the call to modernize Arabic poetry, pressing poets to abandon the single meter and the rigidity of rhymed verse for the expressiveness of free verse.

The Mauritanian novel made its first appearance with Ahmad Weld Abd al-Qader (b. 1941), a poet turned novelist, with *Al-Asma al-mutaghayyera* (*The Changing Names*) in 1981, followed in 1984 by his novel *Al-Qabr al-majhul aw al-usul* (*The Unknown Tomb or the Origins*). Musa Ould Ebnou wrote in both Arabic and French and took the novel into the direction of science fiction in *Madinat al-riyah* (*The City of Winds*, 1996), published in French with a different title, *Barzakh* (*Isthmus*), in 1993. Other prose writings appeared in the form of letters and *maqamat* (assemblies), a genre using rhymed prose known as *saja'* in Arabic and immortalized by the classical Arab writers, al-Hariri (1054–1122) and al-Hamadhani (969–1008). The form, which offers a critical outlook on any society masked by humor and irony, suited Mauritanian writers' preference for satire in addressing political and social issues. In its search for national identity, independent Mauritania revived its folk literature, particularly a poetic form reserved exclusively for women and known as the *tibra'*, consisting of short poems revolving around love themes. Few poets succeeded in publishing independent collections, and most of

their poems are scattered in the Mauritanian and Arab press.

It was the Association of the Muslim Ulama (clergy, legal scholars) of Algeria, established in 1931 by Abd al-Hamid Ben Badis (1889–1940), which struggled to reinstate Algeria's Arab-Islamic identity. It opened modern schools and published two papers, *al-Shihab* (1925–1939) and *al-Basa'ir* (1935–1956), which contributed to the literary and cultural revival in the country. Attention turned first to classical Arabic poetry, but soon fiction began to appear in the form of short stories, championed by Ahmad Reda Huhu (1911–1953), in the pages of *al-Shihab* and in his collections of short stories, including *Sahibat al-Wahy* (*The Source of Inspiration*, 1954), and his political satire, *Ma' Himar al-Hakim* (*With al-Hakim's Donkey*, 1953). Huhu was a strong defender of women's rights, but recommended education for women before emancipation. He was a strong critic of the Algerian bourgeoisie, which put him at odds often with the Association of Ulama, who received donations from rich Algerians.

The postindependence years were dominated by two novelists, Abd al-Hamid ibn Haduqa (1928–1996) and Al-Taher Wattar (b. 1936), two prolific writers whose early works revolved around the Algerian war of independence. Both Ibn Haduqa in *Rih al-Janub* (*The Southern Wind*, 1971) and Wattar in *Al-Laz* (*The Ace*, 1974) denounced the abuses that took place during the war. Among the new generation of young writers the most prolific novelist is Al-A'raj Wasini (b. 1954), whose fiction works mark a turning point in writing techniques and depict his country's pressing social and political issues. The author relies on Arabic folk heritage in *Faji'at al-Layla al-Sabi'a Ba'da al-alf* (*The Tragedy of the One Thousand and Seventh Night*, 1993), inspired by *The Arabian Nights*, and famous historical figures for the symbolic portrayal of events. His latest book, *Kitab Al-Amir* (*The Book of the Emir*, 2004), is a rewriting of the national struggle of Emir 'Abd al-Qādir (1808–1883) against the French army in the 1830s.

Poetry never stopped, but most young poets, despite their admiration for Algeria's prominent poet in the classical mode, Muhammad al-Eid al-Khalifa, turned to free verse. Still missing in the field of fiction writing and poetry are the voices of women writers; Ahlam Mustaghanmi remains the dominant female writer with three published novels: *Dhakirat al-Jasad* (*Memory of the Flesh*, 1996), *Fawda al-Hawas* (*The Chaos of the Senses*, 2004), and *'Aber Sarir* (*A Passing Sleeper*, 2003). Her trilogy is a strongly critical assessment of the events of the black decade of the 1990s in Algeria. In the early 2000s the poet, novelist, and painter Ina'am Bayyud (b. 1953) attracted attention with her collection of poetry *Rasa'il lam tursal* (*Letters that Were Not Sent*, 2003) and novel *Al-Samak La Ubali* (*The Fish Do Not Care*, 2004).

Algeria has a rich oral tradition that received a great deal of interest in the country's search for its identity in the postindependence period. During the colonial period oral poetry provided an outlet for the people's frustrations; its transmission orally allowed it to circulate freely despite the restrictions placed by the colonial administration on any traceable, written expression of national feelings. The Boqala is a feminine genre of oral poetry composed by women around love themes and recited in exclusively feminine gatherings. It has a magical component as it predicts the future through a complex setting. It presents similarities with the Tibra' in Mauritania and the western Sahara. A similar genre in Morocco is known as the 'Urubiyyat.

Tunisia experienced fewer restrictions on its cultural policies and had a stronger Arabic cultural tradition, so that writers there managed to maintain a balanced bilingual trajectory. The poet who launched the romantic movement in the Arab world is the Tunisian Abu al-Qasem al-Shabi (1909–1934), as a poet and a theoretician, in his book *al-Khayal al-shi'ri 'enda al-Arab* (*The Poetic Imagination of the Arabs*, second edition, 1975). He was influenced by Jubran Khalil Jubran's book *Al-Ajniha al-Mutakassira* (*The Broken Wings*, 1904). A fiction writer, Ali al-Dua'ji (1909–1949), a member of a group of young disillusioned writers known as "jama'at that al-sur" (The Taht al-sur Group), revolutionized the genre of the short story in his collections *Sahirtu minhu al-layali* (*Sleepless Nights*, 1969) and *Jawlatun hawla hanat al-bahr al-abyad al-mutawassit* (*A Trip around the Bars of the Mediterranean Sea*, 1962). He depicted peoples' shortcomings, displayed them in a humorous manner, using appropriate allusions and subtle hints, much in the style of a caricaturist. Women writers were active participants in this literary movement both in

prose and poetry, but their contributions were sometimes curtailed due to the pressures of society and the concerns of their families for their daughters' reputation. Some—like the poet Fadila al-Shabi (b. 1946) and the fiction writer Hayat ben al-Shakh (b. 1943)—weathered the storm and continued their literary activities. The literary name that dominated the twentieth century is that of Mahmoud al-Mes'adi (1911–2005), a writer apart among his peers, with a style that defies simplicity and a philosophy concerned with humankind's purpose in life, in the tradition of the existentialists. The author of the well-known play *Al-Sudd* (*The Dam*, 1955), he also wrote *Haddatha Abu Hurayra Qala* (*Abu Hurayra, Said*, 1973) and *Min Ayyam Umran* (*Of Umran's Days*, 2002).

Despite Morocco's proximity to the West and its historical connection to Andalusia, Arabic culture continued to flourish with other Western cultures, primarily French. The city of Fez was the cultural capital of the country, and most of Morocco's writers grew up there. The press offered an excellent venue for literary writings, the best example being the writer 'Abd al-Karim Ghallab (b. 1919), longtime editor of the daily paper *al-'Alam* (*The Flag*). His numerous fiction works promoted the use of Arabic language as in *Wa Akhrajaha min al-Janna* (*He Led Her Out of Paradise*, 1977), and highlight the struggle of the Moroccan national struggle for independence from the French. His book *Sab'at Abwab* (*Seven Gates*, 1965) relates his own experience in jail.

The strong Francophone trend was balanced by works of great literary value written in Arabic, unhindered by the difficulties of publication. Some writers such as Muhammad Shukri (1953–2003) achieved notoriety thanks to the translation, into French, of his autobiographical first novel, *al-Khubz al-Hafi* (*For Bread Alone*, 1982), by another Moroccan novelist, Taher Ben Jelloun, as *Le Pain nu*. The second half of the twentieth century witnessed a profusion of novelists, short story writers, and poets, many such as the poet Muhammad Bennis and the fiction writers Muhammad Berrada (b. 1938) achieving renown beyond the borders of their own country. Berrada's innovative style and technique led to the selection of his novel *Lu'bat al-Nisyan* (*The Game of Forgetfulness*, 1987) for the Moroccan secondary school curriculum.

Another writer, Bensalem Himmish (b. 1948), won the Najib Mahfuz award for his novel *Majnun al-Hukm* (*The Polymath*, 1990). Mubarak Rabiʿ (b. 1940), a psychologist by training and profession, is concerned with the human being and the struggle between good and evil. His novels reflect a deep interest in and knowledge of his country's traditions, as is obvious also in a collection of his short stories, *Sayyidna Qadr* (*Saint Destiny*, 1969). The minister of religious affairs Ahmad at-Tawfiq (b. 1943), a historian by formation and profession, has published four novels. His writings develop strong female characters, visible in *As-Sayl* (*The Flood*, 1998), and promote the coexistence of Arabs and Berbers in *Shujayrat Hinna wa Qamar* (*Henne, Shrubs, and the Moon*, 1998). There is a subtle Sufi feeling that underlines most of his novels, especially *Jarat Abu Musa* (*Abu Musa Women Neighbors*, 1997). Layla Abu Zayd (b. 1950) defends women's place in the Moroccan society, denouncing men's self-centered behaviors in *al-Fasl a-l Akheer* (*The Last Chapter*, 2000). Among the most outspoken women writers of Morocco is the poet Malika al-ʿAsimi (b. 1945), author of two collections of poetry, *Kitabat Kharej Aswat al-ʿAlam* (*Writings Outside the Walls of the World*, 1988) and *Aswat Hanjara Mayyeta* (*Voices of a Dead Throat*, 1989). A staunch feminist, al-ʿAsimi is blunt in her rejection of exploitation and defense of human dignity.

The literary scene in Libya is dominated by the names of two major novelists, Ahmad al-Faqih and Ibrahim al-Kuni. Their writings reflect the feeling of loss following the discovery of petroleum in their country, a situation admirably portrayed by the Saudi Arabian novelist, ʿAbd al-Rahman Munif in his five-volume novel *Mudun al-Malh* (*Cities of Salt*, 1984). The prospect of oil production raised people's hopes for a better life in a dream world that Faqih portrays in *Hadaʾiq al-Layl* (*Gardens of the Night*, 1991). Al-Kawni's deep love for his country pushed him to revive Libya's Berber roots in *al-Majus* (*The Magi*, 1992) and in *Kharif al-Darwish* (*The Dervish's Autumn*, 1994). He is enamored of desert life, and many of his novels evoke life in the pre-oil era. He uses symbolic characters from the Old Testament and moves the action in an atmosphere of spirituality, for which he uses a semi-Sufi style, best portrayed in his novel *Hakadha Taʾammaltu al-Kahina Mim* (*Thus I Meditated on the Priestess Mim*, 2006). A similar interest in local traditions characterizes the Libyan

short story, to which writers such as Ali Mustapha al-Misrati, Abd Allah al-Quwayri and Zaʾimah al-Barni contributed works of great interest.

This profusion of Arabic literary works and the participation of Maghribi writers in the cultural activities of the Arab world have strengthened the bonds between the Maghrib, the "far west" from the perspective of the Levantine heartlands of Islam, and the Mashriq, the southwest Asian land where Islam was born. It put an end to the isolation of the Arab writers of the Maghrib, who long felt the victims of a misconception on the part of the Mash-riqis about their contribution to Arabic scholarship.

See also ʿAbd al-Qādir; Art, Regional Styles: Northern Africa; Literatures in European Languages: Francophone Northern Africa; Theater: Northern Africa.

BIBLIOGRAPHY

Bamia, Aida. "Northern Africa-African Novel." In *Encyclopedia of the Novel*, Vol. 1, ed. Paul Schellinger. Chicago: Fitzroy Dearborn Publishers, 1998.

Cox, Debbie. *Politics, Language and Gender in the Algerian Novel.* New York: Edwin Press, 2002.

Fontaine, Jean. *Le Roman Tunisien de Langue Arabe 1956–2001.* Tunis: Cérès Editions, 2002.

Hamil, Mustapha. "Mohamed Zafzaf's al-Marʾa wa-l-Warda or the Voyage North in the Postcolonial Era." *International Journal of Middle East Studies* 38, no. 3 (2006): 417–430.

Meisami, Julie, and Paul Starkey, eds. *Encyclopedia of Arabic Literature*, Vol. 1. New York: Routledge, 1998.

AIDA A. BAMIA

BERBER

Berber (or Amazigh) is an Afro-Asiatic language that is genetically related to Old Egyptian (Coptic), Kushistic, Chadic, and Semitic. It is the oldest language in North Africa. Unlike Arabic, Berber is a secular language in the sense that it is not backed by a religious book. The largest Berberophone population is found in Morocco. Unlike other North African nations, Morocco has been largely occupied by one group of people for as long as recorded history can recall. The Berbers, or Imazighen (men of the land or free men), settled in the area thousands of years ago and at one time controlled all of the land between Morocco and Egypt. The early Berbers were unmoved by the colonizing Phoenicians; the Romans did little to upset their way of life after the sack of Carthage in 146 BCE. All the same, the Romans ushered in a long period of peace during which many cities were founded, and the Berbers of the coastal plains became city dwellers. Christians arrived in the third century CE, and again the Berbers asserted their traditional dislike of centralized authority by following Donatus (a Christian sect leader who claimed that the Donatists alone constituted the true church).

Arabs brought Islam to Morocco when the Arab armies swept out of Arabia in the seventh century. Quickly conquering Egypt, the Arabs controlled all of North Africa by the start of the eigth century. By the following century, much of North Africa had fragmented, with the move toward a united Morocco steadily growing. A fundamentalist Berber movement emerged from the chaos caused by the Arab invasion, overrunning Morocco and Muslim Andalusia (in Spain). The Almoravids founded Marrakesh as their capital, but they were soon replaced by the Almohads, another Berber dynasty.

Four major varieties of Berber are still in use in North Africa: Tashelhit in the south of Morocco, Tamazight in the center of Morocco, Tarifit in the north of Morocco, and Kabyle in Algeria. Berber has survived mainly because of its historicity and its status as a mother tongue. Berber is only recently acknowledged officially as a part of Moroccan heritage. By the end of the twentieth century, Berber has started to transit from a purely oral language to a written one. This language is being written in Tifinagh (its original alphabet), as well as in the Latin and Arabic scripts. In September 2004, Berber started to be taught in 300 Moroccan primary schools. This initiative was preceded by the creation of the Royal Institute of the Amazigh Culture in October 2001.

See also **Carthage; Languages.**

BIBLIOGRAPHY

Ayache, Albert. *Histoire Ancienne de l'Afrique du Nord.* Paris: Editions Sociales, 1964.

Ennaji, M., ed. *International Journal of the Sociology of Language 123.* New York: Mouton de Gruyter, 1997.

Laroui, A. *Les origines culturelles du nationalisme marocain.* Paris: F. Maspero, 1977.

Sadiqi, Fatima. *Grammaire du Berbère.* Paris: L'Harmattan, 1997.

FATIMA SADIQI

ETHIOPIC

Ethiopic literature refers to works preserved in the Gǝʕǝz language; most of them are the literature of the Ethiopian Orthodox Church. The Gǝʕǝz language has served the Christian nation since the introduction of Christianity in the fourth century. Gǝʕǝz is a Semitic language related to Arabic, Hebrew, Syriac and, most of all, South Arabic. Although Ethiopia is a country of many languages, until the nineteenth century the local literature flourished almost exclusively in Gǝʕǝz.

A literary language with its own writing system, Gǝʕǝz is no longer spoken, but no one is sure when it ceased to be a spoken language—it may have been in the tenth century. It would have disappeared long ago, like many other extinct Ethiopic languages, had it not been for the Christian religion. Because of its literature and the fact that the church services are still conducted in Gǝʕǝz in the twenty-first century, scholars and the clergy have to learn it. Scholars study Gǝʕǝz because of its relation to the other Semitic languages and its Christian literature.

CHARACTERISTICS OF ETHIOPIC LITERATURE

The content of Ethiopic literature is basically religious; even the royal chronicles, intended to be records of the national events that took place at and around the mobile royal court, have religious meaning. Historical incidents (victories of the monarch and his army, suppression of revolts, disgraceful defeats) happen not because the king or any agent makes them happen but because God, using the agent, wants them to happen. However, all religious books written in the Gǝʕǝz language are not, as some assume, sanctioned by the Ethiopian Orthodox Church.

A considerable part of the literature consists of translations that came mostly from Coptic (Christian) Arabic. From its beginning in the fourth century to the middle of the twentieth, the Ethiopian Orthodox Church was closely related to the Coptic Church of Alexandria. Until 1951, the spiritual head of the Church, the metropolitan (*abun*), was a Copt (Egyptian). Knowledge from and about the Christian world came to Ethiopia via the Coptic Church and Ethiopian and Coptic monasteries in Egypt and Palestine. But by using the Gǝʕǝz language and locally composed liturgical materials, as well as music by native musicians, the Ethiopian Orthodox Church has preserved its cultural independence throughout its history.

CONTRIBUTION OF ETHIOPIC LITERATURE

Gǝʿǝz literature has preserved a relatively high number of apocryphal, especially inter-Testamental, works no longer extant in other languages. Biblical scholars and church historians believe that even though such works are excluded from the biblical canon in the West, their contribution to the understanding of Christianity is uniquely significant. The Book of Enoch (*Henok*), the Book of Jubilees (*Kufale*), the Ascension of Isaiah (*ʾǝrgätäIsayǝyyas*), and the Synodicon (*Sinodos*) are considered to be the most important of these works.

Ethiopians' interest in writing down the hagiographic stories (*gädl*, "contending" or "strife" with the evil spirit) of their saints produced a class of literature of great value for the study of the social and political history of the Horn of Africa. The "contendings" include reports of clashes between the spiritual and political leaders on questions of national significance, and between Christianity and African religions.

THE AKSUMITE PERIOD: FOURTH TO NINTH CENTURIES

The literature of the Aksumite period is, primarily, from foreign sources. The origin of the very first books of the new Church was the Mediterranean or Byzantine world. As such, they were translations from the Greek language. They include the Gospel of St. Matthew (some believe the Gospel of John) and the Psalter. These must have been followed by the other Gospels and the remaining books of the Bible. Scholars are more or less certain that the Physiologus, a collection of fables; the monastic rules of Pachomius, the Egyptian monk who started cenobitism or communal Christian monastic life in the fourth century; the Qerǝlos, a collection of Christological treatises by early church fathers; The Ascension of Isaiah; The Paralipomena of Baruch; and The Shepherd of Hermas were translated into Gǝʿǝz during this period.

The coming to Ethiopia of the Pachomian rules during this period indicates that Ethiopian Christianity was shaped by monastic principles from the beginning. Some scholars suggest that the translation of the Qerǝlos into Gǝʿǝz so early must have been inspired by the need to defend the young Church from heresies of the time, especially the Christological formula adopted at the Council of Chalcedon (451), defining the mode of the union of the divine and human natures in Christ.

This period is most noted for the Aksumite Priest St. Yared's laying the foundation of the Ethiopian hymnody. His composition of hymns in honor of God and the saints form the nucleus of the *dǝggwa*, the Church's antiphonary of the year. Yared is credited not only with the composition of the first hymns of the *dǝggwa*, which has grown huge in the course of time, but also with supplying three types of melodies for them.

THE EARLY SOLOMONIC DYNASTY: 1270–1434

No work of any significance from the decline of Aksum in the ninth century to the rise of the so-called Solomonic dynasty in 1270 has come to light, even though a spiritually dynamic dynasty, the Zagwe, ruled during part of the period (1137–1270). In stark contrast, the times of Yǝkunno Amlak (who established or restored the Solomonic dynasty in 1270) and his descendants must have been highly conducive to the flourishing of literature.

The dynamic Metropolitan Sälama II (1348–1388) brought with him from Egypt a significant collection of religious books used by the Coptic Church. These, which included Arabic versions of some rituals and a number of hagiographical accounts of the desert fathers and of the Diocletian martyrs, were translated into Gǝʿǝz at the metropolitan's palace and at the monasteries of Ḥayq ʾǝsfanos in Amhara (modern Welo) and Däbrä Libanos in Šäwa (Shewa).

One of the first works to appear during this period was the Kǝbrä Nägäśt (Glory of the Kings, written or translated in 1314/1322), a legend by means of which the Solomonic dynasty of Ethiopia acquired its legitimacy. According to the legend, Makǝdda (the Queen of Sheba or the South—"Ethiopia," I Kings 10:1–13, and Matthew 12:42) visited Jerusalem to admire the Solomon's wisdom, converted to Judaism, and bore a son to him. When the son, called later Mənilək I, reached maturity, he visited his father. On his return to Sheba, Solomon sent with him priests and people of the law to help him set up a "Jewish" state. His mother abdicated in favor of her son Mənilək, who brought with him the Ark of the Covenant, which he and his new entourage had stolen.

THE PERIOD OF EMPEROR ZÄR'A YAʿƎQOB: 1434–1468

No single native author is known to have produced as much as King Zär'a Yaʿəqob did. His extraordinary devotion to the Virgin Mary and his determination to keep the Church and his empire united drove him to become a prolific writer. First, he substantially increased his father's collection of the miracles of Mary (*Tä 'ərä Maryam*) by importing more stories and composing new ones. His zeal to keep the Christian community united lead him to suppress dissention. The effect was the contrary; his strong devotion to Mary and his firm view on the meaning of the Trinity had created schism (rather than unity) in the church.

The translation of the account of the Arab conquest of Egypt by John, bishop of Nikiu, *Yohannəs Mädebbər* (ca. 690), now preserved only in Gəʿəz, must have taken place at the end of this period (1602). Historians say that this unique Ethiopic source has made it possible for them to write a history of the Arab conquest of Egypt.

THE GONDÄRITE PERIOD: 1607–1755

Ethiopians are great lovers of poetry. The hymns of the *dəggʷa* (the antiphonary for the year) and the two collections titled *Ǝgzi'abher Nägśä* (The Lord Reigneth) are all poetic. In the course of time, the synaxary entries and the hundreds of miracles of Mary have each been supplied, at their conclusions, with a hymn of about five rhyming lines.

A special class of poems called *qəne* is used primarily to praise God and the saint of the day during a church service. *Qəne* poems have to be new composition designed for the occasion and composed by one of the clergy on that day or the day before. This means that almost every day, in each major church, an individual *qəne* poem is sung—freshly composed for that particular day, following Psalms 96:1 and 98:1, "O Sing unto the Lord a new song." A *qəne* poem cannot be used more than once. Some scholars have published collections of the most memorable ones. Although the practice is very old, *qəne* gained popularity during the Gondärite period of 1607–1755, and since then has been used to eulogize heroes and flatter authorities.

Literature in Amharic. Amharic, which was (and still is) widely used as a national means of communication, or *lingua franca*, gradually became the principal tool for literary production as well. Amharic literature, perhaps the most extensive in any African language, deserves a special treatment. The themes treated by the first authors in Amharic were, predictably, controversial theological themes and Christian ethics. This was soon followed, interestingly, by a criticism of tradition as an impediment to progress.

The traditional style of composing poems is being replaced by that of the West. Young writers are increasingly strangers to traditional learning, which is steadily being displaced by Western education. The influence of English expression on Amharic has produced virtually an independent Amharic dialect. The circulation of a work written in this "dialect" has to be limited to a relatively small sector of the otherwise large literate population of the country.

The Amharic literature in the diaspora, especially in the United States, has reached a comparatively respectable level. Several types of Amharic computer software programs created by engineers of Ethiopian nationality have greatly facilitated its growth. This development is due to several factors. The political exiles and refugees who have been forced to leave Ethiopia by the hundreds of thousands (some sources say in the millions) since 1974 belong to the county's educated class—readers and writers of ideas dealing with contemporary issues. Nostalgia for Ethiopian life, hardships suffered by refugees, and twenty-first-century political issues are the themes of the Amharic literature produced in the diaspora. However, because the succeeding generations will inevitably assume the local cultures, this literature's future does not seem very bright.

See also **Aksum; Christianity: Ethiopian Church; Gondär; Literature; Literature and the Study of Africa; Writing Systems.**

BIBLIOGRAPHY

Bausi, Alessandro, ed. and trans. *Il Sēnodos etiopico CSCO* Scriptores Aethiopici (text) 552/101, (trans.) 553/102 (1995). Throughout bibliography, *CSCO = Corpus Scriptorum Christianorum Orientalium*, Louvain, Belgium.

Bezold, Carl, ed. and trans. *Kebra Nagast: Die Herrlichkeit der Könige. Abhandlungen der Philosophisch-Philologischen Klasse der königlich bayerischen Akademie der Wissenschaften.* Munich: Verlag der K. B. Akademie der Wissenschaften in Kommission des G. Franz'schen Verlags (J. Both), 1909.

Budge, Ernest A. W., trans. *The Queen of Sheba and Her Only Son Menyelek: A Complete Translation of the Kebra Nagast.* London: The Medici Society Limited, 1922.

Cerulli, Enrico. *Il libro etiopico dei Miracoli di Mario e le sue fonti nelle letterature del medio evo latino.* R. Università di Roma Studi orientali publicata, Vol. 1. Rome: Dott. Giovanni Bardi Editore, 1943.

Cerulli, Enrico. *La letteratura etiopica: L'oriente cristianao nell'unit à delle sue tradizioni.* Florence: Sansoni-Accademia, 1968.

Conti Rossini, Carlo, and Lanfranco Ricci, eds. and trans. *Il libro della luce del negus Zarʾa Yaʿᵊqob (Maṣḥafa Berhān) CSCO* Scriptores Aethiopici (text) Pt. I, 250/47 (1964), Pt. II 261/51 (1965), (trans.) Pt. I, 251/48, Pt. II, 262/52 (1965).

Haile, Getatchew. "Religious Controversies and the Growth of Ethiopic Literature in the Fourteenth and Fifteenth Centuries." *Oriens Christianus* 65 (1981): 102–136.

Haile, Getatchew, ed. and trans. "*Fᵊkkare Haymanot* or the Faith of Abba Giorgis Säglawi." *Le Muséon* 94, no. 3–4 (1981): 235–258.

Haile, Getatchew, ed. and trans. *The Epistle of Humanity of Emperor Zärʾa Yaʿᵊqob (Tomarä Tᵊsbᵊʾt). CSCO* Scriptores Aethiopici (text) 522/95, (trans.) 523/96 (1991).

Haile, Getatchew. *The Mariology of Emperor Zärʾa Yaʿᵊqob of Ethiopia: Texts and Translations. Orientalia Christiana Analecta 242.* Rome: Pontificium Institutum Studiorum Orientalium, 1992.

Kane, Thomas L. *Ethiopian Literature in Amharic.* Wiesbaden: Otto Harrassowitz, 1975.

Molvaer, Reidulf. *Tradition and Change in Ethiopia: Social and Cultural Life as Reflected in Amharic Fictional Literature ca. 1930–1974.* Leiden: E. J. Brill, 1980.

Ricci, Lanfranco. "Letterature dell'Etiopia." In *Storia delle letterature d'Oriente*, ed. Oscar Botto. Sotto il Patrocinio della Commissione Nazionale Italiana dell'UNESCO. Casa Editrice Dr. Francesco Vallardi, Vol. 1 Milan: Società Editrice Libraria, 1969.

Tamrat, Taddesse. "The Abbots of Däbrä-Hayq, 1248–1535." *Journal of Ethiopian Studies* 8, no. 1 (1970): 87–117.

Ullendorff, Edward. *Ethiopia and the Bible.* The Schweich Lectures of the British Academy. London: Oxford University Press, 1968.

van den Oudenrijn, Marcus, ed. and trans. *Helenae Aethiopicum Reginae quae Peruntur Preces et Carmina. CSCO* Scriptores Aethiopici (text) 208/39 (1960), (trans.) 211/40 (1961).

Wendt, Kurt, ed. and trans. *Das Maṣḥafa Milād (Liber Nativitatis) und Maṣḥafa Sellāsē (Liber Trinitatis) des Kaizers Zarʾa Yaʿqob CSCO* Scriptores Aethiopici (text) pt. I, 221/41 (1962), pt. II, 235/43 (1963), (trans.) pt. I, 222/42 (1962), pt. II, 236/44 (1963).

Yacob, Beyene, ed. and trans. *Giyorgis di Saglā, Il libro del Mistero (Maṣḥafa Meṭir). CSCO* Scriptores Aethiopici (text) pt. I, 515/89 (1990), pt. II, 532/97 (1993), (trans.) pt. I, 516/90 (1990), pt. II, 533/98 (1993).

GETATCHEW HAILE

HAUSA

Original forms of Hausa literature include praise singing, oral narrative, poetry, and dramatic performance. The novel genre became popular only during the twentieth century, when works ranging from literary classics to romance novels and pulp fiction appeared. Some Hausa literature is available in English or French translation, but it remains best known in its original form, available only to Hausa speakers and those familiar with the culture, which is concentrated in central northern Nigeria and Niger. In the tenth century Islam began to influence Hausa culture, bringing with it literacy, and leading to the development of *ajami*, the practice of writing Hausa language manuscripts in Arabic script. Hausa culture has long enjoyed a wealth of oral narrative, but literacy appears to have been restricted to Islamic scholars until the establishment of British colonial rule in Nigeria. The turn of the twentieth century marked the beginning of active Hausa literary production in Latin script. In Nigeria the colonial government held writing contests early in the century to promote English and Hausa literacy, both in Latin script. As English and French became the official colonial languages of Nigeria and Niger, works of Hausa literature have been published in English and French translation as well as in Hausa since the mid-nineteenth century.

Praise singing, the declamation of an individual's attributes, is a popular traditional mode of literary expression among all levels of Hausa society. The late M. G. Smith studied the social functions of male Hausa praise singers (1957), clarifying the role of the praise singer as one who maintains the status quo by declaiming laudatory features of a wealthy patron's character or social standing. Both men and women earn a living as praise singers by performing for festivals, holidays, political rallies, weddings, or naming celebrations. Royal praise singers extol the king's praises as they stride before him in procession. The nature of a praise song demands that this be a public performance.

Written poetry became an integral part of Hausa culture with the period of religious reform known as the Sokoto jihad (1804–1830), when it was used as a principle instrument of influence over the masses. Although appearing initially in written form, it was popularized through oral transmission, its rhyme and meter allowing for ease of memorization. Jihad leader Shehu 'Uthman dan Fodio was a prolific author of both prose and poetry, but it was his daughter, Nana Asma'u (1793–1864), who produced a vast collection of topical and religious poetry written in Arabic, Fulfulde, or Hausa, all in Arabic script (*ajami*). Her poetic works were central to the resocialization of refugee women, instructing them in orthodox Islamic practices, as well as recounting historical events of the period and positive character traits of its principle figures, who are remembered in eulogy.

Contemporary poets like Akilu Aliyu, Hauwa Gwaram, Hajiya 'Yar Shehu, Mudi Sipikin, and Sa'adu Zungur have published their works in small chap books that are popular in secondary school curricula. Their topics range from politics and history to current events and contemporary problems between the generations. Some poets are better known as pure entertainers. Their extemporaneous performances often are bawdy, and usually are ephemeral. Although the best of them may earn a living wage from their artistry, their social status is not high.

Oral narrative (*tatsunyoyi*, pl.; *tatsuniya*, s.) has long been the voice of Hausa culture. In 1913 Frank Edgar wrote down in *ajami* the earliest comprehensive collection of oral narrative. It was translated into English by Neil Skinner in 1969. These tales offer a window into Hausa culture, including observations on cultural origins, relations between the sexes, trickster tales, heroes and villains, and histories, running the gamut from morality tales to mysteries.

The novel is a relatively new literary form in Hausa culture. Gaskiya Corporation, a Hausa-language publishing company established early in the twentieth century, was for much of that period the sole Hausa publisher in the country. The first novels published through Gaskiya were based on oral narrative stories including hero tales and fantasy. During the latter part of the twentieth century, Hausa literary novels reflected the social realism of injustices resulting from oil wealth corruption and political upheaval. S. I. Katsina's novels are particularly representative of this period.

See also **Asma'u, Nana; Bello, Muhammad; Colonial Policies and Practices; Literature: Oral; Literature and the Study of Africa; 'Uthman dan Fodio.**

BIBLIOGRAPHY

Boyd, Jean, and Beverly Mack. *The Collected Works of Nana Asma'u. Daughter of Usman Dan Fodiyo (1793–1864).* East Lansing: Michigan State University Press, 1997.

Furniss, Graham. *Poetry, Prose, and Popular Culture in Hausa.* London: International African Institute Press, 1996.

Hiskett, Mervyn. *A History of Hausa Islamic Verse.* London: School for Oriental and African Studies, 1975.

Mack, Beverly. *Muslim Women Sing: Hausa Popular Song.* Bloomington: Indiana University Press, 2004.

Skinner, A. Neil, trans. *Hausa Tales and Traditions: An English Translation of 'Tatsunyoyi Na Hausa,' originally compiled by Frank Edgar*, Vol. 1. Madison: University of Wisconsin Press, 1969.

BEVERLY B. MACK

ISLAMIC

There is a rich body of African literature that is Islamic in the sense that it reflects Islamic ethos and cultures, whether or not it deals explicitly with Islamic precepts or has been directly inspired by Islamic doctrine. Despite the many images of Islam prevalent in different parts of the continent, there is a core of common beliefs, similar institutional patterns, and shared values which have helped to forge an Islamic culture and literature that is also uniquely African.

The greater part of this literature is in African, and especially in Afro-Islamic, languages ranging from Afar, Somali, Swahili, and Nubi in eastern Africa, to Fufulde, Hausa, Wolof, and Mandingo in western Africa. Afro-Islamic languages are indigenous tongues of predominantly Muslim communities that have absorbed a significant proportion of Islamic idiom. Arabic, the language of Islamic ritual and Qur'anic revelation, has also served as a literary medium in Sudan and in the western African regions of Hausaland, Senegal, and the Gambia, and in the old Mali and Songhay empires. More recently, Islamic literature has also appeared in Western languages, particularly in French and English.

Much of the Islamic literature has tended to be written. Oral literature, often a female domain, has sometimes been frowned upon by the Muslim clergy even when influenced by Islam. Islam regards the written word with tremendous veneration. The advent of the religion and Qur'anic literacy, therefore, inspired the emergence of African versions of the Arabic script that came to be used in the construction of a new creative literature in local languages. The inception of European colonial rule led to the marginalization of these local varieties of the Arabic script and, in some cases, to their eventual replacement with the Latin script.

Despite the primacy accorded to the written word in Islam, however, the oral tradition has proved highly resilient and has remained the dominant mode in some literatures, especially those in Somali and Mandingo languages. But even in these cases, pre-Islamic myths and beliefs were in many instances replaced with new ones that have given oral literature in Muslim Africa a peculiarly Islamic imprint. This, for example, is clearly demonstrated in the works of Amadou Hampate Bâ (b. 1901) of Mali and Abdillahi Suldaan (1920–1973) of Somalia.

In form and substance, the Islamic heritage has perhaps been most influential in the poetic genre and least influential in the area of drama; prose fiction occupies a position between these two. The bulk of Islamic literature has, in fact, been in verse, and its literary masterpieces (including some of the greatest epics) have been overwhelmingly poetic. Some of the most prominent poets, from Sheikh Husayn al-Zahra (1833–1894) of the Sudan to Sheikh Muhammad Abdulle Hassan (1856–1921) of Somalia, from Sayyid Abdallah bin Ali bin Nassir (1735–1810) of Kenya to

Sheikh 'Uthman dan Fodio (1754–1817) of Nigeria and his daughters, have come from the leading ranks of Muslim scholars and clergy. Much of this poetry has been composed in local languages and comprises didactic and homiletic verse in a prosodic style which is strongly reminiscent of the Arabo-Islamic *qasida*.

This classical, poetic dimension of Islamic literature has been concerned with a wide range of themes, including the life histories of prophets and other prominent Muslim figures; odes to the Prophet Muhammad, Muslim saints, and martyrs; Islamic mysticism and philosophy; the transitory and illusory nature of this world; religious, social, and political admonition; and Islamic duties and principles of Islamic conduct and morality. Some of these poems, like the Swahili *Hamziyya* of Sayyid Aidarus bin Athman bin Ali (1705–1775), are direct translations from Arabic sources.

Islamic literature in prose exists in the form of novels and novelettes, but it includes the short stories of al-Tayyib Zaruq (b. 1935) in Arabic, Aliyu Makarfi in Hausa, Ahmed Mgeni (b. 1938) in Swahili, and others. A small proportion of the prose fiction in non-Western languages, like some of the Hausa and Swahili novelettes of Umaru Dembo (b. 1945) and Shaaban Robert (1909–1962), respectively, compare with the narratives of *The Thousand and One Nights* in their use of fantasy. Much of the prose literature that is Islamic in content, however, also tends toward some form of realism.

The thematic substance of this prose literature is quite varied, ranging from marriage in a changing society to tyranny and class struggle. Furthermore, the writers differ substantially in their ideological orientation toward Islam. Some are strongly empathetic and reverent toward it: Jabiru Abdillahi, writing in Hausa; and Muhammed Said Abdulla (b. 1918), writing in Swahili, for example, probably belong to this category. Some are irreverent and stand as reformists of various shades, including the Somali novelist Shire Jamaac Axmed, Swahili novelist Said Ahmed Mohamed (b.1947), and Arabic novelist Tayeb Salih (b.1929). Writers that could be described as cultural apostates, like Nuruddin Farah (b. 1945) of Somalia and the Marxist-oriented Ousmane Sembène (b. 1923) of Senegal, have generally composed in English or French. What gives this literature its common Islamic thrust, then, is merely the Islamic sociocultural background against which it is constituted.

In drama the heritage of Islam is more limited. Traditional forms of drama of parody exist in a number of Afro-Islamic societies and are especially popular in the fasting month of Ramadhan. As in the case of the Hausa *wasan kara-kara*, such parody is often employed to critique the conduct of Muslim leaders and teachers. Islamic culture is also featured in some of the written Hausa plays of Shuaibu Makarfi (b. 1918), the Somali plays of Ahmed Farah Ali (b. 1947), and the Swahili plays of Ebrahim Hussein (b. 1943), among others. Some plays staged by students and theater groups in both eastern and western Africa have also had an Islamic content. But, in general, the Islamic impact on African drama has been weak, both in form and in substance.

Despite many similarities, the regional Islamic literatures of eastern Africa, on the one hand, and western Africa, on the other, show an interesting contrast. Because of its proximity to the Arabian Peninsula and the long-term influx of Arab immigrants, Islam in eastern Africa has retained a strong Arab character. In western Africa, however, the religion became more indigenized since its foundations were laid, mainly by gradual contact with Berbers rather than with Arabs. As a result, while the Islamic literature of eastern Africa is pervaded with cultural Arabisms, a good section of the literature of western Africa projects an interplay of tensions and accommodations between the legacy of Islam and more indigenous traditions.

See also **Camara Laye; Farah, Nuruddin; Islam; Salih, Tayeb; Sembène, Ousmane; ʿUthman dan Fodio.**

BIBLIOGRAPHY

Andrzejewski, B. W.; Stanislaw Pilaszewicz; and Witold Tyloch; eds. *Literatures in African Languages: Theoretical Issues and Sample Surveys.* Cambridge, U.K.: Cambridge University Press, 1985.

Bangura, Ahmed S. *Islam and the West African Novel.* London: Lynne Rienner, 2000.

Gérard, Albert. *African Language Literatures.* Harlow, Essex, U.K.: Longman, 1981.

Harrow, Kenneth W., ed. *Faces of Islam in African Literature.* Portsmouth, NH: Heinemann, 1991.

Harrow, Kenneth W., ed. *The Marabout and the Muse: New Approaches to Islam in African Literature.* Portsmouth, NH: Heinemann, 2000.

ALAMIN MAZRUI

MALAGASY

Unlike many former French colonies in sub-Saharan Africa, Madagascar has a rich tradition of writing in its indigenous language. Starting in the eighteenth century and well before colonization got underway, early Malagasy monarchs such as kings Andrianampoinimerina (1745–1810) and Radama I, as well as Queen Ranavalona I, recognized literacy as an attribute of power. Though Queen Ranavalona I sought to restrict the practice of literacy to particular groups within the society, she was the first Malagasy ruler to promote the transcription of selections of Malagasy oral literature, and especially of *hainteny* (poetry). It was also during her reign that sections of the first major work written in the Malagasy language were published. This was a three-volume work titled *Tantara ny Andriana eto Madagascar* (History of the Kings of Madagascar), composed by a French priest, Reverend Father Callet (1822–1885). It was created on the basis of Malagasy oral texts and published between 1837 and 1881.

By the late nineteenth century, Madagascar already had a substantial number of citizens literate in the Malagasy language who were no longer satisfied with transcribing oral literature. Educated Malagasy, including creative writers, launched a movement of resistance against French colonialism known as the VVS (Vy Vato Sakelika) in the early 1900s. Writers such as Rodlish (Arthur Razakarivony, 1895–1968), Stella (Edouard Andrianjafitrimo, 1881–1972), and Ny Avana Ramanantoanina (1891–1940) participated in this movement and suffered imprisonment by the colonial authorities as a result. A poet, Ny Avana became the most celebrated Malagasy language writer of the early colonial period and his work exemplified the despondency of a generation of writers marked by the loss of Malagasy independence.

Poetry remained the preferred genre of Malagasy-language writers, and many writers of the early twentieth century such as Samuel Ratany (1901–1926), Esther Razandrasoa (1892–1931) and Charles Rajoelisolo (1896–1968) were also poets. Alongside these authors, Jean-Joseph Rabearivelo (1901–1937) achieved fame writing in French, but also contributed to Malagasy-language literature by translating many of his works into Malagasy. The poet Dox (Jean Verdi Razakandriana) (1913–1978) was in some respects a contemporary of Ny Avana, but unlike Ny Avana who died in 1941, Dox's reputation spans much of the twentieth century. This is fairly typical. Malagasy language writers are most famous during their lifetimes, especially because their printed works may be unavailable after they pass away.

Although Dox is the author of many published works, publication is the most important challenge confronting Malagasy language writers. The poems of nationally recognized Ny Avana were published in book form only in 1992, fifty-one years after his death, under the title *Anthologie*. Similarly, Rodlish's play, *Sangy Mahery* (*Violent Games*), written in the 1930s and often performed on stage, was not officially published until 1988. Nonetheless, a new generation of writers began to emerge in the late twentieth century, including the poet Clarisse Ratsifandrihamanana (1926–1987) and the novelist Esther Rasoloarimalala Randriamamonjy (still active as of 2007), among others These newer authors have been more successful in getting their works published. However, books remain expensive commodities in Madagascar, and it is not clear how widely the works of such authors are read.

See also **Andrianampoinimerina; Literacy; Madagascar; Radama I; Ranavalona, Mada.**

BIBLIOGRAPHY

Fox, Leonard. *Hainteny: The Traditional Poetry of Madagascar.* London: Associated University Presses, 1990.

Gérard, Albert. *African Language Literatures.* Washington DC: Three Continents Press, 1981.

MORADEWUN ADEJUNMOBI

SOMALI

For centuries, oral literature, especially poetry, has been the dominant form of cultural representation in Somalia. The absence of an official alphabet for Somali precluded the development of a written tradition. In 1972, President Mohammed Siad Barre announced the adoption of a modified version of the Latin script for the writing of the Somali language.

Soon after, an experimentalist group of fiction writers emerged. The writings of this group created a bridge between the oral and the written forms. For example, characters in the novels of this group are described by their physical appearance and by the kind of clothes they wear. The narrator also describes the character via the ambience. This technique has affinities with traditional Somali narrative.

The two best-known writers of this group are Faarax M. J. Cawl (1937–1991) and Xuseen Sh. Axmed Kaddare (b. 1942). Cawl's *Aqoondarro waa u nacab jacayl* (1974; *Ignorance Is the Enemy of Love*, 1982) is a fictionalization of the dervish wars against British colonialism. The story also dramatizes the importance of mastering the three R's.

Kaddare's *Waasuge Iyo Warsame* (n.d.; Waasuge and Warsame; *Waasuge e Warsame*, 1990) is about a journey to Mogadishu by two old men. The "and" linking the two names of the title heroes alludes to a contradiction between Waasuge (a peasant) and Warsame (a pastoralist). Thus, the reader is introduced to a fictional world marked by counterpoints.

The experimentalists are complemented by another group whose novels exhibit structural, stylistic, and thematic innovations. Nuruddin Farah (b. 1945) and Maxamed Daahir Afrax (b. 1952) are the two best known of this group. In "Tolow waa talee, ma..." (1973–1974), Farah, whose novels in English have internationalized the Somali situation, experiments with stream-of-consciousness writing. The story, a fictionalized account of life under the military regime that brought Barre to power, was serialized in *Xiddigta Oktoobar* (October star). Soon after, the regime's censorship board ordered the serialization to cease. Farah then published the story in English, under the title *A Naked Needle* (1976).

Maxamed Daahir Afrax's novel, *Maana Faay* (1981; repr. 1993), is the story of the eponymous heroine's painful love, complicated by corruption and greed. Serialization of the novel in the government daily was discontinued by the censors.

Ironically, the writing and publishing of novels in the Somali language increased during the civil war. This was the result of: (1) the emergence of a new breed of entrepreneurs engaged in desk-top publishing; and (2) the absence of censorship. Awees Hussein Shiino's novel *Dayaxmadoobaad* (1991; Lunar Eclipse) apocalyptically treats the ravages of the civil war.

The civil war also dominates the imagination of Somali writers in the diaspora. Much of the lexicon and morphology of their work is geared to a post-mortem examination. A representative example includes Faysal Axmed Xasan's *Maandeeq* (2000; The one who gratifies the mind), Bile M. Hashi's *Janno* (2003; Paradise), Abdibashir Ali's *Dumar Talo ma laga Deyey* (2003; Women are the solution to the Somali crisis), Maxamuud Cali Calasow's *Gabar Timo Tidcan* (2002; The braided one), and Cabdillahi Cawed Cige's *Ladh* (2005; Anguish). Sadiq B. (Xawaaji's) *Qurbo Jaceyl* (2002; Diasporic love) mostly explores the resilience of two young lovers charting their own fate in an American city.

Written poetry and drama lag behind prose fiction in Somali. There are, however, a few published volumes of poetry, starting with *Geeddiga Wadaay!* (1973; Lead the trek), by Cabdi Muxumad Amiin (b. 1935), which extols the initial accomplishments of the military regime, and ending with *Hal-Karaan* (1993), by Maxamed Ibraahim Warsame Hadraawi (b. 1943), a collection of his poems from 1970 to 1990.

All in all, both prose writers and poets have succeeded in transforming the linguistic aspect of Somali in such a way that development of the written form and the discussion of new themes are possible.

See also **Farah, Nuruddin; Literature: Oral.**

BIBLIOGRAPHY

Ahmed, Ali Jimale. *Daybreak Is Near …: In Literature, Clans, and the Nation-State in Somalia.* Lawrenceville, NJ: Red Sea Press, 1996.

Andrzejewski, B. W. "Somali Literature." In *Literatures in African Languages*, ed. B. W. Andrzejewski, Stanislaw Pilaszewicz, and Witold Tyloch. Cambridge, U.K.: Cambridge University Press, 1985.

Banti, Giorgio. "Letteratura." In *Aspetti dell'espressione artistica in Somalia*, ed. Annarita Puglielli. Rome: Bagatto Libri, 1987.

ALI JIMALE AHMED

SOUTH AFRICAN LANGUAGES

ORAL LITERATURE

The Nguni (isiZulu, isiXhosa, Siswati, Sindebele) and Sotho (Sesotho, Setswana, Sepedi) languages have a rich oral literary tradition, the major genres of which are praise poetry (Z/X:*izibongo* / S:*lithoko*) and oral narrative (Z: *izinganekwane* / X: *iintsomi* / S: *litsomo*). Other oral forms include proverbs and riddles. Rycroft describes praise poems as "a cumulative series of praise names applying to a single referent; though those of prominent people and royalty are interspersed with concise narrative passages or comments, having been repeatedly expanded and polished by official bards in the course of time" (Rycroft 1988). A typical praise stanza first employs a praise name personifying a quality of the king and then links it to an action employing the same quality in verb form.

The art and tradition of praising both in public and in private continue into the present, and professional praisers performed at the installation ceremonies for Presidents Mandela and Mbeki. The largest collection of Zulu *izibongo* was recorded and transcribed by James Stuart in the 1920s. These nineteenth century royal praises, together with the collection edited by C. L. Sibusiso. Nyembezi in 1958 are the source material for more recent editions such as Trevor Cope's *Izibongo* (1968) and Rycroft and Ngcobo's meticulous *Praises of Dingana* (1988). Gunner and Gwala have added an important collection that includes contemporary praises of political leaders and of ordinary people including some humorous praises of and by women, and some touching praises that children have composed for themselves. Royal Xhosa *izibongo* have been collected by Rubusana, by Ndawo, and by David Yali-Manisi. Harold Scheub's 1975 collection too, includes contemporary praises by men, women, and children. Sotho *lithoko* have been collected by Damane and Sanders, and Kunene analyzes their structure.

Scheub describes the oral narrative as moving outward from the familiar to the unfamiliar and from conflict to resolution. In the course of that movement transformations occur, and the listener's emotions are engaged through symbolizing processes and the patterning of images. Two of the most famous performers of extended narrative were Uskebe Ngubane, whose isiZulu narrative *Umxakaza-wakogingqwayo* was reconstructed from notes by Henry Callaway (1868), and Nongenile Masithathu Zenani, a Gcaleka performer whose narrative, performed in 1975, was over one hundred hours long and took almost a month to complete.

Popular themes in isiZulu and isiXhosa oral narrative are human encounters with the sharp-witted amoral trickster (Z: *uchakijana* / X: *uhlakanyana*) or with the dull-witted ogres *amazimu*. *Uchakijana's* victims accept him in whatever human guise he assumes and are generally unaware of his true identity to the end. The *amazimu* on the other hand, seem to be simultaneously both human and ogre, and the humans they encounter use their knowledge of an *izimu's* weaknesses in planning their escape, which is generally successful. In narratives involving animals a particular human type is associated with each character: the mongoose is clever, the chameleon untrustworthy, the rock rabbit lazy, and so on. Sotho *litsomo* have been collected by Jacottet and by Tlali and Chevrier. Zulu *izinganekwane* were collected by Callaway, Bleek, and Vilakazi, and Canonici has produced an analysis of the form. Xhosa *iintsomi* have been collected by Theal, Ndawo, and Scheub. The first collection of Venda folklore with German translation titled *Midzimu ya Malombo* by C. Endemann was published in 1927.

EARLY LITERATURE

Protestant missionary work in Southern Africa in the nineteenth century laid the foundation for literature in African languages. Missionary linguists first created orthographies and then documented the languages for their own study. They then followed the construction of printing presses and the translation of the Bible and religious materials, thereby fixing a particular dialect as the literary standard. The early converts (Z: *Amakholwa*, S: *Badumeli*) were intimately involved in the translation work and composed hymns and prayers of their own, the earliest known being a hymn of praise in Xhosa *UloThixo omkhulu ngosezulwini* (He, the great God, high in heaven), written in 1820 by Ntsikana, a convert and preacher, and the first of many great writers of Xhosa hymns. A collection of hymns by Isaiah Shembe (c. 1868–1935), Zulu prophet and founder of the church *iBandla lamaNazaretha* was published in 1940.

The earliest text in Zulu appeared in 1901, and was an account by three of Bishop John Colenso's first converts of a journey to the court of King Mphande that they made with him in 1859. Early Sotho articles on folklore were published in the newspaper *Lisedinyana la Lesotho* (Light of Lesotho) founded in 1864 by Rev. A. Mabille of the Paris Evangelical Society. In 1893 Azariele Sekese collected some of his articles into *Mekhoa ea Basotho le maele le litsomo* (Customs and Proverbs of the Basotho), which became the first published literary work in Sesotho. Several Xhosa-language journals newspapers were founded and flourished for short periods in the nineteenth century, and *Imvo Zabantsundu* founded in 1884 by D. D. T. Javabu is still in publication as *Imvo*, as is *Ilanga lase Natal*, the Zulu-language newspaper founded in 1904 by J. L. Dube. This first period in vernacular literature was marked in Zulu by writers such as Magema Fuze, P. Lamula, and T. Z. Masondo, who documented Zulu history and traditions as seen through the new lens of Christianity. Motenda, Mudau, and Dzivhani produced historical accounts of the Venda people.

THE EMERGENCE OF THE NOVEL

The translation of English language works of fiction into isiZulu, isiXhosa, and Sesotho led to the beginnings of imaginative written genres in these languages. John Bunyan's *Pilgrim's Progress* was particularly influential, its theme echoing struggles the Christians were themselves experiencing, and its allegorical theme and character-typing echoing the format of the traditional *iintsomi*. Novels integrating the two themes of challenge of the Christian life and the importance of tradition emerged in all three languages with characters fulfilling single and specific functions. In Sesotho the best-known writer of this period is Thomas Mofolo (1877–1948), who wrote *Moeti oa Bochabela* (The Traveler to the East; 1907), *Pitseng* (1910), and in *Chaka* (1926), an historical novel tracing the life of the Emperor Shaka. Publication of *Chaka* was withheld for fifteen years because the press of the Paris Evangelical Society disapproved of its socalled heathen content.

In isiXhosa, Mqhayi wrote *Ityala lamawele* (1914) and *uDon Jadu* (1929); J. J. R. Jolobe wrote *uZagula* (1923), *Umyezo* (The Orchard; 1944) and *Elundeni loThukela* (On the Rim of the Thukela

Valley; 1959), and A. C. Jordan wrote *Ingqumbo yeminyanya* (The Wrath of the Ancestors; 1940). In isiZulu, James Gumbi wrote *Baba ngixolele* (Father, forgive me; 1965); B. Vilakazi wrote *Noma nini* (No matter how long; 1935) and *Nje nempela* (Just so; 1943), and J. M. Zama wrote *Nigabe ngani?* (On what do you pride yourselves? 1948). In Tshivenda in the 1950s, T. N. Maumela published *Elelwani*, E. S. Madima wrote *A si ene*, W. M. Makumu wrote *Nyabele Muthia-Vivho*, and W. M. D. Phopho published a historical novel titled *Phusuphusu dza Dzimauli* that traced the history of the Rammbuda clan.

In the decades preceding the apartheid era, novelists were producing powerful works on the theme of isolation and self-destruction, and the need to reinterpret tradition to meet the needs of urban life. Christianity remained a strong element, though it was seen as too permissive in its Western form to replace the network of rights and obligations that hold traditional society together. An early exponent of this genre in isiXhosa was Guybon Sinxo who wrote *uNomsa* (1922), *Umfundisi waseMthuqwasi* (The Priest of Mthuqwasi; 1927) and *Umzali wolahleko* (The Prodigal Parent; 1939). Representative of the period in isiZulu were R. R. R. Dhlomo's *Indlela yababi* (The Path of the Evil Ones; 1946) and C. L. S Nyembezi's *Mntanami, mntanami!* (My Child, My Child! 1952).

LITERATURE 1960–1990

Novels. Throughout this period publishers and distributors were closely monitored by the government, so that in works that did reach the public, protest against the increasingly oppressive political forces was muted. Christianity was a less explicit element, and intergenerational conflict was added to the continuing theme of the tension between traditional and Western culture, as in C. L. S. Nyembezi's *Inkinsela yaseMgungundlovu* (The Big Man from Pietermaritzburg; 1962), James Gumbi's *Waysezofika ekhaya* (He Was About to Go Home; 1968), Kenneth Bhengu's *Ubogawula ubheka* (Look Before You Leap; 1968) and O. E. H. Nxumalo's *Ngisinga empumalanga* (I Look to the East; 1969). Works in Sesotho from this period include S. P. Lekeba's *Gauta e Ntjhapile* (Johannesburg Has Ensnared Me; 1961), H. M. Lethoba's *Kgunou le Maria* (Kgunou and Maria; 1962)

and A. T. Maboee's *Menyepetsi ya maswabi* (Tears of Grief; 1962).

Poetry. Literary poetry (as distinguished from oral laudatory poetry) had begun to appear in the isiXhosa journals in the mid-nineteenth century. Nyembezi calls Samuel Mqhayi the father of Xhosa poetry and James Jolobe is recognized as the finest Xhosa poet. Their works presented the suffering of the Xhosa people and evoked happier times where society was ordered by traditional rights and obligations.

Zulu poets of this period wrote in both a traditional and a modern style, with a lively debate about the merits of each continuing throughout. Mazisi Kunene's epic *Emperor Shaka the Great* (1979) is the best-known example of the traditional style, but the original isiZulu version was never widely distributed. B. W. Vilakazi's poetry (*Amal' ezulu* 1942) is written in the modern style. Other poets of the period include P. Myeni whose *Hayani maZulu* (Sing Out, Zulu People; 1969), is a reworking of *izibongo* in literary form, D. B. Z. Ntuli *Amagwevu* (Body Blows; 1969), M. J. Makhaye *Isoka lakwaZulu* (The Young Bachelor from Zululand; 1972), and O. E. H. Nxumalo, whose poetry includes some political material as in *Ikhwezi* (The Morning Star; 1965). In the 1960s M. E. R. Mathivha published a poetic drama in Tshivenda titled *Mabalanganye*.

Drama. During this period the political and financial obstacles facing playwrights were considerable. Plays in isiZulu that dramatized nineteenth century African history and were intended for use in schools include A. H. Dladla's *UNtombazi* (Ntombazi; 1979), M. S. S. Gcumisa's *Inkatha Yabaphansi* (The Headring of the Ancestors; 1978), James N. Gumbi's *KwaBulawayo* (At Bulawayo; 1984) and Eliot Zondi's *Insumansumane* (An Incomprehensible Event) about the Bhambatha uprising of 1906.

One-act plays for radio were popular and *Ukhozi* (IsiZulu radio) broadcast numerous plays by D. B. Z. Ntuli, Lawrence Molefe and E. M. Damane, most with themes of domestic drama. State-controlled television broadcast a long-running isiZulu comedy series called *S'Gudi s'Nayisi* (the slogan of the restaurant chain that funded it; later changed to *Khululeka*, Chill) and another called *Emzini Wezinsizwa* (The Home of the Guys) in which characters from different ethnicities live together in a single sex hostel with dialogue in isiZulu, isiXhosa, and Sesotho/Setswana. Popular long-running television dramas in isiZulu shown during this period included *Kwakhala Nonyini* (What was the Reason?) *Hlala Kwabafileyo* (Live Among the Dead) and *Ubambo Lwami* (My Woman).

In the 1980s a vibrant new form of political drama was developing around the Market Theatre in Johannesburg under the direction of Barney Simon. Though many writers involved in this movement were black (Mbongeni Ngema, Percy Mtwa) and the plays dealt with life in the black community, their productions, deferring to the white community, were in English.

THE EFFECTS OF APARTHEID

The promotion of Nguni, Sotho, and Venda literatures by missionaries in the nineteenth and early twentieth centuries led to a vibrant literary culture that was reinforced through vernacular education policies in the mission schools. Elementary school textbooks contained history and folktales written by well-respected authors such as C. L. S. Nyembezi, and high school libraries were stocked with novels and poetic anthologies. During the four decades of apartheid (1948–1994) the strength of these vernacular literary traditions and of the presses that promoted them became a tool in the grand design to foster ethnic loyalties in order to subvert black solidarity. Strict censorship of all materials produced in African languages prevented the overt development of protest literature under conditions where it would naturally have flourished. Those who wished to be published in African languages had severe restrictions placed upon them, and many writers abandoned African languages and joined the large community already writing in English in order to find publishers abroad and to reach a larger audience.

AFRICAN LANGUAGE LITERATURE IN THE NEW SOUTH AFRICA

Since the democratic elections of 1994 and the new constitution of 1996, African languages have gained official status and speakers of these languages have acquired rights and protections under the law. In practice, however, the influence and prestige of English have only grown. In this climate the market for literature in African languages has declined and new authors are choosing to write in English.

One new area of lively activity is a fluid urban argot incorporating one or more African languages in addition to Afrikaans and English that is being used in the lyrics of *kwaito*, a form of music that has elements of rap, as well as in the poetry recited at popular poetry slams. Referred to variously as Is'camtho, Flaaitaal, and Tsotsitaal, this argot changes from city to city and even from one neighborhood to another. Seen by some as a threat to African languages, it might possibly become the next wave in African literature in South Africa.

See also **Apartheid; Language: Choice in Writing; Literature.**

BIBLIOGRAPHY

Andrzejewski B. W.; S. Pilaszewicz; and W. Tyloch; eds. *Literatures in African Languages: Theoretical Issues and Sample Surveys*. Cambridge, U.K.: Cambridge University Press, 1985.

Cope, Trevor, ed. *Izibongo: Zulu Praise-Poems*. Oxford: Clarendon Press, 1968.

Gérard, Albert. *Four African Literatures: Xhosa, Sotho, Zulu, Amharic*. Berkeley: University of California Press, 1971.

Gunner, Liz, and Mafika Gwala, eds. *Musho: Zulu Popular Praises*. Johannesburg, South Africa: Witwatersrand University Press, 1994.

Kunene, Daniel P. *Heroic Poetry of the Basotho*. Oxford: Clarendon Press, 1971.

Mathivha, M. E. R. "A Outline History of the Development; of Venda as a Written Language." In *Essays on Literature and Language: Presented to Prof. T. M. H. Endemenn by his Colleagues*. Turfloop, South Africa: University of the North, 1973.

Molema, Leloba Sefetogi. *The Image of Christianity in Sesotho Literature*. Hamburg, Germany: Helmut Buske, 1989.

Ngcobo, Mtholeni N. *A Survey of Zulu Literature from 1970–1990*. Lewiston, New York: Edwin Mellen Press, 2002.

Rycroft, D. K., and A. B. Ngcobo, eds. *The Praises of Dingana*. Pietermaritzburg, South Africa: University of Natal Press, 1988.

Scheub, Harold. *The Xhosa Ntsomi*. Oxford: Clarendon Press, 1975.

SANDRA SANNEH

SWAHILI

The development of Swahili literature is linked to two sources in its earlier years. There is, first, its oral provenance, embedded in the Swahili culture of the East African coast. Stories, proverbs, sayings and other literary forms, which fed into the literary genre, are well captured in Steere's *Swahili Tales* (1870, with the subtitle *As Told by Natives of Zanzibar*), and Taylor's *African Aphorisms, or Saws from Swahili-land* (1891). Both Steere and Taylor were missionaries based, respectively, at Zanzibar and Mombasa.

The other source for Swahili literary development, which was more direct and pervasive in its influence, emerged from the tenets, teachings and history of Islam. Since its introduction on the East African coast from the eighth century onwards, Islam provided three major ingredients for the growth of Swahili literary expression. These were: the Arabic script (which was adapted to express Bantu Swahili sounds); a cadre of Swahili poets who were themselves knowledgeable about Arabic literature and prosody; and a reservoir of Muslim stories and legends about the Prophet, his companions and the early history and figures of Islam. A combination of the three gave rise to the first written genre, poetry, whose output between the seventeenth and nineteenth centuries was dominated by religious themes. Of these, the earliest extant wok is the *Hamziyyah*, a poem in praise of the Prophet Muhammad which was originally composed in Arabic by the Egyptian poet, al-Busiri (d. 1296). It was translated into Swahili in a versified form by Aidarus Othman, a resident of Pate in the Lamu archipelago; the earliest extant manuscript of the Swahili *Hamziyyah* is dated 1792. But not all poems from the earlier period were religious in content, as is evidenced by the poems of the legendary Liyongo Fumo and Muyaka bin Haji.

Swahili prose as a written genre developed more substantially during the Colonial period, first German and then British. The spread of Swahili as a *lingua franca*, the introduction of the Latin script in Government administration and schools, and the adoption of the Zanzibari dialect as "standard" Swahili paved the way for the publication and wider dissemination of prose writing: stories, chronicles of coastal city-states, autobiographies, and cultural accounts of ethnic communities,

including their "histories." Missionary schools and the publication of the Bible and its narratives also aided the process which was consolidated by the 1950s through the establishment of commercial publishing houses. An outstanding writer who emerged during this period is Shaaban Robert (d. 1962), a poet, novelist, short-story writer, and essayist. A versatile writer, Robert drew inspiration from diverse sources which included coastal and mainland cultures, Arabian narratives (for example, *The Thousand and One Nights*) and Western stories and folktales. His prose works, and novels in particular, opened the door for later novelists such as Said Ahmed Mohamed and Euphrase Kezilahabi to develop the genre further in other directions.

Western-type plays were introduced in East Africa during the colonial period (though it should be noted that drama was already in existence in Swahili oral literature, e.g. in accompaniments to rituals and as poetic enactment of biographies). The development of this genre owes much to the efforts of the departments of English, drama, and theatre arts of East African universities from the late 1960s, which produced a number of skilled playwrights, among them Ebrahim Hussein, Farouk Topan, Alamin Mazrui, Penina Mlama, Jay Kitsao, Amandina Lihamba and Chacha Nyaigotti-Chacha. Hussein published the first full-length play in Swahili, *Kinjeketile* (1969), which depicts the Maji Maji uprising of 1905 against the Germans in southern Tanganyika. His other plays deal with a variety of social and political issues, including the impact of the Zanzibar Revolution of 1964 on a family which takes refuge in Dar es Salaam at the height of its capitalist phase, when Nyerere's socialist doctrine (*ujamaa*) was still a year or two away (*Mashetani* [The devils], 1971).

With Kezilahabi and Hauli, Hussein was among a group of university students to introduce a new way of writing poetry in Swahili. The "free verse" departed from the traditional norm not only in structure and form—by not adhering to a measured prosodic rhyme—but also in content and theme. Kezilahabi's "A Knife in Hand" and Hussein's "The Drum and the Violin," for example, are deeply personal and individualistic: the former captures moments of suicidal thoughts, while the latter portray an inner turmoil that revolves around culture and faith. The introduction of free verse started an interesting debate among scholars on the nature of poetry in Swahili literature. Many poets, including Abdulatif Abdalla, continue to write using rhyme and meter.

See also **Islam; Literature: Overview; Literature: Modern Poetry; Mombasa; Nyerere, Julius Kambarage; Theater.**

BIBLIOGRAPHY

Abdulaziz, M. H. *Muyaka: Nineteenth Century Swahili Popular Poetry.* Nairobi: Kenya Literature Bureau, 1979.

Hussein, Ebrahim. *Kinjeketile.* Dar es Salaam: Oxford University Press, 1969.

Hussein, Ebrahim. *Mashetani* [The devils]. Dar es Salaam: Oxford University Press, 1971.

Miehe, Gudrun, et al. *Liyongo Songs: Poems Attributed to Fumo Liyongo* Köln: Rüdiger Köpper Verlag, 2004.

Steere, Edward. *Swahili Tales: As Told by Natives of Zanzibar.* London: Bell and Daldy, 1870.

Taylor, W. E. *African Aphorisms, or Saws from Swahililand.* London: Society for Promotion of Christian Knowledge, 1891.

Topan, Farouk. "Modern Swahili Poetry." *Bulletin of the School of Oriental & African Studies* 37, no. 1 (1974): 175–187.

FAROUK TOPAN

YORÙBÁ

The culture of written literature in the Yorùbá language started less than two centuries ago with the publication of Henry Townsend's *Yorùbá Hymns* in 1848. Isaac Thomas published the first prose work, *Ìgbésí Ayé Èmi Sègilolá*, in 1930. The first Yorùbá play—*Pàsán Sìnà*—written by Adébóyè Babalolá was published in 1958.

POETRY

The first set of Yorùbá poems, mostly translations of poems originally written in English, were published between 1848 and 1900 and followed the tunes of the Christian hymns. The second group of poems were written by those who adopted the English poetic style in their compositions. Such poets concentrated more on the rhythm of their poems than on Yorùbá oral poetic devices, such as tonal counterpoint, parallelism, repetition, metaphor, and figurative expressions. Ajayi Ajísafé, David Akítólá Àjàó, and Afolábí Johnson were prominent among the earliest poets in this category. Their style is still evident in the works of contemporary poets such as Afolábí Olábímtán (1932–1992) and Adébóyè Babalolá.

Lastly are the poets who incorporate oral literary materials into their compositions. There are three subcategories of such poets. First are those who adopt the tunes of specific Yorùbá oral genres in their works. Examples are Sóbò Aróbíodu, Joseph Foláhàn Odúnjo, Tóyòsí Arígbábuwó, Àlàbí Ògúndépò, and Ifáyẹmí Elébuìbon. The second group of poets established connections between idioms and proverbs relevant to the theme of their composition. Adétìmíkàn Obasá maximized the use of this style to produce three anthologies. The last group of poets, including Adébáyò Fálétí, Akínwùmí Ìsòlá, Túnbòsún Oládàpò, and Lánrewájú Adépòjù, only employ the features of Yorùbá oral poetry, especially tonal counterpoint. This feature involves the use of contrasting tones through a deliberate choice or distortion of lexical items. It is done in a way that some tones, or the tone on the final syllable, in one lexical item will contrast with the tone(s) in another item.

PLAYS

The first attempt to write a Yorùbá play was the serialization of *Pa Mí n Kú Obìnrin* in the weekly newsprint *Elétí Ofè* in the 1930s. However, the play remained unpublished in book form. If the date of publication is anything to go by, the first Yorùbá plays were Babalolá's *Pàsán Sìnà* and Odúnjo's *Agbàlówóméèrí*; both published in 1958. Ìsòlá proposed three major trends for Yorùbá drama: the historical, the didactic, and the protest. Aside from Olú Owólábí in *Lísàbi Àgbòngbò Àkàlà* (1977) and Láwuyì Ògúnníran in *Ààre Àgò Aríkúyerí* (1978), most Yorùbá historical playwrights are not always loyal to strict historical details. The didactic plays, on the other hand, are simple stories designed to entertain and to teach morals. Such plays comment on matters that affect the society in general without much insightful presentation and discussion of the problems created by the prevailing sociopolitical system in the society. However, the emergence of the protest plays has provided the much-needed revitalization where attempts are made to decry the poor economic condition and the political powerlessness of the working class. These plays expose, discuss, and condemn corruption. Oládèjo Òkédìjí's *Réré Rún* (1973) and Ìsòlá's *Kòseégbé* (1981) are perhaps the most popular in this category.

NOVELS

There are two types of Yorùbá novels: those in which the realism is veiled, as in the novels of Daniel Fágúnwà (1903–1963); and those in which the realism is unveiled. The publication of Fágúnwà's first novel in 1938 evolved a new form of writing in Yorùbá literary history. Its success led to the publication of four more titles between 1949 and 1961. The framework in all of Fágúnwà's novels is very similar. The novels involve a particular adventure into the forest by some heroes. The unveiled realistic novels came into being out of authors' conscious effort to deviate from the Fágúnwà's general pattern. There are three subcategories of these novels: historical, social, and crime stories. The historical novel is a kind of imaginative portrayal of some definite aspects of history. For instance, Isaac Délànò, Adébáyò Fáléti (b. 1935) and Timothy Ládélé presented Yorùbá precolonial life in contrast with colonialism in their novels. The social novels, on the other hand, constitute a satiric portrayal of various evils in the society. The emergence of the crime novel began in 1961 with the publication of Akin Omóyájowó's *Ìtàn Adégbèsan.* Other prominent crime fiction writers are Òkédìjí and Kólá Akínlàdé. Although both novelists deal with crime, certain features in their writings reveal that, whereas Akínlàdé's works are novels of detection, Òkédìjí's are thrillers.

See also **Language: Choice in Writing; Literature: Oral.**

BIBLIOGRAPHY

Hair, Paul E.H. *The Early Study of Nigerian Languages.* Cambridge, U.K.: Cambridge University Press, 1967.

Isola, Akinwumi. "Modern Yoruba Drama." In *Drama and Theatre in Nigeria,* 1981.

Ogunsina, James Adebisi. *The Development of Yoruba Novels.* Ibadan, Nigeria: Gospel Faith Mission, 1992.

Olabimtan, Afolabi. "A Critical Survey of Yoruba Written Poetry 1848–1948." Ph.D. diss., University of Lagos, Nigeria, 1975.

AKÍNTÚNDÉ AKÍNYEMÍ

LITERATURES IN EUROPEAN LANGUAGES

This entry includes the following articles:
AFRIKAANS
ANGLOPHONE CENTRAL AND SOUTHERN AFRICA
ANGLOPHONE EASTERN AFRICA
ANGLOPHONE WESTERN AFRICA
FRANCOPHONE CENTRAL AFRICA
FRANCOPHONE INDIAN OCEAN AFRICA
FRANCOPHONE NORTHERN AFRICA
LUSOPHONE

AFRIKAANS

Afrikaans literature begins with Dutch settlers who came to South Africa in 1652 and ultimately formed the system of apartheid. Literature in Afrikaans, a derivative of the Dutch language, was generally supportive of these racial policies. Some writers opposed the political system, as internal struggles having to do both with form and with history evolved.

Whites and Coloureds have spoken Afrikaans since the late-eighteenth century. Stefanus Jacobus du Toit (1847–1911) led the First Language Movement (1875), an effort to separate Afrikaans from Dutch. Afrikaans ultimately became a significant written language. Eugène Marais (1871–1936) and Jan Celliers (1865–1940) were harbingers of the new literature, along with language organizations such as the Suid-Afrikaanse Akademie (1909). By 1924, Afrikaans was the official language in the Dutch Reformed Church, as, in literature, the earlier didactic writing gave way to other literary forms.

During the Second Language Movement, poets such as Eugéne Marais (1871–1936), Jan Celliers (1865–1940), Jacob D. du Toit (Totius) (1877–1953), C. Louis Leipoldt (1880–1947), Daniel François Malherbe (1881–1969), and Toon van den Heever (1894–1956) became important. Leipoldt, condemned as a traitor to Afrikaners, was the most original poet of his time. There were melodramatic novels by Jan H. De Waal (1852–1931), and drama by Leipoldt, Cornelius Jakob Langenhoven (1873–1943), and H. A. Fagan (1889–1965). A shift to realism was seen in the work of Jochem van Bruggen (1881–1957).

South African writer Deon Meyer (1958–). Born in Paarl, Meyer writes in Afrikaans. His work, ostensibly crime novels, deals with political, cultural, and racial tensions in post-apartheid South Africa. © SOPHIE BASSOULS/CORBIS

In the 1920s, a deepening isolation of Afrikaners led to such partisan organizations as the Broederbond and Federasie van Afrikaanse Kultuurvereniginge. Afrikaner poets, the Dertigers, (Thirty-ers), experimented with poetic form: William Ewart Gladstone Louw (1913–1980), Nicolaas Petrus van Wyk Louw (1906–1970), and Elisabeth Eybers (b. 1915). Later, the Sestigers (Sixty-ers) explored the form of the novel, sometimes questioning the system of apartheid: Jan Rabie (b. 1920), Etienne Leroux (b. 1922), Dolf van Niekerk (b. 1929), André P. Brink (b. 1935), Abraham de Vries (b. 1937), Breyten Breytenbach (b. 1939), and Chris Barnard (b. 1939).

With independence in 1990, writers echoed the new South Africa; Marlene van Niekerk (b. 1954) wrote of Soweto, Lettie Viljoen (Ingrid Winterbach) (b. 1948) of a family engaged in the struggle against apartheid, and Etienne van Heerden (b. 1954) of contemporary South African history. Koos Prinsloo (1957–1995) and Mark Behr (1963) dealt critically with the myths of Afrikanerdom. Some have addressed more controversial issues in their writing. Emma Huismans

(b. 1947) wrote of postcolonial subjects, Antjie Krog (b. 1952) of contemporary politics, and Riana Scheepers (b. 1957) of the colonizing of women in South Africa.

See also **Apartheid; Language; Literature.**

BIBLIOGRAPHY

Brink, André; Breyten Breytenbach; and J. M. Coetzee. *Colonization, Violence, and Narration in White South African Writing.* Athens: Ohio University Press, 1996.

Coetzee, John M. *White Writing: On the Culture of Letters in South Africa.* New Haven, CT: Yale University Press, 1988.

De Lange, Margreet. *The Muzzled Muse: Literature and Censorship in South Africa.* Amsterdam: John Benjamins, 1997.

Gardner, Judy H. *Impaired Vision: Portraits of Black Women in the Afrikaans Novel, 1948–1988.* Amsterdam: Vrije Universiteit Press, 1991.

Kriger, Robert, and Ethel Kriger. *Afrikaans Literature: Recollection, Redefinition, Restitution.* Amsterdam: Rodopi, 1996.

Viljoen, Hein, and Chris N. Van der Merwe. *Storyscapes: South African Perspectives on Literature, Space, and Identity.* New York: Peter Lang, 2004.

HAROLD SCHEUB

ANGLOPHONE CENTRAL AND SOUTHERN AFRICA

Anglophone writing in southern Africa is more commonly—and rather cumbersomely—known as English-language writing, or writing by English speakers. This description used to be understood to have meant writing exclusively by whites or those of European extraction. In the first surveys of this literature—by Ian D. Colvin in his introduction to Sidney Mendelssohn's *South African Bibliography* (1910) and by Manfred Nathan in his book-length *South African Literature* (1925)—this is entirely the case. However, since World War II the meaning of Anglophone writing has shifted to include all writers and performers who choose to write in English rather than in other languages of the region.

The term "southern Africa" needs some clarification because there is no working geopolitical region to which it corresponds. Roughly, "southern Africa" refers to South Africa; Namibia (formerly German Southwest Africa); Lesotho (formerly

Basutoland); Swaziland; Botswana (formerly Bechuanaland); Zimbabwe (formerly Southern Rhodesia); Zambia (formerly Northern Rhodesia); and Malawi (formerly Nyasaland), although these last two are sometimes classified as central African. This cluster of countries, in which British colonialism was a common formative experience, is flanked by Angola and Mozambique of the lusophone sphere of influence. Alternatively, all these countries, South Africa excepted, until 1994 formed the "front-line" states of the Southern African Development Coordinating Conference (SADCC), an association founded in 1980 to reduce economic dependence on South Africa which, at that time, was driven by apartheid policies.

The first English-language descriptions of southern Africa date back to explorers like Sir Francis Drake (c. 1543–1596), who rounded the Cape of Good Hope in the 1570s. The seaward view of the subcontinent was known to William Shakespeare, and John Donne worked a reference to Table Mountain into one of his poems, "Progress of the Soul" (1601). In 1634 Thomas Herbert wrote *Some Yeares Travaile into Afrique*, which first familiarized European readers with the inland aboriginal inhabitants, the San and Khoi peoples, then known as *Bushmen*. Daniel Defoe in *Captain Singleton* (1720) and Jonathan Swift in *Gulliver's Travels* (1726) had their characters make use of the facilities of the Dutch-sponsored entrepôt at Cape Town, the base for ever more penetrating and well-recorded expeditions.

The Cape was first occupied by the British in 1795, and in 1806 their rule became entrenched. The classic pattern of nineteenth-century colonization was applied: from 1820 in the Eastern Cape and from 1824 in Natal. Then hunters and missionaries moved into the interior, followed by transport-riders and administrators. David Livingstone (1813–1873), from his base near Mafeking (present-day Mafikeng), on the border of the Kalahari Desert, caught the popular imagination by opening up the "Dark Continent," contributing to the "scramble" for Africa by other colonial powers. By the end of the Victorian period, the imperial strategist Cecil Rhodes could talk of having started a railway line from the Cape that was destined almost to reach Cairo.

Early surveys of South African poetry, like that of Sir T. Herbert Warren in *The Cambridge History of English Literature*, consider the Scottish romantic, Thomas Pringle (1789–1834) as the father of South African English verse. Rudyard Kipling is quoted there as saying: "it's a case of there's Pringle, and there's Pringle, and after that one must hunt the local papers" (1916, 373). Pringle, the Cape's most influential man of letters, founded the first national library and the first literary review (*The South African Journal*, 1824) and championed the freedom of the press. "Afar in the Desert," his rhapsodic poem about belonging yet feeling alien in the wilderness of the hinterland, is indeed where English literature begins to inscribe Africa from personal experience. Settler mores and the plantation culture with which he clashed forced him to assume a Liberal stance, particularly against the slavery system. His *Narrative of a Residence in South Africa* (1835) chronicles this battle of the individual conscience against the illiberal state-information, a stance that may be said to characterize much of the output of the next century and a half.

In the *London Mercury* (1929), under the heading "South African Literature," Francis Brett Young drew a distinction between the copious documentary scribblers of the frontier press and the popular theater of his day, nominating Olive Schreiner (1855–1920) as the pioneer of "literary art" in Africa. In particular he mentioned her *Story of an African Farm*, first published in London in 1883 to huge and enduring acclaim. As Elaine Showalter remarks in her introduction to a 1993 reprint of the novel, "instead of civilized ladies and gentlemen discussing courtship over tea, it told the story of passionate dreamers arguing about the oppression of women and children, the meaning of life, the battle between good and evil, and the existence of God."

Young correctly places *The Story of an African Farm*, a problematic, contradictory text, at the head of a tradition of realist fiction. From the fringe of the British Empire, writers kept writing back to Britain with challenging and subtle social insight. Sarah Gertrude Millin (1889–1968) followed with *God's Step-children* (1924) and Pauline Smith (1882–1959) with her collection of short stories, *The Little Karoo* (1925).

A parallel tradition of adventure romance began at the same time with the publication of H. Rider Haggard's *King Solomon's Mines* (1885).

Rather than the domestic site dealt with by the realist mode, this kind of fiction takes as its natural material the he-man's urge toward expansion and the inevitable conquest of the weak by warfare. *Jock of the Bushveld* (1907), by J. Percy FitzPatrick (1862–1931), remains the most popular account of the preindustrial days of gold diggers and bushwhackers. The British-Zulu wars of 1879 and the so-called Boer War of 1899–1902 against the Afrikaner republics of the Transvaal and the Orange Free State were widely chronicled in this branch of the literature, which persists to the present in the works of writers like Laurens van der Post (1906–1996) and Wilbur Smith (b. 1933).

With the election of a Liberal government in Britain in 1906, the formation of the Union of South Africa in 1910 was assured (the land eventually acquired dominion status). In *The New Countries*, an anthology edited by Hector Bolitho in 1929, work from Australia, Canada, and New Zealand was included alongside South African pieces—notably by William Plomer (1903–1973), whose novel *Turbott Wolfe* (1925) had shockingly advocated "mixed race" marriages. The categorization of South African English work as part of Commonwealth literature continued even after apartheid South Africa was expelled from the Commonwealth in 1961—William H. New's *Among Worlds: An Introduction to Modern Commonwealth and South African Fiction* (1975) is an example.

The first black African literary figure of note writing in English in South Africa was Sol T. Plaatje (1877–1932). His historical novel, *Mhudi*, subtitled *An Epic of South African Native Life a Hundred Years Ago*, was largely written in 1917 but first published—by the missionary Lovedale Press—in 1930. However, only when it was reprinted in the Heinemann African Writers Series (1978) could it be said to have made any lasting impact. "When I first read this beautiful book," Bessie Head wrote then, "I was absolutely in despair. I needed to copy the whole book out by hand so as to keep it with me" (quoted from the jacket). Written as an attempt to preserve vanishing black versions of southern African history in order to serve the Africanizers of the future, *Mhudi* is now considered a model of resistance to European acculturation.

Among the first attempts at a South African cultural-national initiative was the movement begun in Natal around the satirical journal, *Voorslag*, edited mainly by the poet Roy Campbell (1901–1957). *Voorslag* (1926–1927) gave rise to equally short-lived and embattled efforts: *The Sjambok* of Stephen Black (1880–1931) in Johannesburg in 1929 and *The Touleier* of Herman Charles Bosman (1905–1951), also in Johannesburg (1930). Since then, intermittent journals advocating that South African work be directly presented to South African readers have appeared more reliably; *Contrast*, founded in Cape Town in 1960, remains active in the early 2000s as *New Contrast*. From the 1920s, book publishing has developed into a sophisticated industry as well.

The parallel development of Afrikaans-language culture, given a boost by the accession to power of the Nationalist government in 1948, also has acted as a stimulus, although during the deep apartheid period, English-language work assumed an increasingly oppositional position beginning in the 1960s. The famous novel published the year the Afrikaner nationalists took over, *Cry, the Beloved Country*, by Alan Paton (1903–1988)—still the most read South African work—has come to be taken as the typical protest novel, written against segregatory practices.

In a survey like "The Color of South African Literature" by Martin Tucker (in his *Africa in Modern Literature*, 1967), writers like Doris Lessing (b. 1919) are featured. Although her early work was exclusively about Rhodesia, she is still classified by Tucker as a South African writer. The same often applies to Thomas Mofolo (1877–1948), whose *Chaka* (originally written in Sesotho in 1925), when it first appeared in an English translation in 1931, made a great impact, especially on the Négritude writers elsewhere in Africa.

In 1970, at a Modern Language Association conference on British Commonwealth literature, it became clear that as a result of purges and the censorship system of apartheid, southern African literature had really been split into two (the second part being a diaspora of those driven into exile). The school of urban journalists that formed around *Drum* and other magazines—for example, Can Themba (1924–1967), Lewis Nkosi (b. 1935), and Nat Nakasa (1937–1965)—was disbanded and banned. Many great works were now written overseas in the form of autobiographical testimony—two are *Tell Freedom* (1954), by Peter Abrahams (b. 1919), and *Down Second Avenue* (1959), by Ezekiel (now Es'kia) Mphahlele (b. 1919). Dennis Brutus (b. 1924) wrote poetry within his campaign against racial discrimination and violence while Alex La Guma wrote socialist-realist novels about the same topics. By 1974, in his chapter "South Africa" (in Bruce King's collection, *Literatures of the World in English*), John Povey could remark that the gulf between South African expatriates and those at home was absolute.

With the Chimurenga (War of Liberation) declared in the future Zimbabwe, Lessing was prohibited entry. Writers crucial to the formation of a rapidly expanding Zimbabwean literature were active: Dambudzo Marechera (1955–1986) is the prime example, his novella *The House of Hunger* (1978) being a key work about the displacements of young blacks in the ghetto environment. Another is Shimmer Chinodya (b. 1957), whose panoramic *Harvest of Thorns* (1989) is a near-perfect account of Zimbabwe's transition to independence.

A collection like Colin and O-lan Style's *Mambo Book of Zimbabwean Verse in English* (1986) is an admirable summary of what is now the independent and independent-minded, largely black enterprise of ZimLit. In 1992, when Lessing published her *African Laughter: Four Visits to Zimbabwe*—part history, part cultural commentary, and part reminiscence—she stated her position as one of the major figures of the new literatures in English vis-à-vis the burgeoning land of her youth.

The same may not be said of Zambia, to the north, where restrictive government procedures have inhibited literary growth. The National Educational Company in Lusaka has published a few plays, notably by Kabwe Kasoma (b. 1933), and some poetry collections. The autobiography of former President Kenneth Kaunda (b. 1924), *Zambia Shall Be Free* (1962), remains in print. An early novel promoting unity in the land is *The Tongue of the Dumb* (1971), by Dominic Mulaisho (b. 1933).

The first novel about independent Zambia, *Quills of Desire*, by Binwell Sinyangwe (b. 1956), was not published until 1993, by Baobab Books in neighboring Zimbabwe. There, thanks to enlightened publishing policies, together with the technically advanced

annual book fair, an alternative to the publishing industry in South Africa is being formed.

Only one work by a writer of Swazi origin is noted in *A New Reader's Guide to African Literature* (1983), edited by Hans M. Zell, Carol Bundy, and Virginia Coulon. Only one poem from there—by Oswald Basize Dube (b. 1957), a praise poem in honor of King Sobhuza II—has been included in a regional collection, *The Penguin Book of Southern African Verse* (1989).

Malawi, on the other hand, despite the persecution of intellectuals under the rule of President Hastings Banda, has produced a powerful group of poets, most of them associated with the writers' workshop at Chancellor College in Zomba. These include David Rubardiri (b. 1930), Felix Mnthali (b. 1933), Jack Mapanje (b. 1944), and Frank Chipasula (b. 1949), the latter being the editor of the influential anthology *When My Brothers Come Home: Poems from Central and Southern Africa* (1985). In 1967, a rediscovery akin to that of Plaatje in South Africa occurred when George Simeon Mwase's classic account of the Chilembwe Rising of 1915, *Strike a Blow and Die*, was first published.

A work of similar impact—since it records African history in the making, from the inside point of view—is *A Bewitched Crossroads* (1984). It is about the origins of Botswana, the country of adoption of Bessie Head (1937–1986), who almost alone has made Botswanan literature, beginning with her novel *When Rain Clouds Gather* (1968). By the time of her short-story collection *The Collector of Treasures* (1977), she was hailed as one of Africa's trendsetting women writers. She did not live to see her home country, South Africa, free of apartheid and was never permitted to return to it.

In South Africa in the 1980s, despite the severance of cultural ties with the rest of the region, several major careers continued undiminished, as if challenged to excel by the very bleakness of the situation. One is that of Nadine Gordimer. Born in 1923, she began publishing stories in 1937; in 1991 she was awarded the Nobel Prize for Literature, primarily in recognition of her tireless struggle against censorship. As a founder of the Congress of South African Writers, she has ensured the unfettered publication of many younger figures, particularly through the journal *Staffrider*, now defunct. Another novelist with a sustained and equally distinguished output is J. M. Coetzee (b. 1940), also a winner of the Nobel Prize for Literature.

Another noteworthy career is Athol Fugard's (b. 1932). By 1958 he was writing and directing the plays that would make him one of the most produced dramatists in the English-speaking theater. The techniques used in his collaborative texts—for example, *Sizwe Bansi Is Dead* (1974), devised with his performers—have stimulated much other African drama and numerous imitations. The younger generation of writers includes Tsitsi Dangeremba, Zoë Wicomb, Yvonne Vera, and Zakes Mda.

With the election of the first nonracial majority government in South Africa in 1994, southern Africa has for the first time become integrated as a literary whole.

See also **Apartheid; Banda, Ngwazi Hastings Kamuzu; Coetzee, J. M.; Fugard, Athol; Gordimer, Nadine; Guma, Alex La; Head, Bessie Emery; Human Rights; Johannesburg; Kaunda, Kenneth; Paton, Alan; Plaatje, Sol; Rhodes, Cecil John; Sobhuza I and II.**

BIBLIOGRAPHY

Alvarez-Pereyre, Jacques. *The Poetry of Commitment in South Africa.* London: Heinemann, 1984.

Barnett, Ursula A. *A Vision of Order: A Study of Black South African Literature in English (1914–1980).* Amherst: University of Massachusetts Press, 1983.

The Cambridge History of English Literature. Cambridge, U.K.: Cambridge University Press, 1916.

Chapman, Michael. *Southern African Literatures.* London: Longman, 1996; Pietermaritzburg: University of KZN Press, 2003.

Chapman, Michael; Colin Gardner; and Es'kia Mphahlele; eds. *Perspectives on South African English Literature.* Johannesburg: Donkers, 1992.

Coetzee, J. M. *White Writing: On the Culture of Letters in South Africa.* New Haven, CT: Yale University Press, 1988.

Daymond, M. J., ed. *Women Writing Africa,* Vol. 1: *Southern Africa.* New York: The Feminist Press, 2002.

Driver, Dorothy. "South African Literature: In English." In *Encyclopedia of World Literature in the Twentieth Century,* ed. Leonard S. Klein. New York: Ungar, 1984.

Gérard, Albert S., ed. *European-Language Writing in Sub-Saharan Africa.* 2 vols. Budapest: Akadémiai Kiado, 1986.

Gray, Stephen. *Southern African Literature: An Introduction.* New York: Barnes and Noble, 1979.

Gray, Stephen. "South African Poetry: In English." In *The New Princeton Encyclopedia of Poetry and Poetics,* ed. Alex Preminger and T. V. F. Brogan. Princeton, NJ: Princeton University Press, 1993.

Gray, Stephen, ed. *The Penguin Book of Southern African Stories.* London: Penguin, 1985.

Haarhoff, Dorian. *The Wild South-West: Frontier Myths and Metaphors in Literature Set in Namibia (1760–1988).* Johannesburg: University of the Witwatersrand Press, 1991.

Heywood, Christopher. *A History of South African Literature.* Cambridge, U.K.: Cambridge University Press, 2004.

Mphahlele, Ezekiel. *The African Image,* rev. edition. London: Faber and Faber, 1974.

Ricard, Alain. *The Languages and Literatures of Africa.* Trenton, NJ: Africa World Press, 2004.

Smith, M. van Wyk. *Drummer Hodge: The Poetry of the Anglo-Boer War, 1899–1902.* New York: Oxford University Press, 1978.

Smith, M. van Wyk. *Grounds of Contest: A Survey of South African English Literature.* Cape Town: Juta, 1990.

Veit-Wild, Flora. *Teachers, Preachers, Non-Believers: A Social History of Zimbabwean Literature.* London: Hans Zell, 1992.

STEPHEN GRAY

ANGLOPHONE EASTERN AFRICA

Ngũgĩ wa Thiong'o, Nuruddin Farah, and Okot p'Bitek (1931–1982) are the most well-known East African Anglophone writers. Ngũgĩ wa Thiong'o's novels, particularly *A Grain of Wheat* (1967) and *Petals of Blood* (1977), are the most widely read works of East African literature. Nuruddin Farah's novels, especially *Maps* (1986), those in the three-volume series, *Variations on the Theme of an African Dictatorship* (1979–1983), and four of his other novels, *Gifts* (1993), *Secrets* (1998), *Links* (2004), and *Knots* (2007) have received international critical acclaim. Farah was awarded the 1998 Neustadt International Prize for Literature. Okot p'Bitek's book-length satiric poems, *Song of Lawino* (1966) and *Song of Ocol* (1970), have delighted a wide range of audiences and have had a major impact on East African writing because of the innovative ways in which he drew upon Acoli oral poetic performance.

A number of East African writers began to publish works in English just before and after independence in the early 1960s. The best-known English-language works by East African writers that were published during this period were Ngũgĩ wa Thiong'o's novels *The River Between* (1965), *Weep Not, Child* (1964), and *A Grain of Wheat*, and Okot p'Bitek's *Song of Lawino* and *Song of Ocol*. Grace Ogot's first two novels, *The Promised Land* and *Land without Thunder*, were also published in the 1960s. Taban lo Liyong's first volume of poetry, *Frantz Fanon's Uneven Ribs* was published in 1970. Two Tanzanian novelists also wrote novels in English shortly after independence. Gabriel Ruhumbika's *Village in Uhuru* was published in 1969, and Peter K. Palangyo's *Dying in the Sun* was published in 1968.

Ethiopian novelists also published novels in English during this period. Their works included Tsegaye Gebre-Medhin's *Oda Oak Oracle*, Sahle Sellassie's *The Afersata*, and Danichew Worku's *The Thirteenth Sun*. Among East African novelists who have continued to write in English are Nuruddin Farah, Meja Mwangi (*Going Down River Road*, 1976; *Cockroach Dance*, 1979), Abdulrazak R. Gurnah (*Paradise*, 1994), M. G. Vassanji (*The Gunnysack*, 1989; *Uhuru Street*, 1991), and Marjorie Oludhe Macgoye. One of the major literary events in eastern Africa during the early years of independence was the founding of *Transition*, a journal of literary and social commentary, by Rajat Neogy (1938–1995) at Makerere University in Uganda. *Transition* is now one of Africa's oldest and most influential journals.

Anglophone East African writers have grappled with many of the issues that have engaged their counterparts elsewhere in Africa and the postcolonial world: countering colonial historical fiction, raising questions concerning identity, writing African experiences in western languages, engaging with other literatures, and addressing issues of language and audience. The ways in which they have defined and dealt with these issues provide a general outline of some of the features of this literature.

Many Anglophone eastern African writers have written novels that present colonial and postcolonial history from eastern African perspectives. Historical fiction has been a significant genre, especially for Kenyan writers who have written novels that counter the racist, elitist, and Eurocentric biases of colonial writers of East African history as well as those of earlier historical fiction set in east Africa. For example, the early novels of Ngũgĩ wa Thiong'o treat the historical experience of experiences of Gikuyu peasants during the periods of colonial repression of cultural practices and the genocidal suppression of the Kenya Land Freedom Army's liberation struggle. Other historical novels, including Meja Mwangi's (b. 1948) *Carcase for Hounds* (1974), Marjorie Oludhe Macgoye's (b. 1928) *Coming to Birth* (1986), and Samuel Kahiga's (b. 1946) *Dedan Kimathi: The Real Story* (1990), also addressed what is often referred to as the Mau Mau war and the genocidal suppression of the resistance movement. Kenyan historical novels such as Ngũgĩ's *Petals of Blood* (1977) have also addressed politically sensitive issues such as the neglect of rural communities, neocolonial development, the assassination of opposition politicians, and government fostered ethnic conflict.

Nuruddin Farah's works incorporate feminist viewpoints and problematize notions of national, ethnic, linguistic, and gender identity. His three novels with the series title *Variations on the Theme of an African Dictatorship* (*Sweet and Sour Milk*, 1979; *Sardines*, 1981; and *Close Sesame*, 1983) each critique the violent repression of Siad Barre's (1919–1995) regime in Somalia, as well as comment upon other dictatorships and forms of tyranny. In its focus on independent and creative women, *Sardines* considers dictatorship as patriarchy and patriarchal social structures and behavior as dictatorial.

Anglophone East African writers, often working with writers in other East African languages, have also generally been activist writers and have been persecuted for their writing by the corrupt and violent politicians and governments they criticize. Abdilatif Abdalla (b. 1946) wrote *Sauti ya Dhiki* (1973) while he was imprisoned for three years for having written a pamphlet for the Kenya People's Union, an opposition party. Abdilatif and Ngũgĩ wa Thiong'o worked together through the United Movement for Democracy in Kenya and other organizations to document and draw attention to

1980s human rights struggles in Kenya. Ngũgĩ wrote *Caitaani Mutharaba-ini* (1980; translated as *Devil on the Cross* in 1983), his first novel, in Gikuyu while imprisoned without charge but presumably for coauthoring the play *Ngaahika Ndeenda*. He documented his prison experiences in *Detained: A Writer's Prison Diary* (1981).

Persecuted East African activist writers have also included, among many others, Byron Kawadwa (d. 1977), a Ugandan playwright who was murdered by agents of Idi Amin; Nuruddin Farah, who was forced into exile and sentenced to death in absentia by Somalia's former dictator Mohammed Siad Barre; Gakaara wa Wanjau (d. 2001), who was imprisoned by both the colonial and postindependence governments of Kenya; journalist and novelist Wahome Mutahi (1954–2003); and politician and novelist Koigi wa Wamwere (b. 1949). A number of prison diaries and novels with prison settings have been published by eastern Africans. These include Wahome Mutahi's *Three Days on the Cross* (1991), Ngũgĩ wa Thiong'o's *Detained* (1981), Koigi wa Wamwere's *Conscience on Trial* (1988), J. M. Kariuki's (b. 1929) *Mau Mau Detainee* (1963), and Gakaara wa Wanjau's *Mwandiki wa Mau Mau Ithaa-mirio-ini* (1983; translated as *Mau Mau Author in Detention* in 1988). In their vivid descriptions and careful documentation, these works record the prison experiences of the authors as well as other political detainees and also provide evidence of the violence and tyrannical nature of colonial and postcolonial regimes in Kenya and Uganda.

Anglophone eastern African writers have also addressed questions of personal, gender, ethnic, class, national, regional, and African identity. These topics are central to many of Nuruddin Farah's novels that comment upon the mixture of political and personal struggles in an effort to establish viable personal and political identities. In his novel *Maps*, questions of boundaries and identities take the form of an adolescent narrator, who acts as judge, audience, and witness, and tells his story of violence and murder during the war over the Ogaden region between Ethiopia and Somalia. Askar, the male orphan narrator, is the child of Somali parents but when his adoptive mother, an Ethiopian who brought him up in the Ogaden, is murdered, he tastes blood in his mouth and believes that he is menstruating. His childhood failure to recognize physical boundaries or gender difference between them continues to take physical form even as he matures and struggles to define for himself their ethnic, linguistic and national identities.

Many Anglophone East African writers have explored ways of connecting their works in English to oral literatures in African languages. An important contribution made to literary theory by eastern Africans has been the concept of orature as used by Pio Zirimu and Austin Bukenya to distinguish spoken and performed compositions from written texts. East African study of orature has been particularly informed by their work as evidenced both in the body of research that has been produced and in the importance of orature in East African literature curricula. One of the most notable East African studies of this topic is Wanjiku Mukabi Kabira's *The Oral Artist* (1983), a study of the oral narrative performances of Kabebe, an artist from Kiambu, Kenya. Authors have also incorporated elements of orature into written works. For example, Ngũgĩ's *Matigari ma Njiruungi* (1986; translated as *Matigari*, 1989) utilizes oral tales and is written as a performed narrative. Similarly, his *Caitaani Mutharaba-ini* (1980; translated as *Devil on the Cross*, 1983) employs the figure of the gicaandi player, a performer of oral competitive poetry in Gikuyu.

The perhaps defining issue of Anglophone East African literature has been the question of what language/languages should best be used to communicate with East African audiences. The establishment of Swahili as the official and national language of Tanzania and as the national language of Kenya, and the development of literature in Swahili during the colonial and postcolonial eras, has had a profound impact on East African writing in English, as many writers have chosen to write in Swahili and other East African languages rather than in English. Ngũgĩ wa Thiong'o's 1986 call in *Decolonising the Mind* for "the rediscovery of the real language of humankind: the language of struggle" (Ngũgĩ wa Thiong'o, 108) and his declaration to write only in Gikuyu and Swahili enlarged upon literary and political debates that had been active in East Africa since independence and even earlier. Ngũgĩ ends the preface of this book by quoting a poem by Shaaban Robert, East Africa's most renowned poet, in which the poet explained why he chose to write only in Swahili.

In the early 1960s and 1970s, Kenya, Tanzania, and Uganda were part of what was the East African Community, and at the University of Nairobi Ngũgĩ wa Thiong'o, Okot p'Bitek, and Taban lo Liyong were among those who pressed for curricular revisions that would emphasize works by African writers, oral literature, and works in East African languages, especially Swahili. Similar debates took place at Makerere University and the University of Dar es Salaam. During this period Swahili departments were established at the University of Dar es Salaam and the University of Nairobi. As a result of these curricular revisions and a widely shared commitment to Swahili and Swahili literature, the 1970s and 1980s generation of university-educated Kenyan and Tanzanian writers has produced works written almost exclusively in Swahili. The best-known of this group of writers are playwright Ebrahim Hussein (b. 1943), novelist and poet Said Ahmed Mohamed (b. 1947), novelist E. Kezilahabi (b. 1944), and playwright and poet Alamin Mazrui (b. 1933). The orientation of their works is progressive, generally explicitly socialist, and often highly critical of neocolonialism and of East African government policies and political culture, particularly those of the Moi government (1977–2002) in Kenya. Notable among them are Ebrahim Hussein's play *Kwenye Ukingo wa Thim* (1988), which uses a highly publicized and politicized inheritance case in Kenya as the basis for a complex drama that explores issues of ethnicity, class, and gender, and Said Ahmed Mohamed's novel *Kiza katika Nuru* (1988), which considers the patriarchal and class bases of neocolonial corruption.

In the early twenty-first century, a group of young writers including Binyavanga Wainaina (b. 1971) and Yvonne Adhiambo-Owuor have enlivened the Anglophone literary scene in East Africa by establishing a new literary magazine and by writing and publishing engaging short stories characterized by innovative narrative techniques and attention to contemporary voices. After winning the Caine Prize for African Writing in 2002, Wainaina established the literary magazine, *Kwani?*. Adhiambo-Owuor's story first published in *Kwani?* won the Caine Prize in 2004.

See also **Education, School; Farah, Nuruddin; Human Rights; Kagwa, Apolo; Kenyatta, Jomo; Literature: Oral; Ngũgĩ wa Thiong'o; Shaaban Robert.**

BIBLIOGRAPHY

Farah, Nuruddin. *Maps*. New York: Pantheon Books, 1986.

Gérard, Albert S., ed. *European-Language Writing in Sub-Saharan Africa*. Budapest, Hungary: Akadémiai Kiadó, 1986.

Gikandi, Simon. *Ngugi wa Thiong'o*. Cambridge, U.K.: Cambridge University Press, 2000.

Gikandi, Simon. "East African Literature in English." In *The Cambridge History of African and Caribbean Literature*. Cambridge, U.K.: Cambridge University Press, 2004.

Lihamba, Amandina, et al., eds. *Women Writing Africa: The Eastern Region*. New York: Feminist Press at the City University of New York, 2007.

Lindfors, Bernth, ed. *Mazungumzo: Interviews with East African Writers, Publishers, Editors, and Scholars*. Athens: Ohio University Press, 1980.

Lo Liyong, Taban. *The Last Word: Cultural Synthesism*. Nairobi, Kenya: East African Publishing House, 1969.

Ngugi wa Thiong'o. *Decolonising the Mind: The Politics of Language in African Literature*. London: J. Currey, 1986.

p'Bitek, Okot. *Africa's Cultural Revolution*. Nairobi, Kenya: Macmillan Books for Africa, 1973.

Sicherman, Carol. *Ngugi wa Thiong'o, The Making of a Rebel: A Sourcebook in Kenyan Literature and Resistance*. London: Hans Zell, 1990.

ANN BIERSTEKER

ANGLOPHONE WESTERN AFRICA

Two outstanding writers on the African continent are Chinua Achebe and Wole Soyinka. Their works, *Things Fall Apart* (1958) and *The Interpreters* (1965), vie with A. C. Jordan's *Ingqumbo yeminyanya* (The wrath of the ancestors, 1940), Tayeb Salih's *Mawsim al-Hijra ila al-Shamal* (Season of migration to the north, 1969), and Algerian writer Kateb Yacine's *Nedjma* (1956) as Africa's greatest works.

Anglophone West African writers of significance include Amos Tutuola, whose *The Palm-wine Drinkard* (1952) is a story that owes its inspiration to the Nigerian oral tradition but which is decidedly a literary work. The narrative is composed of a dominant movement: the drinkard goes to Dead's Town to bring his tapster back to the land of the living. Each part of the story is either a restatement or an elaboration of that movement—that is, everything, everyone, in some way or another reflects the basic life-death polarity. A combination of similarity and uniqueness results. In the Ghanaian writer Ayi Kwei Armah's *Fragments* (1971), Baako, a "been-to," upon his return to Ghana, experiences difficulties as he attempts to bridge his experiences in the West with traditional African values. *Efuru* (1966), by the Nigerian writer Flora Nwapa, is a story of a woman who, ambitious, talented, brilliant, and beautiful, is confined by tradition, tied to the idea that blood will tell. A woman is seen to be a child-bearer. She may go beyond that, but child-bearing is the minimal requirement of a woman; her fundamental role is prescribed for her, and she must live up to it or suffer the negative criticism of a segment of her society.

In Ben Okri's *Stars of the New Curfew* (1988), the central character moves to his past, then back to Lagos and the present: Arthur's "own nightmares had ceased. But I had begun to see our lives as a bit of a nightmare. I think I prefer my former condition." Ben Okri blends fantasy and reality in *The Famished Road* (1991), a part of a trilogy. Writing of the reality of post-colonial Nigeria, the storyteller uses myth, the Yoruba *abiku* child, with other fantasy images, to shift between preindependence and postindependence settings. The spiritual and the real worlds are linked, the one a dimension of the other, in a narrative mode that African storytellers have been using for centuries.

Buchi Emecheta's *The Slave Girl* (1977) has these accompanying threads: history (British slavery), marriage, the whites and Christianity, images of the market-place (slave market?); in the end, what difference is there in the relationship between men and women, and domestic slavery? between domestic slavery and international (British) slavery? between slavery and marriage? Secondary patterns tell the story of Ojebeta as a domestic slave. As she grows to womanhood, she moves not to freedom and independence, but from one form of slavery into another.

Other West African writers have similarly distinguished themselves. Cyprian Ekwensi's *Jagua Nana* (1961) grew out of a period of such popular "market" literature as *Mabel the Sweet Honey that Poured Away*, by A. Onwudiwe (pseudonym, Speedy Eric) (n.d.) and Miller Albert's *Rosemary and the Taxi Driver* (1960): "Jagua immediately bridled and swung her hips to delight him and winked at him intimately.... Uncle Taiwo had

become ... taken with her 'provincialness' and marvelous skin.... He said he liked her because she was 'not like Lagos women.'" Echewa, T. Obinkaram's *I Saw the Sky Catch Fire* (1992) is a novel about storytelling: "I marveled at the verve with which Nne-nne told her story. As she spoke, the war seemed to come alive in her face and in her eyes, and even beyond that, her attention seemed to be turned inward as if she were reading the words from a screen somewhere in her mind." *The Voice* (1964) is a not wholly successful experiment with the English language and with the relationship between oral tradition and the written word. It is the story of Okolo and his allegorical return to his roots. "Okolo lay still in the darkness enclosed by darkness, and he his thoughts picked in his inside. Then his picked thoughts his eyes opened but his vision only met a rick-like darkness."

John Pepper Clark-Bekederemo's *Song of a Goat* (1961) is a play on the Greek goat-song tragedy. Zifa's "half-possessed aunt" observes, "I looked for a staff/Long enough to kill a serpent I knew/Was strangling my goat. In my search is my defeat." Christopher Okigbo's *Heavensgate* (1962) is a work lost in the legend of Mother Idoto: "And the spent sea reflects/from his mirrored visage/not my queen,/a broken shadow."

But Chinua Achebe and Wole Soyinka remain West Africa's great writers. In *Things Fall Apart*, Okonkwo is a driven man, his life's struggle rooted in manliness and his fear of being like his father, whom he considers effeminate, not a man. He therefore tears out of himself all human compassion. Okonkwo, then, in his own personal development, and given impetus by the model of his father, selects only those aspects from his society that will not interfere with the vision he has developed as a result of that relationship, selectively including only those aspects of his society that he considers masculine. The tragic story of Okonkwo, some of that story unfolding within the historical experience of colonialism in Nigeria, then moves to its inevitable end.

In Soyinka's *The Interpreters*, Sekoni, an engineer and sculptor, is arrested and forced into a mental hospital. When free, he carves "The Wrestler," a masterpiece. He dies in a motor accident. Sekoni's death brings the other interpreters a sense of their limitations and mortality. Egbo runs away and hides among rocks until the funeral is over; Sagoe locks himself in a room full of beer and vomit; Kola seeks escape in his painting. The moral decay of the world equals the physical decay that surrounds them. The interpreters cynically disapprove of the moral emptiness of their society; they have a common interest in art and a desire to change the world around them.

See also **Achebe, Chinua; Armah, Ayi Kwei; Awolowo, Obafemi; Casely-Hayford, Joseph Ephraim; Emecheta, Buchi; Equiano, Olaudah; Nwapa, Flora; Popular Culture; Soyinka, Wole; Theater.**

BIBLIOGRAPHY

Achebe, Chinua. *Things Fall Apart*. London: Heinemann, 1958.

Armah, Ayi Kwei. *Fragments*. Boston: Houghton Mifflin, 1970.

Clark-Bekederemo, John Pepper. *Song of a Goat*. Ibadan: Mbari, 1961.

Echewa, T. Obinkaram. *I Saw the Sky Catch Fire*. New York: Dutton, 1992.

Ekwensi, Cyprian. *Jagua Nana*. London: Hutchinson, 1961.

Emecheta, Buchi. *The Slave Girl*. London: Allison and Busby, 1977.

Nwapa, Flora. *Efuru*. London: Heinemann, 1966.

Okara, Gabriel Imomotimi Gbaingbain. *The Voice*. London: Andre Deutsch, 1964.

Okigbo, Christopher. *Heavensgate*. Ibadan: Mbari, 1962.

Okri, Ben. *Stars of the New Curfew*. London: Secker and Warburg, 1988.

Okri, Ben. *The Famished Road*. London: Jonathan Cape, 1991.

Soyinka, Wole. *The Interpreters*. London: Andre Deutsch, 1965.

Tutuola, Amos. *The Palm-Wine Drinkard and His Dead Palm-Wine Tapster in the Dead's Town*. New York: Grove Press, 1953.

HAROLD SCHEUB

FRANCOPHONE CENTRAL AFRICA

The colonial legacy is very much alive in the geographical configuration of twenty-first century Africa, as well as in many aspects of Africa's contemporary culture, including languages and literatures. The cultural policy in the French colonies was one of cultural assimilation, carried out mainly through the educational system. In school the

Africans learned and mastered the French language and were introduced to the culture of the colonizer. The Belgian policy was similar to that of France. References and cultural models were the same: the cultural history of the French-speaking region of Belgium (Wallonie) taught in the Belgian Congo's schools was, with few exceptions, the same. Like other former French colonies, after its independence, the Congo maintained French as the major European language, coexisting with several major African languages with the status of national languages. Thus, a context of multilingualism and cultural assimilation through the French or the Belgian educational system enabled the development of a modern African literature in French.

The first manifestations of writing in French can be found in the journal *Liaison*, founded in 1950, the Catholic journal *La voix de l'Ubangui* for the former French colonies, and *La voix du Congolais* in the Belgian Congo. These various colonial newspapers and cultural journals served as vehicles of expression for educated Africans or "évolués," as they were called, a space where African intellectuals could voice their opinions on social and cultural matters, as well as publish a variety of literary texts.

THE CENTRAL AFRICAN REPUBLIC

From the perspective of literary history, the Central African Republic is particularly interesting: it is here that the West Indian writer from Martinique, René Maran, was sent as a colonial administrator and worked for many years. His controversial Goncourt Prize–winning novel, *Batouala*, and some of his other works, like *Djouma, chien de brousse* and *Le livre de la brousse*, drew upon this experience. *Batouala* is particularly important as the first manifestation of a critique by a black person of colonial methodology and is often considered as the precursor of the Francophone novel. The dominant themes of the existing central African literature are not very different from those elsewhere in Africa: the encounter between Africa and the West and its consequences, the conflict or the blending of tradition and modernity, the opposition between the village and the urban environment. They reflect the transformation of African society and the individual's quest to find an identity and a way of life in the new context. There is also a desire to preserve or to adapt tradition, through using folk material or including historical events and characters in the written work.

The young Central African literature is represented by poetry, theater, and fiction. Most plays, even when they have been performed for the local public, remain unpublished. The novel, as elsewhere in Africa, appears to be the more practiced and the more published genre. Some novelists are gaining visibility within the country, and their works have been published in Africa as well as in France: Cyriaque Robert Yavoucko's novel *Crépuscule et défi* (1979); Pierre Sammy-Mackfoy's *L'odyssée de Mongou* (1978, 1983); Étienne Goyémidé's *Le silence de la forêt* (1984) and *Le dernier survivant de la caravane* (1985); and Gabriel Danzi's *Un soleil au bout de la unit* (1984). Pierre Makombo Bamboté remains unquestionably the dominant figure of Central African literature. Two major collections of his poetry, *La poésie est dans l'histoire* (1960) and *Chant funèbre pour un héros d'Afrique* (1962), were followed by other collections of poetry and short stories as well as two novels: *La randonnée de Daba* (1966) and *Princesse Mandapu* (1972), the novel that put him in the spotlight of African literature. Bamboté's *Coup d'état nègre* (1985) concerns the events and the political climate under the dictatorial regime of Jean-Bedel Bokassa, as does a novel by Thierry Jacques Gallo, *N'Garaba maison des morts: Un prisonnier sous Bokassa* (1988).

GABON

In terms of intellectual life, literature, and the conditions of reading, writing, and publishing, the situation in Gabon is similar to that of many African countries. During the colonial period, the journal *Liaison* provided an opportunity to the aspiring writers in equatorial Africa to publish their works in its pages. The publication of an *Anthologie de la littérature gabonaise* (1976) by the Ministry of Education and of a special issue of the journal *Notre librairie* (April–June 1991) raised awareness about Gabonese writers by presenting their works to the public.

As elsewhere in Africa, the first manifestations of a new literature were inspired by oral literature, and very often new works in French are rewritings of the oral literature, in an attempt to recapture and preserve the tradition by communicating it in a

modern context. The major figure in this genre is André Raponda Walker, the Gabonese Catholic priest who collected the folk material and published it as *Contes gabonais* (1953). The new literature in French is represented by works of poetry, theater, and fiction. For the most part, the young authors' reputations do not extend beyond the national borders of Gabon. Authors are very much concerned with the national past, as well as the social and cultural situation of their immediate environment. There has been almost no poetry published, and the majority of the plays are performed without being published. The recurrent themes in fiction are a social critique of colonization, but also of local practices and beliefs such as witchcraft; a critique of modern society embodied by the urban environment and portrayed as inhuman; a questioning of some practices related to family and marriage; the revalorization of the African past; and a quest for identity.

Along with Raponda Walker, Vincent de Paul Nyonda belongs to an older generation. He has published a dramatic play, *La mort de Guykafi* (1981), and a comedy, *Deux albinos à la MPassa* (1971), reenacting in a parodic mode the arrival of the nineteenth-century French explorer Pierre-Paul Savorgnan de Brazza. Young authors include Angèle Ntyugwetondo Rawiri, the major female writer in the country, who has published three novels: *Elonga* (1980), *G'amèrakano* (1983), and *Fureurs et cris de femmes* (1980). The first two offer a general social critique: love of money and physical beauty instead of moral and social qualities; they also denounce witchcraft as a manifestation of human envy, jealousy, and malice. The third novel focuses on the condition of African women caught between tradition and modernity.

Maurice Okumba-Nkoghe has published collections of poetry, *Paroles vives* (1979) and *Le soleil de la misère* (1980). He also has written fiction: *Siana* (1982), an autobiographical novel, and *La mouche et la glue* (1984), a novel of destiny, love, death, and rebellion against the father. The rebellion against the paternal authority symbolizes the daughter's will to break with a tradition that dictates a woman's choice of a husband. *Au bout du silence* (1985) by Laurent Owondo is a novel that recounts, through the use of symbolism, the spiritual itinerary of the hero and his psychological development. From a strictly aesthetic standpoint, Okumba-Nkoghe and Owondo emerge as the most accomplished writers of a Gabonese literature still in the process of formation.

DEMOCRATIC REPUBLIC OF THE CONGO

In the Belgian Congo (present-day Democratic Republic of the Congo [DRC]), the birth of African writing in French, as elsewhere in sub-Saharan Africa, took its inspiration from oral literature, and the works were published in local journals. As the Congolese critic Mukala Kadima-Nzuji shows in his book *La littérature zaïroise de langue française, 1945–1965* (1984), the journal *La voix du Congolais* (1945–1959) was instrumental in the promotion of African writing. Although created and controlled by the colonial administration, the journal provided the Congolese *évolués* with a forum where they could express their views on the social and cultural problems of their society.

At the same time, pieces of oral traditional literature and literary works in French, mainly poems by Africans, also were published. Literary contests organized by the journal were a stimulant for literary creativity. Antoine-Roger Bolamba is considered a pioneer with *Esanzo: Chants pour mon pays* (1955), a collection of poems inspired by the oral tradition of the author's ethnic group, in which the lyric mode veils a political revendication embedded in images of blood and fire. Before Bolamba, Paul Lomami-Tshibamba was a pioneer with his novel *Ngando* (1948), much celebrated at the time of its publication and awarded the Prix Littéraire de la Foire Coloniale de Bruxelles in 1948. The novel, like his later short stories *La récompense de la cruauté* (1972) and *N'Gobila* (1972), is presented in terms of magic realism and embodies a symbolic dimension. One might add Philippe Lisembé Elebé as a bridge between generations, with his volume of poetry, *Orphée rebelle* (1972), and with plays such as *Simon Kimbangu; ou, Le Messie noir* (1972) and *Chant de la terre, chant de l'eau* (1973), a dramatic adaptation of the Haitian writer Jacques Roumain's acclaimed novel *Gouverneurs de la rosée.*

In the late 1960s, and particularly during the 1970s, a generation of writers appeared who were trained in literature and were in contact with the literary production of other black writers and the literary currents that produced them, including the négritude movement. A renewed interest in and enthusiasm for literature accompanied the emergence of this new crop of writers. Although of varying aesthetic value and published modestly, their poems translate the idealistic and generous intentions of the young poets and their desire to not only write about social and cultural matters, but also to create works of art. Among the literary groups (for example, the Union des Écrivains Zaïrois) and poetic movements (for example, concretism), the Pléiade du Congo was a "literary circle" that sought to bring together young poets to share and discuss their works. The Editions du Mont Noir, founded by V. Y. Mudimbe in 1971, wanted to promote a high quality Congolese literature. The publishing house was very selective and has identified some of the most talented poets of the country: Kadima-Nzuji, Faïk-Nzuji, Mudimbe, Sumaïli, and young talents such as Elisabeth Francesca Mueya, Olivier Musangi, and François Mayengo.

This period of creative effervescence saw the rise of poets like Philippe Masegabio (*Somme première*, 1968); Gabriel Sumaïli (*Aux flancs de l'équateur*, 1966; *Testaments*, 1971); and Mukala Kadima-Nzuji (*Les ressacs*, 1969; *Préludes à la terre*, 1971; *Redire les mots anciens*, 1977). These three collections of verses attest to Kadima-Nzuji's poetic evolution. His poetry is one of controlled emotions celebrating telluric forces—earth, water—but also love. Although Mukadi Tshiakatumba Matala has published only one collection of verses, *Réveil dans un nid de flammes* (1969), his poetry is of a remarkable quality, embedded in intense lyricism and metaphors of love and revolt, suffering and death. Another young poet, Tshinday Lukumbi, published *Marche, pays des espoirs* (1968). Madiya (Clémentine) Faïk-Nzuji emerged as a talented poet and the leading female poet with several collections of poetry: *Murmures* (1968); *Kasala* (1969); *Le temps des amants* (1969), a vivid poetic celebration of love and sexual fulfillment; and *Lianes* (1971). V. Y. Mudimbe, with *Déchirures* (1971), *Entretailles précédé de fulgurances d'une lézarde* (1973), and *Les fuseaux parfois* (1974), presents a poetry of philosophical reflection that attenuates the violence of rebellion, suffering, destruction, and death.

In theater, 1970 also inaugurated a period of creativity and innovation. In DRC at this time, as in other African countries, many plays were written and performed without being published. Theater is probably the most popular genre because it is accessible to the public. The themes are very much related to the conditions of life and the current problems of DRC's society quest for the past, loss of traditions, social and moral disintegration, corruption, and social critique. Mikanza Mobiem's acclaimed plays *Pas de feu pour les antilopes* (1970) and *Procès à Makala* (1976) were very successful in Kinshasa in the 1970s. Other plays, such as Pius Nkashama Ngandu's *La délivrance d'Ilunga* (1977) and Bikisi Tandundu's *Quand les Afriques s'affrontent* (1984), represent a "literary theater" that is not necessarily to be performed.

In fiction, Mudimbe, exiled in the 1970s, emerged as a major novelist and scholar, renowned for his literary work as well as for his scholarly production. He has received international recognition and literary prizes, and his novels have been translated into Portuguese, English, German, and Dutch. Mudimbe's novels are intensely introspective: his characters follow an internal, personal quest in an introspective mode, translating their inner conflict and divisions. His novels deal with the problems of contemporary Africa: crisis of identity as well as a spiritual and psychological journey in *Entre les eaux* (1973), *Shaba deux: Les carnets de mère Marie-Gertrude* (1989), and *L'écart* (1979); moral and political degradation in the spheres of political power in *Le bel immonde* (1976); the quest for or the rewriting of African history in *L'écart*. It is particularly in the formal innovations and in a highly sophisticated language and style that Mudimbe manifests his profound originality and his contribution to African letters.

Zamenga Batukezanga situates himself apart from most of the writers in DRC and represents what might be called popular culture. His novels, written in the language of everyday life, are very popular: *Les hauts et les bas* (1971), *Bandoki* (1973), *Souvenirs du village* (1972), *Terre des ancêtres* (1974), *Carte postale* (1974), and *Mille kilomètres à pieds* (1979) are among his first works in an ongoing production of short novels dealing with the meeting of tradition and modernity, urban life and social critique. In the short novel *Giambatista Vico; ou, Le viol du discours africain* (1975), Mbwil a Mpaang Ngal deals with cultural alienation and promotes a revalorization of orality.

This first work is continued by another short novel, *L'errance* (1979), and more recently by *Une saison de symphonie* (1994).

Among the next generation of Congolese novelists of the 1980s and 1990s, the most prolific is Pius Nkashama Ngandu, first exiled in France, living in the first decade of the 2000s in the United States. His production includes literary criticism and creative genres: poetry, theater, and especially novels. After a short story "La Mûlatresse Anna," he began his career as a novelist with *Le fils de la tribu* (1983), followed by novels that include *Le pacte de sang* (1984); *Les étoiles écrasées* (1988), the most accomplished of his novels; the voluminous *Un jour de grand soleil sur les montagnes d'Éthiopie* (1991); and *Yakouta* (1995). Ngandu's novels, sometimes poignant and often written in a poetic language, are dominated by the themes of loss, exile, pain, and death inflicted by a dominant power that crushes and destroys individuals physically and psychologically. Mpoyi Buatu entered the realm of letters with his novel *La reproduction* (1986), while Kamanda Kama is emerging as a promising poet and novelist of a philosophical orientation in which solitude and anguish pervade: *Les myriades des temps vécus* (1992), *Lointaines sont les rives du destin* (1994), and *Oeuvre poétique* (1999). Djungu Simba made some attempt in literature with his novel *Cité quinze* (1988), which depicts the deterioration of urban life and the marginalization of a forgotten urban proletariat.

THE CONGO

The Congo has produced a good number of writers. Between 1950 and 1960, the journal *Liaison* served as a forum for the intellectual elite and civil servants of the central African French colonies and for young literary talents. Locally published anthologies mention numerous young writers who are still learning the craft. Among those who will reach literary prominence are Guy Menga, Sylvain Bemba, and Jean Malonga; the last is noted for two novels, *Coeur d'Aryenne* (1954) and *La légende de M'Pfoumou Ma Mazono* (1954). Guy Menga inaugurated his literary career with two successful comedies, *La marmite de Koka-Mbala* (1969) and *L'oracle* (1969), which became very popular in the country. His narratives include *La palabre stérile* (1968) and the hilarious picaresque tale *Les aventures de Moni Mambou* (1971).

Among the generation immediately following Négritude, Gérard Félix Tchicaya U Tam'si's (1931–1989) literary presence dominates several decades of African literary production. A prolific and polyvalent writer of poetry, theater, and fiction, he is primarily a poet with philosophical concerns. Despite his hermetism, one can discern the political, historical and religious overtones of his poetry. Although he too is concerned with an African past and culture, Tchicaya distanced himself from Négritude. His poetry is made of extremely well crafted meditative poems: *Le mauvais sang* (1955); *Feu de brousse* (1957); *A triche-coeur* (1958); *Epitomé* (1962); *Le ventre* (1964); *L'arc musical* (1970), and *Le pain on la cendre* (1977). In the 1980s Tchicaya turned to theater and to fiction. His plays *Le Zulu* (1977), *Le destin glorieux du Maréchal Nnikon Nniku* (1979), and *Le bal de N'dinga* (1988) are comic and satiric representations of African political power and the disintegration of the people's hopes and expectations. In his trilogy *Les cancrelats* (1980), *Les Méduses ou les orties de mer* (1982), and *Les phalènes* (1984), Tchicaya confronts the African past and present through a nostalgic and bitter social criticism.

Jean-Baptiste Tati-Loutard has also written novels, but poetry is definitely his home. His poems are executed in a calm and measured tone. They celebrate nature—the sea, the sun, the beloved woman—and convey a philosophical meditation on life, death, human destiny, and time. His poetry unfolds like a metaphysical meditation, reflecting with serenity on human suffering, love, and death. His poems, collected in *Poèmes de la mer* (1968), *Normes du temps* (1974), *Le Palmier-lyre: poèmes* (2000), and *L'ordre des phénomènes, suivi de les feux de la planète* (2000), have the fluid rhythm and the beauty of the sea. Théophile Obenga wrote *Stèles pour l'avenir* (1978), a long poem in four movements that culminates in jubilation, in contrast with the melancholic and pessimistic tone of the beginning.

Henri Lopès started his literary career with short stories and short novels: *Tribaliques* (1971) and *Sans tam-tam* (1977) cast a pessimistic and critical gaze on the Congo's social and political practices while *La nouvelle romance* (1976) calls for women's emancipation. Now a prominent Congolese novelist, during the 1980s Lopès left his imprint with the tragic humor of *Le pleurer-rire* (1982), which, in a humorous and satiric mode, presents a critique of African dictatorial regimes, denouncing their excesses, abuses, and violation of human rights. A new phase in his fiction is marked by what might be considered a quest for and an assertion of identity. In *Le xchercheur d'Afrique* (1990), *Dossiers classé* (2002), and *Ma grand-mère bantoue et mes ancêtres les Gaulois* (2003), Lopès reflects on the question of racial and cultural métissage through the individual history of the main character. In his novel, *Le lys et le flamboyant* (1997), he recreates a period in history through the fictional, singular story of a character and oral accounts by other characters, thus emphasizing the role of orality in the process of writing history. *Sur l'autre rive* (1992) reenacts and at the same time subverts the transatlantic slave migration with the story of an African woman who voluntarily migrates to the Antilles and assumes a new name, anxious to find a new identity and to erase Africa from her memory.

The most remarkable of the youngest generation of Congolese writers is doubtless Sony Labou Tansi (1947–1995), a prolific and multifaceted author who produced fiction as well as poetry and drama. Since the late 1980s, Sony Labou Tansi has written and directed several plays. With his Rocado Zulu Theater company, he sought to revitalize performance as an art and reconceptualize staging techniques. Among his own plays *Conscience du tracteur* (1979), *Je soussigné cardiaque* (1981), and *Moi, veuve de l'empire* (1987), and *La parenthèse de sang* (1981) convey Sony's preoccupation: to denounce violent, repressive, and authoritarian regimes. His novels *La vie et demie* (1979), *L'anté-peuple* (1983), *L'état honteux* (1981), *Les sept solitudes de Lorsa Lopez* (1985), and *Les yeux du volcan* (1988) are embedded in baroque and magic realism. At times provocative, humorous, or sarcastic, they incorporate parody and transgressive irony, grotesque and Bakhtinian carnavalesque in order to convey the tragedy of contemporary Africa, calling for a general catharsis.

Emmanuel Dongala's first and acclaimed novel, *Un fusil dans la main, un poème dans la poche* (1973), is the odyssey of an Afro-American romantic revolutionary in Africa. It was followed by a novel with epic overtones, *Le feu des origines* (1987), and *Johnny chien méchant* (2002), a tragic story of war and violence. Alain Mabanckou, a prolific and rising writer of poetry as well as of fiction, represents the current new generation of African authors writing from "Afrique sur Seine." His novels *Les petits-fils nègres de Vercingétorix* (2002), *Bleu-blanc-rouge* (1998), *African Psycho* (2003), *Verre cassé* (2005), and *Mémoires de porc-épic* (2006), which was awarded the prestigious Prix Renaudot in 2006, are the illustration of an écriture of irony, play with words, verve, and satire. Among his numerous books of poetry, *Quand le coq annoncera l'aube d'un autre jour* (1999) and *Tant que les arbres s'enfonceront dans la terre* (2004) display hope and keep open the doors the future.

RWANDA AND BURUNDI

Unlike most African countries in which there are several national African languages, Rwanda and Burundi, like Tanzania, have only one national African language. Creative writing in French is almost nonexistent, and the emergence of a local literature in French has yet to happen. The few literary attempts are limited to single works by the novelist Saverio Naigiziki in the 1950s, the poets Migambi Mutabaraka and Cyprien Rugamba in Ruanda; and the novelist Ndavizigamiye Kayoya in Burundi. The voluminous and epic oeuvre of Alexis Kagame, a Catholic priest from Rwanda, constitutes a major literary monument and manifests Kagame's literary presence. His two masterpieces, *La divine pastorale* (1952) and *La naissance de l'univers* (1955), first written in Kinyaruanda and then translated into French, find their inspiration in the oral tradition of Rwanda as well as in the Catholic theology in which Kagame was trained.

See also **Bokassa, Jean-Bédel; Colonial Policies and Practices; Human Rights; Kagame, Alexis; Kinshasa; Literature and the Study of Africa; Literature: Oral; Lopes, Henri; Sony Labou Tansi; Theater: Francophone Africa.**

BIBLIOGRAPHY

Bakiba, André-Patient. *Henri Lopès: Une lecture d'enracinement et d'universalité.* Paris: L'Harmattan, 2002.

Blair, Dorothy. *African Literature in French.* Cambridge, U.K.: Cambridge University Press, 1976.

Brambilla, Cristina, ed. *Letterature dell'Africa.* Bologna, 1994.

Chemain, Roger, and Arlette Chemain-Degrange. *Panorama critique de la littérature congolaise contemporaine.* Paris: Présence africaine, 1979.

Dabla, Sewanou. *Nouvelles écritures africaines.* Paris: L'Harmattan, 1986.

Dévesa, Jean-Michel. *Sony Labou Tansi: écrivain de la honte et des rives magiques du Kongo.* Paris: L'Harmattan, 1996.

Gerard, Albert S., ed. *European-Language Writing in Sub-Saharan Africa.* 2 vols. Budapest: Akadémiai Kiadó, 1986.

Kadima-Nzuji, Mukala. *La littérature zaïroise de langue française, 1945–1965.* Paris: Editions Karthala, 1984.

Kesteloot, Lilyan. *Black Writers in French: A Literary History of Negritude,* trans. Ellen C. Kennedy. Washington, DC: Howard University Press, 1991.

Kesteloot, Lilyan. *Histoire de la littérature négro-africaine.* Paris: Karthala, 2001.

Kom, Ambroise. *Dictionnaire des oeuvres littéraires négro-africaines de langue française des origines à 1978.* Sherbrooke: Naaman, 1983.

Kom, Ambroise, *Dictionnaire des oeuvres littéraires de langue française en Afrique au Sud du Sahara,* Vol. 2. San Francisco: International Scholars Publications, 1999.

Lawson-Anannisoh, E. *"Le roman nouveau en Afrique francophone (Henri Lopès, Soni Labou Tansi): Eléments d'une poétique.* Villeneuve d'Ascq: Presses Universitaires du Septentrion, 1999.

Malanda, Ange Séverin. *Henri Lopès et l'impératif romanesque.* Paris: Silex, 1987.

Mouralis, Bernard. *V. Y. Mudimbe; ou, Le discours, l'écart et l'écriture.* Paris: Présence Africaine, 1988.

Ngandu, Pius Nkashama. *Les Années littéraires en Afrique, 1987–1992.* Paris: L'Harmattan, 1994.

Nkashama, Pius Ngandu. *Dictionnaire des oeuvres littéraires africaines de langue francaise.* Ivry-sur-Seine, France: Editions Nouvelles du Sud, 1994.

Notre Librairie. No. 63 (January–March 1982), on Zaire; no. 105 (April–June 1991), on Gabon; no. 97 (April–May 1987), on the Central African Republic; nos. 92–93 (March–May 1988), on the Congo.

Quaghebeur, Marc, and Emile Van Balberghe, eds. *Papier blanc, encre noire: cent ans de culture francophone en Afrique centrale.* 2 vols. Brussels, 1992.

Thomas, Dominic. *Nation-Building: Propaganda and Literature in Francophone Africa.* Bloomington: Indiana University Press, 2002.

Thomas, Dominic. *Black France. Colonialism, Immigration, and Transnationalism.* Bloomington: Indiana University Press, 2007.

ELISABETH MUDIMBE-BOYI

FRANCOPHONE INDIAN OCEAN AFRICA

A rather large number of islands have been disseminated by geography east of the Indian Ocean and off the coast of Africa: Madagascar, Seychelles, the Mascarenes (Mauritius, Réunion, and Rodrigues), Comoros, and other smaller islands. Madagascar is the largest of these islands (and the fourth largest in the world), Réunion and Comoros have active volcanoes, and Mauritius is eroded and surrounded by a large lagoon, similar to the Seychelles. However, cultural diversity is what is most striking as recent migrations have shaped these islands in many different ways: the Malagasy people originated from Indonesia and Africa (from the first through the sixteenth centuries) and from the sixteenth century, European travelers were the first to settle on the other uninhabited islands. Bourbon, present-day La Reunion, has been under French sovereignty since 1638 and an overseas department since 1946. Mauritius (Isle de France in the eighteenth century) and the Seychelles (from Moreau de Sechelles) became independent in 1968 and 1976, respectively. The Comoros gained independence from France in 1975, except for the island of Mayotte that decided by referendum to remain French. The French language remains the common denominator between these islands and it is still a major language used in literature.

MADAGASCAR

Aside from the four types of ancient oral literature—the *kabary*, the *hainteny*, the *antsa*, and the *angano*—the Malagasy people had a written literature long before the Négritude movement of the 1930s, which marked the beginning of Francophone African writing. The cultural and linguistic connections between France and Madagascar began well before colonization. A colonial literature—written in French by French authors—had developed initially in the form of travel accounts, and later of novels, tales, and short stories, thus gradually creating an *imaginaire de Madagascar*, the construction of an exotic myth in French consciousness. The French critic and essayist Jean Paulhan (1884–1968) studied traditional Malagasy literature and produced the first translations of Malagasy *hainteny* in French. Jean-Joseph Rabearivelo (1901–1937) was one of Madagascar's greatest poets. He left an abundant literary production; mainly poetry, two novels, numerous essays, and translations of Malagasy poetry into French. Among his best-known collection of poems are *Traduit de la nuit* (*Translations from the Night*, 1935) and *Presque-songes* (*Near-Dreams*, 1934).

Two other important figures dominated the pre-independence period after Rabearivelo: Jacques Rabemananjara and Flavien Ranaivo (1914–1999). Jacques Rabemananjara studied literature in Paris in 1937, where he met the African and Caribbean intellectuals Alioune Diop, Aimé Césaire, and Léopold Senghor.

Following Madagascar's independence from France in 1960 and the attendant period of *malgachisation*, Malagasy authors nearly ceased writing in French in the 1970s. At the start of the 1980s a literary revolution marked the literatures of Southern Africa, including Madagascar. Two talented novelists appeared: Michele Rakotoson (b. 1948) was awarded the *Prix littéraire de Madagascar* in 1984 for *Dadabé* and in 1988 published *Le bain des reliques*. Since then she has continued her literary production. In the 1990s, Charlotte Rafenomanjato (b. 1936) published *Le pétale écarlate* and *Le cinquieme sceau*. Both have also written plays in French. In the first decade of the 2000s, Jean-Luc Raharimanana (b. 1967) has published poetry, short stories (*La Lucarne* and *Rêves sous le linceul*), and two novels *Nour, 1947* (2001) and *L'arbre anthropophage* (2004).

MAURITIUS

The French were the first to populate the island in 1715 where they introduced Bourbon Creole from its neighbor, La Réunion (then Isle Bourbon). *Le voyage à l'île de France* (1773) (Voyage to the Ile de France) and especially *Paul et Virginie* (1788) by Bernardin de St. Pierre (1737–1814) confirmed the myth of the paradisiacal island and profoundly marked Mauritian literature. In the face of the massive influx of Indian immigrants at the end of the nineteenth century, the Creole population (African, Malagasy, or métis) joined the Franco-Mauritians in their attachment to French culture. Léoville Lhomme (1857–1928), a Creole, is considered the major Mauritian poet. His poetry was heavily influenced by Leconte de Lisle.

Loys Masson (1915–1969) enjoyed an international reputation with his novel *Le notaire des noirs*

(1961, *The Black Man's Notary*) in which he presented the social and political revolution in Mauritius that was provoked by segregation, as well as the recurrent Mauritian theme of childhood. The work of Robert Edward-Hart (1891–1954; *L'ombre étoilée*, 1924 [*Starry Darkness*]; *Poèmes: Portique oriental*, 1927 [*Poems, Oriental Gate*]) reflected oriental influences (from India and Asia). Malcolm de Chazal (1902–1981), greeted as a genius by André Breton (1896–1966) in 1947, pursued Hart's work by developing the desire of autochthony of which Jean-Louis Joubert spoke, and the lemurian reveries of Jules Hermann (1845–1924). Malcolm de Chazal is the architect of a Mauritian cosmogony (*Petrusmok*, 1951, *L'île Maurice proto-historique, folklorique et légendaire*, 1973) in which Mauritius is presented as the remnant of the lost continent of Godwana.

Beginning with World War II, several authors wrote of their Chinese or Indian origins: Poets such as Joseph Tsang Mang King (b. 1938) and Hassam Wachill (b. 1939), who won the French Academy's Grand Prix for *Jour après jour* (1987) and novelists such as the rising star of Mauritian literature, Ananda Devi (b. 1957), who explored the condition of Indo-Mauritian women in *Rue la poudrière* (1989), *Moi, l'interdite* (2000), *Pagli* (2001), and *Eve de ses décombres* (2006), for which she was awarded the *Prix des cinq continents 2006*. Edouard Maunick (b. 1931) expresses Négritude and *métissage* (mixings of race) in his *Anthologie personnelle* (1989) and in his collections of poems, such as *Ensoleillé vif*. The mixings of race are also the focus of Marie-Thérèse Humbert's (b. 1940) *A l'autre bout de moi* (1979, The other end of myself), which received the *Elle* Prize. Because of his Franco-Mauritian origins, J.M.G Le Clézio (b. 1940) uses strong Mauritian imaginary, in particular in *Le chercheur d'or* (1985) (The Prospector), *Voyage à Rodrigues* (1986, *Journey to Rodrigues*), *Sirandanes* (1990), and *La Quarantaine* (1995, *The Quarantine*).

LA RÉUNION

La Réunion became a French territory in 1638 and an Overseas Department (DOM) in 1946. The end of slavery in 1848 resulted in hired laborers from India coming to La Réunion, and the present-day population of the island diverse. Two languages are in use, however: Creole and French. The literature

of the island of Bourbon started with travel essays. It was not until the middle of the nineteenth century before there was a body of writing by those who had left the island to study in France: Auguste Lacaussade (1815–1897), Charles Leconte de Lisle (1818–1894), and Léon Dierx (1838–1912).

Marius-Ary Leblond (a pseudonym for two cousins, Georges Athénas [1877–1953] and Aimé Merlo [1880–1958]) launched the colonial novel in 1909 with *En France* that was followed with several other novels in the same vein. The *Roman réunionnais* (*The Novel from La Réunion*) began to assert itself in the 1970s with *Les muselés* (*The Muzzled Ones*) by Anne Chenet (b. 1938), and Axel Gauvin's (b. 1944) *Quartier trois letters* (1980). Gauvin employs a writing style that combines French and Creole in *Faims d'enfance* (1987) and *L'aimé* (1990, *The Loved One*) to express sociocultural conflicts, as well as tenderness and human solidarity. The word *créolie* was forged by Jean Albany (1917–1984) and became an emblem for young poets such as Gilbert Aubry (b. 1942) and Jean-François Samlong (b. 1949) who have published anthologies under the name *Créolie*.

Jean-Claude Carpanin Marimotou (b. 1958) distinguishes the Caribbean notion of *créolité* from Créolie that better suits the situation of La Réunion. Marimotou writes in both Creole and French in a collection of poems in which he expresses his Indian identity, as does Carmen Thue-Tune with *Poésie eurasienne* (1981). Axel Gauvin has advocated a form of bilingualism with his book *Du créole opprimé au créole libéré* (1977), but the 1980s experienced a decline in written work in Creole because of the difficulty of writing in an oral language and finding an audience. The 1990s saw an emergence of works of great quality by Jean-François Samlong (b. 1949; *La nuit cyclone*, 1992; *Hurricane Night*) and Monique Agenor (*Bé-Maho*, 1996; *Comme un vol de papang*, 1998; and *Cocos-de-mer*, 2000).

THE ARCHIPELAGO OF THE COMOROS

The four small islands in the middle of the Mozambique Channel form the archipelago of the Comoros: Grande Comore, Anjouan, Mayotte, and Mohéli. Their location has made it a crossroads between Africa and the Arab-Persian world, as well as Madagascar. Islam constitutes the primary link among the islands. The Comoran language is the mother tongue, Arabic is the language of religion, and French is the language of communication with the outside world. The educational system, dominated by the Qur'anic schools, has delayed the emergence of a Comoran literature in French. The first novel, *La république des imberbes* (*The Republic of the Beardless*) by Mohamed Toihiri (b. 1955) in 1985, followed by *Le kafir du Karthala* (1992), marked the beginning of literary activity in French. Nassur Attoumani (b. 1954), with *Mon mari est plus qu'un fou, c'est un homme* (2006, *My Husband Is More Than Deranged, He Is a Man*), was the first to publish a French language novel in the Comoros.

In the Seychelles, the archipelago was inhabited in the eighteenth century by French colonists who brought their language, which is still in use today: French and Creole. Since independence in 1976, an official trilingualism has been established (French, English, and Creole). A modern literature written in Creole is now being published with *Contes et poèmes des Seychelles* (1977, *Tales and Poems of the Seychelles*) by Antoine Abel (b. 1934) and then *Fler fletri* (1985, *Faded Flower*) by Leu Mancienne (b. 1958), written in both Creole and French.

Despite the ethnic, cultural, and linguistic diversity, a sense of *India-océanité* (Indian Oceanness) is emerging. The position of this part of the world at the crossroads of several continents makes it a place where tomorrow's humankind is being slowly elaborated.

See also **Césaire, Aimé; Creoles; Diop, Alioune; Literature; Madagascar; Mauritius; Réunion; Senghor, Léopold Sédar.**

BIBLIOGRAPHY

Beniamo, Michel. *L'Imaginaire Réunionnais.* St-Denis, France: Editions du Tramail, 1992.

Domenichini-Ramiaramanana, Bakoly. *Du ohabolana au hainteny. Langue, littérature et politique à Madagascar.* Paris: Karthala, 1982.

Issur, Kumari et Hookoomsing, V. *L'océan Indien dans les littératures francophones.* Paris: Karthala, 2001.

Joubert, Jean-Louis. *Littératures francophones de l'océan Indien. Anthologie.* Paris: Editions de l'Océan Indien/ ACCT, 1993.

Mauguière, Bénédicte. "Francophone Literatures of the Indian Ocean." In *The Cambridge History of African and Caribbean Literature,* vol. 2. ed. F. Abiola Irele and Simon Gikandi. Cambridge, U.K.: Cambridge University Press, 2004.

Ramarosoa, Liliane. "Situation actuelle de la littérature malgache d'expression française." *Notre librairie* 104 (January–March 1991): 78–85.

BÉNÉDICTE N. MAUGUIÈRE

FRANCOPHONE NORTHERN AFRICA

Continued use of French in North Africa is the direct result of France's colonial conquests throughout the region, primarily during the nineteenth century. Despite the different colonial regimes maintained in the Maghreb by the French throughout the nineteenth and twentieth centuries, Francophone literature by authors from Algeria, Morocco, and Tunisia shares some commonalities in themes and scope. The most frequent issues raised in contemporary literature of French expression, whether the author is Algerian, Moroccan, or Tunisian, stem from questions surrounding the author's identity and place in Maghrebian society as someone who chooses not to write in an indigenous language.

Francophone authors have often been accused by their countrymen of being elitist and disassociated from their homelands, and condemned for evoking references to the former colonial era by their insistence on writing in French. The authors refute these criticisms, arguing that the use of the French language allows them freedom to express what often cannot be uttered in their indigenous languages (Arabic and/or Berber) because of political or sociocultural repercussions. Many Maghrebian women authors of French expression live in exile in France or other European countries. Since the late twentieth century, Algerians Malika Mokeddem (b. 1949), Leïla Marouane (b. 1960), and Assia Djebar (b. 1936) have chosen to live in exile because of persecution at home. The rise of Islamic fundamentalism, the resulting repressive sociocultural climate for women, and the widespread violence of the 1990s aimed particularly at journalists, authors, academics, and intellectuals, forced many women in these professions to flee to France and elsewhere abroad. The most outspoken Algerian women authors, Assia Djebar (elected in 2006 to the prestigious French Académie Française) and Malika Mokeddem, have repeatedly criticized the postindependent government of Algeria for its failing state infrastructure and lack of sociocultural and economic security for Algerians.

Francophone writers maintain that use of French allows access to a larger audience not only in Europe, but across Africa, the Middle East, and the Caribbean. Some Francophone authors have reverted to using their indigenous languages as a means of claiming their multiethnic heritage and as a way to refute fascist nationalism and racism within the Maghreb. The most notable of these authors is Kateb Yacine (1929–1989) who, toward the end of his life, began to write plays in Algerian Arabic. Rachid Boudjedra (b. 1941), who has written for over four decades in French, has also experimented with prose written in Arabic.

In 1891, the first novella written in French by an indigenous Algerian was published. One of the first French literary critics to seriously study Francophone literature of the Maghreb credited *La vengeance du cheikh* (The sheik's vengeance) to author M'Hamed Ben Rahal. Historically, the stylistic and thematic contours of Francophone Maghrebian literature may be categorized into three succinct stages. The first stage, beginning in 1891 and enduring until the late 1930s, reflects some nationalist writing but is more significantly characterized by indigenous Algerian writers who assimilated and mimicked the literary styles of the colonizer. Mouloud Feraoun (1913–1962), assassinated by the French OAS (Organisation de l'Armée Secrète) on March 15, 1962, shortly before the end of the Algerian war of liberation (1954–1962), was one such author. Although his seminal work, *Le fils du pauvre* (Son of a poor man, 1950), reflects classic French prose, the underlying messages of the novel evoke a burgeoning resistance to colonialism in Algeria.

Francophone authors writing at this time were predominately males, influenced by the French colonial education system that mandated linguistic and cultural indoctrination of indigenous peoples. Although fewer in number, women authors, particularly in Algeria, began to write in the 1940s. Their works also reflected a progression from assimilationist formats that mimicked certain styles and themes of the French colonizers to revolutionary discourse refined during the Algerian revolution. As had their male counterparts, women authors

increasingly questioned the politics and sociocultural indoctrination of colonialism. Marguerite Taos Amrouche (1913–1976) (*Jacinthe noire* [Black hyacinth], 1947) forged a literary voice echoed in later works by Assia Djebar. Djebar's first novel, *La soif* (Thirst, 1957), influenced later women authors who examined the conundrums of women's lives in an Algeria that is caught between traditionalism and modernity.

More obscure authors, such as Djamila Debèche (b. 1926), also began writing in French colonial Algeria in the 1940s. Her books, *Leïla, une fille algérienne* (Leila: An Algerian girl, 1947), followed by *Aziza* (1955), described the tormented lives of young Algerian *evolués* (elites assimilated to French culture) who, nevertheless, had begun to question colonial occupation. Both heroines in these novels profess allegiance to their traditional Algerian roots and wholeheartedly support the burgeoning rumors of revolution. However, the protagonists are also conflicted about what their roles will be as women and citizens of a new postcolonial society and nation.

The second stage of writing in the Francophone Maghreb, beginning in the late 1940s and enduring until the mid-1960s, promoted themes that were militant and nationalist. The massacres at Sétif, Algeria, on May 8, 1945, set off a wave of anticolonial literature definitively commencing resistance to colonial rule. Resistance and independence manifested as principal themes in the celebrated works: *Nedjma* (1956) by Kateb Yacine (1929–1989) and *L'incendie* (The fire, 1954) by Mohamed Dib (1920–2003). This new, young, French–educated cadre of militant authors included Malek Haddad (1927–1978) (*La dernière impression* [The last impression], 1958) and Mouloud Mammeri (1917–1989) (*La colline oubliée* [The forgotten hill], 1958), among others. In the 1950s, they published their works in numerous revues and journals such as *Simoun*, *Forge*, *Terrasses*, *Soleil*, *Progrès*, and *Consiences maghrébines*. Militancy was *de rigueur*, as these authors did not seek to hide their anticolonial agendas and openly struggled for independence.

Kateb Yacine's 1956 novel *Nedjma* foregrounded a definite thematic rupture with former novels by Maghrebian authors of French expression. The novel is filled with allusions to the social struggle going on in Algeria at the time. *Nedjma* is not only the name of the elusive female figure who is a constant object of desire for the four male protagonists, but is also the word for star, the principal symbol of Algerian independence (later reproduced on the Algerian flag). Yacine's work raised crucial questions about the identity of the Algerian people as they transited toward nationhood and self-rule. At the same time, the novel evoked both hope in the possibility of a people emerging from the bondage of colonialism, and the despair of characters caught in waves of conflict (ethnic tensions within Algeria, factionalism, religious fundamentalism). These conflicts continued to plague Algeria in the postindependent era, leading eventually to the civil war of the 1990s.

Earlier theoretical texts by Martinican Frantz Fanon (1925–1961) influenced revolutionary literature across the Maghreb. Fanon, who, as a psychiatrist working in Algeria in the late 1950s, witnessed and wrote on the psychological effects of colonialism on the colonized. His famous *Peau noire, masques blancs* (Black skin, white masks, 1952) and the later *Les damnés de la terre* (The wretched of the earth, 1961) grounded theoretical revolutionary discourse that would later provide an impetus for anticolonial movements across Africa and influence later generations of Francophone African authors. In the late 1950s, Fanon sided with the Algerian Front de la Libération Nationale (FLN, the National Liberation Front) freedom fighters, condemning France for its continued imperialism in the region.

Tunisian Albert Memmi (b. 1921), recognized for his influential *Portrait du colonisé, précédé par Portrait du colonisateur* (Portrait of the colonizer and colonized, 1957), astutely studied colonialism from both the colonizers' and colonizeds' perspectives. He revealed truths about oppression and dehumanization that are still valid in the early twenty-first century. These two influential North African theorists changed the course of colonial discourse and founded postcolonial theoretical frameworks that, decades after their original publication, still influence how Francophone literature is read and studied.

The late 1950s, 1960s, and 1970s produced numerous Maghrebian Francophone authors whose

Fatima Mernissi. Fatima Mernissi, author, feminist, and social activist, at a literary meeting in Rabat, Morocco, January 2007. PHOTOGRAPH BY VALERIE ORLANDO

works are considered the foundation of the Francophone canon. These authors include: Algerians Rachid Boudjedra (*La répudiation* [The Repudiation], 1969), Mourad Bourboune (b. 1938; *Le mont des genêts* [The mount of the broom trees], 1962), Assia Djebar (*Les enfants du nouveau monde* [Children of a new world], 1962), Nabil Farès (b. 1940; *Yahia, pas de chance* [Yahia, no luck], 1970); Moroccans Driss Chraïbi (b. 1926; *Les boucs* [The scapegoats], 1955), Abdelkebir Khatibi (b. 1938; *La mémoire tatouée* [Marked memory], 1971); and Tunisians Albert Memmi (*La statue de sel* [Pillar of salt], 1953) and Mustapha Tlili (b. 1937; *La rage aux tripes* [Gut rage], 1975).

The third stage of Maghrebian Francophone writing, dating from the late 1970s onward, reflects themes that also echo the intricate conundrums of not only the region but the larger postcolonial world. Women's emancipation and shifting roles in contemporary Maghrebian society, immigration, exile, corruption of postcolonial governments, violence, civil war, and ethnic genocide are just some of the topics prevalent in the texts of Francophone novelists, essayists, and poets. From the late 1970s forward, authors have sought to define the parameters of more socioculturally based literature that extends its themes into areas other than those of nationalism, revolution, and the tendentious discourses between colonized and colonizer.

Postrevolutionary novelists such as Algerians Leila Marouane, Malika Mokeddem, Mohamed

Mokeddem, Salim Bachi (b. 1971); Moroccans Tahar Ben Jelloun (b. 1944), Fouad Laouri, Mohammed Khair-Eddine (b. 1941), Bahaa Trabelsi, Abdellah Taïa; Tunisians Abdelaziz Belkhodja, Hajer Djilani, Hédia Baraket, among others, dwell less on the duality between the worlds of the colonizer and the colonized and more on questions of individualism, sociocultural disparity, and economic dilemmas in their respective homelands. Many of these themes surface in the works of notable writers such as Tahar Ben Jelloun, considered one of the most prolific contemporary Moroccan authors of French expression. Ben Jelloun became internationally known in 1987 when he won the prestigious French literary prize, Le Prix Goncourt, for his novel *La nuit sacrée* (Sacred night, 1987).

In recent years, Maghrebian Francophone writing has been shaped by many women authors who are vocal both in and outside the Maghreb. Moroccan Touria Oulehri's (b. 1963) *La repudiée* (The repudiated woman, 2001) challenged the oppressive patriarchal rules and regulations that hinder the emancipation of women in twenty-first century Morocco. Siham Benchekroun enjoyed immense success with her novel *Oser vivre!* (Dare to live!, 2002). Although written in French, a language that only the well-educated elite of Morocco read, the novel's principal theme is pertinent to all women: many societal constraints and traditional mores impede a woman's search for her identity and sense of selfhood in Moroccan society.

Early twenty-first century Francophone authors have fostered dialogue about many issues that were once taboo in their homelands. The themes of Moroccan authors Rachid O. (b. 1970), Nedjma Bahaa Trabelsi, and Abdellah Taïa reflect the rapidly changing contours of Moroccan society. It cannot be denied that the more relaxed nature of the themes of contemporary Moroccan literature in French is due to the increasingly liberal climate of Moroccan politics, evident since King Mohamed VI's ascension to the throne in 1999. Authors, journalists, and scholars increasingly use French to engage what they perceive as the stagnant sociocultural traditions and antiquated politics of contemporary Morocco. These writers particularly challenge the norms and conventions of traditionalism, religious piety, and the

Moroccan author Touria Oulehri, Rabat Morocco, January 2007. Oulehri is a teacher at the École Normale Supérieure in Meknès. Her first two novels, *La répudiée* and *La chambre des nuits blanches*, were released in 2001 and 2002. PHOTOGRAPH BY VALERIE ORLANDO

suffocating mores that disenfranchise women and other marginalized groups in the country. The sexual freedom depicted in novels by authors living abroad and in Morocco such as Rachid O's *L'enfant ébloui* (The dazzled child, 1995), Nedjma's *L'amande* (The almond, 2005), Bahaa Trabelsi *Une vie à trois* (Life as three, 2000) and Abdellah Taïa's *Le rouge du tarbouche* (The red fes, 2004) question traditional Moroccan views on homosexuality and gender. Issues evoked in these works concerning gender, sexual freedom, and women's disenfranchisement challenged patriarchy while positioning French Moroccan literature as a principal contributor to the democratization of the country in the twenty-first century.

In the wake of 9/11, Francophone authors of the Maghreb seek to ground a more global, Pan-Africanist sentiment in their works. They aim to build bridges favoring commonalities between nations and authors of French expression. Writers such as Tunisian Abdelwahab Meddeb (b. 1946) cultivate sociopolitical awareness abroad about the Maghreb in particular and the Arab world in general. His *La maladie de l'islam* (Islam's sickness, 2002) drew on critical moments in Islamic history to explain the failure of Arab nation-states, emphasizing that this failure is a primary contributor to the ills that continue to impede these states' development. The author revealed the similarities between Christian and Islamic religious extremist ideologies as he explained the reasons behind the carnage of late twentieth and early twenty-first century terrorist incidents. He blamed both the Arab and Christian worlds for the erosion of East-West diplomacy. Meddeb equally faulted general ignorance and lack of cultural awareness across the globe as primary contributors to the escalation of religious extremist violence.

See also **Djebar, Assia; Literature; Popular Culture: Northern Africa.**

BIBLIOGRAPHY

Bensmaïa, Réda. *Experimental Nations: Or, the Invention of the Maghreb.* Princeton, NJ: Princeton University Press, 2003.

Déjeux, Jean. *La littérature féminine de langue française au Maghreb.* Paris: Karthala, 1994.

Fanon, Frantz. *Peau noire, masques blancs.* Paris: Seuil, 1971.

Fanon, Frantz. *Les Damnés de la terre.* Paris: La Découverte, 2002.

Jack, Belinda. *Francophone Literatures: An Introductory Survey.* New York: Oxford University Press, 1997.

Memmi, Albert. *Portrait du colonisé, précédé de: Portrait du colonisateur.* Paris: Gallimard, 2002.

Memmi, Albert, and Joëlle Bahloul. *Ecrivains francophones du Maghreb.* Paris: Robert Laffont, 1985.

Mortimer, Mildred. *Journeys through the French African Novel.* Portsmouth, NH: Heinemann, 1990.

Orlando, Valérie. *Nomadic Voices of Exile: Feminine Identity in Francophone Literature.* Athens: Ohio University Press, 1999.

Vogl, Mary. *Picturing the Maghreb: Literature, Photography, (Re)Presentation.* Lanham, MD: Rowman and Littlefield, 2003.

VALÉRIE ORLANDO

LUSOPHONE

The Portuguese were the first Europeans to reach sub-Saharan African. In his *Neo-African Literature: A History of Black Writing* (1968) scholar Janheinz Jahn documented that in 1613 Afonso Álvares, born in Portugal to a black mother and a white father, is possibly the first person of African descent to write and have appear in print literary works, specifically poems, in a European language.

In the lusophone African territories, starting as early as the seventeenth century, there were precursors. But writers and literary movements expressing an African and/or proto-nationalist perspective emerged in the mid-twentieth century, mainly in the post–World War II period. One earlier exception occurred, however, in Cape Verde with the emergence, in 1936, of the *Claridade* (Clarity) movement, named for a literary journal founded in that year. On the island of São Vicente several poets and novelists, notably Jorge Barbosa, Manuel Lopes, Baltasar Lopes, and António A. Gonçalves, produced lyrical and neo-realist works based on Cape Verdean themes and the islands' status as a Creole archetype, meaning a comprehensively racially, socially, and culturally hybrid society. Many of the contributors to subsequent journals, such as *Certeza* (Certainty), would take a line of greater social consciousness as a prelude to the pro-independence movements that would emerge in the early 1950s in the five colonies.

In 1951 Angola's Luanda-based "New Intellectuals" launched *Mensagem* (Message), a landmark literary journal. And in Portugal itself, the Lisbon-based Casa dos Estudantes do Império (House of Students from the Empire) published a journal also titled *Mensagem.* One of the House's most illustrious members was Agostinho Neto, the celebrated poet who would be Angola's first president. In the 1960s, while a political prisoner in Lisbon, Neto clandestinely wrote many of the poems that eventually appeared in a bilingual volume published in Italy. That collection was also published in an English translation titled *Sacred Hope* (1974). Other noteworthy preindependence, *engagé* Angolan writers are António Jacinto, Costa Andrade, and Arnaldo Santos, to name a few. Another writer of note is José Luandino Vieira, author of the classic work published in 1967 and translated into English with the title *Luuanda: Short Stories of Angola* (1980).

In Mozambique the 1950s and 1960s gave rise to a number of socially conscious writers. Of particular note are poets José Craveirinha and Noémia de Sousa. Craveirinha literally transformed Mozambican lusophone poetry with the publication, in 1964, of *Chigubo*, the title being the name of a dance of the Ronga people. Noémia de Sousa, by virtue of her poems that appeared in local journals and newspapers, became southern Africa's first black or mixed-race female published poet. Another historically significant literary event was the publication, in 1964, of *Nós Matamos o Cão-Tinhoso*, a collection of short stories by Luís Bernardo Honwana. The English translation, *We Killed Mangy-Dog and Other Mozambique Stories* (1969), is the first lusophone African work to appear in the prestigious Heinemann African Writers Series. It should be noted that because of their anticolonialist militancy Craveirinha and Honwana were each imprisoned for three years.

From the nineteenth century until independence São Tomé e Príncipe's best-known writers spent most of their adult lives in Portugal. The most prominent of the islands' preindependence poets is Francisco Tenreiro, born to an African mother and Portuguese father on the island of São Tomé but taken as a child to Lisbon. Although Terneiro lived out his short life in Portugal, his posthumously published collection of poems titled *Coração em África* (1964; With my heart in Africa) reinforced the reputation he had gained as the Portuguese language's premier négritude poet.

The then-colony of Portuguese Guinea, present-day Guinea-Bissau, was little more than an entrepôt without the institutional infrastructure needed to give rise to an indigenous acculturated elite. Thus, a characteristic literature would only emerge after political independence.

POSTCOLONIAL LUSOPHONE LITERATURE

Since the Portuguese colonies' independence in 1975 and continuing in the 1980s, 1990s, and the beginning of the twenty-first century, the literary scene in the five new nation-states has been to a degree under the influence of *lusofonia*, which can be defined as a kind of pan-Lusitanianism, with all that the latter implies with respect to language, transnationalism, and cultural hybridity. Many who established themselves as writers during the colonial period, as well as a number who emerged since independence, have produced innovative works that constitute the literary canon of each of the five countries. Moreover, increasingly lusophone African works are being incorporated into the literary corpus of the wider Portuguese-speaking world, including, of course, Portugal and Brazil. Also increasingly lusophone African literary works are being published in other languages, including English.

Among Cape Verdeans who began their literary careers before independence and continue to publish in the postcolonial present are Orlanda Amarílis, Teixeira de Sousa, Corsino Fortes, Oswaldo Osório, Francisco Fragoso, and Arménio Vieira. Some of the outstanding writers among those who published their first literary work after independence are José Luís Hopffer Almada, Vera Duarte, and Dina Salústio. And the postcolonial Cape Verdean writer to attract the most international attention is Germano Almeida. Not only was his first novel, *O testamento do Sr. Napumoceno da Silva Araújo* (1989), translated into several languages including English (1991; *The Last Will & Testament of Senhor da Silva Araújo*), there is also a film based on it. Because the film's producer is Portuguese, and its director and most of its main characters are Brazilian, this quintessentially Cape Verdean movie has been heralded as a most appealing example of pan-Lusitanianism.

Foremost among Angolan writers who established themselves before and continued to publish after independence are Uanhenga Xitu, Henrique Abranches, Manuel Rui, Pepetela, Arlindo Barbeitos, and Ruy Duarte de Carvalho. Among those who published their first work after independence are Paula Tavares, Boaventura Cardoso, E. Bonavena, José Luís Mendonça, João Maimona, Rui Augusto, Ana de Santana, Lopito Feijóo, João Melo, and José E. Agualusa. Pepetela and Agualusa are unquestionably the most prolific among the postcolonial prose fiction writers. Along with his pan-lusophone acclaim, Pepetela, several of whose works have been published in translation, has attracted a significant international readership. Moreover, the Angolan novelist has displayed a penchant for humor, often in the form of sardonic satire as a reflection of the increased "open-endedness" of lusophone African postcolonial literature. The most audacious and internationalist example of this humor first appeared in Pepetela's novel *Jaime Bunda, agente secreto.* (Jaime Bunda, secret agent). This novel, first published in 2001, is in its fourth edition as of 2006. Needless to say, even those with no reading knowledge of Portuguese can easily recognize that "Jaime Bunda" is a play on "James Bond." Those familiar with Portuguese will see even more humor in the protagonist's name, for *Bunda*, a loan word of African origin, translates into English as "buttocks," A follow-up novel, published in

2003, whose title translates as "Jaime Bunda and the death of the American" is another example of amusingly postcolonial "globalization."

Mozambican icons, such as the literary prize–winning Craveirinha, have influenced such postcolonial writers as Calane da Silva, Luís Carlos Patraquim, Ungulani Ba Ka Khosa, Eduardo White, Albino Magaia, Lília Momplé, Paulina Chiziane, and Mia Couto. All of the foregoing have opened new literary space with respect to the form and content of individual works. Two especially innovative and provocative women writers are Lília Momplé, author of *Neighbors* (1998), which despite its title is a novel written in Portuguese, and Paulina Chiziane, author of *Niketche: Uma história de Poligamia* (2002; A dance of love: A story of polygamy). Both of these novelists elaborate, from a "womanist," if not feminist, perspective, themes dealing with precolonial traditions, colonialism, postcolonialism, Mozambicanness, pan-Africanness, and universality. The aforementioned Mia Couto, born in Mozambique to Portuguese parents, is another prolific lusophone African writer whose novels and collections of stories have been translated into several languages.

Postcolonial São Tomé e Príncipe, with fewer that 200,000 inhabitants, has a small but dynamic group of writers, including Alda do Espírito Santo, Francisco Costa Alegre, Conceição Lima, and Frederico Gustavo dos Anjos. The latter is one of a very few of that two-island nation's writers of prose fiction. But Albertino Bragança's *Rosa do Riboque e Outros Contos* (1985; Rosa from Riboque and other stories) appears to be, both at home and abroad, the most acclaimed São Tomense work of fiction.

All of Guinea-Bissau's writers emerged after independence. Among these relatively few postcolonial authors are Vasco Cabral, Hélder Proença, Domingas Samy, Tony Tcheka, and Abdulai Sila. With the appearance of *Eterna paixão* (1994; Eternal passion), Sila became Guinea-Bissau's first published novelist. He also established *Ku Si Mon* (With their own hands), Guinea-Bissau's first privately owned publishing house.

Although still formulated in part from the perspective of cultural revindication and social protest that prevailed during the late colonial period among *engagé* writers, postcolonial lusophone African literature, drawing on a longstanding and rich legacy, has entered a new phase. It is an evolving phase whose thematic and stylistic innovations make for an increasing number of aesthetically and socially compelling works of national, lusophone, pan-African appeal, as well as cosmopolitanism.

See also **Creoles; Literature and the Study of Africa; Neto, Agostinho; Postcolonialism.**

BIBLIOGRAPHY

Chabal, Patrick, et al. *The Postcolonial Literature of Lusophone Africa.* Evanston, IL: Northwestern University Press, 1996.

Chabal, Patrick, et al. *A History of Postcolonial Lusophone Africa.* Bloomington: Indiana University Press, 2002.

Hamilton, Russell G. *Voices from an Empire: A History of Afro-Portuguese Literature.* Minneapolis: University of Minnesota Press, 1975.

Hamilton, Russell G. "Portuguese-Language Literature." In *A History of Twentieth-Century African Literatures*, ed. Oyekan Owomoyela. Lincoln: University of Nebraska Press, 1993.

Jahn, Janheinz. *Neo-African Literature: A History of Black Writing*, trans. Oliver Coburn and Ursula Lehrburger. New York: Grove Press, 1968.

Moser, Gerald M. "African Literature in Portuguese: The First Written, the Last Discovered." *African Forum* 2, no. 4 (Spring 1967): 78–96.

Moser, Gerald M., and Manuel Ferreira. *A New Bibliography of the Lusophone: Literatures of Africa.* London: Hans Zell, 1993.

Peres, Phyllis. *Transculturation and Resistance in Lusophone African Narrative.* Gainesville: University Press of Florida, 1997.

RUSSELL G. HAMILTON

LIVESTOCK

This entry includes the following articles:
DOMESTICATION
SPECIES

DOMESTICATION

Three species of animals are usually assumed to have been domesticated in Africa: the guinea fowl, the cat, and the donkey. Only one of these, the guinea fowl, had a wild progenitor that was restricted to the continent. The cat and the donkey may have been first domesticated by the ancient Egyptians; remains of these animals have also been found on early archaeological sites in western Asia. There may also have been some local domestication of cattle and pigs in North Africa from the endemic wild *Bos primigenius* and *Sus scrofa*. All other domestic species originated from outside Africa.

The process by which wild animals become domesticated is still little understood and there are continuing arguments about the definition of "domestication," although most definitions take into account both culture and biology. The cultural process of domestication begins when animals are incorporated into the social structure of a human community and become objects of ownership, inheritance, purchase, and exchange. The morphological changes that occur in domestic animals come second to this integration into human society. The biological process resembles evolution and begins when a small number of parent animals are separated from the wild species and are habituated to humans. These animals form a founder group, which is changed over successive generations in response to natural selection under the new regime imposed by the human community and its environment, and also by artificial selection for economic, cultural, or aesthetic reasons.

It is essential that the species to be domesticated have social behavioral patterns that are compatible with those of humans. This means that the animals must be gregarious, breed readily in captivity, and have a wide home range and a short flight distance. Goats, sheep, and cattle (which were first domesticated in western Asia around eight thousand years ago) fulfill these conditions, but gazelle and most species of antelope do not. It is probably for this reason that the apparent attempts by the ancient Egyptians to domesticate oryx and other antelope failed. However, mention must be made of the special relationship that held in southern Africa between the San and the eland (*Tragelephus oryx*). Eland were never domesticated, although the San did regard the wild herds of this antelope as personal and valued possessions. Lack of domestication in Africa of indigenous antelope, zebra, and buffalo is also probably due to the great abundance of these animals, which were always available as a source of meat, eliminating the need for herding.

A popular impression has prevailed that most domestic livestock was introduced in Africa within the last few hundred years and that, previous to the first European and Asian contacts, the subsistence of the native peoples south of the Sahara had been based mainly on hunting and gathering. Wide-scale archaeological excavations and linguistic studies show, however, that domestic livestock in Africa have a history that stretches back for several thousand years, and that the herding of flocks has been as important to many of the human societies there as it has been anywhere else in the world.

DOMESTIC SPECIES IN AFRICA

Species of domestic animals have slowly moved south through the African continent since at least the third millennium BCE, according to the earliest archaeological evidence for cattle herding, which was found in northern Kenya.

The guinea fowl is probably the only domestic animal that originated solely in Africa. In modern times, two of the four wild species of *Numida* are bred as domestic fowl: the helmeted guinea fowl, *Numida meleagris*, which is found wild in western Africa, and *Numida ptilorhynca*, which is endemic to eastern Africa. There appear to be no references in Europe to the guinea fowl in the Middle Ages until the Portuguese travelers to the African coast gave the bird its present name in the sixteenth century.

Chickens were domesticated at some time before the sixth millennium BCE in India and Southeast Asia from the red jungle fowl, *Gallus gallus*. Chickens had reached western Africa by 800 CE. In eastern Africa remains of chickens have been identified at two Iron Age sites in Mozambique. In southern Africa, chicken remains have been found at the eighth-century Iron Age site of Ndondondwane in Natal.

As interesting indicators of the movement of people, remains of black rats have been found in Iron Age sites in Zambia and in twelfth- to eighth-century CE sites in southern Africa. The black rat (*Rattus rattus*) is native to western Asia and the Orient; it was never domesticated but traveled the world with humans as an unwanted commensal. In twentieth-century western Africa, the grasscutter or cane rat (*Thryonomys swinderianus*) and the African giant rat (*Cricetomys gambianus*) have been bred in captivity for their meat.

The wild progenitor of the domestic cat, *Felis catus*, was most probably *Felis silvestris lybica*, which is the southern form of the widespread species *Felis silvestris*. *Felis silvestris lybica* is the common wildcat of Africa, and it is found over most of the continent from the Mediterranean to the Cape, except in the tropical rainforest belt. There is no information on the history of the domestic cat in Africa, outside Egypt. At the present day in Africa, the wild cat will interbreed with feral and house cats, which makes difficult the separation of even the living cats into wild and domestic forms.

Archaeological evidence indicates that the dog, *Canis familiaris*, was first domesticated in western Asia and Europe around twelve thousand years ago and that the progenitor of the dog was the wolf, *Canis lupus*. In the early twenty-first century, the dog is found throughout Africa, but as with all other domestic animals, it was a latecomer south of the Sahara.

How far dogs moved south in the prehistoric period is difficult to ascertain, as there are very few records from early sites. One find has been reported from the ancient city of Kerma in northern Sudan, dated to the second millennium BCE, and another from the neolithic site of Esh Shaheinab, also in Sudan (c. 3300 BCE). South of the equator, dogs have been dated to the first millennium CE; their remains have been identified at Iron Age sites in eastern and southern Africa.

The domestic pig, *Sus domesticus*, is descended from the Eurasian wild boar, *Sus scrofa*. Despite taboos against the eating of pork, pigs were common animals in ancient Egypt. A number of distinctive breeds are still kept in many parts of the continent, but their history is little known.

The ancestor of the domestic donkey, *Equus asinus*, was the wild ass of northern Africa and Arabia, *Equus africanus*. The Hyksos are held responsible for bringing the first domestic horses, *Equus caballus*, into ancient Egypt in the mid-second millennium BCE. Horses may have reached western Africa by two thousand years ago, and they became very important in the power struggles between different states. However, perhaps because of their susceptibility to disease, donkeys and horses were never widespread south of the equator before the nineteenth century.

The dromedary, or one-humped camel, *Camelus dromedarius*, is perfectly adapted to life in hot arid deserts where it will migrate over huge areas, browsing on the sparsest vegetation and surviving without water for longer than any other mammal. There are no wild dromedaries in existence, and it is not known when they became extinct. By following their herds of camels and using water from ancient wells, the nomads of the Sahel have exploited a huge region that cannot be used for traditional agriculture. Camels cannot survive south of the Sahel because they are highly susceptible to trypanosomiasis, the disease carried by the tsetse fly.

For at least three thousand years Africa has been a melting pot for many different breeds of cattle, with unhumped cattle (*Bos taurus*) brought in from Eurasia and humped cattle (*Bos indicus*) from western Asia and India. There may also have been autochthonous domestication of cattle in northern Africa.

By six thousand years ago it is probable that pastoralism was well established throughout northern Africa and that with the increasing desertification of the Sahara, people began to move south with their cattle. The archaeological evidence for the presence of cattle in western Africa is provided by the small, humpless N'Dama breed, which has evolved a natural immunity to trypanosomiasis.

Throughout Africa, cattle have played a crucial role in the social, economic, and religious lives of the local peoples for at least two thousand years. These cattle have evolved into many distinctive breeds that have not only yielded meat, hides, and manure, but have also been used as draft oxen for plowing, and for providing blood and milk.

Domestic sheep, *Ovis aries*, are descended from the wild Asiatic mouflon, *Ovis orientalis*. By 3000 BCE there were well-defined breeds of sheep in ancient Egypt. The mummified remains of a large number of hairy, thin-tailed sheep have been excavated from the tombs at Kerma in northern Sudan, ranging in date from 2400 to 1500 BCE. By about 200 BCE sheep were probably spreading down the western side of southern Africa from present-day Angola to the Cape; their remains have been recorded at Iron Age sites dating to two thousand years ago.

The best evidence for the kinds of livestock owned throughout Africa in the past comes from rock art, which is often extremely detailed although difficult to date. Both fat- and thin-tailed sheep are seen on rock paintings from Zimbabwe, while fat-tailed sheep have been recorded at eleven sites in the western Cape and at two in western Natal.

The fat tail of the sheep was an extremely valuable resource throughout the continent, as it was to the early European immigrants. In the early nineteenth century, English travelers such as William Burchell described the Cape sheep as hairy and having a tail that weighed from six to twelve pounds. The fat was semi-fluid, like thick oil, and was frequently used for tallow and for cooking.

Domestic goats, *Capra hircus*, are descended from the scimitar-horned goat of western Asia, *Capra aegagrus*. Breeds include the dwarf goats of ancient origin, which are found across equatorial Africa from southern Sudan to western Africa.

Goats had reached the Iron Age sites of South Africa by the fourth century CE, but it seems that the goat was always a less important livestock animal in the south than the sheep and there are few archaeological records of its remains.

CROSSBREEDING OF DOMESTIC BREEDS

All the species of domestic livestock that are commonly found in present-day Africa were living in ancient Egypt, as were the dog and cat. Their diffusion southward took a long time, probably because it only became essential to keep domestic animals when the local peoples, who lived in settlements and had the use of iron, expanded beyond the numbers that could be supplied from hunted meat.

Over the last two thousand years the cattle, sheep, goats, pigs, and dogs, as well as ponies in western Africa, were all crossbred with foreign breeds brought in by Arab and Asian traders, and by successive waves of colonialism from Europe. However, the most important factor in their history was the combination of natural and artificial selection, which led to the evolution of distinctive breeds, sometimes with unique characteristics such as the bulbous horns of the Kuri cattle from the Lake Chad region.

During the twentieth century many of these breeds have been greatly altered by the pervasive demand for "improvement." Thus the native cattle of southern Ethiopia, the humped Boran, whose minimal water needs are in perfect adaptation to their semi-desert environment, have been improved by crossing with northern European breeds. Similarly the ancient Mashona breed from Zimbabwe has been improved by crossing with Hereford beef cattle. In the short term, this improvement leads to high productivity, but there is a loss of the unique genetic constitution of the breed that has evolved in adaptation to the local environment. Susceptibility to stress and to disease is increased and the need to protect these vulnerable herds has led to such misguided policies as the game-eradication schemes of the 1960s, in attempts to control tsetse flies. Researchers and environmentalists realize that the anciently established breeds of livestock are as much a part of the biotope as the wildlife, and if the balance of their management is upset, the entire ecosystem will suffer. Many of the projects for so-called improvement have been halted, and efforts are being made to conserve the remaining purebred, indigenous herds of livestock, including the Boran and the Mashona cattle. In South Africa a society has been established for the conservation of indigenous breeds of all domestic species, including the dog.

See also **Agriculture; Archaeology and Prehistory; History of Africa; Kerma; Production Strategies: Agriculture; Travel and Exploration: European.**

BIBLIOGRAPHY

Blench, Roger. "Ethnographic and Linguistic Evidence for the Prehistory of African Ruminant Livestock, Horses, and Ponies." In *The Archaeology of Africa: Food, Metals, and Towns*, ed. Thurstan Shaw et al. New York: Routledge, 1993.

Burchell, William J. *Travels in the Interior of Southern Africa*. New York: Johnson Reprint Co., 1967.

Chaix, Louis, and Annie Grant. "Study of a Prehistoric Population of Sheep (*Ovis aries* L.) from Kerma (Sudan): Archaeozoological and Archaeological Implications." *Archaeozoologia* 1, no. 1 (1987): 77–92.

Clark, J. Desmond, and Steven A. Brandt, eds. *From Hunters to Farmers: The Causes and Consequences of Food Production in Africa*. Berkeley: University of California Press, 1984.

Clutton-Brock, Juliet. *A Natural History of Domesticated Mammals*. Cambridge, U.K.: Cambridge University Press, 1987.

Clutton-Brock, Juliette. "The Process of Domestication." *Mammal Review* 22, no. 2 (1992): 79–85.

Clutton-Brock, Juliette. "The Spread of Domestic Animals in Africa." In *The Archaeology of Africa: Food, Metals, and Towns*, ed. Thurstan Shaw et al. New York: Routledge, 1993.

Epstein, H. *The Origin of the Domestic Animals of Africa*, 2 vols. New York: Africana Pub. Corp., 1971.

Galaty, John G. "Cattle and Cognition: Aspects of Maasai Practical Reasoning." In *The Walking Larder: Patterns of Domestication, Pastoralism, and Predation*, ed. Juliet Clutton-Brock. London and Boston: Unwin Hyman, 1989.

MacDonald, Kevin C., and David N. Edwards. "Chickens in Africa: The Importance of Qasr Ibrim." *Antiquity* 67 (1993): 584–590.

Robertshaw, Peter. "The Beginnings of Food Production in Southwestern Kenya." In *The Archaeology of Africa: Food, Metals, and Towns*, ed. Thurstan Shaw et al. New York: Routledge, 1993.

Tewe, O. O.; S. S. Ajayi; and E. O. Faturoti. "Giant Rat and Cane Rat." In *Evolution of Domesticated Animals*, ed. Ian L. Mason. London and New York: Longman, 1984.

Voigt, Elizabeth A., and Angela von den Driesch. "Preliminary Report on the Faunal Assemblage from Ndondondwane, Natal." *Annals of the Natal Museum* 26, no. 1 (1984):95–104.

JULIET CLUTTON-BROCK

SPECIES

Transition from hunting to food production gave way to domestication of animals during the Neolithic Age. Indeed, culture, sociopolitical relationships, and environment influenced not only food production but agro-pastoralism. Animal domestication marks great advancement of human progress. Animal rearing and agriculture formed the basis of civilization in many parts of the ancient world. According to a *Scientific Monthly* article published by Walter Hough in 1934, four distinct phases could be discerned on human experience with animals: Animals as human congeners; humans as distinct from other animals; animals selected and controlled by domestication; and the invention of economic use of animals. Domestication connotes the formation of symbiotic relations between humans and animals. In 1984 E. O. Price viewed domestication as both an evolutionary process and an experimental phenomenon. Domestication was not merely taming but included the processes of breeding animals in captivity, which is goal oriented and increases the subjugation of animal to human.

Humans domesticated animals from their natural limits, changing their habits and adapting them to their socioeconomic uses. Domestication marked humanity's new phase of culture, adaptation for the art and embracing the psychology of the animals. As Andrew B. Smith noted, "Rock engravings and paintings, as well as cultural debris, are found in areas with less than 20 mm annual rainfall today. This rock art shows giraffe, hartebeest, and ostrich, all of which, though dry-area adapted, need vegetation to survive even if water is not available. Cattle paintings indicate that water had to exist, at least seasonally" (p. 126). Rock paintings have been found in southern Algeria and Jebel Uweinat, Egypt, Sudan, and Libya.

Cattle were domesticated around regions endowed with aquatic resources, including the Nile Valley, Niger, Mali, Chad, and northern Kenya. Smith observed that the first pastoral culture in present-day Sahel occurred around 2000 BCE; seasonal fishing settlements were occupied by herders at Karkarichinkat in the Tilemsi Valley, Mali, north of Gao.

In East Africa, Lake Turkana in northern Kenya has been identified as the earliest site of pastoralism. New economies of pastoralism also developed in Ethiopia. Herding became a full-time trade and developed relations between two economic groups. As Smith noted, "it is probable that domestic stock were transferred into agricultural economics, with the farmers storing their wealth in the form of cattle" (134). In many parts of Africa cattle became symbols of wealth and prestige.

Hunter-herder groups aided the spread of pastoralism in many parts of southern Africa. Early domestic stock was traced to Bambata in Zimbabwe, where sheep remains were dated to circa 100 BCE. There was an interface and constant shift between hunting and herding. Some animals were more abundant, easily captured and raised in captivity. Hunting provided background for domestication and control of animals. The horse, wild cattle, and smaller mammals were hunted for meat, skins, and other useful products. The horse and dog after domestication were used for riding and controlling herd animals respectively.

Some scholars underscored the importance of culture history while others emphasized the inevitability of symbiotic relationships developing between animals and humans. In both zoology and history, it has been recognized that the idea of domestication was motivated not necessarily by economics but by religion. Animal domestication has been linked to humanity's social and economic development. In 1962 Erich Isaac suggested that no fundamental opposition exists between zoology and culture history with regard to how domestic breeds of cattle developed. However, the question of religious motive remains an unattractive explanation to zoologists. There are assumptions in zoology that the Urus voluntarily joined human society. Other important factors include the degree of control and selection.

In many parts of Africa, cattle have ritual significance. The purpose of domestication was to have an available supply for sacrificial purposes, of animals sacred to gods and goddesses worshipped in the ancient world. It was argued that the economic use of animals was a by-product of domestication, which was religious in origin. Cattle and other homed animals such as sheep and goats were domesticated for their crescent-shaped horns. Animals were domesticated not merely for food or economic uses. Sacrificial stocks were kept away from predators and allowed to develop and reproduce. Cattle were used for secular labor. Neck yoke was practiced in Egypt in about 1600 BCE. As Isaac observed, "Castration of the bull which led to one of the most significant of agricultural developments, the ox, also had a religious origin. . . . Human ritual castration, a reenactment of the fate of the deity in certain cults of Near Eastern ritual mythology (Tammuz, Attis, and so on) probably served as the model for the castration of bulls" (199).

Animals domesticated between 2000 BCE and the twentieth century are noted to be of monophyletic origin. They include the cat, rabbit, silver fox, and nutria. Cattle and other old domestic animals belong to the polyphyletic origin.

The history of the domestic rabbit demonstrates the influence of change in a wild animal due to domestication. Domestic rabbit is derived from wild rabbit. By the seventeenth century, it acquired the attributes of tameness.

In 1986 D. L. Coppock, J. E. Ellis, and D. M. Swift described livestock feeding ecology and resource utilization as follows:

1. Livestock feeding ecology is largely influenced by seasonal patterns of forage selection, diet diversity, and habitat use. The objective was to characterize the trophic niche segregation of livestock and their potential; harvesting capacity for the heterogeneous vegetation resources of the ecosystem.

2. Cattle and camels were grazing and browsing specialists, respectively, while goats, sheep, and donkeys were generalists for both herbaceous and non-herbaceous.

3. Diet and habitat use were greatly influenced by season. Relative to brief rainy periods of resource abundance, long dry intervals of resource scarcity were times of reduced diet diversities (forage-class basis) for most species and greatly increased variation in habitat use.

4. The livestock in aggregate provided a very broad, opportunistic, and temporarily stable trophic niche that resulted from equitable use of all forage classes, and their mobility provided a means to exploit the entire region. These attributes are essential for the persistence of nomads in this harsh, unpredictable environment, and are inimical to development tactics that were to reduce livestock species diversity or restrict mobility. (573)

Animal breeding procedures involve the application of basic sciences, notably reproductive, physiology, genetics, and statistics.

As previously noted, cattle were one of the earliest and most widely domesticated livestock animal species in Africa. They supply about 50 percent of the world's meat and 95 percent of the world's milk. Hides from cattle are used for shoes, bags, and other valuable products. Domestic cattle are members of the genus *Bos* of the Bovidae cattle family. The gestation period of cattle is about 280 days. On the average, each cow has a calf per year. The raising and marketing of beef cattle depends on the socioeconomic environment. Peasant farmers often domesticate one or two cows and utilize them for both beef and milk. Huge ranches keep breeding herds of several thousand head. Some pastoralists held up to 15,000 head of cattle at one time. Beef cattle producers operate breeding herds and sell their calves as feeders while others buy the feeders, grow, and fatten them. The breeding patterns depend on the level of capital, investment, and managerial capacity.

The breeding herd consists of cattle that are usually either pregnant or nursing a calf. The cattle are turned out to pasture or range during summer. The winter season is the most important period for managing the breeding herd. The mothers nurse their calves until they are weaned. The calves could be fattened on pasture or may be sold as feeders to cattlemen who specialize in fattening them for slaughter. The feeders are sold on classes according to set, age, weight, and grade.

Dairy cows are milked twice a day in highly sanitary conditions. In large farms, cows are milked with machines. Some of the dairy cows produce approximately 5,000 kilograms of milk a year. Drought and desertification have been great challenges to cattle breeding in Africa. In most cases, pastoralists have clashed with farmers over grazing rights. This has led to the migration and displacement of pastoral groups. In the central Sudan, pastoralism suffers from overgrazing, overcultivation, and excessive firewood collection. Added to the environmental challenge is the spread of livestock diseases. Breeds from western Sudan bring diseases such as contagious bovine pleuro-pneumonia (CBPP, also known as lung plague).

CHICKEN BREEDING

Chickens are presumably the most abundant birds in the world and used for human food. *Gallus domesticus* was the species of fowl early domesticated by humans. It belongs to the Phasianidae family. There are differences in comb, plumage, color, beard, and other features. There are basically two distinctive categories: egg-producing breeds and broiler breeders. Breeds used for egg production differ from those that are preserved for meat. Hens lay eggs at about twenty-two weeks of age. After a full year of egg production, many are sold and replaced by young hens. The average production per layer is approximately 220 eggs per year. Under good management and facilities, some hen lay 260 eggs per year.

Broiler Breeds. Broiler chickens are often allowed to grow into market size very rapidly, often within eight to nine weeks. Modern broiler environments often possess facilities for heat and ventilation. The energy sources used in poultry feeding include grains such as corn, milo, barley, wheat, and waste fats from meat processing as well as vegetable oil. Soybean meal, meat meals, fish meal, cotton seed meal, and peanut meal are equally important.

Beginning in the late twentieth century, an outbreak of avian influenza (bird flu) and the avian influenza A virus (H5N1) affected large proportions of domesticated birds, including chickens, ducks, and turkeys. The avian influenza was devastating to the poultry sector, affecting the health and livelihoods of both poultry and poultry consumers. In Nigeria about 140 million domesticated birds were threatened. The spread of the bird flu from Asia was facilitated through migrating birds and the poultry trade. Indeed, the outbreak of the bird flu was a setback to Nigeria's effort to ban poultry importation in order to boost local production and trade. The bird flu was first reported in a commercial chicken farm in Jaji, Kaduna. At the farm, which was comprised of 46,000 birds, 42,000 were infected; 40,000 of those infected died. This was followed by an outbreak in Kano state. The Nigerian federal authorities imposed quarantine measures to control the movement of the infected birds.

PIGGERY

Pigs belong to the Suidae family and specifically to the domestic animal scientifically termed *Sus Scrofa*. The domestic pig is stout bodied and short legged, with a coarse coat and short tail. Pigs produce bacon, meat, or pork. Pigs become sexually active at about five to seven months of age. The boars breed throughout the year. After a gestation period of slightly less than four months, the sow farrows give birth to usually six to twelve pigs. At birth an average pig will weigh from 2.4 to 3 pounds. At three weeks of age pigs can usually be expected to average 10 to 12 pounds; at five weeks, 18 to 20 pounds; and at eight weeks 35 to 40 pounds. Commercially produced pigs are predominantly crossbreeds that are usually weaned at about four to eight weeks of age. The housing and sanitation required for breeding pigs involve indoor, enclosed, environmentally controlled units where pigs spend much of their life. The pigs are automatically fed and their manure automatically removed. Pigs often require shelter that provides a dry bedding area, free from drafts. During hot, humid weather, pigs require shelter from direct sunlight during the hottest part of the day and may require a wallow to keep their body temperature normal. Pig breeding requires subjecting them to periodic disinfection.

GOATS

Archaeological findings and phylogeographic analysis suggest that goats and other farm animals have multiple maternal origins, possibly in Asia and the Fertile Crescent region of the Near East, about 10,000 years ago. Researchers have also shown that domestic goats (*capra hircus*) played a central role in the Neolithic agricultural revolution and the spread of human civilization. Goats are considered to be the most adaptable and geographically widespread livestock species in many parts of Africa. In addition, goats constitute the main economic resource in several developing countries and remarkably too in the advanced nations. Goats provide sources of fresh milk and meat. Clutton-Brock suggested that goats have been transported more often than other livestock because "goats are perhaps the most versatile of all ruminants in their feeding habits, a factor that has greatly affected their success as domestic animals... [goats] are also extremely hardy and will thrive and breed on the minimum of food and under extremes of temperature and humidity" (Luikart et al., 5931). The industrial use of goat skin is quite popular in the production of shoes and other leather products.

CAMELS

Camels are strategic to the sociocultural, political, and economic livelihood in the Middle East and northern Africa. Socially, the Tuarges of the Sahara trust the camel as a symbol of love. Indeed, the Afar tribe in Ethiopia values their camels more their sons, and the Arabs hold the belief that only the camel knows the hundredth name of Allah (God). Camels have significantly shaped the trajectory of Near Eastern history in terms of regional human development, political, economic and ecological development. The camel, as a transport animal, launched the Arab into world history and reinvigorated warfare in the desert. Camels were indispensable to the long-distance trade across the Sahara and the forest zone. The widespread use of camels

opened up unoccupied desert to human exploitation and food production.

There are two main types of camels: the one-humped or dromedary camel (*Camelus dromedariu*) and the two-humped or Bactrian camel (*Camelus bactrianus*). They are generically similar but their climatic adaptations differ. The Bactrian camel thrives in the high-altitude deserts of Central Asia, while the dromedary survives in the hot deserts of northern Africa and western Asia. It is, however, sensitive to humidity and low temperatures. The Bactrian is shorter-limbed, more compactly built, and has longer shaggy hair and a longer gestation period. The dromedaries produce no wool. It has been suggested that dromedary and Bactrian camels were first domesticated in Iran and Turkmenistan.

See also **Agriculture; Climate; Famine; Food; Interlacustrine Region, History of (1000 BCE to 1500 CE); Production Strategies.**

BIBLIOGRAPHY

Clutton-Brock, J. *Domestic Animals From Early Times.* London: Heinemman, 1981.

Coppock, D. L.; J. E. Ellis; and D. M. Swift. "Livestock Feeding Ecology and Resource Utilization in a Nomadic Pastoral Ecosystem." *Journal of Applied Ecology* 23 (1986): 573–583.

Hall, S. J. G., and J. Ruane. "Livestock Breeds and Their Conservation: A Global Overview." *Conservation Biology* 7, no. 4 (1993): 815–825.

Hough, Walter. "The Domestication of Animals." *The Scientific Monthly* 39, no. 2 (1934): 144–150.

Isaac, Erich. "On the Domestication of Cattle." *Science, New Series* 137, no. 3525 (1962): 195–204.

Kohler-Bollefson. "Camels and Camel Pastoralism in Arabia," *Biblica Archaeologist* 56, no. 4 (1993): 180–188.

Luikart, G., et al. "Multiple Material Origins and Weak Phylogeographic Structure in Domestic Goats." *Proceedings of the National Academy of Sciences of the United States of America* 98, no. 10 (2001): 5927–5932.

Price, E. O. "Behavioural Aspects of Animal Domestication." *Quarterly Review of Biology* 59, no. 1 (1984): 1–32.

Smith, Andrew B. "Origins and Spread of Pastoralism in Africa." *Annual Review of Anthropology* 21 (1992): 125–141.

Trilsbach, A., and S. Wood. "Livestock Markets and the Semi-Arid Environment: A Case Study from Sudan." *Human Geography* 68, no. 1 (1986): 51–58.

RASHEED OLANIYI

LIVINGSTONE, DAVID (1813–1873).

David Livingstone, of Scottish working-class origins, became an icon of British civilization, Christianity, and commerce in Africa for his own times as well as for later generations. His importance lies, first, in his impact on popular and official European thinking about missionary work, the abolition of the slave trade, and other matters of African policy; much unofficial and official activity was stimulated during and after his lifetime. Second—although he failed to find the source of the Nile River, which he sought for many years, amidst great publicity—he was a great practical geographer and field scientist. Third, refusing to accept stereotypes of either servility or barbarism, albeit with some ambivalence, he championed Africans as potential full members of the modern civilization he exemplified. Fourth, in voluminous notebooks, journals, and letters he gathered an enormous amount of information on the condition of central and southern Africa and the lives of its peoples in his times (1850s–1860s), much of which he published in three major works: *Missionary Travels and Researches in South Africa* (1857); *Narrative of an Expedition to the Zambesi and Its Tributaries, and of the Discovery of the Lakes Sherwa and Nyassa, 1858–1864* (1865); and the posthumous *Last Journals of David Livingstone in Central Africa, from 1865 to His Death* (1874).

From 1841 to 1857 Livingstone was employed by the London Missionary Society and initially worked mainly among the Tswana peoples in southern Africa. But from 1849 he showed an increasing desire to travel into unexplored areas to the north in order to find new fields for missionary work, preparing the way by his own geographical exploration. Thus, longer-term goals became more important to him than immediate conversions to Christianity in one place; Livingstone came to believe that missionary work embraced secular objects such as the promotion of trade as well as religious evangelism. He discovered Lake Ngami (in present-day Botswana) in 1849 and then, from 1853 to 1856, made one of the greatest exploratory journeys ever, from Linyanti (Botswana) to Luanda, the Portuguese port and colonial capital on the Atlantic coast, and then eastward across the continent to the mouth of the Zambezi River and the Indian Ocean.

Explorer David Livingstone (1813–1873). Livingstone was the first European to see Victoria Falls, which he then named. The Livingstone Falls on the Congo River is one of many sites named in his honor. CORBIS

Despite the success in locating Lake Malawi in 1859, Livingstone proved a rather poor leader of the official British Government Zambesi Expedition of 1858–1864, which tried to introduce "legitimate" trade as an alternative to slave trading rampant in the region by finding raw materials for export to Britain. From 1865 to 1873 he explored and reported on the slave trade mainly in present-day Zambia and Tanzania, refused to be "rescued" by the journalist Henry Morton Stanley who sought him out in the eastern Congo in 1871, and resumed his search for the Nile along what were really the headwaters of the Congo (Zaire) River in northeastern Zambia, far to the south of the true sources of the river in present-day Uganda. In this wrongheaded search, he drove himself to death near Lake Bangweulu. His African porters preserved and carried his body to the coast, whence it was transported back to Britain for burial in Westminster Abbey.

See also **Christianity; Colonial Policies and Practices: British Central Africa; Stanley, Henry Morton; Travel and Exploration: European (Since 1800).**

BIBLIOGRAPHY

Clendennen, Gary W., and Ian C. Cunningham, eds. *David Livingstone: A Catalogue of Documents.* Edinburgh: National Library of Scotland for the David Livingstone Documentation Project, 1979.

Huxley, Elspeth. *Livingstone and His African Journeys.* London: Weidenfeld and Nicolson, 1974.

Livingstone, David. *The African Journal, 1853–1856,* ed. with an introduction by Isaac Schapera. Berkeley: University of California Press, 1963.

Simmons, Jack. *Livingstone and Africa.* London: English Universities Press, 1955.

ROY C. BRIDGES

LOBENGULA (1836–1894). Lobengula inherited an Ndebele (Matabele) kingdom in western Zimbabwe in disarray. He spent much of his reign trying to strike a balance between rebellious factions among his own people and the demands of settlers, under the auspices of Cecil Rhodes' British South Africa Company, who were moving north of the Limpopo River. Lobengula's father, Mzilikazi, a fearsome fighter, had moved to the region and founded the Ndebele kingdom after splitting with Shaka, the Zulu founder and warrior king, in the 1820s. Mzilikazi died in 1868, just one year after European prospectors discovered gold on the edge of his domain. Following Mzilikazi's death, a civil war of succession ensued. Two years passed before Lobengula emerged victorious from that war to claim the throne.

Lobengula ruled Matabeleland, the southwestern portion of the land between the Zambezi and Limpopo Rivers. Settlers and prospectors from the English and Afrikaner areas to the south wanted the area and accompanying mineral rights for their own. Lobengula was never as strong as his father in dealing with internal and external threats. In the face of European demands he made some concessions regarding farming and mining rights, and signed an agreement in 1888 stating he would conduct territorial negotiations only with the British.

Cecil Rhodes, who thought Matabeleland contained the next big gold reef after the fabulously rich strikes on the Witwatersrand (modern Johannesburg), formed the British South Africa Company in 1889, and Lobengula granted him a mining concession in the southwestern part of the country. The company's 1890 expedition found very little in the way of mineral wealth and faced big losses. After an Ndebele attack on a company outpost in 1893, the company decided to retaliate harshly despite Lobengula's repeated requests for peace. As Rhodes's adviser Dr. Leander Starr Jameson noted, "Getting Matabeleland open would give us a tremendous lift in shares and everything else." An army made up of the company's police force, settler irregulars, and off-duty imperial regiments attacked the Ndebele capital at Bulawayo in 1893 and razed it. Lobengula died of smallpox while retreating.

See also **Colonialism and Imperialism: Concessionary Companies; Rhodes, Cecil John.**

BIBLIOGRAPHY

Bhebe, Ngwabi. *Lobengula of Zimbabwe.* London: Heinemann Educational, 1977.

Oliver, Roland, ed. *Cambridge History of Africa.* Volume 6. Cambridge, U.K.: Cambridge University Press, 1985.

THOMAS F. McDOW

LOMÉ. The capital and main port of Togo, Lomé was founded in the late eighteenth century on the site of an Ewe settlement. The city's name was derived from a local word meaning "little market." The Germans selected Lomé as the colonial capital of their colony of Togoland in 1897, and during German colonial rule (until World War I) much of the city's infrastructure was built. Located in the southwest corner of the country, Lomé is linked by rail to Palimé in the northwest, to Sokodé in the north, and to Anecho along the coast in the east; cash crops are transported by rail to Lome's port, from which they are exported. Cocoa, coffee, palm products, and cotton account for two-thirds of Togo's export earnings.

Lomé's industrial sector is essentially of post-independence origins. Limestone and phosphate exports and tourism contributed to its commercial expansion in the 1970s. Massive infrastructural building, a liberal investment code, and extensive smuggling across the Ghanaian border by Lomé's entrepreneurial marketwomen contributed to the city's growth. An economic collapse in the 1980s, however, led to drastic economic restructuring that continued into the 1990s. Structural adjustment policies have raised prices for foodstuffs and have been accompanied by paralyzing strikes and riots. In 1993, one-third of Lomé's estimated 600,000 people fled to Ghana during the political violence and social tumult following the economic collapse. The city expanded in the years that followed, and in 2004 the population was estimated at 800,000.

See also **Colonial Policies and Practices: German; Togo.**

KATHARYN CALDERA

LOPES, HENRI (1937–). Author, politician, and diplomat Henri Lopes was born in Leopoldville (present-day Kinshasa) and grew up in Brazzaville. His high school and university studies were in France where he studied literature and history at the Sorbonne. He served as Foreign Minister of Congo-Brazzaville from 1971–1973 and as Prime Minister from 1973–1976. He then became Assistant Director-General and later the Deputy Director-General of UNESCO. He has also served as the Congo-Brazzaville ambassador to France and to the U.K. He is the author of six novels and has published two collections of short stories and a volume of essays. His most well-known novel is *Le pleurer-rire* (The Laughing Cry: An African Cock and Bull Story), a hilarious and biting satirical novel about a corrupt dictator. The primary narrator of the novel is the dictator's most observant and outrageous French-trained valet. Unfortunately, the only other work of Lopes that has been translated into English is his collection of short stories *Tribaliques: Novelles* (Tribaliks: Contemporary Congolese Stories). His 2003 collection of essays is titled *Ma Grand-mère bantoue et mes ancêtres les Gaulois* (author's translation of the title: "My Bantu Grandmother and my Gallic ancestors").

See also **Brazzaville; Kinshasa; Literature.**

BIBLIOGRAPHY

Lopes, Henri. *Tribaliques: Novelles.* Yaounde, Cameroon: Éditions Clé, 1971.

Lopes, Henri. *Le pleurer-rire.* Paris: Présence africaine, 1982.

Lopes, Henri. *Ma Grand-mère bantoue et mes ancêtres les Gaulois.* Paris: Gallimard, 2003.

ANNE ADAMS

LUANDA. Paulo Dias de Novais of Portugal fortified the headland at the bay of Luanda, site of the modern city, in 1575. The city's name derives from the word *loanda*, meaning "tax" or "duty," referring to the small marine shells found in the sheltered, shallow bay there, which the king of nearby Kongo claimed as tribute and used as currency. The subsequent colonial town from 1627 was the military and administrative headquarters of the Portuguese government in its *reino e conquista* (kingdom and conquest) of Angola. It was also the principal seaport of the colony and perhaps the largest shipping point for slaves in Africa, nearly all of whom were taken to Brazil. Although the town drew its political identification from Portugal, with the exception of a brief period of occupation by Dutch forces (1641–1648), it drew most of its population from the local Africans, many of them enslaved. Over the centuries Luanda, like nearly every other nominally "Portuguese" trading town in Africa (e.g., Bissau, Moçambique), developed a distinctive Creole culture which reflecting Afro-Portuguese (or Luso-African) population. Luanda thrived on the commerce in slaves until 1850, when Brazil abolished the slave trade.

Luanda's Creole inhabitants, many of them Catholics and literate, protested articulately the growing immigration from Portugal at the end of the nineteenth century and gradually became politically marginalized under the Portuguese Republic (from 1910), although they maintained a significant artistic and literary community. The city thrived as the modern colony's administrative center and main port, connected by rail and road with coffee, cotton, and other commodity-producing regions to the east, and by an international airport with Portugal and South Africa. With growth of the independence struggles in the 1960s, led significantly by Creole-descended nationalist politicians organized in the Movimento Popular de Libertação de Angola (MPLA), it also became the military headquarters of Portugal's occupying armed forces.

In the 1920s the city's *baixa* district was transformed into a European-style business center. The Africans living there were removed to shantytowns known as *musseques*, a Kimbundu word referring to the red-clay fields in which manioc is grown. Several hundred thousand, mostly impoverished immigrant Portuguese settlers arrived from Portugal, sent to develop and defend the city and the colony from African fighters for independence; they numbered several hundred thousand among an urban population of a half million people. They fled en masse in 1975, leaving the city's infrastructure in a near ruined state. Since the mid-1970s the *musseques* have grown rapidly, their numbers swollen by refugees fleeing the fighting in the countryside. The city became almost dysfunctional, except for the informal economy centered on the huge Roque Santeiro market, one of the largest in Africa. In 1995 an estimated 2.25 million people lived in Luanda, about 70 to 80 percent in the *musseques*, overwhelming urban infrastructure and services such as water and food supply, sanitation, schools, and health facilities. The population pressure on such services has only increased over the years since then, and in 2004 estimates of the city's total population grew to more than 2.8 million.

Luanda is the political base of the Movimento Popular de Libertação de Angola (MPLA), the governing party since independence in 1975, and the administrative capital of the country. Civil war erupted between the MPLA and rival rural parties erupted with independence, and in the ensuing years of struggles (until 2003), the highway networks linking Luanda to provincial capitals were mined and some two hundred bridges destroyed or damaged. All rail service from Luanda to the interior was halted in 1992. Luanda's manufacturing sector—oil refining, cement production, vehicle assembly, and metalworking—functioned below capacity or not at all.

See also **Angola; Colonial Policies and Practices: Portuguese; Colonialism and Imperialism; Slave Trades: Atlantic, Central Africa.**

BIBLIOGRAPHY

Monteiro, Ramiro Ladeiro. "From Extended to Residual Family: Aspects of Social Change in the *Musseques* of Luanda." In *Social Change in Angola*, ed. Franz-Wilhelm Heimer. Munich: Weltforum Verlag, 1973.

Venâncio, José Carlos. *A economia de Luanda e hinterland no século XVIII: um estudo de sociologia histórica.* Lisboa: Editorial Estampa, 1996.

Vieira, José Luandino. *Luuanda*, trans. Tamara L. Bender with Donna S. Hill. Exeter, NH: Heinemann Educational Books, 1980.

KATHARYN CALDERA

LUBUMBASHI. Known as Elisabethville during the Belgian colonial occupation, Lubumbashi is the capital of Katanga Province, in the Democratic Republic of the Congo (formerly Zaire). The city derives its name from the Luba kingdom—currently the Luba are one of the two largest ethnic groups in Zaire—which dominated the Shaba region (in the south of the country) from the fifteenth to nineteenth centuries. Lubumbashi is currently the second largest industrial center in the nation, a result of its proximity to the extraordinarily rich deposits of copper and cobalt in southern Shaba.

Open-pit and underground mines, as well as refineries and smelters, are found throughout the city. Mining has been the cornerstone of the city since 1906, when the Union Minière du Haut-Katanga was formed as a joint endeavor of the Société Générale de Belgique and British Tanganyika Concessions, Ltd., to extract copper and other minerals from Lubumbashi and surrounding areas. In 1967, it began operating as the government-owned GEOMINES, later renamed GECAMINES, the Générale des Carrières et des Mines. It is the largest corporation in the country, providing half of the nation's total revenues and two-thirds of its foreign exchange. The twentieth-century history of Lubumbashi is inseparable from the company, which has effectively acted as a state within a state and which thoroughly dominates the economic affairs of the city. The production of copper has declined steadily since the 1970s, and the industry all but collapsed in the wake of neglect throughout the political upheavals of the 1990s.

Lubumbashi also serves as a manufacturing center for tobacco products, textiles, shoes, metalwork, palm oil, and food processing. The city was the capital of the secessionist state of Katanga from 1961 to 1963. In May 1990, students were murdered on the campus of the University of Lubumbashi in what appeared to be a government-ordered killing. The exact population and ethnic composition of the city are difficult to determine with any accuracy, but scholars estimate the population reached 1 million by the year 2004. Essential services have been strained to the limits, but the government has begun a series of programs aimed at rebuilding key infrastructure. This effort is hampered by the severe economic disarray facing the nation as a whole.

See also **Colonial Policies and Practices: Belgian; Congo, Democratic Republic of the; Metals and Minerals.**

BIBLIOGRAPHY

Fetter, Bruce. *The Creation of Elizabethville, 1910–1940.* Stanford, CA: Hoover Institution Press, 1976.

Jewsiewicki, Bogumil, J. Hoover, and Donatien dia Mwenbu. *Recits de Liberation d'Une Ville.* Paris: Harmattan, 1990.

MICHAEL WATTS

LUGARD, FREDERICK JOHN DEALTRY (1858–1945).

Frederick Lugard was born in India to missionary parents in 1858 and served in the British army in India from 1879 to 1886. From the late 1880s through the 1890s he led military expeditions in eastern and western Africa, most notably intervening in Buganda and neighboring states to bring the territory under British rule as the Protectorate of Uganda in 1893. In 1897, on behalf of the Royal Niger Company, he led a mission in the Sokoto Caliphate in the interior of West Africa. Married to the influential journalist, Flora Shaw (1852–1929), Lugard became one of the most important theorists of British colonial rule in Africa. Lugard's conception of empire followed an imperial model developed in India, by which Britain would rule in collaboration with indigenous officials. Lugard popularized this system as Indirect Rule, but it in fact depended upon direct British intervention in local affairs.

From 1900 to 1906, Lugard served as High Commissioner of the Protectorate of Northern Nigeria that effectively included the core emirates of the Sokoto Caliphate and adjacent Muslim and non-Muslim regions. In consolidating British rule in the region, Lugard introduced administrative reforms that effectively increased the power of the Muslim emirates in regulating economic and social changes in a large and wealthy region of the colony. Lugard's policies were directed at reforming taxation, managing the gradual emancipation of the large slave population, and promoting economic development through the growth in agricultural exports, especially cotton and peanuts. The reliance on traditional authorities in the implementation of colonial policies subsequently became the pattern for the others parts of British colonial Africa where there were no European settlers, and the policy specifically became the model for an amalgamated Protectorate of Northern and Southern Nigeria after 1912.

Although Lugard served as governor of Hong Kong from 1907 to 1912, his principal impact in British colonial history was in Africa. Back in Nigeria as governor from 1912 to 1919, he oversaw the consolidation of Northern and Southern Nigeria and extended Indirect Rule to non-Muslim areas, which resulted in popular protests against the introduction of centralized government and taxation to regions that had previously been autonomous. The demands of World War I and the failure to invest sufficiently in the colonial economy undermined these administrative efforts at political consolidation, despite the rapid expansion in the export economy.

After 1919, Lugard continued his influential role in setting British colonial policy. In 1922, he published his text on colonial administration, *The Dual Mandate in British Tropical Africa.* In 1923, he was appointed British representative on the League of Nations Permanent Mandates Commission and served on the League's commission on slavery and forced labor. He also was a member of the International Labour Organization and served as the first chairman of the London-based International Institute of African Languages and Cultures. Although his policies on slavery were gradualist and effectively maintained the conservative status quo under colonialism, Lugard became recognized as an authority on anti-slavery and on economic development. His commitment to Indirect Rule led him to oppose the transfer of power to European settlers in Kenya and the Italian invasion of Ethiopia. His vision of African dependency was elitist and ultimately ineffective in the face of poor economic performance and growing dissatisfaction among educated Africans. In practice, the implementation of Indirect Rule resulted in marginal investment in colonial development and correspondingly a drain on the resources of the colonies in the interests of Britain.

See also **Colonial Policies and Practices: British West Africa.**

BIBLIOGRAPHY

Flint, John E. "Frederick Lugard: The Making of an Autocrat." In *African Proconsuls: European Governors in Africa*, ed. L. H. Gann and Peter Duignan. New York: Free Press, 1978.

Lovejoy, Paul E., and Hogendorn, Jan. *Slow Death for Slavery: The Course of Abolition in Northern Nigeria, 1897–1936.* Cambridge, U.K.: Cambridge University Press, 1993.

Lugard, Frederick D. *The Dual Mandate in British Tropical Africa.* Fifth Edition. London: Frank Cass, 1965.

Perham, Margery. *Lugard.* 2 vols. London: Collins, 1956–1960.

PAUL E. LOVEJOY

LUMUMBA, PATRICE (1925–1961). Born in Katako Kombe in the Sankuru district of the Kasai province of the Belgian Congo, Patrice Emery Lumumba obtained his primary education at both Catholic and Protestant mission schools. Despite his limited formal training, he found work as a clerk, first in a small Belgian post, Kindu, and then in the post office in Stanleyville (now Kisangani), the provincial capital. Through voracious reading and taking courses by correspondence with European professors, he improved both his formal education and his standing in various biracial sociocultural organizations in Stanleyville. He founded and chaired the Post Office Workers

Society (Amicale des Postiers), cofounded the Belgo-Congolese Union, and became the general secretary of the Association of Native Public Servants. One of the first *évolués*, a colonial status attained by educated members of the local population through *immatriculation* (a juridical act of assimilation of European culture), Lumumba wrote, in 1956, *Congo, My Country* (published posthumously) in which he expounded his views of the future of the colonial society as a non-racial collaboration between Congo nationalists and enlightened Europeans. After serving a jail term for a seemingly concocted charge of embezzlement of post office funds, he moved to Léopoldville (now Kinshasa), the colonial capital, where he became a successful sales manager for the Bracongo brewery.

In 1958 as the Belgian colony suddenly began to move toward independence, Lumumba founded the Mouvement National Congolais (MNC; Congolese

Patrice Lumumba (1925–1961). The first legally elected prime minister of the Democratic Republic of the Congo, Lumumba, was overthrown after ten weeks. Subsequently, Lumumba was imprisoned and assassinated. He had helped the country gain its independence from Belgium in June 1960. GETTY IMAGES

National Movement), which differed from other parties in its broad nationalist and Pan-African appeals. Shifting from his earlier support for recognition of Congo within a Belgo-Congolese union, Lumumba called for immediate and total independence. He attended the Accra (Ghana) first All-African People's Conference in 1958 and, after serving a jail term in Democratic Republic of the Congo for political agitation, participated in the 1960 Brussels Round Table to discuss the Congo's independence. Lumumba emerged as the most important leader of the fractured political parties contending for leadership in the nationalist movement because of his assertive views, oratorical skills, and his ability to form coalitions with groups from all the provinces of the colony. Lumumba's MNC party obtained a relatively sweeping victory in the 1960 general elections. Despite opposition from Belgium, Lumumba became prime minister of the transitional government and led the new nation to independence on June 30, 1960.

As prime minister, Lumumba immediately faced a series of crises: army mutinies and secessions by Katanga and Kasai provinces—and consequent Belgian and United Nations interventions—and Colonel Joseph Mobutu's military coup. Provoked by domestic anti-Lumumba forces and external powers, including Belgium, these crises led to Lumumba's arrest and murder in Elisabethville (now Lubumbashi) on February 12, 1961.

Lumumba's legacy and importance lie in his staunch anti-imperialism, Pan-Africanism (for example, an accord with Kwame Nkrumah to form a union of Ghana and Zaire), antiracist and antitribalist nationalism, and uncompromising commitment to the unity of the country and the nonviolent liberation of colonized people. In Zaire, present-day Democratic Republic of the Congo, these commitments have been observed since his death, mostly in the breach.

See also **Colonial Policies and Practices: Belgian; Congo, Republic of: History and Politics; Mobutu Sese Seko.**

BIBLIOGRAPHY

Kanza, Thomas. *The Rise and Fall of Patrice Lumumba: Conflict in the Congo.* Boston: G. K. Hall, 1979.

Lumumba, Patrice. *Congo, My Country.* New York: Praeger, 1962.

Patrice Lumumba. London: Panaf, 1973.

Sangmpam, S. N. *Pseudocapitalism and the Overpoliticized State: Reconciling Politics and Anthropology in Zaire.* Aldershot, U.K.: Hants, 1994.

Tshonda Omasombo, Jean. *Patrice Lumumba: jeunesse et apprentissage politique 1925–1956.* Bruxelles: Institut africain/CEDAF; Paris; L'Harmattan, 1998.

Witte, Ludo de. *The Assassination of Lumumba.* London, New York: Verso, 2001.

S. N. Sangmpam

LUSAKA.

The Zambian capital of Lusaka was once known as a meeting place for African political leaders challenging European rule in southern Africa. During the colonial period Lusaka was the hub of campaigns against British colonialism, and in the 1970s and 1980s it became the headquarters of the African National Congress and other liberation movements fighting the remaining white-dominated regimes just to the south in Zimbabwe, Mozambique, and South Africa. An anticolonial center is an ironic identity for a city built as a British colonial capital and intended to remind the African population of European superiority. In the 1930s the city and its large Government House were planned by a student of the renowned colonial architect Sir Herbert Baker (famous for his work in South African cities as well as New Delhi) at a time when Africans outnumbered the Europeans in the colony by a hundred to one. The architecture and plan of Lusaka were meant to demonstrate European dominance and to "be the outward and visible sign at all times of the dignity of the Crown."

Cecil Rhodes's British South Africa Company took control of the area that included the site of Lusaka in the 1890s, hoping to find mineral wealth and a source of labor for the mines to the south of the Zambezi. In the 1920s copper was discovered in the northwest part of what, in 1924, became British protectorate of Northern Rhodesia (present day Zambia). The capital of Northern Rhodesia at the time was Livingstone, near Victoria Falls, but Lusaka was built up in the 1930s and became the capital in 1935. Lusaka was more centrally located, and the British considered its altitude and climate healthier than Livingstone's near the Zambezi River.

The "outward and visible sign" of the colonial capital did not quell notions of African independence.

Although the African population of the European city was not large, the Federation of African Societies met in Lusaka in 1948 to found the Northern Rhodesia African Congress, a group that agitated for African rights. Lusaka was also the center point of a 1960 civil disobedience campaign aimed at undermining the Central African Confederation, a politico-economic consolidation of Northern Rhodesia, Southern Rhodesia, and Nyasaland set up in 1953 and administered from Salisbury in Southern Rhodesia. The disobedience campaign led to the breakup of the confederation in 1963 and to Zambia's independence in 1964.

Lusaka grew rapidly after independence, gaining 148,000 people between 1963 and 1969, an increase of over 75 percent. Because of the rapid increase in population in Lusaka, Kenneth Kaunda's government tried to shift growth away from the capital and encourage settlement in Kafue, to the west. Even with these efforts, Lusaka's population in 2004 had grown to more than 1.2 million.

The plain around Lusaka is home to two major ethnic groups, the Nyanja and the Soli, and supports ranches and farms. The city is multiethnic and produces cement, textiles, and shoes, and processes food. The town is roughly separated into the new section, which houses the government offices, and the old town, much more humble and lying along the rail line. Railways are an important mode of transportation in Zambia: In the 1970s, with Chinese assistance, Tanzania and Zambia built the Tan-Zam Railroad connecting Kapiri Mposhi (on the Zambia-Copper Belt line) with Dar es Salaam in order to give Zambia an outlet to an independent African country. Lusaka is linked by lines to Livingstone, the Copper Belt, and Tanzania.

Lusaka's role as an anticolonial, frontline capital dwindled after African-led governments took power in Mozambique in 1975 and Zimbabwe in 1980. In the 1990s the challenges that faced the city were environmental, economic, and demographic. Lusaka's population has continued unabated, even though the region has endured drought, massive unemployment, and runaway inflation of as much as 500 percent in the 1990s and into the twenty-first century.

See also **Colonial Policies and Practices: British Central Africa; Rhodes, Cecil John; Zambia: History and Politics.**

BIBLIOGRAPHY

Fage, J. D., and Roland Oliver, eds. *The Cambridge History of Africa*, Vol. 7, ed. A. D. Roberts. New York: Cambridge University Press, 1986.

Griffiths, Ieuan Ll. *The Atlas of African Affairs*, 2nd edition. New York: Routledge, 1994.

THOMAS F. MCDOW

LUTHULI, ALBERT JOHN MAVUMBI

(1898–1961). Born in Salisbury, Southern Rhodesia (later Zimbabwe), Albert John Mavumbi Luthuli grew up in Groutville, Natal, South Africa. The son of a preacher, he taught in a primary school before becoming an instructor at Adams College in Natal, in 1921. Elected as chief of the Abasemaklolweni Zulu in 1935, he returned to Groutville to administer local justice and organize peasant cane growers.

Albert Luthuli (1898–1961). Luthuli was the first South African and only the second black man to win the Nobel Peace Prize. He led the African National Congress, as president, in nonviolent protests against apartheid laws. AP IMAGES

Luthuli joined the African National Congress (ANC), the leading African political party in the Union of South Africa, in 1945. In 1952 he was deposed from his chieftancy and elected ANC president, both consequences of his contribution to the ANC's Defiance Campaign against the introduction of apartheid. With Luthuli at its head, the ANC completed its transformation from an assembly of notables into a popular movement. Confined to Groutville by government banning orders most of the time, Luthuli was unable to play an assertive part in ANC mass organizing campaigns, and he was not involved in the decision to initiate sabotage operations in 1961. His importance lay in his moral stature. Less patrician than any of his predecessors in the ANC leadership, Luthuli was a figure who commanded widespread loyalty. He was awarded the Nobel Peace Prize for 1960. At the time of his death in 1961, Luthuli's nonviolence and "middle of the road" socialism seemed to be eclipsed by the more radical programs of exiled ANC guerrillas. His gentle vision embodies an African liberal tradition that remains relevant in twenty-first century democratic South Africa.

See also **Apartheid; South Africa Republic of.**

BIBLIOGRAPHY

Callan, Edward. *Albert John Luthuli and the South African Race Conflict*. Kalamazoo: Western Michigan University, 1965.

Gordimer, Nadine. "Chief." *Atlantic Monthly* 203, no. 4 (1959): 34–39.

Luthuli, Albert. *Let My People Go*. New York: Meridian, 1962.

Pillay, Gerald J. *Voices of Liberation*, Vol. 1: *Albert Lutuli*. Pretoria, South Africa: HSRC Publishers, 1993.

THOMAS LODGE

M

MAATHAI, WANGARI (1940–).

Renowned environmentalist, feminist, and political activist Wangari Muta Maathai was born in Nyeri, Kenya. She was awarded the Nobel Peace Prize in 2004. The Nobel Committee cited "her contribution to sustainable development, democracy and peace." Maathai earned a doctorate in anatomy in 1971, and when she became chair of the Department of Veterinary Anatomy at the University of Nairobi she was the first woman to chair a university department in Kenya. She directed the Kenya Red Cross from 1973 to 1980.

In 1977 she began the Greenbelt Movement, a grassroots environmental group that plants trees, establishes nurseries, and educates local groups—especially women's groups—on environmental issues. The Greenbelt Movement has planted more than 300 million trees and established more than 6,000 nurseries in Kenya and has educated many in Kenya, Africa, and the world about the environment and sustainable development. In 2002 Maathai was elected member of Parliament (MP) for the Tetu District in central Kenya. She subsequently was selected to be Kenya's assistant minister for the environment, natural resources, and wildlife. In 2004 Kenya's Parliament named her envoy to the world for the environment, human rights, and democracy. In 2005 she became the first president of the Economic, Social and Cultural Council of the African Union.

See also **Aid and Development: Environmental Impact; Ecology; Ecosystems; Wildlife: Preservation and Destruction.**

Wangari Maathai during her visit to an environmental project in Cape Town, July 21, 2005. Maathai was Kenya's assistant minister, Environment, Natural Resources, and Wildlife. She was the first African woman to win the Nobel Peace prize. GIANLUIGI GUERCIA/AFP/GETTY IMAGES

BIBLIOGRAPHY

Maathai, Wangari Muta. *The Green Belt Movement: Sharing the Approach and the Experience*, rev. edition. New York: Lantern Books. 2003.

Maathai, Wangari Muta. *Unbowed: A Memoir.* New York: Knopf, 2006.

ANN BIERSTEKER

Sklar, Richard L. *Nigerian Political Parties: Power in an Emergent African Nation.* Princeton, NJ: Princeton University Press, 1963.

Uwechue, Ralph. *Know Africa: Profiles in History: Makers of Modern Africa.* London: Africa Books, 1991.

OLATUNJI OJO

MACAULAY, HERBERT SAMUEL HEELAS

(1864–1946). Herbert Macaulay was the son of Reverend Thomas Babington and Abigail Macaulay, and grandson of Bishop Samuel Ajayi Crowther, the first black African bishop of the modern era. After his graduation from the Lagos Grammar School at age fourteen, he worked as a clerk with the Public Works Department. From 1891 to 1894, he studied land surveying and engineering in England. Upon his return, he took appointment with the Lagos colonial administration as a surveyor. He resigned his appointment in 1898 and set up his own private practice.

In 1923, he founded the first political party in Nigeria, the Nigerian National Democratic Party (NNDP) and a newspaper, the *Lagos Daily News*, both of which had as their goals local self-government, economic development, and social justice. At a public rally in 1944, the NNDP and other mass organizations formed the National Council of Nigeria and the Cameroons (NCNC) with Macaulay as its president. In 1946, at eighty-two years of age, he led the NCNC on a nationwide mobilization against certain sections of the newly promulgated Richards Constitution. He fell sick on tour and died on May 7. In appreciation of his contributions, some public buildings and roads are named after him, and his portrait is on the Nigerian one naira coin.

See also **Macaulay, Thomas Babington; Macaulay, Zachary; Nigeria.**

BIBLIOGRAPHY

Coleman, James S. *Nigeria: Background to Nationalism.* Berkeley: University of California Press, 1971.

Kopytoff, Jean H. *A Preface to Modern Nigeria: The Sierra Leonians in Yoruba, 1830-1890.* Madison: University of Wisconsin Press, 1965.

MACAULAY, THOMAS BABINGTON

(1826–1879). The Sierra Leonean minister and school administrator Thomas Babington Macaulay was born at Kissy, Sierra Leone, the son of liberated slaves from Yorubaland. He was educated in Sierra Leone at Kissy Local Primary School, the Church Missionary Society (CMS) Grammar School and Fourah Bay College, and the Islington College, London, where he graduated in 1848. In 1852, he was sent to the Yoruba CMS Mission, where he worked at Igbein and Owu in Abeokuta. He was ordained in 1854 and married Abigail Crowther, daughter of Bishop Samuel Ajayi Crowther.

The dispute between the emigrants from Sierra Leone and Rev. Henry Townsend on Anglican political influence at Abeokuta led to a confrontation between the Crowthers, Macaulay, and Townsend. Townsend posted Macaulay first to Owu and thereafter transferred him out of Abeokuta. Eventually, with the support of Reverend Crowther, Macaulay pleaded that he be allowed to start a grammar school in Lagos. This was accepted and the CMS Grammar School, Lagos, was founded by Macaulay in December 1859.

Macaulay was the principal of CMS Grammar School in Lagos from 1859 until his death. He was the father of seven children, including Herbert Macaulay, considered the father of modern Nigerian nationalism.

See also **Crowther, Samuel Ajayi; Macaulay, Herbert Samuel Heelas; Macaulay, Zachary; Sierra Leone: Society and Cultures.**

BIBLIOGRAPHY

Ajayi, J. F. Ade. *Christian Missions in Nigeria, 1841–1891: The Making of a New Elite.* Evanston, IL: Northwestern University Press, 1965.

Kopytoff, Jean H. *A Preface to Modern Nigeria: The "Sierra Leonians" in Yoruba, 1830–1890.* Madison: University of Wisconsin Press, 1965.

OLATUNJI OJO

MACAULAY, ZACHARY (1768–1838).

The Sierra Leonean abolitionist Zachary Macaulay was a plantation overseer in Jamaica (1784–1792), where he learned management and developed a hatred for the slave trade and slavery. He was sent by the Sierra Leone Company to Freetown, first to serve as a councilor (1792–1794), then as acting governor (1794–1795) and governor (1796–1799). He was serving as acting governor when, in 1794, French Jacobins invaded and destroyed the nascent colony, and he embarked on the process of rebuilding it. A firm, courageous, and caring leader, when returning to Britain in 1799 he took with him to be educated there twenty-one African boys and four African girls from Sierra Leone.

Zachary Macaulay (1768–1838). In addition to being the colonial governor of Sierra Leone, Macaulay was an anti-slavery campaigner. Many liberated Africans adopted his surname in gratitude for his work. HULTON ARCHIVE/GETTY IMAGES

Macaulay became a member of the famous Evangelical Clapham sect and through it was active in the abolitionist movement, the British and Foreign Bible Society, the Church Missionary Society, and the National Society for the Education of the Poor (promoters of Andrew Bell's teaching method, which was widely adopted in Sierra Leone). He was secretary to the Sierra Leone Company and honorary secretary to the African Institution, which replaced the Sierra Leone Company when Sierra Leone became a Crown colony in 1808. He founded the firm of Macaulay & Babington, through which he traded in Sierra Leone. His reputation explains the popularity of Macaulay as a surname adopted by liberated Africans in the colony.

See also **Christianity; Macaulay, Herbert Samuel Heelas; Macaulay, Thomas Babington; Sierra Leone: Society and Cultures.**

BIBLIOGRAPHY

Booth, Charles. *Zachary Macaulay: His Part in the Movement for the Abolition of the Slave Trade and of Slavery.* London: Longmans, Green, and Co., 1934.

Groves, Charles P. *The Planting of Christianity in Africa,* Vol. 1: *To 1840.* London: Lutterworth Press, 1948.

Kup, Alexander P. *Sierra Leone: A Concise History.* New York: St. Martin's Press, 1975.

Schwarz, Suzanne. *Zachary Macaulay and the Development of the Sierra Leone Company, 1793–1794.* Leipzig: Institut für Afrikanistik, Universität Leipzig, 2000.

J. F. ADE. AJAYI

MACHEL, GRAÇA (1945–).

Graça Simbine Machel was born in 1945 in rural Gaza, Mozambique; her father, a pastor, died just three weeks before her birth. She attended mission boarding school and the Liceu António Enes in Maputo. In 1967 she won a scholarship to study modern languages at Lisbon University in Portugal, where she joined the anticolonial struggle in 1969 and became an activist in the Frente de Libertação de Moçambique (Mozambique Liberation Front, Frelimo). When the Portuguese secret police discovered her Frelimo cell in 1972, she fled to Tanzania, where she received military training and worked in the Frelimo secondary school. She married Samora Machel shortly after he became Mozambique's first president in 1975.

Graça Machel (1945–), in her offices in Maputo, Mozambique. Widowed by the late Mozambique president Samora Machel, Graça married former South African president Nelson Mandela. Once a school teacher, she is fluent in many languages. She is the only woman in history to become the first lady of two nations. Per-Anders Pettersson/Getty Images

Machel was appointed minister of Education and Culture in 1975; a separate Ministry of Culture was formed in 1987, though she continued as minister of Education until 1990. She was the only female government minister in Mozambique during those years. She also served on the national secretariat of the Organização da Mulher Moçambicana (Organization of Mozambican Women, OMM) and on the Frelimo Central Committee. She was widowed in October 1986 when Samora Machel was killed in a plane crash that was engineered by the apartheid regime in South Africa.

Motivated by her concern for children who had been orphaned and traumatized during the long war with Renamo, Machel formed a nongovernmental organization, the Fundação para o Desenvolvimento da Comunidade (Foundation for Community Development), in 1990. Working with the United Nations, she was appointed the Secretary-General's Expert on the Impact of Armed Conflict on Children.

In 1998 Machel married Nelson Mandela while he was president of South Africa. She maintained her wide-ranging political activities and divided her time between South Africa and Maputo. Machel's Foundation spearheaded the women's groups that advocated for the Protocol on the Rights of Women in Africa in 2003. She was appointed chancellor of South Africa's University of Cape Town (UCT) in 1999. Among her many awards are the Hunger Project's Africa Prize in 1992, the 1995 Nansen Medal for her work with refugee children, and the 1998 North-South Prize from the Council of Europe's North-South Centre, in recognition of her work as president of the National Organization of Children of Mozambique. She served in 2005 as patron for the World Congress on Family Law and Children's Rights.

See also **Machel, Samora Moises; Mandela, Nelson.**

BIBLIOGRAPHY

Machel, Graça. *Impact of Armed Conflict on Children*. New York: United Nations, 1996.

Machel, Graça. "Graça Machel," by Felicia Cabrita. *Revista Expresso* (December 4, 1999). Available from http://expresso.clix.pt/.

"Mozambique's First Private Foundation under Discussion," *Mozambiquefile* 170 (September 1990), 10–11. A report on the conference that introduced the Foundation for Community Development.

KATHLEEN SHELDON

MACHEL, SAMORA MOISES (1933–1986).

Samora Moises Machel was an anticolonial military strategist and president of the Republic of Mozambique. After primary schooling in the Portuguese colonial system, Machel became a hospital nurse in the colonial capital of Lourenço Marques (Maputo), and he early embraced anticolonial activism, having been inspired by the African spirit of the times and, more directly, by the example of the

Samora Machel (1933–1986). Samora Machel was the first president of Mozambique and a strong follower of Marxist thought. He was awarded the Lenin Peace Prize in 1975. GETTY IMAGES

See also **Colonial Policies and Practices; Mondlane, Eduardo Chivambo; Mozambique.**

BIBLIOGRAPHY

Christie, Iain. *Machel of Mozambique.* Harare, Zimbabwe: Zimbabwe Publishing House, 1988.

Munslow, Barry, ed. *Samora Machel, an African Revolutionary: Selected Speeches and Writings.* London: Zed Books, 1985.

BASIL DAVIDSON

MADAGASCAR

This entry includes the following articles:
GEOGRAPHY AND ECONOMY
SOCIETY AND CULTURES
HISTORY AND POLITICS (1895–2006)

GEOGRAPHY AND ECONOMY

The Mozambique Channel, which is 242 miles wide, separates Madagascar from the coast of eastern Africa. It is possible that Madagascar was once connected to southern Africa and India; together they would have formed the continent known to theory as Gondwana Land. With an area of 226,658 square miles, Madagascar is the fourth largest island in the world. Long and thin, it stretches over a distance of 994 miles from Cape Bobaomby in the north to Cape Vohimena in the south; its width does not exceed 360 miles.

CLIMATE
Trade winds blow throughout the year. Those from the southeast meet the monsoon from the northwest during the warm season from December to May, which is followed by the southerly movement of the Intertropical Convergence Zone (ICZ). One side of this mountainous island is exposed to the winds and has an annual rainfall between 118 and 196 inches. On the other side the winds are less moist, even relatively dry, due to the foehn. Because of its topography and orography—its highest peak is 29,455 feet—the country is known for the extreme variety of its climate. The east is warm and humid, the south has vast tracts of semidesert, the west is warm and dry, and the high central area has a cool climate. Climatic change in Madagascar is so sudden that one can go from a warm and humid area to a

Mozambican anticolonial activist Eduardo Mondlane in 1949 and later. After the formation of Frente de Libertação de Moçambique (FRELIMO) at Dar es Salaam (in Tanganyika, about to become Tanzania) during 1962, Machel joined Mondlane and others and volunteered for military training under FRELIMO. FRELIMO secured training for volunteers in Algeria (independent from France in 1962) and then, in handfuls, sent them into northern Mozambique. There they shaped a military strategy that soon began to have success.

In 1969, after Mondlane's assassination, Machel took over the FRELIMO leadership and proved a capable military strategist as well as an inspired leader. His clinching success in these roles came in 1974–1975, when his forces contained and then outflanked the Portuguese army in central Mozambique. The country won independence in 1975, and Machel was elected president. His later years were spent in launching the new republic while defending it from banditries sent into Mozambique from Rhodesia and South Africa. He was killed in 1986 in an aircraft crash in circumstances strongly indicative of external sabotage. Consistently effective as a man of action rather than an ideologist, he achieved widespread admiration, at home and abroad, as a wise unifier of the diverse strands of opinion gathered in the independence movement that he led to victory.

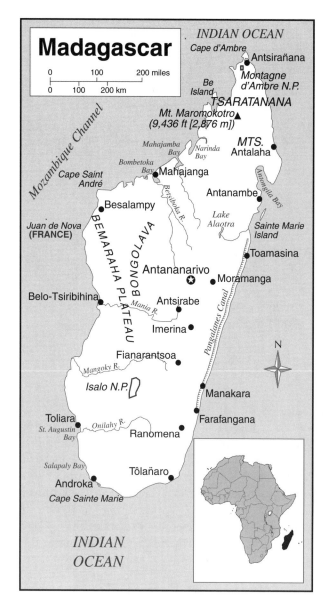

pine trees to the area since the beginning of the twentieth century. The south has thorny xerophytes (*Didierea* and *Alluaudia*).

GEOLOGY

Madagascar's crystalline insular shelf, composed of granite and gneiss, is broken in several places by magma intrusions. In the central highlands, erosion has created a countryside of bare hills, called *tanety*, dotted with huge gullies called *lavaka* and swampy lowlands now used for rice farming. Large flat areas, known as *tampoketsa*, tend to have a bauxite or ferrous shell that is evidence of severe past erosion.

This crystalline base extends westward under a series of sedimentary strata from the northwest (Mahajanga [Majungal Basin) to the west (Morondava Basin), and in a fringing reef along the east coast. In the calcareous parts of these sedimentary strata there are cuestas and rough karstic regions. Erosion has fashioned spectacular sights in several places: ruinlike shapes in the Isalo massif, needles of rock in Tsingy of Bemaraha, and vast grottoes in Ankarana at Ambilobe.

Sand dunes dominate the landscape of the extreme south. The three series of dunes—tatsimian, karimbolian, and flandrian—can be differentiated by their degree of redness, which is caused by age. The red tatsimian sands contrast sharply with the more recent, white flandrian dunes. The flandrian dunes make magnificent beaches that are protected by coral reefs.

POPULATION AND CITIES

Madagascar has a population of about 19 million, unevenly distributed, but with an average density of twenty people per square mile. This population has a growth rate of 3 percent per year, a life expectancy of fifty-seven years, and a gross national product (GNP) of $240 per person.

The eastern and central areas, especially between Antananarivo and Fianarantsoa, are densely populated, and the west and south are sparsely populated (two or three people per square mile). Some parts of the west have nearly no population at all. The majority of Malagasy people (80%) live in rural areas; the capital, Antananarivo, and its suburbs have

cool and dry one in just a few miles. Violent cyclones occur between January and April.

The quantity and type of vegetation depend on the local rainfall. The great rain forest now exists only on the eastern slopes and in the extreme northwest. The west is filled with savannas dominated by the baobab tree (*Andasonia*) in the south and by satrana palms (*Medemia*) in the north. In the central highlands there are still a few areas of forest that are protected from destruction because they are sacred, and there are gallery forests in river valleys. The hills are covered with sparse steppe vegetation (*Hyparrhenia* and *Aristida*), and reforestation programs have returned eucalyptus and

10 percent of the population, and the balance live in provincial and regional towns.

Toamasina, capital of the eastern province and the most important port of Madagascar, is connected to Antananarivo by railway. Toliary and Tolagnaro are the two great cities of the southwest. Fianarantsoa, in Betsileo territory, is the capital of the south. Mahajanga is an important port for coastal trade where even large ships can moor safely. It is not as significant a port as Toamasina, but the establishment of new industries there is important.

Antseranana, in the extreme north, was the last city to become a provincial capital. It has never been a commercial center because it lacks a connection to the interior, but has compensated for this by specializing in two economic activities unique in Madagascar: naval dockyards and saltworks.

These are the administrative and economic centers of Madagascar. With the exception of Antananarivo, their activities are determined by their location and the local agricultural, fishing, or mining potential. The occupations of the inhabitants vary accordingly.

THE ECONOMY

In the eastern forested regions, the people first cleared the land by means of the ancient practice of *tavy*, an itinerant method of cultivation that requires burned land. On this hastily prepared soil, they planted rice, manioc, and bananas. On sloping land, this practice caused massive deforestation. Had the government not protected the remaining forest, rain would have eroded the soil completely in just a few years. As it is, the soil lacks the fertility to produce an acceptable yield. Although the people understand its negative effects, they continue to practice *tavy* because the alternatives require an investment, albeit minimal, that they cannot afford.

The east has always produced valuable crops: vanilla, coffee, cloves, pepper, and various fruits. In the past they were cultivated by foreign colonizers, but in the early twenty-first century they are grown by small national producers who suffer greatly from the worldwide instability of agricultural prices. In addition, frequent cyclones disrupt the economy of the region.

In the central highlands, rice farming is a tradition. Gravity-fed irrigation of carefully arranged rice fields, with as many as eighty levels of terraces, employs a hydraulic system that has not changed over time.

In sharp contrast to the laborious farming methods of the central highlands are those of the vast marshy plains such as those of Lake Alaotra and of the Betsiboka River, known as the rice granaries of Madagascar. Their average yield is similar to that of the plain of Betsimitatatra. These marshes were drained by the first kings of Antananarivo in the eighteenth century.

In the midwest and west, vast open spaces allow those who raise zebu (*Bos indicus*) to have large herds, but this commerce is sometimes limited by the affectionate tie that can arise between the zebu raiser and his herd. Zebu are as numerous as people and have always represented a natural wealth to be exploited.

The Tandroy herders (originally from the south) have created a network of *rabatteurs* throughout the island. They walk hundreds of miles to bring livestock to market. The most important livestock markets are Tsiroanomandidy, about sixty-two miles west of Antananarivo, and Ambalavao, which is thirty-one miles south of Fianarantsoa.

The floodplains of the river deltas in the west have extremely fertile soil, called *baiboho*. Agriculture in these areas is mechanized, and the crops vary according to national and global market conditions. When cotton promised more profit than the cape pea, cotton was grown. More recently tobacco, after a difficult period, became profitable. In the northeast the crop is sugarcane, which is grown along with other export crops such as cocoa and the perfume plant ylang-ylang.

On any island one would expect to find an active fishing culture. In fact, only the Vezu of the southwest coast are true fisherfolk, able to venture onto the high seas. Other inhabitants of the island practice occasional subsistence fishing.

The south has always been the least favored area of Madagascar because of its semiarid climate. In spite of its sparse vegetation, the south is a significant area for the raising of cattle and goats. During the dry season (July to September) the livestock must be moved constantly in search of pasturage and water.

The difference in living conditions between the cities and the country is a serious problem. The state has attempted to solve it though a policy of decentralization. However, the globalization of the economy has placed great strains on Madagascar. It must now find industries that can ameliorate its economic disparities. The most important problem is assuring the survival of a population of which the majority lives below the poverty line. Since the enactment of the structural adjustment program that the international financial institutions demanded, a multitude of informal businesses have appeared, and these ensure the survival of many families.

In the long term, capital investment aimed at developing industrial fishing, mining, and food crops, among others, will surely improve the standard of living. The most significant trend is the growth of the tourist industry, which is based on the fauna and flora of Madagascar.

See also **Agriculture; Antananarivo; Climate; Economic History; Ecosystems; Geography and the Study of Africa; Production Systems: Agriculture.**

BIBLIOGRAPHY

Battistini, Rene, and G. Richard-Vindard, eds. *Biogeography and Ecology in Madagascar*. The Hague: Junk, 1973.

Cowell, Maureen. *Madagascar: Politics, Economics, and Society*. London: F. Pinter, 1987.

Heseltine, Nigel. *Madagascar*. London: Pall Mall Press, 1971.

Jolly, Alison, Philippe Oberle, and Roland Albignac, eds. *Madagascar*. Oxford: Pergamon Press, 1984.

JEAN-AIMÉ RAKOTOARISOA

SOCIETY AND CULTURES

Madagascar currently has an estimated 19 million inhabitants. The overwhelming majority are speakers of a single language: Malagasy, an Austronesian language whose closest current relatives are spoken in the Barito river valley in Borneo, though Malagasy also shows signs of significant Bantu influence, especially in vocabulary. Recent genetic evidence confirms that the current Malagasy population traces back about equally to the Barito valley and East Africa. There are also speakers of Chinese, French, Urdu, Arabic, and Comoran-Swahili on the island, descended from more recent arrivals, although these are all very small minorities.

In the past, scholars trying to explain the uniformity of the Malagasy population proposed a fairly simple story: sometime in the first millennium a group of Austronesian migrants arrived and settled Madagascar and perhaps parts of nearby East Africa. There they gradually absorbed African elements, resulting in the current mix. Sometimes, later Indonesian migrations were also proposed to explain the more Malay-looking inhabitants of the Northern Highlands. More recent archeological work has complicated this picture considerably, though. In fact, the evidence suggests that during the five centuries or so following 700 CE, the population of Madagascar was more likely to be a heterogeneous collection of people of different origins, languages, and ways of life, coexisting in different parts of the island. Between the eleventh and thirteenth centuries, they included the population of a substantial and powerful mercantile city-state on the northeast coast known as Mahilaka—one that appears to have been part of the larger Swahili-speaking Islamic world. Archeologists speak of a moment of synthesis sometime around 1000 or even 1200 CE when current Malagasy culture was born, one that apparently united most of the island in an altogether different cultural tradition. This suggests the intriguing possibility that, just as contemporary Malagasy tend to constantly define everything *gasy*, or Malagasy, against everything *Vazaha* (a term that can be translated to mean foreign, French, or white), Malagasy culture as it is known in the early twenty-first century might have originated in opposition to the dominant culture of Mahilaka—and later, similar Swahili-speaking enclaves—as an explicit rejection of the world of cosmopolitan elites and universalistic religions it represented.

THE HISTORICAL GRID

The subsequent cultural history of Madagascar was marked by a constant tension between openness and withdrawal. On the one hand, Malagasy populations were from the beginning integrated into the larger cosmopolitan trading world of the Indian Ocean, marked as it was by the endless movement of people, products, and ideas. On the other, they maintained a distinctive Malagasy cultural grid that was always to some degree defined against the Indian Ocean world. Malagasy culture showed a remarkable ability to absorb foreign influences and even foreign settlers, and to effectively make them Malagasy. This occurred to any number of Swahili-speaking enclaves such as those in the city of Mahilaka, and possibly to Arabs, Persians, and Indians, as well. Before the colonial period, Europeans were the only settlers who resisted assimilation: as a result, various European attempts to settle the island (the most significant being the French colony at Fort Dauphin in the seventeenth century) faced systematic hostility and were all eventually driven out.

During the colonial period, a number of overseas Chinese and South Asians from what is now Pakistan migrated to Madagascar where they became shopkeepers and mostly small-scale merchants; their descendents remain and have not, for the most part, intermarried with or been absorbed by the Malagasy population any more than the Europeans who sponsored them. But their numbers are few and this seems to have again been something of an exception to the larger historical pattern, and in some cases this caste system as it is sometimes called has begun breaking down since independence.

This is not to say that the presence of foreigners was not important in differentiating Malagasy populations. However, this differentiation seems to have begun by people defining themselves against one or another elite that almost invariably claimed foreign origins. When Portuguese explorers first encountered the rulers of the Antemoro and Antanosy kingdoms of southeast Madagascar in the sixteenth and seventeenth centuries, the latter claimed to be Muslims originally from Mangalore and Mecca. Although they did employ Arabic script, they used it to write ritual tracts in Malagasy and were unfamiliar with the Qur'an. Their dynasties have since disappeared—the Antemoro elite were overthrown in a popular insurrection in the nineteenth century—but the descendants of their subjects still think of themselves Antemoro and Antanosy. Similarly most of the population of Madagascar's west coast consider themselves to be Sakalava: the descendants of subjects of the Maroseraña dynasty that conquered most of western Madagascar over the course of the seventeenth and eighteenth centuries. The Maroseraña too claimed

ultimately to be of foreign stock (they claimed descent from the Antemoro rulers), and although during their days in power they maintained close ties with foreign (Arab and European) traders, they too became thoroughly Malagasy.

One of the most curious cases is that of the notoriously egalitarian Betsimisaraka who inhabit much of eastern coast of the island. They appear to have come into being, as a unified, named group, under the aegis of an elite called the Zana-Malata, descendants of European pirates who settled the area at the end of the seventeenth century (the only precolonial European settlers who managed to avoid being massacred or driven off the island.) The Zana-Malata presided over the creation of a loose confederation of previously scattered groups in the early eighteenth century, calling them the Betsimisaraka. The confederation was short-lived, but the Zana-Malata still exist, now largely assimilated, and the descendants of those who formed part of the confederation still refer to themselves as Betsimisaraka. The term is now applied to a wide variety of eastern peoples who speak a broadly similar dialect, maintain broadly similar settlement patterns (living in scattered forest hamlets of wood houses often set atop poles, presided over by ritual specialists called *tangalamena*), share a proclivity for *tavy* (swidden) agriculture, but are otherwise heterogeneous.

In all of these cases, there is the same pattern: a Malagasy group forms in opposition to a local elite who they see as foreigners (and often are descended at least partly from foreigners); that group eventually either disappears or becomes a culturally assimilated minority; the group identity, however, endures.

Many of what are now considered ethnic identities originated from political projects of this kind. Others turn out to be economic or geographical. The Tanala, for instance, are the forest people of the southern part of the east coast; the Vezo are the fisherfolk of the west coast. The latter case refers not to a geographically contiguous group, because the Vezo are scattered in coastal fishing villages mixed with others who consider themselves Sakalava. The same is true of the Mikea, a population of hunter-gatherers in the same area. Other geographic names include the Antandroy (people of the thorn bush), Antanosy (people of the island), Sihanaka (around the lake), Tefasi (of the sands), and Antankarana (people of the rocks).

Even the name Sakalava is originally geographical in meaning: it literally means [people] of the long valley, though it has come to be employed to refer to subjects of kingdoms formed by the old Maroseraña dynasty. The Sakalava are those who continue to acknowledge the power of their royal ancestors by rebuilding their ancient tombs, guarding their sacred relics, and respecting mediums possessed by royal spirits (*tromba*). This combination of geographical and political definition is quite common.

The Tsimihety, another notoriously egalitarian population, now occupy much of the northern interior of Madagascar; they have over the course of the twentieth century been expanding against both the Sakalava to the west and Betsimisaraka to the east. The name Tsimihety is said to mean those who do not cut their hair, reputedly because the Tsimihety were hill people of the interior who refused to crop their hair as a sign of mourning at the death of a Maroseraña king, and thereby declared their political independence. The Vezo similarly claim they were not just any fisherfolk, but those who managed to use the mobility afforded by their fishing boats to avoid any contact with representatives of the Sakalava kingdoms. This is how they managed to avoid ever being subjects of the Maroseraña, and are hence Vezo and not Sakalava.

THE COLONIAL PERIOD

Until the colonial period, then, it is best to imagine a complex and shifting ethnic grid, with the power of dynasties (claiming descent from some line of distant, half-mythical foreigners) endlessly waxing and waning as they battled one another for influence, seeking alliances as they did so with powerful foreign merchants and ritual specialists. Some would extend their ability to raid or exact tribute over broad areas before splitting or dissolving, or else, being overthrown by somewhat regular popular insurrections. Most ordinary Malagasy appear to have defined themselves in a variety of ways depending on the context—either geographically, by mode of livelihood, or by subjugation to or defiance of some local dynasty—and all such identities were shifting and unstable. It was only after the French

conquest in 1895 that ethnic groups came to be fixed by scholarly and then bureaucratic fiat.

General Gallieni (1849–1916), the French conqueror and first French governor-general of Madagascar, proposed to rule by what he called a *politique de races*—a policy explicitly designed to set the Highlands people (especially the Merina) against the Lowlands (*cotier*) populations, the French having justified their conquest largely by claims to have liberated the coastal populations from Merina domination. Ethnographic surveys were conducted and Madagascar was officially divided into a number of recognized tribes. These were, in order of numerical importance, the Merina, Betsimisaraka, Betsileo, Tsimihety, Sakalava, Antandroy, Antaisaka, Tanala, Antemoro, Mahafaly, Antaifotsy, Makoa, Bezanozano, Antankarana, and Antambahoaka.

All Malagasy were issued identity cards that indicated ethnic origin. Each group was assigned its own contiguous territory, and a traditional ethnic elite was identified—or in the case of societies such as the Tsimihety, manufactured—to fill the lowest rungs of the administrative apparatus and serve as intermediaries with colonial authorities.

In the end, though, the political project of playing Highlanders against cotiers was only sporadically maintained. The Merina, Christianized over the course of the nineteenth century, had powerful advantages in education as the Imerina had a law of universal compulsory primary schooling since 1878. Colonial efforts to foster educational projects in the coastal provinces to create an alternative educated elite proved prohibitively expensive for a colony that was expected to pay for itself. For most of early twentieth century, therefore, the colonial regime ended up relying on the Merina bourgeoisie for much of its staff, teachers, and professionals. This meant that many Highlanders continued to live scattered in the provinces, and often inspired resentment among those they had earlier conquered militarily. It was only after the 1947 revolt that the colonial regime once again seriously revived pro-cotier policies.

The first Malagasy president, Philibert Tsiranana (ruled 1960–1972)—Tsimihety in origin—was the most famous product of this last effort to create a coastal elite whose power would be dependent on the French presence. Tsiranana was overthrown by protests largely in the Highlands, but the eventual beneficiary of the revolution of 1972, Didier Ratsiraka (ruled 1975–1992 and 1996–2002) was himself of Betsimisaraka origin. During the contested elections of 2002, Ratsiraka and his supporters made a blatant appeal to longstanding Highland-cotier antagonisms, characterizing their opponents in the *Forces Vives* as Merina imperialists, and demanding a form of federalism that would have made these largely colonial-origin tribal divisions the effective units of government. Although Ratsiraka eventually lost the struggle and his supporters remain politically eclipsed five years later, the issue is far from settled.

AMBIGUITIES OF IDENTITY IN CONTEMPORARY MADAGASCAR

Madagascar's largest ethnic group, generally referred to as the Merina, are an example of the complexities involved in speaking about identity in a Malagasy context. In 2007, the Merina comprise some three million people and occupy the northern part of the central plateau of Madagascar. At the time of eighteenth-century historical records, this region presently known as Imerina was broken into a number of tiny warring principalities. During most of the nineteenth century the inhabitants of the region were known largely as hova. This was, technically, the name of the commoner class, as the population was divided into three broad castes: *andriana* (nobles), *hova* (commoners), and *andevo* (slaves). The name Merina came into use later, especially in written texts.

Even in the early twenty-first century, however, most inhabitants of the northern highlands do not refer to themselves as Merina, but as Malagasy, or inhabitants of the province of Antananarivo, or as andriana or hova, or by some similar nonethnic term. At the same time, since the mid-nineteenth century some 30–40 percent of the population of Imerina are considered *andevo*: that is, descendants of Malagasy captured from other parts of the island and brought to Imerina as slaves. They are sometimes referred to as *olona mainty* (black people; other Merina in contrast to *olona fotsy* or white people, because of their purportedly more Asian features). However, most, when asked, will insist they are Betsileo: this being the name for the inhabitants of the southern part of the central highlands of which Imerina forms the northern portion. There is no clear line between Merina

and Betsileo: Betsileo are simply descendants of those Highlanders who were not incorporated into Andrianampoinimerina's original kingdom.

No doubt many *olona mainty* do have Betsileo ancestors, but they are descended from people drawn from every part of Madagascar. Betsileo identity appears to be attractive largely because, in the northern highlands, Betsileo are famous for being hardworking and skilful agriculturalists who travel across the island in harvesttime labor migrations; and because many Betsileo have as result married into Merina villages. Betsileo are thus essentially similar to the mainty (many Merina would say Betsileo are a kind of mainty) except that, whereas most descendants of andriana or hova will insist that their ancestors expressly forbade marrying descendants of slaves and threatened terrible punishments if they did, Betsileo are seen as legitimate marriage partners.

Ethnic identities, then, are still shifting, contextual, and relational. Inhabitants of a village near Antananarivo may refer to themselves as white or black in relation to their neighbors, will claim generically Malagasy status in relation to foreigners, still be hova in the eyes of coastal people, and will think of themselves as Merina only when reading schoolbooks, or perhaps, listening to radio addresses by certain nationalist politicians. If they are of mainty descent, they might in other contexts equally well insist that they are not Merina at all but noble descendants of the Betsileo king Andriamanalina.

THE CULTURAL GRID IN THE EARLY TWENTY-FIRST CENTURY

Malagasy culture can be seen as an amalgam of elements imported from across the Indian Ocean— and now, from the world as a whole—yet at the same time, absorbed into the terms of an underlying cultural grid that seems to have emerged at that moment of synthesis between 1000 and 1200. Music and oral literature show influences from Africa to Southeast Asia, yet the same instruments, motifs, and stories occur everywhere across the island. Similarly, when it comes to lifecycle rituals, everywhere the most elaborate of these tend to be circumcision ceremonies and funerals. The former, remarkably uniform throughout the island, seem inspired by Islamic practice; mortuary ritual, on the other hand, takes an almost kaleidoscopic

Republic of Madagascar

Population:	19,448,815 (2007 est.)
Area:	587,044 sq. km (226,658 sq. mi.)
Official language:	Malagasy
Languages:	Malagasy, French
National currency:	Madagascar ariary
Principal religions:	traditional 48%, Christian 45%, Muslim 7%
Capital:	Antananarivo (est. pop. 1,300,000 in 2006)
Other urban centers:	Antsirabe, Mahajanga, Toamasina
Annual rainfall:	Varies from 3,000 to 4,980 mm (118–196 in.) on the east coast to 510 mm (20 in.) in the southwest
Principal geographical features:	*Rivers:* Sambirano, Betsiboka, Ikopa, Tsiribihina, Mangoky, Onilahy, Menarandra, Mandrare, Mananara, Mananjary, Mangoro, Maningory, Fiherenana *Lakes:* Alaotra, Ihotry, Itasy, Tsiazompaniry, Mantasoa, Kikony *Islands:* Nossi-Bé, Sainte-Marie
Economy:	*GDP per capita:* US$900 (2006)
Principal products and exports:	*Agricultural:* coffee, vanilla, sugarcane, cloves, cocoa, rice, cassava (tapioca), beans, bananas, peanuts, livestock products *Manufacturing:* meat processing, soap, breweries, tanneries, sugar, textiles, glassware, cement, automobile assembly plant, paper *Mining:* chromium ore, petroleum, graphite, mica, bauxite, copper, nickel, some gold *Tourism:* Tourism is also important to the country's economy.
Government:	Independence from France, 1960. Constitution adopted in 1959, enacted 1960. New constitution adopted in 1975, replaced in 1992. Multiparty democracy. Under 1992 constitution, the president is elected by universal suffrage for 5-year-term, limited to 2 terms. Bicameral national legislature consists of the 160-member Assemblée Nationale, elected by universal suffrage according to proportional representation, and the 90-member Senate, one-third of whose seats are filled by appointment. The president appoints the prime minister from candidates selected by the Assemblée Nationale. For purposes of local government there are 6 provinces, headed by Secretary of State delegates; 18 prefectures; 92 subprefects; and 705 cantons, headed by cantonal chiefs.
Heads of state since independence:	1960–1972: President Philibert Tsiranana 1972–1975: Prime Minister Major General Gabriel Ramanantsoa Feb. 1975: Colonel Richard Ratsimandrava Feb.–June 1975: General Gilles Andriamahazo 1975–1993: President Didier Ratsiraka 1993–1996: President Albert Zafy 1996–1997: Interim president Norbert Ratsirahonana 1997–2002: President Didier Ratsiraka 2002–: President Marc Ravalomanana
Armed Forces:	Voluntary enlistment *Army:* 20,000 *Navy:* 500 *Air Force:* 500 *Paramilitary:* 7,500
Transportation:	*Rail:* 1,095 km (679 mi.), railways are state owned. *Ports:* Toamasina, Mahajanga *Roads:* 49,827 km (30,961 mi.), 12% paved *National airline:* Air Madagascar *Airports:* Ivato at Antananarivo for international flights. There are 116 airfields throughout the country.
Media:	5 daily newspapers, including *Midi Madagascar,* 24 periodicals. Strong book publishing industry. Television (since 1967) and radio provided through Radiodiffusion Nationale Malgache.
Literacy and Education:	*Total literacy rate:* 70.7% (2006) Education is free, universal, and compulsory for ages 6–13. Postsecondary education provided at Université d'Antananarivo, Université de Fianarantsoa, Université de Toamasina, Imadefolk-Institut Malgache des Arts Dramatiques et Folkloriques, Institut National des Sciences Comptables et de l'Administration.

variety of forms. In its broad themes it always seems to trace back to the secondary burial complex of insular Southeast Asia, distinguishing immediate, dangerous, temporary burial with a later, joyous reinterment that marks the deceased's emergence as a purified ancestor.

Malagasy astrology is also practiced throughout the island; originally the specialty of Antemoro scribes who peddled their magical knowledge at courts throughout the island, it has become popularized and integrated with traditions of magic and medicine that clearly hearken back to East Africa. The same processes of openness and incorporation can be seen operating in more recent cultural phenomenon: for instance, in the remarkable cosmopolitanism of contemporary Malagasy pop music. Malagasy culture came into being in the midst of an Indian Ocean ecuméne that was, economic and culturally, the center of the world at the time; it has been the product of a play of global forces, and of an endlessly resourceful ability to trap and capture those forces and put them to work for local projects of creating autonomous and meaningful lives for Madagascar's inhabitants from the start.

See also **Colonial Policies and Practices; Death, Mourning, and Ancestors; Ethnicity; Language; Literature; Nationalism; Slave Trades.**

BIBLIOGRAPHY

Althabe, Gérard. *Oppression et libération dans l'imaginaire: les communautés villageoises de la côte orientale de Madagascar.* Paris: F. Maspero, 1969.

Astuti, Rita. *People of the Sea: Identity and Descent among the Vezo of Madagascar.* Cambridge, U.K.: Cambridge University Press, 2006.

Bloch, Maurice. *Placing the Dead: Tombs, Ancestral Villages, and Kinship Organization in Madagascar.* London: Seminar Press, 1971.

Cole, Jennifer. *Forget Colonialism? Sacrifice and the Art of Memory in Madagascar.* Berkeley: University of California Press, 2000.

Feeley-Harnik, Gillian. *A Green Estate: Restoring Independence in Madagascar.* Washington, DC: Smithsonian Institution Press, 1991.

Lambek, Michael. *The Weight of the Past: Living with History in Mahajanga, Madagascar.* New York: Palgrave Macmillan, 2002.

Larson, Pier Martin. *History and Memory in the Age of Enslavement: Becoming Merina in Highland Madagascar, 1770–1822.* Portsmouth, NH: Heinemann, 2000.

DAVID GRAEBER

HISTORY AND POLITICS (1895–2006)

In 1817, Madagascar embarked upon the process of nation-state modernity during the reign of King Radama I. That year, the king, ruling over only part of an island two-and-a-half times the size of Britain, with some 2.5 million inhabitants, signed a treaty with a representative of the British Crown, the governor of Mauritius. This was to have long-term consequences.

THE KINGDOM OF RADAMA I

In return for a ban on slave exports from Madagascar, the treaty of 1817 recognized Radama I as king of Madagascar and provided him with the capacity to submit the whole island to a single political authority. This he was to achieve by means of a permanent administration, a standing army, and continuous diplomatic efforts. An opening to European culture marked Radama I's reign. To varying degrees, Radama's successors pursued the same strategy by an assortment of means including deception, diplomacy, and military conquest. For almost seventy years, the kingdom survived the rise of rival imperialisms in the region. But the social cost of this policy, as well as the rapacity of the local oligarchy, induced a deep social crisis.

It was a kingdom on the verge of collapse that French troops set out to conquer in 1894. The expeditionary force lost as many as 40 percent of its men, largely as a result of fever, before it took the capital, Antananarivo, on September 30, 1895. A series of anticolonial revolts followed almost until the eve of World War I. One of the most important insurrections was the rising of the Menalamba (1895–1899), led by minor notables of the old monarchy. All the revolts were put down one by one. At the end of the process, the French colonizers had succeeded in submitting the whole of Madagascar to a single political authority, thus realizing the ambition of King Radama I. After first attempting to govern through a protectorate, the new authorities opted for direct colonial government.

For nine years, from 1896 to 1905, General Gallieni (1849–1916) and his government concentrated their efforts on the construction of a modern state, setting out the main lines of French colonial policy in Madagascar. The eighteen civil governors who followed (1905–1946) were to follow these same broad lines, some of which are still evident in the early twenty-first century. The hallmark of this system was the central role played by the state. It absorbed most of the available resources that it needed to pay its functionaries, carry out public works, and build schools and clinics. These resources came from the poll tax and from the weeks of forced labor that each adult male was required to perform annually for the state.

It was only as a result of World War I that the metropolitan authorities discovered the potential the colonies offered and pushed them to abandon the law of 1900 that obliged France's colonies to be self-financing. The new policy of *mise en valeur* had its beginnings in the interwar period. It witnessed the opening of an ambitious program of public works financed by loans, the starting point of the massive indebtedness of later years. Thanks to these loans, the budget of the health service was increased by a factor of ten, with spectacular effects on population statistics. Madagascar's population rose from two and a half million in 1900 to four million in 1940.

The government also encouraged the cultivation of export crops. Madagascar became the number one world vanilla producer for several decades, which lasted until after the end of the colonial period. The main colonial companies (Marseillaise, Lyonnaise, Rochefortaise, Emyrne, and others), however, put their funds into activities that required little capital yet produced rapid and significant profits that, in effect, meant the cultivation of tree crops and mining. This structure was to outlive the end of colonial rule.

In the main towns, a secret society, the *Vy, Vato, Sakelika*—Iron, Stone, Branch (VVS)—emerged in 1913–1915. Its members were largely young intellectuals who aspired to create a synthesis between traditional Malagasy culture and modernity. The authorities regarded the VVS as a conspiracy and proceeded to make hundreds of arrests. A return to calm, and amnesty for those imprisoned, did not come about until 1921. Then, a movement animated by war veterans and French democrats demanded the abolition of the *Code de l'indigénat*, the law code that denied Malagasy rights of citizenship. Malagasy was not to obtain French citizenship until 1948—too late to bring much change to its underlying relationship with the colonial government.

At the head of the citizenship movement was Jean Ralaimongo (1884–1943), a former schoolteacher who made use of the colonial system of law and of the newspapers as instruments to confront the colonial government. Members of this movement were the pioneers of a modern civil society. The inauguration of the Popular Front government in France (1936–1938) sped the legalization of trade unions and local political parties. For a time, this moderated the course of the anticolonial movement toward a full-fledged nationalist and pro-independence ideology.

During World War II, the colonial administration in Madagascar chose to align itself with the Vichy government in France. In response, the Allies enforced an economic blockade. In 1942, fearing that the island could be used by the Germans or Japanese, British and East and South African troops landed in Madagascar. In 1943, the government of the island was handed over to representatives of the Free French. During these war years, a number of secret societies waited for a favorable moment to pass into action. They infiltrated the Mouvement démocratique pour la rénovation malgache (MDRM), a new nationalist party, formally established in 1946. The MDRM succeeded in getting three of its members elected as deputies to the French National Assembly. Its chief rival in Madagascar was the Parti des déshérités de Madagascar (PADESM), a pro-government party.

But the MDRM's political base, along with the secret societies, was impatient. During the night of March 28–29, 1947, an insurrection broke out in several parts of the island simultaneously; it was eventually to result in the loss of some 80,000 lives. The government accused the MDRM of responsibility and declared the party illegal. The MDRM's leading members were arrested, including the three deputies previously elected to the National Assembly.

Colonial authorities encouraged, even organized, a return to national sovereignty about fifteen years after the uprising. Transformed in 1956 into the Parti social démocrate (PSD), the PADESM was the main beneficiary of Madagascar's political independence, consecrated by the signature of a Franco-Malagasy cooperation agreement on June 26, 1960.

Three republics succeeded one another, interspersed with chaotic transitional periods in 1972–1975 and 1990–1992, and finally by the aftermath of a bitterly contested election in 2001–2002.

THE FIRST REPUBLIC (1960–1972)

For twelve years, Madagascar's First Republic (1960–1972), under the presidency of Philibert Tsiranana (1912–1978), enjoyed a substantial institutional stability that may be largely attributed to its close links to the former colonial power. Several French nationals served as ministers in Madagascar's government, and France maintained two military bases on the island. The Malagasy franc was tied to the French currency. The economic structure of the colonial period was hardly modified. Political life was dominated by the PSD, which enjoyed a majority in a parliament dominated by the executive branch. Several opposition parties were allowed to exist, but their influence became increasingly limited as time went by. Vote-rigging, manipulation of state institutions, and various other means encouraged the PSD in its steady drift toward authoritarianism. Unanimously elected as head of state in May 1959 by a parliamentary college, Tsiranana was reelected as president of the First Republic in 1965 and in January 1972 (99%) by popular vote, but always with the support of the government machine. In international affairs, the First Republic was strongly anticommunist and firmly pro-Western.

Its crisis started in 1971, with the outbreak of a peasant rising in the south, led by the nationalist Madagascar for the Malagasy (MONIMA) party. Several thousands were killed in the subsequent bout of repression. The arrest of Tsiranana's designated successor, André Resampa (b. 1924), who was accused of plotting a coup, followed. Finally, a student strike spread into a general strike that brought down the government after a bloody day of repression on May 13, 1972. It would take three years (1972–1975) before Madagascar regained a degree of stability.

Tsiranana handed power to his chief of staff, General Gabriel Ramanantsoa (1906–1978). The latter, however, resigned after some months in favor of another officer, Colonel Richard Ratsimandrava (1931–1975), who was assassinated just a week after taking power. A military directorate, dominated by Captain Didier Ratsiraka (b. 1936), then ruled Madagascar. Advocating a nationalist and socialist

political program, this naval officer was approved by 96 percent of the voters in a plebiscite in 1975.

THE SECOND REPUBLIC (1975–1991)

The new regime attached a high priority to distinguishing itself from its predecessor, and yet it shared many of the same characteristics. The Avant Garde de la révolution malgache (AREMA) party, created after Ratsiraka's accession to power, bore a strange resemblance to the PSD, from which it inherited many of its personnel and a number of its methods. In foreign policy, the new government tried to put some distance between itself and France. But the island's diplomatic overtures to socialist bloc countries did nothing to improve its development performance. In fact, relations with the European Economic Community were retained, and France continued to be the island's main aid donor and trade partner.

In domestic matters, democratic socialism promoted popular participation. One of the effects of this initiative, however, was to increase the number of state functionaries. Revolution administered from above was an expensive undertaking. The government intended to finance its programs in part by nationalizing key sectors of the economy, but this measure produced disappointingly small sums, while profoundly disturbing the country's economy. In particular, distribution networks were disrupted, leading to shortages of consumer goods and the emergence of queuing. Various tensions developed beneath a superficial appearance of social calm. Nevertheless, Ratsiraka was reelected in 1981.

In 1984, reeling from the effects of its economic and financial crisis, the government reached agreement with the international financial institutions that required implementation of a structural adjustment program. To draw foreign investment, the government created free trade zones that attracted companies active in the textile sector. The benefits of these new measures were slow in reaching the general population, 85 percent of whom were living in rural areas.

In 1989, presidential elections saw the emergence of an opposition Democratic Alliance that was unable to agree on a single candidate to contest the election. Ratsiraka was reelected with the help of widespread vote rigging, according to the leading election observation body. The opposition called for a dialogue in the form of a national conference, and the Federation of Christian Churches (FFKM) in Madagascar, a powerful moral force, offered to serve as mediator. The authorities refused. The National Conference of the Living Forces of the Nation, better known as the *Forces vives*, became the central platform of the opposition, backed by the FFKM. The Forces vives launched a general strike on May 1, 1991. It lasted six months, and at the end Ratsiraka agreed to establish a transitional government charged with organizing new elections. This agreement was reached after the president had responded to the Forces vives by encouraging ethnic agitation and by the violent repression of an opposition demonstration on August 10, 1991.

Albert Zafy (b. 1927), an opposition candidate, won the eventual 1992 presidential elections. A plebiscite approved a new constitution, and the Forces vives deputies formed a majority in the new National Assembly. The new constitution was closer to a system of parliamentary government than its predecessor.

THE THIRD REPUBLIC (1991–2005)

The Forces vives was a broad coalition united in opposition to Ratsiraka. It soon dissolved into factional squabbles between rival leaders. Some were in favor of structural adjustment and remaining in dialogue with the international donors, but a populist faction that included President Zafy wished to raise money from parallel international financial circuits that turned out to include fraudsters. There was a series of financial scandals. International donors suspended negotiations in 1994–1995.

Parliament began a process of impeachment against President Zafy in 1997, calling for fresh elections. Although ageing and in poor health, Ratsiraka presented himself as a candidate and succeeded in getting elected, again under rather dubious circumstances. Legislative elections produced a parliamentary majority for Ratsiraka's AREMA party. The government resumed relations with aid donors. The newly liberalized economy encouraged the emergence of a wealthy new middle class and the first signs of industrialization, even though the majority of the population continued to live in poverty. Ratsiraka and members of his immediate family developed their own commercial interests. In regard to political matters, as a gesture to his more extreme supporters, Ratsiraka changed the constitution to give rights of self-government to Madagascar's six provinces. The opposition, traumatized by its experience with the Forces vives, was ineffective. Ratsiraka's reelection in 2001 seemed to be a mere formality.

During municipal elections in 1999, voters in Antananarivo had chosen as mayor a young industrialist running as an independent candidate, Marc Ravalomanana (b. 1949). His youth and novelty, allied with his considerable business success, made Ravalomanana an attractive figure in comparison to rivals. He announced that he was running for the 2001 presidential elections and succeeded in rallying the support of various opposition factions. Before the interior ministry had announced the official returns, Ravalomanana's campaign organizers declared the results of the elections, based on a systematic collection of results and the mobilization of substantial resources. When the official figures were revealed, Ravalomanana's supporters demanded a public inquest to resolve the differing statistics. With the authorities' refusal, a battle of wills was inevitable.

The resulting confrontation lasted six months and resulted in the deaths of 100 people. The African Union attempted to mediate, but was unsuccessful. President Abdoulaye Wade (b. 1926) of Senegal managed to persuade the two protagonists to meet in Dakar, but their meeting failed to resolve the issue. By July 2002, Ravalomanana emerged victorious only after he had won part of the armed forces to his side.

Legislative elections produced a majority for the party that Ravalomanana had now established, known as *Tiako I Madagasikara*. The senate, however, retained an AREMA majority. The new president announced his intention of launching a new economic initiative based in the rural areas. He successfully launched a program of road and infrastructure development, and raised the prices of agricultural products as an incentive for peasant producers. Some policy mistakes, such as the rapid abolition of tax on various products, fuelled a price inflation, and corruption was still present. The opposition was now led by the septuagenarian Albert Zafy, once the object of a parliamentary impeachment process, and by a Protestant pastor whose political career had begun in 1958.

See also **Andrianampoinimerina; Antananarivo; Colonial Policies and Practices; Dakar; Decolonization; Ethnicity; Kings and Kingdoms; Labor: Trades Unions and Associations; Literature; Political Systems; Postcolonialism; Radama I; Ranavalona, Mada; Ravalomanana, Marc; World War I; World War II.**

BIBLIOGRAPHY

Allen, Philip M. *Madagascar: Conflicts of Authority in the Great Island (Nations of Contemporary Africa).* Boulder, CO: Westview Press, 1995.

Brown, Mervyn. *A History of Madagascar.* Princeton, NJ: Markus Wiener Publishers, 2002.

Covell, Maureen. *Madagascar: Politics, Economics, and Society.* London: Pinter, 1987.

Ellis, Stephen. *The Rising of the Red Shawls: A Revolt in Madagascar, 1895–1899.* Cambridge, UK: Cambridge University Press, 1985.

Kottak, Conrad Phillip, ed. *Madagascar: Society and History.* Durham, NC: Carolina Academic Press, 1986.

Lambek, Michael. *The Weight of the Past: Living with History in Mahajanga, Madagascar.* New York: Palgrave Macmillan, 2003.

Larson, Pier. *History and Memory in the Age of Enslavement: Becoming Merina in Highland Madagascar, 1770–1822.* Portsmouth, NH: Heinemann, 2000.

Middleton, Karen, ed. *Ancestors, Power and History in Madagascar.* Studies of Religion in Africa. Leiden, The Netherlands: Brill Academic Publishers, 1999.

Raison Jourde, Françoise. *Bible et Pouvoir à Madagascar au XIXe siècle.* Paris: Karthala, 1991.

Randrianja, Solofo. *Sociétés et Luttes anticoloniales à Madagascar: 1896-1946.* Paris: Karthala, 2003.

Vérin, Pierre. *Madagascar.* Leipzig, Germany: Leipziger Universitätsvlg, 2005.

SOLOFO RANDRIANJA

MADAGASCAR: EARLY SETTLEMENT.

The early settlement of Madagascar remains enigmatic and controversial, but the broad outlines are becoming clearer. The Malagasy people derive from ancestors from many lands bordering the Indian Ocean, yet when, how and why, their ancestors settled is still a mystery. Adding to the enigma is that Madagascar, the fourth-largest island in the world, was apparently one of the last great islands to be settled. Over the less than two millennia of human occupation, the Malagasy have forged a fundamental unity of language and culture. At the same time, however, populations in different regions have developed distinctive economies and distinct political, social, and ethnic identities.

In twenty-first-century Madagascar there is a shared common language. Malagasy, however, displays regional variation in phonology and vocabulary. It is usually described as having twenty or so dialects, each associated with a particular ethnicity or region. The languages most closely related to Malagasy are in the Austronesian family and are found today in southeast Borneo, but Malagasy has been greatly altered by influence from Bantu languages. Some scholars believe the Bantu influence derived from early Indonesian residence along the African coast, but others suspect that it was the product of interaction of two language communities in Madagascar. Malagasy has been enriched as well by borrowings from other languages of the periphery of the Indian Ocean.

The diversity of physical appearance of Malagasy stands in contrast to their linguistic unity. To the earliest European observers, some populations seemed "Malay" and others "African." Oral histories sometimes point to "Arab" or "Persian" origins. For some authors, African populations first settled the island, to be joined later by Asian immigrants; others argue for the reverse, and still others imagine the Malagasy as scions of a population of Afro-Indonesians originally found on the east coast of Africa. No archaeological evidence exists to sort out this issue.

Limited, but increasing, genetic research indicates that modern Malagasy gene frequencies reflect substantial contributions from both East Africa and island Southeast Asia. African and Asian genes are not evenly mixed—some local populations are more Asian in origin, and others more African. However, there is much local diversity in ancestry and appearance in all regions. Recent studies suggest that both the Asian and African immigrant communities were composed men and women in roughly equal proportions. Immigrants from other lands bordering the Indian Ocean—such as the Persian Gulf and India—have contributed to Malagasy ancestry, as have, more recently, Europeans and East Asians.

There is no evidence, direct or indirect, of human arrival in Madagascar before about 2,300 years ago. No Stone Age archaeological sites have been found, and even the earliest known settlers used iron tools. Recent paleoecological research documenting the history of the island's vegetation gives no clear signal of human impact more than about 2,000 years ago, although it is unmistakable by the fourteenth century. Some of Madagascar's giant lemurs, elephant birds and pygmy hippos, whose extinction is usually connected with human settlement, may have survived in certain areas until the sixteenth century CE.

The first limited evidence of human presence on the island appears in the arid southwest. A long bone of an extinct lemur bearing the traces of butchery has recently been radiocarbon dated to 300 BCE. It was collected from a paleontological site almost a century ago, and there are no associated artifacts. From nearby coastal swamps, three apparently butchered pygmy hippo bones, also collected in the first years of the twentieth century, have radiocarbon dates of the first to fourth centuries CE. Once again, there are no associated artifacts. If these dates are reliable, they may be traces of early visits to the island, rather than the establishment of settlements.

The oldest dated level with archaeological artifacts comes from a rock shelter in the far north of the island, located only a few miles from the coast. Here the deepest layer seems to date to between the fifth and eighth centuries CE, but the occupation was brief, and may not reflect permanent occupation of the island.

The site of Madagascar's oldest known hamlet or village is on the east coast islet of Nosy Mangabe; it dates to the eighth century, which is also the age of the oldest known sites on the Comoros Islands. About fifty miles south of Nosy Mangabe, a village and a string of small hamlets along the Mananara River valley date to the late eighth through the twelfth centuries. These sites have yielded earthenware ceramics, iron slag, and traces of the manufacture of chlorite schist (soapstone) vessels. In addition, Nosy Mangabe has yielded shards of ninth to tenth century Near Eastern pottery, and at one Mananara site, what appears to be a necklace with beads of silver, gold, carnelian, and glass has been found. The presence of trade goods in these earliest

of settlements suggests that participation in the Western Indian Ocean trade networks was always a factor in Madagascar's historical development.

Between the tenth and the mid-fourteenth centuries there were settlements at nearly all well-studied areas along Madagascar's coasts. Near the end if this period, the earliest known occupations of the interior were established. During this period there is solid evidence for nearly all three hallmarks of traditional Malagasy economies: rice farming; cattle, sheep and goat herding; and coastal fishing. As in the early twenty-first century, economic activities varied in response to local environmental conditions. In the arid south, for example, the eleventh-century site of Andranosoa was a wall-enclosed village of cattle-herders. In terms of settlements, this was a period of great diversity. Sites ranged from small farming hamlets to the urban trading city of Mahilaka on the northwest coast, which had a wall enclosing seventy hectares of masonry residences, workshop areas, at least one mosque, and an inner precinct. Mahilaka's 5,000 to 10,000 residents imported Near Eastern and Far Eastern ceramics that have also been found at contemporary communities on the East African coast. Mahilaka was a trading center where island products such as tortoiseshell, chlorite schist, gold, crystal quartz, and possibly wood, tree gum, and iron were exchanged for ceramics, glass vessels, glass beads, and possibly cloth.

The earthenware ceramics of the coastal sites are probably regional variants of a common tradition, although the earliest earthenware of the central highlands are stylistically distinctive and their origins are unknown. The coastal ceramics, particularly along the northern coasts, bear strong resemblance to the ceramics of contemporary settlements of the Comoros Islands, and in some respects they resemble contemporary ceramics of East African coastal communities. However there is no clear archaeological evidence of direct contact between Madagascar and the eastern Indian Ocean; given the genetic and linguistic evidence, this is paradoxical.

In the subsequent centuries leading up to the European visits of the sixteenth century, Mahilaka was succeeded by a series of trading centers along the northwestern and northeastern coasts, though none quite so large. In other regions, settlement patterns often took the form of five to ten villages surrounding a regional center of perhaps 1,000 residents. All these centers contained concentrations of trade goods, suggesting that they may also have been centers of wealth and political authority.

Soon after the arrival of Europeans, there was a series of dramatic changes across the island. The slave trade and the import of guns led to increasing levels of military conflict, population relocations, and reorganizations of political power. In the Imerina region of the central highlands there was a swift increase in population density, with concurrent increases in political complexity. Along the northwest and east coasts there were similar political developments, but these are not well documented archaeologically. In many areas, however, the basic patterns established in the fourteenth and fifteenth centuries continued with little apparent change.

See also **Andrianampoinimerina; Archaeology and Prehistory; Ceramics; Madagascar; Madagascar and Western Indian Ocean, History of; Radama I; Ranavalona, Mada; Trade and Exploration: Europe.**

BIBLIOGRAPHY

Burney, D. A., et al. "A Chronology for Late Prehistoric Madagascar." *Journal of Human Evolution* 47 (2004): 25–63.

Deschamps, Hubert. *Histoire de Madagascar*, 3rd edition. Paris: Berger-Levrault, 1965.

Dewar, Robert E. "Were People Responsible for the Extinctions of Madagascar's Subfossils, and How Will We Ever Know?" In *Natural Change and Human Impact in Madagascar*, ed. Steven M. Goodman and Bruce D. Patterson. Washington, DC: Smithsonian Institution Press, 1997.

Dewar, Robert E., and Henry T. Wright. "The Culture History of Madagascar." *Journal of World Prehistory* 7 (1993): 417–466.

Radimilahy, Chantal. *Mahilaka: An Archaeological Investigation of an Early Town in Northwestern Madagascar.* Uppsala: Department of Archaeology and Ancient History, 1998.

Vérin, Pierre. *The History of Civilization in North Madagascar*, trans. David Smith. Rotterdam and Boston: A. A. Balkema, 1986.

Vérin, Pierre. *Madagascar*, 2nd edition. Paris, 1990.

ROBERT E. DEWAR

MADAGASCAR: RELIGION IN.

Madagascar presents unique challenges for the historical and contemporary study of religious systems in their social, political, and ecological complexity. This article outlines some of the major contributions of Malagasy studies to scholarship on death, burial, ancestry, and spirit mediumship; the relationship of religion to politics and history; and the ecology of religious experience.

The diversity of Malagasy "ways of the ancestors" (*fomban-drazana*) are honored throughout the island. Over the centuries, Madagascar's peoples have also adopted religious faiths introduced by traders, missionaries, and new immigrants to the island, beginning with Islam as early as the twelfth century CE. Between 7 and 10 percent of Malagasy, residing mainly in the northern and western provinces of Antseranana and Mahajanga, now identify themselves as Muslims, most of them Sunni, but some Shia, including Bhora and other Indian Shiites called Karana. Christian missions were established from the sixteenth century onward. Some 49 percent of Malagasy are Christians, about evenly divided between Catholicism and Protestantism. Hindus (Baniany) and Buddhists (Sinoa), descendants of immigrants from Gujarat and south China in the late nineteenth and early twentieth centuries, comprise about 1 percent of the population.

THE WAYS OF THE ANCESTORS

Whether or not they identify with an established religion, Malagasy throughout the island recognize through ritual what they consider to be the interdependence of living and ancestral people. Explorers' accounts from the eighteenth century onward document the veneration by the Malagasy people of ancestors, their own and those of others. According to the evolutionary theories of the nineteenth century, "ancestor worship" was a lower form of polytheistic religion, to be abandoned upon conversion to a monotheistic faith. Ethnographic and historical research in Madagascar, as in Africa, has since shown this assumption to be false. Respect for ancestors derives from ontological convictions about the changing social-somatic nature of a person as he or she is created and reformed through interpersonal relations between the living and the dead that extends throughout life into death and ancestry;

ancestors are conceived as the riverine "spring" or arboreal "root" of future life. The common phrase "ancestral custom" (*fombandrazana*) refers especially to rituals of childbirth, circumcision, naming, marriage, burial, and reburial that affect the creation and transformation of persons.

Although nineteenth-century missionaries tried to forbid Malagasy practices involving ancestors, like the invocation of ancestors at funerals, or spirit possession, Françoise Raison-Jourde shows how highlanders had integrated Christianity into ancestral custom well before the colonial era. The nationalization of missions after independence, together with doctrinal changes (for example, Vatican II), has contributed to the vitality of contemporary religious life. Some churches have grown by specializing in the exorcism of spirits, whereas others have developed new integrated forms of religious worship. *Le prince charmant* (Jacques Lombard and Michèle Fiéloux, 1989) is a powerful video documentary of the personal, as well as social, dimensions of religious pluralism in southwestern Madagascar told through the life story of a Malagasy woman, raised as a Catholic, who became the medium of a Sakalava royal ancestor from the colonial period and is now recognized as a great healer. *Les dieux au service du peuple* (a book and CD-ROM edited by Sophie Blanchy, Jean-Aimé-Rakotoarisoa, Philippe Beaujard, and Marie de Chantal Radimilahy, 2006) provides an excellent overview of the diversity of religious movements and their relationship to contemporary social and political-economic life in Madagascar.

MALAGASY BURIALS AS RELIGIOUS AS WELL AS POLITICAL AND HISTORICAL PRACTICES

In Madagascar, death and ancestry, like life, are not abstract states of being, but the historical outcome of social relations over generations. Numerous scholars have documented the grand size and substantiality of tombs compared to ordinary Malagasy houses. Burials—and reburials in some parts of Madagascar—are among the most important of all religious rituals because they are the occasion for kin who have moved away to reunite around one or more ancestral tombs. In the words of an orator at a Betsileo funeral speaking of the silk and cotton shrouds that guests bring as gifts to the bereaved family, "the dead are wrapped in remembering," in awareness of the many layers of relationships, old and new, that have brought the living together with the ancestors at the burial site.

Except for some memorials for individuals whose bodies could not be returned to their homelands (for example, soldiers killed in European wars), most Malagasy tombs contain more than one forebear and are created out of descendants' combined resources, carefully calculated and including their labor, which is interpreted as ancestral service. The impoverishment that the living will endure to assure their own burial as remembered ancestors is well documented. One of the most important purposes of the regional or hometown associations formed by migrants in towns throughout Madagascar is to provide for the funerals of their members, especially the cost of returning the deceased's bones to his or her selected burial place.

The salience of burials and reburials in Malagasy religious practices, together with population decline during the colonial period, suggested to some scholars that Madagascar was a "civilization of death." Historians know, for example, that the Malagasy have been writing about "the ways of the ancestors," their historical origins, and their practices of medicine, divination, astrology, and geomancy since Arabic script was first adopted to make "great writings" (*sorabe*) in southeastern Madagascar beginning in the fifteenth century, followed by Roman orthography in the early 1820s. Raombana, a Merina nobleman who wrote a nine-thousand-page *History, Annals, and Journal* of Imerina in English from 1845 to 1854, including information from his archaeological research on Merina tombs, expressed the intensity of Malagasy interest in "the ways of the ancestors" past and present. Raombana's written history coexisted with numerous oral narratives in the highlands and on the coasts. The enduring importance of ancestors is expressed in many other forms besides writing and speaking; for example, in the structure and adornment of houses and tombs, the historical pageantry surrounding contemporary spirit possession ceremonies, and the use of personal taboos that commemorate relations between ancestors and living people.

These practices demonstrate that Madagascar is not so much a "civilization of death," but rather that Malagasy have used "ancestral practices" to keep alive an historical consciousness of themselves as sovereign peoples in the face of efforts to subordinate

Members of a Betsimisaraka family in Mananara-Nord region of Madagascar gathered at their familial tombs in a montane forest. In the foreground sit two boxes of bones (*serkay*, from the French *cerceuille*) awaiting placement in the dug-out hole sealed with stones. The deceased kin had been buried at another village in the south. PHOTOGRAPH BY GENESE SODIKOFF, 2001

them—such as harsh labor practices or the deadly military reprisals following the rebellion of 1947–1948, in which an estimated 100,000 people died. Raombana wrote his history during the reign of the

Merina queen Ranavalona I (r. 1828–1861), who repeatedly had to force French and English diplomats, merchants, and missionaries to respect Malagasy ancestral ways and the political autonomy

A Sunni Muslim teacher (*fondy Silamo*) on the veranda of her home in Analalava, teaching girls to read and recite the Qur' an (*mijoro*). In this coastal town of 14,000 in northwestern Madagascar, four *fondy* teach children in their homes. Sunnis also have a Friday mosque (*moskeriny zoma*) and a smaller Thursday mosque (*moskeriny kamisy*). PHOTOGRAPH BY GILLIAN FEELEY-HARNIK, NOVEMBER 1989

with which they were associated. Yet the ancestral ways of Merina royalty, critical to the creation of a Merina state in the nineteenth century, were themselves the historical outcome of repeated efforts to appropriate the ancestral practices of other Malagasy, thereby redefining them as "commoners" or "slaves" by comparison to "nobles." At least one other "kind" of people emerged during this same period from refusing the subordination entailed in conforming to royal mourning practices. One of the striking historical ironies of the colonial and postcolonial periods is the widespread adoption of royal "ancestral custom" in popular protests throughout Madagascar against French colonial officials and the

Malagasy elites who succeeded them and also in everyday negotiations for access to resources like land or labor.

Although Malagasy rituals of birth, death, and ancestry are very diverse, they commonly involve the use of organic materials like water, leaves, stones, and trees to represent processes of growth, decay, death, and regeneration that are considered to be common to all forms of life. The controversy that has long surrounded the unique fauna and flora of the island—ranging from allegedly man-eating trees in the nineteenth century to contemporary debates about conservation and development—should be examined in terms of Malagasy ideas and practices of life and death in religion and philosophy as well as in ecology and political-economy.

See also **Christianity; Death, Mourning, and Ancestors; Islam; Myth and Cosmology; Queens and Queen Mothers; Ranavalona, Mada; Religion and Ritual.**

BIBLIOGRAPHY

Astuti, Rita. *People of the Sea: Identity and Descent among the Vezo of Madagascar.* Cambridge, U.K.: Cambridge University Press, 1995.

Blanchy, Sophie. *Karana et Banians: Les communautés commerçantes d'origine indienne à Madagascar.* Paris: L'Harmattan, 1995.

Blanchy, Sophie, et al., eds. *Ancestralité et identité à Madagascar.* Études océan Indien, no. 30. Paris: Publications INALCO, 2001.

Blanchy, Sophie; Jean-Aimé Rakotoarisoa; Philippe Beaujard; and Marie de Chantal Radimilahy; eds. *Les dieux au service du peuple: Itinéraires religieux, médiations, syncrétisme à Madagascar.* Accompagné d'un CD-ROM. Paris: Karthala, 2006.

Bloch, Maurice. *From Blessing to Violence: History and Ideology in the Circumcision Ritual of the Merina of Madagascar.* Cambridge, U.K.: Cambridge University Press, 1986.

Cole, Jennifer. *Forget Colonialism? Sacrifice and the Art of Memory in Madagascar.* Berkeley: University of California Press, 2001.

Cole, Jennifer, and Karen Middleton. "Rethinking Ancestors and Colonial Power in Madagascar." *Africa* 7, no. 1 (2001): 1–37.

Decary, Raymond. *La mort et les coutumes funéraires à Madagascar.* Paris: G.-P. Maisonneuve et Larose, 1962.

Emoff, Ron. *Recollecting from the Past: Musical Practice and Spirit Possession on the East Coast of Madagascar.* Middletown, CT: Wesleyan University Press, 2002.

Feeley-Harnik, Gillian. *A Green Estate: Restoring Independence in Madagascar.* Washington, DC: Smithsonian Institution Press, 1991.

Feeley-Harnik, Gillian. "*Ravenala Madagascarienesis* Sonnerat: The Historical Ecology of a 'Flagship Species' in Madagascar." In "Emerging Histories in Madagascar," ed. Jeffrey C. Kaufmann, spec. issue, *Ethnohistory* 48, nos. 1–2 (2001): 31–86.

Graeber, David. "Dancing with Corpses Reconsidered: An Interpretation of *Famadihana* (in Arivonimamo, Madagascar)." *American Ethnologist* 22 (1995): 258–278.

Kottak, Conrad P. *The Past in the Present: History, Ecology, and Social Organization in Highland Madagascar.* Ann Arbor: University of Michigan Press, 1980.

Lambek, Michael J. "Taboo as Cultural Practice among Malagasy Speakers." *Man (N.S.)* 27 (1992): 245–266.

Lambek, Michael J. *The Weight of the Past: Living with History in Mahajanga, Madagascar.* New York: Palgrave Macmillan, 2002.

Larson, Pier. "Austronesian Mortuary Ritual in History: Transformations of Secondary Burial (*Famadihana*) in Highland Madagascar." In "Emerging Histories in Madagascar," ed. Jeffrey C. Kaufmann, spec. issue, *Ethnohistory* 48, no. 1–2 (2001): 31–86.

Middleton, Karen, ed. *Ancestors, Power and History in Madagascar.* Leiden, the Netherlands: Brill, 1999.

Raison-Jourde, Françoise. *Bible et pouvoir à Madagascar au XIXe siècle: Invention d'une identité chrétienne et construction de l'état (1780–1880).* Paris: Karthala, 1991.

Rakotomalala, Malanjaona M.; Sophie Blanchy-Daurel; and Françoise Raison-Jourde; eds. *Madagascar: Les ancêtres au quotidian: Usages sociaux du religieux sur les Hautes-Terres malgaches.* Paris: L'Harmattan, 2001.

Sharp, Lesley A. *The Possessed and the Dispossessed: Spirits, Identity, and Power in a Madagascar Migrant Town.* Berkeley: University of California Press, 1993.

Vérin, Pierre. *Madagascar.* Revised edition. Paris: Karthala, 2000.

Walsh, Andrew. "Responsibility, Taboos and the 'Freedom to Do Otherwise' in Ankarana, Northern Madagascar." *Journal of the Royal Anthropological Institute* 8, no. 3 (2002): 451–468.

Walsh, Andrew. "'Nobody Has a Money Taboo': Situating Ethics in a Northern Malagasy Sapphire Mining Town." *Anthropology Today* 22, no. 4 (2006): 4–8.

GILLIAN FEELEY-HARNIK

MADAGASCAR AND WESTERN INDIAN OCEAN, HISTORY OF (EARLY TO 1500). The pre–Vasco da Gama history of the Western Indian Ocean is bound up with that region's relationship with the wider Indian Ocean world (IOW), a vast area running from East Africa and the Red Sea to the Persian Gulf, South India, Southeast Asia, and China, as well as with the IOW's relationship to the Mediterranean world via both the Red Sea and the Tigris-Euphrates River corridor to Syria.

Since the 1980s Asiacentric historians have mounted a sustained attack on the formerly dominant Eurocentric view that the first global economy arose in Europe at the time of the European discoveries of the Americas and Asia. Adopting Fernand Braudel's concept of a Mediterranean maritime economy and civilization, historians such as K. N. Chaudhuri have argued that an Asia-Indian Ocean global economy emerged alongside Islam from the seventh century, and that Europeans achieved global dominance only in the eighteenth century. Others date the start of the Asia-Indian Ocean global economy to between the tenth and thirteenth centuries. Andre Gunder Frank considers that it may well have arisen much earlier, and that European dominance was achieved only in the nineteenth century with industrialization and the emergence of a truly international economy. These revisionists largely omitted Africa from their analysis, although Africanists and historians of the Middle East and of India have long demonstrated that eastern and northeastern Africa possessed strong linkages to Arabia, the Persian Gulf, and South Asia. Michael Pearson and others have also emphasized East African linkages further afield, to Southeast Asia and the Far East as well as the Mediterranean. It has become recognized that the entire Western Indian Ocean region, including East Africa and the islands (the Comoros, Mascarenes, Seychelles, and Madagascar) formed an integral part of the pre-1500 IOW economy.

Two developments formed the context for the rise of the IOW global economy: the emergence and consolidation of powerful centralized states by 1000 BCE in China, India, and Middle East, and significant global warming from 500 to 300 BCE. The economies of the centralized states were based on highly productive agricultural systems and small but significant craft and trading sectors. Global warming led to an expansion in settlement and cultivation of previously inhospitable areas throughout the northern hemisphere, thus establishing the conditions for demographic growth, enhanced agricultural and craft production, and long-distance trade.

While overland trade routes were initially dominant, forged around the Silk Road linking Mesopotamia to China, maritime routes became increasingly important due to improvements in shipbuilding and navigational techniques. These enabled indigenous merchants to take advantage of the monsoons, an alternating system of strong winds unique to the northern sector of the Indian Ocean and South China Sea that, supplemented by a perennial system of southern hemisphere trade and equatorial winds, offered a potential for regular transoceanic sail unparalleled in other oceans. As a result, by the BCE/CE changeover, a transoceanic trading network had emerged in the IOW to supplement the Silk Road.

There appear to have been two periods of major expansion in the IOW trade network before 1500, the first in the centuries around the BCE/CE changeover, and the second from the tenth to the thirteenth centuries CE. These are clearly reflected in the history of the western Indian Ocean. Manuals largely compiled from merchant sources in Alexandria—Strabo's *Geography* (c. 23 CE), the *Periplus* (c. 50–60 CE), and Pliny the Elder's *Natural History* (c. 77 CE)—indicate that by the BCE/CE changeover, East Africa was a major source of valuable commodities such as gold, ivory, and rhinoceros horn and possessed in Rhapta, probably situated in the Rufiji River delta in Tanzania, a major IOW emporium.

The vibrancy of IOW trade played a significant role in the Bantu-speaking settlement of the East African littoral, while the vitality of East African trade attracted merchants from Egypt, Arabia, the Persian Gulf, India, and Indonesia. Traditional Eurocentric and Asiacentric accounts have accredited to these the foundation of the first coastal and island civilizations in East Africa that burgeoned from the eleventh century during the second major period of expansion in the IOW global economy. Thus settlers chiefly from the Persian Gulf from the seventh and eight centuries established the culturally vibrant city-states along the islands and littoral of the East African coast, the Comoros and northwest Madagascar, ruled by sultans who looked to Islamic models of state formation, government, jurisprudence, education, and architecture, that formed the Swahili maritime civilization. In a separate migratory pattern, Austronesians crossed the Indian Ocean to form the first permanent human settlements in Madagascar, possibly from as early as the BCE/CE changeover, certainly from the late eighth century CE into the second millennium (indigenous traditions report continued contact until as late as the start of the sixteenth century). Some historians consider that such migrants sailed directly to Madagascar, others argue that they first visited East Africa and traveled to Madagascar via the Comoro islands where some settled.

However, Afrocentric revisionists have countered the conventional view. The consensus among Afrocentrists is that the Swahili civilization is based essentially upon the Bantu-speaking culture. Felix Chami even advances the thesis that Bantu-speakers founded Rhapta and subsequently developed the oceangoing skills that enabled them to establish the basis for the Swahili maritime civilization. Afrocentrists also reject the idea that Indonesians inhabited East Africa prior to their colonization of Madagascar because of the absence of any archaeological evidence of such a presence. Indeed, some historians argue that Bantu-speaking Africans formed some of the earliest, if not the earliest, migrant groups to Madagascar: genetics studies have shown that all of the twenty-first-century population of Madagascar are of a mixed African and Austronesian genetic makeup.

The Swahili civilization, which peaked from the twelfth century, formed an integral part of the IOW economy, forging commercial links deep into the east African and Malagasy interiors as well as across the Indian Ocean. From this time, East Africa produced both valuable raw materials and semi-processed and processed goods. Traditional historiography has emphasised the export of slaves, but it is probable that slaves remained secondary in quantity, value, and range of distribution to east African gold and ivory. Other significant exports included construction timber (teak and mangrove poles) and Malagasy crystal quartz to Persia, and rhinoceros horn, tortoise/turtleshell, ambergris, yellow sandalwood, leopard skins, iron, and Malagasy chlorite slate (soapstone) to India and (mostly indirectly) to China. In exchange, annual Gujarati fleets brought Indian copper and white and red cloth and Chinese porcelain. By 1500, when the first European navigators were rounding the Cape of Good Horn, the elites of the Swahili city ports lived in luxury, importing fine silk and cotton clothes from Cambay, Sofala gold jewelry, and Chinese plates and bowls. It was in Malindi, one of the major Swahili ports, that navigator Vasco da Gama found a pilot who guided the Portuguese fleet directly across the Indian Ocean to the west coast of India. Only subsequently were the other Western Indian Ocean island groups of the Mascarenes (Réunion and Mauritius) and the Seychelles permanently settled by Europeans.

See also **Bantu, Eastern, Southern, and Western, History of (1000 BCE to 1500); Economics and the Study of Africa; Gama, Vasco da; Indian Ocean, African, History of (1000 BCE to 600 CE); Madagascar and Western Indian Ocean, History of (1500 to 1895); Transportation.**

BIBLIOGRAPHY

Abu-Lughod, Janet L. *Before European Hegemony: The World System A.D. 1250–1350.* New York: Oxford University Press, 1989.

Allen, James de Vere. *Swahili Origins: Swahili Culture and the Shungwaya Phenomenon.* London: James Currey, 1993.

Campbell, Gwyn. "Theories Concerning the Origins of the Malagasy." In *Australes,* ed. Marc Michel and Yvan Paillard. Paris: Harmattan, 1996.

Casson, Lionel, trans. *The Periplus Maris Erythraei.* Princeton, NJ: Princeton University Press, 1989.

Chami, Felix A. "Roman Beads from the Rufiji Delta, Tanzania: First Incontrovertible Archeological Link with the *Periplus.*" *Current Anthropology* 40, no. 2 (1999): 237–241.

Chaudhuri, K. N. *Trade and Civilization in the Indian Ocean: An Economic History from the Rise of Islam to 1750.* Cambridge, U.K.: Cambridge University Press, 1985.

Dewar, R. E., and H. T. Wright. "The Culture History of Madagascar." *Journal of World Prehistory* 7 (1993): 417–466.

Ehret, Christopher. *An African Classical Age: Eastern and Southern Africa in World History, 1000 BC to 400 AD.* Charlottesville: University Press of Virginia, 1998.

Frank, Andre Gunder. *ReORIENT: Global Economy in the Asian Age.* Berkeley: University of California Press, 1998.

Horton, Mark. *Shanga: The Archeology of a Muslim Trading Community on the Coast of East Africa.* London: British Institute in Eastern Africa, 1996.

Kottak, Conrad Phillip, eds. *Madagascar: Society and History.* Durham, NC: Carolina Academic Press, 1986.

Nurse, Derek, and Thomas Spear. *The Swahili: Reconstructing the History and Language of an African Society, 800–1500.* Philadelphia: University of Philadelphia Press, 1985.

Pearson, Michael. *The Indian Ocean.* London and New York: Routledge, 2003.

Pearson, Michael. *The World of the Indian Ocean, 1500–1800: Studies in Economic, Social and Cultural History.* Aldershot: Ashgate, 2005.

Sutton, John. *A Thousand Years of East Africa.* Nairobi: British Institute in Eastern Africa, 1990.

Vérin, Pierre. *The History of Civilization in North Madagascar.* Boston: A. Balkema, 1986.

GWYN CAMPBELL

MADAGASCAR AND WESTERN INDIAN OCEAN, HISTORY OF (1500 TO 1895).

The Western Indian Ocean is generally regarded as including the island of Madagascar and the Comoros, Mascarene, and Seychelles archipelagos. In 1500 the Portuguese were the first Europeans to make inroads into this area. At that time, Madagascar and the Comoros Islands had been inhabited since ancient times with established societies that were the product of an age-old mix of peoples from all sides of the Indian Ocean. The Mascarenes and the Seychelles were by contrast uninhabited, and were only recently populated as a result of European colonization during the seventeenth and eighteenth centuries, following the numerous setbacks in the attempted European colonization of Madagascar. However, between 1500 and 1895, extensive and varied links were formed between these islands. In 1895 the entire region was colonized and divided between France and Britain.

From the end of the fifteenth century, the people of Madagascar, who had up to that time been organized along ancestral lines, either regrouped themselves into confederations or became united in an inland kingdom. Under the rule of different dynasties that emerged from the last waves of immigrants to integrate with the native inhabitants, these political entities, whose development owed a great deal to the Islamic elements of the southeast, contributed to the spread of monarchical state structures that extended inland over a clearly defined geographical area. The people of Madagascar were thus split into distinct segments of land and, as a result, established stable states that rivaled each other, with some seeking to ensure their supremacy over the others.

With the arrival of European powers in the Indian Ocean during the sixteenth century, the introduction of firearms and the intensification of the slave trade, the history of Madagascar became linked to Europe. European navigators looked for ports of call on the route to the Indies or for refueling points; European settlers were massacred or wore themselves out in endless conflicts; pirates made marriage alliances on the northeast coast giving rise to a new dynasty of rulers, or simply left the colonies they had established (Île Bourbon in 1663 and Île de France in 1721).

If many of the kingdoms were frequently at war with each other, several made attempts to unite. Ratsimilaho (1694–1754), the son of an English pirate, educated in England, created a kingdom on the east coast—actually a confederation—which broke apart after his death. The concrete result of his actions however remains: the name Betsimisaraka, which was taken under his rule by the east coast inhabitants who decided to remain united.

Other peoples on the island also unified successfully. In the west, during the seventeenth and eighteenth centuries, the Maroseraña established two kingdoms (Menabe and Boina), which were well organized and rich thanks to the flourishing trade at their ports. Using the resources that came from this trade, the Sakalava kings maintained an army that quickly became an effective instrument of political unification in the west. This army also allowed them to undertake raids into the Betsileo or Imerina. However the fundamental purpose of these ventures during this period of expanding commerce seems to have been the pursuit of cattle and slaves in order to trade with the Europeans and Arab merchants who also operated in the region. And yet the damaging effect of alcohol, introduced to Madagascar by foreigners along with gunpowder and the gun, the disastrous consequences of the strict endogamy practiced by the royal family, and the luxury and debauchery of the powerful, all weakened the warlike passion of the Sakalava, explaining the decline of their kingdom and their inability to finally complete the unification process. But they had shown the path to follow. In the highlands, the Merina had managed to establish themselves in small rival chiefdoms.

Andriamasinavalona (c. 1675–c. 1710) united the majority of these principalities into a huge kingdom. After his lifetime, however, his kingdom was divided between his four sons. It was during this period that the Merina were surrounded by warlike neighbors (Sakalava, Sihanaka, Bezanozano) who enslaved them, raided their herds, or destroyed their crops. While subject to these difficulties, they had had to deal with chronic famines. Their response to this latter concern involved the Merina undertaking large-scale agricultural irrigation to increase rice production. Draining the marshes, irrigating the paddy fields, and the consequent control of the water supply required a population that was disciplined and united in purpose. Fear of an enemy attack or a bad harvest meant living with a permanent feeling of insecurity, increasing social cohesion. For this reason, at the end of the eighteenth century, the Merina peasants were willing to accept a king who could command the support of everyone, along with the discipline and unity of purpose necessary for their own survival.

Andrianampoinimerina (c. 1787–1810) fulfilled these expectations. His wars, in the interior and outside of Imerina territory, were intended to safeguard his kingdom, thus satisfying the peasants, but these wars also had the effect of bringing about the wishes of the Merina merchants who wanted control of the ports and the creation of a grand market in which they could conduct their business in peace. The concerns of his subjects thus coincided with the unifying ambitions of the king.

At the start of the nineteenth century, profound changes occurred in the political situation in Madagascar. On the east coast, torn apart by internal strife, the political unity of Betsimisaraka was a mere memory. On the west coast, the power of the Sakalava kingdoms had given way to a slow but inexorable decline. In the highlands, on the other hand, the united Merina kingdom annexed the Betsileo, cast jealous glances at Sakalava territory and had intentions to rule the entire island.

During this period, the Comoros, once described as an archipelago of warring sultans, was riven by wars caused by incessant rivalry between the noble families. Nonetheless, the sixteenth and seventeenth centuries were marked by a certain level of commercial prosperity as a result of their location, which enabled them to control a proportion of the trade between Madagascar and Africa, or between the latter and the Mascarene Islands, which required a labor force of slaves for their plantations. In the second half of the eighteenth century, the towns of the archipelago were ravaged by periodic raids carried out by the Betsimisaraka and Sakalava.

The Mascarene Islands and the Seychelles, previously uninhabited, began to be settled in the second half of the seventeenth century and particularly during the eighteenth century. Initially calling ports on the route to the Indies, under enlightened governors such as Mahé de la Bourdonnais (1735–1746) they became interdependent colonies (Île

Bourbon with its agricultural possibilities and Île de France with its access to the sea). However the Napoleonic Wars ended in 1814 with the political dismantling of the Mascarene Islands: Bourbon/La Réunion remained French, while Île de France/Mauritius and the Seychelles became British.

During the course of the nineteenth century, the rivalry between France and Britain for control of the Indian Ocean set in motion a new period in the history of the islands. Farquhar, the first British governor of Mauritius, supported the Merina king Radama I (1810–1828), the son of Andrianampoinimerina, in his annexation of a large part of Madagascar in return for the abolition of the slave trade. It was due to him that the British recognized the "Kingdom of Madagascar" that Radama attempted to create. The extensive and varied activities of the London Missionary Society during this period are also evidence of the extent to which European influence had penetrated the island.

With the reign of Ranavalona I (1828–1861), however, who opposed the political views of her husband, all but a few select Europeans were expelled; she also persecuted Christians in Madagascar and imposed a policy of dominating and exploiting subject peoples instead of the policy of integration and assimilation established by Radama. This policy, in turn, was reversed by her son Radama II (1861–1863), who reopened the country to European influence. It was Rainilaiarivony, the prime minister from 1864 to 1895 and husband of three queens in succession, who then established the foundations of a Christian monarchy in 1869, governed and modernized the state in many regards, and attempted to maintain a balance between France and Britain in order to retain its independence.

However, after the Zanzibar Agreement of 1890, in which the British recognized the French protectorate over Madagascar, the country was conquered by Duchesne in 1895 and declared a colony in 1896. This conquest had been particularly campaigned for by Réunion, the "colony turned colonizer," and it was at its urging that the Comoros were made a French protectorate in 1886 and then declared a colony in 1912.

See also **Andrianampoinimerina; Comoro Islands: History and Politics; Kings and Kingdoms; Madagascar and Western Indian Ocean, History of (Early to 1500); Madagascar: Early Settlement; Mauritius: History**

and Politics; Radama I; Ranavalona, Mada; Réunion; Seychelles: History and Politics; Travel and Exploration: European (1500 to 1800).

BIBLIOGRAPHY

Addison, John, and Kissoonsingh Hazareesingh. *A New History of Mauritius.* Paris: Editions de l'océan Indien, 1993.

Chane-Kune, Sonia. *Aux origines de l'identité réunionnaise.* Paris: L'Harmattan, 1993.

Deschamps, Hubert. *Histoire de Madagascar.* Paris: Berger-Levrault, 1972.

Filliot, Jean-Michel. *Histoire des Seychelles.* Paris: Karthala, 1982.

Fontaine, Guy. *Mayotte.* Paris: Karthala, 1995.

Guerbourg, Jean-Louis. *Les Seychelles.* Paris: Karthala, 2004.

Toussaint, Auguste. *Histoire des Iles Mascareignes.* Paris: Berger-Levrault, 1972.

Verin, Pierre. *Madagascar.* Paris: Karthala, 1990.

Widmer, Isabelle. *La Réunion et Maurice.* Paris: INED, 2005.

MANASSÉ ESOAVELOMANDROSO

MÃE AURÉLIA CORREIA. *See* Correia, Mãe Aurélia.

MAGHILI, MUHAMMAD IBN 'ABD AL-KARIM AL- (??–1504).

After early study in Tlemcen in present-day northwestern Algeria, the Islamic scholar and political activist Muhammad ibn 'Abd al-Karim al-Maghili took up residence in Tamantit, the chief town of the central Saharan oasis of Tuwat. There he conducted a vigorous campaign against what he saw as the unwarranted privileges of the Jewish community in their capacity as a community protected or tolerated within the Islamic body politic. In particular, al-Maghili argued that it was unlawful for them to maintain a place of worship of their own. Although opposed by the local *qadi* (judge), he obtained legal opinions (*fatwas*) from North African scholars, some of whom gave strong support to his stance. He led an attack on the Jewish community and destroyed their synagogue, causing many of them to leave Tamantit

permanently. Subsequently, al-Maghili spent some years in western Africa, where he was well received by the sultan of Kano (in present-day northern Nigeria), Muhammad Rumfa (reigned c. 1463–1499), and the ruler of the Songhay empire, Askiya al-Hajj Muhammad (Abi Bakr; r. 1493–1528), whose capital was at Gao (in what is now Mali). For both of these rulers al-Maghili wrote treatises of advice on Islamic rulership, and his replies to the *askiya*'s questions became an authoritative text for later Muslim reformers, such as 'Uthman dan Fodio (1754–1817), as he sought to establish a state in the region of present-day Nigeria.

See also **Islam: Western Africa.**

BIBLIOGRAPHY

Hunwick, John, ed. and trans. *Shara in Songhay: The Replies of al-Maghili to the Questions of Askia al-Hajj Muhammed.* New York: Oxford University Press, 1985.

Hunwick, John O. *West Africa and the Arab World: Historical and Contemporary Perspectives.* Accra: Ghana Academy of Arts and Sciences, 1991.

JOHN O. HUNWICK

MAHDI, MUHAMMAD AHMAD AL-. *See* Ahmad, Mahdi Muhammad.

MAHERERO, SAMUEL (c. 1854–1923).

Samuel Maherero was the son of Maherero Tjamuaha, the first Herero chief of Okahandja in present-day central Namibia, and succeeded his father as chief in 1891. Named Uereani at birth, he was baptized as Samuel in 1868 by Rhenish missionaries, from whom he received his schooling. Samuel's elder brother and missionary protégé Wilhelm (Uaita) was originally intended to succeed his father as chief, but Wilhelm was killed in 1880 in a battle against the Nama. Following his father's death in 1890, Samuel Maherero cooperated with the German colonial rulers then arriving to claim German Southwest Africa. Through the sale of confiscated lands, he was able to mobilize German support in overthrowing and subduing rival Herero chiefs. In the aftermath of the rinderpest epizootic, which in the late 1890s killed most of the livestock at the base of the Herero economy, Maherero retained his power and influence through the sale of land and the supply of labor to the German colonial administration and the South African gold mines.

In 1904, following a series of misunderstandings and the German settlers' self-fulfilling prophecies of war, Maherero led the Herero in a war against the forces of Imperial Germany in the colony. After a string of battles, Maherero and his followers were driven into the Omaheke region of the Kalahari Desert. Many of the Herero died of hunger and thirst as they struggled to reach water and the safety of the Bechuanaland Protectorate (present-day Botswana), where British authorities there granted sanctuary to Maherero and a handful of his followers. After a short sojourn in Bechuanaland, Maherero crossed over into South Africa, where he and his followers were permitted to live on a farm near Groenfontein in the northern Transvaal in exchange for supplying labor to the gold mines of the Rand. Prohibited from returning to the land of his birth and also from buying land in South Africa, Maherero returned to the town of Serowe in Bechuanaland in 1921, where he died of stomach cancer. His body was taken by rail to Okahandja and buried next to the graves of his father and grandfather.

See also **Colonial Policies and Practices: German; Namibia.**

BIBLIOGRAPHY

Dierks, Klaus. *Chronology of Namibian History: From Pre-Historical Times to Independent Namibia.* Windhoek, Namibia: Namibia Scientific Society, 2002.

Heywood, Annemarie; Brigitte Lau; and Raimund Ohly; eds. *Warriors, Leaders, Sages, and Outcasts in the Namibian Past.* Windhoek: Michael Scott Oral Research Project, 1992.

JAN BART GEWALD

MAHFOUZ, NAGUIB (1911–2006). Winner of the 1988 Nobel Prize for Literature, Naguib Mahfouz, who wrote his first novel, *Abath al-aqdár*, in 1938, is by far the most famous Arab writer. Well known amongst the Arab public, particularly for the films that his works have inspired, the so-called Egyptian Balzac dedicated

himself to writing at a relatively late stage in his life. He was a civil servant for many years. Subsequently, he had a regular column in the daily newspaper *al-Ahram*. Representing the rationalist strain of thought of the Arab renaissance (*nahda*), he survived an assassination attempt in 1994. His attacker, an Islamic extremist, criticized Mahfouz in particular for his controversial novel, *Awlad haratna* (*The Children of Gebalawi*), written at the start of the 1960s.

The novel is an allegorical history of the human race that calls for the foundation texts of the great revealed religions to be reread. After Mahfouz's first historical novels, his social period, including the celebrated *Cairo Trilogy* published in the mid-1950s, marks his development as the founder of modern Arab fiction. Also a writer of short stories

Egyptian novelist Naguib Mahfouz (1911–2006). Subjects of Mahfouz's writing include socialism, existentialism, God, and homosexuality. Some of these subjects were prohibited in Egyptian literature at the time they were composed. CORBIS

(*Zaʿbalawi*, one of the most famous, was written in 1962), Naguib Mahfouz had more than fifty works to his name at the time of his death. At one time motivated by the philosophers of the absurd, his work remains essentially Egyptian, both in terms of his subject and in his quest to produce an authentic Arab fiction.

See also **Literature.**

BIBLIOGRAPHY

El-Enany, Rasheed. *Naguib Mahfouz: The Pursuit of Meaning.* London, Routledge, 1993.

Le Gassick, Trevor, ed. *Critical Perspectives on Naguib Mahfouz.* Washington, DC: Three Continents Press, 1991.

Mahfouz, Naguib. *Naguib Mahfouz at Sidi Gaber: Reflections of a Nobel Laureate 1994–2001, from Conversations with Mohamed Salmawy.* Cairo, Egypt: The American University in Cairo Press, 2001.

YVES GONZALEZ-QUIJANO

This history is reflected in the physical and social layout of present day Maiduguri and gives the town—at least in some areas—the look of an old Sudanic city, with ethnic and occupational quarters, markets, a central mosque, and a huge open road, *dandal*, leading towards the Shehu's palace, an area that was initially surrounded by town walls.

BIBLIOGRAPHY

Kawka, Rupert, ed. *Westafrikanische Studien*, Vol. 24: *From Bulamari to Yerwa to Metropolitain Maiduguri. Interdisciplinary Studies on the Capital of Borno State, Nigeria.* Cologne, Germany: Rüdiger Köppe Verlag, 2002.

Koroma, David, and Ibrahim M. Waziri. "A Brief History of Yerwa/Maiduguri." In *Hallmarks of Academic Excellence: University of Maiduguri, 1975–2001,* ed. David Koroma. Lagos: CSS Bookshop, 2004.

Seidensticker, Wilhelm. "Notes on the History of Yerwa (Maiduguri)." *Annals of Borno,* 1 (1983): 5–15.

EDITHA PLATTE

MAIDUGURI. Maiduguri, also known as Yerwa, was founded by the British in 1907 as the residence of the traditional ruler, the Shehu of Borno. Situated close to a colonial military post (Mafoni) and an established marketplace (Maiduguri), the original place name was Kalwa Bulamari. Whereas the inhabitants in precolonial times were mainly Malgwa (Gamergu), Kanuri, and Shuwa, Maiduguri's selection as the capital of North Eastern State in 1967 and its present status as the capital of Borno State and Borno Emirate, made the town a modern multiethnic city, with 800,000 people and thirty-eight languages. Situated at the northern fringes of the Sudan Belt and within the proximity of two rivers and the largest water reservoir of the Sudan (Lake Chad), Maiduguri is one of the hottest cities of Nigeria. The economic status of the town is closely related to its location near three international borders (Niger, Cameroon, and Republic of Chad), and its accessibility by tarred roads (since 1950) and the railway (since 1964). Although hardly any industry can be found, two main markets and a cattle market attract thousands of people weekly.

Despite the fact that Maiduguri is a colonial creation, its foundation is based within the nearly thousand-year-old history of Kanem-Borno Empire.

MAKEBA, MIRIAM (1932–). Born to Caswell and Nomkomndelo "Christina" Makeba on March 4, 1932, Miriam "Zenzi" Makeba, also known as Mama Afrika, began singing with Johannesburg's Cuban Brothers. She later joined the famous Manhattan Brothers, with which she toured Southern African and recorded the South African jazz standard, "Lakutshon'Ilanga." She started and recorded with the Skylarks, an all female close harmony group, and toured Southern Africa with African Jazz and Variety. In 1956 she performed in Lionel Rogosin's (1924–2000) secretly made film, *Come Back Africa,* before playing the lead role in South African's first jazz opera, *King Kong.*

She traveled to Europe and the United States, where Harry Belafonte (b. 1927) helped launch her international career. In 1960 she sang at the Village Gate in New York City—popularizing South African traditional songs including the "Click Song," "Patha Patha," and the Tanzanian "Malaika." Makeba testified about apartheid before the United Nations in 1964, and was subsequently denied her South African citizenship. She married and divorced activist Stokley Carmichael (1941–1998), and later wed musician Hugh Masekela. Makeba performed with Paul Simon's (b. 1941) African Tour of the Graceland

South African singer Miriam Makeba (1932–) at Wembly Stadium in London. Makeba, also known as Mama Afrika, held a 14-month worldwide farewell tour in 2005. AP IMAGES

project. She has recorded extensively, and lived, and been given honorary citizenship in, several countries. In 1990 she returned to South Africa, where she continues to record and perform.

See also **Apartheid; Masekela, Hugh; Music, Modern Popular.**

BIBLIOGRAPHY

Makeba, Miriam. *Makeba: My Story.* New York: New American Library, 1987.

CAROL MULLER

MALAGASY REPUBLIC. *See* Madagascar.

MALARIA. *See* Disease.

MALAWI

This entry includes the following articles:
GEOGRAPHY AND ECONOMY
SOCIETY AND CULTURES
HISTORY AND POLITICS

GEOGRAPHY AND ECONOMY

Malawi is bordered by Tanzania to the north, Zambia to the west, and is engulfed to the south and east by Mozambique. Malawi's dominant geographic features, Lake Malawi and the highland plateau regions, are part of the East African Rift Valley. The plateau regions vary from 2,297 to 4,593 feet above sea level, and include broad plains interspersed with rolling hills and steep mountain ranges. With a subtropical climate, rain comes in a single wet season from November to April. The country's dominant red-brown clay and sandy-clay latosols are among the most fertile soils in the region, but much soil has been depleted by continuous cultivation.

British missionaries and settlers who arrived in the 1860s met a densely populated, predominantly agricultural population, including people speaking the Bantu languages known in the early twenty-first century as Chewa, Nyanja, Lomwe, Yao, Ngoni, and Tumbuka. As they still do, these people grew millet, sorghum, peanuts, beans, pumpkins, cassava, and (beginning around the eighteenth century) maize—the modern country's staple food crop—using forms of shifting cultivation.

Seeing little strategic or economic value in Malawi (then Nyasaland), the nineteenth-century British government was not enthusiastic about committing resources to a formal presence, but extended protectorate status to Nyasaland in 1891 to block Portuguese hegemony in the region. As a minor outpost of the Empire, the nation struggled to define its course. The government of Nyasaland planned development based on large-scale European estate agriculture. The first consul-general of Nyasaland, Harry Johnson, set aside about 45 percent of all arable land for the European estates. The impact on small farmers was enormous. By the 1930s Nyasaland had a much higher proportion of its land under the control of Europeans than Kenya, Uganda, Tanganyika, or Northern Rhodesia. This imbalance defined relations between Europeans and

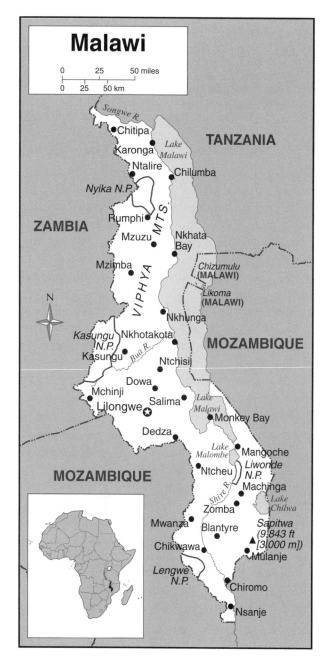

Africans throughout the colonial period and, since independence, between Malawian estate owners and smallholder farmers.

Hut taxes were used to generate revenue and to force African labor onto the estates. African labor was manipulated through the despised labor tenancy arrangement known as *thangata*. Formal credit institutions for small farmers were virtually nonexistent, African non-farm wages were suppressed, and small farmers were forbidden from growing the most profitable types of crops. These policies protected estates by restricting competition from African farmers for labor and markets. Despite these advantages for the estate owners, the envisioned large-scale immigration of European settlers never materialized. By the close of the colonial period, many of the large estates were barely breaking even, and the exodus of Europeans from Nyasaland in the 1950s reflected the financial as well as political realities.

Nationalist sentiment increased after World War II, and by the time of formal independence in 1964 there was (unlike Kenya or Rhodesia) little European resistance to giving Malawi back to Malawians. But after seventy-three years of colonial rule that failed to develop a successful estate sector and deliberately suppressed smallholder farmers, independent Malawi emerged as a poor and forgotten backwater country that has been aptly described as an imperial slum. Making matters worse, the political economy the colonial government left behind was inherited by an African government that proved more interested in positioning itself at the top of a postcolonial hierarchy than in reforming the failed strategies of the Europeans.

The independent government that took power in 1964 not only maintained the estate-led structure of the economy, but actually intensified policies to benefit of a new class of African estate owners. By the early 1970s the nation's first independent leader, the "Life President" Dr. Hastings Kamuzu Banda, established firm control. Banda infamously promised to make his enemies into meat for crocodiles. He used his power to alienate even more land from small farmers to the (now African-owned) estates, and used a government marketing board to tax small farmer production while channeling the revenue into the estate sector. In the mid-1980s, new policies restricted migration outside the country, eliminating one of the few opportunities Malawian small farmers had to break out of poverty. The consequences were grim. During the period 1979 to 1991, for example, per capita smallholder farm production declined by an average of 2.7 percent.

Yet, Malawi was a darling of the West. Western donors rewarded Banda's fierce pro-capitalist (and even pro-apartheid South Africa) regime with favorable treatment. By the late 1980s, however, with the end of Cold War politics, several influential reports discovered that growth in Malawi's estate sector masked severe structural poverty.

In the early 1990s, a conjunction of forces that included pressures from Western donors and church leaders forced Banda to accept a public referendum that ultimately led to multiparty elections and the end of his rule in 1994. Tragically, Banda's successor, Bakili Muluzi (b. 1943, himself a wealthy estate owner), only further entrenched elite power. Worse, under Muluzi, corruption at every level positions exploded. Urgent matters of public policy became paralyzed. Muluzi won reelection in 1999, but failed in a bid to change the new (1995) constitution to allow himself a third term of office in 2004. The winner of the 2004 election, Bingu wa Mutharika (b. 1934), has fought courageously against corruption since becoming president, but his efforts have been blocked by incessant political opposition from former president Bakili Muluzi and other rivals.

Malawi's future would appear to rely on the capacity to break away from the long-established dualistic, estate-oriented economy that is highly dependent on production of a single export crop, tobacco. The political leadership and vision to break the entrenched power that supports the status quo has not yet appeared, and there appear to be few alternatives to the almost exclusive dependence on corn as a food staple and tobacco as an export cash crop, despite stagnating tobacco prices. Malawi received a major boost with relief from most of its international debt in 2006; yet the problems of entrenched poverty, inequality, illiteracy, and the modern catastrophic public health crisis (especially the HIV/AIDS pandemic) pose enormous challenges.

See also **Banda, Ngwazi Hastings Kamuzu; Boundaries, Colonial and Modern; Ivory; Labor: Migration; Naturalism; Plantation Economies and Societies; Postcolonialism; Slave Trades.**

BIBLIOGRAPHY

Kydd, Jonathan, and Robert E. Christiansen. "Structural Change in Malawi since Independence: Consequences of a Development Strategy Based on Large Scale Agriculture." *World Development* 10, no. 5 (1982): 355–375.

Mhone, Guy C. Z. *Malawi at the Crossroads: The Post-Colonial Political Economy.* Harare, Zimbabwe: SAPES Books, 1992.

Vail, Leroy. "The Making of an Imperial Slum: Nyasaland and its Railways, 1895–1935." *Journal of African History* 16, no. 1 (1974): 89–112.

White, Landeg. *Magomero: Portrait of an African Village.* Cambridge, U.K.: Cambridge University Press, 1985.

World Bank. *World Development Report 1993.* Oxford: Oxford University Press, 1993.

PETER WALKER

SOCIETY AND CULTURES

Malawi began as a colonial invention. Its geographic boundaries were first shaped in 1891 when it became the Central African Protectorate under the British Foreign Office. It was renamed Nyasaland (land of the lake) in 1907 when responsibility for it was transferred to the Colonial Office. It is a long sliver of territory that runs north-south between 33 and 37 degrees longitude and 9 and 17 degrees latitude. It covers 45,747 square miles, just over 36,324 of which is land. Lakes Malawi and Chilwa account for most of the remaining area. It is landlocked and borders present-day Tanzania to the north, Zambia to the west, and Mozambique to the east and southwest. It is a tropical country, but its climate varies according to elevation, ranging from hot and humid in the low-lying Shire Valley in the south to the cool semitropical environment of the Shire Highlands farther north, and the Nyika and Vipya Plateaus and the Msukwu Hills farther north still.

The ancestors of many Malawians can be traced back to ironworking farmers of the second or third century CE who coexisted with Late Stone Age hunter-gatherers. By the fourteenth or fifteenth centuries, migrants from the eastern Congo had come to settle in the central and southern parts of the country. Known collectively as the Maravi peoples, they ultimately became the matrilineal Chewa, Mang'anja, and Nyanja ethnic groups. Some scholars argue that the Tumbuka are related to these peoples as well. There seems to be little agreement as to when the Sena (closely related linguistically to the Mang'anja of the Shire Valley) arrived in the southern part of the country from the Zambezi region, but they observe many of the same cultural practices as the Amang'anja and were *in situ* by the nineteenth century.

The northern region is the most heterogeneous linguistically and ethnically and was an area of in-migration from Zambia, eastern Congo, southern Tanzania, and east of Lake Malawi. The main ethnic groups are the patrilineal Tumbuka, Ngonde-Nyakyusa Sukwa-Lambya-Nyiha groups, and the matrilineal Tonga. Chitipa District on the Tanzania-Malawi border country is the most heterogeneous linguistically with some thirteen languages or dialects being spoken. The history of these peoples (and arguably the Maravi as well) reflects a tension between centralizing political forces and the desire for local autonomy revolving around clan governance. In the nineteenth century, more immigrants arrived, most notably the Ngoni (from Natal), Swahili Arabs (from the Indian Ocean coast), the Yao and Lomwe (from Mozambique), and the first European settlers. South Asian immigrants followed European settlement at the end of that century.

By the nineteenth century then, ancestors of the country's main modern residents were in place. The 1998 census results reported a population of 9.9 million. The estimated 2007 population is 13.6 million. The most populous of the three regions is the south (47%), followed by the center (41%), then the north (12%). Most people live in rural areas as compared to towns (only 14%) and a full 78 percent are subsistence farmers, albeit who occasionally sell some surplus crops or specialty cash crops such as tobacco or cotton.

The most commonly spoken languages are Chichewa (officially reported as the first language of some 57% of the population in 1998), Chinyanja (12.8%), Chiyao (10%), Chitumbuka (9.5%), Chilomwe (2.4%), Chisena (2.7%), and Chitonga (1.7%). Chingoni, Kyangonde, Chilambya, Chisukwa, Chindali, and languages spoken by various South Asian and European minorities account for the remaining 3.6 percent. These linguistic designations correspond roughly to the territory's various ethnic groups, although in some cases such as that of the Ngoni, the traditional language has all but died out and those who self-identify as Ngoni speak Chitumbuka or Chichewa. This is the result of mixed marriages (between ethnic groups) between the politically dominant (Ngoni) invaders and the more populous conquered.

Ethnic ambiguity was also furthered by the British colonial policy of Indirect Rule and its concomitant emphasis on tribal membership that privileged some groups over others and hence made certain ethnic designations more desirable. This was further complicated in the postcolonial period by the language policy of the Malawi Congress Party regime (1964–1994) that made Chichewa (the mother tongue of the late President Hastings Kamuzu Banda) one of the two languages of state (English being the other) in 1968.

Most people identify with corporate kin groups (clans and lineages) that reckon membership through the female line (matrilineal) or male line (patrilineal), although marriages between people of different ethnic groups makes observance of custom less than straightforward. Clan and the lineage are important for determining access to land, but it is less clear what practice should be in the case of access to modern resources (such as houses and movable property such as automobiles). Similarly, responsibility for children's upkeep (for example, school fees, medical care, and clothing) is often hotly contested. This is more pronounced in towns than in rural areas.

These tensions are the product of the introduction of the cash economy to the territory during the colonial period. Cash-cropping, labor migration (within the country and beyond), and small business made it possible for individuals to accumulate wealth on their own part, which often led to intergenerational conflict as youth asserted its autonomy vis-à-vis elders. Given that wage employment in the colonial economy favored males over females, opportunities for the accumulation of wealth also antagonized gender conflict.

Most Malawians before (and many after) the nineteenth century venerated their ancestors and acknowledged a High God. Some were adherents of territorial earth and rain cults that were to ensure health and fertility through rainmaking. By 1998, 79.9 percent of Malawians identified themselves as Christians, 12.8 percent as Muslims, and the remainder claiming other or no religious affiliation. The predominance of Christianity is attributable to European missionary activity. The Protestant missions of the Universities Mission to Central Africa in 1875 (Anglican), the Free Church of Scotland, and the Established Church of Scotland (both Presbyterian denominations) were first to established permanent missions in the country. Others

Republic of Malawi

Population:	13,603,181 (2007 est.)
Area:	118,484 sq. km (45,747 sq. mi.)
Official languages:	English, Chichewa
Languages:	Chichewa, English, Tonga, Yao, Tumbuka
National currency:	Malawi kwacha
Principal religions:	Protestant 55%, Roman Catholic 20%, Muslim 20%, indigenous beliefs 3%, other 2%
Capital:	Lilongwe (est. pop. 598,000 in 2003)
Other urban centers:	Blantyre, Zomba, Mzuzu
Average annual rainfall:	760–1,015 mm (30–40 in.)
Principal geographical features:	*Mountains:* Mulanje, and Zomba mountain ranges, Dedza, Sapitwa Peak, Nyika Plateau, Vipya Plateau *Rivers:* Shire, Lilongwe, Bua, Dwangwa, Kasitu, South Rukuru *Lakes:* Marawi (also called Nyasa), Malombe, Chilwa
Economy:	*GDP per capita:* US$600 (2006)
Principal products and exports:	*Agricultural:* tobacco, sugarcane, cotton, tea, corn, potatoes, cassava (tapioca), sorghum, pulses, groundnuts, Macadamia nuts, cattle, goats *Manufacturing:* sawmill products, cement, consumer goods *Mining:* lime, coal; exploitation of bauxite deposits may be feasible in the future.
Government:	Independence from Great Britain, 1964. Republican constitution approved in 1966. New constitution, 1995. Multiparty democracy. President elected by direct universal suffrage for 5-year term. 193-seat National Assembly elected for 5-year term by direct universal suffrage. 1995 constitution calls for formation of a senate; however, elections to fill it have not yet taken place. For purposes of local government, the country is divided into 3 regions, 24 districts, and 8 municipalities.
Heads of state since independence:	1964–1966: Prime Minister Hastings Kamuzu Banda 1966–1994: President-for-Life Hastings Kamuzu Banda 1994–2004: President Bakili Muluzi 2004–: President Bingu wa Mutharika
Armed forces:	President is commander in chief. Enlistment is voluntary. *Army:* 10,000 *Navy:* 200 *Air Force:* 200 *Paramilitary:* 1,500
Transportation:	*Rail:* 797 km (495 mi.), owned by Malawi Railways and its subsidiary, Central African Railway Company *Roads:* 15,451 km (9,601 mi.), 45% paved *Lake ports:* Chipoka, Bandawe, Karonga *National airline:* Air Malawi *Airports:* Kamuzu International Airport in Lilongwe, former international airport at Blantyre, 4 others with paved runways
Media:	2 daily newspapers: *Daily Times, Malawi News.* 5 weeklies, 43 periodicals. Radio service provided by Malawi Broadcasting Corporation. 1 television station.
Education and literacy:	*Total literacy rate:* 63%. Schooling is free and about 80% of children receive some formal education. Postsecondary education provided by thirteen 2-year teacher-training colleges, Banda College of Agriculture, Malawi Polytechnic, Chancellor College, Kamuzu College of Nursing, Malawi Institute of Education, and University of Malawi.

followed, including the Dutch Reformed Church, the Zambezi Industrial Mission, the Seventh Day Adventist Mission, and the Nyasa Baptist Industrial Mission.

Roman Catholics did not begin mission work in the region until the latter part of the century and laid no permanent foundation until the early years of the twentieth. They have since overtaken the various Protestant denominations to become the largest and fastest growing of Malawi's Christian churches. The missions funded and shaped Western education from the inception of colonial rule until after World War II. This produced, on the one hand, generations of white-collar workers who would staff the colonial civil service and private sector jobs. On the other, it produced a tradition of debate and enquiry that often challenged the colonial regime both violently and peacefully (for example, through the establishment of Native Associations, and of Ethiopian or independent churches and missions). Churches continued to play an important role in forcing the pace of political change after independence. The Roman Catholic Bishops' Lenten letter of 1992, for example, has been credited with being among the first critiques of the Banda regime to be publicly enunciated since 1964.

In the modern era, missions, churches, and nongovernmental organizations play an important role in providing spiritual and material support to the country's people. Malawi is still one of the world's poorest countries and has been severely hit by the HIV/AIDS pandemic. It is estimated that just under one million people are either HIV positive or living with AIDS (or 14% of the population in 2005), with higher reported rates of infection in urban over rural areas (21% of people in towns and 12.1% of rural dwellers in 2005).

See also **Archaeology and Prehistory; Ethnicity; Kinship and Descent; Postcolonialism; Religion and Ritual; Secret Societies; Travel and Exploration: European.**

BIBLIOGRAPHY

Department of Nutrition HIV and AIDS, Government of Malawi. "Malawi HIV and AIDS Monitoring and Evaluation Report 2005." December 2005. Available from http://www.plusnews.org/aids/.

Kayambazinthu, Edrinnie. "The Language Planning Situation in Malawi." *Journal of Multilingual and Multicultural Development* 19, nos. 5 & 6 (1998): 369–439.

National Statistical Office. "1998 Population and Housing Census, Final Report." 1998. Available from http://www.nso.malawi.net/data_on_line/.

National Statistical Office. "Malawi Population Projections 1999–2025." Available from http://www.nso.malawi.net/data_on_line/.

Phiri, Kings M.; Owen Kalinga; and H. H. K. Bhila. "The Northern Zambezia-Lake Malawi Region." In *UNESCO General History of Africa V: Africa from the Sixteenth to the Eighteenth Century*, ed. Bethwell A. Ogot. Los Angeles: Heinemann, 1992.

Vail, Leroy, and Landeg White. "Tribalism in the Political History of Malawi." In *The Creation of Tribalism in Southern Africa*, ed. Leroy Vail. Berkeley: University of California Press, 1991.

JOEY POWER

HISTORY AND POLITICS

The history of the colonial territory of Malawi in many ways begins with the arrival of European missionaries, among them David Livingstone, who were active in the region from the 1850s. The area of what would become known as Nyasaland was subsequently closely associated with missionary work, and the mission stations and schools there were among the most famous in Africa. The Free Church of Scotland operated in the Shire Highlands from 1876, and further north from 1881. Missionaries played a key role, too, in the founding of a colonial administration, notably Dr. Robert Laws, who was also instrumental in the establishment of the Livingstonia mission station in northern Nyasaland. While missionary activity flourished, the British South Africa Company (BSAC) was developing an economic interest in the territory north of the Limpopo. Headed by Cecil Rhodes, the BSAC was convinced of the existence of great mineral wealth in central Africa; at the same time, the British government was prepared to support the BSAC in order to protect its strategic interests against other European powers in the area, notably the Portuguese at Mozambique.

The eastern frontier of the BSAC's influence was represented by Lake Nyasa and the highlands to the south. Harry Johnston, the British consul at Mozambique, was responsible for the creation of a colonial infrastructure in the region, and he secured a series of treaties with chiefs in the Lake Nyasa area, treaties, which (however dubious) formed the basis of the British Central Africa Protectorate. Missionary lobbying also contributed to the assumption of Foreign Office control. The Colonial Office took over responsibility in 1904, and the territory was renamed Nyasaland in 1907.

COLONIAL RULE

Unlike British territories to the west and south, Nyasaland was lacking in the mineral resources that had prompted BSAC expansion into the region. As in these other colonies, however, Nyasaland witnessed the alienation of land to white farmers who settled and developed plantations in the favorable Shire Highlands. Even so, the settler community never approached the proportions of those in Northern and Southern Rhodesia. Rather, the mining economies of the Rhodesias and South Africa increasingly drew large numbers of workers from Nyasaland to those regions, often for many years at a time. In particular, the Rhodesian Native

Labor Bureau began recruiting labor in Nyasaland from 1903 and was later joined by the South Africa-based Witwatersrand Native Labor Association. The outward flow of migrant labor continued even after the governor of the territory passed legislation restricting the practice in 1911. There were relatively few economic incentives for Africans to remain within the territory; although some African farmers later became pioneers of cash-crop production, notably of tobacco, such activity often had to be carried out on white-owned land where the price for such produce was fixed and Africans had to provide labor in lieu of rent and taxes. The sustained migration of labor further impoverished many rural communities already displaced by land alienation. Notably, Nyasa migrant workers based in Southern Rhodesia later formed the nuclei of nationalist and protest movements in that territory.

Economic conditions for white farmers improved markedly prior to World War I. They turned to the production of cotton and tobacco, and the value of their exports more than doubled between 1905 and 1913 following the extension of a railway link from Blantyre to Port Herald. The growth of the plantation system contributed to the eruption of African armed rebellion in 1915. An African clergyman, John Chilembwe, led an uprising of plantation laborers bonded by their Christian faith; they harbored grievances against their white employers, and were further motivated by the brutality experienced by African soldiers in the service of the colonial state. The rebellion was brief but intense, failing to gather widespread support before being crushed. It did, however, provide Africans in Nyasaland with a "tradition of resistance" in the latter stages of colonial rule.

Nyasa workers in other territories contributed to the growth of protest movements. Nowhere was this more clearly demonstrated than in the growth of the Jehovah's Witnesses–based Watchtower movement, which originated in northern Nyasaland and took root in the mining compounds of Northern and Southern Rhodesia. The Nyasaland African Congress (NAC), established in 1944, extended its influence into Southern Rhodesia via more than one hundred thousand Nyasa migrant workers in that territory, as well as being the main engine of protest in Nyasaland itself. In particular, the NAC, in common with other African political organizations in the region,

protested against the movement toward a Central African Federation. This federation would join Nyasaland in an administrative block with Northern and Southern Rhodesia. The colonial authorities attempted to calm African fears by offering African politicians a greater stake in government. In 1949, for example, a number of Africans were given seats on the Legislative Council in Zomba, the capital.

The colonial authorities, however, were determined to establish the Federation, which duly came into being in 1953. Britain was convinced that such an administrative unit was the best way to secure the long-term economic and political development of the region, while also creating a pluralist and multiracial society. But Africans, in Nyasaland as elsewhere, saw the Federation as reinforcing white minority rule and opposed it bitterly. During the 1950s the NAC expanded and protest became increasingly forceful. In particular, there was a sharp increase in rural unrest as a result of government interference in agricultural practice. This was undoubtedly critical to the success of the NAC which, like other such movements, required widespread rural support if it was seriously to challenge colonial rule. Civil disobedience in Nyasaland in 1959 led to widespread arrests and a crackdown on protests; among those incarcerated was the prominent NAC leader, Dr. Hastings Kamuzu Banda. Simultaneously, however, the strength of the opposition led the colonial authorities to reconsider the viability of the Federation, and by 1960 colonial governments were forced to concede the necessity of offering enfranchisement to the African majority. In 1961, the newly formed Malawi Congress Party (MCP) under Banda rallied mass support and won a majority of seats in the local assembly. Nyasaland became internally self-governing in January 1963 and won independence as Malawi in July 1964.

THE INDEPENDENT STATE

Throughout the thirty years of his rule, Banda was synonymous with Malawi itself. Prime minister from 1964, he became president when Malawi became a republic in 1966. He was life president from 1971, and also held the posts of president of the MCP and minister of external affairs, works and supplies, agriculture, and justice. Charismatic and religious, he was revered for much of his time in office, being regarded as something of a father figure. An elder of the Church of Scotland, he clearly regarded his role as extending beyond the conventional confines of secular government, issuing decrees on matters such as hairstyles and the length of women's skirts, and strictly censoring books, magazines, and films. To some extent his conservative domestic politics were mirrored abroad, where he cultivated amicable relations with apartheid South Africa, much to the frustration of his immediate neighbors.

His rule was also ruthless with regard to opposition and dissension within government ranks. He dismissed three government ministers for opposing him in September 1964, with others resigning in protest; crushed the armed revolt led by former colleague Henry Chipembere in the south of the country in early 1965; and suppressed another insurrection led by Yatuta Chisiza in 1967. Thereafter Banda faced no serious challenge until the early 1990s. Opponents were either driven into exile, imprisoned (for example Gwanda Chakuamba in 1981), or killed (Albert Nqumayo in 1977). One potential successor, Dick Matenje, was killed in a suspicious car crash in 1983. For many years the government harassed Jehovah's Witnesses who refused to join the MCP, and thousands of Witnesses fled into exile in 1970, 1972, and 1976. A number of opposition groups operated in exile, most prominently the Socialist League of Malawi and the Malawi Freedom Movement.

By the early 1990s Banda's regime was coming under increasing criticism for human rights abuses from Amnesty International and the Roman Catholic Church in Malawi. In September 1992, opposition politicians formed the Alliance for Democracy and another pressure group for political reform, the United Democratic Front (UDF). In October 1992, Banda finally and reluctantly agreed to a national referendum on the transition to multiparty democracy. The referendum took place in June 1993, and although the opposition was strongly supported in the north and south of the country, the MCP retained its support in the central region. Banda remained in power following an amnesty for political exiles and a cabinet reshuffle. In May 1994, however, a general election saw Banda finally relinquish political office. In the presidential election, Banda won some 34 percent of the vote, but Bakili Muluzi of the UDF won 47 percent and was quickly inaugurated as the

country's new head of state. In early 1995 Banda, whose health was deteriorating, and several former colleagues in the MCP government were arrested for their alleged involvement in the killing of opposition politicians in 1983. All the accused, however, were acquitted in December 1995.

Muluzi oversaw substantial political liberalization during his decade in office, winning re-election in 1999, but Malawians continued to struggle under the hardships of poverty, food shortage, and the high rate of HIV/AIDS infection. Political problems, moreover, remained, with accusations of corruption rife during Muluzi's presidency. In 2004 Muluzi stepped down and the presidential election was won by Bingu wa Mutharika, who swiftly announced an anticorruption drive; but events took a dramatic turn in 2005 when Mutharika resigned from the UDF, accusing the party (and his predecessor) of opposing his anticorruption program. Impeachment proceedings, meanwhile, were launched against Mutharika against a backdrop of growing social and economic despair in Malawi.

See also **Banda, Ngwazi Hastings Kamuzu; Chilembwe, John; Colonial Policies and Practices; Livingstone, David; Political Systems; Rhodes, Cecil John.**

BIBLIOGRAPHY

Cullen, Trevor. *Malawi: A Turning Point.* Edinburgh: Pentland Press, 1994.

Gertzel, C. "East and Central Africa." In *The Cambridge History of Africa*, Vol. 8: *From c. 1940–c. 1975*, ed. Michael Crowder. Cambridge, U.K.: Cambridge University Press, 1984.

Harrigan, Jane. *From Dictatorship to Democracy: Economic Policy in Malawi, 1964–2000.* Ashgate, U.K.: Aldershot, 2000.

McCracken, John. *Politics and Christianity in Malawi, 1875–1940: The Impact of the Livingstonia Mission in the Northern Province.* Cambridge, U.K.: Cambridge University Press, 1977.

McCracken, John. "British Central Africa." In *The Cambridge History of Africa*, Vol 7: *From 1905–1940*, ed. A. D. Roberts. Cambridge, U.K.: Cambridge University Press, 1986.

Nzunda, Matembo S., and Kenneth R. Ross, eds. *Church, Law and Political Transition in Malawi 1992–1994.* Gweru: Mambo Press, 1995.

Pachai, Bridglal. *Malawi: The History of the Nation.* Longman: London, 1973.

Phiri, Kings M., and Kenneth R. Ross, eds. *Democratization in Malawi: A Stocktaking*. Blantyre: Christian Literature Association in Malawi, 1998.

Shepperson, George, and Thomas Price. *Independent African: John Chilembwe and the Origins, Setting, and Significance of the Nyasaland Native Rising of 1915*. Edinburgh: Edinburgh University Press, 1958.

Williams, T. David. *Malawi: The Politics of Despair*. Ithaca, NY: Cornell University Press, 1978.

RICHARD REID

MALAYO-POLYNESIAN LANGUAGES.   *See* **Languages: Malayo-Polynesian.**

MALI

This entry includes the following articles:
GEOGRAPHY AND ECONOMY
SOCIETY AND CULTURES
HISTORY AND POLITICS

GEOGRAPHY AND ECONOMY

Covering approximately 478,767 square miles (slightly less than twice the size of Texas), the landlocked Republic of Mali is positioned in the center of western Africa. The former French colony (1892–1960) shares borders with seven neighboring states (Mauritania, Algeria, Niger, Burkina Faso, Côte d'Ivoire, Guinea, and Senegal) and geographical, cultural, and economic patterns tend to flow easily across these colonial era political divides. Indeed, the territory that is present-day Mali has long served as a crossroad connecting the diverse peoples and cultures of the region.

In terms of climate and vegetation, the loose sands of the Saharan zone in northern Mali grade into the open savanna of the Sahelian environment of the central part of the country, which flows into the woodland Sudanic landscape of south. There are two principal seasons: the dry and the wet. The dry season, which runs from October to May, is characterized by an early cool period and a later period during which the hot *harmattan* winds blow into the region from the north. The wet season runs from roughly June through September. Annual rainfall accumulation ranges from almost nil in the north to 55 inches in the extreme south. Temperatures in the north can vary from 117 degrees Fahrenheit during the day to 39 degrees Fahrenheit at night. The Sahelian region experiences an average temperature range of 73 to 97 degrees Fahrenheit, and the Sudanic zone sees an annual temperature range from 75 to 86 degrees Fahrenheit. With the exception of the Bandiagara Plateau in the east, the Adrar des Iforas in the northeast, and the foothills of Guinea's Fouta Djallon in the south, the terrain is relatively flat with alternating plains and minor plateaus.

Two river systems dominate Mali's landscape. Originating in the highlands of Guinea, the mighty Niger River runs northeasterly through the center of the country to the legendary city of Tombouctou (Timbuktu/Timbuctoo) and on to Bourem where it shifts dramatically to a southeasterly flow. From there it makes its way into Niger, onward into Nigeria, and eventually out into the Gulf of Guinea. In the area around Mopti, the Niger forms a dramatic floodplain known as the Inland Niger Delta. The Senegal River is a key feature in the west. It originates at the junction of the Bafing and Bakoye Rivers near the town of Bafoulabé and runs in a northwesterly direction into neighboring Senegal and Mauritania and eventually into the Atlantic Ocean. These riverine environments have played an important role in Mali in the realms of agriculture and trade for generations.

Almost 12 million people live in Mali, per a 2007 estimate. The population density increases from north to south, with the vast majority of the nation living in the southern third of the country. Roughly 90 percent of the overall population lives in rural areas. Bamako, the capital city on the banks of the Niger River, is home to approximately 1 million residents. It has been estimated that 2 million more Malians live abroad as migrant workers. Mali is a culturally diverse country with several major ethnic groups: the Bamana (roughly one-third of the population), the Maninka, and the Fula, and a large set of smaller ethnic groups.

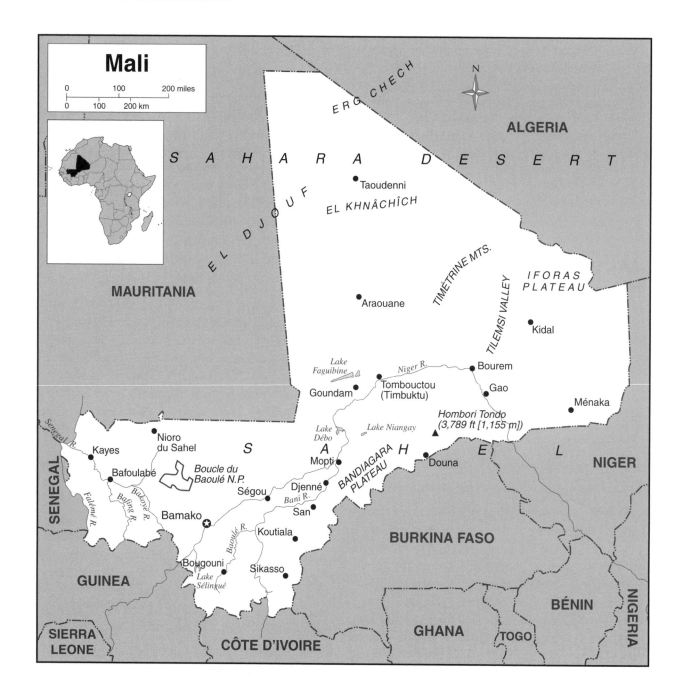

For Mali's people, the task of making a living is a challenging one. The overall geography presents real obstacles for the nation's subsistence-oriented herders and farmers with such environmental factors as poor soil quality and drought playing major roles. For commercial producers, global terms of trade are disadvantageous at best. As a result of these combined factors, Mali is one of the poorest countries in the world with a gross national income per person of roughly US$290 in 2003. However, over the millennia, the diverse peoples of this country who have a rich cultural history have developed livelihood strategies that are sensitive to their homeland's daunting geography and difficult niche in the global economy.

The shifting sands of the northern region have witnessed the rise of a well-developed pastoral economy, one that typically meets subsistence needs while also contributing to one of the country's dominant export arenas: livestock. A 2005 estimate suggests that animal husbandry accounts for about a third of the primary sector's contribution to the gross domestic product. Likewise, the farming peoples of the southern tier have managed to construct a viable agrarian system based on the cultivation of millet, sorghum, and rice for direct consumption, and have added commercial production of cotton for foreign markets. The agricultural sector engages roughly 80 percent of the population. Since the colonial period when commercial production was widely expanded, cotton has become the country's chief agricultural export, accounting for approximately 22 percent of all export earnings in 2003. With strong government support, Mali has become the second leading producer of cotton on the African continent, following Egypt. It is notable that Mali was among the strongest proponents of cotton subsidy reform during recent debates within the World Trade Organization (WTO). In fact, the WTO ruled in favor of Mali and its allies against the United States and the European Union, although the ruling has not translated into action.

In the industrial and business sectors, new entrepreneurs have launched successful enterprises that engage a growing number of formal wage earners. Gold, which played a major role in precolonial trade dynamics in the region, has recently moved into a primary position within Mali's national economy. Industrial gold mining operations have expanded considerably, to a level where the precious metal has become Mali's leading export. In 2001 Mali was Africa's third largest producer, behind South Africa and Ghana respectively. At the same time, more and more people enter the informal labor sector in Bamako, Segou, and other smaller urban areas. Malians have also left their homeland in record numbers to find employment abroad in Europe, Asia, and North America.

Upon gaining its independence from France in 1960, Mali, under its first president Modibo Keita, followed a socialist development pathway with the state playing a central role in ownership and planning. In 1968 Moussa Traore took power in a coup d'etat and, until 1992, led a one-party government that increasingly oriented its development agenda toward a more pro-Western approach. With the ousting of the longstanding dictator and installation of Alpha Oumar Konare in the early 1990s, the country's transition to multiparty democracy and a free market economy was in full swing.

In 2002 Amadou Toumani Touré took the reigns of power and, as of 2007, he continued to lead Mali toward a Western-style government and economy. From a statistical standpoint, the results along this road have been mixed. In the 1980s, GDP increased at an annual rate of 2.8 percent. The 1990s saw ups and downs. In 1994 Mali went through a 50 percent devaluation of its currency (the CFA franc), a move that was paralleled by a fall in global commodity prices. This checked the rate of growth significantly. However, between 1996 and 1999 the economy rebounded with an average 5.7 percent growth in GDP. The early years of the new millennium were marked by drought that once again hindered economic growth, with rates falling to 2–3 percent. Since 2000, as gold production has expanded, the growth rate has been rising.

See also **Climate; Desertification, Modern; Famine; Metals and Minerals; Niger River; Sahara Desert; Timbuktu; Touré, Amadou Toumani; Transportation.**

BIBLIOGRAPHY

Bingen, R. James; David Robinson; and John M. Staatz; eds. *Democracy and Development in Mali.* East Lansing: Michigan State University Press, 2000.

Imperato, Pascal James. *Historical Dictionary of Mali.* Lanham, MD: Scarecrow Press, 1996.

Koenig, Dolores. *Innovation and Individuality in African Development: Changing Production Strategies in Rural Mali.* Ann Arbor: University of Michigan Press, 1998.

Wooten, Stephen, ed. *Wari Matters: Ethnographic Explorations of Money in the Mande World.* Berlin: Lit Verlag, 2005.

STEPHEN WOOTEN

SOCIETY AND CULTURES

For more than six hundred years Mali has been at the center of multiple networks of trade and social exchange between the peoples of the southwestern rain forest zone and those of the Sahel and the Sahara to the north. The Niger River has been critical to the formation of those networks. Flowing north from the Fouta Djallon mountain range (in present-day Guinea) through the center of Mali just over the border of the Sahel and then bending south (through Niger and Nigeria), ultimately emptying into the Bight of Bénin, the Niger River has served for centuries as a principal artery of traffic and long-distance trade—and sometimes warfare. Beginning in medieval times, the Niger gave rise to an urban culture, including such cities as Jenné, Mopti, and Segu, the economies of which were originally based on warfare and trade in slaves, salt, gold, and other goods. Standing in sharp contrast to those are Malian cities dating from the premodern period that have achieved their importance since French colonial rule, such as the capital, Bamako.

The characteristically high mobility of the Malian people has created a web of social relations and commercial networks that crisscrosses the country and transcends national boundaries. These networks are based on kinship, alliance, and common regional origin. Families are organized hierarchically not only in terms of sex but also age and generation, and they are generally patrilineal, patrilocal, and polygynous. Since the late nineteenth century, urbanization and the migration of youth in search of labor have weakened the family's authoritarian structure. Nevertheless, especially in rural areas, authority and control within the family remains in the hands of the eldest male of the senior generation. In contrast, in the regions to the north of Mali, authority within many families of the Tuareg, Moors, and others has been substantially undermined by ecological degradation and concomitant migration, and also by the political crises that made refugees of numerous groups beginning in the 1970s.

The family is the principal unit of production in Mali, engaged primarily in subsistence farming. Similar to many other African societies, children participate in the family production starting at an early age: in 2003, about 52 percent of all Malian children aged ten to fourteen were estimated to work full- or part-time. Considering the extremely limited number of job opportunities for people with a school education, many parents, in particular farmers, have little incentive to send their children to public school. From the early 1990s, considerable governmental effort has been directed toward increasing literacy rates and primary school enrollment to as much as 50 percent by the year 2000. As a result of these efforts, the rate of public school enrollment in Mali has been growing (with approximately 49% of Malian children of primary school age attending public school in 1997). Still, adult illiteracy rates continue to figure above 50 percent. A 2003 estimate indicates a literacy rate of 46.4

percent among people over the age of fourteen (men 53%, women 39%).

One reason primary and secondary school enrollment has been growing so slowly is that, because of the rudimentary labor market, the public educational system offers little guarantee of employment. In the meantime, many parents, particularly in rural Mali, prefer to enroll their children at traditional Qur'anic schools or at reformed Islamic educational institutions. The latter only offer training in worldly affairs but promises to form ethically responsible members of society.

Many Malian cultural groups distinguish between different categories of people according to their social origins: first, those who are of free or noble birth; second, the descendants of serfs; and third, professional specialists, called *nyamakala* (in Bambara), who perform specialized services for free-born patrons. Historically, those born into a nyamakala family worked as blacksmiths, potters, leathermakers, as specialists of elaborate speech and musical performance, and as mediators in cases of conflict. They have attracted considerable scholarly attention because of their seemingly ambiguous social status: On the one hand, free-born people both fear and respect them because they are said to control *nyama*, a powerful albeit impure occult force; on the other hand, nobles hold them in contempt because of their contamination with nyama. As a consequence of radical social and political change under colonial rule, in the early twenty-first century many people of nyamakala descent no longer pursue the trade traditionally associated with their origin. Yet they are still considered a distinct social category and occasionally are called upon to engage in social mediation. Some women of nyamakala descent capitalize on the recent introduction of various media technologies to turn their considerable musical skills into a source of income. They perform their traditional music in front of national and international audiences and, in the process, become pop icons of a modern and cosmopolitan female African identity.

Mali is composed of a number of what have often been considered distinct ethnic groups. Each so-called ethnic group does have its own language and particular cultural practices. In any given region, however, networks of commerce and migration that promote cultural and commercial exchange often mitigate the differences between the cultural practices, languages, and economic activities of these groups. In the past, when families or individuals moved from one area to another, they integrated themselves into the sociopolitical hierarchy of their new community where they would acquire a newly fashioned ethnic identity. They often also learned new skills to practice a novel profession, and adopted the predominant language of their new home, sometimes favoring it over their native language. For this reason, a person's family name, clan identity, and place of origin play a greater role in forming his or her identity than that person's ethnic or linguistic affiliation.

Other social institutions support the blurring of ethnic divisions. These include hunter organizations and, in town, Islamic associations. Hunters' organizations, most of which exist in the rural areas of southern Mali, assimilate people of diverse ethnic origins into single, overarching social units. Historically, hunting, associated with knowledge of magic and other powers necessary to dominate the forces of the wilderness, has been of marginal economic importance though of great symbolic significance. Not surprisingly, then, oral accounts portray the legendary kings of the medieval southern empires as hunter-heroes who relied on supernatural powers to establish and maintain their rule. In contemporary Mali, city dwellers still reminisce about hunter organizations that, in the context of a state-promoted politics of cultural authenticity, have become a dominant symbol of a heroic past.

Islamic associations, in contrast, tend to be associated by their members with an urban, anonymous society and a modern Muslim identity. Similar to hunters' associations, Islamic associations cut across social and ethnic divisions. Unlike hunters' associations, however, they are primarily an urban phenomenon; and they mobilize numerous female members who regularly meet in neighborhood groups to acquire Arabic literacy and religious knowledge.

Although trade networks, migration, hunters' organizations, and Islamic associations foster the fluidity of ethnic boundaries, it is common both in and outside the country to refer to Malian peoples by ethnic names. Ethnic identity also plays a vital part in contemporary Malian national politics.

REGIONAL CULTURAL PRACTICES AND ETHNIC GROUPS

Islam spread to the area of contemporary Mali in several historical movements. Peoples in the north of Mali were exposed to Islamic influence brought to them across the Saharan desert by the Almoravid warriors since the eleventh century. Under the kingdom of Mali in the thirteenth and fourteenth centuries, Dyula traders created islands of Muslim faith and practice in the savanna towns of southern Mali and northern Côte d'Ivoire. In the fifteenth and sixteenth centuries, the northern cities of Timbuktu, Jenné, and Gao turned into centers of Islamic erudition and into nodal points not only for trade in salt, slaves, and gold, but also for scholarly intellectual exchange across the Sahara. From there, Islamic culture expanded southward as the Songhay Empire extended its control to Segu in the sixteenth century. But only in the colonial period did broad segments of the rural population, especially in Mali's southern triangle, convert to Islam.

In the early twenty-first century, Islam is the religion of 90 percent of the total Malian population, rural and urban. Because local practices and institutions of Islam are infused with traditional understandings of esoteric knowledge and power, there exists considerable debate among Muslims about proper religious observance. The few Christians, primarily Catholic, are mostly Dogon and Bobo, and comprise only 1 percent of the total Malian population. Traditional religious practices that are still mostly unaffected by Islam are to be found among the Bobo, the Senufo-Minianka, and the Dogon.

People who speak Mande-related languages native to the country's southern and central regions—approximately 50 percent of the total population—dominate Mali politically. These people live in the core areas of the former kingdoms of Ghana, Mali, Segu, and Kaarta and are strongly represented, both locally and nationally, in political and administrative positions. Among them, the Bambara (or Bamana, as they call themselves), who cultivate mainly millet and sorghum in a northward-pointing triangle located between the borders of the Côte d'Ivoire and Mauritania, form the largest group. Their language, Bambara, is the lingua franca of commerce throughout Mali. Together with French, Bambara is used in public

République du Mali (Republic of Mali)

Population:	11,995,402 (2007 est.)
Area:	1,240,007 sq. km (478,767 sq. mi.)
Official language:	French
Languages:	Bambara, French
National currency:	CFA franc
Principal religions:	Muslim 90%, indigenous 9%, Christian 1%
Capital:	Bamako (est. pop. 1,000,000 in 2006)
Other urban centers:	Segou, Sikasso, Mopti, Gao, Kayes, Timbuktu
Annual rainfall:	varies from 500–1,500 mm (20–60 in.) in south to 175–500 mm (7–20 in.) in sahelian zone to 0–175 mm (0–7 in.) in saharan zone
Principal geographical features:	*Mountains:* Adrar des Iforas, Timetrine Mountains, Manding Mountains, Bandiagara Plateau, Hombori Mountains *Lakes:* Faguibine, Garou, Do, Niangay, Debo, Sélingue, Télé, Oro, Fati, Haribomo, Aougoundou, Kabara, Tanda, and other seasonal lakes *Rivers:* Senegal, Niger (Joliba), Bafing, Bakoye, Bani, Baoulé, Bagoé, Falémé, Sankarani
Economy:	*GDP per capita:* US$1,300 (2006)
Principal products and exports:	*Agricultural:* cotton, millet, rice, corn, vegetables, peanuts, cattle, sheep, goats *Manufacturing:* food and beverage processing, textiles, cement, cigarettes, pharmaceuticals, plastics, soap, farm implements *Mining:* gold, phosphates, salt, limestone, marble
Government:	Independence from France, 1960. Constitution, 1960. New constitution approved 1974, enacted 1979. New constitution approved in 1992. Multiparty democracy. President elected for 5-year term by universal suffrage. 147-member Assemblée Nationale elected for 5-year terms by universal suffrage. President appoints prime minister and cabinet. For purposes of local government there are 6 regions divided into 42 cercles (counties).
Heads of state since independence:	1960–1968: President Modibo Keita 1968: Lieutenant Moussa Traoré and Captain Yoro Diakité 1968–1969: Captain Yoro Diakité, acting chairman of Comité Militaire pour la Libération Nationale (CMLN) 1969–1979: Colonel Moussa Traoré, chairman of the CMLN 1979–1991: President Moussa Traoré 1991–1992: Lieutenant Colonel Amadou Toumani Touré, chairman of the Comité de Transition pour le Salut du Peuple 1992–2002: President Alpha Oumar Konaré 2002–: President Amadou Toumani Touré
Armed forces:	*Army:* 6,900 *Navy:* 50 *Air force:* 400 *Paramilitary:* 1,800
Transportation:	*Rail:* 729 km (453 mi.) *Roads:* 18,709 km (11,625 mi.), 18% paved *Airlines:* International flights by Air Afrique and privately owned Trans Air Mali; domestic flights by national Mali Tombouctou Air Service, Air Mali *Airports:* International facilities at Bamako, 7 domestic airports throughout the country
Media:	2 daily newspapers: *L'Essor-La Voix du Peuple, Bulletin Quotidien de la Chambre de Commerce et d'Industrie du Mali ;* 13 other main periodicals. No publishing. Radiodiffusion Nationale du Mali provides radio. There is 1 television station.
Literacy and Education:	*Total literacy rate:* 46.4% Education is universal, free, and compulsory from ages 6–15. About half of children receive primary education. Postsecondary education provided by École Nationale d'Administration, École Nationale d'Ingénieurs, École de Médecine et Dentisterie, École Normale Supérieure, Centre Pédagogique Supérieur, Institut Polytechnique Rural de Katibougou. There is no university.

administration and in national media broadcasting. Closely related to the Bambara people in language and traditions are the Malinke, agriculturists who are concentrated in the southwest, and the Dyula, who as traders cover Mali's entire southern triangle. The Soninké, who inhabit central Mali, also speak a Mande-related language. They live primarily in the regions of Nioro and Segu and are involved in both agriculture and livestock raising, as well as in national and international trade.

The Dogon, the Bobo, and the Senufo-Minianka live in southwestern Mali. Although their ancestors had once been under the sway of the medieval Mande emperors, they still maintain some traditions and practices that clearly distinguish them from the Mande-speaking societies. Similar to some people from the north, they are underrepresented in political and administrative positions. Nevertheless, they have been well integrated into Mali's cotton export economy since colonial times.

In the northeast, the Songhay and the Fulani (or Peulh) dominate the Niger Bend. The Songhay, descendants of those people who built the Songhay Empire, grow millet and sorghum and raise livestock. Many of the Fulani were originally nomadic cattle herders who became sedentary as a result of serious cattle losses during the extended droughts of the 1970s and 1980s. The Fulani are especially numerous in the Mopti, Segu, Sikasso, and Nioro regions where they herd not only their own livestock but also that of other ethnic groups. Another group inhabiting the Niger Bend is the Bozo, who are predominantly agriculturists and fishers.

The droughts of the 1970s and 1980s have also seriously impaired the subsistence activities of the Tuareg and the Moors, northern people who are made up of both Berber groups and former slaves captured from among the people of southern Mali. The Tuareg and the Moors are mainly pastoralists and traders, and inhabit the vast areas of the northern Sahel and the Sahara. The lifestyle of the Tuareg, more than that of the Moors, was strongly affected by colonization, which the Tuareg resisted vigorously. Moreover, since independence, these northern peoples have benefited comparatively little from the government's investment in infrastructure and, in general, have been denied political participation at the national level. Largely as a consequence of these two disadvantages—that had devastating ramifications for the northern people during the droughts—many Tuareg and the Moors have cast their opposition specifically as a matter of ethnic conflict between themselves and the southern, Mande-speaking peoples. Some of them capitalized on the winds of change brought by the end of single party-rule in 1991 to engage in an armed rebellion, which ended in an, albeit shaky, truce in 1996.

Another consequence of the droughts and of the precarious living conditions in the Sahelian zone has been the migration of young men to work as wage laborers in Bamako and other countries in western Africa, such as Côte d'Ivoire, Ghana, Sierra Leone, and Gabon; some have even migrated to France. Between the 1970s and 1990s, Malians formed large expatriate communities (up to 20% of the foreign population of other countries in western Africa) while maintaining strong ties to their families in Mali through letters, radio messages, and cash remissions. Some of these expatriate communities have been disrupted by civil strife in the respective countries that often led to the forceful expulsion of Malian migrant workers. In other West African countries and in France and the United States, expatriate Malians continue to create cultural organizations that allow them to preserve and partly recreate the cultural traditions of their home communities, and to reassess the importance of safeguarding a Muslim identity in a diasporic situation. Thus, the high mobility and cultural flexibility that have in the past characterized Malians continue within and beyond the borders of the present nation-state.

See also **Bamako; Côte d'Ivoire; Ethnicity; Famine; Gao; Jenné and Jenné-jeno; Moors in African History; Niger River; Timbuktu.**

BIBLIOGRAPHY

Amselle, Jean-Loup. *Mestizo Logics. Anthropology of Identity in Africa and Elsewhere.* Stanford, CA: Stanford University Press, 1998.

Brenner, Louis. *Controlling Knowledge. Religion, Power, and Schooling in a West African Muslim Society.* Bloomington: Indiana University Press, 2001.

Conrad, David. *Empires of Medieval West Africa: Ghana, Mali, and Songhay.* New York: Facts on File, 2005.

Jansen, Jan, and Clemens Zobel, eds. *The Younger Brother in Mande: Kinship and Politics in West Africa.* Selected papers from the Third International Conference on Mande Studies, Leiden, 1995. Leiden, the Netherlands: The Research School of Asian, African, and Amerindian Studies, 1996.

McNaughton, Patrick. *The Mande Blacksmiths: Knowledge, Power, and Art in West Africa.* Bloomington: Indiana University Press, 1988.

Schulz, Dorothea E. "Music Videos and the Effeminate Vices of Urban Culture in Mali." *Africa* 71, no. 3 (2001).

DOROTHEA E. SCHULZ

HISTORY AND POLITICS

Mali sits at the crossroads of regional, continental, and global history dating back more than 1200 years. The Ghana Empire (or Wagadu), centered in southern Mauritania/northwestern Mali, flourished between the ninth and twelfth centuries due to control over long distance trade in salt, gold, slaves, and other commodities. These routes connected coasts east and south with trans-Saharan traders and, through these traders, to Europe and the Middle East. An eleventh-century invasion by Muslim Berbers based in the Sahara (the Almoravid invasion) focused on Ghana's gold mines and weakened the Empire. In the twelfth century the Mali Empire supplanted Ghana. At its height, the Mali Empire extended from Fouta Djallon in the west to Gao in the east. The Empire's rulers represented a new configuration of elite power: long-distance traders, a rising qUlama intelligentsia that grew in influence as Islam spread into West Africa, slavers, and a large, permanent military establishment. In 1468 the Songhay Empire, based in Gao, supplanted Mali. Songhay represented an intensification of both the role of military might and Islam in the control of the region's economy.

The decline of Mali and rise of Songhay turned the middle Niger River Valley into a contested buffer that linked the Sahara and North Africa with the savanna and forest regions in the south. In 1591 a Moroccan invasion destroyed Songhay and produced disarray in the zone. Seizing this opportunity, Bamana farmers organized the Segu kingdom around 1660. Segu relied on warfare, slave-taking, and pillage for its force, and its power grew along with the Atlantic slave trade. Around 1818 a Fulani Islamic caliphate, Macina, arose in the inner Niger Delta and challenged Segu's power. Macina was one of several jihadist movements in West Africa in the eighteenth and nineteenth centuries. It received important support from Sokoto Caliphate to the east and represented a rejection of both the militarism and brutality of Segu and the long-standing dominance of Timbuktu's Islamic scholars. Macina then fell in 1862 to the Tukulor army led by Al-Hajj Umar Tal.

MALI UNDER COLONIALISM

The Tukulor conquest coincided with French colonial penetration into the interior of West Africa.

In Mali, the Tukulor period was a time of brutality, economic decline, and anarchy. When the French moved decisively into the interior of West Africa in the 1870s, much of the population welcomed them in the hopes of an end to Tukulor violence. France defeated the Tukulors and in 1892 established the colony of French Sudan. Over the next forty-five years the colony would change boundaries, names, and forms of affiliation with the French West Africa federation headquartered in Dakar.

The French hold on the Sudanese countryside was tenuous. They underinvested in the colony, found no high-value natural resources, and failed at cotton and rice exportation. France's greatest impacts on the population were social. Forced labor disrupted local production systems and increased generational tensions as elder males—relied upon by colonial administrators—were given the authority to produce lists of laborers. Recruitment for World Wars I and II resulted in the death of thousands of Sudanese subjects but was also important for generating resistance to both colonial and customary authorities when the soldiers returned home.

Colonialism produced a new urban elite that was French educated and that looked to salaried colonial jobs as status symbols and as an escape from customary hierarchies. It was from this group that Mali's earliest colonial resistance movements emerged, centered in cultural organizations. One such organization was the Arts et Travail society founded in 1937 by Modibo Keita (1915–1977). It later gained greater political traction through Keita's affiliation with the Communist Party, and from support from one of West Africa's earliest women's movements led by Aoua Keita (1912–1980).

Keita later made savvy use of the French effort to install limited democratic party politics from the mid-1940s onward. Two lead parties emerged in the Sudan: the Union Soudanaise-Rassemblement Démocratique Africain (USRDA) and the Parti Soudanais Progressiste (PSP). The two represented a split between an urbanized, educated, unionized new generation (the USRDA) and a rural, conservative old guard (the PSP) supported by rural chiefs. Keita's USRDA won local elections in the late 1950s.

MALI AFTER INDEPENDENCE

Mali gained independence in 1960 and adopted a single party state. Keita repudiated the currency in use throughout much of Francophone West Africa (the franc de la Communauté Financière de l'Afrique, or CFA franc), created the Mali franc, and saw GDP decline by 2 percent annually between 1963–1968 while smuggling and the black market grew. The state became ever more repressive as it scrambled for economic stability and in 1968 the army overthrew Keita.

The new regime, led by President Moussa Traoré (b. 1936), maintained centralized control of the economy. In 1979 Traoré declared the Union Démocratique du Peuple Malien (UDPM) the sole legal political party, and the country became more deeply divided by patrimonial networks. The late 1970s witnessed important resistance to Traoré and the UDPM, resistance especially rooted in the higher education sector.

The 1980s saw a deepening of Mali's debt problems and the government grudgingly signed a series of structural adjustment accords. Resistance to the state arose—as during the colonial period—in the cultural and arts sector. This time, Alpha Oumar Konaré (b. 1946), a former UDPM Minister, was at its center. By 1990, the Traoré government was in crisis and a second coup, led by a coalition of workers, students, and intellectuals ensued in 1991.

Multiparty democratic elections led to the selection of Konaré as president. A vibrant and free press arose. The government negotiated an important peace settlement in the mid-1990s with leaders of a Tuareg uprising in the north, an achievement that included significant devolution of decision-making authority and resources. The economy grew at about 4.6 percent throughout the decade, foreign direct investment increased quickly, and Mali became the leading cotton exporter in sub-Saharan Africa and one of the leaders in gold production. National elections in 1992, 1997, and 2002 led to peaceful transitions between officeholders and majority political parties. The state instituted decentralization that devolved much decision-making and, in principle, resources to 701 newly created communes; communal elections in 1999 and 2004 were widely praised as free and fair.

Both the economy and political momentum have slowed since the election of Amadou Toumani Touré as president in 2002. Few benefits from either economic liberalization or democratic decentralization have reached Mali's rural masses, and important limits to growth loom in both the cotton and gold sectors. The country's biggest challenge in the coming years will be to find ways to extend the potential economic and political benefits to a much wider population

See also **Colonial Polocies and Practices; Desertification, Modern; Gao; Hamallah of Nioro; Postcolonialism; Senghor, Léopold Sédar; Slave Trades; Slavery and Servile Institutions; Timbuktu; Touré, Amadou Toumani; World War I; World War II.**

BIBLIOGRAPHY

Bingen, R. James; David Robinson; and John M. Staatz; eds. *Democracy and Development in Mali.* East Lansing: Michigan State University Press, 2000.

Hunwick, John O., ed. *Timbuktu and the Songhay Empire: Al-Sa'di's Ta'rikh al-Sudan down to 1613, and Other Contemporary Documents.* Leiden, The Netherlands: Brill, 1999.

Levtzion, Nehemia. *Ancient Ghana and Mali.* New York: Africana Publishing, 1980.

McIntosh, Roderick James. *The Peoples of the Middle Niger: The Island of Gold.* Malden, MA: Blackwell Publishers, Inc., 1998.

Roberts, Richard L. *Two Worlds of Cotton: Colonialism and the Regional Economy in the French Sudan, 1800-1946.* Stanford, CA: Stanford University Press, 1996.

Robinson, David. *The Holy War of Umar Tal: The Western Sudan in the Mid-Nineteenth Century.* Oxford: Clarendon Press, 1985.

KENT GLENZER

MAMI WATA.

One of the most widely known icons in Democratic Republic of the Congo's popular culture is the mermaid, called Mami Wata (mammy water) in the west and Mamba Muntu (crocodile/snake person) in the east. The imagery of Mami Wata provides commentary upon the world in which money and commodities mediate social relations. Paintings of her are related to the painted portrait (in Congo-Kinshasa, always based upon a photograph) that serves as a declaration of the social legitimacy of the individual. Mami Wata tells how to succeed in the world of postcolonial modernity and, at the same time, is a reminder of the social price of such success. The acceptance of Mami Wata in Congo-Kinshasa was matched by social commentary that condemned association with her because the wealth she provides is not shared. The Mami Wata icon divides the world into two spheres, the masculine and the feminine, which are strictly distinct but irrevocably linked. The image recalls the opposition of these spheres with regard to access to social power, mimicking the opposites of nature and culture, tradition and modernity. In purely European and North American terms, Mami Wata is a representation of the liberal world of winners and losers who partake unequally in a finite stock of wealth where everything has a price.

In postcolonial Congo-Kinshasa, the mermaid symbolically reproduces the colonial universe of race/gender relations, in which the white woman was kept outside the world of the colonized common people. The artists give her those attributes of her sex that the colonial culture publicly acknowledged, but deprived her of the attributes that make a fecund woman, a mother of children, sexually attractive. Her ample nude breasts are displayed, but her buttocks are encased in the tail of a fish. Mami Wata stands in opposition to the legitimate wife, who guarantees the continuity and prosperity of the group, and whose representation emphasizes attributes of fertility.

She is painted black only when representing the so-called free woman, the one with whom man stays for pleasure, but not to perpetuate a group. Their contractual relationship is based on seduction and an exchange of services between two individuals. This seduction, at the core of Congolese urban music of the 1950s and 1960s, is the central

Mami Wata as spirit/lover who offers success to her man. Chéri Benga plays with the traditional image, presenting himself as Mami Wata's protégé who has the advantage of publicizing his professional skills without offending anyone else because he is crediting his success to a Mami Wata. FROM THE COLLECTION OF BOGUMIL JEWSIEWICKI.

issue in Mami Wata imagery, alongside the question of modern wealth (access to commodities and services). Contrary to a co-wife, a free woman as the lover of an urban man is resented by wives as one who, in preventing a man from sharing all his wealth with the family, undermines social order. Mami Wata does the same; the wealth and power she provides to her lover is to be enjoyed personally, renouncement of procreation or death by sorcery of family members is the price to pay.

It is difficult to establish a solid link between the image of Mami Wata and the colonial Christian missionary culture. The Marian cult, and the Catholic organization Légion Marie, came to the Belgian Congo relatively late. Before the 1950s, images of the Virgin and explicit references to her as one who interceded between believers and God were rare. As elsewhere, women available to participate in organized parish activities were limited to the towns, where African women did not become numerous until after World War II. The establishment of the Légion Marie appears to coincide with an increase in the number of Christian women, and to have shortly preceded the popularity of Mami Wata.

In the Belgian Congo, the white woman was a powerful sexual object of desire, strictly reserved for white men. Most white women lived in urban centers. With the few exceptions of nuns, they performed no work; even in domestic spaces black men were those who worked. Until the 1950s, when white women settled in the colony in greater numbers, it was common for a white man to keep an African mistress, but not to accept the paternity of children. Interracial desire and seduction were experienced as matters of power between political bodies so separated that sexual relationship had to remain socially sterile. These elements, combined with the Marian cult, explain how the mermaid came to be symbolically represented as a non-black (white, Asian) woman; not even a woman but the pure object of man's desire for power. Mami Wata lures men to modernity but wealth and the powers she procures are used to the detriment of the social group.

The idea of a half-woman, half-fish aquatic being combines many elements: precolonial beliefs in aquatic spirits, the partly empirically based conviction that whites were ghosts who came from beyond the sea (their white skin called to mind the appearance of a drowning victim), and elements of West African folklore. Anglophone West Africans played

an important role in the construction of urban society and culture, particularly in western Congo-Kinshasa. Soldiers came first, then educated agents of commercial and industrial companies, and finally sailors. They were the founders of the first dance clubs, introducing European styles and the first social dance music. They also imported the name Mami Wata. By contrast, in southeastern Congo-Kinshasa, she is called Mamba Muntu (snake/crocodile person), referring to the sorcery with which the crocodile is associated and to sin represented by the snake. It appears that these two symbols of evil—ancestral sorcery and Christian sin—contributed in the 1970s to the spread of the image of Mami Wata all over Congo-Kinshasa.

In northeastern Congo-Kinshasa, artists pictured a Muslim adoring the mermaid as she emerges from the water. The few local Muslims are either descendants of the Swahili-speaking nineteenth-century traders or businessmen from the Levant. Their striking economic success and their exclusive relations with politicians and army officers gave rise to the conviction that their power comes from Mami Wata.

Visually, the representation of Mami Wata owes much to colonial imagery that widely published images of black women in which they were treated as ethnographic and sexual objects. Many curios postcards, modestly entitled young woman from such a tribe (such as Mangbetu young woman or Mongo girl), made her bared breasts face the viewer, whereas the lower part of the body remained outside of the visual field. Some of these images depicted her holding a mirror, a sorcery and divination device in Congo-Kinshasa.

A hybrid form of her representation makes visually explicit the paradigm of access to wealth and power in postcolonial modernity. The paintings of Mami Wata, which could be purchased in the 1960s and 1970s for the price of three or four bottles of beer, expressed in public space the paradigm for social success for all men. In this image, an honorary white woman, since she is white only from outside, opened the way through the great gulf that separated blacks from whites, the powerful from those condemned to being exploited, the modern from the traditional, and so on. Since these two worlds could not be merged, the prosperity of an individual's community of origin became the price of his success. A man who benefited from her favors repaid Mami Wata with the lives of his kin.

Kinshasa inhabitants dreaming of emigrating to the West while virtually getting letters and drinks from relatives already living there. A TV set is now taking the place of Mami Wata's image in inspiring people's dreams about modernity. Painting by Shula, Kinshasa, 2002. FROM THE COLLECTION OF BOGUMIL JEWSIEWICKI.

The mermaid is usually accompanied by a snake and sometimes holds a cup into which the latter dips its tongue. She carries a watch, some jewels, a comb and a mirror, and sometimes a book that represents the Bible. Like Eve, she seduces black men with the promise of knowledge and power. This promise of access to knowledge is underlined by the mirror she carries; it is a widely recognized divination tool in both the non-Christian cults and the syncretic churches. Sometimes Mami Wata wears glasses, initially associated with whites, then with educated people, and perceived as a tool that permits better sight with which to conspire on the side of power.

Since the 1980s, Christian imagery, especially images of Christ and scenes from the Old Testament, are replacing Mami Wata as an evocative protective force, a promise of divine intercession. In the parlor of the urban home where one once found a Mami Wata, in the early twenty-first century one sees the Christian religious images that painters mass produce.

There have long been rumors that all the powerful men who arose as religious or political leaders, including Mobutu Sese Seko, had a Mami Wata. Yet by the end of the 1980s, the mermaid had lost her popularity, replaced by West African marabouts (Islamic holy men) and numerous secret societies, satanic cults, and eastern cults, all fueled by mysticism.

In Congolese culture, Mami Wata was, and still is, the representation of the relationship between power and the individual male. She speaks with great clarity about the political culture of

Mami Wata brings business success. In the eastern part of the Congo, Muslim traders' success in business is attributed to the connection between Islamic magic and Mami Wata's powers. Painting by Londa, Bunia, 1986. FROM THE COLLECTION OF BOGUMIL JEWSIEWICKI.

Mobutu's regime. Success in life, money, women, and power could not come without the arbitrary power of the president or one of the vassals who acted in his name. To attract the attention of one of the powerful, just as to attract the attention of a Mami Wata by stealing her comb or her mirror, might just as well open the doors to prosperity as the doors of hell. Like that of Mami Wata, the generosity of the president was capricious and unpredictable; the least disloyalty, the slightest attempt at autonomy, became punishable by exclusion from his inner circle.

Henry Drewal's edited book and Fowler Museum for Cultural History exhibit present a broad, comparative, panorama of water spirits worshipped all over the Black Atlantic. In West Africa, a Mami Wata spirit is worshipped by many believers

at once; the same Mami Wata can do a favor for many believers, unlike in the Democratic Republic of the Congo where a Mami Wata cannot have a relationship with more than one man.

There is no Mami Wata for women; instead, the successes of market women are attributed to sleeping with the serpent, the Christian symbol of evil, that, after each copulation, vomits up money. It should be noted that if the image of the mermaid is beautiful, that of *nguma* (the serpent) is ugly. From a male point of view there is a double contradiction. The first is that a rich woman holds power while she is supposed be a mediator between a man and power. The second contradiction is she that has money that properly belongs only to a man, because in a colonial society he was the only salaried worker. The black woman should have access to money only through a man, whose power in the city resides in his access to and control over modernity.

See also **Religion and Ritual; Symbols and Symbolism.**

BIBLIOGRAPHY

Drewal, Henry. "Performing the Other: Mami Wata Worship in Africa." *Drama Review* 32, no. 2 (1988): 160–185.

Drewal, Henry, ed. *Sacred Waters: Arts for Mami Wata*. Bloomington: Indiana University Press, 2007.

Jewsiewicki, Bogumil. *Mami Wata. La peinture urbaine au Congo*. Paris: Editions Gallimard, 2003.

BOGUMIL JEWSIEWICKI

MANDELA, NELSON (1918–). Nelson Mandela was born to Henry Gadla Mphakanyiswa (1880–1928) and Nosekeni Fanny Mandela at Mbhashe in the Umtata district of the Transkei. Henry Gadla, a scion of the Thembu royal house and a chief, was not in line for the succession and was later deposed for insubordination. Fanny Mandela, a devout Methodist, was his third wife. This meant that her son, Nelson, could not inherit the chieftainship. His exclusion from local prospects set the young Mandela on the course of education. He took up urban politics and that paved the way for his interest in the presidency of South Africa.

The nine-year-old Nelson Mandela, as arranged by his father, traveled to Mqekezweni after his father's death, where the acting chief of the Ama-Thembu, Jongintaba David Dalindyebo (d. 1942), took charge of his education. He enrolled at the local school and eventually gained admission in 1938 to Fort Hare College, the missionary-run educational center for the most promising African youths of the era, but was expelled in 1940 for engaging in a strike action. In 1941 he traveled to Johannesburg, where he took up temporary employment as a policeman at the mines and met Walter Sisulu (1912–2003), then among the founders of the nascent African National Congress (ANC), who encouraged him to study law. Mandela simultaneously enrolled for a BA by correspondence, which he obtained in 1942, and went on to study law at Witwatersrand University. Here he

was exposed to Indian and white students and to radical, liberal, and Africanist thought. He joined the African National Congress and in 1944 founded the ANC Youth League with Walter Sisulu and Oliver Tambo (1917–1993).

In 1948 the Afrikaner National Party came into power and began institutionalizing racism as apartheid. A spate of racist laws were passed in quick succession, among them the Group Areas Act of 1950, which ultimately resulted in the uprooting of millions of Black, Coloured, and Indian people, and the Bantu Education Act of 1953, designed to make sure that Africans remained menial laborers.

The ANC, with Mandela on its executive committee, responded by adopting a program of militant action against the Nationalists. In 1951 the ANC organized a national work stoppage in cooperation with the Indian Congress. This was followed in 1952 with the Defiance of Unjust Laws Campaign, in which 8,577 volunteers defied racist laws and were subsequently imprisoned. The outbreak of violence and the six-month banning of fifty-two leaders, among them Mandela and the newly elected president-general of the ANC, Albert Luthuli (c. 1898–1967), ended that campaign. Banning orders restricted the rights of movement and association. In 1953 Mandela was served with his second such banning order, this one for two years. A third, five-year, banning order came in 1956.

On June 25–26, 1955, the ANC and other anti-apartheid organizations convened the Congress of the People in Kliptown, just outside Johannesburg, at which some three thousand delegates adopted the Freedom Charter as a blueprint for a nonracial, democratic South Africa. Discontent over the charter within the ANC and alleged white and communist influence resulted in a split in 1958 and led to the formation of the Pan-African Congress (PAC) under the leadership of Robert Sobukwe (1924–1978). Meanwhile, the government declared the Freedom Charter a treasonable document and in 1956 brought to trial 156 key figures, among them Mandela and Luthuli. The trial continued until March 1961, when all of the accused against whom charges had not already been dropped were acquitted.

In 1960 a peaceful anti-Pass demonstration organized by the PAC resulted in a massacre at Sharpeville, in which police killed 69 protestors and injured 180. Blacks responded with a massive

Nelson Mandela (1918–). Mandela was the first South African president to be elected into office in a fully democratic election. Prior to his term, he was a leader of the African National Congress (ANC) and was imprisoned for twenty-seven years for initiating the ANC's armed struggle. AP IMAGES

work stoppage; the government retaliated by declaring a state of emergency, banning the ANC and PAC and detaining thousands throughout the country, among them Mandela. After his release, he participated in the organization of a national conference of anti-apartheid groupings against the government's intention to leave the British Commonwealth and establish a racist republic. In the campaign that followed the conference, he went underground to facilitate his work and avoid arrest and came to be known as the Black Pimpernel.

In 1961 Mandela, having reached the conclusion that the power of the Nationalists would never be broken through mass civil action alone, initiated Umkhonto we Sizwe (the Spear of the Nation) to organize sabotage against key state installations. December 1961 saw the first bomb blasts in South Africa against apartheid. Mandela left the country secretly and traveled incognito to African

nations to raise funds and set up training bases for Umkhonto cadres. He himself underwent military training in Algeria and Tunisia.

Mandela returned to South Africa in July 1962, was arrested in August, and was sentenced in November to five years imprisonment, three for incitement to strike and two for leaving the country without a passport. In June 1964, he was sentenced to life imprisonment for sabotage and for attempting to overthrow the state through violent revolution.

Mandela's personal life had seen drastic changes from 1957 to 1960. He and his first wife, Evelyn Ntoko (1922–2004), divorced in 1957. He married Winnie Madikizela in 1958, and by early 1960 they had two daughters. Imprisoned numerous times beginning in the late 1950s and subjected to a long series of bans, Winnie nonetheless persisted in her anti-apartheid activities and contributed significantly to keeping her husband in the public eye.

The anti-apartheid struggle escalated in 1976 when African youth in the township of Soweto revolted against the enforcement of Afrikaans as a medium of instruction. The revolt spread to other parts of the country and brought out the workers. By 1985 the government was in crisis. In 1988 Mandela's condition of imprisonment improved significantly, and the government began negotiating with him. The last Afrikaner president, Frederik Willem de Klerk, unbanned the ANC, PAC, and the South African Communist Party, and released Mandela in 1990. The two men shared the Nobel Prize for peace in 1993. The first nonracial democratic elections followed in 1994, and Mandela was returned as the first democratically elected president of the country. He served in that office until June 1999, after which he retired from public life to make his home in Qunu, Transkei, near the place of his birth.

See also **Apartheid; De Klerk, Frederik Willem; Mandela, Winnie; South Africa, Republic of: History and Politics (1850-2006).**

BIBLIOGRAPHY

Johns, Sheridan, and R. Hunt Davis, Jr., eds. *Mandela, Tambo, and the African National Congress: The Struggle against Apartheid, 1948–1990, a Documentary Survey.* New York: Oxford University Press, 1991.

Mandela, Nelson. *No Easy Walk to Freedom.* New York: Basic Books, 1965.

Mandela, Nelson. *Long Walk to Freedom: The Autobiography of Nelson Mandela.* Boston: Little Brown, 1994.

Meer, Fatima. *Higher Than Hope: The Authorized Biography of Nelson Mandela.* New York: Harper and Row, 1990.

Vail, John. *Nelson and Winnie Mandela.* New York: Chelsea House Publishers, 1989.

FATIMA MEER

MANDELA, WINNIE (1934–). A symbol of the sufferings of black women in South Africa under apartheid, Winnie Mandela was born in rural Transkei and studied social work in Johannesburg as a young woman. She married Nelson Mandela in 1955 at the height of the National Congress mass mobilization against apartheid. After Nelson Mandela's incarceration for life in 1964, she became a political leader in her own right. She was detained many times between 1958 and 1989, including being tried for terrorism in 1967. She was banned (excluded from meeting with more than one person and from political activity), listed (could not be quoted), and banished (sent to the isolated rural town of Brandfort in 1977). She aligned herself with the Black Consciousness Movement in the 1970s despite her restrictions and waged a personal political battle against petty apartheid in Brandfort where she established a crèche and a clinic. Friends who visited her, including Helen Joseph, were harassed and detained.

Winnie became a legendary national and international symbol of strength and courage: the Mother of the Nation. In 1985 Winnie's house in Brandfort was burned down when she was visiting a doctor in Johannesburg. She refused to return to Brandfort. An international campaign pressured the South African government to relent. In January 1986, Winnie formed the Mandela United Football Club. Members acted as her bodyguards but behaved as warlords in the strife-torn wards of Soweto. Township youth, angered at the role of the Football Club, raided Mandela's house in Orlando in 1987 and burned it down in 1988. She was unaware that some members of the Club were police *agents provocateurs*. Her role became increasingly contested by the African National Congress (ANC). She was implicated, tried, and

South African anti-apartheid leader Winnie Madikizela-Mandela (1934–), Pretoria High Court, July 5, 2004. After a conviction for fraud and other charges in April 2003, Mandela resigned from all leadership positions in the African National Congress. In July 2004, the court overturned part of her conviction but upheld the fraud charge. © SIPHIWE SIBEKO/ REUTERS/CORBIS

convicted for the abduction and torture of youths who had been accused of being spies, one of whom, Stompie Seipei, was killed. The Mandelas divorced in 1994. She was the center of fraud accusations as leader of the ANC Women's League. But neither personal nor political scandal ended her career. She became a member of parliament in 1994, was a deputy minister of social development, and held leading positions in the Women's League and on the national executive committee of the ANC. Winnie Mandela left public life in 2003.

See also **Apartheid; Johannesburg; Joseph, Helen; Mandela, Nelson; South Africa, Republic of.**

BIBLIOGRAPHY

Bezdrob, Anne Marie du Preez. *Winnie Mandela: A Life.* Cape Town, South Africa: Zebra Press, 2003.

Gilbey, Emma. *The Lady: The Life and Times of Winnie Mandela.* London: Vintage, 1994.

Mandela, Winnie. *Part of My Soul Went with Him,* ed. Anne Benjamin. New York: W. W. Norton, 1985.

SHEILA MEINTJES

MANSA MUSA

MANSA MUSA (r.c. 1312–1337). Mansa Musa is the most famed among Europeans of the Malinke kings, under whom the Malian empire reached its maximum size in the early fourteenth century. He owes his fame outside of western Africa to the pilgrimage he made to the holy places of Islam in 1325.

Ascending the throne after his predecessor, Abobakar II, died (allegedly, in some accounts) in a maritime expedition in the Atlantic Ocean, Mansa Musa endeavored to consolidate the borders of the empire. He was assisted in this by a brilliant general, Saran Mandian.

A prince educated in Arabic, he resumed the tradition followed by Malian sovereigns of making a pilgrimage to Mecca. He prepared painstakingly for the journey and, following tradition, required the towns and provinces of the empire to make a contribution. He left Niani with a large retinue, taking with him a great quantity of gold drawn from the treasure accumulated by several generations of sovereigns.

Mansa Musa dazzled the inhabitants and the court of Cairo upon his arrival in 1324. According to an historian of the time, he came on horseback superbly clothed, with over ten thousand subjects of his empire, and distributed gorgeous gifts magnificent to behold. In Cairo the Malian sovereign and his companions distributed so much gold that the price of that precious metal dropped. This largesse added to his fame; several decades after his trip to Cairo, chroniclers were still writing about the splendor and the generosity of the Malians.

Mansa Musa returned home from the holy places with an architect, the famous Ishaq El Teudjin, who constructed for him several buildings. Among these were the Gao mosque; the Djinguereber, which is the well-known Timbuktu mosque; and a palace, named the Madougou, in the same city. In Niani itself, the capital of the Malian regime, the Arab architect built a mosque and a remarkable "audience room," a square room topped by a dome and decorated with arabesques of bright colors. Of these monuments, all built with earthen bricks, none survive except the Djinguereber in Timbuktu.

A patron sovereign, Mansa Musa attracted poets and other people of letters to his court. He built several libraries and supported education in the Qur'an.

Under his reign Mali reached its greatest size. The empire extended from Teghazza in the Saharan plain in the north to the Guineo-Ivorian forest in the south; from (modern) Banjul on the Gambia River in the west to Azelik (in present Niger) in the east. At the end of the fourteenth century, a portrait of Mansa Musa holding a large nugget of gold in his hands appeared on the first European maps showing the kingdoms and peoples of Africa.

Despite his fame, however, Mansa Musa is not favorably remembered in Mandinka oral traditions. He is reproached for squandering the gold of the Crown and thus weakening the empire. Yet his work is long lasting. All Malian cities bear his mark. To him are owed their monuments of hard-packed earth spiked with wood, a style so characteristic of Sudanese architecture.

See also **Communications: Oral; Mali; Niani; Timbuktu.**

BIBLIOGRAPHY

Lainé, Daniel. *African Kings,* trans. Charles Philips. Berkeley, CA: Ten Speed Press, 2000.

Levtzion, Nehemia. *Ancient Ghana and Mali.* London: Methuen, 1973.

Ly Tall, Madina. *Contributions de l'histoire de l'empire du Mali (XIIIe–XVIe siècles).* Dakar, Senegal: Nouvelles Editions Africaines, 1977.

Niane, Djibril Tamsir. *Recherche sur l'empire du Mali au moyen âge.* Paris: Presence Africaine, 1975.

DJIBRIL TAMSIR NIANE

MAPONDERA, PAITANDO KADUNGURE

MAPONDERA, PAITANDO KADUNGURE (??–1904). Mapondera, whose name means "he who vanquishes the stronghold of his enemy," was the son of Gorenjena, a member of the Changamire Rozvi royal family in eastern Rhodesia (present-day Zimbabwe) and famed ruler and warrior of the Negomos in the late nineteenth century. Mapondera earned the praise name "Hugumu" for his leadership in battles against both European settlers and other Africans who impinged on the Mazoe district in the 1890s. His first distinction came during a struggle against Ndebele invaders, during which he killed their leader, Chiyama Mikomo.

With his reputation and the relative security of his territory against other Africans established, Mapondera concentrated on relations with Portuguese and British merchants who were coming into the area in the last quarter of the nineteenth century. In 1891, Mapondera entered into a mineral concession with the Portuguese Selous Exploitation Syndicate, intending to benefit from trade with Europeans without threatening his people's independence. The following year, British South Africa Company (BSA) police were eager to institute their administration in the area. To this end, they attacked Mapondera's village, captured his half brother, and put him in prison, where he committed suicide. BSA dominion grew in what was becoming Southern Rhodesia, and inhabitants of the Mazoe were forced to pay taxes to their "sovereigns." Mapondera, disillusioned, began to see Europeans as enemies.

Publicly denouncing the Southern Rhodesia Native Commission and encouraging Africans to resist all forms of European authority, Mapondera formulated his belief that blacks must band together to fight colonialists. In 1895 he led some forty men to ambush European settlements and patrols. The conflict continued to escalate, and Africans from the Mazoe district, as well as the Tete district in neighboring Portuguese Mozambique, conspired to organize forces and to share resources and information regarding the activities of Europeans. Mapondera's guerrilla attacks continued while his movement grew in numbers and succeeded, to some extent, in disrupting trade. When two Mozambican leaders, King Muenemutapa Chioco and Makombe Hanga, the Barue monarch, resisted partnership with the Portuguese, Mapondera openly supported them by decrying not only colonialists in Africa but also Africans who made concessions to Europeans. He once said to a Shona chief who disagreed with his idea of unity among African peoples, "You have no

excuse now, as we warned you years ago against being friendly with White men in the country. We will kill you when we have killed the White chief."

As Mapondera's following grew, Europeans came to regard him as a key enemy. In 1902 the Portuguese occupied his headquarters. Caught crossing from Mozambique into Southern Rhodesia, Mapondera surrendered and was sentenced to seven years' imprisonment. He died in prison in 1904 as the result of a hunger strike.

See also **Colonial Policies and Practices: British Central Africa; Mozambique: History and Politics; Zimbabwe: History and Politics.**

BIBLIOGRAPHY

Mutswairo, Solomon M. *Mapondera, Soldier of Zimbabwe.* Harare: Longman Zimbabwe, 1983.

SARAH VALDEZ

MAPS AND MAPMAKING. *See* Cartography.

MAPUTO.

Maputo, the capital city of Mozambique, was founded in 1721 when Dutch traders established a trading port to gain access to a protected deepwater bay. British traders settled there in the late eighteenth century, and the Portuguese made their own settlement on the site in 1781. Local people called it Xilunguine, or white man's place, though the British called it Delagoa Bay, and the Portuguese called it Lourenço Marques, after a Portuguese explorer who visited the area in 1544. Following independence in 1975, the city's name was changed to Maputo in recognition of a local chief.

Ivory was initially the primary export, but it was the discovery of gold and diamonds in South Africa in the 1870s that transformed the role of the city in the region after a railroad was built connecting South Africa to the port to accommodate the export of minerals. The Portuguese moved their capital from Mozambique Island in the north to the developing industrial center in the south at Lourenço Marques in 1898. By 1928, the census reported 28,568 Africans and 9,001 Europeans in residence in the new capital. The city was marked by a division between the European sector, home to cement office buildings, paved streets, electricity, and running water, and the surrounding African neighborhoods that featured makeshift reed houses and a lack of amenities.

During the last half of the twentieth century, Maputo remained the political capital under the Portuguese colonial administration and the succeeding independent government, and was designated as a separate political entity equal to the ten provinces. It developed into the primary industrial center of Mozambique, with cement, shoes, tobacco, cashews, and rubber among the key goods. A large aluminum smelting plant, Mozal, was opened in 2000. Major cultural centers, including the Universidade Eduardo Mondlane, were established in the city. By the turn of the twenty-first century, the population was nearly one million (989,386 in 1997, with a further 440,927 residing in Matola, the adjacent city that some consider a neighborhood of Maputo) with tens of thousands uncounted and living in the surrounding sprawl of African neighborhoods.

See also **Mozambique.**

BIBLIOGRAPHY

Jenkins, Paul. "Image of the City in Mozambique: Civilization, Parasite, Engine of Growth or Place of Opportunity?" In *African Urban Economies: Viability, Vitality or Vitiation?* ed. Deborah Fahy Bryceson and Deborah Potts. New York: Palgrave Macmillan, 2006.

Newitt, Malyn. *A History of Mozambique.* Bloomington: Indiana University Press, 1995.

Penvenne, Jeanne Marie. *African Workers and Colonial Racism: Mozambican Strategies and Struggles in Lourenço Marques, 1877–1962.* Portsmouth, New Hampshire: Heinemann, 1995.

KATHLEEN SHELDON

MARANKE, JOHN (1912–1963). The Rhodesian religious leader John Maranke was born in the Bondwe area of the Maranke Tribal Trust land of Southern Rhodesia (present-day Zimbabwe) under the name of Muchabaya Ngomberume. He was a descendant on his father's side of the royal Sithole lineage. His mother was daughter of the Shona chief Maranke, whose clan name he adopted after a dramatic spiritual calling to found a Christian church.

Little accurate information is available about Maranke's childhood. According to local missionaries, Maranke attended the American Methodist mission school under the name of Roston, after which he migrated as a laborer to the town of Umtali in eastern Zimbabwe. Close family and church members, however, dispute Maranke's affiliation with the Methodist mission.

In the official testament of the church, *Humbowo Hutswa we Vapostori* (The New Revelation of the Apostles), Maranke recounted his first spiritual vision, which took place in 1917, when he was five. Over the years, he experienced a series of mysterious illnesses and dreams, culminating in a near-death experience in 1932. On July 17, 1932, Maranke claimed to have seen a sudden flash of lightning and to have heard a booming voice dubbing him John the Baptist, instructing him to preach and seek converts from many nations. Maranke began by proselytizing within his immediate family, converting his older brothers, Conorio (Cornelius) and Anrod, and his uncle, Peter Mupako. He held his first public sabbath ceremony on July 20, 1932, in the Maranke Reserve near the Murozi River (dubbed the Jordan). Approximately 150 people joined the new group.

Maranke used visionary experiences as the inspiration for establishing the ritual practices and social hierarchy of the church. These practices drew heavily on Old Testament doctrines and showed evidence of influences from Methodist liturgy, Seventh-Day Adventism, and traditional Shona religion. By 1934 the social organization of the group was firmly in place. Maranke, who considered himself to be a *mutumwa*, or holy messenger and reinterpreter of Christian doctrines, devised a Saturday sabbath ceremony (*kerek*) consisting of prophetic readings, preaching, and hymns in Shona, interspersed with songs in various local dialects. Other ritual practices included a Eucharist or Passover celebration (*paseka* or *pendi*), mountain prayer retreats (*masowe*), and healing rituals. Maranke maintained tight control over the group's leadership hierarchy by bestowing the spiritual gifts (*bipedi*) of preaching, baptism, healing, and prophecy, and a series of ranks (*mianza*) at the annual Passover ceremony. He further elaborated this leadership structure following minor internal conflicts in local congregations during the 1940s and 1950s.

Until his death in 1963, Maranke and his immediate relatives controlled the *paseka* and the leadership hierarchy from Bocha, Zimbabwe. Maranke's eldest sons, Abel and Makebo, initiated a traveling *paseka* to neighboring countries in 1957. After Maranke's death, leadership was passed to Abel and Makebo. There was a brief schism resulting in the founding of a spin-off Apostolic group under Simon Mushati, Maranke's maternal cousin.

After Makebo's death in the late 1980s, Abel assumed leadership until his death in 1992. The church expanded rapidly across several African nations, establishing large congregations in Zaire, Zambia, Malawi, Mozambique, and Botswana, and with some European converts within and outside of Africa. The 1992 succession was initially smooth, and leadership was transferred, by spiritual consensus, to Mambo Noah, a ranking healer in the Zimbabwean congregation. For a short period, Clement Sithole, one of Maranke's younger sons who had briefly studied in England, challenged Noah and attempted to reform the church but eventually returned to the fold with his followers. The fundamental leadership structure established by Maranke has demonstrated longevity, and the church continues to grow, with more than 500,000 members across Africa.

See also **Christianity.**

BIBLIOGRAPHY

Daneel, M. L. *Old and New in Southern Shona Independent Churches*, Vol. 1: *Background and Rise of the Major Movements*. The Hague: Mouton, 1971.

Jules-Rosette, Bennetta. *African Apostles: Ritual and Conversion in the Church of John Maranke*. Ithaca, NY: Cornell University Press, 1975.

Maranke, John. *The New Witness of the Apostles*, trans. J. S. Kusotera. Bocha, Zimbabwe: 1953.

Mariotti, Luciana. *Il millennio in Africa: "L'Apostolic Church of John Maranke."* Rome: Euroma La Goliardica, 1991.

Mary Aquina, O. P. "The People of the Spirit: An Independent Church in Rhodesia." *Africa* 37 (January 1967): 203–219.

Murphree, Marshall W. *Christianity and the Shona*. New York: Humanities Press, 1969.

BENNETTA JULES-ROSETTE

MARGAI, MILTON AUGUSTUS STRIERY

(1895–1964). Milton Augustus Striery Margai was born of slave descent to a rural paramount chief in the British Sierra Leone Protectorate and overcame Creole prejudices in Freetown to become the first "protectorate native" to graduate from the Fourah Bay College there. He went on to study medicine in England, becoming the first physician from the protectorate. Margai practiced medicine for twenty-five years in the colonial service, working with secret societies to professionalize midwifery in rural areas. He published books on the subject, gaining wide support with womens' groups and the trust of local chiefs for his efforts. Margai formed the Sierra Leone People's Liberation Party (SLPP) in 1951.

He won the elections held that year inaugurating the process of decolonization, becoming minister while diffusing urban-rural ethnic tensions by including Creoles in his administration. Margai's

Milton Augustus Striery Margai (1895–1964). Margai, the first prime minister of Sierra Leone, oversaw the creation of Sierra Leone's constitution, which was adopted in 1958. He was knighted the following year. AP IMAGES

brother, Albert Margai, challenged his careful leadership style, becoming prime minister in 1958. In 1959 Milton Margai was knighted and the same year appointed parliamentary leader. He led an all-party independence delegation to London in 1960 for independence negotiations, proving to be a conservative pro-British leader. His acceptability in Britain, combined with the popular support he had garnered in Sierra Leone, led him to become prime minister in 1961 when independence was granted. Margai remained committed to democracy and encouraged foreign investment until his death only three years later. He was succeeded by his brother, Albert Margai.

See also **Creoles; Sierra Leone; History and Politics.**

BIBLIOGRAPHY

Cartwright, John R. *Political Leadership in Sierra Leone.* London: Croom Helm, 1978.

Conteh-Morgan, Earl, and Mac Dixon-Fyle. *Sierra Leone at the End of the Twentieth Century: History, Politics, and Society.* New York: P. Lang, 1999.

RICHARD R. MARCUS

MARKET SYSTEMS. *See* Economic Systems.

MARKETS. *See* Agriculture: World Markets; Trade, National and International Systems.

MARRAKESH. The founding of Marrakesh is associated with the Almoravid conquest of Morocco around the middle of the eleventh century CE. Marrakesh is located on a wide and open plateau with few physical obstacles, with all the basic requirements for human settlement nearby: the Atlas valleys to the south and east provided the city with water, vegetables, and fruit; and the plains to the west and northwest became the bread basket of the new capital. The Almoravids had also strategic considerations in mind since from Marrakesh; they could keep the Masmouda Berbers of the High Atlas under control.

Under the Almohad dynasty (1147–1269), Marrakesh witnessed further expansion. The Almohads built the *qasba*, or fortress, where the royal family and the government took residence, as well as the famous Qutubiyya mosque and its splendid minaret. During the Almohad period Marrakesh also became an active intellectual center attracting scholars and thinkers from Muslim Spain such as Averroes, Ibn Tufayl, and others. It became also the residence of many famous saints such as Abu al-'Abbas al-Sabti, and Sidi Yusuf ibn 'Ali, who later became part of the "seven saints" for which Marrakesh has been known ever since.

After the Marinid dynasty (1244–1465) chose Fez as its capital, Marrakesh witnessed a period of decline that lasted until the middle of the sixteenth century. In 1557 Marrakesh became the capital city of the new Sa'adi dynasty (1515–1659), which originated in Morocco's south. By choosing Marrakesh as their capital, the Sa'adis expressed two main strategic concerns. The first was to have a capital far from the threat of Ottoman Algeria, which succeeded for a while in controlling the city of Fez. The other motivation was to orient their territorial ambitions southward as a reaction against the encirclement of Morocco by the Ottomans to the east and the Iberians (Spanish and Portuguese) to the north.

The successor 'Alawi dynasty (1666–present) also had its origin in the south of the Morocco, but decided to situate its new capital, Meknes, in the northern part of the country. This time Marrakesh suffered not only because of the transfer of the capital elsewhere, but also because of the global changes witnessed by the world economy. By the eighteenth century much of the world's trade had shifted to the Atlantic at the expense of continental and trans-Saharan trade. The foundation in 1765 of the new port of Essaouira (al-Swira) on the Atlantic coast, just over 100 miles west of Marrakesh, diverted to the sea a sizable part of Marrakesh's caravan trade. The Jewish merchants of Marrakesh and other trading places in the south of the country were also encouraged to settle in the new coastal city. As a result Marrakesh experienced a long period of economic decline during the nineteenth and twentieth centuries. In the twenty-first century the city relies heavily on tourism but the flow of rural migrants and the uncontrolled urbanization resulting from it will continue to upset any significant effort of economic and social development.

See also **Fez; Judaism in Africa; Moors in African History; Morocco; Morocco, History of (1000 to 1900).**

BIBLIOGRAPHY

Deverdun, Gaston. *Marrakech des origines à 1912.* Casablanca: Éditions Frontispice, 2004.

Ibn Al Muwwaqit, Muhammad. *Al Sa'ada Al Abadiya fi Mashahir Al Hadhra Al Murrakushiya.* 2 vols. Marrakesh: n.p., 2002.

Ibn Khalid Al Nasiri, Ahmad. *Kitab Al Istiqsa fi Akhbar Al Maghrib Al Aqsa.* 9 vols. Rabat: Ministry of Culture, 2001.

MOHAMED EL MANSOUR

MARRIAGE SYSTEMS. The study of African systems of marriage has always been influenced by the evolution of anthropology as a discipline. Interpretations of marriage practices have been, and continue to be, shaped by the dominant theory of a period.

The diversity of forms that marriage assumes in Africa bars any monolithic interpretation. However, it can be characterized by certain traits, the most striking of which is the transfer of material and symbolic goods that always accompanies a marriage. It can be said that these transfers, called either bride price or bride service, according to circumstances, signify in legal terms the passage of a woman from one group to another, with all concomitant consequences for the social membership of the children resulting from the union.

As elsewhere, marriage in Africa is a matter between familial groups, narrowly or widely extended, as much as between individuals. It lies at the center of a social and symbolic display that invokes ancestors as witnesses to the coming offspring; fixes the relations between the social groups of the new spouses, among which individuals, goods, and symbols will circulate; assigns social membership and social status to offspring; seals an alliance between groups; and, finally, gives rise to a series of rituals that only death will end.

African systems of marriage are well known for the numerous forms they can assume. Beyond the classic polygamy that can be considered the second great constant in Africa, one can find the following types of marriage: (1) levirate (union of a widow with the younger brother of the late husband); (2) sororate (union of a man with the younger sister of his wife, either while his wife is alive or after her death); (3) union between close blood relatives (union of a man with his niece, first cousin, second cousin, or even half sister or granddaughter); and (4) union with in-laws, relatives whose relationships have been formed by previous marriages (union of a man with his wife's brother's daughter or with the widow of his maternal uncle). One also finds "ghost marriages," often involving two women, designed to mitigate a lack of offspring; two women may marry to counteract a problem resulting from sterility, to maintain the status of a woman of wealth, or to allow queens to retain their dominant position in the social hierarchy. These types of marriages do not all occur within the same society; each culture selects some and forbids others, which suggests that the choice is not random but obeys a logic coherent with the social organization of the culture. The resulting ensemble of marriages forms a matrimonial system specific to the society.

Beyond these general considerations, interpretations begin to diverge, especially when marriage is viewed in the context of other aspects of kinship and society: filiation (descent); lineage; residence; inheritance; the composition and nature of familial groups; economy; and politics. Debates on the subject have occupied African studies, but thanks to them and the diverse theories they have produced, scholars can now view the matter with some clarity.

The theory of descent groups, elaborated by British anthropologists, has tended to interpret marriage and its judicial and legal aspects, such as rights over children, by the patri-, matri-, or bilinear descent groups by which societies are organized. However, no broad generalizations can be advanced. The theory of alliance advanced by Claude Lévi-Strauss has long stumbled over matrimonial systems that do not present mechanical regularities which can be deduced from uniformly applied rules: although marriages between certain types of cousins are preferred, unions between other types of cousins are not necessarily prohibited, preventing the creation of unidimensional models that would structure society as a whole. Finally, marriages are often accompanied by the payment of bride price, which complicates the idea of the simple exchange of a sister for a wife, as is postulated in Lévi-Strauss's theory.

PATRILINEAL SOCIETIES

The best examples of the societies in which marriage between cousins is preferred are found in Central and southern Africa. The Bantu societies of the south, such as the Tswana, Sotho, and Venda, which practice pastoralism and agriculture, are characterized by patrilineal descent. Marriage is sanctioned by a heavy bride price in cattle paid by the close agnatic (i.e., paternally related) kin of the husband to the kin of the fiancée. The preferred marriage is between a man and his mother's brother's daughter, or matrilateral cross-cousin marriage. Another type of favored marriage is between a man and his father's brother's daughter, or patrilateral parallel cousin marriage. In the local social hierarchy, the former type of marriage occurs among the common classes, while the latter—and the union of a man with his brother's daughter or even his half sister—is favored by the elites.

In the first case, a permanent relation is created between the two parties to the matrimonial exchange; the transferred cattle circulate from group to group, and the stable relations between them are reproduced with each generation. The transfer of cattle bonds a brother with his sister because her marriage provides the cows that he can give to the brother of his (female) cousin in order to marry her. Their children will reenact similar marriages, which will have the effect of bonding their groups through payments of cattle. In the second case, marriage with the father's brother's daughter offers two advantages: it keeps the animals within the patrilineage and reenforces the political status of the two participating families.

The two types of marriage have opposite effects, one leading to the circulation of cattle and women, the other to their retention, but each allows the reproduction of the social and political hierarchy. The Lovedu accomplish the same thing by emphasizing the responsibilities of brother and sister. The sister's marriage and the cattle transfer create for her brother a right to claim her daughter as a wife for his son. This right is also tied to the elevated status of women in this society. The scarcity of cattle, in combination with high bride price, constrains the average man to a single choice: to give his sister in marriage in order to acquire the cattle needed for him to negotiate his own marriage.

Other peoples in southern Africa make different marriage choices. The Tsonga, while maintaining a high bride price, forbid marriage with first and second cousins, as well as with a great many other relatives. Although this would presumably lead to the dispersal of siblings, a brother and sister are in fact bonded together because the marriage of one depends on that of the other: the cattle obtained by the marriage of the sister enables the brother to marry. In this case, only the circulation of bride price bonds groups together, for the network does not allow the same marriage alliances to be reenacted in successive generations. The Zulu also insist on setting a high bride price. The payment of cattle confers rights of paternity over the children, as is manifest in certain types of unions. In a ghost marriage, for example, even after his death a man is still considered to be the father of any children that his widow will have with a male relative of the husband (in the levirate form). Similarly, when an unmarried man dies, another will marry a woman in his name and produce children on his account. Finally, a rich woman of high status may marry another woman, giving cattle for her. Her wife will then have children with a member of the cattle-giving woman's kin group, but the cattle-giver is the socially recognized father.

The Lozi of Central Africa, agriculturalists and fishers as well as pastoralists, constantly reshape their villages and mode of residence. Unlike many other patrilineal peoples, they do not have extended descent groups. Like the Tsonga and the Zulu, they forbid marriage with cousins, but their interdictions reach even further, including any type of blood relative (patrilineal, matrilineal, or cognatic). They also forbid sororal polygyny and any type of marriage of a man to a woman of the same descent group as any of his other wives or of his father's or brothers' wives. Dispersion is thus assured, but marriage remains unstable. In the late nineteenth century the bride price was largely symbolic, consisting of hoes, mats, and only one or two head of cattle, before being largely replaced by money in the early twentieth century. Unlike the Tsonga and Zulu, the Lozi did not believe that the payment of bride price allowed the children to be assigned to a social father rather than the biological father, but it did give the husband rights over his wife. Matrimonial interdictions were associated with a biological recognition of paternity. Cognatic and alliance relationships were extended by forming structured networks based on factors other than bride price.

MATRILINEAL STUDIES

The rules of marriage and bride price follow a different logic in the matrilineal societies of Central Africa, which face different issues regarding the type of marriage, rights of the children, and modes of residence of the married couple. In many cases, one cannot speak of marriage compensation in the sense of bride price, but rather of "bride service," made by the son-in-law. This is the case with the Bemba of Zambia, agriculturalists in a poor region. After many years of "service" (working for his wife's kin), a Bemba man is finally allowed to bring his wife and children home, and eventually to marry his wife's sister as well. This arrangement, a sort of trial marriage, is performed after ritual activities and the wife's agreement to follow her husband into his village. He also chooses his place of residence, which may be that of his father, maternal uncle, or father-in-law, depending on the personality and status of the head of the household. The marriages of a brother and sister are not linked by the need to acquire bride-price cattle, but marriage between matri- or patrilateral cousins occurs widely. This offers the couple the advantage of remaining in a familiar village and provides a temporary stability to groups that regularly undergo restructuring. In sum, the reasons for preferring certain types of marriages are opposite to those of heavily patrilinear societies.

The situation is different when the mode of residence tends to be patrilocal, as with the Ila of Zambia or the Kongo of west-central Africa. Kongo children go to live with their maternal uncle at puberty, where they constitute a group of homogenous brothers. Ila children remain explicitly with their father. Bride price for both these groups

is high and favors the departure of the wife for her husband's home. Ila marriage between cross cousins, notably with the daughter of the father's sister, counterbalances matrilineal descent and reinforces agnatic authority.

To summarize, the customs relating to cousin marriage and bride price in Central and southern Africa follow their own internally consistent logic and, depending on various contexts (kinship, economy, politics), one phenomenon may complement, substitute for, or oppose the other. This is not the case in other parts of Africa, where in certain societies all types of cousin-marriage are allowed, whereas in others, all are forbidden, or where there is an ambiguous relation between matrimonial exchange and bride price.

In western Africa, Fulani pastoralists, whether nomadic or sedentary, apply two criteria to the possibilities of marriage and bride price: consanguinity and proximity. Residential endogamy accompanies consanguinial endogamy, but the importance of bride price paid in cattle varies among the different Fulani societies. There are three most common types of marriages—the union of a man with the father's brother's daughter, the mother's brother's daughter, or the father's sister's daughter. Only one possibility is favored statistically by a given society, and that possibility is contingent upon the extent to which the society is patrilineal or cognatic. Only two societies acknowledge all three types of unions without preference, in addition to that of a man with the mother's sister's daughter. This situation reflects the tension between kin groups: the father seeks a daughter-in-law from his relatives, the mother from hers.

The residency alternative ultimately followed in any given case is completely based on concerns about retaining or restricting the circulation of cattle. As a rule, the more numerous the consanguineous marriages within a society, the lower the bride price, even to the point where none is paid at all. Thus, the relation between the size of the bride price and the marriage of cousins is not the same as that observed in southern Africa. Furthermore, matrimonial strategies are tightly linked to political motivations that alternate between endogamy (marriage with a cross cousin) and exogamy (parallel cousin marriage)—according to whether the lineages of each society are primarily concerned with expansion or consolidation. Historical processes are thus introduced into matrimonial systems. The choice of a particular mate, however, cannot be as easily summarized in terms of simple strategies because it is based on preestablished models of marriage favored according to what is at stake at the particular moment. This point is subject to discussion, and other examples may enrich the debate.

The Asante of Ghana have what is known as a double descent system. In such systems social groups are organized according to the principle of matrifiliation, but the patrilineal line perpetuates itself through several generations in another manner, by the masculine transmission of the spirit (*ntoro*) of the father. Each individual is composed of the blood of his mother and the spirit of his father. Marriage of a man with the daughter of his maternal uncle, a matrilateral cross cousin, is recommended (leading to a de facto residence with the maternal uncle of the man) though seldom carried out between true first cousins, whereas marriage of a man with the father's sister's daughter has been the privilege of the Asante princes since the eighteenth century. It offers the double advantage of producing presumptive heirs belonging at the same time to the royal matrilineage and to the other two or three agnatic lineage groups issuing from the first sovereigns but also from individuals who carry in their blood their mother's lineage and their paternal grandfather's spirit, serving in effect as his reincarnation.

Marriage between cousins is not the only type of matrimonial system, and systems representing an opposite tendency occur widely in many societies. Within them, marriage between first and often second cousins is prohibited, but the exchange of sisters, or marriage by exchange, is favored. In the marriage of cousins, the circulation of wives and bride prices among kin groups is replaced by a sort of direct reciprocity—one that is not renewed in future generations. This system is clearly illustrated in Nigeria, where marriage with bride price takes place only when a man has no sister to give in exchange for his bride, and so has none of the rights to progeny, who will belong to his wife's group. Only the exchange of sisters sanctions the affiliation of the children to their father. This is the case with the Tiv, the Mambila, and many others.

With the Tiv, the reciprocity of the double marriage must also extend to the number of children they create; if one of the marriages results in more offspring than the other, the surplus is given to the other couple to equilibrate the two lineages. With the Mossi of Burkina Faso, when the reciprocity is not immediately assured, the daughters from the first marriage belong to the chief, who will redistribute them at the appropriate moment, thereby assuring a deferred reciprocity. Thus, the exchange of sisters that is not renewable in the following generation (meaning that it cannot be reproduced by a marriage between cousins) can be seen as opposed to bride price, which is thus nothing more than a remedy for the lack of a sister. Similar substitution can evolve toward a system of marriage by purchase in which the exchange of sisters is preeminent in the ideology, but no longer in the practice, of marriage.

However, even in the simplest models of reciprocity, other means are employed that act against direct exchange. The Tiv, after reequilibrating children between two couples, use the wards for inaugurating new exchanges. The daughters resulting from marriage with a stranger are utilized in this manner. This is a well-known way of circumventing the norm and adding to a personal network of matrimonial alliances. All the same, in matrilinear societies, one expected strategy is to keep for oneself, secure from one's wife's brother, one's own children resulting from secondary marriages with slaves or with patrilinear neighbors who will find it normal that the husband take his wife with him. Marriage by exchange is therefore rarely simple and is often quite complex.

This is also the case with systems of secondary marriage found on the plateau of Jos in Nigeria. It applies at the same time to the multiplicity of marriages, the principle of nondoubling, and the rejection of divorce. Women must achieve marriages with many men from different exogamous groups. When a first marriage takes place within a group, the next ones, which are all secondary marriages, must never occur within the groups required for the preceding unions. Each time two groups exchange their daughters, they cannot do so again, either in primary or secondary marriage. The forced dispersion of these multiple alliances structures the constituent groups by multiple, but different, bonds. Women, therefore, have many husbands, never divorce (thus, there is no reimbursement of bride price), and change their residence each time they go or return to one of their husbands. Young children follow their mother, then rejoin the group to which they belong, whether it be that of their father or their maternal uncle. This occurs according to the principle of reequilibration of children in marriages of sister exchange or even according to whether the father has "bought back" the child of his brother-in-law; sometimes, the children rejoin one of their mother's other husbands. In sum, these systems organize a complex structure of relations between groups, a multicirculation of women despite direct exchange, and finally a redistribution of children in a manner relatively independent from the principle of descent. It militates against the simple ideology of exchange and descent.

Other systems widely extend the matrimonial interdictions, even to the point of nonrenewable exchange of sisters, accompanied by matrimonial payments. These are the so-called semicomplex systems, in which matrimonial prohibitions are so numerous as to overflow the categories of blood relative and unilineal descent. The Samo of Burkina Faso; the Kako, Gbaya, and Beti of Cameroon; and the Minyanka of Mali, all patrilinear, enact three types of marriage prohibitions: (1) lineage interdictions, including relatives belonging to the patrilineages of an individual's four grandparents; (2) cognatic interdictions, with all cognatic blood relatives for four generations beginning with great-grandparents; and (3) interdictions against doubled alliance in all lines where close blood relatives of the same sex (for a man: father, father's brother, and brother; for a woman, mother, mother's sister, and sister) are already married. These sanctions apparently lead to the dispersion of marriages, but within the context of communities practicing endogamy the choice of spouse comes closer to the possibilities of marriage once the interdictions cease.

Among the Samo, Françoise Héritier has proved, thanks to the use of an informative treatment of genealogies, that the circulation of women used two models at the same time, that of nonrenewed exchange of sisters and that of consanguineally perpetuated exchange up to the fifth generation, which is to say the marriage between third cousins (between great-great-grandchildren). These systems

are independent of unifiliation, for one finds them among both the matrilinear Senufo and the bilinear Gagu of Côte d'Ivoire. The variations in bride price complicate marriage systems to a greater or lesser extent without transforming them radically. On the other hand, the renewal of marriage by direct exchange largely utilizes the possibilities offered by the effects of polygamy, which attributes different marriage prohibitions among half cousins and half siblings and thus permits more rapid returns.

The particularity of African marriage systems is the way in which the simplest rules of alliance are complicated by the use of bride price, polygamy, and the multiple orientation of marriages. To the "mechanical" rules of marriage and individual strategies must be added a veritable matrimonial politics.

POLYGAMY

Polygamy (or polygyny, inasmuch as it concerns a man's marriages) constitutes another general characteristic of African marriage. Used broadly, it varies from a limited polygamy practiced only by certain members of the community to a general norm, or even to the extended polygamy of chiefs and kings. In all cases, it is a means for the enlargement of the family and a sign of power and prestige of the head of household, while also reinforcing the productive capacity of familial groups. One consequence, from the point of view of matrimonial systems, is always the complication of models of alliance, however simple they may be, each unit being composed of groups of half-siblings whose matrimonial fate will thus be different. Another consequence is the introduction into patrilinear systems of filiation of feminine stock that differentiates and segments the masculine lines. Within the man's place of residence, matricentric households composed of each co-wife and her children constitute the point of departure of all segmentation (and of the resultant social hierarchy). Polygamy, the manifestation of masculine domination, has its other side: it imposes the feminine principle on masculine preeminence and makes it the means of social differentiation between men.

Polygamy is also a means of diversifying alliances in such a manner that if the first marriage can follow the paths indicated by rules and tradition, the others are more the result of choice and individual strategy. The models of African systems of marriage are always complex from this double point of view. By allowing individual choice, polygamy is subject to transformation and adaptation to new conditions while remaining a means of establishing prestige and power. Indirectly, it is tightly linked to divorce, the sole means for women to decide their matrimonial future. In Africa men never divorce on their own initiative, for it involves renouncing all the goods, alliances, and symbols they had invested in their union. Divorce, initiated by wives, is not always a twenty-first-century phenomenon; often attested traditionally, it testifies to the capacity of women to take the initiative, and many are those who, after a traditional first marriage, make their personal choice. This feminine equivalent to masculine polygamy (polyandry remaining a rare phenomenon, and systems of secondary marriage limited) reflects upon the latter: the divorce of women destabilizes the polygamy of men whose matrimonial life follows a fluctuating course.

The matrimonial systems presented have undergone transformations as a result of modernity; certain systems have dissolved, while others resist or adapt. The greatest changes have occurred in what one might call the complex "bride price, polygamy, divorce, and separation." The rupture between the city and the country is obvious, but often the generalized monetarization of bride price has profoundly changed its meaning, indeed has changed the entire marriage system. One may detect gerontocracies in which the old, or even the ancestors, as holders of power and goods, have trapped the women, leaving little chance to the young of gathering sufficient money to pay bride price. But on the other hand, in the areas in which there is no lack of work, it is through monetarization that the young liberate themselves from the tutelage of their ancestors by providing them compensation, the fruit of their labor. Still elsewhere, a high bride price testifies to the superior status of the woman, and socioeconomic motivations for marriage assume full importance. On the other hand—among the Zulu, for example—the monetarization of bride price has made women more dependent. These variations in the transformations undergone by bride price are linked to marriage systems in which they have occurred, testifying to their weight with respect to current changes. Polygamy and divorce follow the same type of variations.

The fall of polygamy predicted by theoreticians of modernity is only partial; indeed, the opposite

can be observed in some places. The reasons for one situation or the other are sometimes directly opposed. Polygamy may be retained to increase the size of the family or abandoned to have fewer women and children in order to raise the latter in better fashion. The choice of the city dweller may depend on his standard of living. The rich find it hard to resist the prestige and power polygamy offers, especially with women of the elite, who can also be tempted by the advantages provided by such a marriage, even as a second wife. Another common solution is to have a "field woman" and a "city woman," or, among the urban elite, a wife and mistresses.

The change of marriage systems in the context of modernity is inaugurated in particular by women who seek by means of divorce or separation a better matrimonial situation than that of "little wife" or mistress. Their strategies are always limited by the question of economic autonomy and attribution of children, who are rarely granted to them except in specific contexts to be found in matricentric households. The accelerating development of African cities, along with their relations with the countryside, are transforming marriage systems more and more by accentuating the individual strategies of men as well as of women at the expense of the strategies of familial groups traditionally subjected to the domination of men, whether they be father, brother, or maternal uncle. It can be asked whether, in parallel with these changes, the meaning and symbolic foundations of African marriage disappear or continue to resist. The recent realization by observers of the women's point of view has clarified women's matrimonial strategy as well as women's relative independence in their conjugal choices. But polygamy, divorce, and multiple marriage reveal, in any case, the ultimate aim of these feminine strategies, that is, to transform the final suitable marriage into a durable alliance.

See also **Kinship and Affinity; Kinship and Descent; Slavery and Servile Institutions; Women.**

BIBLIOGRAPHY

Bohannan, L. "Dahomean Marriage: A Revaluation." *Africa* 19 (1949): 273–287.

Clignet, Rémi. *Many Wives, Many Powers: Authority and Power in Polygynous Families.* Evanston, IL: Northwestern University Press, 1970.

Comaroff, John. *The Meaning of Marriage Payments.* London: Academic Press, 1980.

Dupire, Marguerite. *Organisation sociale des Peul.* Paris: Plon, 1970.

Fortes, Meyer. "Kinship and Marriage among the Ashanti." In *African Systems of Kinship and Marriage,* ed. A. R. Radcliffe-Brown and Daryll Forde. New York: Oxford University Press, 1960.

Gluckman, Max. "Kinship and Marriage among the Lozi of Northern Rhodesia and the Zulu of the Natal." In *African Systems of Kinship and Marriage,* ed. A. R. Radcliffe-Brown and Daryll Forde. New York: Oxford University Press, 1960.

Goody, Jack, and Stanley Tambiah. *Bridewealth and Dowry.* Cambridge, U.K.: Cambridge University Press, 1973.

Heusch, Luc de. *Why Marry Her? Society and Symbolic Structures.* Cambridge, U.K.: Cambridge University Press, 1981.

Kuper, Adam. *Wives for Cattle: Bridewealth and Marriage in Southern Africa.* Boston: Routledge & Kegan Paul, 1982.

Muller, Jean-Claude. *Du bon usage du sexe et du mariage: Structures matrimoniales du haut plateau nigerian.* Paris: Editions L'Harmattan, 1982.

Ngubane, Harriet. "Marriage, Affinity, and the Ancestral Realm: Zulu Marriage in Female Perspective." In *Essays on African Marriage in Southern Africa,* ed. Eileen J. Krige and John Comaroff. Cape Town: Juta, 1981.

Obbo, C. "The Old and New in East African Elite Marriage." In *Transformation of African Marriage,* ed. David Parkin and David Nyamwaya. Manchester, U.K.: Manchester University Press, 1987.

Richards, A. I. "Some Types of Family Structure amongst the Central Bantu." In *African Systems of Kinship and Marriage,* ed. A. R. Radcliffe-Brown and Daryll Forde. New York: Oxford University Press, 1960.

Smith, M. G. "Secondary Marriage in Northern Nigeria." *Africa* 23 (1953): 298–323.

Tardits, Claude. "Femmes à crédit." In Vol. 1 of *Échanges et communications: Mélanges offerts à Claude Lévi-Strauss,* comp. Jean Pouillon and Pierre Maranda. The Hague: Mouton, 1970.

ELISABETH COPET-ROUGIER

MASCARENE ISLANDS. *See* **Mauritius; Réunion.**

MASCULINITIES. *See* **Gender.**

MASEKELA, HUGH (1939–). Hugh Masekela was born on April 4, 1939, in Witbank, South Africa. Drawn to music as a child, his early influences include the film *Young Man with a Horn,* and performers from Louis Armstrong (1901–1971) to Jelly Roll Morton (1890–1941). He found his instrument in the horn—the trumpet, flugelhorn, and cornet.

He performed and refined his art in South Africa with the Municipal Brass Band. By the time he was nineteen, he was playing in the orchestra of Todd Matshikiza, in his 1958 stage production of *King Kong.* He met his first wife, the singer Miriam Makeba during this time. With Makeba and others, Masekela formed the Jazz Epistles, and landed a recording contract in Johannesburg.

When the apartheid laws banned large (more than ten) public gatherings of blacks, Masekela realized he could not perform in South Africa anymore. With the help of his early mentor, Trevor Huddleston, as well as other musicians of international repute, he fled to London and took up the formal study of music.

Masekela's wife (already in the United States), Harry Belafonte (b. 1927), Dizzy Gillespie (1917–1993), and others encouraged him to come to the United States in the 1960s. He recorded "Trumpet Africaine" in the United States in 1963, then performed with many of the most important, emergent rock bands of the day, including The Byrds and Bob Dylan. In 1968 his release, "Grazin' in the Grass," brought him top-40 acclaim. He later partnered with noted recording impresario Herb Alpert (b. 1935), who guaranteed him work through the 1970s, but he chose to return to Africa to encourage new talent. He went to Ghana to work with Nigerian Fela Ransome Kuti and other African beat proponents, which inspired him to join up with Hedzoleh Sounds, a Ghanaian band, for five years (1973–1978). Nonetheless, he continued to record in the United States for Columbia Records and in collaboration with Alpert.

In the 1980s Masekela established his own mobile recording company based in Botswana. He also formed a new band, Kalahari. Late-stage apartheid violence drove him back to London, and he remained outside Botswana until the end of apartheid. He produced several albums, collaborated

Hugh Masekela (1939–). The South African flugelhorn and cornet player performs during a cultural event in New Delhi, India, March 2004. Upon being exiled to the United States for taking part in an anti-apartheid campaign, Masekela began a jazz career with the famed musician and actor Harry Belafonte. Prakash Singh/AFP/Getty Images

with Mbongeni Ngema (b. 1955) to create the hit Broadway musical *Sarafina!* (1988), and worked with Paul Simon (b. 1941) on the album *Graceland*, which featured other South African artists such as Ladysmith Black Mambazo and his (now former) wife, Miriam Makeba. With the collapse of apartheid in the early 1990s, he was finally able to return home. Masekela remains an active performer and jazz composer.

See also **Apartheid; Huddleston, Trevor; Kuti, Fela; Ladysmith Black Mambazo; Makeba, Miriam; Music, Modern Popular.**

BIBLIOGRAPHY

Masekela, Hugh, and D. Michael Cheers. *Still Grazin': The Musical Journey of Hugh Masekela.* New York: Crown Publishers, 2004.

NANCY E. GRATTON

MASERU. Maseru, the capital of the Kingdom of Lesotho, is situated on the country's western border adjoining the Free State province of South Africa. A bridge across the Mohokare (Caledon) River links the two. The population in 2006 was approximately 350,000. The settlement was founded in 1869 as the capital soon after British annexation and remained its administrative and trading center throughout British colonial rule, which ended in 1966. Subsequent growth has been rapid, fueled since 1990 in part by the development of a textile industry. Its factories, mainly Chinese owned, employ in Maseru some 30,000 people, mostly women. Maseru is the seat of Parliament (120-member National Assembly and 33-member Senate) and site of the headquarters of all government ministries. It has two large international hotels (Lesotho Sun, formerly Lesotho Hilton, and Maseru Sun) and a number of smaller hotels and bed-and-breakfast establishments. The State Library and National Archives opened in 2006 in a new Chinese-funded building. China (Beijing), Ireland, Libya, South Africa, and the United States all have resident diplomatic missions at the ambassadorial level in Maseru. Local government falls under the elected Maseru City Council. The main street is Kingsway, on or close to which are most government offices and main shops and some hotels, as well as the Basotho Hat Handicrafts Centre, built in the shape of a comical Basotho hat, a national emblem. The second business area is situated to the east near the Pitso Ground, a traditional public assembly place.

See also **Colonial Policies and Practices; Lesotho.**

BIBLIOGRAPHY

Ambrose, David. *Maseru: An Illustrated History.* Morija, Lesotho: Morija Museum and Archives, 1993.

DAVID AMBROSE

MASKS AND MASQUERADES

This entry includes the following articles:
NORTHERN AFRICA
SUB-SAHARAN AFRICA

NORTHERN AFRICA

Throughout rural areas of North Africa, Muslims may celebrate the Great Feast (*'id al-adha*) and the Feast of the Muslim New Year (*'Ashura*) with masquerade performances that last from two to seven days. Young men drape animal skins, old rags, and woven carpets over their bodies, paint their faces, and wear masks made from animal skin or cardboard in order to masquerade as Jewish men and women, religious judges, slaves, prostitutes, supernatural spirits, and various animals. Masqueraders chase and tease women and children and perform lewd and obscene acts in public, inverting socially acceptable behavior and suspending all hierarchic distinctions between people. A group of musicians accompanies the masqueraders, collecting offerings of money, eggs, chickens, and other food that they later share among themselves.

The masquerade of the Great Feast, in particular, features the masked character of Bujlud (also called Bilmawn, Buihedar, Bu-Islikhen, Bubtain, and other names in both Arabic and Tamazight that basically mean the one who is dressed in skins). Young men control the masquerade, and older men purposefully remove themselves from their performance. The young men coerce a socially marginal and impoverished man to play the character of Bujlud, who is dressed in the bloody skins of animals sacrificed earlier that day. They are sewn around his nude body, skins are fastened to each

arm, each leg, and the front and back of his body. Often the skins covering the arms hang down so that the hooves dangle below his hands. On his head he may wear an old piece of cloth and attach shoes to either side of his head to represent ears, or cover his face with an animal skin. He may also place the horns of a goat or a cow on his head.

During both the Great Feast and the 'Ashura masquerades, young men also dress as parodies of Muslim religious judges, elder Muslim men, Jewish men and women, and other burlesque characters. Jewish characters wear tattered filthy clothing, a skullcap, skin cardboard masks to which they attach long beards of wool (if dressing as men) and corncobs to make noses. Those who portray elder Muslim men wear white beards, dress in old rags, carry prayer counting beads made of snail shells, and strategically place eggplants and strips of sheepskin to create the impression of having enlarged genitals. Some men cover their faces with black soot and wear black capes, intending to charade as black slaves. Men also mask as pack animals by placing straw mats or rugs over their heads, wearing saddles on their backs, and carrying animal skulls on sticks in order to imitate mules, donkeys, or camels.

Great secrecy surrounds masquerade preparations, and, when masqueraders first emerge, they intentionally scare nearby children, flinging ashes on them. A carnivalesque atmosphere arises when villagers mock and tease the maskers, who respond by chasing the villagers and hitting them with the sticks they carry. The maskers forcefully enter houses, knocking over cooking pots and ceramic water jugs, playfully harassing women with obscene banter, and rudely grabbing whatever food they can. Women often present their children to Bujlud so he can touch them. Although the children are severely frightened by the figure covered with skins, anyone touched by Bujlud is said to receive *baraka* (divine blessing) and be protected from illness. Edward Westermarck (1862–1939) wrote that the act of harassing masked figures who depict beasts of burden and marginalized characters, such as Jews and slaves, functions to expel evil, illnesses, and diseases from a village.

The origins and early history of these masquerades are unknown. An earlier generation of scholars often interpreted them as examples of ancient pre-

Islamic agrarian rites common to the circum-Mediterranean region. Others argue that the masquerades mock the moral values that the Muslim Great Feast legitimizes, such as patriarchal authority, marriage, communal solidarity, and religious obedience, as participants act out lewd behaviors that are forbidden in everyday life. Young men, who are not subject to the disapproval of socially conservative elder men who temporarily leave the village during the masquerades, engage in playful self-directed satire, immodest behavior towards women, and the caricature of socially marginal and authoritative characters, allowing villagers to negotiate and ease the tensions of daily life.

Some Islamic reformers have criticized the act of masquerading and its associated debauchery as pagan and anti-Islamic, and these condemnations have led to masquerading's decline in many parts of North Africa. However, in Berber areas of Morocco, such as the town of Goulmima in southeastern Morocco, the masking performances of 'Ashura intentionally reject Islamist discourse. They are billed as examples of the Judeo-Berber culture that existed in North Africa before the arrival of Islam, and costumed figures carry banners with political messages promoting their Amazigh (Berber) heritage.

Many discussions of North African masks and masquerading fail to recognize that they also share characteristics with West African masquerading. In both regions young men, who prepare the masqueraders in secret, dominate performances. The bodies of the masqueraders are covered so that they lose their individual identities and assume those of the characters they represent. Music accompanies performances, which are held during ritually significant periods dissociated from everyday life. Finally, both West and North African masqueraders engage in playful behavior that often involves social commentary. These similarities between West and North African masquerades suggest that they may also share a historical connection.

See also **Dance: Social Meaning; Festivals and Carnivals; Secret Societies; Symbols and Symbolism; Theater: Northern Africa.**

BIBLIOGRAPHY

Hammoudi, Abdellah. *The Victim and Its Masks: An Essay on Sacrifice and Masquerade in the Maghreb*, trans. Paula Wissing. Chicago: University of Chicago Press, 1993.

Laoust, Emile. "Noms et cérémonies des feux de joie chez les Berbères du Haut et de l'Anti-Atlas." *Hesperis* 1 (1921): 3–66, 253–316, 387–420.

Saul, Mahir. "Islam and West African Anthropology." *Africa Today* 53, no. 1 (2006): 3–33.

Westermarck, Edward. *Ritual and Belief in Morocco*, 2 vols. New York: University Books, 1968.

CYNTHIA BECKER

SUB-SAHARAN AFRICA

Although masking is not universal in Africa, many societies have long and rich traditions of masquerades. In the fourteenth century Ibn Battuta, an Arab geographer, commented upon the use of articulated bird masks in the court of the Mali empire. In 1738 Francis Moore was one of the first Europeans to give an account of an African masquerade, which he encountered in the Senegambia in West Africa. From the mid-nineteenth century through the early decades of the twentieth century many travelers, missionaries, and colonial officials published descriptions of masquerades from diverse regions in Africa. Throughout the twentieth century African masks and the masquerade rituals and ceremonies within which they appear have been the focus of study and exegesis.

Throughout Africa masks take many forms and include a variety of carved wooden constructions, as well as those that are made entirely from bark, animal skins, plant fibers, and woven cloth. Masquerades may be owned collectively by communities, lineages, initiation and other voluntary associations, or by individuals. With few exceptions, women are excluded from performing the masks themselves, although in Gelede masquerades among the Yoruba of Nigeria women play critical roles in the rituals.

Masquerades are well documented among many groups living in West Africa, including the Dogon, Bamana, Bobo, Bwa, Mossi, Senufo, Mende, Dan, Yoruba, Igbo (Ibo), Ijaw, Ibibio, Efik, Idoma, Mambila, and Bamileke. Numerous central African groups, including the Chokwe, Kuba, Luba, Hemba, Teke, and Lega, among many others, also utilize masks. Many of these groups still perform their masquerades in the early twenty-first century. By contrast, masquerades were historically much less significant among groups living in northern, eastern, and southern Africa, although they are performed by some Berber groups living in Morocco, as well as by the Makonde in Tanzania and the Chewa in Malawi.

In many societies masquerades are the visible manifestation of spirits. These spirits may be ancestral or powerful bush, forest, or water spirits. Among the Yoruba of southwestern Nigeria, Egungun ritual society masquerades are embodiments of ancestral spirits. Ancestral spirits also appear as important masquerades among the Okpella and the Igala of Nigeria and among the Chokwe of Congo. Forest and bush spirits among the Senufo and Dan of Côte d'Ivoire and the Igbo of Nigeria are made visible through the vehicle of masquerades. In Ijaw communities in Nigeria, water-spirit masquerades are performed in annual public ceremonies that are intended to honor and propitiate these powerful beings.

In a number of African societies masks were formerly used in a regulatory capacity and played a central role in the governance of the community. Masquerades were used as strategies for social control by warrior associations among the Bamileke in Cameroon and in the Cross River area in Nigeria. Among the Dan of Côte d'Ivoire and the Igala, Idoma, and certain Igbo groups in Nigeria, a masked figure once sat in judgment of criminals, levied and collected fines, and presided over cases involving land disputes. Among the Bamana of Mali, the Komo men's association and its masquerade were charged with eradicating witchcraft.

Masks play central roles in chieftaincy rituals. In contemporary rural Malawi, spirit masks of the Chewa Nyau society perform at the installation of village headmen. This postcolonial ritual, which has its origins in the precolonial installation of divine kings, recalls a heroic past, but also reflects and reconfigures current political realities. In the twentieth century among the Bamileke, regulatory societies have been transformed into prestige titled societies and the distinctive beaded elephant mask has been incorporated into chieftaincy rituals. In Côte d'Ivoire among the Dan, a chief may own several old and important masks. These old masks are no longer used in performance, but are laid beside the chief in ritual contexts as a validation of his political authority. Pectoral and hip masks

have been a long-standing part of leadership regalia and are still worn by the *Oba* of Bénin and the *Attah* of Idah in Nigeria as symbols of political authority.

Masquerades are often material symbols of secret knowledge and serve as ritual separators between various segments of the community, such as men and women, initiated and noninitiated, community members and strangers. Among the Lega of Congo, for example, different ranks within the Bwami initiation association own and use a variety of masks. Miniature wooden and ivory masks are the property of several of the highest ranks within the association. These masks might either be worn on the body or carried by members during various ceremonies, and function as mnemonic devices alluding to the esoteric knowledge that is the purview of each specific rank. Leaders of the men's Poro association in Liberia and Sierra Leone often owned small miniature versions of larger-scale spirit masks to which they have titular rights. These personal masks validated a man's right to sit at Poro counsels and to participate in decision making. They also served as a means of identification and a validation of authority for itinerant Poro leaders.

Throughout Africa masquerades play a central role in coming-of-age ceremonies. During these rituals, the separate realms of bush and village, living and dead converge. Among the Kuba of Congo the novices are sequestered for a period of time outside of the village, in the bush, the domain of the spirits. During this period, the initiates are symbolically reborn as adults under the watchful eye of masked spirits. Masks are often used to orchestrate training in esoteric knowledge, and in the closing ceremonies of initiation, spirit masks appear in public ceremonies when the young people are presented to the community as adults. Among the Chokwe of Angola, masked spirits control the boy's initiation camp and bar women from entry into the ceremonies. Among the Gola, Bassa, and Vai of Liberia and the Mende, Bullom, and Temne of Sierra Leone, the water-spirit guardian of the women's Sande association takes the form of a masquerade. The spirit presides over the initiation camp, protects young girls during their seclusion, participates in their training, and appears with them during their reentry into the community as adult women.

Death produces a dangerous rupture in the social fabric, and it is carefully managed through a variety of rituals. In the closing phase of many societies' funeral ceremonies, including those of the Dogon of Mali, the Mossi of Burkina Faso, the Dan of Côte d'Ivoire, and the Chewa of Malawi, masks play an important role. Among the Hemba of Congo, the final phase of the funeral marks the end of mourning for the bereaved and the return of the village to a normal social life. In the ritual, the *so'o* mask, an allegorical figure of death, is used in two performances. The first performance emphasizes the state of disorder caused by death; the second performance restores order to the village. Among the Kuba and Kuba-related peoples of Congo, many of the same masks that play a critical role in boy's initiation appear at the funerals of titled elders. Their use in performance reinforces distinctions in power between titled and nontitled men and between men and women. The masks validate the institution of title-taking and reinforce the authority invested in senior titleholders.

Masks and the performances in which they are used often embody important forms of symbolic classification and the ordering of social experience. Among the Dogon of Mali the towering vertical form of the *sirige* mask represents the multistoried family house, and the graphic motifs engraved and painted on this mask symbolize the history of generations within Dogon communities. The masker's symbolic gestures reenact fundamental episodes of the Dogon creation myth.

In several Berber communities in Morocco, masquerades are performed between the Sunni Muslim feast of sacrifice and the celebration of the New Year. In these masked rituals, characters parody and contest central values, which the Muslim feast of the sacrifice sanctifies.

In the Congo the Teke *kidamu* mask, carved in the shape of a flat disk with clearly articulated bipolar divisions, is symbolically rich. This mask type, first created around 1860, has been continually modified throughout the twentieth century, reflecting a history of shifting and evolving relationships between two competing segments within the Teke political organization. The mask's primary symbolism and its use in performance express the essential nature of Teke society and highlight relationships Teke have had with their neighbors over the centuries.

In Côte d'Ivoire some Dan spirit masks are defined as entertainers. In Mali, youth-association puppet masquerades, which are performed by Bamana, Bozo, Somono, and Maraka troupes, are defined by the participants as play, although the content of these masquerade performances is often quite serious and explores the nature of society and people's relationships with powerful spirit entities.

Multiple masking traditions may exist parallel to one another in a single society. Moreover, every masquerade tradition has its own history, which may be marked by periodic transformations in the material repertoire (the masks and their costumes), in the context of use, and in the universe of interpretations assigned to them. Spirit masks among the Dan operate in a variety of contexts. Many are central to boys' initiation, while others act as messengers, debt collectors, adjudicators, and entertainers. Throughout its life history an individual Dan mask from any of these contexts might acquire prestige as it ages and subsequently its behavior, role, and interpretation is modified accordingly.

Among the Bamana of Mali the Chiwara men's association performs paired male and female antelope masquerades in annual rites which inaugurate the farming season. The form, iconography, and performance of these paired masquerades embody the virtues that the Bamana associate with agriculture. Chiwara is the mythical antelope who introduced farming to the Bamana and the pairing of the male and female mythical antelopes recreates the essential conditions for agricultural fertility symbolizing the union of the sun, the male principle, and the earth and water, the female principle. In those Malian communities where the Chiwara men's association is now defunct, these same antelope masquerades are often incorporated into festivals that the community defines as entertainments. The interpretation of the masquerades in their new performance context clearly resonates with meanings emergent in the older context. However, in many multiethnic communities these same Chiwara masquerades evoke a distinctive Bamana ethnic identity based on Bamana participants' sense of a shared history and a group investment in an agricultural life.

Masquerades have undergone repeated transformations over time and new forms and contexts of use are continually emerging in Africa. In Sierra Leone in the 1950s Ode-Lay masked associations, which were multiethnic and urban, grew up in Creole neighborhoods in Freetown as a response to disruptive social change. The inspiration for the Creole Ode-Lay associations, however, is to be found in Yoruba secret societies which were established in Sierra Leone by Yoruba immigrants after 1807. The Ode-Lay masked performances draw heavily upon Yoruba hunters' association and Egungun society rituals. Other key elements have been borrowed from Mende and Limba masking traditions. The Ode-Lay masquerades are militant and during the performances participants perform martial arts games with each other or with members of competing troupes. By the 1970s members of Sierra Leone's ruling party served as patrons for Freetown's various Ode-Lay associations and, as a way of extending their influence and consolidating their authority outside of the capital, they encouraged the establishment of Ode-Lay associations in more rural areas. Elsewhere in Mali, Congo, Nigeria, and Côte d'Ivoire masquerades have been incorporated into the repertoire of national dance troupes and stand as valued examples of a national cultural patrimony. In Mali masquerades, like those which are still performed today at Dogon funerals, are now occasionally performed in cultural festivals and for tourists while the Chiwara antelope mask has been adopted as a national cultural symbol and its image appears on public monuments, on the masthead of various publications, on locally produced textiles, and on commercial advertising signs.

See also **Dance: Social Meaning; Festivals and Carnivals; Ibn Battuta, Muhammad Abdullah; Secret Societies; Symbols and Symbolism.**

BIBLIOGRAPHY

Anderson, Martha, and Philip Peek. *Ways of the Rivers: Arts and Environment of the Niger Delta.* Los Angeles: UCLA Fowler Museum of Cultural History, 2002.

Arnoldi, Mary Jo. *Playing with Time: Art and Performance in Central Mali.* Bloomington: Indiana University Press, 1995.

Bascom, William. *The Yoruba of Southwestern Nigeria.* New York: Holt, Rinehart, and Winston, 1969.

Bastin, Marie-Louise. "Ritual Masks of the Chokwe." *African Arts* 17, no. 4 (1984): 40–45, 92–93.

Biebuyck, Daniel. *Lega Culture: Art, Initiation, and Moral Philosophy among a Central African People.* Berkeley: University of California Press, 1973.

Binkley, David A. "Avatar of Power: Southern Kuba Masquerade Figures in a Funerary Context." *Africa* 57, no. 1 (1987): 75–97.

Blakely, Thomas D., and Pamela A. R. Blakely. "Masks and Hemba Funerary Festival." *African Arts* 21 (1) 1987: 30–37.

Cole, Herbert. *I Am Not Myself: The Art of African Masquerades.* Los Angeles: Museum of Cultural History, UCLA, 1985.

Drewal, Henry John, and Margaret Thompson Drewal. *Gelede: Art and Female Power among the Yoruba.* Bloomington: Indiana University Press, 1983.

Dupré Marie-Claude. "Le masque *kidumu* maître d'histoire tssayi." In *l'Art et politiques en Afrique noire* [Art and politics in black Africa], ed. Bogumil Jewsiewicki. Ottawa: Canadian Association of African Studies, 1989.

Fischer, Eberhard, and Hans Himmelheber. *The Arts of the Dan in West Africa.* Zurich: Museum Reitberg, 1984.

Geary, Christraud. "Elephants, Ivory, and Chiefs: The Elephant and the Arts of the Cameroon Grassfields." In *The Elephant: The Animal and Its Ivory in African Culture*, ed. Doran H. Ross. Los Angeles: UCLA Fowler Museum of Cultural History, 1992.

Griaule, Marcel. *Masques dogons.* Paris: Institut d'ethnologie, 1938.

Hammoudi, Abdellah. *The Victim and Its Masks: An Essay on Sacrifice and Masquerade in the Maghreb*, trans. Paula Wissing. Chicago: University of Chicago Press, 1993.

Harley, George W. *Masks as Agents of Social Control in Northeast Liberia.* Cambridge, MA: The Museum, 1950.

Ibn Battuta. *Travels in Asia and Africa, 1325–1354*, trans. H. A. R. Gibb. London: Routledge and Kegan Paul, 1984.

Kasfir, Sidney L., ed. *West African Masks and Cultural Systems.* Tervuren, Belgium: Musée Royal de l'Afrique Centrale, 1988.

Kasfir, Sidney L., and Pamela R Franco, eds. "Women's Masquerades in Africa and the Diaspora." Special issue, *African Arts* 31, no. 2 (1998): 18–79.

Kaspin, Deborah. "Chewa Visions and Revision of Power: Transformations of the Nyau Dance in Central Malawi." In *Modernity and its Malcontents: Ritual and Power in Postcolonial Africa*, ed. Jean Comaroff and John Comaroff. Chicago: University of Chicago Press, 1993.

Mark, Peter. *The Wild Bull and the Sacred Forest: Form, Meaning, and Change in Senegambian Initiation Masks.* Cambridge, U.K.: Cambridge University Press, 1992.

Moore, Francis. *Travels into the Inland Parts of Africa.* London: J. Stagg, 1738.

Nunley, John W. *Moving with the Face of the Devil: Art and Politics in Urban West Africa.* Urbana: University of Illinois Press, 1987.

Ottenberg, Simon. *Masked Rituals of Afikpo: The Context of an African Art.* Seattle: University of Washington Press, 1975.

Phillips, Ruth. *Representing Woman: Sande Masquerades of the Mende of Sierra Leone.* Los Angeles: UCLA Fowler Museum of Cultural History, 1995.

Richards, Polly. "'Imina Sangan' or 'Masques à la mode': Contemporary Masquerade in the Dogon Region." In *Re-visions: New Perspectives on the African Collections of the Horniman Museum*, ed. Karel Arnaut. London: Horiman Museum and Gardens, 2000.

Roy, Christopher. "Leaf Masks among the Bobo and the Bwa." In *Material Differences: Art and Identity in Africa*, ed. Frank Herreman. New York: Museum for African Art, 2003.

Sieber, Roy. *Sculpture of Northern Nigeria.* New York: Museum of Primitive Art, 1961.

Steiner, Christopher, and Jane Guyer, eds. *To Dance the Spirit: Masks of Liberia.* Cambridge, MA: Peabody Museum, Harvard University, 1986.

Strother, Zoe. *Inventing Masks: Agency and History in the Art of the Central Pende.* Chicago: University of Chicago Press, 1998.

Weil, Peter. "Women's Masks and the Power of Gender in Mande History." *African Arts* 31, no. 2 (1998): 28–37, 88–91.

Wooten, Stephen. "Antelope Headdresses and Champion Farmers: Negotiating Meaning and Identity through the Bamana Ciwara Complex." *African Arts* 33, no. 2 (2000): 18–33.

Zahan, Dominique. *Sociétés d'initiation bambara, le n'domo, le koré.* Paris: Mouton, 1960.

MARY JO ARNOLDI

MASQUERADES. *See* Masks and Masquerades.

MASSAWA. After the disappearance of the ancient Aksumite-era seaport of Adulis, Massawa (or Məṣəwwa), on the Red Sea, became Ethiopia's main seaport. Massawa was an island separated from the mainland by less than a mile, and fleets would anchor between the island and the mainland. Small boats would then transport goods from the anchored ships to the port of the same name, Massawa, situated on the mainland. During the second half of the nineteenth century, when Egypt controlled the port, a rail causeway was built that connected the island and the mainland port.

Muslims have always inhabited Massawa, a fact evidenced by the Turco-Arabic architecture of its mosque, palace, and bazaars. In 1557, when the Ottoman Turks controlled the Red Sea from Port Said in the north to Aden on the Gulf of Aden in the southeast, they also occupied the port. From 1589 on, the Turks ruled Massawa through a local chieftain to whom they gave the title and authority of a na'ib, Arabic for deputy. In time, this local chieftain made the post hereditary; the original family retained differing degrees of control over the port until 1885, even though actual ownership of the port changed several times during that period.

Ethiopian rulers have consistently been preoccupied with controlling the port, as it was the kingdom's main gateway for trade, the way for Christian pilgrims to access the Holy Land, and a passageway for Muslim pilgrims going to Mecca and Medina. However, the Ethiopian leaders often lacked the power to maintain control. As a result, and despite the port's dependence on the hinterland for its victuals and drinking water, Ethiopians were subjected to a good deal of ill treatment and extortion at the hands of the na'ib and the Islamic community. These groups menaced the envoys the king sent to the Middle East, especially representatives sent to Egypt to bring a new Orthodox metropolitan to Ethiopia.

Despite Ethiopia's claims to Massawa, evidenced by both its geographic situation and historical documents, the port came under direct Ethiopian control only in 1955 when the Italian colony of Eritrea was federated with Ethiopia. Prior to 1955, the port was under the control of Egypt, followed by Great Britain when Egypt became its protectorate, and then Italy. Since Eritrea's independence from Ethiopia in 1994, Massawa has been under Eritrean control.

See also **Eritrea; Ethiopia and the Horn, History of (1600 to 1910).**

BIBLIOGRAPHY

Alvarez, Fransisco. *The Prester John of the Indies: A True Relation of the Lands of the Prester John, Being the Narrative of the Portuguese Embassy to Ethiopia in 1520,* trans. C. F. Beckingham and G.W. B. Huntingford. Cambridge, U.K.: Cambridge University Press, 1961.

Prouty, Chris, and Eugene Rosenfeld. *Historical Dictionary of Ethiopia.* Mentuchen, New Jersey: Scarecrow Press, 1981.

Rubenson, Sven. *The Survival of Ethiopian Independence,* 4th edition. Hollywood, California: Tsehai, 2003.

Zewde Gabre-Sellassie, *Yohannes IV of Ethiopia, A Political Biography.* Lawrenceville, New Jersey: The Red Sea Press, 1997.

GETATCHEW HAILE

MAT MAKING. *See* Arts: Basketry and Mat Making.

MATHEMATICS.

From the earliest times onward humans in Africa have created and developed mathematical ideas. For an annotated bibliography of mathematics in African history and cultures, see Paulus Gerdes and Ahmed Djebbar's *Mathematics in African History and Cultures: An Annotated Bibliography* (2004).

Among the earliest "mathematical artifacts" known worldwide, several are from Africa. A small piece of the fibula of a baboon, marked with twenty-nine notches, was found in a cave in the Lebombo mountains between South Africa and Swaziland. The bone has been dated to approximately 35,000 BCE. Well known and widely discussed is another bone found at Ishango (Congo), dated at 20,000 BCE.

One of the oldest mathematical texts from Ancient Egypt is a collection of problems copied by the scribe Ahmose (c. 1650 BCE), that dates from the Middle Kingdom (2040 to 1782 BCE). Its title contains a vision of mathematics: "Correct method of investigation of nature to know all that exists, each mystery, and all secrets." It contains various methods of approximate solution. For instance, the length of the side of the square that has approximately the same area as that of the circle is determined as 8/9 of the diameter of the circle, which implies 3.1605 as a close approximation for the value of π. The "pinnacle of achievement" of mathematics in Ancient Egypt is the exact result for the volume of a truncated pyramid with square base.

During the Hellenistic period and its aftermath, famous mathematicians worked in Alexandria, like the geometers Euclid (c. 365–300 BCE), Heron (c. 100 CE), Claudius Ptolemeus (second century CE), and the number theorist Diophantus (third century CE). Hypathia of Alexandria (c. 370–415 CE) is the first female mathematician known in history. In the same period, several other mathematicians are known from the Maghreb, like Theodorus (c. 465–398 BCE), Eratosthenes (c. 276–194 BCE), and Nicotelese (c. 250 BCE), all of Cyrene; Theodoses (second century BCE) of Tripoli; and Apuleius of Madaura (c. 124–170 CE).

North Africa played an important role in the genesis of algebra in Islamic culture (for an overview, see Djebbar 2005). North African mathematicians from Egypt to the Maghreb made their contributions, like Abu Kamil (d. 930), Abu Bakr al-Hassan (twelfth century), Samaw'al (d. 1175), Ibn al-Yasamin (d. 1204), Ibn Rashiq (c. 1275), Ibn al-Banna (1256–1321), Uqbani (1320–1408), Ibn Qunfudh (1339–1407), Ibn al-Ha'im (1352–1412), Ibn Haydur (d. 1413), Ibn al-Majdi (1365–1447), Qatrawani (fifteenth century), Sibt al-Maradini (1423–1506), and Ibn Ghazi (1437–1513). Important mathematicians born outside Africa worked for many years in North Africa, like Ibn al-Haytham (965–1041), Al-Qurashi (d. 1184), and Al-Qalasadi (1412–1485). Ibn Mun'im (d. 1228) of Andalusian origin settled in Marrakesh where he laid the foundations of combinatorial analysis, including a presentation of the so-called *triangle of Pascal* (1623–1662). Several mathematical notations used in the early twenty-first century had been conceived in the medieval Maghreb. Since the mid-1970s many mathematical manuscripts from the medieval Maghreb have been discovered, analyzed, and edited, underscoring the mathematical heritage of North Africa.

Mathematical ideas from Ancient Egypt to Islamic Egypt and from the Maghreb during the

Middle Ages found their way to Europe and have contributed substantially to the international development of mathematics. For instance, several Europeans came to North Africa to study mathematics, like Leonardo de Pisa, known as Fibonacci (d. c.1240).

Hundreds of mathematical manuscripts—written in Arabic and in various African languages—from Timbuktu in present-day Mali remain to be analyzed to lift the veil from some of the mathematical connections between Africa south of the Sahara and the north of the continent. The astronomer-mathematician Muhammed ibn Muhammed (c. 1740) from Katsina in present-day Nigeria was well known in Egypt and the Middle East. Thomas Fuller (1710–1790), brought from West Africa as a slave to North America in 1724, became famous in the New World for his mental calculations. Late in his life he was discovered by antislavery campaigners who used him as a demonstration that blacks are not mentally inferior to whites. In southern Central Africa the *sona* drawing and storytelling tradition incorporated various geometrical ideas, such as the conception of various algorithms to compose symmetric figures composed of a single line, and rules to chain these graphs to form bigger symmetric monolinear figures. Some geometrical knowledge from Central Africa has survived until the beginnings of the twentieth century in the Mississippi area among people of African descent. For an overview of geometrical and other mathematical ideas from Africa south of the Sahara, see Claudia Zaslavsky's 1999 study, Ron Eglash's 1999 work, and Gerdes's 1998 and 1999 books.

With the end of the colonial period and the conquest of national independence a period of mathematical revival started on the African continent. Only a few African mathematicians had received a doctorate before independence, like the Egyptians Ali Mostafa Mosharafa (1923) and Mohamed Mursy-Ahmed (1931) (independence in Egypt came in 1937); the Nigerians Chike Obi (1950), Adegoke Olubummo (1955), and James Ezeilo (1959) (independence in Nigeria came in 1960); and the Sierra Leonen Awadagin Williams (1958) (independence in Sierra Leone came in 1961). They received their doctorates from British universities.

Since then, African mathematicians have been awarded doctoral degrees by universities in at least fifty-three different countries, mostly situated in three continents: Africa (44%), Europe (36%), and America (20%). During the second half of the twentieth century more than three thousand Africans earned a doctorate in mathematics. Hundreds have been working as researchers in Europe and North America. As of 2005, the percentage of female doctorate holders was only 11 percent. African mathematicians have organized themselves in national and regional associations. In 1976 the African Mathematical Union (AMU) was created. The AMU regularly holds congresses, organizes mathematical olympiads for the youth, and publishes a research journal titled *Afrika Mathematika*. It has created various commissions to contribute to the quality of mathematics education, to promote the participation of women in mathematics, and to study and disseminate the history of mathematics in Africa. African mathematicians are doing research in various fields of pure and applied mathematics, including applications to urgent problems the continent is facing, like desertification, malaria, and HIV/AIDS.

See also **Geometries; Number Systems.**

BIBLIOGRAPHY

Djebbar, Ahmed. *Une histoire de la science arabe.* Paris: Editions du Seuil, 2001.

Djebbar, Ahmed. *L'algèbre arabe: Naissance d'un art.* Paris: Vuibert, 2005.

Eglash, Ron. *African Fractals. Modern Computing and Indigenous Design.* New Brunswick, NJ: Rutgers University Press, 1999.

Fauvel, John, and Paulus Gerdes. "African Slave and Calculating Prodigy: Bicentenary of the Death of Thomas Fuller." *Historia Mathematica* 17 (1990): 141–151.

Gerdes, Paulus. *Une tradition géométrique en Afrique—Les dessins sur le sable.* 3 vols. Paris: L'Harmattan, 1995.

Gerdes, Paulus. *Women, Art and Geometry in Southern Africa.* Trenton, NJ: Africa World Press, 1998.

Gerdes, Paulus. *Geometry from Africa: Mathematical and Educational Explorations.* Washington, DC: The Mathematical Association of America, 1999.

Gerdes, Paulus. *Sona Geometry from Angola: Mathematics of an African Tradition.* Monza: Polimetrica, 2006.

Gerdes, Paulus. *African Doctorates in Mathematics: A Catalogue.* Nairobi: African Academy of Sciences, 2006.

Gerdes, Paulus, and Ahmed Djebbar. *Mathematics in African History and Cultures: An Annotated Bibliography.* Cape Town: African Mathematical Union, 2004.

Obenga, Théophile. *La géométrie égyptienne. Contribution de l'Afrique antique à la Mathématique mondiale.* Paris: L'Harmattan and Gif-sur-Yvette: Khepera, 1995.

Sica, Giandomenico, ed. *What Mathematics from Africa?* Monza: Polimetrica, 2005.

Zaslavsky, Claudia. *Africa Counts: Number and Pattern in African Cultures.* Chicago: Lawrence Hill Books, 1999.

PAULUS GERDES

MATRIARCHY AND MATRILINY.   *See* Kinship and Affinity; Kinship and Descent; Marriage Systems.

MAURITANIA

This entry includes the following articles:
GEOGRAPHY AND ECONOMY
SOCIETY AND CULTURES
HISTORY AND POLITICS

GEOGRAPHY AND ECONOMY

For Arab geographers, Mauritania was part of the Maghreb, or West, but the French attached it to French West Africa when they placed it under the military command headquartered in Saint-Louis, in present-day Senegal. Since independence in 1960, Mauritania has made political use of its ambiguous position between North Africa and what is known as black Africa. It maintained this position even after the Senegal River became its southern border and a large number of black Mauritanians (about a third of its population—the number is a politically sensitive subject and consequently no official figures are given) joined the *bidan* (white Moors) to all become citizens of the new nation. Being at the crossroads between North and South Africa has augmented the cultural and racial tensions that marked the country's history before, during, and after French colonization. Mauritania also shares a border with Algeria and Western Sahara, and a longer border with Mali. The country is divided administratively into 13 regions (*wilaya*), 53 prefectures (*mughata*), and 216 municipalities (*beldia*).

Mauritania has always been a land of transit: trade caravans and pilgrimages to Mecca, nomadic groups following their herds, Romantic explorers such as Odette du Puigaudeau (b. 1894) or Théodore Monod (b. 1902) in times past, now replaced by tourists on their way to deep Africa, exporters of old cars going south, and emigrants going north on their way to Europe.

Most of the irrigated area and arable land (0.2%) is concentrated along the Senegal River, which makes this region the most densely populated of the country. The rest of its 397,953 square miles consists mainly of flat desert landscape with a scattering of small oases and some central hills whose highest point is Kediet Ijill (3,002 feet). Geological formations, such as the Gelb er-Richat (Adrar), attracted naturalists such as Théodore Monod, who interpreted it as a meteoritic crater.

The capital Nouakchott, which was a tiny fishing town until 1958, is doubly threatened by the advancing sand dunes and the rising sea that endangers neighborhoods that lie below sea level. A majority (708,000) of Mauritania's population (3,270,065 in 2007) lives in Nouakchott and Nouadhibou, a fishing town in the north. These high population densities as well as the swelling population in other smaller towns were further increased as a result of drought in the 1970s and 1980s and, in the north, because of conflict with Morocco over the Western Sahara. Mauritania's extensive Atlantic coast (469 miles) provides one of its leading resources, fishing, which has been shared with a large number of foreign fishing fleets.

Ecological tourism is taking its first timid steps in the Banc d'Arguin National Park on the northern coast and the Diawling National Park on the mouth of the Senegal River. There is also some tourism in Adrar (north central area) across the sand dunes and towns on the ancient caravan routes of the Sahara (Chinguetti, Ouadane) that stretch down to Oualata in the south.

Apart from fishing, Mauritania's key resources are iron ore (in decreasing demand worldwide) followed by gypsum, copper, and phosphate. International companies and Société Nationale Industrielle et Minière (SNIM) are exploring for diamonds and gold. European, Chinese, and Australian companies have

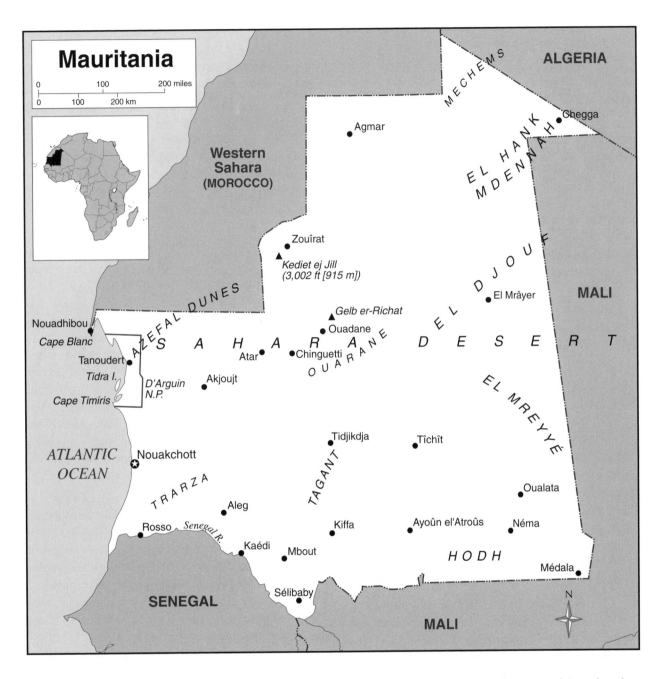

contracts to explore for oil and promise substantial production and exports in the following years.

With a weak industrial base (fish processing and mining of iron ore and gypsum), Mauritania has been particularly vulnerable to the periods of drought it periodically suffers. Natural freshwater resources other than the Senegal River are scarce. The climate is nearly always hot, with the highest temperatures occurring between June and August, a time of great social activity as that is when dates (*getna*) are harvested. Wind- and sandstorms occur primarily in March and April.

All these natural constraints explain why the majority of those who still live on the land and depend on it for crops (dates, millet, sorghum, rice, and corn) and raising livestock (goat and camels) for survival live below the international poverty line. Desertification has led to growing urban immigration and the resulting development of informal work and self-employment (trade, handicraft, and small services), mostly among women (for whom the government is practically the only employer) and the more disfavored groups, usually *haratin* (descendants of slaves).

See also **Pilgrimages: Islamic; Slave Trades; Travel and Exploration; Transportation: Caravan.**

BIBLIOGRAPHY

Cheikh, Abdel W. O., et al. *Sahara, L'Adrar de Mauritanie, Sur les traces de Théodore Monod.* Paris: Vents de Sable, 2002.

Puigaudeau, Odette du. *Pieds nus à travers la Mauritanie.* Paris: Phébus, 1993.

Salem, Zekeria Ould Ahmed, ed. *Les trajectoires d'un Etat-frontière: Espaces, évolution politique et transformations sociales en Mauritanie.* Dakar: CODESRIA, 2004.

Seddon, David. "The Political Economy of Mauritania: An Introduction." *Review of Political Economy* 23, no. 68 (1996): 97–214.

MARIA CARDEIRA DA SILVA

SOCIETY AND CULTURES

The current population of Mauritania is around three million people, spread over an area of over 600,000 square miles, three-quarters of which is desert. In the 1950s, most Mauritanians were mainly nomadic and rural, whereas in the early 2000s the majority is concentrated in built-up areas with populations of more than five thousand. The two main cities of Mauritania, Nouakchott, the capital, and Nouadhibou, contain more than a quarter of the country's population. Poverty remains a significant factor. The estimated GNP is US$480 per capita and more than half of Mauritanians over the age of fifteen are illiterate.

The result of a colonial demarcation of boundaries that have been reshaped several times since independence in 1960, Mauritania is the home of a variety of ethnic and linguistic groups: Arabic-speaking Moors, Pulaar speakers, Soninke, and Wolof. The relative size of these groups is still a matter of dispute that is complicated by around half of the Moor population consisting of former black slaves (*haratin*), sometimes called black Africans by the nationalists, as being part of the black peoples of Mauritania (Pulaar, Soninke, and Wolof), as opposed to the Moors (whites). At the time of independence, statistics from the colonial era indicated that the ethnic makeup of the population was 80 percent Arabic speakers, 14 percent Pulaar, 4 percent Soninke, and around 1 to 2 percent Wolof. The black African community make their living mostly from agriculture and live in the south of the country, whereas the Arabic-speaking population, formerly consisting mainly of livestock-owning nomads, live in the central and northern part.

Since the 1960s, a variety of reasons, including climate change, war in the Sahara, and the construction of the southern trans-Mauritania highway, have resulted in widespread migration to Mauritania's southern borders where the last remaining ecological areas capable of being developed are located. Ethnic rivalry over these areas has persisted, intensified by the conflicting Arab and black African national identities.

This ethnic diversity goes hand in hand with strong similarities between the different ethnic groups: adherence to Maliki Islam and broadly similar traditional hierarchical structures that clearly contrast free men (warriors, marabouts) and individuals of a particular caste, variously designated as tributaries, *griots*, craftsmen, freed slaves, and slaves. French colonization and the changes that have occurred since independence have clearly reduced the importance of these structures, but they remain pervasive. Evidence of this can be seen in the continuing debate concerning slavery, which in 1980 was officially abolished for the third time since 1902.

In the Moorish (or Maure) society to which the majority of the Mauritanian population belongs, the vertical structure of the statutory groups just described is coupled with a horizontal subdivision of the entire society into tribes (Arabic *qabila*, plural *qaba'il*). Sharing the same territory, with a common interest in livestock, various common obligations (particularly the fixing of a blood price for a murder committed by a member of the tribe), the existence of a recognized system of chiefdoms, and an assembly (*jama'a*) speaking on behalf of the masses, are among the characteristics that mark the tribe as a political force. Although now removed from their territory and sedentarized, tribal identity nonetheless continues in the early twenty-first century to represent a formidable political and social force.

Ethnic group, tribe, and caste, seemingly the most meaningful method of classifying Mauritanian society, are intertwined and overlap with the social distinctions that are the product of its precolonial and colonial inheritance and modern capitalism. Employment in the modern sense is only relevant

République Islamique de Mauritanie (Islamic Republic of Mauritania)

Population:	3,270,065 (2007 est.)
Area:	Area: 1,030,700 sq. km (397,953 sq. mi.)
Official language:	Arabic, French
Languages:	Arabic, French, Poular, Soninke, Wolof
National currency:	ouguiya
Principal religions:	Muslim 100%
Capital:	Nouakchott (est. pop. 708,000 in 2006)
Other urban centers:	Nouadhibou, Rosso, Kiffa, Atar, Zouérate, Kaédi,
Annual rainfall:	varies from less than 500 mm (20 in.) in south to less than 100 mm (4 in.) in desert northern half of the country
Principal geographical features:	*Plateaus:* Adrar, Tagant, Assaba *Rivers:* Senegal, other small seasonal rivers *Lakes:* R'Kiz, d'Aleg (seasonal)
Economy:	*GDP per capita:* US$2,600 (2006)
Principal products and exports:	*Agricultural:* dates, millet, sorghum, rice, corn, cattle, sheep *Manufacturing:* petroleum refining, plastics and chemicals production, food and beverage processing, paper manufacturing, textiles, smelting, fish processing *Mining:* iron ore, some gold, gypsum
Government:	Independence from France, 1960. Republic proclaimed in 1961. Constitution, 1961. New constitution adopted in 1991, calls for bicameral national assembly. Multiparty presidential elections of 1990s seen as flawed. Bloodless coup in 2005 replaced president with military council with intentions of establishing democratic institutions and organized elections. Country remains an autocratic state until next election.
Heads of state since independence:	1960–1961: Prime Minister Mukhtar ould Daddah 1961–1978: President Mukhtar ould Daddah 1978–1979: Lieutenant Colonel Mustapha Ould Mohammed Salek, chairman of the Comité Militaire de Redressement National (CMRN) 1979: Lieutenant Colonel Mustapha Ould Mohammed Salek, chairman of the Comité Militaire Salut National (CMSN) 1979–1980: Prime Minister Lieutenant Colonel Mohammed Khouna Ould Haidalla 1979–1980: Lieutenant Colonel Mohammed Mahmoud Ould Louly, chairman of the CMSN 1980–1984: Lieutenant Colonel Mohammed Khouna Ould Haidalla, chairman of the CMSN 1984–2005: President Colonel Maaouya Sid Ahmed ould Taya 2005–2007: Colonel Ely Ould Mohamed Vall 2007–: Prime Minister Zeine ould Zeidane
Armed forces:	*Army:* 15,000 *Navy:* 500 *Air force:* 150 *Paramilitary:* 6,000
Transportation:	*Rail:* 717 km (446 mi.) *Ports:* Port Autenome at Nouadhibou, Port de l'Amité at Nouakchott, Bogue, Kaédi, Rosso *Roads:* 7,660 km (4,760 mi.), 11% paved *Airline:* Served by Air Afrique *Airports:* International facilities at Nouakchott and Nouadhibou; 23 smaller airports and airstrips throughout the country
Media:	Main periodicals: *Ach-Chaab, Al-Bayane, Le Calame, Eveil-Hebdo, Mauritanie Demain, Le Peuple, Journal Officiel.* 15 radio stations and 1 television station.
Literacy and education:	*Total literacy rate:* 59% (2006). Attendance is compulsory for 6 years; about 80% of children receive formal education. Postsecondary education is provided by Université de Nouakchott, Institu National des Hautes Études Islamiques, École Nationale d'Administration, Institut Supérieur Scientifique.

to 4 percent of the working population, according to official statistics from 2000. The public sector is the leading employer, followed by mining, industrial fishing, and small business. Although this shows the existence of a nascent class structure (office and industrial workers), it is impossible to ignore the marginal nature of these middle classes in comparison with the traditional subdivisions and distinctions of Mauritanian society. It is these ethnic frameworks, both statutory and tribal, harnessed and channeled by the state with all the powers and resources at its disposal, that continue to be central to Mauritanian society.

See also **Livestock; Moors in African History; Nouakchott; Slavery and Servile Institutions.**

BIBLIOGRAPHY

Cheikh, Abdel W. O.; Bruno Lamarche; Robert Vernet; and Jean-Marc Durou. *Sahara. L'Adrar de Mauritanie. Sur les Traces de Théodore Monod.* Paris: Vents de Sable, 2002.

Zekeria, Ould Ahmed Salem, ed. *Les Trajectoires d'un Etat-Frontiere: Espaces, Evolution Politique et Transformations Sociales en Mauritanie.* Dakar, Senegal: Council for the Development of Social Science Research in Africa, 2004.

ABDEL WEDOUD OULD CHEIKH

HISTORY AND POLITICS

The Islamic Republic of Mauritania, stretching north from the Senegal River and composed of Saharan *bidan* (white, Arab) and Sahelian *sudan* (black, African) peoples, shares nothing but its name with the Roman Mediterranean province of Mauretania once populated by Mauri (darker skinned) Berbers. Europeans facilitated this continuity by associating Maures (Moors) with Africans, and in early modern times pushing their geographical home from the Maghreb, deep into the Sahara. Colonial ethnographers saw the nomadic pastoralists in the area extending from the Atlantic to Timbuktu and present-day southern Morocco/Algeria to Senegal, as sharing a common language (*hassaniya*, an Arabic-Berber dialect), religion (Islam), and desert economy, and therefore constituting a distinct Maure culture. French administrator Xavier Coppolani (1866–1905) originally envisaged this vast domain as Mauritanie occidentale in a proposal to the French Ministry of Colonies in 1897.

This vision was soon challenged. In 1891, emirs with whom the French had long-standing commercial treaties on the left bank of the Senegal River saw the right bank, where they traditionally exercised political and religious influence, annexed definitively to Senegal. The northern boundary negotiated with Spain (1900) excluded valued Atlantic pastures and fertile northern *wadis*. The central regions of oasis agriculture and commerce, Tagant and Adrar, resisted Coppolani's initiative. The support of Morocco's fiercely anti-French Shaykh Ma al-ʾAinin augmented the resistance. Although the civil territory of Mauritania was promulgated in 1904, the boundaries of what became the French West African colony of Mauritania were secured only in 1920.

For Ma al-ʾAinin's successors, the Moroccan sultanate and powerful northern tribes such as the Regueibat, Mauritania's borders did not exist. They continued to demand allegiance from the Adrar-Tagant, enticed emirs into dissidence, claimed customary rights to pastures and wells, exploited client relationships (protection payments, religious dues), and launched raids (*ghazis*) against French convoys and camel patrols. These ended only with a severe drought in 1933–1934, and coordinated military activity brought an end to resistance against colonial rule.

Pacification had consequences. It necessitated heavy requisitions of food and animals, and severely damaged fragile local economies. Peace permitted the development of education (the Franco-Arab *madrasa*), agriculture (especially dates and grain), and commerce—traditionally the joint responsibilities of clerical clans and students (Arabic plural, *talamid*), and slaves and freed slaves (*haratin*). Saharan warriors and regional emirs depended on instability to justify their livelihood—extracting protection payments from sedentary cultivators and caravans and levying taxes on the spoils of war. Security threatened this political economy even as former dependents prospered. There were few opportunities for unemployed warriors.

Social changes reflected regional economic opportunities. The best agricultural land bordered the Senegal River. Development was thwarted by land being worked by the haratin, whose masters annually claimed the bulk of the harvest. This relationship fed large desert populations. French attempts to free haratin in order to market more of their produce in the colonial economy undermined an economic as well as a social network. The Adrar-Tagant traditionally exchanged slaves, desert salts, and animals for manufactured items (Morocco) and grain (the French Sudan). Mauritania's new boundaries decapitated the slave trade (as political policy intended) and distorted these trajectories to reorient merchants to Senegal for food and commercial goods (including industrial salts) and for marketing animals and animal products (milk, meat, skins). Administrative centers (south and central) attracted new groups of merchants, suppliers, and transporters, as well as haratin wage laborers.

The more distant eastern and northern regions were marginalized. As a result, impoverished nomads emigrated permanently to Sudan or Morocco, attached themselves as clients to prosperous town-dwellers, became sedentary in the process, or defied French patrols by resurrecting the once-prosperous trans-Saharan slave trade. Wherever possible, chiefs were threatened with fines and imprisonment if they did not comply with orders to expand cultivation (grain, vegetables, and dates). These policies generated a demand for what was traditionally slave labor and conflicted directly with efforts to end slave trading. Masters responded to their predicament by creating a dependent haratin of male slaves and increasing control over female slaves—assuring Mauritanian slavery a future.

World War II initiated significant political changes. In 1946, Mauritania became a French overseas territory and elected deputies to the national parliament. Political parties were formed and elections fought in the 1950s; the key question shaping politics derived from the colonial experience: should Mauritania look to Morocco and the Arab world for its future, or to Senegal (from where it was still administered) and Francophone black Africa? During the 1956–1960 era of decolonization, future president Mukhtar ould Daddah (b. 1924) hinted at the answer. Although a French-trained lawyer, as vice-president of the Government Council he initiated the decree that moved Mauritania's capital to Nouakchott in 1957. In 1958, the new Parti du regroupement mauritanien (that became the Parti du people mauritanien in 1961) was directing an autonomous territory and, in 1959, adopting a parliamentary-style constitution and electing members to its own first National Assembly (with ould Daddah as prime minister). The Islamic Republic of Mauritania became independent in 1960.

This political direction was not unopposed: Mauritanian politicians self-exiled in Morocco encouraged a Moroccan Liberation Army attempt to reconstitute greater Morocco by sending troops to liberate the Adrar in 1958. Morocco did not formally recognize Mauritania until forced to by the United Nations in 1969. A few years later, a compromise over the northern border issue was reached by dividing the former Spanish Sahara between them. Natives of the region, largely Ragibat with tribal connections in Algeria and Mauritania, organized violent opposition. The Algeria-backed Polisario Front successfully exploited Mauritania's weaknesses,

twice attacking Nouakchott itself. French and Moroccan forces were increased on Mauritanian soil, inciting local resentment and unease. Compounded by the costs of war and a decade of drought, the situation climaxed in a coup d'etat in 1978 that marked the end of Mauritania's Saharan claims. It initiated more than twenty-five years of palace-coup politics.

Mukhtar ould Daddah's vision of Mauritania, as Coppolani's, was as a hyphen between north and south. But once again, it was a vision doomed to failure, never fully shared by white (bidan) Arabic-speakers who felt their Mauritania wrongly belonged to the Maures or black (sudan). The non-Arabic-speakers (the majority being Halpulaar) did not feel fully incorporated in ould Daddah's vision and instead favored southern autonomy. Hapulaar resistance to perceived government Arabization in the 1960s and 1970s escalated in the 1980s. A series of post-coup regimes, tarnished by international accusations that slavery was alive and well in spite of a recent law prohibiting it (1980), courted Middle Eastern development aid: Mauritania became Arab and Islamic in law, education, and administration. A two-tiered system increasingly separated white Arab from black African students. Haratin who spoke *hassanyia* because of their relations with bidan families had more economic and professional opportunities than free black Africans.

In 1986, the Front de Libération des Africains de Mauritanie (FLAM), led mostly by Halpulaar, circulated a manifesto in Nouakchott opposing this Arab orientation; the government's response saw two-thirds of the signers arrested and tortured, with three killed. In 1987, accusations that the Halpulaar planned a coup d'état triggered a purge of black Africans in the army. In April 1989, a localized incident in the Senegal River Valley sparked a war with Senegal in which Maures living in Dakar were attacked and forcibly repatriated, and hundreds of black Africans in Mauritania accused of being Senegalese were killed. In total, at least 80,000 fled to Senegal (where UN refugee camps were set up) and Mali, family and property were left behind, and identity papers were lost or destroyed. The Halpulaar continued to suffer persecution through 1991 and 1992. This state-sponsored violence ended in amnesty for those who had perpetrated it (1993) and an invitation for Mauritanians abroad to return. But without recognition of their refugee status, those who returned faced violence when reclaiming their property and harassment over missing identity papers (without which they could neither vote nor legally work). It is believed that as of 2006, 15,000 to 20,000 Mauritanian refugees remain in exile, an ongoing reminder of Mauritania's fragile unity.

Mauritania rejected the liberal institutions embedded in the decolonization process by opting for a one-party regime tightly controlled by the then-President Mukhtar ould Daddah. Antislave and human right activists groups joined opponents in Marxist, Islamist and Baathist camps in the 1980s and 1990s. The state (after 1978, a military regime) combined repression and co-optation to control them. In the context of Africa-wide democratization, Colonel Maaouya Sid Ahmed ould Taya (in power since a coup d'état in 1984) installed a civilian liberal democratic regime in 1991: a democratic constitution was adopted, multi-party elections were organized. But in this façade democracy, opposition parties and civic organizations were often shut down, and independent newspapers were censored; an oligarchy of military officers, wealthy businessmen, and relations of the president monopolized economic and political advantages. Ironically, although an Islamic state, religious-based parties were prohibited; their followers were labeled Islamists and jailed without trial. In recent years, North American and European fear of terrorism has assisted the government in its prohibitions: in the guise of assisting international antiterrorist efforts, Mauritania simultaneously clamped down on domestic political opposition and leveraged foreign (mainly U.S.) military aid. Combined with controversial recognition of Israel (1999), the government's Islamist policy contributed to a significant loss of legitimacy. A serious attempt to overthrow the regime in 2003 revealed its vulnerability; in August 2005, members of the president's own security forces exercised a successful coup d'état. The current military leadership held a referendum on a new constitution in June 2006, and promised truly democratic elections in 2007. But it continues to prosecute Islamists and procrastinate on social reform (slavery, racism, refugees).

See also **Colonial Policies and Practices; Dakar; Moors in African History; Nouakchott; Refugees; Slave Trades; Slavery and Servile Institutions.**

BIBLIOGRAPHY

International Crisis Group. *Islamism in North Africa IV: The Islamist Challenge in Mauritani: Threat or Scapegoat?* Middle East/North Africa Report No. 41, May 11, 2005.

International Crisis Group. *Political Transition in Mauritania: Assessment and Horizons.* Middle East/North Africa Report No. 53, April 24, 2006.

Jourde, Cédric, "Mauritania." In *Countries at the Crossroads 2005: A Survey of Democratic Governance*, eds. Sarah Repucci and Christopher Walker. New York: Freedom House and Rowman and Littlefield, 2005.

Magistro, John V. "Crossing Over: Ethnicity and Transboundary Conflict in the Senegal River Valley." *Cahiers d'études africaines* 33, no. 130 (1993): 201–231.

McDougall, E Ann. "A Topsy-Turvy World: Slaves and Freed Slaves in Colonial Mauritania." In *The End of Slavery*, eds. Suzanne Miers and Richard Roberts. Madison: University of Wisconsin Press, 1989.

McDougall, E Ann, Mesky Brhane, and Urs Peter Ruf, "Legacy of Slavery; Promise of Democracy: Mauritania Enters the 21st Century." In *Globalizing Africa*, ed. Malinda Smith. Trenton, New Jersey: Africa World Press, 2003.

Robinson, David. *Paths of Accommodation: Muslim Societies and French Colonial Authorities in Senegal and Mauritania, 1880–1920.* Athens: Ohio University Press, 2000.

Stewart, Charles C. *Islam and the Social Order in Mauritania: A Case Study from the 19th Century.* Oxford: Oxford University Press, 1973.

Stewart, Charles C. "Political Authority and Social Stratification in Mauritania." In *Arabs and Berbers: From Tribe to Nation in North Africa*, eds. Ernest Gellner and Charles Micaud. London: Gerald Duckworth, 1973.

Stewart, Charles C. "North-South Dialectic in Mauritania: An Update." *Maghreb Review* 2, no. 1 (1986): 40-45.

E. ANN MCDOUGALL
CÉDRIC JOURDE

MAURITIUS

This entry includes the following articles:
GEOGRAPHY AND ECONOMY
SOCIETY AND CULTURES
HISTORY AND POLITICS

GEOGRAPHY AND ECONOMY

Mauritius, an island of volcanic origin located almost 500 miles east of Madagascar, at 20 degrees

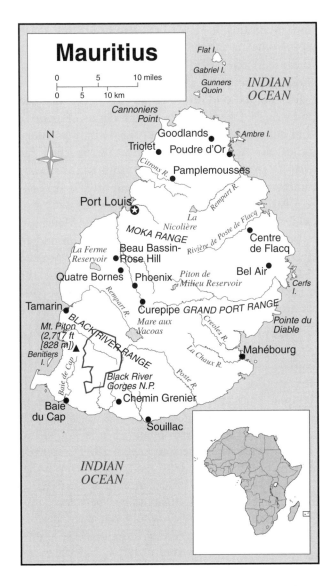

The focus and structure of the Mauritian economy has changed substantially since the island was settled permanently in 1721. Bertrand François Mahé de La Bourdonnais, governor from 1735 to 1746, envisioned the Mascarenes as a naval base from which French interests in India could be supported. In keeping with La Bourdonnais' vision, Mauritian colonists concentrated throughout much of the eighteenth century on the production of the foodstuffs and naval stores needed by the squadrons and privateers that operated in the Indian Ocean during France's wars with Great Britain. Pierre Poivre, the colony's first royal comptroller (1767–1772), encouraged the production of commodities such as cotton, indigo, and spices, but these attempts to develop export-oriented plantation agriculture failed.

The late eighteenth century also witnessed the development of a significant commercial sector in the island's economy. Beginning in 1769, the island was opened to free trade by all French nationals. The extension of similar privileges to American merchants in 1784 and to all other foreign nationals in 1787, coupled with the success of Mauritian based privateers who preyed on enemy shipping during the wars that Britain and France fought during this era, made the island an increasingly important commercial entrepôt in the western Indian Ocean that attracted shipping from as far away as northern Europe and the United States. The island's capture by a British expeditionary force in 1810 and subsequent inclusion in the British Empire in 1814 undermined its position as a commercial center with the result that Mauritian colonists turned increasingly to the production of sugar.

The Dutch had first introduced sugar cane onto the island during the seventeenth century. Cane cultivation was reintroduced by La Bourdonnais, but the local sugar industry languished until the first decade of the nineteenth century when the interruption of French sugar supplies caused by the great slave revolt in Saint Domingue (later Haiti) encouraged Mauritian colonists to begin expanding production. The abolition in 1825 of the preferential tariff on West Indian sugar entering Great Britain revolutionized the local sugar industry and from the mid-1830s onward sugar accounted for

south latitude and 57 degrees east longitude, is one of the three Mascarene Islands situated in the southwestern Indian Ocean. The island consists of a plain that rises from the northeast toward the southwest and is broken by gorges, small rivers, and peaks that are the remnants of an ancient volcanic crater. The climate is subtropical but moderated by the southeast trade winds. Annual rainfall varies widely, from more than 196 inches on the windward slopes of the central plateau to only 35 inches on the west coast. The Republic of Mauritius includes the island of Rodrigues as well as the dependencies of Agalega and the Cargados Carajos Shoals (or Saint Brandon Islands), giving the country a total land area of 788 square miles.

85 percent or more of the value of Mauritian exports.

Sugar continued to dominate Mauritian life until the early 1980s. Following independence in 1968, the Mauritian government sought to diversify the country's economy. To this end, an Export Processing Zone was established in 1971 to encourage the development of export-oriented industries, especially textiles and clothing. Tourism has also been developed and become another important source of foreign exchange. In the face of growing competition from other countries producing clothing and textiles, the Mauritian government is seeking to diversify the country's economy still further by encouraging the development of financial services and information technology.

See also **Plantation Economies and Societies; Slave Trades.**

BIBLIOGRAPHY

Allen, Richard B. *Slaves, Freedmen, and Indentured Laborers in Colonial Mauritius.* Cambridge, U.K.: Cambridge University Press, 1999.

Paturau, J. Maurice. *Histoire économique de l'Ile Maurice.* Les Pailles, Mauritius: Henry et Cie Ltée, 1988.

Storey, William Kelleher. *Science and Power in Colonial Mauritius.* Rochester, NY: University of Rochester Press, 1997.

RICHARD B. ALLEN

SOCIETY AND CULTURES

Mauritian society and culture has been characterized by considerable diversity since the island was colonized in 1721. Mauritius houses four principal communities—Franco-Mauritian, Creole (i.e., of African and Malagasy descent), Indo-Mauritian, and Sino-Mauritian—that are frequently further subdivided along class, ethnic, linguistic, and religious lines.

Many Franco-Mauritians trace their ancestry to the European (mostly French) artisans, government officials, merchants, soldiers, and sailors who settled on the island during the eighteenth century. The origins of the Creole population stem from the local demand for servile labor during the eighteenth and early nineteenth centuries. Perhaps as many as 101,000 men, women, and children were imported into Mauritius as slaves between 1721 and 1810, approximately three-fourths of whom reached the island after 1769. Most of these slaves came from Madagascar and eastern Africa, especially Mozambique and the Swahili coast, and included individuals taken from a broad range of peoples and cultures. Smaller numbers of slaves from India, Southeast Asia, and West Africa also reached the island's shores during the eighteenth and very early nineteenth centuries; like those imported from eastern Africa and Madagascar, these slaves came from a wide variety of societies and cultures. Mauritius' capture by the British in 1810 brought an end to the legal importation of slaves, but an estimated 52,550 slaves were introduced illegally onto the island from Madagascar and the East African coast between 1811 and circa 1827.

However, this servile workforce proved to be inadequate to meet the labor needs of the island's rapidly expanding sugar industry during the first decades of the nineteenth century. This fact, coupled with the formal abolition of slavery in 1835 and the subsequent withdrawal of the colony's former slaves from estate labor at the end of the apprenticeship period (1835–1839), spurred the introduction of indentured laborers from India. More than 451,000 Indian immigrants arrived to work on the island's sugar estates between 1834 and 1910, two-thirds of whom remained permanently in the colony. Three-fifths of these immigrants came from northern India, especially the provinces of Bengal and Bihar, while one-third arrived from Tamil- and Telegu-speaking areas in the Madras Presidency in southern India. Smaller numbers of immigrants also arrived from central and western India via the port of Bombay. Small numbers of Chinese immigrants likewise began to reach the island in the mid-nineteenth century, most of whom were Hakka speakers from the province of Hunan.

The modern Mauritian population of approximately 1.2 million people reflects the sociocultural complexity that has been a hallmark of local life since the eighteenth century. The 2000 census reported, for example, that almost one-third of all Mauritians are Christians (both Roman Catholic and Protestant), one-half are Hindus, and 16.6 percent are Muslims, with other faiths (e.g., Buddhism) accounting for the balance of the population. Economic growth and development has

---

République de Maurice (Republic of Mauritius)

Population:	1,250,882 (2007 est.)
Area:	2,040 sq. km (788 sq. mi.)
Official language:	English
Languages:	Creole (common), French, English, Hindi, Urdu, Hakka, Bhojpuri
National currency:	Mauritian rupee
Principal religions:	Hindu 48%, Roman Catholic 24%, other Christian 9%, Muslim 17%, other 2%
Capital:	Port Louis (est. pop. 146,319 in 2006)
Other urban centers:	Beau Bassin and Rose Hill, Vacoas-Phoenix, Curepipe, Quatre Bornes
Annual rainfall:	Varies from less than 900 mm (36 in.) on the west coast to 5,000 mm (200 in.) or more in the central region.
Principal geographical features:	*Mountains:* Moka Range, Grand Port Range, Black River Range *Rivers:* Grande Rivière Sud-Est, on Mauritius
Economy:	*GDP per capita:* US$13,700 (2006)
Principal products and exports:	*Agricultural:* sugarcane, tea, corn, potatoes, bananas, pulses; cattle, goats, fish *Manufacturing:* food processing (largely sugar milling), textiles, clothing, chemicals, metal products, transport equipment, nonelectrical machinery
Government:	Became an independent parliamentary democracy within the British Commonwealth in 1968; became a republic within the Commonwealth in 1992. Multiparty parliamentary democracy. Prime minister is head of government and of the Council of Ministers, which is responsible to the National Assembly. The unicameral National Assembly, elected by universal suffrage, consists of 70 members who serve 5-year terms. The prime minister nominates the president, who serves a 5-year term. For purposes of local government there are 9 administrative districts and urban-rural councils. The island of Rodrigues has considerable autonomy and has 2 elected representatives to the National Assembly and a minister in the Cabinet.
Heads of state since independence:	1968–1982: Prime Minister Sir Seewoosagur Ramgoolam 1982–1995: Prime Minister Sir Anerood Jugnauth 1992: President Sir Veeraswamy Ringadoo 1992–2002: President Cassam Uteem 1995–2000: Prime Minister Navin Ramgoolam 2000–2003: Prime Minister Sir Anerood Jugnauth 2003–: President Sir Anerood Jugnauth
Armed forces:	The United Kingdom has treaty obligations for defense of Mauritius. There are no regular military forces. *Paramilitary:* 1,300
Transportation:	*Port:* Port Louis *Roads:* 2,020 km (1,255 mi.), 100% paved. *National airline:* Air Mauritius *Airport:* Sir Seewoosagur Ramgoolam International Airport at Plaisance
Media:	7 daily newspapers in French and English, including *Le Mauricien, The Sun, L'Express.* 2 daily publications in Chinese: *Chinese Daily News* and the *China Times.* 26 weekly, bi-weekly, or monthly newspapers in English and/or French. There is an active book publishing industry. Television (2 stations) and radio (13 stations) are government controlled, provided by Mauritius Broadcasting Corporation.
Literacy and education:	*Total Adult Literacy rate:* 85%. Education is free and compulsory for ages 5–12. Secondary schools are predominantly religious or private; matriculation to them is on a competitive basis and only 50% of students go on. Postsecondary education provided by University of Mauritius, the Mauritius Institute of Education, the Mahatma Gandhi Institute, the Mauritius College of the Air (television and radio), and Institut Africain et Mauricien de Bilinguisme.

---

done much to lessen the poverty that afflicted many segments of Mauritian society at independence in 1968, but the gap that continues to exist between the country's poor and those who are well-to-do remains a source of social and political tension. Although the government emphasizes the extent to which Mauritius is a peaceful, tolerant, and multicultural "rainbow" society, all segments of society have become increasingly aware of their ethnic and cultural heritage, and ethnically based communalism remains a significant feature of Mauritian life, especially in politics.

See also **Creoles; Slave Trades.**

BIBLIOGRAPHY

Allen, Richard B. "The Mascarene Slave-Trade and Labor Migration in the Indian Ocean during the Eighteenth and Nineteenth Centuries." In *The Structure of Slavery in Indian Ocean, Africa and Asia*, ed. Gwyn Campbell. London: Frank Cass, 2004.

Bowman, Larry W. *Mauritius: Democracy and Development in the Indian Ocean.* Boulder, CO: Westview Press, 1991.

Carter, Marina. *Servants, Sirdars and Settlers: Indians in Mauritius, 1834–1874.* Delhi: Oxford University Press, 1995.

Ly-Tio-Fane Pineo, Huguette. *Chinese Diaspora in Western Indian Ocean.* Bell Village, Mauritius: Editions de l'Océan Indien, 1985.

RICHARD B. ALLEN

HISTORY AND POLITICS

The island of Mauritius, located in the South West Indian Ocean, is one of the few countries whose history begins in the colonial era. There were no indigenous inhabitants and the first settlers arrived in the 1720s. As of the early twenty-first century, there is no written record available of any arrival preceding that of the Portuguese. Because of its location and its use as a base by pirates and French corsairs, the island was the focus of inter-European rivalry in the Indian Ocean in the seventeenth and eighteenth centuries. The Dutch took possession in 1638 and abandoned it in 1719 when the Cape became the preferred location.

French possession of the island occurred in 1715; the French ruled for nearly one hundred years until they were defeated in 1810 by the British. There were four successive administrations: the French East India Company ruled from 1715 to 1765; the Royal government from 1765 to 1790; a revolutionary government from 1790 to 1803; and a Napoleonic government from 1803 to 1810. Agriculture stagnated and trade proved the most lucrative activity for the island's French population. This population became a very vocal minority by the end of the eighteenth century and demanded political rights. It temporarily broke away from France when slavery was abolished in French colonies in 1794. Slavery was officially restored when Napoleon I took over in France and slave owners' rights reestablished. The importation of an extremely ethnically varied slave population created a unique society composed of Indian, Malagasy, African, and French persons by the end of the eighteenth century.

A racially mixed free population also emerged, demanding equal civil and political rights with people of European descent. They obtained greater equality in 1826 when the British takeover removed discrimination against free people of color. This "little rock," as the first British governor Robert Farquhar described Mauritius, had potential as a strategic "spot" in extending British influence in the South West Indian Ocean. Rather than establish "representative government" as in the Caribbean, the British chose to implement a Crown colony system. Sugar cultivation was encouraged partly in order to stave off the cost of maintaining the colony.

However, unlike the Caribbean, there was no major influx of British settlers. Instead the British local colonial administration attempted to woo the French colonists while at the same time pursuing a seemingly contradictory policy of abolishing slavery (the lifeblood of the French colonists) and of anglicizing Mauritius. French colonists found unlikely allies in the few British merchants settled there. Both groups of planters and merchants were at the forefront of political demands for municipal elections, then later for representation on the Council of Government, and eventually for elections.

It was the British governor, Sir John Pope Hennessy, who coined the phrase "Mauritius for Mauritians," which became the slogan of the Mauritian elite. However those who qualified as electors were the large property owners and those who could speak English or French well. This disqualified the bulk of the population. With the rise of trade unionism, colonial policy softened toward the activities of workers' associations and the elite politics characterizing late-nineteenth-century Mauritius slowly gave way to mass participation in politics. The Labour Party was formed in 1936 by Dr. Maurice Cure; its leaders campaigned for an improvement in workers' lives and for pension benefits decades later. It was also the leaders of this party, especially Sir Seewoosagur Ramgoolam, a British-trained medical doctor, who led the country to independence in 1968.

Independent Mauritius inherited a large unemployed population, a rapidly growing population, and unstable ethnic situation. Riots occurred in 1967 and British troops had to be urgently called in. Nevertheless the welfare state was established and alternatives to the predominance of sugar in the economy were envisaged. Despite these attempts, a crisis situation culminated in 1971. A new political party, the

Mouvement Militant Mauricien (MMM), emerged with Paul Bérenger at its head; it supplanted the main opposition party, the Parti Mauricien Social Démocrate. It launched a series of nationwide strikes in 1971 but its leaders were imprisoned and a state of emergency declared. Although socialist in outlook, once the MMM finally came to power nearly thirty years later in 2000, it followed a neoliberal capitalist philosophy, indicating how much the party had changed in ideological orientation.

The Labour Party and the MMM are the main political parties in the early 2000s. Democratic participation is active. There is an absence of women from politics and the voice of the youth is barely heard. Despite these weaknesses, Mauritius' evolution since independence in terms of its management of ethnic relations and the economy is considered a success story on the African continent.

See also **Slave Trades.**

BIBLIOGRAPHY

Burrenchobay, Sir Dayanand. *Let the People Think: A Compilation of the Thoughts of Sir Dayendranath Burrenchobay.* Mauritius: Stanley Rose-Hill, 2000.

Bowman, Larry W. *Mauritius: Democracy and Development in the Indian Ocean.* Boulder, CO: Westview Press, 1991.

Simmons, Adele. *Modern Mauritius: The Politics of Decolonization.* Bloomington: Indiana University Press, 1982.

Unienville, Raymond. *Histoire politique de l'Isle de France.* Ile Maurice: L.C. Achille, 1975–1989. Mauritius Archives Publications.

VIJAYA TEELOCK

MBABANE. Mbabane is the administrative capital of Swaziland, Africa's remaining absolute monarchy. Though legislative functions are carried out at Lobamba, most administrative offices are situated in Mbabane.

Founded as the capital in 1902 after the British replaced Bremersdorp (present-day Manzini) as the administrative center, the town has grown into Swaziland's second largest city (pop. 60,000 in 2000) and is a major commercial and trading center. It is the home of most foreign embassies, government offices, the main government hospital, radio and television facilities, the main banking center of the country, as well as the location of numerous parastatals.

Situated in the Dlangeni Hills (amid the oldest rocks in Africa) of Swaziland's highveld, Mbabane's setting is stunning, with rugged mountains to the north and west and steep valleys to the east and south. At an elevation of 3,700 feet, the city boasts a malaria-free climate and is well watered. Major deposits of tin and iron ore have been extracted from the hills.

Mbabane is thought to be named after a local area chief, Mbabane Kunene, in the location of King Mbandzeni's main cattle kraal. In the mid-to late 1800s, numerous white adventurers and/or concession seekers began arriving. One of the most prominent early settlers was Allister Miller, who arrived in 1888 and died in 1951. The main thoroughfare in Mbabane is named after him and he was by all accounts a man with considerable talents and interests, founding the country's first newspaper, *The Times of Swaziland,* in 1897, as well as establishing many of the country's major agricultural activities.

See also **Swaziland.**

BIBLIOGRAPHY

Booth, Alan R. *Historical Dictionary of Swaziland,* 2nd edition. Lanham, MD: Scarecrow Press, 2000.

Thompson, Christina Forsyth. *Mbabane into the Millennium: The Story of a City.* Mbabane: UNDP Swaziland, 1999.

DOROTHY C. WOODSON

MBEKI, THABO (1942–). The second South African president, Thabo Mvuyelwa Mbeki was born on 18 June 1942 in Idutywa, Transkei. His parents were Epainette and Govan Mbeki (the latter one of Nelson Mandela's comrades in the 1960s). At the age of fourteen he joined the African National Congress (ANC) Youth League and in 1962 he left the country after the ANC was banned by the South African government. In 1966 he completed a masters degree in economics at Sussex. In 1970 he received military training in the Soviet Union and then became the assistant secretary of the ANC's Revolutionary Council in Lusaka. In 1974 he married Zanele Dlamini; and the following

Thabo Mbeki (1942–). The president of South Africa arrives at the Jose Marti airport, Havana, Cuba, September 14, 2006. He was there to meet with representatives of over one hundred countries for the fourteenth nonaligned summit. AP IMAGES

negotiations that culminated in the first democratic constitution in 1993 and accompanying national elections in April 1994. In 1993 he was elected as the ANC's national chairperson and in 1997 as ANC president. In South Africa's first democratic government he served as the first deputy executive president between 1994 and 1999. In 1999 he succeeded Nelson Mandela as president.

Mbeki is known as a political strategist and a manager in government. In addition to his mission to implement the policies designed in the Mandela period as a framework to overturn all the effects of apartheid (including the Reconstruction and Development Programme), he also developed the vision for an African Renaissance for the twenty-first century. It envisaged a revival of Africa in this century similar to the European Renaissance, and included renewal in the economic, political, cultural, linguistic and scientific fields. Mbeki is therefore one of the architects of the African Union and its development plan: the New Partnership for Africa's Development (NEPAD), which has been adopted as the African Union's macro-economic framework with the objective to create an environment in which African economies can participate in the different dimensions of globalization. For Mbeki NEPAD is a vital instrument in promoting the interests of Africa internationally and pursuing the goal that the twenty-first century should be "Africa's Century."

See also **Apartheid; Mandela, Nelson; South Africa, Republic of: History and Politics (1850-2006).**

BIBLIOGRAPHY

Gumede, William Mervin. *Thabo Mbeki and the Battle for the Soul of the ANC.* Cape Town: Zebra Press, 2005.

Hadland, Adrian, and Jovial Rantao. *Thabo Mbeki.* Cape Town: Maskew Miller Longman, 2000.

Jacobs, Sean, and Richard Callard, eds. *Thabo Mbeki's World: The Politics Andideology of the South African President.* Scottsville: University of Natal Press, 2002.

Makgoba, Malegapuru William, ed. *African Renaissance: The New Struggle.* Cape Town: Tafelberg and Mafube, 1999.

Mbeki, Thabo. *Africa: The Time Has Come: Selected Speeches.* Cape Town: Tafelberg and Mafube, 1998.

Mbeki, Thabo. *Mahube: The Dawning of the Dawn: Speeches, Lectures and Tributes.* Braamfontein, South Africa: Skotaville Media, 2001.

DIRK KOTZE

year he became a member of the ANC's National Executive Committee. From 1975 to 1978 he represented the ANC in Swaziland and Nigeria and then returned to Lusaka as the political secretary in the president's office. During the period 1984–1989 he directed the ANC's Department of Information and Publicity and thereafter the Department of International Affairs. He also spearheaded the secret talks with the South African government in Europe in the late 1980s in preparation of the ANC's unbanning and the release of political prisoners (such as Nelson Mandela) as a precursor of the constitutional negotiations and democratization.

In the early 1990s, Mbeki was one of the ANC's strategists during the constitutional

MEDIA

This entry includes the following articles:
OVERVIEW
BOOK PUBLISHING
CINEMA
COMIC ART
JOURNALISM
LANGUAGE
POLITICS
RADIO AND TV
RELIGION

OVERVIEW

The continent of Africa incorporates fifty-three countries, each with an individual set of media institutions, histories, and practices that is somewhat unique. This is equally true of the media of all regions of Africa including Arab North Africa (which is often discussed as part of Middle East/North Africa [MENA]), Sub-Saharan Black Africa, Island Africa (the islands off the coasts of the continent), and South Africa (the industrial giant in the far south of the continent).

RADIO AND DEVELOPMENT COMMUNICATION

With a few notable print exceptions, the modern mass media in Africa was introduced by the colonial powers during the latter portion of the colonial era, chiefly to link Europeans living in the colonies to the metropoles. In broadcasting, the British and the French were the most important powers. In 1927 the British East Africa Company began a British Broadcasting Company (BBC) relay service for settlers, broadcasting from Nairobi, Kenya. They also introduced radio in Cairo in 1928, a move that would help make Egypt, already a regional powerhouse in the cinema and theatre, a leader in Middle Eastern broadcasting. The French began the first radio service in Madagascar in 1931. To some extent radio broadcasting policies in Africa were mirrors of colonial policies, the British allowing some decentralization and use of vernacular, the French advocating a centralized broadcasting model with mainly services in the French language. In most of their colonies, the British eventually established broadcasting systems designed along the public corporation model of the BBC. Belgian policy tended to leave broadcasting to interested parties, religious groups, or the private sector. The Portuguese, inactive in the radio sector and other social services, failed to establish broadcasting in their colonies until the 1970s.

African radio stations, still too new and still too controlled by colonial governments, participated little in the struggles for independence that marked the 1950s and 1960s. Still, during the 1960s, the newly independent governments were cognizant of the power of the media as tools in the forging of national consciousness among the diverse ethnic groups in these new states. In this spirit, they introduced television into their respective countries. About half of the African nations acquired television broadcasting systems within a decade of their independence. In the other less significant 50 percent, installation of television systems was delayed until the 1970s. But in most nations both the United Nations Educational Cultural and Scientific Organization (UNESCO) and Western multinationals were eager to encourage the development of broadcasting in Africa. In this convergence of interests, the concept of "development media" flourished. Within this paradigm, mass media were to be used as tools to motivate and empower society to strive for changes to improve people's lives.

But development and the means of achieving it are endlessly debatable. For African broadcasters in newly independent states, members of the civil service, national development meant focusing on national concerns and national activities of their nascent states and their rulers, conveniently sidestepping opposition as counterproductive. Thus was born in Africa what critics have called "protocol journalism," ritual coverage of pronouncements, speeches, and activities of ruling party officials, particularly the head of state. By the 1970s, with insecure one-party states and military rule dominating the continent, redundant news and ritualistic current events were the mainstay of much African broadcasting and would remain so until the early 1990s. In the early twenty-first century, even in an African media situation marked by far more pluralism, protocol journalism—somewhat of an established style—is still a staple of the state owned media.

Despite these failings, media use for positive social purposes is an important trope in African media and culture. Initially, some nations launched radio distribution schemes designed to awaken peasants to their new governments through radio. Some projects introduced listening clubs to promote discussion among audiences of media content. Other important milestones in African development broadcasting were tied directly to schools broadcasting, such as the Ivorian *Projet télévisuelle* supported by UNESCO and the government of France or the Kenyan Schools Broadcasting project funded by USAID, both in the 1970s. Indeed "development media," as it is known in media theoretical circles, has always been the provenance of Western academics. And Western media scholars and practitioners, through their involvement in international aid projects and international nongovernmental organizations (NGOs) have continued to influence development communication and to refine its theories.

In the early 2000s the techniques of "edutainment" are used to embed messages about attitudes and behaviors deemed appropriate into storylines of television and radio dramas. The genre uses audience parasocial interaction and role modeling to help audience members develop new ways of being and interacting. South African Broadcasting (SABC)'s flagship TV serial drama, *Soul City*, represents a milestone in the development of high quality edutainment. Edutainment including *Soul City* is heavily involved in the struggle against HIV/AIDS. On a continent where one in nine is infected with the virus, a great deal of media talent in Africa is necessarily devoted to the project of stemming the course of this infection through information, education, and communication.

To a great extent, the introduction of mass media in Africa has led, according to some scholars, to an enormous shift from group to individual consciousness. This process of individuation is a means by which an individual awakens and recognizes that he or she has a self that is separate from the group, allowing one to engage in self-analysis and self-criticism. Historically, in Western societies at least, individuation has been associated with the development of literacy. But scholars have also argued that mass media are "mobility multipliers," introducing unknown worlds into the lives of rural peasants, thereby aiding them to imagine alternative lifestyles outside of their own situations. Individuation has also been associated with melodramatic media genres that provide ordinary individuals with a means to perceive and articulate a heightened sense of the drama of their own lives; in effect, their personhood.

Clearly the mass media in Africa have been bound up in very direct ways with the project of urbanization that has been part and parcel of the colonial era. Indeed, Africa, the least urbanized continent, is the continent that is urbanizing the most rapidly. The perceived availability of paid employment, another aspect of individuation implicated in modernity, has always drawn Africans away from their rural villages into cities. Here the mass media, with its host of alternate realities, helped new arrivals to negotiate the professional and emotional demands of urban landscapes and lifestyles that are much less regulated by kin and custom. For these reasons, "advice aunties," call-in or write in programs that give counsel on human relationships, have long been popular.

But old Africa dies hard. Despite the cell phone revolution, radio is still sometimes used as a loudspeaker system, announcing important events, especially births and deaths, to family members scattered by urban migration, to other parts of a given country or region). Programs like "Newspaper on Air" or "Pick of the Dailies," which are broadcasts that summarize some of what is locally available in print, provide some of the one in two non-literates on the continent with access to the written word through radio.

Compared to other parts of the world, distribution of radio receivers in Africa is low. There were 216 radio receivers per 1,000 persons in 1997, as compared to the world average, which was almost double at 418. Only southern Asia had a lower radio receiver rate at 118 per 1,000, while North America had 1,017 per 1,000 persons. While radio is not available in all the 1,000-plus African languages, radio programs are broadcast in hundreds of African languages, making radio the medium of choice of the subsistence farmer, still the most common occupation of the African despite very rapid urbanization.

Deregulation of broadcasting across the African continent in the 1990s has given way to a plethora of radio stations, easily well over 1,000. It has also made possible the transmission over FM of such international radio services as the BBC World Service or Radio France Internationale (RFI), once popular on short wave. Deregulation opened up the media landscape to a whole host of new media services, information and communication technologies (ICTs), and transnational broadcasting. The latter is having a significant impact on African television.

TELEVISION AND INFORMATION AND COMMUNICATION TECHNOLOGIES (ICTS)

In contrast to radio, television in Africa since its inception has largely been an urban phenomenon. Even in the twenty-first century, several African countries still have only one terrestrial domestic broadcaster. Moreover, it is not uncommon to find that satisfactory television reception is limited to the vicinity of major urban areas. TV set distribution is also the lowest in the world with Africa averaging 60 per 1,000 as compared to the world average of 240 and the North American rate of 429. Television, far more than radio, is dominated by state control, replete with foreign fare, and disseminated in the European languages of English, French, or Portuguese. In Arab-speaking North Africa, however, Arabic-speaking broadcasts have always been a mainstay program importation from Egypt or the Middle East. In the early 2000s an ever- increasing amount of television content is supplied to broadcasters in North Africa by regional Middle Eastern satellite-based services. These services emerged in the mid-1990s, partly in response to the Gulf War's so-called CNN effect. They are seen by North Africans as local, and are clearly preferred by broadcasters and increasingly by audiences, to imported European or American fare.

Throughout Africa, a rapidly growing proportion of urban televiewers have access to transnational television through expanding forms of distribution available since the mid- 1990s. These forms include private satellite reception dishes, subscriptions to cable television or multipoint multichannel distribution systems (MMDS systems) or retransmission of transnational television by terrestrial services. The Francophone African countries enjoy the most access to transnational television in sub-Saharan Africa because the government of France helps to subsidize Francophone satellite programming as a matter of foreign policy. Research figures show that almost one in two television viewers has access to transnational broadcasts in some Francophone African cities. Access to this costly programming is possible because of the communal nature of television viewing in Africa. Open-air viewing is common with less well off neighbors and family members allowed to benefit from a nearby TV receiving set, a paid TV subscription, or a satellite dish.

The new information and communication technologies, considered personal technologies in the Western world, are also sites of shared use. As of October 2005, Internet World Statistics reported a 2.7 percent Internet penetration rate for Africa, the lowest of any region in the world. North America's Internet penetration rate is 68.2 percent for the same period; the world's rate was 15.2 percent. But on a continent where connectivity is difficult and expensive, Internet account owners, like cell phone users, share their resources with networks of friends, neighbors, and relatives. And these ICTs make it possible for African kin, among them, growing numbers of labor migrants in the global economy, to remain connected to one another across continents.

NEWSPAPERS AND PRESS FREEDOM

The written press across the African continent involves a broad range of newspapers, from single broadsheets disseminated by war lords engaged in Africa's multiple conflicts to large elite urban dailies such as the Egyptian *Al Akbar* with circulation topping half a million. Despite their enormous differences, the press on the African continent is not without its similarities. Throughout this vast continent, journalism was introduced either by missionaries or by the colonial powers. During France's brief colonial adventure in Egypt, Napoleon introduced the first newspaper to Africa in 1800. On the other side of the continent, in Liberia and Sierra Leone, early presses were created by and for Negroes returning to Africa from America or Europe. Unlike the situation in broadcasting, a private written press was tolerated by colonial governments, although France remained leery of local press entrepreneurs in its colonies until after the 1930s. The press in Francophone Africa has since suffered from a tendency toward officialdom and history of undercapitalization.

In Anglophone East and southern Africa, a private press was created largely for a European settler class. Such papers established somewhat of a standard for quality, writing, editing, and layout. Anglophone West Africa's press has always been the most lively, and because of the absence of a European settler class, some have said, the most "African." Indeed some theorists have argued that advocacy journalism and a partisan press find a natural home on the African continent. It is thought such journalistic styles derive from older forms of informative discourse that still circulates in areas of low literacy. Among these include news provided by town criers, imams, court poets, and gossip or rumor networks, alternatively termed "pavement radio" (in Anglophone countries), *radio trottoir* (in Francophone countries), or news of the *suq* (in the Arab world).

Indeed the manner in which newspapers are used in Africa is somewhat indicative of the continent's poverty and its low levels of literacy. A single copy of a newspaper is often passed from reader to reader, from city to town, to the countryside. And it is not uncommon for a literate reader to read articles aloud for his illiterate companions or family members. These observations suggest that although circulation figures are low—16 newspapers in Africa for every 1,000 persons compared to 96 per 1,000 in the world as a whole or 141 per 1,000 in North America—there is still considerable access to the printed word.

Recognizing the importance of the printed press, both actual and symbolic, most African countries have maintained government-owned newspapers since independence, staffed by civil servants. These papers still persist, often supplying readers with "officialese" so decried by critics. The press, especially its private sector, has enjoyed somewhat of a renaissance since the mid-1990s. New methods of Internet distribution have aided many papers to survive by connecting local African newspapers to the widening worldwide African diaspora. These media outlets played important roles in mobilizing their respective electorates in the elections that took place throughout Africa in the early 1990s. In 2006 one of the best sources of news about the African continent is All Africa News.com, a nonprofit African news agency that aggregates and distributes news from more than 125 African-based and Africa-interested

organizations. The service is the flagship of All Africa Global Media, a multimedia content service provider, a systems technology developer, and the largest distributor of African news worldwide.

Given the situation of media pluralism that emerged in the 1990s, African media are struggling to improve the rights of journalists and the freedom of the press. The Freedom House's annual survey of press freedom in 2004 reported that only 15 percent of sub-Saharan African countries had free media. It rated another 35 percent as partly free, and the remaining 50 percent as not free. Around the continent, a bevy of press controls hamper the media including insult laws enforcement, arbitrary arrest/harassment of journalists, and preferential treatment of media outlets favorable to governments/ruling parties, all of which lead to self-censorship. The African media, thought to be strongest since independence, still remain relatively weak brokers of democracy. With much of the continent embroiled in conflict or mired in economic despair, the media situation remains exceedingly fluid. The only constant for the foreseeable future is change.

See also **Communications; Education, School; Education, University and College; Literacy.**

BIBLIOGRAPHY

Berenger, Ralph. "Media in the Middle East and North Africa." In *Global Communication: Theories, Stakeholders, and Trends*, ed. Thomas L. McPhail. 2nd edition. Malden, MA: Blackwell, 2005.

Bourgault, Louise M. *Mass Media in Sub-Saharan Africa*. Bloomington: Indiana University Press, 1995.

Bourgault, Louise M. *Playing for Life: Performance in Africa in the Age of AIDS*. Durham, NC: Carolina Academic Press, 2003.

Freedom House. *Freedom of the Press 2004: A Global Survey of Media Independence*. Lanham, MD: Rowman & Littlefield, 2004.

Ginsberg, Faye D.; Lila Abu-Lughod; and Brian Larkin, eds. *Media Worlds: Anthropology on New Terrain*. Berkeley: University of California Press, 2002.

Hasty, Jennifer. *The Press and Political Culture in Ghana*. Bloomington: Indiana University Press, 2005.

Hyden, Goran; Michael Leslie; and Folu Ogundimu, eds. *Media and Democracy in Africa*. New Brunswick, NJ, and London: Transaction Press, 2002.

Mellor, Noha. *The Making of Arab News*. Lanham, MD: Rowman & Littlefield, 2005.

Mytton, Graham; Ruth Teer-Tomaselli; and André-Jean Tudesq. "Transnational Television in Sub-Saharan Africa." In *Transnational Television Worldwide*, ed. Jean K. Chalaby. London: I. B. Taurus, 2005.

LOUISE M. BOURGAULT

BOOK PUBLISHING

The independence period of the 1960s was one of anticipation. The big British- and French-based companies dominated the market with schoolbook imports. The establishment of examination boards in Anglophone Africa led to an explosion of new textbooks. Mbari Publications in Ibadan, EAPH's New Africa Library in Nairobi, and Heinemann's African Writers Series revealed that there was a general as well as an educational market for literature. However British prime minister Harold Macmillan's family firm managed to set up neocolonial state publishing houses in several newly independent countries.

Publishing in Francophone Africa was dominated by Les Nouvelles Éditions Africaines (NEA), a joint undertaking by the governments of Sénégal, Côte d'Ivoire, and Togo together with French firms. Its near monopoly stifled the growth of independent publishers and by the 1990s publishing in these countries was in decline.

The Nigerian Indigenization Decree demanded a majority local shareholding. The oil boom paid for containers full of imported books for Universal Primary Education (UPE) when development economists believed the country should have spent the money on paper and machines to reprint the books in the country under license. Zambia had copper and began producing its own books. Kenya had "black gold," as coffee was called, and new Nairobi publishers sprang up.

The good fortune of these countries disguised the fact that other African countries were running out of money and books. In April 1982 the Nigerian foreign exchanges closed. The 1980s were the years of a "book famine." Liberalization in the 1990s made books, paper, printing machines, and ink available again, but at a high price.

Since the turn of the twenty-first century, publishing in western and eastern Africa has been even more dominated by school textbooks, often distorted by tranches of World Bank money, which has favored the branches of multinationals rather than totally national companies. Kenyan publishers believe that the state Jomo Kenyatta Foundation in Kenya should have encouraged local production. Elsewhere in East Africa there are home-grown publishers such as Fountain Publishers in Uganda and Mkuki na Nyota in Tanzania.

Egypt and South Africa have the best established publishing industries in Africa. Egyptian publishers market their books to the Arabic-speaking world, especially outside Africa. Arabic has made inroads into the French language industry in the Maghreb.

Publishers such as Juta started in South Africa in the nineteenth century. In the early twentieth century mission presses such as Lovedale in the eastern Cape set out to meet the needs of education and religion, often in the African languages. Under apartheid Afrikaner firms made fortunes from the Bantu Education Department. As of the early 2000s these cash-rich companies are still in textbook publishing under the ANC and are buying media companies further north in Africa.

Under censorship the well-established English language publishers were supine. During the 1970s and 1980s heroic firms such as David Philip and Ravan brought out work by African writers. The revived university presses of KwaZulu-Natal and Witwatersrand again provide informed criticism of how society is developing after apartheid. There is a big entertainment market, though international firms can outbid the local publishers with their advances.

The African Books Collective (www.africanbooks collective.com) is a self-help initiative by more than one hundred publishers from Anglophone Africa that promotes and distributes books in the rest of the world. The African Publishers Network (www.apnet.org) brings together about forty national publishers associations.

See also **Education, School; Education, University and College; Literacy; Literature; Postcolonialism.**

BIBLIOGRAPHY

Chakava, Henry. *Publishing in Africa: One Man's Perspective.* Oxford: Bellagio Publishing Network, 1996.

Gibbs, James, and Jack Mapanje. *The African Writers' Handbook.* Oxford: African Books Collective, 1999.

Zell, Hans M., ed. *The African Studies Companion: A Guide to Information Sources*, 4th edition. Glais Bheinn, Scotland: Hans Zell Publishing, 2006.

JAMES CURREY

CINEMA

Africa has always been part of the global network of film culture: there were film screenings in South Africa in 1896, Lagos in 1903, and Dakar in 1905. British, French, and Belgian colonial authorities were acutely aware of the power of cinema. They sometimes deliberately exploited the "magic" of photography to dazzle natives, and they established film units that made instructional or propagandistic films especially tailored for the supposed mentality of Africans (Diawara, Burns). The association of cinema with nation building and the often paternalistic attitudes introduced by the colonial authorities have had a durable afterlife in African national film policies, in the ideologies governing state-controlled television, and in the sponsorship of African filmmaking by European governments and nongovernmental organizations.

During the colonial period, commercial cinemas were established in African cities and became integral to the African experience of modernity, along with electric lights, recorded music, trains, motor cars, and factory work. Commercial cinema provoked intense anxieties in the colonial authorities. France prevented the importation of Arabic films into its sub-Saharan colonies for fear that Islamic sentiments would be inflamed. British authorities worried that the sight of white men being shot and—worse—white women removing bits of their clothing in American films would undermine the psycho-social basis of colonial rule. African cultures also had to come to terms with this new social institution; in a pioneering study, Brian Larkin traced the intense debates within Hausa culture around the establishment of cinemas in northern Nigeria, where some Islamic authorities saw cinema as the work of the devil ("Theatres of the Profane").

Foreign commercial cinema has had ubiquitous effects on African popular culture. Fraternities of young men dressed up as cowboys and paraded through the streets of Lagos, Enugu, and other southern Nigerian cities in the 1940s. Jean

Idrissa Ouédraogo. One of the leading talents of the second generation of African filmmakers, Ouédraogo springs from the remarkable cinematic tradition of Burkina Faso. His fables of village life in Yaaba and Tilai found a worldwide audience. THE KOBAL COLLECTION

Rouch's documentary *Moi, un noir* (1958) follows migrant workers in colonial Abidjan who call themselves Edgar G. Robinson, Eddie Constantine, and Dorothy Lamour. Among the first films made by Africans in Niger was an imitation of an American western, Mustapha Alassane's *Le retour d'un aventurier* (1966). In the 1990s the image of Rambo lured the child soldiers of Liberia and Sierra Leone to mayhem and death.

Such transplanted cultural forms take root because they serve African purposes. Often foreign cinema cultures have provided styles that young Africans use to resist the oppressive control of elders. From Kano (Larkin, "Indian Films") to the Swahili coast of Kenya (Fuglesang), Indian and American films have provided idioms for reconceiving sexual attractiveness, love, and marriage. African audiences are extremely active, creating a constant noisy reaction to what is happening on screen. Sometimes an interpreter for a local language stands near the screen, perhaps utterly transforming the story in the process. The once-flourishing Ghanaian tradition of locally produced painted film posters is another example of local institutions that mediate international cinema culture.

Cinema houses in Africa are often owned by Lebanese or Indian businessmen and are serviced by European or American distribution companies. It is normal to show three different films per

Ousmane Sembène. The great founding figure of African cinema, Ousmane Sembène was already a major novelist when he turned to filmmaking in the 1960s. A Marxist perspective and mordant humor inform his cinematic investigations of Senegalese society. FILMS TERRE AFRICAINE, LES/ THE KOBAL COLLECTION

day and change the program frequently. American action films, Hong Kong martial arts films, and Bollywood Indian films are the standard fare, to the exclusion of almost anything else. Video sales or rental shops and television broadcasts provide a somewhat expanded generic range, including American comedies and romances. In general, cinema theaters across Africa have grown dilapidated and many have gone out of business, while video viewership has boomed. Videos are often screened in small, informal video parlors and by itinerant entrepreneurs who visit the remotest villages with a generator, television monitor, and VCR or DVD player. Satellite and cable television channels stream films into more prosperous urban homes. The ability to watch films at home has had some dramatic social effects, particularly in places where women were restricted from going out to cinemas but now avidly watch films in private.

It is always cheaper for film distributors to rent second-run foreign films than African-made films that need to recover their production costs on the local market. This iron law, coupled with insufficient support from African national governments,

has prevented African filmmaking from achieving a true industrial structure. Hundreds of African films have been made, but always on an ad hoc basis, with individual filmmakers forced to raise the money for each project themselves (often from European governmental and nongovernmental sources) and to act as their own distributors, carrying their films abroad to a circuit of international film festivals, universities, and a few art cinema houses. In Africa, they may rent theaters and personally supervise the ticket receipts, but the established distribution channels remain closed to them.

Films have been produced all over Africa on this rickety basis. The strongest cinematic traditions have been established in Senegal, Mali, and Burkina Faso. The aesthetic and political radicalism of the pioneers in the 1960s and 1970s (Ousmane Sembène, Med Hondo, Djibril Diop Mambety, and Souleymane Cissé) has been continued but also sometimes qualified in the work of the next generation, including figures such as Cheick Oumar Sissoko, Idrissa Ouédraogo, and Jean-Marie Teno. This is very much a director's cinema, and it has produced a number of world-class talents; in general, remarkably interesting work has been created with meager means and amidst great difficulties. But in spite of some local successes, African films are seldom seen on African screens.

Video technology has fundamentally altered this situation, however. Beginning in the late 1980s, in Ghana and Nigeria low-budget feature films began to be shot directly on video and sold as video cassettes as well as being screened in rented halls. By 2000, Nigeria was producing well over a thousand such films per year, in English, Yoruba, Hausa, Igbo, and other languages. Because such productions do not require much technical training or capital, they have an immediate relationship with urban popular culture. They tend to be full of melodrama, violence, and witchcraft. The films are sold and rented primarily as video compact discs; they are screened in humble video parlors and broadcast on television. They have become the dominant form of audio-visual entertainment in Nigeria and Ghana and have won huge audiences across Africa and in the African diaspora in Europe and the United States.

South Africa has also begun to emerge as a major force, after its long isolation caused by apartheid. Its television programming is more important than its cinematic output, but its capital and technical infrastructure are spreading their influence across the continent through such means as satellite television channels broadcasting African films, chains of modern multiplex cinemas, and the marketplace at the Sithengi Film Festival.

See also **Colonial Policies and Practices; Communications; Dakar; Film and Cinema; Lagos; Rouch, Jean; Sembène, Ousmane.**

BIBLIOGRAPHY

Barlet, Olivier. *African Cinemas: Decolonizing the Gaze.* New York: Zed, 2000.

Burns, J. M. *Flickering Shadows: Cinema and Identity in Colonial Zimbabwe.* Athens: Ohio University Press, 2002.

Diawara, Manthia. *African Cinema: Politics and Culture.* Bloomington: Indiana University Press, 1992.

Fuglesang, Minou. *Veils and Videos: Female Youth Culture on the Kenyan Coast.* Stockholm: Stockholm Studies in Social Anthropology, 1994.

Haynes, Jonathan, ed. *Nigerian Video Films*, 2nd edition. Athens: Ohio University Press, 2000.

Larkin, Brian. "Indian Films and Nigerian Lovers: Media and the Creation of Parallel Modernities." *Africa* 67, no. 3 (1997): 406–440.

Larkin, Brian. "Theatres of the Profane: Cinema and Colonial Urbanism." *Visual Anthropology Review* 14, no. 2 (1998–1999): 46–62.

Larkin, Brian. *Media and Urban Form: Technology, Infrastructure and Culture in Northern Nigeria.* Chapel Hill, NC: Duke University Press, 2007.

Ukadike, Nwachukwu Frank. *Black African Cinema.* Berkeley: University of California Press, 1994.

JONATHAN HAYNES

COMIC ART

Comic art in Africa is an informational medium and a form of mass-cultural entertainment that crosses literary, leisure, and developmental boundaries. Facets of contemporary life that deal with the retention of traditional customs, migratory fluxes, and gender relations are addressed through a high level of technical facility in the wake of important societal changes such as democratization and various development initiatives that concern the empowerment of women at local, national and international levels. Comic art categorically occupies a space within the postcolonial terrain and aids in changing perceptions of social values for an African readership that includes both youth and adults. The popular reach of the medium is evident in diverse representations, from childhood immunization posters to cyber-magazines. The latter counterbalances strong themes of tradition and modernity in illustrating cultural phenomena that espouse African popular beliefs.

Comic art typically comprises detailed images, as well as text housed in speech balloons or thought boxes. Primarily, these images are used to communicate a political or social anecdote with the text engaging the visual. Three distinct categories of comic art—the vignette, the sequential narrative, and the graphic novel—embolden the communicative premise of the medium. In the first category, the vignette is an evocative sketch of a brief incident, as seen in satirical and didactic cartoons published in periodicals and on educational posters. Zapiro (b. 1958, Jonathan Shapiro), a popular editorial cartoonist of South African publications such as *Mail & Guardian* and *Sunday Times*, crafts the vignette as a sardonic critique of structural adjustment policies applied to Africa that have neither significantly increased formal employment nor comprehensively reduced rates of poverty. Rich in caricature, the single-panel illustrations maintain narrative coherence through loose symbolic representations based on the motivations and actions of characters in prescribing to any singular plot.

The second category of comic art, the sequential narrative, is structured by an arrangement of several illustrative panels to create a pictorial story. The sequential narrative references a lexicon of both prose and illustration that is demonstrated in a relationship that fashions a deliberate and ordered string of events. The Cameroonian cyber-magazine *Gbich!* features several models of the narrative device to index the adversities encountered in daily life through humor and parody. Examples include the well-liked series *Jo Bleck* by Karlos Guédé Gou (b. 1966, Liadé Guédé Carlos Digbeu) and *Sergent DeuTogo* by Bob Destin Zinga Kanza (b. 1977).

Graphic novels, the third category of comic art, represent a collection of sequential narratives into an album or book that is formally marketed as an educational tool or a medium of entertainment, but often the two forms overlap. The graphic novel, *A l'ombre du Baobob* is a compilation of comics stories authored by Francophone African artists, and it is utilized in educative forums such as functional literacy and life-skills training programs centered on child welfare and public health campaigns. This type of informational graphic novel deepens social dimensions by attending to topics such as female genital excision, child soldiers, and universal human rights. The graphic novel has also successfully engaged South African communities by presenting a candid and historical account of the life of celebrated political dignitary Nelson Mandela in a Madiba Legacy Series. Other comics of the postapartheid nation often explore the influence of women on South African society, in addition to historical figures that include Steve Biko and Shaka Zulu. In Senegal, comic art that entertains, such as *Goorgoorlou* by T. T. Fons (b. 1957, Alphonse Mendy), has been syndicated in daily newspapers, broadcasted on primetime television as an animated sitcom, and anthologized into several albums.

Graphic novels conventionally are long, complex narratives; however, because of scarce material and financial resources, many African graphic novels are published in Europe under the auspices of intermediary institutions, European cooperations, and commercial entities, and then are distributed in Africa. According to research conducted on comic book production in Africa, there are many publishing houses, albeit with poor distribution, that have participated in the comic art business since the 1970s. Sasa Sema Publishing (Nairobi, Kenya), Nouvelles Éditions Ivoriennes (Abidjan, Côte d'Ivoire), Afrique Éditions (Kinshasa, Democratic Republic of the Congo), and Sogedit (Dakar, Senegal) have all actively promoted vignettes, sequential narratives, and graphic novels through a dynamic cultural industry.

Comic art is by and large a cultural product branded by African sartorial and geographic idiosyncrasies created through diverse artistic techniques. There are archetypes of conventional superhero fantasies, but these exemplars are specifically located in urban South Africa where advanced developmental conditions allow for more technological innovation in the graphic production of comic art on computers, instead of by hand. A large amount of comic art is produced in the equatorial region of Africa, where antecedents such as Congolese popular style painting follow a similar set of aesthetic imperatives through caricature and speech balloons.

The capacity of comic art to inform and simultaneously be conceptually imaginative comes from its ability to mine parallel genres from across the world. Comic art is popular art appropriating aesthetics from global varieties that include Manga (Japan), Manhwa (Korea), Manhua (Chinese) and Disney (United States). Yet despite the multiplicity of comic art styles, stylistic tropes are quintessentially African by rescinding presumptions about African morality and intellect conceived in the non-Western cultural conscious, with iconography that critiques the political escapades of notorious figures such as the Congolese dictator Mobutu Sese Seko and former Nigerian president Sani Abacha. Characters appear authentically African through dress and demeanor, whereas geographical landscapes of rural and urban realities convey visual representations of Africa that are free of the historical implications of stereotype and marginalization.

The plight of women under the helm of spouses and fathers, in addition to the persecution of young, uneducated domestics by their female bourgeoisie employers, are special foci for comic art. In this regard, the number of male comic artists drastically exceeds the amount of female practitioners in the industry. Fifi Mukuna (b. 1968, Ntumba Fifi Mukuna), from the Democratic of Republic of Congo is part of a small list of female comic artists currently working in the field. Conversely, the social position of men in Africa affords them the opportunity to pursue advanced professional training in journalism or the social sciences, resulting in a sensitized approach to subject matter that concerns women in Africa.

Images of the Maghreb are mainly produced by first- and second-generation comic artists who reside in Belgium or France, but whose origins are in countries that include Algeria, Morocco, Tunisia, and Libya. Farid Boudjellal (b. 1953), an artist of Algerian heritage who negotiates dual identities of Africans and Europeans, creates the most popular comic art that illustrates the rich tradition of the North African region. Boudjellal documents Mahgrebian culture in a state of transition, and depicts Arab Muslim and Jewish relations, and the politics of Islam in a country where nationality laws regularly delay the French citizenship of North African émigrés. The abundant linguistic diversity in Africa has made language an important topic of comic art. Its textual production ranges from Francophone, to Lusophone, to Anglophone narratives. Comic art is also written in languages frequently spoken in Africa, some of which include Malagasy, Swahili, Wolof, and Arabic, which are enriched by a highly expressive combination of Western slogans that are on occasion peppered with savvy slang words. This streetwise appeal presents comic art as a desirable educational medium to inform youth and adults who are literate and semi-literate in a direct and entertaining way.

See also **Art, Genres and Periods; Literacy; Mandela, Nelson; Popular Culture; Shaka Zulu.**

BIBLIOGRAPHY

A l'ombre du Baobab: Des auteurs de bandes dessinée africains parlent d'éducation et de santé. Equilibres et Population, 2001.

Barnard, Rita. "Note from the Post-apartheid Underground." *The South Atlantic Quarterly* 102, no. 4 (Fall 2004): 719–754.

Eisner, Will. *Comics and Sequential Art: Principles and Practice of the World's Most Popular Art Form.* Florida: Poorhouse Press, 1985.

"Gbich! Online." Available from www.gbichonline.com

Jewsiewicki, Bogumil. *Cheri Samba: The Hybridity of Art.* Montreal, Canada: Galerie Amrad African Art Publications, 1995.

Kruger, Loren, and Patricia Watson Shariff. "'Shoo—This Book Makes Me to Think!" Education, Entertainment, and 'Life-Skills' Comics in South Africa." *Poetics Today* 22, no 2 (Summer 2001): 475–513.

Lumbala, Hilaire Mbiye. "Émergence de la bandes dessinée africaine." *Notre Libraire: Revue de la littérature du sud* 145, *La bande dessinée* (July–September 2001): 18–23.

Nelson Mandela: A Son of the Eastern Cape. South Africa: Umlando Wezithombe Publishing, 2005.

Olaniyan, Tejumola. "Cartooning Nigerian Anti-Colonial Nationalism." *Images and Empires: Visuality in Colonial and Post-Colonial Africa*, ed. Paul S. Landau and Deborah D. Kaspin. Berkeley: University of California Press, 2002.

KENYETTA LOVINGS

JOURNALISM

Africa's print media have been shaped by centuries of colonialism, ownership and control by postindependence autocratic governments, and in the twenty-first century, by democratization, privatization, and the Internet. Only one country, South Africa, consistently gets high marks for its healthy, free press. The various imperial histories and quality of media development and the differing realities of north and sub-Saharan Africa, make generalizations difficult. Africa's print journalists do, however, face common problems. These include self-censorship due to continuing implicit and explicit government threats, low audience literacy rates and purchasing power, the difficulty of circulating materials over decaying infrastructure and across vast differences, and limited training resources.

Historically, scholarship indicates an early healthy press in Anglophone countries, especially in West Africa, while the limited press in Francophone countries was chronically underfunded and harshly restrained. In the nineteenth century, newspapers in sub-Saharan Africa served the informational

Newspaper stand in the medina of Rabat, Morocco, December 2006. The Moroccan government had recently prohibited publication of the Arabic-language magazine *Nichane* for insulting Islam, after the publication of an article titled "Jokes: How Moroccans Joke about Religion, Sex, and Politics." ABDELHAK SENNA/AFP/GETTY IMAGES

and entertainment needs of European settlers. Missionaries were an important driving force for an indigenous press with an evangelical agenda. Newspapers in Arabic-speaking North Africa were often mouthpieces for the government, while others played a role in the agitation against the Ottoman occupation before World War I.

In the first half of the twentieth century, an indigenous press that had a specific meaning beyond just the local indigenous press, advanced freedom, and presses often were closed down or harassed by colonial authorities. After independence in the 1960s, most nations nationalized their press and passed repressive laws. In the 1990s, with the end of the Cold War, a trend toward multiparty democracy supported by Western interests led to some media pluralism. Press laws were eased, national systems privatized, and new papers launched. Some of these new publications are reputable and professional, while others are unethical and irresponsible. The increased competition in the media marketplace has been a boon to young women entering a previously male-dominated field.

The realities of a competitive news marketplace in the twenty-first century exposed a press often unable to meet the interests of its paying customers and the demands of its advertisers. The transition from government-owned to market-driven also has

been stunted by a growing, but still limited, private advertising sector. Some papers are still dependent upon government advertising, while others have not been weaned from Western donor funding. Due to low salaries and meager resources overall, it is difficult to maintain high professional standards. Journalists are influenced by the promise of money from vested interests and cowed by government threats of arrest. There is concern over the increasing concentration of ownership and control by global media conglomerates. The market for indigenous papers in local languages has yet to be fully exploited.

All African countries are wired to the Internet at various levels, and online editions of publications are proliferating to meet the needs of local readers and those in the global diaspora. While this eliminates the circulation and costly paper problems of old media such as newspapers, the digital divide is still expansive. Meanwhile, journalists are only starting to access the vast amount of information online, due to a general lack of training opportunities, the expense of subscribing to databases, and technical difficulties that cause unreliable connectivity.

See also **Colonial Policies and Practices; Communications; Literacy; Photography.**

BIBLIOGRAPHY

Bourgault, Louise. *Mass Media in Sub-Saharan Africa.* Bloomington: Indiana University Press, 1995.

Nyamnjoh, Francis B. *Africa's Media, Democracy and the Politics of Belonging.* New York: Zed Books, 2005.

MELINDA B. ROBINS

LANGUAGE

The patterns, politics, and policies of language use in the African media today are part of the legacy of European colonial rule. German colonizers generally tended to favor the use of local African languages in the colonial media. In what was then German East Africa, for example, the Germans established Swahili periodicals as early as the 1890s. The French and the Portuguese, on the other hand, often discouraged and even prohibited African language media, even though when African resistance to colonial rule became stiff, they both incorporated African languages in their radio programming. Media under the British generally maintained a greater balance between English and a few African languages. In Southern Africa, for instance, Cecil Rhodes' Bantu Press produced Ndebele and Lozi versions of the *Bantu Mirror* and Shona and Chinyanja editions of its *African Weekly* and in what had become Tanganyika the British published *Mambo Leo* in Swahili. In spite of these differences in colonial language policies in the media, however, their ultimate objective was the same. In different ways they were all intended to promote the colonial agenda of command and control.

The nationalist response to the colonial media was also not monolithic linguistically. The open anti-Islamic hostility of the Germans in East Africa, for example, inspired the Swahili anticolonial journalistic venture, *El-Najah*, using the Arabic script. Later, after the British had replaced the Germans, the Tanganyika African National Union (TANU) produced its own *Sauti ya TANU* (Voice of TANU), a Swahili paper in the Roman script under the editorship of Julius Nyerere. In neighboring Kenya, Jomo Kenyatta of the Kenya Central Association released its anticolonial organ, *Muiguithania*, in Gikuyu. In the French colonies, on the other hand, French continued to dominate much of the nationalist media. Even the *Voice of Fighting Algeria*, the radio transmission of the Algerian anticolonial combatants who had considered the use of French as anathema, ultimately introduced programs in this same colonial language to consolidate its anticolonial efforts.

After independence, media control continued to be in the hands of the state and, at least in the print media, there was often little change in language use. In the 1970s, UNESCO tried to stimulate "rural newspapers" in African languages with mixed results. In many countries, some attempts were made to increase the number of African languages in the electronic media and especially in radio programming. Due to the high cost involved in such multilingual programming, the period of time devoted to each program became necessarily limited. In addition, because these programs targeted specific ethnoregional audiences, they became less national in perspective. In this case, the medium affected the presentation of the message.

State control and censorship of the media made the short-wave radio extremely popular in many African countries. Citizens could turn to European radio services like the British Broadcasting Company and Radio France to learn the "truth" about important political developments in their own countries. These European stations included transmissions not only in English and French, but also in select African languages, especially Arabic, Hausa, and Swahili.

The momentum for democratization that swept the continent in the 1990s led to the expansion of privately owned media and to a flowering of the press. The ethno-nationalist expression of this democratic trend, however, also triggered the development of new periodicals and radio stations operating entirely in ethnic-based languages. There are many variations in this development, from region to region, from one form of media to another. Francophone African countries, for example, are behind their Anglophone counterparts in newspaper production in African languages. Lusophone African nations have the least amount of print media in African languages. Television in Africa is still far less multilingual than radio. In spite of these differences, however, there is little doubt that the media in African languages received a boost from the opening up of the space of the politics of pluralism in many African nations.

Equally important has been the decline in protectionist state-nationalist ideologies precipitated by post–Cold War globalization, resulting in greater media liberalization. American access to African audiences, especially in Africa, is no longer confined to English-language magazines or the multilingual radio broadcasts of Voice of America. In the early twenty-first century it includes the power of Cable News Network and other television programs, all contributing to the growing Americanization of English in Africa. It is true that American newspapers like the *New York Times* and the *Washington Post* have less influence in Africa than the British *Financial Times* and the *Manchester Guardian*. Similarly, British English is heard more widely on radio in Anglophone Africa than American English. On television, however, it is American English that is dominant because American television occupies a disproportionate share of the African electronic space.

The expanding networks of communication fostered by globalization, however, have also made African languages more dependent on Western ones. Much of the international news that is transmitted in African languages by the African media is, in fact, based on translations of texts in European languages, especially English, released by media syndicates. This dependence has posed new challenges to African languages. The translation project has to respond to a whole range of the vocabulary of world politics, from the Cold War and the Iron Curtain to nuclear proliferation and the ozone layer. There is also the challenge of translating euphemisms: How can one discuss "homosexuality" without being morally judgmental? In this process, African languages have found a new source of lexical enrichment.

At the same time, however, the media is helping to stabilize African languages, many of which have yet to develop a widely acceptable standard variety. The electronic media (and especially radio and television) are a major force behind the standardization of pronunciation and promoting an accent. The print media, on the other hand, especially newspapers and magazines, constitute major forces behind the standardization of spelling. Both forms of media will help in standardizing usage.

In the final analysis, the relationship between language and the media in Africa is one of symbiosis and interdependence.

See also **Colonial Policies and Practices; Communications; Globalization; Kenyatta, Jomo; Language; Rhodes, Cecil John.**

BIBLIOGRAPHY

Bourgault, Louise M. *Mass Media in Sub-Saharan Africa.* Bloomington: Indiana University Press, 1995.

Eribo, Festus, and William Jong-Ebot, eds. *Press Freedom and Communication in Africa.* Trenton, NJ: Africa World Press, 1997.

Hatchen, William. *The Growth of the Media in the Third World: African Failures, Asian Successes.* Ames: Iowa State University Press, 1993.

ALAMIN MAZRUI

POLITICS

Reliable and up-to-date figures on media penetration in Africa are hard to come by, but in the late 1990s UNESCO estimated there were least 224 daily newspapers with a combined circulation of 12 million published in Africa. That was up from 199 newspapers in 1970 with a combined circulation of 4 million. Radio still dominated communications with up to 158 million radio broadcasting receivers (up from 33 million in 1970). According to the World Development Indicators 2006 of the World Bank, by 2004 at least 20 out of every 1,000 people had access to the Internet, up from 5.1 percent four years earlier. The number of mobile phone subscribers was up from 7.5 million in 1999 to 76.8 million by 2004. It is therefore no surprise that the late 1990s onward has seen an explosion of interest into the role of media and information in democratization and democratic politics in Africa.

The media configuration in the early the twenty-first century remains marked by its origins in the colonial order. Traces of these regimes remain most visible in the form of linguistic limitations (the newspapers are published mostly in the languages of the former colonial masters). Other characteristics are restricted ownership, an urban bias, a focus on white settler populations (particularly in southern Africa), and lack of independence from government or state power. Commercial mass media in Africa, both under colonialism and since independence, have generally operated without much regard for the majority of the continent's people. Nevertheless, ordinary Africans—acting together with more organized political actors—have accessed and utilized media for communication, mobilization around basic freedoms, or for substantive political rights and cultural change.

COLONIALISM

The earliest dated publication in Africa was the 1798 French-language *Courier de l'Egypte* for troops engaged in Napoleon's invasion of Egypt. In southern Africa, white settlers in Cape Town inaugurated the *South African Journal* (simultaneously published in Dutch as the *Zuid-Afrikaansche Tijdschrift*) in 1824.

Most publications aimed at the African population were published by mission societies, such as the *Umshumayeli Wendaba* (Publisher of the News) on the southeastern coast of South Africa. Exceptions were the *Sierra Leone Royal Gazette,*

Nmandi Azikiwe (1904–1996), right, with Matthew Mbu (1929–), 1966. Former Nigerian president Azikiwe attended college in West Virginia before returning to Africa and becoming founding editor of the *West African Pilot*, a publication that led him to a career in politics. Mbu was his naval defense minister from 1960 to 1966. DAVID CAIRNS/EXPRESS/GETTY IMAGES

published by former slaves repatriated from North America (established in 1801), the *Royal Gold Coast Gazette* established in Freetown 1822, and *Koranta ea Becoana* (Bechuana Gazette) that was published both in English and Tswana between 1901 and 1908 in Mafikeng, South Africa.

In the first quarter of the twentieth century, newspapers aimed at a small minority of elite Africans proliferated around the continent, with the most active in West Africa (especially southern Nigeria), North Africa (Egypt, Morocco, and Tunisia), and southern Africa. These publications often served as the springboard for a number of proto-nationalist or independence movements whose leaders often started their political careers as

journalists or newspaper publishers. Examples include Sol Plaatje (1876–1932, South Africa), Nnamdi Azikiwe (1904–1996, Nigeria), Habib Bourguiba (1903–2000, Tunisia) and Félix Houphouët-Boigny (Côte d'Ivoire). Plaatje, for example, used his newspapers to agitate for equal rights for all civilized men. Azikiwe, who, similar to Plaatje, had visited the United States and met early black radicals there, introduced a militant, partisan tone to his journalism and his publication, the *West African Pilot*, which had a lasting effect on Nigerian journalism.

Britain was the first to introduce radio to its colonies in southern and eastern Africa—ostensibly to connect settlers to keep in touch with the motherland. France soon followed by introducing radio services in its colonies in West and North Africa.

DECOLONIZATION

Post–World War II reforms—most significantly attempts by colonial regimes to liberalize colonialism—accelerated the establishment of print media presses in some colonies such as Kenya, Rhodesia, and apartheid South Africa. Private enterprise also took notice of this opportunity. An example is the publication of the news magazine *Drum* in Johannesburg in 1951. An earlier version of the magazine, owned by a British journalist, largely played to white stereotypes of Africans as rural and tribal. Following the intervention of an African editorial advisory board and with an eye on the bottom line, the (still white) owners and editor hired a staff of capable black journalists who changed for a brief time how black people were represented in print and provided a welcome space for nationalist, anti-apartheid voices. *Drum* soon introduced separate editions for West and East Africa that had similar impacts on those societies' cultural and political life. *Drum* ceased being published in 1965, but was revived in the mid-1980s as a downmarket celebrity and lifestyle magazine in Southern Africa.

Other publications such as *Transition* (initially based in Uganda, later in Nigeria, and then in the United States) and *Présence Africaine* (in Paris) provided space for African intellectual, cultural, and political writers (mainly those exiled to operating out of Western Europe) to challenge stereotypes of Africans and engage in forums with European elites.

The most significant use of radio in the nationalist struggles of the 1950s and 1960s occurred in the context of the Algerian war of independence. There the guerrilla movement used underground radio (*The Voice of Algeria*) not only to taunt the French, but also to inform the local community and build national identity among Algerians.

INDEPENDENCE

Rather than extensive restructuring of media systems, rulers after independence in many cases saw consolidation and extension of colonial public spheres. Dictatorships and one-party states—with few exceptions the norm—nationalized private media in the name of unity, introduced laws to control media (outright censorship, repressive ministries of information), purchased controlling stock in media companies, or informally affected journalists' work environment (by withholding state advertising contracts from critical newspapers, for example). Journalists faced arrest and incarceration, publications have been banned and confiscated, and in some instances printing presses were destroyed. Radio and television often became the sole preserve of the state.

In Cameroon, for example, for much of the postindependence period, the country's official media (the state broadcasting institutions, and the state print media and publishing corporations) have effectively served as the propaganda of the ruling party and the country's president, Paul Biya, who has ruled since 1982. Biya treated the state television service CRTV as his personal property, manipulated state print media, and shut private media out of discussions of political power. Unable to intervene effectively in substantive issues, private media have been reduced to a public relations arm of the government as well as serving as a site for ethnically-based contests between national and local politicians, usually taking the focus away from the state's failings.

Meanwhile in southern Africa where white settler regimes (South Africa, Rhodesia, Angola, and Mozambique) rejected any gradual reforms of race-based or colonial rule after 1960, the state maintained free, democratic media only for whites, and harassed or banned media aimed at the black population or that were critical of those regimes.

In the interim, television had also made its arrival (making its debut in 1959 in Nigeria). But television would suffer the same fate as radio—controlled by the state, effectively serving as propaganda tools, and insufficiently funded, often recycling mainly cheap American, British, and French entertainment programming.

DEMOCRATIZATION AND THE PRESENT

The third democratic revolution that swept Africa in the wake of the end of the Cold War in the late 1980s and 1990s had a profound impact on the continent's media. Although in places such as Cameroon the state was successful in containing the spread and impact of the new media freedoms, elsewhere the media was crucial in sweeping aside dictatorial regimes, aiding popular uprisings, exposing human rights abuses, or compelling elections. Regulation of media systems—often under the pressure of World Bank directives on good governance and restructuring—resulted in this period also witnessing the sprouting of new media outlets, especially private radio, private presses and, for better or worse, the reentry of multinational news corporations into these media markets (in some cases resulting in domination of the media landscape by the British Broadcasting Corporation [BBC], the French Radio France Internationale [RFI], and Canal Plus or the U.S.-based Cable News Network [CNN].).

The early 1990s democratization of South Africa, the most technologically advanced country on the continent and the country with the largest economy, was a crucial landmark. The country's media were transformed, and in the process expanded to control significant shares of other continental media markets. By 2006 Multichoice, the South African-based multinational cable subscription and satellite television company, dominated television schedules on the continent, partly through deals with local broadcasters.

Despite the growth of cell phone use and the slow increase of Internet access, new technologies have not had the same effect on African politics as elsewhere (in Asia for example). Although media repression is less overt and state control of media not as acute, many of the information inequalities inherited from colonialism still persist. As a result, diversity of media does not necessarily translate into diversity of perspectives.

To a large extent, poor, ordinary Africans—especially rural inhabitants, the illiterate, and the residents of urban slums—are still essentially excluded from mass media, both as consumers and as subjects for reporting.

See also **Azikiwe, Benjamin Nnamdi; Bourguiba, Habib bin 'Ali; Cape Town; Colonial Policies and Practices; Decolonization; Houphouët-Boigny, Félix; Johannesburg; Plaatje, Sol; Political Science and the Study of Africa; Postcolonialism; World Bank.**

BIBLIOGRAPHY

Bourgault, Louise. *Mass Media in Sub-Saharan Africa.* Bloomington: Indiana University Press, 1996.

Fanon, Franz. *A Dying Colonialism.* New York: Monthly Review Press, 1965.

Horwitz, Robert. *Communication and Democratic Reform in South Africa.* New York: Cambridge University Press, 2001.

Martin, Phyllis M., and Patrick O'Meara. *Africa,* 3rd edition. Bloomington: Indiana University Press, 1995.

Nyamnjoh, Francis. *Africa's Media: Democracy and the Politics of Belonging.* London: Zed Books, 2005.

Shillington, Kevin, ed. *Encyclopedia of African History,* Vols. 2 and 3. New York: Fitzroy Dearborn, 2004.

Sean Jacobs

RADIO AND TV

Throughout their history, broadcasting operations in Africa have been central in the establishment of colonial rule, in the formation of independent nations, and in the processes of democratization and globalization. In both colonial and postcolonial contexts, they have served as powerful sources for the development of shared identity, for transmitting key information to subjects and citizens, and for the development of cultural and political consensus. Broadcast media in Africa have also been, and in the early twenty-first century still are, key sites for encounters with Western culture, values, and behavior.

POLITICS

Concerns about political bias, political access, language choice, and cultural coverage are some of the most volatile and delicate issues surrounding broadcast media in Africa. Due to their tremendous influence and widespread reach across African populations, broadcasting stations have been closely controlled and monitored by both colonial and postcolonial governments. Until the early 1990s, nearly all television and radio stations in Africa were government owned and operated. Starting in the late twentieth century, African airwaves have begun opening up some, with a few governments allowing the creation of privately owned and local community stations. Bénin, Burkina Faso, Mali, South Africa, and Uganda, for example, each have dozens of different community radio stations. In moments of political crisis, broadcasting stations are often among the first sites for intensified state surveillance or military control, a testament to the continuing power of broadcasting, particularly radio, as the main vehicle for mass communication in African nations.

Relations between broadcast media and democratic processes vary widely across different African nations. In Burundi, South Africa, and many West African nations, for example, independent radio stations play a significant role in informing people about electoral processes, signaling abuses by those in power, debating political issues, and allowing citizens to air their views. In these cases, radio—particularly talk show and call-in radio formats—gives greater voice to the concerns of ordinary citizens and helps create a more vibrant civil society. One case of radio in the service of democracy in Africa has been that of HornAfrik, Somali's first independent radio and television station. This Mogadishu-based station was founded in 1999 by three Somali-Canadians who returned to their war-torn nation in an effort to give Mogadishu residents an effective means to communicate with each other and with the various warring factions across the city.

By contrast, there are many cases where independent media have been restricted or banned altogether. In Zimbabwe, privately owned radio stations are illegal; the only operating radio system is run by the state. In such climates, state media are typically filled with pro-government coverage, whereas opposing political viewpoints and alternative voices are granted little, if any, visibility, due to various forms of direct and indirect censorship and intimidation. Lying between these two poles are cases such as in Cameroon and Zambia where independent stations exist, but their operations are restricted by government censorship or by threats to revoke or fail to renew their broadcasting licenses. Critical political voices, vibrant debate, and investigative reporting within independent media are thus limited. Instead, most independent broadcasters may remain active only if they pursue more politically neutral content, such as religious broadcasting, music, sports, and community news. Within this context, media freedom violations in Africa are closely monitored by several different organizations such as the International Committee to Protect Journalists, an independent

nonprofit organization based in New York, and the Media Institute of Southern Africa (MISA), based in Windhoek, Namibia, which serves eleven different nations in Southern Africa and issues regular reports on violations of journalistic freedom.

HISTORY, OWNERSHIP, AND AUDIENCES

There are currently over sixty different television providers and nearly five hundred different radio stations in Africa. The first official radio station in Africa was established in 1924 in South Africa. In 1926, Algeria's first radio station was created, and in the following year radio broadcasting was set up in Kenya. Africa's first television operation was established in Algeria in 1956. The first television station in sub-Saharan Africa was established in Ibadan, Nigeria in 1959. A year later, Egypt introduced its television system. South Africa, in 1976, was among the last African nations to begin television broadcasting. In 1973 the first color television service on the continent was introduced on the Tanzanian island of Zanzibar. On the Tanzanian mainland, however, television was not brought in until 1994.

Radio is by far the most pervasive medium in Africa, reaching 50 to nearly 100 percent of the population in any given African nation. There are an estimated 150 million radio sets in Africa, and 44 million televisions. Television ownership tends to be urban and middle to upper class; radio ownership is more broadly based. Radio listening frequently occurs outdoors and is an occasion for collective activity and socializing. Media broadcasts reach African listeners and viewers via both internal and external sources. People in Africa may choose to listen to their own national or local radio channels, or to international shortwave broadcasts from foreign stations such as the British Broadcasting Corporation, Voice of America, Radio Moscow, or Deutsche Welle. In addition, in some cases listeners are also able to receive radio broadcasts emanating from neighboring countries. In nearly every African nation there is a state owned and operated television station. A small number of African countries have privately owned independent televisions stations, cable networks, and digital satellite providers. African radio has also become available via the Internet, either in the form of streaming audio or downloadable audio segments. Stations such as Addis Live! (Ethiopia), Channel Africa (South Africa), and Radio

Phoenix and Q-FM (Zambia), have Web sites where one may listen to streaming broadcasts.

PROGRAMMING

Radio and television programming in Africa covers the full spectrum of broadcast genres: news, documentaries, features, dramatic serials, talk shows, comedy, music, folklore, children's programs, and religious programs. On the whole, radio programs tend to be locally produced in most African countries, whereas a high percentage of television programming is imported, due to high local production costs. Imported programs include talk shows, documentaries, dramatic serials, and soap operas from the United Kingdom, the United States, Mexico, and India. American-produced programs such as *The Oprah Winfrey Show*, *Dr. Phil*, *The Bold and the Beautiful*, *Days of our Lives*, *Barney and Friends*, and *Buffy the Vampire Slayer* may be found on many different African stations.

African radio and television drama is one of the most vibrant broadcast genres on the continent, drawing devoted audiences. In addition, electronic media in Africa has adapted various oral traditions, such as advising and storytelling, with great success. The form and content of dramatic broadcasts are diverse, as are their inspirational sources. Some dramatize traditional folktales and myths, some are versions of productions that were first written for theatre or novels, and some are directly modeled after a Western-style soap opera format. Examples of African dramatic productions include the South African-produced soap operas *Isidingo* and *Soul City*, both of which are exported to several neighboring African nations, and Zambia's long-running radio dramas *Ifyabukaya* (in the Bemba language) and *Malikopo* (in the Tonga language). Other programs that enjoy great popularity throughout the continent include religious sermons from various Islamic, Pentecostal, and evangelical leaders.

A large portion of radio broadcasting in Africa consists of musical programming. Music types span the entire spectrum from traditional to modern, from Western to African. Many stations feature of blend of indigenous traditional music, locally recorded popular or urban music, religious music, and imported music such as reggae, country and western, rock, hip hop, classical, and music from other African countries. Other stations cater strictly to a single musical niche such as hip hop or religious music. Types of music-centered programming include disc jockey-hosted top hits formats, uninterrupted block music formats, music request programs, and early morning commute time formats which are a blend of news, weather, music, and talk. Since the introduction of radio in Africa, Africa broadcasting institutions have been important agents in the promotion and archiving of both traditional music and new musical genres. Many radio stations have close links to the music recording industries in their respective countries and have been key catalysts for establishing new musical talents and new musical sounds.

Given the high degree of multilingualism in most African nations, as well as the legacy of a dominant colonial language (English, French, or Portuguese), decisions about which languages to use in broadcasting are often politically charged and have far-reaching consequences. In most cases, the former colonial language is the official government language, and state radio and television have a high percentage of their programming in the official language. For example, the state-run Zambia National Broadcasting Corporation uses English and seven different indigenous Zambian languages. Several dozen other native languages in Zambia receive little to no airtime in the dominant broadcast media, although the recent rise of community radio stations has counteracted this imbalance to a small degree.

Across the continent, broadcasting is used as a key tool for health education, farming education, voter education, and literacy campaigns. The format of Entertainment Education (or Edutainment), which combines dramatic, entertaining formats with educational messages to help encourage behavior change, has been effective in HIV/AIDS education and prevention campaigns throughout Africa. Examples of particular programs include the radio drama *Journey of Life* (Ethiopia), *Centre 4 TV Medical Drama* (Uganda), and the multimedia (radio, television, and comic book) campaign *Soul City* (South Africa).

PROSPECTS

These programs will continue be important vehicles for bringing about positive change in Africa. The capacity of radio and television in Africa to enrich lives, foster civil society, and promote a diverse range

Kenneth Maduma. Africa broadcasting institutions play major roles in introducing and promoting local and imported music among African listening audiences. In this image from the late 1980s, Zambia National Broadcasting Corporation's senior producer Kenneth Maduma plays selections from American rhythm and blues artist Bobby Brown and pop artist Gloria Estafan. PHOTOGRAPH BY DEBRA SPITULNIK

of cultural, linguistic, and political expression is immense. This potential will be more fully realized with increased possibilities for community input in media production, and when media professionals in Africa are able to operate with greater journalistic freedom and infrastructural support.

See also **Communications; Political Systems; Mogadishu; Namibia; Popular Culture; Windhoek.**

BIBLIOGRAPHY

Abu-Lughod, Lila. *Dramas of Nationhood: The Politics of Television in Egypt.* Chicago: Chicago University Press, 2005.

Bourgault, Louise Manon. *Mass Media in Sub-Saharan Africa.* Bloomington: Indiana University Press, 1995.

Curran, James, and Myung-Jin Park, eds. *De-Westernizing Media Studies.* New York: Routledge, 2000.

Fardon, Richard, and Graham Furniss, eds. *African Broadcast Cultures: Radio in Transition.* Oxford: James Currey, 2000.

Hyden, Goran; Michael Leslie; and Folu F. Ogundimu; eds. *Media and Democracy in Africa.* New Brunswick, NJ: Transaction, 2002.

Nyamnjoh, Francis B. *Africa's Media: Democracy and the Politics of Belonging.* London: ZED Books, 2005.

Singhal, Arvind; Michael J. Cody; Everett M. Rogers; and Miguel Sabido; eds. *Entertainment-Education and Social Change: History, Research, and Practice.* Mahwah, NJ: Lawrence Erlbaum, 2003.

DEBRA SPITULNIK

RELIGION

The move to public prominence of religious movements and idioms throughout Africa in the era of post-authoritarian politics, and the enormous success with which they mobilize various media technologies, practices, and designs, demonstrates that the relationship between religion and media, in Africa as elsewhere, is not one of simple instrumentality or message transmission. Nor should the novelty of the intertwining of religion and media be overemphasized, and this for two reasons.

First, many examples illustrate the long-standing history of the intertwining of religion and technologies and practices of mediation in

African societies. Ancestor cults and mortuary rites, for instance, manifest and dramatize the ongoing relevance of deceased members of the household for the moral topography of the living world. In many African societies, it is ritual experts who ensure the communication across the boundary constituted by death. Sacrificial rites, too, are often about mediating the living world and that of the dead, such as among the Dinka in Sudan, where animal sacrifice establishes communication between the two worlds while simultaneously demarcating and emphasizing their separateness, and the temporary victory of the living over death.

Second, on a more ontological level, religion, as well as communication, refers to the act of establishing contact, of binding together two different entities or realities. By its very nature, religion renders palpable and perceptible that what eludes human cognition, and thus mediates between what can be physically and sensually known and verified on one side, and the metaphysical on the other. In this sense, religion always entails a range of materials and techniques (media), and relies on specialists holding authority in questions relating to the proper use of technologies of mediation. Religious traditions, in order to persist, need to be constantly translated or trans-mediated into new material form and practice. It is therefore useful to explore from a historical angle how individual media intervene as means in processes of communication, and how they help reproduce or rework existing channels, by generating opportunities for religious practitioners to engage in spiritual and religious experience. Rather than assuming that the adoption of new media effect clear-cut shifts from one mode of religious mediation to another, their repercussions should be seen as being more fragmentary and unsystematic in nature, affecting particular messages and practices and engendering new conflicts over authority, proper religious practice, and experience.

Individual religious traditions importantly shape the ways in which media are represented and acknowledged as actual channels of conveying a message, experience, or mediating between this world and the realm of the transcendental. Muslims and Christians, for instance, differ in their approaches to what The Book actually entails, what it communicates, and how it should be employed in ritual

and everyday practice. In Islam, reciting and listening to God's word has conventionally figured as the orthopractic form of submitting to God's will. In Christian history, there has been a stronger propensity toward seeing as the authentic and authenticating form of religious experience, illustrated, for example, by iconic representations of saintly piety in Catholicism.

Religious traditions not only differ in how they organize the mediation of religion and the sacred power of mediation. They also interlock in various and changing ways with regionally and culturally specific hierarchies of perception—definitions of which sensory impressions provide the most reliable and authoritative knowledge about the sacred. The emphasis on hearing in Muslim religious practice has not precluded the emergence of visual forms of Muslim piety in areas of West Africa. Followers of the Muride Sufi order in Senegal, for instance, engage in visual tokens and representations of their spiritual leaders and their divine blessing (*baraka*) in ways that disprove generalizing assumptions about the allegedly strong anti-iconic bent in Islam. Because of these regionally divergent hierarchies of authentic spiritual perception and engagement, there sometimes exist fierce debates within particular religious traditions as to which mode of sensual and embodied mediation is the most truthful and effective one.

Depending on what venues of communication with the transcendental a particular religious tradition privileges, its teachings and objectives are often articulated and promoted through the interlocking of various media and media practices. Some religious traditions privilege media that are external to the body. In others, the body itself becomes the primary means of mediating the world of the transcendental. Yet most religious traditions encompass and embrace a combination of different media, techniques and understandings of communicating with the transcendent world. Numerous adherents of Islam and Christianity in Africa, in addition to practices centering on The Book, also engage in trance rituals associated with spirit possession. Here the body becomes the principal means of communication with the realm of the metaphysical—the various spirits that, once they enter the body of the host, materialize different layers of historical experience and social consciousness. This embodied engagement with the world and will of the spirits is combined with other materials and modes of mediation, such as particular fabrics and materials that the spirits ask their hosts to don, and the particular rhythmic and melodic patterns used to invoke the spirit.

Similar to rites surrounding ancestor worship, trance associated with spirit possession dramatizes the complex relationship between people's recognition of the effects that of the supernatural on their daily dealings and the instable, transient ways in which these metaphysical forces are represented. This suggests that, rather than contrasting traditional means of mediating religious experience from electronic and digital ones, it is useful to examine points of convergence as much as differences between them. For instance, although spirit possession provides a primarily embodied means of representing spirits or of giving material form to their ever-present importance to people's lives, some of its effects resemble those of visual media technologies, such as video film. Ghanaian and Nigerian video films enable a paradoxical recognition of the relevance of the supernatural to everyday experience by making room for a representation of occult practices in a double sense. Not only do stories of the hero's renouncement of and victory over the forces of evil acknowledge the latter's very existence, but the films also show the effects of occult practices in gruesome detail and therefore render visible what in everyday life remains arcane.

Yet film may intervene as a medium of religious experience and identity that sets it apart from conventional means, institutions, and practices of religious mediation. Examples range from Indian Bollywood movies to Latin American *telenovelas*, all of which are avidly consumed by heterogeneous television audiences in Africa. By circulating at a transnational scale, these diverse film genres help telespectators to reflect on their identity as modern Muslims, on their place in a global *umma* (the community of believers), and in a world of normative diversity.

Electronic and digital technologies may play yet a different role in mediating religious experience. Once religious movements and their leaders adopt them, in combination with innovative styles of proselytizing and public presentation, the technologies feed into ongoing reformulations of spiritual experience and religious practice and introduce new dynamics into struggles over authoritative knowledge and religious leadership. Moreover, depending on the ways the production and consumption of their religious media products are organized, and whether their circulation is effected outside state control and beyond national borders, they may encourage the articulation of new, religiously inspired idioms and identities, and the emergence of communities formulated as an alternative to the national political community.

See also **Communications; Death, Mourning, and Ancestors; Film and Cinema; Religion and Ritual; Spirit Possession.**

BIBLIOGRAPHY

Fortes, Meyer. *Religion, Morality and the Person: Essays on Tallensi Religion.* Cambridge, U.K.: Cambridge University Press, 1987.

Fuglesang, Minou. *Veils and Videos. Female Youth Culture on the Kenyan Coast.* Stockholm, Sweden: Stockholm Studies in Social Anthropology, 1994.

Larkin, Brian. "Indian Films and Nigerian Lovers: Media and the Creation of Parallel Modernities." *Africa* 67, no. 3 (1997): 419–440.

Larkin, Brian. "Notes on Media and the Materiality of Qur'an Recitation." Paper presented at the Media, Religion, and the Public Sphere Conference, Amsterdam, December 2001.

Lienhardt, Godfrey. *Divinity and Experience. The Religion of the Dinka.* Oxford: Clarendon Press, 1961.

Meyer, Birgit. "Ghanaian Popular Cinema and the Magic in and of Film." In *Magic and Modernity. Interfaces of Revelation and Concealment,* eds. Birgit Meyer and Peter Pels. Stanford, CA: Stanford University Press, 2003.

Meyer, Birgit. "Religious Remediations. Pentecostal Views in Ghanaian Video-Movies." *Postscripts* 1, no. 2/3 (2005): 155–181.

Meyer, Birgit, and Annelies Moors. *Religion, Media, and the Public Sphere.* Bloomington: Indiana University Press, 2006.

Middleton, John. *Lugbara Religion. Ritual and Authority among an East African People,* 2nd edition. Hamburg, Germany: Lit Verlag, 1999.

Plate, Brent. "Introduction: Film Making, Mythmaking, Culture Making." In *Representing Religion in World*

Cinema: Film Making, Mythmaking, Culture Making, ed. Brent Plate. New York: Palgrave, 2003.

Schulz, Dorothea. "Promises of (Im)mediate Salvation. Islam, Broadcast Media, and the Remaking of Religious Experience in Mali." *American Ethnologist* 33, no. 2 (2006): 210–229.

Schulz, Dorothea. "Drama, Desire, and Debate. Mass-Mediated Subjectivities in Urban Mali." *Visual Anthropology* 19 (2007): 1–23.

Stolow, Jeremy. "Religion and/as Media." *Theory, Culture, and Society* 22, no. 4 (2004): 119–145.

Vries, Hent de, and Samuel Weber, eds. *Religion and Media*. Stanford, CA: Stanford University Press, 2001.

DOROTHEA E. SCHULZ

MEDICINE. *See* Disease; Healing and Health Care: Islamic Medicine; Healing and Health Care: Medicine and Drugs.

MEKKI, AICHA (1952–1992). Aicha Mekki was a Moroccan journalist. French for her was a language of freedom, inspiration, and evasion, and she loved the West and its culture. In her writing, she was committed to revealing the plight of the marginalized and excluded segments of the population in Morocco, and wrote articles about battered wives, maids, drug addicts, alcoholics, prostitutes, and the poor.

Mekki was dead for a week before her body was found in her small, shabby apartment in Casablanca on May 16, 1992. Her death was an enigma, for those who knew her felt that she loved life too much to commit suicide. Colleagues, readers, and the media recognized her as a journalist with a great sense of professionalism and dedication. Her writings on social issues spanned seventeen years in the Moroccan Francophone daily *L'Opinion*, depicting the hardships of the poorest and most disadvantaged segments of society.

See also **Literature: Women Writers, Northern Africa; Media: Journalism.**

BIBLIOGRAPHY

Lahjomri, Abdeljlil. *Pleure Aicha tes chroniques égarées.* Casablanca: Malika Editons, 2001.

Sadiqi, Fatima; Amira Noaira; and Moha Ennaji. *Women Writing Africa: The Northern Volume.* New York: Feminist Press at the City University of New York, 2007.

MOHA ENNAJI

MENELIK II (1844–1913). Mənilək, or Menelik II, was the king of Šäwa (Shewa) from 1865 to 1889, and King of Kings, or Emperor, of Ethiopia from 1889 to 1913. He is remembered as the founder of modern Ethiopia and a leader of the only third world country that successfully resisted European colonialism. He was an astute politician and a benevolent monarch; his admirers called him *əmməyyä Mənilək* (Motherly Mənilək).

Mənilək was born to King Hˇaylä Mäläkot (or Haile Melekot) of Šäwa (c. 1824–1855) on August 17, 1844, in Angoläla, near Ankobärr, the capital of his grandfather, the famous King Śahlä Śəllase of Šäwa. Mənilək grew up during the period known as *Zämänä Mäsafənt*, or the Era of Princes, when the rulers of Ethiopia's major provinces or principalities, including his father's Šäwa, did not take orders from the monarch in Gondär. Emperor Téwodros II (1818–1868), who made it his mission to put an end to the independence of the princes, overran Šäwa in November 1855; three months later the eleven year-old Mənilək was taken back to Gondär (and later to the fortress of Mäqdäla) as a captive. At Téwodros's court, Mənilək did, however, receive the treatment due a prince: the Emperor even gave Mənilək his daughter in marriage.

On June 30, 1865, Mənilək escaped from the fortress of Mäqdäla and went to Šäwa where he built a strong base that allowed him to aspire to the Ethiopian throne. His first chance at the throne came when Emperor Téwodros took his own life rather than surrender to Great Britain's large military expedition that came from India to free the Europeans who were residing in Ethiopia, including Queen Victoria's envoy whom the Emperor had detained and put in shackles at the fortress of Mäqdäla.

Mənilək's hopes were thwarted by another warlord in the north, Kasa (later Emperor) Yohannəs IV (c. 1831–1889), who was much stronger militarily. Mənilək had to drop the title of King of Kings of

Ethiopia and surrender to Yohann∂s, who crowned M∂nil∂k on March 26, 1878, as his vassal, King of Šäwa.

On March 9, 1889, Yohann∂s died in Mätämma, on the Ethio-Sudanese border in the west, in a war with the Sudanese Mahdists. Yohann∂s's death left M∂nil∂k a power with no rival. M∂nil∂k immediately consolidated his kingdom and was crowned King of Kings of Ethiopia on November 3, 1889.

M∂nil∂k was not strong enough to oust Italy from its colony of Eritrea, the Ethiopian territory north of the River Märäb, which the Italians occupied while Ethiopia was at war with the Mahdists. On May 2, 1889, M∂nil∂k signed a twenty-article treaty of commerce and friendship with Italy in a village called W∂c̆ale (Wichale). The Treaty of W∂c̆ale was prepared in Amharic (the Ethiopian language) and Italian, and the difference in the wording of Article XVII in the two languages carried grave consequences.

As far as Italy was concerned, Article XVII of the treaty made Ethiopia its protectorate. It notified to world powers of the time of its acquisition. For Ethiopian leaders, among them Taytu (1851–1918), M∂nil∂k's consort, the thought of making Ethiopia a protectorate of another nation was abominable. Too embarrassed to withdraw its notification to a world power of the time, Italy threatened to occupy Ethiopia to force it to follow the stipulations of the Italian version of the treaty. A series of protracted skirmishes ended in a fierce fight at Adwa on March 1, 1896, with a glorious victory for Ethiopia and a first and humiliating defeat of colonialism.

M∂nil∂k was indeed the founder of modern Ethiopia, fulfilling to a great extent Emperor Téwodros's dream of united Ethiopia, but he was never able to dislodge the colonial powers from the coastal territories that he claimed to be his ancestral lands. However, by pressing to the southeast and southwest, he doubled the Ethiopian territory he inherited. Since most of these gains in the south and west were achieved though conquest, in those regions M∂nil∂k is also known for the cruel conduct of his armies and the unwelcome garrisons he stationed there.

M∂nil∂k died on December 12, 1913, after a long period of paralysis and declining health due to a stroke.

See also **Taytu, Empress; Téwodros.**

BIBLIOGRAPHY

Bairu Tafla. "Marriage as a Political Device: An Appraisal of a Sociopolitical Aspect of the Menilek Period 1889–1916," *Journal of Ethiopian Studies* 10, no. 1 (1972): 13–21.

Bairu Tafla. *Ethiopian Records of the Menilek Era. Selected Amharic Documents from the Nachlass of Alfred Ilg, 1884–1900.* Wiesbaden, Germany: Harrassowitz, 2000.

Berkeley, George Fritz-Hardinge. *The Campaign of Adowa and the Rise of Menelik.* New York: Negro University Press, 1969.

Darkwah, R. H. Kofi. *Shewa, Menilek and the Ethiopian Empire 1813-1899.* London: Heinemann Educational, 1975.

Marcus, Harold G. *The Life and Times of Menelik II Ethiopia 1844–1913,* reprint edition. Lawrenceville, New Jersey: Red Sea Press, 1995.

Rubenson, Sven. *Wichalé XVII: The Attempt to Establish a Protectorate over Ethiopia.* Addis Ababa, Ethiopia: Addis Ababa University Press (Institute of Ethiopian Studies), 1964.

Rubenson, Sven. *The Survival of Ethiopian Independence,* 4th edition. Hollywood, California: Tsehai Publishers, 2003.

Sellassié, Guèbré. *Chronique du règne de Ménélik II,* trans. Tésfa Sellassié, annotated by Maurice de Coppet. vol. 1. Paris: Maisonneuve frères, 1930.

Sellassié, Guèbré. *Chronique du règne de Ménélik II,* trans. Tésfa Sellassié, annotated by Maurice de Coppet. vol. 2. Paris: Maisonneuve frères, 1932.

GETATCHEW HAILE

MENGISTU, HAILE MARIAM (1942–).

Haile Mariam Mengistu was an Ethiopian military officer and president of the People's Republic of Ethiopia from 1987 to 1991. At the age of fourteen Mengistu joined the juvenile unit of the Ethiopian army under the command of Emperor Haile Selassie, and at eighteen he joined the adult unit. After graduating from officer training school, he was given his army commission, ultimately rising to the rank of colonel.

Mengistu was a charismatic individual with delusions of grandeur. He was a leading figure in the military coup that overthrew the imperial

Haile Mariam Mengistu (1942–). In December 2006, Mengistu, the president of Ethiopia, was convicted and sentenced in absentia to life imprisonment for genocide due to his role in the Red Terror. He has not served his sentence because he fled to Zimbabwe in 1991 and the country refused to extradite him. AP IMAGES

regime of Selassie in 1974. He was rewarded for his efforts with the office of vice chairman within the governing council, called the Provisional Military Administrative Council. He held this position until 1977. Initially he gave the impression of having only the good of the country at heart, but during the first three years of the Ethiopian revolution it became clear that Mengistu had a vision of delivering Ethiopia from its historic backwardness.

By 1977 Mengistu and his supporters had adopted a Marxist-Leninist ideology and had become clients of the Union of Soviet Socialist Republics. In that same year he took over the office of chairman within the Council. Over the next thirteen years, his administration introduced socialist policies. The government's stated aim was to correct historic injustices based upon the ethnic chauvinism of imperial regimes that had been dominated by the Amhara ethnic group. In 1987 he became chairman of the Council of Ministers and, in that same year, he assumed the title of president of the People's Democratic Republic of Ethiopia. Mengistu was primarily committed to the maintenance of Ethiopian unity, and he adopted Marxism-Leninism to minimize the importance of ethnicity and other particularistic affinities. In the end he failed, mainly because of his inability to resolve the demand of the Muslim province of Eritrea for self-determination and because ethnic

opposition emerged against his statist development strategy.

Mengistu's regime was marked by violence, as rebels from the province of Eritrea fought for independence and invaders from neighboring Somalia attacked Ethiopian settlements. His response was harsh, and human rights violations occurred under his orders, including torture, forced relocations of as many as 100,000 people, and state-ordered murders. Mengistu was ultimately forced to flee the country, and he sought refuge in Zimbabwe in 1991.

See also **Eritrea: History and Politics; Ethiopia, Modern: History and Politics; Haile Selassie I; Postcolonialism.**

BIBLIOGRAPHY

Giorgis, Dawit Wolde. *Red Tears: War, Famine, and Revolution in Ethiopia.* Trenton, NJ: Red Sea Press, 1989.

Tekle, Amare. "Mengistu Haile Mariam." In *Political Leaders of Contemporary Africa South of the Sahara: A Biographical Dictionary,* ed. Harvey Glickman. New York: Greenwood Press, 1992.

EDMOND J. KELLER

MENSAH, E. T. (1919–1996). Emmanuel Tetteh Mensah was a Ghanaian highlife musician born in Ussher Town, Accra. His father, an amateur guitarist, was the boy's initial inspiration. However it was the opportunity Teacher Lamptey provided to E. T. and his older brother, Yebuah Mensah, in the fife band at the Government Elementary School in James Town that laid the foundations for his future role as the king of dance band highlife, the father of modern highlife, and the leader of the most influential dance band in West Africa, the Tempos. A singer and composer, he was a multi-instrumentalist but later settled on the strange combination of alto sax (reed instrument) and the trumpet (valve instrument).

Between 1932 and 1940, Mensah was a sideman for the Accra orchestra, the Accra Rhythmic Orchestra, and for Jack Leopard and His Black and White Spots. He enrolled at the School of Pharmacy at Korle Bu Hospital in 1940 and graduated in 1944. He combined his profession as a pharmacist and a musician working for the government before establishing his own pharmacy shop in

1948 and after a series of leadership changes he became the leader of the Tempos.

In the 1950s, in line with the general climate of preindependence Ghana and the massive interest in traditional culture and the patriotic sentiments of the time, Mensah restructured the Tempos with percussion instruments and traditional rhythms as the foundations of the new highlife. He changed their repertoire from jazz and European dances to highlife and Latin sounds including calypsos, rumbas, and cha chas. He composed and performed songs in Twi, Ga, Fante, Ewe, Hausa, and West African pidgin English. These innovations caught on with their teeming fans because they could relate positively to local languages and African melodies and rhythms.

In 1952 Mensah signed a recording contract with Decca and released a series of hits including the ever popular classic, "All for You," followed by "Nkebo Baaya" (I will go with you), "St. Peter's Calypso," "205," and "You Call Me Roko." In 1953 Mensah and his Tempos Band was the first to go professional at a time when most musicians in

Ghana combined their musical careers with other professions to supplement their incomes. In 1956 Mensah performed with the great African-American jazz trumpeter, Louis Armstrong, and the All Stars at his own club, The Paramount in Accra. Throughout the 1950s and 1960s, Mensah and the Tempos traveled widely. They made several successful trips to Nigeria that led to the Grand West African Tour from October 1958 to February 1959. The band also performed in major cities in the larger subregion. Their West African tours during this period inspired generations of musicians including Bobby Benson, Victor Olaiya, Rex Lawson, and Victor Uwaifo, all of Nigeria.

Landmark recordings include the 1969 album *The King of Highlife-African Rhythms* for Decca, and his last, *Highlife Greats* in 1978 with Victor Olaiya, for Afrodisia. In 1986, Off the Record Press in London published his biography, *E. T. Mensah: King of Highlife* to accompany the release of the LP *Tempos All For You* by the London-based RetroAfric label. In the same year, Mensah completed a promotional tour of London and Holland

E. T. Mensah (1919–1996) and his Accra highlife dance band the Tempos. Mensah formed the group in 1948 and toured with the band's members throughout West Africa. JOHN COLLINS/ BAPMAF ARCHIVES

for this release. In the 1970s Mensah was a central figure in establishing the Ghana Musicians Welfare Association and the Musicians Union of Ghana (MUSIGA) and subsequently became an executive member of both associations. In addition to a special concert in Lagos in his honor, he has received various awards from ECRAG in Ghana. In 1989 the Ghanaian government awarded Mensah with its most distinguished award, *Okunini* (The distinguished one).

See also **Music, Modern Popular: Western Africa.**

BIBLIOGRAPHY

Agawu, Kofi. *Representing African Music: Postcolonial Notes, Queries, Positions.* New York: Routledge, 2003.

Bender, Wolfgang. *Sweet Mother: Modern African Music.* Chicago: University of Chicago Press, 1991.

Collins, John. *West African Pop Roots.* Philadelphia: Temple University Press, 1992.

Collins, John. *Highlife Time.* Accra: Anansesem, 1994.

Collins, John. *E. T. Mensah: King of Highlife.* Accra: Anansesem, 1996.

KWASI AMPENE

MERINA. *See* **Madagascar.**

Fatima Mernissi (1940–). The Moroccan feminist writer and socialist speaks at a press conference in Rabat, Morocco, May 7, 2003, after being announced a joint winner (along with Susan Sontag) of the Principe de Asturias Literature Prize. © HOUBAIS MUSTAFA/EPA/CORBIS

MERNISSI, FATIMA (1940–). An internationally recognized authority on feminism and Islam, author Fatima Mernissi was born in Fez, Morocco, in 1940 into a wealthy urban family. Mernissi is one of the few elite women in her region and era to obtain higher education in Arabic, French, and English. In *Dreams of Trespass* (1994), she depicts an account of her childhood, including the secluded harem life she lived in Fez, as well as the freer, happier time at her father's country house where several of his wives lived. At Mohamed V University in Rabat, Mernissi chose political science as her subject, later studied at the Sorbonne, and earned a doctorate at Brandeis University in Massachusetts in 1974. Mernissi is a prolific writer and an important Arab-Muslim intellectual. Many of her books have been translated into English and many other languages.

Mernissi's books on women include *Beyond the Veil* (1975), *The Veil and the Male Elite* (1988), *Forgotten Queens of Islam* (1990), *Doing Daily Battle* (1983), *Islam and Democracy* (1992), and *Scheherazade Goes West* (2001). She realized early that regardless of class, the status of Moroccan (and other Arab-Muslim) women in heavily patriarchal societies silenced their voices. She dedicated her research to relevant questions about Islamic culture. Her investigations ranged from direct studies of the use of religion by men to grassroots militancy among women's nongovernmental organizations.

See also **Literature: Women Writers, Northern Africa; Women: Women and Islam in Northern Africa.**

BIBLIOGRAPHY

Sadiqi, Fatima; Moha Ennaji; and Amira Nowaira, eds. *Women Writing Africa: The Northern Region*. New York: The Feminist Press at the City University of New York, 2008.

FATIMA SADIQI

MEROË. *See* Nubia.

METAL CASTING. *See* Arts.

METALS AND MINERALS

This entry includes the following articles:
RESOURCES
METALLURGY
IRON
COPPER AND ALLOYS
GOLD AND SILVER

RESOURCES

DISTRIBUTION

Africa is resource rich, but mineral and metal deposits, as well as the benefits from this wealth, are unevenly distributed. Sub-Saharan Africa accounts for 8 percent of the world's total mining production. If petroleum is included, the production value is more than $35 billion. However, only nineteen sub-Saharan countries benefit substantially from mineral wealth, and even those that have sizable mineral and metal deposits do not always obtain the benefits of these riches.

The basis for Africa's mineral wealth is the geology of sub-Saharan Africa. The foundation of Africa is a core of stable, continental crust composed of Precambrian rocks. This is the craton, composed mainly of granite, gneiss, and greenstones. In terms of mineral and metal deposits, greenstones are the most favorable rocks for gold and other mineral layers. Such areas include the principal goldfields of Ghana (Ashanti), Ethiopia (Adola), Zimbabwe (Midlands), and the border between Swaziland and South Africa (Barberton Belt). In addition to these known gold deposits, there are undeveloped greenstone belts in Burkina Faso (Boromo, Aribinda, and Dori-Assakan), northwestern Tanzania, and northern Democratic Republic of the Congo (Kilo, Moto, Nagayu, and Isiro). Minerals and metals are also found in depositional basins. Examples are the goldfields of the Witwatersrand in South Africa, Tarkwa in Ghana, and the Copperbelt that runs through Zambia and Democratic Republic of the Congo. Mineral and metal deposits are associated with crustal movements that have led to the formation of sedimentary basins. The Karoo sequence, which holds most of Africa's coal, is a large sedimentary deposit located in Mozambique, Malawi, South Africa, Tanzania, and Zimbabwe.

Furthermore, minerals and metal resources are associated with areas where the crust has fragmented, allowing magma to well up and form what are called kimberlite intrusives. These are the source of diamonds in Angola, Guinea, Botswana, South Africa, Tanzania, and Democratic Republic of the Congo. Mineral and metal deposits are also found in areas where the crustal plates are diverging. One such area is the Great Rift Valley that runs through eastern Africa. This geological activity has led to the formation of nonmetallic minerals such as kaolin clay, bentonite, pozzolana, and fluorite, as well as of salt lakes that contain valuable minerals including salt, soda ash, and potash.

Mineral and metal deposits are also associated with volcanic activity that formed the South African Bushveld Complex and the Great Dyke of Zimbabwe. These areas contain chromium and platinum. Younger volcanic areas contain phosphates (Angola, Uganda, and Tanzania), and under some circumstances copper (South Africa), gold, and nickel. Mineral deposits are also created by erosional processes and chemical weathering, as is the case with bauxite in Guinea; rutile in Madagascar, Mozambique, and Sierra Leone; alluvial gold deposits in southern Ethiopia and northern Democratic Republic of the Congo; and alluvial diamonds in Namibia.

More than half the world's diamonds, platinum, and cobalt are found in Africa. The world relies on African mines for up to a third of its uranium, manganese, and chromium, and a tenth of its rutile, copper, and bauxite. Africa also supplies some 8 percent of the world's phosphates, 7 percent of its iron ore, and 6 percent of its petroleum.

The distribution of mineral wealth is, however, highly uneven. Nineteen countries benefit from commercial-scale mining, but out of these countries only two, South Africa (gold and diamonds) and Nigeria (petroleum), account for more than half the total mineral production. Five other countries—Zambia (copper and cobalt), Democratic Republic of the Congo (copper and cobalt), Botswana (diamonds), Angola (petroleum), and Gabon (petroleum, manganese, and uranium)—are major sources of minerals. Some African countries are important because they are world leaders in the availability of strategic minerals and metals. For example, Zambia is the world's seventh largest producer of copper and second largest producer of cobalt. Guinea has the world's largest bauxite reserves and is the world's second largest bauxite producer; Sierra Leone has one of the world's largest deposits of rutile; Zimbabwe is the fifth largest producer of asbestos; Gabon is the fifth largest manganese producer. Namibia and Niger together produce 16 percent of the world's uranium.

In spite of Africa's mineral wealth, only South Africa has become wealthy as a result of its deposits. This is because most of Africa's mineral wealth is controlled by transnational corporations or parastatal companies. In addition, the majority of minerals and metals are exported as raw ore. Although some ore is exported as finished metal, none of it is used to make manufactured products. As a result, the jobs generated by mining are, for the most part, unskilled or semiskilled, and in several areas, notably South Africa, migrant labor is dominant. Another important reason why Africa's mineral wealth has failed to generate real wealth for African nations is that mining operations are enclaves to the rest of the economy. They have strong ties to the export market but few links to the local economy.

HISTORY OF EXPLOITATION

The history of mineral development in Africa provides clues to modern-day mineral production and the reasons behind the uneven distribution of mineral wealth. Mining has always been an important economic activity in Africa. Gold panned from alluvial deposits and riverbeds was the mainstay of trade in the West African kingdoms of Ghana, Mali, and Songhay. Copper was found in the watersheds of the Congo and Zambezi Rivers in Central Africa and mined in Katanga (Shaba) long before the arrival of Europeans. Iron was worked in the ancient civilization of Meroë, which straddled the banks of the upper reaches of the Nile. Ironworking technology spread slowly south, and Africans closely guarded its secrets from Europeans.

Until the middle of the nineteenth century, Africans maintained control over their mineral resources, but this declined as the slave trade caused social upheaval, and the presence of Europeans on the continent increased. The discovery of diamonds in South Africa, at Kimberley in 1867, marked the beginning of the transfer of Africa's mineral wealth to Europeans. Britain annexed the Kimberley area in 1871 from the Griqua ethnic group and the South African Republic. And whereas the British controlled the production, African miners were the basis of the fortunes made by the likes of Cecil Rhodes (1853–1902), who, along with European financiers, bought up the claims of individual miners and formed mineral giants such as De Beers.

Other mineral discoveries soon followed. Gold was found in the Witwatersrand in the 1880s. From the 1880s to the 1930s, prospectors and financiers from Germany, the United States, Belgium, France, South Africa, and Britain established mines throughout the continent, including Angola, the Belgian Congo (present-day Democratic Republic of the Congo), Southern Rhodesia (present-day Zimbabwe), Northern Rhodesia (present-day Zambia), Nigeria, and Sierra Leone. Mineral production increased dramatically during the twentieth century, displaced agricultural products, and led to the transformation of trading routes. Prior to mining, trading routes ran across the continent to the Indian Ocean, where traders plied between Arabia, India, and China. But new mining trade routes were designed simply to bring the minerals to waiting ships that took them to Europe and the Americas. Railways were built, but they did not connect centers of population. For instance, the route from the Katanga copper mines in the Belgian Congo ran through Angola, not Democratic Republic of the Congo, so this railway provided little economic stimulus to the area. The mines operated as enclave economies until the 1960s.

Independence brought a wave of nationalization to Africa, and mines in Zambia, Sierra Leone, Uganda, Ghana, Tanzania, Democratic Republic of the Congo, Togo, and Mauritania were nationalized following independence. As a result, African mining enterprises in the early twenty-first century are roughly split between privately and state-owned mines. The private mines belong to transnational corporations, or are jointly owned by private companies and the state. The rest are controlled by parastatal mining companies run by national governments. However, the lock that transnational corporations have historically had on African mineral production means that there are few small-scale mining operations. Technology drives this, as well. Mining has become more mechanized and larger-scale. In addition, with marketing and production of key minerals in some cases controlled by a single company, as is the case with De Beers, it is hard for small companies to compete. However, mining does occur on a small, noncommercial scale in more than thirty African countries, and more than 20 million workers depend on artisanal mining for their subsistence.

Africa's share of the world mineral production has slipped since independence. Private companies, wary of political instability and the threat of nationalization, have invested elsewhere, notably in Latin America and Asia. As a result, sub-Saharan Africa's share of the world mineral production has fallen since 1960 and is stagnant with a growth rate of 1 to 2 percent a year. The irony behind this decline is that Africa still contains vast mineral wealth, but much of it has not been tapped, or investments in new mining projects have been curtailed or halted. For example, new deposits have been discovered but have yet to be developed. These include the Tenke Fungerume copper deposits in Democratic Republic of the Congo, and the Adola gold belt in Ethiopia.

As a result of its history and the way in which its minerals and metals are controlled by a few large companies, Africa's mineral assets are largely a source of potential wealth for much of Africa. Without more refining of ore and the creation of finished products, better linkages to local economies, and indigenous capital for investment in new exploration, Africa's mineral wealth will continue to be unevenly distributed and underdeveloped.

Exploration of virgin areas using new technologies is also very promising. Most of the exploration was done during colonial times and is outdated. Countries have had good success in attracting new investment when they revise the mining laws and in enabling environments to stimulate new private sector development. The resulting upturn in investment in the mining sector is impressive, as has been the case with Mali, Tanzania, and Ghana.

See also **Energy; Rhodes, Cecil John.**

BIBLIOGRAPHY

Campbell, Bonnie; Thomas Akabzaa; and Paula Butler. *Regulating Mining in Africa: For Whose Benefit?* Uppsala, Sweden: Nordiska Afrikainstitutet, 2004.

Cunningham, Simon. *The Copper Industry in Zambia: Foreign Mining Companies in a Developing Country.* New York: Praeger, 1981.

European Commission. "Mining in Zambia." Available at http://www.zambiamining.co.zm.

Labys, Walter C. *The Mineral Trade Potential of Africa's Least Developed Countries.* New York: United Nations Industrial Development Organization, 1985.

Ogunbadejo, Oye. *The International Politics of Africa's Strategic Minerals.* Westport, CT: Frances Pinter, 1985.

Stock, Robert. *Africa South of the Sahara: A Geographical Interpretation.* New York: Guildford Press, 1995.

United Nations Programme of Technical Cooperation. "Poverty Eradication and Sustainable Livelihood: Focusing on Artisanal Mining Communities. Available at http://esa.un.org/techcoop.

Wilson, M.G.C., and C.R. Anhaeusser, eds. *The Mineral Resources of South Africa.* Silverton, CO: Council for Geoscience, 1998.

World Bank. *Strategy for African Mining.* World Bank Technical Paper no. 181. Washington, DC, 1992.

DAVID SMETHURST

METALLURGY

Fuel and combustion technology is known from all regions of the world. Many studies show that an open wood or charcoal fire can easily attain 1,000 degrees Celsius. These temperatures can fire pottery to a good hardness, anneal copper, and set in motion solid-state reduction of iron oxide. In essence, there is nothing inherently unique about the reduction of copper or iron that would prevent multiple inventions. Indeed metallurgist J. E. Rehder has stated:

> Copper is very easily melted in a charcoal hearth and a native copper tool or knife inserted for annealing can easily disappear, to be found later as a small ingot in the bottom of the hearth. This would lead to intentionally melting several pieces to make a large one, which is basic metallurgy.

Copper oxide adhering to native copper from a local surface deposit would be automatically reduced when the copper was melted, to yield more metal in the hearth than was apparently added. This is a simple and natural origin of smelting. (1982, 91)

A contrary view supporting a single origin for the invention of metallurgical technology was advanced by the late Theodore Wertime that:

one must doubt that the tangible web of discovery, comprehending the art of reducing oxide and then sulfide ores, the recognition of silver, lead, iron, tin, and possibly arsenic and antimony as distinctive new metallic substances, and the technique of alloying tin with bronze could have been spun twice. (1964, 1266)

Historians of global technology usually ascribe to one of these two models of the development of metallurgy. Likewise, Africanists are still embroiled in the origins debate, with some supporting the diffusionist model and other favoring the multiple independent inventions of iron and copper technology. Diffusionists have maintained that metallurgy—both copper and iron—in Africa must have been introduced from elsewhere, possibly the Near East via North Africa's Nile Corridor, and/or from Near East or the Indian subcontinent via the East Africa Coast, for the following reasons. First, they have asserted, there is little archaeological evidence for pyrotechnologies in sub-Saharan Africa predating the beginning of copper and iron production. Second, they add, no archaeological progression demonstrates the southwestern Asian sequence of development from lithics, to copper, to bronze, and then to iron. Third, they found no African archaeological sites contemporary with or predating the beginning of copper and iron production in the Near East. It is noteworthy to mention that the diffusionist group has taken great pains to discredit any evidence of early production of copper and iron in Africa.

Those favoring multiple independent inventions of metallurgy have argued that Africa indeed has a pyrotechnological tradition of use of native copper, copper smelting, and iron smelting. They point out that the lack of evidence for prehistoric mining of copper in Africa is a result of the continent's scarcity of copper, and not of necessary expertise. They point to a tradition of copper working in the Early Kingdom of Egypt (c. 2686–2181

BCE), where a crucible furnace for casting bronze dating to 2300–1900 BCE was recovered within the temple precinct at Kerma. Several copper mines and a smelting site at Akjout, Mauritania, date from the ninth to third centuries BCE. Copper mining and smelting were practiced in the region west of Agadez, Niger, in the early first millennium BCE, but native copper was melted probably before 3500–2000 BCE. Iron smelting at Agadez began by roughly 500 BCE. The reconstructed metallurgical sequence for the Agadez region has been divided into three phases:

Cuivre I (c. 2000–1000 BCE)—native copper was melted
Cuivre II (c. 900 BCE)—copper was smelted
Fer I (c. 500 BCE)—iron smelting began.

The evidence for metallurgy in Niger prompted a leading diffusionist, R. F. Tylecote, to concede "Clearly we now seem to have some signs of a Copper Age in West Africa" (1982a, 62).

In many regions of tropical Africa, copper and iron production in Africa began roughly contemporaneously. Iron may initially have been produced as by-product of copper "since iron ore can be reduced to cast iron in any furnace capable of smelting copper, simply by adding a little less ore and blowing a little harder" (Rehder 1982, 91). The use of iron in Egypt and northwest Africa between approximately 1200 and 1000 BCE is widely accepted by archaeologists. The production of iron is known to have been undertaken in these areas in the eighth and ninth centuries BCE, respectively. Iron smelting furnaces have been carbon-14 dated to the interval 500–1000 BCE in Nigeria, Niger, Senegal, Tanzania, and Rwanda.

THE TECHNOLOGY OF COPPER AND IRON IN SUB-SAHARAN AFRICA

The basic requirements in metallurgy include ore, water, charcoal for fuel, transport, a reasonable level of furnace technology, and labor. Studies in the thermodynamics of smelting have shown that smelting of iron is much more difficult than the smelting of any other metal, including aluminum, copper, gold, lead, silver, or zinc. Because iron oxides are more stable than those of other metals, high temperatures and low partial pressure of oxygen are required to reduce it. The separation of copper and iron from its oxides requires carbon monoxide (CO) as a reducing agent. Carbon monoxide reacts with the metal oxides to produce the metal and carbon dioxide (CO_2). These conditions are obtained by burning carbon in a very limited supply of oxygen. The minimum temperature at which the reduction of iron from iron oxides and silicates occurs is about 1,100 degrees Celsius.

A successful smelting operation is a delicate balancing act between two opposed requirements. On the one hand, the smelter must maintain a temperature sufficiently high to keep the slag fluid. Furnace temperatures are raised by admitting more air to the furnace, thereby increasing the rate of combustion of the fuel. But too much air will produce more CO_2 than can be reduced to CO. Without an atmosphere rich in CO, metallic iron (and copper) cannot form, and the smelter will be left with only useless slag to show for his efforts.

The invention of kilns and furnaces had two advantages over open fires: it was approachable, less smoky, and had higher internal temperatures for reducing ores. Although the design of furnaces requires skill, greater skill still is required to bring the furnace to produce the metal. These techniques are subtle, take a long time to master, and must be maintained by regular practice. Widespread use of metals occurred only after metal workers could consistently obtain furnace temperatures sufficiently high enough to maintain a fluid slag. This furnace technique is complex and of great interest to archaeometallurgists in Africa and elsewhere.

Many historians of technology are convinced that the use of copper and its alloys preceded that of iron because copper has a lower melting point (1,083 degrees Celsius), which makes it easier to smelt and melt. Copper smelting involved ore cleaning to get rid of waste rock. The ore was then preroasted to expel impurities, including antimony, arsenic, and sulfur. Roasting converted copper sulfite to copper oxide, which was reduced to metal through heating in the furnace.

Through experimentation, copper workers invented and mastered the technique for casting copper from its native or smelted state in molds. Casting using the lost wax technique permitted the casting of complicated objects such as statuettes, figurines, and jewelry. African casters produced brass by the lost wax technique as early as 800 CE at Igbo Ukwu in southeastern Nigeria. Ife casters used copper for bracelets, anklets, rings, collars, ceremonial axes, hoes, and currency from the eleventh century. The famous Bénin bronzes were cast from the thirteenth and fourteenth centuries CE. The object to be cast was first modeled in wax around small clay core. It was then totally enclosed in clay, except for orifices to drain out the melted wax, and baked. The molten wax escaped through the holes, which were then plugged. Molten metal was then poured into the empty space within the mold. After the metal set, the clay core was broken and the cast object removed. Earliest evidence of the lost wax method is at Ur in Mesopotamia around 3,000 BCE.

The best-known copper alloys used by African casters were brass, an alloy of copper and zinc. When containing less than 36 percent of zinc, brasses are ductile when cold and can be worked into complex shapes without the necessity of frequent annealing. Vast deposits of copper in Katanga, Democratic Republic of the Congo, allowed smelters in this region to cast cross-shaped *katanza* ingots, which they traded extensively in West and Central Africa. These ingots were later fashioned into tools and ornamental weapons, including the well-known Luba throwing knives. The Bénin bronzes are technically brasses, as true bronze is an alloy of copper and tin. Prehistoric mining and use of tin in Africa was rare. Other African societies known to have used the lost wax technique include the Dogon of Mali and the Sao of Cameroon.

Both direct and indirect processes of iron smelting were widely used by ancient African smelters. The direct process involves the production of bloomery (relatively soft, wrought) iron by the cementation process (adding charcoal). Bloomery iron was produced in the solid state as a direct result of smelting iron ore. Pure iron melts at 1,537 degrees Celsius, but bloomery iron has rarely been heated above approximately 1,250 degrees Celsius. The carbon content in bloomery is variable, but usually low. High carbon bloomery steel has properties similar to modern carbon steels. Bloomery iron smelted at 1,200 degrees Celsius is usually a spongy mass of iron oxide and iron silicate (or slag) arising from the reaction between the ferrous oxide and the silica gangue (mineral impurities) in the ore in reducing conditions. It is a soft metal with a tensile strength of about 40,000 pounds per square inch (p.s.i), only slightly more than the strength of pure copper which is about 32,000 p.s.i. Hardening, through forging, increases the strength of iron to almost 100,000 p.s.i.

The indirect process involves the production of cast iron in blast furnaces and the manufacture of wrought iron and steel from cast iron by decarburization. In *Pre-Industrial Iron: Its Technology and Ethnology*, William Rostoker and Bennet Bronson explain that decarburization is the process by which the proportion of carbon in a high carbon steel is reduced. Cast iron is iron containing between 2 percent and 4.5 percent of alloyed carbon (C). Cast iron exists in two forms, white and gray, so-called from the appearance of the surface when it is fractured. In gray iron, most of the carbon exists as graphite, and the silicon content usually exceeds 1 percent. In white carbon, most of the carbon exists as cementite. Fast cooling rates and low silicon content favors production of white cast iron. Both cast irons are brittle, gray because of the lack of strength and disposition of the graphite, and white because of the extreme hardness and brittleness of cementite. According to Rostoker and Bronson, cementite is the iron carbide in the microstructure of steel and cast iron. The hardness of steel or cast iron is proportional to the number and close spacing of the cementite crystal present. Cast iron with 4 percent alloyed carbon can be melted at 1,150 degrees Celsius resulting in homogeneous metal with few or no nonmetallic inclusions. This metal is, however, very brittle and impossible to hammer forge until it is decarburized to wrought iron or steel.

Analysis of metallurgical samples from African industrial sites has documented a variety of smelting and forging techniques. African ironworkers produced high carbon steel and even cast iron in their bloomeries. They used two methods to decarburize high carbon steel or cast iron. The first was annealing at the hearth while making the desired object in an oxidizing atmosphere. The second involved consolidating bloom in open crucibles at the hearth. The quality of iron produced and used was quite variable. Both hot and cold forging were undertaken. Cold hammering was evidenced by broken slag inclusions and by the distortion of its microstructure. Cold forging was probably used in

the fine finishing of smaller objects, such as nails and knives. The tool kit was probably simple, including stone hammers, and the artifact may have been held with crude calipers or tongs or even by hand; with such tools cold hammering would have been the easiest way to finish small tools.

Pressure welding technology was systematically employed by African forgers to fabricate desired objects. Pressure welding technology involves heating individual metal pieces at high temperatures in the forge and then quickly hammering the pieces together to join them. The Luba of the Upemba Depression (Katanga), Democratic Republic of the Congo, are known to have used this technique. The indications of hot welding of hypoeutectoid steel to eutectoid or hypereutectoid steel reasonably suggests that the technique of hot hammering or welding probably had the aim of improving the quality of the object forged. According to Rostoker and Bronson, the term "eutectoid" denotes the carbon content of a steel at which the temperature of solid state transformation of iron is minimized. In pure iron this transformation occurs at about 910 degrees Celsius; at the eutectoid composition, with 0.8 percent carbon, it occurs only at 723 degrees Celsius. The terms hypereutectoid and hypoeutectoid refer to steels that are higher or lower in carbon than the eutectoid composition. In general, when heated, hypoeutectoid steels are less wear resistant but tougher, whereas hypereutectoid steels are harder and more brittle.

Analysis of iron artifacts from Swahili sites of the East African coast have revealed crucible steel dated to 630–890 CE. These are the first crucible steel samples known from sub-Saharan Africa. The discovery of crucible steel in East Africa provides evidence of early contact between East Africa and South Asia and points to interactions that involved technological transfer between the two subcontinents. The crucible steel process was adapted in the Near East in the seventh century and in Toledo, Spain a little later. Islamic scholars, including al-Biruni (973–1048) and al-Tarsusi (twelfth century CE), noted the crucible steel process was widely used and understood in the Islamic world. The only other known centers for the production of crucible steel before the eighteenth century were in Arabia, South India, Sri Lanka, China, and Spain.

SIGNIFICANCE OF METALLURGY IN AFRICA
To some archaeologists the African bloomery smelting and brass casting was technologically sophisticated and technically distinct from other Old World bloomery processes. First, African ironworkers developed a method of making steel (the African Direct Steel Process) that was distinct from steelmaking developed elsewhere. Second, African iron and steel were often of superior quality to that imported from Europe. Third, natural draft smelting furnaces (those that operate without bellows or equivalent devices) are an African invention. However, other archaeologists have argued that there is no convincing evidence that African bloomery technology was fundamentally different from that employed elsewhere in the Old World, as the same mechanisms or reduction of the ore and of the formation and carburization of the bloom have been observed in both African and non-African bloomery furnaces.

Metal tools had functional advantages over microlithic stone tools. The possession of iron technology led to prosperity, population increase, and colonization of ecological zones previously difficult to exploit with stone tool technology. It also provided a social role as prestige and social communicator of identity and status.

See also **Economic History; Labor: Trades Unions and Associations; Slave Trades.**

BIBLIOGRAPHY

al-Hassan, Ahmad, and Donald R. Hill. *Islamic Technology.* Cambridge, U.K.: Cambridge University Press, 1992.

Bocoum, Hamady. "La métallurgie du fer en Afrique: Un patrimonie et ene resource au service de développement." In *Aux origins de la métallurgie de fer en Afrique: Un anciennete meconnue. Afrique de l'Ouest et Afrique Centrale*, ed. Hamady Bocoum. Paris: United Nations Educational, Scientific, and Cultural Organization, 2002.

Childs, S. Terry. "Transformations: Iron and Copper Production in Central Africa." In *Recent Advances in Archaeometallurgical Research*, ed. Peter Glumac. Philadelphia: University Museum of Pennsylvania, 1991.

Childs, S. Terry, and David Killick. "African Metallurgy: Nature and Culture." *Annual Review of Anthropology* 22 (1993): 317–337.

Childs, S. Terry, and Eugenia W. Herbert. "Metallurgy and its Consequences." In *African Archaeology: A Critical Introduction*, ed. Ann B. Stahl. Malden, MA: Blackwell, 2005.

Cline, Walter. *Mining and Metallurgy in Negro Africa.* Menasha, WI: George Banta, 1937.

Eggert, Manfred. "The Bantu Problem and African Archaeology." In *African Archaeology: A Critical Introduction*, ed. Ann B. Stahl. Malden, MA: Blackwell, 2005.

Grebenart, Danillo. "Les Métallurgies du Cuivre et du fer autour d'Agadez (Niger), des Origins au Debut de la Période Médiévale. Vues Generales." In *Métallurgies Africaines: Nouvelles Contributions*, ed. Nicole Echard. Paris: Societe des Africanistes, 1983.

Herbert, Eugenia. *Iron, Gender, and Power.* Bloomington: Indiana University Press, 1993.

Holl, Augustin. "Metals and Precolonial African Society." In *Ancient African Metallurgy: The Sociocultural Context*, ed. Joseph O. Vogel. Walnut Creek, CA: Altamira Press, 2000.

Killick, David J. "A Comparative Perspective on African Iron-working Technologies." In *The Culture and Technology of African Iron Production*, ed. Peter Schmidt. Gainesville: University of Florida Press, 1996.

Kusimba, Chapurukha Makokha; David Killick; and R.G. Creswell. "Indigenous and Imported Metals on Swahili Sites of Kenya." In *Technology and Culture in Africa*, ed. Terry S. Childs. Philadelphia: University Museum of Pennsylvania, 1994.

Maddin, Robert; James David Muhly; and Thomas Sherlock Wheeler. "How the Iron Age Began." *Scientific American* 23, no. 4 (1977): 122–131.

Needham, Joseph. *The Development of Iron and Steel Technology in China.* London: The Newcomen Society, 1958.

Okafor, Eze Emmanuel, and Patricia Phillips. "New [14]C Ages from Nsukka, Nigeria and the Origin of African Metallurgy." *Antiquity* 66 (1993): 686–688.

Phillipson, David. *The Later Prehistory and Eastern and Southern Africa.* Nairobi, Kenya: British Institute in Eastern Africa, 1977.

Pleiner, Radomir. *Iron in Archaeology: The European Bloomery Smelters.* Prague, Czech Republic: Archeologicky ustav, 2000.

Rehder, J. E. " Primitive Furnaces and the Development of Metallurgy." *Journal of Historical Metallurgy* 20 (1982): 87–92.

Rostoker, William, and Bennet Bronson. *Pre-Industrial Iron: Its Technology and Ethnology.* Philadelphia: Archaeomaterials, 1990.

Schmidt, Peter R., ed. *The Culture and Technology of African Iron Production.* Gainesville: University of Florida Press, 1996.

Schmidt, Peter, and Betram Mapunda. "Ideology and the Archaeological Record in Africa: Interpreting Symbolism in Iron Smelting Technology." *Journal and Anthropological Archaeology* 16 (1997): 73–102.

Schmidt, Peter, and Donald Avery. "More Evidence for Advanced Prehistoric Iron Technology in Africa." *Journal of Field Archaeology* 10 (1983): 421–434.

Schmidt, Peter, and S. Terry Childs. "Ancient African Iron Production." *American Scientist* 83 (1995): 525–533.

Taylor, S. J., and C. A. Shell. "Social and Historical Implications of Early Chinese Iron Technology." In *The Beginning of the Use of Metals and Alloys*, ed. Robert Maddin. Cambridge, MA: Massachusetts Institute of Technology Press, 1988.

Tylecote, Ronald F. "Early Copper Slags etc. From the Agadez Region of Niger." *Journal of Historical Metallurgy* 16 (1982a): 58–64.

Tylecote, Ronald F. *A History of Metallurgy*. London: Institute of Metals, 1982b.

Van der Merwe, Nikolaas J. "The Advent of Iron in Africa." In *The Coming of the Age of Iron*, ed. Theodore A. Wertime and J. D. Muhly. New Haven, CT: Yale University Press, 1980.

Van der Merwe, Nikolaas J., and Donald H. Avery. "Science and Magic in African Technology: Traditional Iron-smelting in Malawi." In *The Beginning of the Use of Metals and Alloys*, ed. Robert Maddin. Cambridge, MA: Massachusetts Institute of Technology Press, 1988.

Wertime, Theodore A. "Man's First Encounter with Metallurgy." *Science* 146 (1964): 1257–1267.

CHAPURUKHA M. KUSIMBA

IRON

The history of iron use in Africa has been challenged both by continental and global perspectives. The red lateritic soils in Africa attest to iron's ubiquitous distribution. Ores were first exploited for their pigments (known generally by the term ochre) in prehistoric times, and their mostly red and yellow hues were used widely in rock art, face and body painting, and other expressive forms. African metallurgists exploited the rich deposits of hematite, magnetite, or limonite in pyrotechnological processes that required precise control over temperatures and gases. The production of workable metal led to iron's significant role in African history over the past 3,000 years.

Iron in its metallic form was difficult to achieve and the question of diffusion versus independent invention is still being debated. Historians have not abandoned the possibility of independent invention in Africa, given the current paucity of evidence and the unique trajectory of iron's subsequent spread. Although the complexity of iron metallurgy itself argues against multiple sites of innovation, most historians continue to focus attention on the search for distinctive African origins.

Iron use defined the core concepts for the periodization of Africa's past. Markers of Early and Late Iron Age confer eras that may be traced from one end of the continent to the other. However, the technology itself reveals an exceptional variety of techniques and innovative processes, supported by evidence of natural-draft shaft and pit furnaces, bellows, tuyeres (pipes), crucibles, and other archaeological remains.

Unlike other world regions, sub-Saharan Africa's history of ironworking is not clearly preceded by copper or bronze technology. In contrast to the scarcity of copper, iron ores abound. African technological history confounds the Eurasian sequences of Bronze Age followed by Iron Age. Both metal and manufactured products were traded widely, but the knowledge of iron technology affected demography and political evolution.

ORIGINS OF IRONWORKING IN AFRICA

The earliest evidence for exploiting iron comes from the Nile Valley, where ancient Egyptians worked meteoritic iron with its characteristic high nickel content in predynastic times. The iron found in terrestrial ores had to be chemically separated from impurities through the process of iron smelting. Early miners collected surface finds and later exploited underground deposits by digging pits and shafts. Sporadic finds of ritual objects fashioned in iron appear before the first millennium in the Nile Valley, but without early evidence of smelting or large-scale fabrication.

In contrast, the earliest dates for North African iron-smelting sites in Morocco and Mauritania are no earlier than about 810 BCE, suggesting to some historians that diffusion from elsewhere is likely. In smelting, the fusion of the ore's iron with carbon from charcoal fuel produced an iron bloom that could be repeatedly hammered into a workable metal. The possible earlier iron production site Do Dimmi (1,400 miles south of Carthage), together with sites near the Termit Massif, point to a first or second millennium BCE range and require further investigation. Another first millennium BCE iron-smelting site, Taruga (in present-day Nigeria) lies 560 miles south-southwest of Termit and was likely

Binadjoube blacksmiths with smelted iron, Togo 1982. Blacksmiths hold a locally smelted iron bloom. Smelting at Binadjoube (in the Bassar region of present-day Togo) ceased in the early twentieth century under pressure from colonial authorities. PHOTOGRAPH BY CANDICE GOUCHER

representative of the Nok culture, believed to be a settled farming people, who also produced pottery and sculpture. Other iron production sites in Nigeria, Cameroon, Gabon, Central African Republic, and the western Great Lakes region (Rwanda and Burundi) are equally suggestive of the first millennium BCE and attest to the variety of technologies employed by African metallurgists south of the Sahara at roughly the same time, and the need for an integrative continent-wide framework.

The possible first millennium BCE West African sites as yet provide scant evidence for a separate sub-Saharan invention. Firm evidence for diffusion has not materialized either. North Africa's proximity to other early non-African sites for ironworking (in Yemen, Anatolia, and South Asia, for example) suggests that the possibility of diffusion from a point of origin outside the continent cannot be eliminated. Even if iron smelting was practiced first in North Africa, the archaeological arc of iron technology's proposed spread southward is entirely missing.

SPREAD AND IMPACT OF THE IRON AGE
Iron eventually did spread rapidly south of the equator between about 500 BCE and 500 CE.

Linguistic and archaeological evidence suggests multiple routes, as does the diversity of local innovations. Diffusion was once associated with the migration of Bantu agriculturalists. Linguistic evidence reveals a common origin for many Bantu words for iron and has been used to document both a spread from the Great Lakes and from West Africa. Borrowings from Central Sudanic languages complicate the view that iron and agriculture were always linked. Traditional iron smelting is virtually extinct, preventing the detailed analysis of ironworking vocabularies necessary to resolve these questions.

Locally smelted iron blooms were acquired by the African blacksmith, who used a variety of hammering and forging technologies to produce tools and weapons. Blacksmithing skills were prized and their domain sometimes overlapped with healing and divination, surplus accumulation, and highly gendered ideas of political authority. Although women were universally excluded from iron smelting and blacksmithing activities, they sometimes mined the ores and provided necessary quantities of charcoal fuel. Oral traditions confirm the prominence of metallurgists in economy and religions, as

Constructing iron smelting furnace, Banjeli, Togo, 1985. Iron smelters reconstruct the smelting process at Banjeli, Togo. Pieces of an old furnace were incorporated into the new natural draft furnace. PHOTOGRAPH BY CANDICE GOUCHER

well as the dangers of mining faced by women, children, and slaves. That blacksmiths were both revered and despised in their cultural roles suggests the complexity of iron's impact.

IRON TRADE, ENVIRONMENT, AND DECLINE
Early trade in iron has been cited as forging links with the Mediterranean, Red Sea, and Indian Ocean commercial systems. Nomadic pastoralists could have practiced ironworking, spreading both product and knowledge, although iron production is most consistently associated with settled societies and large states. Later large-scale iron smelting, such as found in the Nubian city of Meroe, the capital of the Kushite kingdom, relied on charcoal fuel and led to widespread deforestation. Similar scenarios from Great Zimbabwe to Banjeli (Togo)

attest to the environmental impact of iron technology and the fragile ecological relationships negotiated by Iron Age societies.

In the Later Iron Age, metal was traded as iron blooms, currency, tools, weapons, and other objects. The arrival of Europeans in the fifteenth century CE corresponds to the decline of local industries as iron bars became a staple import. Historians debate the role of trade and deforestation as alternate causes of decline. Iron production could be subverted for warfare and enslavement, as well as appropriated for armed resistance. Gradually, the standing anvil and powered bellows were introduced alongside imported metals of inferior quality and cheaply manufactured iron goods. In all but a few places, the African age of iron came to an end with the European conquest and prohibitions on local mining and manufacture during the colonial period.

See also **Literature, Oral; Production Strategies.**

BIBLIOGRAPHY

Alpern, Stanley B. "Did They or Didn't They Invent It: Iron in Sub-Saharan Africa." *History in Africa* 32 (2005): 41–94.

Aux origines de la métallurgie du fer en Afrique. Une ancienneté méconnue. Afrique de l'Ouest et l'Afrique centrale. Paris: United Nations Educational, Scientific and Cultural Organization, 2002.

Boucom, Hamady, ed. *The Origins of Iron Metallurgy in Africa: New Light on Its Antiquity—West and Central Africa (Memory of Peoples)*. Paris: United Nations Educational, Scientific and Cultural Organization, 2004.

Herbert, Eugenia W. *Iron, Gender, and Power: Rituals of Transformation in African Societies*. Bloomington: Indiana University Press, 1993.

Lawal, Ibironke O., comp. *Metalworking in Africa South of the Sahara: An Annotated Bibliography*. Westport, CT: Greenwood Press, 1995.

Schmidt, Peter R., ed. *The Culture and Technology of African Iron Production*. Gainesville: University Press of Florida, 1996.

Van der Merwe, Nikolaas J. "The Advent of Iron in Africa." In *The Coming of the Age of Iron*, ed Theodore A. Wertime and James D. Muhly. New Haven, CT: Yale University Press, 1980.

Vansina, Jan. "Linguistic Evidence for the Introduction of Ironworking into Bantu-Speaking Africa." *History in Africa* 33 (2006): 321–361.

CANDICE L. GOUCHER

COPPER AND ALLOYS

The story of copper in Africa differs from that of other continents in both its history and its cultural significance. Metallurgy in Africa did not evolve slowly from copper to copper alloys to iron; rather, copper and iron were worked simultaneously from the beginning in most areas south of the Sahara. This has led to the assumption that the technology was imported from outside on the grounds that it would have been difficult to master iron working without a long apprenticeship with copper, which is more easily smelted. There is no agreement about origins or paths of diffusion, however, and indeed some scholars argue for an independent invention on the basis of early dates for metalworking in a number of sites and the lack of demonstrated sources outside the continent.

Copper is relatively scarce in much of sub-Saharan Africa, especially West Africa, although there is evidence of ancient workings at Akjoujt and in Aïr. It occurs more plentifully in regions of central and southern Africa. A discontinuous band of mineralization stretches from the Niari Basin in the present Republic of the Congo to northern Angola. There are even more significant deposits in Namibia, Zimbabwe, the Transvaal, Katanga, and northwestern Zambia. Copper was also worked extensively at Hufrat en-Nahas in the Bahr al-Ghazal (Sudan). Ancient prospectors were remarkably adept at identifying sources of metal: with the exception of some of the ore bodies of the Copperbelt (Zambia), which were not discovered until the 1920s, virtually all of Africa's copper deposits were worked in the precolonial era by indigenous metallurgists, beginning in the first millennium BCE. Miners sought out native copper and copper carbonates such malachite and azurite; they did not work sulphides lying below the water table, which were more difficult to mine and to smelt.

COPPER TECHNOLOGY

Native copper could simply be gathered from surface deposits and melted in an open crucible, like gold, but sources of such ores were soon exhausted. More complex ores were obtained from open cast mines and from shallow pits and deeper shafts dug out with sticks and hoes. Some of the open cast mines were

enormous. It has been estimated that thousands of tons of malachite were extracted over the centuries from Kansanshi (Zambia), for example. In Zimbabwe ancient mining shafts extended some sixty feet below the surface. Mining was carried out by men, women and children; it was always a dangerous occupation, as skeletons found in mines attest. Ore was carried to the surface in baskets (winches were unknown), then broken up before being smelted in small furnaces made of clay, often derived from termite and ant hills. Charcoal fuel was used to achieve temperatures sufficient to separate solid metal from rocky matrix in a reducing atmosphere. Sometimes furnaces were broken down when the smelt was complete and the metal retrieved from the bottom of the bowl; in other cases, they were used over and over and the molten metal run out into ingot molds.

Copper could be worked by a number of techniques to create finished objects. Most commonly it was cold hammered or repeatedly heated and cooled. Copper wire was made both by hammering and, in central and southern Africa, by drawing it through ever-finer plates. The art of lost-wax casting (*cire perdue*) was highly perfected in many cultures of West Africa, extending as far south as the Cameroon Grassfields. Among the best known works are the sculptures of Igbo Ukwu, Ife, Bénin, and Asante. The technique may have originated in ancient Egypt, but African craftsmen adapted it to their needs. Both Akan (Ghana) and Cameroonian artists, for example, attached molds to crucibles when casting smaller objects to reduce the build-up of gases and allow the molten metal to flow more quickly and evenly. Elsewhere sand molds were employed to produce less sophisticated but highly varied objects, especially ingot currencies that were traded over wide areas.

African metallurgists also understood the differing properties of pure and alloyed metals. For lost-wax casting they generally chose alloys of copper such as bronze or brass because of their lower melting temperature and greater ductility; some of the masterpieces of ancient Ife, however, are almost pure copper, representing a remarkable technical accomplishment. Bronze, an alloy of copper and tin, often with varying amounts of lead, was produced in Africa, but brass (an alloy of copper and zinc) was always an imported metal.

COPPER IN AFRICAN CULTURES

In many parts of the world, copper, along with iron, played a primarily utilitarian role. This was not the case in Africa. Partly, no doubt, because of its scarcity but also because of its physical qualities and mythico-religious associations, it was reserved primarily for the social and ritual spheres, with iron functioning as the metal of everyday use. In ancient grave sites, copper is ubiquitous—in contrast to the almost total absence of gold—indicating its valuation as a prestige metal from earliest times. Both archaeological and written records show that it was widely traded within Africa, both from indigenous mines and from abroad. In many societies copper was esteemed more highly than gold, which was readily traded with foreign merchants for copper and brass. As an import from the Mediterranean and then Atlantic worlds, copper and its alloys were second only to textiles in the volume of imports from the early centuries of the trans-Saharan trade (ninth through tenth centuries BCE) to the eve of the colonial era.

Copper and its alloys had a number of uses. First of all, they circulated as currencies in a bewildering variety of forms: lumps, ingots, rods, bars, wire, rings, basins, knives, bullets, "top hats" (*musuku*), and "golf clubs" (*marale*), but almost never as coins. Among the best documented are the copper crosses of Katanga varying in size from less than half an inch to six inches. Copper objects also served as prestige items. In many cases they were part of royal regalia or systems of social stratification. Frequently, too, copper had connotations of fertility, with copper jewelry marking the marital status of the wearer, for example, or the number of children born.

The common use of copper and its alloys in ritual objects reflects beliefs in the distinctive cosmological properties of the metals, culturally specific and subject to change, but part of an overarching "language of metals" that seems to have been nearly universal in precolonial Africa.

COLONIALISM AND AFTER

During the period of colonial rule, two copper mining sectors attracted the greatest investment: Katanga (Belgian Congo) and the Copperbelt of Northern Rhodesia. The Union Minière du Haut Katanga (UMHK) monopolized copper production in the Congo until it was nationalized in 1967 as GECAMINES after the colony won independence as Zaïre. At the peak of world copper prices in the early 1970s, copper was the country's most important export, accounting for half the government's revenues and two-thirds of its foreign exchange. But the dramatic fall in copper prices 1973–1975, high transport costs after civil war in Angola closed the Benguela Railroad, and political turmoil and secessionist wars in Zaïre itself crippled copper production in Katanga. Although the government signed a number of agreements with foreign investors after the fall of President Mobutu in 1997, the industry has not yet recovered.

Zambia also benefited from the copper boom in the first decade after independence in 1964, with copper exports accounting for even more of the country's foreign exchange (95%). In 1969 the government acquired 51 percent of the mining industry. When the world price dropped by almost 40 percent, the government tried to compensate by increasing production, but in the face of increasing costs and transport charges, this meant selling copper at or below the break-even point. This led to serious economic, political, and social problems that the country has tried to solve through partial privatization and other IMF-proposed programs, and an appeal to foreign investors, most notably China, the world's largest importer of copper. Nevertheless in 2004 Zambia's mining sector (primarily copper but also other minerals such as cobalt and emeralds) amounted to only 3.2 percent of gross domestic product (GDP).

See also **Archaeology and Prehistory.**

BIBLIOGRAPHY

Bobb, F. Scott. *Historical Dictionary of Democratic Republic of Congo (Zaïre)*, rev. edition. Lanham, MD: The Scarecrow Press, 1999.

Childs, S. Terry, and Eugenia W. Herbert. "Metallurgy and its Consequences." In *African Archaeology*, ed. Ann Brouwer Stahl. Malden, MA: Blackwell, 2005.

Childs, S. Terry, and David Killick. "Indigenous African Metallurgy: Nature and Culture." *Annual Review of Anthropology* 22 (1993): 317–337.

"Democratic Republic of the Congo" and "Zambia." In *Africa South of the Sahara*. London and New York: Routledge, 2007

Grotpeter, John J.; Brian Siegel; and James R. Pletcher. *Historical Dictionary of Zambia*, 2nd edition. Lanham, MD: The Scarecrow Press, 1998.

Herbert, Eugenia W. *Red Gold of Africa: Copper in Precolonial History and Culture*. Madison: University of Wisconsin Press, 1984.

Lambert, Nicole. "Nouvelle contribution à l'étude du Chalcolithique de Mauritanie. In *Métallurgies Africaines*, ed. Nicole Echard. Paris: Mémoires de la Société des Africanistes, 1983.

Shaw, Thurstan. *Igbo-Ukwu: An Account of Archaeological Discoveries in Eastern Nigeria*. 2 vols. Evanston, IL: Northwestern University Press, 1970.

Shaw, Thurstan. *Nigeria: Its Archaeology and Early History*. London: Thames and Hudson, 1978.

EUGENIA W. HERBERT

GOLD AND SILVER

From pre-dynastic (4000 BCE) times through early Christianity, most of the world's gold came from southern Egypt and Nubia (*nub*, meaning "gold"). Starting in 641 CE, the Islamic advance across North Africa became a catalyst for renewed exploitation and revitalized gold production in Egypt, Nubia, Ethiopia, and the Magreb created a zone of cheap and plentiful gold from the Atlantic to the Red Sea. By the tenth century, extensive East African trading voyages, coalescing at Kilwa, emerged as a key Muslim entrepot for the inland gold of Sofala and south-central Zimbabwe.

The Arab conquest of North Africa also provided information on the gold sources south of the Sahara that had fed the earlier fortunes of Rome and Carthage, and frequent Islamic references to both the anti-Atlas and trans-Saharan gold trade were subsequently reflected in early European references such as Abraham Cresques's *Mappa Mundi* (1375–1377) and explorer Jean de Bethencourt's "River of Gold" (1402). The empires of Ghana and Mali flourished on the gold trade: sub-Saharan gold from sites at Bambouk and Boure, exchanged for salt en route, were transported across the desert and minted into currencies by both the medieval European and Muslim worlds.

Spurred on by these references, the Portuguese, arriving by sea on the West African coast by the fifteenth century, effected a shift in the gold trade to Arguin and the Guinea Coast. The Gold Coast fort of El Mina, involving the Akan traders as key partner-players, became the principal supplier of bullion to the world market, outflanking the trans-Saharan trade. The reputation of Ghana's historic involvement is reflected in its traditional political panoply.

Archaeological evidence for both gold or silver is rare: Tin-Hinan's tomb at Abalessa in the western Ahaggar, the most ancient deposit, dates from the fourth and fifth centuries CE; in East Africa, gold dated to circa 1200 CE has been found in hilltop burials at Mapungubwe; and a quantity of gold jewelry dating from the fifteenth and sixteenth centuries was unearthed at Rao, Senegal.

Responding to the fluctuating demands of both Islamic and European economic history, silver and gold were intertwined in complex ways. Under the Almoravids and the Almohads, Sijilmassa was a primary minter of dinars with gold coming from the Sudan, at the same time that silver was being brought from the mines of the anti-Atlas and the Bani, via Sijilmassa, to the Mediterranean coast and Europe. Although the Mamluks continued the Fatimid policy of minting dinars when they became rulers of Egypt in 1250 CE, silver ducats from Christian countries often had greater value. Concurrently, the expulsion of the Jews from Touat in 1492 effected a shift back from gold to silver and the minting of the North African silver dihram followed. Starting in the fifteenth century, European ships carried silver to Arguin and Portendik, exchanging it against the *tibar*, or gold dust of the Guinea coast, which the English Crown converted into the gold *guinea* in 1663. Continued preference for silver coinage was subsequently reflected in the African conversion of French-introduced Louis Philippe five-franc pieces and Maria Theresa silver thalers into jewelry.

Gold and silver was traded and used in three forms: (1) as a malleable ore without smelting; (2) cast into ingots or bars using a copper amalgam; and (3) as a finished product (coins and jewelry) that was frequently recast, recycled, and further "debased" (e.g., *kakra* gold). The techniques involved in both silver and gold smithing include filigree and granulation, casting (*cire perdue*), beaten sheet metal often with repousse and/or niello decoration, damascene, and gilting. Gold and silver pulled thread

A "Croix du Sud" gold fibula, created with filigree and granulation by the Jewish goldsmith Albert Benadou, Agadir, Morocco, 1999. PRIVATE COLLECTION OF LABELLE PRUSSIN

BIBLIOGRAPHY

Eudel, P. *Dictionnaire des bijoux de l'Afrique du Nord.* Paris: Ernest Leroux, 1906.

Gabus, Jean. *Sahara: Bijoux et techniques.* Neuchatel: A la Baconniere, 1982.

Garrard, Timothy. *Gold of Africa.* Munich: Prestel-Verlag, 1989.

Hazard, Harry W. *The Numismatic History of Late Medieval North Africa.* New York: American Numismatic Society, 1952.

Johnson, Marian. "Black Gold: Goldsmiths, Jewelry and Women in Senegal." Ph.D. diss., Stanford University, 1981.

Mauny, Raymond. "Essai sur l'histoire des metaux en Afrique occidentale." *BullIetin IFAN* 14, no. 2 (1952): 545–595.

Wischnitzer, Mark. *A History of Jewish Crafts and Guilds.* New York: J. David, 1935.

LABELLE PRUSSIN

embroidery is used extensively on textiles and on leather.

Early Jewish involvement in the trade and production of precious metals under Carthaginian, Roman, and Byzantine rule continued to flourish in the wake of the Arab invasion of North Africa and the Iberian peninsula. Their renown as goldsmiths and silversmiths combined with their devotion to alchemy, magic, and demonology and the objects they fashioned for both ritual use and their overlords, both under crescent and cross, traveled in tandem with the extensive Jewish gold trade over which they exercised a virtual monopoly. Combining literacy and trade, they were often ambulant, fulfilling multiple roles as minters, smiths and armorers, musicians and singers, negotiators, interpreters, and tax collectors and, by virtue of Islamic proscription, heavily involved in usury.

The North African adaptation of Malekite law, which proscribed the wearing of gold for men and attributed negative qualities to it, in turn fanned the preference for silver jewelry among Muslims and Berbers, whereas in sub-Saharan Africa, gold continued to be the preferred metal for jewelry among Wolof, Bamana, Songhay, Peul, and Sarakolle women and for the Asante panoply. These differential preferences were ultimately reflected in the practices of both resident sub-Saharan gold smithing castes such as the Songhay *Diam*, the Wolof *Thiam*, the Asante *Kyem*, and the transient Tuareg silver smithing caste, the *enaden*.

See also **Judaism in Africa; Production Strategies; Sijilmasa.**

MIDWIFERY. *See* **Childbearing.**

MILITARY ORGANIZATIONS

This entry includes the following articles:
HISTORY OF MILITARY ORGANIZATIONS
NATIONAL ARMIES
COLONIAL ARMIES
GUERRILLA FORCES
MERCENARIES
MILITIAS

HISTORY OF MILITARY ORGANIZATIONS

Little is known about African armies before about 1200. In the period following 1200, Africa can be divided into several military zones, in each of which a distinct art of war prevailed. One of the first distinctions to be made is between those areas where cavalry was used and those where it was not. The great northern savannas, south of the Sahara and north of the tropical rainforest of western and Central Africa, were the one area in Africa where horses could survive well enough to make cavalries possible. For the cavalries of the western savanna, however, mounts proved to be a problem. The largest and fastest horses, imported from the desert regions, could not reproduce well in western Africa, and the local breeds of horses, established for some time, were smaller and not as powerful. Nomads of the Sahara were notable for their use of the larger horses and camels as mounts. Although they possessed great potential military power as a result of this, as well as social norms that encouraged virtually every male to be a horseman and fighter, their social organization rarely gave rise to disciplined armies. At times, though, when united by a religious leader (Ibn Yasin and the Almoravid movement of the eleventh century, for example; or Nasr al-Din in the Tubenan movement of the late seventeenth century) they could be a formidable force.

Perhaps because of the problem with mounts, western African cavalries relied on missile tactics, rather than shock tactics. Cavalrymen carried javelins or bows, and strategies consisted largely of harrying opponents with these weapons, and charging with the saber only when the opponent was broken.

Coastal societies in Senegambia lacked horses but often encountered horsemen along their interior boundaries, ranging from the Serer in modern Senegal, around to modern Sierra Leone, and then in modern Bénin, where a gap in the rainforest allowed cavalries to operate. Perhaps because of the threat of cavalries, armies in these areas were often organized in tight phalanxes and generally fought in close order, as this was the most effective way for infantry to face horses, because the animals normally will not charge through a compact mass of soldiers. Along the Gold Coast (present-day Ghana), even though cavalry was not present, tight formations, typically of professional soldiers using hand-to-hand weapons, with archery only as support, were the norm. Information on this period is lacking for most of the rest of western Africa.

In Angola, armies also were composed entirely of infantry, but with more loosely organized formations than those of western Africa. Archers were used as skirmishers; most tactics were based on hand-to-hand fighting by highly trained, skilled soldiers. In Kongo some soldiers carried defensive arms, typically shields; in Angola the soldiers did not. Instead, they were trained to dodge weapons and fought in loose formations, with space between members.

The arrival of Europeans initially had little impact on the tactics of African armies. In Senegambia, Europeans supplied horses, generally of the larger and more powerful sort; these were incorporated into existing armies that had long been importing similar horses from the desert. In other societies, Europeans occasionally offered their services as mercenaries during the sixteenth and seventeenth centuries. Although African military leaders purchased European-made firearms in the sixteenth and seventeenth centuries, these were treated as just another sort of missile weapon and did little to displace indigenous missile weapons, such as bows. In Angola, where large numbers of European soldiers were engaged in wars of conquest after 1579, the most significant contribution to the local art of war was the use of European soldiers as a sort of heavy infantry. They bore more defensive arms (body armor and helmets) than their African counterparts, but their skill in hand-to-hand fighting, usually with the sword, was valued more than any technical advantages in weapons.

None of the early African armies had highly developed logistical systems. Most armies were accompanied by large bands of porters who carried food and supplies—in Angola, they were often half as numerous as the army itself—where rivers made transport possible. In other cases, armies resupplied through foraging or looting the countryside. Logistical problems tended to limit the maximum size of armies, as well as their range.

The development of the flintlock musket and its importation into Africa in large numbers after the early eighteenth century had a profound impact on the conduct of war in many African societies. In areas where cavalry played an important role, such as Senegambia and the savanna interior of the Guinea coast, firearms remained relatively unimportant until well into the nineteenth century. But in coastal societies, firearms were incorporated into the armies, displaced bows almost entirely, and resulted in tactical changes. On the Gold Coast, the tight formations of the seventeenth century gave way to more open formations wherein all combatants carried firearms. Instead of closing in on opponents, African generals sought to win through musket fire, often maneuvering to avoid close fighting. Formations were loose, and individual units were small and mobile to accommodate these changes. Similar changes took place both in Kongo, where larger, looser formations equipped with firearms replaced the smaller and more skillful units of professional soldiers of earlier times, and in Angola, where the Portuguese-led armies and their African opponents both fought in the same way.

The Kingdom of Dahomey (modern Bénin) had to make different adaptations to accommodate the potential of firearms. Because its soldiers had to fight horsemen of the interior kingdoms, especially Oyo, they could not use loose formations. Instead, they developed tight groupings of musketeers, drilled the soldiers to maintain a high rate of firing, and rotated the platoons. Without cavalry support, however, Dahomean units were not always effective against opposing cavalry.

Where cost or transportation factors made it impossible to supply African armies with large numbers of firearms, the older art of war remained, even where cavalry did not play a role. In the eighteenth century, the Lunda of Central Africa had good success with the older tactics of rapid closing for hand-to-hand fighting, even against opponents bearing firearms.

Given the uncertain nature of weapons, and the need for solidarity among soldiers, it was common for religious symbols and ideology to play a significant role in African warfare. Islam had a great potential for bringing the nomadic horsemen together for unified attacks on the Western Sudan. Similarly, soldiers in other parts of the continent often tied fetishes and other charmed religious paraphernalia to their clothing in anticipation of war. In Christian Kongo, St. James was the patron saint of the country and its soldiers, and religious dancing accompanied mobilizations.

See also **Taylor, Charles Gahnhay; Warfare.**

BIBLIOGRAPHY

Law, Robin. *The Horse in African History.* Oxford: Oxford University Press, 1981.

Thornton, John. *Warfare in Atlantic Africa, 1500–1800.* London: Taylor and Francis, 2005.

JOHN K. THORNTON

NATIONAL ARMIES

Although most African armies were based upon the colonial forces of the old imperial powers, the Cold War had a tremendous impact on them in the decades following independence. Some countries retained strong European ties, particularly in Francophone Africa, where French military involvement remained strong. Others came under Communist influence, developing large mechanized armies based on the Warsaw Pact model. South Africa maintained its status as a regional military power despite international sanctions, and continues to do so under majority rule.

Unfortunately, many African armies are notorious for corruption, incompetence, and the destabilizing influence they have had on the continent's development. The Zairian Armed Forces (FAZ) provides a classic example. Poorly paid troops resorted to extortion and theft to make ends meet, equipment was poorly maintained, and the government repeatedly relied on mercenaries and foreign intervention to deal with the Katanganese Succession and Simba Rebellion of the 1960s, the Katanganese invasion of Shaba Province in 1978, and conflicts arising from the instability in Central Africa following the Rwandan holocaust. France intervened repeatedly to back up client states such as the Central African Republic, the Côte d'Ivoire, and Rwanda when these countries' own defense forces were not only incapable of maintaining order, but played a major role in fomenting crisis.

Some African armies have established reputations as professional, disciplined forces that are effective international peacekeepers. The Botswanans' excellent service in Somalia earned them praise; their defense force is made up of well-trained, long-service volunteers. Senegal, whose troops fought with distinction during the world wars as part of the French colonial army, also maintains a positive image. The Nigerian army, considered to be excellent at the time of independence, has since gained notoriety in a succession of coups that established military dictatorships. Theoretically well-equipped with tanks and heavy artillery, and supported by a modern air force and navy, Nigeria's large army makes the nation the dominant regional power.

Nigeria played the leading role in West African intervention in Liberia's civil war. The peacekeeping force called Economic Community of West African States Monitoring Group (ECOMOG) arrived in Monrovia in August 1990 and also included troops from Gambia, Ghana, and Sierra Leone. The 2,500-

person force was unable to maintain order—some troops were so poorly supplied that they lacked boots. The conflict continued, spreading into neighboring Sierra Leone and resulting in over a decade of horrific violence.

Liberia originated in 1822 as a haven for freed American slaves, and had strong ties to the United States during the Cold War. A group of noncommissioned officers seized power in a brutal 1980 coup, after which illiterate Master Sergeant Samuel Doe became president. The Armed Forces of Liberia retained support from the American government, but this support declined with the end of the Cold War. When a Libyan-trained insurgent band led by Charles Taylor crossed the Ivorian border on Christmas Eve 1989, the military collapsed. Several competing factions emerged. Inept peacekeepers seemed powerless to restrain many of the fighters, teenage thugs who were fueled by drugs and financed by smuggled diamonds.

Why have some African governments had such trouble with their armies? In many nations, the military was used, not to protect the national interest, but to maintain corrupt regimes in power, which unscrupulous soldiers then seized for themselves. Ethnic rivalry has also been a source of conflict within many armies, leading to not only factionalism but also the eruption of civil war. Although poor equipment and training partially explain poor performance, even well-supplied national armies encountered tremendous difficulties with insurgents. After gaining independence from Portugal in 1974, the Marxist regimes established in both Angola and Mozambique received extensive support from the Communist bloc. Yet the National Union for the Total Independence of Angola (UNITA) and the Mozambican National Resistance (RENAMO), both of which received aid from the West and particularly South Africa, proved to be formidable opponents.

Ironically, the collapse of Communism led not only to the termination of Soviet military aid, but to political realignment and military reorganization in both of the former Portuguese colonies. Mozambique turned its large mechanized army into a smaller, lighter counterinsurgency force that was able to bring that nation's civil war to a peaceful conclusion in 1992. Angola turned to its former foes for assistance: Executive Outcomes, a South African private military company, played a significant role in UNITA's final defeat.

South Africa provides a good example of a professional defense force adapting modern military methods to African conditions. Under the apartheid regime, the country had a light, mobile force of well-trained conscripts and reservists providing the bulk of its manpower. South African industry manufactured light armored vehicles designed for African conditions, as well as excellent artillery in spite of international sanctions. From 1965 to 1989 South African troops regularly defeated Cuban- and Soviet-equipped insurgents from the Southwest Africa People's Organization (SWAPO) in Namibia, and also led forces in Angola. Key elements in their success were an increasing use of black African troops and an extensive civil affairs effort focused on maintaining the support of the local population. Since the establishment of majority rule, the South African military integrated even more fully, with many black Africans—including former African National Congress (ANC) fighters—holding top leadership positions.

Perhaps the most dramatic example of the adaption of modern technology to traditional African military culture comes from Chad. During fighting against Libya in the Aozou Strip in 1987, Chadian forces used four-wheel-drive pick-up trucks equipped with antitank missiles to inflict a series of crushing defeats on the Libyans, who were well equipped with Soviet armored vehicles and aircraft. Over 4,000 Libyan troops were killed, and hundreds of tanks and armored personnel carriers destroyed in what became known as the Toyota Wars. Chadian losses were 77 killed and 123 wounded. Although the Chadians received military assistance from France and the United States, their effective tactics were based on those of nomadic desert horsemen.

See also **Warfare: National and International.**

BIBLIOGRAPHY

Edgerton, Robert B. *Africa's Armies: From Honor to Infamy. A History from 1791 to the Present.* Boulder, CO: Westview Press, 2002.

Ellis, Stephen. *The Mask of Anarchy: The Destruction of Liberia and the Religious Dimension of an African Civil War.* New York: New York University Press, 1999.

Finnegan, William. *A Complicated War: The Harrowing of Mozambique.* Berkeley: University of California Press, 1992.

Reno, William. *Warlord Politics and African States.* Boulder, CO: Lynne Rienner Publishers, 1998.

Turner, John W. *Continent Ablaze: The Insurgency Wars in Africa, 1960 to the Present.* London: Arms and Armour Press, 1997.

FRANK KALESNIK

COLONIAL ARMIES

All colonial powers in Africa maintained locally recruited armies for internal security and in order to extend and guard territory. African colonial armies, mainly infantry who lived off the land, cost less than European troops. Only the French and British employed African troops outside the continent. Officers and senior NCOs (noncommissioned officers) were invariably white, whereas most recruits came from ethnic groups officially identified as martial races.

The earliest British colonial forces were Coloured Corps that fought on the South African frontier, and the West India Regiment, initially recruited from Caribbean slaves, that helped guard the West African settlements. France recruited soldiers in its North African colonies and, from the 1850s, *tirailleurs* in West Africa. In 1912, General Charles Mangin (1866–1925) successfully argued that France, in order to redress its demographic disadvantage with Germany, should conscript *la force noire* in West Africa. In a European war, African troops could be used for garrison work in the colonies, thus releasing white and North African regiments to defend France. However, in World War I, 170,000 *Tirailleurs sénégalais* were recruited for service in France as front line troops against the Germans. Controversially, they were also used as occupation troops in the German Rhineland in 1919–1920. The second largest African colonial army in 1914 was the 20,000 strong *Force publique* in the Belgian Congo, originally raised by the Congo Free State, and which had gained a reputation for harsh behavior.

World War I was fought in Africa mainly by colonial troops who had conquered the two German West African colonies by mid-1916. In the long campaign in German East Africa, German *Schutztruppen* fought British, Belgian, South African, and

Portuguese forces until 1918. In both world wars, British West African troops fought in East Africa. The British policy of confining African forces to the continent changed as manpower shortages grew; by 1918 African troops were employed in Egypt and the Levant, mainly as non-combatant labor, and serious consideration was being given to recruiting a large African army for use in Europe. In both world wars, the South African government opposed arming Africans who were recruited for non-combatant labor corps.

During the interwar years, colonial armies were reduced in size. By 1930, British colonial forces south of Khartum numbered only 12,000 men. Like most colonial armies, the British forces were little more than lightly armed gendarmeries used for internal security. The French, the Belgians, and later the Italians, operated a system of conscription, but other colonial armies relied on volunteers. French colonial troops continued to be conscripted and sent overseas to Europe and North Africa, and to fight in campaigns in Syria and Indochina.

Italy's successful aggression against Ethiopia (1935–1936), and the alliance with Germany, posed a serious threat to the British and French in Africa. The King's African Rifles in East Africa, and the Sudan Defence Force, created in 1925, were strengthened and made more mobile. In September 1939, when war broke out, French colonial regiments again faced the Germans in Europe. When France was defeated by Germany and Italy in mid-1940, some 15,000 colonial troops became prisoners of war. The Free French, led by de Gaulle (1890–1970), continued to fight with their main force being colonial troops in the central African colony of Chad. Italy's colonial army, raised in Eritrea, was expanded for the war against Ethiopia; in 1940 it was claimed to number 250,000 men. However, in the East African campaign of 1940–1941, it suffered from large-scale desertion and was defeated by South Africans and British and Belgian colonial forces.

Nearly one million men from the European colonies in Africa were enlisted in the war years 1939–1945. By 1945, over 500,000 recruits had been through the British forces. Most were volunteers but conscription, often via chiefs, was used. Literate and numerate men were also required for the newly created technical corps. As in 1914–1918, African soldiers were employed as laborers in uniform, building roads and bridges, driving trucks, working in dockyards, and guarding prisoners in North Africa and the Levant. East and West African troops had proved their military worth in the East African campaign, and from 1943 they were recruited as combatant troops and as porters for the Burma campaign against the Japanese. By 1945, over 90,000 African soldiers from British Africa were serving in Asia.

For most African soldiers the war was a remarkable period in which they were exposed to a range of new experiences: new foods, a uniform, regular wages, health care, industrial time, ideas of modern discipline and sanitation, opportunities to learn new skills and languages, and overseas travel. Demobilization of African armies was carefully planned, and undertaken with considerable efficiency, albeit slowly, with most soldiers returning to their homes in the rural areas. Although older literature argued that veterans were prominent in nationalist politics, there is no evidence that they played a larger or more active role than any other group of people. Harsh reactions by colonial authorities in Senegal at Thioroye in 1944, following a soldiers' mutiny over pay and conditions, and to a veterans' protest march in the Gold Coast in February 1948, helped change the face of postwar West African politics, but in neither incident were soldiers or veterans directly challenging colonial rule. In Kenya, a few former soldiers were involved in the Mau Mau revolt, but many more fought against them in the ranks of the King's African Rifles.

After 1945, African colonial armies were reduced in size. African troops were used by the British as labor in the Middle East, and East African troops fought in the Malayan emergency (1952–1954); French colonial troops fought in France's colonial wars in Indochina (1946-54) and Algeria (1954–1962). Colonial authorities were slow to appoint African officers, but the process sped up with the approach of the transfer of power. However, most officers came from the educated elites, not the ethnic groups that formed the bulk of the rank and file. At independence, most African armies expanded but they continued with many of the structural weaknesses that characterized colonial forces, not least an officer class largely divorced from the men they commanded.

See also **Warfare: Colonial; World War I; World War II.**

BIBLIOGRAPHY

Clayton, Anthony. *France, Soldiers and Africa.* London: Brassey's Defence Publications, 1988.

Echenberg, Myron. *Colonial Conscripts: The Tirailleurs Sénégalais in French West Africa, 1857–1960.* Portsmouth, NH: Heinemann, 1991.

Grundlingh, Albert. *Fighting Their Own War: South African Blacks and the First World War.* Johannesburg: Ravan Press, 1987.

Killingray, David, and David Omissi, eds. *Guardians of Empire.* Manchester, U.K.: Manchester University Press, 1999.

Lawler, Nancy Ellen. *Soldiers of Misfortune: Ivorian Tirailleurs in World War II.* Athens: Ohio University Press, 1992.

Lunn, John. *Memoirs of the Maelstrom: A Senegalese Oral History of the First World War.* Portsmouth, NH: Heinemann, 1999.

Michel, Marc. *L'appel a l'Afrique: Contributions et réactions à l'effort de guerre en A.O.F. 1914–1919.* Paris: Publications de la Sorbonne, 1982.

Parsons, Timothy H. *The African Rank-and-File: Social Implications of Colonial Military Service in the King's African Rifles, 1902–1964.* Portsmouth, NH: Heinemann, 1999.

DAVID KILLINGRAY

GUERRILLA FORCES

Africa has the highest incidence of violent conflict of any continent, much of it involving guerrilla forces. The nature, aims, and activities of such forces show great diversity across Africa and through history. Most have engaged in nominally civil conflicts, although these are difficult to distinguish clearly from interstate wars as guerrillas often operate across porous international frontiers and sometimes act as proxy forces for neighboring or more distant states. The apparent lack of political agenda among many recent groups has raised particular problems of analysis and policy, challenging researchers to formulate new understandings of the groups' underlying motivations.

DEVELOPMENT AND DIVERSITY OF GUERRILLA FORCES

The precolonial situation was generally one of low-intensity local or regional conflict between relatively fluid polities. This was further destabilized by European contact, particularly the Atlantic slave trade, which enhanced the militarization of many African societies. Some authors argue that elements of contemporary guerrilla warfare represent a reversion to such precolonial modes of conflict, but this comparison is problematic given different political, social, and material circumstances in the early twenty-first century.

Insurrections by Africans, some substantial, took place throughout the colonial period, such as the Maji-Maji rebellion in German East Africa from 1905 to 1907. But African guerrilla forces fighting recognizably modern, nationalist struggles were first seen in anticolonial rebellions after World War II. During the 1940s and 1950s, France faced uprisings in Madagascar, Tunisia, Morocco, and Algeria, the latter developing into large-scale conflict. The British were meanwhile confronted with insurgency in Gold Coast, Nigeria, Egypt and, most seriously, the Mau Mau revolt in Kenya. Guerrillas also fought liberation struggles against colonial regimes in Southern Africa and Portuguese Guinea in the 1960s and 1970s.

Even after Angola, Mozambique, and Zimbabwe achieved independence, Cold War geopolitics perpetuated proxy conflicts in Southern Africa, with guerrilla groups supported by the United States, the Soviet Union, or their respective allies. Apartheid South Africa, with European and North American backing, was a major destabilizing influence on neighboring states, either through direct military intervention or through support for groups such as Resistência Nacional Moçambicana (RENAMO) and União Nacional para a Independência Total de Angola (UNITA). The Horn of Africa was also drawn into the Cold War through Soviet support to Ethiopia.

Some of these forces continued fighting in the post–Cold War era, with peace arriving in Mozambique in 1992 and Angola in 2002. Similarly, long-term conflict has afflicted southern Sudan, where civil war first began in 1963. In other countries, protracted insurgency has been waged against occupying African states. Eritrea began its independence struggle against Ethiopia in 1961, finally succeeding in 1993. Elements in Western Sahara fought Moroccan rule from 1976 and, despite a ceasefire since 1991, the dispute remains unresolved. Complex, factional guerrilla forces have been embroiled in situations of state collapse in Liberia, Sierra Leone, Somalia, Rwanda, and Democratic Republic of the Congo

(DRC), and significant rebellions continue in Uganda, Côte d'Ivoire, and elsewhere.

The diversity of these guerrilla forces to some extent reflects changing political contexts during and since decolonization. Large, relatively well-organized forces successfully liberated Algeria, Portuguese Guinea, Eritrea, and countries in Southern Africa, but failed to achieve secession for Biafra, the rebel state that existed in southeast Nigeria from 1967 to 1970. By contrast, small, fragmented groups with little or no central command have characterized recent conflict in the Great Lakes region.

African guerrilla strategies have also varied and have been shaped by influences from outside the continent. Mao Zedong's (1873–1976) revolutionary doctrines have been most influential, particularly his idea of people's war, which was widely adopted by African liberation movements. During the Cold War, shared ideology drew support for some African guerrilla forces from the international Left. A notable example was when Ernesto "Che" Guevara (1928–1967), with Cuban backing, went to Congo-Kinshasa in 1965 on an unsuccessful mission to support a revolt by Marxists loyal to the memory of assassinated Prime Minister Patrice Lumumba (1925–1961). In southern Africa, guerrilla training came variously from Eastern bloc or Western countries, or from white minority governments in South Africa and Rhodesia, according to geopolitical alignments and interests. Some African guerrillas benefited from the military experience of former colonial troops who were veterans of the liberation of Europe or decolonization conflicts elsewhere, such as French Indochina. However, as of 2007 many guerrillas receive only basic weapons training.

Tactics used range from conventional pitched battles (such as Biafra), to more diffuse guerrilla techniques, to terrorizing civilians. Sierra Leone's Revolutionary United Front (RUF) became infamous for limb chopping, although instances of civilian mutilation occurred earlier, as in the Mau Mau revolt, and other groups were known for their sometimes extreme brutality, such as RENAMO. In certain cases, narcotic and alcohol use by guerrillas has promoted human rights violations by overcoming inhibitions to undertake brutal acts. However, guerrilla groups often operate in and react to an environment of state or state-sponsored violence against real or perceived opponents. Atrocities are not confined to rebel movements, as evinced by genocide perpetrated by state-backed militias in Rwanda in 1994 and in the Darfur region of Sudan in recent years.

Guerrillas are generally recruited from those for whom expression of political grievances, social aspirations, or economic advancement through peaceful means is blocked. Recruitment is often voluntary, at least initially, through ideological, political, or sometimes religious mobilization, or in response to state repression. Poorly educated young men with few opportunities provide a large pool of potential recruits in the context of demographic growth, limited school provision, and underemployment that characterizes most African countries. Government forces may recruit from the same dispossessed social stratum, sometimes blurring the lines between guerrillas, soldiers, and bandits. Women have fought in some insurgencies—in Portuguese Guinea, Eritrea, Rhodesia, and Liberia—or they have been involved by providing social support or through trading networks. Forced recruitment has been common in some conflicts, and impressment of child soldiers has prompted international concern in Sierra Leone, northern Uganda, and elsewhere.

The leadership of guerrilla forces is usually better educated. The charismatic and politically astute figureheads of some liberation movements, such as Samora Machel (Mozambique) and Nelson Mandela (South Africa), went on to become presidents in their respective countries, and their movements transformed themselves into peacetime political parties. Elsewhere, placing former commanders in positions of power has provoked further violence and plunder, as the cases of Charles Taylor in Liberia and Foday Sankoh (1937–2003) in Sierra Leone show.

For armaments, African guerrilla forces in the early twenty-first century rely mostly on small arms and light weapons, often of Eastern bloc or former Eastern bloc manufacture. These became widespread during liberation struggles and have flooded Africa since the end of the Cold War, facilitated by porous borders and poor international controls on the arms trade. Two portable weapons form the basis of most guerrilla armories. The first is the AK-47 (Kalashnikov) assault rifle, highly durable and light enough to be handled even by child soldiers. The second is the RPG-7 rocket-propelled grenade launcher, designed as an antitank weapon but finding much wider use by African guerrillas. Other commonly-used weapons include light mortars, and some insurgencies have effectively deployed SAM-7 surface-to-air missiles, notably the Partido Africano da Independência da Guiné e Cabo Verde (PAIGC), whose guerrillas downed Portuguese aircraft. Antipersonnel and antivehicle landmines of both European and North American manufacture have been widely used and continue to kill or maim significant numbers of civilians every year.

POLITICS OR PLUNDER?

The financing of guerrilla forces worldwide is a current preoccupation in academic and policy circles. Previously, some movements received support from Cold War actors, whereas others were backed by rogue states such as Libya. In some recent conflicts, particularly in West and Central African countries, neighboring states have supported guerrillas for geopolitical and economic reasons. Humanitarian aid from North American and European governments or nongovernmental organizations (NGOs) has been diverted to some groups, notably in the Horn of Africa, and was important in sustaining the Biafra rebellion. Diasporas have financed certain guerrilla forces, for example the Eritrean People's Liberation Front (EPLF) and Liberians United for Reconciliation and Democracy (LURD). However, claims of wider diasporic support for insurgencies may be overstated and should be placed in the context of the general importance of international remittances to people in developing countries. More importantly, diasporas may nurture grievances or subnationalist sentiments at home through newspapers, Web sites, and other media, or lobby North American and European policymakers for international recognition and support for their cause (e.g., by requesting the imposition of sanctions on home governments).

All guerrilla forces support themselves to some extent from local resources, but reasonable self-provisioning often slips into looting local people for self-enrichment. Exploitation of commercial primary products has been another prominent activity for many recent groups. In Africa, timber, mineral ores, and uncut gemstones have commonly been traded, with guerrillas in Sierra Leone, Angola, and DRC characterized as diamond insurgencies. Such groups often fail to articulate a clear political agenda. Some analysts therefore argue that their insurgency is driven by greed, and that political objectives are abandoned or merely form a façade for wars of plunder. Others challenge this view and the ensuing debate is glossed as greed and grievance. Those supporting the grievance perspective point out that economically motivated violence has always formed part of war, if not initially then as conflict becomes entrenched, and that economic concerns are inseparable from political and social ones. The geography of conflict often relates to the national political economy, with insurrections arising in neglected provincial areas that see little benefit from the export of high-value local resources, as evidenced by the ongoing unrest in the oil-rich Niger Delta. Plunder may thus represent a form of resistance to exploitative, centralized states, whereas entrepreneurialism by guerrillas would have no outlet in times of peace because of their socioeconomic marginalization. Furthermore, even small groups of apparent outlaws may be encouraged, manipulated, or supported by mainstream politicians for their own ends.

This debate has implications for conflict resolution. Seeing guerrillas purely as economic actors may be problematic in peacebuilding. Disarming, demobilizing, and rehabilitating them into civilian life through cash support, as in donor-funded programs in Sierra Leone, Liberia, Angola, and DRC, is costly and difficult. However, these measures may fail to address chronic structural problems in the countries concerned, and instead the prewar political economy, with the inequities that originally provoked the conflict, may be largely reconstructed. Truth and reconciliation commissions or human rights trials may help purge societies of painful histories, but the main beneficiaries still tend to be educated elites.

NEW UNDERSTANDINGS AND RESEARCH DIRECTIONS

Some attempts to move the debate beyond greed and grievance explore psychosocial drivers of guerrilla behavior. Some authors argue that feelings of alienation engender a strong need for redress, expressed in forms of violence that reverse the established order of power, such as humiliation of authority figures.

Concerns have also been raised over the preference of Europe and North America, since the end of the Cold War, for power-sharing agreements to involve all guerrilla factions as a means of resolving civil conflict. Typically, pacified rebels get better access to state power and resources, including positions in the government or army, or development funding for their home areas. However, this may incentivize insurgency as a means of pursuing political power or economic resources, which risks further undermining democratic politics. The peace process may itself be drawn out by guerrilla leaders so that they may continue to tap external resources, as recently witnessed for Somalia and Côte d'Ivoire.

After the September 11, 2001, attacks in the United States, some African guerrilla groups, particularly in certain Saharan and Sahelian countries and Somalia, are viewed by U.S. policymakers in terms of Islamic insurgency, prompting U.S.-led security initiatives involving North and West African states. Other analysts see this characterization of disparate armed groups, often concerned more with local political grievances or banditry than with jihad, as misguided, arguing that the war on terror is being instrumentalized by African governments to leverage donor support, ostensibly for security purposes but, in reality, to repress or repel domestic opponents.

Overall, a proper understanding of the sociology of African guerrillas is needed and their actions, however abhorrent, need to be situated in their national and global politico-economic contexts. Even the most wanton economic violence is not perpetrated in a political vacuum, but in historically inscribed spaces of power and marginalization.

See also **Cold War; Machel, Samora Moises; Mandela, Nelson; Taylor, Charles Gahnhay; Warfare.**

BIBLIOGRAPHY

Berdal, Mats, and David Malone, eds. *Greed and Grievance: Economic Agendas in Civil Wars.* Boulder, CO: Lynne Rienner, 2000.

Clapham, Christopher, ed. *African Guerrillas.* Oxford: James Currey, 1998.

Clayton, Anthony. *Frontiersmen: Warfare in Africa since 1950.* London: Taylor and Francis, 1999.

Hanlon, Joseph. *Beggar Your Neighbours: Apartheid Power in Southern Africa.* London: James Currey, 1986.

Keen, David. *Conflict and Collusion in Sierra Leone.* Oxford: James Currey, 2005.

Tull, Denis M., and Andreas Mehler. "The Hidden Costs of Power-Sharing: Reproducing Insurgent Violence in Africa." *African Affairs* 104, no. 416 (2005): 375–398.

MARTIN EVANS

MERCENARIES

Mercenaries are soldiers specifically recruited by states, insurgent groups, or corporations and paid to engage in armed combat.

Mercenary groups assume two main forms: informal groups of adventurer-mercenaries who often have ideological motivations, and multinational commercial entities that pursue their own corporate economic interests. Adventurer-mercenaries were common during the 1960s and 1970s in Africa. For example, several hundred French, Belgian, British, and Rhodesian mercenaries served in the Democratic Republic of the Congo from 1960–1968. During the Nigerian Civil War, hundreds of mercenaries volunteered to fight for secessionist Biafra. Multinational military corporations, also known as private military companies, have been increasingly common in Africa since the 1990s. For example, Executive Outcomes (EO), a South African private company, was hired by the governments of both Sierra Leone and Angola to assist them in defeating insurgent groups in their territory.

Although mercenaries have been a feature of war since hired 10,000 mercenaries in 1500 BCE, the decolonization of Africa resulted in a resurgence of the use of mercenaries by foreign governments, rebel movements, and commercial companies to carry out military operations.

Mercenaries hired for service in Africa are mostly young veterans of elite armed forces, such as the United States' Green Berets, Britain's Special Air Service, and the South African Defense Force's (SADF) 32 Buffalo Battalion. The end of apartheid in South Africa resulted in a large number of white soldiers leaving the SADF in search of alternative military employment.

Mercenaries are utilized in a variety of ways by their employers, including coups, counterinsurgencies, and economic protection. The most infamous coup in which mercenaries participated was the 1975 overthrow of the Abdallah regime in the Comoros by French mercenary Bob Denard

(b. 1929) and his colleagues. A number of African governments have hired mercenaries to assist them in defeating rebel groups and insurgents. In the 1990s, the government of Sierra Leone hired EO to train infantry units and run intelligence, logistics, and communications. Other private military contractors hired by Sierra Leone included the British-based Sandline and the Gurkha Security Guards (GSG). In the mid-1990s, the Angolan state oil company, Sonangol, hired EO to assist the Angolan army in regaining control of the Soyo oil fields from National Union for the Total Independence of Angola (UNITA) rebels.

Mercenaries are subject to legal control through both domestic and international law. The 1972 Organization of African Unity Convention for the Elimination of Mercenaries in Africa was the first convention prohibiting mercenaries. Mercenaries were defined as men who sold their services to a person, group, or organization engaged in insurgency against a state; thus states were not prohibited from hiring mercenaries by the Convention. Protocol 1 to the Geneva Conventions of August 12, 1949, deprives mercenaries of the status as participants in armed conflict and denies protections afforded to other combatants. Article 4 of the Hague Convention of 1907 on the Rights and Duties of Neutral Powers and Persons in War on Land provides that "corps of combatants cannot be formed nor recruiting agencies opened on the territory of a neutral power to assist the belligerents."

See also **Organization of African Unity; Warfare.**

BIBLIOGRAPHY

Mockler, Anthony. *The New Mercenaries: The History of the Hired Soldier from the Congo to the Seychelles.* New York: Paragon House, 1987.

Sapone, Montgomery. "Have Rifle with Scope, Will Travel: The Global Economy of Mercenary Violence." *California Western International Law Journal* 30, no. 1 (1999): 1–43.

Singer, Peter. *Corporate Warriors: The Rise of the Privatized Military Industry.* Ithaca, NY: Cornell University Press, 2003.

Thomson, Janice E. *Mercenaries, Pirates, and Sovereigns.* Princeton, NJ: Princeton University Press, 2001.

MONTGOMERY MCFATE

MILITIAS

While associations of irregular combatants have been a feature of warfare in Africa for some time, since 1990 "militia" has become an increasingly prominent term in discussions of mass violence and militarization across the continent. This reflects both real changes in the sociopolitical landscape with the end of the Cold War and an inability or unwillingness by many international observers to understand the complexities of post–Cold War violence in countries like Rwanda, Sierra Leone, or Liberia. Militia, in other words, has become a generic term for armed groups whose intentions, motivations, and alliances are not always clear.

In the narrowest definition, a militia is a group of citizens with some level of training mobilized to form a nonprofessional military force in the service of the state. While there are efforts to categorize various types of militias in Africa according to their function and make-up—religious, ethnic, vigilante, or anticrime militias—in the twenty-first century the term is broadly applied to any armed organization that doesn't easily fit the model of a rebel group, an official state army, or a purely criminal gang. This may include organizations comprising members of a single ethnic group fighting for dominance or survival, groups motivated by economic opportunism, community defense forces—or, as is increasingly the case, some combination of these.

Despite the variety of uses of the militia label, the term consistently invokes the sense of an irregular, nonprofessional fighting force and a complex relationship to the state and to other civil society or social networks. As a result, any effort to understand militias in Africa needs to examine a few key elements. First is the nature of the militia's relationship to the state and to governing elites and political parties. This includes understanding how militias are armed and financed. Second is the question of gender. In many cases (though not all) militias are considered to be all male fighting forces, and in some cases membership in a militia is equated with becoming or behaving as an adult male. What is too often left out of discussions about militia activity, however, is that they often rely on gendered divisions of labor to support themselves and gendered violence can be one of the hallmarks of militia activity. The question of violence, both its uses and its forms, is a central one for understanding militias in an African context,

since militias call into question the state's monopoly on the use of force and very often militias employ violence in a way that official armies cannot. Finally, in the contemporary period it is critical to ask how African militias, which are so often thought of as symbols of Africa's retreat from the modern world, are increasingly linked to global networks of finance, trade, and political maneuver.

MILITIAS AND AFRICAN STATES

Post–Cold War literature on militias in Africa has distinguished between so-called first- and second-generation civil militias. Whereas first-generation militias fit more closely the narrow definition of a state sponsored, civilian auxiliary military force, second-generation militias are characterized by the ambiguities and complexities of their relationship to the state. In fact, many observers have argued that it is precisely where the state itself is most in question—countries such as Liberia, Sierra Leone, Somalia, or the Democratic Republic of the Congo, where bureaucratic institutions have crumbled or are especially ineffective—that militias tend to proliferate. This weak state theory suggests that the usual mechanisms for controlling violence may not be sufficient to put a check on those governing elites who would use mass violence as a political or economic tool. Thus, for example, a radical Hutu nationalist faction of the government in Rwanda was able to mobilize the Interahamwe militia for the 1994 genocide despite the official government participation in the peace process.

So-called warlords in resource rich areas of the continent have mobilized militias in an effort to gain and secure access to diamonds, cocoa, rubber, or timber reserves and to facilitate their trade on the global market without interference from the state or other rivals. These militias challenge the state's monopoly on the legitimate use of force, though as in Somalia, Nigeria, or Sierra Leone they may also facilitate alternative networks for the exercise of sovereignty and political control (what has been referred to as the "shadow state" or "private indirect government").

In other cases African leaders fearful of a coup d'etat by the military or a power grab by strong government ministers may deliberately weaken the armed forces and various government ministries, choosing instead to allow the proliferation of armed militia factions to ensure that none becomes

A member of the Liberians United for Reconciliation and Democracy (LURD) in Voinjama, Liberia, 2002. Like many contemporary African conflicts fought by irregular militia forces, Liberia's war was often characterized as a "bush war" at the margins of global forces. Yet the global flows of both small arms and heavy artillery are integral to how such militia forces function. PHOTOGRAPH BY DANNY HOFFMAN

powerful enough to threaten the status quo. This was particularly striking in the case of Liberia under the rule of Charles Taylor (1997–2003), who by some accounts spent 75 percent of the official budget on various loyal militias guaranteeing the president's personal security. Similarly in Sierra Leone, the Sierra Leone People's Party government relied on the Civil Defense Forces militia for much of its security after elections in 1996 when it was clear that many soldiers in the Sierra Leone Army were unhappy with the rise of the party and in some cases were collaborating with rebels to profiteer on the black market trade in diamonds.

GENDER DYNAMICS

The stereotype of the twenty-first-century African militia fighter is of a young, impoverished male combatant. While this is accurate in many cases, it tends to eclipse the complicated gender relationships at work in many African militias and says little about who actually participates in militia activities.

Despite the focus on male combatants and their activities as fighters, many militias include people conscripted, recruited, or forced to serve the noncombat support needs of the organization.

This can include both men and women, though very often women are disproportionately impacted. So-called camp wives, cooks, and baggage and armament carriers are typically not included in disarmament proceedings or other postconflict reintegration efforts, and yet are integral to the functioning of a militia movement and often experience severe social and economic consequences for those roles. This has been a pressing issue in the postconflict period in Sierra Leone and Liberia, where noncombatants were not defined as militia members for the purposes of disarmament and reintegration programs, and yet their association with militias during the war years has made it extremely difficult to resume their prewar lives.

In addition to those people who might live with or travel with a militia force, the support roles for a militia may be filled by communities sympathetic to its cause or coerced into providing assistance. For example, the Inkhata Women's Brigade played an important role, both practically and symbolically (since women were seen as the bearers of the "traditional culture" that the militias were defending) in mobilizations of male Zulu paramilitaries in South Africa from the 1970s to the 1990s.

Fighters in the Kamajor militia movement in Bo, Sierra Leone, 2000. Members of the organization were initiated into the Kamajor "society," a civil defense movement that troubled the line between a social movement and a military organization. Initiation and the use of occult artifacts were said to render the bodies of fighters immune to the bullets of their enemies. PHOTOGRAPH BY DANNY HOFFMAN

Such examples challenge the preconception that a militia is only the male fighters that make up its combat ranks. At the same time, participation in a militia may become a marker of manhood when the discourse of masculine responsibility becomes militarized, as it was in parts of Sierra Leone in the late 1990s; in some rural communities it was considered an obligation of adult men to participate in civil defense units.

VIOLENCE

Though militia movements engaged in their home regions as community defense forces may be notable for higher levels of discipline than unruly state armies or invading rebel forces (the early phase of the kamajor movement in Sierra Leone is one example), in general irregular forces are associated with excessive and often unconventional forms of violence. Conventional wisdom holds that a lack of extensive professional training leads to human rights abuses. No doubt that is sometimes the case. Yet such explanations miss some of the complexities that may be at work in militia activity.

On the one hand, groups like the Sierra Leonean kamajors were affiliated in the early periods of the war with other social bodies such as the poro secret society, which had its own rules of ethical conduct and war time behavior and limited the abuses committed by the organization. At the other extreme, many militia leaders are keenly aware of how international nongovernmental organizations respond to humanitarian emergencies, and in some cases the use of extreme violence may be a strategic gamble to attract the attention of international relief agencies. There is evidence that this was the case for factions in the late stages of the Liberia civil war, which ended with Charles Taylor's overthrow in 2003.

Because of their irregular status, militias may also be a convenient surrogate for state militaries. Such outsourcing of violence allows governments to distance themselves from, and yet still pursue, policies condemned by the international community. The janjaweed militias in the Darfur region of western Sudan seem to have played this role since 2003, when they began a campaign of genocide and forced removal of local communities.

Child soldiers with the Liberians United for Reconciliation and Democracy (LURD) forces, Voinjama, Liberia, 2002. The use of underage combatants has been one of the most remarked-upon features of militia activities in sub-Saharan Africa. The fixed age marking the boundary between childhood and adulthood codified in much of the international anti-child soldier language does not always map easily into local conceptions of the responsibilities and capabilities of youth, especially young men. PHOTOGRAPH BY DANNY HOFFMAN

One of the most notable instances of militia violence in twentieth-century history was the 1994 genocide in Rwanda. Though not unique, the gender violence in that conflict was particularly pronounced. Hutu militias engaged in rape as a strategic form of attack on Tutsi women in an apparent effort to not only terrorize Rwandan Tutsis and moderate Hutus, but symbolically destroy Tutsi ethnic identity as well.

INTERNATIONAL CONTEXTS

In the popular imaginary militias tend to be associated with local conflicts. Yet even the most local organizations may be connected to transnational and even global networks of arms trading, resource extraction, mercenary labor, and expatriate influence. Warlords in Liberia, Côte d'Ivoire, the DRC, and the Horn of Africa are sustained by their connections to global markets and their ability to bypass the regulatory and taxation apparatuses of the state. In the Niger Delta of Nigeria a number of militia groups have sprung up to contest the Nigerian government and foreign oil companies' treatment of local communities in the oil fields

region. Many of the continent's militias are armed through weapons dealers with links in Europe, the former Soviet Union, China, and the United States. Both British and South African security companies have supplied training to pro-government militias in Sierra Leone, Angola, and elsewhere around the continent. And in many cases technologies such as the Internet, cellular telephones, and increased air travel have allowed expatriates to send supplies, information, and financial support to allied militias in their home countries as a way to destabilize or preserve ruling regimes.

See also **Cold War; Labor: Conscript and Forced; Sudan: Wars; Taylor, Charles Gahnhay; Warfare.**

BIBLIOGRAPHY

Ero, Comfort. "Vigilantes, Civil Defense Forces and Militia Groups: The Other Side of the Privatization of Security in Africa." *Conflict Trends* 1 (2000). Available from http://www.accord.org.za/ct/2000-1/CT%201_2000%20pg25-29.pdf.

Francis, David J., ed. *Civil Militia: Africa's Intractable Security Menace?* Hants: Ashgate, 2005.

Hassim, Shireen. "Family, Motherhood and Zulu Nationalism: The Politics of the Inkatha Women's Brigade." *Feminist Review* 43 (1993): 1–25.

Mbembe, Achille. *On the Postcolony.* Berkeley: University of California Press, 2001.

Reno, William. *Corruption and State Politics in Sierra Leone.* Cambridge, U.K.: Cambridge University Press, 1995.

Reno, William. "The Changing Nature of Warfare and the Absence of State-Building in West Africa." In *Irregular Armed Forces and Their Role in Politics and State Formation,* ed. Diane E. Davis and Anthony W. Pereira. Cambridge, U.K.: Cambridge University Press, 2003.

DANNY HOFFMAN

MIRAMBO

MIRAMBO (c. 1840–1884). Legend has it that Mirambo was captured by Ngoni peoples entering the area of present-day western Tanzania when he was young and from them learned spear-fighting techniques and political leadership. As a chief, Mirambo used these methods to build his personal political influence and his own private army. Equipped with firearms and required to undergo vigorous conditioning, his military units became known as a *rugaruga* and were used later by other Nyamwezi leaders.

At the time Swahili-Arabs dominated the flourishing east African ivory trade from their inland post at Tabora, the link between the expanding ivory frontier and Zanzibar, the island entrepôt off the east African coast. In the early nineteenth century various groups inland took part in the ivory trade as Nyamwezi hunters, porters, and caravan leaders. These Nyamwezi were not centrally organized (there were thirty-one Nyamwezi chiefdoms in 1859), and often the Swahili traders would play them off against one another. As elephants became scarcer in Nyamwezi areas, it was necessary for their trading expeditions to travel farther and farther to bring back ivory. Mirambo, whose capital, Urambo, was in the vicinity of Tabora, sought to unify the Nyamwezi in order to better organize trade and deal a blow to the Swahili.

With an army of five thousand, Mirambo began a campaign of bringing Nyamwezi groups under his control and disrupting trade between Zanzibar and the ivory frontier, which at that time had moved to the west and south of Lake Tanganyika. By harassing caravans and making ivory acquisition more difficult, Mirambo and his *rugaruga* caused the price of ivory at the coast to rise. Sultan Barghash of Zanzibar sent a large caravan to make peace with Mirambo in 1875, and after negotiations reached an agreement for a temporary alliance the next year. For the next eight years Mirambo controlled the corridor between Tabora and Lake Tanganyika from Lake Victoria in the north to Lake Rukwa in the south. Mirambo profited greatly from the trade passing through his large sphere of influence by charging tolls, levies, and protection fees, but his empire dissolved shortly after his death in 1884.

See also **Tanzania.**

BIBLIOGRAPHY

Bennett, Norman Robert. *Mirambo of Tanzania: 1840–1884.* New York: Oxford University Press, 1971.

THOMAS F. MCDOW

MISSIONARIES

MISSIONARIES. *See* **Christianity.**

MKAPA, BENJAMIN

MKAPA, BENJAMIN (1938–). Benjamin William Mkapa was born in the Mitwara region of southeastern Tanzania. After his early schooling in Tanzania, he received a bachelor of arts degree from Makerere University in Uganda. During the late 1960s and the 1970s, he held the post of managing editor at several of Tanzania's leading newspapers, *The Nationalist, Uhuru, The Daily News,* and *The Sunday News.*

From 1974 to 1976, Mkapa served as press secretary to Tanzania's first president, Julius Nyerere, leader of the nation's only legal party—the socialist-oriented Revolutionary State Party. Under Nyerere and his successor, Ali Hassan Mwinyi (b. 1925), Mkapa held various cabinet posts—including minister of foreign affairs—between 1977 and 1995. In 1984, Mkapa served as ambassador to the United States.

In 1995 Mkapa was chosen president on the Revolutionary State ticket in the nation's first

Benjamin Mkapa (1938–). Former Tanzanian president Mkapa arrives at the inauguration for South African president Thabo Mbeki on April 27, 2004 in Pretoria. Mkapa was Tanzania's president between 1995 and 2005. AFP/GETTY IMAGES

multiparty national election, receiving 62 percent of the vote. In 2000 he was elected for another five-year term. As president Mkapa continued the privatization of the economy begun by his predecessor and encouraged foreign investment. This policy won the favor of the World Bank and the International Monetary Fund, which forgave some of the nation's foreign debts. Economic growth during his presidency almost doubled to 6.7 percent annually, but critics said that poor Tanzanians were not benefiting from the increase. He was accused of giving aid to Burundian rebels and of involving Tanzania in the civil war in Democratic Republic of the Congo in the late 1990s. President Mkapa made the battle against HIV/AIDS one of his major causes, saying that "AIDS is wiping us out." After leaving office in 2005, he worked to reduce poverty in Tanzania, in part by promoting legalization of the informal economy of the poor.

See also **Nyerere, Julius Kambarage; Tanzania.**

BIBLIOGRAPHY

Maliyamkono, Teddy L., and Fidelis E. Kanyongolo, eds. *When Political Parties Clash.* Dar es Salaam, Tanzania: Tema Publishers, 2003.

Mkapa, Benjamin. *Building a Vision: President Benjamin W. Mkapa.* Dar es Salaam, Tanzania: Southern African Research and Documentation Centre, 1995.

MICHAEL LEVINE

MOBUTU SESE SEKO (1930–1997). Born Joseph-Désiré in Lisala in the remote northern regions of the Belgian Congo, Mobutu Sese Seko attended a succession of schools before his expulsion from junior high school at the age of nineteen for behavioral problems. He was conscripted into the colonial army in 1950, serving for most of the next six years at the noncommissioned officer school in Kananga and then at army headquarters in Léopoldville (present-day Kinshasa). He then became a journalist in Léopoldville. He was sent to the 1958 Brussels World's Fair and spent 1959–1960 in a journalist training program in Brussels.

In the wake of an army mutiny in newly independent Congo in July 1960, Mobutu, then allied to the radical nationalist Congolese leader Patrice Lumumba, was named army chief of staff and was able to gain relative control of the armed forces. On September 14 he initiated his first coup to "neutralize" tensions between Prime Minister Lumumba and President Joseph Kasavubu, appointing an interim government of young university graduates. Enjoying support from Western nations, especially the United States, he participated in the removal of Lumumba to Shaba (Katanga) in January 1961, where he was assassinated.

On November 24, 1965, Mobutu seized power through the army. In 1967 he created a single political party (Mouvement Populaire de la Révolution) to underpin his personal rule and was elected by plebiscite for seven-year presidential terms in 1970, 1977, and 1984. In his early years of rule, he renamed the nation Zaire (in 1971), recentralized an administration dispersed to provincial and local bases, for a time stabilized the economy, and created the illusion of strong development. From 1975, however, the country began a

Mobutu Sese Seko (1930–1997) on May 14, 1997. Seko served as president of Zaire (modern-day Democratic Republic of the Congo) for 32 years. After being overthrown, he was exiled in Togo but lived mostly in Morocco until his death in 1997. ERIC FEFERBERG/AFP/GETTY IMAGES

prolonged decline, and Mobutu's regime became notorious for venality and misrule. Despite legalization of opposition parties in 1990, Mobutu continued to maintain himself in power.

In 1991, after rioting in Kinshasa, he appointed an opponent, Étienne Tshisekedi, prime minister but dismissed him after twelve days. He dissolved the national assembly in 1994. In 1996 Mobutu began treatment for prostate cancer. In September 1996 a revolt led by Laurent Désiré Kabila, head of the Alliance of Democratic Forces for the Liberation of Congo, spread across Zaire from the east. After negotiations with Kabila failed, Mobutu fled Kinshasa in May 1997 for exile, at first in Gabon, as Kabila's forces entered the capital.

See also **Colonial Policies and Practices: Belgian; Congo, Democratic Republic of the: History and Politics; Lumumba, Patrice.**

BIBLIOGRAPHY

Duke, Lynne. *Mandela, Mobutu, and Me: A Newswoman's African Journey.* New York: Doubleday, 2003.

Monheim, Francis. *Mobutu, l'homme seul.* Brussels: Éditions Actuelles, 1962.

Young, Crawford, and Thomas Turner. *The Rise and Decline of the Zairian State.* Madison: University of Wisconsin Press, 1985.

CRAWFORD YOUNG

MODERNITY AND MODERNIZATION: ANTIMODERN AND POSTMODERN MOVEMENTS. There has been a vigorous debate about the nature of "modernity" and of Africa's place in the development of the modern world. Modernity itself has been described in a number of different, sometimes opposing ways, with many scholars suggesting that the term is of little value in asserting anything specific about contemporary Africa (Englund and Leach 2000, Cooper 2005). These debates reflect the slippery character of the very notion of "the modern" as a phenomenon and a category. Is modernity, for example, a distinctive historical "moment," "era" or process in history—and if so, how would it be distinguished from colonialism, or even capitalism; or is the "modern," rather an analytical category, a theoretical framework that enables scholars to grasp the unfolding of long-term historical processes across regions—and indeed the world?

In some accounts, modernity is equated primarily with the use of contemporary technologies and media, from medical resources, to international transport, to satellite television. The study of globalization has devoted a good deal of attention to such substantive changes. Yet modernity can also be understood, not as a set of material features of social life, but as a cultural orientation, or worldview. Such a perspective would include ideas about individualism, wealth accumulation, and consumerism.

There is also a strong dimension of scholarship, influenced in particular by the work of Foucault, that sees modernity as a set of tactical practices that characterize modes and discourse of governance that have become dominant throughout the world in the last three centuries. Here, the emphasis is on examining the ways in which the sovereignty of the state exercises power through the development of new regimes of discipline, individuation, and surveillance. Adding to the challenges of this perspective is the way that scholarship on modernity is at pains to distinguish these processes—material, ideological, governmental—from older notions of "modernization" that suggest a grand historical progress, in which (African) societies "develop" from and "traditional" conditions, only to "take off" as they become "modern" (Rostow 1960). A focus on modernity as a cultural orientation has, rather, demonstrated ways in which the very categories of the "traditional" and the "modern" emerge as part of modernity itself; in this way, the "traditional" and the "modern" are less distinct historical eras than they are contrasting perspectives on contemporary social transformation. This review will focus, in particular, on those approaches that have emphasized the ways that African peoples have been interested in and active participants in the making of the modern world.

One of the important dimensions of the contested nature of modernity is the fact that specific formulations, reformulations, appropriations, and reactions to it are often, themselves, characterized by contradiction and ambiguity. It is, for example, often the case the African movements, projects, and everyday practices can be seen simultaneously to embrace and reject the possibilities of the modern world. An early an influential example of such a perspective can be found in the East African Beni Ngoma (or "Drum Band") societies (Ranger 1975). These competitive dance associations were founded in the coastal, urban Swahili towns of what are now Kenya and Tanzania in the late nineteenth century. They involved young men who adopted the music, uniforms, and instruments of German and British colonial military bands in order to stage performances in which competing factions vied for political and social prominence within their communities. These bands came to incorporate men from across the interior of East Africa, and proved important social vehicles for many Africans to advance their rights to participate in, or oppose the colonial administration. In this way, colonial

authority was both made use of and challenged within African communities.

The form that Beni took proved extremely influential across much of East and Southern Africa. The Kalela dances of Northern Rhodesia (now Zambia's) Copper Belt are a related example of the way that an overt imitation of colonial European clothing and style could be used to transform relations among Africans (Mitchell 1956). In Kalalela, Zambian urbanites, most of them working in grueling conditions of copper mining, asserted their own sense of their creative command of a modern identity, even as they challenged the terms of this modernity through songs, dances, and forms of dress that could be assertively humorous, ribald, and ironic.

A contemporary movement related to both Beni and Kalela are the *sapeurs* of the Republic of Congo. *Sapeurs* are devotees of *haute couture*, often spending enormous sums of money acquired through exhaustive work in the informal, often illegal economy, to purchase clothing in order to establish their reputation as celebrities in their home communities (MacGaffey and Bazenguissa-Ganga 2000). Many *sapeurs* travel to France to facilitate the clothing trade, shipping large quantities of clothing back to Congo, sustained, again, by underground practices that connect Congo and Paris in a circuit of illicit economic exchanges. Here again, such explicit dimensions of modernity as global travel, cosmopolitan, European cultural products, and capital accumulation are embraced, even as *sapeurs* challenge the fact that they feel excluded from the opportunities provided to national and global elites, and often subvert the cosmopolitan standards of taste and fashion through their sartorial performance of the exuberant excesses of consumerism.

Modernist movements such as these raise questions about the significance of mimesis—the attempt to resemble "others" to pursue one's own social projects. Processes of mimesis have also been extremely important in activities surrounding healing, in which communities of the afflicted attempt—often in ritual form—to confront and transform the effects of modernity on their lives.

Foremost among such rituals is the *hauka* "cult," whose activities in the Gold Coast (Accra, Ghana) were famously recorded in the film *Les*

Maîtres Fous by Jean Rouch. In these rites, adepts who feel themselves in some sense unwell, become possessed by sprits, or *hauka*, who are identified with the most powerful colonial, administrative, and military officials of the day. By embodying these spirits, the participants in these healing practices are able to acquire an external perspective on their own position as subjugated, social outcasts that often restores a feeling of competence and well-being.

A similar therapeutic process is found in the *Zar* practices from the Horn of Africa (Boddy 1989). Here, it is especially women in both Muslim and Christian communities across Ethiopia, Sudan, and Somalia who become possessed by Zar spirits, typically in order to overcome problems in reproductive health, such as miscarriage, infertility, or divorce. Women become possessed by *zar* spirit, who are always representatives of modern institutions—district administrators, police officers, school teachers, military officials—with origins outside of local communities. Through possession by these modern powers, women transform their identities as modern subjects, even as they feel that their own reproductive problems have been exacerbated by such modern institutions as the cash economy, the marginalization of local spiritual sources in favor of either Islam or Christianity (or both), labor migration, and the expansion of the nation-state. This pattern of the creative, ritual use of modern symbols to provide redress for the physical and moral transformation of people and communities who feel they have suffered under modernist processes is widespread in Africa, where powers associated with epidemic disease, long-distance travel, and high-tech communication are routinely appropriated as spiritual forces that can restore health and well-being to sufferers.

While these modern responses to modernity's institutions, processes, and cultural categories give evidence of Africans' efforts to restore a sense of order and well-being to disrupted lives, it is also the case that modernity itself is personified in many African communities in the figure of dangerous, malicious, frequently occult forces. The importance of witchcraft in the form of both an imaginative device, a standardized nightmare of the devastation wrought by the excesses of accumulation, apparently unfettered social and physical mobility, and coercive colonial and postcolonial state authority; and the form of social movements meant to discover, punish, or even eradicate witchcraft and related occult practices is widespread throughout Africa.

The notion that some people make use of malevolent, occult forces, whether intentionally or unintentionally, to enhance themselves or destroy others, is probably a taken-for-granted reality in most communities across Africa. It has further been noted that references to these forces, typically in the form of witchcraft accusations, or widely circulating reports of the activities of witches, have increased significantly in the colonial and postcolonial eras throughout the continent. In some instances, the increase in such accusations and fears suggests a collapse of the moral authority of local and regional social relations as communities become incorporated into large-scale modern political processes, from colonial conscription to the bureaucratization of emerging nation-states, through the expansion of globalizing markets.

In most instances, the potency of such modern reforms have generated new "idioms" of witchcraft and sorcery; modernist institutions are imagined to extract the energies of the people they incorporate through nefarious means, and, further, these means must be countered through new modes of ritual protection—modes generally themselves seen to be akin to witchcraft. The *Kamcape* movement, for example, in the Southern Tanzanian, Eastern Zambian, and Malawi region, cleansed villagers of witchcraft and issued "certificates" to demonstrate the efficacy of their techniques. This use of bureaucratic techniques to combat occult forces is part of a widespread pattern, one frequently made use of by young men who have had extensive encounters with the similar state-based institutional practices (e.g., as labor migrants required to possess passes for residence and transit to and from worksites, as patients in health clinics, as civil servants, or as primary and secondary school students), and use these modernist techniques to transform the bases for authority in their home communities (Auslander 1993).

This pattern is especially prevalent in areas of intensive labor migration, where young men are incorporated into industrial work that leaves them vulnerable to both a lack of support from their home communities, and with chronically low wages that do not permit them to be independent and self-sustaining. Such young men, unsuccessful as either wage laborers or as rural peasants, also typically envision older members of their communities as threatening their youthful vitality, and so see a connection between the injustice of their economic misfortune and the malevolent power (characteristically understood to be motivated by "jealousy") of elders who block their advance. It is also more generally the case that witchcraft is seen as a tension that defines urban-rural relations in regions across the continent. Urbanites are thought to establish their town lives by appropriating the support of their kin and neighbors for their own personal advancement (and so denounced as witches consuming the life substance of others), while urban residents fear their rural kin will attack them with nefarious means if they fail to regularly redistribute their earnings.

Witchcraft accusations and eradication are not merely local phenomena; increasingly the state is understood to make use of extractive, occult forces. The 1996 presidential commission on "Satanism" appointed by Kenyan President Daniel arap Moi was intended to allay concerns about the use of "dangerous powers" (symbolically similar to witchcraft and sorcery, but articulated in the distinctly modern, Christian, and Muslim idiom of "Satanism") by state officials; when the release of the report was suppressed in 1999, it inflamed the suspicions of many Kenyans, precipitating widespread accusation across the nation. References to Satanism as a movement on national and transnational scales, often taking a form identical to "local" idioms of sorcery and witchcraft, became widespread across Africa.

RUMORS OF THE MODERN

In addition to accusations of witchcraft at the local, regional, and national level, there are also a host of rumors—often referred to as *radio trottoir*, or "sidewalk radio"—that circulate in most African cities. These rumors describe the ambiguous nature of power and wealth in modern Africa, as accumulation and status are felt to be extremely alluring and evidence of a "modern," cosmopolitan identity, even as they are feared as sources of antagonism and instability.

One of the oldest and most pervasive of such "rumors" is found across West Africa, and refers to a spirit known as Mami Wata (Bastian 1996). Mami Wata is a beguilingly beautiful spirit who promises her devotees—or in some cases, her unsuspecting consorts—enormous wealth, in return for which she may deprive them of their reproductive capacity, or even demand blood sacrifices that require wealthy, modern persons to destroy their kin in order to maintain lifestyles that depend on accumulation.

This logic of a dangerous "Faustian" bargain is embedded in a wide range of practices across the continent. In East Africa, individuals looking to get ahead quickly in business are suspected of making contracts with Islamic spirits, *majini*, who will provide financial support in exchange for (blood) sacrifices. Such *majini* are typically seen to destroy those with whom they make such contracts, as their bloodlust proves insatiable. In West Africa, similar models of business success assume that *juju* is used. *Juju* is popularly conceived of as occult substance, frequently manufactured from the bodies of young people, which permit those who control the substance to extract wealth from the energies of others.

In East Africa, and increasingly in southern Africa, there are long-standing reports of what are variously described, as *mumiani* or *banyama*, individuals who steal human blood for a range of purposes. Generally, these blood-stealers are associated with modern institutions—from firemen in colonial Nairobi, to Catholic clergy in Zambia, to wildlife extension officers in Tanzania (White 2000). Such blood-stealers use their (often high tech) expertise to convert the health of their victims into private sources of wealth and prestige, whether in the form of medicines, sacramental wine, or petrol, all substances rumored to be derived from the blood of victims of these evildoers.

A related rumor (often also described as *mumiani* in Tanzania, and now quite prominent in South Africa) sees victims not as those who have their blood stolen, but as zombified labor. Victims report that they awake from what they thought was sleep to find that their bodies are weak and in pain, and their clothing is soiled. Such accounts are taken as evidence that these people have been turned into zombies, forced to work during their sleep in the industrial or agricultural sector for malevolent employers. The nature of this employment is frequently seen to correspond with new forms of "flexible" and irregular labor, which is increasingly characteristic of contemporary African economies.

In all of these rumors, as in the discourses of witchcraft and mimetic rites, there is a formulation of modernity as an extractive enterprise, which is imagined and grasped as an assault on the physical and moral well being of human victims. Peoples across Africa have responded to these assaults in kind, by attempting to enhance their well-being, and, indeed, their bodily health, through therapeutic practices that appropriate and transform the ambiguous powers of modernity.

See also **Mami Wata; Moi, Daniel arap; Witchcraft.**

BIBLIOGRAPHY

Auslander, Mark. "'Open the Wombs!': The Symbolic Politics of Modern Ngoni Witchfinding." In *Modernity and Its Malcontents: Ritual and Power in Postcolonial Africa*, ed. Jean Comaroff and John L. Comaroff. Chicago: University of Chicago Press, 1993.

Bastian, Misty. "Married in the Water: Spirit Kin and Other Afflictions of Modernity." *The Journal of Religion in Africa* 26 (1996): 1–19.

Boddy, Jannice. *Wombs and Alien Spirits: Women, Men, and the Zar Cult in Northern Sudan.* Madison: University of Wisconsin Press, 1989.

Cooper, Frederick. *Colonialism in Question: Theory, Knowledge, History.* Berkeley: University of California Press, 2005.

Englund, Harri, and James Leach. "Ethnography and the Meta-Narratives of Modernity." *Current Anthropology* 41, no. 2 (2000): 225–248.

Geschiere, Peter. *The Modernity of Witchcraft: Politics and the Occult in Postcolonial Africa.* Charlottesville: University of Virginia Press, 1997.

MacGaffey, Janet, and Rémy Bazenguissa-Ganga. *Congo-Paris: Transnational Traders on the Margins of the Law.* Bloomington: Indiana University Press, 2000.

Mitchell, J. Clyde. *The Kalela Dance: Aspects of Social Relationships among Urban Africans in Northern Rhodesia.* Manchester: Manchester University Press, 1956.

Ranger, Terence O. *Dance and Society in Eastern Africa: 1890–1970: The Beni Ngoma.* Berkeley: University of California Press, 1975.

Rostow, Walt W. *The Stages of Economic Growth.* Cambridge, U.K.: Cambridge University Press, 1960

White, Luise. *Speaking with Vampires: Rumor and History in Colonial Africa.* Berkeley: University of California Press, 2000.

BRAD WEISS

MODES OF PRODUCTION. *See* Production Strategies.

MOGADISHU. Mogadishu, the capital of Somalia, was reduced to rubble and depopulated by violent intraclan fighting in the early 1990s after the fall of the government of Siad Barre. The shelling and gun battles destroyed 600-year-old Islamic secular buildings and mosques as well as the city's modern infrastructure. It remains one of the most dangerous cities in the world, torn by violence that erupts between political and military factions.

Founded in the tenth century as an Arab outpost on the Indian Ocean, Mogadishu had by the thirteenth century become the most important town in East Africa. At the time it was the primary transit point for the gold trade from Sofala, in southern Africa, and was also the northernmost town in the Swahili trading system that carried the gold north. During the fourteenth century the town grew considerably and had a large population of rich merchants and a well-developed court life. The Arab traveler Ibn Battuta visited in the fourteenth century, and a Chinese expedition reached Mogadishu in the 1420s. The old city of Mogadishu, called Hammawein or Xamar Weyne, was very beautiful and rivaled such Swahili towns farther down the coast as Lamu, Mombasa, and Kilwa.

Unlike most east African coastal towns that had to contend with the Portuguese in the early fifteenth century, the city-state of Mogadishu remained under its own sultans until the middle of the nineteenth century, when it came under the suzerainty of the al-Busaid sultans of Oman, who ruled Muscat and Zanzibar. The city remained under the sultan of Zanzibar's control until, under heavy British pressure, the sultan leased (and later sold) Mogadishu to the Italians in 1897.

The Italians made Mogadishu (Mogadiscio) the capital of Italian Somaliland, a territory that covered most of the southern part of what is present-day Somalia. After World War II, the United Nations entrusted Italian territory in the Horn of Africa to the British, and British trusteeship of the city lasted until independence in 1960.

Mogadishu is the largest city and major port of independent Somalia, and it grew rapidly. In 1965 the population was 141,000; by 1974, it was over 250,000. Some estimates place the population in 2004 as high as 1.2 million, and 20 to 25 percent of that figure is believed to be made up of formerly rural people who have been displaced from their homes by the chronic violence afflicting the nation. Many of Somalia's exports, mostly fruits and animal hides, were exported through Mogadishu, and the city supported meat, fish, and milk processing; soft-drink bottling; textile and cosmetics production; and cotton ginning. Trade and industry, however, was seriously disrupted by the ongoing violence.

The city became a battleground in the late 1980s when Siad Barre tried to flush rebels out of Mogadishu by shelling the city for four weeks toward the end of his embattled rule. More than 50,000 people were killed and as much as 75 percent of the city was left in ruins. When Barre fled the country after his regime collapsed in 1991, the city was left with no central authority and dwindling food supplies when fighting broke out between remaining rival factions. Clan leader Mohammed Farah Aidid launched a three-month attack in November 1991 in an attempt to root out supporters of his rival, Ali Mahdi Mohammed, from parts of Mogadishu. The colossal destruction left burned-out buildings and dead bodies scattered throughout the city; 14,000 people were killed, nearly twice as many were injured, and 400,000 people fled to the countryside or abroad. American troops and a United Nations (UN) peacekeeping force attempted to bring order to Mogadishu, but to no avail. The rebuilding of the city looked like a daunting task in the mid-1990s. The UN peacekeeping force pulled out in 1994, leaving no peace, no constitution, no government in power, and virtually no infrastructure.

See also **Colonial Policies and Practices: Italian; Ibn Battuta, Muhammad ibn Abdullah; Somalia: History and Politics; Zanzibar; Zanzibar Sultanate.**

BIBLIOGRAPHY

Kertcher, Chen. *The Search for Peace—or for a State: UN Intervention in Somalia, 1992–95.* Jerusalem: Harry S. Truman Research Institute for the Advancement of Peace, Hebrew University of Jerusalem, 2003.

Samatar, Ahmed I. "The Curse of Allah: Civic Disembowelment and the Collapse of the State in Somalia." In *The Somali Challenge*, ed. Ahmed I. Samatar. Boulder, CO: Lynne Rienner, 1994.

THOMAS F. McDOW

MOHAMMED, BIBI TITI (1926–). Born in Dar es Salaam, Titi studied the Qur'an as a youth and was among the first girls enrolled in the government primary school. First married at the age of fourteen, she began her public career as a lead singer performing *maulid* (poems commemorating the life and teachings of the Prophet Mohammed). Her group later transformed itself into a *ngoma* (drum and dance) troupe. It was in the context of these multiethnic dance organizations that Titi developed her skills as an orator, organizer, and networker—skills she harnessed for the nationalist cause beginning in the 1950s.

In 1955 Titi was recruited by top members of the Tanganyikan African National Union (TANU), then an all-male organization, to spread the nationalist message among women. Titi began speaking before women's ngoma groups in Dar es Salaam, elaborating on the parallels between nationalist rhetoric regarding political independence and women's struggles for respect, equality, and autonomy vis-à-vis husbands, fathers, and the state. In the late 1950s and early 1960s Titi traveled throughout Tanganyika, Africa, and the world, spearheading the movements for decolonization and women's empowerment.

After independence she was appointed president of Umoja Wanawake Tanzania (UWT)—the women's branch of the national party. She also served as an elected member of parliament and junior minister for community development. In 1967 she parted political ways with Tanzania's president Julius Nyerere over his socialist proclamation, *The Arusha Declaration.* In 1969 Titi was arrested, detained, and convicted on charges of treason, a charge she denied. Sentenced to life in prison, she was pardoned by Nyerere and released in 1972.

See also **Dar es Salaam; Nyerere, Julius Kambarage; Tanzania.**

BIBLIOGRAPHY

Geiger, Susan. *TANU Women: Gender and Culture in the Making of Tanganyikan Nationalism, 1955–1965.* Portsmouth, N.H.: Heinemann, 1997.

Meena, Ruth. "Bibi Titi: Traitor or Heroine of *Uhuru?*" *Southern African Political and Economic Monthly* (April 1992).

LAURA FAIR

MOHAMMED V (1909–1961).

Mohammed V, Moroccan monarch, was born in Fez. He was the son of Sultan Muhammad bin Yusef, and succeeded him on his father's death in 1927. He showed resistance to French colonization from the beginning of his reign, and, in 1930, objected to, but ultimately signed, the "Berber decree," enacted by the French to divide Moroccans into Berbers and Arabs.

An ardent nationalist, the French deposed and exiled him from 1953 to 1955, forcing him and his family into exile in Corsica and then to Madagascar. A relative of his, Mohammed Ben 'Arafa, was placed on the throne in his stead. After strong nationalist pressure in 1955, the French brought Mohammed V from exile in Madagascar to France, where he was once again recognized as sultan upon his return. In February 1956 he successfully negotiated Moroccan independence with France. On November 10, 1956, Mohammed V returned to Morocco, and obtained full recognition of Moroccan sovereignty from France and Spain. On March 2, 1956, Morocco obtained independence, and in 1957 he took the title of king. On his death in 1961, he was succeeded by his son, who became Hasan II.

Mohammed V had a great impact not only over his country but throughout the world. His obituary in the *New York Times* (February 27, 1967), reported that "his grandeur was his simplicity."

See also **Hasan II of Morocco; Morocco: History and Politics.**

BIBLIOGRAPHY

Ayache, Albert. *Le Maroc: Bilan d'une Colonisation.* Paris: Editions socials, 1956.

Bidwell, Robin L. *Morocco under Colonial Rule.* London: Penguin, 1973.

Julien, Claude-André. *Histoire de l'Afrique du nord.* Paris: Payot, 1986.

Laroui, Abdallah. *L'histoire du Maroc: Un essai de synthèse.* Paris: François Maspéro, 1980.

MOHA ENNAJI

MOI, DANIEL ARAP (1924–).

Daniel Torotich arap Moi was educated by missionaries at the Kabartonjo Island Mission in the Great Rift Valley in central Kenya colony, and at the Government African School at Kapsabet. He trained to become a teacher and began his first job in 1945 at the local Government African School. There he rose to headmaster and later returned as assistant principal. In 1955, Moi was one of the first Africans nominated to the Legislative Council as the colony began to lurch toward independence in the wake of the Mau Mau revolt. He left the council in 1960 to become the assistant treasurer of the Kenya African National Union (KANU), the major political party. Later that year, he joined the Kenya African Democratic Union (KADU), which had been formed by politicians who feared that the two largest ethnic communities in the colony, Gikuyu and Luo, would dominate KANU. Following the elections of 1961, in which Gikuyu and alleged Mau Mau leader Jomo Kenyatta was elected president-in-absentia and the way was prepared for Kenyan independence, Moi was appointed Minister of Education. He entered local government in 1962 and served for two years.

In 1964, the year following Kenya's official independence, KANU absorbed KADU and Moi became Minister of Home Affairs in President Kenyatta's cabinet. He was appointed vice president in 1967, and succeeded Kenyatta as president upon his death in 1977. He was officially elected to the position a year later. Moi began his term by launching an anticorruption drive, releasing political prisoners who had been held under his predecessor. By 1981, however, when Kenya hosted the Organization of African Unity's (OAU) eighteenth

Daniel arap Moi (1924–) at the Commonwealth Heads of Government meeting in Coolum, Australia, March 4, 2002. Moi served as Kenya's second president from 1978 to 2002, following Jomo Kenyatta's death in 1977. He is widely know to Kenyans as *Nyayo*, a Swahili word for "footsteps." TORSTEN BLACKWOOD/AFP/GETTY IMAGES

politician Charles Njonjo (b. 1920), accusing him of attempting to overthrow the government.

The Law Society of Kenya, joined by groups from universities and churches, continually spoke out against human rights violations committed by Moi's government. In 1986, the underground group Mwakenya (Union of Patriots for the Liberation of Kenya) emerged, while expatriate Kenyans organized to form their own organizations of dissent. These associations came together as the United Movement for Democracy under the leadership of Ngugi wa Thiong'o, a prominent and activist Kenyan writer. Initial foreign response to Moi was varied: President Ronald Reagan (1911–2004) of the United States criticized Kenya's human rights record during an official visit Moi made to America in 1987, yet Margaret Thatcher (b. 1925) received him warmly in London, soon after giving Kenya an aid package of £50 million.

For the 1988 elections in Kenya, Moi replaced secret ballot voting with a new procedure in which voters were required to line up behind larger-than-life photographs of their chosen candidate. Amid accusations of intimidation and rigging, Moi was reelected unopposed. Popular calls for a multiparty political system and rampant frustration with Moi's policies were exacerbated by the 1990 murder of Minister of Foreign Affairs and International Cooperation Robert Ouko, generally considered to be among the few uncorrupted Kenyan politicians remaining in office. The formation of a new, dissenting Kenyan National Democratic Party was announced in 1991, amid growing internal unrest and international pressure to democratize. Later that year, Moi accepted the formation of an opposition party, the Foundation for the Restoration of Democracy (FORD). Despite opponents' persistent charges of voting fraud, Moi was again reelected in 1992, with 36.4 percent of the vote, and was returned to office yet again in 1997. By law, he was barred from running for the presidency in 2002, and threw his support behind Uhuru Kenyatta, the son of Jomo Kenyatta, Kenya's first president. His candidate failed at the polls, however, and Moi was succeeded in office by Mwai Kibaki (b. 1931), who secured a large majority of votes in anticipation, once more, of relief from seemingly endless corruption centered on the office of the president.

summit, there was widespread disillusionment with Moi's initial anticorruption campaign. It had been replaced with more cronyism and corruption than ever and the familiar heavy hand of governmental power.

Moi officially declared Kenya a one-party state in 1982. Later that year the air force staged a coup, accusing Moi's government of widespread corruption and brutality. Shops in Nairobi, the capital, were looted, and masses of people gathered to celebrate the apparent end of the Moi regime. Moi's forces, however, were swift in defeating resistance, and Moi responded by dissolving the air force and jailing those who had participated in the celebrations. Moi suspended his Minister of Home and Constitutional Affairs, the Gikuyu

See also **Kenyatta, Jomo; Ngũgĩ wa Thiong'o; Organization of African Unity.**

BIBLIOGRAPHY

Karimi, Joseph. *The Kenyatta Succession*. Nairobi, Kenya: Transafrica, 1980.

Moi, Daniel Arap. *Kenya African Nationalism: Nyayo Philosophy and Principles* New York: MacMillan, 1986.

Moi, Daniel Arap. *Which Way Africa?*, ed. Lee Njiru and Browne Kutswa. Nairobi: Governmentt Press, 1997.

Morton, Andrew. *Moi: The Making of an African Statesman*. London: Michael O'Mara, 1998.

SARAH VALDEZ

MOMBASA. Mombasa is the largest port in East Africa and Kenya's second largest city. It has been a favorite stop for travelers on the East African coast for centuries. The Arab traveler and writer Ibn Battuta passed through in 1331, and the Portuguese navigator Vasco da Gama launched his initial visit to India from there in 1498.

Founded on an island of 7.5 square miles in the eleventh century by Arab traders, Mombasa was favorably located for coastal trade and succeeded Kilwa in the fifteenth century as the primary Swahili town. From the early sixteenth century, and for more than a hundred years, the Portuguese and Omani Arabs vied for control of the town; the Portuguese built the still-existing massive fort, Fort Jesus, in 1593. The local Mazrui clan captured the fort and the town in the 1740s, challenging Omani rule until the Omani sultan of Zanzibar took the town in 1832. Though Mombasa was under nominal Zanzibari rule until Kenyan independence (1963), British interests predominated after the 1890s.

The British established the capital of their East African Protectorate in Mombasa in 1887. The city was the nexus for the Indian Ocean dhow trade, overland caravans, European explorers, and Indian and Arab businessmen. The completion of a rail line from Mombasa to Lake Victoria in 1902 brought new prosperity to the city, and commercial and light industrial districts began to grow out from the Swahili old town. By 1930, thanks in part to a post–World War I boom, the city had spread to the mainland from the island it originally occupied.

Dockworkers' strikes in Mombasa after World War II upset the port economy and were the beginning tremors of the coastal component of what became the nationalist in Kenya. After independence in 1963, however, the town grew as up-country traders, especially Gikuyuus, arrived to set up businesses. With the dredging of Kilindini harbor, the modern deep-water port on the southwest side of Mombasa Island, the city became the primary port for Kenya, Uganda, Rwanda, and Burundi. In addition to shipbuilding and repair activities around the port, Mombasa is also one of Kenya's primary industrial areas, processing sugar, refining oil, and producing cement and fertilizer.

In the 1950s white settlers from South Africa and Rhodesia began to visit the Kenya coast for vacation, and Mombasa became the center of a growing tourist trade. Tourism exploded in the 1970s, and by the late 1980s luxurious hotels and beachfront resorts lined the coasts north and south of the city. Each year more than a quarter of a million people arrived to take in the warm sun, beautiful coral, and relaxed atmosphere and to visit the old town, Fort Jesus, and nearby game parks.

More than 707,000 people lived in Mombasa in 2002 by United Nations estimates, many of them Swahili Muslims. Others came from the East African interior as labor migrants. Even after the advent of multiparty democracy in Kenya in 1992, Daniel arap Moi (who first assumed the presidency in 1978 by constitutional succession) refused all attempts to register the Mombasa-based Islamic Party of Kenya (IPK) and banned its meetings and deported its leader. Moi's rule was marked by controversy and allegations of widespread corruption. Elections were finally held in 2002, and Moi turned over the office of presidency to the popularly elected Mwai Kibaki, who had run on the anti-corruption platform of a multi-ethnic coalition party. His policies are aimed at coping with many of the factors that threaten Mombasa's tourist sector, notably the spread of AIDS, and overdevelopment. Nonetheless, Mombasa has thrived as a sailors' town for nearly a thousand years and will continue to be the most important port for East Africa in the twenty-first century.

See also Eastern African Coast, History of (Early to 1600); Gama, Vasco da; Ibn Battuta, Muhammad ibn Abdullah; Kenya; Kibaki, Mwai; Labor: Trades Unions and Associations; Moi, Daniel arap; Tourism.

BIBLIOGRAPHY

Willis, Justin. *Mombasa, the Swahili, and the Making of the Mijikenda.* New York: Oxford University Press, 1993.

THOMAS F. MCDOW

MONDLANE, EDUARDO CHIVAMBO

(1920–1969). The Mozambican anticolonial activist Eduardo Chivambo Mondlane was born in Gaza province, Mozambique. Mondlane was educated in South Africa, in Portugal, and in the United States, where he obtained a bachelor of arts degree and then a doctorate from Northwestern University. After working for a time for the United Nations, Mondlane identified himself completely with the anticolonial cause in Mozambique, accepting that Portuguese imperialist intransigence might well make war unavoidable. "We could continue indefinitely living under a repressive imperial rule, or find a means of using force against Portugal which would be effective enough to hurt Portugal without resulting in our own ruin" (Mondlane, 125). Having launched his country's independence movement, Frente de Libertação de Moçambique (FRELIMO), in 1962, Mondlane presided over a gradual enlargement of anticolonial warfare and in 1968 assembled a representative congress, held in Niassa province, at which compromise with the Portuguese empire was rejected. Traveling widely, Mondlane was increasingly accepted as one of the founders of a liberated Africa. In 1969 he was murdered in Dar es Salaam by a parcel bomb of Portuguese or South African provenance. His reputation linked courage with humane tolerance and moderation. But his murder warned prophetically that the mindless terrorism promoted by externally organized banditries, chiefly from racist South Africa, could now prove fatal to the whole project of anticolonial independence.

See also Machel, Samora Moises; Mozambique.

BIBLIOGRAPHY

Isaacman, Allen, and Barbara Isaacman. *Mozambique: From Colonialism to Revolution, 1900–1982.* Boulder, CO: Westview Press, 1983.

Mondlane, Eduardo. *The Struggle for Mozambique.* Baltimore, MD: Penguin Books, 1969.

Munslow, Barry. *Mozambique: The Revolution and Its Origins.* London and New York: Longman, 1983.

BASIL DAVIDSON

MONEY

This entry includes the following articles:
OVERVIEW
COLONIAL CURRENCIES
COMMODITY CURRENCIES
EXCHANGE RATE SYSTEMS

OVERVIEW

Money in one form or another is now used and sought throughout Africa, but its history is uneven, its usefulness sometimes superseded, and its moral implications often debated. On parts of the coasts and near some inland trade routes, cash as minted currency has been familiar for many centuries. In other, less traveled inland areas it came into common use only in the early twentieth century as new European colonial taxation, cash cropping initiatives, and wage labor recruitment sharply increased the needs for and use of cash. But even in most of the latter areas, the idea of money was not new, and other local and regional commodities had long served some of the same purposes.

Money is conventionally defined as something recognized as a standard of value, used for storing, measuring and accounting for wealth, and capable of circulating indefinitely among its users, but useful only or mainly for purposes related to exchange. What translates as money varies widely by language; and financial concepts like income, investment, and capital may have no convenient translation into some African languages—a sign of deeper cultural differences in economic life. Evidence gathered by direct observation in Africa has qualified and challenged assumptions of economists, social philosophers, and the broader public about money's uses, meanings, and effects on society—and even about its very definition.

CURRENCIES AND QUASI-CURRENCIES

Money merges into other categories of things exchanged. Objects that African peoples have used as money or quasi-money (that is, money with some uses beyond exchange) have included items and substances as diverse as cowrie shells, salt blocks, cloth strips, gold dust, iron bars, glass beads, copper croisettes, buttons, company scrip, minted coins and banknotes, checks, and notes and bills of exchange. Money in most African cities and many towns now includes electronic money, that is, credits and debts without paper, coin, or other material specie. Where and whether animals should be deemed money, for instance in marriage payments, is much debated, but these are seldom just that. Cowries have widely served as money but also, in some cultures, have sexual or other symbolic connotations and aesthetic values not so quantifiable. The same commodity may oscillate in and out of use as currency as it changes hands or as times change. No part of Africa has not seen some succession of currencies come and go, whether through trade, conquest, or policy reversals, and people throughout Africa have long understood that what counts as money today may not tomorrow.

Money is a sign of human interdependence, and it suggests trust in, or reliance upon, shared understandings. Money's familiar advantages over other means of exchange are that it can be easily standardized, recognized, counted, transported, divided, and substituted for other money or other things. But some of these same attributes, and others like concealability, make money volatile and contestable in impoverished communities, ones without easy access to banks, or ones not long accustomed to financial calculation on a decimal system. Control over the production and circulation of money is coveted, if not contested, almost anywhere.

IMPORTED AND AFRICANIZED CURRENCIES

Classical assumptions about money's stability of value have proved especially unreliable in Africa south of the Sahara. Before European colonial times, minted moneys came via traders, in waves, from distant parts of the world; and competing traders brought competing moneys. The Indian rupee was traded inland from the East African coast by the early 1800s. The silver Maria Theresia Thaler, minted in Vienna from 1751 and later in Prague, Milan, and Venice, circulated widely by the mid-1800s in East Africa (in Ethiopia in 1893 it became the talari, minted in Paris with the effigy of Menelik II). Numerous other currencies of foreign origin would later be Africanized and nationalized in comparable ways.

Most imperial trading and governance companies and later colonial regimes shifted currencies repeatedly and unpredictably. Some of the European-promoted moneys and quasi-moneys (for instance cowries from the Maldive Islands, which gained value as they traveled west, or metal rods like the *mitako* in the lower Congo in the 1890s) were designed to be unusable in commerce with Europeans themselves. Some, for instance the macuta and reis in Portuguese Angola, had recognized standard equivalencies in cowries (in this case, in multiples in the thousands), for periods. But colonial governments and independent national ones have sought to monopolize the issuance of currencies by illegalizing others. An example is a decree on July 22, 1939, which made the escudo the sole legal tender in Portuguese Mozambique, or the moves of the newly independent Sudan on January 1, 1956, to replace the Egyptian pound with the Sudanese pound at par, and on January 1, 1958, to make Egyptian and British moneys no longer legal tender.

After independence, some African leaders kept the currency names of their former colonizers (for instance Kenyan shilling from Britain, Rwandan franc from Belgium), while others adopted names from other nations (Zimbabwe dollar). Still others used words from African languages spoken within their borders (Botswana *pula*, literally, rain in the Tswana tongue; Ghana *cedi*, from an Akan word for cowry shell). Some yet used African names for main units and European-derived names for subunits (for example the Angola *kwanza*—meaning beginning in some Bantu tongues—with its 100 centimos, a word borrowed from Spanish rather than from the locally spoken Portuguese).

Rulers may dictate what to stamp on money, but they cannot so easily dictate its acceptance at home or abroad. The Krugerrand, a South African coin containing a troy ounce of gold in a copper alloy, was first minted in 1967, bearing on its obverse the likeness of Paul Kruger, first president of the South African Republic, classed as a white (and on the reverse, a springbok antelope). On it, South Africa was written in Afrikaans and English but not Xhosa, Zulu, or any other South African tongue. The Krugerrand was devised mainly to market South African gold to collectors. But numerous other nations prohibited its import until South Africa changed its leadership and ended its policy of apartheid (racial segregation) in the early 1990s.

INTERNATIONAL INVOLVEMENT IN NATIONAL CURRENCY POLICY

Some African money has remained international by design. Several former French colonies have maintained two zones of common currency, each zone using an originally French-issued money called the franc CFA. Initially, this stood for French Colonies of Africa, Colonies françaises d'Afrique, on issuance under colonial authority in 1945; in 2007 it stood for Financial Community of Africa, Communauté financière d'Afrique, for the West African group, and for Financial Cooperation in Central Africa, Coopération financière en Afrique Central, for the Central African one. Francophone Africans call each of these currencies the *franc*, sometimes colloquially the *céfa*. In each group, some nations have individually joined or seceded on occasion. As of January 2007, the members of one group, the West African Economic and Monetary Union (Union Économique et Monétaire Ouest Africaine, UEMOA), were Bénin, Burkina Faso, Côte d'Ivoire, Guinea-Bissau (a former Portuguese colony), Mali, Niger, Sénégal, and Togo. They issued their currency from the Central Bank of the West African States (Banque Centrale des États d'Afrique de l'Ouest, BCEAO), headquartered in Dakar, Sénégal.

The six members of the other group, the Economic and Monetary Community of Central Africa (Communauté Économique et Monétaire de l'Afrique Central, CEMAC), included Cameroon, Central African Republic, Chad, Republic of the Congo, Equatorial Guinea (a former Spanish colony), and Gabon. Their currency was issued from the Bank of the Central African States (Banque des États de l'Afrique Centrale, BEAC), headquartered in Yaoundé, Cameroon. The value of the franc CFA in each zone was pegged to that of the French franc up

to 1999 (with exchange rate changes in 1948 and 1990), and afterward to the euro. Both forms of CFA continued to be guaranteed by the French Treasury, an involvement with not just economic and financial but also political and diplomatic implications.

Exchange rates controlled by national authorities or international agencies affect the flows of food and other necessities between countryside and city. They also affect the balance of trade across borders. Currency price setting, where practiced, thus involves delicate political balances and difficult moral issues. Popular demonstrations protesting high food prices in cities can visibly threaten national regimes, whereas setting crop prices too low can threaten the livelihood of rural producers. But producers are also consumers. Rural people as well as urbanites depend partly on manufactured goods, including some foods, fuels, clothing, and medicine, from cities and abroad. The exchange rates that help them sell crops can also raise the prices they pay to procure these things. Exchange rates at variance with prices determined by supplies and demands open windows for illegal profiteering. That government officials sometimes participate in such activity themselves helps explain why some of them insist on implementing or maintaining exchange controls in the first place.

"Floating" a currency, that is allowing its exchange rates to fluctuate unregulated by government, is one way of cutting such price gaps (to economists, market "distortions") and the opportunities they afford for illegal currency trade. In the late twentieth and early twenty-first centuries, some of the largest international development agencies, notably the World Bank, the International Monetary Fund, and U.S. Agency for International Development, have used their influence (especially the promise of loans or grants or their continuance) to encourage national leaders and finance ministries in numerous African countries to deregulate exchange rates. But not all have followed this advice or yielded to this pressure, for better or worse. Numerous major African currencies, including the South African rand, were largely deregulated in exchange rates over this period; but others, including the Nigerian naira (tied to the U.S. dollar) and the West and Central African CFA (tied to the

French franc, as discussed), remained more tightly regulated after the turn of the century. The increasing involvement of the Republic of South Africa and the People's Republic of China over wider areas of Africa than ever before promised to alter trends of opinion and policy, but those countries' own shifting economic policies made the directions hard to predict. Debates continue on the appropriateness of fixed or floating exchange rates, involving issues as varied as sovereignty, trade balance, and nutrition.

USER ADAPTATIONS

Money, including nationally and internationally issued money, always carries its hazards as well as advantages for users. Independent but unstable state regimes can tax money's earning or spending, overprint it to dispense patronage at election times, and devaluate or abolish it overnight. Inflation erodes its purchasing power. Paper money kept in homes is susceptible to theft, fire, flooding, and insect damage. Banks and other financial institutions' interest rates for savings have generally augmented money's value more slowly than animals multiply by breeding, despite the latter's being subject to sudden major losses periodically through droughts, epizootics, or other causes. Money's versatility and liquidity can make it tempting to spend, and its concealability can limit the influence of kin or neighbors on its prudent use. Hence, wherever money is found, people devise ways to limit its uses.

While some theorists of social evolution have supposed that money tends to acquire new positive functions as time passes, changes in policy and political conditions have sometimes made currencies lose functions. Continued three-digit inflation rates in some settings, as in the Democratic Republic of the Congo toward the end of the twentieth century, have reduced money's convenience to the point where urbanites needed "brick" bundles for daily purchases or even sackfuls of banknotes for larger ones like cars. Many there resorted to bartering food, gasoline, and cigarettes, and in the countryside to passing new local currencies instead, for instance, money made of buttons. There and in areas in Sierra Leone, southern and western Sudan, northern Uganda, during episodes of civil war, national currencies have threatened to lose all meaning and value. Yet much trade has yet continued with bundled money, multiple imported currencies, locally improvised currencies, or no money at all. In and around Somalia during an episode of state collapse in the 1990s and early 2000s, animal mobility has allowed even substantial long-distance trade overland to continue.

Barter can be defined two ways. In the sense of direct exchange of goods, services, or both without using money, barter does not just recede into history as an economy monetizes. It continually reappears where money becomes scarce, inflation high, or polities unstable. Barter in the other sense of negotiated prices does not just steadily yield to fixed prices. Rules or expectations vary from one setting to another, however, about what kinds of exchangeables may be bargained for.

Migration and monetary remittance, between nations and between continents, plays an ever greater role in African economic life as agricultural ecosystems are threatened, terms of trade worsen, and indebtedness increases. Some communities have become heavily dependent on such money sent home across borders, for instance in the cases of some Somalis' circular migrations to Yemen, Lesothoans' to South Africa, or Mauritanians' to Senegal. Border controls and currency exchange restrictions hinder movements of people and money. Despite the rise of international electronic banking and the liberalizing of many nations' currencies over the past few decades, many migrants continue preferring to remit money via trusted friends or relatives in cash, for reasons of security, solidarity, or convenience.

Meanwhile, people in many parts of Africa prefer to save in plural currencies (not always legally) to be able to trade across borders and to guard against abrupt devaluation of any one currency. Economists conventionally divide moneys into "hard" or "soft," hardness usually referring to usefulness in international exchange or in reserves outside national borders. Where rates of inflation have been relatively high (as in Zimbabwe in the early twenty-first century), savers seek legally or illegally to acquire "harder" foreign moneys (over this period, U.S. dollars were popular), known for holding their value, to supplement or substitute for local ones. Legal restrictions on currency exchange open opportunities for profit by persons willing to risk getting caught or able to benefit from special protection. Hence the use of offshore banking by government officials and persons connected to them who enjoy special legal immunities or political protection at home.

LIQUIDITY AND ILLIQUIDITY

Whereas neoclassical economic theory has tended to assume general human preferences for asset liquidity (that is, ease of exchange) and divisibility, observation on the ground reveals many instances where people try to keep or make large parts of their wealth illiquid and indivisible in order to remove it from their own temptation, while keeping enough of it accessible for emergencies. This is particularly so in face-to-face communities where it can be hard for persons with money to refuse requests for sharing, giving, or loan repayment. Commonly in African communities as elsewhere, concern about gossip, witchcraft, or other social sanctions may underlie such decisions about saving or hoarding, mingling with more strictly economic concerns like inflation.

In many parts of the continent, regardless of access to banks or post office saving facilities, many continue to invent their own means of saving. They devise break-open saving receptacles, join self-help contribution clubs like rotating saving and credit associations, or entrust cash to kin or neighbors—most often, it seems, to persons elder to or more solvent than themselves—to save for them. As these strategies suggest, a major concern of savers continentwide is not to appear antisocial. Some rural savers prefer holding large banknotes, rather than their equivalent in smaller ones, precisely because they are harder to break up. Others seek to defer collecting wage or crop earnings to let them accumulate. Gold earrings in coastal West Africa allow women to wear their wealth while they save it and defend it from their men; metalsmiths can add gold as a woman ages. Whatever the merits of saving, it is seldom a lesson that richer peoples can teach poorer ones for the first time. To infer from such practices as gifting, marriage payments, or sacrificial ceremonies that large sections of African populations are merely profligate spenders may be to overlook many ways of saving and investing going on in indirect or diversified forms, or for longer-term rewards than are apparent.

CULTURAL CONDITIONING OF EXCHANGE

Some theorists have supposed that money gradually penetrates all exchanges until nothing remains that cannot be bought or sold, and in certain times and places it has seemed so on the ground. Visiting Tiv in northeastern Nigeria from 1949 to 1953, the anthropologist Paul Bohannan observed morally ranked "exchange spheres" as follows. Foods, small animals, raw materials, and tools were freely exchangeable for each other; they made up what he called a subsistence sphere. A second, higher sphere of "prestige" goods included slaves, cattle, cloth, and brass rods. The supreme third sphere consisted of humans other than slaves, particularly women. "Conveyance" within spheres was a morally neutral act, but strong moral values surrounded "conversion" between spheres. Money, demanded for colonial taxation and made available through cash cropping, provided, in Bohannan's view, a new "common denominator," entering into exchanges in all three spheres and scrambling these together. Restudies in the same and broader region suggest a more complex picture of trade circuits that overlap on the map, and that change over time.

No society's norms permit all things to be bought and sold, and money never penetrates exchange circuits evenly or absolutely. Protected from some kinds of market activity in many and probably most places, by moral discouragement or outright legal or spiritual prohibition, are human bodies (or at least certain ones) and their parts and fluids, and land where blood has been shed in battle or rites of passage. To these may be added sacred human-made objects of particular kinds, and religious, scholastic, and military distinctions and offices. Sale, rental, and mortgaging of rural land have been morally, legally, or religiously prohibited in many parts of Africa south of the Sahara. (Parts of Ghana have long been exceptional in the exchangeability of rural land by sale.) Financiers and legislators with idealistic visions of free markets have attempted, by enacting state land-tenure reforms, to challenge and change these rules in numerous countries in the past century, but their programs have not often produced the intended outcomes. Cattle in many herding societies, for instance among Fulani (Fulbe) in the western Sahel, have in the past been deemed properly saleable only in personal or family crises, and such sales widely stigmatized. Just as land or livestock may not be deemed attachable as liens for cash loans, cash may not be considered an adequate or lasting substitute for appropriated or confiscated land or animals.

Islamic sacred law (*shariʿa*), as most Muslims interpret it, condemns lending and borrowing at interest, while it condones lending repaid at par or profiting by trade with immediate exchange and fairly shared information. It generally condemns gambling, mortgaging, some forms of speculating, and trading with unevenly shared information as being dangerous, unfair, or both. It allows bargaining for particular kinds of commodities or for particular purposes while forbidding or discouraging it for others. It also prescribes proportions of inheritance in cash or kind to be given to male and female heirs. Many local variants on these rules and expectations can be found across northern and Sahelian Africa, along more southerly portions of the eastern coast, and wherever else Muslims live, travel, or trade. All these kinds of permissions and restrictions on exchange are debated in public and private, and nowhere is there a society whose norms about exchange are not sometimes adapted by local judges or contravened in practice.

Whereas classical and neoclassical economic theories assume money to be very often fungible, or readily substitutable for other money, ethnographic findings suggest that many people, across and outside Africa, earmark money derived from particular activities for particular uses. Frequently, such designation has symbolic and moral significance. Thus, in many cultures, money from antisocial activities (which might include murder, theft, or gambling) or from sales of commodities symbolically associated with evil or spiritual pollution, is perceived as dangerous to its earner or holder and others related. Such "tainted" money can take many forms: among Mandinko in the Gambia, it can come from selling hot peppers; among Luo in western Kenya, from selling gold, tobacco, or patrimonial land; among Nuer in southern Sudan, from stigmatized domestic service. In some settings such rewards are scrupulously kept out of sacred activities like marriage or funerals, while in others they and the people associated with them are deemed ritually purifiable. Here again, however, people sometimes break their own cultural rules for profit or convenience.

People who share other commodities do not always share money, or vice versa. Foreigners in Africa sometimes express surprise at sharing or hoarding habits within families that differ from their own. Among Luhya in Kenya, Fulbe and others in the Gambia, and others in many settings in recent decades, unmarried adult sons have often been expected to surrender cash wages directly to fathers in their homesteads. In many of these same settings, however, adults commonly keep locked boxes, partly to conceal and protect cash from their own spouses. Patterns like these give the lie to stereotypes of African individualism or kin communalism. Foreign-based employers and crop buyers have sometimes caused cross-cultural misunderstandings by paying only men as "household heads" for work done by women, children, and attached dependents, when it was not assumed among families that the new cash would be shared.

Money carries messages well beyond the economic. It is always given qualitative as well as quantitative values, and it can be used to symbolize almost anything—good, evil, or morally neutral. Banknotes and coins contain political symbols: portraits of current rulers, slogans and emblems of state or party, or idealized depictions of dress, monuments, or technological or military power. By the languages, names, and images that leaders of new nations pick for their money, they variously evoke autonomy, modernity, endogenous authenticity. In some countries where pictures of heads of state have been printed on money, their names or nicknames can be heard in pop lingo to refer to banknotes, coins, or money in general, in admiration or in ridicule. Money may daily remind users of nationhood, that is, but such messages are unevenly received on a continent where nations are dubiously rooted entities originally demarcated from outside, and where these remain of questionable legitimacy in popular thought. The nationalist symbolism belies the rich local meanings that African people attach to money. It also belies the degree of practical control that foreign and international powers have exerted have exerted over fiscal and monetary policy in African countries in recent decades.

MONEY AND WEALTH

Money does not always mean wealth, or vice versa. Much of rural Africa prefers to keep its main wealth in other, more useful or aesthetically satisfying forms, whether mineral, vegetable, animal, or human. In some areas a wealthy person is someone who, by careful giving or lending, has accumulated not just money but personal obligations in addition or instead. Nor is an influx of cash always helpful in alleviating poverty. If it rescues parts of a population temporarily from destitution it can at the same time impoverish other, disadvantaged parts or an adjacent population through commodity price inflation, a subtle but major contributor to famines in Africa as elsewhere. Or it may stimulate excessive local borrowing and thus lead to interpersonal debts and misunderstandings (a process well fictionalized in Ousmane Sembène's pessimistic 1972 novella of Dakar, *The Money Order*). What is true at the micro level is sometimes true at the macro too. Cash cropping and the production of new industrial exportables like oil may bring big. immediate new rewards to a region or nation but also introduce subtle new risks and dependencies, for instance through currency overvaluation that can disrupt domestic food production, as has happened in Nigeria and Cameroon in recent decades.

Across Africa money is perceived as a mixed blessing, sometimes hidden, sometimes celebrated, but never publicly allowed to take over any economy fully. Policies designed to monetize an economy may both help and hurt the people involved. To discern the effects of financial development and philanthropic relief programs from without or within, there is no substitute for direct and patient local observation.

See also **Apartheid; Debt and Credit; Economic History; Economic Systems; International Monetary Fund; Kruger, Paul; Livestock; Production Strategies; Religion and Ritual; Sembène, Ousmane; Warfare: Civil Wars; World Bank.**

BIBLIOGRAPHY

Bohannan, Paul. "The Impact of Money on an African Subsistence Economy." *Journal of Economic History* 19, no. 4 (1959): 491–503.

Ensminger, Jean. *Making a Market.* Cambridge, U.K.: Cambridge University Press, 1992.

Francis, Elizabeth. *Making a Living: Changing Livelihoods in Rural Africa.* London: Routledge, 2000.

Guyer, Jane I. *Marginal Gains: Marginal Transactions in Atlantic Africa.* Chicago: University of Chicago Press, 2004.

Guyer, Jane I, ed. *Money Matters: Instability, Values and Social Payments in the Modern History of West African Communities.* Portsmouth, NH: Heinemann, 1995.

Hart, Keith. *Money in an Unequal World.* New York: Texere, 2000.

Hill, Polly. *Studies in Rural Capitalism in West Africa.* Cambridge, U.K.: Cambridge University Press, 1970.

Hogendorn, Jan, and Marion Johnson. *The Shell Money of the Slave Trade.* Cambridge, U.K.: Cambridge University Press, 1986.

Hopkins, Anthony G. *An Economic History of West Africa.* London: Longman, 1973.

Hutchinson, Sharon. *Nuer Dilemmas: Coping with Money, War, and the State.* Berkeley: University of California Press, 1996.

Isichei, Elizabeth. *Voices of the African Poor.* Rochester, NY: University of Rochester Press, 2002.

Little, Peter. *Somalia: Economy without State.* Bloomington: Indiana University Press, 2003.

Masson, Paul, and Catherine A. Pattillo. *The Monetary Geography of Africa.* Washington, DC: Brookings Institution Press, 2004.

Meillassoux, Claude. *Maidens, Meal and Money.* Cambridge, U.K.: Cambridge University Press, 1981.

Ousmane, Sembène. *The Money Order.* London: Heinemann, 1987.

Parry, Jonathan. "On the Moral Perils of Exchange." In *Money and the Morality of Exchange*, ed. Jonathan Parry and Maurice Bloch. Cambridge, U.K.: Cambridge University Press, 1989.

Parkin, David. *Palms, Wine and Witnesses: Public Spirit and Private Gain in an African Farming Community.* San Francisco, CA: Chandler, 1972.

Parry, Jonathan, and Maurice Bloch. *Money and the Morality of Exchange.* Cambridge, U.K.: Cambridge University Press, 1989.

Pick, Franz, and René Sédillot. *All the Moneys of the World.* New York: Pick Publishing, 1971.

Rivallain, Josette. *Échanges et pratiques monétaires en Afrique: du Xve au XIXe siècles à travers les récits de voyageurs.* Paris: Musée de l'Homme, 1994.

Rodinson, Maxime. *Islam and Capitalism.* London: Allen Lane, 1974.

Seidman, Ann. *Money, Banking and Public Finance in Africa.* Atlantic Highlands, NJ: Zed Books, 1986.

Shipton, Parker. *Bitter Money: Cultural Economy and Some African Meanings of Forbidden Commodities.* American Ethnological Society Monograph 1. Washington, DC: American Anthropological Association, 1989.

Stiansen, Endre, and Jane I. Guyer, eds. *Credit, Currencies and Culture: Africa Financial Institutions in Comparative Perspective.* Uppsala, Sweden: Nordiska Afrikaninstitutet, 1999.

Verran, Helen. *Science and an African Logic.* Chicago: University of Chicago Press, 2001.

PARKER SHIPTON

COLONIAL CURRENCIES

Although at the beginning of the colonial period in Africa colonial currencies circulated along side domestic African currencies, by the end of the colonial period colonial currencies definitely replaced all precolonial African currencies. Prior to colonization, exchanges in local markets were monetized in key trade African centers. It has been established that Europeans factories in search of other commodities were known to sell goods such as iron bars or slaves to get cowries in Africa. These cowries were subsequently used to buy more goods. By the end of the colonial period, iron bars and colonial currencies progressively replaced cowries. Colonial currencies were issued by the colonies on large geographical spaces of the colonial empires. Each group of colonies associated both geographically and economically had a common currency. Under the standard colonial system, a colony or group or colonies had its own local currency issued by a single local currency authority.

In British East Africa (Kenya, Tanzania, and Uganda), the local currency authority was issued by the East African Currency Board (EACB), established in December 1919 after World War I and originally operating on mainland Tanzania (then Tanganyika), Kenya, and Uganda. The first currency issued was the florin bearing the head of George V. Earlier efforts to replace the Indian rupee as the currency in use in colonial East African territories originated in crisis. The florin was subsequently replaced by the shilling on January 1, 1943, bearing the head of George VI. The shilling was the currency issued for use in Kenya, Tanzania, Uganda, British Somaliland, Italian Somaliland, and parts of

Yemen during the time these areas were British colonies and protectorates. The EACB stopped functioning in 1966 when the Central Banks of Kenya, Tanzania and Uganda came into existence. Suda, during the colonial period, used the Egyptian pound that was in circulation in Egypt and in Northern Sudan since 1834, following a British Royal decree. The Sudan's pound was introduced in 1956 following independence from Britain and Egypt. The Sudanese pound was subsequently replaced by the dinar between 1992 and 2007.

In British West Africa, the West African Currency Board was responsible for issuing currencies in English colonies (Nigeria, Ghana, Sierra Leone, and Gambia). The West African pound was introduced in 1907 for circulation in Nigeria, the Gold Coast (now Ghana), Sierra Leone and the Gambia. From 1912 to 1959, it was issued by the West African Currency Board. The British section of Cameroon adopted the West African currency in 1916 after it was taken from Germany. During the 1958 to 1968 period, the West African pound was replaced by local currencies in the newly independent nations (Ghanaian pound, Nigeria pound, Gambia pound and Leone in Sierra Leone; CFA Franc in the British section of Cameroon.

In Italian Somaliland, the somalo was the currency between 1950 and 1962. The somalo replaced the East African shilling at par, and was replaced by the Somali shilling at par. Italian Somaliland and British Somaliland united in 1960 to form the Republic of Somalia.

In Belgian colonial territories that included the present Democratic Republic of Congo, Burundi, and Rwanda, the Congolese franc, in value equal to the Belgian franc, started circulating in the Belgian Congo in 1887. Its circulation was subsequently extended to Rwanda and Burundi beginning in 1916. Since then, a common currency, issued by a common Central Bank, the Central Bank of Belgian Congo and Rwanda-Burundi, circulated in the three countries. As with Belgium's coins, coins issued in the three countries were minted in two distinct versions, one with French legends, the other with Flemish legends. In Rwanda and Burundi, the Belgian Congo franc became the currency of Burundi and Rwanda in 1916, when Belgium occupied the former German colony and replaced the German East African rupie with the Belgian Congo franc. Burundi and Rwanda used the currency of Belgian Congo until 1960, when they began issuing their own francs that continue in effect in the early twenty-first century. The Congo franc was replaced in 1967 by the Zaire currency.

In Portuguese colonies (Angola, Mozambique, Cape Verde, Guinea-Bissau) the real (réis, pl.) was the currency in circulation until 1914, when it was replaced by the escudo. In Angola, the escudo was the currency from 1914 until 1928 and again between 1958 and 1977. From 1928 to 1958, the angolar was the currency of Angola. Mozambique used the escudo from 1914 to 1980, and Guinea and São Tomé e Príncipe from 1914 to 1975 and 1977 respectively. Until its independence in 1975 Cape Verde's escudo was at par with the Portuguese escudo.

In French colonies, French denominated currencies were introduced in Senegal after 1820 depicting the heads of successive French kings (Louis XVIII, Louis-Philippe, Napoléon III), and initially focused exclusively on two Senegalese main commercial towns (Gorée Island and Saint-Louis). The metropolitan franc was subsequently extended to all French colonies. A West African Bank (*Banque de l'Afrique Occidentale*), previously established as Bank of Senegal, was charged with issuing French denominated currency in all West African French colonies after 1901. A separate currency authority was created for French Central Africa and Cameroon in 1955. In all cases, the local currency authority was charged with the administration of the currency arrangement. This included the ability to buy and sell the local currency at a fixed rate against the foreign currency of the colonial power (sterling pound or French franc).

See also **Colonial Policies and Practices; Gorée; Saint-Louis.**

BIBLIOGRAPHY

Galbraith, John Kenneth. *Money: Whence It Came, Where It Went.* Boston: Houghton Mifflin, 1995.

Weatherford, Jack McIver. *The History of Money: From Sandstone to Cyberspace.* New York: Crown Publishers, 1997.

SALOMON SAMEN

COMMODITY CURRENCIES

"A country's money is, after all, no more than a commodity, well able, under the guidance of supply and demand, to take care of itself," wrote the English economist John Maynard Keynes in 1914 (259). The distinction between "commodity currency" and "currency" proper depends on the definition of each word-concept and the possible ways they might be combined: as concepts and as material forms. In the quotation above, one of the great twentieth century theorists of money implied that conventional definitions might fail; this was in the context of his review of a new book about the most stable, wide-ranging and successful coin currency in modern African history, the silver, Austria-minted Maria-Theresa *thaler*, eternally imprinted with 1780, the date of her death. In this, as in other matters, the African evidence presents challenges to conventional wisdoms.

In the centuries before national monies were mandated by colonial governments, African trade and exchange were mediated through a variety of indigenous and imported objects that fulfilled one or several of the classic "functions of money": as media of exchange, means of payment, units of account, and stores of value. Some—such as cloth, salt, livestock, and various metal objects—were also usable for practical purposes and so became designated loosely by outsiders as commodity currencies. In the past, social evolutionary theorists implied (erroneously) that commodity currencies were "primitive" monies, one step more "advanced" than barter of one good for another, but not yet reaching the purely abstract quality of all-purpose, "modern" money.

In the early twenty-first century, the concept of commodity currency has been used by economists in a new and different way: to designate present-day national currencies whose exchange rates on the world currency markets are measurably influenced by their countries' reliance on the export of products that are referred to as "primary commodities," that is natural resources and agricultural products. Of the fifty-nine countries in the world that have commodity currencies in this sense, twenty-two are in Africa, almost half of all African countries. This specialized sense of the term will not be discussed in this entry, but it does remind one that monetary concepts get redefined in relation to the markets, currencies, and commodities of a particular historical era and set of participants.

These differentiations amongst types of currency are clearly very important for the analysis of African economic history and organization. But they are very tricky. They can be imprecise as well as changing over time. If the concept of commodity means any item that is traded at market-driven prices, then *all* currencies—Western, Eastern, African, past and present—are commodities if and when there are markets for them. Market demand may be patchy. Even currencies of modern Western origin could be treated as commodities at one point in the chain of exchange and as currencies at others. The Maria-Theresa *thaler* was produced in identical form and silver content by the Austrian mint and sold to the Levantine merchants as a commodity. It was not legal tender in Austria for much of its two-hundred-year history. Likewise, the brass manilla and the shell cowry were manufactured and bought by Europeans as commodities and used in Africa to purchase African goods. Then they circulated locally among Africans as all-purpose money. For much of early modern history *all* these currency objects were treated *by Europeans* as commodities once they were in Africa, and therefore deprived of the essential quality of convertibility back into European monies. Gold and silver alone retained convertibility with Europe, but as commodities not as an issued currency.

Within Africa, the concept of commodity currency often designates those objects that served for one or several of the conventional functions of money, but could also have a value for consumption purposes as tools, clothing, livestock, and food. This criterion would then identify as currency proper the gold, silver, shells, manillas, copper croisettes, and all other purely symbolic metal currencies for which no use other than the classic functions of money, including displays of wealth and power, could be clearly identified. Again the definitions are ambiguous. The *thaler* was used as a market weight and fashioned into women's jewelry; the gold dust currency of the Akan of Ghana could be wrought into regalia of state; the copper croisettes of Central Africa, which were possibly the oldest metal currencies indigenous to Africa, were buried with the dead. Are these ceremonial and decorative functions "use," or does one want to restrict that concept to "practicality"?

There is another, different, possible distinction between types of currency in Africa, namely that those objects that historians call currencies proper lent themselves to specialist treatment: strict standardization, numeration and protection from counterfeit, adulteration, deterioration, and consumption. They became literally counted on, over long periods of time, by a wide variety of users, and were monitored by experts. Objects other than metals and shells could hold a stable enough form and quality (in this material sense) to be used as monies but they lent themselves less easily to standardization and preservation over the rough and tumble of transport, storage, and hand-to-hand exchange across ecological boundaries. This, however, does not necessarily make them a kind of second-class or (even less) primitive money. Two important institutions depended on the existence of a kind of monetary multiplicity that was not simple denominational, using the same sort of materials and entailing complete equivalence. Monetary variety allowed (1) "assortment bargaining," whereby *collections* of goods were used as counterparts in exchange, often summarized in stable fictional units of account such as the "trade ounce"; and (2) Muslim *mudaaf*, whereby traders avoided the prohibited monetary gains on financial transactions by repaying a loan in a currency or commodity other than that of the original loan (Webb 1995, 63).

The commodities with the widest use as currencies, in this last sense, were salt, textiles, and cattle:

- Salt: Bars of salt were used throughout the dry areas of the eastern Sudan, Uganda, and south into the Great Lakes region. The salt mines and pans were owned by powerful local leaders, with complex systems of access and distribution that fluctuated according to rainfall as well as currency demand.
- Textiles: The two great regions for cloth currency were the West African Sahel, using woven cotton, and Central Africa, using raffia cloth. In both cases, production of currency grade cloth was restricted enough to prevent massive inflation. In Nigeria, the Tiv were

famous for "Munchi cloth" that they traded out into the whole region. In Central Africa, Lele production of raffia cloth was largely monopolized by the elders.

- Cattle: The centrality of cattle herds in Eastern and Southern African regional systems of valuation has been well documented. In the twenty-first century a fictive cattle unit still mediates some exchanges although no actual cattle change hands.

For scholars of money, it is the relationship between the material goods in circulation and the conceptual definitions—the modes of calculation and recording in accounting and valuation—that is the most challenging aspect of African multiple currency systems.

See also **Economic History; Livestock: Domestication; Metals and Minerals; Salt; Textiles.**

BIBLIOGRAPHY

Barret-Gaines, Kathryn. "The Katwe Salt Industry: A Niche in the Great Lakes Regional Economy." *African Economic History* 32 (2004): 15–49.

Cashin, Paul; Luis Cespedes; and Ratna Sahay. "Commodity Currencies." *Finances and Development* 40, no. 1 (2003). Available from http://www.imf.org/external/pubs/ft/fandd/2003/03/cash.htm.

Dorward, David. "Precolonial Tiv Trade and Cloth Currency." *International Journal of African Historical Studies* 9, no. 4 (1976): 576–591.

Douglas, Mary. "Raffia Cloth Distribution in the Lele Economy." *Africa* 28 (1958): 109–122.

Guyer, Jane I., ed. *Money Matters: Instability, Values, and Social Payments in the Modern History of West African Communities.* Portsmouth, NH: Heinemann, 1995.

Keynes, John Maynard. "Review of *Le Thaler de Marie-Therese: Etude de Sociologie et d'Histoire Economique.*" *The Economic Journal* 24, no. 4 (1914): 257–260.

Semple, Clara. *A Silver Legend: The Story of the Maria Theresa Thaler.* London: Barzan, 2005.

Webb, James A., Jr. 1995. *Desert Frontier: Ecological and Economic Change along the Western Sahel, 1600–1850.* Madison: University of Wisconsin Press.

JANE I. GUYER

EXCHANGE RATE SYSTEMS

Monetary systems in Africa vary depending on the colonial history of each country. In general, the structure of the monetary and banking institutions of the majority of African countries reflect an extension of what exists in their respective metropolitan centers. In fact, most of the present-day African monetary systems institutions were initiated by the colonial powers. Therefore, despite the far-reaching measures that independent African countries have taken in recent years to achieve greater monetary autonomy, a variety of attachments still remain. Generally speaking, African countries can be grouped in two in terms of monetary developments: The first group includes all the countries that decided to consolidate the monetary arrangements that exist before independence and the second is composed of countries that decided to create their own national monetary arrangements.

CONSOLIDATION OF THE CFA FRANC ZONE
The group of countries that decided to keep the monetary arrangements from the colonial period are the countries known as the CFA Zone. They include Bénin, Burkina Faso, Cameroon, CAR, Chad, Congo (republique of), Côte d'Ivoire, Equatorial Guinea, Gabon, Guinea-Bissau, Mali, Niger, Senegal, and Togo.

Originally, the French franc circulated in these counties, but in 1945 France introduced new currency for them. The currency was called the CFA (for Colonies Françaises d'Afrique) franc (see Table 1); in 1948, it was pegged to the French franc at a rate of one CFA franc for two French francs. With the introduction of the new French franc in 1960, the parity became one CFA franc for 0.02 French francs. The CFA franc served as currency for two separate groupings of sub-Saharan countries, French West Africa and French Equatorial Africa. The French treasury guaranteed the exchange rate and ensured transferability to and from France and the other territories through potentially unlimited financing provided by an "Operations Account." Until 1955, the right of bank note issue in the CFA franc zones was vested in certain private banks. In 1955, two new public institutions were given responsibility for note issue in West and Central Africa: the *Institut d'émission de l'Afrique occidentale française et du Togo* (Dahomey, Guinea, Ivory Cost, Mali, Mauritania, Niger, Senegal, Upper Volta, and Togo), and the *Institut d'Émission de l'Afrique*

The currencies of Africa

Region	Countries	Currencies
North Africa	Algeria	Algerian dinar
	Egypt	Egyptian pound
	Libya	Libyan dinar
	Mauritania	Ouguiya
	Morocco	Dirham
	Sudan	Sudanese dinar/pound
	Tunisia	Tunisian dinar
Central Africa	Angola	Kwanza
	Burundi	Burundian franc
	Cameroon	Central African CFA franc
	CAR	Central African CFA franc
	Chad	Central African CFA franc
	Rep. of the Congo	Central African CFA franc
	Equatorial Guinea	Central African CFA franc
	Gabon	Central African CFA franc
	Dem. Rep. Congo	Congolese franc
	Rwanda	Rwandan franc
	São Tomé e Príncipe	Dobra
West Africa	Cape Verde	Cape verdean escudo
	Gambia	Dalasi
	Ghana	Cedi
	Guinea	Guinean franc
	Liberia	Liberian dollar
	Nigeria	Naira
	Sierra Leone	Leone
	Benin	West African CFA franc
	Burkina Faso	West African CFA franc
	Côte d'Ivoire	West African CFA franc
	Guinea-Bissau	West African CFA franc
	Mali	West African CFA franc
	Niger	West African CFA franc
	Senegal	West African CFA franc
	Togo	West African CFA franc
East	Djibouti	Djiboutian franc
	Eritrea	Nakfa
	Ethiopia	Birr
	Kenya	Kenyan shilling
	Somali	Somaliland shilling
	Tanzania	Tanzanian shilling
	Uganda	Ugandan shilling
South	Botswana	Pula
	Lesotho	Loti
	Malawi	Malawian kwacha
	Mozambique	Metical
	Namibia	Namibian dollar
	South Africa	Rand
	Swaziland	Lilangeni
	Zambia	Zambian kwacha
	Zimbabwe	Zimbabwean dollar
Indian Ocean	Comoros	Comorian franc
	Seychelles	Seychelles rupee
	Madagascar	Ariary
	Mauritius	Mauritian rupee

Table 1.

government and issued bank notes for their respective monetary areas. According to the rules of the Franc Zone, all these African countries were obliged to deposit all their earnings in the Operations Account, and had in principle unlimited access to French franc in exchange of their own currency.

With the exception of Guinea and Mali, France's strong influence on monetary policy of the newly independent countries of the CFA zone was maintained. In 1959, the *Instituts d'émission* were transformed into central banks, called the *banque centrale des états de l'Afrique de l'ouest* (BCEAO) and the *banque centrale des états de l'Afrique équatoriale et du Cameroun* (BCEAEC) subsequently renamed *Banque des états de l'Afrique centrale* (BEAC) in 1972. Its headquarters remained in Paris. In addition to issuing currency notes, the two central banks were authorized to extend credit to commercial banks and the treasuries of their member countries. In 1966, each central bank was authorized to grant short term loans to national treasury equal to 10 percent of the country's fiscal receipts. This limit was raised to 15 percent in 1970 and to 20 percent in 1972.

The CFA franc zone was further modified in 1972–1973 by new treaties between France and the African members. In Central Africa, the central bank was renamed the *Banque des Etats de l'Afrique Centrale* (BEAC) its headquarters moved to Yaoundé, Cameroon, as of 1977, and, for the first time, Casimir Oye Mba (Gabon), an African professional, was named as its governor. In West Africa, similarly, the headquarters was transferred to Dakar, Senegal, in 1978 with Abdoulaye Fadiga (Côte d'Ivoire), another African, as Governor. The requirements for holding reserves in the Operations Account were modified and reduced to 65 percent of total reserves, but emergency measures were to be taken if the ratio of reserves to the central bank short term liabilities declined below 20 percent or if the operations account balance became negative. Despite the 1972–1973 reform, Mauritania chose to quit the CFA franc zone rather than sign the new treaties with France and decided to create its own central bank.

In 1985, Equatorial Guinea, a former Spanish colony, joined the BEAC and the central Africa currency zone while Guinea-Bissau, a former Portuguese colony, joined the BCEAO and the West Africa Monetary Union in 1997.

équatoriale fançaise et du Cameroun (Cameroon, Central African republic, Chad, Congo-Brazzaville, and Gabon). These two monetary institutes were based in Paris (France), controlled by the French

"One of the fundamental ills of the CFA franc system is that it had given its member countries an essentially overvalued currency, which has seriously impaired the competitiveness of their export products, and has tied their economies to French markets . . ." (Abdel-Salam 1970, 345). This ill became evident in the course of the 1980s and led to an economic crisis that culminated in the devaluation of the CFA franc in 1994.

The decision to devalue the CFA (taken by the French monetary authorities without prior consultation with their African counterparts) came after years of wrangling; it was advocated early on by the International Monetary Fund and World Bank, but resisted by both French and African authorities who feared that a devaluation will cut the link with the French franc and dismantle the monetary union. The depth of the economic and financial crisis eventually forced France to change in its position at a meeting of the Franc Zone in Paris in September 1993, when it made clear that it would only provide aid to countries having agreed to programs with the Bretton Woods institutions. Therefore, African heads of state had no choice than to accept the fact that there was no alternative to devaluation, and on January 11, 1994, the devaluation the CFA franc by 50 percent was announced.

NATIONAL MONETARY ARRANGEMENTS

Anglophone Africa. Before independence, British colonies were grouped into three currency boards—monetary institutions, which had a fixed exchange rate with the British pound—the West African Currency Board, the Southern Rhodesia Currency Board, and the East African Currency Board, in each of which the quantity of money was linked to the amount of sterling assets held by the currency board. The West African Currency Board included The Gambia, the Gold Coast, Nigeria, Sierra Leone, and later the British Cameroons. The Southern Rhodesia Currency Board (Central African Board after 1954) included southern Rhodesia, northern Rhodesia, and Nyasaland. The East African Currency Board comprised Kenya, Tanganyika, Uganda, and later Zanzibar, Aden, Somalia, and Ethiopia. Each of these currency boards was characterized by a fixed exchange rate with the pound sterling, an automatic system of issue, and a 100 percent conversion of the local currency into sterling.

Classification of exchange regime in Africa

The 53 countries of Africa can be classified today from the monetary point of view into five groups according to the International Monetary Fund (IMF).

1. Exchange arrangements with no separate legal tender (14 countries)

West Africa Economic and Monetary Union (WAEMU): Benin, Burkina Faso, Côte d'Ivoire, Guinea Bissau, Mali, Niger, Senegal, Togo

Central Africa Economic and Monetary Community (CAEMC): Cameroon, CAR, Chad, Congo (Republic of), Equatorial Guinea, Gabon

2. Currency Board arrangements (1)

Djibouti

3. Fixed peg arrangements (12)

Against one currency: Cape Verde, Comoros, Eritrea, Lesotho, Namibia, Seychelles, Swaziland, Zimbabwe

Against a composite: Botswana, Libyan Arab Jamahiriya, Morocco, Tunisia

4. Managed floating (16)

Algeria, Angola, Burundi, Egypt, Ethiopia, Gambia (the), Ghana, Kenya, Mauritania, Mauritius, Mozambique, Nigeria, Rwanda, São Tomé e Príncipe, Sudan, Zambia

5. Independently floating (9)

Congo (Democratic Republic of), Liberia, Madagascar, Malawi, Sierra Leone, Somalia, South Africa, Tanzania, Uganda

Table 2.

The British protectorates in southern Africa were linked to the Union of South Africa, the major economy in the region, which was formed in 1910. It had its own currency, the South African pound, which upon creation of the South Africa's central bank in 1921, became the sole circulating medium and legal tender for the small British protectorates of Bechuanaland (Botswana), Basutoland (Lesotho), and Swaziland, and also for the League of nation's trusteeship territory of South-West Africa (Namibia). The South African pound was replaced by a new currency, the rand, in 1961, and the monetary union became known informally as the rand monetary area. After independence, the British agreed to dismantle the currency boards and set up central banks in each of their colonies.

In West Africa, member countries progressively withdrew from the West African Currency Board: Ghana in 1957, Nigeria in 1959, British Cameroons in 1962 (which joined the central African CFA franc zone as part of Cameroon), Sierra Leone in 1963, and Gambia in 1964. The new currencies in Ghana (the Ghanaian pound, later the cedi) and Nigeria (the Nigerian pound, later the naira) were initially linked at par with the sterling.

In East Africa, the former colonies aimed to retain cohesion among member countries and replace the currency board with some type of monetary union, in the context of a new East African Community linking Kenya, Tanzania, and Uganda. However, after arduous negotiations that failed in 1966, each of the three countries decided to issue its own currency and create its own central bank.

After they became independent in the late 1960s, Botswana, Lesotho, and Swaziland continued to use the rand as the sole currency in circulation, without any formal agreement with the South African government. In 1969, after a customs union agreement was renegotiated with South Africa, attention turned to formalizing and adapting monetary relations between the smaller countries and South Africa. This led eventually, in December 1974, to a formal agreement recognizing the Rand Monetary Area linking Lesotho and Swaziland with South Africa. The agreement provided that the rand would be legal tender and exchangeable at par within Lesotho and Swaziland, but the latter would have the right to issue their own currencies, whose note issue would be backed 100 percent by rand deposits with the South African Reserve Bank. The Rand monetary Area was replaced in July 1986 by the Common Monetary Area as a result of an agreement among the three countries to accommodate certain concerns of Swaziland. Namibia was made an independent member of the area in February 1992, though it had long been a de facto member of the rand zone.

Botswana decided to withdraw from the monetary union. It continued to use the rand on an informal basis until the introduction of the pula in August 1976, which was pegged to the U.S. dollar until 1980, when it was tied to a basket of currencies. The islands of Mauritius and Seychelles, which were members of the sterling area, have their own rupee currency in circulation. With independence, Mauritius established the central Bank of Mauritius.

North Africa. As French territories during colonial times, Algeria, Morocco and Tunisia were originally part of the French franc zone. Following their political independence, the Algerian dinar, the Moroccan dirham, and the Tunisian dinar were introduced as national currencies linked to the

French franc at fixed parity. Tunisia established its first central bank, the *Banque centrale de Tunisie*, in September 1958, and Morocco replaced the former *Banque d'Etat du Maroc* by a new state-owned institution, the *Banque centrale du Maroc*, in July 1959. Algeria established the *Banque centrale d'Algérie* in January 1963. During the 1960s the currencies of these countries were pegged to the French franc at a fixed rate. However, since the 1970s the foreign exchange policy in these countries has aimed at maintaining a stable real exchange rate against a basket of currencies weighted according to their main trading partners and competitors. This policy basically consisted of adopting a constant real exchange rate rule according to which the authorities adjust periodically the nominal exchange rate so as to maintain the real exchange constant.

The Libyan Currency Commission, established in 1952, was replaced in 1956 by the National Bank of Libya, transformed in 1963 into the Bank of Libya. In Egypt, the National Bank of Egypt issued banknotes for the first time on April 3, 1899. Later the Central Bank of Egypt and the National Bank of Egypt were unified into the Central Bank of Egypt. After pegging its currency to the U.S. dollar for many decades, Egypt began a transition to a flexible exchange rate system in 2000. The exit from the peg went through several phases, including a series of step devaluations between 2000 and 2002, a first attempt at a float in January 2003, and a successful transition to a unified, flexible exchange rate system in late 2004. From 2000 to 2004, the Egyptian pound experienced a cumulative depreciation of 68 percent against the U.S. dollar. During this period, there was an active parallel market for foreign exchange with a premium that reached as high as 15 percent over the official rate.

Others. Belgian colonies of the Congo and Rwanda-Urundi formed a monetary union, whose currency, the Congolese franc, was pegged to the Belgian franc. Portuguese and Spanish colonies typically used the escudo or peseta, respectively.

Upon independence in 1960, Rwanda and Burundi ceased using the Congolese franc and responsibility for issuing the new franc of Rwanda and Burundi was given to a joint monetary institution. However, the economic union did not survive the political conflicts that occurred in 1963–1964, and each country subsequently adopted its own currency.

Before independence, Angola, Mozambique, Cape Verde, Guinea-Bissau and São Tomé e Príncipe were part of the Portuguese escudo area. Mozambique adopted a new currency, the metical, in 1980, five years after independence, and initially its official fixed parity was defined in terms of a basket of six currencies.

In Liberia, the national currency, the Liberian dollar, was created in June 1935, but the country has no central bank of its own. The currency in circulation consists of American coins and paper money. The Bank of Monrovia, a subsidiary of the First National City Bank of New York, acts as government banker and administers most of the financial activities. Liberia thus constitutes an extension of the U.S. currency area, not only technically, but also in the view of most exchange authorities. A Central Bank of Liberia (CBL) was later introduced in October 18, 1999, by an Act of the National Legislature of the Republic of Liberia. It became functional in 2000 and succeeds the National Bank of Liberia (NBL). The principal objective of the CBL is to achieve and maintain price stability in the Liberian economy. To this end, it seeks to preserve the purchasing power of the national currency; promote internal and external equilibrium in the national economy; encourage the mobilization of domestic and foreign savings and their efficient allocation for productive economic activities; facilitate the emergence of financial and capital markets that are capable of responding to the needs of the national economy, and foster monetary, credit and financial conditions conducive to orderly, balance and sustain economic growth and development.

See also **Colonial Policies and Practices; Dakar; Debt and Credit; International Monetary Fund; World Bank; Yaoundé.**

BIBLIOGRAPHY

Abdel-Salam, Osman Hashim. "The Evolution of African Monetray Institutions." *Journal of Modern African Studies* 8, no. 3 (1970): 339–362.

Masson, Paul R., and Catherine A Pattillo. *The Monetary Geography of Africa.* Washington, DC: Brookings Institution Press, 2004.

Monga, Celestin, and Jean-Claude Tchatchoung. *Sortir du Piège monétair.* Paris: Economica, 1996.

JEAN-CLAUDE TCHATCHOUANG

MONGELLA, GERTRUDE I. (1945–).

Gertrude Igenbwe Mongella is president of the Pan-African Parliament. Born on the Tanzanian island of Ukewere in Lake Victoria, Mongella is an internationally recognized feminist, politician, diplomat, and advocate for women's rights. She began her education at the age of twelve and graduated in 1970 from the University College of Dar es Salaam with a degree in education. Between 1970 and 1982, she taught at the Teachers Training College and worked as a curriculum developer and school inspector for Tanzanian schools. Mongella's political career began with her appointment in 1975 to the East African Legislative Assembly. Two years later, she was appointed to the National Executive Committee of Tanzania's ruling party, the Chama cha Mapinduzi (Party of the Revolution).

During the 1980s, Mongella held various ministerial positions, including minister of state and minister of lands, tourism, and natural resources. In these capacities and in her subsequent role as Tanzanian high commissioner to India, she became a recognized international figure especially known for her efforts to promote women's rights and

Gertrude Mongella (1945–) at the United Nations' Fourth World Conference on Women in 1992. She was there as president of the Pan-African Parliament. Mongella previously served as goodwill ambassador for the World Health Organization's Africa Region.

improve conditions for women in the developing world. In 1992, UN secretary general Boutros Boutros-Ghali designated Mongella secretary general of the 1995 Fourth World Conference on Women to be held in Beijing, China. Her stewardship of the conference, widely deemed a success, earned her the nickname "Mama Beijing." Mongella was elected as the first president of the Pan-African Parliament in March 2004 for a five-year term. She is married and the mother of four children.

See also **Education, University and College; Tanzania: History and Politics; Tourism; Women.**

KELLY M. ASKEW

MONROVIA. The capital of Liberia, Monrovia is situated on the coast of West Africa. It was founded through the efforts of the American Colonization Society, who were concerned with "repatriating" freed slaves in the United States who, they believed, would cause problems if allowed to remain and live alongside whites. The first boatload of black Americans was sent to Africa in 1822, but no effort was made to return them to their lands of origin, and many were American-born. Instead, they were settled in one spot on the coast, and this settlement became Monrovia. The settlement was named after the U.S. president at the time, James Monroe. The land, a hilly peninsula at the mouth of the Mesurado River, was bought by the American settlers, later known as Americo-Liberians, from a local authority, known as "King Peter." However, the doubtful legality of this purchase, together with the fact that the settlers regarded their African neighbors as less civilized than they, formed the basis for later conflict.

In 1989, Monrovia was a city of about 3.4 million people. This population included a core of long-established Americo-Liberians and a large number of neglected rural people who came to the capital during the postwar economic boom based on rubber and iron ore. The new inhabitants included many foreign traders and merchants, as well as rural Liberians. At this time over 80 percent of Monrovians were Christians.

Many more rural Liberians fled to Monrovia following the outbreak of civil war in 1989. Population estimates have been extremely difficult to acquire since that time. Historians believe that as many as 300,000 persons displaced from the countryside have sought shelter in the city, but the influx of refugees has led to a serious breakdown in public sanitation and health services. A cholera outbreak has claimed many lives, as have dehydration, disease, and starvation among the city's poorest inhabitants.

In 1992 the National Patriotic Front of Liberia under the leadership of Charles Taylor ravaged the city. The suburbs were mostly destroyed, but the central, old part of the town was defended successfully by the Economic Community of West Africa States Monitoring Group, the United Liberation Movement of Liberia for Democracy, and the Armed Forces of Liberia. In 1996 Monrovia became the site of peace negotiations between the warring military factions. A new, civilian government was elected in 1997, with Charles Taylor as President, but civil strife and rebel action continued to batter the city and the countryside. In 2003, Taylor resigned the presidency and left the country, and his replacement, Moses Blah, assumed office.

See also **Liberia; Taylor, Charles Gahnhay.**

BIBLIOGRAPHY

Fraenkel, Merran. *Tribe and Class in Monrovia.* London: Oxford University Press, 1964.

MARTHA HANNAN

MONTANE ENVIRONMENTS. *See* **Ecosystems: Montane Environments.**

MOORS IN AFRICAN HISTORY. The name Moor derives from the region in northwestern Africa known in Roman times as Mauretania. It comprised the present countries of Morocco and Algeria and was a narrow strip along the Mediterranean and Atlantic coasts, never extending more than 300 miles inland. The name has gone through many mutations of meaning over the past

2,500 years as a result of indiscriminate usage, often motivated by the growing emotionality of the term's racial overtones. During this time the ethnonym has always been an external one, applied by Europeans to designate a variety of African peoples; at no time has an African people designated itself as Moor.

A summary of the word's history explains its meaning. The Greek word Μαψροι (Mauroi), the root of the Latin word Mauretania and therefore of Moors, is first attested in a poem by Pindar (d. c. 435 BCE) and in a play by Aeschylus (d. 456 BCE). Neither Mauretania nor Mauroi is mentioned in Herodotus's (d. c. 425 BCE) *Histories*, composed around 439 BCE, the earliest known account of the peoples of northern Africa. By common consensus Mauroi means dark skinned; it should not be confused with μυλαζ (*melas*, black).

In 27 BCE, Emperor Augustus (d. 14 CE) extended the Province of Africa (present-day Tunisia) to include Numidia (present-day eastern Algeria). The rest of Algeria and northern Morocco, to the west, were nominally independent under a vassal king of Mauretania. In 40 CE its last king, Ptolemy, son of Juba II (d. 23 BCE), was assassinated on the orders of Emperor Caligula (d. 41 CE), and his possessions were divided into two imperial provinces: Mauritania Caesariensis (capital at Cherchell), and Mauritania Tingitana whose capital was Tingis (modern Tangier), opposite the Iberian promontory that formed the Pillars of Hercules at the straits leading to the Atlantic Ocean (the present-day Straits of Gibraltar). By the third century most of Morocco had ceased to be administered; Emperor Diocletian (d. c. 312 CE) did not control more than the immediate vicinity of Tangier, which was administered from Iberia. The Vandals controlled the country from 429 until 534, when Belisarius took it for Byzantium.

After the Arabs had conquered Egypt in 640, they made no effort before 670 to penetrate farther west than adjoining Libya. Northwestern Africa was not subdued by the caliphate until the end of the century. In 712 a majority Berber army crossed into Spain, seizing the country in what was almost a ceremonial parade. The army continued into France but in 732 turned back, south of Poitiers without engaging in battle, an event that marks the limit of Muslim expansion in western Europe.

By 756 the Islamic state of al-Andalus had been constituted in Spain by an Umayyad dynasty of Syrian descent. The incomers, to whom the term Moors was now more broadly used by Christians in Western Europe, included not only Berbers from northern Africa but also Syrians, Yemenis, and Jews. For some four hundred years these Moors left monuments that attest to a marvelous flowering of Islamic civilization unequaled in the Christian Europe of its time. In law and learning, in art and poetry, in religious writing, in architecture, in its supreme expressions in the Mesquita, the Great Mosque of Córdoba, and in the architecture of the Alhambra palaces and the exquisite Generalife palace in Granada, the Moors reached incomparable heights of taste and elegance, only to collapse politically in the eleventh century.

A further invasion by the Moroccan Berber Almoravids in 1088 lasted only half a century. In its turn a new Berber group, the Almohads, overthrew it in 1145. Thereafter the Christian kingdoms, first Portugal and then Castille, slowly eroded Moorish power, culminating in the fall of Granada and the unification of present-day Spain in 1492. In the following year all Jews who would not convert to Christianity were expelled, followed by the expulsion of the Moors (Muslims) in 1502.

The term Moors slowly penetrated European languages outside the Iberian Peninsula. In French it is first found as *mor* in a work of Chrétien de Troyes in 1175. The spelling *maure* occurs first in 1636.

The Moors who were expelled from the kingdom of Granada first returned to their ancestral homelands in northern Africa, particularly Morocco. Fez was a particular center of attraction. Many had emigrated long before, including Jews of Arab culture; one was Musa ibn Maymun (Mosheh ben Maimon; in English, Maimonides), the personal physician and confidant of Saladin (1138–1193, Egyptian opponent of the Crusaders in Palestine) and outstanding astronomer, philosopher, and theologian. In art and architecture, Islamic influences persisted in the exuberant *mudjedar* styles of architecture in Portugal and Spain. A similar eclectic Moorish style became fashionable again in the late nineteenth and early twentieth centuries, when it was used, among other things, for the design of synagogues in Europe and America.

Averroes (Abu al-Walid Muhammad ibn Ahmad ibn Rushd, 1126-1198 CE), as portrayed by Raphael in "The School of Athens," 1509. Active as a philosopher, physician, mathematician, and adviser at the court of the Almohad sultan Abu Yusuf al-Mansur (r. 1184-1199), he wrote commentaries and treatises on a wide range of topics, including Aristotle, Galen, and defenses of rationality and the analytical method. KEAN COLLECTION/HULTON ARCHIVE/GETTY IMAGES

The relatively narrow original sense of the word Moor was extended through usage over time. In Jerusalem in 1480 and in Sinai in 1483, a German friar, Felix Fabri (c. 1441–1502), drew a clear distinction between those he counted as Moors and those he regarded as Saracens. The Moors were from the Iberian Peninsula and northern Africa; the Saracens were Muslims of eastern origin, from the Arabic word *sharq* (east). By the time Vasco da Gama (c. 1469–1524) wrote his *Voyages*, he used the term to refer to the Muslims he encountered along the eastern African coast after rounding the Cape of Good Hope. His usage was followed by João de Barros (1496–1570), the distinguished head of the Casa da India (the India Office in Lisbon), and thereafter indiscriminately by European writers of all nations to designate African, or black, Muslims wherever

they were encountered, even as far as the Moros of the Philippines.

The term has also had a no less promiscuous career in the United States. Muslims from West Africa enslaved in the United States were sometimes called Moors, especially if they happened to be literate in Arabic. This designation was turned into a mark of distinction by Nobel Drew Ali (d. 1929), the charismatic spiritual leader and forerunner of Elija Muhammad. Ali founded the Moorish Science Temple in 1913. A combination of black empowerment, syncretistic Sufism, and orientalism, the Moorish Science Temple claimed that African Americans were descendents of Moors, illegally enslaved, and were thus effectively citizens of the Empire of Morocco. Meanwhile, in French, the term *maure* is still used to designate that segment of modern Mauritania's population that calls itself white (colloquial Arabic: *bidân*).

See also **Gama, Vasco da; Immigration and Immigrant Groups: Arab; Judaism in Africa; Northern Africa: Historical Links with Mediterranean; Northern Africa: Historical Links with Sub-Saharan Africa.**

BIBLIOGRAPHY

Cornevin, Robert. *Histoire de l'Afrique.* Vol. 1. Paris: Payot, 1962.

Diouf, Sylviane. *Servants of Allah: African Muslims Enslaved in the Americas.* New York: New York University Press, 1998.

Freeman-Grenville, Greville S. P. *The East African Coast: Select Documents from the First to the Earlier Nineteenth Century.* Oxford: Clarendon Press, 1962.

Freeman-Grenville, Greville S. P. *The New Atlas of African History.* London: Simon and Schuster, 1991.

Freeman-Grenville, Greville S. P. *Historical Atlas of the Middle East.* New York: Simon and Schuster, 1993.

Gomez, Michael *Black Crescent: The Experience and Legacy of African Muslims in the Americas.* New York: Cambridge University Press, 2005.

G. S. P. FREEMAN-GRENVILLE
REVISED BY ERIC ROSS

MORALITY. *See* **Civil Society.**

MOROCCO

This entry includes the following articles:
GEOGRAPHY AND ECONOMY
SOCIETY AND CULTURES
HISTORY AND POLITICS

GEOGRAPHY AND ECONOMY

Morocco is the only country in Africa to contain all of the Mediterranean bioclimatic and vegetation zones and the only country north of the Sahel to have a signed a bilateral free trade agreement with the United States of America. Its exceptional geographical setting facilitated the development of an extensive export-oriented agriculturally based economy under French colonial rule. This legacy continues to shape agricultural and economic development in the kingdom to this day. The underlying weaknesses of this economy and subsequent economic developments, including several decades of neoliberal restructuring, have left a large and growing number of Moroccans living in poverty and increasingly difficult conditions.

Morocco's 171,731 square miles (excluding the Western Sahara) boast four imposing mountain ranges, including the Rif Mountains in the north and the Atlas mountains (the Anti-Atlas, the High Atlas, and the Middle Atlas) that run from the southwest to the northeast of the country (see map). These mountains intercept moisture-laden air masses coming from the north and west, producing significant orographic precipitation, most of which falls in the winter. Precipitation is highest in the north, where it averages 79 inches or more annually, and lowest in the south, where it averages 4 inches or less each year. Precipitation is also greater in the western part of the country than in the eastern part due to the rain shadow created by the Atlas mountains. Morocco's climate ranges from Mediterranean (north and west) to desert (south and east). This, combined with its highly variable topography, has created conditions that support high species diversity.

As a result of its northwesterly location and its extensive mountain ranges, Morocco receives the highest levels of precipitation in North Africa; it also possesses the most extensive river system. Morocco has eight major perennial rivers and several minor streams. Most of these rivers flow from the Atlas mountains toward the western coastal plains, creating favorable agricultural conditions. Aggressive damming of these rivers has allowed for the development of a sophisticated system of irrigated agriculture. Without irrigation, agriculture in Morocco is precarious because many of the agricultural areas receive 16 inches or less of precipitation annually, and rainfall is highly irregular and unpredictable throughout the country. Rain-fed cereal harvests, for example, vary enormously from year to year, mirroring the irregularities in rainfall as shown in Figure 1.

In order to harness the region's valuable but unreliable precipitation for agricultural development, the French constructed fourteen dams and a series of canals and irrigation perimeters during the colonial period. At independence, the primary exports—and largest contributors to the economy—were agricultural products and phosphates. Since independence, Morocco has largely followed colonial agricultural plans, built more than twenty new dams, and expanded irrigation to cover more than 2,400,000 acres. As it did during the colonial period, this valuable land produces primarily citrus and vegetables for export to Europe, although European countries strictly limit Moroccan imports. As the French before them, the Moroccan government has largely ignored the traditional, rain-fed agricultural sector that employs and feeds a large number of Moroccans.

Morocco began to borrow money from international institutions such as the World Bank to finance its development plans soon after gaining independence in 1956. Following a brief period of large profits from phosphate exports during the 1970s, Morocco accumulated a large external debt and developed a growing economic crisis. This crisis resulted in its entering a succession of structural adjustment agreements with the International Monetary Fund (IMF) beginning in 1983 and lasting a decade. Further liberalization of the economy followed during the 1990s, with privatization of state industries, currency devaluation, and the encouragement of imports. In 2006 the service sector accounted for just over 50 percent of the gross domestic product (GDP) and employed about 25 percent of the workforce, whereas agriculture employed approximately 45 percent of the

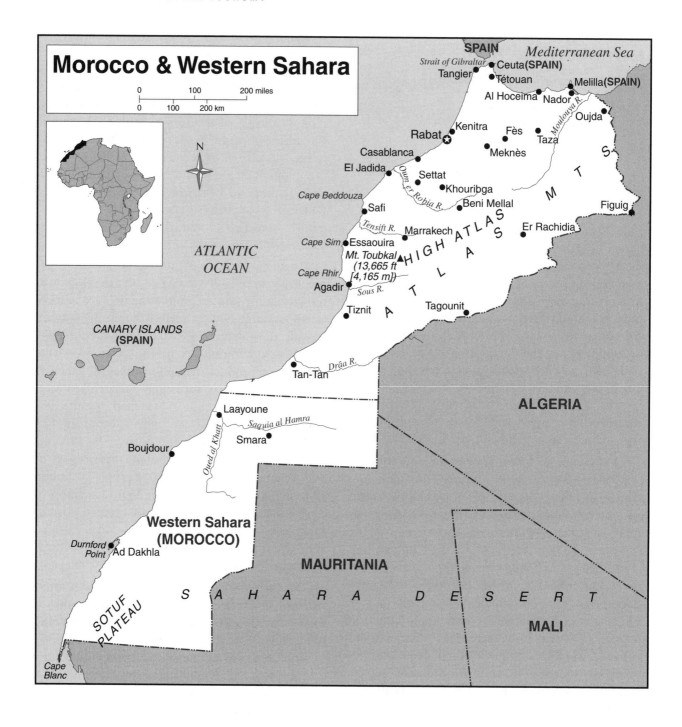

workforce and contributed approximately 17 percent of the GDP. Manufacturing now dominates exports, and the GDP was approximately 44 billion U.S. dollars in 2004, growing at 3.5 percent annually.

Despite predictions of improved economic health, total government debt in Morocco has grown and debt service payments continue to rise. Since 1992, living standards have been declining, largely as a result of neoliberal policies. Poverty and unemployment have increased to about 20 percent, and literacy rates actually fell during the 1990s. Morocco ranks well below its neighbors in North Africa, most of the Middle East, and other middle income countries, in terms of GDP/capita, life expectancy, literacy, infant survival, and many other basic development indicators as shown in Table 1.

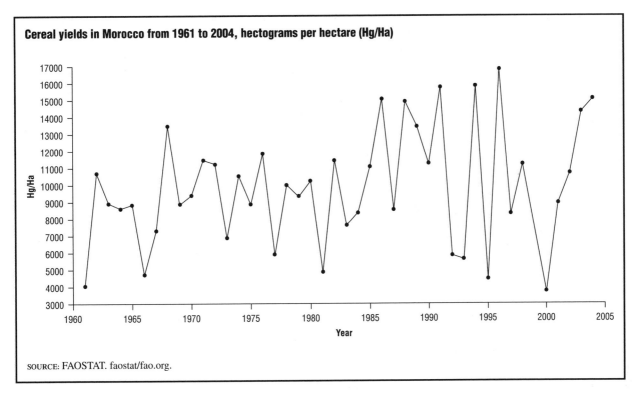

Cereal yields in Morocco from 1961 to 2004, hectograms per hectare (Hg/Ha)

SOURCE: FAOSTAT. faostat/fao.org.

Figure 1.

Development indicators for the Maghreb, 2003–2004

	HDI	Literacy	Life expect.	Infant mort.	GDP/ capita	Debt serv.*
Algeria	0.72	70%	71	35/1000	$6,107	6.5
Morocco	**0.63**	**51%**	**70**	**36/1000**	**$4,004**	**9.8**
Tunisia	0.75	72%	74	19/1000	$7,161	6.4
Arab states	0.68	64%	67	48/1000	$5,685	2.5
Mid-income	0.77	90%	70	29/1000	$6,104	6.4

*Debt service as percent of GDP.

SOURCE: United Nations Development Programme. *Human Development Report 2005*. New York: Oxford University Press, 2005.

Table 1.

The challenges facing Morocco are many. An effort was made by the government to make improvements was the signing of the bilateral free trade agreement with the United States in July 2004. Unfortunately, original project documents recognized that this agreement will disrupt rural agricultural production due to the importation of cheap American grains, potentially dispossess millions of Moroccans of their livelihoods, and exacerbate poverty in rural areas.

See also **Climate; Debt and Credit; Ecosystems; International Monetary Fund; World Bank.**

BIBLIOGRAPHY

Despois, Jean and Raynal, René. *Géographie de l'Afrique du Nord-Ouest*. Paris: Payot, 1967.

Economist Intelligence Unit. *Morocco: Country Profile, 2005*. London: Economist Intelligence Unit, 2005.

Pennell, C. R. *Morocco since 1830: A History*. New York: New York University Press, 2000.

Swearingen, Will D. *Moroccan Mirages: Agrarian Dreams and Deceptions, 1912-1986*. Princeton, New Jersey: Princeton University Press, 1987.

United Nations Development Programme. *Human Development Report 2005*. New York: Oxford University Press, 2005.

DIANA K. DAVIS

SOCIETY AND CULTURES

Situated at the northwest corner of Africa and about the size of California, Morocco has long been a crossroads of peoples and civilizations, bridging northern and sub-Saharan Africa, the Mediterranean, and the Muslim worlds to the east. The Kingdom of Morocco's name in Arabic, *al-mamlaka al-maghribiyya*, literally means the western kingdom. Prior to French (and Spanish) rule over Morocco (1912–1956) it was known as the Sherifian Empire—Sherifian referring to the claimed descent of its rulers from the Prophet Muhammad. Morocco's native peoples, especially those living in its vast mountainous regions of the Rif, the Middle Atlas, and the High Atlas mountains, have offered strong resistance to invaders over the centuries, yet Punic, Roman, and Christian conquerors have left their marks. In the seventh and eighth centuries, Arabs introduced Islam and the language of the Qur'an on North Africa and gradually began the task of absorbing North Africa, including present-day Morocco, into the orbit of Islamic civilization. A second wave of Arab invasions in the eleventh and twelfth centuries, primarily consisting of bedouin nomads from the Arabian Peninsula, further intensified the Arab presence.

Nonetheless, Morocco has maintained a distinctive cultural identity. One aspect of this identity has been a vibrant Jewish community that has included Berber-speaking Jews in the Atlas mountains and the pre-Saharan south, and Arabic-speaking Jews in most of the major towns and cities. Some leading Jewish families in urban Morocco, similar to their Muslim counterparts, trace their origins to Spain, from which they sought refuge after the collapse of Muslim rule in 1492. In 1948 Morocco's Jewish community numbered 225,000; 160,000 Jews remained in 1960 although since then their number has declined to under 5,000. Nonetheless, Moroccan Jews abroad, including those who have emigrated to Israel, retain strong ties with Morocco and are proud of their Moroccan identity.

Of all the countries of North Africa, Morocco shows the most ecological diversity. Its three main geographical regions are the Riffian and Atlas mountain chains, the coastal and interior plains situated roughly between Marrakesh and Fez, and the semiarid pre-Sahara of the south. Except for Marrakesh, Morocco's most important towns and cities—Casablanca, Rabat, Fez, Meknes, and Tangier—are located on the plains to the northwest. These plains have traditionally had the heaviest rainfall and the richest agricultural land, and also the highest population density.

ETHNIC AND LINGUISTIC DIVERSITY

Moroccans are both Berbers and Arabs, terms that are based on language and cultural characteristics because there are no clear physical or biological distinctions between these two ethnic categories. Many Moroccans claim both identities, emphasizing one or the other according to social and political circumstances. Arabic is the dominant language of the region, although there are still communities in the mountainous regions and in some of the oases in Morocco's pre-Saharan regions where the everyday use of Arabic outside the classroom is rare. Nearly half of Morocco's population speaks one of the three major (and interrelated) Berber languages, although most Moroccan Berbers, especially men, speak Arabic as a second language. The most important dialect clusters are *tashilhit*, spoken in the Middle Atlas mountains; *tariffit*, spoken in the Riffian mountains in Morocco's north; and *tamazight* in the High Atlas mountains and the Sus Valley to their south. From the mid-1990s, Moroccan radio and television have significantly expanded broadcasting in the Berber languages, making the Berber cultural movement an integral part of Berber cultural identity.

At the turn of the twentieth century, Morocco's population of nearly three million was roughly 90 percent rural. In 2007, with a population of 33.7 million, about 70 percent of Moroccans live in towns and cities, including the shantytowns (*bidonvilles*) that house large numbers of unemployed and underemployed rural immigrants. Half the population is under twenty-four years old. Sixty percent of males are literate and 39 percent of females are literate. Continued population growth and budget constraints mean that the eradication of illiteracy, especially in rural areas, will not occur soon.

RELIGION AND SOCIETY

Islam in Morocco is distinctively marked by respect for the *salih*s (pious ones). For educated Muslims, pious ones, also known as marabouts, are revered

Kingdom of Morocco

Population:	33,757,175 (2007 est.)
Area:	446,550 sq. km (172,413 sq. mi.)
Official language:	Arabic
Languages:	Berber dialects, French, Arabic
National currency:	Moroccan dirham
Principal religions:	Muslim almost 100%, nominal numbers of Jewish and Christian
Capital:	Rabat (est. pop. 1,200,000 in 2005)
Other urban centers:	Casablanca, Marrakesh, Fez, Meknes, Tangier
Annual rainfall:	200 mm (8 in.) on the northern coast; up to 400 mm (16 in.) north of Casablanca
Principal geographical features:	*Mountains:* Rif Mountains (range), Atlas Mountains (range), Jbel Ayachi, Jebel Musa, Jebel Toubkal, Zarhon *Rivers:* Bou Regreg, Dadés, Draa, Imini, Moulouya, Oued Laou, Oum Er-Rbia, Ourika, Sebou, Ziz *Lakes:* Al Massira, Al Wahda, Bin El Ouidane, D'Afennourir, Idriss, Larache, Mohammed V *Other:* Sahara Desert, Rock of Gibraltar
Economy:	*GDP per capita:* US$4,600 (2006)
Principal products and exports:	*Agricultural:* barley, wheat, citrus, wine, vegetables, olives, livestock *Manufacturing:* food processing, leather goods, textiles, construction *Mining:* phosphates (largest industry), anthracite, antimony, barite, cobalt, copper, fluorspar, iron ore, lead, manganese, salt, silver, zinc *Tourism:* Tourism is important to Morocco's economy.
Government:	Independence from France, 1956. Constitution, 1972; revised in 1992 and 1996. Constitutional monarchy. Bicameral Parliament consists of Chamber of Counselors (270 seats, elected indirectly by local councils, professional organizations, and labor syndicates; 9-year terms) and Chamber of Representatives (325 seats, elected by popular vote; 5-year terms). Prime minister and council of ministers appointed by monarchy. For purposes of local government, there are 16 regions, further divided into provinces and prefectures.
Heads of state since independence:	1956–1961: Mohammad V 1961–1999: King Hasan II 1999–: King Muhammad VI
Armed forces:	18-month conscription obligation. *Army:* 175,000 *Air force:* 13,500 *Navy:* 7,800 *Paramilitary:* 50,000
Transportation:	*Rail:* 1,907 km (1,185 mi.) *Waterways:* Strait of Gibraltar *Ports:* Agadir, Casablanca, Mohammedia, Nador, Safi, Tangier *Roads:* 57,493 km (35,724 mi.) 57% paved *National airline:* Royal Air Maroc *Airports:* International facilities at Casablanca, Marrakesh, and Tangier. 57 other airports and airstrips throughout the country
Media:	The daily newspaper *Al-Anbaa* is the official organ of the government. There are many other newspapers. Weekly magazines include *Le Journal Hebdomadaire* and *Tel Quel*. The 52 radio stations and 5 television stations are government-controlled.
Literacy and education:	*Total literacy rate:* 52.6% (2006). Education is compulsory for 9 years. There are 17 universities.

for their piety, and some of these are also linked to religious brotherhoods (*tariqa*s). Many other Moroccans impute miracle-working powers (*baraka*) to the pious ones, and every quarter in every town and rural community have shrines dedicated to the *salihs'* memory. The legitimacy of Morocco's monarchy has also traditionally been imputed with such powers as God's deputy on earth (*khalifat Allah fi-l-'ard*).

Rising educational levels contribute to causing many, at least in private, to challenge the monarchy's religious claims. Morocco's rapidly rising population growth, population shifts from rural areas to towns, diminishing prospects for economic emigration, a stagnant economy, and dramatically increasing levels of unemployment have created a politically volatile situation in which Islamic radicalism has appealed increasingly to some Moroccans.

One of the most powerful religious movements, the Justice and Welfare movement (*al-ʿadl wa-l-ihsan*), with ʿAbd al-Salam Yasin as its spiritual leader, uses modern media technology to spread its message but has many structural features of a traditional religious brotherhood.

Morocco's current king, Muhammad VI (r. since 1999), as his father Hasan II (r. 1961–1999), emphasizes his religious credentials through carefully orchestrated visits to mosques and shrines and participation in religious events. Increasingly, however, most Moroccans now judge the monarchy less on its claims to religious authority than its ability to lead reform, govern effectively, and improve Morocco's difficult economic situation. A weak economy, a deteriorating environment, and a growing disparity between in income levels challenge Morocco, as do these factors in Morocco's neighbors. However, these issues are played out in a Moroccan way, in which the country's religious and political forms of popular expression, and mix of Arabic, Berber, and widespread use of French, Spanish, and, increasingly, English, make it culturally and socially distinct.

See also **Fez; Hasan II of Morocco; Islam; Marrakesh; Morocco, History of (1000 to 1900).**

BIBLIOGRAPHY

Bennani-Chraïbi, Mounia. *Soumis et rebelles: Les jeunes au Maroc.* Casablanca, Morocco: Editions Le Fennec, 1995.

Eickelman, Dale F. *Knowledge and Power in Morocco.* Princeton, NJ: Princeton University Press, 1985.

Geertz, Clifford. *Islam Observed.* New Haven, CT: Yale University Press, 1968.

Gottreich, Emily. *The Mellah of Marrakesh: Jewish and Muslim Space in Morocco's Red City.* Bloomington: Indiana University Press, 2007.

Troin, Jean-François. *Le Maghreb: Hommes et espaces.* Paris: A. Colin, 1985.

DALE F. EICKELMAN

HISTORY AND POLITICS

Morocco, or the kingdom of Morocco (in Arabic *al-mamlaka al-maghribiyya*), is located in northwest Morocco and is about the size of the state of California. Also like California the country has a marked ecological diversity. Geographers divide the country into four major regions, the Rif and Atlas Mountain chains, the coastal and interior plains situated roughly between Marrakesh and Fez, the semiarid pre-Sahara region to the south, and the Moroccan Sahara—as Moroccans have considered the Western Sahara their land since King Hasan II (r. 1961–1999) led the peaceful November 1975 "Green March" into what was then the Spanish Sahara. After a few months of joint Spanish, Mauritanian, and Moroccan rule, Morocco assumed de facto control over the region, although the international status of the Western Sahara remains contested.

Morocco's population as of 2007 was 34 million. With the exception of a small community of Moroccan Jews, currently estimated at 5,000 (down from 225,000 in 1948), Moroccans are entirely Sunni Muslims. The first language of more than half of Moroccans is one of the country's three major Berber languages, although many people are bilingual in Arabic. In the cities, French is widely spoken, as is Spanish in the northern part of the country. In all cities and in higher education, English is becoming increasingly common. Many Berbers claim a distinct ethnic identity, and the Berber language with its own script is used in primary education in areas of Morocco where Berber-speakers predominate. For the most part, however, Berber ethnic identity is social and not political.

THE COLONIAL ERA IN MOROCCO

Although Morocco fell under colonial rule only in 1912, since the mid-nineteenth century it was subject to financial controls by European powers, and other comprises with its sovereignty, including the incremental occupation of certain parts of the country beginning in 1907. Finally, the French occupied all but the northern zone of Morocco in 1912, with the Spanish occupying northern Morocco, including the mountainous Riffian region, and the far south, including several enclaves along the Atlantic coast and the Spanish Sahara. Resistance to the French rule was fierce in some parts of Morocco, so that the country was not fully "pacified" until 1932. Spanish control over its territories was even more tenuous, with the Spanish unable to defeat the short-lived Riffian Republic (1921–1926) of a religious judge (*qadi*), ʿAbd al-Karim al-Khattabi (c. 1880–1963) until aided by French forces. The city of Tangier, where most foreign embassies were located until Morocco's independence, was declared an International Zone from 1912 until 1956, the year of Morocco's independence and the end of colonial rule.

RELIGION AND POLITICS IN TWENTY-FIRST-CENTURY MOROCCO

Morocco has had a distinct political identity since 788, when it was ruled by the Idrisi dynasty (788–1016). Like the current 'Alawi dynasty, which has ruled Morocco continuously since 1666, the Idrisi dynasty claimed legitimacy through descent from the Prophet Muhammad. Morocco's king (*malik*), called "sultan" until 1957, is "commander of the faithful" (*amir al-mu'minin*), a concept with profound Islamic roots and enshrined since 1962 in successive Moroccan constitutions. Until the 1970s, peasants and tribespeople still referred to Hasan II as caliph, or "God's deputy on earth" (*khalifat Allah fi-l-'ard*), assured of God's special blessings and protection, a notion powerfully reinforced by Moroccan popular understandings of Islam until recently.

Morocco's recognized political parties, which acquired legal status after independence, were obliged to work within the framework of monarchic rule. As Hasan II said before parliament in 1984—Morocco has had local and parliamentary elections at irregular intervals since the early 1960s—his "school" of politics directly follows from that of the Prophet Muhammad. Political parties are banned from using Islamic symbols or speaking in the name of Islam, as the monarchy reserves to itself appeals to religious legitimacy. Hasan II's "dark side" complemented these claims to religious legitimacy. Many Moroccans know the period from the 1960s to the 1980s as *les années du plomb*, the "years of lead," of states of emergency, disappearances, the suppression of dissent, and a judiciary almost entirely subservient to the political will. Following two coup attempts in 1971 and 1972, the monarch took direct control of the military. Only in the 1990s did the political situation open up, with the release of political prisoners and monarch-led efforts to run elections that were more open and to allow opposition voices, albeit circumscribed.

The monarchy's claims to religious legitimacy have steadily eroded but remain strong. Most Moroccans, especially younger and educated ones, now judge the monarchy less on its claims to religious legitimacy than on its ability to reform, govern effectively, and improve worsening economic conditions. The monarchy is no longer unchallenged in claims to speak for Islam.

Rising educational levels contribute to causing many youth, at least in private, to challenge the monarchy's religious claims. Morocco's rapidly increasing population (notwithstanding new attitudes toward limiting the size of families), population shifts from rural areas to towns, diminishing prospects of economic emigration, a stagnant economy, and increasing levels of unemployment, especially among Morocco's educated youth, have created a politically volatile situation in which Islamic radicalism has appealed increasingly to some Moroccans. Since a May 16, 2003, terrorist attack in Casablanca, there have been several other successive ones in 2007 and others that have been averted. Moroccans have become aware that they are not immune to terrorist acts. The state response has been a vigorous campaign against religious radicalism and renewed efforts to address Morocco's long-standing deficiencies in education, public housing, rural and urban development, and health.

In his speeches and public acts, Muhammad VI (r. 1999–), like his father before him, does not hesitate to explain how the state, in becoming more open and accountable, also fulfills an Islamic mandate, sometimes by co-opting Islamist language. The monarchy's claims to religious legitimacy remain strong although not unchallenged, and its policies are sufficiently adaptable to changing political and economic circumstances to continue to offer more hope for the immediate future to most Moroccans than do alternative ideas of political rule.

See also **Colonial Policies and Practices; Ecosystems; Fez; Hasan II of Morocco; Judaism in Africa; Kings and Kingdoms; Literatures in African Languages: Berber; Marrakesh; Moors in African History; Morocco, History of (1000 to 1900).**

BIBLIOGRAPHY

Bennani-Chraïbi, Mounia. *Soumis et rebelles: Les jeunes au Maroc.* Paris: CNRS Éditions, 1994.

Eickelman, Dale F. "Muslim Politics: The Prospects for Democracy in North Africa and the Middle East." In *Islam, Democracy, and the State in North Africa,* ed.

John Entelis. Bloomington: Indiana University Press, 1997.

Hammoudi, Abdellah. *Master and Disciple: The Cultural Foundations of Moroccan Authoritarianism.* Chicago: University of Chicago Press, 1997.

Pennell, C. R. *Morocco since 1830.* New York: New York University Press, 2000.

Slyomovics, Susan. *The Performance of Human Rights in Morocco.* Philadelphia: University of Pennsylvania Press, 2005.

DALE EICKELMAN

MOROCCO, HISTORY OF (1000 TO 1900).

Morocco, occupying the northwest corner of the African continent and separated from Europe by only seven miles, has been a crossroads of Europe's intense interaction with the Muslim world through trade, occupations, military victories, and defeats.

Morocco was at the fringes of the first Muslim empires, and it sought independence from them similar to Al-Andalus in the Iberian Peninsula. From the first centuries of the Islamic era, it was part of the implosion of the early Islamic empires into different, regional dynasties. Morocco's history was inextricably related to that of its seven partly overlapping dynasties, the Idrisis (789–926), Almoravids (1056–1147), Almohads (1130–1269), Merinids (1196–1549), Wattasids (1498–1549), Saadians (1511–1659), and Alawis (1631–present).

That fact that Morocco's inhabitants were Berber (*Amazigh*) prior to the Islamic conquests that began in the seventh century relates to Morocco's historical specificity combining Berber tribal autonomy with Islamic notions of rule through the caliphate. After the Islamic conquests, Morocco was the homeland of two great Berber empires that also grew to include rule over Andalusia (al-Andalus) in present-day Spain, the Almoravids (conquest from 1086–1106), and the Almohads (conquest in 1145). Both of these dynasties had their origins in the southwestern desert and had their later center in Marrakesh. The original founder of the first dynasty, Idris I (d. 791), who assembled a coalition of Berber tribes in 786 at the former Roman city Volubilis, however, was of Arab descent from Ali, the son-in-law of the Prophet Muhammad who was married to the Prophet's daughter, Fatima. His son, Idris II (791–828), established the city of Fez as the capital, which was founded in 789 by his father. Fez soon became the spiritual and trading center, linking al-Andalus in the north with the Arab East. A second north-south trading route passed through Sijilmasa, through which much of the gold trade passed.

Competition, especially between the Fatimids (from Ifriqia [Tunisia]/Egypt) and the Umayyads (from al-Andalus since 711) brought a final end to Idrisi rule in 985. The dynasty had already been fragmented after Idris II's death in 828 when his descendants vied for power. When these external powers fought for supremacy in the tenth-century Maghreb, this increased trade and the Islamization of Morocco. One consequence was that cities such as Fez began to prosper, another that different coexisting statelets, influenced amongst others by Fatimids and the Kharijis, evolved and created a certain stability that was marked by religious heterodoxy. But this relative stability and trade was contingent on the fragile stability in al-Andalus under the Ummayad dynasty. In return, in Cordoba the Ummayad military largely depended on an unruly Berber army, which sacked the palace in 1031, ending the caliphate period in al-Andalus and also the relative stability of the Moroccan-ruled principalities.

It was the first Moroccan empire of the Almoravids that started the expansionary period toward Muslim Spain in the North and toward much of North Africa including Tunis (*Ifriqia*) in the East. At the height of Almoravid rule from about 1086 to 1143, all of al-Andalus was under the dynasty's direct rule. The Almoravids founded Marrakesh as a military post and later as a capital at around 1070 (the exact date is unknown). Yusuf Ibn Tashfin took his troops over the Straits in 1086, and occupied the whole of al-Andalus in 1100 (except Zaragoza) and the east until Algiers. However, the Berber rulers alienated the more liberal Muslim principalities in al-Andalus that previously had asked for help from the Almoravids against the Christians.

The Almoravids, similar to their successors the Almohads (mid-twelfth to mid-thirteenth century), took their strength from Muslim orthodoxy and tribal loyalty. The fragility was due to its interference in Spain that absorbed manpower and finance, leaving the south unprotected and vulnerable to new dynastic pretenders. The implicit vulnerability was even more important because both dynasties relied on local tribes to collect taxes, thereby constantly creating autonomous power zones and potential contenders to their own rule. Under the Marinids from the tribe Banu Marin (mid-thirteenth to mid-fourteenth century), Andalusian affairs continued to attract military and political attention, but the Marinids had no resources to stage similar takeovers as their predecessors. In the end, when Algeciras fell to Christian armies in 1344, this was the end of Moroccan involvement in Muslim Spain.

The period of Moroccan direct involvement in Spain came to a halt toward the end of Marinid period from around 1350, when the Marinids were weakened due to internal rivalries. In the fifteenth century, Morocco in turn came under pressure from Castilla, the Christians, and especially Portugal, which established important trade outposts on Morocco's Atlantic and Mediterranean coasts (in Ceuta in 1415, Tanger in 1471, Azila in 1471, Safi in 1481, El Ksar el Sghir in 1458, and Melilla in 1497). The Marinids disintegrated and a rival tribe, the Bani Wattas, established the Wattasid dynasty in 1498. Sharifian, an alternative to tribal rule, also characterized this period. The Sharifian claim to rule was that, as descendants from the Prophet Muhammad they were superior to other claimants to religious and political authority. The Wattasids, however, ruled through their tribal military power and tribalism as a crucial source of power became clear when the city of Fez, in which Sharifian rule had been proclaimed, was conquered in 1472. It is noteworthy that the most famous observer of the ups and downs of the dynasties in that period was Ibn Khaldun (1332–1406) who, in the introduction *Muqaddima* to his book *Kitab al-Ibar*, explained that tribal solidarity, *'assabiyya*, is at the origin of the state in North Africa and accounts for the many dynastic changes that occurred. Even the Saadians were of tribal origin, but they added something that became the rule ever since: Sharifian background and the religious prestige attached to it. The new basis of state power was no longer solely based on tribal loyalty, but also on alliances with local Islam that organized in largely autonomous *zawiyas*, and with Islamic clerics, *'ulama*. Nevertheless, *'assabiyya* was still paramount.

During the height of the Ottoman Empire in the fifteenth to sixteenth century toward and increasing European domination to the north, Morocco entered a period of relative decline, with long periods of civil war constantly threatening its stability. This was also due to the relative decline of the trans-Saharan trade that was the source of wealth for Sultans, as part of the overall change in trade routes by Ottoman, and especially Portuguese, sailors. After the longest and most important civil war (1603–c. 1672), the present 'Alawi dynasty from the southern oasis of Tafilalet established its supremacy toward the end of the seventeenth century. Isma'il I (1672–1727), seeking a stable base of military power, introduced a black slave army, thereby avoiding the pitfalls of unruly tribal alliances that had worked against all of the previous dynasties. Meanwhile, interactions with Europe increased through trade with Isma'il. He even asked for the hand of Louis XIV's daughter, who kindly refused.

Europe's increasing economic, scientific, and technological superiority became an imminent threat as imperialism became a primary driving force. With France's Algeria campaign that started 1830 and Morocco's military weakness as experienced in the military defeat at Isly in 1844, a new wave of Islamic reformism, the *salafiyya* movement, which aspired to reinforce Islamic authenticity and return to authentic Islamic teachings, arose in order to keep up with European technology. This abstract political movement, however, failed because of tribal autonomy in the countryside. Later 'Alawi rulers, especially Mohamed IV (1859–1873) and Hassan I (1873–1894), attempted to modernize the army by increasing taxation, which failed for the same reason as the previous salafiyya movement.

Rebellion in the countryside (*siba*) increased especially when nineteenth-century rulers attempted to secure Morocco's independence by playing the three great powers against each other: Britain, France, and Germany. This meant granting privileges to traders from each nationality (such as the status of protégés meaning that national law could not be applied to citizens from these countries), which in turn created hostility among city dwellers, 'ulama, and tribes. Increasing contact with the Europeans therefore created ever more domestic instability, as did external debts as one of the means of paying for Morocco's modernization campaigns. It was the issue of debt and domestic instability that made

France force a protectorate regime on Morocco in 1912, with Spain assuming a parallel role in northern Morocco and in the Sahara.

See also **Fez; Marrakesh; Morocco: History and Politics; Northwestern Africa, Classical Period, History of (1000 BCE to 600 CE); Sijilmasa.**

BIBLIOGRAPHY

Lugan, Bernard. *Histoire du Maroc.* Paris: Critérion, 1992.

Pennel, C. *Morocco Since 1830: A History.* New York: New York University Press, 2000.

Pennel, C. *Morocco—From Empire to Independence.* Oxford: One World, 2003.

JAMES SATER

MOROCCO AND SUB-SAHARAN AFRICA.

Contact between North Africa and the rest of the African continent dates from the earliest historically known periods. Herodotus in the sixth century BCE reported that the pastoralist Libyans (Berbers of North Africa) were in the habit of raiding the Ethiopians (black populations of sub-Saharan Africa). However, relations were not limited to conflict. Historical evidence clearly demonstrates the existence of intense trade relations between the two sides, carried by horse chariots along the same caravan routes that emerged later.

The agents of this contact were the pastoralist Berbers who, long before the Christian era, were drifting into western and Central Africa. Controlling the supply of horses, and later of camels, the Berbers were able to push deeper into the Sahara and reach as far as the Niger region. It is assumed that the southward Berber movement may have encouraged African societies south of the Sahara to better organize themselves and develop supratribal political institutions that would allow them to resist incursions coming from the north.

THE MAGHREB AND SUB-SAHARAN AFRICA AFTER ISLAM

Islamization of Sudan, or the land of the blacks (to the Arabs), seems to have begun immediately after the Muslim conquest of North Africa in the seventh century. Ibn ʿAbd al Hakam (d. 871) in the ninth century mentions an expedition from southern Morocco to Sudan as early as 734 CE.

However, the spread of Islam in West and Central Africa was not the result of military conquest but of a slow process based on the movement of Muslim North African merchants to the region and their residence in the trading centers there.

Ibadi merchants from Maghrebi cities such as Tahert or Sijilmasa seem to have played a leading role not only in trans-Saharan trade but also in the spread of Islam in western Sudan. Al Masʿudi (d. 957) records that the city of Sijilmasa in southeast Morocco had commercial relations with western Sudan and that, on the route from Sijilmasa to present-day Senegal, Ibadi Muslim merchants controlled the gold trade. The extent of Islamization in sub-Saharan Africa before the eleventh century cannot be accurately determined, but it is clear from early Arabic sources about the region that Islam began to have a deep impact in western Sudan societies as early as the eighth and ninth centuries, even if the new religion was limited at the beginning to the trading and ruling elites.

In Maghrebi-Sudanese relations, the Almoravid experience stands as the major development that brought large parts of the Maghreb and Sudan under the same rule at the same time. The Sanhaja Berbers, who dominated the western part of the Sahara and also the Morocco-Ghana caravan trade, in the eleventh century initiated a politico-religious movement. The outcome of this was the emergence of a vast empire extending from the Senegal River to Muslim Spain.

The Almoravids had a deep influence on western Sudan, and their impact survived the fall of their empire in the twelfth century. Probably the most important aspect of the Almoravid legacy was the consolidation of the Maliki doctrine on both sides of the Sahara. Among the Soninke states that emerged from the former Ghana empire, Sunni Islam became firmly rooted and the Almoravid way of life was adopted by the new political entities. Politically, the breakup of the Almoravid movement between the Maghreb and the Sahara during its early stages allowed the Sanhaja of the Western Sahara to turn to Ghana, which they weakened, if not invaded, before it gave way to much lesser local states.

CARAVAN TRADE

In the commercial network that linked North Africa to Sudan, Morocco assumed a prominent role. On the Saharan fringes of Morocco emerged a number of trading cities or caravan terminals such as Sijilmasa, Noul Lamta, and Tamdoult.

Starting with the eighth century CE, Sijilmasa, the capital of a Kharij principality in southeast Morocco, became an important relay in the caravan trade. For several centuries after that, Sijilmasa appears to have been an important port, enjoying regular links with the trading posts of the other side of the Sahara. The wealth accumulated by the city in the tenth century made it a tempting prize for the Fatimid dynasty, which aimed to create an empire extending from Egypt to the Atlantic coast. In the eleventh century the emerging Almoravids made its control one of their main objectives. Under their rule, Sijilmasa used to receive large quantities of Sudanese gold. The golden coin al-murabit, associated with this place, became the most appreciated currency of international trade in the Mediterranean. In contemporary sources, the city is referred to as the gate of gold. The Maghrebi geographer, al-Idrisi (thirteenth century), describes the city as a prosperous place where merchants and travelers to Sudan gathered before they set out for the trans-Saharan journey.

In fact, the Almoravids, by controlling a large empire that included Muslim Spain, much of North Africa, and the western part of Sudan, created favorable conditions for the intensification of trade relations between Morocco and the rest of the Maghreb on one hand, and sub-Saharan Africa on the other. The trade routes that developed between north and south became channels of commercial exchange for centuries. Caravans made up of hundreds of pack camels linked the commercial ports of the Sahara and the Sahel, such as Sijilmasa and Timbuktu. The trans-Saharan trade turned essentially around salt and gold, but North Africans exported many other commodities such as leather products, textiles, and books as Islamization and literacy spread among the Sudanese. In return they received ivory, gum arabic, and large numbers of slaves, in addition to gold or gold dust.

Although the volume of the caravan trade is difficult to assess in the absence of documentation, it is assumed that, with the arrival of Europeans to the West African coast starting in the fifteenth century, much of the trans-Saharan trade shifted to the Atlantic. The Moroccan conquest of the Songhay Empire at the end of the sixteenth century also contributed to the disruption of the traditional trade routes between northwest Africa and Sudan with a clear shift of caravan routes to the east. In the eighteenth century Morocco's control over its southern Saharan provinces weakened, and the country's economy became increasingly geared to the Atlantic. By the end of the nineteenth century, the French and Spanish occupation of much of the Western Sahara and the Touat dealt the final blow to centuries of commercial intercourse between the Maghreb and Sudan.

A COMMON RELIGIOUS TRADITION

In the historical experience that both North and West Africa share, it is not possible to disassociate Islam from trade. The new religion arrived in sub-Saharan Africa as a result of Maghrebi merchants settling in the commercial and urban centers of Sudan. This explains why Islam was initially adopted by the trading and political sub-Saharan elites before it spread to other strata of society. It also explains why Maghrebi Ibadi merchants were instrumental in the transmission of Ibadi ideas to the Sudan.

However, Ibadism as a doctrine was later wiped out or reduced to isolated pockets, not only in Sudan and sub-Saharan Africa, but also in the Maghreb as a result of the Puritan Almoravid movement that made Maliki Sunni jurisprudence its official dogma. That the Maliki doctrine took hold in the domains under Almoravid rule or influence meant that the Maghreb and western Sudan were brought together under a single Islamic tradition that covered the whole Islamic west from Andalusia to the banks of the Senegal River. In fact, the Almoravid control over such a large empire created conditions and channels for the transmission of Andalusian and Maghrebi cultural influences to the southern shores of the Sahara and beyond. The fall of the Almoravids in the twelfth century did not affect their cultural and religious legacy, which brought together the Maghreb and Sudan in what became known as the Islamic West.

After the Almoravids, the spread of Islam in West Africa continued under Malian influence. Arabic literacy accompanied this process of Islamization, and over the centuries many students and scholars from the region headed to Fes in Morocco and Qayrawan in Tunisia to acquire knowledge in the famous mosque-universities of the Maghreb. Many sub-Saharan Africans who chose to make their journey to the holy land through North Africa were able to visit local saints and *ulama* (religious scholars) and to build up spiritual links with Maghrebi Sufi masters.

Strangely enough, political discontinuities such as the Moroccan conquest of the Songhay in 1591 do not seem to have affected the religious tradition shared by the Maghreb and Sudan. In the field of Sufism, for instance, the ideas of the famous Maghrebi shaikh Al Jazuli (d. 1465) became widespread in the Niger Bend area, and his book of prayers, *Dala'il al-Khayrat*, remained for centuries the second-most read book after the Qur'an in Timbuktu. In the nineteenth century, spiritual links with western Sudan were strengthened by the spread of the Tijani Sufi order in the region. This Maghrebi Sufi movement acquired thousands of disciples in Senegal and western Sudan, and the shrine of its founder in Fez became a venerated place of pilgrimage for his sub-Saharan followers. In the second half of the nineteenth century some of its local leaders in West Africa played an important role in organizing resistance to colonial domination.

THE MOROCCAN SA'DI CONQUEST OF THE SONGHAY EMPIRE (1591)

Before the 1591 Sa'di invasion of the Songhay there had been close political relations between Marrakesh and Gao, and trans-Saharan trade between the two sides was prosperous. In the religious domain, the Moroccan *ulama* succeeded in building strong links with their counterparts in Timbuktu, thus enhancing the Maliki tradition in the region.

The Sa'di decision to invade the Songhay was the result of many complex considerations, including international strategic motivations as Morocco attempted to break up its encirclement by the Iberians in the north and the Ottomans in the east. Economically, the lavish spending of Ahmad al-Mansur (d. 1603) had put his treasury under extreme strain even with the overtaxation of his subjects, who showed signs of disaffection by lending support to political uprisings in different parts of the country. The control of the Taghaza salt mines, then under Songhay control even if in al-

Mansur's view they were closer to Marrakesh than to Gao, seemed to offer the answer to the sultan's financial problems.

To provide legal grounds for his military adventure, al-Mansur put forward two claims, both based on religion. According to the first one, al-Mansur asserted that he was the only caliph and *imam* by virtue of his prophetic lineage, and therefore all rulers in the Islamic west, at least, owed him allegiance. This claim was a direct challenge to the *askyas* (kings) of Gao who, by submitting to the demands of the Moroccan monarch, would lose much of the taxation revenues they imposed on the gold-salt trade. The second argument—that of jihad—was commonly used by Muslim African rulers, including the Songhay kings, whenever they needed a cover for their expansionist schemes. Al-Mansur claimed that his enterprise against the Songhay would result in the spread of Islam among sub-Saharan unbelievers and would provide his treasury with enough funds to resist or defeat Christian threats coming from Spain. These justifications failed to convince domestic public opinion, and the *ulama* in particular. The scholars strongly refused to endorse his claims, according to which the Sudan campaign would be justified as a jihad action against unbelievers, because the land of the Songhay was well-known to be predominantly Muslim.

Once the Songhay lands were brought under control, the Sa'dis found out that the only way to administer such distant territories was through a combination of two rules. One was military rule through a local *makhzan* (government; literally, storehouse) modeled on the Moroccan pattern, and the other was a system of indirect rule by which the *askya* continued to be the nominal head, but with little real power. After the death of al-Mansur in 1603, the Moroccan military and administrative presence weakened and Moroccan soldiers married with Songhay women. There developed in Timbuktu a class of *arma* (musketeers) who replaced the Sa'di Makhzan and became the real rulers of the Niger Bend areas for many generations.

For a long time, the Moroccan invasion of 1591 and the subsequent downfall of the Songhay Empire was portrayed as a political and economic disaster for the West African region. This view was adopted for different reasons by colonial historiographers and then by a whole generation of post-independence historians from sub-Saharan Africa.

For the first the aim was to support the view that between Arab North and black West Africa the dominant relation was that of antagonism, and just as colonial ideology attempted to do in Maghribi countries themselves, the "villain" to be blamed was "the Muslim Arab." Within this colonial perspective even sub-Saharan Islam came to be known as "black Islam," with little resemblance to the "white Islam" of the conquering Arabs of the north. Many postindependence African historians continued to hold this view as a result of the die-hard colonial interpretation on one hand and the lack of a serious reassessment of African history on the other.

Since the late twentieth century, European historians have begun to question the foundations of colonial historiography. They no longer view the Moroccan invasion of the Niger Bend in 1591 as catastrophic, as was assumed by historians during much of the twentieth century. Politically, the Songhay Empire was already in decay, with acute succession rivalries after 1528 and even outbreaks of civil war. Economically, the Moroccan invasion contributed to the eastward shift of trade, but the process was already under way with the imperial growth of Borno and the emergence of better-organized Hausa kingdoms. "What the Songhays lost," writes Mervyn Hiskett, "the Hausa and Bornoese gained and Sudanic trade sustained no setback, only a partial change of management" (1984, 152).

The Moroccan presence in the Niger Bend regions was not accompanied by any significant intellectual contributions. On the contrary, scholarly activity was disrupted after many 'ulama were forced into exile or sought refuge outside the main urban centers. However, one may also argue that the exile of an eminent scholar, Ahmad Baba of Timbuktu (d. 1627), to Marrakesh resulted in stronger religious ties between Maliki 'ulama on both sides of the Sahara and allowed Sudanic scholarship to gain recognition throughout the Maghreb and the Islamic world. Still, the disintegration of the Songhay Empire and the reorientation of trade along new routes may have contributed to the spread of Islam to new areas.

THE EUROPEAN CHALLENGE (NINETEENTH CENTURY)

For the Moroccan successors of the Sa'dis, the Sahara and western Sudan continued to have a high strategic and economic value, especially after the Europeans embarked on their overseas expansion during the nineteenth century. Much of the Sudanese trade was diverted to the European settlements on the Atlantic coast, and the Spanish or Portuguese occupation of many Moroccan ports on both the Mediterranean and the Atlantic amounted to a real maritime blockade. With the Ottomans firmly established in the rest of North Africa, the sultans of the 'Alawid dynasty (1666–present) considered on several occasions the possibility of southward expansion as the only way to break the Ottoman-Iberian encirclement.

During the early eighteenth century, sultan Isma'il dispatched troops to the Western Sahara and Shinguit (present-day Mauritania) with the aim of establishing some form of Moroccan presence there to secure trade relations with Sudan and to acquire slaves for his black army (*jaysh 'Abid al-Bukhari*). Moulay Isma'il provided military support to the Trarza emir in Shinguit and supported his action against the French settlements in Senegal. The Moroccan sultan was more successful in Touat, where he appointed governors without interruption between 1676 and 1727. The aim was to maintain the trade route linking Timbuktu to southern Morocco. However, no sultan among Isma'il's successors was able to preserve even a symbolic presence in these territories as the country sank into a long civil war between 1727 and 1757.

During most of the eighteenth and nineteenth centuries, Morocco was confronted with severe domestic problems and growing military pressure from the European powers, especially after the French conquest of Algeria in 1830. As French and Spanish colonial designs on the country became clear, the Moroccan Makhzan mobilized all its energies to resist French and Spanish territorial encroachments. Relying on British diplomatic support, Morocco was able to stave off European domination until 1912, but in the meantime it lost all the territories that allowed it in the past to be in contact with sub-Saharan Africa. In 1885 the Spanish imposed their protection on the Western Sahara, and in 1901 the French occupied the Touat provinces in the southeast. The local populations in these territories, and even in Timbuktu where the sultan of Morocco was still recognized as caliph (religious leader), appealed to the Makhzan for help against occupation. However, this ruler was in no position to provide any significant assistance. In the Western Sahara, shaykh Ma al-ʿAynayn (d. 1910) led a resistance against the Spanish and the French with limited support from Moroccan sultans to whom they nevertheless swore allegiance.

However, the regression of Moroccan political influence in the Sahara and Sudan between the seventeenth and nineteenth centuries seems to have been compensated in the spiritual field by the spread of Sufi ideas and movements originating in Morocco. Jazuli Sufism is the oldest, given that it seems to have made its way to the Sudan as early as the sixteenth century. More recent is the Tijani Sufi order that, in the nineteenth century, gained a wide audience in West Africa.

MOROCCO IN AFRICA SINCE INDEPENDENCE (1956–PRESENT)

Since its independence in 1956, Morocco's relations with the rest of the African continent have been dominated by the colonial legacy in terms of frontiers and territorial claims. Throughout the colonial period (1912–1956), the Moroccan nationalist movement conceived the country's independence as a return to the precolonial situation, in which the territories that were declared independent in 1956 constituted part only of a much greater historical Morocco. According to this view, Morocco would have to regain French-colonized Mauritania, the Spanish Sahara, and the territories in southwest Algeria that the French had amputated from the Sharifian Empire during colonial rule.

Moroccan nationalist claims were in direct conflict with the principle adopted by the Organization of African Unity (OAU), according to which territorial borders as inherited from the colonial past were intangible. At its first meeting in 1963, the OAU dismissed Moroccan territorial claims and admitted the newly independent Mauritania as a full member. Until then, Morocco proved to be an active player on the African scene. In 1960 the Moroccan government dispatched troops to the Republic of the Congo under the United Nations flag in a concerted effort to prevent the secession of the Katanga province. In 1961 Morocco convened the first Pan-African meeting in Casablanca to discuss the Congolese crisis and adopt a strategy by which the newly independent states of Africa would oppose neocolonialism and lend their support to the liberation movements across the continent.

However, after 1963 Morocco found itself increasingly isolated within the OAU, especially after Algeria's independence in 1962 and that country's emergence as the leading revolutionary country on the continent. Henceforth, Moroccan-Algerian tensions, largely motivated by territorial conflicts inherited from colonial times, tended to overshadow Morocco's relations with the OAU and the dominant group of revolutionary countries. The major challenge to Morocco, as far as its relations with the African countries are concerned, came in 1975, when Spain decided to leave the former Spanish Sahara and hand it over to both Morocco and Mauritania (Madrid Agreement of November 1975). This settlement was immediately challenged by the Polisario independence movement, supported and armed by Algeria.

Efforts by the OAU to find a political solution to the question were hampered by military confrontation between Morocco and Algeria, either directly or indirectly through the Polisario. With the diplomatic backing of Algiers, many countries from Africa and elsewhere recognized the Polisario as an independence movement. Within the OAU, Morocco came under increasing pressure to start negotiations with the Polisario and grant the Saharan populations the right of self-determination. At the Nairobi summit of the OAU in 1981, Morocco finally accepted the organization of a referendum by which the Saharans would decide their political future.

The Western Sahara crisis reached its apex in 1982 when the OAU admitted the République Arabe Sahraouie Démocratique (RASD) as a member of the organization, even if the quasi-totality of the west Saharan territories were under Moroccan control. Morocco saw in this admission a provocation and a diplomatic hold up. Considering that this recognition was contrary to the referendum solution adopted during the previous year, Morocco decided to leave the African organization. This decision meant that the OAU became irrelevant as a peace broker, and the whole issue was then transferred to the United Nations with a mandate to organize a referendum of self-determination in the contested territories. Such a referendum proved to be an impossible task, as the two parties to the conflict, Morocco and the Polisario, could not agree on the identity criteria of a nomadic population that has always freely moved across the political boundaries. After more than twenty years of United Nations efforts to find a solution that would be something less than total independence for the territory and more than direct Moroccan administration, the situation can still be characterized as a deadlock. The only glimmer of hope lies in the 2006 Moroccan proposal of autonomy, by which the Saharans would be granted large powers for the management of their domestic affairs while remaining within the bounds of Moroccan sovereignty.

As far as Moroccan-African relations are concerned, Morocco tried through various means to minimize the negative effects of the Sahara conflict on these relations. It strengthened bilateral relations and intensified economic and cultural cooperation with many sub-Saharan countries. Morocco tried also to bypass the OAU through active participation in the Francophone movement and by joining the Libyan-inspired Community of Sahel and Sahara (COMESSA; better known by its Arabic acronym, SINSAD). Morocco has also succeeded in maintaining close relations with moderate African countries such as Senegal, Congo (former Zaire), Gabon, Côte d'Ivoire, and others.

See also **Baba, Ahmad; Morocco; Sahara Desert: Caravan Routes; Sijilmasa; Transportation: Caravan.**

BIBLIOGRAPHY

Barre, Abdelaziz. "Les relations entre le Maroc et les pays d'Afrique subsaharienne." In *Les Relations Transsahariennes: l'Epoque Contemporaine*, ed. Laurence Marfaing and Steffen Wippel. Paris: Karthala, 2004.

Bovill, Edward W. *The Golden Trade of the Moors*, 2nd revised edition. London: Oxford University Press, 1968.

Harrak, F., and Houssain El Moujahid, eds. *Le Maroc et l'Afrique subsaharienne aux débuts des temps modernes.* Rabat, Morocco: Institute of African Studies, 1995.

Hiskett, Mervyn. *The Development of Islam in West Africa.* London: Longman, 1984.

Oliver, Roland, and John D. Fage. *A Short History of Africa.* Harmondsworth, U.K.: Penguin Books, 1975.

Saaf, Abdallah, ed. *Le Maroc et l'Afrique aprés l'indépendance.* Rabat, Morocco: Institute of African Studies, 1996.

Willis, John Ralph, ed. *Studies in West African Islamic History*, vol. 1: *The Cultivators of Islam.* London: Frank Cass, 1979.

Yahya, Dahiru. *Morocco in the Sixteenth Century: Problems and Patterns in African Foreign Policy.* Atlantic Highlands, NJ: Humanities Press, 1981.

MOHAMED EL MANSOUR

MOSHOESHOE I

MOSHOESHOE I (1786–1870). Moshoeshoe was born Lepoqo (meaning "disasters") in the village of Menkhoaneng in the Sotho-speaking southern African highveld. His parents were Mokhachane (Libenyane) (1765–1855), a minor Kuena chief, and Kholu, daughter of Ntsukunyane, a neighboring Fokeng chief. From an early age, Moshoeshoe aspired to be a great chief. However, he was an impatient, hot-tempered youth who killed his followers for offenses as trivial as slowness in carrying out his orders. He sought advice from Mohlomi, a doctor, sage, and Kuena kinsman, on how to become a successful leader. Mohlomi counseled Moshoeshoe to be humane and just, to form alliances by marrying into different lineages, and to fight only if peaceful means failed. Mohlomi's advice and Moshoeshoe's own realization that peace, not war, would earn him more followers, changed him into a mature, dignified personality. From 1830 to 1870, he was able to grasp and deal with the complex changes resulting from the interaction of black and white populations as Dutch settlers claimed the land. His firm defense of Sotho speakers who were displaced by these intrusions earned him the respect of contemporary African rulers, colonial officials, and European commentators.

The greatest challenges facing Moshoeshoe during his reign were European settlers' military attempts to conquer and seize Basotho. Britain, the dominant political power in the region, sided with the settlers, owing to economic and political pressures at home. Despite the modernity and sophistication of the British and the settlers' weaponry, Moshoeshoe vanquished an invading British forces in 1852. In two other wars in 1858 and 1865–1867, the settlers failed to defeat him. Such was his diplomatic skill that, by 1868, he was able to pry the British government's loyalty from the settlers' side and bring it firmly onto his side—an act that saved war-weary Basotho from total conquest by the settlers. By doing so, Moshoeshoe achieved his lifelong dream of making an ally of Britain, and securing for Basotho the protection of

Moshoeshoe I (c. 1786–1870). Every March 11, Moshoeshoe Day is a federal holiday celebrated in Lesotho, the area in which the chief was born.

the only superpower then existing. It is therefore not an exaggeration to say that the existence of an independent Lesotho in the early twenty-first century is a result of his statesmanship.

See also **Lesotho: History and Politics.**

BIBLIOGRAPHY

Casalis, Eugene. *The Basutos, or, Twenty-Three Years in South Africa.* Morija, Lesotho: Morija Museum and Archives, 1992.

Ellenberger, D. Fred. *History of the Basuto, Ancient and Modern.* Morija, Lesotho: Morija Museum and Archives, 1993.

Grant, Neville J. H. *Moshoeshoe: Founder of a Nation.* London: Longman, 1981.

Sanders, Peter B. "Sekonyela and Moshweshwe: Failure and Success in the Aftermath of Difaqane." *Journal of African History* 10, no. 3 (1969): 439–455.

Thompson, Leonard. *Survival in Two Worlds: Moshoeshoe of Lesotho, 1786–1870.* Oxford: Clarendon Press, 1975.

MOTLATSI THABANE

MOURNING. *See* Death, Mourning, and Ancestors.

MOVEMENTS, POLITICAL. *See* Government; Independence and Freedom, Early African Writers; Nationalism; Political Science and the Study of Africa.

MOZAMBIQUE

This entry includes the following articles:
GEOGRAPHY AND ECONOMY
SOCIETY AND CULTURES
HISTORY AND POLITICS

GEOGRAPHY AND ECONOMY

Mozambique is situated on the southeast coast of Africa bordering South Africa and Swaziland in the south, Zimbabwe, Zambia, and Malawi in the west, and Tanzania in the north. The country is endowed with abundant land, water, forest, and wildlife resources. Its topography displays three distinct features. First are the coastal areas, rising to 650 feet above sea level, that cover about 42 percent of the country's land, of which over 50 percent is susceptible to flooding (as shown in the disastrous floods in the southern provinces in 2000). Next is the middle plateau (between 650 and 1,625 feet), mostly in the northern region, extending westward to the Zambezi valley and covering about 29 percent of the area. Third is the upland plateau (1,625 to 3,300 feet), which is mostly situated in the northern part and covers some 25 percent of the nation's area. In addition, highland and mountain areas (3,300 feet and above) near the borders with Malawi and Zimbabwe cover 4 percent of the land area.

Climatically, the country is divided into two main regions. North of the Save River, the rainy season lasts from November/December to March/April with annual precipitation ranging between about 39 to 55 inches, but reaching nearly 80 inches in the mountainous regions. South of the Save River the average rainfall is significantly less, about 23 to 31 inches, with even less rain in the

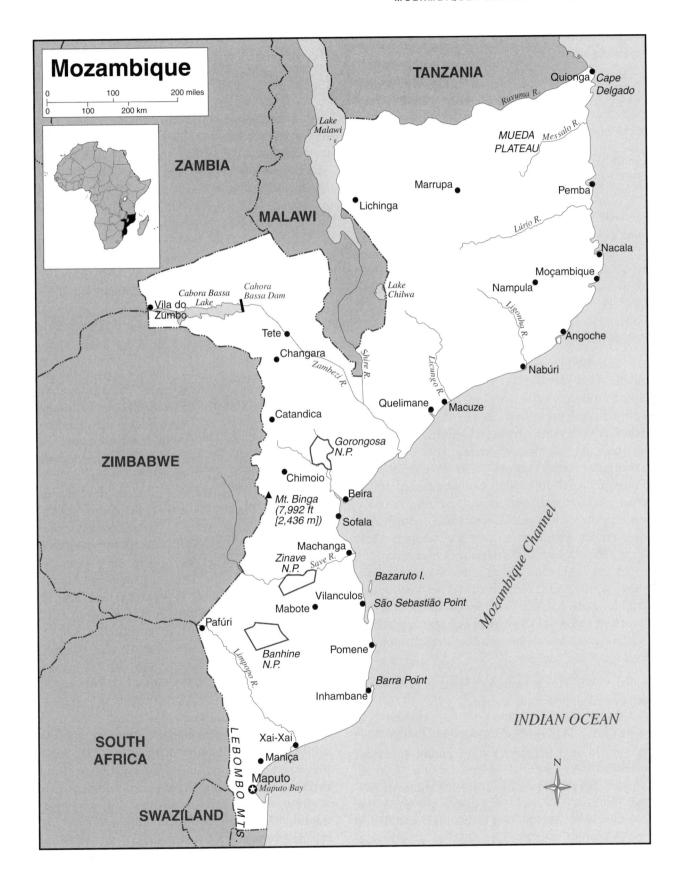

Mozambique

| 0 | 100 | 200 miles |
| 0 | 100 | 200 km |

ZAMBIA

TANZANIA

Quionga · Cape Delgado

Ruvuma R.

Lake Malawi

MUEDA PLATEAU

Messalo R.

MALAWI

Marrupa

Pemba

Lichinga

Lúrio R.

Nacala

Moçambique

Nampula

Cabora Bassa Lake

Cahora Bassa Dam

Vila do Zumbo

Lake Chilwa

Ligonha R.

Angoche

Tete

Zambezi R.

Shire R.

Nabúri

Changara

Licungo R.

Quelimane · Macuze

Catandica

Gorongosa N.P.

ZIMBABWE

Chimoio

Beira

▲ *Mt. Binga (7,992 ft [2,436 m])*

Sofala

Machanga

Zinave N.P.

Save R.

Bazaruto I.

Vilanculos

São Sebastião Point

Mabote

Pafúri

Pomene

Banhine N.P.

Limpopo R.

Barra Point

Inhambane

MOZAMBIQUE CHANNEL

INDIAN OCEAN

SOUTH AFRICA

Xai-Xai

Maniça

LEBOMBO MTS.

Maputo

Maputo Bay

N

SWAZILAND

western regions; long spells of drought occur intermittently there.

Vasco da Gama (1460–1524) claimed this area for the Portuguese empire in 1498, competing with Arab merchants who had traded with the Bantu-speaking coastal populations since the eighth century. Portuguese administrative control never reached far inland until the establishment of António de Oliveira Salazar's (1889–1970) dictatorial Estado Novo in 1926; instead, governments in Lisbon allowed private interests to hold concessions (prazos) to exploit the interior of the country, particularly along the valley of the Zambezi River, the principal waterway flowing through the region. These private merchants sent nearly a half million slaves to Brazil (nearly all of them after 1775), and perhaps as many others into the Indian Ocean trade between the seventeenth and mid-nineteenth centuries.

The Salazar regime in Portugal (1926–1970) modernized colonization in the region and established a mixture of compulsory labor, forced agricultural production, and coerced migrant labor to South African mines (to collect remittances of their earnings there), thus effectively continuing the Portuguese estate system. After World War II, Portugal further intensified its colonization efforts, channeled international capital to Mozambique (in projects such as the Cabora Bassa hydroelectric dam on the middle reaches of the Zambezi), and increased subsidized Portuguese settlement, thus expelling numerous indigenous occupants from their good agricultural lands. The Portuguese regime made few efforts to invest in social infrastructure and sought to extract as much as possible; the living conditions for the Mozambican population remained very poor.

In 1975 Mozambique won independence after an extended liberation struggle (1962–1975) led by the Frente de Libertação de Moçambique (FRELIMO—Mozambique Liberation Front). The majority of the Portuguese settlers, fearing an anticolonial backlash and the Marxist-Leninist doctrine adopted by the new FRELIMO government, fled the country. This rapid withdrawal paralyzed the commercial sector, the civil service, and the health and education systems. The fledgling government intervened by nationalizing land, health care, and education, and attempted to take over operation of the abandoned farms, factories, and companies.

However, FRELIMO's ambitious plans to develop the agricultural sector rapidly through centralized planning and large commercialized state farms were unrealistic and eventually failed.

Mozambique's postindependence economic problems were compounded by deep-rooted unpopularity in many rural areas. In 1977 Resistência Nacional Moçambicana (RENAMO, or Mozambican National Resistance) started a war of destabilization that was sponsored by the white extremist government in Rhodesia and later supported by the apartheid regime in South Africa. This brutal civil war lasted fifteen years and resulted in an estimated one million deaths, over five million displaced people, destruction of infrastructure, and widespread economic and social hardship. The opposing parties signed a peace accord in 1992, and in 1994 Mozambique held its first multiparty elections with FRELIMO winning the majority of votes.

The economy was in ruins as Mozambique emerged from the civil war. In 1992 the per capita GDP was only US$87.00, making the country one of the poorest in the world. Mozambique has experienced unprecedented rates of economic growth since then, albeit from a low starting point, and GDP per capita was estimated in 2006 at US$1,500. One of the features of Mozambique's economic growth is that it has proceeded along relatively diverse lines. Agriculture is still the major employer with over 80 percent of the population working in the sector, although they earned only 32 percent of the GDP (1999) for their efforts. Old labor emigration links with South Africa have re-emerged, and there are an estimated 1 million Mozambicans working across the border illegally and legally. Mozambique is also rich in marine resources, and seafood, particularly prawns, is one of the country's largest exports. With an extensive coastline and wildlife resources inland, tourism is another growing sector of the economy. The year 2000 saw the completion of the MOZAL aluminum smelter, Mozambique's largest foreign (British, South African, and Japanese) investment, not far from the country's capital and largest city, Maputo. Although the plant employs relatively few people, in 2004 aluminum from MOZAL accounted for nearly two thirds of all export revenue. Other growing sectors are mineral extraction and semiprecious stones.

Despite recent growth and often being hailed as one of Africa's economic success stories, Mozambique remains one of the poorest and most aid-dependent countries in the world. It is highly indebted, despite qualifying for International Monetary Fund/World Bank Highly Indebted Poor Countries (HIPC) relief, and international donors and agencies wield considerable power in how the country's economy is managed. The benefits of the economic growth have only reached a small minority of its citizens, and the majority of rural Mozambicans live in poverty. There is the growing problem of unemployment, and the devastating HIV/AIDS pandemic has the real potential to halt any growth. Although Mozambique has escaped war and economic chaos, this troubled country has a long way to go before its people see true prosperity.

See also **Climate; Ecosystems; Gama, Vasco da; International Monetary Fund; Machel, Samora Moises; Mondlane, Eduardo Chivambo; Postcolonialism; World Bank; Zambezi River.**

BIBLIOGRAPHY

Hall, Margaret, and Tom Young. *Confronting Leviathan: Mozambique since Independence.* Athens: Ohio University Press, 1997.

Hanlon, Joseph. *Peace without Profit: How the IMF Blocks Rebuilding in Mozambique.* Oxford: James Currey, 1996.

Isaacman, Allen. *Mozambique: From Colonialism to Revolution, 1900–1982.* Boulder, CO: Westview Press, 1983.

Newitt, Malyn. *A History of Mozambique.* Bloomington: Indiana University Press, 1995.

WILLIAM NORMAN

SOCIETY AND CULTURES

Mozambique is inhabited by approximately 19 million people (2005 estimate), about 70 percent of whom live in rural areas. The national population contains a great diversity of cultures and ethnolinguistic groups. Census data detailing ethnic affiliation have not been collected in Mozambique since the Portuguese colonial era that ended in 1975. Estimates from the 1970 census identified the Makua-Lomwe ethnic group concentrated in the area north of the Zambezi River as the largest (38%); the Thonga living in the area south of the Save River as the second largest (23%); and the

Makonde, Yao, Ngoni, Malawi (or Maravi), Sena, Shona, Chope and Tonga as other groups of politically significant size.

In the nonethnic 1997 census, 23.1 percent of the population stated that they held no religious beliefs, partly reflecting the legacy of Mozambique's recent socialist past. Christianity is the most widely practiced religion, with 23.8 percent of the population identified themselves as Catholics, 17.5 percent as Zionist Christians, and 7.8 percent as Protestants. There is a sizeable number of Muslims (17.8%), mainly from the northern coastal areas influenced by Arab traders prior to the arrival of the Portuguese in the sixteenth century and continuing into the late nineteenth. A further 9.9 percent practice other religions, including indigenous African beliefs centered on deceased ancestors. Rituals and practices associated with these local community spirits are more commonplace than the census data suggest, as many of those who have accepted Christianity continue to respect the influence of their ancestors.

COLONIAL-ERA ETHNOGRAPHIES

There is little depth to the ethnographic literature on the peoples of Mozambique. The Portuguese administration was reluctant to host researchers in rural areas who might question the often harsh colonial policies in force there, as had occurred in neighboring British colonies. Missionaries and administrators, most without academic training, were the main producers of the ethnographic record of the colonial period that does exist. The ethnologist Antonio Jorge Dias (1907–1973) wrote the only ethnography based on substantial field research conducted among a Mozambican people, the northerly Makonde, during the colonial period.

The work of Dias on the Makonde richly describes an agrarian society centered on the Mueda Plateau near the Ruvuma River, Mozambique's border with Tanganyika (present-day Tanzania). In the late 1950s, when Dias studied them, the Makonde traced descent through the mother's line, and young men, upon marriage, took up residence and asserted claims to land in the settlements of their mothers' brothers, their maternal uncles. Scholars, including Dias, however, divided the population of Mozambique into two groupings, with matrilineal peoples such as the Makonde occupying the territory north of the Zambezi, and patrilineal peoples generally occupying the territory to the south. The settlements of the Shona-speaking peoples of central Mozambique, south of the Zambezi, for example, consisted of a male lineage head, his wives and children, and their dependents, thus contrasting sharply with those of the Makonde. The authority of a Shona lineage head rested in his control over the cattle necessary both for the mixed pastoralist-agricultural economy and for the negotiation of marriages.

Dias theorized that the varied kinship systems found in Mozambique represented historical adaptations accomplished by different communities in response to the possibilities afforded them by their natural environments: patrilineal systems tended to emerge where the soil provided a poor base for agriculture but where controllable levels of tsetse fly (a vector for a disease fatal to cattle) made the keeping of bovine livestock possible, requiring warriors, mostly sons, to defend the herd; matrilineal systems predominated where tsetse made cattle raising impossible but where soils provided a rich agricultural substrate. The natural environment was by no means determinant of social organization, however. The Swiss missionary Henri Junod speculated that the Thonga in the far southern parts of the then-colony, among whom he lived in the late nineteenth and early twentieth centuries, had once been a matrilineal people despite the patrilineal forms of organization he witnessed. Continuing to the present day, in fact, prolonged and intensifying exposure of societies everywhere in Mozambique to mercantile capitalism have shifted local social organization toward economic, political, and social practices congruent with patrilineal kinship.

Nature has been no more determining of ethnic identities in Mozambique than of kinship systems; notwithstanding the colonial perspective that took tribal groupings as natural categories. Ethnicity in Mozambique, as elsewhere in the world, has been the dynamic product of peoples' historical engagement with social forces, both local and foreign. Scholars seeking to fill in the ethnographic record on Mozambique consequently look to the histories of its peoples for points of departure. Although delayed by a postindependence government as suspicious of anthropology as its colonial predecessor

had been, the academic project proceeds on the foundation of a historical record generated by historians such as Edward Alpers, Allen Isaacman, Patrick Harries, Leroy Vail, and Landeg White, and the numerous contributors to the three-volume history of Mozambique produced by the history department at the Eduardo Mondlane University in Maputo, all of whom have produced textured social histories of the peoples they have studied.

The earliest residents of the territory were most probably nomadic bands of hunter-gatherers, like the San-speakers found elsewhere in the southern African region into historical times, who shared little in common with any of Mozambique's present-day peoples. According to archaeological evidence, East Bantu agriculturalists began to arrive in the region in small groups around 250 CE. Over the next century and a half, successive waves of migrants either displaced or absorbed earlier residents (including previous migrants) of the areas they came to occupy, laying the foundations of a shared Bantu heritage reflected in the uniformly Bantu contemporary languages of Mozambique. Bantu migrants also brought with them the knowledge of ironworking, allowing them to make tools and to become sedentary farmers. The cultural innovations of these agrarian societies included systems of inheritance, ancestral cults, and the sexual division of labor, and they were able to produce agricultural surpluses and to carry on trade with one another, although on scales limited by the similarities of their economies.

ETHNOHISTORIES

When Portuguese explorers arrived off the coast of eastern Africa around 1500, they found Swahili, Arab, and Indian merchants already trading there for ivory and for gold from the plateau inland. Small-scale chiefdoms had become concentrated into states of increasing dimensions that coordinated caravans to the coast and levied tariffs on the trade routes passing through their territories. Two principal states flanked the middle Zambezi River to the west: the *mwene mutapa* controlled the gold trade in the area between the Zambezi and Save Rivers, and the Malawi (or Marave) exercised dominion over the trade in ivory in the area between the Zambezi and Lake Nyasa (present-day Lake Malawi). Within these states, local chiefs and councils of elders often maintained claims to the lands occupied by their forebears, overseeing their distribution among family members and performing ritual functions to ensure the benevolent oversight of the group's ancestral spirits, but these chiefs and their peoples were subject to demands for tribute from the larger state.

Portuguese interference in the coastal trade after 1525 led to the greater incorporation of the region into the world economy, where ivory and, later, slaves were in increasing demand. The emergence of the Yao ethnic group along the southeastern margins of Lake Nyasa in the seventeenth century was closely bound up with their embrace of caravan trade to the coast that differentiated them from fellow descendants of the Malawi, including the Cewa and Manganja. Headmen of the residential communities—generally the eldest brother of the sorority group (*mbumba*) around which settlements were constituted—who had once controlled the hunt among these predominantly agricultural peoples took responsibility for organizing the caravan. Yao chieftaincies grew in size and strength as they specialized in the overland transport of ivory tusks and slaves gathered by neighboring peoples, and travel to distant lands came to be considered as an essential rite of passage into manhood.

In the eighteenth century, Makua chieftaincies closer to the coast gained increasing power by brokering the commerce in slaves to ports in the vicinity of the island of Mozambique, the nominal administrative seat of the Portuguese officials in the area, thereby procuring arms, ammunition, and powder with which they could sponsor more wide-ranging slaving parties in the interior. Settlements on the periphery of strong chiefdoms, doubtless restive, often entered into mutual security arrangements with those who would otherwise have taken them as captives, further augmenting the power of the influential chiefs (*mwenes*) around whom the Makua ethnic identity was constructed. The small-scale matrilineal origins of these conglomerate communities were preserved in strong female councilors to the mwene (called *apwia-mwene*). In addition to producing militarized, centralized chiefs with expansive tendencies, these reactions to slave trading also created margins around the chiefdoms where fragmented populations moved constantly in search of refuge; from this shared experience, new ethnic identities such as that of the Makonde were born.

In the Zambezi River valley, the Portuguese monarchy granted Crown estates (*prazos de coroa*) in the first half of the seventeenth century in an effort to establish a permanent European presence along the route to the gold of the Mutapa area. As the Portuguese settlers (*prazeiros*) who held these estates attempted to gain hegemony over local sultans and chiefs, however, they formed alliances with local families, through the negotiation of marriages, producing a mixed Afro-Portuguese culture. Although continuing to dwell on European-style estates, prazeiros had limited access to European churches and schools, and as they made more regular use of African languages they became increasingly illiterate. Most eventually adopted African agricultural technologies as well as such local practices as polygyny and beliefs in witchcraft.

Ironically, the trade in slaves from which the Portuguese benefited so greatly—as many as one million people were exported from the area by the Portuguese, Arabs, Indians, Africans, and others over more than a century (from the mid-eighteenth to mid-nineteenth century)—ultimately limited Portuguese influence by empowering African slave-lords in the northern and central Mozambican interior, including later generations of prazeiros who asserted their autonomy from the Portuguese governor. In the eighteenth century, Banyan (Goan Christian) Indian merchants took advantage of Portuguese administrative weakness to establish a stronger presence on the Mozambican coast and even to move into the Makua-speaking interior, where greater Islamization of the population followed.

In southern Mozambique, where the peoples of the region lived in intermediate-sized chieftaincies established in the first half of the second millennium around migrant conquerors from the Sotho- and Shona-speaking areas of the interior, the trade in ivory and slaves was more limited. Dramatic changes would be wrought there, however, by mobile Nguni regiments scattering northward throughout the region in the wake of the disturbances of the 1820s centered on Zulu to the south, in modern Natal. Several Nguni regiments moved through southern Mozambique and settled farther north (creating, for example, the Angoni ethnicity found there today), but the most notable group of raiders was that of the warleader, Soshangane (d. c. 1856), who took up residence in southern central Mozambique near the Save River. At the time of his death in 1858, Soshangane's Gaza empire reached as far north as the Zambezi.

The Gaza Nguni referred to those they had conquered as Tsonga—meaning slave, or servant— and they appropriated their cattle, conscripted their young men into service in the Gaza military regiments, and gave captured women as brides to the warriors. Whereas the Nguni invasion introduced a pronounced class division between the agricultural residents of the southern half of Mozambique and the Nguni warrior elite, the Nguni strategy of integrating the peoples they conquered by claiming local women in marriage led to adoption of the mothers' local cultural practices and languages by the sons who became rulers of the empire. As a result, the Shangaan peoples of the Limpopo River Valley in the far south—originally called so because they had been subjected to the rule of Soshangane—eventually came to be considered as assimilated aristocracy (*mabulundlela*) within the ruling houses of the Gaza empire. The nineteenth century thus saw a final formative round of creating new ethnic communities out of the turbulent flows of people through the region at the time.

Only in the final decade of the nineteenth century and in the first two decades of the twentieth did the Portuguese succeed in subjecting these changing societies of the Mozambican interior to colonial overrule. In doing so, they found allies and military conscripts among smaller populations who had resisted the powerful kingdoms then forming throughout Mozambique, such as the Chopi (Chope) of Inhambane. Notwithstanding this divide and conquer strategy, Portuguese colonialism did little in comparison with other forms of European colonialism to consolidate the identities they found among African populations in Mozambique as rigid tribes. Although stronger senses of modern ethnic affiliations of this stable sort did emerge among many of those forced to leave Mozambique to work abroad, within the colony the Portuguese mobilized labor and collected taxes through localized native authorities (*autoridades gentilicas*). The small scale of these communities, as well as Portuguese oversight of these activities at the level of the local administrative post, eroded the integrity of the nineteenth-century communities and forestalled the emergence of ethnic power

brokers with broad geographical reach. The colonial requirement that religious missions provide education in the Portuguese language in order to encourage the nationalization (meaning lusofication) and cultural assimilation of native populations to the Portuguese Christian civilizing mission also inhibited consolidation of strong ethnic identities in the colony.

SOCIETY AND ECONOMY SINCE INDEPENDENCE

When Mozambique gained independence in 1975, over 90 percent of the Portuguese population, fearing an anticolonial backlash, left the former colony. The Frente de Libertação de Moçambique (FRELIMO) party that had led the struggle for liberation formed a government and sought to create a new society in which neither race nor ethnicity would be salient. With over twelve major languages (or groups of dialects) being used within Mozambique, the potentially divisive issue of language was overcome by adopting Portuguese as the official tongue. FRELIMO foresaw rapid modernization driven by a centralized socialist state as the key to developing the impoverished country it had inherited from the Portuguese. The party and government dismissed the exercise of political authority and religious rituals associated with kin-based social institutions as backwards, and the government undertook an aggressive antiobscurantist campaign in rural areas. Constraints were also applied to Christian and Muslim clerics.

FRELIMO's antiethnic, antireligious nation-building agenda, however, generated considerable hostilities in regions where the party was not well established and alienated traditional authorities who, despite having cooperated with the colonial administration, sometimes retained a degree of legitimacy among their communities. Historians of Mozambique's ensuing civil war (1977–1992) trace the root of the Resistência Nacional de Moçambique (RENAMO) insurgency to Rhodesian and, later, South African attempts to destabilize Mozambique. RENAMO did, however, have substantial ethnic support among the Ndau subgroup of the Shona people in the central provinces and among Makua-speaking groups in northern Mozambique. Although neither the war nor the elections that followed the peace agreement can be characterized as tribally determined, RENAMO has achieved electoral majorities in the

Republic of Mozambique

Population:	20,905,585 (2007 est.)
Area:	801,590 sq. km (309,495 sq. mi.)
Official language:	Portuguese
Languages:	Portuguese, Sena, Shona, Makua, Thonga, Shangana, Swahili
National currency:	metical
Principal religions:	Christian 49%, Muslim 18%, indigenous African and other beliefs 33%
Capital:	Maputo (est. pop. 1,200,000 in 2006)
Other urban centers:	Beira, Matola, Nampula, Quelimane, Tete, Nacala
Annual rainfall:	1,420 mm (55 in.) in center, less in the north and south
Principal geographical features:	*Mountains:* Livingstone-Nyasa Highlands, Tete Highlands, Gorongosa Highlands, Lebombo Mountains, Mount Namuli, Mount Binga, Serra Zuira, Serra Mecula, Mount Jesi, Mount Mabu, Mount Chiperone *Lakes:* Malawi (Nyasa), Cabora Bassa, Chilwa, Amaramba, Chuita, Barride Chicamba Real, Marrangua, Barride de Massingir *Rivers:* Zambezi, Messinge, Chiulezi, Lugenda, Lurio, Maracoleta, Luleio, Limpopo, Gorongosa, Changane, Save, Revue, Pungue, Rovuma, Licungo, Buzi, Molocue, Monapo, Messalu, Ligonha
Economy:	*GDP per capita:* US$1,500 (2006)
Principal products and exports:	*Agricultural:* cotton, cashew nuts, sugarcane, tea, cassava (tapioca), corn, coconuts, sisal, citrus and tropical fruits, potatoes, sunflowers, beef, poultry *Manufacturing:* food, beverages, chemicals (fertilizer, soap, paints), aluminum, petroleum products, textiles, cement, glass, asbestos, tobacco *Mining:* tantalite, some gold, mineral sands, titanium, iron ore, nepheline syenite, oil and natural gas
Government:	Independence from Portugal, 1975. Constitution, 1975. New constitution approved in 1990. Multiparty democracy. President elected for up to 3 consecutive 5-year terms by direct universal suffrage. 250-member Assembleia Nacional elected for 5-year terms by direct universal suffrage. President appoints prime minister and cabinet. The office of prime minister was created in 1986. For purposes of local government there are 10 provinces headed by elected local assemblies, and each province is subdivided into districts.
Heads of state since independence:	1975–1986: President Samora Machel 1986–2005: President Joaquim Alberto Chissano 2005–: President Armando Guebuza
Armed forces:	President is commander in chief. 2-year compulsory military service. *Army:* 30,000 *Navy:* 750 *Air force:* 4,000
Transportation:	*Rail:* 3,512 km (2,177 mi.) *Ports:* Maputo, Quelimane, Mozambique, Nacala, Beira, Inhambane, Porto Amelia *Roads:* 30,400 km (18,890 mi.), 19% paved *National airline:* Linhas Aereas de Moçambique *Airports:* International facilities at Aeroporto International de Maputo. Other main airports at Beira and Mozambique. Numerous other airports and airstrips along the coast and in the interior.
Media:	2 daily newspapers: *Diario de Moçambique, Noticias.* 2 weeklies: *Domingo, Tempo.* Numerous other publications. Approximately 30 books are published annually. Radio is nationalized, provided through Radio Mozambique, Radio Pax, Emissora do Aero Clube. Televisão Experimental was established in 1981.
Literacy and education:	*Total literacy rate:* 53.6% (2006). Education is compulsory for 7 years. Since the end of the civil war, the government has placed a strong emphasis on education, particularly primary. Postsecondary education provided at Universidade Eduardo Mondlane, Centro de Estudos Africanos, Instituto de Línguas, Instituto do Desenvolvimento da Educação, Instituto–Ciencias da Saúde, Instituto Nacional de Investigação Agronómica, University Teaching Hospital.

1994, 1999 and 2004 general elections in the provinces of Sofala, Zambezia, Manica and Nampula, where Makua and Ndau are most numerous.

A surge in ethnographic research in Mozambique since the end of the war, in keeping with the global trend, has shifted from attempting to study entire societies in terms of ethnicity to looking at specific issues and themes within them. For example, following the liberalization of the Mozambican political system and the move toward multiparty democracy, the role of so-called traditional authorities has attracted interest. Harry West and Scott Kloeck-Jensen (1999) examined whether traditional authorities in the rural areas of contemporary

Mozambique have popular political legitimacy or are simply relics of the colonial past. West and Kloeck-Jensen warn against the tendency to generalize and argue that those claiming to be traditional authorities have little historical legitimacy, but must be seen as political actors whose claims of tradition and to power must be understood within their own local political contexts.

The role of women in Mozambican societies, having been overlooked in the classic ethnographies, has become another focus of contemporary research. Kathleen Sheldon's book (2002) addresses this gender imbalance by documenting the changing role of Mozambican women in households and in economic production over the last 150 years and charting the important role that women have played in political life in Mozambique since the beginning of the liberation struggle in the 1960s.

Arguably the most important change that has followed the end of the war in Mozambique has been the shift from an interventionist socialist state to market capitalism. Huge economic investment has occurred, but it has been unevenly distributed among the country's peoples. The principal beneficiaries have been the urban-based elites, whereas the vast rural majority continues to live in poverty. This economic differentiation is the starkest division that exists between the peoples of Mozambique today, and addressing these inequalities remains the biggest challenge facing the nation.

See also **Bantu, Eastern, Southern, and Western, History of (1000 BCE to 1500 CE); Colonial Policies and Practices; Ethnicity; Gender; Household and Domestic Groups; Machel, Samora Moises; Postcolonialism; Slave Trades; Zambezi River.**

BIBLIOGRAPHY

Alpers, Edward A. *Ivory and Slaves: Changing Pattern of International Trade in East Central Africa to the Later Nineteenth Century.* Berkeley: University of California Press, 1975.

Departamento de História. *História de Moçambique,* 3 vols. 2nd edition. Maputo, Mozambique: Tempo, sob autorizacção da Universidade Eduardo Mondlane, 1988–1993.

Dias, A. Jorge; Margot Dias; and Manuel Guerreiro. *Os Macondes de Moçambique* 4 vols. Lisbon, Portugal: Centro de Estudos de Antropologia Cultural, 1964–1970.

Geffray, Christian. *La cause des armes au Mozambique: Anthropologie d'une guerre civile.* Paris: Karthala, 1990.

Geffray, Christian. *Ni père ni mère: Critique de la parenté, le cas Makhuwa.* Paris: Seuil, 1990.

Harries, Patrick. *Work, Culture, and Identity: Migrant Laborers in Mozambique and South Africa, c. 1860–1910.* Portsmouth, NH: Heinemann, 1994.

Isaacman, Allen. *Mozambique: The Africanization of a European Institution, the Zambesi Prazos, 1750–1902.* Madison: University of Wisconsin Press, 1972.

Junod, Henri Alexandre. *The Life of a South African Tribe.* New Hyde Park, NY: University Books, 1962.

Pitcher, M. Anne. *Transforming Mozambique: The Politics of Privatization, 1975–2000.* Cambridge, U.K.: Cambridge University Press, 2006.

Rita-Ferreira, Antônio. *Agrupamento e caracterização étnica does indígenas de Moçambique.* Lisbon: n.p., 1958.

Rita-Ferreira, Antônio. *Povos de Moçambique: História e cultura.* Porto, Portugal: Afrontamento, 1975.

Sheldon, Kathleen E. *Pounders of Grain: A History of Women, Work, and Politics in Mozambique.* Portsmouth, NH: Heinemann, 2002.

Smith, Alan Kent. "The Peoples of Southern Mozambique: An Historical Survey." *Journal of African History* 14, no. 4 (1973): 565–580.

Vail, Leroy, and Landeg White. *Capitalism and Colonialism in Mozambique: A Study of Quelimane District.* Minneapolis: University of Minnesota Press, 1980.

West, Harry, and Scott Kloeck-Jenson. "Bewixt and Between: 'Traditional Authority' and Democratic Decentralization in Post-War Mozambique." *African Affairs* 98, no. 393 (1999): 455–484.

WILL NORMAN

HISTORY AND POLITICS

The modern Mozambican state has its roots in a radical nationalist movement that developed in the 1950s, resisting Portuguese colonial rule. Long before this there had been armed rebellions against the Portuguese colonial authorities, but these were regional rather than national in character. Groups of workers staged strikes and various peasant communities resisted forced labor, but in the first half of the twentieth century a unitary, independent Mozambican state had been little more than the dream of a few intellectuals.

Nationalist consciousness and organized resistance on a national scale was slow in developing, mainly as a result of Portuguese repression of political activity and of the enormous difficulties of communication in a country with many indigenous languages and few opportunities for travel, contact, and the sharing of ideas. An early pathbreaking organization was the Nucleus of Secondary Students of Mozambique (NESAM), created in Lourenco Marques in 1949 by a new generation of students who were fluent in Portuguese. One of the founders of NESAM, Eduardo Mondlane, wrote later: "Under cover of social and cultural activities, [it] conducted among the youth a political campaign to spread the idea of national independence and encourage resistance to the cultural subjugation which the Portuguese imposed" (*The Struggle for Mozambique*, 113).

By cementing personal contacts, NESAM established a nationwide network of communications that extended among former members, as well as those still in school, and that could be used by a future underground. NESAM was significant not only for its forthright nationalistic stance, but also because it produced some of the most important Mozambican political leaders of the second half of the century who gained experience and contacts through it. They included Mondlane, who would lead the independence war from 1964 until his death in 1969; Joaquim Chissano (b.1939), who became president of Mozambique in 1986; and Pascoal Mocumbi (b.1941), Chissano's prime minister.

The students were strongly influenced by nationalist intellectuals, such as the poets Marcelino dos Santos (b.1929), José Craveirinha (1922–2003), and Noémia de Sousa (1926–2003). Then came separate attempts to create a nationwide radical nationalist movement by Mozambicans working in neighboring countries. Three main exile groups were formed in the early 1960s in Rhodesia, Malawi, Tanganyika (present-day Tanzania), and Kenya. These groups had predominantly ethnic or regional bases in the adjoining areas of Mozambique and, being exiled in different countries, offered little hope for the creation of a genuine nationalist front. But when Tanganyika became independent from Britain, all three moved their headquarters to Dar es Salaam.

It was there, on June 25, 1962, that they came together to form FRELIMO (Frente de Libertação de Moçambique) with the blessing of Julius Nyerere, the Tanganyikan independence leader. But the rivalries between the groups were bitter, and no one party would accept the leadership of another. They found a means to unify under a universally respected and internationally experienced outsider during the first FRELIMO congress in September 1962. Eduardo Mondlane was elected president. By then an anthropologist and sociologist, with a Ph.D. from Northwestern University in the United States, he was not associated with any of the exiled parties. He had worked as a research officer in the trusteeship department of the United Nations, preparing background papers on the trust territories of Tanganyika, Cameroon, and Southwest Africa.

The movement he headed was united in name but not in practice. Mondlane, Joaquim Chissano, Marcelino dos Santos, and other intellectuals soon learned that some of the founders still saw the independence movement from narrowly ethnic points of view and did not grasp the potential efficacy of a front that embraced all Mozambicans. In addition, some saw the struggle as a war against the whites, a racialist view that Mondlane did not share. Another bone of contention was what form the fight for independence would take. The first congress declared that all means of struggle would be used, which meant that they would resort to violence unless the Portuguese agreed to negotiate independence peacefully. Some of the former exiles were unprepared for anything except the peaceful resistance they had witnessed succeeding in eastern Africa and Malawi.

Some of these members of the three former proto-nationalist groups abandoned FRELIMO and tried to form new groups dedicated to their diverging strategies, but their efforts were largely in vain. As it turned out, the Portuguese government refused all FRELIMO's offers of negotiation. Soon after the foundation of FRELIMO, authorities arrested thousands of people in Mozambique because of their alleged support for the movement. In January 1963, Mondlane began sending recruits to Algeria for military training. A second group that included a young man named Samora Machel, who would become the independent Mozambique's first president, went for training later in the year. On September 25, 1964, Mondlane proclaimed the beginning of the armed struggle for national independence. He was not giving the Portuguese a polite warning: FRELIMO fighters fired the first shots the same day.

THE INDEPENDENCE WAR

FRELIMO's plan was to launch a widespread popular uprising. Clandestine militants had been sent to seven of the nine provinces, covering the south, center, and north of the country, to mobilize the rural residents of the colony for war. Soon, however, this plan began to crumble. Before the end of 1964, guerrilla fronts that had opened in the central Tete and Zambezia provinces were forced to close. It had been thought that Zambia and Malawi, with the coming of independence in these countries, would become rear bases for FRELIMO fighters in Zambezia and Tete. But this did not happen. Zambian independence was still being consolidated, and President Hastings Banda of Malawi openly collaborated with the Portuguese.

The situation in the south was even worse. The authorities in South Africa and Rhodesia, and the British police in Swaziland, prevented arms supplies from getting through and assisted in catching young Mozambican patriots as they slipped across the border en route to Tanzania to volunteer for military training. By the end of 1964, fifteen hundred FRELIMO sympathizers had been arrested. By 1965, the war had been confined to the two northern provinces of Cabo Delgado and Niassa, separated from Tanzania by the Ruvuma River. The Cabo Delgado front was a classic people's war. Just before the struggle began, fifteen thousand Mozambicans fled across the Ruvuma to escape the Portuguese repression. When the flight stopped, the people moved into Mozambican guerrilla-controlled areas. The people were no longer forced to produce cash crops and were able to grow food for themselves and the guerrillas. Liberated areas were rapidly established.

Niassa posed far more serious problems for the movement. This province is about the size of England and at the time had a population of a little more than a quarter of a million. A mobile guerrilla army such as FRELIMO needed food supplies from the peasants, but residents in the region were few and far between. Nevertheless, the struggle advanced. In 1968, FRELIMO reopened its front in the western region of Tete province, crossing in from a now stronger and more confident Zambia. With its military advance, FRELIMO developed egalitarian economic policies and social services for its expanding liberated areas. FRELIMO leaders were forbidden to have employees, and they established rural clinics, schools, and orphanages that provided their services for free. Collective crop production became the norm. A socialist orientation was apparent, if not stated.

A massive setback for FRELIMO came in February 1969, when Eduardo Mondlane was assassinated by a book bomb delivered to him at his office in Dar es Salaam. Tanzanian police investigated the case with the help of Interpol and concluded that the bomb had been sent by the Portuguese secret police, with the help of traitors inside FRELIMO. After a brief internal struggle, Samora Machel, the movement's military commander, was elected president of FRELIMO in 1970. Under his leadership, the guerrillas thrust south across the Zambezi River, into the central heartland of Manica and Sofala.

By 1973, many Portuguese military officers were tired of fighting what increasingly appeared to be hopeless wars in Mozambique, Angola, and Guinea-Bissau. Plotting began, and on April 25, 1974, the Armed Forces Movement overthrew the fascist government in Lisbon, restoring democracy and paving the way for independence for Portugal's African colonies. On the seventh of September that year, at a ceremony in Lusaka, the new Portuguese government agreed to hand over power to FRELIMO, and a transitional government was set up with Joaquim Chissano as prime minister. Independence day was set for June 25, 1975. Machel stayed outside Mozambique during the transition, returning in May to make a triumphal tour of the country and to be sworn in as president of the People's Republic of Mozambique on independence day.

FRELIMO came to power on the crest of a wave of popular support so high that a one-party state was inevitable. Single-party governance was nothing new for Mozambicans, who had never been given the chance to vote in multiparty elections in the past. They were happy, and the international community offered no protest. The new government had support across a broad international spectrum. The Soviet bloc and China, which had provided military hardware and training for the guerrillas, and the Scandinavian countries and Holland, which had given humanitarian assistance, were particularly delighted. Europe and North America in general were supportive.

Looking on apprehensively, however, were the white minority regimes of Rhodesia and South Africa. FRELIMO was allied with the liberation movements active in their own countries, and Mozambique's first cabinet's inclusion of people of all races did little to alleviate their anxiety. That anxiety, and the concomitant security threat, were clear enough to the new government in Lourenço Marques, soon to be renamed Maputo. But FRELIMO faced more pressing problems at home.

The Mozambicans inherited a bankrupt country. Colonial Mozambique could not feed itself and had imported food from both South Africa and Rhodesia. The colony had run a balance of payments deficit every year after 1957. By 1970, exports covered less than half of the cost of imports, and the annual trade deficit had grown to US$50 million. A small industrial base included an oil refinery, sugar and cashew processing plants, and textile, chemical, and metal industries. But the industries were not integrated and were largely dependent on imported raw materials. The industrial base, as well as agricultural marketing, had been held tightly in Portuguese hands. Virtually all skilled jobs had been reserved for the Portuguese, while the Mozambicans were left with one of the lowest educational levels in the world: 90 percent illiteracy.

With FRELIMO's victory, 90 percent of the two hundred thousand Portuguese residents in the colony had fled in panic, leaving behind half-finished apartment blocks and expensive, uninstalled new machinery. Some simply left, but others sabotaged the economy before they went. They killed cattle, disabled machinery, and smuggled capital out of the country. Thus, 1975 to 1977 was a period of desperately trying to keep the economy going, with the aid of workers' committees in the workplace. In rural areas the larger settler farms were abandoned, and the trading network collapsed. Few industries were nationalized as a policy, but the government took over all the abandoned enterprises—mostly small businesses and shops. Run-down larger firms were increasingly "intervened," a process similar to bankruptcy under which the firm remained officially private but the government appointed the management. By 1980 the state owned the bulk of the economy, but in some areas, such as textiles, agriculture, and banking, the state and private enterprises were competing. During these heady revolutionary days,

reliable statistics were hard to come by. It appears that during 1974–1976, Mozambique's total payments balanced for the first time in twenty years. Exports had dropped, but imports had dropped farther because of the industrial collapse and the drop in demand for imported consumer goods after the Portuguese left.

Alongside the economic reorganization of the period, dramatic political events were taking place. On March 3, 1976, Machel's government closed the border with Rhodesia, in compliance with United Nations sanctions that the Portuguese had never observed. As Rhodesia was dependent on rail and road links running through Mozambique to ports on the Indian Ocean, this ended its use of the Beira and Maputo ports, a serious blow to a landlocked economy. After his border-closure speech, Machel allowed the armed Zimbabwean liberation movement to resume using facilities in western Mozambique. In 1972, the Zimbabwe African National Union (ZANU) had started to move men and arms into Rhodesia over the border from FRELIMO's liberated areas, but this support had been suspended because of peace moves in the region. Machel's decisions changed the face of southern Africa. The relentless assault on the Rhodesians by ZANU forces operating out of bases in Mozambique played a major part in the winning of Zimbabwean independence in 1980.

Even before the outset of this conflict, the Rhodesians had been involved in the creation of a new force that would wreak havoc in Mozambique: the Mozambique National Resistance (RENAMO). Between 1976 and 1980, RENAMO attacks were pinpricks in remote areas that caused no serious problems for Mozambique. The Rhodesians used RENAMO as a backup for their own operations against Mozambique and ZANU. Ken Flower, head of the Rhodesian Central Intelligence Organization (CIO), explained the origins of RENAMO in an interview three months before his death in July 1987. "I myself went twice to see the Portuguese Prime Minister on that subject in 1971 and 1972 and got only half-hearted acceptance. But still, they allowed us, as it were, to do our own thing. And we in turn [developed] this movement, which we ourselves generated, it is true, but to a certain extent was self-generating, and we called it then the Mozambique Resistance.... Certainly, we armed them" (Human Rights Watch, 1992).

It was a low-key operation, but the picture changed in 1980 when Rhodesia gained independence as Zimbabwe, and there was no place for RENAMO on Zimbabwean soil. Ken Flower asked the South Africans to assume sponsorship of RENAMO, and they agreed. Machel's government was either unaware of this development, or considered RENAMO an insignificant threat. With Zimbabwe independent and the conflict apparently over, Mozambique turned its attention to the economy. In 1981 the government unveiled a ten-year plan that called for US$10 billion in finance for big development projects, including more investment in heavily mechanized state farms that were already buckling under their own weight, becoming liabilities rather than a boost to the economy.

Although the government concentrated on the state farming sector, it paid scant attention to the peasants—the majority of the population—who found few consumer goods to buy in rural shops. The peasants stopped producing surpluses and this withdrawal from the market, coupled with a devastating drought between 1982 and 1984, led to a severe economic depression. By the start of the drought, RENAMO had increased its strength from between five hundred and one thousand members to eight thousand in two years, and was receiving ample supplies and training from the South Africans. It was regularly resupplied by air and sea from South Africa to such an extent that, according to some military experts, it was better equipped than the Mozambican army. RENAMO carried out a major military onslaught, claiming it was fighting an oppressive regime. A major focus for RENAMO was FRELIMO's adoption of Marxism-Leninism as its ideology at a congress in 1977.

THE PEACE PROCESS

In 1984 Machel and South African president Pieter Willem Botha (1916–2006) signed the Nkomati Accord, a nonaggression pact under which South Africa was to end its support for RENAMO and Mozambique was to ban African National Congress guerrillas from using its territory as a base. Most analysts believe that Mozambique stuck to its side of the bargain whereas South Africa did not. South African foreign minister Roelof (Pik) Botha (b. 1932) admitted as much in 1985. The war escalated and in 1986 Mozambique suffered another blow. While returning from a summit in Zambia on the nineteenth of October, Machel's plane crashed into a hillside just inside South Africa, killing the president and thirty-four others. There were widespread allegations at the time that the South Africans had lured the plane off course with a phony radio beacon. Joaquim Chissano, foreign minister since independence, took office in November.

By late 1988 it had become clear that there was no military solution to the war. With Chissano's permission, a delegation of Mozambican Catholic and Anglican bishops traveled to Kenya, where they met two senior RENAMO leaders. The churchmen returned to Maputo to tell Chissano that they believed RENAMO too was tired of the war, and that peace negotiations were possible. Proximity talks continued until 1990. In that year, Chissano unveiled a new, multiparty constitution, and in July the first round of direct negotiations between the government and RENAMO began in Rome. On the thirtieth of November the new constitution came into effect, and the People's Republic of Mozambique became the Republic of Mozambique.

In October, 1992 the two sides signed an agreement ending the war. A United Nations peacekeeping force was sent to supervise the peace process that ended with general and presidential elections in October 1994. FRELIMO won an overall majority in the parliament, the Assembly of the Republic, and Chissano defeated RENAMO leader Afonso Dhlakama (b. 1953) in the presidential poll. The United Nations declared the election free and fair.

The total cost of the war to Mozambique is beyond calculation. Tens of thousands were killed in the fighting, and far larger numbers died from ensuing hunger and disease. One estimate of the total number of the war dead is six hundred thousand. Mozambique was left bankrupt, and the government wholly dependent on foreign aid. In March 1996, the Bank of Mozambique said that the country's foreign debt was US$5.4 billion. Shortly before Machel's death in 1986, the government decided to move away from centralized state planning and build a market economy. The following year the World Bank's Structural Adjustment Program was adopted. Implementation was accompanied by widespread privatization, massive currency devaluations, growing unemployment, and the spread of corruption.

The transition from a socialist agenda to capitalism caused considerable hardships. The state itself was an agent of reform in the 1980s and 1990s when privatization and democratization transformed Mozambique. In subsequent elections, FRELIMO has retained its majority in parliament and has thwarted efforts of RENAMO, the main opposition party. Chissano was reelected president in 1999, and in the 2004 national election FRELIMO's candidate, Armando Guebuza (b. 1943), succeeded Chissano as president with 63 percent of all votes. Once again, the people of Mozambique look to FRELIMO for a better future.

See also **Banda, Ngwazi Hastings Kamuzu; Colonial Policies and Practices: Portuguese; Dar es Salaam; Machel, Samora Moises; Malawi: History and Politics; Maputo; Military Organizations: Guerrilla Forces; Mondlane, Eduardo Chivambo; Nyerere, Julius Kambarage; Postcolonialism; South Africa, Republic of: History and Politics (1850-2006); Tanzania: History and Politics; United Nations; World Bank; Zimbabwe, Great.**

BIBLIOGRAPHY

Christie, Iain. *Machel of Mozambique.* Harare, Zimbabwe: Simbabwe Publishing House, 1988.

Conspicuous Destruction: War, Famine, and the Reform Process in Mozambique. New York: Human Rights Watch, 1992.

Hall, Margaret, and Tom Young. *Confronting Leviathan: Mozambique Since Independence.* Athens: Ohio University Press, 1997.

Manning, Carrie L. *The Politics of Peace in Mozambique: Post-Conflict Democratization, 1992–2000.* Westport, CT: Praeger Publishers, 2002.

Mondlane, Eduardo. *The Struggle for Mozambique*, 2nd edition. London: St. Martin's Press, 1983.

Munslow, Barry. *Mozambique: The Revolution and Its Origins.* London: Longman Group United Kingdom, 1983.

Pitcher, M. Anne. *Transforming Mozambique: The Politics of Privatization, 1975–2000.* Cambridge, U.K.: Cambridge University Press, 2003.

Sheldon, Kathleen E. *Pounders of Grain: A History of Women, Work, and Politics in Mozambique.* Portsmouth, NH: Heinemann, 2002.

IAN CHRISTIE
REVISED BY ELIZABETH MACGONAGLE

MSWATI II (1826–1868).

Mswati II was the first son and heir of King Sobhuza I of the Swazi, the founder of Lobamba City (present-day as Old Lobamba, in Swaziland). Assuming the kingship in 1839, he gained fame throughout southern Africa as a great soldier during the widespread violence generally known as the Mfecane, second only to the Zulu leader Shaka. He modeled his own armies after the efficient Zulu regiments, recruiting non-Swazi fighters, including Sotho- and Nguni-speakers, to fight for him. In part due to the coeval decline of the Zulu empire, Mswati was successful in his raids of nearby Zulu territories, as well as his domination of other surrounding terrain. His kingdom came to be known as Swaziland, after a European corruption of his name (Swazi).

By exerting his influence through diplomacy with the Europeans advancing into the region in the 1840s, Mswati avoided conflict with the bordering South African Republic and the province of Natal, and sent his soldiers to settle disputes among neighboring chiefs. He signed a nonbelligerence treaty with the Afrikaner Voortrekkers who then occupied the South African Republic in the high veld, and openly defended his own kingdom against European influences. Mswati died in Hhohho in 1868. His son, Mbandzeni (1855–1889), succeeded him and, through a series of grazing and mineral concessions to Europeans, began to lose control of Swaziland; the kingdom became a British protectorate in 1893, and a High Commission Territory in 1902.

See also **Shaka Zulu; Swaziland: History and Politics.**

BIBLIOGRAPHY

Bonner, Philip. "Mswati II, c. 1826–65." In *Black Leaders in Southern African History*, ed. Christopher Saunders. London: Heinemann Educational, 1979.

SARAH VALDEZ

MUBARAK, HUSNI (1928–).

Born in Minufiya province, Egypt, Husni Mubarak joined the Egyptian Air Force Academy in 1950 and later received further training in the Soviet Union. In 1972 as commander of the air force and deputy

Husni Mubarak (1928–) with Israeli prime minister Ehud Olmert (1945–). The Egyptian president condemned an Israeli raid in the West Bank, pushed Israel to hold talks with Syria, and urged it to pursue peace with the Palestinians during a joint press conference following a meeting in Sharm el-Sheikh, Egypt, January 4, 2007. AP Images

minister of war, he planned Egypt's opening moves in the 1973 Arab-Israeli war. In 1975 he became vice president under Anwar al-Sadat. Following Sadat's assassination by Islamic radicals on October 14, 1981, he became president. Since then, his major achievement has been to balance maintaining relations with Israel while sustaining Egypt's role as the most influential of Arab state. He has accomplished this mainly through the suppression of internal dissent.

The rise of radical Islamic movements appeared to weaken his power base in the 1990s, but this threat has been largely contained. In spite of sporadic efforts by the United States and Europe to promote democracy and civil society, Mubarak's rule has become increasingly autocratic. He won single-candidate reelections in 1987, 1993, and 1999 and, following international pressure, asked parliament to permit multi-party elections in 2005, which he also won by an ample margin amid accusations of widespread electoral fraud. His son, Gamal Mubarak (b. 1963), appears his likely successor.

See also **Civil Society; Egypt, Modern; Sadat, Anwar al-.**

BIBLIOGRAPHY

Marsot, Afaf Lutfi Al-Sayyid. *A History of Egypt: From the Arab Conquest to the Present*, 2nd edition. Cambridge, U.K.: Cambridge University Press, 2007.

Tripp, Charles, and Roger Owen, eds. *Egypt under Mubarak.* London: Routledge, 1989.

DALE F. EICKELMAN

MUGABE, ROBERT (1924–). A member of the Shona ethnic cluster, which comprises roughly 80 percent of the population of Zimbabwe, Mugabe was born at the Kutanma Catholic Mission at Zvimba, Rhodesia, and attended a Jesuit school there. He became a teacher and worked in Ghana when it became the first state in sub-Saharan Africa to free itself from colonial rule. There he married his Ghanaian wife, Sally Hayfron. After their marriage in 1961 the couple returned to what was then white-settler-controlled Southern Rhodesia and entered politics.

When his party, the Zimbabwe African Peoples Union (ZAPU), split along ethnic lines, he stayed

Robert Mugabe (1924–). Zimbabwe president Robert Mugabe delivers a speech during Armed Forces Day commemorations in Harare, August 15, 2006. Mugabe vowed to clamp down on corruption in his ailing economy, accusing Zimbabweans of falling under the spell of greed. AP IMAGES

Mugabe retained part of Rhodesian prime minister Smith's constitution that allowed him to appoint part of the legislature, which continues to ensure that his party dominates the parliament. He faces no real opposition from within his party because it is riven by factionalism, which runs along both ethnic and regional lines. One focus for this factionalism is rivalry to be named as Mugabe's successor, whom Mugabe had not chosen by mid-2007. That there were no public calls for him to nominate one was an indication of his great personal power within the party—he has made it clear that he does not wish to nominate a successor or to retire soon. It is also possible that he has allowed the party to remain weak so that his own influence within the party would be greater. Mugabe was re-elected to office in 2002. In March 2007, the ZANU-PF central committee chose Mugabe as their candidate for the 2008 election.

See also **Zimbabwe: History and Politics.**

BIBLIOGRAPHY

Chan, Stephen. *Robert Mugabe: A Life of Power and Violence.* Ann Arbor, University of Michigan Press, 2003.

Smith, David; Colin Simpson; and Ian Davies. *Mugabe.* London: Sphere Books, 1981.

ALEXANDER GOLDMAN

with the Shona-dominated Zimbabwe African National Union (ZANU). Mugabe was charged by the Central African Federation authorities with "subversive speech" in 1963 and fled into exile in Tanzania. He returned and was jailed in 1964. He spent approximately ten years in detention while Ian Smith and his white administration ruled Southern Rhodesia; their rule brought an international boycott and sanctions, which eventually drove Smith from power.

As leader of ZANU-PF (ZANU-Patriotic Front) Mugabe won Zimbabwe's first free elections, which were held in 1980. The only effective opposition came from the minority Ndebele party, Joshua Nkomo's ZAPU. Their political rivalry deteriorated into civil war that ended with Nkomo's surrender. Throughout his career, Mugabe has incorporated rivals into his government; Nkomo became a vice president of Zimbabwe.

MUHAMMAD VI (1963–). Muhammad VI became king of Morocco on July 30, 1999, a week after the death of his father, Hassan II. Like his father, Muhammad VI was educated in a palace school with fourteen classmates carefully chosen to represent a cross-section of Moroccan society, including Berbers, Arabs, and the sons of urban merchants, a rural preacher from the pre-Saharan south, a judge of Berber origin, and a palace gardener. These classmates continued their studies with the crown prince at Muhammad V University, and many occupied significant posts in the Moroccan government.

Soon after his coronation, Muhammad VI announced on television that his priority was to reduce poverty and corruption. He began to visit all parts of the country to initiate development projects, including the Rif and northern Morocco,

Muhammad VI (Ben Al-Hassan; 1963–). Upon taking the crown, Muhammad VI promised to battle poverty and corruption in Morocco while creating jobs and improving human rights. In 2004, he created a new family code, which granted more power to Moroccan women. AP IMAGES

regions neglected by his father. Muhammad VI is a strong advocate of an expanded civil society. He improved the "transparency" of Moroccan elections; in January 2004 established a "truth" commission (Instance Equité et Réconciliation) to recognize human rights abuses committed from the 1960s through the 1980s and to compensate victims; and in February 2004 implemented a new family code, the *Mudawwana*, which significantly improved the status of women.

See also **Hasan II of Morocco; King Lists and Chronologies; Kings and Kingdoms; Morocco.**

BIBLIOGRAPHY

El Ghissassi, Hakim. *Regard sur le Maroc de Mohammed VI.* Paris: Michel Lafon, 2006.

Tuquoi, Jean-Pierre. *Majesté, je dois beaucoup à votre père … France-Maroc, une affaire de famille.* Paris: Albin Michel, 2006.

DALE F. EICKELMAN

MUHAMMAD ʿABDALLAH HASAN. *See* Hasan, Muhammad ʿAbdallah.

MUHAMMAD AHMAD AL-MAHDI. *See* Ahmad, Mahdi Muhammad.

MUHAMMAD AL-AMIN AL-KANEMI. *See* Kanemi, Muhammad al-Amin al-.

MUKHTAR, SIDI AL- (1729–1811). Descended from a prominent scholarly and saintly lineage, the Sufi scholar and leader Sidi al-Mukhtar (also known as Sidi al-Mukhtar al-Kunti) is considered by many Muslims to be the most important *mujaddid*, or rejuvenator of Islam, to appear in the central Sahara during the eighteenth century. He was a prolific scholar, authoring more than eighty works, and was recognized as a *wali* ("friend of God") whose *baraka*, or spiritual grace, was said to protect all those who placed themselves under his spiritual authority. He was acclaimed as the shaikh of the Qadiriyya Sufi order in the central Sahara and was the founder of his own branch of that order, known as the Qadiriyya-Mukhtariyya. Through the expansion of this Sufi order, made possible by the renown of his scholarship and his spiritual stature, he built a network of clientage links with Muslim scholars that extended his religious authority throughout the region and into Sudanic western Africa.

Al-Mukhtar was the first Muslim leader in the region to encourage a sense of exclusive identity in a Sufi order; he claimed that the Qadiriyya-Mukhtariyya was the only "pure" Muslim community that existed at the time and that the spiritual benefits it offered were superior to all others.

The same mystical Islamic ideology also enabled him to extend both his political and commercial hegemony throughout the region and thus establish a voluntarist basis of social and political authority that contrasted with the Islamic statist models which were also emerging at the time, such as in the Sokoto Caliphate.

See also **Islam.**

BIBLIOGRAPHY

Batran, A. A. "The Qadiriyya-Mukhtariyya Brotherhood in West Africa: The Concept of *Tassawwuf* in the Writings of Sidi al-Mukhtar al-Kunti (1729–1811)." *Transafrican Journal of History* 4, nos. 1–2 (1974): 41–70.

Batran, A. A. "The Kunta, Sīdī al-Mukhtā al-Kuntī, and the Office of *Shaykh al-Tarqa'l-Qādiriyya*." In *Studies in West African Islamic History*, ed. John Ralph Willis. London: F. Cass, 1979.

LOUIS BRENNER

MULTIPARTY SYSTEMS. *See* **Political Systems.**

MUSEUMS

This entry includes the following articles:
HISTORY
MEMORY

HISTORY

Precolonial sub-Saharan Africa had traditions of keeping objects and knowledge that were important to the political systems and to the performance of social and religious functions. However, the Western-type museum was introduced from the nineteenth century by the European colonial powers in order to advance their colonial agendas, and for the enlightenment of the colonial elites. Therefore, the backgrounds of the colonial museums reflected diverse agendas aimed at a better comprehension of the natural resources and of the peoples in the colonies, and/or at disseminating the ideology of the European superiority and settlement. Some museums were also driven by archaeological and paleontological research, or set up as memorial monuments.

In British southern Africa, the first museums, focused on natural history, were the South African Museum, Cape Town (1825) and the Albany Museum, Grahamstown (1855). In southern Rhodesia (later Zimbabwe), museums with Eurocentric backgrounds and an emphasis on white settlers' culture were established in Bulawayo and Salisbury in 1901.

In British East Africa, the Uganda Museum was founded in Kampala (1908) with an ethnography and natural history background. The Nairobi Museum (Kenya) was initiated in 1910, focused on natural history, and later on palaeontology and archaeology. In Tanganyika, the King George V Memorial Museum was opened in Dar es Salaam (1940), and later received excavated material from the Olduvai Gorge site.

In British Nigeria, the first museums were opened in Jos (1952)—linked to the discovery of the Nok Culture—and in Lagos (1957). In Ghana, the National Museum (Accra) was opened in 1957 during the Independence celebration.

Museums in the French colonies were generally linked to the Institut Français d'Afrique Noire (IFAN), focused on colonial ethnography, archaeology, history, and natural resources. The main IFAN museum started in Dakar, Senegal (1941), and branch museums were later established in several colonies, such as Bamako (French Sudan, later Mali), Abidjan (Côte d'Ivoire), Niamey (Niger), Ouagadougou (Haute Volta, later Burkina Faso), Douala, Foumban (Cameroon), and Libreville (Gabon).

No major museums had been established in Leopoldville in the Belgian Congo; however, small, public university and missionary museums—most ethnographic—were opened in different localities.

In Angola, the Museum of Angola was established in Luanda (1938). During the same period a diamond-mining firm sponsored the development of ethnography collections, leading to open an ethnography museum in 1949. A number of provincial museums were opened later.

After their independences, most of the new African nation-states had established national museums either by re-orientating the colonial institutions, or by creating new museums that were to become custodians of the national heritage. The majority of museums came under the aegis of governments, with new nationalistic orientations determined by the political agenda to build up national unity through national identity.

Some countries have developed national heritage agencies administering country-wide networks, such as the Nigerian National Commission of Museums and Monuments, with major museums in Lagos and Jos (history, archaeology, and cultural history); the National Museums of Kenya with main museums in Nairobi, Mombasa, Lamu, and Kisumu (palaeontology, zoology, botany, archaeology, history, cultural history, and contemporary art); and the National Museums and Monuments of Zimbabwe including several museums and historical sites (zoology, botany, geology, archaeology, history, cultural history, and contemporary art).

Among the individual museums that had undergone radical growth in the postindependence period, the National Museum of Niger in Niamey (palaeontology, geology, zoology, archaeology, and cultural history) and the National Museum of Mali in Bamako (archaeology, history, cultural history, and audio-visual collections) became major institutions in West Africa.

Museums have become more diversified, too. Examples include the Museum of Science and Technology in Accra (Ghana), the National War Museum in Umuahia (Nigeria), the Railway Museums in Kenya and Zimbabwe, and the Army Museum in Zimbabwe.

Though the nationalistic orientation remained predominant, there were initiatives to develop wider approaches, such as the initial pan-African scope of the Ghana National Museum and the Museum of the Centre International des Civilisations Bantou (CICIBA) in Gabon, that involved several countries with Bantu-speaking populations.

Museum development faced obstacles, including weakness of institutional capacities, insufficient funding, and inadequate legal and administrative systems. Some museums had been severely damaged by civil wars (Liberia, Sierra Leone, Congo, and Guinea-Bissau), with their collections looted and/or their buildings destroyed.

South African museums were dominated by the ideology of apartheid, with a distinction between exhibitions focusing on European history and culture, and those dealing with natural history and indigenous cultures. Since the end of apartheid, radical changes and tremendous growth occurred, enabling museums to reflect the new democracy. A different relation was established to African history and culture, and to the history of apartheid. Robben Island, in particular, was opened as a museum in 1997.

Starting around 1990, major developments occurred in African museums. The role of museums was reshaped to address developmental and environmental issues, political life, health, peace, and memory. The purpose, research, collections, and displays, were re-addressed to fit with the educational, social, and political needs of people, and to integrate contemporary culture into the collections. The scope of the collections and the relation to the object were reconsidered, with increasing focus on intangible culture as a primary resource.

Owing to these developments, non-state-managed museums have expanded. Private museums sponsored by wealthy individuals were established in several countries, mostly with art focuses (Nigeria, Burkina Faso, Kenya, and Bénin). Community-based museums have expanded, generally addressing issues pertaining to identified social groups (South Africa, Kenya, Zimbabwe, and Mali). Women's museums were established in Senegal and Mali to address women-related cultural, social, and developmental issues.

New growth stressed the needs for institutional- and professional-capacity development, and for appropriate legal and administrative frameworks. The issue of sustainability remains acute within insufficient funding contexts in the early twenty-first century.

Nonetheless, professionalism grew with the professional environment. Professional organizations, training institutions, and museum associations provide support to capacity-building, such as the International Council of African Museums (AFRICOM, Kenya), the West African Museums Programme (WAMP, Senegal), the Centre for Heritage Development in Africa (Kenya), Ecole du Patrimoine Africain (Bénin), the Robben Island Training Course, and the South African Museum Association (SAMA). Museums in the north are also seeing increasing international cooperation.

See also **Abidjan; Accra; Apartheid; Cape Town; Dar es Salaam; Douala; Education, School; Education, University and College; Kampala; Lagos; Libraries; Libreville; Niamey; Warfare: Civil Wars.**

BIBLIOGRAPHY

Ardouin, Claude. "What Models for African Museums? West African Prospects." In *Culture and Development in Africa*, eds. Ismail Serageldin and June Taboroff. Proceedings of an International Conference held at the World Bank, Washington, DC, April 2 and 3, 1992. Washington, DC: 1993.

Gaugue, Anne. *Les états africains et leurs musées. La mise en scène de la nation.* Paris : L'Harmattan, 1997.

Guide du Musée historique de l'AOF à Gorée. Dakar: Institut Français d'Afrique Noire, 1955.

Munjeri, Dawson. "Towards an Integrated Approach: South African Museums Map Out Strategies." In *Culture and Development in Africa*, eds. Ismail Serageldin and June Taboroff. Proceedings of an International Conference held at the World Bank, Washington, DC, April 2 and 3, 1992. Washington, DC: 1993.

Ravenhill, Philip L. "Public Education, National Collections, and Museum Scholarship in Africa." In *Culture and Development in Africa*, eds. Ismail Serageldin and June Taboroff. Proceedings of an International Conference held at the World Bank, Washington, DC, April 2 and 3, 1992. Washington, DC: 1993.

Strandgaard Kirsten. *Introducing Tanzania through the National Museum.* Dar es Salaam: The Museum, 1974.

What Museums for Africa? Heritage in the Future. Paris: International Council of Museums, 1992.

CLAUDE ARDOUIN

MEMORY

Museums are sites of memory. However, memory is not static but changes over time depending on the experiences and perceptions of individuals and communities. Memories are created in museums through identity politics or to redress past wrongs. Also memory is not unitary; it has subnarratives, transitional periods, and contests over dominance. Thus, one group's positive memory may represent another group's painful past. Memories are also recreated through myths to authenticate the present where monuments and museums help to connect the past to the present. This connection sometimes leads to controversy where people see differences between their expectations and their personal experiences.

GENESIS OF THE AFRICAN MUSEUM

The twenty-first-century African museum is a result of a global phenomenon that started with European explorations in the fifteenth century, when African material culture was systematically hauled to Europe. The process was further crystallized when major European museums and antique dealers collected, exhibited, and traded African objects, which culminated in the establishment of museums in Africa during the colonial period. By the latter part of the nineteenth century, Britain and France organized international and colonial exhibitions where they re-presented "their" African peoples. Tony Bennet argued that "the Exhibitionary complex" was a means to put culture into practical use. He compared museums to institutions of power, punishment, and spectacle developed in the eighteenth century. Exhibitions he claimed were "a power made manifest not in its ability to inflect pain but by its ability to organize and co-ordinate an order of things and to produce a place for the peoples in relations to that order" (p. 73). Through the organizational principles of progress, whereby objects were classified by time and race, the viewers were convinced of the position of their nations in history. Exhibitions became time machines as well as a yardstick for races and empires, emphasizing the rhetoric of "us" versus "them" or the civilized as opposed to the uncivilized.

Colonial collection policy, however, was not guided by a particular standard— scientific or aesthetic. Although collections were largely determined by the availability of funds and gifts from colonial officials, there was also intensive collecting among peoples whose resistance to colonialism was enduring and peoples who were deemed artistic in contrast with others. Such unwritten policies turned some museums into storehouses of miscellanies. They constituted the nucleus collections for the future independent African museums.

POSTINDEPENDENCE MUSEUMS

If colonial museums were monuments to the glory of the colonialists, after independence they were transformed to glorify the colonized. Facing the realities of independence in the early 1960s, most African leaders noticed the destructive political and

Musée de la Femme–Henriette Bathily, Gorée Island, Senegal. Founded in 1994, it is the first women's museum in Africa. Its collections and exhibitions are devoted entirely to the lives and material culture of women in Senegal. It was named after Henriette Bathily, a renowned journalist of Senegal. PHOTOGRAPH BY AGBENYEGA ADEDZE

cultural impact of half a century of colonial rule on their societies. To remedy the situation, one of their first acts was to recreate or reinvent the African past that was interrupted by colonialism. Authentic African cultures were defined in opposition to foreign values. Half a century of colonialism's denial of the existence of authentic African

cultures would compel the postindependence leaders to construct an account of the unique culture and history that united the nation. The result was the creation of numerous national and regional museums throughout Africa with the sole mission of reinventing a past usable to the politicians of the present.

How can the new nations be reconstructed through culture? Whose version of the national culture is being shown? What is shown? And why? What is not shown?

The extent to which museums and monuments contribute to national bonding is a debatable issue, given the many competing answers to these questions. Exhibits do not attract national support as do the national soccer team. Most museum exhibitions present the material culture of the dominant ethnic groups or a people whose artifacts are appreciated in the West: Asante (Ghana), Bamileke (Cameroon), Baule (Côte d'Ivoire), Kota (Gabon), Kuba (Democratic Republic of the Congo), and Yoruba (Nigeria). What about the other ethnic groups, since almost all African states are multiethnic?

Cultures in an era of one-party states or dictatorships could become symbols of repression or social control whereby events and representations are doctored to suit the ideology of the ruling power, for example the Eyademas (authoritarian ruler in Togo) and Mobutus (perhaps the most notorious kleptocrat of the 1980s and 1990s).

Perhaps the reason for the myopic collecting and exhibition of some cultures in the multiethnic nations to the detriment of others is that the curators, the cultural elite, and the political leaders have been trained in similar techniques of the political uses of culture in the West and they just adapt it to their local situations. And often they have acted in concert with the former colonial governments and international organizations of the West.

African museums are caught up in the colonial ethnographic and the postcolonial nationalist mode from which they must extricate themselves. They have and continue to define themselves and their institutions in opposition to Western values. The African museum curator must emulate the example of African writers, who have evolved from the immediate postindependence literature of precolonial nostalgia and a nationalist euphoria to the criticism of contemporary issues in their societies and nations. This does not mean that they should ignore the past, but they must learn to incorporate the past into contemporary realities. African culture is not static; it is as dynamic as ever. Also, for far too long, African curators have made the same mistake as their colonial predecessors who preferred

"traditional" artifacts to the detriment of the contemporary ones. Today's artifacts could become tomorrow's masterpieces.

Museums have a vital role to play in education, environment, community development, and local culture. Museums equally promote national and local histories and art. The future of African museums, however, depends on economic, social, and political developments in each state as well as effective leadership and curatorial vision. A museum must develop a sense of community through its lectures, exhibitions, courses, concerts, archives, and collections so that all members of the community feel their memories are preserved and exhibited.

See also **Colonial Traditions and Inventions; Heritage, Cultural; Literature; Nationalism; Postcolonialism.**

BIBLIOGRAPHY

Adedze, Agbenyega. "Museums as a Tool for Nationalism in Africa." *Museum Anthropology* 19, no. 2 (1995): 58–64.

Bennet, Tony. "The Exhibitionary Complex." *New Formations* 4 (spring 1988): 73–102.

Olick, Jeffrey, K., ed. *States of Memory: Continuities, Conflicts, and Transformations in National Retrospection.* Durham, NC: Duke University Press, 2003.

AGBENYEGA ADEDZE

MUSEVENI, YOWERI (1944–).

Museveni's political activism began in 1966, when he was a student in secondary school in Uganda. At that time he organized Rwanda pastoralists in the Mbarara district of western Uganda against eviction from their lands. He attended the University of Dar es Salaam in Tanzania, which he helped to form, from 1967 to 1970 and led the University Students' African Revolutionary Front there. He spent September of 1968 in areas of northern Mozambique that the FRELIMO freedom fighters had liberated from Portuguese control. There he gained his first experiences of guerrilla organization.

After graduation, he worked at the office of the then-Ugandan president, Milton Obote, until Idi Amin's coup d'état in 1971. Museveni fled to Tanzania and soon after formed the Front for

Yoweri Museveni (1944–) at a press conference, Rwakatira, February 2005. The president of Uganda since 1986, Museveni was involved in the war that ended Idi Amin's rule and the rebellion that took Milton Obote out of office. In February 2006, Museveni won election to another five-year term. TUGELA RIDLEY/AFP/GETTY IMAGES

National Salvation (FRONASA), training guerrillas to disrupt Amin's rule. As leader of FRONASA, he returned in 1979 to Uganda with the Tanzanian People's Defense Forces to help overthrow Amin. He served as minister of defense, minister of regional cooperation, and vice chairman of the military commission in the transitional Ugandan National Liberation Front government that replaced Amin.

Claiming that fraud invalidated the 1980 election of the Uganda Peoples Congress Party that returned Obote to the presidency, Museveni left Kampala, the capital of Uganda, in February of 1981 to again organize a guerrilla army, the National Resistance Army. This force was one of only two in Africa to successfully overthrow an independent government with no more than minimal external assistance.

Museveni became president of Uganda in January 1986, when his National Resistance Army seized control of Kampala. As of 2006, his most important achievement has been creation of a new and disciplined army that respected civilians and civilian rule. Under the leadership of his National Resistance Movement and with a manifesto called the Ten Point Program (written during the guerrilla campaign), Museveni reconciled several opposing factions by welcoming them into the broad-based interim government he formed upon taking power. In 1987 he committed the government to a program to liberalize and privatize the economy, and he consistently supported and

expanded these policies over the years that followed. In 1988 he launched the process of writing a new constitution to restore democratic civilian rule, and served as chairman of the Organization of African Unity during 1990–1991. He promulgated a new Ugandan constitution in 1995.

Museveni's rule has not gone unchallenged. Rebel factions, the largest of which is called the Lord's Resistance Army (LRA), led by Joseph Kony (b. 1962), have sprung up in the remoter reaches of the country. The LRA in particular has waged a violent campaign in the north against Museveni's forces, and has severely abused local civilian populations. It met with an equally violent response by government troops.

Opposition candidates who wish to avoid violence by running for office are handicapped by Uganda's political system, which forces them to run as individuals, rather than as representatives of a supporting party. This has facilitated Museveni's reelection efforts, and he was returned to the presidency in 1996 and again in 2001 in spite of widespread allegations of vote rigging in the latter election. By law, he is prohibited from running again in 2006, but his followers have initiated challenges to that legal barrier.

See also **Amin Dada, Idi; Obote, Milton; Uganda: History and Politics.**

BIBLIOGRAPHY

Museveni, Yoweri K. *Selected Articles on the Uganda Resistance War.* Kampala, Uganda: National Resistance Movement Publications, 1985.

Museveni, Yoweri K. *What Is Africa's Problem?* ed. Elizabeth Kanyogonya. Minneapolis: University of Minnesota Press, 2000.

Mutibwa, Phares. *Uganda since Independence.* Trenton, New Jersey: Africa World Press, 1992.

Shamuyarira, Nathan M., ed. *Essays on the Liberation of Southern Africa.* Dar es Salaam: Tanzania Publishing House, 1971.

NELSON KASFIR

MUSIC

This entry includes the following articles:
OVERVIEW
STRUCTURES
ISLAMIC

OVERVIEW

Neither geographical boundaries nor physical characteristics of populations may be taken as determinants of culture. However, music in Africa is intimately linked with language, to the extent that much of its content and structure is difficult for linguistic outsiders to understand, and any appearance of comprehension occurs only by reinterpretation. This holds true regarding both extra-African contacts and cross-cultural exchanges within Africa. In view of the close link between language and music in Africa, language may be identified as the most relevant parameter within which music operates. Speaking at a UNESCO gathering in 1972, J. H. Kwabena Nketia even postulated an analogy, speaking of the "musical languages of sub-Saharan Africa." Accordingly, the geographical notion of Africa is correlated here as much as possible with the broad linguistic picture of the continent.

Using his cantometrics scheme, Alan Lomax divided Africa, including Madagascar, into fourteen broad style areas: North Africa, Sahara, Western Sudan, Muslim Sudan, Guinea Coast, Equatorial Bantu, Eastern Sudan, Upper Nile, Ethiopia, Northeast Bantu, Central Bantu, South Africa Bantu, African Hunters, and Madagascar. Lomax did not, however, postulate rigid boundaries. In fact, the world of African song and dance styles appears in fluctuating and often overlapping configurations.

Although Lomax's cantometrics project was criticized by some on methodological grounds, it has merit as the only attempt at a broad, comparative, stylistic sampling of vocal music across Africa. Certainly, it has produced some interesting, albeit controversial, results. His stylistic examination of single traits of a vast sample suggests the Guinea Coast and Equatorial Bantu as a sort of nucleus, if not dispersal center, of a formative African style world.

A remarkable characteristic in the early twenty-first century African cultural picture is the extremely interruptive, dissected contours of cultural-trait distribution areas. Often, areas geographically distant from each other and separated by divergent cultures show stylistic affinities. In music, notable examples are the similarities between log xylophone music in northern Mozambique, Liberia, and Côte d'Ivoire. Strange likenesses in harmonic part-singing style—with a tendency to equiheptatonic intonation—link

the Chokwe, Luchazi, Mbwela, and others of eastern Angola to the Baule of Côte d'Ivoire. In Namibia, the musical culture of the pastoral Herero is worlds apart from that of surrounding peoples. But in eastern Africa, especially in Nkore (western Uganda), western Tanzania, Rwanda, and Burundi, one finds compelling similarities to the Herero approach to song and movement.

This demonstrates the complex crisscrossing of the migratory paths of people and cultural influences in Africa's history. Some of the affinities may result from eighteenth- and nineteenth-century contacts; for example, northern Mozambique's log xylophone styles could have been transplanted to coastal western Africa after 1815, when liberated slaves from many parts of Africa were dumped in Sierra Leone and Liberia. But other analogies cannot be explained by recent contacts, such as the Baule-Chokwe affinities in homophonic multipart singing, particularly when associated with initiation.

THE HISTORY OF AFRICAN MUSIC

It is legitimate to reconstruct certain aspects of African music history by inference from a twentieth-century sample of sound recordings. Hypotheses, however, must be distinguished from verified historical facts.

Iconological Sources. The oldest iconological sources relating to African music history are rock paintings such as those in the Tassili N' Ajjer of the Sahara (in early twenty-first century Algeria), with many motifs depicting music and dance practices. A famous Tassili rock painting shows a six-string harp played in vertical position by a musician for a person in authority. It has been tentatively dated to around 700 BCE, in the so-called Period of the Horse. The picture suggests the presence of the harp in the central Sahara at that time and also, through componential analysis, the presence of a stratified society, with musicians who played for nobles, chiefs, or perhaps kings. The culture history of Saharan populations, as displayed in the rock art galleries of the Tassili, is of direct relevance to that of peoples south of the Sahara at a later period.

Linguistic reconstructions suggest that around 2500 BCE, Nilo-Saharan languages were spoken in areas much farther north than they are in the early twenty-first century. From about 8000 to 3000 BCE, much of the present Sahara passed through a wet period that gave rise to the development of what has been called an aquatic lifestyle. There are several indications that some of the Green Sahara population, speaking early forms of the Nilo-Saharan languages, gradually migrated southward as the Sahara became drier, continuing an aquatic lifestyle with modifications (such as the introduction of elements of a pastoral economy), as at Lake Chad, along the Upper Niger, and in the swamps of the *sudd* region of the Upper Nile in early twenty-first century Sudan. A number of the visual aspects of music and dance depicted in some of the oldest Saharan frescoes, such as a dance scene from the period of the Neolithic hunters (approximately 6000–4000 BCE) showing elaborated body decoration, seem to be perpetuated in certain areas of present-day sub-Saharan Africa. In the case cited, perpetuation is as remote as in the *ndlamu* stamping dance of the Zulu of South Africa. The Sahara frescoes also include what could be representations of masks and initiation dances. The extensive resources of rock art in southern Africa also contain, to a lesser extent, motifs that could be interpreted as relevant to music and dance history in the areas concerned.

Whereas the iconographic testimonies cited fall under the category of internal African sources because their authors were indigenous, many external pictographic documents are available from the fifteenth century to the present. One of the most interesting early illustrations in color is by traveler and explorer Jan Huyghen van Linschoten (1563–1611) that depicts a player of a braced musical bow, with the bowstick (not the string) passed by the lips. Linschoten saw the performer somewhere on the coast of Mozambique where he landed during his passage to India, either at Sofala or close to Mozambique Island. It is the first record of a mouth-bow tradition that survives in several areas of central and southern Mozambique; it persists in the *chipendani*, an instrument among the Chopi in the south; the *xipendani* among the Tsonga; the *chibendane* in Manica Province; the *chipindano* in Tete Province; and elsewhere.

The illustrations of Linschoten and others—in particular the original watercolors of Giovanni Antonio Cavazzi in 1687 from his stay in the kingdoms of Kongo, Ndongo, and Matamba—can be analyzed for information about the organology of sixteenth- and seventeenth-century African musical instruments. Knowledge about their social settings, playing methods, and sometimes even the tuning layouts may also be derived.

Iconological sources also include more recent materials, such as nineteenth- and twentieth-century illustrations: drawings, paintings, photographs, and so on. An example is the early-twentieth-century photographic collection from southern Angola kept at the Royal Anthropological Institute in London.

Archaeological Artifacts. There is a wide spectrum of artifacts related to African music history from Iron Age cultures. They include single and double bells, such as those excavated at Great Zimbabwe, Inyanga, and elsewhere, and even lamellae of lamellophones. Some of the earliest sources on music history in western, central, and southern Africa are archaeological. In western Nigeria, Frank Willett excavated several terra-cotta pots at a site in Ife, dated to between the eleventh or twelfth and fourteenth centuries, with reliefs depicting musical instruments. The Yoruba instruments depicted include drums of the *gbedù* type, demonstrating the early presence of a characteristic Guinea Coast method of creating drum-skin tension, the so-called cord-and-peg tension (prevalent today in drums of southern Ghana such as the *atumpan* and in *vodu* drums among the Fõ of Togo and Dahomey). The artifacts also include horns (*edon*) and a Guinea-type double bell (a smaller bell attached to the back of a larger bell, such as a mother carrying her child).

Willett's finds also reveal that between the tenth and fourteenth centuries, another ritual Yoruba drum, the *igbin*, was present in Ife. Even today this type of drum is used in religious contexts, for example at the shrine for *òrìṣàńla* or Obatala, the creator God. These artifacts demonstrate the relative antiquity of certain Yoruba musical instruments. Equally conclusive is negative evidence, such as the absence of the hourglass-shaped drums of the *dùndún* type, so prominent in Yoruba culture today and associated with the performance of praise poetry (*oriki*). There is no indication that these drums were used in Yorubaland during the so-called Classical period of Ife, corroborating the opinion that they were introduced from the Hausa speakers north of Nigeria during a much later period.

The most famous artifacts relevant to the study of musical instruments and musical practice are Bénin bronze plaques. They show the presence of a great variety of musical instruments, such as drums, including slit drums; bells; and even the pluriarc (or bow lute), still used in Bénin culture. Archaeology has also contributed to the history of music in central and southeastern Africa, notably in southern Congo, Zambia, Zimbabwe, and Mozambique. In excavations near Kisale, Democratic Republic of Congo, artifacts dating from the tenth to the fourteenth centuries were recovered. Among these were several types of metal bells, an aerophone made of copper, and what may be the tongues of lamellophones.

Iron Age technology produced notable innovations in the repertoire of musical instruments in Africa, particularly during the period from the eighth to the fourteenth centuries. The history of the iron single and double bell in West, West-Central, and Southeast Africa has already been reconstructed in some detail, with new data added that close some area gaps in the sequence of diffusion, such as the Upper Sangha area in the early twenty-first century Central African Republic and the Congo. Iron bells are often associated with chiefship or kinship, and in music their distribution across sub-Saharan Africa largely corresponds with the distribution of time-line patterns, another significant correlation. The proliferation of innovative types of lamellophones with iron lamellae from a dispersal center in southeast Africa (in Zimbabwe and the Lower Zambezi Valley) is another development to be ascribed to the rise of new technology during the later Iron Age. David W. Phillipson postulates that its inception occurred in 1000–1100 CE. In the ruins of Great Zimbabwe, several specimens of single and double bells have been excavated since Karl Mauch's first visit to the ruins in 1871. Also found were what could be lamellae of lamellophones, demonstrating the effects of the later stages of the Iron Age industrial complex on musical practice.

Written Sources.

There is an abundance of external, and more recently internal, written sources relevant to African music and its history. These include some New World sources, such as Alexandre Rodrigues Ferreira's account of the presence of a certain Angolan lamellophone type and a pluriarc—all from Huila Province—in northeastern Brazil toward the end of the eighteenth century. Yet contemporary written sources, especially from the era of the European discoveries and the subsequent colonial period, require critical evaluation by ethnomusicologists trained in historical methodology. It is important to distinguish between primary source material, including the so-called proto-testimonies, and secondary sources. Also, in each case, the place, date, and circumstances of the writings and the author's sociopsychological background, opinions, and value judgments have to be scrutinized in order to separate factual information from personal opinions.

Written sources also include musical notations. Examples are the nineteenth-century attempts at notations of Asante and Fante music in Ghana by Thomas Edward Bowdich in *Mission from Cape Coast Castle to Ashantee* (1819), and notational outlines of Cape Hottentot music by Peter Kolb in *Caput Bonae Spei Hodiernum* (1719).

Sound Recordings.

Recordings of sound are limited to the last decade of the nineteenth century and into the twentieth century. These include wax cylinder recordings such as those made in Uganda by Sir Harry Johnston at the end of the nineteenth century, stored in the British Library in London; the famous recordings of multipart singing from Missahöhe, Togo, made in 1905 by the German lieutenant J. von Smend and stored in the Ethnological Museum in Berlin; acetate disc recordings; and analog tape recordings up to the more recent videotape and digital audiotape recordings. Sound-synchronized films and videos fall into the category of iconological as well as sound sources.

Students of African music history, proceeding from factual sources, cannot subscribe to the early twentieth-century views of musicologists and cultural historians who, arguing from the theoretical position of unilinear evolutionism, relegated African musical practice to a stage of universal cultural history. On the same methodological grounds, the historical study of African music cannot proceed from binary models such as the traditional-versus-modern dichotomy. The axiom of all historical research is the notion of history as a continuous process of datable change. Consequently, all African music documented on sound carriers in the twentieth century is, first of all, twentieth-century African music. Because there are no age-old, absolutely stable traditions, conclusions about earlier forms of African music drawn from a twentieth-century sample are possible only by inference and only to a limited extent. The historian's perception of African music history is that musical cultures in Africa have interacted, innovated, adapted, fused, and split from their beginnings—not just since the impact of colonialism or the introduction of industrially manufactured Western instruments.

AFRICAN MUSIC IN ITS PRESENT SOCIOCULTURAL CONTEXT

Any musical practice exists within a sociocultural context, and Africa is no exception. Some authors have stressed the contextual nature of African music, and elaborated on the functions and roles of music in African social life. Some have postulated that African music is invariably a collective phenomenon, rigidly bound to social events such as rituals, religious ceremonies, and salient events in the life cycle. Although applying to certain musical genres, this does not hold true as a generalization. African musical practice is no more and no less determined by sociocultural contexts than is the musical practice in any other region of the world. The researcher's objective, therefore, can only be to discover the specific contexts of specific genres of African music.

Of course, those contexts vary with the cultural profile of a society. For example, in societies where male or female puberty initiation is practiced, one is likely to encounter specific types of music linked to initiation ceremonies. These include the *myaso yakumukanda*, songs of the *mukanda* boys' initiation school as found in the large eastern Angolan culture area, and *nyimbo za chinamwali* girls' initiation songs in Chewa- and Nyanja-speaking communities of Malawi and Zambia. Without the social context of initiation, these types of music would not exist. In urban societies with a tradition of ballroom dancing, as at the *rebita* clubs in Luanda, Angola, or of gatherings around a radio or record player for dancing, as in many urban and semi-urban areas of southern Africa, further divisions by age and sex may come into play. Class structures had a selective effect upon the composition of dancers and audiences in beer gardens or taverns in western Africa during the highlife era in the 1950s. Such spots attracted a certain social

stratum of the population of cities such as Accra, Ghana.

Religious beliefs, along with general ideas about the shape of musical instruments and their components that are derived from religious concepts, constitute another important cultural context of musical practice in sub-Saharan Africa. Frequently, anthropomorphic or zoomorphic ideas are projected onto instrumental shapes. Thus, instruments usually have a head, a body, and a back. For example, the harp (*ngombi*) in cult music among the Faŋ of Gabon is considered by priests to be the "house" of a female divinity.

Music and oral literature are so closely connected in many African societies that it is impossible to separate the two. This includes not only song texts or special traditions such as the *talking drum*—the drumming of poetry based on the tonality of languages—but any genres that combine these forms of expression. That music also evokes strong nonmusical associations—various feelings, for example—confirms that it is difficult in many cases to delineate borders. Storytelling with integrated songs, for example, seems to display remarkably unified behavioral patterns across sub-Saharan Africa, from western Africa to speakers of Bantu languages in eastern and southern Africa. It is not by chance, therefore, that some word roots for "story" in the Bantu languages recur in comparable form in areas often distant from each other. For example, the root *simo* appears as *simo* in the Kigogo language of Tanzania and *visimo* in the Ngangela languages of Angola; and *ntano* (or its variant *ngano*) appears in several languages of eastern and southern Africa, even as far west as the Bantu language zone R in Malcolm Guthrie's classification scheme in northern Namibia and Angola.

Storytelling with songs is a community-oriented event involving relatively few people. It is somewhere halfway between large community gatherings and self-delectative music, such as the solo performance of a forager on his hunting bow that has been transformed into a musical bow. Hugh Tracey was one of the first researchers to pay attention to the kinds of African music that are strictly individual in concept and performance. It was he who coined the term "self-delectative songs." Some music requires audience response, whereas other music does not. The lonely honey

patterns not actually played by the musician, such as the voices of spirits.

The orality of African musical traditions requires from the field researcher an approach that is adapted to the circumstances. Orality implies that a certain range of variation may often be expected from performance to performance of the same song. However, this does not mean that the songs are not composed. In the past, African music was often called folk music, as if anonymous persons were its originators and everyone was a singer. Pointing to the contrary is the evidence emerging from some of the largest collections of field documentation now available, such as that of the International Library of African Music in Grahamstown, South Africa, or the one at the Ethnological Museum in Berlin. Every single piece of recorded African music was at one time composed by some individual, and occasionally with the help of group members. In most cases the original composer of a song is soon forgotten by the community because of a lack of historical consciousness in rural communities (political hierarchies excluded); the work, however, is transmitted independently of the creator, to be picked up, adapted, and reinterpreted by other musician-composers.

As much as African musical practice is connected inseparably with the verbal realm of expression, equally there are cross-parallels to other forms of expression, notably in the visual arts. Costume patterning and decoration, as well as body paint in initiation ceremonies and masked dancing, often contain coded instructions for transforming musical patterns into movement. Early twenty-first century research has revealed that some abstract geometrical designs of sub-Saharan Africa contain structures identical to those prevailing in music. For example, duple-, triple-, and quadruple-division interlockings are found in mat plaitings of various areas of sub-Saharan Africa.

In eastern Angola and northwestern Zambia a tradition of writing ideographs in the sand survives. Many of them, called *sona* in Chokwe and *tusona* in Luchazi, are constructed by interlocking two grids of dots that are laid out equidistantly. First, the *mukwakusona* (the writer of a *kasona* ideograph) impresses a series of equidistant parallel dots into the sand by using the first and third fingers of his

Kweku Cordrington. Musician and instrument maker Kweku Cordrington introduces people to West African culture at Alley Fest, Texas, 2005. Music in Africa is so intimately linked with the various native languages, to the extent that much of its content and structure is difficult for linguistic outsiders to understand. AP Photo/Tyler Morning Telegraphy, Tom Worner

collector in a central African forest, the worker in the field, the *likembe* (lamellophone) player walking by himself to a mining center in the province of Shaba (formerly Katanga) in Congo, all used to play for their own delight and for stress relief. Playing in solitude is often a dialogue with the instrument, from which strange oscillating voice lines seem to emerge from inherent instrumental

right hand. Next, the writer inscribes into this basic grid a second series of dots that interlock in duple division. Finally, the ideographer inscribes and circumscribes the structure with diagonal lines. Inherent patterns emerge from the final product as in a picture puzzle, analogous to a similar phenomenon in some forms of African music. The inventors of these ideographs projected various ideas into their drawings, interpreting them, perceiving dream images, responding with metaphors, proverbial text lines, stories, and the like. Many of these interpretive texts have become a standard tradition associated with each ideograph, such as the text lines of a song.

See also **Archaeology and Prehistory; Dance; Language: Sociolinguistics; Linguistics and the Study of Africa; Literature: Oral; Music, Modern Popular; Musical Instruments; Religion and Ritual; Tracey, Hugh; Zimbabwe, Great.**

BIBLIOGRAPHY

Agawu, Kofi. *Representing African Music. Postcolonial Notes, Queries, Positions.* London: Routledge, 2003.

Avorgbedor, Daniel, ed. *The Interrelatedness of Music, Religion, and Ritual in African Performance Practice.* Leviston, NY: Edwin Mellen Press, 2003.

Charry, Eric. "Plucked Lutes in West Africa: A Historical Overview." *Galpin Society Journal* 49 (1996): 3-37.

DjeDje, Jacqueline Cogdell, ed. *Turn Up the Volume! A Celebration of African Music.* Los Angeles: UCLA Fowler Museum of Cultural History, 1999.

Guthrie, R. Malcolm. *The Classification of the Bantu Languages.* London: Oxford University Press, 1948.

Kubik, Gerhard. *Africa and the Blues.* Jackson: University of Mississippi Press, 1999.

Kubik, Gerhard. *Tusona—Luchazi Ideographs. A Graphic Tradition of West-Central Africa.* Münster, Germany: LIT Verlag, 2005.

Lomax, Alan. *Cantometrics: A Method in Musical Anthropology.* Berkeley: University of California Extension Media Center, 1976.

Phillipson, David W. *The Later Prehistory of Eastern and Southern Africa.* London: Heinemann, 1977.

Rouget, Gilbert. *Initiatique vôdoun. Imiages du ritual.* Saint-Maur, France: Editions Sépia, 2001.

Stone, Ruth M., ed. *The Garland Encyclopedia of World Music,* Vol. 1: *Africa.* New York; London: Garland Publishing, 1998.

Thompson, Robert Farris. *Flash of the Spirit: African and Afro-American Art and Philosophy.* New York: Vintage Books, 1984.

Tracey, Hugh. *Chopi Musicians.* 2nd edition. London: International African Institute, 1970.

Willett, Frank. "A Contribution to the History of Musical Instruments among the Yoruba." In *Essays for a Humanist: An Offering to Klaus Wachsmann,* pp. 350–389. New York: The Town House Press, 1977.

GERHARD KUBIK

STRUCTURES

COGNITION AND THE STRUCTURE OF MUSIC

Although there is no such thing as "African music" as a singular, unified, pan-African expression, there are structural principles and patterns of behavior common to many musical cultures across the continent. These connecting threads are the result, first, of partly common histories of large agglomerations of people, especially within the Niger-Kordofanian superfamily of languages and even more pronounced within so-called Bantu languages, and, second, of cross-cultural exchanges between peoples, with varying intensity, for hundreds and even thousands of years.

Some of these basic structural principles, encountered in various configurations and with varying degrees of intensity in different cultures, can be described. However, the conventional vocabulary of European and North American music theory is insufficient for doing so and therefore has been largely replaced by a new terminology that comes as close as possible to the underlying African concepts and perceptual facts of its music. In some African languages these concepts are expressed by a vernacular term (of analogous meaning, although different etymology), whereas in others they are not expressed verbally but are silently implied.

In African studies, when most of the results are published in European languages, the term "music" is still universally used as a blanket descriptive label. It is important, however, to keep in mind that the Latin word *musica* has no equivalent in African languages that would be congruent in its semantic field. Instead, most African languages have a term that can be translated as "song" (*oluyimbo* in Luganda, *mwaso* in the Ngangela languages of Angola, for example), but with a somewhat wider semantic field because it includes instrumental representations of a "song." This reflects an idea found in most African cultures: that instrumental melodies "speak," that they can be verbalized—meaning that performances and listeners attach verbal patterns and often syllables with no verbal content—to sound structures. From the verbal interpretation of birds' "speech," as in eastern Angola, where *mwekuhandeka tuzila* refers to "what the birds speak," to the projection of text lines into inherent patterns emanating from an *ennanga* (bow harp) performance in Buganda's court music, there is a broad spectrum of verbalization permeating musical practice in sub-Saharan Africa.

Verbalization of musical patterns is also a tool in the educational transmission of African musical practices. It was only a matter of time until someone (Arthur M. Jones and J. H. Kwabena Nketia were among the pioneers) discovered the use of what has come to be called mnemonic syllables and verbal mnemonics (formerly called "nonsense syllables") in teaching. There is a never-ending opportunity for students of African music, by analyzing mnemonics, to discover how musical patterns are conceptualized by the African musicians who are the carriers of those mnemonic traditions. In many teaching situations, musical patterns are taught by saying to the learner syllables or verbal phrases that, in their kinetic structure and timbre sequences, closely follow the pattern the student is supposed to play. Among the patterns that have been published are some of those used for teaching melodic rhythmic phrases on an *akadinda* seventeen-key log xylophone in the kingdom of Buganda and the *kora* bridge harp in Gambia and Senegal, as well as other Mandinka instruments. Other examples include the patterns for teaching a time line. Mnemonic syllables convey accent values and also express something about dance-beat relationships. For example, *cha* is a syllable used in many African musical cultures to transmit the notion of a rattle beat, always marking on-beat units. Nasals convey the idea of mute or empty pulses, and plosive sounds (such as *k*, *p*, and *t*) may convey strong timbre accents.

PRINCIPLES OF TIMING

Attractive as the word "timing" sounds, it may be misleading. In few African languages, if any, is music described in terms of time. To do so seems to be a characteristic European mode of thought. Nketia coined the term in connection with Ghanaian music, and although it is applicable to European music, there is doubt that any comparable concept existed in the languages of Ghana before he introduced it. In two languages intensively researched—Cinyanja-Chichewa of Malawi and Zambia and Luchazi of Angola and Zambia—no trace of any temporal concept connected to music was found, except as related to performance speed. For example, when a rattle player in a musical group in southern Malawi is slow with his strokes, band members may say "*muku-chedwa!*" (You are getting late! You are delaying!). "Timing," therefore, is merely a crutch to express some observational facts relating to depth structures in African music.

ELEMENTARY PULSATION

Some forms of African music can be placed between song and speech, because they are in free rhythm. Examples are some forms of praise poetry, such as *izibongo* Zulu praise poetry in South Africa and *omuhiva* praise poetry of the Herero in Namibia. But most African music that is accompanied by some body movement (hand clapping, work movement, and dance) is based on an orientation screen that may be described in English as the elementary pulsation. A. M. Jones, speaking of "smallest units," and Richard A. Waterman, speaking of a "metronome sense," were the first musicologists to express this concept, the former in terms of structure and the latter in terms of an inner experience.

The elementary pulsation is a fast, infinite series of pulses, a sort of inner grid made up of the smallest units of orientation. These pulses form an unconscious orientation screen in the mind of performers (including singers, dancers, and instrumentalists) and audiences. In some kinds of instrumental playing, as with xylophone music from southern Uganda (*amadinda*, *akadinda*, and *embaire* music), it runs at the enormous speed of 600 (Maeltzel's metronome) and even more. Enculturation into African music begins with the gradual development of such an inner orientation screen, making the candidate capable of instantly recognizing the pulse units in a piece of music, even when the pulses are not objectified by any action such as strokes, but barely form a silent reference line in the back of the mind.

The elementary pulsation is not necessarily identical to the "smallest rhythmic units" in a piece of African music, although in most cases it does match perfectly. There are traditions and musical styles—in Yoruba religious music, for example—where the line of elementary pulse units is at some points further divided by certain (in between) drum strokes. However, such subdivisions have no orientation function for the performers and often are merely ornamental; moreover, they are transient. The rule of thumb is that the elementary pulsation is made up only of those action units that suggest an uninterrupted flow; conceptually, the elementary pulsation is the line of reference that serves as a grid in the mind of the musicians to tell them where they are in relation to each other. Its function as an orientation screen promotes the development of what has been called the metronome sense in individuals.

THE BEAT

Whereas the elementary pulsation is the primary reference level of "timing" in most forms of African music, of no less importance is the second reference level. In English it is called the beat or ground beat, derived from jazz terminology.

An infinite series of pulse units (such as the elementary pulsation) has no pattern quality. However, the human perceptual apparatus superimposes patterns by grouping the infinite series into distinctive entities. These groups have a starting or inception point, a kind of "1," although it is not necessarily expressed that way in the languages concerned. In African music two, three, four, or, more rarely, five pulses are usually grouped together to constitute what can be called the beat.

The beat has several main structural characteristics. Although the beat in African (as in European and North American) music is an equidistant series of reference points, it is not in itself accented; that is, there is no notion of "strong" and "weak" parts of the meter. Melodic accents of a song may fall anywhere on elementary pulse units to form autonomous phrase structures, on-beat or off-beat, a phenomenon for which Richard A. Waterman introduced the term "off-beat phrasing of melodic accents." In many forms of African music, melodic accents tend to fall on beat units two and four of a four-beat meter, which may give the impression of metrical accents on the "weak parts" of the meter. An example is South African *mbaqanga* music. Accentuation of such an intensity creates a strongly disorienting effect in listeners not used to those particular styles.

In principle, the beat in African music is a non-sonic concept as much as is the elementary pulsation; it is merely an inner reference scheme. But like the latter it can be objectified by action: sometimes it is, sometimes it is not. As much as performers, dancers, and the audience in African music must have internalized the perception of an elementary pulsation in order to operate, so is it necessary for dancers to internalize the beat for finding their steps. The steps may coincide with the beat; they may come in an even way, such as 1-2-3-4, and may take a binary form, such as left-right, left-right (or the reverse). But there are also traditions in which the beat is lifted; for example, in certain dance styles a dancer may lift a leg on beat units 1 and 3, and put it down on 2 and 4. In some central African dance traditions, particularly in certain forms of masked dancing of eastern Angola, the feet sometimes do not move during certain episodes, while the pelvis and shoulders are moved in isolation. In such cases, one of the kinemes (the smallest intra-culturally conceptualized motional units) in the movement style coincides with the beat. Beat unit 1 (the point of inception) is often deliberately veiled through sound attenuation. For this reason, listeners to African music who are from other cultures often reverse African metrical schemes, perceiving, for example, beat units 2 and 4 as 3 and 1.

THE INTERLOCKING OR RELATIVE BEAT

Many kinds of African music have a common beat to which all the performers, including dancers, refer. But there are also many kinds of African music with an interlocking or relative beat, where individual performers in the same ensemble operate from inner reference schemes that do not coincide with those of the other performers. There may be two or three different beat relationships among performers in one ensemble.

Jones discovered the existence of the interlocking or relative beat in some kinds of African music, and in the 1930s he vividly demonstrated an example in the *ngwayi* dance drumming of the Bemba musical culture in Zambia. At that time he called this phenomenon cross rhythm. However, it is not just rhythms that are crossed: what really cross are the internal reference schemes of the musicians playing together. In the *amadinda* xylophone music of Buganda, for example, or in the *mangwilo* xylophone music of northern Mozambique, performers who sit opposite each other at log xylophones placed over a banana-stem base could interlock with each other were they to stomp their feet, which they do not. This first type of interlocking is referred to as "duple-division interlocking."

THE CYCLES

The third reference level engraved in the mind of performers of African music is the cycle. Most African music is cyclic in form. The cycle is simply an entity created by the combination of elementary pulsation, beat, and the basic theme of a musical piece. For example, in a Yoruba story song the cycle is formed by the leader's phrase plus the chorus's response, against the orientation screen of the elementary pulsation, with the beat objectified by hand claps. The cycle number expresses repeating units, such as themes, by the number of elementary pulses that it covers. In notations of African music, cycle numbers replaced the conventional time signatures (as in European and North American music) beginning in 1960.

Another important structural element in African music is the tonal or tonal-harmonic segmentation of a cycle. In most African music the cycles are subdivided into two, four, or eight segments. Thus, a sixteen-pulse cycle will typically cover four or eight hand claps, dance steps, and/or tonal-harmonic progressions. For a twelve-pulse or twenty-four-pulse cycle, the segmentation will equally be 4×3 or 4×6 elementary pulses to form the segments. There are, however, notable exceptions—particularly, it seems, in some *mbira* and other music of the Shona of Zimbabwe, as studied by Andrew Tracey and Paul Berliner, and in the music of the Ganda, Soga, and related peoples in southern Uganda. For example, a cycle of thirty-six pulses in a song may be divided into three tonality segments, each covering twelve pulses. This is the so-called 3×12 segmentation. Post 1960 urban musical styles display the common four-segment division of cycles almost exclusively.

However, in Namibia, among the Nama and Damara, speakers of a Khoesan language, there is an urban dance style known as the Nama step; here the music is often constructed to form cycles that are divided into three or six segments.

TIME-LINE PATTERNS

Time-line patterns are structured, short cycles of strokes, mostly at one pitch level. These patterns are used in some forms of music along the western African coast, in west-central Africa, and in parts of southeast Africa as a complex steering device. In contrast to the simple repeating beat of a bass drum, time-line patterns have an asymmetric structure. They are struck on instruments of penetrating sound, so that all members of the musical group, including the dancers, can hear them. Iron bells, the rim of a drum, or a glass bottle may be used for that purpose, but time-line patterns may also be produced by hand clapping.

Time-line patterns were first correctly written down by Jones (with the help of a transcription machine) from an African who tapped them out on a copper plate. Although their structure is clear, there is still some controversy about how performers visualize these patterns. Some scholars have formed the impression that West African musicians think of time-line patterns merely in relationship to the mnemonic syllables (and perhaps the elementary pulsation), but never in relation to a beat. However, recent comparative studies across western, west-central, and southeastern Africa suggest that, intraculturally, time-line patterns are conceptualized in relation to multiple reference levels: the mnemonic syllables, the elementary pulsation, their own complementary images, and the performer's or dancer's inner beat. In those cases where the concept of a relative or interlocking beat steers a performance, different instrumentalists conceive of the permeating time-line pattern from their own relative viewpoints. That is, the time-line pattern is "hooked" on the inner beat of each ensemble member differently.

TONAL SYSTEMS

The European tonal system of twelve equidistant notes within an octave was imported into most parts of Africa with factory-manufactured instruments, and earlier with religious and school choir teaching. Although this system of scaling has been widely accepted in Africa, there are still pockets of African cultures with tonal systems different from the tempered European twelve-note scale, and also large areas in Africa where the latter has been reinterpreted.

It is important, however, to distinguish between tonal systems and pitch intervals. Pitch intervals of nearly identical Cents values—such as perfect fourths of 498 and fifths of 702 Cents (Cents is a measuring unit to express intervals in any music)—can be found across the most diverse musical cultures of the world, let alone the octave, which seems to be universal. But the relationships of pitch intervals to each other—their layout (in the form of a scale or other arrangement), their number, and so on—may form different tonal systems in the various cultures under study.

An inventory of indigenous tonal systems across Africa suggests that, broadly, three families may be distinguished: (1) tonal systems derived from the experience of sections of the natural harmonic series; (2) tonal systems derived from the experience of speech in tone languages (and, in some cases, the experience of lower partials); and (3) tonal systems following the idea of temperament, meaning that they tend toward an equidistant layout of the tonal material (that is, equipentatonic and equiheptatonic tunings).

Family 1. An important characteristic of family 1 is the presence of simultaneous sounds (besides unisons and octaves) suggesting interval sizes that are known from the natural harmonic series, such as bichords involving fourths or fifths, a somewhat flat major third (of 386 Cents), and a very flat minor seventh (of 969 Cents). In Africa, there are several types of tonal systems that are derived from the experience of the harmonic series, depending on whether their basis is one or two (more rarely three) fundamentals, and which section of the natural harmonic series is used to form the tonal system and, in particular, how high up.

For example, the tonal system of the !Kung (a Khoesan-speaking group found in southeast Angola and northeast Namibia) is derived from the experience of the mouth bow and the selective reinforcement of partials not higher than the fourth harmonic over two fundamentals. A !Kung performer can transform his hunting bow into either a vessel-resonated musical bow or a mouth bow by dividing the string by a tuning noose so that the two fundamentals give any interval that suits the performer—for example, an approximate major third.

Family 2. The relationship between language and music, particularly with regard to intonation of so-called speech tones in tone languages of western Africa's Kwa-speaking linguistic area, is still being investigated, despite considerable work already done on "tone and tune." Yoruba language and music are a case in point. With the exception of the Ijesha and Ekiti, most Yoruba-speaking people in Nigeria and neighboring countries have used (since their music was put on record) an anhemitonic pentatonic scale with apparently perfect fourths and fifths, and seconds and minor thirds as the constituent intervals. In this style, which is sometimes referred to as the Ò.yò. style because it was concentrated in the Yoruba kingdom of Ò.yò., no multipart techniques are found that would accommodate simultaneous sounds other than octaves, unisons, and the occasional heterophony rising from overlapping call-and-response patterns in leader-chorus singing. This style is well preserved in chantefables called àlò..

The question is how the ancestors of the Yoruba, the Fõ, and other western Africans who share this tonal system, arrived at it. In view of the absence of any particular partials-reinforcing techniques, at least in the Ò.yò. Yoruba style and among the Fõ, it may be assumed that the genesis of their common anhemitonic pentatonic system must have been different from that, for example, in southern Africa among various San groups. Data on language-music relationships suggest a vague relationship between the three acknowledged Yoruba tones in language (plus slides and perhaps intermediate tones) and musical pitch, but not in such a strict manner that a tonal step in language would neatly correspond to a musical interval. There is evidence demonstrating the intervals that, in one performance of a Yoruba song appear as seconds, may be intoned as minor thirds in the next. More important than the intervals is the direction of pitch movement for making the text understood. This would suggest that, besides the factor of the tonal language, there should be another, language-independent formative factor as the evolutionary basis of the specific anhemitonic pentatonic system shared by the Yoruba and many others in western Africa.

Family 3. In several areas of sub-Saharan Africa, field researchers have documented tempered instrumental tunings. These temperaments proceed from either a pentatonic or a heptatonic base. Therefore, they have been described as equipentatonic and equiheptatonic tunings in which the octave (a universal interval) is divided by ear into five or seven approximately equal steps.

Equidistant tunings proceed from audible pitch, not from the sound spectrum of a note. Therefore, the study of spectrograms is inconclusive with regard to equidistant tunings. Because instruments of different type, such as flutes and xylophones, or notes of the same instrument without uniform timbre, are tuned together by musicians, the auditory principle is always pitch abstraction, not timbre comparison.

In equipentatonic systems the octave (1,200 Cents) is divided by five, resulting in a standard interval of 240 Cents (plus or minus 20 Cents margin of tolerance); in equiheptatonic systems, 1,200 divided by seven equals 171.4 Cents (again with plus or minus 20 Cents, on the average, as a margin of tolerance). Musicians who tune their xylophones, lamellophones, zithers, and other instruments by ear cannot, of course, achieve accuracy down to decimal values. For structural reasons as well—such as the deliberate attempt at friction octaves (that is, octaves arbitrarily sharp or flat), as in tunings of southern Uganda—they would not aim for arithmetical accuracy. Therefore, equidistance in African instrumental tunings is always approximate. Klaus Wachsmann used to speak of pen-equidistance.

How African instrumentalists eventually arrived at tempered instrumental tunings is an interesting historical issue. Some authors, including Erich M. von Hornbostel, Jaap Kunst, and Jones, have postulated that the idea was imported from Southeast Asia with instruments such as xylophones. Such claims are difficult to verify, however, in the absence of factual sources. There may also be intra-culturally valid motivations, such as the need for shifting patterns across the keyboard of a xylophone

without risking a loss of identity. In the music of southern Uganda, musicians transpose the tone rows that constitute the instrumental themes through any of the five steps of a pentatonically tuned xylophone, without any modal concept. In *amadinda* music these shifts are referred to as the *emiko* of a theme. The unwritten compositional rules also only deal with standard intervals; they are valid irrespective of the *omuko* (pitch-level transposition) at which a theme is played on the xylophone. Obviously, musician-composers of the ancient court music tradition of the Buganda Kingdom (established in the fifteenth century) must have felt a need to create compromised tunings that would allow them to play the same songs in any transposition without losing their identities.

There are some large areas in Africa with tempered instrumental tunings: southern Uganda (among the Ganda and Soga) and the southwestern Central African Republic for equipentatonic tunings; for equiheptatonic tunings, the Lower Zambezi Valley (among the Sena), southern Mozambique (among the Chopi), parts of eastern Angola, some parts of Mandinka-speaking western Africa (in Guinea, Mali, the Gambia, and elsewhere), and some cultures of Côte d'Ivoire. These are some of the prominent areas. Even in the vocal music of some of these regions, musicians often seek a kind of compromise intonation. The most famous example of this is the Chokwe in Angola: in their three-to-four-part singing style, long-held sounds in thirds are corrected constantly in their intonation by the singers, in the sense that minor thirds, where they would appear, are intoned toward neutral thirds. A similar phenomenon is found among the Baule of Côte d'Ivoire.

MULTIPART SINGING

Closely related to the study of tonal systems in African music is the study of multipart patterns in vocal and instrumental performances. As suggested by Jones's harmony map, different styles and techniques of multipart singing exist in sub-Saharan Africa with a somewhat patchy distribution. It has also been demonstrated that the tonal systems and multipart singing found in many African cultures are functionally linked. For example, parallelism in thirds is often associated with heptatonic systems, whereas in pentatonic traditions, fourth parallelism (sometimes interrupted by a single, structurally determined major third) often plays an important role.

There are two entirely different approaches to multipart singing in Africa. One is homophonic, in which a group of people sing the same text together at different pitch levels. The emerging pitch lines then display an identical structure. The different voices usually move in intervals perceived as consonant (i.e., sounding well together). In some cases all the voices move together in parallel, but there are also many instances (particularly in eastern Angola) where parallel, oblique, and contrary motion are all applied alternately within a song. The extent to which contrary motion is acceptable in a tradition depends on the degree to which a language is tonal. Languages with extreme tonality, such as those within the Kwa family of languages in western Africa, would not favor these kinds of motion, whereas other languages, such as Chokwe, Luchazi, and other Bantu languages in Angola, accommodate contrary motion by singers. Regarding form, homophonic multipart singing by vocal groups is often combined with a leader-chorus responsorial scheme.

The other approach is polyphonic. In this case a group of people sing different text phrases (sometimes only syllables) without any common starting and ending points. Singing together, they interlock in various ways. Where the voices meet and produce simultaneous sounds, they are consonant. Polyphonic singing occurs among various San groups—particularly women—and among the central African pygmies. Contrary to earlier claims, these polyphonic styles are historically unrelated. More impressive polyphonic singing styles are found in Zimbabwe and central Mozambique, as in the threshing songs collected by Hugh Tracey among the Shona during the 1920s. In some cultures, polyphonic singing styles are practiced by children in particular, as among the Nyakyusa of Tanzania and other ethnic groups.

SOUND AND BODY MOVEMENT

A common stereotype of African music is that it is rich in rhythm. However, in all the better-known African languages, there is no term that would be congruent in its semantic field with the Greek notion of "rhythm." Rhythm as a concept in isolation is probably not an African concept at all. If one analyzes instrumental performance in sub-Saharan Africa, such as "drumming" (to use a popular label), considering detectable kinemes (intraculturally significant motional-timbral units), one will discover that "drumming" in Africa is not merely "rhythm," but that the basic aim of a hand-drummer (as opposed to a single-pitched bell) is to create language-related motional-timbral patterns. And the drummer conceptualizes, in terms of timbre, units of discernible pitch rather than "rhythms." These units, according to which part of the drum skin or drum's body is struck, constitute a repertoire of sounds and phrases (patterns) often identified with mnemonic or teaching syllables. Therefore, to describe, let alone transcribe, drumming in Africa merely in terms of "rhythm" almost always misses essentials, an idea that is supported by the theoretical vocabulary in African languages referring to drumming.

A kinemic analysis of music and dance originates from the idea that motional patterns can be dissected into intraculturally conceptualized smallest units, called kinemes. Once these have been isolated, they can be explained in drawings and given notational symbols. Kinemic examination embraces and connects the two areas of expression that are intimately linked in many African genres: sound production and body movement. In kinemic analysis one first isolates and lists the action units according to the musicians' own taxonomies. In many African musical traditions, each kineme has a specific syllable or mnemonic phrase attached to identify it. An example is an accompanying drum pattern used in *vipwali* drumming among the Nkhangala, Mbwela, Luchazi, Nyemba, and related peoples in southeastern Angola: *ma-cha-ki-li ma-cha-ki-li*, and so on. In order to discover these kinemes, one often may simply count the number of syllables in a mnemonic phrase; in the case cited, there are four. Therefore, the drummer must have conceptualized at least four different motional-timbral units. Next, one can attempt to check that result by watching the drummer's hands and discovering how those units are produced. For example, they may by produced by striking different areas of the drum skin, or by employing different parts of the hand for a stroke, or both. Finally, each kineme, thus isolated, is given a notational symbol—in the above case, the mnemonic syllables themselves. Then transcription can start, using these symbols and accompanied by an explanatory key.

Kinemic analysis may be employed for the structural analysis of dance movement, as well. It follows the same principle. In contrast to conventional notation systems for dance, such as Laban or Benesh notations, it proceeds from an emic standpoint, using symbols adapted to the dance culture, and being analyzed, just as different languages use different orthographic systems and not a single set of universal symbols.

In structural dance analysis, one first isolates the body areas that are acting, and then represents each area (like each drum) with a horizontal line (vertical lines represent the elementary pulsation.). Next, one identifies the number of kinemes used within each body area. For example, in a certain movement pattern used in various dance cultures of central Africa over a twelve-pulse cycle, two body areas (motional centers) are acting: first, the legs, and second, the pelvis (affecting the arms and upper torso).

Whereas there is extensive and descriptive literature on dance in Africa, including several attempts at dance notation, sometimes under the ideological blanket of "dance literacy," few emically relevant dance studies have been published. One of them is Azuka Tuburu's work on Igbo (Ibo) music and dance. Comparative works on dance in Africa include attempts at delineating broad geographical dance-style areas. Detailed stylistic analysis on a comparative basis is found in Alan Lomax's choreometrics scheme. A third area of attention was the cognitional dimension as reflected in verbalized concepts such as Robert Farris Thompson's "esthetics of the cool" and the study of behavioral patterns embracing body language.

See also **Dance; Language: Sociolinguistics; Languages; Musical Instruments; Tracey, Hugh.**

BIBLIOGRAPHY

Berliner, Paul. *The Soul of* Mbira: *Music and Traditions of the Shona People of Zimbabwe.* Berkeley: University of California Press, 1978.

Ekman, Paul. "Movements with Precise Meanings." *Journal of Communication* 26, no. 3 (1976): 14–26.

Euba, Akin. *Yoruba Drumming: The Dùndún Tradition.* Bayreuth African Studies. Bayreuth, Germany: Bayreuth University, 1990.

Hornbostel, Erich Moritz von. "The Ethnology of African Sound-Instruments." *Africa* 6 (1933): 129–157, 277–311.

Jones, Arthur M. *Studies in African Music.* 2 vols. London: Oxford University Press, 1959.

Kubik, Gerhard. *Theory of African Music*, volume 1. Wilhelmshaven: Noetzel, 1994.

Lomax, Alan, et al. "Choremetrics: A Method for the Study of Cross-Cultural Pattern in Film." *Research Film* 6, no. 6 (1969).

Malamusi, Moya Aliya. *From Lake Malawi to the Zambezi. Aspects of Music and Oral Literature in South-East Africa in the 1990s.* CD with pamphlet, pamap 602, LC 07203 Frankfurt/Mainz: Popular African Music/ African Music Archive, 1999.

Rouget, Gilbert. *Un roi africain et sa musique de cour. Chants et danses du palais à Porto-Novo sous le règne de Gbèfa (1948-1976).* Paris: CNRS Eds., 1996.

Thompson, Robert Farris. *African Art in Motion.* Los Angeles: University of California Press, 1974.

Tuburu, Azuka. "Kinetik und sociale Funktion des Tanzes bei den Igbo." Ph.D. diss., University of Salzburg, 1987.

Waterman, Richard A. "African Influences on the Music of the Americas." In *Acculturation in the Americas*, edited by Sol Tax. Chicago, 1952.

Zemp, Hugo. *Masters of the Balafon: Funeral Festivities. Film.* Paris: Sélénium Films, 2001.

GERHARD KUBIK

ISLAMIC

Islamic music is taken to comprise sound-centric public performance practices imbued—via text, context, associations, or intentions—with Islamic meanings. The category of Islamic music in Africa is problematic. Music is often a misleading concept in Africa, where sonic, verbal, and kinetic performances are closely connected, and where aesthetic and ritual practices are often inseparable. Based on conservative interpretations of Qur'an and hadith, many Muslims regard music as sinful (*haram*), and may reject the notion of Islamic music altogether. Nevertheless, there are continuities between Islamic sonic practices, and broader musical ones. Although the diversity of Islam in Africa renders the category of music unwieldy, Islamic influence has induced striking musical similarities across a broad region.

Throughout Islamic history there has been disagreement over the legitimacy of public musical practice—as entertainment or as devotion—and such disputes have also flared in Muslim Africa. In many areas, musicians' social status appears to have declined with introduction of Islam. Given respectable text and context, male vocal forms are most acceptable; accompanying frame drums (Ar. *tar, duff*) and flutes (Ar. *nay*), are often sanctioned, according to Islamic traditions; other instruments are frequently rejected in Islamic contexts. Usually Sufi orders (*tariqas*) are more tolerant of spiritual audition (*sama'*). But even reformers such as 'Uthman dan Fodio (1754–1813) recognized the effectiveness of chant in calling people to Islam.

Islamic music in Africa encompasses a broad spectrum of practices. Throughout the Muslim world, three recurring sonic contexts may be discerned. In order of increasing sonic diversity and localization these are: ritual contexts (such as *salah*, prayer), holiday/festival contexts (such as 'Id), and life-cycle contexts (such as marriage). Beyond these are nonrecurring contexts expressing particular interpretations of Islam (such as Sufi and syncretic rituals). Finally, one must consider relatively decontextualized popular music genres carrying Islamic themes and embedded in media systems.

A performance genre comprises sonic, textual, and contextual features. Formal ritual genres, prescribed by Islamic law, center on Arabic text, often at the expense of musical sound. Less formal festival genres are supererogatory, and hence exhibit sonic and textual diversity, drawing upon local languages, poetic genres, and musical traditions. Life-cycle genres are still more diverse and open to local sources.

Festival contexts often foster religio-musical specialists who may cross over as entertainer-singers; life-cycle contexts frequently draw upon the broader category of musician. Conversely, religious performers and genres may cross over to the popular music world while retaining religious associations.

Text is central in Islamic music, and so vocalists (among Arabic speakers, *munshid*, hymnodist, or *madda*, praise-singer) are as well. Performers may also be known as singers as religious shades into popular music. Outside the Arab world, an Islamic poem in Arabic is frequently known as a *qasida* (poem).

Throughout the Muslim world certain thematic elements recur: petitions, praise, and loving devotion (to Allah, the prophet Muhammad, and the saints), exhortations to the community, and expressions of religious experience or knowledge. These themes are primarily expressed in religious sung poetry (*inshad dini*).

The most common forms of sung poetry are glorification of God (*tasbih*), petitions to God (*ibtihalat*), and praise (*madih*) for the Prophet. In Egypt, supplication (ibtihalat) and madih are the primary themes of sung devotional poetry; classical and colloquial (*zajal, mawwal*) forms are widely used. Thematically parallel forms are found elsewhere in Africa.

Praise for Muhammad is believed to confer spiritual benefits on singer and listener alike. Although African oral literary traditions of praise exist apart from (and prior to) Islamic ones, the two sets of traditions clearly harmonized. For instance, traditional Manding griots (praise singers) of West Africa trace their ancestry to Surakata, a quasi-legendary praise singer to the Prophet himself who flourished during the period 610–632. Likewise, Fulani Muslim reformer 'Uthman dan Fodio, although banning some music and dance, wrote: Singer, stop, do not waste your time//In singing the praise of men. Sing the praises of the Prophet and be content (Erlmann 1986).

Certain African madih texts exerted global influence, especially the invocation *Dala'il al-Khayrat* by the Moroccan al-Jazuli (d. 1465), and two poems (*Burda* and *Hamziyya*) by Sharaf al-Din al-Busiri (b. 1212), an Egyptian of Berber origin, that became models for composers in local idioms throughout North, East, and West Africa.

RITUAL CONTEXTS

Ordinary congregational prayer (salah) comprises a suite of public sonic genres, including the preliminary call to prayer (*adhan*) performed by the *mu'adhdhin* (muezzin), Qur'anic recitation (*tilawa*) performed by the *qari', du'a'*, and other short, intoned devotional texts. Such performances are a-metric, and strictly vocal. Being obligatory (*fard*), salah is highly regulated in its textual and contextual aspects, though locally inflected sonic differences can be identified. Adhan and tilawa have also infused Arab melisma, ornament, modality, and vocal timbre throughout music of Muslim African. The adhan's musical origins are African, as the first mu'adhdhin, Bilal ibn Rabah (c. 578–c. 638), was an Ethiopian.

Outside prayer, a specialized reciter (Ar. qari') publicly recites the holy Qur'an for a variety of occasions, especially during Ramadan. The text itself is fixed (though variant readings [qira'at] are used in particular regions), as are recitational rules (ahkam al-tajwid) governing phonetics, phrasing, syllable length, and tempo. However, timbral, melodic, and contextual aspects are quite variable. A solo ametric voice is most common, but metered or corporate chanting occurs, too (such as among Berber tolba). There are two principal named styles: elaborate (mujawwad) and simpler (murattal); the latter is increasingly perceived as more proper.

HOLIDAY/FESTIVAL CONTEXTS

Ramadan. Ramadan subsumes two temporal contexts. Evenings feature religious songs celebrating Ramadan, the Qur'an, and the Prophet, and supplicating God. Ibtihalat, tawashih, and tilawa are heard on Egyptian radio. In the Comoro islands, mrenge (boxing matches) are accompanied by drumming after the evening meal. In Kano, Nigeria, royal Hausa musicians (maroka) perform during the holy final ten nights. At dawn, performers rouse the devout for their predawn meal (sahur). In Marrakesh, the ghaita (oboe) and nfir (trumpet) play melodies based on religious chants from mosque minarets. The itinerant Egyptian masahharati awakens the faithful with chanting, accompanied by a small drum (baza). Among the Dagbamba in northern Ghana, a jenjili (musical bow) player circulates, playing and singing. Yoruba youth perform were or ajisaari, vocal genres influenced by ritual cantillations.

Mawlid al-Nab. The season surrounding the Prophet's birthday (12 Rabi' al-Awwal) is celebrated via musical performances of biographical and panegyric texts (also called mawlid) and madih. In Arabic, Busiri's Burda, and the mawlid of Barzanji (d. 1765) are widely distributed in Africa, with variable musical treatments. Mawlid is also expressed in local idioms. Desert Berbers (Zenatas) of Gourara perform ahallil, vocal-flute-percussion praise songs. The Damba festival of the Dagbamba people includes singing, drumming, and dancing honoring the Prophet and the chief. The Dyula (Côte d'Ivoire) celebrate Donba with sermons (kalan) interspersed with song.

Elaborate mawlid performances are found in coastal East Africa. In Lamu, Kenya, the maulidi is observed as series of solo readings (kusoma) interspersed with collective madih (qasida) sometimes accompanied by drum (tari, kigoma) and flute (nay). Many Sufi shaikhs compose mawlids for use in their orders. The Tivaouane lodge of the Senegalese Tijaniyya tariqa performs a yearly gammu celebrating the Prophet's birth with sung devotional poetry.

Pilgrimage to Mecca (Hajj). The embarkation and return of pilgrims is a joyous annual celebration. Among Yoruba, sakara praise singers, accompanied by the molo or goje lutes and sakara clay drum, performed at hajj celebrations; women welcomed returning pilgrims with waka songs. Nubian women sing call/response songs for pilgrims, accompanied by handclaps. Among illiterate Hausa women pilgrims, composition and performance of personal hajj songs reenacting their journey confers cultural capital. These genres reveal Arab influence.

'Id Festivals. Musical content of 'Id festivals varies from monophonic songs in Egypt to the polyphony of the Rasha'ida tribe in Eritrea; Yoruba dundun drum orchestras accompany processions of chiefs to and from prayer ground, while the Dagbamba perform spectacular all-night drum history narrations.

'Ashura. The Shi'a in East Africa (primarily of South Asian origin) commemorate the martyrdom of Husayn with a majlis, including sung elegies and dirges. Sunnis also commemorate various prophetic events on this day; in Morocco, religious chants (ait) and trumpets (neffar) accompany polyrhythmic drumming (daqqa).

LIFE-CYCLE CONTEXTS

Life-cycle contexts include a rich variety of musical features and genres, not all explicitly Islamic. Particularly at weddings, one observes greater liberality in use of music, dance, and mixing of the sexes. Religious songs, especially madih, are commonly performed. In Egypt, inshad incorporates popular Arabic songs and instruments. Hausa Bandiri music transforms Hindi film songs into madih. In East Africa, births and weddings are celebrated with mawlid. Comorians celebrate weddings with music and dance called tari, filled with praise of the Prophet. The Songhoi (Niger) circumcision ritual fuses Islamic with pre-Islamic performance elements.

Sufi Contexts. Active Sufi tariqas gather at least weekly to perform a devotional liturgy (*hadra*), which can be highly musical, including tilawa, madih, and mawlid. But the most distinctive Sufi genre is *dhikr* (remembrance of God), comprising collective rhythmic (sometimes melodic) chanting of divine names, commonly accompanied by movement, accelerating to a climax, and sometimes leading to trance (*wajd, hal*). Alongside dhikr, a munshid may sing Sufi poetry, often composed by tariqa founders in local languages. Regional or tariqa-specific musical traditions may figure prominently. Thus Qadiris in Sudan exhibit Sudanese musical influence; in Senegal they deploy Wolof rhythms on Arab-influenced kettledrums. Shaykh Amadou Bamba (1850–1927), who composed numerous qasidas praising the Prophet, founded the Senegalese Muridiyya. A subgroup, the Baye Fall, employ Senegalese drums devotionally. North African and Egyptian liturgies are melodically similar to Arabic music.

Saint Festival Contexts. With no formal procedure for canonization, the Muslim saint (*wali*) is ubiquitous. While several are widely revered (for example, 'Abd al-Qādir al-Jilani d. 1166), local saints are everywhere. As for the Prophet, the saint is celebrated in an annual public festival (Ar. mawlid) that is literally and spiritually centered on the saint's shrine. Ritual activities take place within the building housing the shrine, and also outdoors in the surrounding area, in nearby buildings.

Most saint festivals are freer than tariqa hadras; instruments and people exhibiting ecstatic behavior frequently appear. Enormous mawlids in Egypt encompass musical diversity. Accompanied by Arab music, Shaykh Yasin al-Tuhami (b. 1948) performs for thousands at the mawlid of al-Husayn in Cairo. Shaykh Amadou Bamba is musically lauded during the Grand Maggal, an annual pilgrimage to his birthplace, Touba.

Spirit Ritual Contexts. Rituals featuring spirit possession, music, and dance are widely distributed throughout Africa. In Muslim areas, such rituals often display Islamic syncretism by assimilating spirit practices within tariqa-like social groups, or by recognizing a special class of Muslim spirits. Women, peripheral in most tariqas, are frequently principals here. Incorporating sub-Saharan instruments and music, these rituals center on trance and spiritual therapy. Typically, musical patterns placate particular spirits, thus enabling diagnosis and therapy. Tariqa-like groups include the North African Gnawa and the Hamadsha. In Egypt, Sudan, and Ethiopia, *zar* performances invoke Muslim spirits; similar rituals in East Africa feature Muslim (*ki-islamu*) spirits, requiring mawlidi performances.

Sectarian Contexts. Whereas Muslim African is predominantly Sunni, isolated sectarian groups perform special genres in unique contexts, including the aforementioned Shiite majlis, the chants of Algerian Ibadi Berbers in Algeria, and Ismaili *ginan* of East Africa, featuring poetry of founder-saints, and a South Asian melodic ethos, often with *tabla* and *harmonium* accompaniment.

INFLUENCE UPON POPULAR MUSIC

Disengaged from religious contexts, sacred sounds of Islam enter mass music media. Besides providing sonic resources, Islamic sounds may confer artistic legitimacy, ethical propriety, and cultural prestige, tap powerful religious feeling and nostalgia, and serve as a touchstone of cultural authenticity. Until the latter twentieth century, many popular Arab singers, such as Umm Kulthum (1904–1975), trained on religious material, such as tilawa, mawlid, or Sufi inshad. Such religious-vocal training bestowed upon these artists both a striking stylistic imprint and elevated cultural status.

Islamic styles and genres may be restaged as live entertainment, such as the Gnawa and 'Isawiyya spectacles in Marrakesh, or secularized (such as Nigerian waka, *were*, *apala*, and sakara), via musical, textual, and contextual changes.

The 1970s witnessed emergence of popular Moroccan groups such as Nass el-Ghiwane that drew upon folk and Sufi heritage, mixed with western popular music. In Senegal's bustling music scene, star singers such as Youssou N'dour and Ismaël Lô (b. 1956) record pop songs praising and invoking local Sufi saints, especially Amadou Bamba.

Western consumption generates at least three distinctive categories of African Islamic popular music: ethnographic performances of authentic Islamic cultural traditions; world beat hybrids incorporating African-Islamic styles (such as the *gnawa*-jazz fusions of Hassan Hakmoun; b. 1963); and the uptake of popular Islamic music into the global industry. In 2004, Youssou N'Dour won a Grammy award for *Egypt*, a Sufi album combining Egyptian, Senegalese, and Western music. Promising artistic and financial rewards, international markets push African Islamic music in new directions, inducing creative experimentation with new styles and fusions.

See also **'Abd al-Qādir**; **Festivals and Carnivals**; **Islam**; **Kano**; **Literature**; **Musical Instruments**; **N'Dour, Youssou**; **Religion and Ritual**.

BIBLIOGRAPHY

Adegbite, Ademola. "The Influence of Islam on Yoruba Music." *Orita* 21, no. 1 (1989): 32–43.

al-Shahi, Ahmed. "Spirit Possession and Healing: The ZAR among the Shaygiyya of the Northern Sudan." *British Society for Middle Eastern Studies Bulletin* 11, no. 1 (1984): 28–44.

Ames, David W. "Igbo and Hausa Musicians: A Comparative Examination." *Ethnomusicology* 17, no. 2 (1973): 250–278.

Anderson, Lois Ann. "The Interrelation of African and Arab Musics: Some Preliminary Considerations." In *Essays on Music and History in Africa*, ed. Klaus Wachsmann. Evanston: Northwestern University Press, 1971.

Boyd, Alan. "Music in Islam: Lamu, Kenya, a Case Study." In *Discourse in Ethnomusicology II: A Tribute to Alan P. Merriam*, ed. Caroline Card, et al. Bloomington: Indiana University Ethnomusicology Publications Group, 1981.

Charry, Eric S. "Music and Islam in Sub-Saharan Africa." In *The History of Islam in Africa*, ed. Nehemia Levtzion and Randall Lee Pouwels. Athens: Ohio University Press, 2000.

Chernoff, John Miller. "The Drums of Dagbon." In *Repercussions: A Celebration of African-American Music*, ed. Geoffrey Haydon and Dennis Marks. London: Century Company, 1985.

Conrad, David. "Islam in the Oral Traditions of Mali: Bilali and Surakata." *Journal of African History* 26, no. 1 (1985): 33–49.

Danielson, Virginia. "Min al-Mashayikh: A View of Egyptian Musical Tradition." *Asian Music* 22, no. 1 (1991): 113–127.

Erlmann, Veit. *Music and the Islamic Reform in the Early Sokoto Empire: Sources, Ideology, Effects.* Marburg, Stuttgart: Deutsche Morgenländische Gesellschaft, 1986.

Euba, Akin. "Islamic Musical Culture Among the Yoruba: A Preliminary Survey." In *Essays on Music and History in Africa*, ed. Klaus Wachsmann. Evanston, IL: Northwestern University Press, 1971.

Giles, Linda L. "Sociocultural Change and Spirit Possession on the Swahili Coast of East Africa." *Anthropological Quarterly* 68, no. 2 (1995): 89–106.

Grame, Theodore C. "Music in the Jma al-Fna of Marrakesh." *The Musical Quarterly* LVI, no. 1 (1970): 74–87.

Kenyon, Susan M. "Zar as Modernization in Contemporary Sudan." *Anthropological Quarterly* 68, no. 2 (1995): 107–120.

Kinney, Sylvia. "Drummers in Dagbon: The Role of Drummer in Damba Festival." *Ethnomusicology* 14, no. 2 (1970): 258–265.

Langlois, Tony. "The Gnawa of Oujda: Music at the Margins in Morocco." *World of Music* 40, no. 1 (1998): 135-56.

Larkin, Brian. "Bandiri Music, Globalization and Urban Experience in Nigeria." *Social Text* 22, no. 4 (2004): 91–112.

Launay, Robert. "Spirit Media: The Electronic Media and Islam Among the Dyula of Northern Cote d'Ivoire." *Africa* 67, no. 3 (1997): 441–453.

McLaughlin, Fiona. "Islam and Popular Music in Senegal: The Emergence of a 'New Tradition.'" *Africa* 67, no. 4 (1997): 560–581.

Nelson, Kristina. *The Art of Reciting the Qur'an.* Austin: University of Texas Press, 1985.

Orwin, Martin. "Language Use in Three Somali Religious Poems." *Journal of African Cultural Studies* 14, no. 1 (2001): 69–87.

Ottenheimer, Harriet J. "Culture Contact and Musical Style: Ethnomusicology in the Comoro Islands." *Ethnomusicology* 14, no. 3 (1970): 458–462.

Scheub, Harold. "A Review of African Oral Traditions and Literature." *African Studies Review* 28, no. 2/3 (1985): 1–72.

Schuyler, Philip D. "Music and Meaning among the Gnawa Religious Brotherhood of Morocco." *World of Music* 23, no. 1 (1981): 3–13.

Schuyler, Philip D. "A Folk Revival in Morocco." In *Everyday Life in the Muslim Middle East*, 2nd edition, ed. Donna Lee Bowen and Evelyn A. Early. Bloomington: Indiana University Press, 2002.

Shiloah, Amnon. "Music and Religion in Islam." *Acta Musicologica* 69, no. 2 (1997): 143–155.

Waugh, Earle H. *The Munshidin of Egypt: Their World and Their Song.* Columbia: University of South Carolina Press, 1989.

Waugh, Earle H. *Memory, Music, and Religion Morocco's Mystical Chanters.* Columbia: University of South Carolina Press, 2005.

MICHAEL FRISHKOPF

MUSIC, MODERN POPULAR

This entry includes the following articles:
OVERVIEW
CENTRAL AFRICA
EASTERN AFRICA
EGYPT
ETHIOPIA
NORTHERN AFRICA
SOUTHERN AFRICA
WESTERN AFRICA

OVERVIEW

Modern African music has a history stretching back more than a century. Although early visitors and travelers brought hitherto unknown musical conventions to Africa, colonization was the main means for the introduction of Western musical instruments and concepts in Africa.

From the first half of the nineteenth century on, European musical traditions spread throughout the continent. In addition, Afro-American music (mainly in western and central Africa) and Arabic (which had arrived even earlier) and Indian music (both in eastern Africa) inspired new music. Brass bands—forerunners were the fifteenth-century drum and fife bands on the West African coast—accompanied the arrival of the colonial armies and administration. After military music came the church music of the various Western denominations: the Protestants with hymns, the Catholics with liturgical chants. Next came the introduction of dance music, as well as the theatrical forms arising from the vaudeville and minstrelsy of North America.

With schools providing increasingly educated musicians, Africans performed in all spheres of musical activity. Soon they realized that imported musical forms could be adapted to local musical traditions, whether by providing fitting lyrics or by adding local percussive rhythmic structure or background, and they joined with the indigenist movements and what later became the nationalist or independence movements. Church hymns were sung in many of the African languages, and new compositions by African composers were drawing on local traditions. In the popular music context the amalgamation of different musical traditions resulted in many kinds of syntheses. They range from local folk music including Western instruments to Western instruments playing local folk music—or local instruments being used to play modern compositions. Western instruments were imitated—for example in Beni *ngoma*, for which gourds are grown to function as horns.

MUSICAL REGIONS

The Sahel. The Sahel is dominated by what is called griot-style or Mandingo rock. (The Sahel covers more or less the area of the ancient Mandinka empire, from Senegal to Mali.) In the 1960s the popular dance orchestras, playing mainly Latin music, increasingly created a sound reminiscent of local string instruments (*kora*), xylophones (*balafon*), or drums. Local instruments were gradually reintegrated in the 1980s, such as the *tama*, a Senegalese drum. The vocal style took on the characteristics of the griots or griottes. Since the 1960s female singers have become stars, especially in Mali.

Since the 1960s national musical cultures have developed from similar roots. In Senegal, Youssou N'Dour created the *mbalax*. In Mali the Rail Band de Bamako produced some of the most famous African musicians: Salif Keita, singer; Mory Kante, singer and *kora* player; and Kante Manfila, guitarist. Both of them originally came from Guinea.

Coastal Francophone West Africa. In Guinea's national competitions Bembeya Jazz was crowned the best band in 1964; it subsequently became one of the favorite bands in West Africa. In Côte d'Ivoire Ernesto Djedje formulated *ziglibithy* in the late 1970s—a mix of Zairian rumba, Afro-beat, and Francophone West African music. In the early 1980s Alpha Blondy presented Afro reggae. In the 1990s a new acoustic music, the Zouglou, sparked off a new movement of "neo-African" bands, especially at the university. By the end of the 1990s the highly percussive *Mapouka* dance—originally from the southwestern coastal region—

sparked of ambivalent reactions because of its "obscene" or even "pornographic" appearance.

Anglophone West Africa. The Anglophone West African states—mainly Sierra Leone, Ghana, and Nigeria—historically are strongly linked by their common British colonial past. They produced guitar bands and dance bands that played "highlife" after World War II. In Ghana, E. T. Mensah is considered the "King of Highlife." The guitar bands have Nana Ampadou as their greatest representative. In Nigeria, Bobby Benson was the leading artist of Nigerian highlife. Fela Anikulapo Kuti created the Afrobeat in the 1970s. Juju music, a Yoruba guitar band style, has been the prevailing sound since independence. After I. K. Dairo, Ebenezer Obey and Sunny Adé are the leading artists. Many other popular styles can be attributed to individual artists. Since the 1970s these have increasingly been female singers, mainly from a middle-class background.

Central Africa. After an initial period of copying Cuban rumba music, the Congo rumba began to evolve; Le Grand Kalle, Franco Luambo Makiadi, and Tabu Ley Rochereau produced hundreds of records. The big dance orchestras were musically questioned by the Zaiko Langa Langa guitar band in the 1970s. Zaiko developed into a "dynasty" and today competes with various classic formations. *Ndombolo* with its emphasized belly movements became the dance style of the late 1990s.

Horn of Africa. Ethiopia's popular dance music in the 1960s drew a lot from both jazz and soul. The sound was strongly Amharic based on the style of the *Azmari* minstrel. In the late 1980s and early 1990s, Aster Aweke and Mahmoud Ahmed became the first Ethiopian artists to achieve international fame.

East Africa. East African music had its own guitar traditions connected with the Katanga/Shaba guitar-picking styles of the 1950s, such as those of Jean Bosco Mwenda, John Mwale, and George Mukabi in Kenya. In the 1980s the Luo-derived Benga beat began to evolve, thereby diminishing the importance of Zairian *soukous* bands. Singing was primarily in local languages—in Tanzania, in Swahili. *Taarab* is Swahili music (along

the coast and on the islands, especially Zanzibar), played at all types of social events. Although seemingly Arabic, it draws its main roots from the mainland East African music. The beginning of the twenty-first century is characterized by the growth of *bongo flava* in Tanzania. This is a new Swahili style mainly in the hip-hop vein but also integrating other mainstream global sounds.

Central Southern Africa. In Zambia local neo-traditional acoustic *kalindula* music was adopted in the 1980s by the electric bands, and Zamrock disappeared. Angolan and Mozambican styles developed, as did the music of the other African Portuguese colonies, under the influence of Portuguese folk music, including fado. In Mozambique, *marrabenta* became the name for modern dance music.

South Africa. In the townships, beginning in the 1950s, the music of the young boys was *kwela*. Electrified, it became *simanje-manje* and in the early twenty-first century is generally called jive or *mbaqanga*. With the liberation of South Africa *kwaito* evolved. It comprises many modern styles and sounds, including hip-hop, but stands apart from the South African version of hip-hop. Its lyrics can be highly critical of the political situation. The global rap craze is conquering the African continent.

Beginning in Senegal in the early 1990s with the famous PBS (Positive Black Soul) and with the South African People of Da City hip-hop spread all over Africa. In the early twenty-first century there is no country where one cannot find a hip-hop group. In Senegal it is termed Senerap, in Ghana it is called Hiplife (highlife and hip-hop), and on Zanzibar it is Taarap (Taarab and rap).

RECORDED AFRICAN MUSIC

The first commercial recordings were made, in various parts of the continent, early in the 1920s. EMI chose West and South Africa; Odeon, East Africa. The musicians at that time were brought to Britain. In the 1940s and 1950s, mobile recording units or local studios within Africa supplied the musical products for the record companies in Europe. The projected market was Africa itself. The gramophone proved to be a practical implement, not requiring any electricity. As it became popular, a cross section of Euro-American popular and classical, as well as religious, music received the widest possible circulation. African record shop owners began to record local artists, and a small local record production started, though the technical side was still done in Europe.

The 45 rpm single and the 33 rpm LP were introduced at the beginning of the 1960s. Local entrepreneurs started their own recording businesses—including pressing—and their labels competed with those of international companies. In the 1970s large modern studios were constructed in a number of countries, but in the 1980s the economic crisis hit most of them, and recording and producing returned to Europe. Paris has become the main center for the production of African music, even for formerly London-based Anglophone artists. In South Africa the situation has been somewhat different. The large record companies operating there since the 1930s have survived. Nigeria, Senegal, Côte d'Ivoire, and Kenya still have their own recording industries. The main medium is the audiocassette although compact discs (CDs) are beginning to appear. The vinyl record has largely disappeared. In Europe and America, African music is mainly distributed on CDs. Video has become another important carrier of African music; commercially produced videocassettes are available everywhere. The cheaper video-CD spread and has been followed by the more expensive and refined DVD.

ORGANIZATION OF MODERN AFRICAN MUSIC

Modern African orchestras generally have a leader who is at the same time the owner of the instruments, the manager, the copyright owner of all the material produced, the director, the main instrumentalist, the main vocalist, and the main composer and lyricist. The bandsmen—women are absent as instrumentalists except in a few all-female orchestras (e.g., Les Amazones de Guinée)—usually own nothing, are paid an hourly or weekly rate, and may be fired at any time. In some cases the hotel or bar owns the instruments and hires a bandleader to handle the rest.

COPYRIGHT, PIRACY, AND THE ADAPTATION TO NEW POVERTY

Copyright is one of the biggest problems facing modern African musicians. Even though many

states are signatories of international copyright conventions, governments do not support the execution of the rights. In Ghana, for instance, special legislation has been introduced to protect copyrights. Only on this basis can royalties be collected and musicians benefit from their work. Piracy is a common practice, much to the detriment of some musical cultures. In Sierra Leone it has led to the total disappearance of the orchestras. The increasing poverty following the economic decline in many countries since 1977 has had the same effect. Electric bands relying on expensive equipment and instruments could hardly survive. New acoustic groups started to operate in increasing numbers. Adapting to new economic conditions, they played local instruments that needed no amplification though some might be required for the vocalist. Their repertoire is a condensation of local popular tunes from various sources. The main aim is to provide a dense rythmic pattern for dancing. Examples are Milo Jazz (in Sierra Leone), Zouglou (Côte d'Ivoire), and Suede Suede (Zaire).

SONG LYRICS

In African music there is rarely a piece that is solely instrumental. The lyrics are of utmost importance. It is the message of a song that the listeners are interested in. Most lyrics are in African languages, including Creole and pidgin. English, French, or Portuguese songs are mostly signs of music in exile (for a foreign audience). In the case of tonal languages, such as Yoruba, the tonal pattern follows the melody. Lyrics are composed mainly by the vocalists themselves. The content varies greatly, from historical epos to love song, but seldom is overtly political, though hints may be hidden in cryptic expressions or familiar proverbs. Many songs are filled with religious references, even though they are not classified as religious.

See also **Adé, Sunny; Communications; Education, University and College; Keita, Salif; Kuti, Fela; Mensah, E. T.; Music; N'Dour, Youssou; Popular Culture.**

BIBLIOGRAPHY

Askew, Kelly M. *Performing the Nation. Swahili Music and Cultural Politics in Tanzania.* Chicago: University of Chicago Press, 2002.

Bender, Wolfgang. *Sweet Mother: Modern African Music,* trans. Wolfgang Fries. Chicago: University of Chicago Press, 1991. Revised as *Sweet Mother: Moderne afrikanische*

Musik. Wuppertal: Edition Trickster im Peter Hammer Verlag, 2000.

Broughton, Simon, Mark Ellingham, and Richard Trillo. *World Music*, Vol. 1: *Africa, Europe and the Middle East.* London: The Rough Guides, 1999.

Charry, Eric. *Mande Music: Traditional and Modern Music of the Maninka and Mandinka of Western Africa.* Chicago: University of Chicago Press, 2000.

Collins, John. *West African Pop Roots.* Philadelphia: Conrath, Philippe, 1992.

Coplan, David B. *In Township Tonight! South Africa's Black City Music and Theatre.* Johannesburg: Ravan Press, 1985.

Erlmann, Veit. *Nightsong. Performance, Power, and Practice in South Africa.* Chicago: University of Chicago Press, 1996.

Ewens, Graeme. *Congo Colossus: The Life and Legacy of Franco and O.K. Jazz.* London: Buku Press, 1986.

Falceto, Francis. *Abyssinie Swing: A Pictorial History of Modern Ethiopian Music.* Addis Ababa: Shama Books, 2001.

Kubik, Gerhard. *Africa and the Blues.* Jackson: University Press of Mississippi, 1999.

Lahana, Michelle. *Youssou Ndour: La voix de la Médina.* Paris: Patrick Robin Editions, 2005.

Makeba, Miriam, in conversation with Nomsa Mwamuka. *Makeba: The Miriam Makeba Story.* Johannesburg: STE Publishers, 2004.

Musiques du Monde. *Cahiers d'études Africaines* 168, XLII, no. 4 (2002).

Palmberg, Mai, Annemette Kirkegaard, eds. *Playing with Identities in Contemporary Music in Africa.* Uppsala: Nordiska Afrikainstitutet, 2002.

Stewart, Gary. *Rumba on the River: A History of the Popular Music of the Two Congos.* London: Verso, 2000.

Tenaille, Frank. *Le Swing Du Caméléon. Musiques et chansons africaines 1950–2000.* Paris: Actes Sud, 2000.

Thorsen, Stig-Magnus. "Sounds of Change—Social and Political Features of Music in Africa." *Sida Studies* 12 (2004).

Turino, Thomas. *Nationalists: Cosmopolitans, and Popular Music in Zimbabwe.* Chicago: University of Chicago Press, 2000.

Veal, Michael E. *Fela: The Life and Times of an African Musical Icon.* Philadelphia: Temple University Press, 2000.

Waterman, Chris. *Juju: A Social History and Ethnography of an African Popular Music.* Chicago: University of Chicago Press, 1990.

WOLFGANG BENDER

CENTRAL AFRICA

Modern Central African music refers to the music that was conceived in the days of Léopoldville (Belgian Congo) and Brazzaville (French Congo) near the end of the 1920s and into the early 1930s. This music is a hybrid product born in colonial cities and is the result of several cultural exchanges, most notably those of Central African, West African, European, Caribbean, and Latin American origin. Since its birth, this popular music has enabled listeners to better understand Congolese and African societies and the African diaspora. Its themes evoke diverse domains of daily life, such as love, human relations, colonization, and independence, as well as human reaction to situations of suffering and inequality. In order to better understand the nature of this music, it is important to revisit the history of colonization in the Congo, the history of the African workforce in Central Africa, and explore the role of the "évolués," or the emerging Congolese elite class.

The Belgian colonial project in the Congo commenced during the second half of the nineteenth century. It consisted of integrating new territories in Central Africa in order to engage them in service to the metropolis. During the first years of colonization, the implementation process encountered difficulty because many strata within the Congolese population refused to cooperate with Belgian power. Since Congolese populations were hostile to the colonization of their territories, the Congo Free State (CFS) found itself relying heavily on foreign labor from Europe, Asia, and other areas of Africa. The CFS recruited non-Congolese African workers from the enclaves of Cabinda and Angola, as well as from Freetown (Sierra Leone), Accra and Elmina (Ghana), Lagos (Nigeria), Monrovia (Liberia), and Dakar (Senegal).

The West African contribution to the Congo was not only economic, but also cultural. West Africans contributed to the emergence of new fashions and a unique musical style. In the 1930s, the Coast men (i.e., West Africans) contributed to what constitutes the most vibrant aspect of Congolese culture: its music. Ghanaian "highlife," European rhythms, as well as the Latin/Caribbean meringue, rumba, and tango, all contributed to the birth of Congolese popular music. The Latin American music brought to the Congo during this period derived from Central African and West African musical traditions. In fact, it marked a type of return to older musical origins. In 1940, at Leopoldville, the Coast men founded the first African orchestra using "new" instruments, and inspired a group of Congolese to form their own orchestra two years later.

At the end of the 1930s through the early 1940s, in bars in Leopoldville and Brazzaville, Henri Bowane, Camille Feruzi, Antoine Kasongo (Congo-Kinshasa), and Paul Kamba (Congo-Brazzaville) created the first Congolese orchestras. They sang in the languages of the Congo and used modern instruments such as the guitar, the piano, the saxophone, and the accordion. These musical pioneers were followed, in the years thereafter, by a number of prestigious musicians, including Antoine Wendo Kolosoyi, Joseph Kabasele, Franco Luambo, Nico Kasanda, Rochereau Tabu Ley, Verkys Kiamuangana, Abeti Masikini, Tshala Muana, Mbilia Bel, and others, whose music conquered Africa, then the world.

Very rapidly, popular Congolese music became the predominant media for social, political, and cultural expression. Its portrayal of the lives of ordinary African people in Africa and in the Diaspora allows us to better understand human societies as well as human reaction to situations of suffering and inequality. In songs dedicated to Congolese women, liberal and conservative visions of femininity were combined. Alternately, they praised the qualities of "modern, educated" Congolese women while still honoring and promoting established moral, familial, and traditional values. This "conservative" vision manifested itself through intolerance of female prostitution.

During the 1950s, popular music was appropriated by the évolués Congolese to further their political ends. The évolués constituted a new social class of Congolese who went to colonial school and occupied an intermediary position between their Belgian colonizers and the Congolese masses. They desired the attainment of a special status that would differentiate them from their Congolese countrymen and afford them a new social level almost equal to that of Europeans. Music would furnish them an outlet and a privileged space for expression and political protest. In the song *Ata ndélé ata ndélé mokili ekobaluka* ("Sooner or later,

the world is going to change, and the White man will be swept aside"), Adou Elenga clearly voices messages of political resistance. This song aptly expresses the Congolese desire for political reform, which, eventually, would lead to the end of the Belgian Colonial regime in 1960.

In 1960 popular music would also go on to celebrate the Congo's independence with the song "Independence cha cha" by the orchestra African Jazz. It would lament the assassination of Lumumba with the song "Liwa ya Lumumba" ("The death of Lumumba") by the OK Jazz in 1961. Between 1965 and 1997, the political dictatorship of Zairean president Mobutu Sese Seko reigned supreme, a one-party political system was implemented, and popular song inhabited an ambivalent role. In an era when Mobutu advocated a return to authenticity, musicians such as Franco Luambo and Tabu Ley became spokesmen for the Mobutist revolution. However, despite this close proximity to the Mobutu regime, these musicians, along with many others, employed a subtle language to describe the daily hardships experienced by the Congolese (ex-Zairians).

During the end of the 1980s and into the early 1990s, Congolese music came to the banks of the Seine in Paris and the Meuse in Brussels. After Rochereau Tabu Ley appeared at the Olympia in Paris in 1970, Papa Wemba, Koffi Olomidé, Tshala Muana, Mbilia Bel, Werra Son, J. B. Mpiana, and other Congolese musicians settled in Paris and Brussels. They started appearing regularly on such noteworthy stages as the Olympia, the Sports Palace of Bercy, and the Zénith (Paris) as well as at similarly prestigious musical centers in Brussels, London, and Los Angeles. As a result, these cities have become important centers for popular Congolese music known as rumba, soukouss, or ndombolo.

During the 1940s, four recording studios played an essential role in the diffusion of popular music. These include the Olympia led by Belgians, and Ngoma, Loningisa, and Opika, led by Greeks. Throughout Mobutu's era, the studio Veve of Verkys Kiamuangana served to support the diffusion of this music. In the early twenty-first century the studio Sonodisc in Paris is the principal distributor of popular Central African music in Paris and throughout Europe.

Koffi Olomidé performs at the Iba Mar Diop stadium in Dakar, April 2005. Olomidé, from Congo of the Quarter Latin group, was taking part in the Ebony Music Festival dedicated to the fight against malaria. Seyllou/AFP/Getty Images

See also **Brazzaville; Mobutu Sese Seko; Music; Popular Culture: Central Africa.**

BIBLIOGRAPHY

Bemba, Sylvain. *Cinquante ans de musique du Congo-Zaïre (1920–1970). De Paul Kamba à Tabu Ley.* Paris and Dakar: Présence Africaine, 1984.

Gondola, Didier. "Musique moderne et identités citadines en ville africaine: Le cas du Congo-Zaïre." *Afrique contemporaine* 168 (1993): 155–168.

Stewart, Gary. *Rumba on the River: A History of the Popular Music of the Two Congos.* London: Verso, 2000.

CHARLES TSHIMANGA-KASHAMA

EASTERN AFRICA

If one takes the term *popular* to mean translocal and appealing to heterogeneous audiences, then popular music in eastern Africa emerged prior to the advent of radio broadcasting and commercial sound recording. The *beni ngoma*, a synthesis of autochtonous competitive dance traditions and timbral and sartorial elements from European military parades, radiated out from the coast early on in the twentieth century, carrying with it the emergent regional lingua franca of Swahili. The ramification of the beni ngoma throughout Kenya and Tanzania laid important pathways and precedents for mass mediated popular music that emerged later, especially after World War II.

COASTAL *TAARAB*

The first gramophone recordings aimed at a consumer base in eastern Africa were of coastal Swahili *taarab* music in the 1920s; and the first popular music "star" was a Zanzibari woman named Siti binti Saad, who rose from being a lowly pottery seller to become a beloved singer and cultural icon of the Swahili coast. Taarab finds its origins in nineteenth-century Arabic court music on the island of Zanzibar—the word itself is derived from the Arabic root for "musical ecstasy"—but Siti binti Saad and her fellow musicians turned it into something else: a Swahili wedding music combining the Arabic *maqam* tradition with local rhythms and vocal styles.

In the twenty-first century the most popular of the many variegated forms of taarab is so-called "modern taarab," performed by Tanzanian groups such as East African Melody and Tanzania One

Prince Adio and Stinky D. Kenyan hip hop/taarab singer Prince Adio performs live on stage with rapper Stinky D in Mombasa, Kenya. March 6, 2005. PHOTOGRAPH BY ANDREW EISENBERG

Theatre. Modern taarab's backbiting (*mipasho*) lyrics, as well as its characteristic synthesized string sounds, have come to dominate taarab even on the Kenyan coast. This situation of uneven musical exchange is largely due to the radio play that Tanzanian taarab has enjoyed in Kenya, a by-product of the fact that modern taarab has served as the soundtrack for Tanzania's national political parties.

Other styles of East African taarab include Egyptian-influenced orchestral taarab—a form that has died in Kenya but persists on Zanzibar, where the now internationally marketed Culture Musical Club and Ikhwani Safaa are based—and the Hadhrami (Southern Yemeni) taarab of men's wedding celebrations. Also, since at least the 1940s, Swahili musicians have utilized South

Asian timbres and melodies (especially Hindi film tunes) to such an extent that an entire genre of Hindi film-based taarab (exemplified in the oeuvre of Mombasan singer "*Profesa*" Juma Bhalo) has developed.

SWAHILI AND RUMBA: TWO LINGUA FRANCAS

The 1950s saw the circulation of guitar-based, Swahili language songs—often topical and narrative in nature, like their beni ngoma counterparts—on radio, on gramophone records, and in urban dance clubs. The timbres, textures, and rhythms of this music departed radically from beni ngoma, drawing heavily on North American jazz as well as Latin American styles, especially the Cuban *son*, which is better known as rumba in Africa and elsewhere. Africans serving in the military and police during World War II, some of whom traveled as far as Burma, played a key role in importing the listening tastes and performance skills of these "foreign" styles into eastern African popular culture. At the same time, as ethnomusicologist Gerhard Kubik has pointed out, the rhythmic aspects of these styles have African roots and may thus have been received as a variation on the familiar. Indeed, by the 1950s the major rumba influence was coming not from across the globe but from the musicians of the Belgian Congo. In particular, the guitar-based rumba of Mwenda Jean Bosco and others (sung in a variant of Swahili) captured the imagination of listeners in Kenya, Tanzania, and Uganda.

POSTCOLONIAL GROOVES

The 1970s was a period of great creativity for Kenyan and Tanzanian popular music. It was during this decade that Radio Tanzania Dar es Salaam began recording and broadcasting Tanzanian popular music as part of the government's nationalist agenda. Much of this music fell under the rubric of jazz or *muziki wa dansi* (literally translated as "dance music"), a rumba-influenced genre involving shimmering electric guitar lines, powerful brass punches, and, most importantly, Swahili lyrics on social issues of urban life. Muziki wa dansi bands (or "clubs" in local parlance) such as Mlimani Park and NUTA Jazz (now OTTU Jazz) were the darlings of Dar es Salaam nightlife through the 1970s and 1980s. By the turn of the twenty-first century

Nyota Ndogo. Kenyan hip hop/R & B singer Nyota Ndogo performs live on stage in Mombasa, Kenya, March 6, 2005. PHOTOGRAPH BY ANDREW EISENBERG

the popularity of these groups had declined; however, their stylistic legacy began to be heard among Tanzanian church choir (*kwaya*) groups.

In the 1970s Kenya also had its share of music groups in the muziki wa dansi mold—for example, Simba Wanyika Original, which began performing in Mombasa 1971 before recording with Phonogram (now Polygram) Records in 1972. What would prove to be a more important trend at this time in Kenya, however, was the development of ethnically defined guitar-based music known as *benga*, which is often sung in other Kenyan languages besides Swahili. In the early 2000s the Kalenjin, Kamba, Kikuyu, Luo, and Luhya all boast of having their own thriving benga scenes. It was the Luo, however, who began this trend by translating the complex rhythmic techniques associated with their *nyatiti* lyre onto the guitar. The acclaimed King of Luo Benga Daniel Owino Misani, leader of Shirati Jazz, still performs in the early 2000s.

The 1960s and 1970s were also golden years for Ethiopian popular music. With the government loosening its grip on artistic production, musicians trained in government-sponsored brass bands began to forge new genres influenced by African American music styles. Since 1998 much of the music recorded in Ethiopia during the 1970s has been re-released for international consumption by the French record label Buda Musique.

YOUTH MUSIC IN THE AGE OF HIP HOP

Just when gospel music appeared to have taken over as the commercial juggernaut of trans-ethnic East African popular music, the 1990s saw an explosion of new youth music genres in Kenya, Tanzania, and Uganda, inspired by African American hip hop as well as Jamaican reggae and ragga. Given that close contact with foreign music presupposes access to media and a degree of cosmopolitan education, it is not surprising that these new youth genres were largely born out of the upper classes. What this has meant is that despite the tendency of such music to index notions of "street life," it has been able to move with relative ease into the domain of what might be called national culture in both Kenya and Tanzania. In Kenya's 2002 presidential election, for instance, the song *Unbwogable* (a Luo-English neologism for "unshakeable") by the duo GidiGidi and MajiMaji played a central role in the victorious campaign of the National Rainbow Coalition.

The biggest success story in eastern Africa's hip hop revolution is to be found in Tanzania's thriving "*bongo flava*" scene, which has produced Swahili rappers like Juma Nature, a household name in urban Kenya as well as Tanzania. The high rate of music piracy in Kenya has failed to scuttle dreams of popular music stardom among that country's youth. The most successful Kenyan artists are just beginning to find ways to make money by such strategies as performing for corporate events or selling the rights to release their album in Tanzania, where piracy has largely been put under control.

See also **Music; Musical Instruments; Popular Culture: Eastern Africa.**

BIBLIOGRAPHY

Askew, Kelly. *Performing the Nation: Swahili Music and Cultural Politics in Tanzania*. Chicago: University of Chicago Press, 2002.

Barz, Gregory. *Performing Religion: Negotiating Past and Present in Kwaya Music of Tanzania*. Amsterdam: Editions Rodopi B.V., 2003.

Brennan, James R., and Andrew Burton, eds. *Dar es Salaam: Histories from an Emerging African Metropolis*. Dar es Salaam/Nairobi: Mkuki na Nyota/British Institute in Eastern Africa, 2007.

Gunderson, Frank D., and Gregory Barz, eds. *Mashindano!: Competitive Music Performance in East Africa*. Dar es Salaam: Mkuki na Nyota Publishers, 2000.

Kubik, Gerhard. "Neo-Traditional Popular Music in East Africa Since 1945." *Popular Music* 1 (1981): 83–104.

Nyairo, Joyce, and James Ogude. "Popular Music, Popular Politics: *Unbwogable* and the Idioms of Freedom in Kenyan Popular Music." *African Affairs* 104, no. 415 (2005): 225–249.

Paterson, Doug, with Jens Finke and Werner Graebner. "Music." In *The Rough Guide to Kenya*, ed. Richard Trillo. London: Rough Guides, 2002.

Ranger, T. O. *Dance and Society in Eastern Africa 1890–1970: The Beni Ngoma*. Berkeley: University of California Press, 1975.

ANDREW EISENBERG

EGYPT

As genre distinctions based upon North American and European categories (such as pop, classical, and folk) cannot be easily transferred to Egyptian music, popular music is here defined as that which is marketed to a mass audience. For at least the last 100 years, the popularity of Egyptian artists has depended upon their ability to be simultaneously innovative and grounded in Egyptian tradition. Egyptian musicians, composers, producers, and media executives strive to create music that is embraced as both modern and authentically Egyptian.

Although traditionalist critics complain that modern Egyptian music is indistinguishable from a globalized, homogenous pop sound, it is important to note some distinguishing characteristics. Almost all types of Egyptian music, just as other genres of Arab music, give primacy to the voice. Typically, the melodic complexity of Arab sound arts (exemplified by the recitation of the Qur'an) finds its ideal expression in vocal rendition; musical instruments support, respond to, and at times translate the melodic lines of a singer. Whereas vocal style is recognizably similar among many genres of Arab music, instrumentation is more variable. Contemporary songs frequently feature the sounds of the *'ud* (eleven-stringed lute), the *qanun* (seventy-eight-stringed zither), the *nay* (end-blown reed flute), and percussion in a mix that includes synthesizers, drum machines, and electronically-modified voices. The use of Arab musical scales (*maqamat*), especially those with quarter tones that fall between the notes of the European twelve-semitone scale, and characteristic rhythms (*iqa'at*) also serve to differentiate much Arab pop music from its North American and European counterparts. Artists may emphasize their Egyptian roots through the use of Egyptian dialect in song lyrics, the naming of Egyptian locations, the sounds of Egyptian folk instruments such as the *kawla* (wide end-blown reed flute), and the use of specific local images in videoclips.

Egyptian music witnessed a golden age in the mid-twentieth century, and even in the early twenty-first century beloved singers of that earlier time remain popular across generations of Egyptians. The unparalleled vocal artistry of Umm Kulthum (1904–1975) represents the standard by which other female singers are judged. Innovative artists of the 1940s–1970s, such as Muhammad 'Abd al-Wahhab (c. 1901–1991), Layla Murad (d. 1995), the Syrian emigrant Farid al-Atrash (d. 1974) and his sister Asmahan (1918–1944), and 'Abd al-Halim Hafiz (1929–1977), have come to represent the heritage (*turath*) of Arab music; their recordings—and contemporary renditions of their songs and styles by other artists—proliferate today.

Egyptian music of the twentieth century has been shaped by the mass media. In the early twentieth century, Cairo became a center for artistic and media production in the Middle East and North Africa. The enormous popularity of Egyptian singers such as Umm Kulthum and Muhammad 'Abd al-Wahhab resulted in large part from their skillful use of Cairo's developing media: recordings, radio, film, and eventually television. Under President Gamal Abdel Nasser, state-owned radio and television broadcast Egyptian programs throughout Northern Africa and the Arab world, where these media had enormous influence. Privatization of the media since the 1970s has led to the consolidation of a few large corporations. Today, Cairo, along with Beirut and Dubai, remains a media capital in the Arab world. Talent scouts and recording studios carefully cultivate the sound and the image of media stars. The videoclip has become perhaps the most ubiquitous format for mediated music in the region. In the early twenty-first century, profit generated from recordings comes not only from CD and cassette sales, but from live performances, video and song downloads, and sales of ringtones for mobile phones.

Similar to their predecessors, contemporary musical artists including 'Amr Diyab (b. 1961), Hisham Abbas (b. 1963), Hakim (b. 1962) and Angham (b. 1972) mix Egyptian elements with those of other musical styles: borrowings from Latin, Indian, Turkish, Arab Gulf, and hip-hop music are prevalent. In the 1990s and the first decade of the 2000s, Egyptian popular music charts have been

Hakim (1962–). Hakim, the Egyptian sheikh of "shaabi," or popular music, performs at Lebanon's Beiteddine festival, July 2002. Hakim and other contemporary musical artists mix Egyptian elements with those of other musical styles, including Latin, Indian, Turkish, Arab Gulf, and hip-hop beats. RAMZI HAIDAR/AFP/GETTY IMAGES

dominated by 'Amr Diyab, known both in Egypt and internationally for his polished songs in the romantic tradition that feature the sounds of Egyptian percussion, flamenco guitar, and rap vocals. Muhammad Munir (b. 1954) has met with great success for his unique style that blends the musical forms, scales, and lyric themes of traditional Nubian music with the harmony and rhythms of keyboards and electric guitars. Another stream of popular music is the *sha'bi* (literally: of the people) style that was pioneered by Ahmad al-'Adawiyya and continued by Sha'ban 'Abd al-Rahim. These singers use repetitive formulas and coarse vocal delivery to express streetwise sentiments and no-nonsense politics with which working-class Egyptians identify. Sha'bi singers have met with criticism from middle-class Egyptians and have been denounced by the government for politically sensitive lyrics. Idioms of sha'bi music are adapted for the Egyptian mainstream and the international market in the music of Hakim (b. 1962), an immensely popular contemporary singer whose dance remixes have had a significant impact in Europe and who has collaborated with American soul/funk superstar James Brown (1933–2007) and Puerto Rican songstress Olga Tañón (b. 1967).

Still another broad category of popular music is Islamic music, including the Sufi *anashid* performed at saints' festivals throughout the country. Exceptional singers of this primarily local genre, such as Shaykh Yasin al-Tuhami and Ahmad al-Tunni, are well-known throughout Egypt and internationally. Live recordings of these singers are distributed via cassette (and, less frequently, CD and VCD). The recent popularity of singers in the tradition of the anashid but with more polished production and distribution, such as British-born Albanian émigré Sami Yusuf (b. 1980), suggests a greater commercial presence for Islamic musical performers in the years to come.

See also **Cairo; Music; Nasser, Gamal Abdel; Popular Culture.**

BIBLIOGRAPHY

Armbrust, Walter. "What Would Sayyid Qutb Say? Some Reflections on Video Clips." *Transnational Broadcast Studies* (Spring 2005). Available from http://www.tbsjournal.com/Archives.

Danielson, Virginia K. "New Nightingales of the Nile: Popular Music in Egypt since the 1970s." *Popular Music* 15, no. 3 (1996): 299–312.

Danielson, Virginia K. *The Voice of Egypt: Umm Kulthum, Arabic Song, and Egyptian Society in the Twentieth Century.* Chicago: University of Chicago Press, 1997.

Frishkopf, Michael. "Some Meanings of the Spanish Tinge in Contemporary Egyptian Music." In *Mediterranean Mosaic: Popular Music and Global Sounds*, ed. Goffredo Plastino. New York: Routledge, 2003.

Gordon, Joel. "Singing the Pulse of the Egyptian-Arab Street: Shaaban Abd al-Rahim and the Geo-pop-politicsof Fast Food." *Popular Music* 22, no. 1 (2003): 73–88.

Racy, Ali Jihad. *Making Music in the Arab World: The Culture and Artistry of Tarab.* Cambridge, U.K.: Cambridge University Press, 2003.

ANNE ELISE THOMAS

ETHIOPIA

Throughout Africa, it was the incursion of European instruments that dominated the progressive emergence of "modern" local music (sometimes called "urban" because it developed essentially around garrison towns and new capitals). The case of Ethiopia is unusual in that this country is the only one on the African continent to have resisted all European expansionism, despite many longing glances cast its way. Aside from five years of Italian occupation (1935–1941), ancient Abyssinia in fact remained uncolonized over three millennia. This centuries-long capacity for resistance, which has given rise to a very firm sense of national belonging, strongly contributed to the development and maintenance of a specific musical identity, whereas many African musical cultures, steamrolled by their neighbors or, since the late twentieth century, sucked into the globalist whirlwind of world music, have completely forfeited their identities.

It was just after the stunning victory at Adwa (on March 1, 1896, Emperor Menelik II defeated the Italians in battle, the one and only example of an African victory against a European army bent on colonization) that the first Western instruments arrived in Ethiopia. In 1897, Tsar Nicholas II of Russia presented forty wind instruments to the victor of Adwa. A musical director (Milewski) came along with the musical tribute. The first European brass band's repertoire was limited to the national anthems of a few foreign delegations that had taken up quarters in the new Abyssinian capital, Addis Ababa ("The New Flower").

Soon after Abyssinia was admitted to the League of Nations the prince regent Ras Tafari (the future Emperor Haile Sellassie) traveled to Europe for a lengthy diplomatic tour. The first leg of his journey led him to Jerusalem, where he was so impressed with the brass band that greeted him that he decided to hire the band members and make them the official band of Ethiopia. The ensemble was composed entirely of young Armenian orphans who had escaped the Turkish genocide of 1915. A musical director, Kevork Nalbandian, also Armenian, was recruited as well. He had a truly remarkable musical background and training (harmonium, khanoun, violin, European musical theory, wind instruments, and brass band music). To this day the memory lives on of the *Arba Lidjotch* (the "Forty Kids"), as they were popularly known in Ethiopia, those teenage musicians who arrived at the Addis train station via Djibouti on September 6, 1924.

It was with Nalbandian that modern Ethiopian music really began to take shape. He composed the Ethiopian national anthem (lyrics by Yoftahe Negussie), which remained the national anthem until the fall of the emperor in 1974, as well as marches in honor of Tafari himself and the members of the imperial family. But above all he took on the Ethiopianization of the repertoire by composing or arranging Ethiopian songs, a first decisive step toward an appropriation of European musical ways. Other marching bands were already springing up, such as the *Arada Zèbègna* (the policemen of the capital city), under the direction of another Armenian, Garabed Hakalmazian, and the Imperial Body Guard Band, led by the Swiss André Nicod. Nicod added colorful tunes from the French operettas then in vogue, but also worked in "melodies of the native land as practical exercises for the outdoor music theory lessons," little by little reinforcing the development of the truly Ethiopian repertoire (Nicod 1937, 51). Starting in 1924–1925 and until the fall of Haile Selassie, there was to be a veritable continuum in the development of Ethiopian music—barely interrupted by five years of occupation under Benito Mussolini. And just before the Italian invasion, some 250 practitioners could be counted among the country's various garrison towns.

Just after the liberation, returning from his exile in Britain, the emperor undertook the country's reorganization. He again called upon foreign instructors to take charge of musical education. The Pole Alexander Kontorowicz (1944–1948) and the Austrian Franz Zelwecker (1950–1957) were the dominant figures in this renaissance, along with the Armenian Nersès Nalbandian (Kevork's nephew) who, from the postwar period until his death in 1977, made a decisive and lasting contribution to the vitality of modern Ethiopian music. The Haile Sellassie I Theatre (today the National Theatre) was to become, from its inauguration in 1955 (under the direction of Franz Zelwecker) and until the end of the empire (1974), the epicenter of this musical revolution.

The institutional bands, which depended directly upon imperial power, provided the impetus for creative evolution: the Imperial Body Guard Band, the Police Band, the Army Band, the Addis Ababa Municipality Orchestra, and the Agher Feqer Mahber Orchestra (the orchestra of the Patriotic Theatre, originally dedicated to the defense of traditional musical culture). These big ensembles' impressive brass sections lent their color to the new music. Resolutely closed off from African influences, this modern tradition is inherited from the American big bands, the format adopted was that of western-style songs with verses and refrains, but the melodic lines were profoundly Ethiopian. The greatest Ethiopian vocalists all got their start with the institutional bands: Tlahoun Gèssèssè, Bzunesh Bèqèlè, Mahmoud Ahmed, Alèmayèhu Eshèté, Menelik Wesnatchèw, Hirout Bèqèlè, Muluqèn Mèllèssè, Ali Birra, and Ayaléw Mesfin. Renowned and prolific arrangers also came to the fore, including Sahlé Degago, Girma Hadgu, Tèfera Mekonnen, Ashiné Haylé, Lemma Demissèw, and Ayaléw Abbèbè, as well as exceptional saxophone players: Gétatchèw Mèkurya, Mèrawi Setot, Tesfa-Maryam Kidané, Seyoum Gèbrèyès, Moges Habté, Téwodros Meteku, Telaye Gebré, Feqadu, and Feqadu Amdè-Mesqel. The American military base at Kagnew, near Asmara, and several thousand Peace Corps Volunteers were also the source of considerable influence.

It was only around 1968–1969 that the Soul Echos, the first truly independent group devoid of any institutional ties, was to emerge thanks to the young producer Amha Eshèté (Amha Records), soon to be followed by the All Star Band, Alem

Girma Band, Venus Band, Ibex Band, Wallias Band, and Dahlak Band, pop groups with five to seven musicians and rarely more than two saxophones. From then on Girma Bèyènè and Mulatu Astatqé were to become the master arrangers of this so-called Golden Age.

During the revolutionary period (1974–1991), only three bands remained active to accompany the old stars and the crop of new talent: the Roha Band, the Wallias Band, and the Ethio Star Band. Decimated by eighteen years of uninterrupted curfew, censorship, and the strictures of "socialist realism" imposed by the Derg (the military dictatorship) modern music is in the twenty-first century dominated by synthesizers. Few real bands manage to survive for long. The same can be observed among the many artists exiled since the revolution (mostly in North America). Financial constraints lead to the proliferation of "one-man bands" and despite its large numbers the Ethiopian-American diaspora, very closed in upon itself, has produced few talents capable of reaching a broader American audience.

See also **Halle Selassie I; Menelik II; Music; Popular Culture: Music.**

BIBLIOGRAPHY

Falceto, Francis. *Abyssinie Swing: A Pictorial History of Modern Ethiopian Music/Images de la musique éthiopienne moderne.* Addis Ababa, Ethiopia: Shama Books, 2001.

Falceto, Francis. "Un siècle de musique moderne en Ethiopie (précédée d'une hypothèse *baroque*)." *Cahiers d'Etudes Africaines* 168 (2002): 711–738.

Falceto, Francis. "1955–2005—Splendeurs et misères de la musique éthiopienne." *L'Éthiopie Contemporaine* (2007): 349–367.

Nicod, André. "La musique éthiopienne." In *L'Éthiopie telle qu'elle était en septembre 1935*, ed. Athens: Adrien Zervos, 1936.

Nicod, André. *Et in Etiopia Ego.* Avignon/Monte Carlo: Maison Aubanel Père, 1937.

West, Stephen. "Musical Development in Ethiopia—A Conference with Alexander Kontorowicz." *Etude: The Musical Magazine* 67, no. 2 (February 1949): 69; 127.

Workaferahu, Kebede. "Soul Music Invades Ethiopia." *Addis Reporter* 2, no. 4 (1970): 16–19.

FRANCIS FALCETO

NORTHERN AFRICA

As a geographic region, northern Africa includes the countries Egypt, Libya, Tunisia, Algeria, and Morocco. However, as a musical and cultural region, Egypt is typically grouped with the Middle East and not with its four neighbors to the west that make up the area referred to in Arabic as the *Maghreb* (place of the sunset). Since ancient times, the Maghreb has been a site of cultural interaction that has dramatically influenced its musical life. The music of four groups provided the primary roots of the musical culture: the original Amazight (Berber) residents; Arab conquerors from the East; Muslim and Jewish refuges from al Andalus (medieval Spain); and West Africans brought to the Maghreb as slaves and mercenaries. This mix of cultures is reflected in the rhythms, melodic modes, and instruments of North African traditional and popular music.

URBANIZATION

A massive relocation, beginning in the 1920s, of the rural poor into the cities was instrumental in the development of North African popular music. Over succeeding decades, rural styles modernized and interacted with other musical styles, including indigenous urban music (together with elite Andalusian genres), and European popular music. Numerous hybrid urban genres emerged out of this interchange, including *rai* (Algeria), *mizwid* (Tunisia) and *cha'abi* ("popular," referring to different styles in each country). Rai, arguably the most influential North African popular genre, developed in the western Algerian city of Oran during the 1920s. A new class of professional female entertainers, *cheikhas*, blended the sung poetry of the rural *cheikhs* (religious leaders) with the music of the *meddahas* (female performers for private gatherings of women). Accompanied by traditional instruments—*gasba* (flute), *tar* (frame drum), and *guellal* (earthenware drum)—cheikhas sang earthy, rhythmically driving songs that addressed the everyday concerns of urban life. During the 1930s performers such as the famous Cheikha Remitti (b. 1923) made the first rai recordings and began to incorporate influences from other genres, including French cabaret music and Spanish popular songs.

TRANSNATIONAL CONNECTIONS

Transnational musical connections have significantly influenced the development of North

African popular music. By the early twentieth century, musicians had begun to employ European and North American instruments, such as the guitar and banjo, alongside traditional instruments, and professional musicians from throughout the Maghreb and Egypt regularly performed in public spaces and cafes. The influence of Egyptian music intensified during the 1930s with the growing popularity of Egyptian musical films and the emergence of pan-Arabism as the dominant force in North African movements for national liberation. Local stars who performed in the Egyptian style included Morocco's Ahmed el Bidawi (1918–1989) and Algeria's Ahmed Wahby (1921–1993). By the 1960s Egyptian-style song was widely popular in the Maghreb and was the dominant popular genre in Morocco and Tunisia.

Other transnational connections influenced the development of a number of popular genres. The roots of Algerian cha'abi lie in the blending of Algerian melodies with Moroccan *qasidas* (poems) by Sheikh Mustapha Nador (1874–1926) and the addition of the Egyptian *darbukha* (goblet-shaped drum) to his ensemble by his protégé Mohammed el Anka (1907–1978). El Anka's cha'abi recordings, made during the late 1920s, were the first recordings of North African popular music. Later artists, such as Dahmane Harachi (1925–1980), the first Algerian cha'abi star based in France, modernized cha'abi by adding foreign instruments and introducing colloquial language. In Morocco artists such as Houcine Slaoui (1918–1951) created an identifiable urban-based, national style (cha'abi) during the late 1940s by mixing regional Moroccan, Middle Eastern, and European music.

In Algeria after World War II, musicians brought together elements of rai with Egyptian, Latin, and African American musical styles and instruments to create a more danceable style (labeled pop rai in the 1960s). Bands of stars, such as Bellemou Messaoud (b. 1947) and Belkacem Bouteldja (b. 1953), which featured singers known as *cheb* (young man) or *chaba* (young woman), set the template for modern rai. Rai continued to incorporate influences from a diverse collection of musical styles, and during the 1980s stars such as Chaba Fadela (b. 1962), Cheb Hasni (1968–1994), and Cheb Khaled (b. 1960; the "king of rai"), were instrumental in rai's becoming an

international phenomenon. During the 1960s and 1970s European rock and pop influenced numerous musicians throughout North Africa (Moroccan pop of the Megri Brothers, and rock rai of Algeria's Raina Rai); from the 1980s local rap scenes have developed throughout North Africa. The beginning of the twenty-first century has seen the emergence of different forms of fusion and North African rock as significant musical forces. Inspired by the success of North African French fusion bands, such as Gnawa Diffusion, fusion musicians create cosmopolitan music that also seeks to rediscover local musical traditions, particularly of marginalized groups, such as the Gnawa (descendants of West African slaves).

Scholarship. Research by scholars on North African popular music, a subject previously neglected, has increased dramatically since the 1990s. Most scholarship to emerge on North African—particularly Moroccan and Algerian—popular music has been published in French. Because of its rise to international prominence during the 1980s, rai is the one popular genre to receive significant scholarly attention, both in French and English.

POLITICAL FORCES

Beginning in the 1930s, Tunisian authorities encouraged the creation of an artistic style of popular music, *ughniya* (song), based on modernization of *Mal'uf*, an Andalusian genre. Following independence (1956), the Moroccan state supported the development of Egyptian-style song (*chanson moderne*) as a national style. During the 1970s the Moroccan band Nass el Ghiwane catalyzed a rediscovery of traditional musics mixed with messages of cultural and political critique. Nass el Ghiwane emphasized the rediscovery of folk genres and instruments, such the *sentir* (Gnawa lute), *lotar* (Amazight lute), and *t'bel* (drum), and wrote songs that addressed contemporary social concerns. Their success sparked the creation of Ghiwanien or progressive bands throughout the Maghreb (Morocco's Jil Jilala and Izenzaren, and Libya's Nasser Midawi). The 1970s also saw a reassertion of Amazight cultural identity in Morocco and Algeria. This movement was strongest in Kabylia in Algeria, where the development of new Berber song was sparked by the success of the singer Idir's song "A vava inouva."

Since its emergence during the 1920s and 1930s, popular music has been a subject of political controversy in North Africa. Censorship of popular musicians has continued since the 1930s when colonial authorities banned some early rai recordings. During different periods, the Algerian state has censored rai and promoted it as a national music. Ghiwanien music and modern rai developed in climates of political repression; the use of Thamazight (the Amazight language) in public life was suppressed throughout the Maghreb; numerous Algerian popular musicians were threatened or assassinated during the political turmoil of the 1980s and 1990s; and popular music, particularly rock and rap, continues to be periodically attacked by governments and political movements.

See also **Music; Musical Instruments; Popular Culture: Northern Africa.**

BIBLIOGRAPHY

Aydoun, Ahmed. *Musiques du Maroc.* Paris and Casablanca: Editions Eddif et Editions Autres Temps, 2001.

Baldassarre, Antonio. "Moroccan World Beat Through the Media." In *Mediterranean Mosaic: Popular Music and Global Sounds*, ed. G. Plastino. New York and London: Routledge, 2003.

Bouziane, Daoudi, and Hadj Miliani. *L'aventure du raï.* Paris: Éditions du Seuil, 1996.

Dernouny, Mohamed, and Boujemâa Zoulef. "Naissance d'un chant protestataire: Le groupe marocaine Nass el Ghiwane." *Peuples méditerranées* 12 (1980): 3–31.

Langlois, Tony. 1996. "The Local and Global in North African Popular Music." *Popular Music* 15, no. 3 (1996): 259–274.

Rosen, Miriam. "On Rai." *Artforum* 29, no. 1 (1990): 22.

Schade-Poulsen, Marc. *Men and Popular Music in Algeria: The Social Significance of Rai.* Austin: University of Texas Press, 1999.

Schuyler, Philip D. 1993. "A Folk Revival in Morocco." In *Everyday Life in the Muslim Middle East*, ed. Donna Lee Bowen and Evelyn A. Early. Bloomington: Indiana University Press, 1993.

JEFFREY CALLEN

SOUTHERN AFRICA

The popular music of southern Africa reflects the region's integration into the modern world-system during the twentieth century. The evolution of performance genres, the changing social roles of performers, and the place of music-making and dance in the cultural practices of rapidly changing societies and communities of southern Africa are all closely linked with the transition from predominantly agrarian, precapitalist social formations to commodity-producing, industrialized, or semi-industrialized modern nation-states. The impact of Western folk, sacred, and popular musical styles has been profound throughout the region, possibly even more so than in other parts of sub-Saharan Africa. Because of South Africa's economic and political dominance in the region, some of this music has, in addition, been influenced by styles originating from that country's major urban centers. In countries such as Malawi, Zambia, and Mozambique, as well as in parts of Angola, various styles of Zairian *soukous* have also been a major influence. However, despite these homogenizing factors, the continuity of resilient local indigenous performance practices remains an important distinguishing element of the popular music on the subcontinent.

HISTORY

Among the earliest and most consequential agents of modernization and cultural innovation in southern Africa were the Christian missions. Seconded in part by the colonial military, the missionaries introduced European instruments and basic compositional techniques embodied in the Wesleyan church hymn. In addition to assimilating hymns, around World War I early popular performers, such as South African Reuben T. Caluza (1895–1969), eagerly absorbed what was available to them of the most advanced European and North American popular music: syncopated rhythms, ragtime, and vaudeville tunes. Labor migrants were responsible for blending these urban idioms with the rural traditions of their respective home areas, thus producing a wealth of local popular genres such as the *famo* dances of Basotho women, the *mbube* choral songs of Zulu-speaking men, the *kiba* songs of Pedi migrants, and a rich variety of guitar and concertina styles.

From the 1930s, South Africa also developed its own variant of jazz. Absorbing the best of American jazz, often under extremely restricted conditions, bands such as the Merry Blackbirds and the vocal quartet Manhattan Brothers blended swing with a local hymn-based style known as *marabi*. The influence of *marabi* is largely responsible for the strong local flavor in South African jazz, most clearly represented in the music of pianist Abdullah Ibrahim (b. 1934). During the 1960s, fleeing ever more restrictive legislation and racial oppression, the most talented of these performers went into exile in Europe and the United States, where some—trumpeter Hugh Masekela (b. 1939) and singer Miriam Makeba (b. 1932), for example—embarked on major international careers. An offshoot of the swing era, albeit in combination with elements of rock and roll, is the *kwela* music of the 1960s. Performed on tin whistles, *kwela* and its derivatives, such as sax-jive, influenced musical forms in Zimbabwe (*tsaba-tsaba*), Zambia (*kalindula*), and Malawi (*simanje-manje*).

The predominant style of the 1950s through 1980s was *mbaqanga*. Created from the guitar music of Zulu-speaking migrants, the evolution of this style owes much to the work of pioneers such as John "Phuzushukela" Bhengu (1930–1985), the all-female group Mahotella Queens, and the Soul Brothers. *Mbaqanga* is also at the root of a number of related styles elsewhere. In Zimbabwe, Oliver Mutukudzi has become popular for his *jit* music, a blend of *mbaqanga* and local Shona traditions, while in Zambia guitarist Alick Nkhata (d. 1978) pioneered *kalindula*, containing strong admixtures of Bemba music.

The 1970s saw the increasing influence of rock, pop, and a number of black styles, such as soul. Fusing the former with *mbaqanga* and elements of Zulu migrant music, Juluka (later renamed Savuka), led by Johnny Clegg and Sipho Mchunu, emerged as one of the major recording groups of the 1980s. Clegg, who was also a prominent anti-apartheid activist and a moving force in the formation of a South African musician's union, provided powerful images through his mixed-race band of a nonracial South Africa that had great appeal both within the country and internationally, particularly in France.

Another major historical turning point was the release in 1986 of *Graceland*. The Grammy Award-winning album by U.S. pop star Paul Simon showcased a wide range of musicians from west and southern Africa, most notably the *mbube* choir Ladysmith Black Mambazo, which in 1987 with the album *Shaka Zulu* became the first southern African group to win a Grammy. Equally influential in focusing international attention on the struggle against apartheid and thereby making South African popular music known to wider audiences were musicals such as *Sarafina*! by Mbongeni Ngema (b. 1955).

The renewed international interest in southern African popular music coincided with the demand for "world music," a term describing the growing commercialization beginning in the mid-1980s of traditional native music and its production for European and North American consumption. Many of the performers, besides those already mentioned, who contributed to (and benefited from) this new expression of global culture are from southern Africa, especially Zimbabwe and South Africa.

Beginning with the visit by Bob Marley to Zimbabwe's independence celebrations in 1980, reggae became a major factor in the southern African popular music scene. Some of the world's most celebrated reggae performers, such as the South African Lucky Dube, probably the biggest-selling artist in his country, come from this part of Africa. In the 1990s, other major genres of African American popular performance, such as hip-hop, have also caught on in South Africa.

IMPACT OF THE STATE AND MASS MEDIA

As elsewhere in Africa, the development of the popular performing arts was for a long time dependent on colonial policies. Certain dance forms considered bellicose or vaguely oppositional by the authorities, such as the *ingoma* dances of migrant workers in South Africa and certain forms of *mbira* music during the early colonial phase in Rhodesia, were banned. Other performance activities regarded as being conducive to the control of the labor force and the maintenance of public order, such as the *kalela* dances in the Zambian Copperbelt, were actively encouraged by the colonial state and mining companies.

The practice continued, in more subtle form, in the more autocratic postcolonial regimes such as that in Mozambique, where the ruling party, Frente de Libertação de Moçambique (FRELIMO), for a long time sought to gain control over the large Chopi *timbila* xylophone orchestras that had formerly been linked with the structures of colonial chieftaincy. In South Africa, apartheid legislation hampered the careers of an entire generation of exceedingly talented performers, and effectively crippled the development of a solid institutional framework (such as music schools) and a healthy informal network of performance venues (such as clubs) open to performers of all races.

Equally obstructive with regard to the development of African popular performance were colonial broadcasting policies. With the exception of South Africa, where rudimentary forms of broadcasting for African audiences in both colonial and native languages started as early as the 1920s, most countries to the north only introduced broadcasting after World War II. While in large areas of Angola transistor radios were virtually unknown even until well into the 1960s, African-language programs in most of the British colonies featured a highly selective range of music, usually of rural origin. In South Africa by the 1960s, more than 90 percent of the population had access to a transistor radio, but with the institution of "Radio Bantu" (African-language services of the South African Broadcasting Corporation), until the mid-1970s and in line with the ideology of separate development, airplay was almost exclusively restricted to traditional music of an allegedly pure "ethnic" character.

The deregulation and democratization (and simultaneously the commercialization) of the media in the 1990s is moving apace in countries such as South Africa and Zambia, thus opening the local markets up to an even greater influence of the international (i.e., U.S. and European) music industries.

Commercial recording on the subcontinent began in 1908 in South Africa and expanded with the opening of the first vinyl-record pressing plant in Johannesburg in 1932. During these years Gallo (now part of the media and entertainment giant Millennium Entertainment Group Africa [MEGA]) established itself as the leading record company in the region. As of the early twenty-first century, Gallo, together with a number of labels owned by the major international companies (such as EMI and BMG) controls virtually the entire southern African market. Smaller companies used to operate in Zimbabwe (Gramma Records) and Zambia, but due to economic and political crises the music industry in these countries has all but collapsed. South Africa is home to numerous state-of-the-art recording studios

(Down Town Studios-Gallo, Powerhouse Studios-EMI, Sunset Recording Studios), but outside South Africa comparable facilities have all closed down in recent years. In countries with a once-flourishing music industry of their own, such as Mozambique, national radio stations also provide studio space, but shortages of vinyl and locally manufactured affordable audio equipment have brought record production to a standstill.

Despite the considerable international acclaim southern African performers have gained, the situation of the vast majority remains precarious in their respective home countries. A combination of factors, among them the lack of a functioning infrastructure controlled by the musicians (such as studios and marketing networks), the ongoing dependence on South Africa for studio space and recording technology, massive bootlegging, and a general disregard by the state for popular musicians, has severely impacted the growth of truly democratic and viable local music industries. Thus in Zimbabwe, high import duties on musical instruments and unsupportive authorities have made it difficult for musicians, despite their role as cultural innovators, to survive as professional performers. The civil war in Mozambique from the mid-1970s to the early 1990s and a declining economy in Zambia in the 1980s have had an even more disastrous impact on the popular music scene.

SOCIAL CONTEXT OF POPULAR MUSIC

As a result of southern Africa's rapid economic growth, urbanization, and industrialization, the social occasions for popular performance reflect growing class and group differentiations, as well as the constant readjustments of social identity, meaning, and values within the evolving modern societies. At the same time, some of these social contexts remain rooted—in modified form—in older forms of social interaction, many of them connected with the exercise of chiefly power and indigenous religious traditions. Thus, in Zimbabwe, the *chimurenga* music of Thomas Mapfumo (b. 1945) has been influential in expressing the nationalist aspirations of the liberation movement, and because of its anchorage in the *mbira* music of the Shona ancestral spirit-possession cult, it has been a significant factor in the selective reworking of precolonial traditions and in the revival of traditional performance practices.

Likewise, in South Africa, popular performers played a crucial role in the antiapartheid struggle, either by directly confronting the minority regime in outspoken lyrics or, much more frequently, by providing images of black power and identity. Numerous performers openly declared their allegiance to the African National Congress and other antiapartheid organizations. Others, such as Ladysmith Black Mambazo, while never directly attacking the system, furthered African mass resistance by providing social commentary and by highlighting the resilience and indefatigability of black popular expression. At the same time, such broadly antihegemonic functions of popular music do not exclude a concern with gender issues and more narrow topics such as the assertion of local and ethnic identities.

See also **Ladysmith Black Mambazo; Makeba, Miriam; Masekela; Hugh; Media; Music; Popular Culture: Southern Africa.**

BIBLIOGRAPHY

Ballantine, Christopher. *Marabi Nights: Early South African Jazz and Vaudeville.* Johannesburg, South Africa: Ravan Press, 1993.

Coplan, David. *In Township Tonight! South Africa's Black City Music and Theatre.* London; New York: Longman, 1985.

Erlmann, Veit. *African Stars: Studies in Black South African Performance.* Chicago: University of Chicago Press, 1991.

Erlmann, Veit. *Nightsong: Performance, Power, and Practice in South Africa.* Chicago: University of Chicago Press, 1996.

Graham, Ronnie. *The Da Capo Guide to Contemporary African Music.* New York: Da Capo Press, 1988.

Hamm, Charles. "'The Constant Companion of Man': Separate Development, Radio Bantu, and Music." *Popular Music* 10 (1991): 147–174.

Kubik, Gerhard. "Donald Kachamba's Montage Recordings: Aspects of Urban Music History in Malawi." *African Urban Studies* 6 (1979–1980): 89–122.

Kubik, Gerhard. "The Southern African Periphery: Banjo Traditions in Zambia and Malawi." *World of Music* 31 (1989): 3–30.

Kubik, Gerhard. "Muxima Ngola—Veränderungen und Strömungen in den Musikkulturen Angolas in 20

Jahrhundert." In *Populäre Musik in Afrika,* ed. Veit Erlmann. Berlin: SMPK, 1991.

Turino, Thomas. *Nationalists, Cosmopolitans, and Popular Music in Zimbabwe.* Chicago: University of Chicago Press, 2000.

Vail, Leroy, and Landeg White. *Power and the Praise Poem: Southern African Voices in History.* Charlottesville: University of Virginia Press, 1991.

VEIT ERLMANN

WESTERN AFRICA

Popular trans-cultural urban music in Anglophone West Africa emerged from the late nineteenth century as a fusion of indigenous music with that of colonial regimental brass bands (including those of West Indian regimental troops), the guitar (and concertina) groups of visiting (including Liberian Kru) seamen, and prestigious ballroom dance orchestras of the local African elites such as the Excelsior Orchestra, the Jazz Kings and the Cape Coast Sugar Babies of Ghana, the Dapa Jazz Band and Triumph Orchestra of Sierra Leone and Lagos City Orchestra of Nigeria. Between the two world wars, the local sales of this early Anglophone West African popular music was so profitable that the HMV, Zonophone, and Odeon sold 800,000 "Native Artists" records, mainly of the guitar band variety known as Akan blues, odonson, native blues, and palmwine (*maringa*) music. During the inter-war period, local forms of popular theater and comic opera also appeared that borrowed ideas from black minstrelsy, silent movies, and church bible-plays such as the Ghanaian "concert parties" and Nigerian "traveling theater."

During and immediately after World War II, American swing, Afro-Cuban rumbas, and Trinidadian calypsos became popular and influenced the growth of urban highlife, juju and maringa music. In Ghana there were the highlife dance bands E. T. Mensah, the Black Beats, Ramblers, and Uhuru, as well as the highlife guitar bands E. K. Nyame, Kakaiku, the Jaguar Jokers, and African Brothers that integrated highlife music into concert party plays. Nigeria had the juju-music bands of Ayinde Bakare and I. K. Dairo, and the highlife bands (influenced by the Ghanaian genre) of Bobby Benson, Victor Olaiya, Rex Lawson, and Victor Uwaifo. Sierra

Excelsior Orchestra. Surviving members of Frank Torto's Excelsior Orchestra of Accra, Ghana's first dance orchestra, formed in 1914. Torto is in the center holding the conductor's baton. JOHN COLLINS/BAPMAF ARCHIVES

Leone's maringa music was played by Ebenezer Calender, the Ticklers, and S. E. Rogie.

Acculturated popular music began to take off in the Francophone areas only after independence. In the 1960s a fusion of Latin, Afro-Cuban, and indigenous dance music occurred in Senegal, Guinea, and Mali where there is a long tradition of professional *griot*, or *jail*, performers. Modern bands and artists that absorbed jali influences include Bembeya Jazz and Mory Kante of Guinea; the Rail Band (with Salif Keita), Les Ambassadeurs (with Kante Manfila), and the musicians Ali Farka Touré of Mali; Ifang Bondi and Foday Musa Suso of Gambia; Super Mama Djombo of Guinea-Bissau; and Groupe Carnaval of Niger. In Senegal, Afro-Cuban and local music were blended by bands such as Xalam, Touré Kunda, and Super Étoile. Youssou N'Dour, the leader of Super Étoile, created his electro-Wolof mbalax dance style in the 1980s and went on to work with many of the world's top music stars.

However, independence acted as a general catalyst throughout the whole of West Africa, not only through the establishment of indigenous mass communications and entertainment industries, but also through women being encouraged to appear on the popular stage and the independence ethos stimulating artistic indigenization. Besides the effect of international pop stars (including South Africa's Miriam Makeba), women were encouraged to become popular entertainers from the late 1950s through the cultural and educational policies of the newly independent west African nations. Ghana's President Kwame Nkrumah set up Workers Brigade bands and concert parties that employed women singers and actresses. The Nigerian government formed Maggie Aghumo's all-female Armed Forces Band, and Guinea's President Sékou Touré established a female gendarmerie band, Les Amazones de Guinée, that included the famous singer Sonia Diabate. Liberia's Fatu Gayflor rose to fame through her country's National Ballet Troupe, and Mali's cultural

E. K. Nyame (1927–1977) and his famous Ghanaian band. Nyame, the composer and singer, is holding his clarinet in this posed shot from 1955. He formed the group in 1950 in order to popularize highlife music with the use of various instruments, including guitars, clips, string bass, and bongo drums. JOHN COLLINS/BAPMAF ARCHIVES

policy abetted a wave of female jalis or *djely mousso* such as Fanta Damba, Fanta Sacko, and Tata Bambo Kouyate. Other top West African popular female performers of the post independence 1960s and 1970s period include Liberia's Miatta Fahnbulleh, Côte d'Ivoire's Aicha Koné, Cameroon's Tity Edima, Cape Verde's Césaria Évora, and Bella Bellow of Togo. In Ghana there was Asabea Cropper, Charlotte Dada, Efua Dokonu, Lola Everett, and Grace Omaboe, and in Nigeria the Lijadu Sisters, Patti Boulaye, and Onyeka Onwenu.

Decolonization also brought more indigenous forms of popular entertainment to the fore. A striking example is the Portuguese *morna* music of Cape Verde, which was eclipsed after independence in 1975 by the local *batuco* and *furaca* polyrhythmic dance music styles that had earlier been denounced by the Portuguese authorities. Independence institutionalized the African personality, négritude, and pan-Africanism. These, together with the contemporaneous African American and Caribbean black consciousness, Afrocentrism and back to roots ideals, led to a self-conscious Africanization by many entertainers. Ghana's Koo Nimo and Cameroon's Francis Bebey have become renowned for combining the acoustic guitar with traditional instruments.

Nigeria's Duro Lapido helped pioneer the use of Yoruba myth and legend in popular traveling theater. "Doctor" Olah's *mailo* jazz, an acoustic folk form of maringa band music, became the rage in Sierra Leone. In the early 1970s the Ga group Wulomei created a folk form of highlife in Ghana using guitar and local instruments, whilst Ernesto Djedje of the Côte d'Ivoire became successful with his electric ziglibithy rendition of local Bebe music.

Also in the early 1970s Afro-rock, Afro-soul, and Afro-beat were blended by Ghana's Osibisa, Cameroon's Manu Dibango, Nigeria's Segun Bucknor, and the late Fela Anikulapo-Kuti. The lyrics of the latter were particularly antiestablishment. Since the late 1970s another acculturated local pop style developed influenced by the imported reggae music (particularly Bob Marley) of Jamaica. This Afro-reggae style is performed by Ghana's City Boys, KK Kabobo, Rocky Dawuni and Kojo Entwi; Côte d'Ivoire's Alpha Blondy; and Nigeria's Sonny Okosun, Majek Fashek, Ras Kimono, and reggae queen Evi Edna-Ogholi.

Since the 1980s, two new musical styles emerged in West Africa; namely local gospel and hi-tech

Victor Uwaifo (1941–). The Nigerian highlife musician of Edo State plays his guitar in the early 1970s. Uwaifo was famous for his joromi music, a style of highlife music that he popularized throughout Africa. JOHN COLLINS/BAPMAF ARCHIVES

forms of popular music. Many of the thousands of separatist Christian churches in Africa allow (unlike North American and European ones) dance for worship, and are utilizing local popular dance bands and their recorded music as part of their outreach programs. Examples of such bands are Nigeria's Charismatic Singers, Imole Ayo's Christian Singers, Sonny Okosun's gospel band, Gladis Ugwakah-Lambah, and Princess Ifeoma. Since 2002, two Gospel and Roots Festivals have been organized in the Bénin Republic and the gospel-highlife bands that sprang up in Ghana during the 1980s now supply 60 percent of the commercial popular music output of the country. These festivals are also paving the way for many women artists to enter the local dance and music profession (such as Mary Ghansah, the Tagoe Sisters, Stella Dugan, and Cindy Thompson and the Daughters of Glorious Jesus).

Disco music, using drum-machines and synthesizers, became fashionable in the 1980s and many West African artists have created local versions of this imported techno-pop (e.g., Nigeria's Bolarin Dawadu, Guinea's Mory Kante, Côte d'Ivoire's Magic System, Cameroon's Mone Bile, and Ghana's burgher highlife created by George Darko and Daddy Lumba while living in Hamburg, Germany, in the 1980s). In the 1990s there was an local upsurge of hip-hop, rap, and ragga, often sung in indigenous languages. There are Nigerian artists such as Tony Tertuila, 2 Face Idibio, Weird MC, Zakky, and Styl-plus. Ghana's numerous performers of hip-life (i.e., hip-hop highlife) include Reggae Rockstone, Lord Kenya, Tic Tac, VIP, Sydney, and Obour. Positive Black Soul, Wa BMG 44, Da Brains, and Rap'Adio are just some of the estimated two thousand local rap groups operating in Senegal.

During the 1980s, African popular music (coined World Music in 1987) became, for the first time, internationally commercially viable, and a number of West African performers have become internationally recognized, such as Nigeria's Fela Anikulapo-Kuti and Sunny Adé (juju music), and the Pan African Orchestra of Ghana's Nana Danso Abiam. There is also interest among World Music fans abroad in the dance music of Francophone West African artists, and particularly well known is Senegal's Youssou N'Dour. Others are Salif Keita and Ali Farka Toure of Mali, Mory Kanta and Bembeya Jazz of Guinea, Baba Mal and Touré Kunda of Senegal, and Angelique Kidjo of the Republic of Bénin. The current focus of World Music fans is on *wassoulou* music, a Malian genre of urban music, based on the pentatonic music and instruments of traditional hunters that, in the early twenty-first century, has become dominated by female artists such as Sali Sidibe, Nahawa Doumbia, and Oumou Sangare.

See also **Adé, Sunny; Évora, Césaria; Keita, Salif; Kuti, Fela; Makeba, Miriam; Music; Popular Culture:** **Western Africa; N'Dour, Youssou; Nkrumah, Francis Nwia Kofi; Touré, Sékou.**

BIBLIOGRAPHY

Barber, Karen; John Collins; and Alain Ricard. *West African Popular Theatre.* Bloomington: Indiana University Press, 1997.

Bender. Wolfgang. *Sweet Mother: Modern African Music,* trans. Wolfgang Freis. Chicago: University of Chicago Press, 1991.

Collins, E. John. "Post-War Popular Band Music in West Africa." *African Arts* 10, no. 3 (1977).

Collins, E. John. *Music Makers of West Africa.* Washington, DC: Three Continents Press, 1985.

Collins, E. John. "Jazz Feedback to Africa." *American Music* 15, no. 2 (1987): 176–193.

Collins, E. John. *West African Pop Roots.* Philadelphia: Temple University Press, 1992.

Coplan, David. "Go to My Town, Cape Coast! The Social History of Ghanaian Highlife." In *Eight Urban Musical Cultures: Tradition and Change,* ed. Bruno Nettl. Urbana: University of Illinois Press, 1978.

Fosu-Mensah, Kwabena; Lucy Duran; and Chris Stapleton. "On Music in Contemporary West Africa." *African Affairs* (London) 86, no. 343 (1987): 227–240.

Graham, Ronnie. *Stern's Guide to Contemporary African Music,* Vol. 2: *The World of African Music.* London: LPC Group, 1992.

Horton, Christian Dowa. "Popular Bands in Sierra Leone: 1920 to the Present." *Black Perspective in Music* 12, no. 2 (1984): 183–192.

Jegede, Dele. "Popular Culture and Popular Music: The Nigerian Experience." *Présence africaine* n.s., no. 144 (1987): 59–72.

Kala-Lobe, Henri. "Music in Cameroon." *West Africa* (London) no. 3405 (November 1982): 2281–2283.

Mensah, Atta Annan. "Jazz: The Round Trip." *Jazz Forschung/Jazz Research* 3/4 (1971/1972).

Stapleton, Chris, and Chris May. *African All Stars: The Pop Music of a Continent.* London: Quartet Books Limited, 1987.

Ware, Naomi. "Popular Music and African Identity in Freetown, Sierra Leone." In *Eight Urban Cultures: Tradition and Change,* ed. Bruno Nettl. Urbana: University of Illinois Press, 1978.

Waterman, Christopher Alan. *Jùjú: A Social History and Ethnography of an African Popular Music.* Chicago: University of Chicago Press, 1990.

E. JOHN COLLINS

MUSICAL INSTRUMENTS.

African traditional instruments are designed and built to express African ideas and musical values. Although many of these instruments belong to the same families as other world instruments, and in some cases share common origins, their construction and use are linked with specific African conditions—the musical principles of the continent and its ecology, history, and social organization.

Some of the values reflected in African music are the importance of human relationships, cooperation, independence, and rhythmic contrast between parts. African instruments have developed to express these values, and as a result have diverged significantly from the instruments of other parts of the world.

TONE QUALITY

In most African instrumental ensembles, it is important that every instrument be distinctly audible, keeping is own independent part. The concept of "blend" is largely subservient to that of "contrast." Given the structural principles of African music, where meaning depends to a great extent on the conflict of rhythms and meters, and on the interplay between musicians and between instruments, African musicians are strongly aware of tone quality and subtle differences in tone. Instruments are thus both carefully chosen and tuned so that each has its own recognizable "voice." This applies in mixed ensembles such as those including drums, rattles, and bells, and in groups of similar instruments like xylophones, mbiras, panpipes, horns, or steel drums; musicians try to fill up the whole sound spectrum. For example, drums are tuned to different pitches with heat, water, wax, or their own tensioning systems; idiophones of different types are chosen for their contrast; individual musicians blow or sound different pitches. The principle is also evident in vocal music in many parts of Africa, where each singer's voice is distinct from his or her neighbor's, and voice tone is open and "characterful" rather than sweet and blending.

In music which depends on rhythmic relationships, it is the exact moment of entry that is important, so most African instruments give a sharp, distinct onset of sound. Likewise, duration is largely of little importance, so even if capable of it, few instruments hold on long notes.

A widespread method of adding contrast and "bite" to instruments in Africa is to add buzzing devices. These vibrate sympathetically with the instrument, or with its individual notes. They can also act to amplify, prolong, or help carry the sound of an instrument, for instance in the open air or in noisy surroundings. Another effect is to selectively emphasize, either methodically or arbitrarily, certain notes or sounds, which can encourage the perception of inherent patterns. Buzz tone is an integral part of the tone quality of many African instruments, although generally considered irritating by Western musicians. It is found not only in Africa but also in some Indian and Chinese instruments, in the Guatemalan marimba, a xylophone of African ancestry, and in certain Western instruments of the Middle Ages, such as the flute and the tromba marina.

Buzzers are made of diverse materials, including loosely attached metal rings, bells, snail shells and other seashells, beads, seeds, lizard skin, string, grass, and bottle tops. Perhaps the most typical African buzz-tone is achieved with membranes known as mirlitons, found on most resonated xylophones, on some instruments of the mbira family, and on some drums. Wherever air moves as a result of the vibration of the body of an instrument, a mirliton can be used. On a resonated xylophone such as the *valimba* of the Sena of Malawi, a hole on the side of each resonator gourd is fitted with a fine membrane affixed with wax. The membrane is tensioned to respond to the pitch of the wooden key and its equally tuned resonator.

A mbira soundboard such as that of the *kankobela* of the Tonga of Zambia has a central hole, with the membrane on the underside. When the mbira is played over its resonating gourd, the air movement in the gourd, induced by the vibrating soundboard, operates the membrane. On a drum, which must have an enclosed airspace, such as the *ditumba da ndanya* of the Luba of Zaire, a membrane is pushed, using a piece of cylindrical calabash neck, into a hole below the pegs, until it is held in place by the calabash neck's tight fit into the hole and then tensioned with a finger. Typical substances for the membrane have included animal tissues such as from cow intestine, jerboa, bat, spider egg sac, cigarette paper, office carbon paper, and plastic bags.

ECOLOGY AND HISTORY

The distribution of African instruments gives a marbled map, the result of the interplay of the physical environment with social organization and the currents of history. Traditional instruments are largely made by the player, using materials growing or living at hand. Makers have an intimate knowledge of the properties of the local flora and fauna, not only for food, medicine, and other purposes but also for music. The ecology therefore determines to a large extent what instruments can be made. Wood determines the sound quality of many instruments; kiaat (*Pterocarpus angolensis*) and sneezewood (*Ptaeroxylon obliquum*) are commonly chosen in central and southern Africa for their resonance. African music is well suited to the varied sounds of many natural or found objects, from calabashes to pods to bottle tops and tins. The Chopi *timbila* xylophone of southern Mozambique is an ecological masterpiece, being constructed of at least fifteen natural materials, including gourds, beeswax, palm leaf, and rubber.

Two poles of African social organization can be distinguished that have a bearing on musical styles and instruments: the pastoral, centralized, hierarchical, living in grassy plains, where instruments are few and singing predominates, and the agricultural small-scale egalitarian, where more instruments can be expected. The scale of the society likewise affects the scale of music making. Organized kingdoms, such as those of the Ganda, Yoruba, Zulu, and Asante, could have large and varied instrumental or vocal groups.

The chance contacts of a people's history affect their instrumentarium. Arabic music has made a deep impression on the west African savanna and on the Swahili east coast. The centuries-long association of the Nguni and Sotho peoples of southern Africa with the Khoesan led to their adopting the latter's bows and song and dance styles. The many invaders of Africa all brought their own musical instruments; Western instruments dominated urban music in Africa in the twentieth century.

CLASSIFICATION

Africa has several unique instruments, including those of the mbira family. All African instruments can be classed in the same families as other world instruments, however, revealing their wider connections.

While African peoples have their own classification systems, based in most cases on the social uses of the instrument, the universal Sachs-Hornbostel classification considers the part of the instrument that vibrates to create the sound.

Aerophones, or Wind Instruments. Typical African examples of wind instruments are the widespread one-note reed-pipe or horn bands, where each player puts his or her one note into the total pattern at the right moments; panpipes, where more notes are available to the player; and end-, side-blown, and gourd flutes. Flutes, often associated, as in Hellenic times, with herdsmen, are now rare. Aerophones with vibrating reeds and finger holes, such as the oboe and clarinet, are rare, except in regions subjected to North African or Arabic influence.

Groups consisting of a number of instruments each of which gives only one note demonstrate a particularly African approach toward music making, one which demands a high degree of cooperation. Such groups, which may be formed of reed, bamboo, or metal tubes blown flute-style across the open end, or of animal, calabash, or wooden horns blown trumpet-style through a side mouthpiece near the tip, are widespread in Africa. The musicians often dance intricate step patterns while playing. As they involve the coordination of a large number of performers, they are often associated with important social occasions. The sound itself is not necessarily the only point of the performance; the entire attention of the dancer-musicians is given to the complexity of coordinating their correct note entries, which are different for each player, with the normally irregular dance steps that are shared by all as they move around in a circle. Such a musical group invariably accompanies a circle dance progressing to the right.

The *tshikona* bamboo-pipe dance of the Venda of northern South Africa is a formal men's dance, performed at the behest of royalty at both ritual and secular occasions, such as the installation of a chief or the opening of a store. It is also popular in Johannesburg, where Venda men play *tshikona* as a sign of their ethnic identity. The instruments are tuned heptatonically, and women play three drums in the center of the ring. Only one tune exists for *tshikona*, but there are many dance steps. The *dinaka* dance of the Pedi, neighbors of the Venda in South Africa, is similar in many ways to *tshikona*, but this dance employs reed-pipes tuned pentatonically, and a number of tunes exist for the ensemble.

The *nyanga* bamboo-panpipe dance of the Nyungwe in central Mozambique uses instruments of up to four notes each, and the technique involves both playing and singing. The principle is otherwise the same. This dance is performed on both ritual and secular occasions, especially when called to do so by the government of the day. Numerous named dance steps accompany only one *nyanga* tune. The women's part consists of singing selected inherent patterns arising out of the total sound of the men's pipe and voice parts, of which there may be over thirty, covering a range of three and a half heptatonic octaves.

The *amakondere* horn bands of the former and current kings of the Great Lakes region of east Africa use composite instruments of horn and calabash, which together with drums accompany formal duties of the ruler. Hutu horn bands in Rwanda used to accompany the dancing of the Tutsi. Some of the higher horns give two adjacent notes of the pentatonic scale, by means of a finger hole at the sharp end.

Chordophones, or Stringed Instruments. Africa shares with Europe the tradition of a singer accompanied by a chordophone. The instrument holds an ostinato pattern, often of great virtuosity, while a player sings against it in a musical dialogue. All four basic chordophone types, harp, lyre, zither, and lute, are present in Africa.

The harp has a body with a skin stretched over it for a soundboard, and one neck (or more than one in the "pluriarc" harp of the west-central coast); the strings are attached to the neck and come down into the soundboard, entering it perpendicularly without any intervening bridge. Harps are played in a long arc from the Great Lakes in the east to the savanna of west Africa. Some of them, such as the Ganda *ennanga*, show a remarkable resemblance to ancient Egyptian harps.

The lyre has a body normally covered in skin, two necks, and a yoke connecting the ends of the necks. The strings are attached to the yoke, pass parallel to the body over a bridge, and are fastened to the base of the body. Lyres are played in Ethiopia and neighboring countries of east Africa.

The Ganda *endongo* lyre lacks a bridge; the strings buzz against the skin of the body. Both African harps and lyres are plucked, while some lyres, such as the *kibugandet* of the Kipsigis in Kenya, may also be strummed.

The zither has a body with the strings stretched parallel to it from end to end. A large family of zithers, known by names such as *bangwe*, *pango*, *ligombo*, and *nanga*, is found in Tanzania, Malawi, and northern and central Mozambique. They may be plucked or strummed. The strumming technique, as with the strummed lyres, is the same as that surmised for the ancient Egyptian lyre: the stretched fingers of the left hand are held between the strings, damping those strings that are not required at any given moment, while the right hand strums all the strings.

The lute has a skin-covered body with a neck extending from it. The strings are attached to the neck and pass parallel to the body over a bridge, being fastened to the base of the body. They may be plucked or bowed. The strings are stopped with the fingers of the left hand, not in most cases by pressing onto the neck, but simply by touching with the front or back of the fingertip. The plucked west African lutes from the savanna regions are fingered onto the neck; a connection with the American banjo has been proposed. The bowed lutes, such as the *molo* of the west African savanna and the many east African examples, including the Ugandan *endingidi*, are associated with North African or Arab influence.

The *kora* of Guinea and neighboring countries is perhaps the most magnificent of all African chordophones. Strictly a lute, it is usually called a "harplute" because of its visual resemblance to a harp, the twenty-one or so strings being stretched in two banks over a double-sided bridge. The body is a large spherical calabash, covered in skin. This is the prime instrument of the *jali* or griot, hereditary professional musicians formerly attached to rulers' courts.

The *zeze* lute of the Swahili coast and inland, now rare, may have had Indonesian connections. Played by itinerant entertainers, it consists of a narrow wooden body with three large built-in frets for the melody string, and one or two strings on the side which serve as drones, fitted with a chicken quill buzzer, and resonated by an attached half gourd.

Bows could technically be subsumed under the above types but are better considered separately. They may be curved or straight, with one string, or occasionally more, stretched from end to end, and may either have a gourd or other resonator attached or be mouth-resonated. They may be struck, plucked, bowed, rubbed—in the case of the southern African *chizambi* friction bow, where the notched bowstick is rubbed with another stick—or even blown, in the case of the *gora* mouthbow of the former Khoe of southern Africa. Unlike the musical bows of the Orient or North America, African bows give at least two fundamentals, either by bracing the string into two segments or by fingering. The harmonic series of each fundamental is selectively resonated in the gourd or mouth to produce melody.

Membranophones, or Drums.

Drums are considered to be the quintessential African instrument and are found almost everywhere, highly developed in west Africa, less so toward the south. There are significant areas, however, where drums were used little if at all, for instance in much of the southern African and other grasslands.

There is an enormous variety of shapes and sizes of drums, falling into two general acoustic types, the closed drum, with one or two membranes, which has a clearer musical pitch but little variety of sound, and the open drum, with one membrane, which is capable of more variety. The shape and materials of every drum body affect its timbre.

A drum plays patterns that are melodic as well as rhythmic; different hand, or stick, strokes give a variety of sounds, which are allotted "drum syllables" in some areas. An average drum group would consist of about three drums of different pitch. The leader, who is allowed more freedom, normally plays the lowest drum. The higher drums play more fixed patterns, and the highest of all often plays repeating "time-line" patterns, coordinating time-keeping devices for the group. These patterns may also be played on other high-pitched idiophones such as a bell, rattle, scraper, clapper, or a stick on the side of a drum.

Most villages have one set of drums for all purposes, but west African villages may possess several distinct drum families, each for a different social or ritual purpose. Drums often become symbols of political or ritual power. In the east African kingdoms, royal drums, some many centuries old, were considered the "crown jewels."

Some well-known examples of drums include the *djembe*, an open, goblet-shaped drum of Guinea and neighboring countries, which has spread worldwide with new-age youth; the hourglass-shaped, double-skinned pressure or "talking" drum, widely used in west Africa; the large, closed, laced, royal four-drum group of the Tutsi *omwami*, or ruler, of Rwanda; the *entenga* royal fifteen-drum chime, tuned to a pentatonic scale, of the Ganda of Uganda; the closed, goblet-shaped buzzing drums of the Luba of southern Zaire; the wax-weighted drums with cutout sides used for the *nyau* masked dance in Malawi; and the large, closed, bowl-shaped *ngoma* drum of Venda chiefs in South Africa.

Idiophones or "Self-Sounding" Instruments.

Idiophones are instruments whose body itself, or parts of it, vibrates to produce sound. They include two of Africa's most important families of tuned instruments, those of the mbira or lamellophone (from *lamella*, thin plate) and of the xylophone. Otherwise, this family comprises most other instruments that are not included under the previous classes, such as the huge variety of rattles, bells, scapers, slit drums, and other small instruments which African musicians have a distinct talent for inventing and making.

The Mbira. The mbira family, of which more than two hundred types have been recorded, is widespread from northern South Africa through to Uganda and across to Sierra Leone, although not played everywhere. The name "lamellophone" has been coined to refer to the family, as no adequate Western word exists for it. However, proponents of an African name have suggested "mbira," "sansa," "likembe," and other names. In this article the name "mbira" is used, that of the Shona peoples of Zimbabwe and their neighbors, in whose hands the instrument reaches probably its greatest complexity, backed by five centuries of tradition.

A mbira consists of a wooden soundboard with several narrow metal tongues or keys fixed to it by means of a "backrest" and a "bridge"—which hold the tongue away from the soundboard—and a "bar" between the two, which presses the tongue toward the soundboard. The tongues are free to be plucked at one end by thumbs or fingers, each giving a different note of the local scale. The soundboard may be a single board, a hollow box, a bell shape (hollowed out from the bottom end), sometimes made of a tin can or other metal, in numerous inventive designs according to the region. In parts of the Zambezi area the tongues may be arranged in up to three "manuals"—that is, bent up so the tips form separate rows. The playing ends of the tongues are commonly arranged in a V-shape layout (lowest notes at the center) but may also be made "low-on-left" or in many local variants.

The mbira is mostly art informal solo instrument accompanying the voice, played while walking, at parties, to pass the time, as a paid entertainment, or as a solace for the player. Zimbabwe and the Zambezi valley seem to be the only region where it has a structured religious function, supporting the hypothesis of its great age and possibly even its origin here. It is played at all-night ceremonies during which ancestral spirits possess the bodies of mediums. Some songs for the *mbira dza vadzimu* are associated with Mutota, a historical ruler of the Zimbabwe kingdom in about the fifteenth century.

Examples of mbira types include the *dipela* of the Pedi of northern South Africa, the southernmost of all mbiras, tuned pentatonically in a V-shaped layout. This is one of the two known exceptions in the mbira family which are played not with the thumbs but with the fingers only, for instance with the instrument hanging from the neck and resting against the stomach of the player. The *mbira dza vadzimu* (mbira of the ancestors), of the Shona/Zezuru of Zimbabwe, is a large instrument of twenty-two keys, V-shaped layout, and heptatonic scale. It is played inside a large calabash for resonance, in order to put mediums in touch with ancestral spirits. This ancient mbira type, with a three-octave range, is not only highly popular within Zimbabwe because of its prominence during the fight for independence but also has a considerable New Age following on the United States and Canadian west coast. Its music is based on complex harmonic sequences. It is normally played in pairs, with each player playing a complementary rhythm.

The *kalimba*, a small mbira with a fan-shaped body equipped with a buzzer mirliton and a minimum of eight keys, V-shaped layout, and hexatonic or heptatonic scale, is played over a small gourd for informal entertainment and walking songs in countries along the Zambezi valley. This instrument, it has been suggested, may be the most ancient form of the mbira in Africa. The *malimba* is a box-bodied mbira with V-shaped layout and pentatonic scale with several central sympathetic keys (keys that are not played but sound on their own when similar pitches are sounded), used in Tanzania by itinerant musician/entertainers.

The *likembe* is a box-bodied mbira with a vibrato hole or holes for the fingers on the reverse side. The keys are often tuned so that to play the descending heptatonic scale one would pluck alternately from left to right down toward the tip of the V-shaped layout. It has the widest distribution of all mbira types. Originating in the area of the Congo (Zaire) River mouth, it has spread, originally by means of colonial porters who played as they walked, to most parts of central Africa as far as Uganda and Tanzania. The *kadongo*, a box-bodied mbira of the Soga of Uganda, is a variant of the *likembe* that is pentatonic, with a V-shaped layout, played in ensembles of four or more instruments of different sizes and pitch ranges. Smaller instruments are sometimes made of metal.

The *timbrh* is a large box-bodied mbira from southern Cameroon with bamboo keys tuned tetratonically, and a unique buzzing system consisting of a piece of stiff grass resting on top of the key, held in place at one end with wax. Like many other west coast mbiras from here down to Namibia, the keys are tuned with varying weights of black bee propolis attached under their tips. The *agidigbo* of the Yoruba of Nigeria, and other similar types of mbira played along the west African coast, are large box instruments often with no more than three or four keys, used less melodically than rhythmically. It is likely that the mbira reached west Africa relatively late. The *kondi* is one of several pentatonic and hexatonic V-shaped-layout mbiras played informally by individuals in Sierra Leone, the northwest limit of the mbira's distribution. This type has the distinction of being the only one played upside down as other African players would see it—that is, with the thumbs, the tongues pointing away from the player. Lastly among the mbiras is the *marímbula* of Cuba and other Caribbean countries, whither it was taken from west Africa during the slave trade. The *marímbula* is a large bass instrument with few keys.

The Xylophone. The xylophone is also widely played in Africa, with slightly less distribution than the mbira. It is a more social instrument than the mbira, strongly linked in many places with public events, rulers, dancing, and often with drums.

Some confusion exists between the words "xylophone" and "marimba." The latter is an African word used colloquially, under the influence of the Central and North American usage. They are in fact synonyms. "Marimba," however, is also used in some parts of Africa to refer to instruments of the mbira family.

Xylophones are idiophones consisting of a row of tuned wooden slats mounted on a frame so that they are supported at the correct nodal points. There are two basic types of xylophones in Africa: those with and those without resonators. The two types are not normally found in proximity.

Xylophones with resonators, which are usually gourds or calabashes but may also be horns, a wooden box, or a pit, are played with rubber-tipped beaters at the center of the key. The resonators usually have buzzing membranes on the sides. They may be played alone but more commonly are found in groups. Most resonated xylophones require a single player, but several styles involve the use of up to four players per instrument.

Some well-known resonated xylophones are the *mbila* of the Chopi of southern Mozambique, played in large orchestras of up to twenty or more players, with as many dancer/singers and several rattle players. The *timbila* are made in up to five different pitch ranges and have a compass of over four heptatonic octaves. Each instrument may have up to twenty keys. The *timbila* dance is one of the artistic peaks of African music/dance performance. Its continuity is currently in severe danger due to postwar conditions in Mozambique and the abolition of chiefs, its former patrons.

A west African xylophone, variously called the *balo, bala,* or *balafon,* is most often associated with the Malinke peoples of the Gambia, Guinea, Côte d'Ivoire, and Mali. This is a heptatonic flame xylophone of about eighteen keys, played by griots, either solo or in duo. The players have bells attached to their wrists as they play. Other instruments are pentatonic, such as the *gyil* of northern Ghana. The *valimba* of the Sena of central Mozambique and southern Malawi is a large instrument of about twenty-two keys, played by three or four boys on one side of the same instrument, accompanied by a drum and rattles, during night-time dances.

Xylophones without resonators are referred to as "log" xylophones because of their large, simple keys, often little more than tuned logs resting on two banana trunks or on a simple wooden frame. The large keys are loud enough not to need resonators. They are struck on the ends with plain sticks by two or more players sitting opposite each other, playing interlocking rhythmic parts. Most log xylophones are pentatonic.

The twelve-key *amadinda* and the seventeen-key *akadinda* xylophones of the Ganda in Uganda have been well studied by several ethonomusicologists and can now be heard as a result in many parts of North America, Europe, and Africa. These former royal court instruments are played at high speed, like most log xylophones, using a duple (*amadinda*) or triple (*akadinda*) interlocking technique between the two primary players. They are accompanied by several drums. The *mangwilo* xylophone of the Ashirima of northern Mozambique is a seven-key instrument played by boys for amusement and to keep birds and animals out of the crops. The *kponingbo* of the Azande of northern Zaire, the Central African Republic, and southwest Sudan is a large party instrument usually played together with a large slit drum and other drums.

INSTRUMENTAL TUNING

Broadly, there are four scale types in use in sub-Saharan African music: tetratonic with four notes per octave, pentatonic with five, hexatonic with six, and heptatonic with seven. In this respect African scales form a single family with those of Europe. Approximately 40 percent of scales are pentatonic, 40 percent heptatonic, and the remaining 20 percent largely hexatonic with some tetratonic, the latter notably among the ancient populations of the Khoesan and Pygmies. The boundaries of scale areas are clearly defined and are closely related to language relationships between the peoples concerned.

The tuning of the notes themselves varies enormously, but two underlying tuning principles can be distinguished, although these by no means cover all African tunings. Firstly, where musical bows and/or the use of harmonics are found, tunings tend to be based on the notes of the natural harmonic series. This is the case for instance among the Gogo of Tanzania, many peoples in Congo, Gabon, and the Central African Republic, and the Nguni peoples of South Africa. Secondly, in several scattered regions such as the heptatonic lower Zambezi valley (mbira, xylophone, zither), Guinea (xylophone, *kora*), eastern Angola (mbira), and the pentatonic Great Lakes kingdoms of Buganda and Busoga (xylophone, harp, lyre, etc.), scales tend to be tuned in close to equal-spaced intervals. In a heptatonic scale this gives a uniform interval size of around 171 cents or six-sevenths of a Western tempered whole tone; in a pentatonic scale around 240 cents or one and one-fifth whole tones.

See also **Music.**

BIBLIOGRAPHY

Hornbostel, E. M. von, and C. Sachs. "Classification of Musical Instruments." *Galpin Society Journal* 14 (1961).

Kirby, Percival R. *The Musical Instruments of the Native Races of South Africa*, 2nd edition. Johannesburg: Witwatersrand University Press, 1965.

Tracey, Andrew. "The Original African Mbira?" *African Music* 5, no. 2 (1972).

Tracey, Andrew. "Kambazithe Makolekole and the Sena Valimba Xylophone." *African Music* 7, no. 1 (1991).

Tracey, Andrew. "The Nyanga Panpipe Dance." *African Music* 5, no. 1 (1971) and 7, no. 2 (1992).

Tracey, Hugh. "Towards an Assessment of African Scales." *African Music* 2, no. 1 (1958).

Tracey, Hugh. "The Mbira Class of Instruments in Zimbabwe." *African Music* 4, no. 3 (1969).

Tracey, Hugh. *Chopi Musicians: Their Music, Poetry, and Instruments.* New York: Oxford University Press, 1970.

ANDREW TRACEY

MUSLIM NORTHERN AFRICA, HISTORY OF (641 TO 1500 CE).

Having completely conquered Egypt and Cyrenaica in 642, the Arab Muslims started turning westward to the lands that they called *bilad al-Maghrib*, the "Lands of the Sunset," or *al-Maghrib*. This region west of Cyrenaica (Barqa), meaning Tripolitania, Africa (present-day Tunisia and the eastern part of Algeria), and *al-Maghrib al-aqsa*, the farther Maghrib, is considered North Africa by Muslims, keeping Egypt apart. By this time, its eastern parts belonged to the Byzantine Empire and were Christianized, with important Jewish communities. The population consisted of rural Berbers, the autochthon populace, and still the landowning descendants of the Romans, together with the Byzantine military and administrative elite in the cities.

In late antiquity, the region had been highly urbanized, but this had already changed in the third century CE. Roman civilization, however, was still observable. The Arab conquest to the West was relatively slow, compared to Arab conquests in other regions, due to the distance to the caliphal capital Damascus where orders had to be passed on by the governor of Egypt. Every crisis, like the murder of the third caliph ʿUthman and the resulting conflicts, stopped the raids until new orders arrived. Thus, after establishing Muslim rule in Tripolitania in 647, only few raids were made further west. No earlier than 670 were the systematic and successful operations started against the Berbers of *Ifriqiya* under the command of ʿUqba ibn Nafiʿ (Sidi Okba) who founded the military city of Kairuan (*Qairawan*, in present-day Tunisia) on a large plateau in the center of the land. ʿUqba decided not to move northward to the coast, but instead to follow the central plateaus to the west. Legend says that he reached the Atlantic. However, in 683 he was defeated and killed in a battle by the Berber chief Kusayla who led the Berber resistance and took Kairuan.

Over the next few years, the Arabs were successful in retaking Kairuan and forced the Byzantines out of the country; they left Karthago in 698. The opposition mounted by the Berbers from the mountains under the *Kahena* (the priestess) would finally be defeated in 698, too. The consolidated authority of the Umaiyads and a change in their perception of the Maghrib in the wider context of their confrontation with the Byzantine Empire allowed Musa ibn Nusayr, the new governor appointed for the first time directly by the caliph in 704, to systematically conquer the central Maghrib and northern Morocco, which became the independent province *Ifriqiya* (*wilaya Ifriqiya*) of the Umaiyad Caliphate. Musa chose a moderate policy of indirect rule, so the Berber chiefs embraced Islam and gave their sons as Arab hostages to Tangier. With the crossing of the straits of Gibraltar (*Jabal Tariq*) in 711 by an Arab-Berber army under the command of the Berber Tariq ibn Ziyad began the intertwined history of North Africa and Muslim Spain (*al-Andalus*).

BERBER RESISTANCE

The Berbers—calling themselves *Imazighen*, or "the noble or free born"—are commonly described as fiercely independent peoples. Their origin is still unclear, but they were the autochthon inhabitants in the Maghrib already before the end of the second millennium BCE, when the Phoenicians settled at the coast. They are divided in several different and named ethnic groups, subdivided in tribes and clans, speaking different Berber languages. Most of them were sedentary agriculturalists, some were living in villages and practicing nomadism (transhumance), and in the plains and the Sahara some were nomads.

After the defeat of the *Kahena*, the Berbers chose religious-doctrinal forms of resistance against the Arab conquest, having mostly embraced Islam.

Being Muslims, they experienced discrimination and exploitation by the Arabs—so they had to provide on a regular basis men, women, and children as slaves to the Arab masters—and considered this un-Islamic. Until the tenth century, the heterodox *Kharijite* form of Islam was a kind of "national religion" (H. Halm) of the Berbers. The *Kharijites* were the Muslim group that abstained from taking side in the conflict between the fourth caliph 'Ali and its rival, the Syrian governor Mu'awiyya. The kernel of its doctrine was the possibility for the Muslim community (the *umma*) to choose the *imam* (leader) or to abandon him in case of unworthiness, abuses of power, or evident incompetence. This allowed it to refuse Arab rule in Kairuan and to elect an Arab or Berber *imam* on its own.

The first *Kharijite* (or *Ibadite* as it is also called) imamate emerged in 757 among Berbers in Tripolitania. In 761 refugees from there founded in the west of present-day Algeria a new city (Tahert) and an *imamate* under the elected Ibn Rustam who united nearly all North African *Kharijites*. The *Rustamid* imams reigned until 909. At the Atlantic coast emerged a Berber state of the *Barghawata* which lasted until the eleventh century, and in the Tafilalt

University-Mosque al-Qarawiyin in Fez, Morocco (6th century AH/12th century CE). The university has remained a center of Islamic learning in North Africa over the centuries. PHOTOGRAPH BY GERHARD ENDRESS, BOCHUM

Ribat of Sousse (Tunisia). The Ribat is a classical fortress of the first Muslim dynasty in North Africa. It was built in the 3rd century AH/9th century CE by the Aghlabids, the rulers of *Ifriqiya* from 184/800 to 297/909. PHOTOGRAPH BY GERHARD ENDRESS, BOCHUM

Kharijite Miknasa Berbers founded the city and Emirate of Sijilmasa which became an important trans-Saharan trade center and succumbed only in 1053 to the Almoravides.

PATTERNS OF CHANGE

The subsequent dynasties and the modes of political change in the Maghrib seem to follow a model already described by the historian and jurist Ibn Khaldun (d. 1406) in his famous *Muqaddima* (Introduction). Besides the *Kharijite* secession, there emerged another possibility of legitimate rule, the *sharifian* type, that is, rule by a *sharif* (noble), a descendant of the prophet Muhammad. The *sharif* would come from outside to a village, city, or tribe with a message; the charisma the *sharif* had as Muhammad's descendant would stand above tribes and clans and therefore he would be able to unite them. When the *sharif* succeeded in being accepted as a religious-political leader, he could start challenging the existing powers. The prototype for North Africa was the dynasty of the *Idrisides* (reigned 789–926), named after Idris I, the great-great-grandson of Muhammad and founder of the city of Fez near the Roman provincial capital of Volubilis where the tomb of *Moulay*

Idris is still venerated. He came from Medina and had to flee Arabia after a failed coup against the Abbasid caliphate. Being welcomed by the Auraba tribe who lived around Volubilis, he conquered all of Morocco.

One hundred years later, the same happened when in 901 a missionary (a *da'i*) of a secret *sh'ite* sect (called *ahl al-haqq*, people of the truth), but known as *Fatimids* or *Ismailites*) came to the Berber tribe of the *Kutama* in Lesser Kabylia (eastern Algeria) preaching the coming of the *mahdi* to establish justice, peace, and unity on earth—and surely having in mind the overthrowing of the Abbasid caliphate. Soon, the *mahdi* would come from Syria where he was hiding and take over the rule. The new dynasty of the *Fatimids* successfully established an empire stretching from Algeria to Egypt and Syria (969), overthrowing the *Aghlabid* state in *Ifriqiya* (800–909). They moved to their new capital, Cairo, and founded the still existing university-mosque *al-Azhar* as their intellectual center (972). In *Ifriqiya* and eastern Algeria, the Berber dynasty of the *Zirids* governed on their behalf until 1049, in allegiance to Abbasid Baghdad (until 1152). The Fatimid caliph al-Mustansir reacted by inciting the Arab tribe of

Banu Hilal to move westward, causing a century of anarchy in the Maghrib. However, the long-term result was an Arabizing of large parts of the Maghrib.

About the same time (1050), the *murabitun* (Almoravids), fighters of faith from the *Sanhaja* Berber in the Sahara, started spreading their Islamic awakening movement in West Africa before first establishing an emirate in the Atlas and then moving north under Yusuf ibn Tashufin (1061–1106) to conquer all of Morocco (until 1082) and Spain (1086). In 1062 they founded Marrakesh as their capital. The first crusade to conquer Jerusalem in 1096 had no direct effect on the region.

The Almoravids were overrun by a very similar movement, the Almohads (*al-muwahhidun*, the proclaimer of the unity of God). In 1120–1121, Muhammad ibn Tumart (d. 1130), who had been a student of the philosopher Ibn Hazm and proclaimed a rigorous orthodoxy, was accepted as *mahdi* by the *Masmuda* Berbers and initiated their fight against the Almoravids which were considered by that time as heretics. In 1147, the Almoravid dynasty ended the with the fall of Marrakesh. The Almohads extended their rule over the whole Maghrib and also over Muslim Spain where at the court of Abu Ya'qub Yusuf (1163–1184) arts and sciences flourished and the celebrated mosque of Sevilla with today's *Giralda* was built. It is here that the philosopher, jurist, and physician Ibn Rushd (Averroës) wrote his commentaries on Aristotle's works. Civil war and throne rivalries led to the decline of the Almohads who left the Iberian Peninsula in 1225.

POLITICAL FRAGMENTATION

In North Africa, the Almohad rule was disputed and the once united Maghrib became politically fragmented under three Berber dynasties: In *Ifriqiya* and eastern Algeria the *Hafsids* came to power (1229–1574). From 1236 until 1554, the *Abdalwadids* or *Zayyanids* reigned in the region of Tlemcen in western Algeria, sometimes occupied by the *Marinids*. Coming from south of the Atlas, the *Marinids* established an empire in Morocco, with Fez as their capital, after having overthrown the Almohads in 1269 (until 1465). The crusade of the French king Louis IX (Saint Louis) against Tunis in 1270 ended with his death there and left no traces. All rulers by this time did not try to impose a single doctrine. Instead, they encouraged the circulation of ideas and founded *madrasas*, residential colleges, and mosques, so that Islamic culture flowered. Military pressures came from the Iberian Peninsula, influencing the relations between the three North African states because the *Zayyanids* and *Hafsids* had commercial relations with Christian Aragon. The confrontation line shifted to North Africa: Between 1458 and 1519, the Portuguese occupied nearly all important places on the Moroccan Atlantic coast, from Tangier to Agadir. The Spaniards, too, established garrisons along the Mediterranean coast at the same time. There was in the whole Maghrib a lack of balance between the unruly tribes in the countryside and the towns and their pacified surroundings under the courts' authority, which lasted until the twentieth century.

See also **Cairo; Egypt, Early; Fez; Ibn Khaldun, Abd al-Rahman; Islam; Kahena; Marrakesh; Northwestern Africa, Classical Period, History of (1000 BCE to 600 CE); Ottoman Northern Africa, History of (1500 to 1850); Slavery and Servile Institutions; Tangier.**

BIBLIOGRAPHY

Abun-Nasr, Jamil M. *A History of the Maghrib in the Islamic Period.* Cambridge, U.K.: Cambridge University Press, 1987.

Halm, Heinz. *The Empire of the Mahdi: The Rise of the Fatimids*, trans. M. Bonner. Leiden, the Netherlands: E. J. Brill, 1996.

Ibn Khaldûn. *The Muqaddima. An Introduction to History*, 3 vols., trans. Franz Rosenthal. London: Routledge and Kegan Paul, 1958.

Julien, Charles André. *History of North Africa: Tunisia, Algeria, Morocco, from the Arab Conquest to 1830.* New York: Praeger, 1970.

Laroui, Abdallah. *The History of the Maghrib: An Interpretive Essay.* Princeton, NJ: Princeton University Press, 1977.

JÖRN THIELMANN

MUTEBI II (1955–). Ronald Muwenda Mutebi II was born in the kingdom of Buganda (northern Uganda) on April 13, 1955, to the then-ruling *Kabaka*, Edward Frederick Walugembe Mutesa II and Sarah Nalule Kisosonkole. After the country's independence in 1962, Mutebi's father

King Mutebi II of Buganda (1955–). Mutebi was crowned the 37th Kabaka, or king of Buganda, a kingdom in Uganda, in 1993. He studied law at Magdalene College, part of the University of Cambridge. AP IMAGES

Politics of Constitution-Making in Uganda, edited by Hansen, Holger Bernt, and Michael Twaddle. London: James Currey, 1997.

NANCY E. GRATTON

became Uganda's first president. In 1966, then-Prime Minister Milton Obote staged a coup, forced the president and his family into exile in the United Kingdom, and established a new constitution that outlawed the traditional kingships of Uganda. Nonetheless, for most Bugandans, Mutesa II was still considered to be kabaka, and when he died in 1969, Mutebi inherited the title.

Obote was deposed in 1971 by Idi Amin, who also continued to disallow the kabaka to return to Uganda. However, in 1986, when Yoweri Museveni assumed the presidency after Amin was forced to flee the country, Mutebi was allowed to return. In 1993, a new constitution recognized the restoration of the Buganda kingdom, and Mutebi II was officially invested as Kabaka. In 1999 Mutebi married Sylvia Nagginda Lusada (b. 1964), and he has four children: three daughters and one son. Since his installation, Mutebi has established the Kabaka Foundation to provide health and education assistance, ease poverty, and address environmental issues in Uganda.

See also **Amin Dada, Idi; Museveni, Yoweri; Obote, Milton.**

BIBLIOGRAPHY

Doornbos, Martin, and Frederick Mwesigye. "The New Politics of Kingmaking." In *From Chaos to Order: The*

MUTESA I (1830–1884). Mukabya Mutesa is regarded by the Ganda people as perhaps the greatest of their kings. At the death of Mutesa's father, King *Kabaka* Suna II, the prime minister, Katikiro Kayira (who formed an alliance with Mutesa's mother, Muganzirwazza (1817–1882), and her Elephant clan), chose Mutesa in 1856 from among sixty-one eligible "princes of the drum." During Mutesa's reign, powerful influences arrived from the outside world, most of which he welcomed. Swahili traders brought imported cloth, guns, and Islam from the Indian Ocean Coast. Mutesa became fluent in Swahili and literate in Arabic. He promoted Islam among his people and, from 1867 to 1876, observed Ramadan. He did not replace the indigenous Lubaale religion, which included the spirits of former kings as deities, but attempted to add Islam to it. The contradictions inherent in this policy led to a crisis of loyalty when young Muslim converts at court rejected Mutesa's leadership because he was uncircumcised and he recognized other gods besides Allah. Mutesa executed more than seventy of the Muslims making them martyrs for their faith and signaling ominous challenges to Ganda unity.

Simultaneously, Egyptian imperialism threatened Buganda from the north. The explorer Henry Morton Stanley visited Buganda in 1875, during the time of Egyptian Muslim military advances far up the Nile toward Buganda and suggested that British Christian missionaries be brought in to counter the Egyptian threat. At Mutesa's invitation, the Church Missionary Society sent several missionaries in 1877. French Catholic "White Fathers" appeared, uninvited, in 1879, but were welcomed by Mutesa to offset the British Protestants. Mutesa then tried to play the external forces in his domain against each other, creating new political-religious groupings that led to civil wars during the reign of his successor, Mwanga II. However, until Mutesa's death of a venereal infection on October 9, 1884, he presided over an era of Ganda power, influence, prosperity, and independence. He is remembered with awe and affection by his people.

See also **Mwanga, Kabaka; Stanley, Henry Morton.**

BIBLIOGRAPHY

Kiwanuka, M. S. M. *A History of Buganda from the Foundation of the Kingdom to 1900.* New York: Holmes and Meier Pub, 1972.

Kiwanuka, M. S. M. *Semakula: The Kings of Buganda.* Nairobi, Kenya, 1971.

Rowe, John A. "Historical Setting." In *Uganda: A Country Study,* edited by R. M. Byrnes. Washington, DC, 1992

Rowe, John A. "Revolution in Buganda 1856–1900. Part 1: The Reign of Kabaka Mukabya Mutesa, 1856–1884." Ph.D diss. University of Wisconsin, Madison, 1966.

JOHN A. ROWE

Portugal is full of biblical references. He sent numerous young relatives and noblemen to study in Lisbon, and his son Henrique was ordained and returned to Kongo as a bishop. During his reign, schools were established in Mbanza Kongo, the capital of the kingdom. He also built a central church on the site of the royal cemetery and had churches erected in the kingdom's provincial capitals.

See also **Ivory; Kongo, Angola, and Western Forests, History of (1500 to 1880).**

BIBLIOGRAPHY

Hilton, Anne. *The Kingdom of Kongo.* Oxford: Oxford University Press, 1985.

Thornton, John. *Africa and Africans in the Making of the Atlantic World, 1400–1680,* 2nd edition. Cambridge, U.K.: Cambridge University Press, 1998.

RICHARD GRAY

MVEMBA NZINGA

MVEMBA NZINGA (c. 1465–1543). A son of the Kongo king at the time of the arrival of the Portuguese at the mouth of the Congo River, he was baptized as Afonso in 1491 by Portuguese priests. As Afonso, he seized the kingdom following the death of his father in 1506. Though some historians have portrayed him as a naive collaborator with the Portuguese, others have argued that he successfully used the Portuguese to strengthen his own position and to expand his kingdom. He controlled the supplies of ivory, copper, raffia cloth, and slaves, which he made available to his European trading partners. By 1520 most slaves were supplied from markets around Malebo Pool on the Congo River, and he used the exotic imports he obtained in return to reward his officials and allies. The Portuguese settlers on São Tomé who brokered this trade, however, frustrated his attempts to open up direct commerce with Lisbon.

Mvemba Nzinga practiced polygamy and adapted Christianity to provide legitimacy for himself and his successors. He claimed miraculous intervention during his political victory in 1506 and developed this legend to strengthen his heirs as a dynasty. He was reported to be a keen student of Christian doctrine, and his correspondence with

MWANGA, KABAKA

MWANGA, KABAKA (1866–1901). Kabaka (King) Mwanga ruled the East African kingdom of Buganda at the moment when Ganda forms of authority utterly dissolved. Mwanga became king when his father Kabaka Mutesa died in 1884, was deposed for ruling badly in 1888, and then was returned to the kabakaship from 1890 to 1899, only because all the more fitting royal heirs had been executed. Remembered by his own followers as weak, cowardly, and enamored of young men in his court, to whom he offered the prestige and even the lands of his senior chiefs, Mwanga came to power at a time when the trade of guns, cloth, and other commodities for ivory and ultimately for people had utterly inverted the Ganda social order. Mwanga failed in his efforts to reassert control over chiefs who had grown rich trading independently of the king and young men with guns who had constituted themselves into armed gangs that secured wealth through violence. The civil war that followed Mwanga's overthrow had religious overtones, because many Ganda chiefs and ordinary people had converted to Islam and to Protestant and Catholic Christianity as enslavement unraveled the social fabric of the kingdom.

Mwanga was nominally returned to the kabaka-ship in 1890 by the Protestant faction of chiefs, but real power over people remained in the hands of king-makers and passed, almost imperceptibly, to British imperial entrepreneurs as they gained control of transportation networks and asserted their right to taxes and forced labor. Urged on by his sister (princesses foment rebellion in Buganda's gendered division of political power) Mwanga raised a rebellion against the British in 1899, a rebellion that helped to rehabilitate his reputation in the late twentieth century.

See also **Ivory; Mutesa I; Uganda.**

BIBLIOGRAPHY

Hanson, Holly Elisabeth. *Landed Obligation: The Practice of Power in Buganda.* Postmouth, NH: Heinemann, 2003.

Twaddle, Michael. *Kakungulu and the Creation of Uganda, 1868–1928.* Athens: Ohio University Press, 1993.

HOLLY HANSON

MYTH AND COSMOLOGY.

Myth and mythologies are conventionally defined in folklore and anthropology as sacred folktales, the content of which concerns the origins or creation of the world, deities, and a particular people or society. African myths and cosmological beliefs may be oral; carved on wood, clay, ivory, or stone; or enacted in dance. Part of oral traditions, these thus express cosmological beliefs about the universe and are acted out in rituals. Mythologies have been of interest to scholars as coded indications of the central values of a society; as a heavily symbolic metaphorical expression of perennial psychic and social tensions—for example, the Oedipus myth; as a charter validating social practices and institutions—for example, in Bronislaw Malinowski's theories; and as revealing, via the logics of myths, universal structures of the human mind—for example, in the structuralist method of Claude Lévi-Strauss. The main poststructural objection to Lévi-Strauss's analysis of mythologies as mental structures is that it is not clear how one may move beyond possible interpretations of the universal [meanings] of myths when many of these interpretations seem arbitrary,

abstracted as they are from social context and agency and leaving open alternate interpretations.

Despite the cultural diversity of Africa and the need for caution against overgeneralizing on continental scales, some motifs or themes appear in many African myths and cosmologies: They concern deities; the creation of the universe, the origin of humans, human institutions, and values; the coming of death; animals; heroes and leaders; and powerful mediating figures (such as tricksters) associated with reproduction, sacred power, and conversion of natural into cultural substances. Interpretation of these motifs requires knowledge of not solely their content but also of their contexts and uses in contemporary society.

Many myths serve an etiological function, that is, explaining ultimate causes, and may justify or critique social practices, as in the case of tricksters, which are often animals but have human appetites and failings. Ananse the Spider among Fante people in Ghana is portrayed as having a large stomach and is associated with greed. Others myths may serve primarily for entertainment, or teach youths who they are, and what their ancestors did. Some trickster figures appear in AIDS education performances (edutainment) in Mali and South Africa in the early twenty-first century. Although defining and unifying groups is one function of origin myths, different variants nonetheless express disagreements, transformations, and contrasts within them. For example, Mande griots (entertainers who function as oral historians) relate historical battles differently, depending on the region they are in and the audience they are addressing.

Scholars have devoted considerable attention to the comparison of myth with history and written with oral expression. In V. Y. Mudimbe's view (1988, 1991), two apparently distinct modes of thought and practice can coexist: One is critical and rational, aimed at mastering nature and its laws; the other is nonrational and unscientific, taking its meaning from objects' irrational investment in mythical propositions. Mudimbe opposes making a rigid dichotomy between oral and written in power, efficiency, and truth. He also attacks the hypothesis of a linear development from myth to history and science because such linear development negates an obvious fact: scientific discourse and practice can coexist with myths.

Situating Mythology and Cosmology in History and Politics. Most scholars in the early 2000s recognize the artificiality of the geographical regions into which the African continent is conventionally divided, and have abandoned ethnocentric and racist ranking schemes. Many scholars also recognize that ethnographic perspectives on Africa are largely, though not exclusively, outgrowths of colonial connections. Recent rethinking questions the old analytic distinction between myth and history, particularly among scholars working in Africa. Many works explore narratives, rituals, and oratory as ways of formulating the history of cultural encounters, such as contacts between Africans and their European colonizers. The anthropological concept of history that began to emerge in the 1980s wove together poststructuralist approaches to symbolic action and political-economic approaches to historical process. Among anthropologists, this renewed interest in history has concentrated on how specific cultural and linguistic traditions shape social consciousness in specific political-economic conditions. In this perspective, local and regional viewpoints are more important than the singled privileged vantage point of North American or European social science. Variants among different myths of origin are in effect mythico-histories or historical knowledge, rather than decontextualized etiological myths.

These mythico-histories often express disputes over autochthonism and legitimate status as true members of the modern nation. In the recent context of ethnic hostilities, Tutsi and Hutu peoples of Rwanda and Burundi, for example, portray differently the origins and past relationships of each group. Hutu refugees in Tanzania tend to emphasize betrayal by the Tutsi in order to seize power from the Hutu in the remote past. In the Hutu refugees' accounts, the Tutsi arrived as foreigners and aliens from their home in the north and allegedly stole power by nefarious means, thereby establishing the imposter status of the Tutsi. As a collective discursive practice concerned with the history of people who have become a community as refugees, this mythico-history constitutes the refugee Hutu as a categorical protagonist people.

Anthropological approaches to African systems of thought developed during the colonial era in the respective political contexts of each metropolitan power. The British school of ethnography, until

recently, concentrated on sociological aspects of African culture (kinship, politics) and tended to devote less attention to the cosmological and the symbolic. When the British did turn to the latter, they were primarily interested in their function of ideas as ideologies within the social systems. Alfred Reginald Radcliffe-Brown (1881–1955) and Sir Edward Evan (E. E.) Evans-Pritchard (1902–1973) shifted the focus from function to meaning. For example, Evans-Pritchard's account for Nuer religion and cosmology concentrated less upon sociological functions and more on linguistic categories.

The French school adopted an approach roughly opposite to early British functionalism: they focused on symbolic-philosophical order, regarding these myths as the determinant of the social structures through universal structures of the human mind. Thus they made early advances in elucidating African cosmological systems and implicit philosophies, particularly in West Africa. This school tended to see social structure as a reflection of cosmology.

Besides these various ethnographic approaches, methodological debates arose as to how much of the appearance of the systematic character of cosmology as a collective system of beliefs may derive from the individual cognitive coherence, or rationalizing, of specific informants. For example, Marcel Griaule's study of the Dogon of Mali relied totally on a single atypical informant: Ogotemmeli, a hunter who had lost his sight as the result of an accident and was endowed with exceptional intelligence and wisdom. In thirty-three days, he introduced Griaule to a profound knowledge of belief that Griaule interpreted as collectively Dogon. Griaule's *Conversations with Ogotemmeli* (1965) is organized around this one man's interwoven monologues on the creation and origin of social organization, a mythical decoding of the universe, and a symbolic interpretation of the foundation of history, culture, and society.

French structuralism has influenced more recent works on African mythology and cosmology. In his *African Religions* (1976), Benjamin Ray reanalyzes Dogon myth structurally, according to its binary pairs of [symbolic] conceptual opposites and correlates it with its content. He shows how the metaphorical structure of the story expresses its central doctrine: the world oscillates between order and disorder. The narrative proceeds through three temporal or diachronic phases: Creation, Revolt, and Restoration. In the first phase, Amma (the creator) brings forth Thought, Signs, Seeds, Words, and Twins: the principles of order. Before this phase can be completed, it is interrupted by an oppositional phase, the revolt of Ogo, which introduces the principles of disorder: emotion, irrationality, sterility, and singularity. A third and final phase that partially mediates the opposition between order and disorder follows, and thus restores the original order. Humans are direct descendants of Nommo, the son of the creator, Amma. Their task is to continually push back the boundaries of disorder, the tides of time and becoming, by spreading out the canopy of civilization over the Earth and by performing periodic rituals to restore its life. This restorative role was predestined for humans from the beginning, and the myth provides the archetypal symbols that the Dogon duplicate on Earth in their organization of society.

In 1965, Meyer Fortes and Germaine Dieterlen's *African Systems of Thought* initiated a collaborative attempt to integrate the British and French emphases as complementing, rather than competing, and to show interconnections between two aspects heretofore separated by them: knowledge/beliefs and social organization. The objective in the early twenty-first century for these anthropologists is to integrate social-functionalist and phenomenological, or experiential, approaches within a unified perspective.

Problems of Translation and Representation.

In approaching African mythology and cosmology in the early twenty-first century, many scholars recognize the distortions arising from the historical and political situation of the academic disciplines as they developed in colonial Africa. European scholars often began by looking at African supreme beings through the prism of Christian soteriology, that is, that salvation is possible through the Christ event. For example, in creation myths about the early contiguity of earth and sky, some European researchers interpreted these themes as equivalent to the idea of the Fall in Christianity. In the colonial era, Christian missionaries believed that they encountered echoes of the Scriptures in the narratives they heard. They attempted to link local African sky-gods, such as Kwoth among the Nuer, to their own deity. They

usually failed to acknowledge the role of Islam in Africa as a source for in disseminating stories echoing from the Biblical tradition: for example, the intersecting themes of Muslim and Judeo-Christian versions of Adama and Hawa (Adam and Eve) among the Hausa of Nigeria and Niger. Another challenge to understanding African mythology and cosmology is that most early collections in Europe were based on published and written sources and so were distanced from their dynamic narrative contexts. Recent work in anthropology and history acknowledges these difficulties and demonstrates an acute consciousness of the conditions under which the disciplines charged with representing the experience of others go about their tasks. The focus is on how the act of representing systems of thought in other cultures has political consequences, and sometimes political motives.

Another issue pertains to the classification of systems of logical thought. The notion of African philosophy is a recent paradigm. At the beginning of the twentieth century, terms such as *primitive philosophy* and *philosophy of the savages* were used to refer to what has come to be called cosmology, modes of thought, or—straightforwardly—philosophy. African thought was considered to be merely a preliminary progressive step toward a more rational human capacity. Missionaries, anthropologists, and colonizers expounded means and techniques of changing Africa toward modern European and Christian standards. In 1959, a Belgian missionary in Central Africa, Placied F. Tempels, published *Bantu Philosophy*, which expressed doubt concerning the supposed spiritual backwardness of Africans in European terms and proposed a new political policy. Yet many of Tempels' African critics such as Hountoundji and Mudimbe, as well as his followers, remained concerned about making African philosophy agree with European philosophical traditions and promoting a cultural integration of African thought with Christianity.

In the late 1960s there was a movement in favor of restoring traditional African philosophies, called ethnophilosophy, with a more secular outlook. Some have objected that ethnophilosophers present a mythologized African philosophy not located in real time, amid real problems, and that its parameters are constructed to a European audience. Thus, philosophy and theology, and mythology and cosmology, are political practices. Knowledge is debated, reformulated, and combined with new historical contexts that emerge over time. Traditions change in the face of new cultural and political-economic needs and new knowledge formulations.

AFRICAN MYTH, COSMOLOGY, AND SOCIETY

Time and Space. Although anthropologists and historians have begun to realize that describing African beliefs may tell more about the European assumptions brought to interpretations of African formulations than it does about the formations themselves, a number of studies of time and space in African myth and cosmology have attempted to avoid these errors of translation. John Middleton (1960), for example, showed the complexities of the worldview of the Lugbara of northwestern Uganda setting beliefs not solely in the content of belief but also in the contexts within which they are invoked and the uses to which the Lugbara put them. In Middleton's portrayal, the Lugbara are overwhelmingly pragmatic and centrally concerned with the evil emergent all around them. The local idiom of evil is inversion (reversal, witches walking on their heads) in myths and cosmological explanations of past and present transformations. Through this idiom the Lugbara display a combination of skepticism and faith in attempting to influence forces they perceived as affecting their lives.

The Lugbara social and cosmological experiences of time and space may reflect a motif of lost paradise widespread in Africa. These serve to categorize complex social and moral relationships. The Lugbara myth states that human society evolved through three social phases: first, a primordial, mythic, paradisal phase, in which the world was the primal unified inverse of the divisions now prevailing (incest was possible; there was no marriage or bridewealth); second, a transitional, mythic-historical phase consisting of both inverse and normal characteristics; and third, the present sociocultural tensions.

Applying myth to recent historical experience, the Lugbara say that the first Europeans they met were cannibals, as the first ancestors who had lived outside Lugbara territory: inverted people who could disappear underground and walk on their heads. Europeans who arrived later were associated with characteristics belonging to the second or mythic-historic phase. Belgians and the first European district commissioner, as Lugbara heroes, were regarded as magical people who performed transformative miracles. In the early twenty-first century, Europeans are regarded as normal people, living and working within the parameters created then. This same scheme applies to contemporary experience. The local group to which the individual Lugbara belongs exists, as it were, at the center of a series of concentric circles, each representing a sphere at greater social and spatial distances. The center is where normal, upright, beleaguered people live, one's kinship community. Outside this central area lies a larger social sphere containing other Lugbara and peoples of other societies who are not regarded as entirely trustworthy and accountable. They possess magical powers and are suspected of sorcery. Further beyond lies the rest of the world, completely inverted and entirely outside the bounds of humanity.

Contrasting cosmologies of time and space are offered by Evans-Pritchard's studies of the Nuer, cattle herders who live in small villages widely dispersed over the flat riverine country of the upper Nile basin in southern Sudan. The Nuer are transhumant, moving about during the dry season in search of grazing for their herds and returning to their villages during the wet season to cultivate their fields. Nuer political organization is noncentralized and segmentary. The alliances characteristic of such systems are mobilized according to recognized genealogical distance, built on kinship relations among dominant or aristocratic lineages on the village, clan, and subtribal levels. Hence the Nuer capacity, despite utilizing this flexible decentralized system, for lengthy resistance against British colonial expansion and, more recently, the northern Sudan government in civil war.

Nuer cosmology is organized in much the same segmentary fashion, except that it is ultimately unified around the supreme god, Kwoth. Spirits of the sky are Kwoth's sons. They are dominant or aristocratic powers, and superior in rank to clan spirits that are said to be children of Kwoth's daughters. Each of these powers operates at a different level of social experience: family, lineage, village, clan, and subtribe. The Nuer conceive of their relation to Kwoth in the idiom of kinship: they are his children and he their unifying ancestor and ultimate shared father. Kwoth is the spirit of the homestead shrine and spirit of the village; he is the ultimate ground of family and village unity beyond divisive spirits of the clans. He is also the spirit of all Nuer, and hence the basis of the widest ethnic unity, surpassing the limited scope of sky spirits.

Thus, the Nuer conceive of Kwoth in intimate, personal terms, as involved in all ritual occasions, and as inspirer of prophets of unification beyond momentary strife. At the same time, however, they also refer to Kwoth in more transcendent terms as creator of the universe and as spirit of the sky, who seems far away to humans, mere "ants" in his eyes. Therefore, although the Nuer see themselves as clearly separated from their creator, they do not experience this separation in radical, irremediable form. The cause of separation is both accidental and natural; it did not stem from a moral breach. Kwoth remains their father and ancestor, transcendent in his authority and power, yet close in moral and ritual terms.

In many African systems of thought, there is close coordination of cosmological time with the underlying dynamics of social context. Likewise, in concepts of space, there is often a close correspondence between humans and the world. Many African peoples organize space in order to situate themselves integrally in the world and express their concern with its renewal. Cosmic forces, for example, determine everything concerning the house. Among the Fali of northern Cameroon, the residence is conceived of and realized on the basis of symbolism that is at once cosmic, anthropomorphic, zoomorphic, and dendromorphic, or ramified, spreading from a single ultimate source. The right side of the house, associated with the east, corresponds to earth and man, to the known world and the tortoise (the animal symbolic of one subgroup of Fali). The left side of the house, associated with sunset, corresponds to water and woman, to the unknown world and the toad (symbolic of the other subgroup of the Fali).

This cosmological arrangement of the Fali home reproduces the successive phases of their myth of origin in terms of establishment, preparation, and possession by a human being of a universe cut to human scale. The single room of the primordial first cosmic house represents the primordial egg from whence issued man's earth, whose square form is reflected in the rectangular

exterior courtyard. The contrastingly round shape of the Fali room suggests an interior, domesticated equilibrium of a nascent but already organized world that contains its own future and whose completion will be marked by a large oval family enclosure divided into four sections, connected two by two. This is the image of a finished world. The cycle will be completed by a circular shelter away from the family residence where the patriarch settles, detached from human activities and marking a return toward the starting point as he prepares to rejoin through death.

References to the primordial myth involve the intervention of a dynamic principle correlative to the right-left symbolic dualism to which the construction of the house is related: the right side is associated with earth and man, the left side, with water and woman. The Fali house is thus likened to a living being, who is born, develops, and dies, expressing the rhythms of the family that forms, reproduces, and dissipates from within it. The buildings are constructed in an order such that the right side of the house goes up at the same time as the left, and the construction of an edifice on the right is necessarily followed by that of another on the left. This back and forth movement is carried out in relation to the central post of the organically growing structure. Once completed and inhabited, the house, as humanity, is suited to procreation; it is also similar to the finished world.

Power. Some anthropologists critique accounts of exercise of power or political relationships, that treat the latter as secularly based, even when it is exercised in religious contexts common in Africa. Such reductionism exhibits a tendency toward a universalizing stance that many African philosophers have decried as ethnocentric and particular to modern Europe and North America. An alternative is to examine power as an aspect of a locally defined cosmos in the form of an immanent force derived from some extrahuman agency. This externalized view of power illuminates African ideas about the nature of society, of nature, and of human actions. For example, much (though not all) illness causation is located in psycho-social disruption and many healing rituals attempt to not solely heal the body, but also redress social tensions.

Smiths among the Tuareg of northern Niger, a seminomadic, stratified, Islamic people, assert informal, rather than official power, because they act as oral historians, artisans, political intermediaries, and ritual specialists; nobles attribute mystical powers to them. Smiths are believed to be closer to the *jinn* (Islamic) spirits. Their powers cut across sacred and secular domains. Because smiths are outsiders of uncertain origins, who marry endogamously within their inherited social stratum they derive freedom to mediate and transform social relationships. For example, in their work with metals and wood, smiths change natural substances into cultural substances. In their praise songs performed at noble weddings, smiths express critical social commentary. In contact between Tuareg society and the outside world of government functionaries and European tourists, smiths often serve as buffers and gatekeepers for nobles.

Bonnie L. Wright, in her work on Wolof griots (included in Arens and Karp, *The Creativity of Power*, 1989), shows that Wolof cultural ideology recognizes distinct external powers held by occupational categories of persons that makes these categories (sometimes described as caste-like, evidently to capture some sense of their separateness) interdependent. Such interdependence limits the exercise of power of any one category over members of any other. Domination by nobles is countered by their dependence on the griot because of powers of speech that nobles require but only griots have. In many African social systems, therefore, the exercise of political influence—both as the source of power to control others and the legitimization for actions—derives from access to and work upon things and people that have natural and supernatural powers.

Mythology, Cosmology, and Social Change. Expressions of power in the language of cosmology provide a useful lens through which to identify African experiences of the social transformations of modernity over the last century or so. A focus upon myth and cosmology need not create the misimpression that African cultures are static or isolated. In *Womunafu's Bunafu* (1977), David Cohen examines how a Soga community in nineteenth-century eastern Uganda was captured by a regional state and transformed into a small-scale version of the state's court. All the cosmological resources of the community's origin myth are put to the ideological purpose of legitimizing the establishment of authority of the king's illegitimate offspring over it. The result is a radical transformation in community structure with corresponding systemic changes in meanings attributed to social forms and spatial arrangements. Hence, reproduction at one level is change at another.

David Lan's *Guns and Rain* (1985) attacks colonialism's ancient régime in the Zimbabwe liberation struggle and portrays religious innovation under the conditions of violent and rapid change prevailing there. Lan builds on Lévi-Strauss's analysis of myth as expressing mental structures and shows that, by expanding the inherited referents of the political symbolism of local spirit mediumship, cult mediums (and perhaps most important among them, a medium associated with the power of war) were able to absorb guerrilla warfare into their mythology and cosmology. In one part of Zimbabwe, at least, the cult incorporated guerrillas, requiring them to conform to its own logic, rather than the other way around, to maintain the integrity and control of the local community of peasants. Lan relates that many *chimurenga* songs of the war of liberation sung by guerrillas and peasants celebrate the (unifying) role of the ancestors and recognize the importance of royal ancestor spirits in myths to the integrity of the community as protectors of its the land and bringers of the rains that enable it to sustain its occupants. Thus, myth may actively influence political and economic changes, even those that others have defined as secular.

SYMBOLISM IN AFRICAN MYTH AND COSMOLOGY

Many studies of African mythological and cosmological symbols have treated the symbols in them as parts of semiological systems related coherently to social structures. Dan Sperber (1975) has questioned the premises of treating African symbolisms as systemic semiologies. He stated that the concepts symbol and meaning, notoriously difficult to define, are categories of European culture, lacking universal or scientific value.

Poststructural approaches to symbols in myth and cosmology attempt to overcome the gap between observers' categories and the experiences of the observed. The Beng people of Côte d'Ivoire, dance, sacrifice, tell folktales, and hold trials beneath kapok trees ritually planted in every village.

The kapok tree symbolizes inconsistencies, oppositions, and contradictions organized around a dominant pair of opposing principles: identity and difference. Although they appear opposed, the Beng do not see them as wholly incompatible. Each principle organizes distinct but complementing aspects of society among them; together, they offer two visions of how the world can be structured (the dualist division of Beng space into village and forest or Earth). However, the Beng do not perceive or experience culture and nature as the rigid oppositions that European culture makes of them. For the Beng, the forest is not formidable, chaotic, and dangerous. Rather, they see it as classified into orderly zones for spirits, for planting, and for hunting and gathering.

Anomaly and Symbolic Mediation. The Beng principles of identity and difference shed additional light on the meanings of key mediating figures in Beng myths: Dog and Hyena. Dog wavers between identifying with and protecting humans, creating disaster for them. Hyena plays the role of buffoon, at whom audiences laugh because of his immoral deeds, but who in life is the object of intense rites aimed at curtailing or counteracting the animal's anomalous identity (he is laughable in one context, lethal in another). In myths, Dog is responsible for both destruction and protection, and perhaps even creation, of humans. Dog is the alter ego for humans, a shadowy embodiment of both hidden hopes and hidden frustrations. He represents positive and negative aspects of being human. Accordingly, the Beng treat dogs inconsistently. They are viewed as witches, or as good and bad, just as human twins and political officeholders.

Hyenas are amusing and dangerous in different realms in Beng oral mythology: they prowl at night, scavenge on other animals' prey, howl irrationally, and are immoral. Hyena is associated with avarice, malice, and stupidity, all inversions of admirable traits. Its greed and stupidity prevent it from indulging to its full satisfaction; because it is foolish, it cannot achieve fully its greedy goals. Beng audiences laugh at recountings of these myths about Hyena. In contrast, the Beng deal with hyenas in life seriously; ritual treatments highlight the hyenas' perceived defects. Thus, myths

concerning Hyena do not reflect rituals focused on hyenas but, rather, distort each other.

Tales contain moral lessons: That is how Hyena is stupid. But perhaps people condemn while secretly admiring Hyena's motives. Attitudes toward real hyenas censure them for monstrous and anomalous features that set them apart. As the pangolin (anteater) of the Lele of Zaire, Hyena crosses boundaries and threatens categories that should remain discrete. Therein he derives anomalous status. By contrast, Dog, to the Beng, is more of a mediator, a bridging figure between domains. Dog and Hyena represent fine distinctions among symbolic anomalies. The Beng enact special rituals when they confront both animals, as the Lele do regarding pangolins, because these animals' similarly anomalous status alternately threatens and bridges categories in the local universe. These animals serve as creative means for making sense of the world and humanity.

Pollution. The Beng observe a number of forest/Earth-related taboos, many of which circumscribe human sexuality: Couples may not have sexual intercourse in the forest or fields; men may not engage in sex the night before they eat meat from animals sacrificed to Earth; pregnant women may not eat food when walking on paths into or out of the forest; women in labor may not deliver in the forest or fields. Married women may not enter the forest or fields during menstruation. Yet, in contrast to some other feminist assertions that menstrual taboos indicate dirt and/or oppression of women, Gottlieb (1988) explores the implications of taboos and rejects these interpretations of sexual pollution and restrictions in African cosmology as androcentric. The Beng attribute joint and mutual responsibility for sexual taboos and pollution on the parts of both men and women. Further, to the Beng, menstrual restrictions do not result from dirty qualities of menstrual blood; rather, they see it as conceived as the symbol of fertility. Keeping it strictly separate from the forest constitutes a ritual statement that human fertility must be separated from the kind of fertility that Earth-forest creates: crops. The Beng fear that offspring and crops may die if they violate these restrictions.

VOICE AND AUTHORITY
Gender Issues in African Mythology and Cosmology. The study of symbolism in African

myth and cosmology raises the issue of voice and authority in ethnography that has been termed the problem of the mute—social groups whose expressions of their models of the world are impeded by those of other, dominant groups in the system. The models of society that women may provide are not always obvious or dominant to men or to ethnographers, but they may, nonetheless, find expression indirectly, or non-verbally. Recognition that women's and other muted groups' models of myth and ritual, for example, may constitute an alternative cultural ethnography has produced important insights. Marie-Claude Dupré describes frustrations of research into a twin cult when the researcher herself is the mother of twins. Batéké women in the (formerly French) Congo appealed to Dupré to help them understand their own experiences.

Access to spiritual knowledge, which is the most fundamental aspect of ritual, appears to be continually weakened, forbidden, and perverted by masculine interventions. Women discover insignia of the rite that men take over from them; moreover, during research, men continually insisted on making their own interpretations of what women's ritual meant. To the Batéké, the parrot is the bird of knowledge, knowledge that is possible but not yet acquired. Thus every mother of twins, who has carried in her body proof of having participated in the unusual, the disordered, wears a few red parrot feathers in her hair on feast days to show that she has been in contact with knowledge but that it has flown away, leaving only that sign of its existence. There is thus a sense that subordinate people are active producers of culture and not merely vehicles of it or victims of a dominant class.

Yet in many African myths, portrayals of women and relations between the sexes appear contradictory. In many origin myths of Khoesan-speaking peoples in the Kalahari Desert, trickster's traits are stereotypically male, antisocial ones: lechery, gluttony, stinginess, boisterousness, bullying. Women characters display more resourcefulness resolve, and courage than men, as well as greater resolve and courage. In other tales, women cause transformations of humans into primal animals, trees, or stones and of cultural objects into their natural forms.

The problem here is how to interpret these tales, their internal contradictions, and their connection to society. Some theorists argue that this symbolic-mythological female dominance holds in check economic-political male dominance, in tales that, as salient features of everyday life, thereby impact persuasively behavior and values in multichannel conversations that are simultaneous, with soliloquies and complaint discourses. Guenther agrees that these themes provide input to social constructions of current reality; women remain important as gatherers, but male tricksters are equally prominent in myths, symbols, and cosmologies. These contradictions may represent male and female versions of mythical themes, or the tenuous, selective, and arbitrary links between myths and reality; some myths are philosophical treatises and cautionary tales, but only indirectly and obliquely. Thus the Khoesan themes do not necessarily imply a symbolic center or ideational core: although female primacy is prominent, men, too, are encountered; mythology contains a wide spectrum of ideas, beings, and events, many are contradictory and opposed, with indeterminacy and ambiguity.

African Responses to Western Scholarship.
During the 1950s in African studies, the impact of anticolonialist movements and African critiques of anthropology resulted in a new discourse that was critical not only of political and economic colonialism but also of all dominant hegemonic colonial culture. Despite liberation movements, some pre- and postindependence African policies seem predicated on the research of European anthropology developed under the dominance of colonial rule. Although local scholars with backgrounds in African cultures have contributed significantly to the study of African myth and cosmology, the paradox and the problem are that most modern African thought is basically the product of Europe and North America. Most thinkers and leaders have received European educations; thus their conceptual frameworks have mirrored their experience of European hegemony and cultural supremacy categories. Key works in cosmology by African thinkers exemplify this hegemony. John Mbiti (1991) has argued that African concepts of the supreme deity spring from an independent reflection on the supreme God recognized in Judeo-Christian tradition. E. Bolaji Idowu (1973) has argued for a monotheistic interpretation of the Yoruba religion. Because of their European educations, they these theologians chose European metaphysics.

African intellectuals acknowledge their estrangement from their own popular cultures and the difficulty of escape from repeating some philosophical dichotomies embedded in European social thought: universalism/relativism; individualism/collectivism; ideal/material. To achieve ideological independence, certain writers have advocated an intra-African philosophic dialogue conducted in African languages. They argue that any practice of European sciences by African scholars tends to reproduce European ideology and that the total rejection of the entire European cosmology is the only way to liberation. In such critiques and debates, Africans are already rewriting their own cosmologies—or intellectual histories—from a non-European stance. In doing do they thereby enable genuine new directions for dialogues between African, European, and North American scholars.

See also **Anthropology and the Study of Africa; Dreams and Dream Interpretation; Literature: Oral; Person, Concepts of; Philosophy and the Study of Africa; Religion and Ritual; Research; Symbols and Symbolism; Time Reckoning and Calendars.**

BIBLIOGRAPHY

Ardener, Edwin. "Belief and the Problem of Women." In *Perceiving Women*, ed. Shirley Ardener. New York: Wiley, 1975.

Arens, William, and Ivan Karp, eds. *The Creativity of Power: Cosmology and Action in African Societies*. Washington, DC: Smithsonian Institution Press, 1989.

Belcher, Stephen. *African Myths of Origin*. New York: Penguin Books, 2005.

Biesele, Megan. *Women Like Meat: The Folklore and Foraging Ideology of the Kalahari Ju'/hoansi*. Bloomington: Indiana University Press, 1993.

Cohen, David William. *Womunafu's Bunafu*. Princeton, NJ: Princeton University Press, 1977.

Comaroff, Jean, and John Comaroff. *Modernity and its Malcontents*. Chicago: University of Chicago Press, 1993.

Dupré, Marie-Claude. "Comment être femme: Un aspect du ritual mukisi chez les Téké de la République populaire du Congo." *Archives de sciences sociales des religions* 46, no. 1 (1978): 57–84.

Evans-Pritchard, Sir Edward E. *Nuer Religion*. Oxford: Clarendon Press, 1956.

Fortes, Meyer. "The Concept of the Person." In *La notion de la personne en Afrique noire*, ed. Germaine Dieterlen. Paris: L'Harmattan, 1973. Reprinted in *Religion, Morality, and the Person*, ed. Jack Goody. Cambridge, U.K.: Cambridge University Press, 1987.

Gottlieb, Alma. "Menstrual Cosmology among the Beng of Ivory Coast." In *Blood Magic: The Anthropology of Menstruation*, ed. Thomas Buckley and Alma Gottlieb. Berkeley: University of California Press, 1988.

Gottlieb, Alma. *Under the Kapok Tree: Identity and Difference in Beng Thought*. Bloomington: Indiana University Press, 1992.

Griaule, Marcel. *Conversations with Ogotemmeli*. London: Oxford University Press, 1965.

Guenther, Mathias. *Tricksters and Trancers: Bushman Religion and Society*. Bloomington: Indiana University Press, 1999.

Hill, Jonathan. *Rethinking History and Myth: Indigenous South American Perspectives on the Past*. Urbana, IL: University of Chicago Press, 1988.

Hountoundji, Paulin. *On African Philosophy*. Bloomington: Indiana University Press, 1983.

Idowu, E. Bolaji. *African Traditional Religion: A Definition*. Maryknoll, New York: Orbis Books, 1973.

Jackson, Michael, and Ivan Karp, eds. *Personhood and Agency: The Experience of Self and Other in African Cultures*. Washington, DC: Smithsonian Institution Press, 1990.

Jacobson-Widding, Anita. "The Shadow as an Expression of Individuality in Congolese Conceptions of Personhood." In *Personhood and Agency: The Experience of Self and Other in African Cultures*, ed. Michael Jackson and Ivan Karp. Washington, DC: Smithsonian Institution Press, 1990.

Lan, David. *Guns and Rain: Guerrillas and Spirit Mediums in Zimbabwe*. London: James Currey, 1985.

Malkki, Liisa H. *Purity and Exile*. Chicago: University of Chicago Press, 1995.

Mbiti, John. *Introduction to African Religion*. Oxford: Heinemann Educational, 1991.

Middleton, John. *Lugbara Religion*. London and New York: Oxford University Press, 1960.

Mudimbe, Vumbi Yoka. *The Invention of Africa*. Bloomington: Indiana University Press, 1988.

Mudimbe, Vumbi Yoka. *Parables and Fables: Exegesis, Textuality, and Politics in Central Africa*. Madison: University of Wisconsin Press, 1991.

Rasmussen, Susan. "Ritual Specialists, Ambiguity, and Power in Tuareg Society." *Man: The Journal of the Royal Anthropological Institute* 27, no. 1 (1992): 105–128.

Rasmussen, Susan. *Healing in Community: Medicine, Contested Terrains, and Cultural Encounters among the Tuareg*. Westport, CT: Bergin & Garvey Press, 2001.

Ray, Benjamin. *African Religions: Symbol, Ritual, and Community.* Englewood Cliffs, NJ: Prentice Hall, 1976.

Sperber, Dan. *Rethinking Symbolism.* Cambridge, U.K.: Cambridge University Press, 1975.

Tempels, Placide F. *Bantu Philosophy*, trans. A. Rubbens. Paris: Editions Africaines, 1961.

Weiss, Brad, ed. *Producing African Futures.* Boston: Brill, 2004.

Zahan, Dominique. *The Religion, Spirituality, and Thought of Traditional Africa*, trans. Kate Ezra Martin and Lawrence M. Martin. Chicago: University of Chicago Press, 1979.

SUSAN RASMUSSEN

MZILIKAZI (c. 1790–1868). Mzilikazi, as the most feared African leader after Shaka in early nineteenth-century southeastern Africa, was the moving force behind the great military violence (sometimes termed *mfecane*, literally: the crushing) and mass population movements in the mid-1800s north of the Vaal River. In the early 1820s, Mzilikazi served briefly as a lieutenant in Shaka Zulu's army. After winning a battle, Mzilikazi decided to herd the cattle captured back to his own kraal rather than send them as tribute to Shaka. The Zulu king sent men to investigate, and Mzilikazi cut the feathers from their headdresses, a grave insult.

To avoid Shaka's retaliation, Mzilikazi fled with a few hundred followers northwest from Zululand to the Transvaal. There he built up a kingdom, incorporating Zulu refugees and conquering local Sotho clans to form an Ndebele people. Mzilikazi's military methods were devastating: his army surrounded villages at night and attacked at dawn, rhythmically beating their shields, killing all but young men and women, and burning the villages to the ground. The captured men were forced to join the age-set regiments (*amabutho*) that made up his army, and the women were taken as wives for his Ndebele warriors.

Mzilikazi built a strong, centralized kingdom, governed by an extensive law code that covered farming, war, marriage, and taxation. Refugees joining the Ndebele for protection performed forced labor, and young men were not allowed to marry until they had served in an *amabutho*.

Mzilikazi moved the Ndebele often (1827, 1832, and 1837) in order to escape pursuing forces and to expand his base. By 1830 the Ndebele numbered six- to eight thousand people and were a strong fighting force. When Shaka's successor, Dingane, sent the entire Zulu army in pursuit of Mzilikazi in 1832, the Zulu returned with some cows but lost three regiments in the fighting. In 1836 the Ndebele attacked the Afrikaners, who had just entered the high veld, at Vegkop. The Afrikaners lost 430 of their force of 6,000, and the Ndebele took or killed thousands of Afrikaner sheep, cattle, and trek oxen. Mzilikazi moved his people from the area after attacks by an Afrikan-Griqua-Rolong alliance and other attacks by the Zulu.

Around 1840 Mzilikazi and the Ndebele (by then fifteen- to twenty thousand strong) founded a permanent capital, Bulawayo, in what is now southwestern Zimbabwe. From there Mzilikazi enlarged and protected his domain by conquering neighboring Shona groups and fending off attacks from "trek-Boers" who were heading further north (1847–1851). He forced the Afrikaners to sign a peace treaty in 1852 that brought stability to the area until the 1860s when gold prospecting ushered in a flood of European immigrants. Subsequent fights over land rights brought an end to the Ndebele kingdom under Mzilikazi's son, Lobengula.

See also **Lobengula; Shaka Zulu.**

BIBLIOGRAPHY

Rasmussen, R. Kent. *Migrant Kingdom: Mzilikazi's Ndebele in South Africa.* London: Rex Collings; Cape Town: David Philip, 1978.

THOMAS F. McDOW